BOUNDARIES OF INFORMATION PROPERTY

The Common Core of European Private Law Series

Common Core of European Private Law

1. *Interpretation of Commercial Contracts in European Private Law*, C.J.W. Baaij, D. Cabrelli and L. Macgregor (eds.)
2. *Immoral Contracts in Europe*, A. Colombi Ciacchi, C. Mak, Z. Mansoor (eds.)
3. *The Acquisition of Immovables through Long-Term Use*, B. Hoops and E.J. Marais (eds.)

This book is sponsored by Banca Intesa Sanpaolo.

BOUNDARIES OF INFORMATION PROPERTY

Edited by
Christine Godt
Geertrui Van Overwalle
Lucie Guibault
Deryck Beyleveld

INTERSENTIA
Cambridge – Antwerp – Chicago

Intersentia Ltd
8 Wellington Mews
Wellington Street | Cambridge
CB1 1HW | United Kingdom
Tel: +44 1223 736 170
Email: mail@intersentia.co.uk
www.intersentia.com | www.intersentia.co.uk

Distribution for the UK and
Rest of the World (incl. Eastern Europe)
NBN International
1 Deltic Avenue, Rooksley
Milton Keynes MK13 8LD
United Kingdom
Tel: +44 1752 202 301 | Fax: +44 1752 202 331
Email: orders@nbninternational.com

Distribution for Europe
Lefebvre Sarrut Belgium NV
Hoogstraat 139/6
1000 Brussels
Belgium
Tel: +32 (0)800 39 067
Email: mail@intersentia.be

Distribution for the USA and Canada
Independent Publishers Group
Order Department
814 North Franklin Street
Chicago, IL 60610
USA
Tel: +1 800 888 4741 (toll free) | Fax: +1 312 337 5985
Email: orders@ipgbook.com

Boundaries of Information Property

Artwork on cover: Detail of 'Arbre' by Antonius van der Pas (1972). Photographed by Fabiane Lange.

ISBN 978-1-83970-230-3
D/2022/7849/29
NUR 822

British Library Cataloguing in Publication Data. A catalogue record for this book is available from the British Library.

FOREWORD FROM A PROPERTY COMPARATIST'S PERSPECTIVE

This project has quite a long history. It goes back to an idea, presented some 25 years ago, that information could, as such, be an economically valuable, identifiable object to which a subject could have rights vis-à-vis a relevant and considerable group of other subjects. In other words, that information as such could be the object of a property right.[1] The question proved to be almost unexpected and was met with reluctance as to whether this could be a relevant research question at all. At that time, information was generally considered to only be legally relevant in cases where intellectual property rights, including a database right, could be found, and where information qualified as a protected trade secret. To understand this reluctance better, we should realise that this idea was presented before the rise of the data economy, with its Big Data and a new profession – data scientists – and before new developments that have simultaneously and radically changed how we look at data, such as distributed ledger technology, blockchain, smart contracts, the sensorisation of society, the Internet of Things, machine learning and artificial intelligence. All these developments have transformed our society fundamentally, but they are all also very recent. Within a relatively limited time frame, we find ourselves no longer living in just one (i.e. real) world, but in a mixture of spheres where the physical world and the virtual world not only meet, but indeed come together as interwoven and interdependent, creating a hybrid world, particularly in our minds. Twenty-five years ago, there was also not the same awareness as now that there are more sources of valuable information than we tended to recognise, such as information hidden in customs and traditions. Arguing, as is done in traditional common law cases, that pure information can never be property is, therefore, from today's perspective, an open-ended statement that is just too far-reaching to be true, and at the end of the day even meaningless.[2] What is pure information? Is not all information 'pure', whatever its contents and shape? We need to accept that, in our present society, information, laid down in data, is so

---

1 Cf. Sjef van Erp, 'Ownership of digital assets (editorial)', *European Property Law Journal* (2016), 73 ff.

2 Cf. the report by the UK Jurisdiction Task Force, 'Legal statement on cryptoassets and smart contracts' (published November 2019 and available at: https://resources.lawtechuk.io/files/4.%20Cryptoasset%20and%20Smart%20Contract%20Statement.pdf).

omnipresent, affecting both our view of what it means to be a person and what we consider to be an object of economic value, that we cannot and should not deny its legal relevance. We are now data subjects, recognising that personal data tell something about ourselves, but also shape us in terms of how the outside world creates its image about us, and those very same data are economically highly valuable objects which are traded. At the same time, we could not go further without information and the gathering of data. We need information about the physical world in which we live to understand – and combat – climate change. Without adequate data and data analysis, we cannot properly understand how our climate is changing and what any possible effects of, for example, the reduction of CO_2 and greenhouse gas emissions could be.[3] We also need information about our physical self and diseases, for example to stop or at least contain the spread of highly contagious viruses such as COVID-19. In other words, over the past 25 years our vision of the legal relevance of information has shifted dramatically. This book is the outcome of that fundamental change in vision, which is shown in its theoretical underpinnings and analyses, as can be found in both the opening chapters and the presentation and examination of the various case studies. The project followed the Common Core method (initially called the Trento Common Core method, named after the university where the team met in the beginning), which has again proven to result in highly innovative and productive insights.

At the heart, it is submitted, of all debates surrounding information as a legal object – be it from a contractual or a proprietary perspective – is the question of to whom any rights could be attributed and how these rights could and should be distributed, particularly if those rights would allow the rightholder control over, and entitlement to the economic benefits of, that information, as far as it is laid down in data. Control then means access to the data, with at a minimum being able to see the data on a screen, the right to make changes and even to delete, and the right to portability and the right to transfer. Taking these elements (access, deleting, etc.) together, we can now do two things when attempting to legally qualify control of information as laid down in data. We can either analyse these elements from a traditional point of view on what 'ownership' means, attempting to restructure ownership such that it may comprise entitlements regarding data, or accept that the object of any right to data is so fundamentally different from existing legal categories (focusing on physical and intangible property, including intellectual property) that a new category of legal relations needs to be developed. That area we could then call data law and the rights which are attributed and distributed concerning information laid down in data we could then call data rights. The first approach demands a thorough comparative legal analysis, which

3 Cf. for example the data gathered by the Intergovernmental Panel on Climate Change (IPCC, see https://www.ipcc.ch/data/) and the World Bank (https://data.worldbank.org/topic/19).

would already be difficult by itself. Unlike what we see in contract and tort law, property law is characterised by fundamental differences in legal analysis, depending on the legal tradition. Civil law and common law differ considerably in both their history and theoretical structure, with considerable implications from a practical viewpoint. And even within the civil law tradition there is no unity. The German definition of ownership is far stricter than the French notion of ownership and the Scandinavian countries follow their own path. Within the common law tradition, unlike in the civil law tradition, no unified theory on the structure and essential characteristics of property law can be found. A distinction must be made between land, movables and claims. The doctrine of estates only applies to land and not movables. For movables, the doctrine of title is important. In other words, the common law tradition is by nature more object-oriented and theoretically disintegrated. The civil law tradition, however, is more subject-oriented, focusing on what constitutes a person's patrimony as that person's 'shadow' in the physical world, and offers a theoretically integrated system.

Focusing on what 'ownership' means, even a superficial examination shows that the object of the right constitutes an essential characteristic of it, as it binds what the right contains. The object qualifies the property right.[4] This is why the disintegrated nature of property law in the common law tradition results in a disintegrated analysis of property rights. That is what, essentially, Hohfeld's theory with its distinction between rights, powers, privileges and immunities comes down to.[5] It cannot, therefore, come as a surprise that we see more and more acceptance of the second above-mentioned approach, namely that we must admit that data are of such a fundamentally different nature compared to the more traditional objects of property rights that we cannot but accept a new category of rights as part of a new legal area: data rights. This acceptance can be found in both the European Union and China. The European Law Institute recently published its Principles for a Data Economy, Part III of which devotes several pages to data rights.[6] Principle 16 of the ALI-ELI project gives the following overview of what constitutes this new category:

> (1) Data rights may include the right to (a) be provided access to data by means that may, in appropriate circumstances, include porting the data; (b) require the controller to desist from data activities; (c) require the controller to correct data; or (d) receive an economic share in profits derived from the use of data. (2) The data rights set

---

4 Sjef van Erp, 'Ownership of data. The numerus clausus of legal objects', *Brigham-Kanner Property Rights Conference Journal* (2017), 235 ff.

5 Wesley Newcomb Hohfeld, 'Some Fundamental Legal Conceptions as Applied in Judicial Reasoning', *Yale Law Journal* (1913), 16 ff. and *Yale Law Journal* (1917), 710 ff.

6 ALI-ELI Principles for a Data Economy: Data Transactions and Data Rights, available at: https://principlesforadataeconomy.org/fileadmin/user_upload/p_principlesforadataeconomy/Files/Principles_for_a_Data_Economy_ELI_Final_Council_Draft.pdf.

> out in Part III are not exhaustive; rather, a legal system may conclude that parties should have additional rights of this sort. Accordingly, no negative inference should be drawn from the absence of those rights in Part III.[7]

In China, the idea of data rights is also being developed.[8] In essence, such data rights cannot be qualified in a more traditional way. They are a mixture of public law (fundamental human rights, data and privacy protection) and private law (for example providing access). From a private law viewpoint, they are even more of a mixture. Although these rights might be contractual in nature, at the same time they may have a far-reaching effect against third parties and could, consequently, also qualify as being of a proprietary nature. This third-party effect could be the result of the public law character of these rights (one can think of data protection law, which gives the data subject a right to withdraw consent to use the data) or their private law character, as data are frequently at the heart of a web of contracts where a particular contractual arrangement regulating the transfer and further use of data may have an impact on other contracts 'downstream' concluded by the data transferees under the initial contract.[9]

Twenty-five years ago, asking the question 'can you own information?' might have raised eyebrows, but today it is at the heart of a fundamental debate on the nature and value of traditional legal conceptions as to what it means to 'own' something in an environment which is both physical and algorithmic, based on information flows as laid down in data. It will be clear that what constitutes property, property rights and, consequently, boundaries to property all evolve, as this project has clearly shown!

Sjef van Erp
Prof. Dr. em. University of Maastricht

---

7 See also Principle 16 under (3): 'The rights set out in Part III are without prejudice to rights other than data rights that a person may have against a controller of data with regard to that data, such as rights arising from breach of contract, unjust enrichment, conversion of property rights, or tort law.'

8 Cf. Lian Yuming (ed.), *Data Rights Law 1.0, The Theoretical Basis. Key Laboratory of Big Data Strategy* (Oxford: 2019), examining in Chapter 3 the concept of data rights.

9 See on data as the spider in a web of contracts my valedictory address at Maastricht University, entitled 'All good things come to an end, but access remains' (Oisterwijk: 2021), 32 ff.

GENERAL EDITORS' PREFACE

It is a special pleasure to welcome the 21st book in the series The Common Core of European Private Law. This book is edited by four scholars, who together represent four different legal cultures: the German, the Belgian, the Netherlands and the English. Their works are already renowned and appreciated well beyond the 'Common Core' circles.

The Common Core project was launched in 1993 at the University of Trento under the auspices of the late Professor Rudolf B. Schlesinger. The methodology used in the Common Core project, then novel, is now a classic. By making use of case studies, it goes beyond mere description to detailed inquiry into how most European Union legal systems resolve specific legal questions in practice, and to thorough comparisons between those systems. It is our hope that these volumes will provide scholars with a valuable tool for research in comparative law and in their own national legal systems. The collection of materials that the Common Core project is offering to the scholarly community is already quite extensive and will become even more so as more volumes are published. The availability of materials attempting a genuine analysis of how things seem to be is, in our opinion, a prerequisite for an intelligent and critical discussion on how they should be. Perhaps in the future European private law will be authoritatively restated or even codified. As of today, the Common Core project is the longest-running scholarly enterprise in the field. The analytical work carried out by the more than 300 scholars that have so far joined us in the Common Core project is also a precious asset of knowledge and legitimisation for any such a normative enterprise.

We must thank the editors and contributors for their work. With a sense of deep gratitude, we also wish to recall our late Honorary Editor, Professor Rudolf B. Schlesinger. We are sad that we have not been able to present him with the results of a project in which he believed so firmly.

No scholarly project can survive without committed sponsors. The International University College of Turin allows us to organise the General Meetings together with the Centro Studi di Diritto Comparato of Trieste. The European Commission has partially sponsored some of our past General Meetings, having included them in their High Level Conferences Program. The Italian Ministry of Scientific Research, the University of Turin, the University of Trieste, the University of Salento, the University of Gothenburg, the Fromm Chair in International and Comparative Law at the University of California and the Hastings College of the Law, the University of Trento, the Collegio Carlo

Alberto and the Consiglio Nazionale del Notariato all contributed to, or are still contributing to, the funding of this Project. Last but not least, we must thank all those involved in our ongoing Common Core projects in contract law, property, tort and other areas, whose results will be the subject of future published volumes.

Our website home page can be found at www.common-core.org. There you can follow our progress in mapping the common core of European private law.

General Editors

Mauro Bussani, University of Trieste – University of Macao
Ugo Mattei, University of Turin – University of California, Hastings College of the Law

Late Honorary Editors

Rudolf B. Schlesinger, Cornell University – University of California, Hastings College of the Law
Rodolfo Sacco, Emeritus, University of Turin

PREFACE

This book presents the results of a long-term comparative research project on information property which has accompanied us for 20 years (2001–2021). The project covers 16 European jurisdictions, and has brought us together with many collaborators with whom we are united in the spirit of a multinational research project, unfunded by third-stream money, powered exclusively by intrinsic scientific motivations.

The central research question is: How do boundaries to information property evolve? In the light of comparatively few legislative interventions in intellectual property law (IP), the following questions arise: Are boundaries set elsewhere? Do industrial practices or legal intervention in other fields of the law set boundaries? The methodology of the project ('the Trento method') and the research results are laid down in Part I. Our academic learnings have taken shape as four individual chapters, which form Part II of the book. They focus on regulatory theory, conflict configuration in IP law, the European Public Domain, and morality in IP Law.

Part III documents the empirical foundation of the project (cases and national reports). When, in individual cases, no answer is given by the country reporter(s), the lacuna is indicated.

We are grateful to numerous supporters. All the contributors of country reports are listed below. We have indicated the contributors' affiliation at the time the respective country report was submitted. We are thankful to each one of them. Updates were invited, but only the editors used the option. Beyond our reporters, without the loyal research assistants who encouraged us while working on the project over the years, and who contributed valuable insights, the project would not have come to an end. In this respect, Dr Anja Balitzki deserves special gratitude. She prepared valuable texts which helped two of the editors to write their comparative remarks while she was employed at the University of Oldenburg (2010–2013). We are indebted to Jakob Rustige who supported us in 2018–2019 to master the technical side of the manuscript while we worked on revisions simultaneously; along the way, he made many corrections to the texts. We thank Ugo Mattei and Antonio Gambaro for their initial encouragement and accepting the Boundaries of Information Property project as additional project in 2004 in the 'property' section under the umbrella of the 'The Common Core of European Private Law' (CCEPL). The chair of the CCEPL-property working group, Filippo Valguarnera, deserves our gratitude for his engagement in the final editing process in 2021. We also thank the publisher for the expeditious publication, especially Rebecca Bryan and Rebecca Moffat for their thoughtful language reviews. Those interested in the sociology of a collaborative legal research project which brings together lawyers from various jurisdictions can read the writings of Agnes M. Schreiner. We, in turn, were the object of her research during our meetings in Trento and Turin.

Bremen, November 2021
Christine Godt, Geertrui Van Overwalle,
Lucie Guibault and Deryck Beyleveld

CONTENTS

PART II. THEORY AND INFORMATION PROPERTY

OVERVIEW OF COUNTRY REPORTS AND ANALYSIS

COUNTRY REPORTS

Country Reports	Year of Submission	Country Reporters (as affiliated when report was submitted)
Belgium	2008	Prof. Geertrui Van Overwalle, University of Leuven - Matthias Coppens, dto. - Dr. Esther van Zimmeren, dto.
Czech Republic	2007	Jan Mates, LL.M., Charles University of Prague (staff scientist at the chair of Prof. Luboš Tichý)
Denmark	2010	Prof. Jens Schovsbo, University of Copenhagen
Estonia	2008	- Prof. Dr. Aleksei Kelli, University of Tartu - Dr. Tobias Schulte in den Bäumen, University of Bremen
France	2010	Prof. Dr. Christophe Geiger (CEIPI, University of Strasbourg) and the following members of the CEIPI's Research Department: - Clarisse de Bailliencourt, dto. (case 12) - Yann Basire, dto. (case 5) - Dr. Vanessa Diebold-Rossoni, dto. (cases 3 and 4) - Hsiao-Fen Hsu, dto. (cases 7 and 8) - Thibaud Lelong, dto. (cases 1 and 9) - Associate Prof. Dr. Franck Macrez, dto. (case 14) - Associate Prof. Dr. Emmanuel Py, dto. (cases 6 and 11) - Caroline Roda, dto. (cases 2 and 10) - Associate Prof. Dr. Christel Simler, dto. (case 13)
Germany	2007	PD Dr. Christine Godt, University of Bremen, Center for European Law and Policy
Greece	2009	Prof. Konstantinos Christodoulou, University of Athens - Constantinos Antonopoulos, dto.
Ireland	2011	Dr. Maureen O'Sullivan, NUI Galway
Italy	2007	Cases 1–6 - Dr. Andrea Pradi, University of Trento - Prof. Andrea Rossato, dto. Cases 7–10 - Prof. Giorgio Resta, University of Bari Cases 11–14 - Dr. Thomas Margoni, University of Trento

(continued)

continued

Country Reports	Year of Submission	Country Reporters (as affiliated when report was submitted)
Lithuania	2008 (cases 3, 5, 7) 2021 (other cases)	Cases 3, 5, 7 – Laura Ratautaite, University of Vilnius (cases 3 and 5) – Gabriele Venskaityte, dto. (case 7) Cases 2, 4, 6, 8, 9, 10, 13, 14, revising cases 3, 5, 7 – Prof. Ramūnas Birštonas, Vilnius University
Netherlands	2008	– Dr. Lucie Guibault, University of Amsterdam – Dr. Agnes Schreiner, dto. – Dr. Stefan Dimitro, dto. – Stefan Kulk, dto. – Lodewijk Pessers, dto. – David Korteweg, dto.
Norway	2009	– Prof. Ole-Andreas Rognstad, University of Oslo
Poland	2008	– Prof. Elżbieta Traple, Jagiellonian University Krakow – Dr. Tomasz Targosz, dto.
Slovenia	2009	– Dr. Maja Bogataj Jančič, LL.M., LL.M., Intellectual Property Institute, Ljubljana – Prof. Dr. Martina Repas, University of Maribor – Prof. Dr. Tomaž Keresteš, University of Maribor – Mag. Simona Štrancar, University of Maribor – Maja Lubarda, LL.M., Lawyer, Ljubljana
Spain	2007	– Dr. Cristina Roy Pérez, University of Barcelona – Dr. Sílvia Gómez Trinidad, dto. – Dr. Mariona Gual Dalmau, dto. – Dr. M. Teresa Franquet Sugrañes, University Rovira i Virgili. – Pablo Garrido Pérez, Lawyer at AddVANTE legal department and Associate Professor at the University of Barcelona
United Kingdom	2010 (2021)	Cases 1–2, 4–6 (2010) – Prof. Dr. Deryck Beyleveld, University of Durham – Dr. Mike Adcock, dto. Case 3 (2010/2021) – Prof. Dr. Deryck Beyleveld, University of Durham – Dr. Mike Adcock, dto. – Dr. Simone Schroff, Plymouth University Cases 7, 8, 9, 11–13 (2021) – Prof. Dr. Christine Godt, University of Oldenburg – with the support of Prof. Dr. Kathleen Liddell, University of Cambridge Case 10 (2021) – Emeritus Prof. Alison Clarke, University of Surrey Case 14 (2021) – Dr. Simone Schroff, Plymouth University

(continued)

ANALYSIS

Editorial Notes and Comparative Remarks	2020, 2021	Cases 1, 7, 8, 9, 11, 12, 13 – Prof. Dr. Christine Godt, University of Oldenburg
		Cases 2, 6, 10 – Prof. Geertrui Van Overwalle, University of Leuven
		Cases 3, 4, 5, 14 – Dr. Lucie Guibault, Dalhousie University

LIST OF LEAD CONTRIBUTORS AND COORDINATORS*

Mike Adcock
Assistant Professor, Department of Law, University of Durham

Deryck Beyleveld
Professor of Law and Bioethics, University of Durham

Ramūnas Birštonas
Professor of Law, Vilnius University

Maja Bogataj Jančič
Dr., Director, Intellectual Property Institute, Ljubljana

Konstantinos Christodoulou
Professor of Private Law, University of Athens

Teresa Franquet Sugrañes
Senior Lecturer, University Rovira i Virgili

Pablo Garrido Pérez
Lawyer, AddVANTE legal department and Associate Professor, University of Barcelona

Christophe Geiger
Professor of Law, Luiss Guido Carli University, Rome

Christine Godt
Professor of European and International Economic Law, Private Law, Carl von Ossietzky University of Oldenburg

Silvia Gómez Trinidad
Senior Lecturer, Professora Agregada Serra Hunter, University of Barcelona

Mariona Gual Dalmau
Senior Lecturer of Law, University of Barcelona

Lucie Guibault
Professor of Law, Schulich School of Law, Associate Director of the Law & Technology Institute, Dalhousie University

---

* As affiliated in 2021.

Aleksei Kelli
Professor of Intellectual Property Law, University of Tartu

Tomaž Keresteš
Professor of Law, University of Maribor

Maja Lubarda, LL.M.
Lawyer, Ljubljana

Thomas Margoni
Research Professor, Centre for IT & IP Law (CiTiP), University of Leuven

Jan Mates
Dr., Attorney-at-Law, Prague

Maureen O'Sullivan
Lecturer of Law, NUI Galway

Andrea Pradi
Adjunct Professor of Law, University of Trento

Martina Repas
Professor of Law, University of Maribor

Giorgio Resta
Professor of Private Law, University of Rome 3

Ole-Andreas Rognstad
Professor of Law and Intellectual Property, University of Oslo

Cristina Roy Pérez
Senior Lecturer of Law, University of Barcelona

Jens Schovsbo
Professor of Law, Center for Information and Innovation Law, University of Copenhagen

Agnes Schreiner
Assistant Professor and Researcher, Department of Jurisprudence, University of Amsterdam

Simone Schroff
Lecturer in Law, School of Law, Plymouth University

Tobias Schulte in den Bäumen
Dr., Corporate Data Protection Officer, Hapag-Lloyd, Hamburg

Simona Štrancar
Mag. University of Maribor

Tomasz Targosz
Chair of Intellectual Property Law, Law Faculty, Jagiellonian University, Kraków

Elżbieta Traple (†2021)
Chair of Civil Law, Law Faculty, Jagiellonian University, Kraków

Geertrui Van Overwalle
Professor of IP Law, Centre for IT & IP Law (CiTiP), University of Leuven

Gabriele Venskaityte
Case handler at DG Competition, European Commission, Brussels

PART I

THE PROJECT 'BOUNDARIES OF INFORMATION PROPERTY' (BIP)

INTRODUCTION

Background, Methodology and Results of the Boundaries of Information Property Project

Christine Godt, Geertrui Van Overwalle, Lucie Guibault and Deryck Beyleveld

The similarity of rules is in most cases an unreliable indicator of the convergence of legal systems. The rule ordinarily symbolizes far more than its bare text states.

J. H. Merryman, *The Loneliness of the Comparative Lawyer*, 2007, p. 47

I. THE BOUNDARIES OF INFORMATION PROPERTY PROJECT

How do boundaries with regard to information property take form? The answer to this question is essential since boundaries define the content of the right to exclude. The standard answer refers to the statutory elements of immaterial property rights, like patentability requirements and the conditions for copyrights and exceptions ('boundaries of information property'). These elements define *ex ante* what can be appropriated; the rest belongs to the public domain. The underlying concept is the property paradigm: once the right has emerged, it absorbs all powers and privileges (Art. 17(2) EU Charter of Fundamental Rights). The role of *ex post* regulation as a matter of *property* restriction has been neglected ('boundaries to information property'); instead, the discourse refers to the 'regulation of use' (e.g. rules regarding research and release of biotechnology and data protection).

Yet at the time when the Boundaries to Information Property (BIP) project was initiated in 2000, tension was rising in relation to ever-growing information property. As a quantitative indicator, the number of patents granted and copyrights claimed was growing exponentially. New rights were acknowledged, the scope of subject matter broadened and the scope of protection expanded.

Qualitatively, various legal principles have served to expand the scope of property as defined by the language of the claims or the visible or audible 'work' (e.g. equivalence; absolute product protection; a restrictive interpretation of exceptions; 'contracting out' of statutory boundaries). Overall, the expansion is well understood as a mirror of the transformation from an industrial into an information society. Yet conflicts around information have become increasingly political. Numerous regulations around adjacent problems have emerged, and a growing number of contracts do not simply 'exploit' IP, but embrace the conflicts between 'information providers' and 'information seekers'. The mantra of beneficial, ever-increasing IP protection has given way to contentious discussions about 'patent quality', 'IP trolls', and various 'patent wars'. Yet *these* much-debated conflicts are not at the centre of the present inquiry for two reasons. Those discussions focus on conflicts between potential 'economic equals'. And they approach the question of conflict as a binary question of property or no-property.

This book, in contrast, is interested in conflicts between IP holders and other interests. IP conflicts do not exhaust with the acknowledgement of title. Many only emerge after legitimate property assignment, then resemble distributional conflicts, and require arrangements which can take either regulatory or contractual forms. In contrast to land and natural resources, information property was for a long time denied a distributional function, since only 'new' information could become the object of property. Conflicts were only acknowledged in relation to commodification as such (e.g. linked to the argument of dignity of life). Yet there are almost always conflicts of control. Therefore, central questions arose: How do we conceptualise these? Do the existing statutory limitations cover all modern conflicts about information? Do the differences between IP laws sufficiently mirror the societal balance in each societal sector? Do public regulations concretise *internal* limits or do they limit property as *external* boundaries? How is the balancing of interests to be conceived? Can information property be equated with standard property, replicating the division of private property and public regulation? Or does private property respond to the equally legitimate rights of others? Can 'the rights of others', which limit internally, and 'public regulation', which limits externally, be distinguished? Which conceptual basis suits the balancing exercise? And what role do contracts play in this balancing exercise?

The BIP project took on the challenge of finding answers to these questions. It grew out of the research interests of the participating editors and focused these on one novel specific issue: the editors have been united in their scepticism about the common dogmas around IP property being uniform and harmonised worldwide, formed by *ex ante* preconditions, preceding regulation, open to unbounded contractual autonomy. Our initial hypothesis became that limits are not only set *ex ante* (respecting at the same time differences in theory between patents and copyrights), but also emerge *ex post* – not only in the form of explicit restrictions.

Conflicting interests require mitigation in one way or another. Conflicting rights limit the scope of IP rights by remedial limitations, by way of defence rights, by way of limits to contractual freedoms, or by regulation in other fields of the law. While the observation of expanding rights is taken for granted, the premise that limits can only be set by statutory law is not. The editors' common persuasion is that property is internally limited, not necessarily by written requirements *inside* IP laws and their underlying principles. Therefore, cases on exhaustion or compulsory licences are not at the centre of the BIP project. The interest is in those *types* of boundaries which strike a balance between the rightholders and other interested parties, be they competitors, patients, farmers, pupils, readers, academic researchers, etc. These conflicts are not new. Exemptions in various IP laws take them into account (private use, educational exemption, citation, medical therapies). Yet contemporary public discussions do not revolve around these conflicts, but around 'access'. The project sets out to explore these conflicts.

We deliberately chose the 'factual approach' of the Common Core project as our methodology to unearth these changes: how do civil courts argue in a given case of conflict? The research hypothesis is that in IP law, even if the 'epistemic communities'[1] do not easily give way to the pressures of change, legislators and courts will find ways to limit the scope of property rights in socially acceptable ways. The question is, how will this be achieved? How will this be argued? Our ultimate goal was to describe the societal and legal changes which we expected to be able to identify in the national reporters' responses to our cases (for the methodology, see infra II.2.).

While the BIP project was being conceptualised, three schools of thought were emerging, and all editors were involved in these discussions. Two of the concepts claim to improve 'access'. First, the human rights discourse began to push for a 'constitutionalisation of IP'.[2] Second, a new debate about the 'commensurabilisation' of economic and non-economic interests (or 'incommensurability') emerged, and novel forms of societal arrangements challenged the legitimacy of the traditional set-up of IP, especially in digital

1 Professional groups which govern a sectorial discourse which comprises practitioners, civil servants, courts, etc. For a social science description see esp. I. Schneider, *Das Europäische Patentsystem* (Frankfurt/New York: 2010), 666 ff.; on patent epistemic communities: C. Godt, 'Experts and Politics in Patent Policy', *International Review of Intellectual Property and Competition Law* (2016), 960, 976.

2 *Inter alia*, C. Geiger, '"Constitutionalising" Intellectual Property Law?', *International Review of Intellectual Property and Competition Law* (2006), 371; L. R. Helfer, 'Towards a Human Rights Framework for Intellectual Property', Vanderbilt University Law School Public Law and Legal Theory, Working Paper No. 06-03 (2007); G. Van Overwalle, 'Human Right Limitations in Patent Law', in: F. W. Grosheide (ed.), *Intellectual Property and Human Rights: A Paradox* (Cheltenham: 2010), 236; C. Godt, 'Intellectual Property and European Fundamental Rights', in: H.-W. Micklitz (ed.), *Constitutionalization of European Private Law* (Oxford: 2014), 210.

fora such as FLOSS and Creative Commons.[3] They aimed at more flexibility and legitimacy operating across the lines of IP law, public law, property law and contract law. A third concept proposed moral limits to property.[4] Thus, the central question for the BIP project became: How does the framing of IP conflicts exactly materialise in practice?

II. STUDY DESIGN

1. RESEARCH QUESTION AND HYPOTHESIS

The default research question is: Are boundaries only set *inside* IP law or also *outside* it? In other words, do contemporary societies configure conflicts inside property law or outside it by regulation (e.g. competition law, data protection, medical law, data law)? Is the discourse dependent on national traditions or does it universally reflect modern conflicts – taking into account the fact that IP rights are widely harmonised globally? Do boundaries which occur within the borders of a nation give IP rights a different scope across Europe? Assuming that the observed expansion is to the detriment of information providers and users, the initial hypothesis is that conflicts are not ultimately resolved by statutory IP law, but are relegated to other areas of law. The research interest was first directed at the repercussions inside IP law, and the aim was to detect the repercussions and novel forms of external property conflict resolution.

At the end of the project, we witness a broad discussion about the need for a new balance in IP. The public discourse in 2022 is different from what it was in the year 2000. Information technology has instigated the contradictory development of a shrinking public domain and, at the same time, a new communication space with unprecedented freedom. The debate revolves around 'information objects' as *topoi* to grasp the changes in modern society which are linked to catchwords like the information or knowledge society. Technology and the economic importance of information have caused an expanding commodification of information and corporate control which challenges the equilibrium of the private–public mix.

In this move towards more private control and private governing structures, the quest for values attached to democracy and liberal freedoms has risen. Modern thinkers like John Rawls and Jürgen Habermas proposed that private rights and

---

[3] L. Guibault/O. L. van Daalen, *Unravelling the myth around open source licences: An analysis from a Dutch and European law perspective* (The Hague: 2006); B. Hugenholtz/L. Guibault, *The Future of the Public Domain: Identifying the Public Domain in Information Law* (The Hague: 2006).

[4] D. Beyleveld, *Dialectical Necessity of Morality: An Analysis and Defense of Alan Gewirth's Argument to the Principle of Generic Consistency* (Chicago: 1991); D. Beyleveld/R. Brownsword, *Law as a Moral Judgement* (London: 1986).

regulation depend on a variety of collective and individual preconditions which secure a proper public–private mix. Democracy builds on individual access to information, coupled with the freedom of expression. A liberal society is unthinkable without personal autonomy, which includes data protection and freedom to control one's own data. Participatory rights link collective rights with purely private ones. In this framework, the exact content of contractual freedom emerges as a result of a deliberate public discourse.

Thus, there is a need to re-conceptualise information property. Deliberate philosophy in the tradition of Habermas proposes the reciprocity of individual freedoms and public regulation. Property theory, to a large extent, is still confined to the considerations about the exclusive right. This is true for both patent law and copyright law, although copyright law departs from a much more elaborate concept. We understand our task as being to conceptualise boundaries to information property, regardless of where they materialise – in property, contracts or torts. To our understanding, this conceptualisation requires empirical and comparative groundwork. The compelling methodology became the factual approach, also called the 'formants analysis', used by the Common Core of European Private Law project,[5] at that time based in Trento.

2. THE 'COMMON CORE' METHODOLOGY: 'THE FACTUAL APPROACH'

a) *The 'Founding Fathers'*

The Common Core project stands in the tradition of projects conceptualised and conducted by Schlesinger, Kessler, Ehrenzweig and Riesenfeld.[6] Their common conviction was that comparative legal research is a contribution to peace. The focus is on the various possibilities of social ordering ('legal pluralism'),[7] not on functional equivalents with the prospect of harmonisation. Their aspiration was 'analytical', not theoretical, which translated into an 'empirical' approach. They rejected the comparison of 'black-letter laws'. The three-level 'formants analysis' is today ascribed to Rodolfo Sacco.[8] This methodology strives for a 'middle theoretic level', which Ralf Michaels today labels 'modern functionalism'.[9]

---

5 http://www.common-core.org/.

6 Concisely M. Bussani/U. Mattei, 'The Common Core Approach to European Private Law', *Columbia Journal of European Law* (1997/98), 339; on the so-called 'Cornell Project' (1957–1968) R. Sacco/P. Rossi, *Einführung in die Rechtsvergleichung* (Baden-Baden: 2017), 77–81.

7 M. Siems, *Comparative Law* (Cambridge: 2018), 119 f.

8 U. Kischel, *Rechtsvergleichung* (Munich: 2015), 113; R. Sacco, 'Legal Formants – A dynamic approach to comparative law', 39 *American Journal of Comparative Law* (1991), 1–34 and 343–401; also R. Sacco/P. Rossi, *Einführung in die Rechtsvergleichung* (Baden-Baden: 2017), 81–86.

9 R. Michaels, 'The Functionalist Method of Comparative Law', in: M. Reimann/R. Zimmermann (eds.), *The Oxford Handbook on Comparative Law* (Oxford: 2006), 340.

The idea is that the law's functions are, at the same time, stabilisation, distribution and efficient resource allocation.

At the centre of the method are construed (hypothetical) cases and country reports. The cases are built around recognisable situations (some on famous precedents) but adapted the diverse legal reality in several jurisdictions so that answers are possible for each jurisdiction. These cases are the conceptual heart of the project, aiming at rich facts and at answers that at their best reveal underlying connotations, which are not necessarily evident to the national author, but which become identifiable from a bird's-eye view.

b) BIP and the Common Core Methodology

The editors of *Boundaries of Information Property* under the umbrella of the Common Core project composed a questionnaire of 14 cases (see the questionnaire), approved by the heads of the Common Core's property section, Antonio Gambaro and Ugo Mattei, in 2001. All of the cases revolve around the question of extended private rights: How are rights and interests construed in situations of conflict? We framed individual rights of competitors, users, patients, researchers and costumers, but also general public interests like environmental protection, public research and cultural heritage conservation. Do these interests translate into effective counter-rights? How do the various European jurisdictions juggle these new tensions?

The hermeneutical challenge was to identify old conflicts in modern configurations. The dissolution of the public–private distinction is at the heart of the problem, rendering the old distinction between private property as *dominium* and public regulation as restriction inefficient. Our interest was to search for competing interests that are making their way back into the law, either in terms of (newly emerging) colliding rights (autonomy, personality right, right to one's own data) or counteracting policies, wherever these were to be found. The methodology of comparative law and of formants analysis was a promising way to identify those novel configurations. A team from different jurisdictions has higher chances of detecting conflicts in remote areas of law and making sense of national differences.

The methodology, however, has serious shortcomings. The most serious is that the project lasted a very long time. The search for committed reporters took a long time; some then dropped out along the way and needed to be replaced. The 16 country reports were first submitted between 2007 and 2010, with some profoundly revised in 2020/21. As with all projects of this scope (many contributors, no external funding), submissions are seldom on time, are not always complete, and differ remarkably in substance. In 2012, the editors decided that the country reporters would have no further obligation to update the reports. The commenting editors, in turn, wrote their comparative remarks on the material as submitted, ignored individual reports which they deemed to be of inferior quality, and took into account recent developments, building on their own knowledge.

c) *Structure of the BIP Questionnaire*

The questionnaire revolves around three core conflicts: IP and competing interests; IP and collective interests; and IP and research. In order to grasp some of the legislative intent in differences between sectorial IP laws, the questionnaire spans several IP rights. We restricted ourselves, however, to patents, copyright and copyright-related rights. We deliberately left aside trademarks and designs. Out of the wealth of newly emerging rights, we chose the discussion about traditional knowledge and the expanding notion of personality rights in one's own genes, but we left other rights, like football transmission rights, aside. To bridge the specialisation gap between patents and copyright, we relied on collegiality and collaboration. However, the questionnaire is not focused on the boundary between information that can claim legal protection and information that does not – usually a central question for IP lawyers. We deliberately neglected cases revolving around statutory requirements. Instead, the questionnaire aims to shed light on colliding interests in *protected* information. The scope of the property claim is at the heart of the research interest. The questionnaire aims at identifying the diverging and converging public policy responses to information conflicts. The academic interest is the identification of emerging rules and principles which were formerly hosted *inside* the statutory rules of IP law. Thus, we look out for a re-description of seemingly new colliding interests. Therefore, a broad enough range of colliding interests is addressed. We acknowledge that contemporary information law is regulated in a 'multi-level' way by statutes on the international, European and national levels. Yet, while statutory laws focus on the creation of rights and the relation between competitors, we are interested in conflicting user interests upstream and downstream.

The first part of the questionnaire is intended to set the scene by presenting commonly occurring cases. Its focus is on conflicts of regulatory goals in laws competing for conflict resolution in connection to IP. Case 1 focuses on a bilateral competitive relationship, the essential facilities doctrine and access to IP (modelled on the famous *Magill* case –only not aimed at injunction, but reasonable compensation). Case 2 is about a 'patent thicket' in gene patents, modelled on the *Myriad* dispute. Case 3 is modelled on a peer-to-peer file-sharing platform; it focuses on 'third' party access to digital works, and investigates the conditions for consumer access (the private copy paradigm). Case 4 examines Europe's unique database right and raises the question of how the public interest in gaining access to government data is affected through licensing. Cases 5 and 6 are 'reach-through' constellations: the first is about control of and access to inventions of others; the second about the control of business freedoms through contracts.

The second part of the questionnaire focuses on potential future conflicts of personal interests in genetic information. It designs the conflict of private and collective interests, regardless of whether voiced as a human right or as a community right: at the time of drafting, it was clear that no cases exist yet. The interest was to find out how country reporters would answer, and which principles they would employ to find a solution. Not all reporters mastered the task, and thus the return was meagre and very much dependent on the reporters' personality, skills and degree of eagerness to contribute. The questions implied are the followings: If an invention builds on information protected by personality/cultural rights, does the person/group who is/are entitled enjoy/s a veto position, a right to be named (or not to be named), a right to control (or condition) research being carried out with this information, or a right to a share in benefits? With respect to personality rights, how to conceive of connected/colliding group/family interests? With respect to the discussion about biobanking, it seems important to reflect on inherent interest collision – especially to provide structure to the distinctive cases.

The third part of the questionnaire focuses on research conflicts, which we deem to be of prime importance for modern societies transforming into information and knowledge societies. The research sector was also chosen for analytical reasons: in research, a distinction is possible between property in commodified information on the one hand, and other constitutionally protected interests on the other hand, like rights of researchers and information providers (data protection, data source).

Table 1. The Questionnaire's Structure

Case number		**IP regime**	**Main interest protected**	**Conflicting interest**	**Use of licence**	**Direct or indirect EU harmonisation**
First Part						
Case 1	Base	Copyright	Software developer	Competing developer	No	Yes (*Magill* case)
	Mod. 1				Yes	
Case 2		Patent	Initial gene	Improvement gene	No	Yes (Biotechnology Directive)
Case 3	Base	Copyright	Music publisher	User	No	Yes (Copyright in the Information Society Directive and *Promusicae* case)
	Mod. 1		Music publisher	Internet service provider/User	No	
	Mod. 2		Music publisher	User	Yes	
	Mod. 3		Collective management	Author	Yes	
	Mod. 4		Collective management	User	Yes	

(continued)

Table 1 *continued*

Case number		**IP regime**	**Main interest protected**	**Conflicting interest**	**Use of licence**	**Direct or indirect EU harmonisation**
Case 4		Database right	Government data	Commercial use	Yes	Yes (Database Directive)
Case 5		Copyright	Author of software	Author of modification to software	Yes	No
Case 6		Patent/Plant breeders' right	Owner of patent on seed	Farmer	Yes	Yes (IP law; competition law) No (contract law)
Second Part						
Case 7	Base	None	Vaccine developer	Patient's consent to use of gene	No	Yes (data protection)
	Mod. 1–4	Patent				Yes (Biotechnology Directive)
Case 8		Patent	Patent owner on cell	Patient's interest in own body material	No	Yes (Biotechnology Directive)
Case 9 (Base and Mod. 1)		None	Individual's right on own genetic material	Other group members' rights on same genetic material (family or region)	No (not between the 2 interested parties)	No
Case 10 (Base and Mods. 1–2)		Patent	Indigenous knowledge	Biological weapon developer; patent owner	No (not between the two interested parties)	No (except Recital 27 Biotechnology Directive)
Third Part						
Case 11 (Base and Mods. 1–2)		Patent	Initial developer	Subsequent acquirer; patent owner	Yes	No
Case 12		Patent	Patent licensee (using invention)	Patent licensor (restricting use)	Yes	Yes (block exemptions from competition law)
Case 13		Patent	Patent owner	Research sponsor (false inventor claim)	No (not between the two interested parties)	No
Case 14	Base	Copyright	Scientific publisher	Author	Yes	No
	Mod. 1			Third party		

III. LESSONS LEARNED: 12 RESEARCH RESULTS

The central lesson learned is that the narrative of information property as *dominium* is fundamentally flawed. *Dominium* extended from public sovereignty and was transposed into 'private autonomy'. The idea flourished in the 19th century, when societies became riddled by societal conflicts around property and capitalism. Today's conflicts revolve around technological and social transformations. Property receded as being the central contested institution. Conflicts in the information society are framed around what to 'commodify' and under what conditions 'access' is required. In this way, property has lost some of its pre-eminent function for contracts, which in their turn have grown in importance. Discussions have shifted back to the old question of 'how property organizes the society', as put by the former Chair of the Common Core Property Division, Prof. Antonio Gambaro, in his key opening speech at the BIP conference in Munich on 11 September 2008.

1. INTERNAL REFORM POTENTIAL OF IP LAW

In contrast to one of our initial hypotheses, conflict resolution is not relegated to non-IP legal arenas. While copyright law has always been more prone to internalise conflicts, even patent law appears able to respond to change. As illustrated by many cases, both the European and the national levels react to change. Thus, boundaries are continuously set and revised *inside* IP laws. This is the first insight of the BIP project. However, it requires strong public pressure, which can be articulated by academia[10] or by the professional community, formulated as frustration about systematic inefficiencies,[11] or criticised for 'lack of patent quality'.[12] An example of the enormous public pressures from

10 Influential became the small book of W. Cornish, *Intellectual Property – Omnipotent, Distracting, Irrelevant* (Oxford: 2004).

11 Two examples might suffice here. (1) For the UK: CIPR: Commission on Intellectual Property Rights, Integrating Intellectual Property Rights and Development Policy, UK Commission on Intellectual Property Rights, 2002. For Germany: the Ministry for Economy published a paper in 2007 raising concerns about the weakened innovation incentive set by the patent system under the title 'Patentschutz und Innovation', discussed by C. Engel, 'Geistiges Eigentum als Anreiz für Innovation – Die Grenzen des Arguments', in: W. Hoffmann-Riem/M. Eifert (eds.), *Geistiges Eigentum und Innovation I* (Berlin: 2008), 43. (2) H. Ullrich, 'Intellectual Property, Access to Information, and Antitrust: Harmony, Disharmony, and International Harmonization', in: R. Dreyfuss/D. L. Zimmerman/H. First (eds.), *Expanding the Boundaries of Intellectual Property* (Oxford: 2001), 365, at 402.

12 Discussed by European Patent Office, *Scenarios for the Future* (2007); however, the argument appears ubiquitously and is voiced by opponents and proponents of the patent system; for an early voice of this argument see J. Straus, 'Produktpatente auf DNA-Sequenzen – Eine aktuelle Herausforderung des Patentrechts', *GRUR* (2001), 1016, 1021.

all interested sides is the European Biotechnology Directive: the deliberations lasted 10 years before it was enacted in 1998;[13] the numerous recitals indicate the many compromises negotiated. However, reform initiatives often fail.[14] Societal conflicts find their way into the lion's den when conflicts acquire a high profile, like the stem cell debate in relation to gene patents.[15] In this regard, we find our hypothesis rebutted. However, we also find evidence of how difficult it is to put other legislative goals (for example, as in Case 2, the restriction of patent claims) into effective law. The technical issues (here functional restriction of patents) appear too technical to survive the political legislative processes, as evidenced by the country reports.

2. EXTERNAL BOUNDARIES

The second research result is that boundaries to information property are also set *outside* IP sectorial laws. 'Outside' boundaries come from three different sources: (1) public law; (2) economic law, such as competition regulation; and (3) individual rights. It is the quadrangle of IP law, public regulation, economic regulation and fundamental rights that forms the 'boundaries' and shapes the scope of modern property. They might overlap, such as regulations on proband data, economic rationales like the principle of non-commodification of the human body, and the individual right to one's own personal data. These

---

13 I. Schneider, (2010, supra n. 1), 265–381.

14 The European Database Directive of 1996 has remained in force despite severe criticism: E. Sheehan, 'Sui Generis Database Protection in the Light of ECJ Caselaw', in: H. Ullrich/ I. Govaere (eds.), *Intellectual Property, Market Power, and the Public Interest* (Brussels: 2007) 241; A. Ohly, 'Urheberrecht zwischen Innovationsstimulierung und -verhinderung', in: W. Hoffmann-Riem/M. Eifert (eds.), *Geistiges Eigentum und Innovation* (Berlin: 2008), 279; M. Vivant, 'La Privatisation de l'Information par la Propriété Intellectuelle', *Review Internationale de Droit Economique* (2006), 361, 388. Furthermore, the proposal to differentiate between the scope of patents depending on the field of technology, a proposal often put forward by economists, was not pursued. European Patent Office, *Scenarios for the Future* (2007); M. Lemley, 'The Economics of Improvement in Intellectual Property Law', 75 *Texas Law Review* (1997), 989, 1084. Reform initiatives for the Biotechnology Directive remained equally unsuccessful, C. Godt, 'Experts and Politics in Patent Policy: The Final Report of the Expert Group on the Development and Implications of Patent Law in the Field of Biotechnology and Genetic Engineering of the European Commission', *International Review of Intellectual Property and Competition Law* (2016), 960.

15 Biotechnology Directive; on the political process, I. Schneider, (2010, supra n. 1), 265 et seq.; for the corresponding policy move in the US see the so-called Utility Guidelines 2001, DoC, Fed. Reg., Vol. 66, No. 4 (05.01.2001), 1092–1099; discussed by C. Godt, *Eigentum an Information* (Tübingen: 2007), 57 f., and later changes of 2007 to reduce patent claims, 'Proposed Changes to Patent Code Loom over Biotech Industry', 25(12) *Nature Biotechnology* (2007), 1333, 1334; also C. Godt, 'Bio-patente in der Medizin – Zur Bedeutung der Auseinandersetzungen um "Myriad" und "Brüstle"', in: M. Jahn/J. H. Kim/L. Knedendorf/ L. Rickli/F. Poll-Wolbeck (eds.), *Medizinrecht* (Tübingen: 2015) 61.

boundaries do not invalidate patents but put limits on their use and require the sharing of benefits. Yet we find strong jurisdictional path dependencies. Some national traditions emphasise that 'public' interests are to be exclusively regulated by the state (Case 7: Germany, Denmark, Norway); others allow their articulation by private individuals, again in different ways (Case 7: compare France, Italy, Greece, Poland, Lithuania).

3. COMPETITION LAW IS COMPLEMENTARY TO IP

The BIP project confirms the intimate relationship between competition law and IP law. At the time of formulating the project results, this observation is no longer ground-breaking.[16] Yet not only did we take one case about the interface of competition law and IP on board in order to fine-tune the concept of 'internal' versus 'external' limits (Case 1), we also specifically designed some of the cases to contain a competition element. In conceptual terms, we have come to understand competition law as an 'internal' boundary to IP. Patents restrict competition, hence *presuppose* competition (H. Ullrich[17]); the exhaustion doctrine common to all IP rights is embedded in competition policy. Yet competition law rests on legislative texts, i.e. 'external' regulation, enforced by competition authorities. Thus, its qualification as an 'internal' or 'external' boundary to IP is fragile. While competition law defines behavioural patent standards,[18] *empirical* case analysis does not help to evaluate whether competition law is either 'external' or 'internal'. What we can state is that competition law is acknowledged as an important boundary. While competition law is largely harmonised by EU law, the BIP reports provide evidence that national courts still find ways to infuse national preferences regarding industrial politics.

---

16 A. Heinemann, *Immaterialgüterschutz in der Wettbewerbsordnung* (Heidelberg: 2002); S. Scotchmer, *Innovation and Incentives* (Cambridge, MA: 2004); H. Ullrich, 'Le Droit de la Concurrence, Propriété Intellectuelle, et Accès à l`Information Technologique', in: M. Buydens/S. Dusollier (eds.), *L'Intéret Général et l'Accès à l'Information et Propriété Intellectuelle* (Brussels: 2007); C.-D. Ehlermann/I. Atanasiu (eds.), *European Competition Law Annual 2005: The Interaction between Competition Law and Intellectual Property Law* (Portland: 2007).

17 Seminal: H. Ullrich, 'GRUR – Teil A'; in: U. Immenga/E.-J. Mestmäcker (eds.), *Wettbewerbsrecht (EU), Teil 2*, 5th edn, (Munich: 2012) 1549; discussed in several contributions in C. Godt/M. Lamping (eds.), *A Critical Mind – Hanns Ullrich's Footprint in Internal Market Law, Antitrust and Intellectual Property* (Berlin: 2022).

18 Three prominent examples may suffice: (1) the patent term cannot be extended by cheating on patent authorities: European Commission, case COMP/A. 37.507/F3 – *AstraZeneca*; (2) the patent term cannot be extended by negotiation with genetic manufacturers ('reverse payments'), T-472/13, T-460/13, T-467/13, T-469/13, T-470/13, T-471/13, General Court confirms on 08.09.2016 the EU Commission decision in *Lundbeck*; (3) 'no hiding of patents in collaborative standard setting', CJEU decision of 16.07.2015, *Huawei*, C-170/13, ECLI:EU:C:2015:477.

4. FUNDAMENTAL RIGHTS LIMIT IP

While we designed the cases around conflicts of interests, we find that the reporters' responses to the BIP cases refer strongly to fundamental rights, fundamental freedoms, human rights and professional freedoms in order to argue for limits on proprietary power. At the time of writing the conclusions (2019), this observation no longer comes as a surprise. It has become standard theory in the meantime. However, the reports reveal that fundamental rights primarily limit claims which aim to stop use (Cases 6, 7–9). Jurisdictions strongly differ as to how these rights are adjudicated (e.g. France (via a general principle of law) and Italy (via data protection law) in Cases 7–9). Professional freedoms may be defined by special laws (Case 6), or by general behavioural standards (Cases 6, 10–13), or they may be protected via competition law (Cases 1, 11, 12).[19]

5. IP REGULATION VIA NON-IP REGULATION

Our inquiry was driven by the question of whether problems of access to IP-protected products (pharmaceuticals, software) are better resolved *ex ante*[20] or by *ex post* means.[21] Our initial hypothesis was that IP conflicts would increasingly be policed by other areas of law. We find this hypothesis only confirmed for

---

19 US Supreme Court, decision of 15.05.2006, *EBay Inc. v. Mercexchange.*

20 Biotech sector: G. Resta, *Autonomia privata e diritti della personalità* (Naples: 2005); S. Simitis, 'Legal Limitations on Genetic Research and the Commercialisation of its Results', in: K. Boele-Woelki/S. van Erp (eds.), *Rapports Généraux du XVIIe Congrès de L'Académie Internationale de Droit Comparé* (Brussels/Utrecht: 2007), 17–30; D. Beyleveld/R. Brownsword, 'Is Patent Law Part of the EC Legal Order? A Critical Commentary on the Interpretation of Article 6 (1) of Directive 98/44/EC in Case C-377/98', in: C. Baumgartner/D. Mieth (eds.), *Patente am Leben? Ethische, Rechtliche und Politische Aspekte der Biopatentierung* (Paderborn: 2003). Digital sector: B. Lutterbeck, 'Sharing – Ein Kampf ums Recht' in: B. Lutterbeck/ M. Bärwolff/R. A. Gehring (eds.), *Open Source Jahrbuch 2007. Zwischen freier Software und Gesellschaftsmodell* (Berlin: 2007); A. Metzger, 'Freie Software, Open Content – Ausgleich expansiver Urheberrechte durch das Vertragsrecht?', in: R. M. Hilty/A. Peukert (eds.), *Interessenausgleich im Urheberrecht* (Baden-Baden: 2004), 253–265; L. M. C. R. Guibault, *Paradigm Shift in European Intellectual Property Law? From Microsoft to Linux,* 10 Lex Electronica (2006), http://www.lex-electronica.org/articles/v10-3/guibault.htm.

21 One example is regulatory social law, which makes the reimbursement of the patent-protected high prices to industry dependent on an 'additional therapeutic value', as in many European countries. While these rules appear to be restrictive on the patent holder, a closer looks reveals an incentivising effect, see D. Chatterjee, *Evergreening – Voraussetzungen der Patentfähigkeit im Deutschen, Europäischen und Indischen Recht,* (Baden-Baden: 2019). A second example is the inclusion of regulatory agencies in the patent examination procedure as a double check of patentability requirements (as in Brazil), for an in-depth inquiry see R. Curzel, *TRIPS and Access to Medicines – Pharmaceutical Patents and the Experience of Brazil* (Alphen/Frederick: 2021).

patents, but not for copyright (see *inter alia* public health policies: Cases 2, 7–9;[22] research policy: Case 13).[23] We submit that the reason for this remarkable difference is the fundamentally different approach to balancing. Copyright law is much more responsive to conflicts, and balances by way of exceptions and limitations. Exceptions and limitations in patent law do not appear as regular but rather as exceptional tools. We observe that public policy concerns about patents are contingently raised either by sectorial laws or by general privacy or data protection laws. In all of these constellations, the purpose is to curtail the negative effects of exclusive rights as far as they encroach on individuals (such as the researcher's freedom) and on institutions (competition or research as institutions of the information society). The goal can be the availability (Case 5) or the non-availability (Case 7) of data to the public. The lesson learned from our cases is that 'IP-induced problems' are *de facto* policed by other areas of law.[24] This result suggests a profound shift in the legal sub-structure of IP law: where boundaries to IP are not set by IP law, they will be set by other areas of law. These interventions will be transposed to contract law. In other words, the centre of gravity of information law might not necessarily be IP law. Information law is cross-cutting. That explains the frequent reference to data protection laws and competition law. These areas of law relate to conflicts in information use. The conflicts become, to adopt system-theoretic language, sector-wise decomposed: regulations interact, are influenced by constitutional guarantees. On the surface, the narrative of 'IP as property' might appear intact. However, judicial reasoning dissolves and replaces it by a constitutional argumentation aiming at a balance of interests. The country reports reveal that solutions are culturally bound, contingent and limited in time.

6. FINE-TUNING OF PROPERTY BY SECTORIAL IP LAWS?

Beyond the fundamental difference between patents and copyright as regards balancing inside IP laws, we find rather little evidence that legislators successfully

---

22 C. Shapiro, *Navigating the Patent Thicket: Cross Licenses, Patent Pools, and Standard-Setting* (2001), http://faculty.haas.berkeley.edu/shapiro/thicket.pdf; K. Jensen/F. Murray, 'Intellectual Property Landscape of the Human Genome', 310 *Science* (2005), 239; E. G. Campbell et al., 'Data Withholding in Academic Genetics', 287 *JAMA* (2002), 473.

23 C. Godt, (2007, supra n. 15), 218 ff; H. Holzapfel, *Das Versuchsprivileg im Patentrecht und der Schutz biotechnologischer Forschungsinstrumente* (Baden-Baden: 2003), I. Schneider, 'Beschleunigung – Merkantilisierung – Entdemokratisierung? Zur Rolle von Patenten in der embryonalen Stammzellenforschung', in: F. S. Oduncu/U. Schroth/W. Vossenkuhl (eds.), *Stammzellenforschung und therapeutisches Klonen* (Göttingen: 2002).

24 M. Albers, 'Patente auf Leben', *JZ* 2003, 275; I. Schneider, 'Governance of the European Patent System – Between Self-Regulation and Legislative Governance: The Case of the EU Biopatent Directive', paper submitted on the Conference 'Frontiers of Regulation' (Panel: 'The Regulation of Intellectual Property', Bath (UK), 05.09.2006; I. Schneider, 'Innovationsfreiheit und -verantwortung: Geistiges Eigentum und öffentliche Ziele', in: W. Hoffmann-Riem/M. Eifert (eds.), *Geistiges Eigentum und Innovation* (Berlin: 2008), 309.

balance societal conflicts by IP differentiation. At least for the analysed conflicts (Case 3: copyright; Case 6: breeders' rights), they are not resolved legislatively. The argument that *lex specialis* IP supports a fine-tuning of proprietary claims is not reflected in the country reports. We see in the reporters' answers how difficult it is to transpose respective reasonings of adjacent regulatory laws into the language of IP law. Considering that most IP conflicts arise between economic equals (and not between IP holders and consumers/patients/probands or representatives of a public/collective interest), this observation says nothing about the potential that those arguments will have an effect on the scope of the right when discussed in a court room.[25]

7. CONTRACTS MATTER

The reports reveal the outstanding relevance of contract law. Many reports argue their national responses in contractual terms. The reports unearth how contracts can translate evolving IP boundaries and shifted values. Yet they may or may not stabilise *de facto* exclusivity (created by technological protection measures: Case 3), they may *discard* liberties (Case 3) or *contract away* duties (Case 5: duty to name the author), or override statutory privileges (private copies, farmers' rights) that are not always and everywhere considered mandatory. Contracts capture the economic potential of property in the digital world by translating the characteristics of information into the legal language. Contracts, on the other hand, may also re-create public space and community values (Cases 9 and 14).

8. NO EUROPEAN CONVERGENCE

The cases provide evidence that European jurisdictions differ *strongly*. This might surprise of many IP lawyers, considering the purported degree of unification and harmonisation in information property. In fact, copyright law, together with plant breeders' rights and database rights, are more harmonised than patent law or any form of rights on a person's body or genetic information. Beyond those differences, we identify three other types of judicial differences. The first two can be illustrated by examples from the German and Italian reports. Firstly, the country reports give technically inverse answers to the same policy goal, which strongly contradicts the expectation of IP convergence. The reports on Case 11 reveal that Germany *abolished* the privilege of professors to be entitled to their

[25] E.g. the CJEU held up the distinction between computer software and the originality standard under general copyright, in CJEU decision of 02.05.2012, *SAS v. WPL*, C-406/10, EU:C:2012:259.

own inventions in 2002, whereas Italy *introduced* it. In both countries, the policy goal was the same: fostering technology transfer. Secondly, the calibration of rights differs. In Italy, the personality right *includes* the right to decide about the commercial use of the genetic information of one's body. This requires the right to be informed about commercial goals. Such prior informed consent encompasses the destination (hence a right to veto commercialisation with one's material). This consent can be revoked. In Germany, in contrast, the personality right has a different content. A proband has the right to be informed about the scientific goals and impact of the study. He/she has *no right* to restrict his/her consent to 'non-commercial uses' only. This is considered an encroachment on the researcher's freedoms. Consent cannot be withdrawn once the study has started. The third type of judicial difference refers to differing general rules of property law. Here, an example from the German and Danish reports on Case 13 is telling: Denmark has no specific legislation on joint ownership, whereas Germany distinguishes two sub-sets of co-ownership, and case law supports the economically active partner in co-ownership situations (as long as the other party does not object, he/she can factually exclusively use the right jointly owned without sharing the profits). These discourses mirror different national preferences, are historically path-dependent and culturally embedded, and fragment the legal uniformity of harmonised property titles. While we expected *some* national differences in transposing the Biotechnology Directive, inherent in its very nature as a Directive, the country reports reveal that the member states took advantage of the opportunity to legislate their national preferences to the largest possible extent – to the detriment of harmonisation.[26] Thus, we can complement the common expression in comparative law that 'different rules may still convey similar results', with its inverse: 'intended harmonisation may result in more differences'. We observe big differences where national specificities are at stake (Case 11: corruption) and little differences where the debate was pre-structured by European harmonisation (Case 2). The transforming force of new legislation is high where it strengthens a preceding reform, like accepted boundaries to the freedom of contract and asymmetric bargaining power (like private copying, exhaustion and Internet service providers in Case 3). The force is weaker where a transformation of values is required (Case 10: indigenous communities; Cases 11 and 12: scientific freedom).

---

26 The fragmenting effect of the (harmonising) Biotechnology Directive is now described by the political scientist I. Schneider, *Das Europäische Patentsystem* (Frankfurt/New York: 2010), 601. On the remaining legal uncertainty and suspicion about the mere *symbolic nature* of the law, see D. Walter, 'Harmonisierung und angemessene Anspruchsbereite bei der Gensequenzierung', *GRUR* (2007), 284; D. R. Schneider/D. Walter, 'Ist der absolute Stoffschutz noch zu retten? Zur Umsetzung der Richtlinie 98/44/EG (Biotechnologie-Richtlinie)', *GRUR* (2007), 831.

9. COMMON LAW/CIVIL LAW DIVIDE?

The fault lines do not run between classical law families, like common law and continental laws, which one would expect, especially with regard to copyright. We find that these former distinctions do play a minor role in our cases. However, the dividing line is instead north/south, emanating from differing concepts of personality rights. The reasons for this distribution are difficult to discern from the reports, since the descriptive formants reveal different legal bases. The reception of international conventions in the public debate plays a role. They shape public expectations and subsequently entitlements, which are adjudicated in contracts. But the reception of the debate on 'access to justice' also seems to have an impact on how civil procedure law allows public interests to be discussed in the court room.

10. PUBLIC-PRIVATE GOVERNANCE SCHEMES

Supplementing our first finding, we find our initial hypothesis – that new conflict constellations cannot simply be absorbed by the old set-up, but require a new conflict resolution design – confirmed. This is giving rise to tentative, tailor-made governance schemes for conflict resolution in one field, which is not necessarily well designed to balance conflicts in another field of law. At best, emerging structures are described as 'open architecture',[27] composed of multiple legal documents, also termed '*greffe*'[28] (Cases 7 and 10). The challenge is the lack of legal rules, and thus the calibration of the balance where the legislator stopped short. 'Non-legal', 'non-binding' documents give guidance with respect to principles and values; however, potential conflicts are not authoritatively resolved. Thus, IP issues are linked to public regulation, and non-legal guidance papers, reflecting the novel legal structures usually referred to as 'governance arrangements'. The clear cut difference between private and public law dissolves; public regulation might inversely instrumentalise private autonomies for its own goals (Case 10: benefit sharing). IP regulation is camouflaged.

---

27 Expression framed by F. M. Abbott, 'Distributed Governance at the WTO-WIPO: An Evolving Model for Open-Architecture Integrated Governance', in: M. C. E. J. Bronckers/R. Quick (eds.), *New Directions in International Law – Essays in Honour of John H. Jackson* (The Hague: 2002), 15–33.

28 M. Amstutz/V. Karavas, 'Weltrecht: Ein Derridasches Monster', in: G.-P. Calliess/A. Fischer-Lescano/D. Wielsch/P. Zumbansen (eds.), *Soziologische Jurisprudenz – Festschrift G. Teubner* (Berlin: 2009), 647, at 648.

11. GROUPS, COLLECTIVES, DIFFUSE INTERESTS, COMMONS

The project included cases which touched on groups (Case 3: users; Case 9: families, ethnic groups, territorially limited groups), indigenous communities (Case 10), diffuse interests (Case 13), and commons (Case 14: Open Access and Creative Commons). The goal was to identify policy-making *in between* an individual right and a public policy orchestrated by the state. The editors were interested in discerning the extent to which the academic reflection about this 'grey area in between' has found its way into IP law. How do jurisdictions distinguish collective interests from public interests? We hoped to identify normative conceptions in the metalegal formants. We found less explicit reflection than we had wished for (the UK being a notable exception). Still, the reports bring out interestingly divergent ideas about how to reflect court principles which one might deem clear and settled, such as the non-commercialisation principle (cf. the Belgian, French and Polish reports on Cases 8 and 9).

12. RE-INDIVIDUALISATION OF PUBLIC INTERESTS

Related to the reflection on different types of collective and public interests is the question of whether collective or individual actors can innovatively use IP to pursue non-traditional purposes. In other words, can public interests be re-framed in an individualised language? Modifications 4 and 5 of Case 3 touch on this question. To what extent do existing collective schemes adapt to the situation of authors or users? Can former 'privileges' of members of the public be transformed into individual rights (Case 3)? Can any member of the group enforce group rights against other individuals of the group (Case 9)? To what extent can non-governmental organisations use property institutions (inventorship, co-ownership: Case 13)? And to what extent can property be transformed to allow for novel social practices (Case 14)? While the reports reveal the subjective unease of reporters in analysing these complicated collisions, the answers reveal the dazzling complexity. Case 13, for example, pits two types of public interests against each other. The country reports reveal that public interests overlap with institutional interests of organisations. These cases challenge doctrinal principles of indirect horizontality; the reference to principles such as separation of power and privity of contract only aggravate the lingering problem of legitimacy. It is the goal of the cases to bring out these novel needs for open deliberation and balancing. While being cautious about arguing for proportionality, the reporters break new ground for the juridical IP discourse, which juggles principles and constitutional values.

QUESTIONNAIRE

CASE 1. ERICA'S IMPROVED BEER MARKET SOFTWARE

A.1. BASE CASE

Frank heads a major beer producing company. In the 1970s, he developed a computer programme which analyses regional patterns of beer distribution and beer consumption. Since then, he has constantly refined the programme and has freely distributed the programme to his traders, trade associations and market analysts. Over time, the programme became the standard instrument to analyse the beer market. Without using it, one cannot be active on this market. Therefore Erica, a former trader of Frank's products and now director of a major competitor of Frank, started to model her own distribution system on Frank's system. Does Frank have a right to an injunction arguing that the computer programme is his?

B.1. CASE MODIFICATION

Frank does license the programme to Erica under the obligation *not to improve it* and not to market the programme without his permission. Can Frank claim an injunction if Erica improves the programme and markets it without Frank's prior consent?

CASE 2. MEDICAL RESEARCH (PUBLIC HEALTH – MODELLED ON BRCA1/2 AND CCR5)

A.1. CASE

Mary, owner of a small biotech company, was granted a patent on the gene BRAU-7. As a utility, the patent accounts for cardiovascular diseases. Five years after the patent was granted, her competitor John found out that the gene BRAU-7, in conjunction with the gene BLIB-5, is responsible for healing wounds.

The proportional relationship to which each gene accounts for the healing process is scientifically unclear. John is also granted a patent on his invention. He sets up a business and starts producing an ointment.

Does Mary have a claim for injunction against John?

CASE 3. CULTURE – THIRD PARTY ACCESS (MODELLED ON P2P FILE-SHARING)

A.1. BASE CASE

Carla, a 15-year-old teenager, downloads and uploads songs from the Internet and exchanges CDs with her girlfriend Karen. She is now sued by the record company 'String'.[1]

Will an injunction be granted?

B.1. MODIFICATION 1

At the same time, 'String' is seeking an injunction against the Internet-based music provider 'Keep Mov'n', whose site has become the most popular music exchange site. 'String' asks the court to oblige 'Keep Mov'n' to prevent the downloading of illegal material and to release the names and addresses of 33 of its subscribers who are suspected of downloading mass quantities of illegal material.

Will 'String' have a successful claim against 'Keep Mov'n'?

C.1. MODIFICATION 2

Carla has a monthly subscription to OD2, an Internet site where you can legally download popular songs for €30 per month. Each song bought via OD2 is encrypted so that no copy can be made nor distributed to anyone else over the Internet. This technological protection measure makes it impossible for Carla to burn a CD of the songs that she just paid for and to listen to them on her way to school every day. Carla finds this unacceptable: she circumvents the technological lock and burns a CD of the songs for her own private use.

Can the record company 'String' object to this?

1 It is a fair assumption to make that the record company 'String' has acquired all the rights from the authors and performers on the songs that it produces or distributes. As such, 'String' is actively legitimated to act against the alleged violators of the rights of which it is the holder.

D.1. MODIFICATION 3

Would Carla have an extra argument by saying that she does not want to pay twice (the subscription price at OD2 and the levy on the blank CD in the framework of the home copying regime) for a song that she cannot copy?

E.1. MODIFICATION 4

Carla downloads and burns onto a CD songs that are distributed under a Creative Commons licence, on a royalty-free basis, allowing users to freely reproduce and distribute the works for non-commercial purposes.

Would Carla have a cause of action for reimbursement of the levy on the blank CD against the collecting society administering the home copying regime?

CASE 4. PUBLIC DATA/DATABASE PROTECTION OF A PUBLIC INSTITUTION

A.1. CASE

The Royal Institute of Meteorology of country X (RIM) is a 100% publicly owned and funded entity whose statutory mission is to gather, organise and interpret meteorological data. In the course of the last century, RIM has developed a comprehensive database, containing all the relevant statistics for the meteorological events that occurred during the period in its own country and across Northern Europe. Realising the immense commercial value of the information included in its database, RIM has recently decided to start licensing its use to the public for a substantial fee. The private research company CLIMATE seeks a licence for use. Referring to its *sui generis* database right, RIM reserves to itself the right to extract and re-utilise substantial and insubstantial parts of its database. CLIMATE objects to this contractual clause, referring to the public financing of the database and claims free and unrestricted access to RIM's data bank.

If CLIMATE proceeds to use the data without the licence, does RIM have a claim for injunction?

CASE 5. THE RIGHT TO BE NAMED (MORAL RIGHTS)

A.1. CASE

Richard, a scientist with the renowned pharmaceutical company IPC, buys a computer programme, the top-selling product of IT-Company (ITC), which organises his article database. The programme has been written by the renowned Professor Higgens at Y-University. A specific algorithm, developed by him, is the core of the programme. This is widely known in the relevant community. In order to strengthen its marketing position, ITC markets the programme enclosing a licence agreement that obliges commercial users to cite the company's name (ITC) when improving the programme; explicitly, any reference to Professor Higgens is forbidden. The contract between Higgens and ITC is silent about the original personality right of Prof. Higgens.

Does Prof. Higgens have the right to be named if Richard adapts ITC's programme to the needs of pharmaceutical companies? Can Higgens claim an injunction if IPC markets the improved product making reference only to ITC?

CASE 6. FARMERS' RIGHTS

A.1. CASE

Assume that your country has accepted GM food: the company CaMon is marketing seeds of a tomato plant that looks fresh on the shelf for longer than others. This feature of the tomato has been patented. Paul, a farmer of vegetables and legumes, is looking for better marketing opportunities. He heard about this plant and hopes to win more customers by expanding his distribution system. It seems that the new tomato plant has the potential to be a building block for his new strategy. He buys the seed – enough to plant 100 acres. However, the delivery of the seed is accompanied by a licence contract that obliges him to sell the whole harvest to a big food processing company (FPC), located 700 km away. Any violation will give rise to contractual penalties.

Paul ignores the licence and sells the harvested tomatoes to regional customers. In September, he receives a letter from CaMon reminding him only to sell to FPC and announcing a lawsuit. Since Paul pursues his own marketing strategies, they meet in court one year later.

Is CaMon entitled to contractual penalties?

CASE 7. PERSONALISED GENOMIC INFORMATION

A.1. BASE CASE

Marc has a unique gene that makes him immune to a specific, but widespread, influenza virus. The Pharmaceutical Company (PhC) screens his genome. As a result of this information, PhC develops a (patented) vaccine against this type of influenza.

Is Marc entitled to veto research on the gene? Does he have *a maiore ad minus* the right not to give consent to experiments that he considers unethical? Could he object to commercial research and restrict the use to 'academic research'?

B.1. MODIFICATION 1

Is Marc entitled to veto the patent application on the grounds of lacking prior informed consent?

C.1. MODIFICATION 2

Is Marc entitled to be named/not to be named in the patent description?

D.1. MODIFICATION 3

Is Marc entitled to a share of the benefits that are generated by marketing the patented products?

E.1. MODIFICATION 4

Is Marc entitled to obtain the product free of charge? Does PhC have a right to claim money from Marc for selling him the product?

CASE 9. CONFLICTING INTERESTS IN FAMILIES AND GROUPS IN GENOMIC INFORMATION

A.1. BASE CASE

The Miller family carries a unique gene that is somehow linked to the development of intelligence. 80% of the family enjoys an IQ of 140. The downside of the gene is shortgevity. Those carrying the gene live no longer than 42 years. Lilly, a carrier of the gene, agreed with a pharmaceutical company Genfix to undertake extended experiments on the gene. As compensation, she was promised a 1% share in all product sales made on the basis of the respective gene. Her brother William, who carries the same gene, objects. Does William have the right to veto the whole contract? Does he have the right to veto the payment of 1%?

B.1. MODIFICATION

Would it make a difference if the gene was not bound to a specific family but was unique to a specific region? Assume the same factual situation as given in the original case; the names are Ricardo and Guillermo, and the name of the company is Genbest. Does Guillermo have a right to veto the payment clause in the contract between Ricardo and Genbest?

CASE 10. TRADITIONAL KNOWLEDGE

A.1. BASE CASE

For centuries, the indigenous community ABC has harboured the knowledge of how to treat a specific eye infection with a specific plant. Plant biologist Tobin bioprospects the country where the ABC live, and he consults with the respective 'council of the elderly'. The 'council of the elderly' agrees to show Tobin the plant and how it is to be grown, prepared and applied – on three conditions. Tobin may only use the plant extract for medicinal purposes and he has to safeguard against anyone else pursuing research for different purposes. Any potential patent application shall name the ABC community. In addition, ABC shall obtain a 2% share in any profits that are generated from exploiting the patent. Tobin accepts these conditions in front of the council in a formal meeting.

Assume that your own country's laws apply and that ABC is a legal entity according to the home country's constitution.

At home, Tobin has a laboratory colleague, Walter, who does contract research for the Army searching for a new poison. Walter discovers that the lead component of the plant is highly toxic with specific 'beneficial' characteristics for warfare (the toxin spreads despite unfavourable wind conditions). Walter files and is granted a patent. Does ABC have the right to veto the patent?

B.1. MODIFICATION 1

If Q does not name the community in his own patent description, does ABC have a right to correction?

C.1. MODIFICATION 2

Q develops a derivative from the substance. The new substance is easily produced chemically in large quantities. Q is granted a patent. Is ABC entitled to a share of the profits?

CASE 11. GRANT-BACK AND REACH-THROUGH (PUBLIC RESEARCH INSTITUTIONS)

A.1. BASE CASE

After years of in-house research, the large IT-Company (ITC) outsourced its research facilities in the beginning of the 1990s. By now, it contracts not only with its own subdivision but also with a diverse range of universities and public and private research institutions, including spin-offs. ITC contractors are obliged to transfer future intellectual property rights to ITC. In breach of this contractual obligation, Prof. Brain of M-University applies for a patent in the name of M-University. M-University transfers the granted patent to a group of students undertaking a start-up.

Can ITC challenge the patent?

B.1. MODIFICATION 1

Would it make a difference if ITC did not demand the transfer of future intellectual property rights but rather demanded to be named as co-inventor?

C.1. MODIFICATION 2

Assume that ITC is a biotech company whose basic business is breeding patented laboratory mice. It licenses 100 mice to Prof. Brain under the condition that he transfer all future inventions resulting from experiments with the mouse model to ITC.

If Brain ignores the clause, which he regards invalid, and applies for a patent for an invention based on experiments with the mouse model, is ITC entitled to challenge the patent on the ground that it is the owner of the patent?

CASE 12. USE RESTRICTIONS

A.1. CASE

Dr Grey, the director of a private research institution, undertakes research projects with a variety of sponsors. She receives a licence for 100 EMC[4] rats from White Corp. for a research project headed by her employee, Dr Black. The licence obliges the institute only to use the rat model in the identified experiment conducted by Dr Black. The use of the rat model in experiments sponsored by White's competitor, Yellow Corp., is expressly forbidden.

Two years later, Dr Black is entrusted with an in-house research project sponsored by Yellow Corp. He continues using the rat model EMC[4] and patents his results.

Does White Corp. have a right to a share in profits as damages on the basis of breach of contract?

CASE 13. CO-INVENTORSHIP, CO-OWNERSHIP (MODELLED ON *PXE*)

A.1. BASE CASE

PXZ is a patient organisation representing 200 families with a disposition of a malignant form of cancer. Its mission is to sponsor wide research on this form of cancer. It raises money, obliges the researchers it sponsors to identify the director of PXZ as a co-inventor in any future filings for patents, and has a strong interest in having a say in future licensing negotiations.

The big pharmaceutical company BPC is close to coming up with a chemotherapy for this form of cancer. A gene-based therapy developed by a researcher sponsored by PXZ could cut profits on the final chemical cocktail. It considers a challenge to the gene patent as part of its business strategy. Can BPC challenge the patent on grounds of false inventorship?

B.1. MODIFICATION 1

PXZ and Prof. Marlow hold a patent as co-inventors, owned jointly by PXZ and M-University. After years have passed and contacts have become less frequent, M-University licenses the invention exclusively to the transnational chemical company TransChem without prior informed consent on the part of PXZ. As TransChem denies any access to third parties, PXZ objects to the licence. Is PXZ entitled to challenge the contract between M-University and TransChem?

C.1. MODIFICATION 2

Would it make a difference if M-University had only granted a simple licence?

D.1. MODIFICATION 3

Assume that an invention has been made jointly. M-University *refuses to patent* the invention because of the University Guidelines on 'Specifically Important Developments'. These require that scientific inventions with the utmost importance and potential broad use be put into the public domain. PXZ and M-University argue about how far these guidelines are binding on PXZ and if the invention is 'scientifically of utmost importance'. Ultimately, PXZ files for a patent on its own. Can M-University challenge the patent?

CASE 14. OPEN ACCESS – CREATIVE COMMONS

A.1. BASE CASE

From 1980 to 2004, Dr Silver and his colleagues have published their scientific articles in the periodicals of 'Big Publishing House, Inc.'. For the publication of each article, 'Big Publishing House, Inc.' required that the authors transfer 'all rights with respect to modes of exploitation now known or to be discovered' to the publisher. In 2004, Dr Silver, along with several of his colleagues, stopped publishing their scientific findings with 'Big Publishing House, Inc.' in reaction to the publisher's very strict licensing conditions. They now decide to make all their publications available on their institute's webpage under a Creative Commons Attribution-NonCommercial-ShareAlike licence. Not only do they make their most recent articles available on the website, they also include the full text of the articles that were previously published by 'Big Publishing House, Inc.'. On the website, the papers are freely accessible, provided that the user accepts the licence conditions by clicking 'I agree' in the dialogue box on their screen. Contrary to the licence used by 'Big Publishing House, Inc.', the Creative Commons licence allows authors to publish their work on the Internet, and to use it for any purpose, including for educational purposes. The licence also allows anyone to reproduce, modify and communicate the paper freely for strictly non-commercial purposes, provided that proper credit is given, and that any redistribution of the paper occurs under the same licence conditions.

'Big Publishing House, Inc.' has got wind of Dr Silver's action and claims an injunction against the making available of the articles on the website. Will an injunction be granted?

B.1. MODIFICATION

Dr Cooper works for a pharmaceutical company. He downloads Dr Silver's latest paper, makes small modifications and publishes it in the company's online newsletter without mentioning the conditions of the Open Access licence. Dr Silver brings a court action for violation of his copyright and breach of contract and demands the removal of the article from the online newsletter. Will he succeed?

PART II

THEORY AND INFORMATION PROPERTY

REGULATION THEORY AND INTELLECTUAL PROPERTY LAW

Geertrui Van Overwalle*

I. INTRODUCTION

Do legislators apply classical command-and-control mechanisms to spur the development of knowledge production? Or do legislators rather regulate by design, using architecture to steer innovative behaviour? Or do they turn to consensus-based tools to achieve a balance between public and private interests? The present chapter aims to shed more light on the wide spectrum of instruments used by national legislators by looking at the findings in the national reports through the prism of regulation theory.

In section II, we dissect the *definition* of regulation. To that end, we first delve into the definition provided in regulation scholarship, and then assess to what extent current intellectual property (IP) law, and patent law in particular, fit this definition. In section III, we focus on the various regulation *theories* which have been set forth in regulation scholarship and in legal discourse and examine the interaction and/or overlap between these two narratives. We then examine the category of regulation theory to which the current patent system belongs. In section IV, we turn to *instruments* which are being put to use to achieve regulatory goals, as described in regulation scholarship. We then turn to the patent system, to investigate what type of regulatory instruments are being applied, illustrating this explorative analysis with cases

* The present research was supported by the Vancraesbeeck Fund (University of Leuven, Belgium) and the Tilburg Institute for Law, Technology and Society (TILT, Tilburg University, the Netherlands), where the author was appointed as part-time research professor from 2008 until 2014. She is grateful for the many inspiring conversations she had at TILT on the topic of regulation, particularly with Bert-Jaap Koops, Ronald Leenes, Maurice Schellekens, Han Somsen and Anton Vedder. The author also wishes to acknowledge the research assistance from Simon Geiregat and Lodewijk Van Dycke (University of Leuven), and insightful suggestions from Michael Neumann (University of Bayreuth) and Ingrid Schneider (University of Hamburg).

from patent law in general, and the cases discussed in the national reports in particular.[1]

The major focus within the present chapter is on information production and patent *law*, even though we might shift to the analysis of the patent *system* at times, as there are overlaps between the two concepts. We define patent *law* as the set of *rules*, promulgated by the (national, European or international) patent legislator and interpreted by (national and/or European) courts. We define the patent *system* as the way in which patent law is being construed, interpreted and implemented by, respectively, legislative, jurisprudential and administrative/executive *institutions*, and the interaction between those distinct branches of government. Some scholars would argue that the patent system also includes *individuals*, who assist within all those institutions in shaping relevant rules, thus encompassing legislators, judges, patent examiners, patent attorneys, etc.[2]

II. DEFINITION OF REGULATION

1. DEFINITION OF REGULATION IN GENERAL

A leading scholar on regulation, Julia Black, defines regulation as the '[s]ustained and focused attempt to alter the behaviour of others according to standards or goals with the intention of producing a broadly identified outcome or outcomes which may involve mechanisms of standard setting, information gathering and behaviour modification'.[3] This concept of regulation puts the change of behaviour front and centre as a key aspiration. This approach has resonated widely in academic literature. In defining regulation, Baldwin refers to '[a]ll forms of social control',[4] Koops refers to '[c]ontrolling human or societal behaviour'[5] and Selznick talks about '[s]ustained and focused control, over activities that are generally regarded as desirable to society'.[6]

1 Examples throughout this chapter have mainly been taken from the cases in the life sciences sector. In particular, Case 2 (medical research), Case 6 (farmers' rights) and Case 10 (traditional knowledge).

2 Cf. P. Drahos, *Information Feudalism* (London: 2002).

3 J. Black, 'Critical reflections on regulation', *Australian Journal of Legal Philosophy* (2002), 1, 35; J. Black, 'What is regulatory innovation?', in: J. Black/M. Lodge/M. Thatcher (eds.), *Regulatory innovation. A comparative analysis* (Cheltenham: 2005), 11. In the same sense, C. Hood/H. Rothstein/R. Baldwin, *The government of risk* (Oxford: 2001); R. Leenes, *Harde lessen. Apologie van technologie als reguleringsinstrument. Rede uitgesproken door R.E. (Ronald) Leenes*, Tilburg University, Tilburg, 16 April 2010, 15, 21, available at: https://pure.uvt.nl/ws/files/1260134/Leenes_Harde_lessen_100826.pdf (last visited 18 July 2017).

4 R. Baldwin/M. Cave, *Understanding regulation* (Oxford: 1999), 91.

5 B.-J. Koops/M. Lips/C. Prins/M. Schellekens (eds.), *Starting Points for ICT Regulations, Deconstructing Prevalent Policy One-liners* (Cambridge: 2006).

6 P. Selznick, 'Focusing Organizational Research on Regulation', in: R. G. Noll (ed.), *Regulatory Policy and the Social Sciences* (Berkeley: 1985).

Disagreement in scholarly literature arises when discussing the scope of regulation. At their narrowest, definitions of regulation tend to centre on deliberate attempts by the *state* to influence socially valuable behaviour by establishing, monitoring and enforcing legal rules. At their broadest, definitions of regulation are seen as encompassing *all* forms of social control, whether intentional or not, whether imposed by the state or other social institutions.[7] Legal scholarship has a tendency to focus on the narrower definitions, in contrast to regulatory scholarship, which leans towards the broader definitions.

2. DEFINITION OF REGULATION AND PATENT LAW

IP law in general, and patent law in particular, respond to the general definition of regulation, in the sense that IP law and patent law can be seen as sustained and focused attempts to alter the behaviour of others according to standards or goals, with the intention of producing a broadly identified outcome or outcomes, which may involve mechanisms of standard setting, information gathering and behaviour modification.

There is wide consensus in legal scholarship that patent law was once introduced to alter the behaviour of others – citizens, groups, firms or communities – and trigger them to develop new goods and services and disclose underlying technologies, thus contributing to the establishment of (social and economic) welfare.[8] Patent law creates incentives by granting the patentee a temporary monopoly on the patented invention in return for the disclosure of the description of the invention. Patent law establishes competent authorities and prescribes patentability criteria, formal requirements and granting procedures. In doing so, patent law regulates two facets. First, by regulating the granting procedure enabling competent patent offices (public authority) to grant patents (exclusive rights) in accordance with the criteria determined in the patent law/treaty, patent law regulates the vertical relationship between the government and the citizen. Second, by defining the contours of the right in the post-grant phase between the patent holder and the potential licensees and the public at large, patent law governs the horizontal relationship (to some extent) amongst citizens.[9]

Notwithstanding the consensus in legal scholarship on the incentive/reward function of the patent system, few legal scholars explicitly endorse the view that

7 B. Morgan/K. Yeung, *An Introduction to Law and Regulation. Text and Materials,* Law in Context Series (Cambridge: 2007), 3–4.

8 G. Van Overwalle/E. van Zimmeren, 'Functions and Limits of Patent Law', in: E. Claes/W. Devroe/B. Keirsbilck (eds.), *Facing the Limits of the Law* (Berlin/Heidelberg: 2009), 415–442 and the literature cited there.

9 The distinction between the horizontal and vertical relationship is especially common in European law, for instance with respect to the effects of different kinds of legislative instruments (Treaty provisions, Regulations, Directives), see Van Overwalle/van Zimmeren (2009, supra n. 8).

the patent law community should introduce a regulatory theory of patents that sees patent law as regulating primary conduct in the innovation process.[10] In contrast, the viewpoint that patent law should be conceived as regulation clearly resonates in the international Declaration on Patent Protection of 2014.[11] The Declaration clearly stipulates that:

> As a framework regulation for innovation markets, the patent system needs to be tailored to the innovation process, which it is supposed to serve, and to the competitive environment, within which it must operate. In order to ensure an efficient functionality of the patent system as an innovation policy tool, patent rights ought to be defined, justified and continually reconsidered by reference to their socio-economic benefits and costs.[12]

The Patent Declaration continues:

> The patent system's primary regulatory purpose is to prevent the market from failing to produce technical knowledge at adequate levels. The overriding rationale is that, absent patent protection, there may be insufficient incentives to invent (*i.e.* to invest in research and development) and to innovate (*i.e.* to exploit the commercial opportunities a new invention makes possible), because others cannot be excluded from appropriating the benefits without sharing the costs.[13]

III. THEORIES OF REGULATION

1. THEORIES OF REGULATION IN GENERAL

Regulation scholarship has developed different theories of regulation over the years. Morgan and Yeung define a theory of regulation as a set of propositions

---

10 See S. Ghosh, 'Patents and the Regulatory State: Rethinking the Patent Bargain Metaphor after Eldred', *Berkeley Technology Law Journal* (2004), 1, available at: www.ssrn.com (last visited 11 September 2015); C. Godt, *Eigentum an Information* (Tübingen: 2007), 415 ff., 572; M. Lemley, 'Faith-Based Intellectual Property', 62 *UCLA Law Review* (2015), 1328, available at: www.ssrn.com (last visited 11 September 2015): 'IP rights are a form of government regulation of the free market designed to serve a useful social end – encouraging innovation and creation' and 'IP rights represent government interventions in the marketplace'.

11 Declaration on Patent Protection. Regulatory Sovereignty under TRIPS, Munich, 15 April 2014, available at: http://www.ip.mpg.de/en/pub/news/patentdeclaration.cfm (last visited 31 March 2015). The Declaration is a well-wrought and solid declaration on patent law, initiated by the Max Planck Institute for Innovation and Competition and prepared by a wide panoply of international patent scholars. The author was one of the members of the Drafting Committee of the Declaration.

12 Declaration on Patent Protection. Regulatory Sovereignty under TRIPS, Munich, 15 April 2014 (ibid.).

13 Declaration on Patent Protection. Regulatory Sovereignty under TRIPS, Munich, 15 April 2014 (ibid.).

or hypotheses about why regulation emerges, which actors contribute to that emergence and the typical patterns of interaction between regulatory actors.[14] Morgan and Yeung point to a *first* prominent theory stream, captured under the term *public interest theories* of regulation. This stream attributes to legislators (and others responsible for the design and implementation of regulation) a desire to pursue collective goals with the aim of promoting the general welfare of the community.[15] One stream within the public interest theory of regulation focuses on welfare economics approaches and articulates regulatory goals in terms of *economic* efficiency.[16] This economic version of public interest theory suggests that regulation is a response to imperfections in the market known as market failures.[17] Regulation is seen here 'as the necessary exercise of collective power through government in order to secure market failures to protect the public from such evils as monopoly behaviour, destructive competition, the abuse of private economic power, or the effects of externalities'.[18] Regulation is justified because regulation can do what the market cannot. The view of regulation here is essentially instrumental: regulation is cast as a social practice that functions as a means to an end, namely as a means to maximise general welfare conceived in terms of maximising allocative efficiency. A second stream within the public interest theory of regulation focuses on *substantive political* approaches and includes other political goals.[19] Whereas the economic version defines collective welfare mainly in terms of efficient resource use, the more political version also entails values such as social justice and redistribution, and places more emphasis on the intrinsic value of participation through a process of dialogue.[20] A third stream within the public interest theory of regulation points to *procedural political* approaches,[21] stressing the need for adequate procedures and minimising the effects of power inequalities, echoing Habermas' 'ideal speech situation'.[22]

A *second* set of theories of regulation encompasses so-called *private interest theories* of regulation. These theories are premised on the assumption that regulation emerges from the actions of individuals or groups motivated to maximise their self-interest. In this approach, regulation has the tendency to

14 Morgan/Yeung (2007, supra n. 7), 16.
15 Morgan/Yeung (2007, supra n. 7), 18.
16 Morgan/Yeung (2007, supra n. 7), 18.
17 A. Ogus, *Regulation: Legal, Form and Economic Theory* (Oxford: 2004).
18 A. Ogus (2004, supra n. 17).
19 Morgan/Yeung (2007, supra n. 7), 26.
20 Morgan/Yeung (2007, supra n. 7), 26. Also see C. Sunstein, *After the Rights Revolution: Reconceiving the Regulatory State* (Cambridge, MA: 1990).
21 Morgan/Yeung (2007, supra n. 7), 36.
22 J. Habermas, 'The Public Sphere: An Encyclopedia Article 1964', 3 *New German Critique* (1974), 49, 55. For more, see T. Prosser, *Nationalised Industries and Public Control: Legal, Constitutional and Political Issues* (Oxford: 1986).

benefit narrow special interests, rather than to promote collective welfare.[23] Private interest theories of regulation gained prominence in the context of the discussion on deregulation. Whereas public interest theories stress market failure and the capacity of regulation to correct such failures, private interest theories instead stress regulatory failure.[24]

A *third* and last category of theories includes *institutionalist theories* of regulation, which give special attention to the increasing role of (public or private) organisations, institutions and systems in regulatory dynamics.[25]

Looking at the role of law in the three categories of theories of regulation, through the lens of regulation scholarship, provides a multi-faceted picture. Public and private interest theories accord a *facilitative* role to law:[26] law functions as an instrument to achieve the chosen public or private interest objectives.[27] In contrast, institutionalist approaches tend to downplay law's role in achieving regulatory goals, and accord to law something of a *coordinating* function:[28] non-legal organisational and systemic dynamics are crucial to regulatory outcomes and law's role is to structure interactions between participants, rather than to shape the substance of the regulatory issue.

Besides regulation scholarship, legal scholarship has also reflected on the role of law and regulation. In contemporary legal theory, it has been argued that the major function of law is the *regulatory* function: law regulates relations between the authorities and the citizens, and amongst citizens.[29] Legislation, provided it is dynamic and customised according to the changes within society, is regarded as a useful instrument to solve complex problems within society. By drafting, applying, interpreting and enforcing the rules, law coordinates the interactions between the authorities and the people (vertical relationship) and between persons (horizontal relationship). In this way, a framework for a coordinated and efficient society may be created. Translating legal scholarship into regulation parlance on this point suggests that law plays a *facilitative* role here: law as an instrument for shaping social behaviour,[30] or as a vehicle for securing (more or less) collective outcomes.

In addition to its regulatory function, law has the function of *providing legal guarantees*.[31] Today's society expects the law to protect its citizens against illegitimate action by the authorities and other citizens. A major aim

23 Morgan/Yeung (2007, supra n. 7), 43.
24 Morgan/Yeung (2007, supra n. 7), 43.
25 Morgan/Yeung (2007, supra n. 7), 53.
26 Morgan/Yeung (2007, supra n. 7), 76.
27 Morgan/Yeung (2007, supra n. 7), 41.
28 Morgan/Yeung (2007, supra n. 7), 76.
29 E. Claes/W. Devroe/B. Keirsbilck, 'The Limits of the Law', in: E. Claes/W. Devroe/ B. Keirsbilck (eds.), *Facing the Limits of the Law* (Berlin/Heidelberg: 2009), 1–24.
30 See Morgan/Yeung (2007, supra n. 7), 6, 51.
31 Claes et al. (2009, supra n. 29), 1–24.

of legislation is to regulate the relations between authorities and citizens and citizens amongst themselves in such a way that the most balanced, effective and defendable coherent set of legal norms is safeguarded. Such a balanced legal system should grant each citizen concerned access to an effective enforcement mechanism and the capacity to act in the public interest. This includes access to the formal, legislative decision-making process and access to the courts. We are inclined to think that law also plays a *facilitative* role here.

Last but not least, law also has a *symbolic* function. Law can additionally be regarded as a mechanism to clarify the binding values within a specific society.[32] It is an instrument to determine, establish and publicly disseminate a statement of the norms valued highly in that society. Regulation scholars prefer to refer to the law's role here as an *expressive* role: law as institutionalising values.[33]

2. THEORIES OF REGULATION AND PATENT LAW

It is generally agreed that patent law aims at serving both the public and the private interest.[34] The *public* interest is served through the development of goods and services to the benefit of customers, citizens, patients, etc. In addition, the public interest is served by the dissemination of the technical information embedded in the patent specification. The *private* interest of the inventor is guaranteed through the grant of a limited monopoly right, as a reward for creativity and inventiveness, including necessary investments in research and development efforts.[35] Although the debate on the legitimation of IP and patent systems has a long and turbulent history, the present consequentialist, utilitarian justification, focusing on both the incentive to invent/innovate and the incentive to disclose argument,[36] is probably most accepted to date.

The *ratio legis* of patent law as described here suggests that the patent system fits within the *public interest theory of regulation*, as its *major* and overriding goal is to pursue collective goals with the aim of promoting the welfare of the community. Even though it is recognised that both the public and the private interest are accommodated in patent law, the idea has gained ground in contemporary legal scholarship that (private) patent rights are not an end in themselves, but are designed to serve a wider (public) interest. Private rights

---

32 Claes et al. (2009, supra n. 29), 1–24.

33 See Morgan/Yeung (2007, supra n. 7), 6.

34 See Van Overwalle/van Zimmeren (2009, supra n. 8) and the many references there.

35 D. Gervais, *The TRIPs Agreement. Drafting History and Analysis* (London: 2003), 81, point 2.10.

36 For more on this theory, as well as the other justifications theories, see S. Sterckx, 'The Ethics of Patenting – Uneasy Justifications', in: P. Drahos (ed.), *Death of Patents* (Oxon: 2005), 175–211.

are subordinate to the public interest: public interest objectives are achieved through accommodating the private interest. The cases under study demonstrate very clearly that the current patent system is premised on an implicit 'social contract', aiming at balancing public and private rights, with some jurisdictions prioritising public interests. In Case 2 (medical research), various jurisdictions supported the view that the public interest function prevails, in recognising patent rights (private interest) to serve as a positive incentive for the production of drugs and therapies important in health care (public interest), but remedying some of the perceived hindering effects via compulsory licences, whenever the exercise of the private rights (e.g. refusals to license) threaten the public interest.

Within the category of the public interest theory of regulation, patent law seems to fit the second sub-school, namely *welfare economics approaches*. Patent law can be seen as a tool to regulate market failures, to provide legal guarantees and – to a lesser extent – to embed values.

a) Remedying Market Failure

Market Failure

It is commonly argued that current patent law institutionalises patents as an instrument for the rightholder to recover his/her *investments* in research and development,[37] and that patent law sets forth goals in terms of responses to imperfections in the market known as market failures.[38]

The cases under study indicate that over the past decades, patent law has expanded in the *pre-grant* arena – more particularly in terms of patentable subject matter – in order to provide incentives to invest and innovate in new technological areas, most notably biotechnology. The scope of patentable subject matter has been considerably stretched by the European Patent Office (EPO) and the EU (Biotechnology Directive of 1998),[39] thereby adapting patent law to the new realities of genetics. In the field of biotechnology, patent protection is now available for micro-organisms, plants, animals and elements isolated from the human body, including genes and stem cells. The trend of extending patentable subject matter to biological material, and the coming into operation

---

37 See D. Guellec/B. van Pottelsberghe de la Potterie, *The Economics of the European Patent System* (Oxford: 2007).

38 Even though it is argued that without a patent system in place, a stimulus would be lacking to do research and development, economic studies on this presumption are inconclusive. In fact, the effect of patents on innovation and diffusion depends on particular features of the *patent regime*. See for a brief explanation: OECD, *Patents and Innovation: Trends and Policy Changes* (Paris: 2004), available at: http://www.oecd.org/science/sci-tech/24508541.pdf (last visited 18 July 2017), 9–10.

39 Directive 98/44/EC of 6 July 1998 of the European Parliament and of the Council on the legal protection of biotechnological inventions, OJ L 213, 30 July 1998, 13.

of the Biotechnology Directive, has been enticed by the concern that without patent protection, research and development in the life sciences would be endangered. The Biotechnology Directive explicitly points to the need for patent protection to stimulate investment and innovation in the biotechnology sector.[40] The far-reaching idea of extending patent protection to human genes, as elements isolated from the human body or otherwise produced by means of a technical process, 'even if the structure of that element is identical to that of a natural element' (Art. 5 Biotechnology Directive) – which has been said to be at odds with the novelty requirement – bears witness to this strong conviction that patents are needed to spur investment and innovation in human biotechnology,[41] and may be inspired by the concern that without patent protection investment and research into genetic diseases and adequate cures would not take place. In the meantime, research has demonstrated that patent protection did not function as a stimulus to conduct (upstream) diagnostic research, but may have played a role in the development of (downstream) therapies and cures.[42]

The cases under study further point to the use of a specific mechanism in the *post-grant* area to respond to particular facets of market failure, notably the exhaustion principle. As is fairly well known, the exhaustion principle entails that once a patented product is put on the market with the consent of the patent owner, that physical object can freely circulate (and be resold), as the patent is exhausted with regard to that specific object. Over time, various legitimation

---

40 Recital 1 states: 'Whereas biotechnology and genetic engineering are playing an increasingly important role in a broad range of industries and the protection of biotechnological inventions will certainly be of fundamental importance for the Community's *industrial development*'. Recital 2 sets forth: 'Whereas, in particular in the field of genetic engineering, research and development require a considerable amount of high-risk *investment* and therefore only adequate legal protection can make them profitable' (emphasis added).

41 During the discussions within the *First* Expert Committee on Biotechnological Inventions of the European Commission (set up in the framework of Art. 16(c) of the Biotechnology Directive to advise the European Commission on patent law in the field of biotechnology and genetic engineering, with an inaugural meeting on 16 December 2002), EPO and EU officials were gradually willing to admit – albeit in a subdued voice or off the record – that the severely contested patentability of human genes as phrased in Art. 5 of the Biotechnology Directive was scientific nonsense, but was strongly inspired by the idea that this provision would spur the European biotech industry. The author was a member of the First Expert Group, and sub-rapporteur on 'Patentability of human stem cells', delivered 13 May 2003 (see https://ec.europa.eu/commission/presscorner/detail/en/IP_03_127, last visited 6 April 2022). For some information on the Second Expert Group, see C. Godt, 'Experts and Politics in Patent Policy: The Final Report of the Expert Group on the Development and Implications of Patent Law in the Field of Biotechnology and Genetic Engineering of the European Commission, 17 May 2016', 47(8) *International Review of Intellectual Property and Competition Law* (2016), 960–980.

42 US Secretary's Advisory Committee on Genetics, Health and Society (SACGHS), Revised Draft Report on Gene Patents and Licensing Practices and Their Impact on Patient Access to Genetic Tests, SACGHS, NIH (Bethesda, MD: 2010).

theories for the enactment of the exhaustion principle have been put forward.[43] First, it has been set forth that exhaustion is introduced to balance the rights of IP owners and the rights *in rem* of holders of related (IP-protected) physical embodiments. Second, it has been argued that the exhaustion provision is based on the idea that the charge for legitimate use of a protected product shall only be paid once, and that after an adequate reward an exclusive right is no longer necessary.[44] Third, it has been said that exhaustion aims at introducing a limit to the exercise of an IP right in order to stimulate free circulation of goods, and to enhance the dynamics of the marketplace. Most recently, the Court of Justice of the EU developed the exhaustion doctrine as an instrument to realise the internal market and the free movement of goods,[45] fully in line with EU law having strong policy goals of market integration. Fourth, the exhaustion theory shields against extension of IP via contracts, thus protecting other values than the effective operation of markets.[46] Based on this rough sketch, one could argue that the exhaustion theory is mainly based on a market (failure) logic, where free circulation and free movement of (once-patented) goods are quintessential.[47]

The cases under study also bring to the fore three additional *post-grant* instruments to deal with market failure. First and foremost, Case 2 (medical research) introduces the experimental use defence. The experimental use defence allows follow-on innovators to be shielded from infringement when modifying patent-protected products and processes, in order to develop and prepare the market entrance of even *better* products.[48] Admittedly, the experimental use defence does not shield such innovators from bringing the improved products onto the market, for which the consent of the patent holder is still needed.[49]

---

43 See G. Bonet, 'Propriété industrielle et libre circulation des produits dans la Communaute economique europeenne: la règle de l'épuisement des droits de propriété industrielle', *Gazette du Palais* (26 March 1994), 345–348; J. Schovsbo, 'The Exhaustion of Rights and Common Principles', in: A. Ohly (ed.), *Common Principles of European Intellectual Property Law* (Tübingen: 2012), 169 ff.; B. Ubertazzi, 'The Principle of Free Movement of Goods', in: I. Stamatoudi/P. Torremans (eds.), *EU Copyright Law. A Commentary* (Cheltenham: 2014), 38.

44 In this regard, the exhaustion principle may well fit within IP allocation theories.

45 The free movement of goods, the first of the four fundamental freedoms of the internal market, see Bonet (1994, supra n. 43).

46 See C. Godt, 'Conflict Configuration in Information Property', in the present book.

47 In this regard, the exhaustion principle might play a role in the prospect theory, see E. W. Kitch, 'The Nature and Function of the Patent System', 20 *Journal of Law and Economics* (1977), 265, 290; E. Hovenkamp, 'Patent Prospect Theory and Competitive Innovation', April 2016, available at: https://papers.ssrn.com/sol3/papers.cfm?abstract_id=2765478 (last visited 24 July 2017).

48 E. Van Zimmeren and G. Van Overwalle, 'A False Sense of Security Offered by Zero-Price Liability Rules? Research Exceptions in the United States, Europe and Japan in an Open Innovation Context', in: R. L. Okediji/M. A. Bagley (eds.), *Patent Law in Global Perspective* (Oxford: 2014), 379–417.

49 There, the initial patent right re-takes its full force, and the consent of the initial patent holder is necessary to exploit the improved products on the market (unless the patent holder is unwilling to do so).

Second, Case 2 (medical research) brings the compulsory licence to the fore. Many national jurisdictions entitle follow-on innovators to manufacture improved products without the consent of the initial innovator/patent holder by way of a compulsory licence for dependency in those cases where the initial patent holder is unwilling to consent to a licence agreement, in order to actually put *better* products on the market. Interestingly, in doing so, most national jurisdictions under study require that the compulsory licence is conditional on a (degree of) *economic* importance.[50] The compulsory licence for dependency also shines some light on how jurisdictions perceive the contribution of first inventors and follow-on inventors in addressing market failure, and on how patent rights are allocated between incumbents and new entrants.[51] This issue is at the heart of patent allocation theories. In a first school of thought, great weight is given to the first inventor, to the extent that the first inventor is entitled to block any follow-on innovator from marketing his/her improved invention. A second school of thought is inclined to share the benefits of innovation between the first inventor and follow-on innovators. This is realised via the concept of compulsory licences for dependency. Analysing Case 2 through the prism of patent allocation theories shows that a minority of member states opt for the first-inventor-takes-all principle and have not introduced a compulsory licence for dependency (the UK). A majority of member states have taken the sharing approach and introduced a compulsory licence for dependency. However, even though those countries seem to celebrate the contribution of follow-on innovators to innovation more, the effect of their intervention is minimised a great deal in practice, as various stringent conditions apply in order to be awarded a compulsory licence for dependency.[52]

Third, Case 2 (medical research) introduces the compulsory licence for public interest or public health. Some of the national jurisdictions under study entitle competitors – equally assuming that they are able to provide the market

50 The dependent invention must represent an 'important technical step/advance of major/considerable economic importance' (Belgium, Denmark, the Netherlands, Germany); 'a technically advanced invention significant for the national economy' (Estonia); or the invention must be of 'public interest' *and* represent 'a technical advance of considerable economic significance' (Slovenia) (see Case 2, medical research).

51 The demand of economic significance – and the many variations on this point – in the area of biotechnological innovation has led to legal uncertainty and has spurred quite some debate in legal scholarship on the legitimation and threshold of this condition. See C. Gielen, 'Algemeen belang: Criterium voor dwanglicenties bij biotechnologische innovatie' [Public interest: Criterion for compulsory licences for biotechnological innovation], *Bijblad Industriële Eigendom* (1997), 23–26 and the references cited there; G. Van Overwalle, 'Klinische proeven en volksgezondheid. Naar een herijking van het algemeen belang in het octrooirecht' [Clinical Trials and Public Health. Reassessing the Notion of Public Interest in Patent Law], *Tijdschrift voor Privaatrecht* [Journal for Private Law] (2000), 899–968.

52 Also see G. Van Overwalle, 'Policy Levers Tailoring Patent Law to Biotechnology. Comparing U.S. and European Approaches', *University of California (UC) Irvine Law Review* (2011), 435–517.

with *better* medicines or treatments – to produce their products without the consent of another innovator/patent holder if he/she is unwilling to exploit at reasonable prices.[53] Here too, various member states have required some degree of *importance* for allowing the compulsory licence to come into operation.[54] This condition has equally spurred debates in policy and academic circles.

Having explained and illustrated that current patent law institutionalises patents as an instrument for the rightholder to recover his/her *investments*, recent economic research indicates, however, that patents are used for a series of other functions than to recoup investment. Blind et al. studied German companies' strategic motives for patenting, and uncovered the following functions of patenting: protection from imitation, blocking competitors, reputation, exchange potential, and incentive/motivation.[55] Even though a strong voice in European patent law has adopted the normative ideal of patents as incentives as its prevailing justification for patent law, in view of the present use of patents as market instruments, it might be argued that patent law has been applied to achieve other functions than the ones initially proclaimed, and in some instances has even been diverted from its main initial objective, possibly leading to new forms of market failure, such as patent thickets.[56]

Property Protection

When reviewing patent discourse and discussing the market failure dynamics, a dissonant view can be witnessed in legal scholarship and practice. In a more traditional account of IP, property is being put front and centre: it is stressed that patent law is intimately interlinked with the concept of property.[57] Academic research stressing the property aspect of patent law often analyses (intangible) IP law and patent law in comparison to tangible property.[58] Such a view is

---

53 See E. Van Zimmeren and G. Van Overwalle, 'A Paper Tiger? Compulsory License Regimes for Public Health in Europe', *International Review of Intellectual Property and Competition Law* (2011), 4, 40.

54 A compulsory licence for reasons of public interest may not always be available in practice as the threshold to acquire such a licence is very high – quite often the licence can only be granted if an 'important' public health issue is at stake (Czech Republic, Denmark) (see Case 2, medical research).

55 See K. Blind/J. Edler/R. Frietsch/U. Schmoch, 'Motives to patent: Empirical evidence from Germany', 35(5) *Research Policy* (2006), 655–672; K. Blind/K. Goluchowicz/J. Rauber, 'Results of the second survey round of the German standardization panel', 8 *DIN Mitteilungen* (2013), 23–25. In the same sense, Guellec/Van Pottelsberghe (2007, supra n. 37).

56 G. Van Overwalle, 'The Impact of Emerging Market Patent Systems on Europe: Awaiting "The Rape of Europa"?', in: F. M. Abbott/C. M. Correa/P. Drahos (eds.), *Emerging Markets and the World Patent Order* (Cheltenham: 2013), 355–368.

57 Also see C. Godt, 'Conflict Configuration in Information Property', in the present book.

58 See J. C. Lai/A. M. Maget (eds.), *Intellectual Property and Access to Im/material Goods* (Cheltenham: 2016); A. Peukert, 'Rethinking the ontology of IP', paper presented at the 8th Annual Workshop of the International Society for the History and Theory of Intellectual Property theme around 'Intellectual Property and Resistance', University of Glasgow, UK, 6–8 July 2016 (paper on file with the author).

often based on human rights theory and practice.[59] At the level of the Council of Europe, the Grand Chamber of the European Court of Human Rights has confirmed that Article 1 of Protocol No. 1 of the European Convention on Human Rights of 1950,[60] guaranteeing the right to the protection of property,[61] equally applies to IP (*Anheuser-Busch Inc. v. Portugal*).[62] In doing so, the Grand Chamber reinforced the case law of the European Commission of Human Rights, noting that 'the holder of a patent is referred to as the proprietor of a patent and that patents are deemed, subject to the provisions of the Patent Act, to be personal property which is transferable and assignable. The Commission finds that a patent accordingly falls within the scope of the term "possessions" in Article 1 of Protocol No.1' (*Smith Kline and French Laboratories Ltd v. the Netherlands*).[63] At the EU level, Article 17 of the Charter of Fundamental Rights of the European Union of 2000 voices a similar viewpoint.[64]

The cases under study illustrate that the property approach is still very dominant in current patent law and practice. In Case 10 (traditional knowledge), it was crystal clear that protection of traditional collective techniques of

59 For the remainder of this section, the reader is reminded that at the European level, a two-layered human rights regime has been developed over time. First and foremost, human rights were recognised in the framework of the Council of Europe, and discussions resulted in constitutional documents such as the European Convention on Human Rights in 1950. The most comprehensive constitutional human rights document at EU level is the Charter of Fundamental Rights of the European Union of 2000, most recently consolidated in 2012. For more on this dual human rights regime, see G. Van Overwalle, 'Gene Patents and Human Rights', in: P. L. C. Torremans (ed.), *Intellectual Property Law and Human Rights* (Alphen aan den Rijn: 2015), 871–914 and the many references cited there.

60 Rome, 4 November 1950, available at: http://www.echr.coe.int/Documents/Convention_ENG.pdf (last visited 25 February 2015).

61 Article 1 of Protocol to the Convention for the Protection of Human Rights and Fundamental Freedoms (Paris, 20 March 1952), entitled 'Protection of property', stipulates: 'Every natural or legal person is entitled to the peaceful enjoyment of his possessions. No one shall be deprived of his possessions except in the public interest and subject to the conditions provided for by law and by the general principles of international law. The preceding provisions shall not, however, in any way impair the right of a State to enforce such laws as it deems necessary to control the use of property in accordance with the general interest or to secure the payment of taxes or other contributions or penalties'.

62 ECHR, Grand Chamber, 11 January 2007, *Anheuser-Busch Inc. v. Portugal* (Application no. 73049/01).

63 ECHR, 4 October 1990, *Smith Kline and French Laboratories Ltd v. the Netherlands* (Application no. 12633/87).

64 Article 17 of the Charter of Fundamental Rights of the European Union of 2000 (most recently consolidated in 2012, see Document 2012/C 326/02, OJ C 326, 26 October 2012, 391) stipulates under the heading 'Right to Property': '1. Everyone has the right to own, use, dispose of and bequeath his or her lawfully acquired possessions. No one may be deprived of his or her possessions, except in the public interest and in the cases and under the conditions provided for by law, subject to fair compensation being paid in good time for their loss. The use of property may be regulated by law in so far as is necessary for the general interest. 2. Intellectual property shall be protected.'

treatment would not be acceptable, because the description of such techniques would be difficult to accept as an item of property. In Case 2 (medical research), despite embracing human genes as object of property, none of the jurisdictions under study even considered transforming the traditional property rule regime (with the right 'to exclude') into a liability rule (with the right 'to take now and pay later'),[65] even though this had already suggested a long time ago to ease the effect of the patents on human genes in upstream research.[66] In contrast, Case 6 (farmers' rights) illustrates that some countries have introduced a farmers' privilege for transgenic plants in their IP laws, which aims at transforming a property rule regime into a liability rule regime, where the intent is not proprietary exclusionary exercise of rights, but remuneration.

b) *Providing Legal Guarantees*

Patent decision-making is a multi-level and multi-institutional governance field: patent law and policy is developed at different levels (global, European and national) and within various institutions at those levels.[67] It is questionable whether the *foreseen* mechanisms and the procedures currently in place *actually* guarantee adequate and wide access to the formal legislative decision-making process and to administrative boards (opposition and appeal) and (national) courts, enabling third parties to challenge the validity of a granted patent, and patent holders to claim infringement of their right.[68]

The cases under study clearly demonstrate that effective procedures are *foreseen* to apply for patent protection, to challenge the validity of patents (albeit only via revocation proceedings, not via opposition proceedings at the national level) (see Case 10: traditional knowledge), and to redress infringement (see Case 2: medical research). A different question, however, is to what extent the procedures foreseen are *actually* accessible. In Case 10 (traditional knowledge), some inconveniences come to the fore. At present, the premises, concepts, interpretation and requirements of patent law are not equipped to accommodate rights to patent protection for communities. Contemporary patent law is premised on the notion of the inventor as an individual, solitary and original

---

65 See G. Calabresi/D. Melamed, 'Property Rules, Liability Rules and Inalienabiliy: One View of the Cathedral', 85 *Harvard Law Review* (1972), 1089–1092.

66 G. Van Overwalle, 'Exclusive Property versus Open Commons. The Case of Gene Patents', 4 *The WIPO Journal: Analysis and Debate of Intellectual Property Issues* (2013), 139–158; G. Van Overwalle, 'Governing Genomic Data: Plea for an "Open Commons"', in: B. Frischmann/M. Madison/K. Strandburg (eds.), *Governing the Knowledge Commons* (Oxford: 2014), 137–153.

67 The current chapter will not address the issue of potential 'regulatory overlap' and duplicative regulation between different administrative agencies. For more, see T. S. Aagaard, 'Regulatory Overlap, Overlapping Legal Fields and Statutory Discontinuities', 29 *Virginia Environmental Law Journal* (2011), available at: www.ssrn.com (last visited 10 September 2015).

68 Van Overwalle/van Zimmeren, (2009, supra n. 8), 415–442.

creator, or a group of individuals (so-called joined inventorship), not collective entities. Since recourse to the patent-granting procedure is not available here, patent law stops short at some point in providing legal guarantees.

c) *Embedding Values*

Patent law is generally considered to be a primarily technical field of law. Many patent experts would even argue in favour of a purely technical, value-free type of (interpretation of) the law. However, the public debate surrounding the patentability of biological material and software has shown that the general public does appreciate a value-driven consideration of patent law.[69]

This approach resonates in the international Patent Declaration of 2014, which underlines that patents have to be regarded as serving a number of objectives, going beyond remedying market failure. The Declaration stressed that for the patent regime to be accepted as a regulatory institution, the operation of the patent system must also accommodate other public policies and interests, such as environmental protection, biological diversity, health care (including managing the risks of pandemics), nutrition, food security, technological and scientific progress, education, and security.[70]

In the cases at hand, notably in Case 2 (medical research), the expansion of subject matter has led to wide concerns. The principal concerns relate to the further appropriation and instrumentalisation of the human body through patents. Legal doctrine has responded to that concern by suggesting the further constitutionalisation of human rights in patent law.[71]

d) *Fostering Coherence*

On top of regulating market failure, providing legal guarantees and echoing values, an additional function of law in general, and IP law in particular, has been set out on the European level. Legislation at the European level is conceived as a tool to foster coherence and harmonisation. Coherence in multi-level regulation

---

69 Van Overwalle/van Zimmeren (2009, supra n. 8).

70 Declaration on Patent Protection. Regulatory Sovereignty under TRIPS, Munich, 15 April 2014, available at: http://www.ip.mpg.de/en/pub/news/patentdeclaration.cfm (last visited 31 March 2015).

71 C. Geiger, '"Constitutionalising" Intellectual Property Law? – The Influence of Fundamental Rights on Intellectual Property in the European Union', 37 *International Review of Intellectual Property and Competition Law* (2006), 371–406; G. Van Overwalle, 'Gene Patents and Human Rights', in: P. L. C. Torremans (ed.), *Intellectual Property Law and Human Rights* (Alphen aan den Rijn: 2015), 871–914; G. Van Overwalle, 'Human Rights' Limitations in Patent Law', in: W. Grosheide (ed.), *Intellectual Property and Human Rights. A Paradox* (Cheltenham: 2010), 236–271; C. Godt, 'Intellectual Property and European Fundamental Rights', in: H.-W. Micklitz (ed.), *Constitutionalization of European Private Law* (Oxford: 2014), 210–235.

has become a priority in the EU. Regulation at the European level is meant to coordinate and harmonise diverging (and possibly inadequate) regulatory policies and practices at the national level, to prevent national measures negatively impacting on the performance of economies and on business and citizens' activities. More positively, following certain principles and good practices for high-quality regulation in a coherent way, as well as facilitating coordination among regulatory institutions at different levels of government, can bring about improvements to the regulatory system as a whole.[72]

The EU's aspiration to establish regulatory coherence is enshrined in its foundational treaties, which proclaim that the EU is determined to be an ever-closer union of the nations of Europe (Art. 1 Treaty on European Union (TEU)), and which set forth that the main goals of the EU are peace, safety and an internal market (Art. 3 TEU). The Union enacts the measures to operationalise the internal market (Art. 26 Treaty on the Functioning of the European Union (TFEU)). The EU's legal tools to achieve regulatory coherence in the area of patent law have their basis in Articles 114 and 118 TFEU, which proclaim that the EU always serves the goal of harmonisation in the sense of approximation of laws.

As discussed in various cases under study, a prominent testament to the desire for harmonisation is the establishment of the Biotechnology Directive in 1998, which came about within the parliamentary machinery of the EU.[73] It has become clear that the Biotechnology Directive created a measure of uniformity between the patent laws of the various member states in the field of innovation in the life sciences. In terms of its vertical regulatory function – regulating the relationship between patent authorities and patent applicants – the Biotechnology Directive has undeniably had a normative effect and an 'upward' push,[74] in the member states, resulting in a certain *acquis communautaire*. The

[72] D. Rodrigo/L. Allio/P. Andres-Amo, 'Multi-Level Regulatory Governance. Policies. Institutions and Tools for Regulatory Quality and Policy Coherence', OECD Working Paper (2009), available at: http://www.oecd-ilibrary.org/governance/multi-level-regulatory-governance_224074617147 (last visited 10 September 2015).

[73] It goes without saying that the very *first* testimony of the harmonisation desire in the patent area is the development of the European Patent Convention in 1973 within the Council of Europe, putting an end to procedural differentiation amongst European member states, by establishing a centralised uniform patent application procedure.

[74] Harmonised norms often surpass average levels of protection that existed in the member states prior to implementation. This phenomenon of 'upwards' approximation is inherent in the process of harmonisation by Directive. A constant expansion of IP rights due to 'upwards' harmonisation is likely to create new obstacles to the establishment of the internal market, rather than remove them, see B. Hugenholtz, 'Copyright Harmonisation in the Digital Age: Looking Ahead', in: M.-C. Janssens/G. Van Overwalle (eds.), *Harmonisation of European IP Law. From European Rules to Belgian Law and Practice. Contributions in honour of Frank Gotzen*, CIR-Reeks vol. 23 (Brussels: 2012), 55–71.

Biotechnology Directive has led to fairly uniform rules throughout the EU with regard to patentable subject matter. As regards patent protection for genes from human origin, Case 2 (medical research) illustrates that harmonisation was achieved with regard to the protection of human genes (Art. 5 Biotechnology Directive) after a long and strenuous implementation saga in the member states. As regards patent protection for plants and animals, Case 6 (farmers' rights) indicates that harmonisation was accomplished concerning patent protection of transgenic plants and animals (Arts. 3 and 4 of the Biotechnology Directive) as all EU member states transposed the patentability in their national patent legislation. However, the Biotechnology Directive equally resulted in a certain degree of differentiation. As Case 2 illustrates, fragmentation arose amongst member states with regard to the scope of gene patents. A first and dominant approach was to grant absolute patent protection for human genes, whereas a second approach was to adopt purpose-bound protection for human genes.[75] These differing styles of interpretation result in legal uncertainty. Rather than enhancing the level of legal certainty, the harmonisation process temporarily resulted in lower levels of legal certainty, in other words in a 'short-term negative effect on legal certainty'.[76] And as Case 6 makes clear, differentiation amongst jurisdictions equally emerged with regard to the scope of protection offered to the holder of a patent on transgenic plants or animals. As Case 10 (traditional knowledge) shows, harmonisation efforts sometimes totally fail, and do not unify the law between member states at all, especially when the Directive in question leaves a broad measure of discretion to the member states as a result of political compromise.

In terms of its horizontal regulatory function – regulating the relationship amongst patent owners, and between patent owners and third parties, such as potential licensees or patients – the Biotechnology Directive had hardly any effect in the member states. The impetus for introducing a compulsory licence for dependency and a compulsory licence for public health in the patent laws of the member states did not stem from the Biotechnology Directive. On the other hand, the initiative to implement a compulsory cross-licensing regime between the patent regime and the plant breeders' rights system did originate in the Biotechnology Directive (Art. 11).

On balance, the EU harmonisation effort in the field of patent law and life sciences has produced mixed results.

---

75 As explained in the synthesis report on Case 2, absolute patent protection is provided in Belgium, Denmark, the Netherlands, Norway and Spain. In contrast, purpose-bound protection is available in France, Germany and Italy.

76 Hugenholtz (2012, supra n. 74).

IV. INSTRUMENTS OF REGULATION

1. INSTRUMENTS OF REGULATION IN GENERAL

Within regulation scholarship, instruments and techniques to regulate behaviour have been studied, and a variety of classification schemes have been suggested. The criterion for classification which is commonly adopted is the underlying modality through which behaviour is sought to be controlled.[77] Morgan and Yeung have identified five mechanisms to regulate behaviour: command, competition, consensus, communication and code.[78] Other scholars have introduced similar[79] or divergent[80] categorisations, but in our view, the work of Morgan and Yeung surpasses those analyses in the way their analysis assists in understanding the relationship between regulation and law. They recognise the facilitative and/or coordinative role of law in putting regulatory instruments to work.[81] Studying the typology of Morgan and Yeung in more depth, and examining their taxonomy and the specificities of regulatory instruments reveals that regulation mostly involves the promulgation of legal rules.

Let us now take a closer look at the five mechanisms Morgan and Yeung have recognised. In doing so, close attention is paid to the role law plays in accommodating those techniques, and in allowing them to be performant instruments.

A first set of mechanisms encompasses *command* mechanisms, also referred to as 'classical' regulation[82] or 'command-and-control' regulation.[83] Command mechanisms involve the promulgation of legal rules prohibiting specified conduct, underpinned by coercive (civil/criminal) sanctions.[84] Command usually encompasses legal rules prohibiting specified conduct, underpinned by civil/criminal sanctions.[85] The law plays a *facilitative* role here and operates in its 'classical' form, through rule-based coercion (active facilitation of regulation).[86]

A second type of mechanisms includes *competition*. Competition arises from rivalry between competing units on the market.[87] There is increasing interest in

---

77 Morgan/Yeung (2007, supra n. 7).

78 Morgan/Yeung (2007, supra n. 7), 80, 92, 103.

79 See e.g. L. Lessig, *Code. Version 2.0* (New York: 2006), suggesting that regulation can take four different forms: law, market, norms and architecture.

80 See e.g. N. Moloney, *The Oxford Book of Regulation* (Oxford: 2010), 447, with his distinction between regulatory and non-regulatory tools. Or A. Estache/L. Wren-Lewis, *The Oxford Book of Regulation* (Oxford: 2010), 373.

81 See supra section III.1.

82 Morgan/Yeung (2007, supra n. 7), 80.

83 Morgan/Yeung (2007, supra n. 7), 80.

84 Morgan/Yeung (2007, supra n. 7), 80, 91.

85 Morgan/Yeung (2007, supra n. 7), 80, 91.

86 Morgan/Yeung (2007, supra n. 7), 80.

87 Morgan/Yeung (2007, supra n. 7), 85.

other regulatory tools than legal compulsion to harness the competitive forces arising from rivalry between competing units, and in financial incentives to encourage desired behaviour.[88] Such incentives can be either negative (conduct is legally unconstrained, but if a firm chooses to act in an undesired way it must pay a charge) or positive (if a firm chooses to act in a desired way it is awarded a subsidy).[89] The wide variety of tools available are commonly referred to as economic instruments, and include charges, taxes, subsidies, tradeable emission/property rights and changes in liability regimes.[90] Such economic instruments are intended to elicit the desired behavioural change through the operation of the competitive forces in the market, hence the term competition-based tools.[91] The law plays a *facilitative* role here as well, albeit more subdued and less visible as compared to command-based tools: the law provides a stable institutional framework that ensures the freedom and security of economic transactions in the market.[92]

A third category of instruments includes *consensus*. Consensus relies on cooperation and rests primarily on the consent of the participants to regulate behaviour.[93] This category includes regulatory tools ranging from self-regulation to techniques involving various forms of cooperative partnerships between state and non-state actors to seek to regulate behaviour.[94] They can be distinguished from other types of regulatory tools on the basis that these mechanisms rest primarily on the consent of participants. As said, self-regulation is relevant in this regard:[95] the stereotypical or 'classical' form of self-regulation is generally understood as an agreement between those involved in the relevant activity to regulate their own behaviour through the creation of some kind of regulatory body entrusted with the tasks of promulgating and enforcing a code of conduct governing the behaviour of its members. The power of a regulatory body to develop, apply and enforce a code of conduct derives from the agreement of its members in which the ultimate sanction for violation is typically expulsion from membership.[96] Other scholars refer to self-regulation as 'principles-based regulation', characterised by 'thinning back the extensive rulebook'.[97] Here too, the law plays a *facilitative* role: the law provides a stable institutional framework within which the security of

88 Ogus (2004, supra n. 17).
89 Ogus (2004, supra n. 17).
90 Morgan/Yeung (2007, supra n. 7), 85.
91 For more, see S. Breyer, *Regulation and its Reforms* (Cambridge, MA: 1982), 156–181.
92 Morgan/Yeung (2007, supra n. 7), 91, also see 92.
93 Morgan/Yeung (2007, supra n. 7), 92.
94 Morgan/Yeung (2007, supra n. 7), 92.
95 See A. Ogus, 'Rethinking Self-Regulation', 15 *Oxford Journal of Legal Studies* (1995), 97–108.
96 See Ogus (1995, ibid.).
97 Moloney (2010, supra n. 80), 447. True as this may be, even a 'thin' rulebook is still a rulebook, which involves the law to be enforced.

contractual agreements or institutional arrangements is ensured,[98] and in which citizens' freedom of contract is respected, enabling them to enlist its coercive force to safeguard the security of agreements to which they have freely consented.[99]

A fourth set of tools relates to *communication*-based techniques. Such techniques include attempts to persuade and educate members of the regulated community.[100] Government-backed public education campaigns are the most familiar form of communication-based instruments.[101] Law plays a *facilitative* role here too, insofar as it confers a constitutional right on all persons to express ideas and opinions.[102]

A fifth and final category includes *code*, also referred to as 'architecture'[103] or 'techno-regulation'.[104] Code refers to design-based instruments that force regulatees to act in the desired manner.[105] Although at first sight the use of code or architecture appears to avoid the reach of law, law equally plays a *facilitative* and permissive role here. On closer inspection, the capacity to use architecture as a means of shaping and constraining social behaviour relies upon the freedom to mould and manipulate the physical environment through rights of property ownership of local/national authorities.[106]

2. INSTRUMENTS OF REGULATION IN PATENT LAW

Having identified five mechanisms to regulate behaviour – command, competition, consensus, communication and code – we now turn our attention to the type of instruments used in patent law. How did policy-makers in the area of patent law choose between the broad array of instruments in pursuing their chosen regulatory objectives?

---

98 Morgan/Yeung (2007, supra n. 7), 91, also see 95.

99 See Ogus (1995, supra n. 95).

100 Morgan/Yeung (2007, supra n. 7), 96.

101 Morgan/Yeung (2007, supra n. 7), 96. Also see K. Yeung, 'Government by Publicity Management: Sunlight or Spin?', *Public Law* (2005), 360–383.

102 Morgan/Yeung (2007, supra n. 7), 102.

103 Lessig (2006, supra n. 79).

104 Koops refers to techno-regulation in this context: 'technology with intentionally built-in mechanisms to influence people's behaviour', see B. J. Koops, 'Criteria for Normative Technology – The Acceptability of "Code as Law" in Light of Democratic and Constitutional Values', in: R. Brownsword/K. Yeung (eds.), *Regulating Technologies – Legal Futures, Regulatory Frames and Technological Fixes* (Oxford: 2008), 158. Also see R. Brownsword, 'Code, Control and Choice: Why East is East and West is West', 25 *Legal Studies* (2005), 1–21.

105 K. Yeung, 'Can We Employ Design-Based Regulation While Avoiding *Brave New World?*', 3 *Law, Innovation and Technology* (2011), 1–30.

106 Morgan/Yeung (2007, supra n. 7), 102.

Command-and-control mechanisms surface patent law in very specific circumstances. In patent law, the rules relating to enforcement of patent rights – embedded in Part III of the TRIPS Agreement (encompassing Arts. 41–49) and their translation into regional and national law – fit into this category. Article 41 TRIPS Agreement sets forth that '[m]embers shall ensure that enforcement procedures as specified in this Part are available under their law so as to permit effective action against any act of infringement of intellectual property rights covered by this Agreement, including expeditious remedies to prevent infringements and remedies which constitute a deterrent to further infringements'. The Enforcement Directive implements and details this set of international rules.[107]

As we can learn from the cases under study, most national patent laws provide legal guarantees in the area of knowledge production and innovation under the form of command-and-control instruments. A first working example relates to Case 2 (medical research) and patent holders, who want to stand up against alleged infringers: in most jurisdictions under study, they have a claim of injunction, (more or less) conditional on (serious) harm to their private interest. A second working example also relates to Case 2 (medical research) and follow-on dependent inventors, who can stand up to unwilling patent holders who refuse to license: in some jurisdictions under study, they have a compulsory licence at their disposal to temper the behaviour of the unwilling patent holder, conditional on some form of economic importance.[108]

Competition-based mechanisms seem to prevail in patent law. The dominant reading which permeates legal doctrine and jurisprudence is that patents are incentives to innovate, with attention to the policy role of patents as a means to stimulate innovation and recoup investment. Patent law and its rules incentivising particular behaviour (invent/disclose) to cure public problems, underpinned by a reward mechanism (private property rights), may well fall into the category of competition instruments.

As we can learn from the cases under study – most prominently Case 2 (medical research) – most national patent laws provide incentives to fuel knowledge production and innovation in the area of biotechnology, by providing patent protection for biological material – ranging from human genes and human stem cells via plants to animals – and processes.

Consensus-based techniques do pop up in patent law as well. Two types of dynamics can be at play here. The first are informal, consent-based norms which are transformed into formal norms. An example may well be the so-called morality clause (Art. 53(a) European Patent Convention), or the notion of fair and

---

107 Directive 2004/48/EC of the European Parliament and of the Council of 29 April 2004 on the Enforcement of Intellectual Property Rights, OJ L 157, 30 April 2004, 45.

108 For further comments on 'economic' importance, see supra section III.2.a.

equitable sharing (Recital 22 Biotechnology Directive). Both provisions are the result of consensus-making outside the legislative machinery, which later found its way into the formal legal framework. The second type are informal norms which do not result in formal norms, but are governed by way of self-regulation. Examples par excellence are the many patent pools and clearinghouses which are set up in the life sciences sector to deal with patent thickets and/or blocking patents.[109] Patent pools and clearinghouses often are agreements between innovator companies and/or universities, sometimes entailing a regulatory body entrusted with the task of enforcing a code of conduct governing the behaviour of its members. The cases under study do not really illustrate the use of this type of measure.

Code-based mechanisms are also at play in the patent area, most prominently in the agricultural sector. Sometimes inventor companies prefer biological mechanisms to secure exclusivity, rather than legal instruments, such as patents. A first key example is genetic use restriction technology (GURT). GURT, colloquially known as terminator technology or suicide seeds, is the name given to methods for restricting the use of genetically modified plants by causing second-generation seeds to be sterile.[110] A second prominent example are hybrid varieties. When crossing plant varieties, the traits of the resulting hybrid variety are often enhanced or the function of a biological quality is improved, as a result of mixing the genetic contributions of the parents.[111] More often than not, hybrid varieties cannot be further propagated, thus biologically limiting the further use of such plants. The cases under study do not really highlight the use of this type of measure.

V. CONCLUDING REMARKS

In the light of regulation theory, patent law in its vertical and horizontal dimensions encompasses all instruments of modern regulation to stir and

---

109 G. Van Overwalle (ed.), *Gene Patents and Collaborative Licensing Models. Patent Pools, Clearinghouses, Open Source Models and Liability Regimes* (Cambridge: 2009), 477; G. Van Overwalle, 'Patent Pools and Clearinghouses in the Life Sciences: Back to the Future', in: D. Matthews/H. Zech (eds.), *Research Handbook on IP and the Life Sciences* (Cheltenham: 2017), 304–334.

110 The question whether or not, and to what extent, patent law itself could and should be considered a means of socio-political regulation of technological trajectories is a subject which is very highly contested (I. Schneider, 'To Be or not IP? Exploring limits within patent law for the constitutionalization of intellectual property rights and the governance of synthetic biology in human health', 37 *Revista de Derecho y Genoma Humano [Law and the Human Genome Review]* (2012), 193–233) and which will not be discussed here.

111 This phenomenon is called heterosis or hybrid vigour. Hybrid breeding methods are used in maize, sorghum, rice, sugar beet, onion, spinach, sunflowers and broccoli.

control behaviour. Against this background, the BIP cases reveal that the patent mechanisms related to command and control and to competition have been well reflected by legal doctrine. The command-and-control instruments are closely related to the vertical dimension of patents (*ex ante*), since the respective rules are closely related to the defence of the right. The country reports reveal that responses which focus on this dimension are characterised by clear-cut language. While the historic relationship between patents and competition was contentious, the country reports reveal that patent law has come to accept that competition is the central regulatory instrument to shape the horizontal dimension of patents. The country reports consistently refer to the relevant case law in all jurisdictions. However, rules which might foster regulatory instrumentality in the horizontal categories of consensus, communication and code are far less developed. This is reflected by the tentative language in the country reports. Nevertheless, the reports reveal that modern constitutional argumentation is filling the lacuna.

CONFLICT CONFIGURATION IN INFORMATION PROPERTY

Christine GODT

I. INTRODUCTION

How are conflicts around information property[1] construed? This is the central question driving the BIP project. The present chapter focuses on 'information property as an institution', and complements the co-editors' contributions on intellectual property (IP) 'as regulation' (Van Overwalle), on IP 'as means to secure access and the public domain' (Guibault), and 'on limits of morality' (Adcock and Beyleveld). This chapter is interested in how property structures conflicts between information property rights and other interests. In contrast to Geertrui Van Overwalle's contribution, which focuses on the incentive function of IP as an institution of innovation policy, this chapter directs the focus to conflicts between IP and 'other' interests: Do national responses to the BIP questionnaire reveal that property still hierarchically reigns over all types of conflicts? How does the modern world exactly define the content of an IP entitlement? Where do boundaries come from? How is the 'balance' of IP and other interests achieved?

The drive for asking these questions is prompted by the strong resistance in the 1990s to regulating intellectual property.[2] The conceptual backbone of this resistance is to understand IP just as ordinary property. 18th-century scholars transposed the notion of (public) sovereignty to the (private)

1 We conceive of 'information property' as a generic term encompassing all types of appropriation and commodification of information (acknowledging that doctrine considers raw information as – in legal terms – not appropriable). The terms 'intellectual property' or 'industrial property' as legal technical sub-terms indicate the conditions for appropriability. 'IP' abbreviates existing legal forms of 'intellectual and industrial property'.

2 Prime examples were the regulations on biopatents (in Europe and the US), limits on 'evergreening' practices (India), limits to the exclusionary power on standard essential patents (EU), compulsory licences (Thailand), and attempts to improve access and to limit excessive pricing for pharmaceuticals (Brazil, South Africa).

property right,[3] conceptualised as the most comprehensive right (civil law jurisdictions qualify this type of right as 'absolute'). Thus, property became the backbone of market economies in the 19th century, driving trade and industrialisation. All entitlements, control rights and profits are absorbed and channelled to the owner.[4] This rationale was transposed to IP. Its historic embeddedness in mercantilist policies which had assigned commercial privileges as public licences was substituted by the common phrase that 'an IP right is not a privilege, but a right',[5] secured by international public law (Art. 27(2) TRIPS)[6] and EU-law (Art. 17(2) EU CharterFR). This is the very foundation for conceiving of intellectual property rights as the basis for private ordering,[7] which has implications for the vertical relationship to the state and the horizontal one between fellow citizens:[8] once the requirements for the right to emerge are fulfilled, the state has no right to withhold the granting of the right (i.e. there is an 'entitlement' to the right). Vis-à-vis other citizens, property grants full autonomy and hierarchical control: unless mandatory,[9] legislative requirements can be 'contracted out' and courts often hold restrictive licence terms valid. Doctrine picked up this priority by rationalising that public regulation and competition law may steer *the use* of rights but may not interfere with *their existence*.[10] The principle of privity of contract was supposed to take precedence.

The BIP project, in contrast, was built on the understanding that this concept has faded away since the mid-1990s, for three reasons.[11] First, it has

---

3 M. Xifaras. *La propriété – Etude de philosophie du droit* (Paris: 2004), available at 'archives ouvertes' since 2014: https://hal-sciencespo.archives-ouvertes.fr/file/index/docid/1025305/filename/mxlapropriete-etudedephilosophiedudroit.pdf, 191, 437, 490.

4 The idea which goes along with this is not only that property is a 'natural right' (an element of central importance in the era of enlightenment). An element inherited by the *ius commune* is the idea that there are bodies of laws which are 'not created by a legislator', and therefore cannot be abolished – 'never die'. See A. Wijffels, 'Ius commune, Comparative Law and Public Governance', in: M. Adams/D. Heirbaut (eds.), *The Method and Culture of Comparative Law* (Oxford/Portland: 2014), 147, at 152.

5 On the history of this debate, C. Godt, *Eigentum an Information* (Tübingen: 2007), 511 ff.

6 Art. 27(2) TRIPS reads: 'Members may exclude from patentability inventions [for reasons of public policy] including to protect human, animal or plant life or health or to avoid serious prejudice to the environment, *provided that such exclusion is not made merely because the exploitation is prohibited by their law*' (emphasis added).

7 R. M. Hilty, 'Intellectual Property and Private Ordering', in: R. C. Dreyfuss/J. Pila (eds.), *Oxford Handbook of Intellectual Property Law* (Oxford: 2018), 898–930.

8 On these two levels of regulation (vertical and horizontal) see G. Van Overwalle, 'Regulation Theory and Intellectual Property Law', in this volume.

9 L. Guibault, *Copyright Limitations and Contracts* (Amsterdam: 2002) exposed how difficult the determination of 'mandatory' is.

10 Concisely reconstructed by A. Strowel/H.-E. Kim, 'The Balancing Impact of General EU Law on European Intellectual Property Jurisprudence', in: A. Ohly/J. Pila (eds.), *The Europeanisation of Intellectual Property Law* (Oxford: 2013), 121–142.

11 Strowel/Kim (2013, supra n. 10), 121–142.

become understood that IP is an instrument of competition, and does not enjoy priority over competition rules.[12] Second, a constitutional discourse emerged in the 1990s,[13] which gained momentum in the 2010s with the conception of the horizontal tension between rights,[14] and evolved into a reflection about a fully-fledged constitutional framework.[15] Third, modern legal thought strives to acknowledge complexity, and no longer to reduce complexity.[16]

While the BIP project was designed prior to the constitutional turn in IP, it started out with the hypothesis that modern IP adjudication will not simply follow an 'old-fashioned' property approach: modern societal conflict resolution depends on balancing.[17] If not directly embedded *inside* the codes of intellectual

---

12 The leading CJEU case is the joint judgments of 6 April 95, *Magill TV Guide*, C-241/91 P and C-242/91 P, ECLI:EU:C:1995:98. It spells out that misuse of an IP right combined with a dominant market position cannot be justified with reference to the property entitlement, sending the message that property holders are also subject to the rule of law.

13 A crystallising publication was J. Habermas, *Faktizität und Geltung* (Frankfurt am Main: 1992) which elaborated the idea of the *Gleichursprünglichkeit* (equal origin) or *wechselseitige Ergänzung* (129) of human rights and democracy. As a consequence, freedoms are never absolute but determined by the rights of others, though not only by rights of Kantian equals but by all socially recognised rights.

14 C. Geiger, '"Constitutionalising" Intellectual Property Law', *International Review of Intellectual Property and Competition Law* (2006), 371; G. Van Overwalle, 'Human Right Limitations in Patent Law', in: F. W. Grosheide (ed.), *Intellectual Property and Human Rights: A Paradox* (Cheltenham: 2010), 236; C. Godt, 'Intellectual Property and European Fundamental Rights', in: H.-W. Micklitz, *Constitutionalization of European Private Law* (Oxford: 2014), 210–235; L. R. Helfer, 'Intellectual Property and Human Rights: Mapping an Evolving and Contested Relationship', in: R. C. Dreyfuss/J. Pila (eds.), *Oxford Handbook of Intellectual Property Law* (Oxford: 2018), 117–143. An overview is provided by: C. Geiger (ed.), *Research Handbook on Human Rights and Intellectual Property* (Cheltenham: 2016).

15 E. van der Sijde, *Reconsidering the Relationship between Property and Regulation: A systematic constitutional approach*, dissertation, University of Stellenbosch, 2015, available at: https://www.researchgate.net/publication/339795976_Reconsidering_the_relationship_between_property_and_regulation_A_systemic_constitutional_approach; J. Drexl, 'Legal Challenges of the Changing Role of Personal and Non-Personal Data in the Data Economy', Max Planck Institute for Innovation and Competition Research Paper No. 18-23, 2018, 5–19, available at: https://papers.ssrn.com/sol3/papers.cfm?abstract_id=3274519 (in: A. De Franceschi/R. Schulze (eds.), *Digital Revolution – New Challenges for Law* (Cambridge: 2019)); earlier: J. Drexl, 'Les Principes de Protection des intérêts diffuse et des biens collectifs. Quel ordre public pour les marches globalisés?', *Revue Internationale de Droit Economique* (2003), 387–409; the Max Planck Institute's declarations on the 'Three-Step Test' for copyright (2010) and the 'Patent Declaration' (2014) are part of this movement, both available on the webpage of the Max Planck Institute: https://www.ip.mpg.de/fileadmin/ipmpg/content/forschung_aktuell/01_balanced/declaration_three_step_test_final_english1.pdf and https://www.mpg.de/8132986/Patent-Declaration.pdf.

16 L. Llewellyn, 'The Normative, the Legal, and the Law-Job: The Problem of Justice Method', 49 *Yale Law Journal* (1940), 1355; J. Braithwaite/P. Drahos, *Global Business Regulation* (Cambridge: 2000); on the various traditions in this field: R. Brownsword, 'Comparatively Speaking: Law in its Regulatory Environment', in: M. Adams/D. Heirbaut (eds.), *The Method and Culture of Comparative Law* (Oxford/Portland: 2014), 189–205; J. W. Singer, 'Property as the Law of Democracy', 63 *Duke Law Journal* (2014), 1287.

17 C. M. Rose, 'Crystals and Mud in Property Law', 40 *Stanford L.J.* (1988), 577.

rights, either adjacent public regulations or a novel use of proprietary institutions will absorb the necessary balancing and regulate from the *outside*. In order to unearth those structures, the empirical methodology of the factual approach was deliberately chosen: How do civil courts reason and argue a given case of conflict? The research hypothesis was that even if the 'epistemic communities'[18] in IP do not easily give way to the pressures of change, civil society, legislators and courts will find ways to limit the scope of property rights in socially acceptable ways. The question is: How is this achieved? How do jurists argue? How are collective/public/societal interests, which might concur or collide with IP right, accommodated? Our goal was to identify these adaptations to societal pressures, and to find a language to describe the changes. The chosen method is identification by way of comparison.

Parallel to the country reporters writing and revising their national reports (2003–2013), the overall IP discourse became more fine-tuned. Legislative changes were made to IP laws[19] – rebutting the early assumption of an unchangeable IP law. Courts explicitly or implicitly referred to constitutional rights and concurring public policy objectives.[20] These changes are reflected in the country reports. Yet the comparative analysis of the country reports unearths surprising differences in the national answers, and surprising effects of national regulation, both IP laws and adjacent regulation. All this begs the question: How do the findings of the BIP project impact information property theory? What is required to better understand information property?

This chapter aims for an answer in pursuing the following steps. First, it needs a language which steps out of the dominant property discourse but is still connected to the property discourse. It will therefore use the 'Hohfeld language', which will be briefly reiterated in section II. It is through this analytic lens that the conflict configuration in our BIP cases across jurisdictions is re-described in section III. The incremental findings of the BIP project will be re-thought in a modern, progressive framework of constitutional property analysis (section IV). Finally, conclusions will be drawn for modern IP theory (section V).

---

18 For an inquiry in the patent epistemic community see C. Godt, 'Experts and Politics in Patent Policy', *International Review of Intellectual Property and Competition Law* (2016), 960, 976 with further references to the social science literature, esp. I. Schneider, *Das Europäische Patentsystem* (Frankfurt/New York: 2010), 666 ff.

19 *Pars pro toto*: national transpositions of Regulation (EU) No. 511/2014 implementing the Nagoya Protocol, see e.g. §34a German Patent Code.

20 Most noteworthy Court of Justice of the EU in two landmark decisions: judgments of 18 October 2011, *Brüstle*, C-34/10, ECLI:EU:C:2011:669 (on wide interpretation of patent exceptions which protect human rights); and judgment of 6 July 2010, *Monsanto*, C-428/08, ECLI:EU:C:2010:402 (on the limiting function of the term 'function' in Art. 9 Biotechnology Directive).

II. HOHFELD REVISITED

Many modern property textbooks, regardless of whether they come from a common law or a civil law tradition, start with Wesley N. Hohfeld's[21] seminal paper 'Fundamental Legal Conceptions as Applied in Judicial Reasoning' (1913).[22] Here, Hohfeld deconstructs the standard definition of William Blackstone (the standard reference in common law) or of Carl F. von Savigny (the standard reference in civil law) as 'an absolute right to a thing against the rest of the world' (*in rem* right).[23] He re-defines property as a relation between people *with regard to* a thing. He draws up a typology of opposites and correlatives, signalling that the entitlement of the rightholder is equivalent to an *obligation* of another.[24] Hohfeld had a tremendous influence on modern property theory.[25] Not only did he provide a language for a common discourse between common and civil property law scholars,[26] he paved the way for property theory for industrial societies of the 20th century.[27]

---

[21] See only A. Clarke/P. Kohler, *Property Law* (Cambridge: 2005), 19–34; S. van Erp, 'Setting the Scene', in: S. van Erp/B. Akkermans (eds.), *Property Law – Cases, Materials and Text* (Oxford: 2012), 37, at 54 ff.

[22] 23 *Yale Law Journal* (1913), 16.

[23] Equally critical of this '*simplicité*', Xifaras (2004, supra n. 3), 8.

[24] For a profound discussion see Clarke/Kohler (2005, supra n. 21), 19–34.

[25] E. Engle, 'Taking the Right Seriously: Hohfeldian Semiotics and Rights Discourse', 3 *The Crit* (2010), 84–107.

[26] The differences in the reflection of property should not be downplayed. The connotation of the terms 'right', 'title' and 'interest' in English law and in civil law are different. There is even no consensus about the need for clear definitions. B. Holligan, Professor of Property Law at the University of Sussex, explains (e-mail exchange 16 August 2017): 'For Civilian property lawyers, it is of primary importance to find out who holds the right of ownership – the most important right in a thing. English lawyers are less concerned with the existence of rights than with the entitlements that rights generate. English property law is fundamentally organised around competing entitlements to possess land and moveable things. The idea of relativity of title means that the weight given to any right/entitlement is never fixed but always relative to the other rights that may exist. See for example the statement in Waverley Borough Council v Fletcher [1996] QB 334 per Auld LJ at 345: "The English law of ownership and possession, unlike that in Roman law, is not a system of identifying absolute entitlement, but of priority of entitlement." It follows that terms, under English law, are not fixed: While one can distinguish an 'entitlement to' a right or an interest (this would be a right or an interest which belongs to a particular person) from an 'entitlement to' do something (for example to possess land) …, a right may itself be an entitlement e.g. a right in land may give a person title to possess the land. … Where English lawyers speak of 'title to' land or moveable things, they probably mean the person who has the best right to possess the thing, not simply the person who has a particular right. … [Therefore] Sometimes there is no difference between 'right' and 'entitlement'. A right can itself be an 'entitlement'. … English lawyers are generally most concerned to resolve conflict between entitlements, rather than to work out in a deductive manner which persons hold which rights.'

[27] Xifaras (2004, supra n. 3), 9, referring to capitalism, and its complex, multiple interactions.

Lucie Guibault has earlier used Hohfeld's analysis for a qualification of competing rights to IP rights which can or cannot be contracted out.[28] The present contribution pursues different goals. First, it is in search of a comparatists' language understood by both common and civil lawyers;[29] Hohfeld's language serves to adopt a position as an observer of the second order.[30] Second, using his correlatives as a means of analytic description alienates the author's civil law imprint, and distances her from the modern German constitutional approach. Third, the idea of interrelated powers (as opposed to monolithic absolute claims) connects to the concepts of bundled differentiated rights in intellectual property law.[31] Fourth, the correlatives provide space to identify the counter-position to the property interest, which allows for a reasoning about the legitimacy of its interests. These are necessary preparatory steps for a later, more structured approach to balancing.

In 1913, Hohfeld opposed the idea of property as *dominium*, a right most absolute, by a relational reconstruction of a different kind, in which the non-rightholder may or may not have a legitimate legal position. At the time, neither a clear definition of the opposing entitlement nor a political perspective were his primary interests. He aimed at a description of the property entitlement by re-defining the opposing 'rights', in contrast to the preceding monolithic perspective of an *in rem* right. He devised two distinct correlations: jural opposites and jural correlatives, each with groupings of four pairs. The jural opposites are: (1) right/no-right; (2) privilege/duty; (3) power/disability; and (4) immunity/liability. The jural correlatives are: (1) right/duty; (2) privilege/no-right;

28 Guibault (2002, supra n. 9), 97–109. The focus of her book was the question of whether limitations are inherent in or external to property. For this question, she ultimately found no guidance in Hohfeld's re-construction. She found that his formal correlatives do not predetermine the qualitative weight of values behind limitations. Therefore, correlatives can be contracted out.

29 Very similar to the reflections on how the common law trust can be translated to civil law by D. Gruyaert, *The exclusivity of ownership*, dissertation, KU Leuven, 2016, digital copy available at: https://limo.libis.be/primo-explore/fulldisplay?docid=LIRIAS1836206&context=L&vid=Lirias&search_scope=Lirias&tab=default_tab&lang=en_US&fromSitemap=1.

30 Giving space for describing the observation of the observation, as demanded by N. Luhmann, *Die Kunst der Gesellschaft* (Frankfurt am Main: 1997). The essence is the insight that an observer cannot observe him/herself. In our case, the reporters cannot observe themselves, neither can I as an editor observe myself. The inevitable consequence is selective perception and 'blind spots'. The 'observation of second order' has the ambition to make at least the perceptible restrictions (in our case the imprinting by traditions of civil and common law) explicit.

31 Most notable in the 'barrier theory' (*Schrankentheorie*) of copyright. It already caters to an approach to the property entitlement that incorporates modern public interests and human rights. I deliberately stay away from transposing the German constitutional analysis of the three sections of Art. 14 German Constitution to the current context, because of its very specific historic context.

(3) power/liability; and (4) immunity/disability. As Alison Clarke explains,[32] this relational concept opens up the perspective that owners' entitlements are dynamic. While, analytically, perfect liberty is defined by an absence both of a duty and of a right, the concept implies degrees of liberties. Central to our analysis of the BIP cases is Hohfeld's reflection to the emergence of 'duties' and 'liabilities' of non-owners as the 'negative' side of property: while property provides 'privileges' to act, it produces (mirrored) 'duties' of others to endure. As much as property secures 'immunity' for example against a trespasser, the trespasser is 'liable' for his act.

While Hohfeld aimed at describing the liberty conveyed by property, he articulates legitimate restrictions to the obligation. The legitimate position of the non-rightholder is not reduced to foreseeability – as the *numerus clausus* and the publicity principle do.[33] The old property concept is based on the idea that well-defined property rights reduce conflicts to a minimum – as long as people are aware of the scope of the entitlement. Property rights are limited solely by the property rights of other owners. Other rights that relate to property do not, however, in principle qualify as limitations. The projected order is the one of the possessory bourgeois. Societal peace is upheld by mutual respect between economic equals. As long as property is transparent, no conflicts arise. Locke was aware of the conceptual problem. He justified the appropriation by the three famous provisos,[34] and made his democratic vision of this type of social order clear: those who *want* to possess, but do not, might either strive to acquire property by labour or leave the country.[35] Later contests of the 19th century (Lassalle/Marx) became side-stepped. In an un-ideological approach, Hohfeld puts in 1913 the jural relations between property holder and non-holder centre-stage and inquires about the various natures of the resulting relations.

This approach inspires a reflection about the contemporary information problem: with societies transforming from industrial into information societies, information becomes ubiquitous. Digitalisation renders information abundant, but not everyone 'owns' it (or is 'licensed', see Facebook's standard terms). Various statutory property rights in information give an incentive to innovate. Special sectorial laws (like data protection laws) define the conditions under which 'new' information can be appropriated. The basic assumption is that 'information' as such is a public good. IP laws rest on the assumption that property rights will only be attributed to qualified items of information, for example original works

32 Clarke/Kohler (2005, supra n. 21), 25.
33 Rose (1988, supra n. 17), 577.
34 J. Locke, 'On Property', in: *Second Treaty of Government* (1690), re-printed in Clarke/Kohler (2005, supra n. 21), 91–99, explained by Clarke at 87–90.
35 J. Locke, 'On Property', in: *Second Treaty of Government* (1690), re-printed in Clarke/Kohler (2005, supra n. 21), 91–99.

(copyright) and new inventions (patents). The underlying idea is Lockean. The creator/innovator mixes labour with existing things that are either private or in the public domain. Yet, while Locke was thinking primarily of the appropriation of existing resources like land and water, IP law is primarily about not-yet-existing immaterial things. While Locke focused on things to which the access of others was to be restricted (dominance by exclusion, becoming the prerequisite of contracts), IP rights aim at a power to direct others. The primary function of IP rights is to extend influence and to exert power over production and through chains.

It does not come as a surprise, then, that the effects of property in information have become contested in the age of information. Not only have the objects of appropriation become contested (individual DNA information), so too have the rights to information, both upstream (raw data, control of supply chains) and downstream (absolute protection beyond the disclosed industrial applicability; control of the production chain). The problem of justifying information property is similar in the age of Locke: he responded that property is justified by the possibility that anyone can acquire property by means of labour. This is the implicit social contract. Yet the underlying model is linear and builds on material: a manufacturer either buys or legitimately appropriates raw materials, and then sells his/her products. In contrast, the IP model departs from a network from the outset. Ideas *always* build on prior ideas. Innovation propels the ever-ongoing process of progress (new ideas). When transposing the Lockean paradigm to information property, three typical characteristics of 'information property' become clearer. First, the law defines the valuables (the original work, the invention) which society is willing to provide a property right for. Once established, the content of the object defines the scope of the right. Second, IP rules define the relation to preceding ideas upstream (with important differences between copyright and patents). Third, they define who later may use the property downstream. In this regard, tensions have arisen, since 'providers of information' claim continuing rights to pre-existing pieces of information, and 'users' claim legitimate access to information (for reasons of 'adding labour' or for constitutional reasons). They thereby challenge the underlying rationales.

It is obvious that the delimitations have become fragile. The content still predetermines the scope of the rights, but it is not definite, not final, not monolithic. The exact content of individual rights and duties (in the sense of Hohfeld) are not defined by the object, but by secondary law set by legislators or interpreted by practitioners and judges. The Hohfeldean analysis helps to distinguish various ('positive') entitlements, and to differentiate property from IP. While an IP right, as much as property, grants a 'right' to exclude everyone else, it is limited in time and by exhaustion (both characteristics of all IP rights), and submitted to exemptions and exceptions (e.g. private use, experimental use).

The IP holder has the 'liberty' to use it in competition, and has the 'power' to control the entitlement by allowing others to use it. He/she enjoys, in principle, 'immunity' from the legal powers of others. However, it flows from the basic rationale of the patent system that dependent patents are not immune from the dominant patent holder, save compulsory licences.

As regards the 'negative' side of the correlatives which Hohfeld defines as 'no-right', 'duty', 'liability' and 'disability', we had better come to grips with the specific character of information. As in general property law, the rest of the world owes to the owner the 'duty' to respect, has 'no right' to use the protected information, is 'liable' to the owner, and is 'disabled' if the owner refuses a contract. Yet the language of opposites and correlatives helps to describe the characteristics of IP relations that leave 'have-nots' in a more privileged position: in IP, rights are typically conditioned. The most important restriction is time. The rest of the world is free to use the information once the term has expired or the right exhausted. Some users enjoy 'privileges' (the opposite of 'no-right'), for example the right to cite or to use information for satire. Under conditions of market dominance, competitors are not 'disabled' to access the protected information (*Magill*,[36] *Huawei*,[37] infra section III.2).

Hohfeld gives a structure to the BIP analysis: rights and immunities – in the language of Hohfeld – can be 'constrained' by entitlements upstream ('providers'); and privileges and liberties – again in the language of Hohfeld – can be 'constrained' by entitlements downstream ('users'). In legal language, these constraints may not necessarily result in a denial of a property right as the 'better' right. However, recognising the 'interest' helps us to reason about possible justifying grounds. In this sense, we can re-order the 14 BIP cases into two groups, depending on when the IP right emerges in the flow of information, either after 'information providers upstream' have delivered or before 'users of proprietary information downstream' demand access. Information providers may constrain the powers of the property holder *because* the information becomes part of the property holder's subject matter. It neither impedes the emergence of the right because of lack of novelty, nor is the information in the same sense 'proprietary', so that we could draw an analogy to 'patent dependency'. It is to be understood similarly to the preceding proprietary 'raw material'. Yet the Hohfeldean language identifies an interest which is not simply absorbed by the 'public domain' as a proprietary '*nullum*'. Prerequisites become visible under which a tangible or intangible object can be appropriated.

---

36 CJEU judgment of 6 April 1995, *Magill TV Guide*, C-241/91 P and C-242/91 P, ECLI:EU:C:1995:98.

37 CJEU judgment of 16 July 2015, *Huawei*, C-170/13, ECLI:EU:C:2015:477.

III. A HOHFELDEAN DECONSTRUCTION OF THE BIP CASES

As explained in Part I, the 14 cases of the questionnaire are structured around three topical issues: (1) regulatory boundaries set by (non-IP) legislation (Cases 1–6); (2) individual and collective genomic information (Cases 7–10); and (3) innovation conflicts including academic institutions and novel social institutions (Cases 11–14). Adopting a 'Hohfeldean perspective' (correlatives), again, keeps the conflict configuration narrowly to rights. Yet it is this perspective which brings out the flow of information. In six cases, upstream information providers are pitted against IP owners (Cases 4, 5, 7, 8, 9, 10), and in eight cases, downstream access seekers/information users have interests opposed to the IP holders (1, 2, 3, 6, 11, 12, 13, 14). While we are aware that this one-dimensional simplification does not fit modern 'digital prosumers' (a constellation we did not include), the model is functional for the chosen cases because it brings up congruent characteristics for each of these two groups.

1. UPSTREAM INFORMATION PROVIDERS

The cases dealing with 'upstream information providers'[38] articulate the interface of incoming information as part of the later commodified information, thus Hohfeldean conflicts between property power and liberties. No BIP case focuses on classical subsequent *equal* 'dependent patents', or copyrights by which the younger work is inspired the older work. The BIP cases focus on 'incoming' *non-proprietary* information (Cases 5, 7–8, 10), but include one case on parallel property rights (Case 2),[39] and one case where proprietary information will trigger the creation of IP (Case 4). The information is neither 'licensed' nor 'sold'. The interface must be otherwise regulated. We chose conflicts between the property owner and interests mirrored by public funding (Case 4), triangular conflicts between IP, individual persons and group/collective interests (Cases 7–9), and internationally recognised autonomy rights of indigenous communities (Case 10).

Case 4, in Hohfeld's language, is about owners and non-owners ('users'). The question is whether public funding translates into (non-exclusionary) public property. The answers of the country reporters are homogenous: no. All the jurisdictions covered conceive of the information as 'private' (thus exclusionary); access rights are considered to be a question of lowered prices. The differences

[38] Cases 4: publicly funded data; 5: right to be named; 7: personalised genomic information; 8: human body as replicator; 9: family genomic information; 10: traditional knowledge.

[39] Which might be re-construed as dependency.

are not significant, save for the Netherlands and Slovenia. These countries have witnessed a debate about the publicness of data processed by public funds. The claim is that public funding shall translate into access (thus 'burdening' the rightholder and 'privileging' the user). This debate is interesting for the fact that the state is not binarily perceived simply as the owner *or* regulator, but as a promoter of potential future property for the sake of its citizens. The proprietary control of the state is to be subject to obligations.

Case 5, in a Hohfeldean reading, is about the relationship between IP (as an economic right) and the moral rights of authors, software producers and 'algorithm inventors/creators'. Copyright laws and worker inventions laws 'upgrade' the 'disabled' creator after transferring the economic right to a person holding a remaining, defendable moral right. The question the case asks is: What are the remaining rights of scientists? Do they have a different status because of a special constitutional protection, or does simple contract law apply? Interestingly, where reporters argued along the lines of standard copyright law and contract law, the dualistic or monolithic concept of their jurisdictions does not determine the final answer (e.g. because in 'monolithic' England, special law provides protection). Surprisingly, in pursuing the same regulatory goal, legislators install inverse tools (abolish or grant entitlements).

Cases 7–9 are, in Hohfeld's language, on triangular conflicts between IP, the protection of the individual and collective interests in genomic information. The country reports reflect strongly differing values across Europe. Whereas data protection/personality rights and the non-commercialisation principle are everywhere in place, strong differences exist as to how much individual or collective entitlements limit property 'immunities' or preside over group interests (stipulated in sector regulations). We identify a north–south split in relation to the value given to personality rights in biomedical research: the protection of personality rights is much stronger in Southern and Western European countries (due to data protection); the correlated rights of the property holder are consequently smaller. These differences mirror the extent to which the Oviedo Biomedicine Convention of the Council of Europe and the UNESCO Universal Declaration on the Human Genome and Human Rights have been absorbed.[40] Northern and Eastern Europe put – relative to patients and probands – a stronger emphasis on the freedom of research, both as individual freedom and as an institutional guarantee. While contracts in violation of these principles are deemed invalid, it depends on the tradition in procedural law which interests can be enforced. In no jurisdiction do probands and patients have the power to prevent the acquisition of property (copyright, patents). Interests of group

---

[40] Council of Europe, Committee on Bioethics, Chart of signatures and ratifications, 14 November 2017 (CDBI/INF (2017) 7 REV.

members can only be proceduralised if their interest is covered by an individual right or a public interest. The violation of the right to prior informed consent might trigger other remedies.

Case 10 is, on the surface, a case of entitlement and disability. Yet the case invites a reflection on the doctrinal problem of collective interests. The recognition of traditional communities has been in place in international public law since 1992. The editors were interested in whether the reporters were able to take up the challenge and reflect on information assigned to a collective entity. While the reporters were working on their reports, the status of indigenous peoples was strengthened by the UN Declaration on the Rights of Indigenous Peoples (UNDRIP) in 2007. Few reports refer to it, and few took up the challenge to reflect on how those rights could be defended under domestic laws.

Our set of upstream cases accommodates three types of counter-rights: public ones (here state funding = taxpayers), individual personality rights (as the inventor, as a human being (patient), as a research subject)[41] and collective interests of communities (families, indigenous communities, Creative Commons).

As expected, but to a surprising extent, we find that IP ground rules strongly differ across countries. Despite the fact that IP rights are broadly harmonised in Europe, on the country-specific level, both rules and their application differ widely. The popular narrative of 'international IP' emerges as a superficial statement. The comparative differences are due to how correlatives are conceived. Conflicts between proprietary rights and opposing rights are not exclusively governed by IP rules.

The upstream information provided is usually not identical to the later commodified information, only based on it. Despite traditional theory (a good description can be found in the Polish report to Case 9), and despite the lack of court decisions, the country reports cautiously link the incoming information to the IP right. The incoming information is not simply absorbed, as public domain information would be. Some reporters use the thought model of derivatives, to which the rationale of patent dependency is applied (a non-existent principle in copyright). The idea is that a later derivative might or might not be 'dependent' on a preceding chemical formulation. The preceding information neither qualifies as 'public domain' (appropriable 'by mixing labour'), nor is the copyright paradigm applied. Others refer to data protection or personality rights.

---

41 We did not include in our set of cases a case built on the CJEU judgment of 18 October 2011, *Brüstle*, C-34/10, ECR [2011] I-9821. The court decided on what the 'uses of human embryos for industrial or commercial purposes' means as stipulated as an exclusion from patentability in Art. 53 European Patent Convention (EPC) in conjunction with Rule 28(1)(c) EPC Implementing Regulations. The CJEU decided against a narrow interpretation of the rule, and extended the exemption to research experiments prior to the patent application. Thus, the moral value judgement exercises a preventive effect. For an in-depth analysis of morality in patent law, see Mike Adcock/Deryck Beyleveld in this volume.

We find that the upstream information environment influences the content of IP rights. In other words, the regulation of upstream information influences the content of IP rights granted downstream. While upstream information is not assigned as 'property', embedded legitimacies (public funding, moral rights, human autonomy and dignity) influence the set of rights held by the later property holder, for example in the form of 'prior informed consent' rights with (country-specific, and dynamically changing) legal consequences.

In this perspective, Hohfeld's analysis opens property law up to asymmetrical obligations, and paves the way for differentiations: while the patient who provided personal bodily information may not have 'a right' to veto a subsequent patent (although he/she would in some jurisdictions), the patentee might be obliged to inform the information provider (the patient).

2. DOWNSTREAM USERS

The downstream perspective[42] articulates claims of 'access' to information property once it is commodified. The interest in access is the object of various sectorial laws which protect *inter alia* individual occupational freedom and the public interest in competition and food security (Cases 1 and 6), health (Case 2), family, youth, and consumer protection (Case 3), or research freedom (Cases 11–14). These rights are articulated by competitors, patients, music consumers, farmers, universities as institutions, individual scientists, and writers. Yet these rights do not provide 'power' vis-à-vis the property holder. In Hohfeldean terms, they are 'privileges' or 'liberties' which (in theory might) burden the 'power' of the property holder. Yet Hohfeld connected liberties in a Kantian way with 'property', thus shedding light on legitimate liberties of non-owners. In the first four cases (1, 2, 3, 6), we designed conflicts framed by regulation; in the last four cases (11–14), framed by contracts. The boundaries in these eight cases have two characteristics in common: (1) a minus for the owner equals a plus for the access seeker and (2) it is for the sake of someone else's liberty that the property of the other is restricted. We are interested in identifying how modern law deals with this tension.

Case 1 (built on *IMS Health*)[43] was designed as a springboard, a warm-up case, alluding to the stream of cases starting with the famous CJEU decision in *Magill*[44] in 1995. The constellation pits the IP holder against 'disabled'

---

42 Cases 1: *Magill*; 2: *Myriad*; 3: *Napster*; 6: farmers' rights; 11: grant-back/reach-through; 12: use restrictions; 13: co-ownership; 14: Open Access/Creative Commons.

43 CJEU judgment of 29 April 2004, *IMS Health*, C-418/01, ECLI:EU:C:2004:257.

44 CJEU judgment of 6 April 1995, *Magill TV Guide*, C-241/91 P and C-242/91 P, ECLI:EU:C:1995:98.

competitors who depend on the commodified information to market their own idea, and therefore demand *access*. The CJEU grants this right on the conditions that: (1) the business idea of the competitor is novel; (2) it cannot be marketed without using the former; and (3) the competitor cannot reasonably build up its own structures. The decision is based on the (objective) principle of dynamic competition and the (subjective) freedom to operate. These principles apply to the grant-back obligation (in the modification). This reasoning became the primer for accepting IP limits set by 'outside' regulation (here competition law).

Case 2 (*Myriad*), using Hohfeld's lens, is about two entitlements to 'power'. Patent law has fine-tuned *access* rights between subsequent patent holders via various instruments which the country reporters could test when answering the case. The editorial interest was in the divergence of jurisdictions under a European Biotechnology Directive which aimed to harmonise in the first place. Strong tensions between interests (private/private, private/public) are mirrored by subsequent national transposing regulation. Originally, this case was designed to show how IP law regulates itself. In the course of the project, this case become a cornerstone for how interest collisions in IP are mediated. While formulated *inside* IP (and in this case the EC Directive is of little effect due to the European Patent Convention), the boundaries are pushed from *outside* IP laws: human rights implications create pressures – and trigger changes to adjudication.

Case 3 is on copyright. The base case and the first modification are modelled on the famous *Napster* case (downstream use). The core conflict between the IP holder and the users is embedded in constitutional values and various regulations on private use and overlapping levy systems. At the time of drafting the case, copyright had been strengthened by the EC. We expected resistance and the emergence of an *access* right based on constitutional values, *inter alia* developing further the statutory private copy exemption and levy schemes. The editorial interest was in how counter-rights are argued, for example as individual rights or collective interests. The hypothesis was that sharing music among young people would, under certain conditions, be exempt for the sake of youth and family protection. The reports reflect remarkable differences as to how policy-makers reacted.

Case 6 is interested in farmers' rights ('downstream users') in a setting governed by patent law and where plant varieties law is not applicable. Will the case be hierarchically decided by property (Hohfeld: power/disability)? Or will professional liberties be acknowledged (upgraded as 'liberties'), and if so, how are these argued? Can values stipulated in *lex specialis* regulation (here in plant varieties law) be generalised in comparable conflict situations? Does the group which generates the public good in the *lex specialis* (here farmers) play a role? The country reporters answered with great caution. Few discuss the possibility of a constitutional reading or a broadening interpretation of the new farmers' privileges inserted in patent law. Answers remain vague as to the possible result of a court decision.

Case 11 on 'grant-back', 'co-inventorship' and 'reach-through claims' aimed at the conflict between industry and public research institutions (on the surface in Hohfeld's language: 'power and liability') in three variants. However, modern academia is not a 'disabled user' of IP. It enjoys a special status, which is acknowledged in member state constitutions and in Art. 13 EU Charter of Fundamental Rights. The central question of the case is how research liberties are translated into law. The reports delivered two surprises on a very different analytical level. Firstly, as a legal technique, inverse rules were stipulated (the so-called professors' privilege was introduced in Italy, but abolished in Germany) to achieve the same goal (here technology transfer). Secondly, academic freedoms come out as weak, even in jurisdictions with strong constitutional research freedom (such as Germany). The reporters' answers do not mirror the social standing of academics and the economic importance which is assigned to research in information societies. In Modification 1, however, the situation is the inverse. Here, the moral right of inventorship is aligned with the research interest. This result can be explained by the strong individualistic foundation of IP law. In contrast, where only a research tool is licensed (Modification 2), and not the whole research project commissioned, the country reporters' answers mirror ambiguity. Many (but not all) jurisdictions rebut the 'reach-through claim', either based on research freedoms or on competition concerns. The strengthening of the subsequent researcher's right in Modification 2 is in line with the investment rationale of the property paradigm. The result is therefore not too surprising. Research interests and property rationale overlap: in fact, it is the second researcher who holds the power, and the first researcher claims upstream participation in downstream property (but overstretches the claim).

Case 12 complements the research scenarios in Case 11 with common 'use restrictions'. Contractual practice recognises field of use restrictions, territorial restrictions, and supply and distribution restrictions. These are broadly accepted under the property rationale, and only contained by competition law. Case 12 aims at how specific research interests (liberties) are articulated by the law in this legal environment. As is to be expected, the descriptive answers differ widely, as do the reasons given. What can be observed is a strong drive to universalise competition rationales, and to approach research and competition as public policies. This is not surprising considering the growing relevance of research for economic growth. The case – in this respect – complements Case 1, as an example of competition law providing boundaries to IP.

Case 13 focuses on the conflict between property and patients – in other words, the conflict between the individual economic right and the non-economic interest of a collective. The tested design idea is sharing ownership, as proposed by the US patient organisation PXE. The base case and Modification 4 test co-inventorship; Modifications 2 and 3 co-ownership. A strategic property title is difficult to reflect in Hohfeld's language. Two challenges were put to the country reporters: How do jurisdictions deal with collective interests in research (*interesses diffusos*)? How is the legitimate *objective* research interest reflected to put research results in the public domain? The base case and the first modification raise question of PXZ's legitimacy in having a say in the exploitation of the patent in the first place. Yet the legitimacy of the organisation as such was not raised by one country report. This may be due to the fact that the case was construed around a fixed number of identifiable patients; the organisation appears incorporated. Therefore, the spoor of (il)legitimate representation and its consequences on access rights, which, in practice, is a central problem, was not addressed. Answering the base case, most country reports dwell on the procedural eligibility of the inventor. Only few understand the challenge that PXZ's managerial input must first be qualified as part of the intellectual invention. The first modification appears to the majority even less questionable since PXZ is the owner (and not only the inventor). Here the problem was the collision with the internal guidelines of the public research institution. Re-reading the answers to Modification 1 (exclusive licensing) and Modification 2 (simple licensing) from a Hohfeldean perspective reveals the deeper rationales of how 'power' is construed in each jurisdiction in cases of shared ownership. Since in this case the focus is one two equal owners, no correlatives matter; it is just about what the rules are between co-owners: What kind of impairment triggers claims between them? Can public declarations of one partner have an effect on the freedom of the other? For some jurisdictions the all-important differentiation is the one between joint and common ownership. For others, the essential differentiation starts with the type of licensing. Interestingly, most jurisdictions do not differ in Modifications 2 and 3.

Modification 3 is, similarly to the base case, not translatable in Hohfeld's language. The case concerns the collision of two types of non-economic (collective) interests using patents strategically for their cause (patients against research). In fact, no report reveals legal language in the reporter's jurisdiction that makes it possible to identify those strategic interests and to balance them. The given conflict is covered up by the simple application of property law (only). The country reports reveal that contract law may be more absorbent for public policies and a weighing exercise backed up by reference to constitutional values.

The focus of *Case 14* is on digital publication and Creative Commons. In Hohfeld's language: Does a proprietary title ('power') occur always fully, unconditionally and at one point in time (in the base case, the scientist–publisher relationship)? Which rights remain with the author? With regard to Creative Commons, do jurisdictions acknowledge contractually split entitlements, and for dualist copyright jurisdictions, do they accept the quest for revindication of the author's moral right? The reports answers reflect the difficulties law and lawyers across countries have in integrating a legal innovation.

Our set of downstream constellations accommodates counter-rights regarding competition, public health, cultural enjoyment, family protection, research freedom, and food security. The challenge of the cases is that these policies appear to be fostered by the 'freedom to operate' counter-right. These cases therefore open the Pandora's box of policy conflicts.

As with our upstream cases, the Hohfeldean analysis has helped to open ways for differentiation: the 'tomato inventor' may have the 'power' to set restrictive contractual terms at will, but the farmer might be 'immune' to restrictions which overly encroach on his professional freedoms.[45] The IP-holding competitor might not always be able to exclude the other competitor, just as the non-holder cannot always access his/her rival's IP. However, the 'no-IP-holding competitor' might be 'immune' to an unjustified refusal to license under specific conditions (Case 1). Contractors might be 'immune' to proprietary injunctions in complex contract chains when an injunction would overly restrict (subjective) user freedoms and (objective) innovation.[46]

3. INTERIM CONCLUSIONS

While the country reports reflect the strong position of property, opposing rights come out not simply as encroachments, but as rights which demand equal respect. The technical re-description as conflicts between entitlements and counter-rights reveals decisions based on a balancing exercise, not as a binary scheme of right and non-right. The result of the balancing exercise is country-specific and depends on the legal environments in which both property rights and counter-rights are embedded.[47] Whether the differences are based on culture or political preferences is most probably contingent. The diversity of answers reflects, however, the legitimacy of counter-rights. The central point is: the questionnaire unearths that it is actually the 'correlatives' and their legal environment which define the scope of property. The answers reflect that modern sectorial regimes go well beyond the binary schemes of (horizontal) right/no-right or (vertical) right-versus-regulation.[48] In the descriptive formants,

45 Dependent on when 'exhaustion' occurs, recently defining restrictive (patent-holder-friendly) conditions, CJEU judgment of 20 October 2011, *Greenstar Kanzi*, C-140/10, ECLI:EU:C:2011:677.

46 Cases along the line of CJEU case law beginning with judgment of 23 April 2009, *Copad*, C-59/08, ECLI:EU:C:2009:260; judgment of 30 November 2004, *Peak Holding*, C-16/03, ECLI:EU:C:2004:759; to judgment of 20 October 2011, *Greenstar Kanzi*, C-140/10, ECLI:EU:C:2011:677. See C. Godt/J. Simon, '*In Rem* Effects of Non-exclusive Sub-licenses in Insolvency', in: C. Godt (ed.), *Regulatory Property Rights. The Transforming Notion of Property in Transnational Business Regulation* (Leiden/Boston: 2017), 207.

47 On the importance of 'regulatory environments' already: R. Brownsword, 'Comparatively Speaking: Law in its Regulatory Environment', in: M. Adams/D. Heirbaut (eds.), *The Method and Culture of Comparative Law* (Oxford/Portland: 2014), 189–205.

48 On the two visions of regulation (one as infringement of private autonomy justified only by considerations of economic efficiency, and the other as collaborative regulatory enterprise), T. Prosser, *The Regulatory Enterprise* (Oxford: 2010), Chapter 1. In IP law, however, it

we see an overlapping fabric of rules which Marc Amstutz called (in French) '*une greffe*',[49] defined as 'a structure which works off the heterogeneity of its heterogeneous bodies and makes them disappear' (Case 6 refers to the Convention on Biological Diversity (CBD) and UNDRIP, Cases 7–9 to the Oviedo Convention and the UN Declaration on Bioethics and Human Rights). The identified correlatives embed constitutional (public or private) values, while the country-specific answers reveal pluralist orders.[50] *This* modern structure emerges from the cases. In contrast to the dominant narrative in the 1990s, our study reveals that it is not IP law which defines the content of rights.[51] The environment defines the IP content. Since the environment differs from sector to sector, from case to case, from country to country, we see diverging contours of IP across the culturally diverse continent. These (national) regulations embed the (harmonised) property right.

The reports rebut our initial hypothesis that the property paradigm is the source of the inability to set boundaries to IP rights. We find that boundaries get established (once needed). Legislators have been active, despite encountering problems (e.g. Case 2, Recital 25 not transposed into binding law; Case 3). The activity of courts is more difficult to assess. In some cases, they did not set boundaries (Case 3, base case), even though scholarly literature advised doing so. In other cases, courts have actively strengthened counter-rights (e.g. Case 1). As far as possible, courts (also) interpret adjacent laws in other areas, in order to bring the boundaries to property to light (Cases 6, 7–9). This confirms our initial hypothesis that boundaries are (equally) defined by laws external to IP. The external (non-property) laws help to fine-tune the limits of property which *a priori* appear non-existent due to the paradigm of being an absolute right. We find that the nature of modern conflicts is distinct from the property conflicts taught in textbooks. The latter were determined by yes-or-no answers (crystals):[52] by selling a good or securing a credit, a property title is transferred.

---

was always difficult to juxtapose the proprietary right against regulation, since the rights themselves owe their existence to positive regulation. They emerge when the stipulated conditions are fulfilled. The parallel to 'natural property' was never really convincing. In contrast, it is the purpose of regulation and adjudication to (also) safeguard individual freedoms and autonomies, *inter alia* as necessary preconditions for market ordering.

49 M. Amstutz/V. Karavas, 'Weltrecht: Ein Derridasches Monster', in: G.-P. Calliess/A. Fischer-Lescano/D. Wielsch/P. Zumbansen (eds.), *Soziologische Jurisprudenz – Festschrift G. Teubner* (Berlin: 2009), 647–674, at 648. [English version:'Globalising Speenhamland: On the Transnational Metamorphosis of Corporate Social Responsibility', in: C. Joerges/J. Falke (eds.), *Karl Polanyi, Globalisation and the Potential of Law in TransnationalMarkets*, (Oxford/Portland: 2011) 359.

50 Which are still engraved in territorial states; on the sometimes-perceived tension between pluralist orders and positivist constitutionalists, R. Brownsword, 'Framers and Problematisers: Getting to Grips with Global Governance', *International Legal Theory* (2010), 287, 299.

51 This is congruent to Xifaras (2004, supra n. 3), 500: 'Autrement dit, il est impossible d'identifier la propriété modern et la propriété privé.'

52 Rose (1988, supra n. 17).

Depending on the jurisdiction, the remaining right is reduced to a right to claim the title back or to revindication. However, in information cases, the conflict structure is more nuanced. Information *providers* often keep their (or some of their) original rights. Their claims range from obtaining recognition, through ensuring use rights and remuneration, to a share in profits. *Users* claim legitimate access out of their own right either because they engaged in improving (this is basically referring to a property entitlement, Case 2) or because of other self-standing rights (Cases 3, 6). Under the former property paradigm, those user and provider rights appeared weak. Unless they were protected by statutory law (Case 3, private copy exemption), they risked being absorbed by the all-encompassing property right. In those cases, a formal law was needed, justified by end and means. We find that many of the reports take recourse to this form of argumentation. More ambitious reports, however, head out of these confines and advance argumentation which gives credit to the counter-rights and weighs them against the proprietary title.

The reporters often use constitutional language to explain descriptive and metalegal formants. This line of reasoning was long blocked in IP law by the general rejection of horizontal effects of constitutional rights, and by the property dogma. For a long time, constitutional rights were conceived of as operable only against the state. The situation has changed with the European Court of Justice construing European fundamental rights as boundaries equally to regulation *and* to rights of others, thus exerting vertical and horizontal effects. The criticism was that the horizontal effect grants too much power to the judiciary and would impair the principle of private autonomy.[53] Only general clauses in private codifications were to be interpreted by reference to constitutional rights. However, European practice shows that the horizontal effect corresponds to a constitutional reading of private relations, and that individual rights might often be better served by a type of decision which focuses on the individual case.[54] Recently, the CJEU gave guidance on the methodology for how to argue these sorts of cases.[55] The Court applies a three-step method. The national court shall

---

53 Explained by S. Walkila, *Horizontal Effect of Fundamental Rights in EU Law* (Groningen: 2016).

54 A. Colombi Ciacchi, 'European Fundamental Rights, Private Law, and Judicial Governance', in: H.-W. Micklitz (ed.), *Constitutionalization of European Private Law* (Oxford: 2014), 102; H. Collins, 'On the (In)compatibility of Human Rights Discourses and Private Law', in: H.-W. Micklitz (ed.), *Constitutionalization of European Private Law* (Oxford: 2014), 26; R. Mańko, 'The Use of Extra-Legal Arguments in the Judicial Interpretation of European Contract Law: A Case Study on Aziz v Catalunyacaixa (CJEU 14 March 2013, Case C-415/11)', 10 *Law and Forensic Science* (2015), 7; E. Frantziou, 'The Horizontal Effect of the Charter of Fundamental Rights of the EU: Rediscovering the Reasons for Horizontality', 21 *European Law Journal* (2015), 657–679.

55 CJEU judgment of 17 April 2018, *Egenberger*, C-414/16, ECLI:EU:C:2018:257; applauding further guidance: E. Frantziou, 'Mangold Recast? The ECJ's Flirtation with Drittwirkung in Egenberger', European Law Blog, available at: https://europeanlawblog.eu/2018/04/24/mangold-recast-the-ecjs-flirtation-with-drittwirkung-in-egenberger/.

first determine the national constitutional relationship between the legislature and the judiciary, then interpret the secondary national law, and then reflect on potential intrusion of fundamental rights. This is in line with recent literature, which devises concrete frames.

IV. CONSTITUTIONAL FRAMING

Many scholars of tangible and intellectual property law have suggested a constitutional framing of property conflicts. Yet it was Elsabe van der Sijde who submitted the most elaborate design in 2015, primarily with immobile property in mind.[56] Her concept is interesting for two reasons. First, South Africa underwent a profound reflection on property theory in the 1990s, and hence South African scholarship currently provides the most recent deliberation on how to conceptualise property. Second, South Africa's self-perception is as a mixed jurisdiction. South African scholarship therefore looks to civil law (Dutch, French), common law (English, US), and German constitutional interpretation of property protection for guidance. In very similar language, Josef Drexl spelled out a frame analysis for conflicts in personal and non-personal data in 2018.[57] Both approaches absorb the idea that conflicts are regulated not by property but rather by other laws which aim at governing policy issues. I will position my theory of IP conflicts exactly between these two.

Elsabe van der Sijde's dissertation 'Reconsidering the Relationship between Property and Regulation: A systematic constitutional approach' (defended in 2015)[58] is inspired by André van der Walt and modern systems theory.[59] André van der Walt developed 'systemic limitations' on property rights, which he distinguished from 'proportionality-based justification of a limitation that is imposed on an otherwise restricted right'.[60] Early on, he unmasked the familiar differentiation in IP law[61] between (legitimate) use regulation and (illegitimate) regulation of property's existence as one which 'allows property to remain a fundamentally unregulated right'.[62] He expressed that 'exceptions and qualifications to the protection of property are often more important because

56 Van der Sijde (2015, supra n. 15).

57 Van der Sijde (2015, supra n. 15).

58 Available at: https://pdfs.semanticscholar.org/089d/eec8546b2aba15d799b5f73717b93889e8bb.pdf.

59 But also by J. W. Singer and P. M. Gerhart, see van der Sijde (2015, supra n. 15), 268–277.

60 A. J. van der Walt, 'The modest systemic status of property', 1 *Journal of Law, Property, and Society* (2014), 15, 51.

61 For a historic analysis of this formula in IP: Strowel/Kim (2013, supra n. 10).

62 A. J. van der Walt, *Constitutional Property Clauses: A comparative analysis* (Cape Town: 1999), 134.

of the systematic purposes they serve'.[63] Along these lines, van der Sijde calls for a 'systematic thinking' which resists a reductionism to meta-principles.[64] She cautions against 'balancing',[65] prefers 'demarcation issues',[66] and rejects the common conceptual alternative of property being an externally restricted right *or* an inherently limited right.[67] She aims at 'questions about time-and-place specific shape that the limitation takes in legislation or other law that creates it'.[68] Her theoretic grounding is Niklas Luhmann, who taught that 'law determines its own boundaries' as an autopoetic system[69] – which translates in van der Walt's language as 'a process that works itself out in a dialogue'.[70] Her central idea is to understand property and regulation as a system of fragmentary overlap and parallelism.[71] This distinction is based on Quinot and Liebenberg,[72] which serves her to formulate 'a constitutional matrix and contextual considerations'.[73] It is for this reason that she puts emphasis on the interaction 'between the regulation of property (as a subsystem of the property system, which in turn is a component of the constitutional system) and other components of the legal system',[74] acknowledging J. W. Singer, who defends increasing regulation as a response to modern complexity.[75] She argues that 'disputes regarding the protection of entitlements must be addressed with reference to the objectives of the system as a whole'.[76] She states: 'regulation is understood as a mechanism through which

63 Van der Walt (2014, supra n. 60), 27.

64 Van der Sijde (2015, supra n. 15), 277.

65 Following A. van der Walt and P. M. Gerhart, see van der Sijde (2015, supra n. 15), 272, 275.

66 Following A. van der Walt, see van der Sijde (2015, supra n. 15), 273.

67 This debate is specific to the South African debate of the 1990s, van der Sijde (2015, supra n. 15), 158. Van der Sijde links the external concept to 'the absolute concept' of (German) pandectists (who further elaborated the French revolutionary idea of *propreté indivisable et sacré* (van der Sijde, 2015, supra n. 15, 56). On the other hand, she links the 'inherent limitation concept' to the (Dutch) private law theory, starting with Hugo Grotius (van der Sijde, 2015, supra n. 15, 56, 82) elaborated by the Dutch functionalists of the 1970 and 1980s (van der Sijde, 2015, supra n. 15, 74 ff.). She understands the concept of inherent limitations as 'firmly rooted in private law doctrine' (91), which 'remains focused on individual rights, which is fundamentally inconsistent with a systematic constitutional approach' (172 n. 328).

68 Van der Sijde (2015, supra n. 15), 172; as opposed to the notion of property being 'abstract, timeless, universal' (ibid at 92).

69 Van der Sijde (2015, supra n. 15), 257.

70 Van der Sijde (2015, supra n. 15), 92, citing A. van der Walt, 'The fragmentation of land rights', 8 *South African Journal on Human Rights* (1992), 429, 448.

71 Van der Sijde (2015, supra n. 15), 199, 205.

72 Van der Sijde (2015, supra n. 15), 200. She refers to G. Quinot/S. Liebenberg, 'Narrowing the band: Reasonableness review in administrative justice and socio-economic rights jurisprudence in South Africa', 22 *Stellenbosch Law Review* (2011), 639–663.

73 Van der Sijde (2015, supra n. 15), 260.

74 Van der Sijde (2015, supra n. 15), 278.

75 Singer (2014, supra n. 16), 1334, defending regulation as value-enhancing and consistent with a free and equal society, and rejecting Henry Smith's cost reduction model.

76 Van der Sijde (2015, supra n. 15), ii.

constitutional values are promoted. Thus, regulation of the use of property does not erode the institution of private property, because the system provides for constitutional or statutory control over the regulatory process'.[77] In doing so, she mirrors Peter M. Gerhart[78] and Jürgen Habermas.[79] 'Limitations are inherent to the system, rather than inherent to the rights'.[80] For illustration, she critically re-constructs the South African Constitutional Court judges' argumentation in recent decisions in terms of a 'systemic methodology'.[81]

In comparison, Josef Drexl develops for data a compact four-corner system ('key objectives') 'that need to be considered simultaneously'.[82] For his subject, these four objectives are: (1) establishing a functioning and competitive market for the data economy; (2) promoting innovation; (3) protecting consumer interests, with a particular focus on protecting the privacy of natural persons; and (4) promoting additional public interests (free flow of information, freedom of information, democracy).[83] Against this backdrop, he tests the idea of data ownership.[84] The approach is similar to that of van der Sijde. The frame helps to collect all respective interests, relevant regulations and constitutional values. It provides for a frame which pieces together economic and non-economic interests, and individual, collective and public interests. It allows for a distinction to be made between 'overlap and non-overlap cases', and provides language for differentiations.

These theories raise the bar as to what the BIP project can contribute to IP theory, but also help to 'read' the country reporters' answers. While van der Sijde's systemic approach is very general, she encourages looking at unrelated regulation and identifying boundaries 'from within the system'. Drexl's tailor-made proposal for data might be very narrow, but the quadrangle provides a universal frame which can be transposed to IP in general. It links IP to competition *and* innovation policy, to collective interests (such as consumers), to individual basic rights (privacy, life, etc.), and other public policies (food security, democracy, public health). This is exactly the spirit in which the BIP cases were drafted in the first place. The dynamic property model frees property theory from the presumption that IP conflicts are exclusively decided by IP

---

77 Van der Sijde (2015, supra n. 15), ii.

78 P. M. Gerhart, *Property Law and Social Morality* (Cambridge: 2014), 7, argues that the value that should be promoted by the property system is not the value we get out of a resource but rather the value that we want individuals to consider when making decisions about property.

79 Paradigm of the interrelatedness of private and public, Habermas (1992, supra n. 13).

80 Van der Sijde (2015, supra n. 15), 287.

81 *Inter alia Shoprite* (2015, dealing with the question of whether a liquor licence is 'property'), 204, 280, 291–296; *Oudekraal* (2010: a case about a 50-year-old unused construction permit), 132 ff.; *Port Elizabeth* (2005: a case about denied eviction of squatters), 140 ff.

82 Drexl (2018, supra n. 15), 5.

83 Drexl (2018, supra n. 15), 17.

84 Drexl (2018, supra n. 15), 19–30.

laws and their *ex ante* property statute requirements (which corresponds to what van der Sijde calls the 'absolute model'). Instead, it gives judges 'space' to decide cases based on values and related legislation. Modern legislators react to policy conflicts *related to* IP law, not necessarily by changing IP laws. Making 'addressees' (rightholders) subject to additional obligations *ex post* often suffices. This line of thought adds a third dimension that complements the description of the BIP conflict constellations. I return to the cases in numerical order.

Case 1, for us as editors, is a prime example of systemic analysis. As Gerhart and van der Sijde note: 'It makes a difference from where you start'.[85] The core of the *Magill* line of decisions is starting the analysis with competition as a rule to which IP is an exception. This means that 'the freedom to operate' is the rule protected by the economic order and basic rights, restricted by the proprietary injunction, which is justified by innovation policies. This is the inverse to natural law's reading of property. Since *Magill* has the highest court authority and is established case law, all reporters referred to it. The rhetoric of rule and exception, however, depends on how much weight is given to the conditions which the CJEU puts on the access right. Regardless of this, Case 1 marks the watershed of IP theory in the direction of systemic constitutionalisation.

Case 2 (*Myriad*) invited discussions on innovation, competition and various constitutional values, such as public health, allowing various argumentations. A constitutional approach could have discussed Recital 25 Biotechnology Directive as an example of the relative power between the European Parliament and the European Commission, and of compulsory licences as an instrument of public health policies (also discussed in jurisdictions beyond Belgium, which inserted a specific rule). Some transposing national regulations are very conscious of the public health impact and have provided for specific rules. The Biotechnology Directive is a rare example of democratic intervention in IP law, giving room to member states to fine-tune. It rebuts our initial bold hypothesis that IP is not to be regulated. Yet the reporters' answers show how weak the stipulated restrictions of the Directive are. On the other hand, later CJEU case law (*Brüstle*, *Monsanto*) shows that regulatory purpose and human rights are taken seriously by courts.

Case 3 (*Napster*) is a perfect case for quadrangular analysis. Incentive protection competes with constitutional values (culture, youth and family protection, civil procedure principles, data protection) and is embedded in secondary regulation which structures mass relations (collective societies) and technology (levies on products). Despite EU harmonisation, the member states have retained a broad leeway for national legislation. Comparative analysis brings out the wide range of ways in which member states have configured this conflict. These context regulations shape the scope of copyright and private use.

[85] Van der Sijde (2015, supra n. 15), 275.

The reports highlight the dynamic nature of law. Collective conflict resolution crafted at a specific point in time, for a specific technology, might become inconsistent due to technological change. Then, re-regulation is required. Inconsistences do not translate directly in operable subjective rights (e.g. a claim to get money back).

Case 4 (meteorological upstream data financed by the taxpayer) raised the question of whether public funding translates into public access. It does in two countries (the Netherlands and Slovenia). The argument is that many will have an incentive to create new property. This is a Lockean, not a Marxist, response. For these two jurisdictions, the systemic analysis would take the following ideas into consideration. First, property creation is promoted by restrictions on existing property (van der Sijde). Second, the regulation limits/burdens the property entitlement, but does not aim at restricting the institution as such (van der Sijde). Third, sectorial laws are *better* suited to regulate sectorial specificities (Singer).

In *Case 5*, a systemic constitutional reading would integrate three additional aspects into the quadrangle frame: the individual right of researchers, the institutional importance of academia, and the transfer of knowledge. If these constitutional values had been put to the forefront, the national answers might be less ambivalent. The case reflects a need to defend the normative values of research in information societies against parties with strategic interests and against silent contracts. A constitutional reading can openly refer to the societal backgrounds in which a legislative solution is introduced (Italy compared to the majority).

Case 6 is only sensibly argued using a quadrangular frame. The patents' function for innovation has to be related to a complex agricultural production system based on division of labour (historically structured by plant varieties law). The case was designed to address professional freedoms protected by competition law, and farmers' rights under plant varieties acts (protection of individual liberties and the public interest in freedom of agricultural actors and food safety). We framed the case to invite a reflection on an analogy, or an independently argued protection of 'the freedom to operate', resulting in answers based on property or contract law. We find, however, that most country reporters are entangled in the strict private law discipline, and not trained to consider a structured analysis as proposed by van der Sijde and Drexl. Since most of them did not raise the question, they could not discuss modern shifts and prerequisites of judicial restraints.

Cases 7–9 are good examples of the '*greffe*' of layered recognition of interests which should guide the systemic legal interpretation. The reports give evidence of how differently constitutional personality rights and collective interests are framed in the jurisdictions analysed (reflecting the national take on questions addressed by the pertinent international conventions, supra section III.1). The systemic constitutional analysis is apt to integrate each national take on conflicts of interests into an analysis of the scope of IP entitlement. The country reports reveal that boundaries can be spelled by regulations conceived as data protection or sectorial protection of research probands/patients. Interfering group interests (family, ethnic, territory) are dealt with nationally. They can be conceptualised as individual rights or as collective or public interests, all with implications for the legal environment. The systemic analysis helps identify the democratic and culturally imprinted legal framework.

Case 10 was conceptualised as a collective title challenge. The editorial expectation was a solution via conflicts of law, especially after the status of collective rights as a human right was further strengthened by the UNDRIP. From a systemic point of view, the case is a good example of a '*greffe*' (Amstutz[86]), or a 'regime complex' (Raustiala/Victor[87]). The protection of traditional communities is a human rights issue and is in the interest of long-term innovation, values which would form the angles of a quadrangle analysis of the case. Due to the few reports drafting answers to this case, we note a broad insecurity about dealing with constitutional framings.

Cases 11–13 aim at conflicts between IP and research. A systemic constitutional analysis would make the underlying decisions more transparent and possibly different. Patent law's incentive for innovation would be opposed by an academic system with its own rules equally credited with fostering innovation. Research is protected by individual freedoms of researchers and the public interest in the outcomes of science by upholding special rules of science.[88] IP (even if held by a public interest organisation) and research are two complementary systems of innovation which are constitutionally protected. Putting the case question in a quadrangular frame would have impeded most reporters from taking easy refuge in property rules. They would have acknowledged the mixed private/public motivation of both institutions. They would not deny the possibility to transfer the rules of competition law to grant-back clauses, and to activate the protective rationale for research. One could still give preference to contractual freedom (if justified). The reports reflect the fact that the institution of academic research is, in constitutional terms, under-structured. As a knowledge institution, a research institute has a protected interest in continuing research in its area of special competence. These interests are not simply 'transferred' by way of transferring a property title, due to their non-transferable nature. Without legislative or juridical regulation, the constitutional value of research freedom risks being undermined by an old-fashioned property paradigm. The knowledge society of

86 Amstutz (2009/2011, supra n. 49).

87 K. Raustiala/D. G. Victor, 'The Regime Complex for Plant Genetic Resources', 58 *International Organisation* (2004), 277.

88 Encapsulated in the CUDOS formula of Robert Merton (published 1942, *c*ommunity [in his word 'communism'], *u*niversalism, *d*isinterest and *o*rganised *s*cepticism. For a discussion see Godt (2007, supra n. 5) 156 ff; 218 ff.

the future will have to insert more subtleties which respect continuing 'access rights' based on professional and institutional interests in research even if the economic title has been transferred. These subtleties can take various forms and range from narrowing the patent scope and statutory access rights to standards for licensing and codes of conduct.

The focus of *Case 14* is on Creative Commons, thus the 'contractually re-designed public domain'. It pits the individualist conception against a social collective phenomenon which innovatively uses traditional property. The question was whether a social development will be respected by the law. Time has shown that it will.

V. CONCLUSION

Boundaries to information property emerge where conflicting rights so demand; modern conflicts are taken care of *ex ante* and *ex post*. Conflict configuration is, in principle, not left to the proprietary hierarchy, just as modern property theory proclaims. This is the central lesson of the BIP project. Boundaries are set *ex ante* by IP laws and *ex post* by regulation, rights of others, and novel uses of property, prompted by civil society, negotiated by legislators and pieced together by judges as '*la greffe*'. Even where the country reporters had difficulties, due to their doctrinal training, in addressing the question raised by a particular case, the importance of public regulation (especially data protection as a cross-cutting area, see Case 3 and the case complex 7–9) is just as evident as new actors that articulate public or collective interests in a proprietary language (e.g. Cases 10, 14).

The BIP project contributes to IP theory the first empirical material for what can today be identified as the modern turn towards systemic constitutionalism. This lesson is not devalued by the fact that reporters struggled with the formants methodology (explained in Part I), and that the national reports have become outdated over time. The inbuilt consequence of the formants analysis is the focus on 'living law' at a given time. The BIP project was not aimed to be a commentary on actual national laws. From an IP theory point of view, the BIP cases provide a 'language of conflicts', and a structure for systemic analysis. Not all of the conflicts devised need a definite solution. Conflicts might sometimes be better left to the parties to mediate (see for family conflicts with regard to genomic information the chapter by Adcock and Beyleveld in this volume); others might require pre-structuring by legislative means, while others might eventually benefit from a judicial decision. The central finding, which even the more doctrinally oriented BIP reports reveal, is that conflicts are not ultimately pre-structured *ex ante* by the notion of property. The cases reveal a modern, dynamic world with conflicts in need of differentiated, but transparent, deliberation. *Ex ante* regulation cannot, as a matter of principle, anticipate all conflicts, or all novel (public, collective) uses of property. *Ex post* accommodation has become the norm, by regulation close to IP or disconnected from it (like data protection), and put in place by social practices of novel collective actors which employ property for a public or collective cause. This change is correlated with a change in the judge's task. He/she will not 'find the (given) law' but will 'find the right and just answer in the given case'. Modern property law is not confined to a binary legal code of rights and no rights; instead, modern conflicts create 'relations' which come with 'obligations'. The conflicting rights can be economic or non-economic in nature. They are not necessarily of 'subjective' nature. Economic reasons, such as innovation and well-functioning competition or a system which incentivises the use of resources (farmers' rights) and subsequent innovations (breeders' rights), have a place in the structured deliberation (and are not set aside as 'merely political'). Fundamental (non-economic) rights might equally limit the scope of injunctions (privacy, Case 7) or even the acquisition of property (Case 13), or might be the basis for legitimate access (patients' rights, Cases 7-9; traditional rights, Case 10.

The BIP project has three implications for IP theory. First, *ex post* and *ex ante* boundaries are different in texture. *Ex ante* boundaries configure conflicts by limiting the subject matter. This is regulation as well (see the chapter by Van Overwalle in this volume). In an ideal world, courts would identify the legislator's intention to limit intellectual property.[89] We find our initial hypothesis rebutted that 'more or less everything' can be commodified:[90] Patent law, copyright laws, trademark law, geographical indications law, database protection (Case 4) – all of these discriminate between what can and cannot be claimed to be 'intellectual property'.[91] This is, at the same time, their task and their limit. But their wisdom is limited. Therefore, additional boundaries are set *ex post*, effectuated by social processes, legislation and courts.[92] *Ex post* boundaries put in place limits on how property can be exercised and define additional obligations. These limits are set by adjacent areas of regulatory law, fundamental rights, and actors in the public or collective interest. Against the common wisdom of property and IP law, it is not only statutory laws *designated* to limit deliberately the scope of property that fine-tune the rules. Regulatory law and property are on the same footing. Regulation does not require any special justification vis-à-vis property.

89 G. Ghidini, *Innovation, Competition and Consumer Welfare in Intellectual Property Law* (Cheltenham: 2010), 183.

90 This is in line with A. Peukert, 'Vereinheitlichung des Immaterialgüterrechts – Strukturen, Akteure, Zwecke', 81 *RabelsZ* 2017, 158–193: '"Vereinheitlichung" does not equal extension'.

91 Information as distinguished from 'technical teaching/invention/knowledge', 'creation', etc.

92 Seminal paper: H. van den Belt, 'Action at a distance: A.W. Hofmann and the French patent dispute about aniline red (1860–1863), or how a scientist may influence legal decisions without appearing in court', in: B. Smith/B. Wynne (eds.), *Expert Evidence: Interpreting Science in the Law* (London: 1989), 184–209.

IP is regulation in the first place, and depends on further fine-tuning regulation *ex post*. We find our initial assumption of the importance of *ex post* limits confirmed in the reports, as much as in recent adjudication. In the reports, we see that jurisdictions, to a different degree, acknowledge public interests in private procedure rules (e.g. Cases 7 and 13: France, Italy, Poland, Spain). These rules play an important role and translate public regulations into IP conflicts.[93] The important lesson for IP theory is that public and collective interests, via regulation or/and procedural rules, have a strong influence on the content of IP. In addition, novel actors use the term 'property' when pursuing a mixed economic/non-economic interest (Cases 10, 13, 14). In those cases, property claims become a vehicle for competing interests. In the *Facebook* decision of 2018,[94] the Federal German Supreme Court (BGH) curbed the legal and factual power to exclude *ex post*. These iterative follow-on limitations are typical of contemporary conflict configuration in IP. They reveal the intimate correlation between the private and the public in information property.

Second, the BIP reports reveal a complex relationship between IP and regulation. Three observations stand out. Firstly, where those rules exist, they often restrict property for the sake of the creation of new property (Cases 1, 4). Secondly, as earlier identified for tort law,[95] specialised legislation is often not applicable, which accounts for the continuing importance of general rules (property, contracts). In contrast to traditional legal logic, we see that general rules absorb the rationales of the *leges speciales* (Cases 7–9), instead of distinguishing *lex generalis* from *lex specialis*. Rules like *lex specialis derogat lex generalis* or the principle of 'unity of law' will not be applied; sectorial fine-tuning is the reality. Thirdly, adjacent regulation may pursue the same goal with the inverse tool (Case 5: Italy). For example, in pursuit of promoting technology transfer from public research to industry, almost all European jurisdictions abolished the 'professors' privilege' in around 2001. But quite to the contrary, Italy *introduced it* for the same reason.[96] This example teaches IP lawyers a lesson about the relative importance of IP law. What is important is the societal development triggered by the rule. The IP instrument can be, depending on the cultural background, contingently either the introduction or the abolition of the tool.

---

93 Traditions in civil procedure which reflect culturally distinct experiences play an interesting role, as revealed in Cases 3 (e.g. disclosure of third parties) and 7 (France and Italy for different versions of how public interests can be articulated and enforced in civil courts).

94 BGH, decision of 12 July 2018 – III ZR 183/17. Patents 'inherit' the Facebook account of their 15-year-old daughter. Facebook cannot claim ownership and refuse access to the parents. Facebook's reference to (the daughter's) data protection does not overrule the rights of the parents. The court equates the Facebook account to a bequested diary.

95 G. Brüggemeier, *Common Principles of Tort Law* (London: 2004).

96 These 'contrafactual' findings are at the heart of the formants analysis, R. Sacco/P. Rossi, *Einführung in die Rechtsvergleichung* (Baden-Baden: 2017), 80.

Third, in contrast to the dominant discourse on international IP harmonisation, the national imprint remains very strong. Cultural differences sneak in during transposition processes and through civil procedure rules. They turn out to be much stronger than expected. IP-adjacent national regulation gives IP different content in each jurisdiction. On the surface, IP rights might be harmonised, but content-wise they differ to a large degree (Case 4: Netherlands and Slovenia on tax-funded data; Cases 7–9: Italy and France on the protection of the individual in genomic research). National regulations overarch IP; procedural rules configure conflicts differently. This is not an assault on Europe, but provides for democratic conflict configuration and regulatory evolution. This is good news.

DRAWING THE CONTOURS OF THE EUROPEAN PUBLIC DOMAIN

Lucie GUIBAULT

I. INTRODUCTION

No doubt the public domain represents the quintessential boundary of intellectual property (IP). IP rights are sometimes described as islands of protection in a sea of free competition,[1] where the sea of competition stands for the public domain. Remarkably, the concept of public domain is not defined by positive law: neither the international conventions on the topic nor the relevant national legislation give the public domain a precise meaning.[2] As a result, the public domain is commonly understood in a negative way, as everything that is not, or is no longer, protected by IP law.[3] Some recent commentators also include within the ambit of the public domain the uses that the law expressly carves out of the scope of protection.[4] These constitute free spaces allowing for the use of protected material without risk of infringement. Even this broad definition can be called into question, however, as being either too Eurocentric (disregarding the special features of traditional knowledge, for example), too static and formalistic, or too dogmatic.[5] A rigid definition of the public domain is prone to misrepresent reality, in that it risks mischaracterising items or uses that should, or should not,

---

1 J. H. Reichman, 'Nurturing a System of Transnational Innovation', in: I. Govaere/H. Ullrich (eds.), *Intellectual Property, Public Policy and International Trade* (Brussels: 2006), 19.

2 S. Dusollier, *Scoping Study on Copyright and Related Rights and the Public Domain*, WIPO (2010), CDIP/4/3/REV./STUDY/INF/1.

3 A. Samuel Oddi, 'The Tragicomedy of the Public Domain in Intellectual Property Law', 25 *Hastings Comm. & Ent. L.J.* (2002), 1.

4 P. Samuelson, 'Challenges in Mapping the Public Domain', in: L. Guibault/P. B. Hugenholtz (eds.), *The Future of the Public Domain – Identifying the Commons in Information Law* (The Hague: 2006), 9.

5 R. Okediji, *Traditional Knowledge and the Public Domain*, Centre for International Governance Innovation Papers No. 176 (26 June 2018); C. Oguamanam, 'Wandering footloose: Traditional knowledge and the "Public Domain" revisited', 21 *Journal of World Intellectual Property* (2018), 306.

be considered part of it. Moreover, the public domain shifts over time and varies along national border lines.[6]

While its existence is mostly derived from something that is 'not', the public domain carries tremendous significance for the pursuit of innovation and creativity. As part of the free flow of information, it is also essential to the democratic process. Items in the public domain are, in principle, available for use by anyone without restriction. For this reason, the possibility to build on the wealth of prior knowledge contained in the public domain, i.e. the possibility to access and use information, is essential in all fields of intellectual endeavour. However one defines the public domain, its socio-economic value is such that it should be nurtured.[7] The importance of leaving room for further creation and innovation when designing IP rights is uncontested: an overly broad and strictly enforced IP regime risks smothering any second comer's inclination towards ingenuity and progress.[8] By erecting barriers to the access and use of information, full and complete protection would unmistakably stifle innovation.

All IP rights are subject to inherent limits. These concern primarily the determination of the protectable subject matter, the scope and duration of protection. Protection is granted only with respect to certain types of creations that meet the requirements for protection of the respective IP regimes. The same goes for the scope of protection conferred by law on rights owners: ideally, the manner in which the exclusive rights and the exceptions and limitations are defined and interpreted takes account of public interest considerations. IP rights are generally circumscribed in time, thereby enabling unrestricted use by anyone, once the term of protection has lapsed.[9] But the perceived expansion of IP protection – for example through the extension of the term of copyright, the encroachments brought on by technological protection measures or the creation of a database right – puts a definite strain on the public domain.[10]

If the public domain is so essential to society, why does the concept remain so vague and fluid? How are the boundaries to IP rights, and by correlation the content of the public domain, designed at all? And how should conflicts arising around the public domain be solved?

---

6 R. Spoo, 'The Uncoordinated Public Domain', 35 *Cardozo Arts & Ent. L.J.* (2016), 107.

7 R. Pollock, *The Value of the Public Domain*, London Institute for Public Policy Research (2006), 15, available at: https://rufuspollock.com/papers/value_of_public_domain.ippr.pdf.

8 J. Boyle, 'A Manifesto on WIPO and the Future of Intellectual Property', 9 *Duke Law and Technology Review* (2004), 1.

9 Typically, only trademarks and geographical indications do not have a limited duration, as long as they are used. All other rights, including patents, copyrights, plant breeders' rights, industrial designs subsist for a specific length of time.

10 Dusollier (2010, supra n. 2), 4; J. Boyle, 'The Second Enclosure Movement and the Construction of the Public Domain', 66 *Law and Contemporary Problems* (2003), 33, 38.

Analysing IP rights in terms of property entitlements is only one way to contemplate conflicts with or between IP rights.[11] While this approach primarily focuses on the respective rights of the parties to a dispute, it generally provides a satisfactory framework of analysis in cases of conflict between different individual entitlements. However, it is mostly inadequate to analyse conflicts emerging around the definition of the public domain, that is, the free spaces between private entitlements. For example, the parties' entitlements should have no bearing on deciding whether a work, invention or idea deserves protection in the first place. Nor should this line of analysis play a role in cases where the term of protection has lapsed. Although cloaked under the guise of private disputes, these and similar cases that touch on the public domain involve IP policy matters that are best handled by the lawmaker. It cannot be ignored, however, that private interactions between parties can have an impact on accessibility and use of information in the public domain. The arbitration of conflicts dealing with the public domain therefore requires looking beyond the legal nature of the parties' entitlements; it requires examining the broader public interest considerations that shape the respective IP regimes. These public interest considerations should be discernible on the basis of the justifications and objectives of IP law.

In the context of the BIP analysis, the key question that this chapter aims to address is how, and on what ground, conflicts around the public domain are adjudicated in different contexts. In order to answer this question, the first step consists in examining the rationales behind the current European IP regimes, and more specifically behind the European regimes of copyright and database right (section II). In theory, if the goals pursued by a particular legal norm are clear, then the contours of that norm should be easily ascertainable. In other words, the study of the justifications behind the regimes should shed light on the reasons given for the assessment of a conflict between opposing norms. The focus of this chapter is on European Union IP law, specifically copyright and database right, because of its high degree of harmonisation. While the various principles underlying the national copyright regimes may serve as guide for the European lawmaker (section II.1), an in-depth analysis of such national influences would take us beyond the scope of the BIP project. A brief analysis of the underpinnings of EU copyright law (section II.2) leads to a discussion of the place of the public domain in harmonised European copyright law (section II.3). The next section discusses how the rules of European IP law are applied in specific factual situations depicted in the BIP cases that touch on the boundaries of a particular IP regime, in the light of the stated objectives of that IP regime (section III). Specifically, Case 4 (public sector information), Case 3 (private copying exception) and Case 14 (voluntary relinquishment of rights) come

11 See C. Godt, 'Conflict Configuration in Information Property', in the present book.

under review. This approach also allows us to consider the impact of private parties' licensing practices on the subsistence of the public domain.

II. LEGAL FOUNDATIONS OF EUROPEAN COPYRIGHT LAW

Since there is no common international understanding of what forms the public domain, how do the European and national lawmakers make the determination of where and on what grounds the limits of intellectual property rights should be set? As demonstrated below, the answer to this question is not as straightforward as one would hope.

1. RATIONALES UNDERLYING NATIONAL COPYRIGHT LAW

By its very nature, European law is not deeply rooted in any specific legal tradition. European Union law has evolved over the past five decades, through political compromises reached between representatives of the constituent member states. The body of European copyright law is even more recent, as it emerged mostly within the last 30 years.[12] Notwithstanding its recent history, it would be a gross oversimplification to reduce the influences on European law only to the broad concepts carried by the two main legal traditions present in the European Union i.e. common law and civil law. Although the majority of the EU member states belong to the civil law tradition, there exist stark ideological differences between countries that share the same tradition. The same observation holds true with respect to the legal tradition underlying the copyright regime: member states are generally divided between countries that belong either to the *copyright* (UK and Ireland) or the *authors' rights* (continental European countries) tradition.[13] However, even within authors' rights systems, some countries take a dualist approach to authors' economic and personality rights (France, Italy, the Netherlands and Spain), while others take a monist approach to the protection of authors, where economic and personality rights are considered to be inseparable (Germany, Slovenia).[14]

Different theories and philosophies underlie each national system. Without overly generalising, it is fair to say that the UK and Ireland's copyright regime is

---

12 The first Directive in the area of copyright law was Directive 91/250/EEC of 14 May 1991 on the legal protection of computer programs, OJ L 122, 17 May 1991, 42–46.

13 A. Ramalho, *The Competence of the European Union in Copyright Lawmaking – A Normative Perspective of EU Powers for Copyright Harmonization* (Basel: 2016), 175.

14 P. Goldstein/P. B. Hugenholtz, *International Copyright: Principles, law, and practice* (New York: 2013).

based largely on utilitarian principles, whereas the authors' rights regime usually rests on natural rights principles, personality rights theory or labour theory.[15] Within the authors' rights tradition, however, the varying approaches to copyright protection show that other justifications can play a role in the design of the regime than the sole reliance on the natural rights, personality rights theory or labour theory. Such justifications may originate in a different conception of the institution of 'property', but often they reflect an acknowledgment that public interest considerations ought to support the recognition and exercise of rights (Germany, the Netherlands).[16] For example, the copyright system in the Nordic countries (Norway) is strongly influenced by principles of legal realism that present a realistic view of the purpose and the effect of legislation.[17]

The theories and philosophies that underpin a specific national copyright regime serve as a compass guiding the acts of the legislator and the interpretation by the courts. Without a clear understanding of the rationales behind a legal regime, lawmakers can hardly purport to achieve a coherent set of rules. The overall objective sought by the regime, which materialises the regime's theoretical underpinnings, should be traceable not only in the recognition and enforcement of IP rights, but also in the delineation of the boundaries of protection. The choice for a particular set of norms should in principle coincide with the goals to be attained. In practice, a utilitarian approach to copyright will lead to a different solution for a specific problem than a natural rights, personality rights theory or labour theory approach. Issues of delineation of copyright protection, like the criteria for protection and the determination of the scope of protection, provide useful illustrations of this mechanism. Indeed, until the European harmonisation, the originality threshold was markedly lower in the United Kingdom and Ireland than anywhere else in the European Union, while the number of statutory exceptions on authors' rights was noticeably lower in France, Spain and Italy than in the countries following the copyright tradition.[18] Even if the different approaches generally tend towards the recognition of similar rights in practice,[19] there remain significant distinctions between the copyright and the authors' rights systems, like questions of initial ownership and moral rights, to name but these, that still stand in the way of complete harmonisation.

---

15 S. van Gompel, *Formalities in Copyright Law: An Analysis of their History, Rationales and Possible Future* (Alphen aan den Rijn: 2011), Chapter 6, 193 ff.

16 L. Guibault, *Copyright Limitations and Contracts: An Analysis of the Contractual Overridability of Limitations on Copyright* (The Hague: 2002), 27 ff.

17 U. Bernitz, 'What is Scandinavian Law?', in: P. Wahlgren (ed.), *Scandinavian Studies in Law* (Stockholm: 2007), 13–30.

18 Goldstein/Hugenholtz (2013, supra n. 14).

19 J. Ginsburg, 'A Tale of Two Copyrights: Literary Property in Revolutionary France and America', 147 *RIDA* (1991), 289; A. Strowel, *Droit d'auteur et copyright – Divergences et convergences* (Paris: 1993); J. A. L. Sterling, 'Creator's Right and the Bridge between Author's Right and Copyright', 29(3) *IIC* (1998), 302.

2. RATIONALES UNDERLYING HARMONISED EUROPEAN COPYRIGHT LAW

Clearly the member states of the European Union adhere to a mosaic of different philosophies in support of their national copyright regime.[20] Do any of these ideologies inform the harmonising efforts of the European legislator and the Court of Justice of the EU? What goal does European copyright law purport to achieve? Does the pursuit of a particular legislative objective in the area of copyright law help shape the boundaries of the regime?

European copyright law was progressively developed through the adoption of secondary legislation[21] and the CJEU's judicial interpretation. Positive

[20] J. Ginsburg, 'General Report, Justifications for Authors' Rights', in: J. Blomquist (ed.), *Copyright, To Be or Not To Be*, ALAI Study Days (2018), 15–26.

[21] As of 2019, ten Directives and two Regulations have been adopted in the area of copyright law: Directive 2009/24/EC of the European Parliament and of the Council of 23 April 2009 on the legal protection of computer programs (codified version), OJ L 111, 5 May 2009, 16–22; Council Directive 93/83/EEC of 27 September 1993 on the coordination of certain rules concerning copyright and rights related to copyright applicable to satellite broadcasting and cable retransmission, OJ L 248, 6 October 1993, 15–21; Directive 96/9/EC of the European Parliament and of the Council of 11 March 1996 on the legal protection of databases, OJ L 77, 27 March 1996, 20–28; Directive 2006/115/EC of the European Parliament and of the Council of 12 December 2006 on rental right and lending right and on certain rights related to copyright in the field of intellectual property (codified version), OJ L 376, 27 December 2006, 28–35; Directive 2006/116/EC of the European Parliament and of the Council of 12 December 2006 on the term of protection of copyright and certain related rights (codified version), OJ L 372, 27 December 2006, 12–18; Directive 2001/29/EC of the European Parliament and of the Council of 22 May 2001 on the harmonisation of certain aspects of copyright and related rights in the information society, OJ L 167, 22 June 2001, 10–19; Directive 2001/84/EC of the European Parliament and of the Council of 27 September 2001 on the resale right for the benefit of the author of an original work of art, OJ L 272, 13 October 2001, 32–36; Directive 2012/28/EU of the European Parliament and of the Council of 25 October 2012 on certain permitted uses of orphan works, OJ L 299, 27 October 2012, 5–12; Directive 2014/26/EU of the European Parliament and of the Council of 26 February 2014 on collective management of copyright and related rights and multi-territorial licensing of rights in musical works for online use in the internal market, OJ L 84, 20 March 2014, 72–98; Directive (EU) 2019/789 of the European Parliament and of the Council of 17 April 2019 laying down rules on the exercise of copyright and related rights applicable to certain online transmissions of broadcasting organisations and retransmissions of television and radio programmes, and amending Council Directive 93/83/EEC, PE/7/2019/REV/1, OJ L 130, 17 May 2019, 82–91; Directive (EU) 2019/790 of the European Parliament and of the Council of 17 April 2019 on copyright and related rights in the Digital Single Market and amending Directives 96/9/EC and 2001/29/EC, PE/51/2019/REV/1, OJ L 130, 17 May 2019, 92–125; Regulation (EU) No. 2017/1563 of the European Parliament and of the Council of 13 September 2017 on the cross-border exchange between the Union and third countries of accessible format copies of certain works and other subject matter protected by copyright and related rights for the benefit of persons who are blind, visually impaired or otherwise print-disabled, OJ L 242, 20 September 2017, 1–5; Regulation (EU) No. 2017/1128 of the European Parliament and of the Council of 14 June 2017 on cross-border portability of online content services in the internal market, OJ L 168, 30 June 2017, 1–11.

harmonisation through the adoption of Directives and Regulations was achieved in the area of copyright law in roughly three phases: seven Directives were enacted in the period between 1991 and 2001 (not counting the codification efforts of 2006 and 2009);[22] one Directive in 2012 and one in 2014;[23] and the last pieces of legislation, namely two Regulations and one Directive, were adopted in 2017 and 2019 respectively. The majority of the Directives are categorised as 'vertical', in that they concern a specific copyright matter (computer programmes, term of protection, databases, resale rights, orphan works or collective rights management). One is clearly 'horizontal', as it applies across the board, irrespective of the type of work or user involved (information society).

Negative harmonisation through judicial interpretation occurred in a similar three-tiered fashion: the Court of Justice's initial task was to address conflicts between the four fundamental EU freedoms and intellectual property.[24] Once Directives were in place, the CJEU's role then turned towards giving uniform meaning to ambiguous Community concepts. More recently, the CJEU has taken a proactive role in shaping copyright norms, for example by creating a European concept of copyrightable works.[25] Nowadays the CJEU is increasingly called upon to balance copyright rules against competing values that are also protected under EU law.[26] The seemingly haphazard manner in which European copyright law has come about suggests that the main actors in the lawmaking process probably never delved very long into the need to anchor the rules with a solid line of justification or to infuse the entire project with a clear objective.

Throughout this harmonisation exercise, the primary concern in the legal commentaries was to determine whether the European Union had competence to legislate in the area, and if so, on what ground(s). With the exception of Article 36, which allows for exceptions to the principle of free movement of goods and services notably for the protection of industrial and commercial

---

22 P. B. Hugenholtz, 'Copyright in Europe: Twenty Years Ago, Today and What the Future Holds', 23 *Fordham Intell. Prop. Media & Ent. L.J.* (2013), 503.

23 F. Gotzen, 'The European Legislator's Strategy in the Field of Copyright', in: T. E. Synodinou (ed.), *Codification of European Copyright Law – Challenges and Perspectives* (Alphen aan den Rijn: 2012), 43–54.

24 Ramalho (2016, supra n. 13), 59.

25 E. Rosati, *Copyright and the Court of Justice of the European Union* (Oxford: 2019); but see M. Favale et al., 'Is There a EU Copyright Jurisprudence? An Empirical Analysis of the Workings of the European Court of Justice', 79(1) *Modern Law Review* (2016), 31.

26 A. Strowel/K. Hee-Eun, 'The Balancing Impact of General EU Law on European Intellectual Property Jurisprudence', in: J. Pila/A. Ohly (eds.), *The Europeanization of Intellectual Property Law: Towards a European Legal Methodology* (Oxford: 2013), 122–143; see for example T. Snijders/S. van Deursen, 'The Road Not Taken – the CJEU Sheds Light on the Role of Fundamental Rights in the European Copyright Framework – a Case Note on the *Pelham, Spiegel Online* and *Funke Medien* Decisions', 50 *IIC* (2019), 1176.

property, the Treaty of Rome did not originally foresee a specific EU competence to regulate copyright law.[27] For the greater part of the copyright harmonisation process, the competence of the European Union was not explicit: most actions were based on the need to regulate the internal market and to eliminate economic barriers between member states.[28] However, asking whether there exists an explicit basis for legislation in the area of copyright law is different from asking what philosophical principles should guide the legislator's actions. Since 2012, the European Union has express power to legislate in the area of intellectual property on the basis of Article 114 of the Treaty on the Functioning of the European Union (TFEU).[29] This provision reads as follows:

> Save where otherwise provided in the Treaties, the following provisions shall apply for the achievement of the objectives set out in Article 26. The European Parliament and the Council shall, acting in accordance with the ordinary legislative procedure and after consulting the Economic and Social Committee, adopt the measures for the approximation of the provisions laid down by law, regulation or administrative action in Member States which have as their object the establishment and functioning of the internal market.

Article 114 TFEU mentions the approximation of laws and the establishment and functioning of the internal market, but these indications can hardly count as sufficient justification for the adoption of copyright rules. Ana Ramalho is one of the few authors who has examined the European harmonisation from a normative perspective.[30] Since none of the European treaties offer any normative guidance to the European Union lawmakers, Ramalho undertook an in-depth examination of the reasons put forward for the adoption of each Directive in the area of copyright law. On the basis of the recitals contained each Directive, Ramalho identified different categories of objectives: some Treaty-related objectives (e.g. the establishment of the internal market, the promotion of culture), and some specific objectives (e.g. the protection of authors and performers, of the content industries, of intermediaries, and of end users, and

---

27 A. Markowska/N. Meurens/A. Ramalho, *European Implementation Assessment – Review of the EU copyright framework, Annex II, Legal Aspects of Copyright: The added value and options for further harmonisation and efficiency of the EU copyright regime, including the projected impact on other policy areas*, European Parliamentary Research Service (2015), PE 558.762, 234.

28 A. Ramalho, 'Conceptualising the European Union's Competence in Copyright – What Can the EU Do?', *International Review of Intellectual Property and Competition Law* (2014), 179; T. Georgopoulos, 'The Legal Foundations of European Copyright Law', in: T. E. Synodinou (ed.), *Codification of European Copyright Law – Challenges and Perspectives* (Alphen aan den Rijn: 2012), 31–42.

29 Consolidated version of the Treaty on the Functioning of the European Union, OJ C 326, 26 October 2012, 47–390.

30 Ramalho (2016, supra n. 13), 29–32.

the compliance with international obligations). While all these objectives play a fluctuating role in the development of European copyright law, Ramalho nevertheless concludes that the provisions of the TFEU contain no normative statement guiding either the European legislator, the CJEU or the member states on how to weigh opposing interests against one another.[31]

Partly as a result of the absence of normative guidance, the European Commission's initiatives in the area of copyright law have been characterised by piecemeal legislative action. As an illustration of this, the most recent Impact Assessment on the modernisation of EU copyright rules[32] states that the key objective of the new legislative initiative is to ensure the smooth functioning of EU copyright rules in the Digital Single Market. The general objectives identified in the document include:

> (i) allow for wider online access to protected content across the EU, focusing on TV and radio programmes, European audiovisual (AV) works and cultural heritage; (ii) facilitate digital uses of protected content for education, research and preservation in the single market and (iii) achieving a well-functioning market place for copyright where rightholders can set licensing terms and negotiate on a fair basis with those distributing their content (notably as regards new forms of content distribution).

The European lawmaker stresses that the harmonised framework contributes to the proper functioning of the internal market, and stimulates innovation, creativity, investment and production of new content, including in the digital environment, in order to avoid the fragmentation of the internal market. The protection provided by that legal framework also contributes to the Union's objective of respecting and promoting cultural diversity. These measures are a far cry from the call for copyright reform that could be heard in some circles before the presentation of Proposal for a Directive on Copyright in the Digital Single Market in September 2016.[33] In any case, the reasons put forward by the European lawmaker do not amount to what could be considered an overarching set of coherent rationales for the European copyright regime as a whole.

---

31 Ramalho (2016, supra n. 13), 211.

32 Commission Staff Working Document, *Impact Assessment on the modernisation of EU copyright rules Accompanying the document Proposal for a Directive of the European Parliament and of the Council on copyright in the Digital Single Market and Proposal for a Regulation of the European Parliament and of the Council laying down rules on the exercise of copyright and related rights applicable to certain online transmissions of broadcasting organisations and retransmissions of television and radio programmes*, European Commission, Brussels, 14 September 2016, SWD (2016) 301 final, 9.

33 A. Robert, *Commission dilutes copyright reform in digital strategy* (8 May 2015), EurActiv.fr, available at: https://www.euractiv.com/section/languages-culture/news/commission-dilutes-copyright-reform-in-digital-strategy/.

The gaps left by the European legislator are hardly filled by the jurisprudence of the CJEU. Throughout its decisions, the Court repeatedly stresses that the harmonisation effectuated aims to safeguard a fair balance between the interests of the holders of copyright, and the interests and fundamental rights of users, as well as the public interest. In the Court's opinion, the system of exclusive rights of the author and the limitations and exceptions to those rights are the mechanisms that allow for such a fair balancing.[34] The safeguarding of the public interest is but one of the concerns examined in the jurisprudence of the CJEU, however. Other frequently reiterated concerns relate to the need to ensure the good functioning of the internal market and to establish a high level of protection for authors, allowing them to obtain an appropriate reward for the use of their works.[35] In the absence of an overarching European 'copyright rationale', these concerns are weighed against each other on a case-by-case basis in the light of a specific factual situation, just applying a particular piece of secondary legislation. This inevitably leads to varying outcomes. In other words, there is no comprehensive, coherent or explicit set of rationales underlying the European harmonisation in the area of copyright law that can serve to delineate what ought, or ought not, to be part of the rights owners' monopoly.

3. IMPACT OF HARMONISED EUROPEAN COPYRIGHT LAW ON PUBLIC DOMAIN

The progressive harmonisation of European copyright law is bound to affect the public domain in some way. That new copyright rules end up having an impact on the public domain is almost unavoidable in practice, since the preservation of the public domain is never part of the European Commission's impact assessment reports.[36] New copyright rules impact the public domain any time that the term of protection is extended, new subject matter receives protection, new rights are created or new conditions of use are imposed. Such new rules essentially mean that permission to use is needed where none was required before

---

[34] CJEU judgment of 29 July 2019, *Pelham GmbH, Moses Pelham, Martin Haas v. Ralf Hütter, Florian Schneider Esleben*, C-476/17, ECLI:EU:C:2019:624, para. 59; CJEU judgment of 29 July 2019, *Spiegel Online*, C-516/17, ECLI:EU:C:2019:625, para. 42; CJEU judgment of 29 July 2019, *Funke Medien*, C-469/17, ECLI:EU:C:2019:623, para. 56.

[35] CJEU judgment of 7 August 2018, *Land Nordrhein Westfalen v. Renckhoff*, C-161/17, ECLI:EU:C:2018:634, para. 18; CJEU judgment of 1 March 2017, *ITV Broadcasting v. TVCatchup Ltd*, C-275/15, ECLI:EU:C:2017:144, paras. 22 and 23; CJEU judgment of 4 October 2011, *Football Association Premier League and Others*, C-403/08 and C-429/08, ECLI:EU:C:2011:631, para. 186.

[36] See for example Commission Staff Working Document, *Impact Assessment on the modernisation of EU copyright rules*, European Commission, Brussels, 14 September 2016, SWD (2016) 301 final.

their introduction. Besides the price that must now be paid in exchange for the permission to use, new rules generate transaction costs typically associated with the identification of the party from whom permission must be obtained, with the negotiation of an agreement and with the enforcement of that agreement. From a law and economics perspective, the recognition of new rules makes sense if the social welfare exceeds the costs incurred by their introduction and enforcement. A law and economics approach to rulemaking is only one way to justify the introduction of new legal norms, however. It likely does not take account of non-economic considerations, such as the effect of reduced access to culture and the creation of limits on freedom of expression.

Trying to quantify the impact of EU copyright rulemaking on the public domain is a tremendously important project, but one that would go well beyond the bounds of this study.[37] However, a qualitative estimate of the possible impact of the harmonised copyright rules on the public domain would offer a useful contextualisation for the discussion of the BIP cases in the following section. For the purposes of this section, 'public domain' is understood in its broadest sense, i.e. as encompassing not only information that does not meet the threshold for protection or works the copyright term of which has lapsed, but also the free spaces created by limitations on exclusive rights and by the author's voluntary relinquishment of rights.[38] In Jessica Litman's words, the public domain includes 'those aspects of copyrighted works which copyright does not protect'.[39]

The table below lists every Directive and Regulation adopted by the European legislator in the area of copyright law since 1991. In the right column is my own assessment of the impact of the Directive on the public domain. The assessment is based on whether each Directive[40] introduces either or more of the following measures:

- extension of the duration of protection;
- coverage of new subject matter;
- creation of new exclusive right;
- creation of new remuneration right;
- creation of other restrictions on use;
- recognition of exceptions and limitations;

---

37 For an empirical study of the impact of term extension on the exploitation of books, see: J. Flynn/R. Giblin/F. Petitjean, 'What happens when books enter the public domain? Testing copyright's underuse hypothesis across Australia, New Zealand, the United States and Canada', 42(4) *University of New South Wales Law Journal* (2019), 1215–1253. The authors find that even the shortest copyright terms can outlast works' commercial value, even where cultural value remains and that works are priced much higher where they are under copyright than where they in the public domain.

38 Boyle (2003, supra n. 10), 60.

39 J. Litman, 'The Public Domain', 39 *Emory L.J.* (1990), 1010, 1023.

40 For the reference to each Directive and Regulation, see supra n. 21.

Table 1. Comparative Impact of EU Directives on the Public Domain

Directive Title		Impact on the Public Domain
1.	Directive 2009/24/EC on the legal protection of computer programs (former Directive 91/250/EC)	Net neutral effect
2.	Directive 2006/115/EC on rental and lending rights and related rights (former Directive 92/100/EC)	Negative effect
3.	Directive 93/83/EEC on satellite and cable retransmission of copyrighted works	Neutral effect
4.	Directive 2006/116/EC on the term of protection of copyright and related rights (former Directive 93/98/EC)	Negative effect
5.	Directive 96/9/EC on the legal protection of databases	Negative effect
6.	Directive 2001/29/EC on copyright and related rights in the information society	Net negative effect
7.	Directive 2001/84/EC on resale right	Neutral effect
8.	Directive 2012/28/EU on certain permitted uses of orphan works	Net neutral effect
9.	Directive 2014/26/EU on collective management of copyright and related rights	Neutral effect
10.	Regulation (EU) No. 2017/1128 on cross-border portability of digital content	Neutral effect
11.	Regulation (EU) No. 2017/1563 on cross-border exchange of accessible formats for persons with a visual disability	Positive effect
12.	Directive (EU) 2019/790 on copyright in the Digital Single Market	Net negative effect

Source: Compiled by the author.

As explained hereafter, the result is either 'positive', 'neutral', 'net neutral', 'net negative' or 'negative'. Only one Regulation turns out to have a 'positive effect' on the public domain, i.e. Regulation (EU) No. 2017/1563 on the cross-border exchange of accessible formats for persons with a visual disability. The overall aim of this Regulation is to create a regime allowing for the importation and exportation of accessible format copies of books for persons with a visual disability. The Regulation does so without introducing other obstacles or impediments to access and use of copyright-protected works. Three Directives – on satellite and cable retransmission, on resale right, and on the collective management of rights – and the Regulation on the cross-border portability of digital content qualify in my opinion as having a 'neutral effect' on the public domain, because they essentially aim at regulating the exercise of existing rights, without introducing any of the measures mentioned above.

Directive 2009/24/EC on the protection of computer programs (formerly Directive 91/250/EC) is one of two Directives categorised as having a 'net neutral effect' on the public domain. This classification reflects the fact that the

Directive does extend copyright protection to a new type of work and that it recognises exclusive rights to the authors, but that it also builds in exceptions for the benefit of users, including making reproductions for back-up and decompilation purposes. Moreover, Article 9 of the Directive specifies that the exceptions provided for in this Directive cannot be overridden by contract. At the time of adoption back in 1991, the Directive was considered to correspond to industry practice.[41] If it is any indication of the Directive's net neutral effect, the number of court cases that have arisen over a period of almost three decades around the interpretation of the provisions contained therein has remained, comparatively speaking, extremely low.[42]

Directive 2012/24/EC on certain permitted uses of orphan works is the second Directive that falls under the category of norms having a 'net neutral effect' on the public domain, despite its intended objective of facilitating the digitisation and dissemination of orphan works. The Directive creates a legal framework for the recognition of an 'orphan work status' for protected works the rights owner of which cannot be identified or located. The framework is aimed at cultural heritage institutions (publicly accessible libraries, educational establishments and museums, as well as archives, film or audio heritage institutions and public-service broadcasting organisations). The European legislator's strict premise is that prior consent of all rightholders is required before cultural heritage institutions can proceed with digitising and making available to the public any work in their collection.[43] In the case of orphan works, prior consent cannot be obtained. An institution is exempted from obtaining permission under the Directive only if a work acquires 'orphan' status, after a diligent search for the rightholder has been carried out and recorded. A diligent search must be conducted in good faith in respect of each work in an institution's collection by consulting appropriate sources for the category of work in question. In practice, the diligent search obligation is so cumbersome that cultural heritage institutions refrain from relying on this framework to provide access to the works in their collections.[44]

---

41 M. Lehmann (ed.), *Rechtsschutz und Verwertung von Computerprogrammen* (Cologne: 1993), 161 ff.

42 The list of cases involving Directive 91/250/ECC is the following: CJEU judgment of 18 December 2019, *IT Development SAS v. Free Mobile SAS*, C-666/18, ECLI:EU:C:2019:1099; CJEU judgment of 12 October 2016, *Ranks v. Microsoft*, C-166/15, ECLI:EU:C:2016:762; CJEU judgment 3 July 2012, *UsedSoft v. Oracle*, C-128/11, ECLI:EU:C:2012:407; CJEU judgment of 2 May 2012, *SAS Institute Inc. v. World Programming Ltd*, C-406/10, ECLI:EU:C:2012:259; CJEU judgment of 22 December 2010, *BSA v. Ministry of Culture Czech Republic*, C-393/09, ECLI:EU:C:2010:816.

43 Directive 2012/24/EC on certain permitted uses of orphan works, Recital 6.

44 S. Schroff/M. Favale/A. Bertoni, 'The Impossible Quest – Problems with Diligent Search for Orphan Works', 48 *IIC* (2017), 286–304; E. Rosati, 'The Orphan Works Directive, or throwing a stone and hiding the hand', 8(4) *Journal of Intellectual Property Law & Practice* (2013), 303–310.

Two Directives, i.e. Directive 2001/29/EC and Directive 2019/790, qualify in my opinion as having a 'net negative effect' on the public domain. The first one is Directive 2001/29/EC on copyright in the information society. This piece of legislation was very controversial from its inception and has remained so until today, as evidenced by the high number of disputes and referrals that make their way to the CJEU. At its origin, Directive 2001/29/EC pursued a twofold objective: to harmonise certain aspects of copyright and related rights law throughout the internal market, and to implement Europe's international obligations under the WIPO Internet Treaties.[45] While the Directive consolidates the exclusive rights conferred on authors and related rights owners, especially as they apply in the digital networked environment, it also recognises an exhaustive list of exceptions and limitations. Commentators have criticised the lack of clarity with regard the boundaries between the harmonised rights and the scope of each one of them. Rights and exceptions could have balanced each other out, were it not for the fact that in the countless cases that have arisen since the implementation of the Directive, the CJEU has most often given a broad interpretation to the rights and a restrictive interpretation to the exceptions.

The most controversial element of Directive 2001/29/EC, however, is the introduction of legal protection against the circumvention of technological protection measures (TPMs) and the removal of rights management information. Again, although the Directive attempted in Article 6(4) to accommodate the exercise of exceptions with the use of TPMs, the national implementation of this provision has created more legal uncertainty than anything else. Users have generally not been able to benefit from this countervailing measure at all, primarily because Article 6(4) excludes its application to content offered online pursuant to contractual terms. Nowadays, the vast majority of works distributed online are subject to contractual terms of use.[46] Overall, the impediments to the use of copyrighted content enabled through Directive 2001/29/EC in my opinion clearly outweigh the exceptions' potentially positive effect.

Directive 2019/790 on copyright in the Digital Single Market was recently adopted after years of consultation, study and reflection on the part of the European institutions and stakeholders on the direction to give European copyright reform. The final text of this Directive is a far cry from the Commission's once-expressed intention to create a European Copyright Code allowing for a far-reaching overhaul of the EU copyright framework and contributing to the

[45] WIPO Copyright Treaty (WCT) and the WIPO Performers and Phonograms Treaty (WPPT), both signed in Geneva, on 22 December 1996.

[46] M. M. M. van Eechoud et al., *Harmonizing European Copyright Law – The Challenges of Better Lawmaking* (Alphen aan den Rijn: 2009), 162 ff.

development of the Digital Single Market.[47] The stated objective of this Directive does not differ much from that of Directive 2001/29/EC, i.e. 'to adapt EU copyright rules in a context where digital technologies are rapidly changing the way works and other protected subject matter are created, produced, distributed and exploited'. What the Directive gives with one hand, it takes away with the other, with the end result being a 'net negative effect' on the public domain. The Directive creates a number of new exceptions to address different issues arising in the knowledge economy. First, two exceptions permit text and data mining, one mandatory exception for reproductions made by research organisations and cultural heritage institutions for scientific research purposes, and one for general text and data mining in support of the development of data analytics and artificial intelligence. Second, educational establishments will be able to use works in digital and cross-border teaching activities to the extent justified by the non-commercial purpose to be achieved. Third, the Directive introduces a new licensing mechanism, backed with an exception in case no licensing mechanism exists, for the digitisation and dissemination of out-of-commerce works by cultural heritage institutions. In relation to this, the Directive contains one of the very few provisions in the entire *acquis communautaire* that expressly refers to the public domain, at Article 14:

> Member States shall provide that, when the term of protection of a work of visual art has expired, any material resulting from an act of reproduction of that work is not subject to copyright or related rights, unless the material resulting from that act of reproduction is original in the sense that it is the author's own intellectual creation.

Article 14 clearly aims at preserving the public domain, by preventing re-appropriation through copyright or related rights claims over the digitisation of public domain works. This provision essentially reverses the decision of the German Federal Court of Justice, which confirmed that photographs of public domain paintings are, in principle, protected by a copyright-related right under the German Copyright Act.[48] The Reiss Engelhorn Museum in Mannheim had instituted a court proceeding against Wikimedia for having made available to the public online a number of photographs of public domain works of art on display at the museum. Although Article 14 should in principle act as a barrier against

---

47 European Commission, *Communication from the Commission to the European Parliament, the Council, the European Economic and Social Committee and the Committee of the Regions, A Single Market for Intellectual Property Rights Boosting creativity and innovation to provide economic growth, high quality jobs and first class products and services in Europe*, COM (2011) 287.

48 German Federal Court of Justice, decision of 20 December 2018, Case No. I ZR 104/17 (*Museumfotos*).

a museum's copyright claim on 'mere' digital reproductions of public domain works, the Directive leaves the door open to infringement claims whenever a digital reproduction is deemed to meet the European originality requirement. Moreover, nothing in the Directive prevents the holder of a public domain work from disseminating the digital copy pursuant to restrictive contractual terms or subject to technological protection measures.

The 'net negative effect' of Directive 2019/790 is partly attributable to two other intensely debated provisions: (1) the creation of a new right that allows news publishers to claim remuneration for the online use of their publications (Art. 15); and (2) the imposition of content monitoring measures on online platforms such as YouTube, which seeks to resolve the 'value gap' and help rightholders to better monetise and control the distribution of their content online (Art. 17).[49] Both provisions were highly controversial throughout the adoption process, precisely because of the negative impact that they are anticipated to have on the public domain and on the general public's fundamental freedom of expression. In my opinion, the restrictions put on the online distribution of news articles and on the content made available through online platforms have the potential to negatively affect a significantly greater number of people, and in a much broader context, than the number of people who might benefit from the free spaces created by the Directive.

Finally, three Directives have an unmistakably 'negative effect' on the public domain, i.e. Directive 2006/115/EC on rental and lending rights and related rights, Directive 2011/77/EU on the term of protection, and Directive 96/9/EC on the legal protection of databases. The first of the three, as it was initially adopted in 1992,[50] Directive 2006/115/EC on rental and lending rights, was celebrated among rights owner representative groups as a positive step towards greater protection for authors and related rights owners.[51] Not only did it harmonise the commercial rental and public lending rights of authors, it also harmonised the rights of four categories of neighbouring rights owners: performing artists, phonogram producers, film producers and broadcasting organisations.[52] For a number of member states, harmonisation of both categories

---

49 J. P. Quintais, 'Safeguarding User Freedoms in Implementing Article 17 of the Copyright in the Digital Single Market Directive: Recommendations from European Academics', Kluwer Copyright Blog, 12 November 2019, available at: http://copyrightblog.kluweriplaw.com/2019/11/12/safeguarding-user-freedoms-in-implementing-article-17-of-the-copyright-in-the-digital-single-market-directive-recommendations-from-european-academics/.

50 Directive 92/100/EC, OJ L 346, 27 November 1992, 61.

51 R. A. Rosenbloum, 'The Rental Rights Directive: A Step in the Right and Wrong Directions', 15 *Loy. L.A. Ent. L. Rev.* (1995), 547; J. Reinbothe/S. von Lewinski, *The EC Directive on Rental and Lending Rights and on Piracy* (London: 1993).

52 Hugenholtz (2013, supra n. 22), 507.

of rights did not mean the simple adaptation of existing norms to a common European framework, but rather their introduction in national legislation in the first place. The Directive contains only four limitations on neighbouring rights, but leaves it at the discretion of the member state to provide for the same kinds of limitations with regard to the protection of performers, producers of phonograms, broadcasting organisations and of producers of the first fixations of films as it provides for in connection with the protection of copyright in literary and artistic works. As a result, from the date of coming into force of Directive 92/100/EC, the objects covered by the new rights could no longer be used without prior permission, save in circumstances falling within the scope of a limitation.

The Directive with the most direct impact on the public domain – understood in its traditional sense – is Directive 93/98/EC on the term of protection of copyright and related rights, which was first adopted in 1993,[53] codified in 2006, and revised in 2011.[54] On two formal occasions, 1993 and 2011, the European legislator extended the duration of protection to the direct detriment of the public domain. The 1993 Directive effectively prolonged the copyright protection by 20 years, bringing it to the life of the author plus 70 years after death. Spain's longer copyright term of 100 years after the death of the author was grandfathered into the Directive. The 2011 Directive fixed the term of protection with respect to any subject matter other than a phonogram to 50 years from first publication or communication to the public, and brought the term of protection of a lawfully published fixation of the performance in a phonogram in line with copyright, i.e. 70 years after the first publication or first communication to the public. Recital 5 of the Directive states explains that '[w]hereas the minimum term of protection laid down by the Berne Convention, namely the life of the author and 50 years after his death, was intended to provide protection for the author and the first two generations of his descendants; whereas the average lifespan in the Community has grown longer, to the point where this term is no longer sufficient to cover two generations'. So, while the harmonisation of the term of protection is not without gaps and exceptions,[55] the overall effect of this measure

53 Council Directive 93/98/EEC of 29 October 1993 harmonizing the term of protection of copyright and certain related rights, OJ L 290, 24 November 1993, 9–13.

54 Directive 2011/77/EU of the European Parliament and of the Council of 27 September 2011 amending Directive 2006/116/EC on the term of protection of copyright and certain related rights, OJ L 265, 11 October 2011, 1–5.

55 The Term Directive leaves member states free to decide how to regulate the term of protection of previously unpublished works (Art. 4), critical and scientific works (Art. 5) and photographs (Art. 6); the Directive also allows member states that had a longer term of protection prior to the adoption of the Directive to maintain that longer term of protection (Art. 10).

has been to ratchet up the term of protection and actively delay works and other subject matter from entering the public domain.[56]

The last Directive considered as having a negative effect on the public domain is Directive 96/9/EC on the legal protection of databases. This Directive recognises a two-tier regime of protection for databases: one based on the rules of copyright law, for databases that reflect the authors' own intellectual creation, and a second based on *sui generis* rules, granting protection to non-original databases that show a substantial investment, measured qualitatively and/or quantitatively, in either the obtaining, verification or presentation of the contents. The first part of the Directive harmonises the rules of copyright law with respect to databases across the member states, granting protection to databases that show originality in the selection or arrangement of their content. The second part of the Directive, however, creates an entirely new form of protection to the benefit of makers of databases, by subjecting non-original databases to exclusive rights of extraction and re-utilisation for a term of 15 years, renewable upon demonstration of additional substantial investment. Since the Directive contains several ambiguous concepts that are prone to interpretation, the CJEU has been called upon to render preliminary rulings in numerous cases. While the Court has often given a rather narrow interpretation of the type of substantial investment qualifying a database for protection,[57] once protection is admitted, the Court tends to give a rather broad interpretation of the scope of protection conferred under the Directive.[58] Absent this unique protection regime, non-original databases would not be the object of an exclusive right and they would be freely re-usable by anyone. The negative impact on the public domain is all the more deplorable given that, in two separate evaluation studies, the effectiveness of the *sui generis* right as a means to stimulate investment on databases was found to be unproven and still highly contested.[59]

---

56 C. Angelopoulos, 'The Myth of European Term Harmonisation: 27 Public Domains for the 27 Member States', 5 *International Review of Intellectual Property and Competition Law* (2012), 567.

57 CJEU judgment of 9 November 2004, *The British Horseracing Board and Others v. William Hill Organization Ltd*, C-203/02, ECLI:EU:C:2004:695; *Fixtures Marketing v. Organismos prognostikon agonon podosfairou AE (OPAP)*, C-46/02, ECLI:EU:C:2004:694; *Fixtures Marketing v. Svenska Spel AB*, C-338/02, ECLI:EU:C:2004:696; *Fixtures Marketing and Oy Veikkaus Ab*, C-444/02, ECLI:EU:C:2004:697.

58 CJEU judgment of 29 October 2015, *Freistaat Bayern v. Verlag Esterbauer GmbH*, C-490/14, ECLI:EU:C:2015:735; CJEU judgment of 19 December 2013, *Innoweb BV v. Wegener ICT Media BV and Wegener Mediaventions BV*, C-202/12, ECLI:EU:C:2013:850; CJEU judgment of 5 March 2009, *Apis-Hristovich EOOD v. Lakorda AD*, C-545/07, ECLI:EU:C:2009:132; CJEU judgment of 9 October 2008, *Directmedia Publishing GmbH v. Albert-Ludwigs-Universität Freiburg*, C-304/07, ECLI:EU:C:2008:552.

59 JIIP & Technopolis, Study in support of the evaluation of Directive 96/9/EC on the legal protection of databases – final report, European Commission, Brussels, DG Communications Networks, 16 May 2018, SMART number 2017/0084, 140; European Commission, First evaluation of Directive 96/9/EC on the legal protection of databases, DG Internal Market

While half of the secondary legislation put in place by the European lawmaker in the area of copyright can be deemed as having a negative effect on the public domain, the impact of the CJEU's case law on the public domain is more subtle. Only a handful of decisions expressly mention the words 'public domain', all of which in relation to the term of protection.[60] We should keep in mind, however, that if the Court interprets statutory provisions in favour of rights owners, it may ultimately result in a reduction of the public domain. It would go beyond the scope of this chapter to examine in detail how each decision of the Court of Justice in the area of copyright and related rights law might affect the public domain. Suffice it to say that the preservation of the public domain is not a priority of the Court. Perhaps it should not be the Court's priority. But in the absence of any normative guidance on the rationales of the European copyright regime, such a definite position would also be too dismissive.

III. PUBLIC DOMAIN AND THE BIP CASES

Despite international and European harmonisation efforts in the field of intellectual property, significant differences remain in the way member states have drawn the line between protecting rights and accommodating the public interest. The tension between copyright protection and public interest finds its expression in the contours of the public domain, i.e. in the determination of what is, or is not, part of the owner's exclusive rights. Legislators and courts play an important role in defining the public domain, just as private parties play a role in contractually adapting the limits of protection to their own circumstances. Taking a broad and inclusive approach to the interpretation of the public domain, we posit that the spaces left around the islands of IP protection form the public domain. These spaces include not only the 'negative' public domain, i.e. everything that is not, or is no longer, protected by IP, but also the free uses recognised by statutory law and the voluntary uses permitted by rights owners.[61] Considered from a positivist perspective, the public domain comprises all

---

and Services Working Paper, Brussels, 12 December 2005; see A. Beunen, *Protection for Databases: The European Database Directive and Its Effects in the Netherlands, France and the United Kingdom* (Nijmegen: 2007).

60 CJEU judgment of 29 July 2019, *Pelham GmbH, Moses Pelham, Martin Haas v. Ralf Hütter, Florian Schneider Esleben*, C-476/17, ECLI:EU:C:2019:624; CJEU judgment of 20 October 2010, *Montis Design BV v. Goosens Meubelen BV*, C-169/15, ECLI:EU:C:2016:790; CJEU judgment of 24 June 2010, *Flos SPA v. Semeraro Casa e Famiglia SPA*, C-168/09, ECLI:EU:C:2010:371; CJEU judgment of 29 June 1999, *Butterly Music Srl v. Carosello Edizioni Musicali e Discografiche Srl*, C-60/98, ECLI:EU:C:1999:33.

61 P. Samuelson, 'Mapping the digital public domain – Threats and opportunities', 66 *Law & Contemp. Probs* (2003), 147–172.

intellectual works that can be copied, used and re-used without restriction of any kind. 'Open' knowledge falls within this description.[62]

Each of the three BIP cases examined below deals with a different aspect of copyright and related rights protection on the spectrum of the public domain, going from the definition of what is protectable subject matter (Case 4 on public sector information), to the free use recognised in the copyright act (Case 3 on the private copying exception), and the voluntary relinquishment of rights by the author (Case 14 on the voluntary relinquishment of rights). Cases 3 and 14 allow not only for a consideration of the role of statutory provisions in shaping the contours of the European public domain, but also for an examination of the impact of private contracts on such contours.

1. PUBLIC SECTOR INFORMATION (CASE 4)

Traditionally the public domain is understood in a negative way, i.e. everything that is not, or is no longer, protected by IP. A basic tenet of copyright law holds that only original expressions of ideas are susceptible of protection. Raw data, facts and other non-original information fall outside of the copyright regime. Similarly, non-original collections of raw data, facts or any other type of content remained unprotected, until the adoption of Directive 96/9/EC on the legal protection of databases.[63] As mentioned in the previous section, this Directive introduced a *sui generis* right for non-original databases that demonstrate a substantial investment in the collection, verification and presentation of a database. The creation of this new right initially pursued a purely utilitarian objective, as evidenced by two recitals in the Directive which state that 'databases are a vital tool in the development of an information market within the Community' and that 'investment in modern information storage and processing systems will not take place within the Community unless a stable and uniform legal protection regime is introduced for the protection of the rights of makers of databases'.[64]

Case 4 focuses on the practice of a public body, a meteorological institute, around the licensing of meteorological data to third parties for a fee. Meteorological data, as such, is clearly public domain information. Does it matter that this information is produced by a public body, i.e. an organisation financed through public means? Does the public character of the entity producing the

62 Pollock (2006, supra n. 7).

63 There were a few exceptions, like the *geschriftenbescherming* in the Netherlands and the 'catalogue right' in Scandinavian countries, which were progressively repealed following the adoption of Directive 96/9/EC.

64 Directive 96/9/EC on the legal protection of databases, Recital 9.

data reinforce the 'public domain' dimension of the information contained in the database? The hidden question underlying Case 4's factual situation is whether the law of the member states makes any distinction in the level of protection awarded to databases created by a governmental body, as opposed to a private entity. Arguably, the utilitarian objective of the *sui generis* right plays no role for public bodies, as a country's meteorological institute needs no financial incentives to produce weather-related data. Since meteorological data is created in the normal course of operation of the meteorological institute, does a database containing such data meet the Directive's requirement of substantial investment? If it does, would there be any public interest reason to limit a public body's exercise of the database right? Does the purpose for which the content of the database is used influence the outcome?

The vast majority of the national reports conclude that the user of the database would need to obtain a licence from the meteorological institute, without which the institute would have a claim for injunction against the user on the basis of the *sui generis* database right. Only a few country reporters raised the question of whether public bodies are able to qualify as database makers under Directive 96/9/EC. After analysis, the common opinion among the country reporters is that the Directive does not exclude public entities from its scope of application. The next question raised by some was whether the production of a meteorological database meets the criterion of substantial investment in the collection, verification and presentation of the data: is the meteorological institute 'collecting' the data in the sense of the Directive, or is it merely 'creating' the data through daily meteorological observations as in the *British Horseracing Board* and *Fixture Marketing* cases, in which case no substantial investment is recognised?[65] In the absence of sufficient information conveyed in the case description, country reporters erred in favour of recognising protection for the database maker, rather than recognising the public domain nature of the meteorological database. Appropriation of information seems to be the collective default rule in such situations. Several country reporters did remark, however, that the meteorological institute would need to abide by the rules on competition law and avoid abusing its dominant position on the market. This means that the institute would be required to grant a licence under reasonable and non-discriminatory terms.

In two separate decisions, the Court of Justice of the EU confirmed the country reporters' general opinion that Directive 96/9/EC applies to databases

65 CJEU judgment of 9 November 2004, *The British Horseracing Board and Others v. William Hill Organization Ltd*, C-203/02, ECLI:EU:C:2004:695; *Fixtures Marketing v. Organismos prognostikon agonon podosfairou AE (OPAP)*, C-46/02, ECLI:EU:C:2004:694; *Fixtures Marketing v. Svenska Spel AB*, C-338/02, ECLI:EU:C:2004:696; *Fixtures Marketing and Oy Veikkaus Ab*, C-444/02, ECLI:EU:C:2004:697.

created by a public body.[66] The *Compass-Datenbank* case involved a private entity's request for access to the companies register created and maintained by the Republic of Austria and whether Austria's licensing activities qualified as an 'undertaking' within the meaning of Article 102 TFEU. In reaching its conclusion on the competition law issue, the Court accepted Austria's reliance on the *sui generis* database right to protect the information contained in the companies register, but without considering in detail whether the database met the criteria for protection set out in Directive 96/9/EC. In the second case, Freistaat Bayern claimed that Verlag Esterbauer had made an unlawful use of its topographic maps and had appropriated the underlying data in order to produce its own touristic maps. The entire case revolved around the concept of database and the notion of 'independent materials' in a database. Remarkably, the Court took for granted that the Bavarian topographic maps were covered by the database right, without even speaking a word about whether the maps met the substantial investment criterion. The Court has yet to pronounce on what qualifies as a substantial investment in relation to data created by a public body.

With respect to the use of public domain information, Case 4 raises another important issue, that of the intersection between IP protection and the European norms on the re-use of public sector information. A number of country reporters pointed out that the use of the meteorological data could fall within the scope of Directive 2003/98/EC on re-use of public sector information.[67] But this relationship is not necessarily an easy one, as several country reporters highlighted in their reports. Recital 22 of Directive 2003/98/EC on the re-use of public sector information emphasises that 'the Directive does not affect the existence or ownership of intellectual property rights of public sector bodies, nor does it limit the exercise of these rights in any way beyond the boundaries set by this Directive'.[68] Consequently, where a public sector body deals with IP-protected material, whether produced internally or through third parties, the IP protection will prevail over the obligation to allow re-use. On the other hand, Directive 2003/98/EC does lay down principles for the re-use of the public sector information, concerning the fees that may be charged for allowing re-use and the licensing conditions that may not restrain competition.[69] Clearly, letting the public body's IP rights prevail over the possibility to re-use the public sector

66 CJEU judgment of 12 July 2012, *Compass-Datenbank GmbH v. Republik Österreich*, C-138/11, ECLI:EU:C:2012:449; CJEU judgment of 29 October 2015, *Freistaat Bayern v. Verlag Esterbauer GmbH*, C-490/14, ECLI:EU:C:2015:735.

67 Directive 2003/98/EC of the European Parliament and of the Council of 17 November 2003 on the re-use of public sector information, OJ L 345, 31 December 2003, 90–96.

68 Directive 2003/98/EC, Recital 22.

69 Directive 2003/98/EC, Arts. 6 and 8.

information frustrates the goals of Directive 2003/98/EC on the re-use of public sector information. This policy blocks the general public's access to public domain material.

Giving access and allowing re-use of public sector information is essentially a matter of policy. Especially in the age of Big Data and artificial intelligence, the European legislator recently reassessed its position on the matter. Directive 2019/1024 on open data and the re-use of public sector information[70] moves away from the longstanding position described above, at least in respect to specific categories of data produced by government agencies. Article 1(6) of Directive declares that '[t]he right for the maker of a database provided for in Article 7(1) of Directive 96/9/EC shall not be exercised by public sector bodies in order to prevent the re-use of documents or to restrict re-use beyond the limits set by this Directive'. The thematic categories of high-value datasets covered by Article 1(6), as referred to in Article 13(1) of the Directive, are:

1. geospatial;
2. earth observation and environment;
3. meteorological;
4. statistics;
5. companies and company ownership; and
6. mobility.

Interestingly, if this Directive had been adopted a decade ago, neither the *Compass-Datenbank*[71] case nor the *Freistaat Bayern*[72] case would have made their way to the Court of Justice: both types of data concerned in these decisions (geospatial, and companies and company ownership) figure among the 'specific categories of data' for which public sector bodies may not exercise database rights in order to prevent the re-use of documents or to restrict re-use beyond the limits set by the Directive. The same conclusion would have applied to Case 4 on meteorological data. It is worth emphasising, however, that any other collection of research data created or curated by the government would be subject to the new principle of 'as open as possible, as closed as necessary', which means that concerns relating to intellectual property rights, personal data protection and

---

70 Directive (EU) 2019/1024 of the European Parliament and of the Council of 20 June 2019 on open data and the re-use of public sector information, PE/28/2019/REV/1, OJ L 172, 26 June 2019, 56–83.

71 CJEU judgment of 12 July 2012, *Compass-Datenbank GmbH v. Republik Österreich*, C-138/11, ECLI:EU:C:2012:449.

72 Court of Justice of the European Union, Judgment of the Court of 29 October 2015, C-490/14 *Freistaat Bayern v. Verlag Esterbauer GmbH*, ECLI:EU:C:2015:735.

confidentiality, security, and legitimate commercial interests would be taken into account in accordance with this principle.[73]

A final word on the protection of facts and data, to emphasise the possible impact that the CJEU's *Ryanair* decision[74] may have on the public domain. Essentially, the Court of Justice ruled that, despite the fact that Ryanair's dataset (price, flight and timetable information) was not protected by copyright or by the *sui generis* database right, not only could the airline company impose valid contractual re-use restrictions, but the exceptions normally recognised by law did not apply. In the Court's own words:

> it is clear from the purpose and structure of Directive 96/9 that Articles 6(1), 8 and 15 thereof, which establish mandatory rights for lawful users of databases, are not applicable to a database which is not protected either by copyright or by the *sui generis* right under that directive, so that it does not prevent the adoption of contractual clauses concerning the conditions of use of such a database.[75]

This very controversial decision disregards the balance mechanisms built into IP legislation and effectively reinforces the primacy of public ordering through contracts. Were a public body to engage in such licensing practices, one would hope that the rules on competition and the principles laid down in Directive 2003/98/EC on the re-use of public sector information – as later amended – would impose appropriate limits on the public authority, in order to protect the public interest in accessing and re-using public domain information. Although a call for reversing the *Ryanair* case has been heard from all quarters, that correction has yet to occur.[76] In the meantime, private parties may contractually appropriate non-protected, public domain information with little to no impunity.

2. PRIVATE COPYING EXCEPTION (CASE 3)

Beyond the traditional conception of the public domain are the free uses recognised by statutory law. Directive 2001/29/EC on the harmonisation of copyright and related rights in the information society is the main instrument through which the European legislator has purported to harmonise the exceptions on copyright. Statutory exceptions create free spaces that allow,

---

73 Directive (EU) 2019/1024 of the European Parliament and of the Council of 20 June 2019 on open data and the re-use of public sector information, PE/28/2019/REV/1, OJ L 172, 26 June 2019, 56–83, Art. 10(1).

74 CJEU judgment of 15 January 2015, *Ryanair Ltd v. PR Aviation BV*, C-30/14, ECLI:EU:C:2015:1.

75 Ibid., para. 39.

76 JIIP & Technopolis, *Study in support of the evaluation of Directive 96/9/EC on the legal protection of databases – final report*, European Commission, Brussels, DG Communications Networks, 16 May 2018, SMART number 2017/0084, iii.

under specific conditions, for certain uses to lawfully take place without the prior authorisation of the rights owner. Ideally the determination of the types of uses permitted and the conditions for their exercise would be guided by the rationales underlying the copyright regime. As observed in section II.B above, however, there is no comprehensive, coherent or explicit set of rationales at the root of the European copyright framework that can serve to delineate what ought, or ought not, to be part of the rights owners' monopoly. The lack of common justification is discernible in relation to the exceptions contained in Article 5 of Directive 2001/29/EC. As a result, the list of 20-odd optional exceptions does not immediately lead to significant harmonisation.[77] Partly due to the harmonising effect of the case law of the Court of Justice of the EU, the laws of the member states have converged over time. But there are still remarkable outliers. Moreover, harmonisation has occurred primarily with respect to the categories of exceptions, rather than with respect to the precise scope and workings of each exception.

Initially inspired by peer-to-peer file-sharing activities, Case 3 deals at its core with the exercise of the private copying exception. The advent of peer-to-peer file-sharing technology opened the door to widespread copying activities by individuals, though mostly illegal. Base Case 3 and its modifications examine the multiple ways in which peer-to-peer file-sharing technology in particular, and digital technology in general, have put a strain on the boundaries of the private copying exception. The boundaries of the exception shift over time, depending on the interpretation given to the relevant statutory provision, in light of the objectives ascribed to each national copyright regime: a regime grounded on the person of the author gives a narrower interpretation of the private copying exception than a system based on utilitarian or other social principles. The national reports reveal a mosaic of different approaches and solutions to the issue. Notably, the legislation of Ireland and the United Kingdom do not recognise a general private copying exception. As a consequence, peer-to-peer file-sharing activities are in these two countries always unlawful.

The free use space afforded pursuant to the private copying exception is subject to strict conditions, laid down in Article 5(2)(b) of Directive 2001/29/EC:

> Member States may provide for exceptions or limitations to the reproduction right provided for in Article 2 in respect of reproductions on any medium made by a natural person for private use and for ends that are neither directly nor indirectly commercial, on condition that the rightholders receive fair compensation which takes account of the application or non-application of technological measures referred to in Article 6 to the work or subject-matter concerned.

[77] L. Guibault, 'Why Cherry Picking Never Leads to Harmonisation: The Case of the Limitations on Copyright under Directive 2001/29/EC', 2 *JIPITEC* (2010), 55.

Key limitations to the free use space therefore concern the person allowed to make the reproduction, the absence of direct or indirect commercial purpose, the obligation to pay fair compensation and the application of technological protection measures. As transpires from the national reports, other limitations have been imposed on private copying activities through judicial interpretation.

Base Case 3 addresses the issue of the copyright relevant act involved in downloading songs from the Internet, the person permitted to make a private copy, and the final destination of that copy. With respect to the first issue, the technology used has a direct impact on the outcome: songs downloaded from the Internet by using a peer-to-peer file-sharing software nowadays involve not only an act of reproduction, but also an act of communication to the public. Since Article 5(2)(b) Directive 2001/29/EC applies only to acts of reproduction, any act of communication to the public would be an infringement. Although the text of Article 5(2)(b) does not explicitly require it, the national legislation and courts have consistently ruled that the natural person doing the reproduction must do so for their own personal purposes and may not transfer the copy to any third party. An original, tangible copy of the work could be handed over to someone else, however, on the basis of the exhaustion doctrine. Similarly, legislators and courts throughout the European Union have progressively come to agree that, in order for the private copying exception to apply, the copyright-protected works need to be downloaded from a lawful source.[78] Put another way, the statutory exception for private copying does not apply, or no longer applies, to most peer-to-peer file-sharing activities.

Given the illegal character of most peer-to-peer file-sharing activities, the first modification to Case 3 focuses on the potential liability of an intermediary service provider (ISP) who facilitates such activities. A corollary question is whether the ISP can be obliged by law to disclose the personal data of customers alleged to infringe copyright through peer-to-peer file-sharing. The answer to the first question was unanimous among the national reporters: on the basis of the provisions of Directive 2000/31/EC on electronic commerce,[79] the ISP could be held liable in every member state for promoting copyright infringement by its customers. On the second issue, answers varied widely between member states, until the Court of Justice rendered its decision in the *Promusicae v. Telefonica* case.[80] The CJEU acknowledged that copyright enforcement is a legitimate purpose to justify the treatment of personal data. However, such treatment must

---

78 CJEU judgment of 10 April 2014, *ACI Adam and Others v. Stichting de Thuiskopie*, C-435/12, ECLI:EU:C:2014:254.

79 Directive 2000/31/EC of the European Parliament and of the Council of 8 June 2000 on certain legal aspects of information society services, in particular electronic commerce, in the Internal Market ('Directive on electronic commerce'), OJ L 178, 17 July 2000, 1–16.

80 CJEU judgment of 28 January 2008, *Productores de Música de España (Promusicae) v. Telefónica de España SAU*, C-275/06, ECLI:EU:C:2008:54.

be proportionate in order to ensure a balance in the enforcement of conflicting fundamental rights, such as data protection.

Moving on from illegal to legal sources of download, the second modification to Case 3 explores the intersection between the exercise of the private copying exception and the application of technological protection measures (TPMs). The case highlights the different solutions put in place by the member states for the implementation of Article 6(4) of Directive 2001/29/EC. The free use space conferred on users pursuant to Article 5(2)(b) becomes very tenuous in the online environment: where TPMs are applied to a work, the member state may, in the absence of voluntary measures by the rights owner, take appropriate measures to allow users to exercise the private copying exception. There is no obligation on the member states to do so, however, and no accommodation is permitted at all if a reproduction for private use has already been made possible by the rightholders, including where the number of reproductions is limited. Moreover, no obligation exists where works are made available to the public on agreed contractual terms in such a way that members of the public may access them from a place and at a time individually chosen by them. The implementation of these provisions has taken an array of different forms across the member states, giving users variable freedom to make private copies of works made available online. In some countries, the circumvention of TPMs for private purposes is tolerated, in others it is conditional on the intervention of an administrative body, and yet in others it amounts to an unlawful act.[81] The free space left for users largely depends on each country's viewpoint regarding where the balance of interest lies between protecting the rights of owners and encouraging the dissemination of works. This balance is determined, in turn, by the rationales underlying the national copyright regime.

The third modification to Case 3 focuses on the obligation to pay fair compensation to the rights owner for the private copying of their work. There exists an important body of case law emanating from the Court of Justice in relation to the private copying exception. The case law deals almost exclusively with the interpretation of the concept of fair compensation and the administrative burdens related to the payment of such compensation. The Court issued preliminary rulings on questions pertaining to the definition of 'fair compensation',[82] the person or entity liable to pay the compensation,[83] the

81 M. M. M. van Eechoud/P. B. Hugenholtz/L. Guibault/S. van Gompel/N. Helberger, *Harmonizing European Copyright Law: The Challenges of Better Lawmaking*, Information Law Series vol. 19 (Alphen aan den Rijn: 2009), 168.

82 CJEU judgment of 21 October 2010, *Padawan v. SGAE*, C-467/08, ECLI:EU:C:2010:620.

83 CJEU judgment of 10 April 2014, *ACI Adam and Others v. Stichting de Thuiskopie*, C-435/12, ECLI:EU:C:2014:254; CJEU judgment of 11 July 2013, *Amazon.com International Sales Inc. and Others v. Austro-Mechana Gesellschaft*, C-521/11, ECLI:EU:C:2013:515.

country in which the compensation must be paid in the case of cross-border sales,[84] the obligation to pay the compensation where the use is subject to a licence,[85] and the proper basis for calculation of the compensation.[86] However, no court decision has so far examined the difficulties raised by the interplay between the application of TPMs and the obligation to pay fair compensation to the rights owner. No legislator has taken action either. The text of Article 5(2)(b) of Directive 2001/29/EC suggests that the determination of the level of compensation needs to take account of the application or non-application of TPMs to the work. Where TPMs are applied in such a way that private copies are impossible, would it not be logical to waive the payment of the compensation? Early in the development of digital rights management (DRM) systems, the proposition had been made that private copying levies could be phased out with the increased use of DRM systems.[87] Light years further on in terms of computer development, levies are still being collected on a range of digital recording media and devices across Europe, while anti-copy mechanisms or other business models often prevent the making of copies. The country reporters unanimously agree that this discrepancy should be addressed. Admittedly, the underlying copyright rationales would have little influence on the outcome here.

3. VOLUNTARY RELINQUISHMENT OF RIGHTS (CASES 3 AND 14)

This chapter takes a broad understanding of the public domain, which comprises all intellectual works that can be copied, used and re-used without restriction of any kind, whether through the operation of the law or the authorisation of the author.[88] The voluntary relinquishment of rights is therefore the last step on the public domain definition spectrum. In this case, free spaces are created not through the intervention of the legislator, either through the definition of protectable subject matter or the recognition of statutory exceptions, but at the will and discretion of the rights owner. Depending on existing limits

---

84 CJEU judgment of 16 June 2011, *Stichting de Thuiskopie v. Opus Supplies Deutschland*, C-462/09, ECLI:EU:C:2011:397.

85 CJEU judgment of 27 June 2013 *Kyocera and Others* (C-457/11), *Canon Deutschland GmbH* (C-458/11), *Fujitsu Technology Solutions GmbH* (C-459/11) and *Hewlett-Packard GmbH* (C-460/11) *v. Verwertungsgesellschaft Wort (VG Wort)*, Joined Cases C-457/11 to C-460/11, ECLI:EU:C:2013:426; CJEU judgment of 5 March 2015, *Copydan v. Nokia Danmark*, C-463/12, ECLI:EU:C:2015:144.

86 CJEU judgment of 10 April 2014, *ACI Adam v. Stichting de Thuiskopie*, C-435/12, ECLI:EU:C:2014:254

87 P. B. Hugenholtz/L. Guibault/S. van Geffen, *The Future of Levies in a Digital Environment*, Report commissioned by the Business Software Alliance, March 2003.

88 Dusollier (2010, supra n. 2); Pollock (2006, supra n. 7).

set by the legal regime in place, the voluntary relinquishment of rights may take the form of a dedication of works to the public domain, but most likely of a broad authorisation to use works with few to no restrictions. In fact, the dedication of works to the public domain is uncommon in Europe, as this practice is considered to encroach upon the inalienable moral rights of the author.[89] The voluntary relinquishment of rights, therefore, usually takes the form of a unilateral licence from the rights owner, granting permission to widely reproduce and communicate the work to the public.[90] The Creative Commons (CC) licences suite is the most well-known set of terms applicable to copyright-protected content that will achieve this result.[91] The CC licences suite empowers rights owners to choose the conditions under which they wish to disseminate their work. All CC licences are granted on a royalty-free, worldwide and irrevocable basis. The requirement to give attribution (CC-Attribution) is the only mandatory condition. Other optional conditions vary between the right to reserve commercial use (CC-NonCommercial), the right to make derivative works (CC-NoDerivative), and the obligation to share modified works under similar conditions (CC-ShareAlike). Neither the contractual validity of the CC licences or the formation of contract are an issue in the BIP project. The CC licences are considered from two different perspectives: first, from the individual user's perspective in Case 3, Modification 4, and second, from the scientific author's perspective in Case 14.

Continuing on the topic of private copying, the last modification of Case 3 asks whether someone who downloads and burns songs to a CD that are distributed under a CC licence would have a cause of action against the collecting society administering the home copying regime for the reimbursement of the levy on the blank CD. The core issue in this case revolves around the idea that there is in principle no rationale for obliging the user to pay compensation to rights owners, if the latter have authorised the free reproduction of their works. Notwithstanding the rights owner's choice of conditions under the CC licence, all CC licences permit the reproduction of the works licensed for private purposes. If a user buys a blank CD to burn only CC-licensed works, why would the user need to pay the levy on that blank CD? Why would a rights owner who chooses to licence their works under a CC licence wish to receive payment for such a use?

The levy represents the monetary compensation required by Article 5(2)(b) of Directive 2001/29/EC, the amount of which is generally fixed by law and

---

89 A. Guadamuz, *Comparative Analysis of National Approaches on Voluntary Copyright Relinquishment*, WIPO Report CDIP/13/INF/10 (5 June 2014), available at: https://ssrn.com/abstract=2446451.

90 L. Pallas Loren, 'Building a Reliable Semicommons of Creative Works: Enforcement of Creative Commons Licenses and Limited Abandonment of Copyright', (2007) 14 *Geo. Mason L. Rev.* 271.

91 See: https://creativecommons.org/share-your-work/licensing-examples/.

paid by manufacturers and importers of blank media. In most jurisdictions, the money is collected through a collective rights management organisation (CMO), before being distributed to registered rights owners. Rights owners and users are therefore at arm's length from each other, leaving no room for the exercise of their individual preferences. In reality, the levy system created to compensate for private copying activities is a rough justice system. The compensation is payable to the CMO with respect to each blank medium sold on the market that is recognised as capable of recording works for private purposes. The obligation to pay remains, regardless of whether or not the rights owner has granted permission to use the work through a CC licence, or otherwise. Even if a user chooses to only make private copies of CC-licensed music, the system does not provide any means to carve out an amount from the compensation owed that would represent the portion of CC-licensed repertoire.

In fact, any system that foresees the automatic payment of fair compensation is by definition incapable of adjusting to the particular situation of a subgroup of stakeholders. This is also evident in relation to the payment of the non-waivable right to equitable remuneration to the performer and phonogram producer for the communication to the public of commercial phonograms.[92] Unfortunately, the existing CJEU case law interpreting the concept of fair compensation provides no useful insight on the issue of the intersection between the manufacturers' and importers' obligation to pay the levy on blank media and the end user's choice to copy only CC-licensed works.[93] At this point, the only conclusion that we can draw from the last modification of Case 3 is that the free space afforded by rights owners through CC licences cannot fully benefit users, because of the inherent workings of the levy system.

The voluntary relinquishment of rights in the sector of scientific publishing is the topic of Case 14. The initial question posed in the case concerns the ownership of rights on scientific articles. Scientists must typically agree to a broad transfer of their rights to the publisher, which covers 'all rights with respect to modes of exploitation now known or to be discovered'. Was this transfer of rights, including with respect to articles written before the Internet had become a viable mode of exploitation for works, valid? Authors' contract law is not harmonised across the European Union. Member states therefore follow widely diverging approaches in the regulation and interpretation of authors' contracts. The legislation of a few member states expressly regulates the transfer of rights

92 C. Angelopoulos, 'Creative Commons and Related Rights in Sound Recordings: Are the Two Systems Compatible?', in: L. Guibault/ C. Angelopoulos (eds.), *Open Content Licensing: From Theory to Practice* (Amsterdam: 2011), 243–295; French Cour de Cassation, decision of 11 December 2019, No. 18-21211, ECLI:FR:CCASS:2019:C101021.

93 CJEU judgment of 21 October 2010, *Padawan v. SGAE*, C-467/08, ECLI:EU:C:2010:620; CJEU judgment of 10 April 2014, *ACI Adam and Others v. Stichting de Thuiskopie*, C-435/12, ECLI:EU:C:2014:254.

relating to forms of exploitation that are not known or foreseeable at the time the copyright contract was concluded.[94] In those member states, the rights on works with respect to unknown modes of exploitation are presumed not to have been transferred, or at least not without additional remuneration or consent. In practice, a distinction is made between older and newer articles: the rights on the pre-Internet-age articles will be deemed to belong to the author, while the rights on the more recent articles will have been assigned to the publisher. In other member states, the only protection conferred on the author are the general principles of contract law, in deference to the principle of freedom of contract. In these countries, all rights will be deemed to have been transferred to the publisher. As a result, the scientist may or may not own the rights on some or all of the articles disseminated online, depending on the jurisdiction.[95]

Clearly, only rights owners are entitled to attach a CC licence to their articles. Depending on the outcome of base Case 14, the author may have infringed the publisher's right by attaching a CC licence to his articles. Turning to the use of the CC-licensed scientific article, the modification to Case 14 then asks whether by the scientist at the employment of a pharmaceutical company violated the CC-Attribution-NonCommercial-ShareAlike licence by publishing a slightly modified version of the article in a company newsletter. The licence indeed allows anyone to reproduce, modify and communicate the paper freely for strictly non-commercial purposes, provided that proper credit is given and that any redistribution of the paper occurs under the same licence conditions. The vast majority of country reporters recognised the legal validity of the contractual obligations arising from the CC licence. They also considered that this use contravened the non-commercial and share-alike terms of the licence. The French response stands out, however, by suggesting that authorising the making of derivative works might encroach upon the author's moral rights and that the share-alike clause is an invalid attempt to transfer rights on future works. While there is no case law in France discussing the validity of CC licences, this position may now be considered too harsh. A French court could come to a different conclusion on these two points.

Case 14 highlights the role contracts can play in creating free use spaces in the scientific publishing industry. The idea of publishing publicly funded scientific articles under Open Access conditions has gained incredible ground over the past decade. The European Research Council, followed closely by the

[94] Europe Economics/L. Guibault/O. M. Salamanca, *Study on the remuneration of authors of books and scientific articles, translators, journalists, and visual artists for the use of their works (final report)*, Study prepared for the European Commission, DG Internal Market, MARKT/2014/088/D, Luxembourg, Publications Office of the European Union, 2016, 322.

[95] L. Guibault, 'Owning the Right to Open Up Access to Scientific Publications', in: L. Guibault/ C. Angelopoulos (eds.), *Open Content Licensing: From Theory to Practice* (Amsterdam: 2011), 137–168.

national research councils of the member states, has adopted an Open Access policy based on the assumption that, for the greater good of science and the public interest, publicly funded research should be made accessible without restriction.[96] The principle of unfettered access also entails the freedom to use and re-use publicly funded scientific research. CC licences are the main vehicle used to accomplish the goals of Open Access publishing. Where the authors have nevertheless transferred their rights to the publisher, they are encouraged to self-archive their articles in an institutional repository after the expiration of a reasonable embargo period. To facilitate this process, some member states have implemented legislation stating that the author of a work of science for which the research was funded in whole or in part by public funds has the right, at the expiration of a reasonable period after its first publication, to make that work available to the public for free, provided that the source of the first publication is clearly stated.[97]

IV. CONCLUSION

This chapter has attempted to draw the contours of the European public domain. This is no easy task, as the public domain is a fluid notion meant to reflect the tension between copyright protection and public interest. In view of the breadth of the BIP project, a broad and inclusive approach to the interpretation of the public domain is justified. Accordingly, the public domain examined in this chapter is deemed to cover not only the 'negative' public domain, i.e. everything that is not, or is no longer, protected by IP law, but also the free uses recognised by statutory law and the voluntary uses permitted by rights owners.

The absence of common understanding about the public domain's nature and content is partly due to the fact that no normative guidelines direct the European legislator's efforts in determining where to draw the line between what ought, or ought not, to be part of the rights owners' monopoly. The European legislative efforts are driven by considerations relating to the proper functioning of the internal market, the stimulation of innovation, creativity and investment, and the production of new content. The preservation of the public domain is never part of these considerations. Whereas there is no uniform 'European' public

96 See: https://erc.europa.eu/managing-project/open-access.

97 Netherlands Act of 30 June 2015 modifying the Copyright Act and the Neighbouring Rights Act for the strengthening of the position of the author and the performing artist in contractual relations about copyright and neighbouring rights (Authors' Contract Law Act), Art. 25fa; French Act No. 2016-1321 of 7 October 2016 for a Digital Republic, Art. 30 adding Art. L.533-4 to the Research Code; Italian Law of 7 October 2013, n. 112, G.U. n. 236, 8 October 2013; German Law of 1 October 2013 Gesetz zur Nutzung verwaister und vergriffener Werke und einer weiteren Änderung des Urheberrechtsgesetzes (BGBl. I S. 3714).

domain, the progressive harmonisation of European copyright law has had a definite impact on the public domain in Europe. According to our assessment, more than half of the Directives adopted in the area of copyright and related rights law have reduced the wealth of the public domain, either by extending the term of protection, by protecting new subject matter, by creating new rights or by imposing new conditions of use. Such new rules essentially mean that permission to use is needed where none was required prior to their introduction. Ultimately, the determination of what forms the public domain is in the remit of the national legislator and courts, which implement and interpret the European rules according to their own legal traditions and normative framework.

Private parties also play a role in the determination of the public domain, by contractually adapting the limits of protection to their own circumstances. Through Cases 4 and 14, we have seen that contracts can be used to withdraw material from the public domain, to impose extra restrictions on the use of material, or, on the contrary, to broaden the user's access to and use of copyright-protected works. Some contracts could be open for challenge according to the general principles of either contract law or competition law, but hardly ever on the basis of their failure to abide by the rationales underlying the copyright regime. Other contracts, although valid, have little to no practical effect, as demonstrated in the last modification to Case 3 on the private copying exception.

Finally, it must be emphasised that the public domain is not static: it evolves over time and in line with renewed insight and changes in policy. Remarkably, in the recent past, the measures that have had the most positive effect on the public domain were not part of the copyright reform, but rather those dealing with open government data and the re-use of public sector information, or with the requirement to publish publicly funded scientific research results under Open Access conditions. If the public domain is not preserved from within the copyright regime, it might very well obtain protection from outside.

MORALITY AND INTELLECTUAL PROPERTY LAW THROUGH THE LENS OF HUMAN RIGHTS

Mike Adcock and Deryck Beyleveld

I. INTRODUCTION

The exclusion from patentability on the ground of immorality specified in Article 53(a) of the European Patent Convention (EPC) and in Article 6(1) of Directive 98/44/EC on the Legal Protection of Biotechnological Inventions (Biotechnology Directive) has proved highly controversial. While, for example, UK trademark law excludes the registration of marks that are contrary to public policy or to accepted principles of morality (s. 3(3)(a) Trade Mark Act 1994), copyright law generally has no explicit immorality exclusions. However, we argue that commitment to human rights as conceived in the United Nations Declaration of Human Rights 1948 (UDHR) constitutes a commitment to the existence of morality conceived of as a system of practical rules governed by a categorical impartial imperative, the principle of generic consistency (PGC) of the American moral philosopher Alan Gewirth:[1]

> All agents ought to act in accord with the generic rights (rights to the generic conditions of agency)[2] of all agents.[3]

Thought of as the categorical imperative, the PGC is a principle with which all actions and rules for action must be consistent unconditionally, with the

---

1 A. Gewirth, *Reason and Morality* (Chicago: 1978).

2 Generic conditions of agency (GCAs) are needs of agency in the sense that the absence of them reduces the ability of an agent to act, or at least to achieve the agent's chosen purposes, to at least some extent, *regardless of what these purposes are or might be*. For further explanation, see below.

3 An agent is a being who has the capacity and disposition to act for reasons, and an action is voluntary behaviour in order to achieve an end that the agent has chosen to pursue. The term 'moral rights' applied to the generic rights is distinct from the term 'moral rights' used in copyright law (where the contrast is primarily with the author's pecuniary or economic rights).

implication that no rules or actions inconsistent with the PGC may be regarded as valid by any legal system that professes adherence to human rights per the conception thereof in the UDHR.

This chapter has five main sections. In the first (section II), we discuss the concept of morality and provide reasons to focus on the conception of it as consisting of rules governed by a categorical impartial imperative in any system of rules that recognises that there are human rights per the UDHR. In section III, we briefly outline Gewirth's argument for the PGC being the categorical imperative, and argue that, whether or not Gewirth's argument is valid, the PGC must be taken to be the supreme principle of any system of rules built around the idea that there are human rights per the UDHR. In section IV, we explain the implications of this for the relationship between law and morality in any legal system that professes adherence to human rights per the UDHR. In section V, we explain the content of the PGC and outline rules for its application.[4] In section VI, we apply the PGC to the some of the cases reported on elsewhere in this volume (Cases 1, 2, 7, 9 and 10).

II. THE CONCEPT OF MORALITY

The relationship between morality and law depends on what we understand by morality. Traditionally, at least in moral philosophy, moral rules (as against non-moral ones) are thought of as rules governed by a categorical *impartial* imperative. By its very idea, a categorical imperative is one that all rules for action and all actions must comply with unconditionally in order to have any normative validity. A categorical *impartial* imperative imposes duties and confers powers (authorisations and rights) equally on all agents in the sense that it requires all agents to be treated with equal concern and respect in relation to the duties it imposes and the rights it confers.

So conceived, the very existence of morality is highly controversial, even though many persons adopt normative viewpoints that they treat as having the characteristics of morality. While various philosophers, such as Immanuel Kant,[5] Alan Gewirth,[6] and discourse theorists like Karl Otto Apel[7] and

4 A different presentation of the theoretical framework of this chapter is to be found in M. Adcock/D. Beyleveld, 'Morality in Intellectual Property Law: A Concept-Theoretic Framework', 4 *Intellectual Property Rights* (2016), 154.

5 I. Kant, *Groundwork of the Metaphysics of Morals* (Cambridge: 1997), Chapter III.

6 Gewirth (1978, supra n. 1).

7 K. O. Apel, 'The A Priori of Communication and the Foundation of the Humanities', 5(1) *Man and World* (1972), 3–37.

Jürgen Habermas,[8] together with various intuitionists (e.g. Jonathan Dancy),[9] maintain that morality can be shown to exist as what it purports to be, many others maintain that a commitment to morality (as such) cannot be justified. While some of these (e.g. David Gauthier)[10] maintain that prudential reasons can be given for most agents to accept an impartial governing imperative, such reasons do not provide unconditional reasons to accept such an imperative, so many philosophers (e.g. Bernard Gert)[11] maintain that the best we can do is show that anyone who considers that there is a categorically binding impartial imperative must accept that it has a specific content.[12]

We consider that Alan Gewirth has shown that the PGC is the categorical imperative.[13] However, we will not rely on his argument for this here. Instead we will argue (see section III) that anyone who considers that there is a categorical impartial imperative must accept the PGC. But we will do so from the perspective of anyone who (or any system of rules that) accepts that there are human rights per the conception thereof of the UDHR, and we are able to do this because the UDHR portrays human rights as moral rights in line with the conception of morality with which we are operating.

That the UDHR conceives of human rights as conferred by a categorical imperative is implied by Article 2 UDHR, according to which

> Everyone is entitled to all the rights and freedoms set forth in this Declaration, without distinction of any kind, such as race, colour, sex, religion, political or other opinion, national or social origin, property, birth or other status. Furthermore, no distinction shall be made on the basis of the political, jurisdictional or international status of the country or territory to which the person belongs, whether it be independent, trust, non-self-governing or under any other limitation of sovereignty.

This is reinforced by Article 28, according to which

> Everyone is entitled to a social and international order in which the rights and freedoms set forth in this Declaration can be fully realised

---

8 J. Habermas, 'Discourse Ethics: Notes on a Program of Philosophical Justification', in: J. Habermas, *Moral Consciousness and Communicative Action* (Cambridge: 1990), 43–115.

9 J. Dancy, *Moral Reasons* (Oxford/Cambridge, MA: 1993).

10 D. Gauthier, *Morals by Agreement* (Oxford: 1986).

11 B. Gert, *Morality – Its Nature and Justification* (Oxford: 1998).

12 That understanding the concept of a categorical imperative requires it to be assigned a particular content is also argued by Immanuel Kant (Kant (1997, supra n. 5), Chapter II).

13 See especially D. Beyleveld, *The Dialectical Necessity of Morality: An Analysis and Defense of Alan Gewirth's Argument to the Principle of Generic Consistency* (Chicago: 1991).

together with Article 30, according to which

> Nothing in this Declaration may be interpreted as implying for any State, group or person any right to engage in any activity or to perform any act aimed at the destruction of any of the rights and freedoms set forth herein.[14]

That the UDHR conceives of the categorical imperative as *impartial* (hence, as a moral imperative) is revealed by Article 1 UDHR, according to which

> All human beings are born free and equal in dignity and rights. They are endowed with reason and conscience and should act towards one another in a spirit of brotherhood.

To this it might be objected that, while the UDHR conceives of human rights as categorically and impartially possessed by human beings, this does not mean that it conceives of them as governed by a categorical imperative, rather than as a set of categorical imperatives.

But this cannot be so. It is not coherent to think of each human right as implying a duty on others that holds categorically (unconditionally). As Immanuel Kant says, there can be only one categorical imperative,[15] and this is because if there are different rules that are categorical imperatives, then they cancel each other out and there is no categorical imperative, *unless they are consistent with each other*, in which case they are combinable into a single imperative or reveal different aspects of a single imperative. Thus, any human rights that are capable of coming into conflict with each other can only be thought to hold categorically in the circumstances of their application, i.e. when the categorical imperative requires them to be recognised. In consequence, any categorical imperative must itself specify a criterion to resolve conflicts between the various human rights that it recognises as having at least *prima facie* application.[16]

From this it follows that all human rights instruments that purport to give legal effect to the UDHR (such as the International Covenant on Civil and Political Rights (ICCPR), the International Covenant on Economic, Social and Cultural Rights (ICECSR), and regional conventions such as the European

---

14 Art. 30 is arguably prompted by Art. 29(2) according to which '[i]n the exercise of his rights and freedoms, everyone shall be subject only to such limitations as are determined by law solely for the purpose of securing due recognition and respect for the rights and freedoms of others and of meeting the just requirements of morality, public order and the general welfare in a democratic society', and has the implication that the requirements of morality, public order and general welfare in a democratic society must themselves be conceived of in a way that is consistent with the rights set forth in the Declaration.

15 Kant (1997, supra n. 5), 4:421.

16 It is possible for more than one human right to apply absolutely only if such rights are incapable of coming into conflict with each other.

Convention on Human Rights (ECHR)) must be held to conceive of human rights as moral rights: for they can only sincerely claim to be giving effect to the UDHR if they conceive of the human rights they grant in the terms of the UDHR.

The conception of human rights as categorical possessions of human beings is also in line with the doctrine of the Court of Justice of the European Union (CJEU) that human rights are fundamental principles of EU law[17] (which status has recently been formalised by the incorporation of the EU's Charter of Fundamental Rights and Freedoms into the Constitution of the EU).[18] This is because fundamental principles of EU law set requirements that all Directives and Regulations of the EU must comply with.[19] In other words, all EU law that does not comply with morality (specified through the lens of human rights per the UDHR and the international instruments that purport to give effect to it) must be held to be null and void.

III. HUMAN RIGHTS' CONTENT

On this basis, we may conclude that morality in relation to, for example, EU law and the law of any country that purports to recognise human rights per the UDHR must, if this recognition is to be sincere, operate in accordance with the conception of a human right contained in the UDHR. But we can do better than this, because, as we will show, this conception, by itself (and independently of the rights that are specified in Arts. 3–28 UDHR), entails a principle that specifies the content that human rights must have.

The argument for this begins with the idea that human rights are, and can only be, specified in rules for action, which, by their nature, prescribe reasons for agents to act, and that it is not coherent to think of something, S, as a reason for an agent to act if, by accepting S, the agent implies that the agent is not an agent.

With this in mind, we contend that any agent (call her 'Agnes') must, on pain of implying that she is not an agent, accept that all her actions (and those of

17 S. Morano-Foadi/S. Andreadakis, 'Reflections on the Architecture of the EU after the Treaty of Lisbon: The European Judicial Approach to Fundamental Rights', 17 *European Law Journal* (2011), 595–610.

18 J. Neyer, 'The Constitution's Gift. A Constitutional Theory for a Democratic European Union', 17 *European Law Journal* (2011), 716–719.

19 D. Leczykiewicz, 'Effective Judicial Protection of Human Rights after Lisbon: Should National Courts Be Empowered to Review EU Secondary Law?', 35 *European Law Review* (2010), 326–348. Indeed, by the concept of a fundamental principle, even the EU treaties must comply with fundamental principles of EU law.

any other agent) must be governed by the principle of hypothetical imperatives (PHI), according to which

> If an agent wishes to achieve an end E (or act in accord with a rule R), then the agent must act to secure whatever means are necessary to achieve E (or to comply with R) or give up E (or R).

The PHI is not a hypothetical imperative because it does not depend on what E or R might be. It is not conditional on any specific purposes that an agent might have, nor upon an agent's desire to be an agent. Its acceptance is required in order for an agent to understand what it is for the agent to act, and hence to understand what it is for *the* agent to be *an* agent. In the language used by Alan Gewirth, it is dialectically necessary for Agnes to accept the PHI. For Agnes not to accept the PHI is for Agnes to imply that she is not an agent (under which implication it is unintelligible for Agnes to think of herself as acting for any E or R).

Now, since there are generic conditions of agency (GCAs) (see below), it follows that it is dialectically necessary for Agnes to accept that she ought to act to secure her possession of the GCAs unless she is willing to suffer generic damage to her ability to act (i.e. unless she is willing to accept damage to her ability to achieve, or even to pursue, any E or to comply with any R). We will abbreviate this as $\{AoGa^A\}_A$.[20]

This is the conclusion of the first stage of Gewirth's argument for the PGC, and it is uncontroversial apart from Gewirth's claim that $AoGa^A$ is rendered categorically binding on Agnes because it is dialectically necessary for her to accept it.

It is, of course, possible that Agnes might not care whether or not she implies that she is not an agent, and so might not act in accord with $AoGa^A$. Some philosophers seem to think that this shows that even if it is dialectically necessary for Agnes to accept a practical precept, this does not show that Agnes is categorically bound to accept the precept.[21]

This, however, supposes that an unconditional reason to act (a categorically binding one) is one that Agnes *necessarily will* act in accordance with, when (in fact) it is one that she *unconditionally ought* to act in accordance with. Given that it makes no sense to say that Agnes ought to do something that she either necessarily will or necessarily will not do, the very idea that Agnes is categorically bound to accept $AoGa^A$ implies that she might not care whether

---

20 'Ao' = 'Agnes ought to act in accord with. 'Ga' = 'Agnes' GCAs'. $^{\text{'A'}}$ = 'unless Agnes is willing to suffer generic damage to her ability to act'. '$\{ \ldots \}_A$' = whatever is contained within { } is dialectically necessary for Agnes to accept.

21 See e.g. D. Enoch, 'Agency, Shmagency: Why Normativity Won't Come From What is Constitutive of Agency', 115(2) *Philosophical Review* (2006), 169–198.

or not she acts in accord with $AoGa^A$. Furthermore, as Kant says, if there is a categorical imperative, then it must already be connected entirely *a priori* with the concept of the will of a rational being as such (an agent),[22] but not contained in this concept.[23] In our opinion, this only makes sense if a categorically binding rule is not a construct of agency but one of agential self-understanding (i.e. of dialectical necessity).[24]

Gewirth goes on to argue that, *from Agnes' dialectically necessary point of view*, $AoGa^A$ is normatively equivalent to the claim that Agnes has rights to the GCAs (AGR), so that $\{AoGa^A\}_A$ entails $\{AGR\}_A$, and furthermore that $\{AGR\}_A$ entails not only that it is dialectically necessary for every other agent, e.g. Brian (B), to consider that he has the generic rights (i.e. that $\{BGR\}_B$, which is wholly uncontroversial), but that it is also dialectically necessary for Agnes to accept that Brian also has the generic rights (i.e. that $\{BGR\}_A$), from which it follows that it is dialectically necessary for every agent to accept the PGC.[25]

However, whether or not Gewirth is right about this, anyone who accepts that all agents must categorically be treated with equal concern and respect *as agents* must, given $\{AoGa^A\}_A$, accept that the PGC is categorically binding on all agents, and this idea of impartiality is built into the concept of human rights per the UDHR. So, anyone who accepts that there are human rights per the UDHR must accept the PGC as the supreme principle all practical reasoning, hence of all systems of rules (and hence of all law).

This can be shown slightly differently. Anyone who holds that there are human rights per the UDHR must accept that, because human agents are human beings, all human agents have human rights. Since having the GCAs is necessary to be able to act at all/act successfully regardless of the purposes involved, having the GCAs is necessary to exercise any right/to respect any right, which means that no grant of a human right can be sincere unless accompanied by recognition that all human agents have human rights to possess the GCAs. Because it must be recognised that $\{AoGa^A\}_A$, from which it then follows that $\{BoGb^B\}_B$, it follows that these rights must be interpreted in the way in which the PGC recognises them[26] (on which see further in section V).

This argument has the effect of placing a degree of distance between acceptance of the UDHR (which essentially provides the concept of a human right with which the international order of human rights operates) and the

22 Kant (1997, supra n. 5), 4:426.

23 Kant (1997, supra n. 5), 4:420 footnote.

24 D. Beyleveld, 'What Is Gewirth and What Is Beyleveld: A Retrospect with Comments on the Contributions?', in: P. Capps/S. D. Pattinson (eds.), *Ethical Rationalism and the Law* (Portland: 2017), 233–255.

25 D. Beyleveld (1991, supra n. 13), 24–46.

26 D. Beyleveld, 'The Principle of Generic Consistency as the Supreme Principle of Human Rights', 13(1) *Human Rights Review* (2011), 1–18.

content of the rights recognised by Articles 3–28 UDHR, to which the ICCPR, the ICESCR, and the ECHR, etc., give effect. Specifically, it shows that all these instruments must be interpreted in accordance with the requirements of the PGC if they are to implement the UDHR under its conception of a human right. Consequently, if their various provisions, and the provisions of the UDHR itself, cannot be so interpreted, then they must be rejected or Articles 1 and 2 of the UDHR revised.

If we are to make use of this, however, then we need to explain the content and nature of the PGC more fully, which we will do in section V.

But first, we will outline what we see to be the implications for the way in which legal systems recognising human rights must, perforce, view the relationship between positive law and morality generally and IP law and morality more specifically.

IV. HUMAN RIGHTS' EFFECT

In any legal system recognising human rights as conceived by the UDHR:

1. Any actions or rules not compatible with the PGC must be considered normatively invalid.
2. Where laws exist to confer powers, the issue of their normative validity must focus on the powers conferred. Thus, the focus of morality provisions (governed by the PGC) must, in the case of patents, be on the legitimacy of granting a patent, i.e. the legitimacy of conferring the power on the patent holder to prevent others from using the patented invention. Consequently, Article 6(1) of the Biotechnology Directive, which states that inventions are unpatentable if their commercial exploitation is contrary to *ordre public* or morality, is mistaken, unless the conditions under which commercial exploitation is contrary to morality are those under which granting the monopoly right that holding a patent confers is contrary to the PGC.
3. Compatibility with morality (the PGC) must be read into any law of the system.[27] Thus, even if Article 6(1) (properly interpreted) were not in the Biotechnology Directive, it would have to be read in.[28] One way of reading

[27] It follows that Art. 27(2) of the World Trade Organisation's General Agreement on Trades and Tariffs (Trade Related Aspects of Intellectual Property Rights), which states that member states *may* prohibit patents on grounds of immorality, is unacceptable.

[28] It is worth noting that the unpatentability of 'methods for treatment of the human or animal body by surgery or therapy and diagnostic methods practised on the human or animal body'

morality provisions into, say copyright laws, which contain no explicit immorality exclusion, is to read their exclusions on grounds of public policy and public interest, as grounds of morality. This dovetails with the closing remarks of Bingham LJ in the English Court of Appeal case of *W v. Egdell*,[29] who implies that human rights may be analysed in terms of public interest requirements.[30]

4. Exclusions for the purpose of morality must, like violations of fundamental principles, be interpreted broadly, not narrowly. This has not always been recognised in judgments of the European Patent Office (EPO).[31] However, it must be borne in mind that there can be moral (PGC) reasons to confer legal powers, which must also be interpreted broadly. Given that protecting the GCAs of one agent can come into conflict with the GCAs of another agent (indeed of the same agent), to find out what this means in practice requires case-by-case assessment according to rules for doing so provided by the PGC (see section V), and neither morality-driven exclusions nor morality-driven inclusions can be given priority as a general rule. The only general rule that can be applied is that the PGC's application be interpreted broadly. The opinion of the EPO's Board of Appeal in *WARF* is in line with this. According to the Board of Appeal

> [t]he frequently cited principle according to which exclusion clauses from patentability laid down in the EPC were to be construed in a restrictive manner, did not apply without exception (point 33, T-1374/04).

Provisions must be considered in the light of their

> wording, the object and purpose of the provision, the interests involved, the consequences of a narrow or broad interpretation, respectively, and the aspect of legal certainty (point 33, T-1374/04).

---

of Art. 53(c) EPC (previously Art. 52(4)) is readily read as an exclusion on the grounds of morality. Indeed, it is difficult to read it in any other way.

29 [1990] 2 WLR 471.

30 Correlatively the public interest must be defined as what is needed to protect the GCAs of any agent. It follows from this that no reservations, derogations or exceptions to any human right are permissible unless in the service (directly or indirectly) of protecting agents' possession of the GCAs. This means, for example, that all the exceptions to Art. 8(1) ECHR (the right to private life) in Art. 8(2) must be for the protection of the GCAs of agents other than the subject whose right under Art. 8(1) is engaged. (See also n. 16 supra.)

31 See European Patent Office, Guidelines for Examination in the European Patent Office, pt. G, Chapter II 4.1 (2012), available at: http://www.epo.org/law-practice/legal-texts/html/guidelines/e/g_ii_4_1.htm (last accessed 20 October 2017).

V. CONTENT AND RULES FOR ITS APPLICATION

1. CONTENT

The PGC, directly, grants rights to agents (and only agents)[32] to possess the GCAs. Gewirth divides GCAs into two main categories: those necessary for an agent to be able even to try to act, and those that are necessary for an agent to act successfully (i.e. to achieve the agent's purposes). The former are designated as basic GCAs (or basic goods). The latter, in turn, are divided into two categories: those necessary to enable an agent to maintain the agent's general ability to achieve the agent's purposes (non-subtractive GCAs); and those necessary for an agent to be able to improve the agent's general ability to achieve the agent's purposes (additive GCAs). GCAs of all three kinds are also divided into substantive ones (related to the purposivity of agency) (constituted by needs for physical, emotional and psychological integrity, and informational needs) and procedural ones (related to the voluntariness involved in action) (constituted by various freedoms to pursue purposes). In all three cases, a GCA is something needed regardless of what the agent's purposes might be. It is beyond the scope of this chapter to characterise all the GCAs that there are. Suffice it to say that life is a basic GCA for all mortal agents, as is physical health, and emotional and mental stability, insofar as not having them has at least some negative effect on an agent's ability to pursue purposes voluntarily at all. Accurate information and the ability to rely on promises are non-subtractive GCAs, whereas further education (education which better enables an agent to achieve the agent's purposes than the education an agent already possesses) is an additive GCA. Expressed in this way, GCAs are universal for all finite agents (those whose ability to achieve their purposes can be interfered with).[33] However, what might instantiate interference with a GCA or satisfy an agent's need for a GCA can vary. For example, if Agnes is allergic to peanuts, then feeding her peanuts can interfere with her possession of life, while it can be necessary to preserve Brian's life (when no other food is available to him) because he is not allergic to peanuts.[34]

It should be noted, however, that GCAs are to be distinguished from conditions needed for agents to become agents, as this is one corollary of the fact that the PGC grants rights directly only to agents.

---

32 This, see further below, is simply because the generic rights are rights under the will conception, and only agents can have such rights.

33 Gewirth (1978, supra n. 1), 52–56.

34 D. Beyleveld, 'Transcendental Arguments for a Categorical Imperative as Arguments from Agential Self-Understanding', in: J. P. Brune/R. Stern/M. Werner (eds.), *Transcendental Arguments in Moral Theory* (Berlin: 2017), 141–159.

Because Agnes' possession of the GCAs is governed normatively by the PHI, rights to the GCAs under the PGC are rights under the will conception. This is to say that Agnes' right to, for example, life, is the right for her to enjoy life *if she so wishes*. In other words, Agnes may release other agents from their duties in relation to her right to life, if she is (freely) willing to die. Because Agnes is required to recognise that all other agents have rights to possess the GCAs, this release must, however, satisfy the requirement that Agnes not, by releasing others from their duties in relation to her right to life, interfere with rights of others to possess their GCAs when they are unwilling to suffer generic damage to their ability to act. Thus, Agnes may commit suicide and others may assist her to die, indeed, may kill her, if this is not against her will and does not threaten the GCAs of others against their will.[35]

Because the PGC grants rights to possess the GCAs, and the GCAs are instrumental needs of agency, these rights are both positive and negative, which is to say that the PGC not only imposes duties on Brian not to interfere with Agnes' possession of the GCAs against her will, but also imposes duties on Brian to assist Agnes to possess the GCAs (*if* she so wishes) *when* she is unable to do so by her own unaided efforts, *and* assisting her does not threaten disproportionate damage[36] to Brian's possession of the GCAs (against his will).[37] However, because agents cannot, in many cases, act positively to secure the GCAs of others without disproportionate risk to their own possession of the GCAs, positive protection of GCAs is, in practice, the responsibility of collectives rather than individuals, beyond the responsibilities of individuals to try to set up the necessary collectives.[38]

2. RULES FOR APPLICATION

Direct applications of the PGC simply involve assessing which GCAs of an agent/agents are engaged by a particular action/actions or in a particular situation/situations, and determining what needs to be done, by whom, so as to ensure, as

---

35 In this, the PGC differs from Kant's Formula of Humanity (FoH) for the categorical imperative, according to which Agnes may only cause or agree to generic damage to herself in order to prevent greater such damage to others or herself (see Kant (1997, supra n. 5), 4:429). While the PGC, like the FoH, requires an agent never to be treated solely as a means, but always at the same time as an end in itself, a different conception of what it is to treat an agent as an end in itself is involved. For a systematic comparison between Gewirth and Kant, see D. Beyleveld, 'Gewirth and Kant on Kant's Maxim of Reason: Towards a Gewirthian Philosophical Anthropology', in: P. Bauhn (ed.), *Gewirthian Perspectives on Human Rights* (London: 2016), 13–29.

36 Assessed by the criterion of needfulness for agency (see below).

37 D. Beyleveld (1991, supra n. 13), Chapter 10.

38 A. Gewirth, *The Community of Rights* (Chicago: 1996), 59.

far as possible, that the least damage to anyone's[39] GCAs results. Protecting the GCAs of Agnes can come into conflict with protecting the GCAs of Brian, and such conflicts are dealt with by Gewirth's criterion of needfulness for agency,[40] according to which basic GCAs outrank non-subtractive GCAs, which outrank additive GCAs; and similar discriminations can be made within these categories according to the extent of damage or the immediacy of damage (when this affects chances of being able to reverse the damage) caused to possession of a GCA by interference with it. The general idea here is that having some GCAs is necessary for the possession of others but not vice versa, and some kinds of damage to a GCA can be reversed more easily than others or involve less generic damage than others. These considerations are derived from understanding the PHI, and so do not constitute principles additional to the PGC itself.

However, applying the PGC directly is not always able to resolve questions about the legitimacy of actions. There are a number of reasons for this. First, direct application can be exceedingly complex, as it requires knowledge of what actions will affect the GCAs of which agents (which sometimes requires complex empirical research), and judging, for example, the immediacy of generic damage against the extent of generic damage is not always straightforward (and there might, in fact, be no clear rule for it). Secondly, some choices that the PGC requires to be made (e.g. between driving on the left and driving on the right) are not determinable by the PGC itself. Thirdly, choices that the PGC permits agents to make for themselves might come into conflict with other choices that the PGC permits agents to make for themselves.

In all these cases, the PGC requires choices to be made procedurally, i.e. by delegating the decision to a process that it authorises. Processes can range from tossing a coin, to decisions of experts, to decisions of neutral arbiters, to decisions by democratic vote. The appropriate procedure depends on the reason why the PGC cannot determine an answer directly. However, both the requirement to appeal to procedures and the requirement to accept the results of the procedures are to be justified as requirements of the PGC and this presupposes that clear direct applications of the PGC cannot legitimately be overridden by the indirect applications of the PGC.

It is also worth noting that, in its support of positive rights, the PGC accords with the Marxist dictum: 'From each according to his abilities, to each according to his needs'.[41] Marxism, however, is essentially an economics-based theory of means to establish a society regulated by this maxim, and commitment to the

[39] The PGC applies distributively rather than in aggregation, which is to say that two lesser generic harms cannot outweigh a greater generic harm.

[40] Gewirth (1978, supra n. 1), 62–63, 342–344.

[41] K. Marx, 'Critique of the Gotha Programme', in: *Marx/Engels Selected Works, Volume Three* (Moscow: 1970), 13–30.

PGC does not, by itself, entail any commitment to Marxist theory as such. To appreciate the significance of this, at least four further points must be noted, which complicate considerably judgment under the PGC about the permissibility of existing regulations and positive laws.

- The PGC *ideally* requires that no one enjoy surplus value (goods that are not GCAs) at the expense of anyone being deprived of their GCAs. At the same time, it permits the enjoyment of surplus values when the GCAs are satisfied, only requiring (as an additive GCA) that all have opportunity within their abilities to strive for surplus value.
- However, in non-ideal circumstances (i.e. where current social and political circumstances are not in accord with the PGC, yet have considerable support), it must be recognised that enforcement of the ideal requirements is impracticable and attempts at enforcement could lead to very undesirable outcomes under the PGC. Thus, the PGC will not require more than a commitment to practicable outcomes designed to be as close to the ideal requirements as feasible and also designed to facilitate gradual progression to the ideal.
- Nationalism, *as such*, is contrary to the PGC (as it is to human rights), and may be regarded as, at most, an instrumental good when needed to defend against attacks from non-PGC-compliant regimes.
- Whether or not the PGC is compatible with capitalism is debatable. But it is certainly not compatible with a form of capitalism that recognises only negative rights unfettered by social welfare principles. While it does not rule out *a priori* the idea that, in non-ideal circumstances, the PGC's ideals can be best achieved by an unfettered free market with low taxes on the rich, such a claim must be proved and, in our opinion, is not sustainable.[42] It is, however, worth noting that forms of capitalism that are premised on the idea that it is illegitimate to regulate the operation of the free market by any principles other than those of supply and demand rest on the idea that a free market is one in which all are equal in knowledge and power, and this is simply not the case in the real world.[43] Under the PGC, the idea that a free market may only be regulated by principles of supply and demand is acceptable only on the understanding that a free market is one in which agents are equal with respect to their own possession and control of the GCAs, which is to say that a free market is defined by conformity to principles external to those of supply and demand. In other words, under the PGC, a free market, one

---

42 For further discussion of all these matters see Gewirth (1996, supra n. 38), and D. Beyleveld/ R. Brownsword, *Consent in the Law* (Oxford: 2007), Chapter Ten.

43 An interesting non-Gewirthian (utility maximising) analysis of this is to be found in Gauthier (1986, supra n. 10).

that may (and, perhaps, ought to) be regulated only by the principles of supply and demand, is defined as the zone of behaviour that the PGC neither commands nor prohibits.

3. APPLICATION TO NON-AGENTS

What of human non-agents? On the basis of the reasoning presented here, human non-agents and other non-agents cannot be granted the generic rights, simply because the generic rights are rights under the will conception. But this does not mean that agents do not have, or may not be charged with, duties to protect interests of humans and non-humans who do not display the capacities of agency.

First of all, agents might have duties to protect non-agents in order to protect the rights of agents.[44]

Secondly, a community might decide to impose duties on its members by democratic procedures to protect the interests of non-agents simply because it wishes to do so, provided only that this does not entail interference with the generic rights of those who do not wish to do so.

Thirdly, and perhaps most importantly, the PGC imposes duties on agents to apparent non-agents on the ground that the only creature that Agnes can be certain is an agent is herself and cannot be certain that any other creature is not an agent (because agents necessarily have self-consciousness and only Agnes can know that she has self-consciousness). At most Agnes can know that Brian behaves as though he is an agent (i.e. that he is an apparent agent). So, confronted with an apparent agent, like Brian, Agnes has a choice: she can presume that Brian is an agent, in line with which she will be required to treat him as having the generic rights, or she can presume that he is not an agent, consistent with which she will not only not be required to treat him as having the generic rights, but may not do so. Whichever presumption she makes, she *might* be mistaken, but cannot know whether or not she is mistaken. However, if Brian happens to be an agent, and she fails to treat him as an agent, she has violated the PGC by failing to act in accord with Brian's generic rights, whereas if she treats him as an agent (which she can do, simply because he is an apparent agent), she has not violated the PGC (because she has not, thereby, failed to act in accord with any agent's generic rights). Because the PGC is categorically binding, Agnes may not risk violating the PGC *when she is able to avoid the risk without violating the*

44 For a good discussion of this, see P. Carruthers, *The Animals Issue: Moral Theory in Practice* (Cambridge: 1992), 98–121. Although this is from a contractualist view, Carruthers' discussion has relevance for Gewirthian theory because contractualism also accords direct moral status only to agents.

PGC, which she can do when Brian is an apparent agent. Therefore, Agnes must treat apparent agents as agents for all practical purposes.

But, just as Agnes cannot know whether Brian, an apparent agent, is an agent, she also cannot know whether or not (for example) her cat Felix, who is an apparent non-agent, is an agent. Because Felix is not an apparent agent, Agnes cannot treat Felix as an agent, in consequence of which she cannot treat him as having the generic rights. This is because, to repeat, the generic rights are rights under the will conception, and, *as such*, can be attributed intelligibly only to those who display the capacity (i.e. those that are able to behave as though they have the capacity) to release Agnes from any duties she has to respect their need for GCAs. This, however, is not to say that Felix lacks interests that are generic needs for Felix *to act* if Felix happens to be an agent. So, for example, Felix can be killed, he can be starved, he can be caused severe pain, he can display what in human agents would be taken to be signs of distress as well as signs of a need for affection, all of which signify interests that Felix has as a cat that are GCAs if Felix happens to be an agent. Again, Agnes can presume that Felix is an agent or that he is not. If she acts against Felix's generic interests as a cat, and he is an agent, then she will have violated the PGC. If she acts in accord with Felix's generic interests as a cat, and he is not an agent, she will not have violated the PGC. Because the PGC is the categorical imperative, Agnes may not risk violating the PGC when she is able to avoid doing so. Consequently, it is dialectically necessary for Agnes to accept that she has duties to Felix not to act contrary to his generic interests as a cat. These precautionary duties are owed, in the final analysis, not to Felix *as an agent*, but *to* Felix *as a possible agent*, and *to him as a cat* because as a cat he is, as far as Agnes can know, a possible agent.[45]

To this it has been objected by Holm and Coggon[46] that this entails that Agnes owes duties to tables, chairs and rocks, in fact to everything she can identify, because anything she can identify could possibly be an agent.

However, while anything that Agnes can identify *could be* an agent, not everything that Agnes can identify has the behavioural capacity to display interests that correspond to the GCAs of agents. The difference between the coat in Agnes's cupboard and Felix is that Felix has behavioural capacities that indicate that he has generic needs that correspond to Agnes's GCAs, whereas Agnes' coat does not. This means that it is possible for Agnes to relate to Felix as a possible agent in a way that generates identifiable duties, but not possible for her to relate to her coat as a possible agent in this way.

---

45 D. Beyleveld/S. D. Pattinson, 'Precautionary Reasoning as a Link to Moral Action', in: M. Boylan (ed.), *Medical Ethics* (New Jersey: 2000), 39–53.

46 S. Holm/J. Coggon, 'A Cautionary Note Against "Precautionary Reasoning" in Action Guiding Morality', 22 *Ratio Juris* (2009), 295–309 (305).

It follows from this that Agnes has duties to apparent non-agents only in proportion to the extent to which they have behavioural capacities that display generic interests that correspond to the GCAs of agents. Agnes' coat does not have these behavioural capacities to any extent, whereas Felix has them to some extent.[47]

How this proportionality is to be assessed is beyond the scope of this chapter.[48]

4. IMPLICATIONS FOR INTERPRETATION OF HUMAN RIGHTS

Finally, there are four implications for the interpretation of human rights that are important for purposes of this chapter that should be noted.

First, the precautionary reasoning outlined above entails that, insofar as the UDHR may be held to apply to all human beings (if defined in distinction from human agents), the UDHR and other human rights instruments claiming concordance with the UDHR must be held to comprise two kinds of rights: rights of (apparent) agents under the will conception and rights of (apparent) non-agents (correlatives of duties of agents to apparent non-agents) under the interest conception, both of which are, however, justified by the PGC under precautionary reasoning.[49]

Secondly, as already explained, unless being human equates with being a human agent, possessing human rights equally must be interpreted as being equally under the protection of the PGC (per this precautionary reasoning), and it is only through such thinking that we consider the UN Convention on the Rights of the Child 1989 and the UN Convention on the Rights of Persons with Disabilities 2006 (which do not grant all the rights of the UDHR to all their subjects, simply because all their subjects cannot exercise all these rights) to be coherent given the UDHR declaration that all humans are equal in human rights.

Thirdly, the fact that the PGC grants rights under the will conception implies that the kind of control that Agnes has over her possession of the GCAs is essentially the type of control over something that is granted when someone holds property in a thing, insofar as an essential aspect of a property right is that

[47] D. Beyleveld/S. D. Pattinson, 'Defending Moral Precaution as a Solution to the Problem of Other Minds: A Reply to Holm and Coggon', 23(2) *Ratio Juris* (2010), 258–273.

[48] But for the issues involved see e.g. D. Beyleveld/R. Brownsword, *Human Dignity in Bioethics and Biolaw* (Oxford: 2001), 117–134.

[49] While duties to apparent non-agents can, as we have said, be justified in two other ways, these justifications rest on contingencies that do not fit the characterisation of a human right per the UDHR.

the default position, albeit defeasible in special circumstances, is that the owner does not need to justify use of the property or to prevent others from using it. With this in mind, one of us has argued elsewhere[50] that a property right is best understood as a 'rule-preclusionary right', which is to say that what characterises a claim to a right as a property right is not centrally the claim to have some specific bundle of powers to control an object, though the power to use and to prevent others' use of the object of the right is essentially involved. Rather, it is the claim that if X is A's property, then A does not, *as a presumptive rule*, need to justify A's power to use and to prevent others from using the object of the right even when A does not need to use it and others do.

Premised on this, it was argued that there is only one object that Agnes clearly has a right to in these terms. This is Agnes' body as an instantiation or vehicle of Agnes' person. The reason for this is that Agnes' body is so related to Agnes's existence as a person that for Agnes to be required to justify Agnes' control over Agnes' body on a case-by-case basis before the powers Agnes claims over it can be exercised would disproportionately threaten Agnes' very existence. This does not mean that Agnes' claim can never be overridden. The central point is that the default position must always be that, failing the case being made by others for the moral rights of others conflicting with and overriding (in PGC terms) Agnes' right to control Agnes' body, Agnes must be granted, without having to justify this, the essential powers of control over Agnes' body. So (and contrary to much received bioethical wisdom), unless one can own one's body, one cannot own anything. In these terms, a claim to have some object as one's property that is not physically part of one's body is the claim that it is normatively to be regarded as part of one's body (i.e. as having the same normative significance it would have if it were physically part of one's body). Because the PGC operates with the will conception of rights, Agnes' powers must also be extended to a power to commodify her body.

Now, things that Agnes has created, whether they be works of art or inventions, are naturally viewed as expressions, indeed, as instantiations, of Agnes' person; the further thought being that, as such, to use such instantiations, especially for another's personal profit, without Agnes' consent is to use Agnes' person (at least putatively) to Agnes' detriment. As such, rights to control such works have the hallmarks that would enable them to be assimilated under what in German jurisprudence are thought of as personality rights (to be distinguished from, though related to, such rights in IP law).[51] Here it is to be observed that the jurisprudence of the ECtHR has been in the direction of construing the right to

50 Beyleveld/Brownsword (2001, supra n. 48), Chapter 8.

51 The general right of personality is constitutionally guaranteed by Arts. 1 and 2 of the German Basic Law. It is held against 'all the world' and guarantees protection of human dignity and the right to free development of the personality.

private life under Article 8 ECHR as just such a right.[52] It follows from this that IP rights should be viewed as falling under the Article 8 ECHR right to private life, which in turn is to be analysed as a property right in rule-preclusionary terms.

This is important, because, as we have already noted, there can be moral reasons for granting rights (including IP rights), and moral reasons for preventing these rights from being exercised must take these reasons into account.

VI. APPLICATION TO SELECTED BIP CASES

Case 1: Competitor's Access to IP

In the 1970s, Frank (who heads a major beer producing company) developed a computer programme to analyse regional patterns of beer distribution and beer consumption. Since then, he has constantly refined the programme and has freely distributed it to his traders, trade associations and market analysts. The programme has become the standard instrument to analyse the beer market, and one cannot be active in this market without using it. Frank holds the copyright in the programme, which grants him negative and positive rights to:

- copy the copyrighted work (reproduction right);
- issue copies of the work to the public (distribution right);
- rent or lend the work to the public;
- perform, show or play the work in public (performing right);
- communicate the work to the public;
- make adaptations of the work;
- authorise others to carry out any of above through issuing a licence.[53]

In copyright law, if the programme is used by others without a licence, or contrary to its terms, Frank may obtain an injunction and make claims for damages.

[52] According to I. Roagna, 'Protection of the Right to Respect for Private and Family Life under the European Convention on Human Rights', Council of Europe, Strasbourg, 2012, 12: '[T]he notion of private life [under Art. 8 ECHR in the jurisprudence of the ECtHR] is much wider than that of privacy, encompassing a sphere within which every individual can freely develop and fulfil his personality, both in relation to others and with the outside world ... [For example,] over the years the notion of private life has been applied to a variety of situations, including bearing a name, the protection of one's image or reputation, awareness of family origins, physical and moral integrity, sexual and social identity, sexual life and orientation, a healthy environment, self-determination and personal autonomy, protection from search and seizure and privacy of telephone conversations'.

[53] See for example s. 16(1) of the UK Copyright, Designs and Patents Act 1988.

However, competition law permits the use of copyrighted work by others under specific circumstances:

1. the use of the right (infrastructure) is a precondition for activities on a secondary market and the refusal to use excludes any competition ('indispensability'); and/or
2. the undertaking requesting a licence has not only imitated those products but produces essentially 'different' ones ('innovation test').[54]

Frank will therefore be forced into licensing the use of his computer programme to Erica, but only to the extent of allowing Erica to operate within the relevant market.

Consequently, if Erica, a former trader of Frank's products and now director of a major competitor of Frank, starts to model her own distribution system on Frank's system without a licence, Frank has a right to an injunction arguing that the computer programme is his. If the terms of the licence contain an obligation not to improve it and market the programme without Frank's permission, Erica may not improve and market the programme without Frank's prior consent.

It might be thought that this case does not raise issues under the PGC because the production of beer is not necessary to protect GCAs. However, while this is so, Frank does have a right to earn a livelihood, and this generates a right to recoup investment needed to earn that livelihood. And because the same considerations apply to Erica, there is a case to be made for conditions under which Frank must permit Erica to make use of Frank's copyrighted work without his consent. So, structurally, the legal position seems fine from the perspective of the PGC. What is questionable about the legal position is the restriction (as a matter of principle) of exemptions from licensing requirements for someone who wishes to use a copyrighted work solely in relation to purposes of entering the market. No other rights, such as the right of adaptation, are permitted.

Case 2: Dependency on the Use of a Patented Invention in Medical Research

Mary, owner of a small biotech company, was granted a patent on the gene BRAU-7 (patent 1). As a utility, the patent accounts for cardiovascular diseases. Five years after the patent was granted, her competitor John found out that the gene BRAU-7, in conjunction with the gene BLIB-5 (patent 2), is responsible for healing wounds. The proportional relationship to which each gene accounts for the healing process is scientifically unclear. John is also granted a patent on his invention. He sets up a business and starts producing an ointment.

[54] See for example s. 18 of the UK Competition Act 1998.

Does Mary have a claim of injunction against John?

As EU law stands, a patent may be granted if the gene

- is novel;
- involves an inventive step;
- is susceptible of industrial application;
- has (per Art. 6(1) of the Biotechnology Directive) a commercial exploitation that is not contrary to *ordre public* or morality;[55] and
- has a known function.

At the time Mary was granted patent 1, it is very unlikely she was aware of the gene's role in wound healing. What is clear is that Mary was able to demonstrate an industrial application that is 'specific, substantial and credible' in the patent application. The patent thus granted provides absolute protection covering all later discovered functions, including the wound healing function.

Although Recital 25[56] of the Biotechnology Directive addresses the interpretation of claims when sequences overlap, this narrow exclusion only applies to those parts of the sequence that are not essential to the invention. This is not the case here.

Therefore, the current legal position is that Mary has a claim of injunction against John and also to damages if the interpretation of the claims shows that there is an overlap between John's invention and Mary's invention.[57]

In this situation, patent 2 will be termed a dependant patent as a matter of patent law if it cannot be worked without falling within the scope of protection of patent 1. John may then seek a compulsory licence in order to work his invention.[58] Under the compulsory licence provisions, John will need to

---

55 In relation to this, Art. 6(2) states, as examples only, that the following are also unpatentable: processes for the cloning of human beings; processes for modifying the germ line genetic identity of human beings; uses of embryos for industrial or commercial purposes; and processes for modifying the genetic identity of animals that are likely to cause them suffering without any substantial medical benefit to man or animals, and also animals resulting from such processes. To this Recital 38 adds that any uses that offend 'against human dignity, such as processes to produce chimeras from germ cells or totipotent cells of humans and animals, are obviously also excluded from patentability'. Because the preamble to ICCPR (to which all EU member states are party) states that human dignity is the ground of human rights (which implies that any violation of human rights is a violation of human dignity), and Recital 39 of the Directive states that morality refers to moral principles recognised in the member states, it follows logically that any use of biotechnological material or product of such use that violates human rights is also unpatentable.

56 Whereas, for the purposes of interpreting rights conferred by a patent, when sequences overlap only in parts which are not essential to the invention, each sequence will be considered as an independent sequence in patent law terms.

57 An overlap would exist if a person skilled in the art interpreted the claims of patent 1 broadly to as to cover all uses of the gene.

58 See for example s. 48 UK Patents Act 1977.

demonstrate that he has made efforts to obtain a licence under reasonable terms and conditions, has not been successful within a reasonable period and will be required to pay adequate remuneration.

Under the PGC, ideally, patients should not have to pay for health care (which raises questions about the patentability of all medical treatments). Health care and medical treatment should be provided by the state and paid for by proportionate taxes on surplus income. Granted, developing treatments costs money, and this, too, needs to be funded. On the assumption that it is at least permissible to fund this on capitalist principles via patents, there still remains the question of how much profit developers may legitimately extract. And it is also arguable that, in principle, treatments should not be made available to persons simply on the basis of their ability to pay.[59] This background must be understood in assessing this case and any other case involving medical treatments; but for present purposes, we will assume that nothing in this case on these points violates the PGC.

At any rate, it should be clear that Mary should at least be required to license patent 2 under equitable terms, and that this should not be solely on the grounds of a compulsory licence regime.

Case 7: Boundaries of Personality Rights in Genetic Information in Regard to Research and Patents

Marc is immune to a specific, but widespread, influenza virus. A Pharmaceutical Company (PhC), obtains a sample of tissue from Marc, which it uses to screen Marc's genome. PhC finds that he has a unique gene that is responsible for his immunity and (on the basis of the information obtained) develops a vaccine against this type of influenza, for which it obtains a patent.

The UK Human Tissue Act 2004, for example, requires PhC to obtain Marc's informed consent to the removal of his tissue for the purpose of having his DNA analysed. If Marc considers that the purposes for which it will be used are unethical, he can refuse to provide a sample of his tissue. If PhC wishes to use the tissue for research purposes that go beyond those to which Marc has consented, then approval must be obtained from an officially recognised ethics committee. However, as regards patent applications, the situation is complex. UK patent law (and, indeed, the Biotechnology Directive *as currently interpreted* – see further below) does not require Marc to have given his consent to patenting of his gene. Nor does it give Marc the right to be named in the patent description. Whether Marc is entitled to any share of the benefits that are generated by marketing the

59 D. Beyleveld/S. D. Pattinson, 'Individual Rights, Social Justice, and the Allocation of Advances in Biotechnology', in: M. Boylan (ed.), *Public Health, Policy and Ethics* (The Hague: 2004), 59–72.

patented products, or whether Marc is entitled to obtain these products free of charge, will depend entirely on any contractual agreement between Marc and PhC, and will not affect the grant of the patent. Similarly, any deviation from the terms of the informed consent form will not affect the grant of the patent.

Before we comment on this from the perspective of the PGC, it should be noted that according to Recital 26 of the Biotechnology Directive:

> Whereas if an invention is based on biological material of human origin or if it uses such material, where a patent application is filed, the person from whose body the material is taken must have had an opportunity of expressing free and informed consent thereto, in accordance with national law.

Surely this means that if Marc has not given his consent to patenting of any of his genes that PhC isolates from his tissue, then no patents may be granted on these genes. However, in his opinion on Case C-377/98, Advocate General Jacobs states that, although such a requirement to obtain informed consent is a fundamental principle of EU law, enforcement of the requirement is the preserve of law other than patent law, and that, in any event, many gene patents involve the taking of blood samples from thousands of people and it is impractical to require patent offices to check that everyone from whom a sample was taken gave their consent.[60] We consider this to be untenable for the following reasons:

- it is not impractical for patent offices in cases like Marc's to check on his consent;
- even where a patent is taken on something developed from samples taken from thousands, all the patent office needs to do is require certification that consent has been obtained on the understanding that if this is proved to be false then any patent granted will be revoked and penalties applied;
- as a fundamental principle of EU law, informed consent must apply to all activities regulated by EU law; and
- Recital 26 refers to what must be ascertained where a patent is filed, not where a patent is to be filed.[61]

It follows that if the patentability of Marc's gene is not to rest on his informed consent to patenting, then it needs to be the case that the PGC does not require or even permit such consent to be a fundamental principle of EU law.

---

60 Opinion of Advocate General Jacobs, (2001) Case C-377/98 *Kingdom of the Netherlands v. European Parliament and Council of the European Union.*

61 See further D. Beyleveld, 'Why Recital 26 of the EC Directive on the Legal Protection of Biotechnological Inventions Should Be Implemented in National Law', *Intellectual Property Quarterly* (2000), 1–26, and D. Beyleveld/R. Brownsword, 'Is Patent Law Part of the EC Legal Order? A Critical Commentary on the Interpretation of Article 6(1) of Directive 98/44/EC in Case C-377/98', *Intellectual Property Quarterly* (2002), 129–143.

However, regardless of what Recital 26 requires, there can be no doubt that the PGC grants Marc a right to control the use of his body (and use of a gene obtained from Marc's body is undoubtedly a use of his body) by his informed consent. Furthermore, there is no doubt that research on this gene, products obtained from this research, patents on such products, and profits made from marketing of these products are uses of Marc's body.

This does not, however, mean that this right is absolute, that it cannot be overridden by the rights of others. The circumstances in which this applies are, of course, those in which it is *necessary* to do so for the protection of the GCAs of other agents. And, on this basis, other agents certainly have a right to protection against influenza. On this basis, even if PhC's use of Marc's gene were necessary to protect the basic GCAs of other agents, it would not follow that Marc should not be entitled to some profits from the marketing of the products: if this were true, then PhC should not be entitled to any profits (merely to recoupment of its investment). And, though Marc should (under the PGC) have a case on the grounds of unconsented screening/patenting under domestic legislation, like the UK Human Tissue Act 2004, that governs the removal and use of human tissue, it is certainly not the case that Marc's consent should not be at least a *prima facie* requirement for patentability as well. It is beyond the scope of this chapter to analyse in detail the conditions under which Marc's *prima facie* right to give his consent for patenting may be overridden *in patent law*, but it should at least be clear that the existence of such a right is as much a concern of patent grant as it is of other applicable laws. To put it differently, within the context of the ECHR, Article 8 ECHR applies as much to patent law as to any other EU law. It should, however, be noted that the situation is different where the tissue is removed purely for research, where it is removed in the course of clinical research offering a possible treatment, and where it is removed in the course of treatment. This is because, in the latter two cases, it should be clear that, in general, Marc must be able to refuse to allow a patent without this compromising his participation in a trial or receiving treatment. We can say no more here than that if use of Marc's DNA is *necessary* to be able to cure influenza (a big if) or at least the best way (arguable), then it will be legitimate (or arguably legitimate) to override the requirement to obtain his consent, given that the risks to Marc of removal of his tissue are minimal.

Case 9: Conflicting Interests of Families and Groups in Genomic Information

The Miller family carries a unique gene that is linked to the development of intelligence. 80% of the family enjoys an IQ of at least 140. The downside of the gene is 'shortgevity'. Those carrying the gene live on average no longer than 42 years. Lilly, a carrier of the gene, agreed with a pharmaceutical company Genfix that Genfix may undertake extended experiments on the gene. As compensation, she was promised a 1% share in all product sales made on the basis of the responsible gene. Her brother William, who carries the same gene, objects on the grounds (presumably) that he owns the gene as much as Lilly does.

Under general contract law, the default position is that that no one who is not a party to the contract between Lilly and Genfix has either a right to veto the contract between Lilly and Genfix or the right to veto the payment arrangement.[62] Consequently, coupled with considerations we have discussed in Case 7, William also cannot

- demand payment;
- stop Genfix taking out a patent; or
- prevent direct research on the gene.

We will not comment on whether the PGC permits Lilly to contract with Genfix for a share of the profits, nor on the powers Lilly has in contract law versus patent law (as these are already covered in our comments on Cases 3 and 7). The sole issues are whether the fact that Lilly shares the gene with William and other members of the Miller family means that they should have a say in the contract that Lilly may make with Genfix and whether they too are entitled to a share in the profits. Most pointedly, should they be able to veto Lilly's contract if it does not grant them a share of the profits? Because the research bears on William's generic interests as much as on Lilly's (and they will, presumably gather personal data *a fortiori* on William as well as Lilly), we think that Lilly, ideally, should have consulted with her family about the proposed contract and asked for their opinions. Ideally, the contract she made would have been a contract between the family and Genfix, with Lilly having the greater say only because of the inconvenience to her as the subject of the experiments. The precise details here will, however, depend on just what the experiments involve. What is required/permitted will also depend on the extent of Lilly's knowledge of, contact with, and relations with her family. The PGC cannot require the impossible, and variations in relevant circumstances can affect the practicability as well as the consequences of various arrangements that are not PGC-neutral.

Case 10: Collective, Cultural Rights. 'Reach-Through'

For centuries, the indigenous community ABC has harboured knowledge of how to treat a specific eye infection with a specific plant. Plant biologist Tobin bio-prospects the country of the ABC and its 'council of the elderly' agrees

62 *Dunlop Tyre Co v. Selfridge* [1915] AC 847 or Contracts (Rights of Third Parties) Act 1999.

to show Tobin how the plant is grown, prepared and applied – under three conditions:

- Tobin may only use plant extracts for medicinal purposes and must safeguard against anyone else pursuing research for different purposes;
- any potential patent application must name the ABC community; and
- ABC will obtain a 2% share in any profits that are generated from exploiting the patent.

Tobin accepts these conditions in front of the council in a formal meeting.

Thereafter, Walter, a laboratory colleague of Tobin (who does contract research for the Army, which is searching for a new poison for purposes of biological warfare) discovers that the main component of the plant is highly toxic with specific 'beneficial' characteristics for warfare. Walter files and is granted a patent on the poison that can be produced chemically in large quantities. In addition, Tobin does not name ABC in his own patent.

As all the country reports show, the universal answer under all patent law jurisdictions is that ABC can seek to be named as joint inventor on Tobin's patent. ABC would need to show that it has contributed to the inventive step.[63] In seeking being named as joint inventor and being included as one of the proprietors of the patent, revocation of the patent does not appear to be possible. In addition, in patent law, being named on the patent is generally seen as an adequate remedy.

Under contract law, ABC has an enforceable contract with Tobin, and he is clearly in violation of his contractual agreement with ABC by not naming ABC as a joint inventor on the patent. ABC are likely to get remedies under contract law, but this is unlikely to lead to Tobin's patent being revoked.

In addition, if Tobin has permitted Walter to use the material he obtained from ABC for non-medicinal purposes (or has not taken adequate steps to prevent him from doing so) further remedies under contract law will be available to ABC. But suing for breach of a contract or licence agreement does not involve the risk of patent invalidation.

If Tobin has not permitted Walter to use the material for Walter's patent, then a remedy may be available under criminal law. However, Tobin can only seek to revoke Walter's patent on certain grounds. These grounds are generally limited to the fact that the invention is not a patentable invention.

All of this said, it should be noted that it is surely extremely unlikely that Walter would have been granted a patent. The development and use of biological weapons is prohibited by the UN Convention on the Prohibition of

63 See for example s. 7(a) UK Patents Act 1977.

the Development, Production and Stockpiling of Bacteriological (Biological) and Toxin Weapons and Their Destruction of 1975 for (as stated in the Preamble) 'the sake of all mankind' and because 'such use would be repugnant to the conscience of mankind'. Since all EU member states are party to this Convention, patenting such weapons would almost certainly be considered to violate Article 53(a) EPC and Article 6(1) of the Biotechnology Directive, even on the highly narrow interpretation of these clauses operated by patent offices.

Although the last part of Article 6(1) of the Biotechnology Directive[64] states that 'exploitation shall not be deemed to be so contrary merely because it is prohibited by law or regulation', this caveat does not apply here. The Convention on the Prohibition on the Development, Production and Stockpiling of Bacteriological (Biological) and Toxin Weapons and Their Destruction was enacted as it would be 'repugnant to the conscience of mankind' to permit such activity and therefore against human dignity. These are precisely the grounds which engage directly with the first part of Article 6(1), prohibiting the patenting of inventions which would be contrary to human dignity.

Under the PGC, it should by now be clear that insulation of the conditions of patentability from the immoral use of an invention (involved in the narrow and very odd interpretation of Art. 6(1) of the Biotechnology Directive) just is not tenable. Because ABC is the source of the material from which Walter's invention is developed, on the presumption that the material may be commodified, and ABC would not have consented to a patent on Walter's invention, the PGC requires an analogue of Recital 26 of the Directive to be read in, rendering inventions developed from the source's property (as normatively part of the source's body) not to be patented without the source's consent. On this ground alone, granting a patent to Walter's invention is a clear violation of Article 6(1).

Finally, it should be noted that in relation to plant genetic material, the 2010 Nagoya Protocol on Access and Benefit Sharing, which is a supplementary agreement to the 1992 Convention on Biological Diversity, to which all EU member states are party, provides a number of options for member states, one of which (not adopted by the UK) is that the origin of the material must be disclosed and a patent will not be granted if there is no disclosure. This, under the PGC, should not be an option but a compulsory requirement.

64 Art. 6(1) of the Biotechnology Directive: Inventions shall be considered unpatentable where their commercial exploitation would be contrary to *ordre public* or morality; however, exploitation shall not be deemed to be so contrary merely because it is prohibited by law or regulation.

VII. CONCLUDING REMARKS

Limitations of space have prevented us from commenting on the other cases reported on in this volume, and we have not been able to do much more than suggest or outline how the PGC is to be applied to the cases we have considered. It should, however, be clear that the consequences of recognition of the PGC as the supreme principle of human rights has radical consequences for the interpretation and validity of IP laws in countries that claim to recognise the existence of human rights per the UDHR.[65]

---

65 For a detailed examination of the application to the PGC to the EPO case of *Warf* and the CJEU case of *Brüstle*, see Adcock/Beyleveld (2016, supra n. 4).

PART III

CASES

Country Reports, Editorial Notes and Comparative Remarks

CASE 1. ERICA'S IMPROVED BEER MARKET SOFTWARE

A.1. BASE CASE

Frank heads a major beer producing company. In the 1970s, he developed a computer programme which analyses regional patterns of beer distribution and beer consumption. Since then, he has constantly refined the programme and has freely distributed the programme to his traders, trade associations and market analysts. Over time, the programme became the standard instrument to analyse the beer market. Without using it, one cannot be active on this market. Therefore Erica, a former trader of Frank's products and now director of a major competitor of Frank, started to model her own distribution system on Frank's system. Does Frank have a right to an injunction arguing that the computer programme is his?

A.2. EDITORIAL NOTE: THE EUROPEAN FRAMEWORK

The base case is modelled on the famous CJEU cases *IMS Health*[1] and *Magill*[2] (later in line: *Huawei*[3]) but EU law does not apply to the designed case (no transborder/Community element). The research interest is directed towards national deviations from these cases (under the condition that a national antitrust control exists). Three aspects of European law are important for the national case analyses:

1. European legislation provides for copyright protection of computer programmes.[4] Due to the member states' duty to transform directives into national law, most national statutes will have a corresponding provision.
2. The relationship between European and national competition law is stipulated by Regulation (EC) No. 1/2003.[5] Its Article 3(1) emphasises that

---

1 CJEU judgment of 29 April 2004, *IMS Health*, C-418/01, ECLI:EU:C:2004:257.

2 CJEU judgment of 6 April 1995, *Magill TV Guide*, C-241/91 P and C-242/91 P, ECLI:EU:C:1995:98.

3 CJEU judgment of 16 July 2015, *Huawei*, C-170/13, ECLI:EU:C:2015:477.

4 Art. 1 Directive 91/250/EEC on the legal protection of computer programs, OJ L 122, 17 May 1991, 42, replaced by Directive 2009/24/EC, OJ L 111, 5 May 2009, 16.

5 Council Regulation (EC) No. 1/2003 of 16 December 2002 on the implementation of the rules on competition laid down in Arts. 81 and 82 of the Treaty, OJ L 1, 1–25.

national competition authorities, which apply national competition law to any abuse prohibited by Article 102 TFEU (former Art. 82 EC), must also apply Article 102 TFEU. National and European law are applied in parallel. Furthermore, Article 3(2) Regulation (EC) No. 1/2003 states that member states may adopt and apply stricter national law for prohibiting and sanctioning unilateral conduct engaged in by undertakings. Thus, national rules may qualify a certain conduct by a dominant undertaking as abuse, even if European law does not.

3. Early on, the European Court of Justice based restrictions on IP rights on Article 102 TFEU[6] and reversed the former doctrine that IP law takes precedence over competition law, thus acknowledging IP as an important factor for the analysis of market dominance.[7] Building, and distinguishing, the refusal-to-license case from earlier case law on 'essential facilities', it was the *Magill* court[8] which first established a licence justified under 'exceptional circumstances', defined by three additional requirements which the Court refined over time: (a) the refusal prevents the emergence of a new product for which there is a potential consumer demand; (b) the refusal excludes any competition on a secondary market; and (c) the refusal cannot be objectively justified.[9]

In *IMS Health*, the Court confirmed the requirements as cumulative, and added as a criterion that the licence must be indispensable to be active on a market.[10]

Thus, while it already had been a determining factor to establish dominance, the Court established indispensability as a condition on its own for a refusal to license to constitute an abuse of dominance. An IP right will be indispensable if

---

6 Art. 102(2) TFEU: 'Any abuse by one or more undertakings of a dominant position within the internal market or in a substantial part of it shall be prohibited as incompatible with the internal market in so far as it may affect trade between Member States'.

7 Although an IP holder is not automatically in a dominant position, V. Emmerich, in: M. Dauses (ed.), *Handbuch des Europäischen Wirtschaftsrechts* (Munich: 2011), H.I. §3. Art. 102 AEUV, para. 41 et seq.

8 The company Magill wanted to produce a weekly TV guide for Ireland which displays the programmes of different broadcasters. Such a TV guide did not exist on the Irish market. According to Irish law, broadcasters had copyrights concerning the programme lists, and forbade Magill to publish them.

9 CJEU judgment of 6 April 1995, *Magill TV Guide*, C-241/91 P and C-242/91 P, ECLI:EU:C:1995:98, paras. 54 et seq.

10 CJEU judgment of 29 April 2004, *IMS Health*, C-418/01, ECLI:EU:C:2004:257, para. 38. The facts of the *IMS Health* case are close to Case 1: IMS Health had developed a data bank with a special 'brick structure' in order to collect territorial market information (copyright-protected), and produced reports for the pharmaceutical industry. Two competitors tried to be active on the market with different structures, but did not succeed, since customers preferred the 1860 brick structure, fearing high switching costs. The CJEU concluded that the structure could be seen as a *de facto* standard for the pharmaceutical industry, on which future product development depended.

it is not possible for competitors to turn to any workable alternative technology or to 'invent around' the IP right.

The indispensability criterion was refined in the *Bronner* case.[11] Another important duty to license judgment is *Microsoft*,[12] in which the Court of First Instance (now the General Court) extended the new product requirement. The Court held that a licence can also be sought even if it is not sought to directly incorporate the technology in clearly identifiable new goods and services.

Applying these criteria to the case, it becomes clear that the base case was designed to meet the CJEU requirements (new product requirement: 'Erica intend to model her own programme'; indispensability of Frank's system (no 'inventing around'), 'high switching costs for users', emerging indispensability due to the *de facto* standard which evolved by earlier free distribution; market distorting foreclosure effect having a negative impact on competition on the downstream market). That means excluding Erica in the individual case is indicative of an overall significant hampering of innovation downstream.

The central question is: Do national laws concur with or deviate from these arguments, or do they employ different sets of law (here IP law for a dependent patent-compulsory licence, although the question insinuates an answer inside the private law system: 'Does Frank have a right to an injunction' (not: 'What can Erica do?'))?

A.3. COUNTRY REPORTS

(1) BELGIUM

I. Operative Rules

Frank has no right to an injunction against Erica.

II. Descriptive Formants

Belgian competition law (Belgian Competition Act (BCtA), now Book IV and Book V of the Belgian Code of Economic Law (BCEL)) mirrors European

11 CJEU judgment of 26 November 1998, *Bronner*, C-7/97, ECLI:EU:C:1998:569, paras. 41 and 44 et seq. A newspaper producer sought access to the home-delivery service of a competitor. The CJEU defined a facility as indispensable if there is no actual or potential substitute for it and if there are technical, legal or economic obstacles which make it impossible or unreasonably difficult to establish such a facility oneself – which would not be the case with regard to the home delivery.

12 CFI judgment of 17 September 2007, *Microsoft*, T-201/04, ECR II-3601, paras. 643 and 647. Microsoft had refused to disclose some interoperability information that was presumed to be covered by IP rights.

competition law and its case law to a great extent. We have not found any typical Belgian approaches concerning the debate on refusal to license.

In principle, Frank has the right as the owner, to authorise or forbid the use, distribution and adaptation of his computer programme, based on Article 5 Belgian Software Act (BSA)[13] (now Art. XI.298 BCEL – the Belgian legislation on intellectual property rights, including computer programmes, is now stipulated in Book XI BCEL), which implements Article 4 of Directive 91/250/EEC.

However, in exceptional circumstances an IP rightholder cannot refuse a licence on reasonable terms without the refusal constituting an abuse of dominance and thus violating Article 102 TFEU/Article 3 BCtA (Art. IV.2 BCEL), as established by European case law.

Since Belgian law and jurisdiction follows the CJEU case law, no national deviation has occurred.

In conclusion, if Frank were to refuse a licence to Erica's company, his behaviour would constitute an abuse of dominance under Article 102 TFEU and Article 3 BCtA (Art. IV.2 BCEL), since the conditions set out in *Magill*, *IMS Health* and *Microsoft* might be met.

There is an interesting Belgian parallel case, although neither the facts nor the legal questions are entirely comparable, i.e. *Source Belgium v. Febelco*,[14] which concerned a dispute between Source Belgium (a competitor of IMS Health on the Belgian market for delivering market analysis information on the sales of pharmaceutical products) and Febelco (a major wholesale distributor of pharmaceutical products). The case differs from the questionnaire case since it was agreed that the respective information as such was not covered by an IP right.[15] When Febelco decided not to provide Source Belgium with its sales information anymore, Source Belgium filed a complaint with the Belgian Competition Council and asked for preliminary measures, arguing that the Febelco's refusal to supply sales information to Source Belgium constituted an abuse of dominance and therefore violated Article 3 BCtA (Art. IV.2 BCEL).

The president of the Belgian Competition Authority considered *prima facie* that Febelco's refusal to supply the sales information indeed constituted an infringement of Article 3 BCtA (Art. IV.2 BCEL) and obliged Febelco to continue delivering the sales information. The president argued that Febelco was in a dominant position on the market of the delivery of its own sales information. A refusal to supply would prevent Source Belgium from carrying

---

13 Software Act of 30 June 1994, *Official Journal*, 27 July 1994 [Wet 30 juni 1994 houdende omzetting in Belgisch recht van de Europese richtlijn van 14 mei 1991 betreffende de rechtsbescherming van computerprogramma's, *B.S.*, 27 juli 1994].

14 Pres. Competition Council [Voorz. Raad voor de Mededinging], 25 March 2004, no. MEDE-V/M-04/0003, Source Belgium v. Febelco, Driem. Tijdschr. RM 2004/01, 160–175.

15 J. Ysewyn, *Tien jaar Belgisch Mededingingsrecht. Rechtspraakoverzicht [Ten Years of Belgian Competition Law. Overview of the Case Law]* (Brussels: 2007), 343–344.

on with its activities (a market analysis without the sales information of a major distributor is not complete and therefore not useful) and would completely destroy all competition on the market for analysis of the pharmaceutical market, since only IMS Health would still be able to continue with its activities on this market. The case is more complex, however, since other competition law issues were at stake as well, such as a possible cartel, excessive pricing, possible abuse of dominance of IMS Health itself (paying Febelco very high prices for the sales information and imposing exclusivity clauses), etc. Still, the interesting fact remains that Febelco was obliged to supply its sales information.

Thus, Belgian law does not depart from European case law in this regard.

III. Metalegal Formants

As a matter of principle, one is free to contract or not. However, the freedom to contract is limited.[16] If certain conditions are met, a refusal to contract can violate certain legal provisions, for example non-discrimination legislation or competition law.

With respect to competition law, the objective is to guarantee the existence of real competition, and by doing so, add to general welfare. In this context, monopolists' actions (mergers and acquisitions, cartels, etc.) are scrutinised for anti-competitive behaviour.

The argument becomes more complex, however, when IP is concerned. The essence of an IP right is the grant of an exclusive right on the exploitation of a certain invention, sign or another intellectual asset. Nevertheless, 'the fact that intellectual property laws grant exclusive rights of exploitation does not imply that intellectual property rights are immune from competition law intervention'.[17] Striking a proper balance between IP protection and competition law has proven to be quite challenging. The objective is to obtain more consumer welfare and more innovation. However, every intervention of the (by definition not perfectly informed) courts or institutions can have downsides for this very purpose. It has been suggested by Microsoft that obliging it to 'give' its interoperability information would completely chill its incentive to innovate. Empirical information is quite scarce, and it would seem that a lot of decisions are based on 'default presumptions' concerning the likely effect on competition, innovation and general welfare.[18]

---

16 E. Ballon, 'Hoofdstuk VIII. Onrechtmatige mededinging: Capita Selecta', in: J. Stuyck (ed.), *Handelspraktijken anno 1996 [Trade Practices anno 1996]* (Antwerpen: 1996), 213–216; S. Stijns, *Verbintenissenrecht [Contract Law]* (Brugge: 2005), 44–50.

17 Commission Notice: Guidelines on the application of Article 81 of the EC Treaty to technology transfer agreements, OJ C 101, 27 April 2004, 2, para. 7.

18 E.M. Fox, 'Monopolization, Abuse of Dominance, and Refusal to License Intellectual Property to Competitors – Do Antitrust Duties Help or Hurt Competition and Innovation? How Do We Know?', in: C.D. Ehlermann and I. Atanasiu (eds.), *European Competition Law Annual 2005: The Interaction between Competition Law and Intellectual Property* (Oxford/Portland, Ore.: 2007), 633–645.

Refusal-to-deal or refusal-to-license situations highlight the tension between static and dynamic competition. Requiring a dominant player to give access to its essential facilities may lead to an increase in static competition but a decrease in dynamic competition. The latter, i.e. Schumpetarian competition, is often considered more important.[19] The European courts only consider a refusal to license to be a competition law infringement in very exceptional circumstances. For a refusal to license IP, a special condition needs to be met, i.e. the 'new product' criterion, prevention of follow-on innovation or the denial of interoperability information.[20]

(2) CZECH REPUBLIC

I. *Operative Rules*

Frank has no right to an injunction against Erica.

II. *Descriptive Formants*

According to the provisions of section 2(2) Copyright Act 121/2000 Coll., a computer programme is protected as a work. According to section 12(1) Copyright Act an author has the right to use a work and to grant authorisation to exercise this right. Thus, Frank has the right to refuse to grant a licence to Erica. However, Frank is distributing the computer programme to everybody without any licence condition. Sections 65 and 66 Copyright Act also apply to computer programmes. In section 66 Copyright Act, there are restrictions on the rights of the author of the computer programme. *Inter alia*, in section 66(1) Copyright Act an authorised user is allowed to arrange and transform a computer programme, if this is necessary for utilisation of the computer programme for his/her purpose. Even though this provision must be applied restrictively,[21] Erica shall be allowed to transform the computer programme for her own distribution system.

However, in this case the Act on Protection of Economic Competition 143/2001 Coll. would also apply. According to section 11(1)(f) Competition Act, an abuse of dominant position is *inter alia* the refusal of an intellectual property holder to licence his/her right to other competitors, who cannot operate on

---

19 V. Korah, *Intellectual Property Rights and the EC Competition Rules* (Oxford/Portland, Ore.: 2006), 135.

20 DG Competition Discussion Paper on the Application of Article 82 of the Treaty to Exclusionary Abuses, paras. 237–240.

21 See J. Kříž, I. Holcová, J. Kordač, V. Křesťanová, *Autorský zákon komentář a předpisy související* (Copyright Act, Commentary and related regulations) (2nd ed., Prague: 2005), p. 198.

the same market without such a licence, unless such a licence cannot be fairly required.[22]

If the computer programme is a standard tool for analysis of the beer market, then Frank's refusal to license his computer programme is, according to section 11 Competition Act, an abuse of a dominant position, because there is no justification for Frank to refuse a licence. Frank is distributing the computer programme freely to other parties and his refusal is only based on competition reasons.[23]

Frank will not succeed, and Erica will be allowed to use the computer programme. Of course, Frank may ask for reasonable reimbursement for utilisation of his computer programme.

III. Metalegal Formants

Since the Czech Competition Act directly incorporates the CJEU's case law, there is no deviation with regard to the metalegal formats from European law.

(3) DENMARK[24]

I. Operative Rules

Frank has a right to an injunction.

II. Descriptive Formants

The relevant Danish rules are §§6 and 11 of the Danish Competition Act (DCompA, 21 August 2007). They are modelled on the TFEU. According to

22 See more P. Svoboda, in: J. Munková, P. Svoboda, J. Kindl (eds.), *Soutěžní právo* (Competition law), (1st ed., Prague: 2006), p. 238 et seq.

23 There is no information on proceedings taking place in a court up to 25 March 2007 in relation to section 11 and abuse of dominant position by a refusal to license to intellectual property in the legal database ASPI. Neither was there any information on the webpage of the Office for the Protection of Competition (www.compet.cz) up to 25 March 2007 that any proceeding has taken place because of abuse of dominant position by a refusal to license intellectual property.

24 The national report for Denmark is, to a large extent, based on (and, to some extent, even copied from) the Norwegian national report. Thanks to the author of the Norwegian report, Professor, dr.juris Ole-Andreas Rognstad, University of Oslo, for accepting this and in this way also giving an example of Scandinavian legal uniformity and Norwegian generosity. The reader should be aware, however, that on some points the rules in the two countries differ greatly. Thanks also to my colleagues at the University of Copenhagen, Professor, dr.jur. Mette Hartlev and Assistant Professor, cand.jur. Clement Petersen PhD for their valuable input. The analyses of Danish law are based on the law as it was understood in the spring of 2009.

the Danish Copyright Act (DCA, 20 June 2008), Frank holds exclusive rights to reproduce and to make the computer programme available to the public (DCA §2). According to Danish law, holders of copyright can rely on injunctions to prevent infringement of their rights.

Given that Erica's programme violates Frank's rights according to DCA §2, the next question is whether competition law limits Frank's ability to rely on his copyright to prevent Erica from modelling her own programme 'on Frank's system'. As seen from a competition law point of view, this is a 'refusal to license' case. Danish courts would construe the competition rules in accordance with the case law of the CJEU and the General Court. Erica would seem to be able to base a competition law defence on the suppression-of-innovation argument developed from *Magill* and *IMS Health*. The facts of the case are few but suggest that Erica does *not* intend to develop a 'new product' in the sense of *Magill/IMS Health*, but rather a *substitute* one 'modelled on Frank's programme'. Such a programme would be expected to serve the same functions as Frank's and would probably basically copy the existing programme. Such a substitute would potentially benefit competition (static efficiency) by lowering prices (more in section III below) but not by stimulating innovation (dynamic efficiency). In this situation where there is no 'new product' (or innovation, see more in section III below) the indispensability test from *IMS* would most likely not support Erica, and Frank would retain his right to an injunction to prevent the copying of the programme.

III. Metalegal Formants

The case is about finding the right balance between incentivising Frank without restricting innovation unreasonably. The case law of the CJEU demonstrates that competition law may sometimes serve as a 'second tier' to fine-tune the exercise of IP rights in special situations where rightholders, by relying on special market conditions, are able to claim a reward which has no basis in the IP rights system. Normally the 'internal balancing' mechanisms of IP rights – such as the rules defining the protected subject matter of the limitations – make sure that a correct balance between static efficiency (notably price) and dynamic efficiency (innovation) is maintained.

(4) ESTONIA

I. Operative Rules

The unauthorised use of Frank's computer programme would presumably be punished as a crime or a misdemeanour. Frank can use civil remedies (claim compensation for damages, termination of the unlawful use). Additionally, there is a non-performance of obligations of an undertaking in control of an essential facility on the part of Frank, which can be punished as a misdemeanour. Erica could claim compensation for damages.

II. Descriptive Formants

The case concentrates on complex issues of copyright and competition law. Frank has developed a computer programme, which would be protected under §4(3) clause 3 Copyright Act[25] as a literary work. The author of a work has both economic and moral rights. This means that Frank has the right to use his computer programme himself and exclude others from using it. In this case, Frank has licensed the programme to many companies and individuals (including Erica). The case does not reflect the specific terms of Frank's licensing strategy, but it could be assumed that the programme was licensed to Frank's business partners. From a copyright perspective, it is up to Frank to decide who is allowed to use his programme.

It is assumed that 'modelling a distribution system on Frank's system' constitutes the use of Frank's programme. Unauthorised use of a computer programme may have different legal consequences.

Subsection $222^1(1)$ of the Penal Code[26] provides that '[u]nlawful physical use or possession of a computer programme for commercial purposes is punishable by a pecuniary punishment or up to 3 years' imprisonment'. The provision is the result of legislative changes[27] *inter alia* reviewing the system of sanctions in the field of intellectual property, and it became effective as of 15 March 2007. Consequently, it is hard to predict how this provision will be applied by the Estonian court system.

Erica uses and remodels Frank's computer programme for commercial purposes. Without Frank's consent, the use referred to could constitute a punishable criminal act. However, if the licensing agreement is not very clear about where the right to use the programme ends, then it is possible that the use of the programme by Erica will not qualify as a criminal offence. Frank should have been very clear when the right to use the programme ends.

Unauthorised use of a programme also violates the economic rights of an author, which is punishable as a misdemeanour.[28] According to $\S81^4(1)$

---

25 Autoriõiguse seadus. Entered into force on 12 December 1992 – RT 1992, 49, 615; 2008, 59, 330.

26 Karistusseadustik. Entered into force on 1 September 2002 – RT I 2001, 61, 364; 2008, 54, 305.

27 Karistusseadustiku ja selle muutmisega seonduvate seaduste muutmise seadus. Entered into force on 15 March 2007 – RT I 2007, 13, 69 (in Estonian). Official text available at https://www.riigiteataja.ee/ert/act.jsp?id=12789872 (4 May 2019).

28 Subsection 3(5) of the Penal Code provides: '[i]f a person commits an act which comprises the necessary elements of both a misdemeanour and a criminal offence, the person shall be punished only for the criminal offence. If a punishment is not imposed for the criminal offence, the same act may be punished for the misdemeanour'.

Copyright Act, violation of the economic rights is punishable by a fine of up to 300 fine units.[29]

If we say that 'modelling a distribution system on Frank's system' involves changing and improving Frank's programme, moral rights are infringed as well. The catalogue of the moral rights includes the right of integrity of the work, the right of additions to the work and the right of supplementation of the work. According to §81^3(1) Copyright Act, violation of the moral rights is punishable by a fine of up to 300 fine units.

Competition law aspects are relevant to the case as well. It is said that without using the computer programme an entrepreneur cannot be active on the market. This means that Frank has an essential facility. §15 Competition Act[30] provides:

> An undertaking is deemed to control essential facilities or to have a natural monopoly if it owns, possesses or operates a network, infrastructure or any other essential facility which other persons cannot duplicate or for whom it is economically inexpedient to duplicate but without access to which or the existence of which it is impossible to operate in the goods market.

Undertakings in control of essential facilities are undertakings in a dominant position (§13(2) Competition Act).

These have specific obligations. Pursuant to §18(1) clause 1 Competition Act, an undertaking in control of an essential facility is obliged to 'permit other undertakings to gain access to the network, infrastructure or other essential facility under reasonable and non-discriminatory conditions for the purposes of the supply or sale of goods'. The denial of access to an essential facility constitutes a misdemeanour. Subsection 73(1) Competition Act provides:

> A person who denies other undertakings access to a network, infrastructure or other essential facility under reasonable and non-discriminatory conditions, or engages in other activities which create violation of the obligations provided by law for an undertaking with special or exclusive rights or essential facilities shall be punished by a fine of up to 300 fine units or by detention.

The Competition Board is the competent authority for conducting proceedings in matters of misdemeanours provided for in §73 Competition Act.[31] In addition, the Competition Board has the right to issue a precept if the person breached the obligations of an undertaking in control of an essential facility (§62(1) clause 7 Competition Act). The Competition Board may impose an obligation to perform

29 Pursuant to §47(1) of the Penal Code, a fine unit is equal to 60 Estonian kroons.

30 Konkurentsiseadus. Entered into force on 1 October 2001 – RT I 2001, 56, 332; 2007, 66, 408 (in Estonian).

31 Competition Act §73^8(2).

the act required by the precept (§62(2) clause 1 Competition Act). Damage caused by acts prohibited by the Competition Act is subject to compensation by way of civil procedure (§78 Competition Act).

Erica, however, did not follow the procedure described in the Competition Act in order to get access to the essential facility (the computer programme), but instead decided to use the computer programme without any authorisation. Legal acts do not allow such use.[32] Consequently, Erica infringed Frank's rights on the programme. The fact that Frank is obliged to license his programme does not justify Erica's act. As said above, Erica's act is punishable as a crime or misdemeanour.

III. Metalegal Formants

The Estonian law focuses on criminal sanctions with regard to copyright infringements, based on a strong notion of the double nature of intellectual property. Therefore, little room is provided for competition remedies, which are bound to a strict formal regime.

(5) FRANCE

I. Operative Rules

Frank has no right to an injunction because he holds an essential facility.

II. Descriptive Formants

French case law has more or less followed the CJEU decisions recognising the freedom of access to information. This was stated in the case of stock market listings, private appropriation is unlikely.[33] Similarly, in the case of weather

---

32 Erica cannot also claim that she acted out of necessity. Section 29 of the Penal Code defines the concept of necessity as follows: '[a]n act is not unlawful if the person commits the act in order to avert a direct or immediate danger to the legal rights of the person or of another person, and if the means chosen by the person are necessary for the aversion of the danger and the interest protected is evidently of higher importance than the interest subject to damage. In considering interests, the importance of the legal rights, the degree of the danger by which they are threatened and the danger arising from the act shall be taken into account'. It is emphasised in Estonian legal literature that the concept of necessity is not applicable if there is a specific legal procedure to protect one's rights – J. Sootak, P. Pikamäe, *Karistusseadustik. Kommenteeritud väljaanne* (The Penal Code. Commented Edition) (Tallinn: 2004), p. 135 (in Estonian).

33 Commercial Court of Compiegne, 2 June 1989: Droit informatique et télécoms 1989, n°4, p. 60, obs. N. Poujol.

forecasting, the Court of Paris insisted that the French National Weather Forecasting Office had no copyright claims concerning their databases since they are presented 'without any original contribution' and that such a right would not serve its essential purpose if used to 'justify the systematic access interdiction of available weather forecasting information to a category of operators'.[34] Nevertheless, it was considered that the Agence France Presse (AFP) could require more substantial royalties from a broadcaster – which was publishing an electronic journal likely to challenge the AFP – than from a consumer.[35] Finally, the Court of Cassation (French Supreme Court) stated that merely compiling figures would not be grounds for the protection of copyright.[36]

Since Frank's software has become the standard instrument to analyse the beer market, another CJEU theory has to be applied. In fact, even if these later cases show that competition law has prevailed over IP in the last decade in France, giving CJEU competition law cases a real national impact, it seems that the case we are presented with has to be seen under the scope of the essential facilities doctrine.

The essential facilities doctrine appeared first in the United States in 1912 in the *Terminal Railroad Association* judgment.[37] In this judgment, the plaintiffs argued that the only three possible railway crossings over the Mississippi River belonged to only one association, which was comprised mostly of railway companies. The Supreme Court declared that these crossings were essential facilities and that the association should provide access. However, only the lower courts, in the US, have explicitly adopted an 'essential facilities' doctrine.

The European Court of Justice has never applied the essential facilities doctrine and even in *Bronner*, the first case which really dealt with essential facilities, the term was not used.

The criteria according to which certain facilities are considered essential were given in the judgment regarding the European Night Services agreement between different European railway companies that operate night passenger services through the Channel Tunnel.[38] The three criteria are that:

> first, such infrastructure, products or services cannot be interchangeable and second there must not exist viable alternatives to potential competitors. Finally,

---

34 Paris Court of Appeal, 18 March 1993: Droit informatique et télécoms 1993, n°1, p. 23, obs. P. De Brousse; overruled by Court of Cassation (commercial section), 12 December 1995.

35 Paris Court of Appeal, 17 May 1990: Droit informatique et télécoms 1992, n°3, p. 31, obs. P. Gaudrat.

36 Court of Cassation (1st chamber, civil section), 2 May 1989, Jurisclasseur Général 1990, II, 21392, obs. A. Lucas.

37 224 U.S. 383, 56 L. Ed. 810, 32 S.Ct. 507 (1912) – *United States v. Terminal Railroad Association of St Louis*' B. Doherty, 'Just What Are Essential Facilities?', 38 *CML Rev* 2001, pp. 397–436.

38 CJEU judgment of 15 September 1998, *European Night Services Ltd (ENS), Eurostar (UK) Ltd, UIC, NV Nederlandse Spoorwegen and SNCF v. Commission*, T-374/94, T-375/94, T-384/94 and T-388/94, ECLI:EU:T:1998:198.

without getting access to such facilities, the latter would be excluded from the market.[39]

Therefore, both definitions give an overview of what the doctrine means. *Bronner* used different expressions such as the 'dominant position' of a company and the 'abuse' of this dominant position to describe it. It seems important, then, in the description of the essential facilities doctrine to describe what a dominant position and an abuse of this position mean.

European authorities do not use the expression 'essential facilities' and prefer to use the concept of abuse of a dominant position, which is, as has been seen, a component of the definition of the essential facilities doctrine and which is defined in Article 102 TFEU.

In contrast to the CJEU's reluctance to apply the essential facility doctrine, the French Conseil/Direction National de la Concurrence (the commission charged with prosecuting and sanctioning anti-competitive trading practices) has applied the doctrine in several cases, especially concerning software.

Its first opinion was given in 2002 regarding access to a computer programme that analyses newspaper distribution. In its opinion of 22 May 2002,[40] the Commission specified to conditions according to which software may be considered as an essential facility:

- the facility must be owned by an undertaking with a dominant position;
- access to the facility must be strictly necessary for the competing industry to access the market, whichever stage of the market it wants to access; and
- the competing undertaking must be able to reproduce the facility under reasonable economic conditions.

The Court of Cassation applied the essential facilities doctrine in 2001 to a database that it qualified as being an 'essential resource'.[41] With this decision, the judges considered that the financial conditions of access to these databases were excessive and unjustified, constituting an abuse of dominant position.

The Court of Cassation also stressed this notion of abuse of dominant position in another decision.[42] In this case, two companies were in conflict, one

39 O. Stehmann, 'Applying "Essential Facility" Reasoning to Passenger Rail Services in the EU – The Commission Decision in the Case GVG', case comment: 25 *E.C.L.R.* 2004, pp. 290–394.

40 Advice n°02-A08, 22 May 2002 relatif à la saisine de l'association pour la défense de la distribution de la presse: http://www.conseil.conc.fr. S. Lemarchand, 'L'affaire NMPP : s'oriente-t-on vers une nouvelle limite au droit d'auteur du logiciel au nom de la libre concurrence?', *Propriété Intellectuelle* 2004, n°11, p. 626.

41 Court of Cassation (commercial section), 4 December 2001, France Telecom Lectiel, JurisData n°2001-012012, obs. S. Poillot-Peruzzeto; Revue Contrats, Concurrence et consommation 2001, commentaire n°46, obs. M. Malaurie Vignal.

42 Court of Cassation, 12 July 2005, n°04-12.388, JurisData n°2005-029484; Revue Contrats, Consommation, Concurrence 2005, commentaire n°190.

arguing that the other abused its dominant position on the market of newspaper distribution, refusing to grant a licence of the software '*Presse 2000*' used by every distributor to analyse and follow the distribution of newspapers by retailers. The Court of Cassation overruled the decision of the Court of Appeal using the arguments developed by the French Conseil National de la Concurrence in its opinion of 2002 (described above). The Court of Appeal judged that the software used constituted an 'essential facility the copy of which, for commercial purposes, at reasonable costs, was not possible'.

Therefore, the Court of Cassation highlighted the fact that the essential facilities doctrine can be applied only if the software in question can be considered as being absolutely necessary/essential.

In our case, if the software is considered as being absolutely necessary, it seems that an injunction could not be granted to Frank.

III. Metalegal Formants

The solution of this case depends on the CJEU cases of *IMS Health* and *Magill*. In fact, prior to these cases, even though IP rights in France and everywhere else in Europe were considered to be stronger than competition law rules, a generation of subsequent innovators claimed access to prior IP without 'working around' initial inventions. In view of the constant broadening of the scope of IP rights, these innovators considered IP protection to be too constraining on further innovation, which came to cover even trivial innovations. As a result, a lot of past innovations cannot be improved or refreshed.

A question then arose: how are the interests of society best served? Are they served by rewarding innovation economically through broad protection of IP rights or are they served by requiring access to the intellectual property of the original inventor[43] (thus rewarding him/her only once)?

Effectively, the restriction of access to products protected by IP rights may be challenged through the application of competition law. Therefore, it is argued that most often, competition law must be applied whereby companies cannot save their monopoly in the European Union, except in relation to IP rights. Consequently, it is unfair to protect something only one person or company has created for which it obtained intellectual property protection where, by contrast, a third party can be punished because it is the sole provider of a product or a service that cannot be protected.

According to Barton,[44] during the 1970s, intellectual property was weak and competition law very strong, whereas in the 1990s intellectual property

[43] See S. Scotchmer, 'Standing on the Shoulders of Giants: Cumulative Research and the Patent Law', 5(1) *Journal of Economic Perspectives* 1991, pp. 29–41.

[44] Hearings on Global Competition and Innovation, 1996, pp. 3409–20, FTC Proceedings.

became strong and competition law weak. For Barton this raised a problem: 'if broad patents and patents covering basic research encourage primary R&D activity, they may discourage subsequent improvements or substitute products by reducing spill-overs'.

The CJEU changed the trend and decided to give a chance to competition law over IP. The French courts followed suit.

(6) GERMANY

I. *Operative Rules*

Frank has no right to an injunction.

II. *Descriptive Formants*

Frank has a right to his computer programme under German copyright law (§2 I 1 Urheberrechtsgesetz (UrhG)).[45] The scope of the right enshrines the right to modify it (§69c No 2 UrhG). Although copyright law provides for several statutory barriers to the author's right (§§44a et seq. UrhG), none of those is applicable to the case.

Until 2005, the central paradigm of German competition law (former §19 German Antitrust Law (GWB)) was that IP rights prevail over competition law. According to the so-called *Inhaltstheorie*, competition law was not applicable as far as the scope of intellectual property right reaches. In addition, no statutory moral right ('fair use') in copyright applied (conclusive list in §§44a–63a UrhG). The CJEU judgments of *Magill* (1995) and *IMS* (2004) demanded a conceptual change, resulting in a reform of §19 GWB in 2005, and again in 2021.

§19 German Antitrust Law (GWB) regulates the 'misuse of market dominance' and stipulates the case of 'refusal to license' in §19 sec. 4 No. 4 GWB. However, the legislator limited the rule to 'access to networks and other infrastructures', and explicitly declared it not to be applicable to IP rights.[46] One may argue

---

45 If he also created the database, he is entitled to the rights under §87 b German Copyright Law: 'The maker of the database has the exclusive right to reproduce, to distribute and to communicate to the public the whole database or a qualitatively or quantitatively substantial part thereof. The repeated or systematical reproduction, distribution or communication to the public of qualitatively and quantitatively insubstantial parts of the database shall be deemed as equivalent to the reproduction, distribution or communication of a qualitatively or quantitatively substantial part of the database provided that these acts run counter to a normal exploitation of the database or unreasonably prejudice the legitimate interests of the maker of the database.'

46 Entwurf eines Sechsten Gesetzes zur Änderung des Gesetzes gegen Wettbewerbsbeschränkungen, BT-Dr. 13/9720 of 29 January 1998, p. 37; some authors nevertheless demand an application to IP rights (e.g. S. Maaßen, *Normung, Standardisierung und Immaterialgüterrechte* (Köln: 2006) 238 et seq.).

that Frank's programme has evolved into an infrastructure for distribution ('essential facility'). It became a 'standard instrument' and is thus indispensable for Erica to be active on the market. In exploiting his right, he prevents Erica from marketing a different product. However, Frank's digital infrastructure is primarily essential for legal reasons. Erica could devise an alternative. The programme is not a 'natural monopoly' in the sense of §19 sec. 4 No. 4 GWB, and thus §19 sec. 4 GWB does not apply. The same applies to §§19 IV No. 1 and 20 I alt. 1 GWB being a 'hindrance of competitors' (*Behinderungsmissbrauch*), in order to not circumvent the legislator's intention.

Frank, however, might be obliged to grant a licence under the conditions developed by the judiciary known as 'competition law defence' (*kartellrechtlicher Zwanslizenzeinwand*, technically §242 German Civil Code (Bürgerliches Gesetzbuch (BGB)) in conjunction with §§19, 20 GWB). The German Supreme Court (Bundesgerichtshof (BGH)) refined the CJEU jurisprudence (supra section A.2) in its *Spundfass* decision in 2004[47] (published the same year the *IMS* case was decided), and in *Orange Book Standard* in 2009.[48] Regional courts have further developed the case law.[49] Until the CJEU *Huawei* decision in 2015,[50] this national case line differed from the CJEU 'duty to licence' cases *Magill–IMS–Bronner* in that it draws on industrial standards which are not set by market dominance but by a communicative process of industry guided by administrations. Whereas the prior CJEU cases gave resonance to the 'different market' precondition of the 'essential facilities' doctrine, the BGH cases saw the justification of the 'duty to licence' in the fact that the indispensability rests on collective corporate behaviour (not primarily on supreme technical performance). Although this corporatist reasoning of the German High Court does not apply in the given case, these cases are discussed as mirroring more fundamental principles of competition law.[51] The core is market access for 'new' products, a prerequisite of innovation. Arguing that Erica's programme is 'new', she would qualify to be granted a licence – if she meets the requirements as set out by the court (prior unconditional and concrete offer for a licence agreement, money deposited to a secure account).

Finally, one may argue the given case by referring to the general principle of *venire contra factum proprium*. Frank had freely distributed the programme for some time. He contributed to the wide application of the instrument

---

47 BGH judgment of 13 July 2004 (KZR 40/02), BGHZ 160, 67 – *Standard Spundfass*.

48 BGH judgment of 6 May 2009 (KZR 39/06), BGHZ 180, 312 – *Orange Book Standard*.

49 For transferred standard-essential patents: Higher Regional Court (Oberlandesgericht) Düsseldorf, 22 March 2019, I-2 U 31/16 – for a comment see P.G. Picht, '*In rem* of effect licensing declarations', in: C. Godt and M. Lamping (eds.), *A Critical Mind – Hanns Ullrich's Footprint in Internal Market Law, Antitrust and Intellectual Property* (Berlin: 2022).

50 CJEU judgment of 16 July 2015, C-170/13, ECLI:EU:C:2015:477.

51 The requirements of the *Orange Book Standard* decision are applied not only to *de facto* standards but also to standards set by standard-setting organisations (*de jure* standards).

(without remuneration), and thus bound himself. It would be contrary to his previous behaviour, which the market could legitimately expect. Therefore, Frank's refusal to license would be unfair and amount to a misuse of market dominance. He has no right to an injunction.

III. Metalegal Formants

While traditional German IP theory upheld that IP rights prevail over competition law, EU competition law forced German law to acknowledge the dispensability of IP rights in specific circumstances. Gradually, competition law's self-understanding has shifted from an antipode of IP to a complementary order fostering innovation and progress. Whereas the Anglo-American debate has revolved around the idea of network industries forging the transformation of IP rules, the German debate has gained momentum with the idea of an industry standard which owed its monopoly power not to intellectual supremacy but to corporate–administrative cooperation (*Standard Spundfass*).

The central question of the case is, however, how far exactly IP rights reach. What are the conditions set by competition law? IP rights are important in order to promote innovation and therefore enjoy a considerable status in today's legal systems. However, the more indispensable they get for following improvers, and the more they are (mis)used for other purposes than promoting and protecting innovation, namely to constrain competitors, the more actively competition law will restrain IP rights. In contrast to the EU's explicit innovation-driven approach (especially emphasised by the 'new product' criterion), German law (*Orange Book Standard*) still focuses on the reasons why an IP right restricts market access. At the core of *Spundfass* and *Orange Book Standard* is a corporatist rationale of a modern economy. Therefore, access is not broadly granted, but is constructed on a fictional contractual relationship between the IP rightholder and the licence seeker. The licensee must fulfil his/her contractual duties (namely paying fees and royalties), before he/she is entitled to use the right. The conceptual core is the intricacies of (an ultimately judicial) fixing of a remuneration for the statutory duty to license. The licence seeker is allowed to use the IP right after requesting a licence, awaiting the denial, and depositing a fair licence fee. It is questionable whether this jurisprudence complies with European competition law.[52] It is more difficult to acquire a compulsory licence under German law than under European law. However, German law may only deviate from European law by providing stricter rules for unilateral conduct of dominant undertakings, not stricter rules for their competitors or other market participants. It is not clear in which way the German version of *kartellrechtlicher*

---

52 See e.g. the article of G.-K. De Bronett, 'Gemeinschaftsrechtliche Anmerkungen zum "Orange-Book-Standard"- Urteil des BGH', *WuW* 2009, 899–908.

Zwangslizenzeinwand is to be classified. Some authors argue that the European criteria (*Magill, IMS Health, Microsoft*) would only be applicable in general 'refusal to license' cases (not in cases, in which the rightholder demands unreasonable royalties or discriminates against someone).[53] The German *Zwangslizenzeinwand* may only be applicable in cases of unreasonable licensing practices.[54] There is unease about the different standards and rationales applied by the German Supreme Court and the CJEU.[55]

(7) GREECE

I. Operative Rules

Erica may object to Frank's claim for an injunction by claiming a compulsory licence.

II. Descriptive Formants

Community and Greek national law (Arts. 2 para. 3, 40–45 Law 2121/1993 = Directive 1991/250/EEC) recognise the right to intellectual property of the creator of a software programme. Nevertheless, if this right gives him/her a dominant position in the relevant market (here, 'the standard instrument to analyse the beer market') then he/she must not exploit that position abusively (Art. 2 Law 703/1977; Art. 102 TFEU).

Greek courts will have to follow CJEU case law in this respect and especially *Magill, Ladbroke, Oscar Bronner* and *IMS Health*. On the basis of the aforementioned cases it can be noted that IP rights enjoy a special treatment under competition law. Therefore, they are not 'immune'. Each case depends on the 'special circumstances' at issue. However, the CJEU has interpreted the 'special circumstances' doctrine in a very narrow way, allaying the fear that had been created by *Magill*.

---

53 J. Herr, 'Patent Litigation and Industry Standards', (2009) 21 *Intellectual Property & Technology Law Journal*, 10 at 11; W. Erdmann, S. Rojahn and O. Sosnitza, *Handbuch des Fachanwalts, Gewerblicher Rechtsschutz* (2nd ed., Köln: 2011), 1.E.VIII., para. 263; T. Kühnen, *Handbuch der Patentverletzung* (5th ed., Köln: 2011), E.III.5.b) aa), paras. 1254 et seq.

54 T. Kühnen, *Handbuch der Patentverletzung* (5th ed., Köln: 2011), E.III.5.b) aa), paras. 1253 et seq.; of different opinion: P. Maume, *Der kartellrechtliche Zwangslizenzeinwand im Patentverletzungsprozess* (Köln: 2010), pp. 22 ff., who argues for an application of European criteria in German law in cases of a general refusal.

55 Demanding clarification for the sake of legal certainty, T. Nägele and S. Jacobs, 'Zwangslizenzen im Patentrecht – unter besonderer Berücksichtigung des kartellrechtlichen Zwangslizenzeinwands im Patentverletzungsverfahren', *WRP* 2009, 1062 at 1067 f.; A. Balitzki, 'Der kartellrechtliche Zwangslizenzeinwand bei standardessentiellen Patenten im deutsch-niederländischen Vergleich', in: S. Behrends, C. Bick, G. Brandt and A. Eiselt (eds.), *Integration im Prozess der Internationalisierung* (Oldenburg: 2012), pp. 49–60.

In the given case, the 'work', though original and meriting copyright protection, works as a useful and utilitarian tool for a commercial product. The tool is necessary for everyone who wants to become active on the market. This could have two readings: one has to use the very same tool to sell the very same product, or one could develop one's own product only by using Frank's tool as a necessary basis (if this product is considered to constitute an essential facility, although the CJEU has never referred to it as such expressly) in order to be generally active on the market and not sell the same product as it is.

Furthermore, of central importance in the present case is the choice of the criterion of abusiveness. If the supply of the public with a market analysis programme is crucial, then the abusiveness of Frank's acts is unquestionable, to the extent that the needs of the public seem to be already met by his (initial) programme. A contrary solution would perhaps be fitting only in the event of Erica's programme providing substantively new possibilities for its user. The criterion should not be identified with the question of whether the new programme constitutes a product of Erica's own work, a fact, if established, which suffices simply to give grounds for its own separate intellectual property (or possibly joint property) involving it.

If, again, the prevention of freedom of competition is crucial, then Frank's claim will always be abusive, together with his entailed refusal to cede to Erica the licence for use and further improvement. This is so, given that the insistence of Frank on his claim that anyone else should abstain from the exploitation and further development of his programme excludes by definition the contestability of the relevant market by any third party. This approach – probably the more convincing one – is also in keeping with the position established by the case law of CJEU that (beyond the moral right of the author) the 'main function' and the 'specific object' of the right of intellectual property is the power of the beneficiary to exploit it economically, that is, to assign its use for a consideration, and not the power totally to preclude this use.[56]

In every other respect, it should be noted that the correctness of the above solution is supported, naturally, in the present instance by the fact that Frank has already made the use of his programme available to all his distributors, and moreover free of charge. Of course, this concession does not deprive him totally and definitely of his right of intellectual property over it, that is, of the right, in accordance with the preceding paragraph to gain economically from its exploitation (Art. 13 para. 5 Law 2121/1993: 'purpose principle')[57]

---

56 See CJEU judgment of 20 October 1993, *Phil Collins v. Imtrat Handelsgesellschaft MBH a.o. & Leif Emmanuel Kranel v. EMI Electrola GmbH*, C-92/92, ECLI:EU:C:1993:847; see also CJEU judgment of 6 April 1995, *Magill*, C-241/91 P and C-242/91 P, ECLI:EU:C:1995:98.

57 Koumantos, *Copyright Law* (1991), pp. 57, 169, 204–205, 228; Kotsiris, *Copyright Law* (2017), p. 75; Kallinikou, *The Fundamental Issues of L. 2121/1993 for the Law of Copyright* (1994), nos. 121, 128; Goldbaum, *Urheberrecht und Urhebervertragsrecht* (1961), pp. 75 ff.

However, his subsequent unjustified refusal to cede the use of it against a consideration is contrary to good faith, as it constitutes at the same time an illegitimate retraction (*venire contra factum proprium*, Art. 281 Civil Code).

In any case, Frank has the right to be recognised as the creator of the programme (the so-called 'moral' right), but no injunction, unless Erica refuses to pay a consideration for the use of his programme.

III. Metalegal Formants

The aforementioned analysis of course does not necessarily imply that the case law in this area is settled. According to the information provided, it is very likely that the courts will make Frank license his product not for it to be used as such but as a basis for a similar (but not substantially similar) product which will allow one to be active on the same market. This licensing would be even easier if the product to be marketed did not coincide with the product marketed by Frank on the basis of the software at issue. In order to reach the aforementioned conclusion, courts would also consider whether the creation of similar softwaretech would be possible or would be extremely costly, as well as whether the creation of a similar product and the adaptation of the market to it would be a realistic aim.[58]

(8) IRELAND

I. Operative Rules

In principle, Frank's behaviour will be seen as hindering competition, but this must be balanced with his strong copyright and an absence of litigation in this area.

II. Descriptive Formants

In Ireland, computer programmes are protected under section 2(1) Copyright and Related Rights Act 2000 (as amended) as literary works. Whilst copyright is a statutory right, it is also a property right under the property law provisions of the Constitution,[59] as recognised in case law.[60] A rather curious feature of

---

58 Stamatoudi, *Community Competition Law and Intellectual Property. Abuse of Dominant Position* (2006), and Stamatoudi, 'The hidden agenda in *Magill* and its impact on new technologies', *World Intellectual Property*, 1998, vol. 1, 153–176.

59 Art. 43 of the Irish Constitution, together with Art. 40.3.2.

60 *Phonographic Performance Ltd v. Cody* [1994] 2 ILRM 241, appealed successfully on other grounds [1998] 4 IR 504.

Irish copyright law is that its scope is potentially broader than the statutory framework. In the case *Phonographic Performance Ireland v. Cody*,[61] Keane J. recognised that copyright, in addition to being a statutory right, was also a property right with constitutional protection. This part of the dictum has since been approved in the High Court by Charleton, J., in *EMI v. Eircom*.[62] Furthermore, Keane J. observed that unlike other common law jurisdictions, the common law copyright in Ireland had not necessarily ceased to exist in the wake of the introduction of statutory protection.[63] The potential significance of this statement should not be underestimated – the notion of a common law copyright has long been disapproved of in other common law jurisdictions, such as the US, the UK, Australia and Canada. These countries claim that copyright only exists as a statutory right or, in legal theory terminology, a positivist right. The claim that the contrary may be the case in Ireland could mean that copyright exists as a natural right, whose scope could be much greater than that recognised by statute. Moreover, in the case of *EMI Records [Ireland] Ltd v. Eircom PLC*,[64] the judge stated that in addition to being a legal right which arises under statute and vests in the author, 'a natural human expectation arises that there should be such a right as a matter of simple fairness', giving some weight to the hypothesis that some form of common law copyright may survive statutory enactments. Whether either of these *obiter* statements is ever relied upon in court proceedings remains to be seen: most of the little copyright case law in Ireland gets frozen on the grant of an interlocutory injunction and thus fully fledged cases are few and far between. The author's rights are therefore significant in breadth and length. Moreover, section 4(5) Copyright and Related Rights Act 2000 (as amended) provides that references in the Act to copyright include references to copyright under any previous enactment conferring copyright, suggesting that other sources of copyright may co-exist with the statutory provisions.

Another issue that relates to the protection of computer programmes is that in Ireland computer programmers do have moral rights over their software and in order for this to be waived, such right must be relinquished in writing[65] and cannot be assigned or alienated.[66] In reference to computer programmes, the rights of paternity,[67] integrity[68] and against false attribution[69] all apply and the

---

61 Ibid.

62 [2010] IEHC 108.

63 *Phonographic Performance Ltd v. Cody* [1994] 2 ILRM 241, appealed successfully on other grounds [1998] 4 IR 504.

64 [2009] IEHC 411.

65 Chapter 7, section 116(1) and (2) of the Copyright and Related Rights Act 2004 (as amended).

66 Ibid., section 118.

67 Ibid., section 107(1).

68 Ibid., section 109(1).

69 Ibid., section 113(1).

former two rights last for the length of the copyright.[70] The latter right lasts for 20 years after the rightholder's death.[71]

The starting point would appear to be that a refusal to licence is the right of the author of the work and, moreover, moral rights could be relied upon to prevent any alteration of the work. Thus, an injunction could certainly be sought.[72]

National competition law is on a statutory footing but is also subject to the constitutional guarantees in relation to property, and, by extension intellectual property rights, in Articles 40.2.3 and 43 of the Constitution. Wherever property rights are restricted, this must be done with the exigencies of the common good in mind, under Article 45, and this will involve the court in a balancing exercise.

Irish competition law, which arises under the Competition Act 2002, is modelled closely on European law. Whilst dominance itself in a market is not problematic, abuse of such dominance is not allowed under section 5. There is very little litigation on competition matters, not helped by the fact that the Competition Authority experienced a large cut in funding and resources, as detailed in its 2009 Report.[73] The Competition Commission has since been dissolved and been superseded by the Competition and Consumer Protection Commission.

Generally speaking, software development is perceived by the Competition and Consumer Protection Authority as a form of R&D and licensing to third parties is regarded as socially beneficial with a market with low entry barriers. Conflicts, whilst unlikely, may arise in cases where there is a refusal to license, given that this would involve abuse of a dominant position. Frank is in a dominant position and has refused to license, and this refusal is likely to be regarded as unjustified. According to Dr Stanley Wong, formerly of the Irish Competition Authority,[74] a refusal to license intellectual property rights is an example of an abusive refusal to deal. Such conduct may be exemplified as either a refusal to start dealing or a unilateral termination of an ongoing deal. The latter is more likely to raise the spectre of abusive behaviour rather than a refusal to deal *de novo*. The essential facilities doctrine may be raised if Frank's refusal

---

70 Ibid., section 115(1).

71 Ibid., section 115(2).

72 Under section 127(2) in relation to copyright infringement and under section 137(3) in relation to an infringement of the integrity right. Injunctive relief is not specifically prescribed for infringement of the paternity right – instead the statute provides a remedy of 'damages or other relief', under section 137(2). Moral rights are not protected in the same way as copyright – the principal difference in terms of the remedies available to the aggrieved party is that copyright is a property right, moral rights are not.

73 https://www.ccpc.ie/business/wp-content/uploads/sites/3/2017/03/2009-Annual-Report-FINAL_0.pdf, accessed 27 February 2022.

74 See the Competition Authority website: http://www.tca.ie/search.aspx?q=stanley%20wong%20intellectual, accessed 2 June 2010.

to license is not objectively justifiable. However, in the opinion of Dr Vincent J.G. Power: 'many economists would suggest judges in Ireland are unwilling to find the existence of dominance, and therefore the abuse of dominance would appear to be a very difficult case to mount in an Irish court'.[75]

Under the *Magill* guidelines, it is questionable whether the 'exceptional circumstances' would be satisfied in Irish law, given the aforementioned strong copyright and the dearth of competition cases in relevant areas before the courts. Moreover, in the instant case, no new product is being produced: the complainant seeks to compete in an existing market.

A Guidance Note, published by the Competition Authority in 2005, treats refusal to supply involving intellectual property rights and other refusal to deal cases identically. It states that a refusal to supply will not amount to a breach of section 5 of the Act unless the following criteria are satisfied:

1. the firm is 'dominant' in the relevant market;
2. the refusal can be categorised as an abuse; and
3. there is no objective justification for the refusal.

It further states that a refusal to supply may constitute dominance but only in a limited number of circumstances.[76] Relevant examples given include, in extreme cases, if a dominant firm is the only source for the relevant product or service, or where it ceases to supply an existing customer, then it may have to justify any refusal to supply. No guidance is given on what constitutes an 'extreme' case, but Erica may be able to argue that without access to the software, she will be excluded from the market.

As an example of an 'objective justification', where a *de novo* refusal to supply is based on 'clear, transparent and internationally accepted criteria', then the refusal must be applied in a non-discriminatory manner. The Irish courts have recognised that a refusal to supply can constitute an abuse of dominance in the following cases: *A. & N. Pharmacy Ltd v. United Drug Ltd*[77] and *Authority v. O'Regan and Others*.[78] Whether this would apply to cases involving intellectual property rights remains an open question.

III. Metalegal Formants

There are a number of competing factors to consider in the application of Irish competition law to intellectual property rights. On the one hand, the Competition

75 V.J.G. Power, 'Reflections on Irish Competition Law 1991–2005' (2004) 4(1) *Hibernian Law Journal*, p. 195.

76 http://www.tca.ie/images/uploaded/documents/Booklet%20-%20Guide%20to%20Competition%20Law%20and%20Policy%20for%20Businesses.pdf, accessed 2 June 2010.

77 [1996] 2 ILRM 42.

78 [2007] IESC 22.

and Consumer Protection Authority is under-resourced, proving dominance is not an easy task in Irish courts, there is very little litigation in this area, and there is strong protection of IP rights. On the other hand, the Competition and Consumer Protection Authority has specifically stated that it will intervene in cases where IP rightholders abuse their dominant position.

(9) ITALY

I. *Operative Rules*

Frank has no right to an injunction, on the argument that by denying access through his claim he is abusing his dominant position on a secondary market.

II. *Descriptive Formants*

The Italian Copyright Law (ICL, l. 633/1941) reserves to the original author of a computer programme or a database the exclusive right to produce, to improve and to market his/her creation (Art. 64bis and 64quinquies ICL). The exceptions to the exclusive right are very narrow and limited to the possibility of modification for the purposes of study, teaching or scientific research (Art. 64sexies c. 1 let. a ICL) and for public security reasons (Art. 64sexies c. 1 let. b ICL). Under the ICL, Frank has a right to an injunction to stop Erica from using his programme in order to model her own distribution system.

However, the fact that the programme has become a standard instrument suggests that the case should also be analysed in terms of competition. Even though there are no previous specific cases on the point in the Italian legal system, a systematic reconstruction of the case law on similar circumstances might suggest a peculiar way in which Italian courts set boundaries on IP rights via antitrust.[79] Earlier decisions of the Antitrust Authority have followed the same line of thought expressed by the CJEU case law. Through a broad interpretation of the rule which provides for coordination between the EU and the Italian antitrust systems (Art. 1 c. 4 Italian Antitrust Law (IAL, l. 287/1990), the Antitrust Authority has pushed for a law that is as different as possible from the principles developed by the CJEU.[80] Indeed, case law shows an effort to enhance the essential facilities doctrine as a tool to inhibit the refusal to give access to information resources held by an operator who controls a source for which there are no market alternatives.

---

79 See Bertani, *Proprietà intellettuale, antitrust e rifiuto di licenza* (Milan: 2004), pp. 117 ff.

80 The Antitrust Authority in the case *Sign v. Stet-Sip* applied the *Magill* test elaborated by the CJEU in order to allow competitors (Sign) of the former legal monopolist (Stet-Sip) to have access to the information contained in Stet-Sip's phone directory; see AGCM 27 April 1995 no. 2970, in *Bollettino*, 1995, 17/5.

This interpretation is slightly different from the one suggested by ordinary (administrative) courts in the famous *Panini* case.[81] In that case, the courts applied to IP rights, by analogy, the special exemption provided for legal monopolies by Article 8 c. 2 IAL. This provision states that antitrust law does not apply to companies that manage services of general economic interest or to legal monopolies in relation to everything that is closely linked to performance of specific tasks assigned to them (Art. 8 c. 2 IAL). The exemption was codified in a special regulation by the legislature in 2001. With statute no. 57/2001, Parliament added to Article 8 c. 2 IAL five new paragraphs through which it introduced a specific duty to share informational goods (Art. 8 c. 2quater IAL), and considered the refusal to give access to these goods in a secondary market to be an abuse of dominant position prohibited by Article 3 IAL (Art. 8 c. 2quinquies IAL).

Applied to our case, it seems that both interpretations will lead to the same conclusion: Frank cannot claim an injunction because it would be deemed to be an abuse of a dominant position. However, the two interpretations are slightly different on evidentiary grounds: following the essential facility doctrine, Erica should demonstrate Frank's dominant position and the abuse (the *Magill* test restricted in *IMS Health*); in the other case, we may find a *per se* rule both on the dominant position (legal monopolies are *per se* in a dominant position) and on the abuse due to Frank's refusal to give access.

III. Metalegal Formants

Italian case law is split with regard to setting the boundaries on IP rights stemming from competition law. On the one hand, administrative courts suggest that the boundaries to IP rights stem directly from their special status as a legal monopoly, thus applying the special regime provided in Article 8 c. 2bis to sexies IAL. On the other hand, the position of the Antitrust Authority is to apply EU antitrust law, specifically the test set out by the CJEU in *Magill* and *IMS Health*. This position is supported by the majority of scholars, who criticise the first interpretation by arguing that it is consistent neither with European legal principles (Art. 106(2) TFEU does not mention legal monopolies as one of the recipients of the exemption) nor with the nature of IP rights, as they do not automatically give the IP holder a dominant position.

Although neither line of interpretation has been confirmed, the legal discourse seems to support those who consider EU law good law, including in the Italian system.

---

81 See TAR Lazio, 8 January 1998, in *AIDA*, 1998, p. 554 with a comment by Sarti; Consiglio di Stato, 17 February 1999, no. 172, in *AIDA*, 1990, p. 590.

(10) LITHUANIA

Answer omitted.

(11) NETHERLANDS

I. Operative Rules

Frank presumably has a right of injunction against Erica.

II. Descriptive Formants

Pursuant to Articles 10(1) and 45h Dutch Copyright Act, Erica's unauthorised use of the software gives rise in the present circumstances to a right of injunction to the benefit of Frank.[82] Whereas Frank's computer programme is protected by copyright pursuant to Article 10(1) Dutch Copyright Act, Frank has the exclusive right to authorise or prohibit the reproduction and communication to the public of his work. He is therefore entitled to institute an injunctive action in order to stop anyone from infringing his right. Since Erica's use of the software does not fall under any of the limitations on copyright provided for in Articles 45j–45n of the Dutch Copyright Act, Frank has a right to start an injunction to prevent her from further using the programme.

However, since Frank's computer programme has become a standard in the market, we can assume that his company occupies a dominant position in the market. The question is whether his refusal to license his software to Erica constitutes an abuse of such dominant position, contrary to Article 24 Dutch Competition Act. Cases of abuse of dominant position in relation to the refusal to license an intellectual property right have reached the Dutch courts as well as the Dutch Competition Authority (Nederlandse Mededingingsautoriteit).[83] In the presence of exceptional circumstances calling for it, even the Supreme Court of the Netherlands did conclude that such refusal to license constituted an abuse of dominant position and ordered the grant of a compulsory licence.[84]

In reaching their decision, the Dutch courts have closely followed the jurisprudence of the European Court of Justice. Since 1995, the CJEU has

---

82 Rb. Utrecht, 8 augustus 2007, nr. 220843/HA ZA 06-2471, *Computerrecht* 2007, 176.

83 Hof 's-Gravenhage, 30 januari 2000, *AMI* 2000, p. 73, m.nt. H. Cohen Jehoram; CBB, 8 januari 2003, LJN: AF2794 (*KPN v. Denda*); see J. Houtdijk, 'De strijd om de programmagegevens in Nederland: een nieuwe episode in een bekend omroepfeuillton', *Mediaforum* 2005, Nr. 11 /12, pp. 356–365.

84 HR, 6 juni 2003, *AMI* 2003, p. 141, m.nt. K.J. Koelman, *AA Katern* 2003, 89, p. 4801, m.nt. M.S.C. Bakker and A.A. Quaedvlieg, *Mediaforum* 2003, pp. 247–256.

developed a series of criteria against which the exercise of intellectual property rights can be tested to determine whether the rights owner is engaging in anti-competitive behaviour, contrary to Article 102 TFEU. According to the settled case law of the CJEU and as summarised in the *Microsoft* decision, a compulsory licence will be ordered only in exceptional circumstances.

In the present case, the first question to address is whether Frank's refusal to license relates to a product that is indispensable to the exercise of a particular activity on a neighbouring market. In order to determine whether the computer programme is indispensable for enabling the undertaking by which Erica is employed to carry on business in the relevant market, 'it must be determined whether there are products or services which constitute alternative solutions, even if they are less advantageous, and whether there are technical, legal or economic obstacles capable of making it impossible or at least unreasonably difficult for any undertaking seeking to operate in the market to create, possibly in cooperation with other operators, the alternative products or services.'[85] Whereas Frank's software has become the standard instrument in the field, its use could probably be considered indispensable for any enterprise wishing to carry out activities on a neighbouring market.

However, it remains unclear from the description of the case whether Erica's use of Frank's software concerns activities in the same or a neighbouring market. According to the case, Erica is a former trader of Frank's products and is now director of a major competitor of Frank. This leads us to believe that her activities directly compete with Frank's. Similarly, there is no evidence that Frank's refusal to license actually prevents Erica from bringing a new product to the market for which there is potential consumer demand. In this regard, the CJEU recalled in the *Microsoft* case that a 'new product' is a product which does not limit itself essentially to duplicating the products already offered on the market by the owner of the copyright. It is sufficient, therefore, that the product concerned contains substantial elements that result from the licensee's own efforts. For these two reasons, it is conceivable that Frank could successfully obtain an injunction to prevent Erica from using his software without authorisation.

In this context it is interesting to mention the judgment of the District Court in The Hague in the case *Philips v. SK Kassetten*. In this judgment, the position of the so-called Fair, Reasonable and Non-Discriminatory (FRAND) standards was discussed. FRAND standards are used in the standard-setting process to ensure compatibility and interoperability. Standard setting organisations involved in this process obligate their members to license according to FRAND standards.

85 CJEU judgment of 29 April 2004, *IMS v. NDC Health*, C-418/01, ECLI:EU:C:2004:257, para. 28.

Although the case from the District Court in The Hague was about patent law and the above-mentioned case is not about FRAND standards, the case may be interesting for future case law in the Netherlands relating to competition law and intellectual property law.

The case involved CD and DVD technology which Philips patented. The opposing party argued that they had not infringed the patent of Philips because according to the FRAND standards they were entitled to a licence. The court did not agree with this line of reasoning. The opposing party did not obtain a licence; therefore, they were infringing the patent right of Philips. The court did not exclude the possibility that, in special circumstances, a party which is entitled to a licence according to the FRAND standards but did not obtain one could be exonerated of an infringement. However, in this case there were no such special circumstances. In this case, there is therefore no abuse of a dominant position. The opposing party knew Philips had patented the technology in question and even then decided not to obtain a licence according to the FRAND standards. Therefore, they infringed the patent right of Philips.

The court acknowledges that this judgment differs from the German case law in FRAND defence cases (for example *Orange-Book-Standard*). According to the German Bundesgerichtshof, a FRAND defence succeeds when a licence is not actually obtained if the opposing party unconditionally offered to obtain a FRAND licence, which the patent holder could not refuse without discriminating against or constraining the other party, and to already live up to the conditions of the licensing agreement (for example to already pay royalties). The Dutch court does not agree, because this is not in compliance with the rules of patent law, it creates legal uncertainty and it is unnecessary for the protection of the legitimate interests of the opposing party.[86]

III. Metalegal Formants

Modern competition law recognises that its goal is best served by protecting the competitive process rather than individual competitors. Since the rationales of competition law are thus to promote welfare by stimulating static and dynamic efficiency, it can be concluded that competition and intellectual property laws are largely complementary: both aim to maximise welfare. Intellectual property laws accomplish this goal by enabling firms to recoup their investments in innovation through a temporary period of exclusivity granted *ex ante*. Competition laws accomplish this goal by incentivising firms to innovate and set their prices lower, and, where necessary, by sanctioning anti-competitive behaviour *ex post*.

---

[86] Rb. 's-Gravenhage, 17 maart 2010, HA ZA 08-2522 and HA ZA 08-2524 (*Koninklijke Philips Electronics N.V. v. SK Kassetten GmbH & Co. KG*) – r.o. 6.19–6.25.

However, intellectual property rights can, in some instances, result in protection of creations with anti-competitive consequences. The freedom to refuse access is especially (but not exclusively)[87] relevant where the facility that the competitor seeks access to comprises an intellectual property right.[88] Exclusivity is the very essence of an intellectual property right.[89] Hence, forced access to competitors undermines the certainty intellectual property rights aim to create. The result could be a substantial impediment to innovation.

(12) NORWAY

I. Operative Rules

Frank possibly does not have a right to an injunction, but this depends partly on the interpretation of the *Magill/IMS* rule and partly on the further facts of the case.

II. Descriptive Formants

There are two sets of relevant rules: Articles 53 and 54 EEA Agreement and §§10 and 11 Norwegian Competition Act (NCompA, 5 March 2004). The former set of rules applies to arrangements that affect trade between the states parties to the EEA Agreement (i.e. the EU member states and the EFTA states Norway, Iceland and Liechtenstein). Both sets of rules are phrased according to Articles 101 and 102 TFEU and are to be interpreted in the same way as these provisions.[90]

The case at hand concerns Frank's potential right to refuse to grant Erica a licence to use the programme. If he has such right, he will be granted an injunction. If the computer programme fulfils the originality criteria and constitutes a work under §1 of the Norwegian Copyright Act (NCA, 12 May 1961; replaced by New Act 28 May 2018 §2), Frank holds exclusive rights to

87 F. Lévêque, 'Innovation, leveraging and essential facilities: Interoperability licensing in the EU Microsoft case', *World Competition: Law and Economics Review* (2005) 80.

88 W.E. Kovacic and A.P. Reindl, 'An Interdisciplinary Approach to Improving Competition Policy and Intellectual Property Policy', *Fordham International Law Journal* (2005) 1062; H. Hovenkamp, M.D. Janis and M.A. Lemley, 'Unilateral Refusals to License in the U.S.', Stanford Law School (John M. Olin Program in Law and Economics Working Paper No. 303), 2005, p. 20; R.P. Merges, P.S. Menell and M.A. Lemley, *Intellectual Property in the New Technological Age* (New York: 2003), p. 1022. But see: C. Ritter, 'Refusal to Deal and Essential Facilities: Does Intellectual Property Require Special Deference Compared to Tangible Property?', 28(3) *World Competition: Law and Economics Review* (2005) 281–298.

89 J. Turney, 'Defining the Limits of the EU Essential Facilities Doctrine on Intellectual Property Rights: The Primacy of Securing Optimal Innovation', 2 *Northwestern Journal of Technology and Intellectual Property* (2005) 184.

90 Cf. Arts. 1 and 6 of the EEA Agreement.

reproduction and to make the computer programme available to the public (NCA §2; New Act §3). Consequently, the question is whether Frank's refusal to license his rights to the computer programme contravenes the competition rules. This depends on whether the refusal constitutes an abuse of a dominant position on the relevant market. The situation on this point is no different in Norway than in the EU member states, as the *Magill/IMS* doctrine is also relevant under the Norwegian competition rules. There is reason to believe that Norwegian courts would intend to apply the doctrine in accordance with the case law of the CJEU and the General Court.

The key issue seems to be whether Erica will create a 'new product' in the sense of the doctrine, including the impact of the statement of the General Court in *Microsoft* that the appearance of a new product cannot be the only parameter determining whether a refusal to license an intellectual property right is capable of causing prejudice to consumers within the meaning of Article 102(b) TFEU).[91] Since the CJEU has not yet confirmed the appropriateness of the statement, the legal situation remains unclear. Based on the information that we have, it is not unlikely that a Norwegian court would deny Frank an injunction with reference to Article 54 EEA Agreement or NCompA §10, but an absolute and certain answer cannot be given.

III. Metalegal Formants

As in European law, the issue at stake is striking the balance between creating incentives for innovation on the one hand and safeguarding effective competition on the other hand.

(13) POLAND

I. Operative Rules

Frank will probably succeed in obtaining the injunction.

II. Descriptive Formants

It is not clear whether in Poland one would also have to get to the stage where competition law should be deployed in order to curb the alleged abuse of dominant position by Frank. First, it is doubtful under the given facts whether Erica uses Frank's programme. It is perfectly possible that Erica has taken over the ideas behind Frank's computer programme but has not copied or

---

[91] CJEU judgment of the Court of First Instance (Grand Chamber) of 17 September 2007, *Microsoft*, T-201/04, ECLI:EU:T:2007:289, para. 687.

used the programme itself in any other way. If this is the case, Frank would not be able invoke his copyright in the computer programme and there would be no infringement of his exclusive rights. Under Polish law, the only remedy possibly available to Frank in this situation would be the law on combating unfair competition.[92] The Polish law on unfair competition contains a general clause according to which an act of unfair competition consists in any action contrary to the law or good morals and which infringes, or threatens to infringe, legitimate interests of other entrepreneurs or clients. Apart from the general clause, the Polish law recognises specific torts of unfair competition listed in the second part of the statute.

The question therefore arises whether taking over a competitor's achievements, ideas, etc., when they are not protected by exclusive rights such as copyright or patents, may amount to an act of unfair competition. No specific tort of unfair competition seems to apply to such circumstances; however, it is commonly accepted that 'unnamed' torts of unfair competition may be created (or more precisely 'discovered') by courts and the doctrine on the basis of Article 3 of the Unfair Competition Act.[93] It has also been generally accepted that certain ways of exploiting somebody else's achievements may be treated as unfair competition even if there are no exclusive IP rights involved[94] (e.g. TV formats).[95] Nevertheless, this is a very complicated matter and it is usually decided by courts on the circumstances of the case. What would be required would be an 'additional' element of unfairness in the defendant's actions, such as abuse of trust, break-up of a long professional relationship, etc., so that unfair competition law would not replace intellectual property law precisely in those areas where some of the most fundamental conditions of IP protection are not met.

In this scenario, an injunction does not seem probable because although there clearly is an act of exploitation of Frank's achievements, a sufficient degree of unfairness seems to be lacking. True, Erica is Frank's former tradesman but Frank himself has made his system the industry standard and, it seems, has never opposed the use of it by other persons (on the contrary, he has encouraged it). Consequently, the mere use of this system as a model after which a similar system is to be created would have nothing unfair in it. If this is the right

---

92 Law of April 16, 1993 on Combating of Unfair Competition, Consolidated text, Journal of Laws 2003, No. 153, pos. 1503 with further amendments.

93 J. Szwaja, in: J. Szwaja (ed.), *Ustawa o zwalczaniu nieuczciwej konkurencji. Komentarz* (Warsaw: 2006), pp. 170 ff.

94 Supreme Court, 2 January 2007, V CSK 311/03.

95 Supreme Court, 23 February 1995, III CZP 12/95; E. Traple, P. Podrecki, 'Wybrane aspekty tzw. formatów telewizyjnych', *ZNUJ PWiOWI*, vol. 80, 2001, pp. 173 ff.; A.J. Schoen, 'Poszukiwanie prawnej ochrony tzw. formatów telewizyjnych na gruncie prawa autorskiego oraz prawa zwalczania nieuczciwej konkurencji', *PIPWI UJ*, vol. 98, 2007, pp. 155 ff.

evaluation there would be no tort of unfair competition and no injunction available to Frank.[96]

Computer programmes are protected by copyright in Poland in the same manner as other types of works. Frank would therefore be in a position to demand an injunction against Erica and to pursue other claims provided for by the Copyright Act. As copyright law does not provide for any kind of compulsory licence, the only reasonable means of defence for Erica would be to claim that Frank is abusing his dominant position. It is common practice in Poland to refer to the relevant decisions or doctrinal views based on European competition law. This is especially helpful when no national decisions or court judgments have been issued.

To our knowledge, there has not been in Poland a case resembling the well-known CJEU cases concerning the interaction of competition law and intellectual property law.[97] It seems rather certain that Frank enjoys a dominant position on the market. In order to find Frank's reliance on the copyright abusive, one would have to establish not only that Frank's software has become a standard tool on the market but also that by refusing to grant a licence Frank stymies competition and especially makes it impossible for a new innovative product to enter the market. It is rather difficult to assume that a computer programme (protected by copyright) meets these requirements for at least two reasons: first, as already mentioned, a computer programme cannot be confused with a database, i.e. in this case the information Frank has gathered through all those years using the programme. It is true that building such a database is an immense task involving time and considerable amounts of money (see the facts in *IMS Health*). Under such conditions, the owner of the database has obvious advantages over his/her competitors because the creation of a comparable database would be hindered by prohibitively high costs. A computer programme may achieve a comparable position but in a different context (the *Microsoft* example). It may be so widely used that it becomes indispensable for others to have it or to make their products compatible with it. On the other hand, it would be difficult to show why third parties should be allowed to use the programme and modify it to produce a different and competing computer programme. What Erica has done was to create another computer programme fulfilling the same function as Frank's software (i.e. analysing patterns of beer distribution). Consequently, antitrust law would not help Erica, as the exercise of copyright by Frank could not be regarded as abusive and as a result of this unlawful.

---

96 Art. 18 of the Law on Unfair Competition grants essentially the same rights that may be found in typical intellectual property regulations, such as a claim to cease and desist.

97 Art. 2 of the Act on the Protection of Competition and Consumers of 16 February 2007, Journal of Laws 2007, No. 50, pos. 331 states that the Act is without prejudice to IP rights. However, this is not understood as meaning that the exercise of IP rights may never come under scrutiny of the competition authorities but only that the very fact such rights exist does not constitute a competition law problem.

III. Metalegal Formants

Depending on the facts of the case, there are in our opinion three issues that are of general relevance for almost all legal systems. First, there is the question of the scope of IP protection. As *Magill* demonstrates, sometimes the problem lies in the overly broad interoperation of IP statutes, very often contrary to the basic rules of IP protection. It is of utmost importance to avoid protecting ideas by means of copyright. When one remembers that copyright does not in itself protect efforts or investments of time and money, one preserves the adequate scope of the public domain, including above all free access to information.

The second question is the legal protection of efforts and investment by other means. Very often unfair competition law can be deployed, but there are other examples too, notably the protection of databases by *sui generis* rights. This results from the observation that sometimes exclusive rights fall short of protecting impressive market achievements. It may feel simply 'wrong' to accept this state of affairs but there is also another reason: as our economy is more and more based on information[98] and ideas, it is understandable to seek legal remedies to protect information. However, information as such is ill-suited to protection based on exclusive rights. This dilemma has nowhere been satisfactorily solved and it exists also in Poland. As already mentioned, the most common instrument in Poland is to rely on the general unfair competition clause.

The third issue is the one actually addressed in *Magill* and other CJEU judgments, namely the misuse of IP rights and the abuse of a dominant position under copyright law. In fact, the problem is on the one hand obvious and on the other hand difficult to grasp. Intellectual property rights by their very nature create monopolies. Competition law has been set up in order to contain monopolies.[99] The question is therefore to what extent and on what conditions competition law delineates the scope of protection granted by IP rights. It is useless and harmful to try to solve this problem by referring to false clichés, such as the famous differentiation between the existence and exercise of IP rights. It is obvious that the courts, including the CJEU, have no right to question the existence of IP rights and therefore it contributes nothing to the debate to say that competition law acknowledges the existence of rights but may interfere with their exercise. The Polish law has not solved the problem either, and it is likely that it will wait for European directions.

---

98 Even the legal acts, such as Directive 2001/29/EC, use the term 'information society'.

99 Although it may be argued that this is a misconception, as competition law markets are very different from IP subject matter – E. Traple, 'Oddziaływanie przepisów gwarantujących wolność konkurencji na wykonywanie majątkowych praw autorskich. Uwagi na tle orzeczenia Europejskiego Trybunału Sprawiedliwości z 6 kwietnia 1995 r. w sprawie "Magill"', *ZNUJ PWiOWI*, vol. 67, 1996, pp. 134 f.

(14) SLOVENIA

I. Operative Rules

Frank will not succeed with his claim to an injunction if his conduct has not been in accordance with the rules of competition law.

II. Descriptive Formants

The Copyright and Related Rights Act (CRRA),[100] in accordance with Directive 91/250/EEC on the legal protection of computer programmes, recognises copyright on computer programmes, as long as they represent individual work and the author's own intellectual creation (Art. 111 CRRA). As regards computer programmes, the CRRA contains specific provisions in the second section of the fourth chapter (Arts. 111–117 CRRA). These provisions are *leges speciales* in relation to other provisions of the CRRA. Consequently, for questions not covered in these special provisions, other provisions of the CRRA are applicable.

In accordance with Article 113 CRRA, the author has exclusive rights on computer programmes, which can be categorised as copyright work. These rights include the right to reproduce, transform and distribute the computer programme. The author has the right to decide whether he/she will authorise a third party to use his/her copyright work. Consequently, he/she may also decide to prohibit a person from using the computer programme. This decision is generally completely in the domain of the holder of the copyright.

It can be derived from the case at hand that Frank distributes the computer programme to everyone. This means that the lawful acquirers of this programme or entitled users have specific rights under the limitations of the scope of the author's right on the computer programme, as regulated in Article 114 CRRA. Lawful acquirers are entitled to these rights if an additional requirement is fulfilled. Reproduction of the entire computer programme or component parts of it and adaptations and other transformations of the computer programme are admissible within the framework of the limitations of copyright, if necessary to use the programme in accordance with its intended purpose. The authorisation of the author of the computer programme is not required in such a case. It can therefore be said that Erica may make alterations to the existing computer programme for her own needs (for the needs of her own distribution programme), as long as it is necessary for using the computer programme for its intended purpose. We assume that Erica is a lawful acquirer of Frank's computer programme, since Frank licensed the computer programme to all his traders (therefore to Erica as well).

---

100 Official Gazette RS, nos. 21/1995, 9/2001, 30/2001, 43/2004, 17/2006, 139/2006, 68/2008.

If the additional, aforementioned requirement in Article 114 CRRA has not been met (it has to be stressed that restrictive interpretation is required), Erica must obtain authorisation from the copyright holder of the computer programme. Since Frank's computer programme is a standard instrument for analysing the beer market, and without it, such business activity would not be possible, access to this programme is essential and Frank can be deemed to have a dominant or monopoly position on the relevant market. In this regard, a conflict occurs between the intellectual property right and the protection of competition. Although the existence of intellectual property rights does not oppose the protection of competition *per se*, their exercise can have an impact on distortion of competition. In such (otherwise exceptional) cases, intellectual property rights do not have priority over competition. It seems that in such situations the protection of effective competition is more important. As a consequence, the rules of competition law may be used in cases where exercise of intellectual property rights can be characterised as a distortion of effective competition. If Frank holds a dominant position on the relevant product and geographic market, he has special responsibilities under the rules of competition law not to allow his conduct to restrict competition on the market. This means that Frank is not authorised to act in a manner which is otherwise usual for non-dominant undertakings. Accordingly, the refusal to grant the licence could mean conduct which violates the rules of competition law.

Article 9 of the Prevention of Restriction of Competition Act (PRCA) forbids the abuse of a dominant position within the market of the Republic of Slovenia. The provision is very similar to Article 102 TFEU. According to the rules of the PRCA, an undertaking is any legal or natural person performing an economic activity, which is defined as any activity performed on the market for payment (Art. 3(1) and (2) of the PRCA). Refusal to grant a licence is not explicitly mentioned among the types of abuses listed in the PRCA; however, it must be considered that the types of abuses are only listed as examples. Any conduct of a dominant undertaking that restricts competition, including refusal to grant licences to its competitors, can therefore be characterised as abuse, according to the case law of the European Court of Justice. Above all, the Competition Authority will determine the existence of abuse of a dominant position, if refusal to grant the licence means closing the market and, through this, excluding competitors.

The Slovenian Competition Authority refers to decisions made by the European Commission and the CJEU. Consequently, it is our opinion that the decision of the Slovenian authorities in this case would not differ from the decisions of the CJEU in cases like *Magill*, *IMS Health* and others.

Considering the facts of the case, Frank's programme is necessary to access the market. If Frank refuses to grant Erica the licence without an objectively justifiable reason, this could mean the abuse of his dominant position and therefore the infringement of competition law, if all the criteria established by European law are fulfilled.

III. Metalegal Formants

Answer omitted.

(15) SPAIN

I. Operative Rules

Frank has no right to an injunction.

II. Descriptive Formants

Frank, being the author of the computer programme, has an authors' right under Spain's Law of Copyright (LPI).[101] The LPI determines the contents of the authors' rights in its Articles 95–103. In consequence, the rights granted by the authorship of a computer programme mean that: (1) a violation of these rights should be prosecuted (Art. 96 LPI); (2) interim measures could be adopted (Art. 138 LPI); (3) the conduct that violates the copyright should be terminated (Art. 139 LPI); and (4) injunctions could be requested (Art. 140 LPI). However, competition is protected by the Spanish Competition Law (LDC). Competition could be infringed as a consequence of (1) the dominant position conferred by the exclusive intellectual property right and (2) its abuse due to the licence refusal. The effects of the refusal to license could affect a downstream market or a service provided by a potential competitor. The absence of a licence could lead to the infringement of Article 2 LDC.

Frank's company, as an intellectual property rightholder (with an exclusive right), has a dominant position in the relevant market of the product (the computer programme for analysing the regional characteristics of beer consumption and distribution). A refusal to license the programme means that this position could be considered to be abusive, if the service provided by Frank's company has become a standard for its sector. Consequently, as will be analysed below, the injunction requested by Frank's company would probably be refused.

The fact that Frank's company developed a service that over time has become a standard instrument in the sector may mean that there is a need to grant compulsory licences. In that case, third parties could provide other products and

---

101 Royal Decree 1/1996 of 12 April. Consolidated text of the Law on Intellectual Property.

services that may be connected to those protected by the exclusive right. These products and services could be part of a downstream market that would be developed by a potential competitor to Frank's company. In addition, we have to keep in mind that Frank distributed his programme freely to his traders. When a new product introduced by a (potential) competitor could appear, the refusal to license seems to be a protection that could have negative effects on the market.

Spanish regulation on competition law has mostly the same content as European law, so the analysis according to Spanish law would lead to similar solutions to the latter (supra section A.2).

This last assumption is closely connected to the *essential facilities* doctrine originally laid down in the *Commercial Solvents* case and in the *Oscar Bronner* and *IMS Health* cases[102] (supra section A.2).

The service provided by Frank will only be indispensable if it is required to create a subsequent product or service. The situation differs when the service has become a standard in the sector. Then, a compulsory licence could be requested. The standardisation of a system is an exceptional situation in the copyright system and the refusal to grant a licence could restrict the possibilities of innovating or creating new standards; in consequence, competition would be limited. In this context, if Frank refuses to give a licence to a product that has become standard or is needed to develop new products, as seems to be the case, there is a foreclosure in a downstream market and it is possible that competition is infringed. Probably, Frank would not receive an injunction.

III. Metalegal Formants

The relation between IP rights and competition law is not clearly delimited. An exclusive right involves a power position on the part of its rightholder. That position does not mean misuse or anti-competitive behaviour. An exclusive right only shows the existence of a legal monopoly on the part of its rightholder. Legal considerations or trends on IP rights protection and competition rules do not pursue different goals. It is agreed that both fields of law promote the increase of innovation and consumer welfare. Therefore, it could be stated that although they protect different interests – authors' rights (private interest) and competition in the market (public interest) – these two fields of law should be balanced to achieve the major goals indicated.

Finally, it should be noted, in a broader perspective, that economic policies in a concrete historical moment could be the origin of changes in

102 B. Gallego, 'La negativa unilateral de una empresa en posición de dominio a conceder una licencia para la utilización ce un derecho de propiedad intelectual (Comentario a la Sentencia del TJCE de 29 de abril de 2004, asunto C-418/01, *IMS Health GMBH &Co. OHG v. NDC Health GMBH & Co. KG*)', *ADI* 26 (2005–2006).

certain general principles. For instance, in an economic crisis context,[103] some liberal economy principles based on the theory of the free market have been reviewed. This unexpected economic situation has shown that self-regulation of the markets has been called into question, greater state intervention in the economy has been pointed out, and the adoption of measures to increase innovation and industry activities has been the objective of economic policies in the decade of the 2000s. In particular, these last measures could entail major protection of innovation versus a certain limit on free competition, although the last goal for both policies is focused on promoting significant development in the economy. In consequence, in a concrete history moment, some economic policies could throw out of balance the relation between the exclusive rights and competition rules regarding how to better achieve major goals.

(16) UNITED KINGDOM

I. *Operative Rules*

Frank cannot claim an injunction.

II. *Descriptive Formants*

This problem deals with copyright protection of a computer programme developed by Frank as regulated by the Copyright, Designs and Patents Act 1988 (CDPA 1988). If this is the case, Frank will be considered as the author of the work in question as he has created it (s. 9 CDPA 1988). This also makes Frank the first owner of the copyright in the work as it is stated in section 11 CDPA 1988.

Assuming that Frank holds such a copyright, it can be argued that Erica is potentially infringing his rights by using Frank's distribution system based on the computer programme to model her own. Secondly, it is necessary to show that Erica's work was derived from Frank's computer programme, i.e. that there is a causal connection between the two works. Erica derives her own distribution system from Frank's by using it as a model which is sufficient to satisfy this requirement.

Finally, it has to be demonstrated that Erica copied or adapted the whole or any substantial part of the copyrighted work (s. 16(3) CDPA 1988). This normally depends on the facts of the case and factors such as the parameter of the work,[104]

---

103 Like the economic and financial crisis that began in 2007 in the United States and followed in Europe.

104 *Hyperion Records v. Warner Music* (unreported).

the depth of the protection afforded and the importance/originality[105] of the part of the work that was interfered with in relation to the work as a whole. In this case it can be argued that Erica would have most probably had to copy the whole of the computer programme, as it is an essential instrument in analysing the beer market, and adapt it for her own needs. It can therefore be argued that Erica is most likely infringing Frank's copyright in the computer programme by using it for her own distribution system, which would normally give him a right to an injunction (s. 96 CDPA 1988).

However, it has to be noted that Frank has freely distributed the programme to the market participants, which rendered it a standard instrument in the beer market without which it is difficult to actively participate in the market. It is therefore necessary to examine whether Frank's refusal to allow Erica, one of his former traders and a participant in the market, to use the computer programme amounts to an unjustified abuse of his beneficial position in the market. In order to determine the approach, the UK courts take into account case law arising in front of the European Court of Justice.

The underlying principle behind the European judgments is the 'essential facilities' doctrine, which is a European competition law doctrine. It establishes that if a facility controlled by a dominant undertaking is indispensable in order to operate in a particular market, access to that facility will be mandatory in the interests of maintaining or developing competition.[106] The CJEU furthered this notion in the important case of *IMS Health*.

Presuming that the UK courts will follow the *IMS Health* judgment, it can be argued that Frank will most likely be forced into licensing the use of his computer programme to Erica. This statement is further based on the requirement that Erica intends to produce a new product, different from that offered by Frank. Moreover, the computer programme is indispensable for any operator in the market and it is unjustifiable to refuse its availability to Erica because Frank has already made it freely available. Finally, bearing in mind that one cannot be active on the beer market without the use of the computer programme, it can be argued that the refusal to license it has the potential to effectively eliminate all competition on this market. Bearing this in mind, Frank is unlikely to be allowed the right to an injunction.

III. *Metalegal Formants*

There exists a discrepancy between the CJEU's approach in *IMS Health* and the approach of the Commission and the General Court in *Microsoft*. Many

---

105 *Designers Guild v. Williams* [2000] 1 WLR 2416; *Kenrick v. Lawrence* [1890] 25 QBD 99.

106 J. Turney, 'Defining the Limits of the EU Essential Facilities Doctrine on Intellectual Property Rights: The Primacy of Securing Optimal Innovation' (2005) 3 *North Western Journal of Technology and Intellectual Property* 187.

commentators[107] side with the CJEU's decision in *IMS Health* due to the fact that it is a lot more certain and rational.

A.4. COMPARATIVE REMARKS

Case 1 explores the relationship between IP law and competition law: Does competition law set barriers to IPRs if they adversely affect competition? Which requirements have been established for competition law to intervene? The base case broadly aims at a non-contractual relationship between a former and a subsequent innovator.

The case departs from a computer programme which is protected under all EU member state copyright laws due to Directive 91/250/EEC. Belgium is the only country which has chosen to adopt a specific law (Software Act), whereas France has one single statute which contains different forms of IPR (Code de la Propriété Intellectuelle). Therefore, Frank will – as a point of departure – enjoy a right to injunction, because the use and adaptation of the programme fall within the scope of his exclusive right. Considering that a solution might already be found in IP law itself,[108] some reports reflect on entitlements for access, but no statutory exception applies.[109]

The core question of the base case is whether countries allow competition law to override IP law once the use of IP rights raises competition concerns. What are the prerequisites, and do national laws differ from the standard set by the CJEU?

Overall, all countries have come to accept competition law as a barrier to IP rights. Not all member states have introduced special legislative wording for IP rights (only the Czech Republic, Estonia and Italy). However, all countries apply, as a matter of 'abuse of a dominant position', the *criteria* developed by the CJEU and the General Court in the *Magill*, *IMS Health* and *Microsoft* cases.

The reports differ in *evaluating* the facts of the case. Answers are contingent (1) on whether Erica creates a 'new' product in the sense of European case law and (2) on whether she wants to be active 'on the same or on a different market' than Frank. These differences are due to case ambiguities and remaining open questions with regard to the CJEU's adjudication, especially since the statements of the General Court in the *Microsoft* judgment are controversial.

Some national legal differences remain. Some countries have issued special regulation for refusal-to-license constellations and seem to be more inclined

107 K. Brimsted and C. Rees, 'Refusal by dominant undertaking to grant copyright licence' [2004] *European Intellectual Property Review*, N-133; D. McCann, 'European Union: Competition Law – Abuse of Dominant Position' (2006) *International Company and Commercial Law Review* 27.

108 See also the further remarks in the Polish report.

109 See the reports of Germany, Italy, Netherlands and Poland.

to grant access to information goods than other countries (Czech Republic, Estonia, Italy). A curious aspect is that the Czech rule gives the licence seeker the possibility to operate on the same market as the IPR holder. As discussed above, European law requires a derivative market or at least two different stages of production which are interconnected.[110] In Estonia, a special procedure must be followed after a refusal to license in order to be able to use the IPR. It seems that the Estonian rule resembles the principles regarding access to physical property. This is interesting because many authors have criticised special requirements established by the CJEU for intellectual property and demanded a uniform approach for property in general. In Italy, two different standards apply at the same time. Whereas the Competition Authority applies European criteria, some administrative courts qualify IPRs as a legal monopoly linked to a special task assigned to the rightholder by the state. Comparing the reports, it is Italy which has the most explicit policy to make information widely available.

The opposite position has been taken by Germany and the Netherlands. In Germany, a special set of rules has been developed for so-called 'standard essential patents'. These patents must be necessary to use a technical standard (especially in information and communication technologies). The legitimation for limiting the IP right is seen in that the dominant position does not rest on superior technology but on the market effects of the setting of standards. Cast as a defence, licence seekers are required to meet several conditions which mimic a contractual pursuit if negotiations have failed. As known, this reasoning has survived the scrutiny of the CJEU in a line of cases. Dutch law is more restrictive, building on the inverse argument. The Dutch Rechtbank 's-Gravenhage emphasised the general rule that a licence has to be obtained prior to the use of a patent (on a bilateral basis or through a court decision). Nevertheless, the court has opened up a little by stating that special circumstances might demand instant access. Unfortunately, the court did not specify what these special circumstances might be. A similar approach seems to exist in Estonia. It is necessary for the licensee to follow a specific procedure established by the Competition Board. Consequently, in the Netherlands and in Estonia one is not allowed to just use the licence, even if the IP owner has a duty to license.

The reports on the base case mirror the balancing exercise the courts are faced with: two interests are at stake, namely the interest of the IP owner and the general interest concerning free competition. The consequence of strong IPR protection is that the owner may (also) keep a secondary market to him/herself and can exclude any competition. In such a situation, EU law makes the proprietary injunction subject to additional requirements. In this case, the law assumes that competition as a general interest should have a higher priority and might limit the scope of the IPR. Competition law is used as an effective barrier in order to reach this aim, securing 'access'.

---

110 CJEU judgment of 29 April 2004, *IMS Health*, C-418/01, ECLI:EU:C:2004:257, para. 45.

Whereas information and innovation have both gained in importance in recent years, courts have had difficulties in coming to grips with IP restrictions. The novel characteristic of 'indispensability' in network technology has rendered the old paradigm of 'inventing around' non-functional. It further remains contested how exactly the innovation element of the 'new product' can be operationalised. The difficulties that have evolved in IP law in the face of this challenge are hardly surprising, and it took the European Court of Justice to question the old paradigm of the preceding IP law (*Magill*). The reports display the disagreement about the leading principles and the exact delineations of the 'new balance'.[111] Jurisdictions approach the task on a case-by-case basis, manoeuvring between stressing the importance of IPR protection[112] and opening up the possibility of follow-on innovations through mandatory licensing.

B.1. CASE MODIFICATION

Frank does license the programme to Erica under the obligation *not to improve it* and not to market the programme without his permission. Can Frank claim an injunction if Erica improves the programme and markets it without Frank's prior consent?

B.2. EDITORIAL NOTE

Compared to Case 1 (base case), the modification aims to identify a potential conceptual turn in competition law which safeguards the innovation potential of competitors.

B.3. COUNTRY REPORTS

(1) BELGIUM

I. Operative Rules

Frank may claim an injunction if the licensing clauses do not run counter to competition law.

---

[111] An aspect highlighted by A. Balitzki, 'Der Kartellrechtliche Zwangslizenzeinwand bei Standardessentiellen Patenten im Deutsch-Niederländischen Vergleich', in: S. Behrends, C. Bick, G. Brandt and A. Eiselt (eds.), *Integration im Prozess der Internationalisierung* (Oldenburg: 2012), 49–60, discussing the German and Dutch decisions.

[112] The Dutch and the Spanish reports rightfully emphasise this point.

II. *Descriptive Formants*

According to Article 5(b) Belgian Software Act (Art. XI.298(b) BCEL) (implementing Art. 4(b) Software Directive), the author of a computer programme has the right to authorise (or not) the adaptation of a computer programme. Frank will therefore have an injunction on the basis of Articles 86ter or 87 Belgian Copyright Act (BCA)[113] (Arts. XI.334 or XVII.14 BCEL).

It is interesting to analyse this solution from a competition law perspective. Article 4(1)(d) of Regulation (EC) No. 772/2004[114] (now Regulation (EU) No. 316/2014)[115] considers as a hardcore restriction the 'restriction of the ability of any parties to the agreement to carry out research and development, unless such latter restriction is indispensable to prevent the disclosure of the licensed know-how to third parties'. The Commission further elaborates this provision by stating that:

> both parties must be free to carry out independent research and development. This rule applies irrespective of whether the restriction applies to a field covered by the license or to other fields. However, the mere fact that the parties agree to provide each other with future improvements of their respective technologies does not amount to a restriction on independent research and development. The effect on competition of such agreements must be assessed in light of the circumstances of the individual case.[116]

Admittedly, a hardcore restriction will merely lead to the block exemption not being applicable. The hardcore restrictions in block exemption Regulations and guidelines, however, are generally considered to be 'restrictions by object'. Although these infringe *per se* Article 101(1) TFEU, they are not automatically excluded from the application of Article 101(3) TFEU, i.e. exemption, but it is quite unlikely that the four conditions for exemption would be met.[117]

In the context of Article 102 TFEU, we can refer to paragraph 240 of the Draft Guidelines on Article 82:

> A refusal to licence an IPR protected technology which is indispensable as a basis for follow-on innovation by competitors may be abusive even if the licence is not sought

---

113 Act on Copyright and Neighbouring Rights, 30 June 1994, *Official Gazette*, 27 July 1994 [Wet 30 juni 1994 betreffende het auteursrecht en de naburige rechten, *B.S.*, 27 juli 1994].

114 Commission Regulation (EC) No. 772/2004 of 27 April 2004 on the application of Article 81(3) of the Treaty to categories of technology transfer agreements, OJ L 123, 27 April 2004, 11–17.

115 Commission Regulation (EU) No. 316/2014 of 21 March 2014 on the application of Article 101(3) of the Treaty on the Functioning of the European Union to categories of technology transfer agreements, OJ L 93, 28 March 2014, 17–23.

116 Commission Notice: Guidelines on the application of Article 81 of the EC Treaty to technology transfer agreements, OJ C 101/2, 27 April 2004.

117 Commission Notice: Guidelines on the application of Article 81(3) of the Treaty, OJ C 101, 7 April 2004, 97–118, paras. 20 and 46; I. Van Bael and J.F. Bellis, *Competition Law of the European Community* (The Hague: 2005), 69–71.

> to directly incorporate the technology in clearly identifiable new goods and services. The refusal of licensing an IPR protected technology should not impair consumers' ability to benefit from innovation brought about by the dominant undertaking's competitors.[118]

We can also refer to paragraphs 75 et seq. of the Guidance on the Commission's enforcement priorities in applying Article 82 (i.e. refusal to supply and margin squeeze; see in particular paragraph 78 for the refusal to license IP rights).[119]

With this in mind, Frank's attitude *in casu* might raise some concerns with regard to the negative effects of his behaviour on innovation. The restrictive licence conditions completely chill Erica's incentive to innovate the computer programme. Considering that this programme is as such indispensable for entering the beer analysis market, it is certainly conceivable that the incentives for Frank to innovate on the programme would be completely stifled as well. A comparison can be drawn with the Commission's reasoning in *Microsoft* (approved by the General Court), where it was suggested that if no interoperability information were provided in order to ensure follow-on innovation, Microsoft's incentives to innovate would also diminish.[120]

III. Metalegal Formants

Answer omitted.

(2) CZECH REPUBLIC

I. Operative Rules

Frank can successfully claim an injunction.

II. Descriptive Formants

The above-mentioned provision of section 66(1)(a) Czech Copyright Act, which allows the adaptation of the programme if this is necessary to use it for its purpose, is a non-mandatory provision and can be excluded by the agreement

---

118 DG Competition Discussion Paper on the Application of Article 82 of the Treaty to Exclusionary Abuses, December 2005, available at: ec.europa.eu/competition/antitrust/art82/discpaper2005.pdf (last consulted 5 May 2019).

119 Communication from the Commission – Guidance on the Commission's enforcement priorities in applying Article 82 of the EC Treaty to abusive exclusionary conduct by dominant undertakings, OJ C 45, 24 February 2009, 7–20.

120 Commission Decision of 24 March 2004, *Microsoft*, COMP/C-3/37.792, paras. 709 et seq.

of the parties.[121] If Frank licences the computer programme to Erica under the obligation not to improve it, then Erica is breaching the licence contract and infringing Frank's copyright.

According to the above-mentioned section 12(1) Czech Copyright Act, an author has the exclusive right to use his/her work or authorise another person to use his/her work. *Inter alia*, the right to use a work also includes the right to distribute the work (section 12(4)(b) Copyright Act). If Erica is distributing the computer programme without prior authorisation, then she is breaching Frank's copyright.

There is no refusal to licence the computer software, because Erica is allowed to use the computer programme, and so the facts of the case do not meet the definition of an abuse of a dominant position according to section 12(1)(f) Czech Competition Act.

The injunction will be granted to Frank.

III. Metalegal Formants

Answer omitted.

(3) DENMARK

I. Operative Rules

It is difficult to say, but compared to the base case, the case is tilting in Erica's favour.

II. Descriptive Formants

Applying the *IMS/Magill* doctrine, Erica is in a better position in this case than in the one discussed above. This is because here she does not intend to copy Frank's programme to offer a substitute programme, but engages in the innovative activity of 'improving' the programme to offer an alternative/improved programme.

Unlike with the situation described above, one may, therefore, consider whether the improved version of Frank's programme constitutes a 'new product' within the meaning of *IMS*. This would very much depend on the facts and the case offers too little information to support any clear conclusions. It would seem,

[121] See J. Kříž, I. Holcová, J. Kordač, V. Křesťanová, *Autorský zákon komentář a předpisy související* (Copyright Act, Commentary and related regulations) (2nd ed., Prague: 2005), p. 198.

however, that the reference to a 'new product or service' should be construed in a rather broad sense to also include products or services which are presently unknown. In this way, access to upstream technology which is indispensable to follow-on *innovation* (and not just concrete 'new products') would also be considered an abuse. Erica, therefore, in principle would be able to claim a defence both in the situation where the improvements amount to what is in reality a new, freestanding product, and where the improvements only result in a product which is only 'better' than Frank's. Arguably, Erica's position would be (much) stronger in the first situation than in the latter.

If the 'new product' criterion has been satisfied, the next step would be to determine whether or not Frank has any objective justification for the refusal. He can sue for breach of contract and even infringement of his exclusive right to the computer programme, which includes the right to adaptation, provided that the programme is protected as a work.

III. Metalegal Formants

Answer omitted.

(4) ESTONIA

I. Operative Rules

Frank can claim an injunction because of copyright infringement.

II. Descriptive Formants

According to §13(1) Copyright Act, '[a]n author shall enjoy the exclusive right to use the author's work in any manner, to authorise or prohibit the use of the work in a similar manner by other persons'. Since Frank is the author of the computer programme, it is up to him to decide under which conditions he licenses the programme. However, the situation in Modification 1 is somewhat different. As was determined above, Frank is considered to be an undertaking[122] controlling an essential facility for the purposes of §15 Competition Act. One of the obligations of undertakings in control of essential facilities is to 'permit other undertakings to gain access to the network, infrastructure or other essential

[122] Subsection 2(1) of the Competition Act gives the following definition: 'a company, sole proprietor, any other person engaged in economic or professional activities, an association which is not a legal person, or a person acting in the interests of an undertaking'.

facility under reasonable and non-discriminatory conditions for the purposes of the supply or sale of goods' (§18(1) clause 1 Competition Act). Nothing in the case indicates that Frank licensed the programme to Erica under unreasonable and discriminatory conditions. Consequently, it can be said that the licensing agreement is valid and can be enforced.

The licensing agreement explicitly stipulates that Erica is not allowed to improve and to market the programme. Improving and marketing the programme would infringe some moral rights (right of integrity of the work, right of additions to the work; §12(1) clauses 3 and 4 Copyright Act) and economic rights (distribution right, right of alteration of the work; §13(1) clauses 2 and 5 Copyright Act). Both infringements are punished as misdemeanours.[123]

Subsection $81^7(1)$ Copyright Act provides that in the case of the unlawful use of a work or an object of related rights, the author or holder of related rights may, *inter alia*, claim compensation for damages, termination of the unlawful use of a work or an object of related rights, and delivery of that which was received by way of the unlawful use of a work or an object of related rights. These claims are made pursuant to the Law of Obligations Act.

III. Metalegal Formants

The Estonian Copyright Act is based on the *droit d'auteur* tradition, which enshrines an author's moral rights. The moral and economic rights sometimes overlap. For instance, the right of alteration of the work (§13(1) clause 5 Copyright Act) is an economic right, while the right of integrity of the work, the right of additions to the work and the right of supplementation of the work (§12(1) clauses 3, 4 and 7 Copyright Act) are moral rights. This overlap makes the development of limitations on an author's rights very complicated, since it would be necessary to limit some of the moral rights. The construction of voluntary licensing structures is also time-consuming and therefore expensive.[124] W. Kingston's suggestion that the intellectual property system 'is "frozen" into a dual patent-copyright paradigm, into which new ways of inventing and new kinds of information have to be fitted somehow'[125] holds true in respect of Estonia as well. The problem becomes especially evident when analysing the protection of functional works such as computer programmes.

---

123 Violation of the moral rights is punishable by a fine of up to 300 fine units – Copyright Act §$81^3(1)$. Violation of the economic rights is punishable by a fine of up to 300 fine units – Copyright Act §$81^4(1)$.

124 See the Estonian commentaries on Case 5.

125 W. Kingston, 'Unlocking the Potential of Intellectual Property', in: O. Granstrand, *Economics, Law and Intellectual Property. Seeking Strategies for Research and Teaching in a Developing Field* (Boston/Dordrecht/London: 2003), pp. 311–329, p. 312.

The Competition Act facilitates the access to essential facilities. Still, there are provisions which could enhance innovation to some extent. Undertakings in control of essential facilities are considered undertakings in a dominant position (§13(2) Competition Act). The Competition Act provides that '[a]ny direct or indirect abuse by an undertaking or several undertakings of the dominant position in the goods market is prohibited, including limiting production, service, goods markets, technical development or investment' (§16 clause 2 Competition Act). It is not clear whether the restrictive licensing agreement not allowing improving and marketing the programme would constitute an abuse of a dominant position (limiting technical development) for the purposes of the Competition Act. Future case law must give the answer to that question. Currently the interrelation of intellectual property and competition law is not extensively analysed in court cases. The Estonian legal literature on the subject is also very limited.

(5) FRANCE

I. Operative Rules

Frank has a right to an injunction.

II. Descriptive Formants

Articles L. 112-2 and L. 112-3 of the French Intellectual Property Code[126] reveal that Frank's software, which is considered to be a database rather than software, is protected by the French *droit d'auteur* (copyright) and that the improvement thereof and other modifications to databases are protected by copyright. Therefore, Erica will not obtain protection for the entire software but only for her modifications.

Nevertheless, Frank retains the copyright over the software/database, regardless of the fact that there is a contract for a licence binding Frank and Erica and regardless of the restrictions stipulated in this contract. The major part of the work is protected as being designed and created by Frank. Therefore, Erica is not entitled to market the software without Frank's permission, on the same grounds that Frank is not entitled to market Erica's version of the software without the prior consent and agreement of Erica.

[126] Intellectual Property Code, Art. L.112-2 and L 112-3 as enacted and later modified by Act No. 94-361, 10 May 1994, Art. 2, Journal Officiel, 11 May 1994; Act No. 96-1106, 18 December 1996, Art. 1, Journal Officiel, 19 December 1996; and Act No. 98-536, 1 July 1998, Art. 1, Journal Officiel, 2 July 1998.

Marketing the software is considered an act of infringement and counterfeiting of copyright under Articles L. 335-2 et seq.[127] It can be sanctioned by up to three years of imprisonment and €300,000 in damages.

III. *Metalegal Formants*

Answer omitted.

(6) GERMANY

I. *Operative Rules*

Frank has a right to an injunction against Erica.

II. *Descriptive Formants*

Whereas the contractual duty only would result in damages, Frank has a right to an injunction due to Erica's violation of his copyright. She is infringing Frank's right under §69c No. 2 UrhG in that she 'transformed' i.e. worked on Frank's work by improving it. On the other hand (explicitly §69c No. 2 UrhG), Erica's own copyright in respect of her achieved improvement is not touched upon. However, one could consider generalising the standard prohibitions of Article 4(1)(d) Technology Transfer Block Exemption Regulation (TT-BER), and applying them as fairness standards, which might trigger the invalidity of contractual terms under §242 BGB.[128] Article 4(1)(d) states that the following is a hardcore restriction: 'the restriction of the licensee's ability to exploit its own technology or the restriction of the ability of any of the parties to the agreement to carry out research and development, unless such latter restriction is indispensable to prevent the disclosure of the licensed know-how to third parties'. Thus, Frank's contractual clause could be invalid.[129]

---

127 Intellectual Property Code, Art. L.335-2 and following, as enacted and later modified by Act No. 94-102, 5 February 1994, Art. 1, Journal Officiel, 8 February 1994; Act No. 98-536, 1 July 1998, Art. 4, Journal Officiel, 2 July 1998; Order No. 2004-916, 19 September 2000, Art. 3, Journal Officiel, 22 September 2000, effective 1 January 2002; and Act No. 2004-204, 9 March 2004, Art. 34 I, Journal Officiel, 10 March 2004.

128 This would be possible by analogy, as the Block Exemption Regulation is not applicable according to the market share threshold (Art. 3).

129 A. Fuchs and W. Möschel, 'Art. 102 AEUV', in: F. Immenga and E.-J. Mestmäcker, *EU-Wettbewerbsrecht* (5th ed., Munich: 2012), para. 367; H. Lutz, 'Technologie-, Patent- und Knowhow-Lizenzverträge im EG-Recht', *RIW* 1996, 269; R.M. Winkler and H.-P. Jugel, 'Die neue EG-Gruppenfreistellungsverordnung für Technologietransfer-Vereinbarungen', *EuZW* 1996, 364; different opinion: J.B. Nordemann, in: U. Loewenheim, K.M. Meessen and A. Riesenkampff (eds.), *Kartellrecht*, (2nd ed., Munich: 2009), §1 GWB para. 220.

III. Metalegal Formants

In contrast to contractual non-competition clauses, non-improvement duties are allowed under competition law – despite their negative impacts on innovation. But under certain circumstances there are restrictions in that regard, as shown by Article 4(1)(d) Technology Transfer Block Exemption Regulation. The reasoning is basically that of patent law's dependency construct: 'Whoever may improve the pioneer's product has an own right on his improvement. But he/she is not allowed to market the improvement without permission of the pioneer.' This mechanism upholds the incentive to invent resp. to create. However, the open question is how much leeway is needed for competitive innovation. European patent laws have competed for centuries for the 'best' solution in respect of legal preconditions for compulsory licences (e.g. the tight German property model vs. the broad, competition-friendly English model). No equivalent has developed in the field of general copyright. Therefore, high-profile cases like the *Microsoft* case continue to revolve around the re-definition of the boundaries between IP (in that case copyright) and competition law, considering anew the tension between the necessary incentive structure of property on the one hand and the necessary leeway for innovation and economic freedom on the other hand.

(7) GREECE

I. Operative Rules

The clause which forbids any improvement of the programme is not valid. Thus, the answer does not differ. Frank does not have a claim for injunction.

II. Descriptive Formants

The proposed solution does not seem to differ in the modification of the case. This is because the rules of free competition (Arts. 2, 2A Law 703/1977; Art. 102 TFEU) constitute *jus cogens* and cannot be disposed of by an agreement between the parties, an agreement which in the present instance would also have the character of a prohibited vertical cooperation or harmonised practice contrary to Article 101 TFEU and Article 1 Law 703/1977.

III. Metalegal Formants

Answer omitted.

(8) IRELAND

I. Operative Rules

It is more likely that Frank will be granted an injunction, as he is not excluding Erica from the market.

II. Descriptive Formants

Frank could claim a new copyright, in all likelihood, on each derivative of the work, given that the threshold of originality in copyright in Ireland is very low. Interestingly, in the original *Magill*[130] case, tried in the Irish courts before it reached the CJEU, a copyright in TV listings was recognised – something akin to the 'sweat of the brow' test in the US, which was dispensed with in *Feist Publications Inc. v. Rural Telephone Service Co.*[131]

Section 17(5) of the Irish Copyright and Related Rights Act provides that 'copyright shall not subsist in a work which infringes or to the extent that it infringes, the copyright in another work' and, therefore, Erica will not be able to claim a copyright in any modification that she makes without permission.

III. Metalegal Formants

Answer omitted.

(9) ITALY

I. Operative Rules

Yes, Frank probably has an action for contract infringement and a claim for an injunction based on copyright law.

II. Descriptive Formants

As stated above, as far as computer programmes or databases are concerned, Articles 64bis (software) and 64quinquies (database) ICL make any changes to the original work subject to the consent of the copyright holder.[132] Article 18 c. 2 ICL

---

[130] C-241, 242/91P, *R.T.E. v. Commission* [1995] ECR I-743, [1995] 4 CMLR 718.

[131] 499 U.S. 340 (1991).

[132] See Abriani, Cottino, Ricolfi, 'Diritto Industriale', in Cottino (ed.) *Trattato di diritto commerciale* (Padova: 2001), pp. 450 ff. and Marchetti, Ubertazzi, *Commentario breve al diritto della concorrenza* (Padova: 2004), p. 1362, IV, 4.

gives the author veto power over any modification that occurs without his/her consent. As a result, in order to improve and to market the programme, Erica would have had to ask for Frank's permission. *A fortiori*, the use of restrictions imposed contractually on Erica is perfectly lawful and Frank can sue Erica for contract infringement and claim an injunction.

III. Metalegal Formants

Over the years, the rule has been interpreted in an increasingly restrictive way to allow modifications of the product as long as they are done privately and not in a business activity. Only in those cases in which economic exploitation is most likely will authorisation of the author be required. This is the rationale which has guided the Italian legislator in protecting digital works (computer programmes or databases).[133]

(10) LITHUANIA

Answer omitted.

(11) NETHERLANDS

I. Operative Rules

Frank has a right of injunction against Erica.

II. Descriptive Formants

The case relates to the relationship between the exercise of a copyright and an important rule of public competition law. This case is about freedom of contract. The general rules of the Dutch Civil Code (Books 3 and 6) are applicable. It concerns rules about the realisation of contracts, interpretation, the observation in terms of reasonability and fairness, etc. The freedom of contract implies that the parties involved can, within wide margins, agree on what they wish for. The freedom of contract also implies the freedom not to enter into an agreement. The legislator saw this starting point as a

---

133 Art. 5 d.lgs. 29 December 1992, no. 518, implementing Council Directive 91/250/EEC of 14 May 1991 on the legal protection of computer programme, and Art. 4 d.lgs. 6 May 1999, no. 169, implementing Directive 96/9/EC of the European Parliament and of the Council of 11 March 1996 on the legal protection of databases.

sufficient guarantee of the negotiating positions of the author and his/her counterparty.[134]

Frank has entered into a licence agreement under the condition that any possible improvement of Frank's programme by Erica will only be marketed after she has obtained his permission. Only when Erica markets an improved version of Frank's programme without his prior consent will he be able to successfully claim an injunction.

In this case, it could also be argued that Frank's behaviour constitutes abuse of his dominant position on the relevant market. The licence granted to Erica might restrict technological progress. The condition in the licence which forbids improving the computer programme without permission limits (the incentive for) improvement of the programme. Since this programme is indispensable for the market, the restriction of improvement might be a disadvantage for users in the sense of Article 102(b) TFEU. If the licence agreement does not comply with Article 102 TFEU, Frank will not be able to claim an injunction.

III. Metalegal Formants

The same interests as in the base case apply. A balance has to be struck between the interests of the owner of the intellectual property right and the importance of effective competition. In this case, the element of contract freedom is added. As the rightholder, Frank in principle is entitled to give (or not to give) permission to adapt the computer programme. Furthermore, the freedom of contract gives rightholders a lot of freedom to set out the conditions for a licence. However, this freedom can be limited by the rules of competition law.

(12) NORWAY

I. Operative Rules

Frank will probably not be able to claim an injunction, but it depends partly on the interpretation of the *Magill/IMS* rule and partly on the further facts of the case.

II. Descriptive Formants

Again, Frank's success in claiming an injunction will depend on whether his behaviour will be contrary to the competition rules. A contractual obligation

---

134 J.H. Spoor, D.W.F. Verkade and D.J.G. Visser, *Auteursrecht. Auteursrecht, naburige rechten en databankenrecht* (Deventer: 2005), p. 446.

not to improve the programme is tantamount to a refusal to license the right for improvements. The *IMS/Magill* doctrine should likewise be applicable in this case, the result being that Frank abuses his dominant position if improving the programme is indispensable in order to be active on the secondary market and to make the new product – provided that there is no objective justification for the refusal. Frank will be unable to claim an injunction if his behaviour runs contrary to the competition rules – if not, he can sue for breach of contract and even infringement of his exclusive right to the computer programme, which includes the right to adaptation (NCA §§1(2) (13), 2 and 4(2)); New Act §§2(2) m, 3 and 6(1)), provided that the programme is protected as a work.

III. Metalegal Formants

Answer omitted.

(13) POLAND

I. Operative Rules

Frank may obtain an injunction against Erica

II. Descriptive Formants

There are two important legal questions involved: (1) whether there is an obligation not to improve a computer programme valid (e.g. in the light of the provisions of competition law), and so, (2) whether Erica infringes Frank's copyright or only the contractual obligation not to improve and market the new product.

Again, there is no case law in Poland concerning the validity of non-improvement clauses for software. However, it should be assumed that they are valid and enforceable. A modification of the original work may create a derivative work. The modifying party retains copyright in the 'added' part but cannot use (i.e. also market) the work without the permission of the original copyright owner. Moreover, though the very act of creating a derivative work does not require the permission of the copyright owner in the original work,[135] the use of such work (copying, making available to the public, etc.) does.

[135] Prevailing view: E. Traple, in: M. Bukowski et al., *Prawo autorskie i prawa pokrewne. Komentarz* (Kraków: 2005), p. 102.

The rule for computer programmes is different: according to Article 74(4) point 2 Copyright Act the act of modification of a computer programme (regardless of any further acts relating to the modified programme, such as selling, uploading, renting, etc.) also requires the consent of the rightholder. In this light, there may be no doubt that generally a contract clause prohibiting modifications cannot be regarded as invalid, since it is not even necessary, as precisely the same scope of protection follows from the clear wording of the statutory provisions.[136] This cannot be changed by competition law. Competition law can therefore intervene only in special circumstances. As it has been established that Frank would probably not abuse his dominant position if he refused to license the programme to Erica, a prohibition of improvement must *a maiore ad minus* be also accepted as admissible.

Should Erica disregard this prohibition, an infringement of Frank's copyright would take place. This is because under Article 74(4) points 2 and 3 Copyright Act consent of the rightholder is required for the modification and marketing of computer programmes. Since such consent would be lacking, Erica's actions would infringe the copyright, and statutory remedies (Art. 79 Copyright Act) would be available to Frank. Simultaneously, Erica would act in breach of the contract but that would give Frank no real advantage.

III. Metalegal Formants

Here the question is to what extent it is permissible to use IP rights, the rationale for which lies in promoting progress, to in fact stymie progress. However, it would be difficult to challenge the current legal position in this respect as a general rule, as it is certainly not feasible to allow marketing works with some modifications without the consent of the original copyright owner. The problem is therefore in exceptions: it seems that competition law (which as a rule can react in such cases only if abuse of dominant position is proven) is not always the perfect instrument. Because traditional copyright works such as musical or literary works do not require exceptions in this respect, copyright law has not so far thoroughly reflected upon the consequences of introducing software protection under its roof. It seems that when the improvement is vital, and the original rightholder refuses to authorise the use, an equivalent of compulsory licence in industrial property law could be envisaged. One may therefore say that the problem is the result of copyright expansion covering subject matters for which copyright was not designed (the same may apply to databases). Instead we are forced to 'bend' competition law to reach comparable results.

---

136 J. Barta, R. Markiewicz, in: M. Bukowski et al., *Prawo autorskie i prawa pokrewne. Komentarz* (Kraków: 2005), p. 571.

(14) SLOVENIA

I. Operative Rules

In principle, Frank can prohibit Erica from improving the programme, if his conduct does not infringe the rules of competition law.

II. Descriptive Formants

According to the provision of Article 114 CRRA, which regulates the limitations of the scope of copyright, the lawful acquirers of the computer programme may translate, adapt, arrange and otherwise alter a computer programme and reproduce the results thereof without prior authorisation of the author. The following condition must be met: such an action must be necessary to use the computer programme in accordance with its intended purpose. This provision is not mandatory and is used only if parties do not stipulate otherwise.[137] Besides this limitation of the scope of the copyright, the legitimate acquirer of the computer programme may also need the authorisation of the author or owner of the programme to make any translations or adaptations.

In the case concerned, the parties stipulated that Erica is not allowed to either improve the programme or market it without Frank's permission. Frank has the right to damages due to violation of the contract. He also has a prohibition claim due to copyright violation under Article 167 CRRA. Erica is violating Frank's right as designated in Article 113(2) CRRA, according to which the author of a computer programme has exclusive rights to translate, adapt, arrange or otherwise alter the computer programme.

As far as competition law is concerned, Frank's conduct could also represent an abuse of a dominant position, insofar as the conditions named in the report on the base case are fulfilled.

III. Metalegal Formants

Answer omitted.

(15) SPAIN

I. Operative Rules

Frank has no right to an injunction if the licensing clauses infringe competition rules.

137 See also decision of the court II Ips 552/2003.

II. Descriptive Formants

The arguments considered in the report on the base case are the grounds on which the second question can be solved too.

The granting of a compulsory licence for a product that has become a standard in the sector should not involve any restriction on its use. A restriction would inevitably lead to the elimination of competition in a derived market or another market (new product), to the detriment of both competitors and consumers. It would also be contrary to one of the main grounds for which the CJEU considers it necessary to grant licences: to prevent potential competition by creating new products or services from being eliminated. For all these reasons, and taking into account the CJEU's judgments, in this context any prohibition on improvement and any requirement to obtain Frank's permission would be contrary to the rules of competition and, therefore, invalid.

III. Metalegal Formants

Regarding contractual prohibitions on improvements, Spanish law considers these clauses not to be contrary to competition law in principle, but a study is needed. We agree with the Belgian report, which considers a legal analysis focused on Article 101 TFEU (or Art. 1 Spanish LDC in our national context). A possible vertical restraint could be imposed if the improvement must go back to the rightholder in exclusivity and third parties cannot have access to the improvement. In that case, a foreclosure to competition would take place and a broader study should be done.

(16) UNITED KINGDOM

I. Operative Rules

Frank can claim an injunction.

II. Descriptive Formants

In order to prove infringement, it has to be shown on the balance of probabilities that Erica has interfered with the activities that are under Frank's exclusive control as a copyright owner. It can be argued that Erica does this by seeking to improve the programme, which entails adapting it (s. 21 CDPA 1988), and by marketing it, which can amount to infringement, by issuing copies to the public (s. 18 CDPA 1988). The causal link between the new and the copyrighted work can be easily demonstrated due to the fact that Erica sought to make improvements on Frank's computer programme, which entails founding and deriving her work from Frank's. The problem question does not state how much/which parts or whether the whole computer programme was sought to be improved by Erica. Assuming that Erica seeks to improve the whole or a substantial part (s. 18(3) CDPA 1988) of the computer programme, she is most likely to be acting in infringement of Frank's copyright. This is even more so bearing in mind that the licence granted to Erica does not cover improving the computer programme and offering it to the public, which renders her actions unauthorised. Bearing in mind Erica is left without defences, it is highly likely that Frank will be granted a right to an injunction by UK courts under section 96 CDPA 1988.

It is also worthwhile mentioning that the licence is effectively a contract between Erica and Frank. Due to the fact that Erica breaches the contract by failing to comply with its terms, Frank may have a claim in damages under UK contract law for the loss he incurred as a result of the breach.'[138]

III. Metalegal Formants

Even though there are no UK cases expressly resolving the conflicting relationship between preserving intellectual property rights over the need to ensure fair and effective competition in the domestic markets, it is unequivocal that the debate is open and running in the UK. Most commentators and academics argue that the approach the Commission has taken in the *Microsoft* judgment has gone too far by allowing a 'direct competitor access to information in circumstances where a new product was not necessarily being created and getting the intellectual property right meant that considerable effort had to be expended by Microsoft.'[139] Moreover, McCann argues that this is 'dangerous in that it may have the effect of discouraging companies from expending vast sums of money on research and development, which is necessary for the emergence of new products on to the market.'[140]

It is indisputable that it is necessary to establish a fine balance between the protection of IP rights and the need to ensure healthy competition in the market – both factors acting as an incentive towards innovativeness and breakthrough.

UK commentators tend to argue that the *IMS Health* judgment, most likely to be followed by the national courts, is moving towards achieving this balance. It arguably 'tends to avoid eroding the substance of the intellectual property rights itself and instead erodes the "peripheral" rights such as the control over a

138 *Hadley v. Baxendale*, 9 Exch. 341, 156 Eng. Rep. 145 (1854).

139 D. McCann, 'European Union: Competition Law – Abuse of Dominant Position' (2006) *International Company and Commercial Law Review* 5.

140 Ibid., p. 8.

secondary market.'[141] It seems reasonable to suggest that the only way that the national courts and the CJEU will derogate from an intellectual property right is to achieve innovation gain elsewhere. For this reason, the *IMS Health* approach represents the rational and the most satisfactory approach to be taken.

B.4. COMPARATIVE REMARKS

All reports depart from the IP rationale which reserves the right to make modifications to the creator. Therefore, Erica's action is framed as an infringement which is forbidden unless there is a justification. To the surprise of the editors, only few country reports consider possible justifications (e.g. dynamic competition; patent dependency regime; innovation; fundamental freedoms; oppressive contracts). Where they do, competition law is key. Two ideas are put forward. First, the Belgian, Estonian, German and Greek reports refer to Article 101 TFEU and the corresponding national provisions. However, though the agreement is restrictive on Erica, competition law does not forbid the IP holder from demanding permission for improvements and marketing. Complementary to this, the European Block Exemption Regulation only forbids an IP holder from demanding a grant-back of severable improvements made by the licensee.[142] A severable improvement is one that can be exploited without infringing upon the licensed technology.[143] As long as the licensee has to use the licensed technology, the rightholder has leeway to determine how to deal with his/her IP. The second idea put forward by some reports is to test the European requirements for a refusal to license. However, such requirements are not fulfilled.[144]

According to a number of reports, Frank can claim a breach of contract.[145] The Spanish and the Greek reports, however, deviate. The Greek report argues that a term which prohibits any improvement of the programme is forbidden under Greek law. The German report, on the other hand, touches on the idea of generalising the standard prohibitions of the Technology Transfer Block Exemption Regulation, and of qualifying them as standard contract terms.

141 D. Byrne, 'Compulsory licensing of IP rights: has EC Competition Law arrived at a clear and rational analysis following the IMS judgment and the Microsoft decision?', Golding Essay Prize (2006), p. 11, available at: https://www.competitionlawassociation.org.uk/docs/essay06.pdf (last accessed 2019).

142 Art. 5(1)(a) of Commission Regulation (EC) No. 772/2004 on the application of Article 81(3) of the Treaty to categories of technology transfer agreements. For Case 1, Modification 1 the Regulation would not be applicable because of the market-share thresholds (Art. 3).

143 See Commission Notice, Guidelines on the application of Article 81 of the EC Treaty to technology transfer agreements, para. 109.

144 See the reports of Belgium, Czech Republic, Denmark, Greece, the Netherlands, Norway, Slovenia and Spain.

145 See the reports of Germany, Italy, Norway, Poland, Slovenia and the UK.

CASE 2. MEDICAL RESEARCH (PUBLIC HEALTH – MODELLED ON BRCA1/2 AND CCR5)

A.1. CASE

Mary, owner of a small biotech company, was granted a patent on the gene BRAU-7. As a utility, the patent accounts for cardiovascular diseases. Five years after the patent was granted, her competitor John found out that the gene BRAU-7, in conjunction with the gene BLIB-5, is responsible for healing wounds. The proportional relationship to which each gene accounts for the healing process is scientifically unclear. John is also granted a patent on his invention. He sets up a business and starts producing an ointment.

Does Mary have a claim for injunction against John?

A.2. EDITORIAL NOTE

For EU member states, the patentability of human genes and the scope of such patents, as the gene patent regime, is predetermined by EU law since 1998. It determines the action radius of Mary.

1. Patent protection for genes

All selected jurisdictions provide patent protection for human genes. This approach is based on national legislation transposing the Biotechnology Directive of 1998.[1] The approach is based on Article 3 Biotechnology Directive, which allows patentability of inventions which are new, which involve an inventive step and which are susceptible of industrial application even if they concern a product consisting of or containing biological material (e.g. Estonia). Alternatively, the approach is based on Article 5 Biotechnology Directive, allowing patentability of elements isolated from the human body or otherwise produced by means of a technical process, including the sequence or partial sequence of a gene, even if the structure of that element is identical to that of a natural element (e.g. Belgium).

---

[1] Directive 98/44/EC of the European Parliament and of the Council of 6 July 1998 on the Legal Protection of Biotechnological Inventions, OJ L 213, 30 July 1998, 13.

Given the fact that human genes are regarded as inventions in the jurisdictions at hand, and assuming that Mary's invention further fulfils the criteria of novelty, inventive step and industrial application, Mary's patent is not in question.

2. Scope of gene patents

The EU Directive gives leeway to member states as to the exact scope of gene patents. The BIP project is interested in how national legislatures have designed the scope, and how courts have adjudicated. Arguably, absolute patent protection for genes is suggested by Article 9 Biotechnology Directive. The basic idea is to conceive gene patents as product patents. Product patents are commonly awarded absolute patent protection, implying protection for all applications of the patent, including known and new applications (*absoluter Stoffschutz*). Article 9 Biotechnology Directive stipulates that the protection conferred by a patent on a product containing or consisting of genetic information shall extend to all material in which the product is incorporated and in which the genetic information is contained and performs its function. If a country reads this as absolute patent protection, the patent holder may stop anyone not having his/her consent from making or using any product. The counter model is 'purpose-bound patent protection'. That means that the scope of a patent for a gene is restricted to a specific use. Purpose-bound patent protection can be achieved in two ways: either by requiring that the use is formulated in the *claims* (so-called *funktionsgebundener Stoffschutz*), or as matter of principle whereby the scope of the patent is always limited to the industrial use disclosed in the patent *specification* (*zweckgebundener Schutz*).

3. Industrial application

The patent's scope should not be confused with the requirement in Article 5(3) Biotechnology Directive, which stipulates that 'the industrial application of a sequence or a partial sequence of a gene which serves as the basis of an invention has to be concretely exposed in the patent application'. This merely means that gene patents also have to fulfil the classic requirement of *an* industrial application. A gene patent will thus not be granted if no single function of the gene sequence is mentioned in the patent application. In other words, Mary just needed to identify *a* function of the BRAU-7 gene and indicate it relates to the cardiovascular system in her patent *application* in order to obtain an absolute protection covering all later discovered functions, amongst which the wound-healing function.

4. Overlapping gene sequences

In the framework of the purpose of interpreting rights conferred by a patent, Recital 25 Biotechnology Directive stipulates that when sequences overlap only in parts which are not essential to the invention, each sequence will be considered as an independent sequence in patent law terms. This recital envisages the situation where two inventions are related in the sense that two gene sequences are partially overlapping. The recital sets forth that when the common fragment is *not* essential for the later invention, no relationship of dependence exists.

However, the recital is not mirrored by binding regulation of the Directive.

5. Compulsory licences (what can John do?)
Compulsory licences can be applied, in principle, on two different grounds: dependency and public interest. The BIP project is interested in the concrete argumentation on the national level.

6. Defences
Further interest is in what kind of defences may be available to exclude John from liability for patent infringement. A first defence that comes to mind is the experimental use defence. However, it is most unlikely in the given circumstances that this exception will apply, as John is not only investigating but already commercialising the subject matter of the patented invention. A second defence is to challenge the validity of Mary's patent. John may claim that the patent should not have been awarded to Mary in the first place. In the jurisdictions considered here, human genes are regarded as inventions, so Mary's patent cannot be invalidated because it does not meet the invention criterion. However, one could imagine that Mary's patent does not fulfil the further criteria of novelty, inventive step and industrial application. If John is successful in demonstrating shortcomings in any of those criteria, Mary's patent may fail and she will not be able to sue him for infringement.

A.3. COUNTRY REPORTS

(1) BELGIUM

I. *Operative Rules*

Mary will have an injunction against John. However, she might be faced with a compulsory licence on grounds of dependency (of John's invention) or reasons of public health.

II. *Descriptive Formants*

- Article 5(3) Biotechnology Directive;[2]
- Articles 4§4 3°, 27, 31, 31bis, 32–38 and 73 Belgian Patent Act (BPA) (Arts. XI.5§6 3°, XI.29, XI.37, XI. 38, XI.40–46 and XVII.14 BCEL – the Belgian

2 Directive 98/44/EC of the European Parliament and Council of 6 July 1998 on the legal protection of biotechnological inventions, OJ L 213, 30 July 1998, 13–21.

legislation on intellectual property rights, including biotechnological inventions, is now stipulated in Book XI BCEL).

a) What can Mary do?

Mary can prevent anyone not having her consent from using her patent on gene BRAU-7, on the basis of Article 27§1 BPA (Art. XI.29 BCEL). On the basis of Article 73 BPA (Art. XVII.14 BCEL), she can start a lawsuit before the Brussels Commercial Court and ask for an injunction.

b) What can John do?

However, if Mary were to refuse a licence to John on reasonable terms, he can apply for a compulsory licence. John can do so on two different grounds, namely dependency and public health.

Compulsory licences for dependency can be based on Article 31§1 2° BPA (Art. XI.37§1 2° BCEL), which states:

> The Minister may grant, in accordance with Articles 32 to 34 [Arts. XI.40–42 BCEL], a license to exploit covered by a patent when an invention covered by a patent owned by the applicant for the license cannot be exploited without infringing the rights deriving from a patent granted on an earlier filing, insofar as the dependent patent permits an important technical advance of considerable economic significance in relation to the invention claimed in the dominant patent and on condition that the license is given predominantly for the supply of the domestic market.

The detailed procedure can be found in Articles 31§1 2°, 31§2 and 32–38 BPA (Arts. XI.37§1 2°, XI.37§2 and XI.40–46 BCEL). No such licence has ever been granted in Belgium.

Article 31bis BPA (Art. XI.38 BCEL)[3] provides for a compulsory licence[4] 'in the interest of public health'. The Belgian legislator has chosen not to define 'public health', since this concept can evolve in time, but some examples were given: 'when products, processes or diagnostic methods are put at the disposal of the public in insufficient quantity or quality, or at abnormal high prices, or when the patent is exploited under conditions which are contrary to the public health interest or which constitute anti-competitive practices'.[5]

3 As introduced in 2005 by the Act on Biotechnological Inventions, 28 April 2005, *Official Gazette*, 13 May 2005 [Wet 28 april 2005 tot wijziging van de wet van 28 maart 1984 op de uitvindingsoctrooien, wat betreft de octrooieerbaarheid van de biotechnologische uitvindingen, *B.S.*, 13 mei 2005].

4 Note that procedure and conditions of Art. 31 BPA (Art. XI.37 BCEL) and Arts. 32–38 BPA (Arts. XI.40–46 BCEL) are not applicable to this Art. 31bis BPA (Art. XI.38 BCEL), as explicitly stated by para. 12 of Art. 31bis BPA (Art. XI.38 BCEL).

5 Bill, Report, *Parl. Doc.*, Chambre, 2004–2005, DOC 51 1348/006, 62–63 [Wetsontwerp, rapport, *Parl. St.*, Kamer, 2004–2005, DOC 51 1348/006, 62–63], available at: www.dekamer.be (last consulted 5 May 2019). For comments, see G. Van Overwalle, 'The Implementation of the Biotechnology Directive in Belgium and its Aftereffects. The Introduction of a New Research

Diagnostic methods as well as medicines and methods to produce medicines fall under the scope of a public health compulsory licence.[6] The possibility of a public health compulsory licence is not limited to cases were competition law is infringed.[7]

The detailed granting procedure is described in Article 31bis BPA (Art. XI.38 BCEL).[8] A faster procedure for situations of public health *crisis* is foreseen in Article 31bis §6 6° BPA (Art. XI.38§6 6° BCEL). This emphasises that the basic public health compulsory licence has a broader scope than mere crises.

III. Metalegal Formants

Unlike France and to some extent Germany,[9] and disregarding the suggestion in legal doctrine,[10] the Belgian legislator has rejected purpose-bound protection

---

Exemption and a Compulsory License for Public Health', 37 *I.I.C.* 2006, no. 8, 909–910; J. Debrulle, L. De Cort and M. Petit, 'La licence obligatoire belge pour raisons de santé publique' [The Belgian Compulsory Licence for Public Health], in: G. Van Overwalle (ed.), *Gene Patents and Public Health* (Brussels: 2007), 175. For the translation and summary thereof see G. Van Overwalle, 'The Belgian Compulsory Licence for Public Health (Translation and Summary)', in: G. Van Overwalle (ed.), *Gene Patents and Public Health* (Brussels: 2007), 203.

6 G. Van Overwalle, 'The Implementation of the Biotechnology Directive in Belgium and its Aftereffects. The Introduction of a New Research Exemption and a Compulsory License for Public Health', 37 *I.I.C.* 2006, no. 8, 910–911; J. Debrulle, L. De Cort and M. Petit, 'La licence obligatoire belge pour raisons de santé publique' [The Belgian Compulsory Licence for Public Health], in: G. Van Overwalle (ed.), *Gene Patents and Public Health* (Brussels: 2007), 175–178.

7 J. Debrulle, L. De Cort and M. Petit, 'La licence obligatoire belge pour raisons de santé publique' [The Belgian Compulsory Licence for Public Health], in: G. Van Overwalle (ed.), *Gene Patents and Public Health* (Brussels: 2007), 174–175. Also see G. Van Overwalle, 'The Implementation of the Biotechnology Directive in Belgium and its Aftereffects. The Introduction of a New Research Exemption and a Compulsory License for Public Health', 37 *I.I.C.* 2006, no. 8, 910; G. Van Overwalle, 'Zonder trommels en trompetten: EU-Biotechnologierichtlijn in het Belgisch octrooirecht' [Without Drums and Trumpets: the EU Biotechnology Directive in Belgian Patent Law], *I.R.D.I.* 2005, 363–365.

8 And for explanations: G. Van Overwalle, 'The Implementation of the Biotechnology Directive in Belgium and its Aftereffects. The Introduction of a New Research Exemption and a Compulsory License for Public Health', 37 *I.I.C.* 2006, no. 8, 910–916; G. Van Overwalle, 'Zonder trommels en trompetten: EU-Biotechnologierichtlijn in het Belgisch octrooirecht' [Without Drums and Trumpets: the EU Biotechnology Directive in Belgian Patent Law], *I.R.D.I.* 2005, 365–373; J. Debrulle, L. De Cort and M. Petit, 'La licence obligatoire belge pour raisons de santé publique' [The Belgian Compulsory Licence for Public Health], in: G. Van Overwalle (ed.), *Gene Patents and Public Health* (Brussels: 2007), 178–198.

9 G. Van Overwalle, 'The Implementation of the Biotechnology Directive in Belgium and its Aftereffects. The Introduction of a New Research Exemption and a Compulsory License for Public Health', 37 *I.I.C.* 2006, no. 8, 903; G. Van Overwalle, 'Zonder trommels en trompetten: EU-Biotechnologierichtlijn in het Belgisch octrooirecht' [Without Drums and Trumpets: the EU Biotechnology Directive in Belgian Patent Law], *I.R.D.I.* 2005, 354–355.

10 G. Van Overwalle and P. Jacobs, 'Octrooien op genen: een alternatieve benadering' [Gene Patents: an Alternative Approach?], *B.I.E.* 17 April 2001, 115–116; G. Van Overwalle and P. Jacobs, 'Naschrift op de reactie van dr. B. Swinkels', *B.I.E.* 16 July 2001, 221–222; P. Jacobs and G. Van Overwalle, 'Gene Patents: a Different Approach', *E.I.P.R.* 2001, no. 11, 505–506.

for gene patents and opted for absolute protection when implementing Directive 98/44/EC[11] (Biotechnology Directive).[12] This means that a gene patent offers protection for the sequence itself and for later applications using this sequence possibly not foreseen by the 'upstream' patent holder at the time of the application. Hence, Mary's patent on BRAU-7 covers John's invention, even if Mary was not aware at the time of the wound-healing function of the BRAU-7 gene sequence.[13]

The above should not be confused with the requirement of Article 4§4 3° BPA (Art. XI.5§6 3° BCEL): 'The industrial application of a sequence or a partial sequence of a gene which serves as the basis of an invention has to be concretely exposed in the patent application.'[14] Based on Article 5(3) Biotechnology Directive, this merely means that gene patents also have to fulfil the classic requirement of *an* industrial application. A gene patent will thus not be granted if not a single function of the gene sequence is mentioned in the patent application.[15] In other words, Mary just needed to identify a function of the BRAU-7 gene and indicate it related to the cardiovascular system in her patent application in order to obtain absolute protection covering all later-discovered functions, amongst which the wound-healing function, as well.

According to Article 27 BPA (Art. XI.29 BCEL), a patent is a negative right, i.e. it gives the patent holder the right to prevent everybody else from undertaking certain actions that make use or aim to make use of his/her invention.

It is often argued that the unreasonable use of patents could have negative economic and social effects. If, for example, the patent holder refuses to license

---

11 Directive 98/44/EC of the European Parliament and Council of 6 July 1998 on the legal protection of biotechnological inventions, OJ L 213, 30 July 1998, 13–21.

12 Art. 27ter BPA (Art. XI.31 BCEL).

13 Keeping in mind of course Recital 25 of the Biotechnology Directive: 'Whereas, for the purposes of interpreting rights conferred by a patent, when sequences overlap only in parts which are not essential to the invention, each sequence will be considered as an independent sequence in patent law terms.'

14 Note that the minor difference with the text of Art. 5(3) Biotechnology Directive – 'which serves as the basis of an invention' – was added to emphasise that not merely a discovery, but an invention was needed in order to be patentable; see G. Van Overwalle, 'The Implementation of the Biotechnology Directive in Belgium and its Aftereffects. The Introduction of a New Research Exemption and a Compulsory License for Public Health', 37 *I.I.C.* 2006, no. 8, 898–899; G. Van Overwalle, 'Zonder trommels en trompetten: EU-Biotechnologierichtlijn in het Belgisch octrooirecht' [Without Drums and Trumpets: the EU Biotechnology Directive in Belgian Patent Law], *I.R.D.I.* 2005, 355.

15 Explanatory Memorandum, *Parl. Doc.*, Chambre, 2003–2004, DOC 51 1348/001, 13 [M.v.T., *Parl. St.*, Kamer, 2003–2004, DOC 51 1348/001, 13], available at: www.dekamer.be (last consulted 5 May 2019). For comments, see G. Van Overwalle, 'The Implementation of the Biotechnology Directive in Belgium and its Aftereffects. The Introduction of a New Research Exemption and a Compulsory License for Public Health', 37 *I.I.C.* 2006, no. 8, 898–899; G. Van Overwalle, 'De implementatie van de EU-Biotechnologierichtlijn: de Belgische octrooiwet in spreidstand' [The Implementation of the Biotechnology Directive: the Belgian Patent Law in a Straddle], *T.B.H.* 2006, 573.

his/her invention on reasonable terms, other interests might be harmed, such as innovation or public health. This could be even more the case where gene patents offer absolute instead of purpose-bound protection. The fear that too many and too broad upstream gene patents will result in hindering research and innovation has resulted in two instruments in the BPA.

To avoid the 'sterility' of useful and economically important inventions, the Belgian legislator has introduced the compulsory licence for dependency in the 1984 BPA (now Book XI of the BCEL) introducing Article 31§1 2° (Art. XI.37§1 2° BCEL).[16]

Implementing the Biotechnology Directive, the Belgian legislator has chosen to go somewhat further than merely transposing the Directive. In order to find a balance between the patentability of genes and public health, the Belgian legislator seized the opportunity with the already mentioned Article 31bis BPA (Art. XI.38 BCEL) in 2005.[17] Triggered by the *Myriad* case,[18] it was decided that the available compulsory licensing schemes did not suffice to avoid unreasonable use of patents that are important to public health.[19]

Although not a single patent has been licensed via an application for a compulsory licence in Belgium,[20] it is argued that the existence of such mechanisms creates some pressure on reluctant patent holders to convince them into a reasonable agreement.[21]

Now, does John fulfil the requirements of Article 31bis BPA (Art. XI.38 BCEL)? Article 31bis §1 BPA (XI.38 §1 BCEL) explicitly states that a compulsory licence *can* be granted. Bearing in mind the *ratio legis* of Article 31bis BPA (Art. XI.38 BCEL), i.e. finding a delicate balance between the private interests of

16 Explanatory Memorandum, *Parl. Doc.*, Chambre, 1980–1981, no. 9191/1, 21–22 [M.v.T., *Parl. St.*, Kamer, 1980–1981, nr. 919/1, 21–22], available at: www.dekamer.be (last consulted 5 May 2019).

17 J. Debrulle, L. De Cort and M. Petit, 'La licence obligatoire belge pour raisons de santé publique' [The Belgian Compulsory Licence for Public Health], in: G. Van Overwalle (ed.), *Gene Patents and Public Health* (Brussels: 2007), 164.

18 On the *Myriad* case: G. Matthijs, 'Diagnostics in Practice', in: G. Van Overwalle (ed.), *Gene Patents and Public Health* (Brussels: 2007), 35–38.

19 G. Van Overwalle, 'The Implementation of the Biotechnology Directive in Belgium and its Aftereffects. The Introduction of a New Research Exemption and a Compulsory License for Public Health', 37 *I.I.C.* 2006, no. 8, 908–909; J. Debrulle, L. De Cort and M. Petit, 'La licence obligatoire belge pour raisons de santé publique' [The Belgian Compulsory Licence for Public Health], in: G. Van Overwalle (ed.), *Gene Patents and Public Health* (Brussels: 2007), 167–174.

20 G. Van Overwalle, E. Van Zimmeren, E. Verbeure, and G. Matthijs, 'Models for facilitating access to patents on genetic inventions', 7 *Nature Review Genetics*, February 2006, 147.

21 G. Van Overwalle, 'The Implementation of the Biotechnology Directive in Belgium and its Aftereffects. The Introduction of a New Research Exemption and a Compulsory License for Public Health', 37 *I.I.C.* 2006, no. 8, 889–920; E. Van Zimmeren, and G. Requena, 'Ex-Officio Licensing in the Medical Sector: the French Model', in: G. Van Overwalle (ed.), *Gene Patents and Public Health* (Brussels: 2007), 137–140.

the inventors and public health interests,[22] it will come down to a case-by-case analysis and a comparison of the relevant interests at stake.

(2) CZECH REPUBLIC

I. Operative Rules

Mary has a claim for injunction.

II. Descriptive Formants

The patentability of human genes is subject to the Patent Act[23] and the Biotechnological Inventions Act.[24] The Biotechnological Invention Act is a *lex specialis* in relation to the Patent Act. The Biotechnological Inventions Act transposes Directive 98/44/EC on the legal protection of biotechnological inventions into the Czech legal order. The Biotechnological Inventions Act gives basic guidelines on what is patentable under which conditions and also includes provisions on compulsory licences.

Compulsory licences comprised in the Biotechnological Inventions Act are compulsory licences for plant and animal varieties. Such compulsory licences may be granted according to section 9 of the Biotechnological Inventions Act to a breeder who cannot obtain or exploit a plant or animal variety right without infringing a prior patent and if that breeder applied unsuccessfully for a licence from a rightholder.[25] This provision would be helpful for John but is applicable only to plant and animal variety rights.

The Patent Act comprises provisions on compulsory licences in its section 20(1) and (2). According to section 20(1) Patent Act, a compulsory licence may be granted if the proprietor of the patent unreasonably does not exploit the invention (or exploits it insufficiently) after the expiration of four years from the patent application or three years from the grant of the patent. This period has expired but if Mary exploits the invention, then the compulsory licence will not be granted to John.

According to section 20(2) Patent Act, a compulsory licence may also be granted when an important public interest is endangered. According to the explanatory report on the Patent Act, such a public interest is, for example, the

---

22 Bill, Report, *Parl. Doc.*, Chambre, 2004–2005, DOC 51 1348/006, 45 [Wetsontwerp, rapport, *Parl. St.*, Kamer, 2004–2005, DOC 51 1348/006, 45], available at: www.dekamer.be (last consulted 5 May 2019).

23 Act on Inventions and Rationalisations Proposals 527/1990 Coll.

24 Act on the Protection of Biotechnological Inventions 206/2000 Coll.

25 See also Art. 12 Directive 98/44/EC on the legal protection of biotechnological inventions.

health of the people.[26] Such a compulsory licence shall be granted in the case, for example, of an epidemic. If John's substance heals wounds, then it would be possible to apply for a compulsory licence in a time of war, for example, when the necessity of healing wounds dramatically increases.

A compulsory licence under section 20 Patent Act has so far never been granted, and there has only been one application, which was rejected because it was based mainly on economic reasons.[27]

III. Metalegal Formants

Answer omitted.

(3) DENMARK

I. Operative Rules

Yes, Mary has a claim for injunction against John.

II. Descriptive Formants

The fact that Mary is granted a patent on the gene BRAU-7 implies that she has been granted a product patent. Under Danish law, a product patent gives the patent holder absolute product protection, i.e. protection for all applications of the patent, including new applications. It follows from §8(2)(2) of the Danish Patent Act (DPA, 28 January 2009) that the application of the patent need not be included in the patent claims. Consequently, the applicant may claim absolute product protection. Therefore, John's patent on his invention is dependent on Mary's product patent on the gene BRAU-7 and Mary may claim an injunction for breach of her exclusive right to exploit the patent, cf. DPA §3, when John sets up a business and starts producing an ointment.

In principle, John could invoke the rule in DPA §46 on compulsory licensing in situations of dependency. The rule has never been used in practice and the requirements are very strict (John's invention should be 'an important technical step' of 'major economic importance'). Therefore, the rule would seem not to be applicable in this case. Nor would the rule in DPA §47 on compulsory licences in cases of 'important public interests'.

---

26 See also R. Horáček, K. Čada, P. Hajn, *Práva k průmyslovému vlastnictví* (Rights to the Industrial Property) (1st ed., Prague: 2005), p. 73.

27 Ibid.

III. *Metalegal Formants*

The case illustrates the difficulties of finding the balance which best serves the societal interest associated with innovation. On the one hand, the rule of absolute product protection gives inventors a strong right (high incentives). On the other hand, the blocking effect is broad and even covers uses which were not known to the inventor at the time of patenting. Arguably, the public policy reasons for granting protection against uses which were known at the time of patenting are stronger than for granting protection which enables the patent holder to control new downstream/secondary applications of the invention.

(4) ESTONIA

I. *Operative Rules*

Mary has a claim against John.

II. *Descriptive Formants*

According to §6(1) Patent Act,[28] 'the subject of an invention may be a device, process, material, including biological material, or a combination thereof'. It is assumed that in the present case the subject of an invention in both patents is biological material.[29] Subsection 15(1) Patent Act provides that only the proprietor of a patent has the right to use the patented invention. Therefore, John needs Mary's permission to use her invention. This requirement holds true if the patent on the gene BRAU-7 is in force in Estonia and John intends to use his invention in Estonia.

If Mary and John do not conclude a licence agreement, then John is not allowed to use the gene BRAU-7. Of course, John can sue Mary to get a compulsory licence. According to §47(1) 3) Patent Act:

> A person who is interested in using a patented invention and is capable of doing so in the Republic of Estonia, may, upon refusal of the proprietor of the patent to grant a

---

[28] Patendiseadus. Entered into force on 23 May 1994 – RT I 1994, 25, 406; 2008, 59, 330 (in Estonian). Unofficial translation available at https://www.riigiteataja.ee/en/eli/502042019006/consolide (19 January 2009).

[29] Subsection $15^1(3)$ provides: '[i]n the case of an invention containing genetic information, the exclusive right of the proprietor of the patent shall extend to all biological material in which the invention is incorporated and which performs its function according to the said genetic information, except the human body and parts thereof'.

licence, file an action in court for acquiring a compulsory licence if the patent hinders the use of another, technically advanced invention significant for the economy of the Republic of Estonia.

In order to get a compulsory licence, John has to prove *inter alia* that his invention (the ointment) is a technically advanced invention that is significant for the Estonian economy.

III. Metalegal Formants

The case concentrates on the issue of how to guarantee that IP holders do not block each other, and that useful products reach society on affordable terms. The Estonian legal framework is similar to the legal frameworks of other European countries. Estonia is a party to the Paris Convention for the Protection of Industrial Property,[30] the Agreement on Trade-Related Aspects of Intellectual Property Rights[31] and key regional agreements in the field of IP (e.g. the European Patent Convention).[32] Estonia has also harmonised its legislation with the relevant EU Directives in the field of IP.

Therefore, the measures to avoid blocking and to enhance exploitation of IP are almost the same as in other EU member states. As noted above, the Patent Act strictly defines what can and cannot be patented.[33] At the same time, it is necessary to bear in mind that 172 patents were granted under the Patent Act and 1,009 European patents were entered into the European Patent Register valid in Estonia between 1 January 2008 and 31 December 2008.[34] This means that the majority of patents are granted pursuant to the European Patent Convention by the European Patent Office. The limitations of patent owners' rights are provided by the Patent Act. Compulsory licensing could be considered an appropriate tool to address the problems introduced by the case. Currently there is no case law concerning compulsory licensing in Estonia. The relevant literature is also limited.[35]

---

30 Paris Convention for the Protection of Industrial Property. Paris, 20 March 1883, entered into force in respect of Estonia on 24 August 1994 - RT II 1994, 4-5, 19.

31 Agreement on Trade-Related Aspects of Intellectual Property Rights. Marrakech, 15 April 1994, entered into force in respect of Estonia on 13 December 1999 - RT II 1999, 22, 123.

32 Convention on the Grant of European Patents. Munich, 5 October 1973, entered into force in respect of Estonia on 1 July 2002 - RT II 2002, 10, 40.

33 Patent Act §§6, 7.

34 Statistical data available at http://www.epa.ee/client/default.asp?wa_id=525&wa_object_id=1&wa_id_key= (19 January 2009).

35 See e.g. A. Kelli, A. Kalvi, *Compulsory License as a Tool for Limitation of a Patent Owner's Rights* - Intellectual Property and Bioscience. Compendium of Working Papers from ScanBalt IPKN Project (Stuttgart/Berlin: 2007), pp. 83–94.

(5) FRANCE

I. Operative Rules

Under French IP law, Mary has no grounds for a claim against John. However, there are concerns that French law may not be in line with the Biotechnology Directive.

II. Descriptive Formants

Under French patent law, Mary could sue John, providing that John's patent is dependent on Mary's patent. A patent is dependent on another patent when the exploitation of the first involves the reproduction of all or part of the second. This would constitute an infringement.

However, French patent law limits the scope of a patent covering a gene sequence. Article L. 613-2-1 al. 2 of the French Intellectual Property Code provides that: 'The rights created by the delivery of a patent including a gene sequence may not be called upon against a later claim on the same sequence if this claim satisfies the requirements of Article L. 611-18 and if it discloses any other particular application of this sequence'.[36] Consequently, the second patent is totally independent of the first. This article is a result of Amendment 95 of the Bioethics Bill project, which aimed to protect any gene sequence from ownership. Gene sequences are normally always available for any new diagnostic or therapeutic application invented later.

Article L. 613-2-1 al. 2 of the French Intellectual Property Code calls into question the principle that the infringement of the patented product occurs as soon as this product is made, even if it is made by a different process and independently of the industrial application that leads to the invention. Article L. 613-3 of the French Intellectual Property Code provides that: 'The following shall be prohibited, save consent by the owner of the patent: a) Making, offering, putting on the market or using a product which is the subject matter of the patent, or importing or stocking a product for such purposes'. Consequently, the material reproduction of the protected product is the necessary act but sufficient of the infringement by manufacture.

The prohibition of dependence between these patents seems contrary to Directive 98/44/EC of 6 July 1998 on the legal protection of biotechnological inventions.[37] Article 9 of this Directive provides that: 'The protection conferred

---

[36] Art. L. 613-2-1 al. 2, inserted by Act No. 2004-800, 6 August 2004, Art. 17 a III, Journal Officiel, 7 August 2004, p. 14063.

[37] Directive 98/44/EC of the European Parliament and of the Council of 6 July 1998 on the legal protection of biotechnological inventions, OJ L 213, 30 July 1998, 13–21.

by a patent on a product containing or consisting of genetic information shall extend to all material, saved as provided by Article 5(1), in which the product is incorporated and in which the genetic information is contained and performs its function'. French patent law is consequently stricter than the Directive and goes against its objective of harmonisation. But a private individual may put forward a Community standard even without direct effect or incapable of being applied in a dispute between private individuals. Thus, he/she may apply to the national court to set aside the application of any rule of law which would be contrary to a Community standard, whether this is a general rule or an individual measure.[38]

In the aforementioned case, Mary's patent covers a gene sequence. As a utility, this patent accounts for cardiovascular diseases. John's patent covers the combination of Mary's gene sequence with another gene sequence. This combination accounts for the healing process. John has already started to produce an ointment. Under Article L. 613-3 of the French Intellectual Property Code, John has infringed Mary's patent because Mary's product is materially reproduced. But under Article L. 613-2-1 al. 2 of the French Intellectual Property Code, Mary has no grounds to initiate proceedings against John. Her only option is to refer to the Biotechnology Directive and to ask the judge to set aside Article L. 613-2-1 al. 2 of the French Intellectual Property Code. Consequently, the outcome of the proceedings depends on the court's decision on this point.

III. Metalegal Formants

Answer omitted.

(6) GERMANY

I. Operative Rules

Presumably, Mary has a claim for injunction against John.

II. Descriptive Formants

a) Assuming that Mary's patent was granted by the German Patent Office

Mary has a claim for injunction based on §1004 BGB in conjunction with §9 German Patent Code, if John's patent is 'dependent' on Mary's patent. The basic

[38] CJEU judgment of 28 October 1975, *Rutili*, C-36/75, ECLI:EU:C:1975:137, p. 219; CJEU judgment of 30 April 1996, *CIA Security International*, C-194/94, ECLI:EU:C:1996:172, p. 2201.

reason why the patents could be dependent is the overlap in respect of BRAU-7. However, a mere overlap does not necessarily result in dependency: with the aim of reducing dependencies, the legislator introduced §1a sec. 4 German Patent Code in 2005, implementing the Biotechnology Directive. It requires gene sequence patents to indicate the function in the patent claim.

We shall assume that both patents are issued under the new law and take it for granted that the patents are valid. The question of whether Mary's patent dominates John's depends on how the claims were formulated. If Mary's patent included 'the cardiovascular system' as a function of the gene in the claim, then John's patent would not be dependent. However, if Mary's patent indicated 'cardiovascular diseases' as potential therapies somewhere in the description as a 'utility', then John's patent would, in principle, be dependent.[39] Only if the sequence were to overlap 'in parts which are not essential to the invention' in the sense of Recital 25 Biotechnology Directive,[40] not explicitly implemented into German law, could the patents be qualified as non-dependent. In both patents, BRAU-7 is essential. Thus, the exception of Recital 25 of the Biotechnology Directive does not apply. Consequently, Mary would not have a claim for injunction against John.

Therefore, patent attorneys in practice strongly seek to avoid the indication of a function in the claim (unless it is necessary in order to delineate prior art). Thus, any function-related information will be phrased as utility. Then John's patent would be dependent on Mary's. There is no liability rule in German law cutting down on the right to exclude and authorising John to use the patent with equitable compensation. Thus, Mary has a claim for injunction.

b) Assuming that Mary's patent was granted by the European Patent Office

In Germany, gene patents are largely not filed with the German Patent Office, but rather for Germany through the EPC filing procedure. An equivalent rule to §1 sec. 4 German Patent Law does not exist in the EPC. §1 sec. 4 German Patent Law is conceived of as a norm regulating only the claim formulation and not the scope of the patent. Therefore, the rule is not applicable to EPC patents with a German destination.[41] Consequently, John's patent is dependent on Mary's.

---

39 Note: the German Bundestag explicitly rejected the idea of functional restriction (*Funktionsbeschänkung*) as a concept of utility and scope (*gewerbliche Anwendbarkeit* and *Umfang*). For this alternative see the *utility* restriction in the French country report.

40 'Whereas, for the purposes of interpreting rights conferred by a patent, when sequences overlap only in parts which are not essential to the invention, each sequence will be considered as an independent sequence in patent law terms.'

41 H.-P. Götting, 'Stellungnahme zur Einschränkung des absoluten Stoffschutzes nach §1a Abs. 4 PatG' (February 2005), 10; H.-P. Götting, 'Kritische Bemerkungen zum absoluten Stoffschutz', (2009) *GRUR*, 256–260; R. Uhrich, *Stoffschutz* (Tübingen: 2010), 296 et seq.

III. *Metalegal Formants*

The case touches on the contested[42] issue of blocking progress in medical research through patents. It does not refer to the classical patent–public health interface of affordable access to medicines. Neither does it refer to the question of patentability (presumably settled by §1a sec. 2 German Patent Law/ Art. 5(2) Biotechnology Directive).[43] Nor does it resort to the narrow German experimentation resp. research exemptions (§11 No. 2 German Patent Law/ Art. 5 sec. 3 of the Constitution).[44] The focus is on growing dependencies, which have resulted in blockage situations and problems which have become known as 'patent thickets' – a term describing the opaque legal landscape, an effect colliding with patent law principles. The conflict between John and Mary takes up the discussion about research tools defined as marketable research information. As early as 1987, R. Eisenberg[45] had described the problem and advised replacing the property rule (right to exclude/injunction) with the liability rule (compensation). The more recent discussion has revived the debate about the underlying patent equilibrium in respect of modern research. It brings up old discussions about the role of patent law as just one innovation system which is driven by property rights, besides others like competition, scientific curiosity or Aesculapian and research ethics.

In Germany, §1a sec. 4 German Patent Code allegedly introduced an instrument to reduce dependencies. However, as a regulatory instrument, it is about to fail – as gene patents are not filed in Germany and the rule is not applicable to EPC patents.[46] Industry perceives dependency as central to the

---

42 Some perceive no problem at all (J. Straus), some account for a slowing down of research through blockage (R. Eisenberg), first empirical studies suggested that the problem is not so much with patent rights but with access to material (T. Caulfield, S.N. Cohen, R. Cook-Deegan, E.D. Kieff and J. Walsh, 'Evidence and anecdotes: an analysis of human gene patenting controversies', (2005) 24(9) *Nature Biotechnology*, 1091–1094; yet, concerns remained: R. Cook-Deegan and C. Heaney, 'Patents in Genomics and Human Genetics', (2010) Annual Review of Genomics Human Genetics, 383–425.

43 However: (1) Recognise the revocation of the patent EP 699 754, and restriction of the patents EP 0705902 and EP 0705903, three of several patents on BRCA1/BRCA2 (connected to breast cancer) held by Myriad by the EPO (19 May 2004, 25 January 2005). (2) The problem of dependencies rests on the broad protection scope of 'close to discovery' patents and this problem is exacerbated by the limited number of genes and the ever-increasing identification of multifunctional sequences.

44 These exemptions in German law are narrow (BVerfG, decision of 10 May 2000, GRUR 2001, 43; BGHZ 130, 259 and BGHZ 135, 217 – *Klinische Versuche I, II*). However, in practice, public research institutions are shielded by a moral threshold against lawsuits against scientific institutions, low prospects in conjunction with the high costs of lawsuits, and a long-term efficiency rationale.

45 R. Eisenberg, 'Proprietary Rights and the Norms of Science in Biotechnology Research', (1987) 97 *Yale Law Journal*, 177–231.

46 It is alleged that both, the German ministry of justice and the industry ministry intended the loophole and only pretended to give in for the compromise with the German Parliament.

patent system; problems are to be resolved in negotiations. The right to refuse a licence is perceived as inherent to the right to exclude. Compulsory licences are not available in these cases (§24 German Patent Law). No other solution (other than those accompanying public funding of research) has been put in place yet, like a clearinghouse mechanism.[47]

The central metalegal question is how a legal system pursues public health policies to foster progress in medicine: how does it resolve the tension between the idea of progress driven by property and progress driven by exchange (via competition *or* research norms), both geared towards fostering the availability of new therapies? The legal set-up in Germany reflects a strong trust in the property system. Neither are access rules in place which provide access to privileged users (like public research institutions or hospitals), or access rules which secure sequential technological development. No negotiations about clearinghouses have been published nor are guidelines issued by leading scientific societies comparable to those issued by the International Society of Stem Cell Research.[48]

(7) GREECE

I. *Operative Rules*

Unless her interests are not seriously affected, Mary may claim for an injunction, but John may object to it by claiming a compulsory licence.

II. *Descriptive Formants*

This is a case of a dependent patent according to Article 13 para. 4 Law 1733/1987. Since the use of John's patent requires the use of Mary's patented gene, Mary can seek an injunction against John. On the other hand, John can seek a compulsory licence of Mary's patent, if his invention represents significant progress compared to the older patent, according to Article 13 para. 4 Law 1733/1987.

It is obvious that at the very centre of the thinking on the issue is the concept of the 'dependent' invention. Greek law seems to conceive of this in a very broad way, since it contents itself with the fact that the two inventions are 'related', without interesting itself in the specific manner in which they interact; it suffices that 'the productive exploitation of the one is not possible without affecting the rights of [the beneficiaries of the other]' (Art. 13 para. 4

47 See the Belgian country report.

48 See P. Taylor, 'Research Sharing, Ethics, and Public Benefit', (2007) 25 *Nature Biotechnology*, 398–401.

Law 1733/1987). It is not clear whether this constitutes only a procedural rule, i.e. a rebuttable presumption of the interconnection between the two methods. Anyway, though the description of the content of the protection in every patent is important, the relevant formulation of the terms of the patent will always be interpreted in the light of good faith, business ethics and the purpose of the law.

More particularly as concerns bio-inventions, Greek law has been adjusted to the Biotechnology Directive by Presidential Decree 321/2001. According to this enactment, the prerequisites for the acquisition of a dependent patent do not differ from those set, as above, by the general law of Law 1733/1987. Thus, if by any chance the interests of the earlier inventor are not seriously affected, then it is likely that his/her relevant claim for the payment of a consideration for the granting of a compulsory licence in favour of the beneficiary of the dependent invention will be taken to be abusive. The interpreter could base such a judgement on Article 281 of the Civil Code, by way of which only Recital 25 Biotechnology Directive can be taken into account, since the latter – which nevertheless gives expression to a more general spirit – has not been incorporated into Greek law, since it does not form part of the text of the Directive.

III. Metalegal Formants

Within this framework, the question of whether the law wishes to facilitate progress and innovation, even at the expense of previous intellectual achievements, will be decisive. It seems from the very broad formulation of the concept of a dependent invention in Article 13 of Law 1733/1987 and Article 10 of Presidential Decree 321/2001 that the Greek legislator favours compulsory licences over the risk of putting a brake on research and technology. This applies *a fortiori* as any interests of the parties – any *loci* in favour of the exploitation of the new invention licence – are better balanced by the institution of reasonable compensation of the old owner by the new, compensation of which the amount can be perfectly adjusted to the individual circumstances.

In any event, does the support of innovation at the expense of previous innovation perhaps constitute an evaluative contradiction, since the protection accorded to the innovative creator is subsequently cancelled where he/she remains without protection against his/her more creative successors? Does perhaps, on the other hand, such a regulation force the intellectual creator to engage in a constant quest, that is, in constant improvement and updating of his/her creation for reasons of defending it against competition? But is, then, competition in intellectual creation meaningful? Would a science or an art which constantly cancels itself out without feeling any genuine inner scientific or artistic unease about this, but exclusively for reasons of the survival of the creator, have meaning?

(8) IRELAND

Answer omitted.

(9) ITALY

I. Operative Rules

No, Mary will not have a claim for an injunction because John's invention is considered independent from the one for which she was granted a patent. This is due to the difference in use from the one Mary should have claimed in her patent application.

II. Descriptive Formants

As a general rule, for the Industrial Property Code (IPC l. 30/2005) a patent which involves the implementation of previous inventions is protected by patents still in force, and cannot be implemented, or used, without the consent of the patent holders (Art. 68 c. 2 Industrial Property Code).[49] For the purposes of interpreting the rights conferred by a patent, the last sentence of Article 4 c. 1 let. d of statute 22 February 2006, no. 78 on legal protection of biotech inventions states that when gene sequences partially overlap, each sequence will be considered independent if they overlap in parts which are not essential. The rule, taken from Recital 25 of the Biotechnology Directive, concerns the situation in which two inventions are partially related to the same sequence and excludes the dependence when the shared fragment is not essential for the most recent invention. In order to determine whether John's patent is autonomous or dependent on Mary's patent, courts must establish whether the gene BRAU-7 constitutes an essential part of John's invention: in doing so they should evaluate whether the function or the utility of Mary's invention could determine her patent's extension.

The biotech field departs from the traditional rules of patent by providing that the exclusive right conferred by a patent does not cover any possible use of the product.[50] The legal protection of biotechnological inventions is statutorily restricted to those functions specifically claimed in the patent application: this

49 For a comment on this article see Marchetti, Ubertazzi, 'Commentario breve al diritto della concorrenza', *Appendice Aggiornamento* 2005 (Padova: 2005), p. 83.

50 See comment on Art. 66 and 68 Industrial Property Code in Marchetti, Ubertazzi, 'Commentario breve al diritto della concorrenza', *Appendice Aggiornamento* 2005 (Padova: 2005), pp. 443 ff. particularly p. 450.

is the provision of Article 3 c. 1 let. d of statute 22 February 2006, no. 78 on the patentability of elements of the human body. The provision requires that the function and industrial application of the invention should be not only concretely disclosed but also specifically claimed. Furthermore, the provision is extended to DNA by Article 4 c. 1 let. d of statute 22 February 2006, no. 78, which, in its first sentence, explicitly denies the patentability of a sequence or partial sequence of a gene used to produce a protein, unless its function is not claimed. According to Article 52 c. 2 Italian Patent Code,[51] the patent protection for biotechnological inventions will be extended only to the trial use or technical function[52] *specifically claimed in the application* (purpose-bound product claim).

Just because the protection conferred by a patent on a gene sequence is limited, by law, to the functions claimed by the applicant, Mary may prohibit the production of the substance only for the use claimed or for its equivalent. By showing a use of the sequence BRAU-7 for a purpose other than the one which characterises Mary's invention, John could be considered not to be benefiting from an essential part of Mary's invention. Therefore, John's use of gene BRAU-7 will not infringe the patent granted to Mary.

III. Metalegal Formants

The issue involved in this case concerns derivative works and dependency in biotech patents. This is strictly related to the problem of identifying the content of the exclusive right conferred by a patent and the extent of its protection. In the Italian legal system, the general principle that patent protection extends to every possible use of the product has been interpreted in an increasingly restrictive way as the relationship between the product and its function has lost its character of uniqueness and predictability.[53] It has been in the field of chemical/pharmaceutical patents that, in order to foster innovation, patent protection has been reduced in relation to the use specified in the application.[54] This trend has been confirmed by the legislature, which in transposing the Biotechnology Directive used more stringent criteria for the patentability of gene sequences. The relevant rule[55] provides that elements of human origin, as well as nucleic

---

51 Art. 52 c. 2 Industrial Property Code.

52 It has been held that in this case function and industrial application are used as synonyms: see Marchetti, Ubertazzi, 'Commentario breve al diritto della concorrenza', *Appendice Aggiornamento* 2005 (Padova: 2005), p. 1381.

53 See Court of Cassation, 16 November 1990, no. 11094, in *Giur.it*, 1991, I, 1, p. 394 and Court of Cassation, 6 March 1995, no. 2575, 1995, in *Foro. It.*, 1995, I, p. 1828.

54 See Di Cataldo, 'Fra tutela assoluta del prodotto brevettato e limitazioni ai procedimenti descritti e agli usi indicati', (2004) *Riv. Dir. ind.*, p. 111.

55 See Art. 3 c. 1 let. D and Art. 4 c. 1 let. d of statute 22 February 2006, no. 78 on the legal protection of biotech inventions.

acids, are not patentable, unless their function and/or industrial application is not specifically described and claimed. The rule appears well balanced in an economy, such as the Italian one, which invests in (and produces) less basic research (and therefore inventions of new products) and is more focused on finding new applications for existing products. The limit of this rule consists of its national character and there are always fewer patent applications with limited geographic boundaries, especially in biotechnology.

(10) LITHUANIA

I. Operative Rules

Depending on the particular circumstances, Mary may or may not have a claim for injunction against John.

II. Descriptive Formants

Lithuania implemented the Biotechnology Directive not by separate legal act, but by amending and supplementing the pre-existing Lithuanian Patent Act of 1994. Therefore, human gene patents are recognised in Lithuania. Article 4(2) of the Lithuanian Patent Act clearly reflects this possibility, repeating Article 5 of Biotechnology Directive. The general requirements of novelty, inventive step and industrial application apply to such inventions. No Lithuanian case law on biotechnological inventions, let alone on human gene-related patents, is reported at the moment.

Turning to the scope of Mary's rights, one the one hand, Lithuania implemented Article 9 of the Biotechnology Directive without additional changes, which became Article 39 of the Lithuanian Patent Act. Therefore, one may argue that Lithuania conceives of gene patents as product patents. Consequently, Mary – in principle – would be able to claim an injunction against John, because the latter uses the gene BRAU-7 in his invention.

On the other hand, Article 38 of the Lithuanian Patent Act states that the scope of legal protection conferred by a patent shall be determined by the set of claims. As this provision is of general application, it also applies with regard to biotechnological inventions and human genes in particular. Lithuanian Supreme Court has noted on many occasions that:

> the claims are the 'heart' of the patent; only according to the claims of the invention can the exclusive rights of the patent owner be established. Thus, in the case of disputes concerning both the invalidity of a granted patent and disputes concerning the protection of the rights of the patent owner, it is necessary to determine with great

care the claims of the invention protected by that patent, i.e. the limits of the legal protection conferred by a patent.[56]

Therefore, it is important how Mary's patent claim or claims were drafted. If the particular gene function in Mary's claim or claims was indicated and restricted by the curing of cardiovascular diseases, it can be concluded that John's invention, which is related to distinct uses, is outside the scope of Mary's patent. In such a scenario, Mary has no valid claim for injunction against John.

Turning to the issue of *compulsory licences*, Lithuanian law recognises the possibility for the Government of the Republic of Lithuania to issue such a licence for a person to market a patented invention within the territory of the Republic of Lithuania, if an invention protected by a patent is related to public needs, national security and public health protection, or the development of economically important sectors (Art. 50 of the Lithuanian Patent Act). So far, no compulsory licences have been granted in Lithuania. As John's invention is related to public health protection, the compulsory licence in this case is viable.

Lastly, considering possible *defences*, it is unlikely that John could use traditional defences of private use or experimental purposes/scientific research (Art. 35(3) of the Lithuanian Patent Act), as he is clearly involved in commercial activity. Certainly, he has a possibility to challenge the validity of Mary's patent because her invention was not patentable due to the lack of novelty, inventive step and industrial application (Art. 63 of the Lithuanian Patent Act).

III. Metalegal Formants

The balance between the protection of the first inventor's IP rights and individual or collective interest in subsequent useful inventions in Lithuania can be achieved by strictly applying and interpreting the patent claims. Having said that, Lithuania's normative acts do not necessarily require the particular function of biotechnological inventions to be identified in the claims; therefore, this solution not always will be available.

Another solution is to apply compulsory licences. But as practical experience with compulsory licences in Lithuania is non-existent, it is difficult to predict how easy or difficult would be to use this legal instrument. Another, probably more efficient solution could be cross-licensing between both patent holders.

As regards the invalidation of Lithuanian patents, it is worth noting that in Lithuania only formal examination of the patent application is provided for. This leads to the consequence that many national patents can be 'weak' patents and

---

[56] Ruling of 27 June 2016 of the Civil Division of the Supreme Court of Lithuania in case No. 3K-3-325-701/2016.

potentially vulnerable to the attacks based on lack of novelty, inventive step and industrial application.

(11) NETHERLANDS

I. Operative Rules

Presumably Mary does have a claim for injunction against John.

II. Descriptive Formants

Article 2(1) Dutch Patent Act 1995 (DPA) reads: 'Inventions that are new, that involve an inventive step and that are susceptible of industrial application shall be patentable'. Pursuant to Article 3(f) of the Act, however, patents shall not be granted in respect of methods for treatment of the human or animal body by surgery or therapy and diagnostic methods practised on the human or animal body; this provision shall not apply to products, in particular substances or compositions, for use in any of these methods. According to Article 4(5), substances or compositions are patentable subject matter, insofar as they are intended for the application of one of the methods referred to in Article 3(f), provided that the intended application does not belong to the state of the art. Furthermore, notwithstanding Articles 4(1)–(4) of the Act (criterion of novelty), substances or compositions within the meaning of Article 4(5) are patentable subject matter for a specific application in a method as meant in Article 3(f), provided that that application does not belong to the state of the art.

Article 25(3) states that:

> If an invention is related to a sequence or a partial sequence of a gene, the description must contain a concrete description of the function and the industrial application of this sequence or partial sequence. Where a sequence or partial sequence of a gene is used for the production of a protein or partial protein, the description of industrial applicability must specify the protein or partial protein that has been produced as well as its function.

While John's more recent patent cannot be practised effectively without the practice of Mary's older patent, John's patent is dependent on Mary's patent. Consequently, John needs permission to practise Mary's patent, but she refuses to grant a licence. In this case, the ground for a compulsory licence laid down in Article 57(4) DPA might solve the problem. The compulsory licence shall be granted by the court on a claim by John insofar as his patent for which the licence is requested represents an important technical advance of considerable economic importance. Whether or not this criterion has been satisfied has to be considered in the light of the other – unknown – circumstances of this case. But it is certainly possible that the ointment indeed represents such a technical advance.

The licence shall not extend further than is necessary for the application of John's patent. Furthermore, John shall be obliged to grant a reciprocal licence under his patent to Mary. The procedural regulations have been incorporated in Article 58 DPA.

III. Metalegal Formants

In this case, the tension can be seen between the (absolute) protection of intellectual property rights and innovation, which is in this case probably in the interest of public health.

While in general one of the ideas behind intellectual property is to stimulate innovation by protecting inventions, in this case intellectual property has a negative effect on innovation. This may even have negative consequences for public health.

Compulsory licences are meant to prevent excessive use or abuse of a monopoly position of the rightholder of the patent and to overrule the monopoly functioning of the patent in certain exceptional crisis situations.[57]

The Dutch Patent Act provides several possibilities to force a rightholder to grant a (compulsory) licence. The TRIPS Agreement provides rules for the granting of compulsory licences. Because of the sensitivity of the subject and the lack of agreement on this subject between member states, the rules which make compulsory licences possible are limited. Because the options for compulsory licences have been limited since the Dutch Patent Act was adapted in conformity with the TRIPS Agreement, the expectation has been that there will be even fewer successful requests for compulsory licences.[58]

In this case, the compulsory licence for a dependant patent conforming to Article 57(4) of the Dutch Patent Act might be granted. This specific article has changed several times in the Netherlands. In the Dutch Patent Act of 1910, the compulsory licence for dependant patents was unlimited. According to Article 34(4) of the Dutch Patent Act 1910, a licence had to be granted if it was necessary for the application of a younger patent. There was no other condition for this sort of compulsory licence. In the law proposal for the Dutch Patent Act 1995, the provision was restricted. The younger patent now had to embody a substantial/considerable improvement. The provision was changed because there was a lot of criticism of the provision. The criticism was that it was too easy to

---

57 J.L.R.A. Huydecoper and C.J.J.C. van Nispen, *Industriële eigendom. Bescherming van technische innovatie* (Deventer: 2002), p. 311.

58 Ibid., p. 314.

get a compulsory licence. Not only was this a disadvantage for the rightholders, but it was also not in line with other European countries. The provision was changed again because of the implementation of the TRIPS Agreement. The current provision requires that the younger patent has to embody important technical progress of substantial economic meaning. Adding the condition of 'important technical progress of substantial economic meaning' was seen as a further limiting of the possibility of the compulsory licence. The substantial economic significance has to be seen from a collective point of view, not from an individual point of view (meaning not only economic significance for the inventor but for an industry in general).[59]

The former provision was not used frequently after the implementation of the TRIPS Agreement as there was a fear that a younger license would never comply with the new strict condition. The practical use of this provision has been reduced.[60]

In cases like these dealing with a compulsory licence, a balance has to be struck between the rights of the IP rightholder and the public interest, in this case innovation and public health. In the provision in the Dutch Patent Act 1910, the balance leaned more towards the public interest instead of the interests of the rightholders. The current provision requires 'important technical progress of substantial economic meaning'. This criterion is not easily complied with. This leads to a stronger protection of the interests of the rightholders. On the other hand, the article has decreased in practical value and perhaps leaves not enough room for innovation.

(12) NORWAY

I. Operative Rules

Yes, Mary has a claim for an injunction against John.

II. Descriptive Formants

The fact that Mary is granted a patent on the gene BRAU-7 implies that she has been granted a product patent. Under Norwegian law, a product patent gives the patent holder absolute product protection, i.e. protection for all applications of the patent, including new applications. It follows from §8(2)(2) of the Norwegian

59 C. Gielen, 'Algemeen belang: Criterium voor dwanglicenties bij biotechnologische innovatie', *BIE* (1997) 23.

60 J.L.R.A. Huydecoper and C.J.J.C. van Nispen, *Industriële eigendom. Bescherming van technische innovatie* (Deventer: 2002), p. 317.

Patent Act (NPA, 15 December 1967) that the application of the patent need not be included in the patent claims, the consequence being that the applicant may claim absolute product protection. Therefore, John's patent on his invention is dependent on Mary's product patent on the gene BRAU-7 and Mary may claim an injunction for breach of her exclusive right to exploit the patent, cf. NPA §3, when John sets up a business and starts producing an ointment.

III. Metalegal Formants

The provision in NPA §8(2)(2) was introduced in 1979 in order to bring Norwegian patent law in line with what was considered to be the prevailing rule internationally and in accordance with the European Patent Convention. The rule was not amended or modified when Norway implemented the Biotechnology Directive (Directive 98/44/EC) in 2003 as part of its obligation under the EEA Agreement. As the case in question shows, the rule of absolute product protection may have a negative impact on innovation and even public health if the inventor who could not possibly have foreseen the disputed application refuses to grant a licence on reasonable terms.

(13) POLAND

I. Operative Rules

Whether or not Mary will have a claim for injunction depends on the nature of the patent granted.

II. Descriptive Formants

Despite the focus on genes, the underlying legal problem is of a more basic nature. It is necessary to establish whether the patent granted to Mary is a product patent or a patent for use of the gene in a described therapy. In other words, it is essential to establish whether the application has been included in the claim(s) of Mary's patent. John has discovered that the gene in question may be used for another type of therapy (in conjunction with another gene).

The Polish law does not require the function of the gene to be indicated in patent claims[61] and therefore it is unlikely that it has been so done in Mary's application, as this would narrow down the scope of protection. Therefore, if the application is not included in patent claims (but only in the description to

[61] Unlike in §1 a(4) of the German Patentgesetz, it is only required that the technical applicability must be described, but this can be done in the description and not in patent claims.

indicate its industrial applicability), John's patent would have to be regarded as a dependent patent and Mary would have a claim for injunction. If, on the other hand, the function of the gene was included in patent claims, John's invention would not be dependent, as in this invention the gene is used for a different purpose. Thus, no claims (including the right to injunction) would be available to Mary.

The same would be basically true if Mary had applied for a patent before the European Patent Office and designated Poland as one of the states where she wants to have patent protection.

III. Metalegal Formants

The facts of this case highlight a problem that is certainly inherent in all dependent patents but that becomes even more conspicuous and at the same time controversial with regard to biotech patents and in particular patents for gene sequences. In a way, the basic nature of the problem is quite similar to that in the modification to Case 1, i.e. the use of IP rights to create obstacles to scientific progress, which, at first glance, appears to be rather alien to the rationale of IP protection. However, as has already been explained, it has not been so far convincingly shown that the current rules concerning related intellectual subject matter (e.g. a copyright work and a derivative or transformative work, an invention and a dependent invention) should be abandoned, as this would have very serious adverse consequences for the rightholders. Nevertheless, as far as gene sequences are concerned, these difficulties take on an additional element. It is widely known that patenting of gene sequences has not been admitted without controversies. Many arguments have been raised, on one side trying to show that in such cases there is no invention in a classic patent law meaning, but rather a discovery, and on the other side emphasising the social and ethical perils patenting of genes may bring about. In this light, it may be argued that since gene sequences (especially discovered ones) are more akin to discoveries, patents should only be allowed for specific applications (functions), as otherwise there would be a possibility to create an all-encompassing commercial monopoly for genes. In some countries (e.g. in Germany) the law has tried to strike the balance by requiring that the function of a gene be included in patent claims, but this is not a universal solution. Because there is no such requirement in the EPC, national provisions following the German example will not attain their objective, as it will always be possible to obtain patents for gene sequences without specifying the function of a gene in patent claims, taking advantage of the European procedure.

The current state of affairs is clearly unsatisfactory, and the analysed case is only one of the many examples. The very fact that compulsory insurance for patent infringements has been envisaged constitutes the best proof that the current system is ineffective and convoluted. The progress of science also means that there are less and less fully independent patents. Thus, two conflicting interests must be reconciled. The inventor whose invention proves to also be important in other applications than originally expected must be protected against free-riding by other inventors who would have never had the possibility to create their inventions had it not been for the original patent. At the same time, it may be observed that the free-riding may take place in a different direction: where an invention may be used in conjunction with other elements to create a new, qualitatively different invention the owner of the first patent would have never created him/herself, he/she may receive windfall profit, i.e. a profit exceeding his/her 'contribution' to the new, dependent invention. In the highly sensitive area of gene patents, these problems are exacerbated as the public interest in the progress of medicine makes the dangers of blocking new inventions even more conspicuous.

(14) SLOVENIA

I. Operative Rules

Mary indeed has a claim against John, provided that she did not give permission to John and that John is not the owner of the compulsory licence.

II. Descriptive Formants

In Slovenia, patent protection of biotechnological inventions is regulated by the Industrial Property Act (IPA)[62] and the Regulation on Legal Protection of Biotechnological Inventions (RLPBI).[63] The latter implemented Directive 98/44/EC on the legal protection of biotechnological inventions (Biotechnology Directive). The purpose of the RLPBI is to set out more exactly the substantive requirements for obtaining a patent on biotechnological inventions, which must be met in addition to the requirements laid down in the IPA.

It can be derived from the facts of the case that John began to manufacture and sell an ointment for healing wounds. Since he was unable to achieve this solely by using his own patented invention, he also used the patented invention of which Mary was the owner. In the case at hand, it is of great importance to determine whether John's patent has the characteristics of a dependent patent. A dependent patent[64] is a patent where the realisation of one invention also

62 Official Gazette RS, no. 51/2006; ZIL-1-UPB3.
63 Official Gazette RS, no. 81/2003.
64 The concept of a dependent patent is derived from paragraph II of Art. 126 IPA in relation to granting a compulsory licence.

implies the realisation of a previous invention.[65] In such a case, exploitation of the previously patented invention requires the permission of the patent owner. Thus, exploitation of the dependent invention without the permission of the owner of the patent of the previous invention is a violation of the previous patent. In order to determine the dependence of one patent on another, one can refer to Recital 25 of the preamble of the Biotechnology Directive, which was not implemented into Slovenian law, according to which the overlapping of sequences in parts that are not essential to the invention suggests the independence of the patent. Considering the facts of the case, we can determine that BRAU-7 is an essential part of the invention. Therefore, it can be concluded that we are dealing with a dependent patent. As a result, Mary does have a claim for injunction against John, if it is assumed that Mary did not give John permission to use her patented invention.

On the other hand, the case raises the question of the compulsory licence. A compulsory licence is a special kind of licence that enables an individual to exploit a patented invention without prior permission of the owner if certain conditions required by the law are met. In such a case, a licence to exploit a patented invention is not obtained on a voluntary basis. The possibility of obtaining a compulsory licence to exploit a patented biotechnological invention is primarily handled by the RLPBI, although it has to be stressed that its use is restrictive and can be applied only in certain cases. Specifically, the provision of Article 11 handles the question of compulsory licences only in the plant variety right–patent relationship and not in the patent–patent relationship, as in the case at hand. Consequently, the above-mentioned provision of the RLPBI cannot be applied. For this reason, it is necessary to seek a suitable solution that regulates the patent–patent relationship, which can be found within the IPA.

Provisions on compulsory licences are also contained in Articles 125–127 IPA, according to which the granting of such a licence is possible only for a patent, but not for other industrial property rights. A compulsory licence, which differs in many ways from a contractual or voluntary licence, is granted in Slovenia by a competent judicial court[66] without the consent of the patent owner.[67] In this event, for the case at hand, the provision of paragraph II, Article 126 IPA is applicable, which regulates the special case of granting a compulsory licence in the event that the patent cannot be achieved without infringing on another patent. This provision therefore handles the issue of the so-called dependent patent. For the granting of a compulsory licence for a dependent patent, the

---

65 See S.M. Marković, *Patentno pravo* (Beograd: 1997), pp. 78–79.

66 In Slovenia, this is the District Court of Ljubljana (paragraph II, Art. 103 of the Courts Act; Official Gazette RS, no. 23/2005; ZS-UPB1).

67 See M. Janjić, *Prinudna licenca u materiji patenta u uporednom i međunarodnom pravu* (Beograd: 1962), pp. 65 ff.

requirements of Article 125 IPA must be fulfilled, as well as the supplemental requirements defined in Article 126 IPA.

John may obtain a compulsory licence to exploit Mary's patent, as long as the following cumulative requirements are met (Art. 125 IPA):

- if this is required in the public interest, particularly in regard to national security, nutrition, health care or the development of other important sectors of the state economy, or if a judicial court determines that the patent owner is abusing patent rights, particularly by restricting competition;
- the party filing the request for the granting of the licence must prove that measures had been taken conclude agreement with the patent owner under reasonable business conditions and that these measures were not successful within a reasonable period of time.[68]

This means that the use of John's patent would have to be of public interest (insofar as we set aside that Mary is not abusing her patent rights). Health care is also recognised as a public interest, yet a considerable doubt appears as to the fulfilment of this requirement due to the many different types of medicine for healing wounds already present on the market.

Since in the case at hand exploitation of the patented invention was not possible without exploiting the first patent, in order for a compulsory licence to be granted the following additional requirements of Article 126 of the IPC must be met:

- the invention claimed in the second patent must involve a technical advance of considerable economic significance compared to the invention claimed in the first patent;
- the owner of the first patent shall under reasonable conditions be entitled to a cross-licence to use the invention claimed in the second patent;
- the use authorised in respect of the first patent shall not be transferable except with the simultaneous transfer of the second patent.

According to the provision of paragraph I, Article 126 IPA, a compulsory licence shall be granted if the scope and duration of the licence are limited with regard to their purpose and primarily for the supply of the market of the Republic of Slovenia.[69] Such a licence must not be exclusive, which is logical. Otherwise, the owner of the first patent cannot use the invention, which cannot and must not be

68 This condition does not apply if a state of war or similar state of emergency has been declared. Nevertheless, the owner of the patent shall be notified of the decision of the court as soon as possible (paragraph IV, Art. 125 IPA).

69 See Regulation (EC) No. 816/2006 on compulsory licensing of patents relating to the manufacture of pharmaceutical products for export to countries with public health problems.

the object of the compulsory licence. It has to be emphasised that a compulsory licence already means a substantial intervention in the intellectual property rights of the owner due to the existence of public interest. In our opinion, granting an exclusive compulsory licence would exceed the goal or purpose of this licence. In the same way, a compulsory licence cannot be transferable.[70]

As long as the requirements listed from the provisions of Articles 125 and 126 IPA are met and John obtains a compulsory licence to use Mary's invention, Mary cannot stop the use of John's patent for the invention of healing wounds. At the same time, due to paragraph II, Article 126 IPA, Mary also has the right to use John's patent. In addition, Mary is entitled to obligatory remuneration. The amount of remuneration shall be determined with regard to the circumstances of each case and taking into account the economic value of the compulsory licence (Art. 127 IPA).

III. Metalegal Formants

Answer omitted.

(15) SPAIN

I. Operative Rules

Presumably, Mary does have a claim for injunction against John.

II. Descriptive Formants

a) Assuming that Mary's patent was granted by the Spanish Patent Office (OEPM)
The relevant legislation is:

- Patent Law 11/1986 of 20 March;
- Law 29/2006 of 26 July, on guarantees and rational use of medicines and health products;
- Royal Decree 2245/1986 of 10 October, approving the implementing regulations of the Patent Law.

By bringing into force Law 10/2002 of 29 April, Spain has adopted Directive 98/44/EC on the legal protection of biotechnological inventions. The modifications made to Spanish national law make it possible to grant patents on

[70] Transfer of the compulsory licence is only possible with the simultaneous transfer of the part of the business activity of the recipient of the compulsory licence to which the compulsory licence refers (subparagraph c, Art. 126 IPA).

genes if the application fulfils the requirements that are required in general for any kind of invention.

On one hand, assuming that Mary's patent is valid, the question of whether Mary's patent dominates John's depends on the scope of protection of the granted patent. Article 50.4 of the Patent Law stipulates that if the object of a patent is a product containing or consisting of genetic information, the protection shall extend to all material in which the product is incorporated and in which the genetic information is contained and performs its function. Therefore, dependency between the two patents is contingent on the inclusion[71] of 'cardiovascular therapies or cardiovascular treatments' as a function of the gene patented by Mary. The industrial application of a sequence or a partial sequence of a gene must be disclosed in the patent application. Only if the sequence overlaps 'in parts which are not essential to the invention' in the sense of Recital 25 Biotechnology Directive, explicitly implemented into Spanish law,[72] can the patents not be qualified as non-dependent. In both patents, BRAU-7 is essential, so Mary would have a claim for injunction against John.

On the other hand, the question above raises the issue of compulsory licences. Article 86 of the Patent Law envisages granting compulsory licences in specific cases. One of these is when one patent depends on another: that is to say, a patent can only be exploited if access is provided to a previous one. Article 89.1 of the Patent Law, modified by the Biotechnology Directive, expressly stipulates that when the holder of a patent cannot exploit it without infringing a prior patent, he/she may apply for a compulsory licence for non-exclusive use of the prior patent, subject to payment of an appropriate royalty. Applying this article, Mary will be obliged to grant a non-exclusive licence to exploit the patent.

---

71 Art. 26 of Law 11/1986 on Patents states that '[c]laims shall define the object for which protection is sought. They shall be clear and concise and shall be based on the description', in the same way as Art. 84 of the European Patent Convention does. The scope of the protection is defined by the claims; the description only helps to interpret the content of claims in the sense provided by Art. 60: 'The scope of protection conferred by a patent or patent application shall be determined by the content of the claims. The description and drawings shall, however, be used to interpret the claims.' See M. Vidal-Quadras Trias De Bes, *Estudio sobre los requisitos de patentabilidad, el alcance y la violación del derecho de patente* (Barcelona: 2005), p. 113. For case law, see Decision of the Provincial Court of Barcelona of 15 January 2001. Moreover, Art. 28.2 of the Royal Decree 2245/1986 of 10 October 1986, approving the implementing regulations of the Patent Law, provides that if the examiner the (Registry of Industrial Property) considers that 'there is a lack of clarity in the description or in the claims he will notify the applicant so that there is a period of two months to formulate the allegations that are considered appropriate'.

72 See also the implementation process of the Directive in the German country report.

b) Assuming that Mary's patent was granted by the European Patent Office
According to Article 64 EPC, if Mary was granted a patent through the EPC filing procedure, the operative rules would be the same. The majority of biotechnological patent applications in Spain are European.[73]

III. Metalegal Formants

In granting biotechnological patents, Spain has not modified the requirements for patentability but has avoided granting gene patents when their function is not well identified in the application.[74] The scope of compulsory licences is not limited to the cases of interdependence between plant varieties and inventions, because they are available in cases of dependency between patents.

Another possibility would be to apply to patents on genes the 'other uses' allowed by Article 31 TRIPS Agreement. The TRIPS Agreement has direct effect in Spain, as Instruction no. 2/95 of the Spanish Patent and Marks Office states, so it would be possible to prevent 'compulsory licences'[75] in order to strike a balance between promoting access to existing drugs and promoting research and development into new drugs. A compulsory licence could only be obtained if it is not possible to get a voluntary licence from the rightholder on reasonable commercial terms, but unfortunately this is not the case in Spain.

(16) UNITED KINGDOM

I. Operative Rules

Depending on the scope of Mary's patent claim, it may be possible to show infringement, which is necessary to allow Mary to claim an injunction against John. However, several defences may become available to John due to the strong importance of his product and work to the preservation of public health and the furtherance of medical research.

---

73 A.M. Lázaro Andrés, 'Patentes farmacéuticas biotecnológicas en España: un análisis del período 1990–1995, en La patente farmacéutica', *CEFI* 1996, pp. 267–281.

74 This requirement in similar to the 'utility' criterion required by the USPTO.

75 As the WIPO explains: 'the term "compulsory licensing" does not appear in the TRIPS Agreement. Instead, the phrase "other use without authorization of the rightholder" appears in the title of Article 31. Compulsory licensing is only part of this since "other use" includes use by governments for their own purposes'. See WTO, 'TRIPS and pharmaceutical patents', available at https://www.wto.org/english/tratop_e/trips_e/tripsfactsheet_pharma_2006_e.pdf.

II. *Descriptive Formants*

In order to determine whether Mary has a claim for an injunction against John, it has to be presumed that Mary has been granted a patent under UK patent law which is regulated by the Patents Act 1977 (PA 1977).

In order to be allowed to claim for an injunction under this Act, it is firstly necessary to establish that patent *infringement* has occurred. Patent infringement requires three criteria to be met: (1) it is necessary to demonstrate the types of activities that constitute infringement; (2) this activity has to fall within the scope of the patent monopoly; and (3) does the defendant have any defences available. Section 60(1)(a) states where the potential infringer 'makes, disposes of, offers to dispose of, uses or imports the product or keeps it whether for disposal or otherwise', he/she is conducting the activities that may constitute infringement. In this particular problem question, the potential infringer John uses gene BRAU-7 in conjunction with gene BLIB-5 to produce a product that will account for healing wounds. This activity is likely to fall under the type of activities that may constitute infringement, thereby satisfying the first step in demonstrating patent infringement.

The second criterion requires us to look at the scope of the patent claims and the way their language is interpreted under the current UK patent law. The scope of the claims is undoubtedly the most important step in determining whether infringement has occurred as they define the scope of the legal protection conferred, they demarcate and define the patented invention and delineate the nature, breadth and scope of the monopoly conferred to the patent holder. The courts have moved from granting a strict literal interpretation to the language of the claims (*Rodi & Wienberger AG*)[76] to allowing a purposive construction of the claim where the question is 'whether persons with practical knowledge and experience of the kind of work in which the invention was intended to be used, would understand that strict compliance with a particular … word … was intended by the patentee' (as per Lord Diplock in *Catnic*).[77] It also has to be borne in mind that the UK is signatory to the European Patent Convention (EPC), which supports the purposive approach, as stated in Article 69 EPC and the Protocol to Article 69. According to the House of Lords in *Kirin-Amgen*,[78] the literal approach is wrong, and the main question is 'what would a person skilled in the art understand the patentee to have used the language of the claim to mean?' *Actavis v. Eli Lilly*,[79] introduced a doctrine of equivalents approach via a reformulated Improver questions which seeks to find a balance between

---

[76] *Rodi&Wienberger AG v. Bamfords Ltd* [1963] RPC 61.
[77] *Catnic Components v. Hill & Smith Ltd* [1992] RPC (HL).
[78] *Kirin-Amgen v. TKT* [2004] UKHL 46.
[79] *Actavis v. Eli Lilly* [2017] UKSC 48.

fair protection for the patentee with a reasonable degree of certainty for third parties.

The main issue that arises in this problem question is whether John's use of the BRAU-7 gene in the way described in this case will amount to interference with the monopoly, i.e. the patent claim Mary holds as a patentee. In order to determine this, it is necessary to look at the similarities and differences between the composition and purpose of the products. Mary uses only BRAU-7 towards curing cardiovascular diseases. On the other hand, John uses BRAU-7 in conjunction with BLIB-5 and for an arguably different purpose – for healing wounds. Moreover, it is scientifically unclear to what extent BRAU-7 is responsible for the healing process, thereby making it difficult to determine whether this gene has a material effect on the way John's product functions. However, it can be argued that due to the fact that the purposes of the two products are different (for cardiovascular diseases and healing wounds) and the fact that John uses BLIB-5 in conjunction with BRAU-7 (a method presumably responsible for the healing effect of the product), John cannot be infringing Mary's patent.

On the other hand, by applying the *Actavis* test and presuming that BRAU-7 is of a material effect on the ointment's healing power and that the person skilled in the art thought that Mary intended the patent claim to be interpreted broadly (in the way that it covers all uses of BRAU-7 for curing medical conditions), it can be argued that John is infringing Mary's patent. Assuming that the UK courts decide to take the latter approach, infringement may be established.

It is now necessary to look at the potential *defences* that may be available to John and that may exclude him from liability for patent infringement. Section 60(5)(b) states that 'an act which would constitute an infringement of a patent for an invention shall not do so if it is done for *experimental purposes* relating to the subject-matter of the invention.' The main issue that arises in claiming this defence is what will amount to 'experimental purposes' and whether experimental use with a predominately commercial benefit will fall under this defence. In *Kline & French Laboratories Ltd v. Attorney-General*,[80] it was stated that:

> experimentation will usually have an ultimate commercial objective; where it ends, and infringement begins must often be a matter of degree. If the person concerned keeps his activities to himself and does no more than further his own knowledge or skill, even though commercial advantage may be his final goal, he does not infringe. But if he goes beyond that, and uses the invention or makes it available to others, in a way that serves to advance in the actual market place, then he infringes.[81]

Bible explains that 'In defining experimental use, the courts will hold any apparent experimental use that shows any advancement within the commercial

[80] *Kline & French Laboratories Ltd v. Attorney-General* [1989] 1 NZLR 385.

[81] Ibid.

sector to constitute an infringement.'[82] An example of where experimental use led to commercial advantage and then infringement is *Monsanto v. Stauffer Chemicals*,[83] where the experimentation put the defendant into a better position to market the product rather than purely expanding their knowledge.

Even though there have been several proposals to develop this defence further, the UK has seen a limited application of it. According to the UK Intellectual Property Office's consultation paper, 'the exception only extends to experiments which generate genuinely new information; it does not extend to experiments which are designed to verify existing knowledge.'[84] Moreover, the exception is further qualified by Aldous J in *Smith Kline French Laboratories Limited v. Evans Medical Limited*,[85] where he stated that 'the experiments had to have a real and direct connection with the subject matter of the invention and be within the claims of the patent if s.60 (5) (b) is to apply.'[86]

Therefore, bearing the above in mind, it is necessary to have several factors taken into account whilst determining whether John will be allowed to claim this defence. This defence is limited under UK law and if earning pure commercial advances in the market place through experimental use outweighs the knowledge and information contributed to the research area, this is unlikely to be exempted by way of the research exemption defence.

Whether John will be allowed to claim this defence is a matter of degree. On one hand, John has already secured a patent over the use of BRAU-7 and BLIB-5 for healing wounds, which will, undoubtedly, bring him commercial advantage in that sector and, realistically, act as a strong incentive for many inventors to innovate further. On the other hand, depending on the state of the art prior to his invention, John may be indeed contributing to the area by demonstrating a way for these two genes to be used together to make this useful and important ointment. The application of this defence in this particular problem question will depend on which approach the courts take. Nevertheless, it is important to mention that most current academics believe that it is necessary to expand the concept of this defence to cover experimental use even where commercial advantage results,[87] 'along the lines of a defence of fair dealing or fair use in

---

82 Sonya J. Bible, 'Does the Experimental-Use Defense to Patent Infringement Still Exist', available at: https://scholar.smu.edu/cgi/viewcontent.cgi?article=1113&context=scitech (last accessed 2022).

83 *Monsanto v. Stauffer Chemicals* [1985] RFC 515.

84 Patent research exception, available at: https://www.gov.uk/government/news/changes-to-the-patents-research-exceptions (last accessed 2022).

85 *Smith Kline & French Laboratories Ltd v. Evans Medical Ltd* [1989] FSR 513.

86 Ibid.

87 M. Rimmer, 'Myriad Genetics and patent law and genetic testing' [2003] *European Intellectual Property Review* 17.

copyright law',[88] because of the great importance of contributing to and furthering medical research and preserving public health. The BRCA1/2 gene is used as an example of this where 'the patents held by Myriad Genetics have the potential to hinder significant research currently underway in a number of leading genetics laboratories.'[89]

Therefore, even though there are strong arguments that John *should* be allowed to claim this defence, this will significantly depend on the extent to which his innovation contributes new information to the state of the art of that particular area and whether the courts will be able to overlook the fact that he will achieve significant commercial benefit.

The next defence that may be available to John is to *challenge the validity of Mary's patent*, i.e. to claim that the patent should not have been awarded to Mary in the first place. This defence is available under section 74(1) PA 1977, which states that 'the validity of a patent may be put in issue by way of defence in proceedings for infringement of the patent.' In order to determine whether Mary's patent can be challenged, it is necessary to look at the criteria for granting a patent. Section 1(1) PA 1977 states that a patent may be granted only for an *invention* that is *new*, involves an *inventive step*, is capable of *industrial application* and is not excluded as a *non-patentable invention.*

Genes can be considered as inventions if an industrial application can be found for them. This is regulated by Article 5(2) and 5(3) of Directive 98/44/EC on the legal protection of biotechnological inventions (Biotechnology Directive), which state:

> (2) An element isolated from the human body or otherwise produced by means of a technical process, including the sequence or partial sequence of a gene, may constitute a patentable invention, even if the structure of that element is identical to that of a natural element.
>
> (3) The industrial application of a sequence or a partial sequence of a gene must be disclosed in the patent application.

Therefore, Mary's patent cannot be challenged on these grounds, as it satisfies the invention criteria.

Secondly, the invention has to satisfy the novelty criteria. Section 2(1) PA 1977 states that 'an invention shall be taken to be new if it does not from part of the state of the art.' What amounts to 'state of the art' is defined in section 2(2) 'as all matter ... which has at any time before the priority date ... been made

[88] K. Davies and M. White, *Breakthrough: The Quest to Isolate the Gene for Hereditary Breast Cancer* (London: 1995).

[89] M. Rimmer, 'Myriad Genetics and patent law and genetic testing' [2003] *European Intellectual Property Review* 17.

available to the public … by written or oral description, by use or in any other way.' The same argument was raised in the *BRCA2* case, where the Institut Curie argued that the patent held by Myriad Genetics is invalid because it suffers from lack of novelty arising from the availability of a number of predisposition tests based on indirect methods. Moreover, they argued that where there are a variety of technology combinations that allow for 'invention' duplication that are already fairly widespread and therefore available to the 'non-lay person', they cannot possibly be out of the state of the art and therefore new. Assuming that similar research and tests for using BRAU-7 have been used as a method towards preventing cardiovascular diseases, as was the case in *BRCA2*, there may be an argument that Mary's patent fails on the novelty requirement. If this is also the decision of the court, the fact that the patent fails on only one criterion will be sufficient to revoke that patent.

Nevertheless, in case that the court decides to take a different decision, it is necessary to examine whether Mary's patent satisfies the other criteria. Section 3 PA 1977 states that 'an invention shall be taken to involve an inventive step if it is *not obvious* to a person skilled in the art'. Qualities of a person skilled in the art are defined in the *Dyson Appliances Ltd*[90] case, where it was held that that person has to have common general knowledge, be unimaginative, have no inventive capacity or ingenuity, be capable of making routine developments and be an ordinary member of the field who is aware of everything in the state of the art. Opposition to the BCRA1 gene raised this argument by stating that 'the international public consortium had already located the BRCA1 gene and had already provided considerable information regarding the gene and its relevance for the detection of breast and ovarian cancer.'[91] Moreover, they stated that:

> [the] identification of a gene like BRCA 1 and 2 is the culmination of many years of work requiring the input of activities and information from many, many different groups. And awarding the patent, in other words the full rewards to those individuals, to that group that has put that last brick in the wall, is unfair because it does not recognise the contribution of others.[92]

Therefore, whether Mary's patent could fail because it does not involve an inventive step will depend on the situation in the relevant state of the art. Applying the arguments from the *BRCA1/2* cases and assuming that, due to

---

90 *Dyson Appliances Ltd v. Hoover Ltd* [2001] RFC 47.

91 M. Rimmer, 'Myriad Genetics and patent law and genetic testing' [2003] *European Intellectual Property Review* 12.

92 CBC, 'The Impact of Gene Patents on Health Care and Medical Research: The Case of Breast Cancer Genetic Screening' (21 March 2000), available at: www.radio.cbc.ca/programs/thismorning/features.html (last accessed 2017). See also 'U.S. gene patents: Patient care stymied in Canada, hospital claims', available at https://www.cbc.ca/news/health/u-s-gene-patents-patient-care-stymied-in-canada-hospital-claims-1.2820211 (last accessed 2022).

accumulation of Mary's and other researchers' work, the use of BRAU-7 for cardiovascular diseases was obvious to a person skilled in the art, Mary cannot and should not be allowed to be the only person to commercially benefit from the patent. This argument can provide solid grounds to challenge Mary's patent and its revocation.

Finally, it is necessary to examine whether Mary's patent satisfied industrial applicability criteria. Section 4(1) PA 1977 states that 'an invention shall be taken to be capable of industrial application if it can be made or used in any kind of industry, including agriculture.' Using the *BRCA1/2* cases as an analogy once again, Institut Curie contented that the patents held by Myriad Genetics are 'insufficiently descriptive and lacking in industrial character and utility.'[93] Moreover, it can be also argued that Mary's use for the BRAU-7 patent (for cardiovascular diseases) can be seen as 'overly broad' (House of Lords in the *Biogen* case)[94] or not 'specific' enough (*Icos Corporation*).[95] Therefore, even though Mary's invention can be used in the medical industry, its patent can be challenged on grounds of the use not being specific enough, as it will account for all cardiovascular diseases. If this is the approach taken by the courts, this may also be a potential ground for challenging the validity of Mary's patent.

It has to be noted that this defence has limited use under UK IP law. John will not be able to raise this defence if Mary brings infringement proceedings against him in front of the European Patent Office because of the nine-month limitation period from the day of granting the patent during which it can be challenged. Seeing that five years have passed since Mary has received a patent for his invention, John will not be allowed to claim this defence. However, if Mary brings infringement proceedings in front of a domestic court, John can claim that the patent should not have been granted to Mary in the first place on the basis of the above arguments: that it is not new, lacks inventive step or does not have specific industrial applicability. If John is successful in demonstrating flaws to any of the above criteria, he cannot infringe, and Mary cannot claim an injunction.

The final concept that may relieve John from liability for infringement of Mary's patent is the doctrine of *compulsory licensing*. This concept is incorporated into the UK law through the Biotechnology Directive and is used in the area of plant breeding. Article 12 Biotechnology Directive states that 'where a breeder cannot acquire or exploit a plant variety right without infringing a prior patent, he may apply for a compulsory licence for non-exclusive use of the invention protected by the patent'. It is unclear to what extent compulsory licensing would

---

93 M. Rimmer, 'Myriad Genetics and patent law and genetic testing' [2003] *European Intellectual Property Review* 9.

94 *Biogen v. Medeva* [1997] RPC 1.

95 *Icos Corporation* [2002] OJEPO 293.

apply in this type of case. Nevertheless, several academics raise valid points towards a strong argument that the doctrine of compulsory licensing should be expanded in the UK to cover gene patenting where there is a strong need to preserve public health. Smith therefore argues that 'work must be done at the European level to develop a system of compulsory and *ex officio* licensing in the interest of society at large and of public health promotion'.[96] 'Moreover, a monopoly with respect to a gene-based treatment may slow the introduction of treatments into clinical practice because companies with an exclusive licence will not have the incentive to develop new technology rapidly.'[97]

Therefore, it can be argued that this doctrine should be developed further to create a legal framework as an incentive for genetic testing and research without having to endure excessive costs. Bearing in mind the useful purpose and contribution of John's product to the preservation of public health, if this doctrine is accordingly developed by the UK courts, he may and arguably should be allowed to claim this defence as a way to exclude him from liability for infringement of Mary's patent and permit further use of BRAU-7 in medical research.

In conclusion, depending on the scope of Mary's patent claim, it may be possible to show infringement, which is necessary to allow Mary to claim an injunction against John. However, as explained above, several defences may become available to John due to the strong importance of his product and work to the preservation of public health and the furtherance of medical research.

III. Metalegal Formants

The case raises a number of arguments with regard to the 'long-standing debate over whether medical diagnostics should be patentable subject-matter'.[98] The main issues that arise are the need to preserve public health through timely access to health care and encourage medical research against an equally pressing need to preserve the value of intellectual property rights and the desire to promote innovation through biotechnological patents.

This debate particularly 'crystallised with the recent controversy over Myriad Genetics relying on patents in respect of genetic testing of breast cancer'[99] and the awarding of the CCR5 patent to Human Genome Sciences, 'declared by

96 D. Smith, 'Patent Battle Looms over Cancer Gene', *The Sydney Morning Herald*, 15 March 2001.

97 M. Rimmer, 'Myriad Genetics and patent law and genetic testing' [2003] *European Intellectual Property Review* 27.

98 P. Loughlan, 'Of Patents and Patients: New Monopolies in Medical Methods' (1995) 6 *Australian Intellectual Property Journal* 5.

99 M. Rimmer, 'Myriad Genetics and patent law and genetic testing' [2003] *European Intellectual Property Review* 1.

some as an outrageous decision by the patent office.'[100] With respect to the latter, several commentators argued that allowing this patent 'created monopolies on the human genome that could impede research on AIDS and other diseases, especially the development of new therapies.'[101] Moreover, when it comes to the BRCA1/2 gene patent, a study has showed that this patent 'inhibits health care systems from choosing the most effective testing strategy.'

On the other hand, it is of utmost importance to have strong intellectual ownership in all industries, and especially so in the medical research industry, where there is strong reliance on patents to attract long-term investments.[102] Patents grant a wide monopoly to the inventors, prohibiting competitors from making, using or selling their invention without a licence, and thereby providing a reward for their hard work and acting as a strong incentive for further innovation and achievements in the field.

However, it is important to bear in mind that this research needs to be done for the public good and not against it. These two competing values are founded on the concept of preserving the public health of a society but also ensuring that sufficient commercial value is attached and awarded to the extremely useful products that result out of the hard work and effort put in by the inventors. Even though a great challenge for policy-makers and researchers, it is necessary to strike the proper balance that maximises incentives for competition and new breakthroughs in the medical research industry, but also ensuring that preservation of public health remains the primary objective throughout.

A.4. COMPARATIVE REMARKS

In most jurisdictions, Mary *has* a claim of injunction against John (Belgium, Denmark, Estonia, Lithuania, Norway, Slovenia, Spain, the UK). In other jurisdictions, Mary *only* has a claim against John *if* her interests are seriously affected (Greece). In some jurisdictions, Mary has *no* firm ground to initiate proceedings against John (France, Italy, Germany). Last but not least, in yet other jurisdictions, there is no straightforward answer: Mary *may* or *may not* have a claim of injunction (UK).

In many jurisdictions, John *may* in principle apply for a compulsory licence for reasons of dependency (Belgium, Denmark, the Netherlands, Slovenia, Spain, in principle Germany). However, in practice John will *not* always be able to acquire a compulsory licence for dependency as the conditions for

100 T. Hollon, 'Gene patent revisions to remove some controversies' (2000) 6 *Nature Medicine* 362–363, available at https://doi.org/10.1038/74591 (last accessed 2022).
101 Ibid.
102 N. Sharpe and R. Carter, 'Genetic Testing' [2006] *Wiley-Interscience* 338.

being awarded such a licence are pretty stringent (the dependent invention must represent an 'important technical step/advance of major/considerable economic importance' – Belgium, Denmark, the Netherlands, Germany; 'a technically advanced invention significant for the national economy' – Estonia; the invention must be of 'public interest' *and* represent 'a technical advance of considerable economic significance' – Slovenia).

In some jurisdictions, under the current state of legislation and case law, John *cannot* apply for a compulsory licence for reasons of dependency (UK). In some jurisdictions John *may* in principle also apply for a compulsory licence for reasons of public interest (Czech Republic, Denmark, Lithuania). However, in practice John will *not* always be able to acquire a compulsory licence for public interest in practice as the threshold to acquire such a licence is very high (licence can only be granted if an 'important' public health issue is at stake – Czech Republic, Denmark). In other jurisdictions, John *may* in principle also apply for a compulsory licence for public health (Belgium, Denmark).

The reports reveal three types of national regimes as to the scope of the patent. First, *absolute* patent protection is granted for human genes in Belgium, Denmark, Germany, Lithuania, the Netherlands, Norway and Spain. Second, *purpose-bound* protection for human genes is granted in France and Italy. Some jurisdictions require the function to be explicitly indicated in the patent *claims* (Germany, Italy). In such cases, the scope depends on how the claims were formulated. If Mary's patent included the cardiovascular system as a function of the gene in a claim, then John's patent would not infringe. If, however, Mary's patent did not mention cardiovascular diseases in the claims, but only as potential therapies somewhere in the description, then John's patent would infringe. Mary may only prohibit the production of the substance for the use *claimed* or its equivalent, but may not stop the use of the BRAU-7 gene for a purpose other than the one claimed in her patent, and may thus not stop John from producing his ointment, as John's patent does not infringe Mary's patent. Other jurisdictions restrict the scope of the patent to the purpose described in the patent *specification*, independent of the formulation of the claim (France). Providing a more restrictive protection than the one foreseen in Article 9 Biotechnology Directive seems to go against the harmonisation objective of the Directive. Can a patent holder in a country applying a purpose-bound patent regime turn to a court to demand the setting aside of the restricting clause and claim infringement? In other words, can Mary demand the abolition of the purpose-bound protection approach?

Third, departing from these models, some countries (e.g. Poland) have introduced a *hybrid* regime (Poland). In those jurisdictions, applicants are free to claim a certain function in their patent claims. If an inventor chooses *not* to refer to the specific function in the patent claims, but just mention it in the patent specification, then the inventor will be awarded *absolute* patent protection. Thus, if Mary did not mention any specific function in her patent claims, she will have absolute patent protection and, hence, a right of injunction against John. If, on the other hand, an inventor chooses to take up the specific function in the patent claims, a purpose-bound and *restricted* scope will apply. Had Mary included the specific function of her gene in the claims, John's invention would be considered as having a distinct purpose and not dependent, and Mary will not have an injunction against John.

However, legal uncertainty seems to prevail in some other countries. Depending on the interpretation method applied in court, the outcome of the case may well be different (UK). If the courts interpret Mary's claim *narrowly*, they may take the view that the purpose of the two products is different (cardiovascular diseases and healing wounds), thus John is not infringing Mary's patent and Mary has no claim for injunction. If, on the other hand, the courts apply a *broad* interpretation and argue that Mary's claim covers all uses of BRAU-7 for curing medical conditions, then John is infringing and Mary has an injunction against John.

As to overlapping sequences, Italy and Spain explicitly inserted Recital 25 into their legislation and stipulate that when gene sequences partially overlap, each sequence will be considered independent if they overlap in parts which are *not* essential. Greece did not insert the recital into its legislation, but has nevertheless taken it to heart. It is agreed that when the interests of a first inventor are not seriously affected by the later invention, it is likely that a claim by the first inventor for payment of remuneration will be considered to be abusive (Greece).

Various jurisdictions would award John a compulsory licence, but only based on a public interest ('important public interest' – Czech Republic; public interest – the Netherlands; or public health – Belgium, France).

Based on dependency, John could *in principle* apply for a compulsory licence in Belgium, Denmark, Estonia, Greece, Slovenia, Spain and Germany. But quite often the requirements for such a compulsory licence for dependency are very strict. Quite often the dependent invention needs to demonstrate 'an important technical step of major economic importance' (Belgium, Denmark), 'technical significance' for the national economy (Estonia), or 'significant progress' (Greece). In some jurisdictions, the threshold for the grant of a compulsory licence is even higher. On top of representing a technical advance of considerable economic significance, the dependent invention needs to contribute to the public interest, particularly in relation to national security, nutrition, health care or the development of other important sectors of the national economy (Slovenia). It is interesting to note that most jurisdictions distinguish between the 'older' or 'dominant' patent versus the 'later' or 'subordinate' patent (e.g. Belgium), whereas some jurisdictions are not interested in qualifying the exact nature of the interaction between two dependent patents; the fact that the exploitation of one patent is not possible without affecting the rights of another patent suffices (Greece). As it is doubtful whether John would be able to live up to these high expectations, it is rather unlikely that John would be awarded a compulsory licence *in practice*. In some jurisdictions (UK), a compulsory licence for dependency does not seem to be available, and compulsory licensing may not relieve John from liability for infringements of Mary's patent. In some jurisdictions, a system of cross-licences applies in the case of compulsory licensing: the first and dominant patent holder is entitled to a cross-licence from the second and dependent inventor (the Netherlands, Slovenia). So, assuming John would be granted a compulsory licence, Mary would also have the right to use John's patent.

Some jurisdictions have introduced a compulsory licence for *important* public interest (Czech Republic, Denmark). Public interest may include the health of the people, and may be granted in the case of an epidemic, or in a time of war where the necessity of healing wounds dramatically increases. As no important interest can be clearly demonstrated, it seems highly unlikely that John will get a compulsory licence (Czech Republic, Denmark). Only few jurisdictions have introduced specific compulsory licence to deal with situations of hold-up in the medical area and to safeguard access to patented subject matter that is vital for *public health* (Belgium, France).

As to metalegal formants, two different issues govern the set-up of jurisdictions. The first, more *general* level is the national take on *patent allocation theories*: How should patent rights be allocated between first inventors and (dependent) follow-on innovators? Some patent regimes give great weight to the first inventor, to the extent that the first inventor is entitled to block any follow-on innovator from marketing his/her improved invention. Such an approach is today taken by the UK. Other patent regimes are inclined to share the benefits of innovation between the first inventor and the follow-on innovators. This is realised via the concept of compulsory licences for dependency. This approach is taken in the majority of jurisdictions in Europe. However, even though those countries seem more inclined to celebrate the contribution of follow-on innovators to innovation, the effect of their intervention is minimised a great deal in practice, as various stringent conditions apply to be awarded a compulsory licence for dependency.

The second metalegal approach is the lens of *social contract theory*. Two distinct phenomena emerge in the field of human genetics. A first phenomenon relates to the nature of patent claims on genes. Claims on genes are generally difficult, if not impossible, to 'invent around'. Problems arise when such gene patents are licensed too restrictively, as this could lead to barriers to future research and development, restricted clinical access and decreased availability of high-quality tests for patients. A second phenomenon relates to the dense and fragmented genetic patent landscape. Problems arise when 'patent thickets' emerge, leading to royalty stacking and resulting in a 'tragedy of the anti-commons', equally affecting further research and development, and harming clinical and patient access in the long run. As yet, empirical data do not confirm the existence of a dense patent thicket in genetics at large, but it is possible that thicket problems in genetic diagnostics are increasing with the turn from monogenetic testing to multifactorial testing (multiplex diagnostics) and the shift towards diagnostics based on genome-wide association studies driven by the high throughput of Single Nucleotide Polymorphism (SNP) platforms and next-generation sequencing possibilities. In itself, the present case is not an illustrative example of this phenomenon, but the case may well invigorate concerns about the potential negative effects of a dispersed patent landscape.

The current patent system is premised on an implicit 'social contract' as it aims at balancing private and public interests. The solutions put forward in the various jurisdictions wish to echo social contract theory and set forth remedies that preserve the current function of the patent system, serving as a (positive) incentive for the production of drugs and therapies that are important in health care, and remedying some of its perceived (hindering) effects in the field of genetic diagnostics. The majority of countries award a strong, wide (absolute) protection in the area of human genetics, the policy argument being that strong protection provides for strong incentives to innovate. Remarkably, however, the same countries often provide legal measures to attenuate the potential blocking effects of strong patents and introduce legal instruments to assist in tackling restrictive licensing practices, such as compulsory licences in the public interest (the Netherlands) or for public health (Belgium, France and Switzerland). Even though none of these new compulsory licence mechanisms have been put to work as yet, they may have an indirect, preventive effect on possible unduly restrictive licensing behaviour by patent owners. A minority of countries have opted for weak, narrow (purpose-bound) protection in the field of human genetics. Interestingly, those countries have not coupled their regime with legal instruments to redress restrictive licensing behaviour. None of the countries, however, have gone so far as to consider transforming the property right granted by patents (including right 'to exclude') into a liability rule (including the right to take now and pay later), even though this already has been suggested a long time ago to ease the effect of the patent system in upstream research.

CASE 3. CULTURE – THIRD PARTY ACCESS (MODELLED ON P2P FILE-SHARING)

A.1. BASE CASE

Carla, a 15-year-old teenager, downloads and uploads songs from the Internet and exchanges CDs with her girlfriend Karen. She is now sued by the record company 'String'.[1]

Will an injunction be granted?

A.2. EDITORIAL NOTE

This case analyses the national provisions implementing Article 5(2)(b) of Directive 2001/29/EC on Copyright and Related Rights in the Information Society. This provision in the Directive is not only optional, but its wording also left member states some latitude to decide on how to implement it. This explains the variations in the member states' implementing legislation.

As the application of copyright rules is always very fact-specific, the simple wording of this question proved to be ambiguous for most country reporters. The question was formulated with the aim of giving respondents greater leeway to describe their national law and how it would apply to this general factual situation. Here, Carla downloads from the Internet, but the case is silent both on the technology she uses and on the source of her download. If Carla downloads songs from the Internet by using peer-to-peer file-sharing software, it is not unreasonable to argue that most file-sharing software nowadays involves not only an act of downloading but also an act of uploading. The source of Carla's download may be legal or illegal. The case also does not specify whether the exchanged CDs are the result of the reproduction of the downloaded songs or if they were lawfully acquired from another (analogue) source. All these technical features matter and are likely to influence the outcome of the case. The answers to the question vary as country reporters have given their own interpretation of the facts and of the applicable law.

---

1 It is a fair assumption to make that the record company 'String' has acquired all the rights from the authors and performers on the songs that it produces or distributes. As such, 'String' is actively legitimated to act against the alleged violators of the rights of which it is the holder.

A.3. COUNTRY REPORTS

(1) BELGIUM

I. *Operative Rules*

Merely downloading songs would fall under the home copy exception. However, exchanging the CDs with a friend would go beyond the scope of this exception. Therefore, an injunction would probably be granted.

II. *Descriptive Formants*

- Article 5(2)(b) Directive 2001/29/EC;[2]
- Articles 22§1 5° BCA (Art. XI.190 9° BCEL) and 46§4 BCA (Art. XI.217 7° BCEL).

Articles 22§1 5° and 46§4 (for the neighbouring rights) BCA (Arts. XI.190 9° and XI.217 7° BCEL) provide a home copy exception. A substantial part of Belgian legal doctrine argues that this exception also applies when the content was illegally distributed or illegally placed on the Internet. Article 22§1 BCA (Art. XI.190 BCEL) only requires that the content was legitimately made public prior to the downloading.[3] This means that Carla is safe when she downloads.

In order to fall under the exception of Article 22§1 5° BCA (Art. XI.190 9° BCEL), the home copy has to be made in the family circle and has to be destined only for this family circle.[4] If Carla were to download songs in order to distribute them among her classmates, she would probably not fall under these conditions, since such behaviour would go beyond the scope of the family circle. The same

---

2 Directive 2001/29/EC of the European Parliament and of the Council of 22 May 2001 on the harmonisation of certain aspects of copyright and related rights in the information society, OJ L 167, 22 June 2001, 10–19.

3 F. de Visscher and B. Michaux, *Précis du droit d'auteur et des droits voisins [Manual Copyright and Neighbouring Rights]* (Brussels: 2000), 114–115; J. Deene and K. Van der Perre, 'Nieuwe Auteurswet – Belang voor de digitale wereld' [A New Copyright Law – Importance for the Digital World], *NjW* 2005, no. 119, 872; M.-C. Janssens, 'De uitzonderingen op het auteursrecht anno 2005 – Een eerste analyse' [The Exceptions on Copyright anno 2005 – A First Analysis], *A&M* 2005, no. 6, 489–490 and 498–499, M.-C. Janssens, 'Art. 22', in: F. Brison and H. Vanhees (eds.), *Huldeboek aan Jan Corbet. De Belgische Auteurswet. Artikelsgewijze Commentaar [Homage to Jan Corbet. The Belgian Copyright Act. Commentaries per article]* (Brussels: 2006), 121. *A contrario* A. Berenboom, *Le nouveau droit d'auteur et les droits voisins [The New Copyright and the Neighbouring Rights]*, collection Création Information Communication [Creation Information Communication] (Brussels: 2005), 313.

4 M.-C. Janssens, 'Art. 22', in: F. Brison and H. Vanhees (eds.), *Huldeboek aan Jan Corbet. De Belgische Auteurswet. Artikelsgewijze Commentaar [Homage to Jan Corbet. The Belgian Copyright Act. Commentaries per article]* (Brussels: 2006), 132–133.

reasoning applies for the situation in the present case where Carla exchanges a CD with a friend.

It is not entirely clear yet what role the three-step test[5] can play in this situation. Can it be applied by the courts as well or is this an exclusive right of the legislator? The majority of the doctrine argues that the courts can apply the test with regard to the 'normal exploitation of the work' and the 'no unreasonable prejudice to the legitimate interests of the rightholder' aspects of it. In other words, if the home copy exception were to prove to have serious effects on the author's interests, the three-step test could limit its application.[6]

III. Metalegal Formants

Before the Internet era the financial loss resulting from home copying was minimal. In addition, controlling copying was difficult, hence a home copy exception was introduced. With the advent of the digital era, the economic impact of home copies did not stop growing and the balance in copyright between the interest of the rightholder and that of the consumer, as expressed in the home copy exception, was thoroughly disturbed.[7] Especially with the advent of the modern Internet and its peer-to-peer networks, the normal exploitation of works is at risk. Since copyright, like any IP right, is constantly searching for a balance between various interests, this evolution could mean that the exception must be re-evaluated.[8] With the Copyright Directive 2001/29/EC and its subsequent implementation, a step has been made to restore the balance.

When implementing Directive 2001/29/EC in 2005, the Belgian legislator did not opt to introduce an extra condition for the home copy exception (although amendments have been proposed).[9] Because of this, Internet users can probably not be prosecuted or held liable when they merely download content.

---

5 As expressed in Art. 5(5) Directive 2001/29/EC.

6 M.-C. Janssens, 'Art. 22', in: F. Brison and H. Vanhees (eds.), *Huldeboek aan Jan Corbet. De Belgische Auteurswet. Artikelsgewijze Commentaar [Homage to Jan Corbet. The Belgian Copyright Act. Commentaries per article]* (Brussels: 2006), 122.

7 However, some famous verdicts against Napster and others proved the music industry was regaining some terrain: C. De Keersmaeker, 'Muziek op het internet: Auteurs- en naburige rechten op het spel? Ontwikkelingen sinds begin 2001' [Music on the Internet: Copyright and Neighbouring Rights at Stake? Developments since the beginning of 2001], *A&M* 2003, no. 3, 186–197.

8 S. Dusollier, *Droit d'auteur et protection des œuvres dans l'univers numérique. Droits et exceptions à la lumière des dispositifs de verrouillage des œuvres [Copyright and the Protection of Works in the Digital Age. Rights and Exceptions in the Light of Technical Protection Measures]*, in collection Création Information Communication [Creation Information Communication] (Brussels: 2005), 463–476.

9 Report, Bill on the implementation of Directive 2001/29/EC, *Parl. Doc.*, Chambre, 2003–2004, DOC 51 1137/013, 25–29 [Verslag Wetsontwerp houdende de omzetting in Belgisch recht

What if Carla was uploading and sharing the songs?
Even though downloading is probably allowed under Belgian law, it is beyond doubt that unauthorised uploading and sharing is not. Belgian case law already confirmed in 1996 that such actions would constitute a communication to the public, which is an exclusive right of the rightholder.[10] The financial consequences of uploading might be severe, as was illustrated when an 'uploader' was sentenced to pay compensatory damages amounting to €1.25 per estimated download of the files he had shared, resulting in damages of more than €100,000 in total.[11]

(2) CZECH REPUBLIC

I. *Operative Rules*

An injunction will be granted only with respect to the sharing of CDs.

II. *Descriptive Formants*

Downloading songs from the Internet is not at present recognised by legal practice as illegal conduct and is usually classified as use of work according to section 30(1) and (2) Copyright Act. Such use is deemed to be free use (or, in common law terminology, *fair use*).[12] However, it is doubtful if such use is in accordance with the three-step test that should be applied to justify free use. The three-step test (section 29 Copyright Act) states that exceptions to and restrictions of the copyright are to be applied only in special cases (provided for by the Copyright Act), if use is consistent with the normal exploitation (of the work) and if legitimate interests of the author are not unreasonably affected. To download work from the Internet is most probably 'normal exploitation of the work' and can be considered to not unreasonably affect the legitimate interests

van de Europese richtlijn 2001/29/EG van 22 mei 2001 betreffende de harmonisatie van bepaalde aspecten van het auteursrecht en de naburige rechten in de informatiemaatschappij, *Parl. St.*, Kamer, 2003–2004, DOC 51 1137/013, 25–29]. In fact, during parliamentary debates no discussion on the matter was held. As we have seen above, this 'freedom to download' reflects the majority opinion in legal doctrine.

10 Recital 25 Directive 2001/29/EC; J. Deene and K. Van der Perre, 'Nieuwe Auteurswet – Belang voor de digitale wereld' [A New Copyright Law – Importance for the Digital World], *NjW* 2005, no. 119, 868–869; Pres. Court Brussels [Voorz. Rb. Brussel], 16 October 1996, *A&M* 1996, 426.

11 Correctional Court Brussels [Corr. Rb. Brussel], 55th Chamber, 25 October 2004, *A&M* 2005, no. 2, 136; *De Juristenkrant* 2005 (note D. Deneuter, T. Verbiest.), no. 105, 13; *NjW* 2004, no. 89, 1246, note J. Deene.

12 See further www.ifpi.cz (last accessed 5 May 2019).

of the author. We believe that under current law downloading songs falls under section 13 Copyright Act. An injunction will not be granted in this case.

Carla is exchanging songs downloaded from the Internet with her friend Karen. This conduct, according to section 14(1) Copyright Act, clearly constitutes distribution of the work. Distribution of work means distributing a work in tangible form by transferring property, irrespective of whether such transfer is made with or without consideration. The distribution is in tangible form because the songs are burned on CD and Carla is transferring property to Karen. An injunction will be granted in this case under the conditions of sections 40 and 41 Copyright Act.

III. Metalegal Formants

Answer omitted.

(3) DENMARK

I. Operative Rules

(a) For the 'exchange' (which is taken to include any private 'lending'/'borrowing'/ 'selling'/'buying') of CDs: no. (b) For the downloading: only if the songs are uploaded illegally. (c) For the uploading: yes, an injunction will be granted.

II. Descriptive Formants

a) The exchange

Provided that the CDs are lawfully made, the exchange of the CDs will not infringe copyright. The exchange of CDs as such is not considered as an act of distribution covered by the DCA, as long as the receiver is Carla's girlfriend (not 'the public'). Therefore, 'String' will not be granted an injunction on the grounds of the exchange alone.

Even if the exchange (not renting) had involved the public, 'String' would not have been able to control it because of the rule of exhaustion of rights ('first sale') in DCA §19.

b) The downloading

Downloading is an act of reproduction to which the rightholder has exclusive rights according to the DCA. However, the exclusive right to reproduction does not cover copying for *personal use*, cf. DCA §12, provided that the conditions laid down in the provision are fulfilled. As the download is supposedly for Carla's own personal use, it will be covered by §12. The application of this rule also presupposes that the copy is made on the basis of a legal version (DCA §11(3)).

This means that if the material Carla downloads is uploaded or in another way made available (e.g. by way of streaming) on the Internet without the permission of the author, her download infringes 'String's' rights in the recording. Penal or civil liability is dependent on Carla's knowing or awareness of the probability that the recordings were illegally uploaded or made available, cf. DCA §§76 and 83.

c) The uploading

Uploading is considered to be both an act of reproduction and (as the site to which the songs are uploaded is supposed to have general access) an act of making the songs available to the public. To such a use no limitation applies. An injunction will therefore be granted for the uploading.

III. Metalegal Formants

Balancing the interests of rightholders in controlling the use of the protected subject matter against the users' interests in free access and use has proven to be a difficult task. The difficulties have been both of a practical nature – stopping infringing actions – and of a political nature – justifying user restrictions on use of protected material on the Internet. The present rules make a distinction between songs which have been made available on physical media and songs which have been acquired online. This distinction makes sense from a practical perspective, but it has made the copyright rules rather complicated and in certain respects also leads to legal positions which can be hard to justify (e.g. the non-applicability of the exhaustion rule to CDs which are the result of legal downloading).

(4) ESTONIA

I. Operative Rules

- Downloading – presumably punished as a misdemeanour, civil remedies presumably available;
- Uploading – punished as a crime, civil remedies available;
- Permanent exchange of original CDs – allowed, no remedy available;
- Temporary exchange of original CDs without commercial purpose – not allowed, punishable as a misdemeanour, civil remedies available.

II. Descriptive Formants

Pursuant to §11(1) Copyright Act the content of copyright is constituted by moral and economic rights. The catalogue of the economic rights of an author includes *inter alia* the right of reproduction of the work and the right of making the work available to the public (§13(1) clauses 1 and 9[1] Copyright Act). Subsection 13(1) clause 1 Copyright Act defines reproduction as 'the making one or several temporary or permanent copies of the work or a part thereof directly or indirectly in any form or by any means'. The right of making the work available to the public is explained as follows: 'making the work available to the public in such a way that persons may access the work from a place and at a time individually chosen by them'. H. Pisuke characterises the right of making the work available to the public as an Internet environment right which was included in the Copyright Act as a requirement of Directive 2001/29/EC.[13] Performers and producers of phonograms are entitled to the same rights (§67(2) clauses 3[1] and 5; §70(1) clauses 1 and 5 Copyright Act).

Based on the above-mentioned provisions of the Copyright Act, it can be concluded that downloading could violate the right of reproduction. Uploading could violate the right of reproduction as well as the right of making the work available to the public.

At the same time, it is important to bear in mind that there is an exemption for private copying in the Copyright Act: '[a] lawfully published work may be reproduced and translated by a natural person for the purposes of personal use without the authorisation of its author and without payment of remuneration on the condition that such activities are not carried out for commercial purposes' (§18(1) Copyright Act). The right of reproduction of a performer and a phonogram producer are limited in the same way.[14] The question remains whether a person is allowed to make a private copy from an illegal reproduction of a work. It has been argued by the Estonian copyright experts that due to the requirements of three-step test, the private use exemption is not applicable to illegal copies of a work.[15] According to the three-step test (§17 Copyright Act), a user is permitted to use a work without the authorisation of its author and without payment of remuneration only in the cases explicitly prescribed in the Copyright Act, provided that this does not conflict with normal exploitation of the work and does not unreasonably prejudice the legitimate interests of the author. In conclusion, it can be said that downloading remains a controversial issue, since the Copyright Act does not provide explicitly that the private use exemption is not applicable to illegal copies.

---

13 H. Pisuke, *Autoriõiguse alused* (Copyright Basics) (Tallinn: 2006), p. 41.

14 Pursuant to §75(1) clause 1, without the authorisation of a performer, producer of phonograms, and without payment of remuneration, it is permitted to use the performance, phonogram, including by reproduction for private use by natural persons, taking account of the provisions of §§26 and 27 of the Copyright Act and on the condition that such reproduction is not carried out for commercial purposes.

15 E. Vasamäe, 'Fonogrammitootja reprodutseerimisõigus ja infoühiskonna mõju sellele' (Right of Reproduction for a Producer of Phonograms, and the Impact of the Information Society Thereon), (2006) 10 *Juridica*, p. 683, pp. 688–689.

As regards uploading, it is important to consider whether it is done on password protected websites or a website which is open to the public. In this case, it is assumed that uploaded songs are available to the general public. This kind of uploading infringes the right of reproduction and right of making the work available to the public.

The rightholder ('String') has several options for how to react. Pursuant to §33 of the Penal Code, '[a] person is capable of guilt if at the time of commission of the act he or she is mentally capable and at least 14 years of age'. According to §3(2) Penal Code, offences are divided into two categories: criminal offences and misdemeanours. If we accept that downloading from an illegal source is not allowed under the private use exemption (currently this is not the general opinion) and that it violates the right of reproduction, then it could be considered to be a misdemeanour. According to §81^{4}(1) Copyright Act, violation of the economic rights is punishable by a fine of up to 300 fine units.[16]

Uploading is deemed to be a criminal offence. Pursuant to §222(1) Penal Code, '[r]eproduction, with the intention of distribution, of a work or an object of copyright without the permission of the author of the work, the holder of the copyright or the holder of the related rights is punishable by a pecuniary punishment or up to 3 years' imprisonment'.

The record company 'String' can also use civil remedies to address the issue of uploading and downloading. Subsection 81^{7}(1) Copyright Act provides that in the case of the unlawful use of a work or an object of related rights, the author or holder of related rights may, *inter alia*, claim compensation for damages, termination of the unlawful use of a work or an object of related rights, and delivery of that which was received by way of the unlawful use of a work or an object of related rights. These claims are made pursuant to the Law of Obligations Act. At the same time, it is necessary to bear in mind that Carla is 15 years old. Subsection 1053(2) of the Law Obligations Act provides:

> The parents or curator of a person of 14 to 18 years of age shall also be liable for damage unlawfully caused to another person by the person of 14 to 18 years of age regardless of the culpability of the parents or curator, unless they prove that they have done everything which could be reasonably expected in order to prevent the damage.

The exchange of CDs can be understood in two different ways. Firstly, the exchange of CDs means that the CDs are exchanged permanently (e.g. Carla gives one CD and receives another in return). Nothing in the description of the case indicates that the exchanged CDs are pirated copies.[17] It is assumed that

[16] Pursuant to §47(1) of the Penal Code, a fine unit is equal to 60 Estonian kroons.

[17] The Copyright Act defines 'pirated copy' as 'a copy, in any form and whether or not with a corresponding packaging, of a work or object of related rights which has been reproduced in any country without the authorisation of the author of the work, holder of copyright or holder of related rights' – §80^{1}(1) Copyright Act.

the CDs are originals sold by the authorised person. Subsection 13(1) clause 2 Copyright Act provides the following principle:

> The first sale or transfer in some other manner of the right of ownership of a copy of a work by the author or with his or her consent in a Member State of the EU or a state which is a contracting party of EEA Agreement shall exhaust the right specified in this clause and copies of the work may be further distributed in the Member States of the EU or the states which are contracting parties of EEA agreement without the consent of the author.

Consequently, due to the principle of exhaustion of rights, the exchange of CDs is legally allowed.

Secondly, the exchange of CDs could also mean that the CDs are temporarily exchanged. In order to decide whether that kind of practice is legally allowed, it is necessary to consider the following provisions. Subsection 13(1) Copyright Act provides: '[a]n author shall enjoy the exclusive right to use the author's work in any manner, to authorise or prohibit the use of the work in a similar manner by other persons'. It can be concluded from the provision that an author can use the work him/herself and authorise the use of the work by others. Additionally, pursuant to §17 Copyright Act, limitations on an author's rights must be directly prescribed in the Copyright Act. The Copyright Act does not have provisions which *expressis verbis* allow the exchange of CDs. The exchange of CDs could be regarded as violation of the economic rights, which is punishable by a fine of up to 300 fine units (§814(1) Copyright Act).

III. Metalegal Formants

The Internet has posed challenges to all copyright regulations around the world. Estonia is no exception. Although Estonia has harmonised its Copyright Act with all relevant EU Directives, there are many issues which have to be addressed. Due to a lack of established case law, the scope of several provisions remains unclear. For instance, pursuant to §18(1) Copyright Act, '[a] lawfully published work may be reproduced and translated by a natural person for the purposes of personal use without the authorisation of its author and without payment of remuneration on the condition that such activities are not carried out for commercial purposes'. This provision, however, does not say whether the private use exception also applies to a copy which was made from an illegal source (e.g. downloaded from the Internet). At present, there is an initiative to develop a new copyright act for Estonia. Some aspects will hopefully be clarified.

(5) FRANCE

I. Operative Rules

Unless Carla knows that the source of the downloads is illicit, the private use exception applies. In this case, an injunction will not be granted.

II. Descriptive Formants

When an Internet user connects to a file-sharing site, he/she is violating copyright on two counts. Any complete or partial performance or reproduction made without the consent of the author or of his/her successors in title or assignees is unlawful (Arts. L. 122-4 – right of the author – and L. 335-3 – right of the producer – of the French Intellectual Property Code). First, he/she copies the downloaded songs onto his/her hard drive. According to the French Intellectual Property Code, reproduction consists in the recording of a work by any process permitting it to be communicated to the public in an indirect way (Arts. L. 122-3 and L. 213-1). Secondly, he/she communicates the downloaded songs, because he/she makes the songs on his/her computer available to other users. Now, according to the French Intellectual Property Code, performance consists in the communication of the work to the public by any process (Arts. L. 122-2 and L. 213-1). It is therefore necessary to differentiate between downloading and uploading.

Carla downloads songs from the Internet. She does not upload. Therefore, she reproduces without the consent of the author.

However, private use is tolerated. Once a work has been disclosed, the author may not prohibit copies or reproductions reserved strictly for private use and not intended for collective use, with the exception of copies of works of art to be used for purposes identical to those for which the original work was created and copies of software other than backup copies (Arts. L. 122-5 2° and L. 211-3 2° of the French Intellectual Property Code). This exception is limited to personal or family use and excludes any use by third parties.[18] Private use must benefit a limited group of persons united by family ties or friendship.[19]

---

18 For loan of copies to third parties, see Court of Cassation (criminal section), 4 January 1991, JurisData n°1991-003606.

19 See Paris Court of Appeal (4th chamber A.), 4 April 2007, C.C.E. 2007, commentaire n°68, note Ch. Caron; Propr. intell. 2007, p. 320 ff., obs. A. Lucas; R.T.D.Com. 2007, p. 357 ff., obs. F. Pollaud-Dulian; R.L.D.I. 2007, n°29, p. 10 ff., obs. N. Craipeau; Montpellier Court of Appeal (3rd correctional chamber), 10 March 2005, J.C.P. G. 2005, II, 10078, note Ch. Caron, Propr. intell. 2005, n°15, p. 165, obs. P. Sirinelli. Contra, Aix-en-Provence Court of Appeal, 5 September 2007, Gaz. Pal., 20 January 2008, p. 34 ff., note L. Tellier-Loniewski and F. Revel de Lambert; R.L.D.I. 2007, n°31, p. 10 ff., obs. L. Thoumyre.

Carla downloads songs from the Internet and exchanges CDs with her girlfriend Karen. The private use exception applies because the downloading is reserved for personal use. Consequently, an injunction would not be granted on the grounds of a violation of the copyright. However, it should be noted that some French jurisdictions exclude this exception when the user knows that the source of the copy is illicit.[20]

III. Metalegal Formants

Answer omitted.

(6) GERMANY

I. Operative Rules

'String' has no claim against Carla.

II. Descriptive Formants

Injunctions against Carla are to be considered under §§16, 17, 19a UrhG (rights of the author) and §85 UrhG (rights of the producer (of CDs)). The downloading and uploading in principle could violate the copyright. However, private use copies are exempt from the scope of the right (§53 UrhG) as long as the copied work was not an 'evident illegal reproduction'. And, as a matter of logic, the private use exemption can only apply to 'downloading'. The original Napster constellation (P2P file-sharing) is technically characterised by the fact that (infringing) 'uploading' is *not* necessary. This constellation provoked the debate arguing that the Napster communication was 'non-public'. In 2003, the German legislator clarified that 'public communication' always requires consent (§§52 sec. 3, 19a UrhG), irrespective of *how* the work was made available: actively uploading or passively making available. Here, Carla does not download as a member of a Napster-type group. She 'downloads' (without making her files simultaneously available). Her use is merely private. The mere 'exchange of a CD' does not violate any copyright.

---

[20] See Versailles Court of Appeal, 16 March 2007, JurisData n°2007-331563, C.C.E. 2007, commentaire n°91, note Ch. Caron, R.T.D.Com. 2007, p. 548, obs. F. Pollaud-Dulian; Court of Cassation (criminal section), 30 May 2006, JurisData n°2006-033837, J.C.P. G. 2006, II, 10124, note Ch. Caron, J.C.P. E. 2007, 1114, n°9, obs. M.-E. Laporte-Legeais, D. 2006, p. 2997, obs. P. Sirinelli, D. 2006, p. 2676, note E. Dreyer. Contra, A. Singh and T. Debiesse, 'Réseaux P2P: pertinence et définition de la source licite', 18 R.L.D.I. 2006, n°554, p. 75 ff.; A. Lucas, note under Court of Bayonne on 15 November 2005, Propr. intell. 2006, n°19, p. 178 ff.

III. Metalegal Formants

The Internet has disrupted the traditional public (commercial)-private use distinction which had evolved as demarcation line between property rights (uses are to be authorised) and free access (*freier Werkgenuss*). The system was built on the idea of an indirect system of end user payment.[21] On the one hand, digital copying has become easy and ubiquitous. On the other hand, digital rights management (DRM) seemingly remedies former market failures in respect of legitimate protection of property rights. Legislators reacted. In transposing the InfoSoc Directive, the German *Bundestag* opted for a technical solution, hence the broad extension of private claims in the Internet in the first place. In respect of competing interests (users' rights and cultural values), it did not vote for broad exemptions, but for a value-loaded formulation ('evidently illegal reproduction'). All communities agree that this solution was an intermediate step.

(7) GREECE

I. Operative Rules

According to the prevailing view, 'String' has the right to claim for an injunction both for uploading and downloading. Yet there is no case law on this matter.

II. Descriptive Formants

The case based on copyright has to be decided between reproduction for private use or infringement of economic rights (reproduction, communication to the public).

Greece was one of the first countries to implement the European Directive 2001/29/EC (InfoSoc Directive). Greece has also ratified the WIPO Internet Treaties. According to them, any author's work protected under copyright constitutes subject matter of protection irrespective of whether it is in an analogue or digital environment. The same is true if the subject matter is protected under neighbouring rights or by the *sui generis* right on databases.

In file-sharing three different acts have to be distinguished: (1) mediating between uploader and downloader, i.e. the profitable offering of the copy to other users of the file-sharing network constitutes an act of making available; (2) uploading a CD or other subject matter on a computer constitutes an act of

[21] 'Stufensystem der mittelbaren Erfassung': BVerfGE 31, 267 – *private Tonträger*.

gratis reproduction because the file must be copied; (3) downloading by other users constitutes an act of reproduction that may prevent the normal exploitation of the song.

The illegality of the first act is clear, since it constitutes a form of exploitation of the song. See Modification 1.

The illegality of the second act is not equally clear. *Gratis* uploading is not, of course, a sort of exploitation of the IP right on the song; nevertheless it harms the exclusive right of the owner to make the song available to the public, since no one has any reason to buy a CD of the song after the song is uploaded in the Internet. The notion of the 'public' typically excludes family members and close personal friends. The millions of simultaneous users of peer-to-peer networks who do not know each other constitute the 'public' under copyright law.

The illegality of the third act is even more dubious. According to the prevailing view, downloading is covered by the exclusive right of reproduction. Greek law on copyright provides explicitly for the right of reproduction and the right of making available to the public (Arts. 3 para. 1 a and h, 46 para. 2 h, 47 paras. l d and 2 d, 48 para. 1 g Law 2121/1993 as amended by Art. 81 Law 30S7/2002). Article 28C of Law 2121/1993 concerns temporary acts of reproduction and contains a clause of general application (three-step test). According to this view, an injunction should be granted on the grounds of the above-mentioned provisions. There is no case law.

However, the opposite view seems more correct. In Article 18 Law 2121/1993, that is, in the case of 'private use', Law 2121/1993 expressly introduces as an exception the power of the creator to permit or prohibit the reproduction of the work, its storage in a material medium, etc. The 'lawful publication' of the work is set as the sole prerequisite for the lawfulness of such a private use (Art. 18 Law 2121/1993), and the prevailing view takes this term to be synonymous with the licensing of the person from whom the user obtained access to the work and the capability of 'downloading' it.[22] This understanding – known as the 'theory of lawful origin'[23] – assimilates publication with licensing, in spite of the fact that their linguistic meaning differs totally. Lawful publication of the work has already taken place once and for all if at least one licence for this has intervened. On the other hand, each use of the work must be expressly permitted.

---

22 In this frame see, for preference, Kaliinikou, *Copyright and Neighbouring Rights* (3rd ed., 2008), no. 183, who requires lawful publication not only once and for all, i.e. not only for the initial copy, but for every copy being used for private reproduction. In this sense 'lawful publication' before private use means actually nothing else than licensing of the private use. See also Stavridou, 'Reproduction for private use and right for a reasonable fee in Marinos', et al., *Information Society and Copyright* (2003), pp. 119–135.

23 See Vagena, 'The dependence of the lawfulness of the private use of the work on the lawfulness of his source of origin' (commentary on the decision Cour d'Appel d'Aix en Provence, Arrêt du 5 Septembre 2007), *DiMEE* 2008, 60–64.

The assimilation of the concepts of 'licensing' and 'publication' cancels out and effectively renders meaningless the rule of Article 18 para. 1 Law 2121/1993, which expressly permits private use of the work 'without the permission of the creator'. In other words, if the permission of the creator for this private use, its storage or reproduction were also needed, then the power of the creator to permit or prohibit the reproduction or storage of the work (and the establishment of the more general right of intellectual property) would suffice for this, and it would not be required for the rule of Article 18, legitimating private use in spite of the lack of the creator's permission, to be established as an exception.

In fact, the balancing of the conflict of interests on both sides – the interests of the creator and of the end user – provided for by Article 18 Law 2121/1993 would seem to be just. If the work escapes from the creator's sphere of power with his/her volition, then the end user reasonably expects that the work is circulating lawfully, in which case it is reasonable that the end user not to be required to check the lawfulness of the source from which the work was obtained. Otherwise – by the same reasoning – he/she would have to ask and check at every bookshop whether it has the relevant permission of the publisher for the marketing of each book, to check the lawfulness and the validity of the publisher's permission, or even of the permission of the sub-licenser to the bookseller for this, and so on; in other words, according to the opposite prevailing opinion, the end user would be under an obligation to carry out the whole *probatio diabolica* of the intellectual property in order to discover the *locus standi* of its assignor to sell the work in question in bulk!

The opinion rebutted is not only disproportionately onerous for the end user, but it also lacks any practical applicability, since it is a known fact that proof of the end user's involvement in the chain of distribution of the work conflicts with the confidentiality of communications in accordance with Article 19 paras. 1–3 of the Greek Constitution (see Modification 1).

III. Metalegal Formants

The reason for the protection of the private use of the work by the third party as against the creator self-evidently goes back to the legal nature of the right of intellectual property and the distinction of the work from its material medium: intellectual property in general is a right to economic exploitation of the work and not material dominion over the medium which (happens to) embody it. Thus, by definition, it does not hinder real changes or amendments to the material of the medium of embodiment, for example storage of the material medium, reproduction, that is, the creation of new material media for it, except if they affect (the 'normal' according to Art. 18 Law 2121/1993) economic exploitation of the whole work (the 'idea').

(8) IRELAND

I. Operative Rules

An injunction is one of the remedies available for copyright infringement and would be granted to prevent further unlawful acts in this case.[24]

II. Descriptive Formants

The Copyright and Related Rights Act 2000 (as amended) (CRRA 2000) provides that the copyright owner or another authorised by the owner has the exclusive right to undertake to copy the work, to make it available to the public and to adapt the work.[25] Liability for primary infringement, which would include direct infringement of the copyright in question, is strict; therefore, knowledge of the law is assumed, and lack thereof is no defence. Nonetheless, it may have some bearing on any damages awarded.

The reader is reminded that the points made in relation to the various sources of copyright in Case 1, i.e. that in Ireland copyright derives from statute, the Constitution and possibly also the common law, apply throughout the cases relating to copyright in this report.

Downloading from the Internet is illegal, as the CRRA 2000 confers a right to control copying upon the owner of the copyright, which the Act refers to as 'the reproduction right'.[26] The Act also defines copying as 'storing the work in any medium'.[27]

The CRRA 2000 specifies that the owner of copyright has the exclusive right to control the uploading of content to the Internet. It provides that the owner has the exclusive right to control 'making available to the public of copies of the work, by wire or wireless means, in such a way that members of the public may access the work from a place and at a time chosen by them (including the making available of copies of works through the Internet)'.[28]

This applies both to the Internet and to proprietary intranets. The uploading of a work to the internal systems of a company or institution might be contrary to the 'making available' right and whether this constituted infringement would depend on how the term 'public' is defined.

Uploading to P2P networks may constitute an offence under section 140(1)(e). An injunction would be granted to prevent further uploading.[29]

---

24 Under section 127(2).
25 Section 37(1).
26 Section 39(2).
27 Section 39(1)(a)(i).
28 Section 40(1)(a).
29 Under section 127(2).

The fair dealing provisions in the CRRA 2000 are quite limited. Section 50(1) of the Act provides that copyright will not be infringed in a musical work by fair dealing if the purpose is for research or private study. Fair dealing will apply where the work has already been lawfully made available to the public and where the interests of the copyright owner are not prejudiced by the purpose and extent of the use.[30] Fair dealing cannot be relied upon as a defence where the person carrying out the copying knows or should know that more than one person will be provided with copies of substantially the same material at the same time and for the same purpose.[31]

Mere possession of infringing copies would not appear to be an offence – copies must be shown to have been made or imported for a commercial purpose. In *Minister for Justice v. Hogyi*,[32] computer programmes and films had been illegally copied and were found on the personal computer and on CDs and DVDs in Hogyi's apartment. Hogyi came to Ireland and the Hungarian authorities applied for a European arrest warrant. However, no offence would have been committed under Irish law – although he had possession of illegally copied material, this was not sufficient for the granting of the arrest warrant.

Making a copyright work available to a P2P network may be a criminal offence if the interests of the owner are prejudiced[33] under section 140(1)(e). Upon conviction on indictment, a maximum penalty may be imposed of a fine not exceeding £100,000 or imprisonment for a term not exceeding five years, or both.[34]

As matters stand under Irish law, courts will most likely distinguish less and less between downloading and uploading. In the words of Charleton J. in *EMI and Others v. Eircom Ltd*,[35] because of the nature of the software which facilitates downloading and uploading:

> Each downloading participant [becomes] an uploading participant whereby others in an active swarm will load from each other participant. This happens because of the peer-to-peer software and it happens whether a participant wants it to happen or not.

Exchanging CDs, provided that they have been made lawfully, is not specifically illegal under the CRRA 2000. It is not clear whether Carla has burned these CDs or whether they have been acquired lawfully. If the former is the case, there is an infringement as she has reproduced the music without permission and she may

---

30 Section 50(3)(b).
31 Section 50(4).
32 [2006] IEHC 373.
33 Section 140(1)(e).
34 Section 140(7)(b).
35 [2010] IEHC 108.

also be infringing the 'making available' right of the author of the work. If the latter is the case, there is no infringement as no copies have been made.

III. Metalegal Formants

Ireland was eager to implement the InfoSoc Directive aiming at fostering the digital economy. At that point in time, the interests of content providers were valued higher than the freedoms of users.

(9) ITALY

I. Operative Rules

Yes, 'String' will be granted an injunction.

II. Descriptive Formants

According to Article 156 ICL, every copyright holder is entitled to injunctive relief to enjoin any infringing activity. A preliminary injunction after a summary judgment is also possible according to Article 163 ICL. According to Article 171 et seq. ICL, Carla's activity is defined as copyright infringement: while the downloading of songs without the copyright holder's authorisation is, according to Article 174ter, a misdemeanour, uploading – that is to say letting others download – is a penal offence (Art. 171 c. 1 let. a-bis). This stands even in cases where a commercial or for-profit intent is not present.

Indeed, Article 171 c. 1 let. a-bis adopts a very broad definition to outlaw all uploading activity: it is a crime to put a protected work at the disposal of the public, by placing it in a network system, with any kind of connection ('*[mettere] a disposizione del pubblico, immettendola in un sistema di reti telematiche, mediante connessioni di qualsiasi genere, un'opera dell'ingegno protetta, o parte di essa*'). This activity may be sentenced with a pecuniary penalty.

If a for-profit intent can be demonstrated, then the activity can be more seriously punished with a jail term of up to four years (Art. 171ter).

III. Metalegal Formants

Legal scholars seem not to be particularly interested in analysing and classifying file-sharing activities and their legal consequences, mostly because the legislature has enacted very specific rules. This is mostly due to the fact that file-sharing through peer-to-peer technologies, and its impact on the entertainment industry, has been the subject of an intense public debate, carried out on the national mass media. This has created a strong pressure on the legislative bodies to react quickly and strongly with a series of *ad hoc* provisions. As usually happens in such situations, a quick reaction, not based on the discussion among legal scholars on the most effective ways of regulating new phenomena, leads to bad rules which must be corrected right after their enactment. And this is exactly what happened in Italy.

In 2004, the Italian government adopted an urgent decree (d.l. 22 March 2004, no. 72, named the *Decreto Urbani* after the Italian Minister of Culture who proposed the decree). According to the decree, the illegal distribution of motion picture works without any intention to profit is a misdemeanour punishable by a fine slightly higher than the one already in force for musical works.

In the process of conversion,[36] the text of the decree was modified by changing the wording of Article 171ter of ICL: instead of '*per scopo di lucro*' (with the purpose of lucre), the use of the formula '*per trarne profitto*' (to obtain profit) was proposed.[37] Even though this seems to be only a minor change, the consequences are profound: according to consolidated case law, while '*lucro*' is a specific financial benefit, '*profitto*' is a much broader concept that encompasses all types of benefits, either financial or solely moral. The amendment was adopted by a majority in Parliament and the decree was adopted as l. 21 May 2004, no. 128. According to the new wording, any sharing of any file protected by the copyright legislation is a major crime to be punished with a jail term of up to three years.

This new statute generated a strong reaction and Parliament adopted a new statute, l. 31 March 2005, no. 43, which restored the original wording of Article 171ter ('*scopo di lucro*') and added Article 171 c. 1 let. a-bis, which has been analysed above.

(10) LITHUANIA

I. *Operative Rules*

As far as the downloading of songs is concerned, the record company has no claim against Carla if the songs were uploaded to the Internet with the consent of the rightholders. If the songs were uploaded without the consent of the rightholders, 'String' has a claim against her.

---

[36] An urgent decree must be converted into an Act of Parliament within 60 days from its enactment and, during this process, Parliament has the power to modify its text.

[37] The amendment was proposed by the representative in charge of following the process of conversion, Gabriella Carlucci, a former show-girl without any legal knowledge. As she later stated, it was intended to make the profit intent requirement, needed to make illegal file-sharing activity a crime, more precise.

II. *Descriptive Formants*

The Lithuanian Law on Copyright and Neighbouring Rights (hereinafter – Copyright Act) regulates two groups of rights: moral rights (Art. 14) and economic rights (Art. 15). In this hypothetical case, the infringement of the economic rights is concerned. Injunctions against Carla are considered under Article 15 (economic rights of the author) and Article 54 (economic rights of the phonogram producers).[38]

The downloading and uploading of songs could violate the right of making a work available to the public over computer networks (on the Internet). The incorporation of Directive 2001/29/EC has extended the scope of the right of reproduction to the digital environment (Arts. 15(1)(8), 54(1)(3)).

The record company is a holder of neighbouring rights. Article 54 regulates the rights of the record company 'String'.[39] It enables the record company to permit or to prohibit copies of the work from being made available to the public. In order to make a copy or to make the work or its copy available to the public, it is necessary to get the express permission of the holder of the neighbouring rights. Carla uploads and downloads the songs without permission.

It should be said that Lithuanian law contains some limitations on copyright and neighbouring rights (under consideration of the so-called 'three-step test').[40]

The 'private use exception' is one of the limitations of copyright which is provided in Article 20. The version of this article since 2012 states: 'It shall be permitted for a natural person, without the authorization of the author of the work or any other owner of copyright in the work, to reproduce, exclusively for his individual use and not for commercial advantage, in a single copy a work lawfully published or communicated to the public.' The 'private use exception' also applies to the neighbouring rights (Art. 58). Therefore, the particular answer depends on whether the songs were posted (i.e. 'lawfully communicated to the public') on the Internet legally, that is, with the rightholders' consent. If the musical files were posted legally, Carla could make a personal copy under Article 20. In such a case, 'String' has no valid claim against Carla.

But if the songs were posted on the Internet illegally, then Article 20 does not apply, Carla's actions of downloading are illegal, and 'String' has a claim for an injunction.

---

38 In Lithuania, neighbouring rights protection has been extended since 10 June 1994.

39 The right of reproduction, publication, making available to the public and distribution of a CD or copies thereof to the public by sale, rental or lending, or any other form of transfer of ownership or possession, as well as by importing or exporting (Art. 54(1)(1)–(4)).

40 The three-step test allows an exception in copyright law to be applied in certain special cases, namely when the application of that exception does not conflict with a normal exploitation of the work and does not unreasonably prejudice the legitimate interests of the rightholder (Art. 5(5) of the European Copyright Directive, Art. 9(2) of the Berne Convention).

Another issue is that Carla also uploads music files. This activity is qualified as public communication (for authors' rights purposes) and making available to the public for related rights (in this case, phonogram producers) purposes. There is no exception allowing uploading without the permission of the rightholder. So either Carla has permission (which is clearly not the case here), or she uploads without permission and thus violates the rightholders' rights.

Regarding the exchange of CDs, an additional qualification of the concept of 'exchange' is necessary, as this concept may imply two different scenarios. From the case, it is not clear whether Carla exchanges CDs legally bought on the market or acquired in another legal way, or alternatively whether she exchanges CDs containing copies of songs she downloaded from the Internet. In the first scenario, i.e. where the CDs were acquired legally, Carla can freely exchange them. She can transfer the ownership to her friend, and the rightholder cannot object because the rights to the sold copy are exhausted (Art. 16).

The situation is different if the CDs under consideration contain downloaded songs, because the exhaustion rule does not apply. Even if the songs were downloaded legally using the private copy exception, this exception does not extend to the further distribution of the copy made under this exception. Therefore, the exchange of CDs in the latter scenario is illegal.

III. Metalegal Formants

Lithuania used to have one of the most restrictive private copying regimes in the EU. A copy for one's parents or friends was not covered; one's private copy was not exchanged among friends or even family members.[41]

The limitation on the reproduction of work and objects of neighbouring rights for personal usage has caused the most controversy, as the application of this limitation in certain cases involves the mechanism of compensation for rightholders.[42] Two situations are to be distinguished. First, in the case of reprography, the compensation shall be paid by the persons providing

---

41 E. Ivanauskienė, N.J. Matulevičienė, 'Autorių teisės ir gretutinės teisės elektroninėje leidyboje', *Atviros Lietuvos fondas* 2000; E. Ivanauskienė, 'Teisė atgaminti kūrinį', *Autorių teisės į literatūros, mokslo ir meno kūrinius: aktualijos ir perspektyvos*, Pranešimų rinkinys (Vilnius: 2004); A. Vileita, *Lietuvos Respublikos Autorių teisiu ir gretutiniu teisiu įstatymo komentaras*, Lietuvos rašytoju sąjungos leidykla (Vilnius: 2000), pp. 77–78. One of the recommended actions for improving Lithuanian copyright law was to allow multiple instances of private copying within family members: M. Kiškis, 'Recommendations for improving Lithuanian intellectual property law, policy and enforcement', published under the auspices of the Internet Research and Innovation Institute, available at: http://inventresearch.weebly.com/uploads/1/0/7/4/10744518/mkiskis_ipr_policy_recommendations_1.pdf (last accessed 23 February 2022).

42 V. Mizaras, 'Lithuanian Copyright: Historical and Modern Aspects and Trends of Development', *Journal of Copyright Society of the USA*, 2006, vol. 54, No. 4, pp. 849–852.

fee-paying services of reprographic reproduction (Art. 23(3)). In the case of a reproduction of audio-visual work or a work recorded on a phonogram, or a copy of a performance, phonogram, film or broadcast, copyright holders have the right to receive fair compensation (a percentage of the wholesale price for blank CDs, CD-ROMs, etc.)

Despite the quite strict regulation and the widespread downloading of copyright-protected materials from the Internet by users, rightholders so far have not initiated litigation against this group of infringers in Lithuania. In part, this can be explained by the difficulty of identifying the possible infringing individuals; in part, because the rightholders seek to avoid the negative publicity which would be caused by targeting end users, including teenagers, as in this hypothetical case. Therefore, the rightholders have focused on the uploaders.

(11) NETHERLANDS

I. Operative Rules

There is no injunction available for the downloading of songs from the Internet, as long as the songs had been put on the Internet with the consent of the rightholder and as long as Carla does not upload them onto the Internet. Assuming that Carla herself makes a copy for her friend, an injunction will be granted as regards the sharing of CDs. If the CDs were bought from a legal source, there is no injunction available.

II. Descriptive Formants

Acts of downloading and uploading songs from/to the Internet fall under the rightholder's exclusive rights pursuant to Article 1 of the Dutch Copyright Act. Without the rights owner's consent, Carla's actions would in principle infringe the copyrights of the rights owner of the songs she is downloading and/or uploading. Downloading songs from the Internet can, under specific conditions, be covered by the exception in Article 16c of the Dutch Copyright Act, which allows her to make a copy for her own private use. Uploading a protected work without permission is always a copyright infringement. An injunction should therefore be granted if she uploads protected material.

Applying the exhaustion doctrine, CDs that are put on the market with the rights owner's consent can be lent or given away freely without permission from the rights owner, pursuant to Article 12b Dutch Copyright Act. If Carla's CDs were purchased legally, the exhaustion doctrine applies and Karen can exchange them with her friend. By contrast, if the CDs were made following the downloading of the songs from the Internet, the Copyright Act provides that copying music for one's own private use is permitted, but the copy must be made by the person herself (Art. 16c(1) Dutch Copyright Act). Carla cannot make private copies for Karen or *vice versa* (Art. 16c(7) Dutch Copyright Act). It will, however, be difficult for the record company to prove who made the copy: Carla or Karen.

III. Metalegal Formants

This case shows the tension between the interest of rightholders to protect their works and the interest of users not to be hindered when using works in the private sphere. The Copyright Commission, whose mandate it is to advise the government on copyright matters, pointed out that, on the one hand, the copying in the private sphere makes it necessary for the rightholder to have a certain amount of control over the private use of protected material. On the other hand, the end user's interest in seeing his/her private sphere respected also exists. The Committee has favoured an approach where the legitimate interests of the rightholders should serve as a guide to determine the amount of control rights owners should have over the copying.[43]

In the Netherlands, the private copy exception applies to downloading in a peer-to-peer context. Difficulties with the private copy exception arise because of the change in technology. Talking about the private copy exception in the context of CDs differs from the exception in the Internet era/peer-to-peer context. Not only is it possible to make perfect copies, it is also relatively easy to make copies from the Internet. The making of private copies of CDs has never happened on the large scale it does today with peer-to-peer networks. Today, the possibility of financial losses for authors becomes more acute. This is especially a problem for audio recordings and audio-visual works. In these cases, individual use in the private sphere becomes the primary form of use. The exploitation of these works becomes problematic. The Committee feared this might endanger the balance between the interests of rightholders and of users.[44]

Another element that has changed is the enforcement of the private copy exception. The copying of CDs at home was more difficult to control than the downloading of songs. With the downloading of songs, it is also difficult to control, but at least online uses of works can be traced. On the other hand, the change in the amount of copying also makes effective enforcement more difficult.[45]

In the 2009–2010 response to the report of the Parliamentary Working Group on Copyright, the changes involving the private copy exception were mentioned. The Minister predicted that the current levy system with regard to private

43 Rapport Commissie Auteursrecht, *Advies over auteursrecht, naburige rechten en de nieuwe media*, August 1998, pp. 11–12.

44 Ibid., pp. 28–30.

45 C. Alberdingk Thijm, *Het nieuwe informatierecht* (The Hague: 2006–2007), pp. 87 f.

copying would not have a long future. In the digital world, the emphasis is on the content itself and not on the device which carries the content. If the industry develops adequate licensing systems, there would be no more justification to still have a levy system for platform-shifting and time-shifting. The Minister suggested that the discussion should therefore be focused on the copying of content (downloading) on the Internet.[46]

Following the CJEU's ruling in the *ACI Adam v. Stiching the Thuiskopie* case,[47] downloading from a peer-to-peer file-sharing system is no longer covered by the private use exception if the works had been uploaded from an evidently illicit source. At the time of implementing Directive 2001/29/EC into Dutch law, the Parliamentary Working Group on Copyright had proposed making downloading from an illegal source through peer-to-peer networks a criminal offence, but only after the industry has worked out a licence system. The Minister had supported this proposal, since this would make setting up a new compensation system unnecessary. Furthermore, in this way the responsibility of coming up with new business models would lie with the industry, where it belongs. However, the Minister also pointed out the potential risks of encroaching upon Internet users' right to privacy.[48] The law should reflect a balance between the protection of intellectual property and privacy interests.[49] The Minister also stated that criminalising the downloading of illegal material could lead to monitoring the Internet use of individuals. This could lead to a decrease in the 'support of society' for copyright in general.[50] Nevertheless, the day that the CJEU handed down its ruling in the *ACI Adam* case meant the official end of downloading from illegal sources like The Pirate Bay. Officially, however, the organisation in charge of representing the interests of music producers in the Netherlands, Stichting Brein, announced shortly thereafter that it would not institute proceedings against individual downloaders.

(12) NORWAY

I. *Operative Rules*

(a) For the exchange of CDs: no. (b) For the downloading: only if the songs are uploaded illegally. (c) For the uploading: yes, an injunction will be granted.

---

46 *Kamerstukken II* 2009–2010, 29 838 Nr. 22, pp. 10–13.

47 CJEU judgment of 10 April 2014, *ACI Adam*, C-435/12, ECLI:EU:C:2014:254.

48 *Kamerstukken II* 2009–2010, 29 838 Nr. 22, p. 13.

49 See M. de Cock Buning and A. Ringnalda, 'Maatregelen tegen auteursrechtinbreuk door P2P-filesharing: wat leert Umfeld ons?', *AMI* (2010) Nr. 1, pp. 7–8.

50 *Kamerstukken II* 2009–2010, 29 838 Nr. 22, p. 13.

II. Descriptive Formants

It should be distinguished whether the exchanged CDs are 'originals', copies made from 'originals' or copies downloaded from the Internet. In the latter case, the question of whether the exchange of the copies is lawful will depend on the legality of the downloading (see below). But provided that the CDs are lawfully made, the exchange of the CDs will not infringe copyright. The exchange of CDs as such is to be considered an act of distribution, but as long as the receiver is Carla's girlfriend, it is not covered by the author's (NCA §2; New Act §3), performing artist's (NCA §42; New Act §16) or phonogram producer's (NCA§45; New Act §20) exclusive right to make the work or recordings available to *the public*. Therefore, 'String' will not be granted an injunction on the grounds of the exchange alone.

Both the downloading and the uploading are acts of reproduction to which the rightholder has exclusive rights, cf. NCA §§2, 42 and 45 (New Act §§3, 16 and 20). However, the exclusive right to reproduction does not cover copying for *private use*, cf. NCA §12 (New Act §26), provided that the conditions laid down in the provision are fulfilled. As the download is supposedly for Carla's own private use, it will be covered by NCA §12 (New Act §26). That is not the case, however, with the uploading on the Internet, which will infringe both the reproduction right and the right of making available to the public. An injunction will therefore be granted for the uploading.

As far as the downloading is concerned, a few copies of a work or recording already made publicly available may be made for private use pursuant to NCA §12, first paragraph (New Act §26, first paragraph. However, since 2005, the private copying provision (§12, fourth paragraph; New Act §26, first paragraph) explicitly states that it is not permitted to make copies for private use on the basis of copies which have been subject to or are the result of an illegal reproduction or unlawful act making them available to the public. This means that if the material Carla downloads is uploaded or in other way made available (e.g. by way of streaming) on the Internet without the permission of the author, her download infringes 'String's' rights in the recording. On the other hand, penal or civil *liability* is dependent on Carla's *knowing* or awareness of the probability that the recordings were illegally uploaded or made available, cf. NCA §§54(2) and 55(3) (New Act §§79(1) and 81(1)).

III. Metalegal Formants

The issue in question is the very balance of rightholders' interests in controlling the use of the protected subject matter and user interests in not having the rightholder interfere in the use of copyrighted material, in particular not within the user's private sphere. Norwegian law has traditionally been very concerned with maintaining the balance between the rightholders' interests and public interests in a broader sense. This is reflected in the fact that Norwegian law does not accept the concept of exceptions or exemptions to copyright which are to be interpreted narrowly. For a long time, it has been accepted that the delimitations to the rights have as much solid legal foundation as the rights themselves.[51] Consequently, the NCA uses the term 'delimitations to the right' instead of 'exceptions' or 'exemptions'.[52]

The introduction of the ban on private copying on the basis of illegal material (NCA §12(4)), which was the Norwegian response to the problems arising from new technologies, in particular peer-to-peer networks, was the subject of intense public debate. The Norwegian legislator chose to introduce the provision with reference to the three-step test in Article 9(2) Berne Convention and Article 5(5) Copyright Directive 2001/29/EC, despite the allegations that the provision would create a whole nation of law infringers. The response of the legislator to the allegations was the requirement for liability, namely that the maker of the private copy knows or holds to be probable that the source of the copy is illegal (cf. above).

(13) POLAND

I. *Operative Rules*

An injunction will be granted with respect to uploading only.

II. *Descriptive Formants*

Assuming 'String' has a copyright in the pieces of music Carla either downloads or shares with her friend, the success of an action against Carla depends on whether Carla, who clearly uses copyrighted music works (by making copies and making the works available to another person), may argue that she has not infringed 'String's' copyright. There would be no infringement if Carla acted within the statutory exceptions and limitations of copyright. The Polish copyright law provides for a fairly extensive scope of copyright exceptions. For the present case, two of them are of relevance. First, Polish copyright law allows making copies for private use (Art. 23 Copyright Act). It is the prevailing view that downloading copyright works (including music) falls under this exception,[53] as downloading is in effect nothing more than making a digital copy. Under Polish law, there is no requirement that a private copy exception be allowed only when

---

[51] Originally expressed by Professor R. Knoph, *Åndsretten* (Oslo: 1936), p. 124 and later confirmed by the parliament committee, Innst. O. (1960–61), pp. 16–17.

[52] Cf. the headline to chapter 2 of the NCA.

[53] J. Barta, R. Markiewicz, *Prawo autorskie* (Kraków: 2008), pp. 119–120.

the 'source' copy is legal or at least its illegality is not manifest to the user.[54] It is also immaterial that even if the source copy is legal, it is still illegal to make the copies available to other persons who may access them at a chosen time and place. Thus, the very act of downloading for private use is legal and does not constitute copyright infringement. If this is the case, no claims can be pursued by the copyright holder.

Uploading works on the Internet will be illegal on the other hand, since this must be qualified as making the work available to the public and such actions do not fall under any known limitations of copyright. If the technical process requires that downloading and uploading are inseparable (as is the case with some P2P networks), then the whole activity will be banned.

Carla sharing copies of works with her girlfriend is covered by the same exception. According to Article 23(2) Copyright Act this is, however, limited to single copies and the circle of persons using works in this way must be limited to persons bound by personal relations (especially family or social relations). While exchanging records, Carla probably copies the records of her friend and lends her own records to her friend. Both types of use are within the copyright limitation referred to in Article 23 Copyright Act. The relationship of friendship is a social relation undoubtedly covered by the said provision.

III. Metalegal Formants

This case is again about the balance of interests, especially in the digital environment. The first question is whether private copies should be allowed at all. If so, what should the limitations be? In Poland there is quite widespread support for the right to make private copies. Interestingly, the issue is not only about access to copyright works and thus to information that is necessary to ensure the creation of new works and consequently indispensable for the development of science and culture. For many works, such noble arguments are clearly not best suited.[55] But there is another interest at stake – the interest of consumers who regard it as legitimate to make a backup CD or a CD with music to listen to in a car or a digital copy for an iPod. It would seem at least artificial to ban such copies. At the same time, the Internet has changed the scale of private copying. What is more, works posted on the Internet for downloading have been mostly put there illegally. It is therefore understandable that rightholders find this situation unsatisfactory. However, on a closer look, it is fairly easy to see that the problem is not really about the scope of protection (and consequently the scope of copyright limitations and exceptions – in this case the right to make

---

54 Ibid., p. 120.

55 Among them many works of 'popular culture'.

a copy for private use) but about the enforcement of the law in force. If the law in force were complied with, there would be no illegally uploaded works on the Internet to download. Then the existence of the right to a private copy would not be perceived as dangerous, as private copies made from exchanged CDs would not have such adverse effects on the profits of copyright owners. What is therefore needed is a new solution for the digital environment that would retain the private copy exception but at the same time remove the inconsistency between illegal uploading and legal downloading.

(14) SLOVENIA

I. Operative Rules

'String' has a claim for injunction against Carla on both accounts.

II. Descriptive Formants

Downloading files from the Internet represents an act of reproduction, governed by Article 23 of the CRRA, while uploading files presents an act of making available, governed by Article 32a CRRA. Both reproduction and making available are exclusive rights held by the rightholder.

If Carla uploads music files without acquiring permission from the rightholders, she infringes the exclusive right of making available.

Carla could argue in her defence that downloading music files represents a form of permitted private use, governed by Article 50 CRRA, and therefore does not infringe the exclusive right of reproduction. Article 50 CRRA introduces an exemption from copyright and defines the situations in which users do not have to acquire the rightholders' permission in order to use the works for private purposes. Consequently, users can under certain circumstances freely reproduce the works, while the rightholders receive corresponding remuneration (Art. 37 CRRA). Notwithstanding this first impression, a more in-depth analysis of the Slovenian copyright arrangement reveals that downloading music files which are not made available under suitable licence terms is most probably not allowed. Specifically, the Slovenian legislator sets very strict conditions for private use to be allowed, since the conditions set by Article 46 CRRA also have to be met.

Where reproductions are made on another medium (not paper or any similar medium), only those reproductions that fulfil all of the following conditions can be considered, under current Slovenian copyright law, to be private reproductions which are permitted and free, and as such subject to 'fair remuneration': that they are (1) reproductions of a disclosed work, (2) made in no more than three copies, (3) on the condition that a natural person reproduces them (4) for private use, (5) that the copies are not made available to the public, and (6) that the reproduction is not done in order to gain direct or indirect economic advantage.[56]

In addition to the above, private reproductions are permitted only if all the additional conditions set out in Article 46 CRRA are fulfilled: the private reproductions have to be (1) limited by the intended purpose, (2) compatible with fair practice, (3) must not conflict with normal use of the work, and (4) must not unreasonably prejudice the legitimate interests of the author.

Only if all the above-mentioned conditions are fulfilled do private reproductions qualify as permitted.

There is no judicial practice regarding the standards of the so-called 'four-step test' introduced by Article 46 CRRA. Downloading works from the Internet would most probably not qualify as compatible with fair practice and would most likely be in conflict with the normal use of the work. As such, it would also unreasonably prejudice the legitimate interests of the author.

Carla burns the downloaded music files onto CDs and exchanges them with her girlfriend Karen. Such an act infringes the exclusive right of distribution, governed by Article 24 CRRA. It qualifies as an infringement, even though the copies are not offered to the public (Karen is Carla's friend), since such copies are not produced lawfully.

III. Metalegal Formants

Answer omitted.

(15) SPAIN

I. Operative Rules

The record company's legal action would not be successful regarding the downloading. It would be possible to have an injunction regarding the uploading.

II. Descriptive Formants

In the present scenario, we add the following assumptions to those stated above in Case 1. The Internet service provider is authorised by the holder of the copyright to distribute music on its server. Consumers or third parties download music for

---

56 These reproductions are not permitted unless otherwise provided by the CRRA or by a contract with respect to: (1) written works to the extent of the whole book, unless such work has been out of print for a minimum of two years; (2) graphic editions of musical works, unless by means of handwritten transcription; (3) electronic databases; (4) computer programmes; and (5) in the form of building of architectural objects.

their own personal use from the website. The music download exchange is done under concrete circumstances (one consumer).

To respond to the issue at hand, we need to study several rights included in the Spanish LPI that are connected to the economic rights of the author or the rightholder.[57] These economic rights are, broadly, the right of reproduction (Art. 18 LPI), the right of distribution (Art. 19 LPI) and the right of 'public communication' (Art. 20 LPI).[58] In particular, Article 18 LPI recognises that the right of reproduction involves: (1) fixing the work by any means or in any form that enables it to be communicated; and (2) making full or partial copies. The definition given in Article 18 LPI is the result of the modification of the LPI by Law 23/2006, which incorporated the provisions of Directive 2001/29/EC into the Spanish legal framework and, in fact, transposes the content of Article 2 of the Directive, thus extending the scope of this right to the digital environment.[59] Therefore, the reproduction of a work by a third party without the permission of the author violates the right of reproduction contained in Article 18 LPI.

As well as the right to reproduce the work, Spanish law also recognises the exclusive right of the author to distribute the work. According to Article 19 LPI, this right enables the author to allow or to prohibit copies of the work from being made available to the public by a particular channel of distribution without the express permission of the rightholder. Both Directive 2001/29/EC and the Spanish LPI recognise that the right of distribution on a national and Community level is exhausted after the work has first been marketed with the copyright holder's permission. However, that fact does not exhaust the international level of protection.

Considering the legal framework explained above, it should be noted that the Spanish LPI places some limitations on the right of reproduction in its Article 31. The first limit on the right of reproduction is how the work is to be used. The work can only be reproduced for the private use of a third party (that is to say, not a collective use). The second limit imposed by the LPI is that the reproduction should not be for the purpose of making a profit. Thus, the private copy exception to the reproduction right according to Article 31.2 LPI is subject to the following requirements: (1) obtaining the copy from a legal source;

---

57 We consider that a holder of the proprietary rights could be the producer or distributor of the protected work.

58 Several civil jurisdiction decisions – e.g. Decision of the Provincial Court of Madrid of 16 November 2004, Decision of the Provincial Court of Madrid of 13 November 2003, Supreme Court Decision of 3 March 2001, and Supreme Court Decision of 12 December 2001, among others – define the scope of the rights of reproduction, distribution and public performance, respectively in different media (analogical, digital or physical).

59 See J.A. Gómez Segade, 'En torno a la Directiva sobre el derecho de autor y los derechos afines en la sociedad de la información', *Actas de Derecho Industrial*, no. 26, 2005–2006, pp. 1430–1447; J.A. Gómez Segade, 'El derecho de autor en el entorno digital', *Revista General de Legislación y Jurisprudencia*, no. 3, 1999, pp. 309–330.

(2) for the purpose of private use; (3) the lack of an economic profit; and (iv) the payment of fair compensation to the author (please see the comments on the levy in Modification 3 below).

From the above, as far as downloading is concerned, it seems clear that Carla does not infringe the intellectual property rights of the record company because she makes private use of the songs she downloads from the server.[60] Neither does she try to make a profit; she does not sell the songs for a profit. In consequence, the record company would not have any right to an economic injunction for infringement of its intellectual property rights according to the private copy exception. Regarding the exchange of CDs, we consider that mere exchange with another user does not mean that a collective use is being made of the songs.

However, as far as uploading the music is concerned, Carla could be infringing the public communication right recognised by Article 20 LPI. The Spanish regulation defines public communication as any activity by means of which people can have direct access to the work without any previous distribution of the work to each one of them. Uploading is defined as a 'public communication' act under Directive 2001/29/EC. If a third party uploads music onto the Internet without the author's consent, it probably would be infringing the above-mentioned author's right. In consequence, Carla could have committed an act of public communication of the work.

III. Metalegal Formants

The protection of copyright holders and third party uses of the author's work is an issue that often has to be dealt on a case-by-case basis. The Spanish LPI distinguishes the author's rights and their limits. At the same time, the LPI tries to combine the rights of the authors with third party rights (users, consumers) in order to benefit access to culture. The balance may come when the author's rights are limited on behalf of the public interest.

To summarise, on the one hand, the lawful acquisition of a work should always be taken into account to decide if there is any infringement of the author's right. This is the main point to consider regarding the downloading of music and the application of the private copy exception and its different requirements. On the other hand, the uploading of music without the consent of the author is difficult to justify in terms of the public communication right of the author.

---

60 For some comments on the *Napster* case: M. Lacruz Mantecón, 'Napster, o como cargarse la propiedad intelectual (tal como la venimos entendiendo)', available at: http://www.unirioja.es/dptos/dd/civil/napster.html (last accessed 5 May 2019); or M.A. Bouza and M. Castro Marques, 'El Caso Napster', *Actas de Derecho Industrial*, no. 26, 2005–2006 pp. 435–449.

(16) UNITED KINGDOM

I. Operative Rules

'String' may apply to the High Court for an injunction against Carla in order to stop her infringing the copyright of the songs. If Carla was aware of the infringement, or had reason to believe she was infringing, 'String' may also apply for damages. In addition to the existing remedies and sanctions, the record company could apply for seizure of the infringing copies.

II. Descriptive Formants

Carla has downloaded and uploaded songs from the Internet without the permission of the various copyright owners. Copyright subsists in sound recordings and in the music and lyrics to a song, pursuant to section 1(1) CDPA 1988.[61] The mixture of songs, downloaded and uploaded, constitute both literary and musical works under the CDPA 1988. The melody of each song constitutes a musical work,[62] while the lyrics of each song will also constitute separate copyright work – literary work: *Redwood Music Ltd v. B. Feldman & Co. Ltd.*[63] The downloaded songs will therefore attract copyright protection as literary works, namely words designed to be sung.[64]

Uploading and downloading the songs from the Internet without the permission of the copyright owner clearly infringes the copyright of the works. For the purposes of this question, it will be assumed that Carla has downloaded and uploaded the songs in their entirety, which means that the questions surrounding whether there was a substantial taking are not in issue. Only the copyright owner has the exclusive right to undertake certain restrictive acts in relation their songs under section 16(1) CDPA 1988. Since Carla has *downloaded* songs from a peer-to-peer file-sharing system on the Internet without the permission of the various owners, she has infringed the owners' exclusive rights to copy their work,[65] issue copies of their work to the public and rent or lend their work as set out in section 16 CDPA 1988. The uploading of files, on the other hand, is a communication to the public, covered by section 20(1). An English case similar

61 The United Kingdom enacted the Copyright and Related Rights Regulations 2003 (SI 2003/2498), in effect as of 31 October 2003, implementing the Copyright Directive 2001/29/EC, which contain strong pro-owner provisions.

62 According to s. 3(1)(a) CDPA 1988, 'musical work' means a work consisting of music, exclusive of any words or action intended to be sung, spoken or performed with the music.

63 [1979] RPC 385.

64 According to s. 3(1) CDPA 1988, a literary work is defined as being 'any work written, spoken or sung, other than a dramatic or musical work.'

65 Section 16(1)(a) CDPA 1988.

to the facts in the question is *Polydor Ltd v. Brown*.[66] The case concerned some children who used peer-to-peer software on the family computer to copy music files containing copies of copyright works onto a shared directory on the home computer. The father of the household, although having no knowledge of his children's actions, was found liable for infringement under section 20 CDPA 1988 because he had installed and used the software, therefore breaching the copyright owner's exclusive right of communication of the work to the public. A notable member of the judiciary, Collins J, held that the 'mere fact that the files were present and were made available' to the public by connecting the computer to the Internet and running the P2P software was sufficient for copyright infringement to have occurred. On this basis, Carla, even though she is only 15 years old, will have infringed the copyright of the works. First Carla has 'reproduced' the whole or a substantial part of the primary work in a different material form without the permission of the copyright owner, violating section 17(2) CDPA 1988. Then, passing the CD to the friend, on the other hand, falls under section 18, which covers the distribution of physical items. In spite of Carla exchanging CDs with her girlfriend Karen, this does not at present constitute personal use.

The CDPA 1988 also imposes secondary liability for copyright infringement upon anyone who transmits songs using a telecommunications system, without the consent of the various copyright owners, and who knows or has reason to believe that infringing copies of the works will be made by recipients (s. 24(2) CDPA 1988). Since both girls are 15 years old and accustomed to downloading and uploading various songs, it is likely that they would be caught within the criteria for secondary liability set out in section 24 CDPA 1988.

The case would look different if the download was authorised by the rightholder. In particular, there is a new private copying exemption in force which allows the user to make copies for personal use (not applicable to software). It explicitly covers downloads (s. 28B(4)) and was introduced in 2014 as a result of the Hargreaves report. It should be noted though that the rule is highly contentious because it does not have a levy system or other remuneration mechanism. While still in force now, it is likely to repealed as this directly contradicts Article 5(2)(b) InfoSoc Directive. Exchanging CDs containing copyright works in the form of illegally copied songs is also an infringement of the copyright works under section 17(2) CDPA 1988, because Carla has reproduced the whole or a substantial part of the primary work in a different material form without the permission of the copyright owner. In spite of Carla exchanging CDs with her girlfriend Karen, this does not at present constitute personal use.

There are a range of remedies and sanctions that the record company 'String' can impose on those who infringe the copyright of the songs. The record company

[66] [2005] EWHC 3191 (Ch).

is able to apply to the High Court for an injunction against Carla in order to stop her infringing the copyright of the songs under section 96 CDPA 1988. 'String' may also apply for damages from Carla for the copyright infringements under section 96 CDPA 1988 as well. However, if Carla states that she was unaware that she was infringing copyright, innocent infringement will not give rise to a right to damages under section 97 CDPA 1988. In addition to the existing remedies and sanctions, the record company could apply for seizure of the infringing copies pursuant to section 100 CDPA 1988.

III. Metalegal Formants

The debate in the UK about peer-to-peer networks has been strongly influenced by the US debate (infra Modification 1), less by continental discussions which led to and resulted from Article 5(2)(b) of Directive 2001/29/EC. The majority of cases brought by record companies, English and American, have resulted in settlements out of court, usually by parents paying on behalf of their children.

A.4. COMPARATIVE REMARKS

The comparative remarks on this case are aggregated in section E.3 below.

B.1. MODIFICATION 1

At the same time, 'String' is seeking an injunction against the Internet-based music provider 'Keep Mov'n', whose site has become the most popular music exchange site. 'String' asks the court to oblige 'Keep Mov'n' to prevent the downloading of illegal material and to release the names and addresses of 33 of its subscribers who are suspected of downloading mass quantities of illegal material.

Will 'String' have a successful claim against 'Keep Mov'n'?

B.2. EDITORIAL NOTE ON EU LAW

This modification of the case focuses on the role of Internet service providers (ISPs) in facilitating online access to illegal content. More specifically, the modification deals with the interconnected questions of whether ISPs can be held liable for, and forced to take action to prevent, the unlawful activities of their customers who use peer-to-peer file-sharing software and whether ISPs can be obliged to divulge the identity of allegedly infringing customers. Besides the substantive copyright rules contained in Directive 2001/29/EC, the relevant legal framework relating to the degree of ISP liability is laid down in the EC Directive on Electronic Commerce,[67] which determines the conditions under which different categories of service providers (mere conduit, caching or hosting services) can be exonerated from liability for the infringing acts of their users.

On the first point, the liability of a hosting service provider, like 'Keep Mov'n', hinges on the service's actual or constructive knowledge that infringing activities are taking place via its platform, pursuant to Article 14 of the E-Commerce Directive. The CJEU had not yet rendered its decision in the recent *Brein v. Ziggo BV* case[68] at the time the reports were written. The Court ruled that the making available and management of an online sharing platform, like 'Keep Mov'n', constitutes a 'communication to the public', within the meaning of Article 3(1) of Directive 2001/29/EC, for which the authorisation of the rights owners is required. In other words, it is clear that an online sharing platform that advertises and profits from providing access to works published without authorisation of the rightholders cannot realistically invoke absence of actual or constructive knowledge to escape liability. The national reports' analyses foresee such a logical finding.

The national reports also predate the CJEU's ruling in the *Scarlet Extended v. SABAM* case,[69] where the Court confirmed that no obligation can be imposed on an ISP to install a filtering system in order to identify and block unlawful use of file-sharing, as this would be incompatible with the EU Directives 2000/31/EC, 2001/29/EC, 2004/48/EC, 95/46/EC and 2002/58/EC, construed in light of the fundamental rights to protection of personal data and freedom of expression. As we shall see below, short of compelling ISPs to take measures to stop infringing activities from occurring on their services, the conditions for holding ISPs liable for copyright infringement seem rather uniform across member states. The situation will soon need to change, however, as member states must proceed with the implementation of Article 17 of the new Directive (EU) 2019/790 on Copyright in the Digital Single Market before the deadline of 7 June 2021.[70]

The second aspect considered in this modification concerns the related issue of the conflict between protecting the interests of IP holders and the right to privacy of Internet users, the latter of which may be protected either according to the principles of civil procedure or by data protection laws. The legal basis for a

---

[67] Directive 2001/31/EC of the European Parliament and of the Council of 8 June 2000 on certain legal aspects of information society services, in particular electronic commerce, in the Internal Market ('Directive on Electronic Commerce'), OJ L 178, 17 July 2000, 1–16.

[68] CJEU judgment of 14 June 2017, *Stichting Brein v. Ziggo BV and XS4All Internet BV*, C-442/79, ECLI:EU:C:2017:456.

[69] CJEU judgment of 24 November 2011, *Scarlet Extended v. SABAM*, C-70/10, ECLI:EU:C:2011:771.

[70] Directive (EU) 2019/790 of the European Parliament and of the Council of 17 April 2019 on copyright and related rights in the Digital Single Market and amending Directives 96/9/EC and 2001/29/EC, OJ L 130, 17 May 2019, 92–125.

request for information by the rights owner lies in Article 15(2) of the E-Commerce Directive, which specifies that 'Member States may establish obligations for information society service providers promptly to inform the competent public authorities of alleged illegal activities undertaken or information provided by recipients of their service or obligations to communicate to the competent authorities, at their request, information enabling the identification of recipients of their service with whom they have storage agreements.' The question is how this permissive language has been implemented at the national level and how has it been interpreted by the courts.

The reports were mostly written before the CJEU issued its ruling in the *Promusicae* case, in which it held that member states can, but are not obliged to, implement a duty to release personal information to enable a rightholder to enforce their rights against ISPs and individual users.[71] The Court called upon the member states to strike a fair balance between the various fundamental rights at stake.[72] The national reports precede the General Data Protection Regulation (EU) No. 2016/679, which supersedes Directive 95/46/EC on Personal Data Protection.

B.3. COUNTRY REPORTS

(1) BELGIUM

I. *Operative Rules*

Yes, 'String' will have a successful claim for preventing the downloading of illegal material (see a) below), but for the release of names and addresses, the situation is not entirely clear (see b) below).

II. *Descriptive Formants*

- Article 8 European Convention of Human Rights;
- Article 6(1)(b) Personal Data Protection Directive[73] (now replaced by Arts. 5 and 6 of the General Data Protection Regulation (GDPR));[74]

---

71 CJEU judgment of 29 January 2008, *Promusicae*, C-275/06, ECLI:EU:C:2008:54, paras. 54 et seq.

72 Ibid., para. 68.

73 Directive 95/46/EC of the European Parliament and of the Council of 24 October 1995 on the protection of individuals with regard to the processing of personal data and on the free movement of such data, OJ L 281, 23 November 1995, 31–50.

74 Regulation (EU) No. 2016/679 of the European Parliament and of the Council of 27 April 2016 on the protection of natural persons with regard to the processing of personal data

- Articles 12–15 Directive on Electronic Commerce;[75]
- Article 8 Enforcement Directive;[76]
- Articles 80 and 86ter BCA (Arts. XI.293 and XI.334 BCEL);
- Articles 3 and 18–22 Belgian E-Commerce Act of 2003[77] (Arts. XII.1§2 and XII.17–20 BCEL);
- Articles 122 and 124–126 Belgian Electronic Communication Act.[78]

Since the case refers to a *site*, it is assumed that the case concerns a hosting provider and not merely a fully decentralised Kazaa-like peer-to-peer programme.

a) Preventing the downloading of illegal material

The Directive on Electronic Commerce has been implemented by the Belgian E-Commerce Act of 2003. Articles 18–22 (Arts. XII.17–20 BCEL) regulate the liability of Internet service providers (ISPs). As the present case seems to be dealing with a *hosting provider*, Article 20 of the Belgian E-Commerce Act (Art. XII.19 BCEL) applies, which states that the provider is not liable for any hosted information, on two conditions. First, he/she may not have effective knowledge of any illegal activity or information nor of any facts and circumstances that indicate the unlawful character of the activity or information. Second, from the moment the ISP is aware of the unlawful character onwards, he/she has to warn the authorities and restrict access to the infringing information (Art. 20(1) and (3) E-Commerce Act).

It is questionable whether 'Keep Mov'n' fulfils the criteria to be exonerated as a hosting provider. Since they might be involved in the content of the site (e.g. proposing the theme), 'Keep Mov'n' might thus become a content provider. In that case, general liability would be the rule, without any possible exoneration for being an ISP. Such a view has been strongly confirmed by the Belgian Supreme Court.[79]

If there is no control and knowledge of the content, the exoneration of liability for ISPs does not limit the possibility for judicial authorities to oblige ISPs to

---

and on the free movement of such data, and repealing Directive 95/46/EC (General Data Protection Regulation), OJ L 119, 4 May 2016, 1–88.

75 Directive 2000/31/EC of the European Parliament and of the Council of 8 June 2000 on certain legal aspects of information society services, in particular electronic commerce, in the Internal Market ('Directive on Electronic Commerce'), OJ L 178, 17 July 2000, 1–16.

76 Directive 2004/48/EC of the European Parliament and of the Council of 29 April 2004 on the enforcement of intellectual property rights, OJ L 157, 30 April 2004, 16–25.

77 Act of 11 March 2003 on Certain Legal Aspects of the Information Society Services, *Official Gazette*, 17 March 2003 ('E-Commerce Act') [Wet 11 maart 2003 betreffende bepaalde juridische aspecten van de diensten van de informatiemaatschappij, *B.S.*, 17 maart 2003].

78 Electronic Communication Act, 13 June 2005, *Official Gazette*, 20 June 2005 [Wet betreffende de elektronische communicatie, 13 juni 2005, *B.S.*, 20 juni 2005].

79 Supreme Court [Cass.] P.03.1427.N, 3 February 2004, www.cass.be, *R.D.T.I.* 2004, no. 19, 51–59, note F. De Patoul and I. Vereecken, 'La responsabilité des intermédiaires de l'internet: première application de la loi belge' [The Responsability of ISPs: First Application of the Belgian Law].

terminate or prevent a specific infringement, if this has been foreseen by law (according to Art. 21§1 E-Commerce Act).[80] Articles 86ter §1 2° and 87§1 2° BCA explicitly provide this possibility for intermediaries since 2007.[81] In other words, irrespective of whether 'Keep Mov'n' should be qualified as a mere transfer hosting or content provider,[82] 'String' can ask for an injunction on the basis of the BCA.

In a number of decisions, hosting or mere conduit providers have been obliged by the courts to stop the downloading of illegal material.[83] In June 2007, the mere conduit provider Scarlet was ordered to install a filter programme, in the hope that this programme would counter peer-to-peer networks.[84] This decision has been criticised, not least because this can come into conflict with the provisions of Article 15 E-Commerce Directive and its Belgian counterpart (Art. 21§1 E-Commerce Act), which explicitly exclude a general obligation to monitor.[85] Although Articles 86ter §1 and 87§1 BCA now explicitly foresee the possibility of an injunction against 'intermediaries whose services are used … to violate copyright', Article 21§1 E-Commerce Act only allows for temporary judiciary injunctions in specific cases. A proper balance should be struck between avoiding a general obligation to monitor and the possibility of injunctions against intermediaries. The *Scarlet* case was appealed all the way up to the EU Court of Justice. The Court found that the obligation imposed on Scarlet to install a filtering system in order to identify and block unlawful use of file-sharing would in effect require the company to carry out a costly

---

80 J. Deene, 'Aansprakelijkheid van internet service providers' [The Liability of Internet Service Providers], *NjW* 2005, no. 115, 729.

81 As introduced by the new enforcement acts of 2007 we have spoken about in Case 1. Before this modification, some doctrine criticised the use of Art. 87 Copyright Act against intermediaries: C. De Preter and T. De Meese, 'Het aansprakelijkheidsregime voor ISP's en andere tussenpersonen in de wet elektronische handel: onbekend en onbemind' [The Liability Regime for ISPs and other Intermediaries in the E-Commerce Law: Unknown is Unloved], *T.B.H.* 2007, no. 3, 240, note under Pres. Court Antwerp [Voorz. Rb. Antwerpen], 5 October 2006.

82 The solution being the same for a possible injunction, this is of course not valid for the criminal and civil liability consequences.

83 Pres. Court Antwerp [Voorz. Rb. Antwerpen], 5 October 2006, *T.B.H.* 2007, no. 3, 233–236, note C. De Preter and T. De Meese, 'Het aansprakelijkheidsregime voor ISP's en andere tussenpersonen in de wet elektronische handel: onbekend en onbemind' [The Liability Regime for ISPs and other Intermediaries in the E-Commerce Law: Unknown is Unloved], *T.B.H.* 2007, no. 3, 237–244; note J. Deene, 'Seniorennet moet inbreuken doen ophouden. Senioren plegen auteursrechtelijke inbreuken' ['Seniorennet' Has to Stop Infractions. Seniors Commit Copyright Infractions], *De Juristenkrant*, 25 October 2006, 7.

84 Pres. Court of 1st Instance Brussels [Voorz. Rb. Brussel], 29 June 2007, commented by J. Deene, 'Scarlet moet illegaal downloaden verhinderen' [Scarlet Must Prevent Illegal Downloading], *De Juristenkrant*, 12 September 2007, 11.

85 C. De Preter and T. De Meese, 'Het aansprakelijkheidsregime voor ISP's en andere tussenpersonen in de wet elektronische handel: onbekend en onbemind' [The Liability Regime for ISPs and other Intermediaries in the E-Commerce Law: Unknown is Unloved], *T.B.H.* 2007, no. 3, 237–244, J. Deene, 'Scarlet moet illegaal downloaden verhinderen' [Scarlet Must Prevent Illegal Downloading], *De Juristenkrant*, 12 September 2007, 11.

general monitoring function for an unspecified period, which would be contrary to Directive 2000/31/EC. The Court also noted that the protection of intellectual property rights 'must be balanced against the protection of other fundamental rights'. While the order to install a filtering system only concerned the interests of copyright holders in musical works, the measure would not only limit Scarlet's right to conduct business, it could also infringe the fundamental rights of Internet users, namely the rights to the protection of personal data and to freedom of expression respectively guaranteed under Articles 8 and 11 of the EU Charter of Fundamental Rights.[86]

b) Release of names and addresses

Article 21§2 E-Commerce Act, implementing Article 15(2) of the Directive on Electronic Commerce, obliges ISPs to provide the judicial and administrative authorities, at their request, with all the information which is useful for the detection of infringements.

In the present case, a discussion could arise about the applicability of this provision, since it is not certain that those 33 people have really stored information on the 'Keep Mov'n' site. The wording of Article 15 E-Commerce Directive concerns the 'identification of recipients of their service with whom they have *storage agreements*'. If those people were merely downloading, no identification data would have to be given. Initially the storage agreement component was transposed in Belgian law (*opslagovereenkomsten*), but this is no longer the case since the E-Commerce Act was amended in 2005 in order to clarify ISPs' obligations.[87] Now, hosting, caching or mere conduit providers are simply obliged to communicate any information that can help to detect infringements. This includes names, postal addresses, IP addresses, etc.[88] Obviously, this is also in line with the right of information established by Article 8 Enforcement Directive, which has been implemented in Article 86ter §3 BCA.

The provisions above do not simply mean that names and addresses should be communicated by 'String' in the present case. Privacy issues and related European and Belgian legislation on the protection of personal data have to be kept in mind as well.

Highly relevant in this regard is the judgment of the CJEU in the *Promusicae* case.[89] In this case, the Court denies that member states are required to introduce an obligation to communicate personal data in order to ensure effective

---

86 CJEU judgment of 24 November 2011, *Scarlet v. SABAM*, C-70/10, ECLI:EU:C:2011:771.

87 Art. 51 Act of 20 July 2005 containing diverse provisions, *Official Gazette*, 29 July 2005 [Wet 20 july 2005 houdende diverse bepalingen, *B.S.*, 29 July 2005].

88 Explanatory Memorandum to the Act of 20 July 2005 containing diverse provisions, *Parl. Doc.*, Chambre, 2004–2005, DOC 51 1845/001, 45–47 [M.v.T bij de Wet van 20 july 2005 houdende diverse bepalingen, *Parl. St.*, Kamer, 2004–2005, DOC 51 1845/001, 45–47].

89 CJEU judgment of 29 January 2008, *Productores de Música de España (Promusicae) v. Telefónica de España SAU*, C-275/06, ECLI:EU:C:2008:54.

protection of copyright in the context of civil proceedings, as requested by 'String' in the present case. Provided that member states transpose the various IP and privacy Directives in such a way as to ensure a proportional balance between the fundamental rights of property, effective judicial protection and privacy, the Court does not exclude the possibility either.

It is interesting to see that Advocate General Kokott seemed inclined to think that an obligation to communicate such personal data for mere civil proceedings concerning copyright infringement would not easily fulfil the proportionality requirement. Also interesting is the emphasis which is put on the foreseeability of legitimate interferences with privacy, derived from Article 8(2) European Convention of Human Rights and Article 6(1)(b) Personal Data Protection Directive, which state that personal data must be collected for specified, explicit and legitimate purposes and may not be further processed in a way that is incompatible with those purposes.[90]

The main articles in the Belgian legislation that impose obligations on ISPs to provide information in infringement cases are Articles 21§2 E-Commerce Act and 86ter §3 BCA.[91] Since Article 3 2° E-Commerce Act excludes all matters which are regulated by privacy and personal data protection regulation from its scope of application, Article 21§2 does not suffice to oblige 'Keep Mov'n' to release names and addresses.[92] As for Article 86ter §3 BCA, this is an implementation of Article 8 Enforcement Directive, which explicitly preserves other statutory provisions governing the protection of confidentiality of information sources or the processing of personal data.

Taking a look at the privacy and personal data protection legislation itself, the relevant *lex specialis* is the Electronic Communication Act. According to Articles 122 and 124–126, traffic data need to be made anonymous as soon as possible and cannot be used or communicated unless the requirements of the explicitly mentioned exceptions to this principle are fulfilled. These exceptions include prescriptions that traffic data be kept and communicated to the administrative and judicial authorities upon request, for the purpose of investigating and prosecuting criminal acts. In the context of civil proceedings, however, no such obligation is foreseen, nor can it be deduced from any other provision, since the exceptions to the basic principles, i.e. confidentiality and anonymity, are to be interpreted restrictively.[93]

---

90 Opinion AG, 18 July 2007, *Productores de Música de España (Promusicae) v. Telefónica de España SAU*, C-275/06, ECLI:EU:C:2007:454, paras. 109–111.

91 As introduced by Art. 14 of the Act on the Civil Law Aspects of the Protection of Intellectual Property Rights, 9 May 2007, *Official Gazette*, 10 May 2007 [Wet 9 mei 2007 betreffende de burgerrechtelijke aspecten van de bescherming van intellectuele eigendomsrechten, *B.S.*, 10 mei 2007].

92 See also Art. 1(5)(b) Electronic Commerce Directive.

93 Explanatory Memorandum [Memorie van Toelichting], Electronic Communication Bill [Wetsontwerp betreffende de elektronische communicatie], *Parl. Doc.*, Chambre, 2004–2005, DOC 51 1425/1, 74.

So, although the European privacy and personal data protection legislation,[94] as interpreted by *Promusicae*, does not forbid member states to legislate to oblige ISPs to release names and addresses in such civil infringement proceedings, it could be argued that the Belgian legislator has not done this. Therefore, 'Keep Mov'n' could not *in casu* be obliged to release names and addresses.

However, this issue has not been extensively dealt with in legal doctrine, nor is there, as far as we know, really clarifying case law.[95] It is not an uncommon opinion that the release of names and addresses in civil proceedings would be allowed.[96] This argument is based on Article 125§1 1° Electronic Communications Act, which allows for communication data to be released 'if the law imposes or allows such actions' (own translation). Article 86ter BCA would then be the act allowing for the release of names and addresses. Although this reasoning might be acceptable, we may ask whether the introduction of a new exception on privacy and personal data legislation should not have been more explicit.

If the release of names and addresses is not possible, we need to keep in mind Article 80 BCA, which states that 'any malicious or fraudulent infringement of copyright and neighbouring rights shall constitute an offense of counterfeiting.' Infringing copyright for commercial purposes will constitute not only a *civil* infringement but also a *criminal* offence, and could therefore fall under the exception for criminal investigation and prosecution (Arts. 122§1 1°, 125§1 1° and 126§1 Electronic Communications Act).

---

94 Art. 13 Directive 95/46/EC of the European Parliament and of the Council of 24 October 1995 on the protection of individuals with regard to the processing of personal data and on the free movement of such data, OJ L 281, 23 November 1995, 31–50, and Art. 15 Directive 2002/58/EC of the European Parliament and of the Council of 12 July 2002 concerning the processing of personal data and the protection of privacy in the electronic communications sector (Directive on privacy and electronic communications), OJ L 201, 31 July 2002, 37–47.

95 In *Sabam v. Tiscali* (Pres. Court of 1st Instance Brussels [Voorz. Rb. Brussel], 29 June 2007) the argument that installing a P2P filter would come down to a violation of privacy and personal data legislation was refuted by the President of the Court on the basis of Art. 5b) of the general Act on the Protection of Personal Data of 8 December 1992, which provides for an exception on the prohibition of the processing of personal data when this is necessary for the execution of the agreement with the concerned party. The President of the Court considered that the standard contract conditions of Scarlet provided that it was forbidden to use the connection for copyright infringements and that Scarlet would have the right to take appropriate sanctions if the contract conditions were violated. Therefore, in the reasoning of the President of the Court, the data protection legislation would not be violated if a filter was installed and thus traffic data processed. This decision dates from before *Promusicae* and, in addition, the case did not specifically concern the situation where this traffic data would be communicated to copyright holders. Therefore, we doubt that this reasoning would be upheld in a situation as described in this modification.

96 So far there is little legal doctrine, but for instance: J. Deene, 'Privacy inbreukpleger kan primeren op handhaving auteursrecht' [Privacy of the Infringer may Prevail over Copyright Enforcement], *De Juristenkrant*, 16 April 2008, 5.

On the other hand, if indeed the release of names and addresses is possible after all, there is a safeguard. According to the wording of Article 86ter BCA, the release of names and addresses can only be ordered if an infringement of copyright has been established. In addition, 'String's' collecting of the traffic data (i.e. the IP addresses) is problematic, as it falls under Article 124 3° Electronic Communications Act, which prohibits intentionally taking cognisance of traffic data concerning other persons, as advised by the Belgian Privacy Commission in 2001.[97]

III. Metalegal Formants

The issues dealt with in this case relate to striking a proper balance between various fundamental interests such as freedom of information, privacy and ownership. Protecting ownership, i.e. protecting the interests of IP rightholders, can have a negative effect on the freedom of information and privacy (and *vice versa*). In this regard, ISPs play a central role: they are best placed to assist in protecting copyright or refusing to intervene where intervention would be detrimental to privacy or the free flow of information on the Internet.[98] This is the reason why IP rightholders' organisations tend to ask for more and more obligations on ISPs in order to ensure their interests. But perhaps taking on ISPs too harshly might have chilling effects. Being afraid of judicial actions, ISPs might act as judges themselves, taking information offline as a precaution. The common interest might be harmed in this way, as freedom of speech or possible legal uses of peer-to-peer networks get restricted.[99]

With both the Electronic Commerce Directive and the Enforcement Directive, Europe has aimed at establishing a proper balance. Rightholders can always ask for judicial injunctions to stop specific infringements, but ISPs still do not have a general obligation to monitor Internet traffic in order to avoid liability. While caching and hosting ISPs have more obligations than mere conduit ISPs, the former still do not risk liability when they take proper action from the moment they know of specific infringements.

---

97 Belgian Privacy Commission, Advice no. 44/2001, 12 November 2001 concerning the Compatibility of Investigating Online Copyright Infringement and the Legislation on Personal Data Protection and Telecommunication [Commissie voor de Bescherming van de Persoonlijke Levenssfeer, advies nr. 44/2001, 12 november 2001, betreffende de verenigbaarheid van het onderzoek naar overtredingen van het auteursrecht op het internet met de wetsbepalingen tot bescherming van persoonsgegevens en van telecommunicatie].

98 F. Coppens, 'Filtrage P2P: possibilités techniques et obstacles juridiques' [Filtering P2P: Technical Possibilities and Legal Obstacles], *R.D.T.I.* 2008, no. 30, 95.

99 F. Coudert and E. Werkers, 'La protection des droits d'auteur face aux réseaux *peer-to-peer*: la levée du secret des communications est-elle justifiée?' [The Protection of Copyright in the Context of *Peer-to-Peer*: is the lifting of Trade Secrets Justified?], *R.D.T.I.* 2008, no. 30, 80.

Even though ISPs are often not held liable for copyright infringements, they have, as intermediaries, a duty to cooperate with the administrative and judicial authorities. In this regard, it seems logical that they can be asked to give useful information on distribution channels, such as names and addresses, as foreseen by Article 8 Enforcement Directive. However, the European Union has kept the third pillar, i.e. privacy, of our fragile balance in mind as well.

Recent case law shows how delicate and uncertain the aforementioned balance is. In *Scarlet*, a Belgian court obliged a mere conduit ISP to install a filter programme. The ordered measure resembles an obligation for the ISP to constantly monitor and screen the traffic that passes through its network. While logic might be respected, since it is only after a specific judicial injunction that the ISP is burdened with this task, the principle excluding a general obligation to monitor is, perhaps, at risk.[100]

In *Promusicae*, the CJEU held that member states were not obliged to force ISPs to release names and addresses in civil proceedings. However, they are allowed to do so, as long as they respect a proper balance between privacy and rightholders' property rights. If society deems the online infringement of IP serious enough to give up such a large chunk of our Internet communication privacy, would those infringements then not be serious enough to justify criminal law sanctions as well? Under Belgian law, the release of names and addresses to the judicial and administrative authorities for criminal proceedings is foreseen. After all, when music companies go after individuals who download or upload content without commercial objectives,[101] is their goal then not mainly to punish and deter, rather than to obtain financial compensation for the damages those specific individuals have caused them?[102]

To conclude, the obligation to constantly screen and filter the Internet for certain content (*Scarlet*), combined with the obligation to release names and addresses in civil proceedings (possibility left open by *Promusicae*) for the mere

---

100 C. De Preter and T. De Meese, 'Het aansprakelijkheidsregime voor ISP's en andere tussenpersonen in de wet elektronische handel: onbekend en onbemind' [The Liability Regime for ISPs and other Intermediaries in the E-Commerce Law: Unknown is Unloved], *T.B.H.* 2007, no. 3, 237–244, J. Deene, 'Scarlet moet illegaal downloaden verhinderen' [Scarlet Must Prevent Illegal Downloading], *De Juristenkrant*, 12 September 2007, 11; F. Coppens, 'Filtrage P2P: possibilités techniques et obstacles juridiques', *R.D.T.I.* 2008, no. 30, 99–100.

101 We recall that under Belgian law, copyright infringement with commercial objectives would constitute a *criminally* sanctioned offence.

102 See also the critique on the position of the CJEU in *Promusicae* for broadening the exceptions on confidentiality of communcations: F. Coudert and E. Werkers, 'La protection des droits d'auteur face aux réseaux *peer-to-peer*: la levée du secret des communications est-elle justifiée?' [The Protection of Copyright in the Context of *Peer-to-Peer*: is the Lifting of Trade Secrets Justified?], *R.D.T.I.* 2008, no. 30, 83.

private interests of music companies, could constitute a challenge to the balance between IP, privacy and freedom of information.[103]

(2) CZECH REPUBLIC

I. Operative Rules

Both claims will be successful.

II. Descriptive Formants

A claim to prevent downloading of illegal materials would be successful under section 40(1)(b) Copyright Act. This provision of the Copyright Act prohibits not only infringement of copyright, but also exposure of infringement of copyright and impending repetition of exposure. It is important to note that the list included in this provision is not exhaustive but only illustrative. We can see this characteristic of the above-mentioned provision from the word 'especially' by which the list of prohibited behaviour starts. The Internet music provider 'Keep Mov'n' provides services which result in exposure of infringement of copyright and impending repetition.

The second claim against 'Keep Mov'n' will also succeed and 'Keep Mov'n' will have to release a list of names and addresses of 33 of its subscribers who are suspected of downloading mass quantities of illegal material. This claim will be granted according to the provisions of section 40(1)(c)(3) Copyright Act. This provision of the Copyright Act was adopted to prevent situations where the provider of the services argues personal data protection and will not release the personal data of subscribers who are infringing copyright. This provision clearly constitutes an obligation for providers such as 'Keep Mov'n' to disclose details of users who are infringing copyright or exposing copyright to infringement.

It is also necessary to say that the Copyright Act grants all rights to authors, so there is a special provision (section 41) to grant the above-mentioned rights to persons who are exclusively authorised by the author to use the work or persons who are entrusted by statute to exercise property rights. If 'String' is neither exclusively authorised to use the work nor entrusted by statute to exercise property rights, then only the author will successfully be able to claim remedies

---

[103] In this regard we would like to mention the careful approach of Committee of Ministers of the Council of Europe, in its Recommendation CM/Rec(2008)6, 26 March 2008, to the Member States on Measures to Promote the Respect for Freedom of Expression and Information with Regard to Internet Filters, available at: https://wcd.coe.int/ViewDoc.jsp?id=1266285&Site=CM&BackColorInternet=9999CC&BackColorIntranet=FFBB55&BackColorLogged=FFAC75 (last consulted 5 May 2019).

against 'Keep Mov'n'. In such a situation, 'String' will not have active legitimacy to the above-mentioned claim.

III. Metalegal Formants

Answer omitted.

(3) DENMARK

I. Operative Rules

'String' may have a successful claim against 'Keep Mov'n' for the prevention of downloading, and possibly for the release of the names and addresses of its subscribers.

II. Descriptive Formants

The Danish E-Commerce Act (DECA, 22 April 2002), which implements the rules of the E-Commerce Directive 2000/31/EC, exempts 'Keep Mov'n' from any liability for copyright infringements which take place on the site. These rules, however, do not rule out 'String's' claim for injunction against 'Keep Mov'n'. The rules on injunctions follow from the general Danish Procedural Act (DPA, 6 November 2008) §642(1).

In order to impose an injunction, 'String' needs to prove that 'Keep Mov'n' has performed an illegal act, for example that it has violated the rules of the DCA. The facts are not entirely clear about the nature of the site and 'Keep Mov'n's' role in it.

If 'Keep Mov'n' carries out the downloading itself, it would be a direct copyright infringement.

If 'Keep Mov'n' operates merely as an 'exchange site', i.e. only facilitates the downloading by independent users, this would not in itself constitute a copyright infringement in the form of a 'reproduction' or a 'making available' of songs. Instead 'Keep Mov'n' would likely be considered liable for complicity in the illegal downloading by users. The DCA does not contain any rules on the liability for complicity but the general principles derived from the Danish Penal Act would apply.

Denmark implemented the Enforcement Directive 2004/48/EC in 2006 and now provides for rules for example on measures regarding rights of information in DPA §306. This rule includes an obligation for infringers to give information containing the names and addresses of a number of different entities, including 'distributors'. This expression may be understood as covering the individual subscribers.

III. *Metalegal Formants*

The liability for operators of P2P and similar services is complicated. Often, the legal position depends very much on the technical character of the system. The DCA only contains specific rules regarding concrete actions in the form of uploading, downloading or making available, but not regarding the role of facilitating copyright infringements. This omission has created a lacuna in the system, which has been filled with the general principles on complicity. The result is a complicated legal situation which may illustrate the difficulties of making the traditional copyright rules fit the modern environment. The position also challenges the traditional copyright dictum that the legislation is 'technology neutral'. For P2P operators, choosing the 'right' technology may constitute the difference between a right and a wrong.

Regarding the passing on of the names etc., the issue at stake is the proper balance between the safeguarding of 'property rights' on the one hand and freedom of information and privacy on the other. The obligation to give information containing names etc. are limited to situations of rather serious copyright violations and it would, therefore, seem to be rather unproblematic.

(4) ESTONIA

I. *Operative Rules*

'String' can ask the court to oblige 'Keep Mov'n' to prevent the downloading of illegal material. The violation of the right of making the work available to the public is punishable as a misdemeanour.

'String' can further ask the court to oblige 'Keep Mov'n' to release the names and addresses of its subscribers.

II. *Descriptive Formants*

According to the description of the case, the Internet music provider 'Keep Mov'n' is violating the right of making the work available to the public (§13(1) clause 9^1 Copyright Act). According to §81^4(1) of the Copyright Act, the described activity (violation of an economic right) is punishable as a misdemeanour with a fine of up to 300 fine units.

'String' can ask the court to oblige 'Keep Mov'n' to prevent the downloading of illegal material. Subsection 81^7(1) Copyright Act provides that in the case of the unlawful use of a work or an object of related rights, the author or holder of related rights may, *inter alia*, claim compensation for damages and termination of the unlawful use of a work or an object of related rights.

'String' can ask the court to oblige 'Keep Mov'n' to release the names and addresses of 33 of its subscribers. Pursuant to §280(1) of the Code of Civil Procedure,[104] if an action is filed due to an infringement of copyright and related rights, the court may require, at the reasoned request of the plaintiff, that the defendant or another person provide written information concerning the origin and distribution systems of the services that infringe a right arising from intellectual property. Subsection 280(3) of the Code of Civil Procedure specifies that the information may include the names and addresses of the persons who ordered the services.

However, in criminal procedure an accused person is not obliged to reveal any information. This principle is established by §22 of the Constitution of the Republic of Estonia:[105] '[n]o one shall be compelled to testify against himself or herself'. Since IP infringement often constitutes a criminal act, there might be some conflict between the obligation to give information and the right not to testify against oneself.

III. Metalegal Formants

Before the changes to the Penal Code[106] which entered into force on 15 March 2007, all moral and economic rights of the author or holder of related rights were protected by criminal law. The explanatory memorandum to Amendment Act of the Penal Code and Related Acts emphasises the need to adopt a more differentiated approach in which only the most serious violations of moral and economic rights are regarded as criminal offences. One consideration for the differentiation was also whether the infringing act was committed for commercial purposes or not.

In our case, 'Keep Mov'n' makes the work available to the public for non-commercial purposes (at least, the text of the case does not imply that 'Keep Mov'n' gets money for its activity). Consequently, its activity does not constitute a criminal offence. However, at the same time, a person who uploads the illegal material commits a crime.[107]

---

104 Tsiviilkohtumenetluse seadustik. Entered into force on 1 January 2006 – RT I 2005, 26, 197; 2008, 59, 330 (in Estonian).

105 Eesti Vabariigi põhiseadus. Entered into force on 3 July 1992 – RT 1992, 26, 349; 2007, 33, 210 (in Estonian).

106 Karistusseadustiku ja selle muutmisega seonduvate seaduste muutmise seadus. Entered into force on 15 March 2007 – RT I 2007, 13, 69.

107 Reproduction, with the intention of distribution, of a work or an object of copyright without the permission of the author of the work, the holder of the copyright or the holder of the related rights is punishable by a pecuniary punishment or up to three years' imprisonment – Penal Code §222(1).

There is not much case law dealing with the obligation to reveal information in such cases.

(5) FRANCE

I. *Operative Rules*

If 'Keep Mov'n' is aware of the copyright violations, the claim to prevent the downloading will succeed.

II. *Descriptive Formants*

According to French law, 'Keep Mov'n' is considered to be a content provider and not a publisher or a service provider.[108] In principle, the content provider can be held liable under civil and criminal law when he/she knows that the content is illicit or when he/she does not remove the illicit content.[109]

If an Internet music provider such as 'Keep Mov'n' does not remove illicit content despite being aware of its illicit character, it can be held responsible under civil and criminal law. If it does not know that the content is illicit, 'String' could ask the provider to remove the content. Again, 'Keep Mov'n' could be held liable under civil and criminal law if it does not comply.

According to Article 6 II of the Law to Support Confidence in the Digital Economy, the content provider must store data allowing for the identification of the persons who have contributed to the infringement of content. If the provider does not respect this obligation, he/she can be condemned to a one-year prison term and a fine of €75,000.[110] The judicial authority can request access to this information under Article 6 II of the Law to Support Confidence in the Digital Economy. It is likely that the same regime will apply with respect to the identification of mass downloaders.

III. *Metalegal Formants*

Answer omitted.

---

[108] See Court of Paris, 15 April 2008, *J.-Y. Lafesse et al. v. Sté DailyMotion et al.*; R.L.D.I. 2008/38, n°1162, obs. J.-B. Auroux; comm. N. Dreyfus, R.L.D.I. 2008/39, n°1297; High Court Paris, 15 April 2008, *J.-Y. Lafesse et al. v. OVH et al.*; Court of Paris, 3 June 2008, *Lafesse et al. v. OVH et al.*

[109] Art. 6-I-2 Act No. 2004-575, 21 June 2004 to Support Confidence in the Digital Economy, *Journal Officiel*, 22 June 2004, p. 11168 ff.

[110] Art. 6-VI-1 Act No. 2004-575, 21 June 2004 to Support Confidence in the Digital Economy, *Journal Officiel* of 22 June 2004, p. 11168 ff.

(6) GERMANY

I. Operative Rules

'String' can claim an injunction against 'Keep Mov'n', but does not have a claim for disclosure of the addresses of subscribers.

II. Descriptive Formants

As in the base case, the claim is to be based on §§16, 17, 19a UrhG (rights of the author) and §85 UrhG (rights of the producer (of CDs)). The difference is the defendant: 'Keep Mov'n' is neither a user nor a mere 'service provider',[111] but a 'content provider'. For the individualistic, liability-based German injunction law (*Störerhaftung*), it is essential that 'Keep Mov'n' is, in one way or another, responsible for the infringement of the copyright by the end users.[112] In contrast to Napster, 'Keep Mov'n' is providing not only computing power and software, but also music. The company controls the content and the system (§44a UrhG[113] does not apply.) Thus, it is liable for the infringement.

However, 'String' is *not* entitled to have the names and addresses of subscribers disclosed, due to data protection, neither under §101a UrhG, nor under data protection laws (Telemediengesetz [In English: Telemedia Act], TelekommunikationsG [Telecommunications Act] data protection laws/GDPR). Early on, lower courts decided this way based on §101 UrhG.[114] These decisions were confirmed by the Bundesgerichtshof (BGH).[115] If, however, the potential infringer is asked for disclosure, the BGH cautioned that the requirements for the burden of proof to be met shall not be overstretched. 'Sufficient probability' shall be sufficient to accept a duty to submit documentation. Again, third party

111 Yet the former ultimate distinction between mere service provider and the responsible content provider does not hold any more. In addition, service providers can be liable for the violation of personality rights by deep-linking, if they violate their inspection duty (Kammergericht (Higher Regional Court Berlin), *Computer und Recht* 6/2006, 413).

112 For the competing concept of vicarious liability compare the UK country report, specifically explaining US law in the *Napster* case. See also M. Gampp, 'Trendwende im US-Urheberrecht: Sind Musiktauschbörsen doch legal?', GRUR Int. 2005, 107–121. The basics of *Störerhaftung* were confirmed by OLG Hamburg, decision of 8 February 2006 (U 78/05), GRUR-RR 2006, 148 – *Cybersky*.

113 '*Zulässige vorübergebende Vervielfältigungshandlungen*'.

114 Hanseatisches OLG decision of 28 April 2005, Jur-PC Web.-Dok. 62/2005; OLG Frankfurt decision of 25 January 2005, K&R 3/2005, 138; LG Köln, ZUM 3/2005, 236; for academic accounts see G. Spindler and J. Dorschel, CR 1/2005, 38; M. Bohne, GRUR-RR 2005, 145; V. Kitz, GRUR 2003, 1014.

115 BGH, GRUR 2013, 509 – *UniBasic-IDOS*.

inquiries are not accepted.[116] This line of argumentation is deemed to be in line with the corridor spelled out by the European Court of Justice in *Promusicae*.[117] The formal principle is that German procedural law does not acknowledge a claim against the defendant to deliver information about third parties which does not directly support the claim against the defendant – it protects the defendant against those claims by which the plaintiff aims at reducing the burden of his/her own inquiry against third parties (no *Ausforschungsanspruch*).[118] Only in cases of close family relations and if the parent is identified as a telephone subscriber is the parent subject to a 'secondary duty to disclose' (*sekundäre Darlegungslast*) the child's name, if the child had admitted the copyright violation.[119]

III. Metalegal Formants

In contrast to the base case, this case revolves around the balance between protection on the one hand, and data protection, freedom of the Internet and civil procedure principles on the other hand. By clearly opting for the 'consent solution' (§19a UrhG), the Bundestag decided on a strong protection design (supra base case) and thus paved the way for DRM systems. Yet powerful opposite interests limit the protection of copyright: individual data protection and civil procedure principles.

Under the principle of civil procedure, nobody shall be compelled by anybody to produce data without the probability of having a legal claim, and nobody shall be compelled by anyone to disclose data of other persons. These liberal standards have survived the transformation to an information society.[120] The German debate revolved around the transposition of Directive 2004/48/EC (more protection for the copyright holder) for a long time, but got overtaken by the EU debate on stronger data protection (eventually becoming GDP Regulation (EU) No. 2016/679). The main issue remains the same: the addressees are Internet service providers. The original attempts to go after the final users had encountered strong academic objection – arguing that this is in conflict with national[121] and European[122] data protection.[123]

---

116 T. Dreier, in: T. Dreier and G. Schulze (eds.), *UrhG-Commentary* (6th ed., Munich: 2018), §101a, para. 3; J. Wimmers, in: U. Loewenheim, M. Leistner and A. Ohly (eds.), *Urheberrecht*, (6th ed., Munich: 2020), paras. 8 and 15.

117 CJEU judgment of 29 January 2008, C-275/06, ECLI:EU:C:2008:54.

118 On this procedural principle in comparative perspective: J. Wimmers, in: U. Loewenheim/ M. Leistner/A. Ohly (eds.), *Urheberrecht*, (6th ed., Munich: 2020), para. 3.

119 BGH judgement of 30 March 2017, I ZR 19/16.

120 One case (AG Darmstadt, 30 June 2005 – 300 C 397/04) is a claim against saving user data (in the forefront of a suit of music distributors).

121 Basic Freedom Art. 10 German Constitution; §88 TKG.

122 Directive 2002/58/EC; Directive 2000/31/EC (E-Commerce Directive).

123 G. Spindler and J. Dorschel, 'Der Auskunftsanspruch gegen den Provider', CR 2005, 38–48.

There is an interesting parallel in breeders' rights litigation. The constellation is similarly triangular: the proprietary breeder, the distributor and the farmers who (after having paid the purchase price) owe equitable remuneration for cultivating certified varieties. How can the breeder investigate whether the farmers pay the fees due? The ECJ ruled that a claim for information against the distributor is only legitimate if there are indications of the violation of rights. But if the breeder has information that the supplier of processing services is providing preparatory services to farmers to whom he/she supplied the propagating material, then the distributor is obliged not only to provide the names of farmers directly indicated, but also to reveal the names of those farmers he/she is also serving.[124]

(7) GREECE

I. Operative Rules

'String' will have a successful claim only for preventing the mediation in the exchanges of the songs, but not for releasing the addresses or names of the subscribers. 'Keep Mov'n' may object, but only after paying a 'reasonable fee'.

II. Descriptive Formants

The Internet music provider is harming the reproduction right of authors and rightholders of neighbouring rights according to the international conventions, the *acquis communautaire* and the national law. 'Keep Mov'n' is obliged to have the permission of the creator and other rightholders, not only since the right of reproduction and the right of making available are exclusive rights, but firstly because 'Keep Mov'n' is profiting from this activity and therefore this company is illegally exploiting the intellectual property of the record company. The latter will have a successful claim against the Internet music provider. The downloading of sound recordings will only be possible after paying a 'reasonable charge' according to Article 18 para. 3 Law 2121/1993 (see also Art. 102 TFEU). Nevertheless, the claim for releasing names and addresses of clients infringes the constitutionally secured secret of communication (Art. 19 of the Greek Constitution).

III. Metalegal Formants

It is a particular characteristic of most networks that, unlike other locations of transactions, in order to move or participate in these, the individual is forced to

124 CJEU judgment of 14 October 2004, *Brangewitz*, C-336/02, ECLI:EU:C:2004:622.

enter into a contract – indirectly or directly – with their provider, and within this framework to inform him/her of a series of his/her personal data concerning his/her transactions in question. For example, for the debiting of any telephonic communication, the disclosure to the provider of the telephone numbers of the parties communicating, the place of installation of the terminal of each, etc., is required. Similarly, for an exchange of electronic messages (e.g. e-mail), the disclosure of the electronic addresses of the parties, the duration of 'entry' or of 'surfing' of the caller on the Internet, the terminals of sending and receipt of the message with the form of its storage in hidden memory, etc., is required.

These necessarily revealed personal data do not constitute the (intellectual) content of the transaction via the network, but only empirically perceived characteristics of it; thus, the parties to the transaction, the time it took place, and the time and place of its performance are its '*external* data'. Successive subcategories of this constitute the so-called '*data of movement*' of the communication (e.g. the parties, the numbers and duration of their call, etc.) and the so-called '*data of position*' (e.g. of the terminals, the installations of each place). Contrasted with the 'external' data of the communication are the '*internal*' data, that is, the content of the communication.

In spite of this, differentiating the legal protection of the external personal data from that of the internal is not justified, since from the elementary or more complex processing of the external data it will usually be possible to make conclusions about the internal data, that is, about the content of the transactions which they concern, and, by extension, about the personal identities of the parties engaging in them. For example, the provider of the network will usually by definition be in a position to acquire a host of information about those engaging in transactions within its network; (particularly by re-combining this information), it will be able to learn about their commercial or consumer habits and preferences, their circle of acquaintances, even about their health problems (in the event of frequent calls to a doctor or hospital), the number of people whom each person is entertaining, as well as when and for how long (e.g. in the event of the multiplication, for example doubling or tripling, of the quantity of electricity or water consumed), and so on. Thus it is to be concluded, in accordance with the prevailing view,[125] that external data (of the communication), that is, also the electronic addresses of the downloaders of the works which are traded by means of the Internet, are also subject to the confidentiality of communication

---

125 See, for preference, Dagtoglou, *Fundamental Rights* (2001), p. 351; Livos, 'Penal Protection of Telecommunication Data', *Penal Chronicles* 37, 737, 753; Chrysogonos, *Fundamental and Social Rights* (2002), p. 240; Kaminis, *Unlawful means of proof and the constitutional safeguarding of civil rights* (1998), p. 205; Tsakyrakis, 'The confidentiality of communication – Absolutely inviolable, or a wish of the legal order?', *NoB* 1993, 998; Voutsakis, 'Comment in Athens District Courts Council 3533/99', *NoB* 2000, 1662 ff.; Tsolias, *DiMEE* 2004, 362 ff., passim; Karakostas, *Law and the Internet* (2nd ed., 2003), p. 141, footnote 8.

under Article 19 of the Constitution.[126] However, the earlier prevailing view that according to Article 19 of the Constitution only the content of the communication (its 'internal data') is confidential has not been entirely abandoned.[127]

Despite that, it should be noted that in cases of vexatious, malicious or emergency calls, the Community legislator (Art. 10a Directive 2002/58/EC) provides for the possibility of the lifting of confidentiality, and that, at least until the voting of the new law on the confidentiality of electronic communications (Law 3471/2006), there arose a debate between the Authority for the Protection of Personal Data[128] and the Authority for the Maintenance of the Confidentiality of Communications[129] concerning the borderline between their responsibilities. The position which the common legislator (Law 3471/2006) attempts to take on the problem of adjustment to Directive 2002/58 seems contradictory. On the one hand, the legislator favours the *en bloc* inclusion 'of any use of electronic communications services' 'in the confidentiality of communications', so that this is lifted 'only on the conditions and with the procedures stipulated in Art. 19 of the Constitution' (Art. 4 para. 1 Law 3471/2006). On the other hand, in the sole – in practical terms – instances where the need to reveal the external data of electronic communication arises, that is, in cases of vexatious, malicious or emergency calls, Article 8 of Law 3471/2006 expressly provides for the lifting of the confidentiality of the call numbers without the fulfilment of the conditions of Article 19 of the Constitution, that is, without evidence of a serious danger to public security or the commission of serious crimes. In this way, the legislator regulates the issue as if it were not subject to Article 19 of the Constitution but proclaims the need for it to be subject to it.

---

126 On the other hand, no practical problem is created by the correctness of the inclusion of external data within the provision, corresponding to Art. 19 of the Constitution, of Art. 8 of the European Human Rights Convention, since the latter makes subject to the same treatment both the confidentiality of correspondence and the confidentiality of the private sphere, pardoning, moreover, the lifting of confidentiality on much broader substantive conditions and without any further specific prerequisites e.g. authorities responsible for lifting the confidentiality, etc. The same applies *a fortiori* to the equivalent Art. 17 of the International Covenant on Civil and Political Rights (Art. 1 Law 2462/1997) and Art. 12 of the Universal Declaration of Human Rights (a text, however, without legal binding force according to the prevailing view, see Roukounas, *International Public Law I* (1980), pp. 203 ff.).

127 See, for preference, Manesis, *Fundamental Rights* (1984), p. 238; Pararas, *1975 Constitution – Corpus I* (1982), p. 293; Karamanos, 'The confidentiality of communication', *NoB* 1968, 16, 1137, and the earlier case law, e.g. Opinion of the AP 38/1959, *PoinChr* 10, 55 ff. The position has also been expressed that the external data of communication, though subject to Art. 19 of the Constitution, are safeguarded to a lesser extent, Dimitropoulos, *Constitutional Rights. Special Part, Lectures on constitutional law III/B* (2005), p. 182; Dimitropoulou, 'The Confidentiality of Letters' in *Aegean University, Marinal Business Sciences* (2006), pp. 90, 99–100 and 103–104.

128 See its Decision No. 79/2000.

129 See Opinion 1/2005, *DiMEE* 2005, 142.

(8) IRELAND

I. Operative Rules

Under Irish case law, it is likely that ISPs and perhaps some other providers will move to put a stop to the practice of illegal downloading and will also reveal names, under a court order. There have been a number of cases on this issue over the past few years, as detailed below.

II. Descriptive Formants

In 2005[130] Kelly J., in the High Court, heard a case in which the plaintiffs, the Irish Recorded Music Association, requested the ISP, Eircom, to reveal the names and addresses of 17 of their subscribers. There was neither a suggestion nor evidence of any wrongdoing on the part of the defendants but, as the ISP, they were aware of the identities of their subscribers. The defendants were concerned with finding out about their obligations of confidentiality to their subscribers. The judge in this case referred to a House of Lords decision[131] in *Norwich Pharmacal Company and Others v. Customs and Excise Commissioners*[132] in which a principle of innocent infringement was established. In that case, Lord Reid stated that where a person got mixed up in another's tortious wrongdoing, even where they were not at fault, although incurring no personal liability, there was still a duty to disclose the identities of the wrongdoers to the wronged party or parties.[133] This principle is a part of the law in several common law jurisdictions and the name given to these orders is 'Norwich Pharmacal Orders'. They obligate the disclosure of identity and other information held by a third party concerning an alleged wrongdoer to the wronged person. A qualifier has been put on the use of these orders in Ireland by Finlay C.J., who stated in *Megaleasing UK Ltd v. Barret*[134] that the proof of wrongdoing would have to be very clear and that only names and identities should be discovered rather than facts concerning the commission of the wrong. The court engaged in a balancing exercise in which it found that the identities would only be publicised if infringement proceedings were taken by the plaintiffs.

---

130 *EMI Records (Ireland) Ltd, Sony BMG Music Entertainment (IRL) Ltd, Universal Music Ireland Ltd and Warner Music Ireland Ltd v. Eircom Ltd and BT Communications Ireland Ltd* [2005] IEHC 233, [2005] 4 IR 148.

131 As a common law jurisdiction, when there is no Irish authority, Irish judges will often refer to other common law jurisdictions to seek guidance on the matter at hand.

132 [1974] AC 133.

133 Ibid., p. 175.

134 [1993] IRLM 497, 504.

In another High Court case, *EMI Records [Ireland] Ltd v. Eircom PLC*,[135] a settlement had already been reached between the parties in the main proceedings, as the defendant had agreed not to oppose the plaintiffs' application. The plaintiffs comprised EMI Records, Sony, Universal and Warner, and their application was to require the ISP, Eircom to block access to The Pirate Bay. Many cases in Ireland do not proceed to a full hearing as an interlocutory injunction is granted, which freezes and ultimately halts any action. In the instant case, the judge did not have the opportunity to hear both sides of the argument, which he acknowledged may have affected the outcome of the order. An injunction, which required the defendant to block or disable Internet subscribers' access to The Pirate Bay, was granted.

The judge was satisfied that section 40(4) of the CRRA 2000 sometimes entitles plaintiffs to seek an order against an innocent party who, nonetheless, transmits infringing material.

In *EMI and Others v. Eircom Ltd*,[136] a 2009 settlement between EMI and Eircom, issues were raised under the Data Protection Acts 1988 and 2003 which required scrutiny by the court to ensure compliance with that legislation.

Among the software devices developed to detect illegal downloaders is DtecNet. Information regarding the IP address where the illegal downloading has taken place is provided by the plaintiffs to the defendant, Eircom. Eircom can identify the bill payer of the account. Eircom then informs its subscriber that they have been detected infringing copyright. If there is a second incident of illegal downloading, Eircom is obliged, when so informed, under the settlement to write to the subscriber warning them that unless the infringement ceases, they will be disconnected from the Internet service. Where there is a third infringement, Eircom then removes Internet service provision from the subscriber. The plaintiffs are not interested in finding out the identities of the copyright infringers and have thus resiled from their earlier practice of seeking orders against individuals – an expensive and time-consuming process. Before they are cut off, the bill payer does have an opportunity to make a representation to Eircom, which has responsibility for reviewing all the evidence. The court was satisfied that the points raised by the Data Protection Commissioner about the lawfulness of the settlement terms were not warranted. The court felt that the graduated response, or three strikes, was lawful and was adamant that no accusations of criminal behaviour were being made.

In *EMI v. UPC*[137] another ISP, UPC was sued by EMI. They had refused to sign up to the 'three strikes' policy of Eircom. They asserted that they were a mere conduit and did not filter Internet traffic. Therefore they could not prevent

---

135 [2009] IEHC 411.

136 [2010] IEHC 108.

137 Unreported, High Court, Charleton J., 11 October, 2010.

copyright infringement. The judge, Charleton J. studied other jurisdictions' laws regarding the legality of cutting off Internet access in Ireland. He found that there was no basis in law for so doing, despite the fact that EMI relied on section 40(4) to seek to establish that innocent infringers could be deemed to be culpable of copyright infringement if they failed to take action to prevent this activity within a reasonable period of time, on being informed of this misuse of their service. No blocking injunctions to prevent access to Pirate Bay were then available in Irish law. The judge reconsidered the previous two EMI cases: the judgment he delivered in 2010 still stood but he observed in the case that Eircom never sought to argue a contrary case, despite having appeared in court. This was part of the settlement terms with EMI, however. He said: 'I regret that my previous judgment in the matter was wrong. The legislative basis enabling me to act in that way does not exist in Irish law as it exists in other European jurisdictions.' Ireland was not yet in compliance with its obligations under European law.

In *EMI Records (Ireland) Ltd & Ors v. Data Protection Commissioner & Anor,*[138] Eircom had been operating a three strikes rule for four months. Its subscribers contracted not to use the Internet to infringe copyright. Three hundred and ninety-one subscribers were wrongly notified that they had uploaded material in breach of contract and one made a complaint to the Data Protection Commissioner about a breach of privacy as the recording companies did not have permission to monitor his Internet activities. In January 2012, the DPC issued a notice to Eircom directing it to cease its scheme with the recording companies. The case in question is a judicial review of the lawfulness of that notice. The DPC argued that in the *SABAM* case,[139] the ECJ ruled that ISPs were not responsible for monitoring copyright infringement of users. Another Belgian referral was made to the ECJ in C-360/10 *Belgische Vereniging van Auteurs, Componisten en Uitgevers CVBA (SABAM) v. Netlog NV,*[140] the outcome of which was that there can be no blanket filters. However, the DPC's enforcement notice was found to be incomplete, and therefore invalid.

EMI Records (Ireland) Ltd & Ors v. Data Protection Commissioner[141] involved an appeal to the Supreme Court by the DPC in which the decision of the trial judge was upheld.

In *EMI Records (Ireland) Ltd & Ors v. UPC Communications Ireland Ltd & Ors,*[142] Digital Rights Ireland unsuccessfully sought to be joined as a friend of the court, having wanted to make a submission regarding Statutory Instrument 59 of 2012. This allowed for the granting of injunctions against Internet service

138 [2012] IEHC 264.
139 Case C-70/10 *Scarlet Extended S.A. v. Societebelge des auteurs, compositeurs et editeurs SCRL,* ECLI:EU:C:2011:771.
140 ECLI:EU:C:2012:85.
141 [2013] IESC 34.
142 [2013] IEHC 204.

providers pursuant to the provisions of Article 8(3) of the Copyright Directive 2001/29/EC. This Directive obliges Member States to provide remedies such as damages and injunctions for copyright owners. They were deemed by the court not to be an objective group.

In *EMI Records (Ireland) Ltd & Ors v. UPC Communications Ireland Ltd & Ors*[143] the applicant applied for an injunction requiring the defendants, the ISP UPC, to block access to The Pirate Bay and this injunction was granted because the legislation had since been approved.

Sony Music Entertainment (Ireland) Ltd v. UPC Communications Ireland Ltd (No 1)[144] involved an application to direct an ISP to enforce a 'graduated response system.' This was similar to the *EMI v. UPC* case in 2010 which was dismissed because the legislation at the time was incomplete, though this had since been rectified. The plaintiff used software to detect infringing users. The defendant would then contact the offending user and if the downloading continued, on the third occasion the plaintiff could apply for a Norwich Pharmacal order to identify the customer. The plaintiff could apply to court to have the customer's connection terminated.

Sony Music Entertainment (Ireland) Ltd. & Ors v. UPC Communications Ireland Ltd.[145] involved an appeal by UPC who claimed that the court had no jurisdiction to make such orders against non-infringing ISPs and that a special regulator should be appointed. The Court of Appeal, however, confirmed that national courts do have jurisdiction to grant graduated response system injunctions against innocent intermediaries if there is an allegation of copyright infringement.

III. Metalegal Formants

Answer omitted.

(9) ITALY

I. Operative Rules

Yes, 'String' will have a successful claim with regard to the illegal downloading activities, but not with regard to the disclosure of the names and addresses of 'Keep Mov'n' subscribers.

According to Article 156 ICL, any infringing activity can be enjoined by a court. Still, the release of the names and addresses of the site's subscribers,

143 [2013] IEHC 274.
144 [2015] IEHC 317.
145 [2016] IECA 231.

regulated by Article 156bis, will not be granted, since, according to case law on the subject, the right to privacy of the site's subscribers' will prevail unless evidence of the commission of a crime can be provided.

II. Descriptive Formants

The first issue, the enjoining of any illegal downloading activities, has a clear and simple solution: Article 156 states that a court order to prohibit any infringing activities can be obtained even against a service provider whose services are used for carrying out copyright violations.[146]

The second issue, the injunction to disclose the names and addresses of 'Keep Mov'n' subscribers, is more problematic since it involves two conflicting rights: on one hand the right to obtain information about infringing activities, granted by Article 156bis ICL, and on the other hand the right to privacy.

According to Article 156bis ICL, a copyright holder may get a court order for the disclosure of the 'elements for the identification' of the individuals involved in said copyright infringement. But according to Article 132 of the Italian Privacy Code (d.lgs. 30 June 2003, no. 196), telephone traffic data may be disclosed only for the repression of crimes, thus requiring a specific crime to be committed.

In an important decision, which has been confirmed by other courts, the Court of First Instance of Rome (Tribunale di Roma)[147] ruled that file-sharing does not necessarily constitute a crime. For this reason, the right to privacy, as a personality right, prevails over copyright and its economic dimension. In this specific situation, downloading music without the copyright holder's consent, while illegal, does not constitute a crime but rather, according to Article 174ter, an administrative infraction.

The case before the court involved an independent German music label who monitored for some time many peer-to-peer networks in order to collect the users' IP addresses. It then asked for a court order to have Internet service providers disclose users' personal information with the intention of suing them. The court, refusing, stated that the monitoring of peer-to-peer networks by a private company, in order to harvest the IP addresses of supposedly infringing users, is an illegal processing of personal data and thus forbidden by the Italian privacy legislation (which is an implementation of Directive 95/46/EC of the European Parliament and of the Council of 24 October 1995 on the protection of individuals with regard to the processing of personal data and on the free movement of such data).

---

146 A similar case was decided by the Tribunale di Bergamo, with a court order no. 3277 of August 1st, 2008.

147 See Tribunale di Roma, 17 March 2008, *Peppermint Jam Records GmbH v. Soc. Tiscali*, in *Giur. it.*, 2008, 1738, with a note by Sirotti Gaudenzi.

This decision was confirmed by the European Court of Justice in the *Promusicae* decision.[148]

It is worth noting that the privacy supervisory authority (Autorità Garante per la Tutela dei Dati Personali) strongly supported this ruling and adopted a decision ordering various private companies to stop their monitoring activities of peer-to-peer networks and to erase any collected data by 31 March 2008.[149]

III. Metalegal Formants

Among scholars there seems to a be a consensus that privacy prevails over copyright protection, since privacy protects the human personality and it is grounded on constitutionally protected rights, while copyright has no constitutional coverage.[150]

(10) LITHUANIA

I. Operative Rules

The record company can claim an injunction against 'Keep Mov'n'. As far as the second request is concerned, this will likely succeed as well.

II. Descriptive Formants

The incorporation of Directive 2004/48/EC has extended the means for protecting intellectual property rights by Law No. X-855, of 12 October 2006.

The exclusive nature of IP rights means that the holder of these rights can prohibit any unauthorised use of the rights he/she enjoys, or any other infringement of such rights. The author or the holder of the neighbouring rights can opt for any of the actions regulated in Article 77.[151]

---

148 CJEU judgment of 29 January 2008, *Promusicae*, C-275/06, ECLI:EU:C:2008:54.

149 See Garante per la protezione dei dati persona, available at http://www.garanteprivacy.it/garante/doc.jsp?ID=1495246 (accessed 28 February 2008).

150 Scorza, Caso, 'Il conflitto tra copyright e privacy nelle reti peer-to-peer: in margine al caso peppermint', (2007) 5 *Diritto dell'Internet*, p. 461.

151 Art. 55 of the Copyright Act lists the actions: (1) recognition of rights; (2) injunction with the aim of prohibiting the continuation of unlawful acts; (3) prevention from carrying out acts because of which the rights may be actually infringed or damage may be actually caused; (4) redress of the infringed moral rights (injunction to make appropriate amendments, to announce the infringement in the press, or in any other way); (5) exaction of unpaid remuneration for unlawful use of a work, objects of related rights or *sui generis* rights; (6) compensation for property damage, including lost income and other expenses, and in the cases provided for in Art. 84 non-pecuniary damage, as well; (7) payment of compensation; and (8) application of other measures for defence of the rights, provided for by this and other laws.

As far as the first question is concerned, it is essential for liability under Lithuanian law that 'Keep Mov'n' was directly or indirectly responsible for the infringement of the copyright (Art. 6.246 of the Civil Code). The Supreme Court has confirmed that the indirect contribution to the infringement of IP rights suffices.[152] Therefore, 'String' could be justified in asking for 'Keep Mov'n' to put an end to its illegal activity.

As regards the second request, according to Article 79 of the Law on Copyright and Neighbouring Rights, the court may order that information on the origin and distribution networks of copies of the works, goods or services which infringe copyright or related rights be provided. The legislative provisions pertaining to the requirements for collecting evidence and provisional measures are also to be attributed to the procedural rules.[153]

Article 79(2) sets out that infringers of the rights who were found to be using the services infringing the rights on a commercial scale, or who were found to be providing on a commercial scale services used by third persons in activities infringing the rights, may be ordered to provide information on the origin and distribution networks of copies of the works, other objects of the rights protected under the Law, or goods or services which infringe copyright. One of the conditions for applying this provision is the protection of confidentiality of sources of personal data. In this hypothetical case, Article 79(2) does not apply because there is a question whether 'String' has a claim against 'Keep Mov'n' to release the names and addresses of its subscribers but not a claim against the subscribers to provide information on the infringement.

The second possibility to gain information about the addresses of subscribers in a form of evidence is Article 80 of the Copyright Act. The court may, on application by a party which has presented reasonably available evidence sufficient to support its claims and has, in substantiating those claims, specified evidence which lies in the control of the opposing party, order that such evidence be presented by the opposing party. The information about the addresses of 33 of its subscribers lies in the control of 'Keep Mov'n' and the record company has no access to that information. For the moment, there is no legal precedent that explains the scope of this provision.[154] As far as the grammatical expression of the provision is concerned, it should apply in this hypothetical case. This alternative should be considered with a great caution with a view to the necessity of protecting confidentiality.

---

152 Supreme Court case No. 3K-3-48/2007, *K.M. leidykla 'Briedis', M.B., V.J., R.M. ir A.L. v. J.K. leidykla 'Saulabrolis', UAB 'Arlila' ir S.D.*

153 As set out in Arts. 6, 7 and 9 Enforcement Directive.

154 CJEU judgment of 29 January 2008, *Promusicae*, C-275/06, ECLI:EU:C:2008:54.

III. Metalegal Formants

Lithuanian legal copyright doctrine recognises injunctions as preventive as well as precautionary measures for intellectual property which can be applied without any claims for damages.[155]

Nevertheless, the enforcement of copyright and related rights cannot always be considered effective due more to social, economic or public character factors, than to legal reasons. Local society is not yet sufficiently mature to recognise this type of ownership, and it is still tolerant of infringements of copyright as well as of other intellectual property rights.[156]

(11) NETHERLANDS

I. Operative Rules

'String' has a claim against 'Keep Mov'n' to prevent the downloading of illegal files, but not for the disclosure of the names and addresses of the subscribers.

II. Descriptive Formants

In principle, a hosting provider is not liable for the actions of its subscribers, under Article 6:196c of the Dutch Civil Code, unless it had actual knowledge of illegal activity and was not aware of facts or circumstances from which illegal activity is apparent. An ISP becomes obliged to prevent the downloading of illegal material as soon as a rights owner informs it of illegal activities by its users. Failure to take measures after being informed will engage its liability for the infringement of copyrights by its users.[157] On the other hand, if there is evidence that the service provider is aware of the illegal nature of its subscribers' activities, rights owners would be entitled to ask the court to put an end to these activities.

In the present case, it could be argued that if 'Keep Mov'n' has become so popular among music lovers, it is because it offers access to illegal content through peer-to-peer software. On the basis of sufficient evidence showing that 'Keep Mov'n' has actual knowledge of the illegal nature of the downloading activities from its service, 'String' could ask the court to put a stop to this practice.

Technically speaking, i.e. even if 'Keep Mov'n' is not directly liable, 'String' would be able to ask for an injunction to stop the illegal activities from taking

155 V. Mizaras, 'Lithuanian Copyright: Historical and Modern Aspects and Trends of Development', *Journal of Copyright Society of the USA*, 2006, vol. 54, No. 4, p. 853.
156 Ibid., p. 859.
157 Rb. Den Haag, 9 juni 1999, *BIE* 1999, 117 (*Scientology v. XS4ALL*).

place via its services on the basis of Article 26d of the Copyright Act. This provision implements Article 8(3) of Directive 2001/29/EC, and states: 'Upon application by the author, the court may order an intermediary whose services are used by a third party to infringe copyright, to cease and desist from providing the services that are used for that infringement'.

A service provider can be ordered to release the names and addresses of its subscribers in order to enable a rightholder to protect his/her rights. There is no obligation for the service provider to actively hand over the names and addresses. However, the Supreme Court of the Netherlands ruled that in certain circumstances the refusal to release such information can be a wrongful act towards the rightholder. The Court gave a broad interpretation of the provisions of Directive 2000/31/EC on Electronic Commerce, as implemented in Article 6:196c Dutch Civil Code, to conclude that Internet service providers may owe a duty of care to rightholders to monitor or prevent unlawful activities.[158] In this sense, the Court considers that the obligation to disclose names and addresses of users is not limited solely to cases where the provider has actual knowledge of unlawful activities taking place. Since names and addresses are personal data, the rules in the Dutch Data Protection Act must be followed. The provisions of this Act prescribe that service providers can only supply the information if the interests of the rightholder are more important than the interests of the persons whose names and addresses are about to be released. In addition, the rightholder who is asking for the information has to process the information in accordance with the Dutch Data Protection Act.[159]

III. Metalegal Formants

The question concerns the role of ISPs in the context of peer-to-peer networks. ISPs can play an important role in the enforcement of intellectual property rights. ISPs are crucial to the freedom of information. Furthermore, ISPs have the obligation to respect the privacy of their clients. In determining the ISPs' obligations in this context, several interests must be weighed against each other. A balance has to be struck between the interests of rightholders, the freedom of information and privacy. A few points can be made about these interests.

From the rightholders' perspective, it is important to point out the difficulty of enforcing their rights. In the peer-to-peer context, the number of infringements of copyright by anonymous users is very high. It is practically impossible to start legal procedures against every individual infringer. The ISPs that facilitate

158 HR, decision of 25 november 2005, *Mediaforum* 2006, Nr. 1 (*Lycos v. Pessers*), m.nt. A.H. Ekker; Rb. Den Haag, 5 januari 2007, nr. 276747 / KG ZA 06-1417, *Computerrecht* 2007, 46.

159 Rb. Utrecht (vzr.), 12 juli 2005, LJN: AT9073 (*Brein et al. v. Service Providers*); HR, decision of 25 november 2005, *Mediaforum* 2006, Nr. 1 (*Lycos v. Pessers*).

these infringements are a much more (financially) attractive and efficient legal opponent than the individual infringers.[160]

The greater the burden on the ISPs to prevent the downloading of illegal material or to disclose the personal information of their clients, the greater the threat to freedom of information. The situation could arise where ISPs, afraid of being held liable, take precautionary measures to remove certain content. An easy finding of liability of ISPs could have chilling effects and encroach upon the freedom of information on the Internet, to the detriment of the public as a whole.[161] In the response to the report of the Parliamentary Working Group on Copyright, the Minister of Justice emphasised the importance of the freedom of information, as well as the need for users to have access to a varied cultural offer.[162]

From the users' perspective, an important interest to protect is their privacy. This is especially the case when an obligation arises for ISPs to provide names and addresses of customers. In principle, customers of ISPs have the right to surf the Internet anonymously. This right is not absolute and must sometimes yield for the interest of rightholders. However, there should always be a fair balance between the rights of users (privacy rights) and the rights of IP owners.

The present case involves two questions: (1) the question of whether the provider can be obliged to prevent the downloading of illegal material; and (2) the question of whether the provider can be obliged to disclose the names and addresses of their subscribers.

Concerning the first question, the situation around the liability of ISPs in facilitating the use of peer-to-peer file-sharing software to access illegal content remained ambiguous in the Netherlands for a number of years.[163] Once it became clear that downloading from illegal sources no longer fell within the private copying exception (see Dutch answer to the base case), the next question was how to deal with platforms offering peer-to-peer file-sharing software that facilitates such illegal activities. As the epic legal battle around the use of The Pirate Bay software later taught us, the problem lies in finding an appropriate remedy in these circumstances.[164] Blocking websites like The Pirate Bay is neither an efficient or workable solution for the service providers.

The second question revolves around the privacy of subscribers. In principle, subscribers need to be able to be peruse the Internet anonymously. When an ISP is obligated to release the names and addresses of subscribers, a fair balance has to be struck.

---

[160] 25 november 2005, *NJ* 2009, Nr. 48 - 550, pp. 5446–5447 (*Lycos v. Pessers*), m.nt. P.B. Hugenholtz.

[161] 25 november 2005, *IER* 2006, Nr. 1 pp. 1–3 (*Lycos v. Pessers*), m.nt. J.J.C. Kabel.

[162] *Kamerstukken II* 2009–2010, 29 838 Nr. 22, p. 2.

[163] Rb. Den Haag, 10 mai 2012 (*Brein v. UPC, KPN et al.*) ECLI:NL:RBSGR:2012:BW5387.

[164] HR, 13 november 2015 (*Brein v. XS4ALL and Ziggo*) ECLI:NL:HR:2015:3307.

The construction whereby ISPs have to decide which interest has to prevail in a certain case has received some criticism. The ISP is forced to make a choice between (human right) interests and is punished with liability when it does this wrong. The criticism basically states that a private enterprise has to make a decision which is normally made by a judge. In most cases, a provider will not be qualified (enough) to make that kind of decision. ISPs will try to avoid liability risks and legal procedures. In the case of the disclosure of personal information, this could lead to ISPs releasing personal information very easily, without a thorough investigation and due process.[165] This could threaten the subscribers' right to privacy.

(12) NORWAY

I. *Operative Rules*

'String' may have a successful claim against 'Keep Mov'n' for the prevention of downloading, and possibly, but not necessarily, for the release of the names and addresses of its subscribers.

II. *Descriptive Formants*

The facts are not entirely clear about the nature of the site and 'Keep Mov'n's' role in it. As pointed out in the Belgian report,[166] it is questionable from the facts whether 'Keep Mov'n' is to be considered only a hosting provider or if it is in reality a content provider. Provided that 'Keep Mov'n' merely has a hosting function, the non-liability rule in §18 of the Norwegian E-Commerce Act (NECA, 23 May 2003), implementing Article 14 E-Commerce Directive 2000/31/EC, applies. This, however, will hardly impact on 'String's' claim for an *injunction* against the downloading, since NECA §20 states that the non-liability rules in §§16–18 shall not prevent a court or a public authority from obliging a service provider to cease or prevent an infringement. It seems clear from the facts that 'Keep Mov'n', notwithstanding whether it is a host or a content provider, carries out the downloading itself. Consequently, an injunction can be claimed pursuant to general procedural rules, against the reproduction and making available of content to the public without the consent of the rightholder in contravention of §§2, 42 and 45 of the NCA.

In current Norwegian law, there are no provisions which explicitly justify the claim for the release of the names and addresses of third parties. The legislator

---

165 25 november 2005, *NJ* 2009, Nr. 48 – 550 (*Lycos v. Pessers*), m.nt. P.B. Hugenholtz.

166 See Belgian report.

refrained from implementing the non-mandatory rule of Article 15(2) of the E-Commerce Directive.[167] Norway is also not bound by the IPR Enforcement Directive 2004/48/EC, as matters of procedural law have been considered to fall outside the scope of the EEA Agreement, the Enforcement Directive consequently being considered not 'EEA-relevant'. Therefore, Norway has to date no obligation to implement the 'information disclosure rule' in Article 8 of the Directive. 'String's' possible success in the claim for the release of the names depends on general civil procedural rules. According to §28–2 of the Civil Procedure Act (17 June 2005), a claim for preservation of evidence outside the course of a trial may be brought before a court if there is a risk that the evidence will be substantially weakened if access to the evidence prior to the trial is not given. In a case before Stavanger City Court, a Norwegian law firm, on behalf of film producers, made a claim for the release of the identity of a subscriber, against the background that the Telecommunication Authority has exempted the access provider from its duty to confidentiality pursuant to §2–9 of the Electronic Communications Act (4 July 2003).

III. Metalegal Formants

The issue at stake is striking the proper balance between safeguarding the 'property rights' on the one hand, and the freedom of information and privacy, on the other. After the Telecommunication Authority's decision mentioned above, concerns have been raised as to whether private undertakings should be entitled to investigate and process confidential information and, in this respect, 'take over' the role of the police.

(13) POLAND

I. Operative Rules

The injunction against 'Keep Mov'n' may be granted. Information about subscribers will not be released.

II. Descriptive Formants

Internet downloading platforms may operate in various ways and the technical differences may prove crucial as far as infringement of copyright is concerned. Here it seems safe to assume that 'Keep Mov'n' operates a centrally controlled website in the Napster style and not a peer-to-peer decentralised network, in

[167] Ministry Proposal, Ot. prp. no. 4 (2003–2004) p. 10.

which it would only provide software used by millions of users storing copies of works on their own personal computers and without any central index controlled by the provider.

There has been no such case before Polish courts, but it may be assumed that an injunction can be granted because 'Keep Mov'n' assists or profits from illegal copyright infringements committed by users. Polish copyright law does not recognise the concept of indirect infringements in the sense of an independent form of infringement of copyright. Under Polish law, the infringer is the person who uses the work illegally (i.e. commits acts encroaching upon the sphere of exclusivity granted by law to the rightholder, e.g. copying, lending, making available to the public, broadcasting, etc.). Copyright infringement is however an illegal act. Using the terminology of civil law, copyright infringements are therefore torts. According to Article 422 of the Civil Code, not only is the direct tortfeasor liable for damages but also the person who abetted the tort, assisted in it or has intentionally taken advantage of the damage incurred by third party. Since copyright infringements are torts, creating a platform used to commit infringements may lead to liability.[168] If 'Keep Mov'n' profits in some way from this activity (e.g. fees, advertising) it may also be intentionally taking advantage of infringements committed by third parties (its users). As 'Keep Mov'n' is a content provider, its liability is not covered by the exception introduced for Internet service providers by the law on providing services by electronic means.[169]

The general rule under Polish law is that the defendant is not obligated to provide information on third parties, even if they are suspected of illegal activities. However, Poland has implemented the Enforcement Directive2004/48/EC. Article 80(1) point 2 Copyright Act grants to the rightholder the right to demand information on third party infringers but only concerning origin, distribution networks, amount and price of goods or services infringing copyright. This provision is new and very poorly drafted. There have been no published court decisions concerning this issue so far and it is to a large extent uncertain how the new instruments will be interpreted in practice.[170] The main doubt concerns the

168 J. Barta, R. Markiewicz, *Prawo autorskie* (Kraków: 2008), p. 176.

169 Law on Providing Services by Electronic Means of 18 July 2002, Journal of Laws 2002, No. 144, pos. 1204, Chapter 3.

170 Since illegally making the works available to the public is also covered by criminal sanctions, copyright owners tend to use this path to obtain information on infringers (i.e. with the assistance of the police or prosecutors). The most common method is to use some available software to trace the IP addresses of Internet users who upload works to P2P platforms. With this information, the rightholder engages the police (notice of a possible criminal act). Criminal proceedings are instituted and in the course of these proceedings, state organs (the police, the Prosecutor's Office) may demand information on the identity of the users with those IP addresses from ISPs. Rightholders gain access to this information as it will be present in case files and the rightholders as victims of the crime in question (persons whose rights have been criminally infringed) may take part in criminal proceedings and may access the files.

apparent limitation of the subject matter of the requested information. Under the current wording of Article 80(1) point 3 Copyright Act, the identity or other personal data of the direct infringer is not covered and could not be requested. It is clear that the said provision was drafted with traditional 'brick and mortar' infringements in mind (e.g. selling illegal CDs or books). However, it may be argued that distribution also means digital distribution. If so, 'Keep Mov'n' users could be covered by this provision. In this case, Article 80 would serve as a legal ground permitting the illegality of providing the plaintiff with the personal data of third parties to be set aside (Art. 23(1) point 2 Data Protection Act). Because users engaged in downloading could defend themselves with the private copy exceptions, any information provided by the content provider would have to be limited to uploaders.

It should be added that the personal data of infringers may be acquired in criminal proceedings as some forms of copyright infringements are sanctioned by criminal law as well.

III. Metalegal Formants

There are two metalegal issues: indirect infringements and data protection. The first issue is not obvious in this case, as we are informed that 'Keep Mov'n' is a content provider. However, we are very well aware of much more complicated situations, especially concerning technologies capable of non-infringing use and the responsibility of their creators. The best examples are seminal court decisions issued in the US[171] and in other countries,[172] sometimes with very different outcomes. As the famous historic examples of cassettes[173] and video tape recorders show,[174] these are not entirely new problems. Nevertheless, where the defendant controls the activities used for infringement, there should be no doubt that legal intervention is justified and necessary. It is also more efficient than concentrating on individual small-scale infringers.

The second issue is data protection. Although the problem is certainly highly sensitive, it seems that the concerns raised against such information rights are somewhat exaggerated, as data protection should not serve to hide tortfeasors and criminals.

---

171 *MGM Studios, Inc. v. Grokster, Ltd.*, 545 U.S. 913 (2005).
172 Hoge Raad, 19 december 2003 (*Buma v. KaZaA*).
173 BGH 22 January 1960 I ZR 41/58.
174 US Supreme Court, *Sony Corp. v. Universal City Studios, Inc.*, 464 U.S. 417 (1984).

(14) SLOVENIA

I. *Operative Rules*

'String' can claim an injunction against 'Keep Mov'n' to prevent illicit downloading. 'String' could further have a claim for disclosure of names and IP addresses of its subscribers.

II. *Descriptive Formants*

The two above-mentioned claims are completely different. The first claim refers to the prohibition of 'Keep Mov'n's' operation. 'String' will succeed if it proves that 'Keep Mov'n' is not only an access provider, but also a content provider (music), and therefore that it does not merely provide access to the computer equipment which enables file-sharing, but has a more active role in such activities. In such cases, it has to be liable for copyright infringements committed by its users.

The second claim concerns disclosure of the personal data of some of 'Keep Mov'n's', users who may be infringing copyrights. There are no express legal provisions in Slovenian legislation which would allow for communication of personal data in the case at hand.

Article 37 of the Constitution of the Republic of Slovenia safeguards privacy of communications and sets very strict conditions for a breach of privacy to be allowed. The provision requires the conditions to be further regulated by legislation.

Accordingly, Article 8 of the Personal Data Protection Act states that personal data can only be processed (i.e. used in any way) if this is allowed by a law or if the person concerned consented to the use of his/her personal data. More specific provisions on the topic at hand are contained in the Electronic Commerce Market Act. Article 8(4) states that service providers have to communicate to any competent authority upon its request data on the basis of which the users of their services can be identified. Service providers have to communicate this data upon an order issued by the court for the purposes of discovering and preventing crimes. In cases provided by sector-specific laws, service providers also have to communicate such data without a court order.

Additionally, Article 10 of the Civil Procedure Act provides that the persons who dispose of personal data are obliged to communicate this data to the court upon its request if this data is important for the court's decision, regardless of the provisions on protection of personal and other data. 'String' could therefore file a lawsuit for copyright infringement and demand disclosure of personal data; however, this demand would eventually be decided on by the court.

III. Metalegal Formants

The Slovenian Copyright Act has traditionally governed limitations on copyright law very narrowly. The particularity of the Slovenian limitations on copyright has been since 1995 that the Copyright Act not only provides a set of specified limitations but also provides a very general rule in Article 46. Article 46 is in fact a Slovenian implementation of the 'three-step test' from Article 9(2) of the Berne Convention. In theory, there is no consensus on whether the 'three-step test' should (1) only represent an instruction for national legislators on how to construct provisions regarding exceptions/limitations in their national copyright law, or (2) also be implemented 'as such', to complement special provisions on exceptions/limitations and serve as a guidance for judges when they decide actual cases. In any case, it is obvious that national legislators can have (at least) two approaches when they construct the system of exceptions/limitations. They can implement (1) 'a general three-step test like instruction' in addition to specific exceptions, or (2) just a set of specific exceptions/limitations. Legislators who take the first approach design a much narrower system of free use than those who take the second approach. Slovenian legislators took the first approach and designed a system of a very narrow limitations: specific limitations set out in Articles 47–57 are accompanied by the general test contained in Article 46 that has to be observed by judge when he/she decides concrete case. In fact, Slovenian legislators went even further and prescribed a 'four-step test'[175] – the above-listed three requirements from Article 9(2) of the Berne Convention are accompanied by an additional requirement, otherwise known from Article 10(1) of the Berne Convention, dealing with permissible/free quotations. The substantial limitations listed in Articles 47–57 of the Copyright Act are permissible only in the cases mentioned in Articles 47–57, provided that the extent of such exploitation of a copyright work (1) is limited by the intended purpose, (2) is compatible with fair practice, (3) does not conflict with normal use of the work, and (4) does not unreasonably prejudice the legitimate interests of the author.

In Slovenia there is no public debate about a 'cultural flat rate', about proposals to legalise P2P file-sharing. There has been a legal case, *Partis v. Telekom*, which was modelled on the *Pirate Bay* case; however, the claims in that case were based only on the provisions of the Copyright Act and not on the Criminal Code.

---

175 Some commentators talk about a five-step test, listing also the wording 'in cases mentioned in this Section' as a special requirement/step; see Analysis of National Levy Schemes and the EU Copyright Directive by Copyright Levies Reform Alliance, April 2006.

(15) SPAIN

I. Operative Rules

As far as the first request is concerned, we consider that 'String' could be justified in asking for 'Keep Mov'n' to put an end to its illegal activity. As far as the second request is concerned, 'Keep Mov'n' is not obliged to hand over the personal data of third parties. What is more, in this context, the Spanish Organic Law 15/1999 on Personal Data Protection should be respected. The only situation in which these data would have to be disclosed would be if the third parties were allegedly using the music illicitly, as we will point out below. In this last case, we consider that 'String' could request this information in a criminal procedure. Otherwise, at this point, the Spanish Law 34/2002 of 11 July, on services of the information society and electronic commerce and after the CJEU *Promusicae* ruling, should be taken into account to determine whether 'String' could ask the service provider 'Keep Mov'n' for these data in order to initiate civil proceedings for violation of intellectual property rights.

II. Descriptive Formants

Following the general assumption, in the present scenario we assume that the website 'Keep Mov'n' is an intermediary that not only enables users to exchange music but also supplies music (we assume we are not in a peer-to-peer scenario). We assume, in turn, that it has not been authorised by the holder of the rights, the record company 'String', to reproduce or distribute this music. Under these two premises, it could be considered that 'Keep Mov'n' violates intellectual property rights and third party users need its website to exchange music.

First, we should review which civil measures are recognised by the Spanish regulation to put an end to alleged IP rights infringement. The LPI cites the actions that can be adopted in a declaratory case (civil proceedings) and those measures that can be requested by the rightholder.[176] As well as the regulation contained in the LPI, we must also bear in mind the content of the Spanish Civil Procedural Law (LEC) and, in this respect, with the transposition of Directive 2004/8/EC of 29 April 2004, the Spanish legal system has extended the means for protecting intellectual property rights by Organic Law 19/2006 of 5 June – this law extends the measures that can be adopted in civil proceedings.[177]

---

176 The modification made by Law 23/2006 of 7 July to the LPI was mainly the transposition of the InfoSoc-Dir. 2001/29/EC into Spanish law and it made possible to request new types of precautionary measures.

177 Organic Law 19/2006 provides for preliminary proceedings at the beginning of a legal process for the violation of an intellectual property right. This regulation involves modifying the LEC, Law 1/2000, particularly in those parts relating to these protecting measures in an intellectual property rights defence.

In response to the reforms implemented in the Spanish legal system, several authors[178] have clearly defined which actions can be taken by the holders of intellectual property rights according to the provisions of the LPI. On the one hand, the LPI accepts applications for precautionary measures in an ordinary procedure for the violation of rights and the cessation of the illegal activity done by a third party. On the other, it also establishes measures for ensuring that information is obtained and evidence gathered so that subsequent legal proceedings can be initiated in the form of preliminary procedures.

On the basis of the legal provisions, and taking account of what has been said above, 'String' could opt for any of the actions regulated in Article 138 LPI, i.e. to apply for an injunction restraining the unlawful activity or to apply for material and moral damages. Likewise, the holder of the allegedly infringed copyright could also request that the offender pay the court costs of making the decision totally or partially public. Without going into the compensation system or the fining options (see Art. 140 LPI), the record company could request immediate suspension of the illegal activity and prevent the offending party from engaging in this offending activity again.[179] We believe that the modifications made by Organic Law 19/2006 to civil procedural law, and which affect the protection of intellectual property rights, mean that these measures could be requested as urgent precautionary measures.[180] As a result, on the basis of the content of Article 141 LPI and Article 721 LEC on procedural matters, 'String' could request both the precautionary cessation of the offending activity and the suspension of Keep Mov'n's Internet services.

However, we should first determine what the Internet provider's duties are regarding the defence of IP rights. The second request made by the record company is not recognised as a right in the LPI and the LEC. However, the reforms carried out by Organic Law 19/2006 mean that the LEC does recognise

---

178 E. González Pillado, 'La protección procesal del derecho de autor tras las reformas operadas por las leyes 19/2006 y 23/2006', *Actas de Derecho Industrial*, no. 27, 2006–2007, pp. 173–202; A. García Vidal, 'Notas sobre la ley 19/2006, de 5 de junio, por la que se amplían los medios de tutela de los derechos de propiedad intelectual e industrial', no. 6518, 2006; R. Castillejo Manzanares and I. Rodíguez Martínez, 'La tutela jurisdiccional de los derechos de autor y la propiedad industrial en el ámbito comunitario y nacional', *Actas de Derecho Industrial*, no. 27, 2006–2007, pp. 39–70.

179 In our approach to the hypothetical case, we regard the 'Keep Mov'n' website not as an Internet service provider but as a violator of the rights of the record company. Therefore, it lies outside the protection of the Spanish LESICE. Despite this, and even if 'Keep Mov'n' was considered an intermediary in terms of the LESICE, the LPI stipulates that the services being provided can be suspended if they enable third parties to infringe the intellectual property rights recognised by the LPI (Art. 139 LPI). In this respect, see the comments by E. González Pillado, 'La protección procesal del derecho de autor tras las reformas operadas por las leyes 19/2006 y 23/2006', *Actas de Derecho Industrial*, no. 27, 2006–2007, pp. 173–202.

180 The conditions required to apply for the ordering of precautionary measures (Art. 728 LEC) are a risk of harm through the lapse of time or *periculum in mora* and the *prima facie* case or *fumus iuris*.

that anyone who starts a lawsuit for violation of an intellectual property right on a 'commercial scale' could ask the civil courts for preliminary proceedings to acquire information and data about the origin and the distribution networks of the services that infringe the intellectual property rights (Art. 256.1.7º LEC). The aim of these preliminary proceedings is to identify possible offenders and, as a result, initiate legal proceedings against them. In our opinion, the alleged offence in this case must be on a 'commercial scale' in accordance with the legal provisions. For the moment, there is no legal precedent that enables the concept of 'commercial scale' to be interpreted. Thus, if the 33 users of the 'Keep Mov'n' website were retailers who download music for sale, hire or distribution for profit, 'String' would be entitled to request these measures. In all cases, it should be borne in mind that these proceedings may involve questioning the users, or taking other measures, to determine whether they have violated intellectual property rights. These proceedings could only be justified if action is subsequently taken against the infringement of intellectual property rights. But this is not a settled issue, even after the CJEU *Promusicae* decision.

To summarise, it could be difficult to affirm that 'String' could ask for the release of the names and addresses of its subscribers in civil proceedings.

III. Metalegal Formants

As far as the second demand[181] is concerned, it should be borne in mind that all comments must be made with great caution. Acquiring data about the users as alleged offenders is a process that must respect the basic principles of the right to a defence and to legal protection that govern the Spanish legal system. As some authors rightly point out, those users who make statements are not taking part in a procedure: they are not under oath and are not considered to be witnesses.[182] And as a result, if no action is ultimately taken, the data acquired under a statement must be totally confidential and cannot be used for any reason other than that for which they were requested. In order to determine the scope of these measures, we will have to wait until there is case law. Even so, the guarantees given by Law 15/1999 on Personal Data Protection must be respected when giving information about these users. At this point, one should consider the court's opinion about the respect for the copyright protection and data protection, especially personal data use.

---

181 The different reports state similar legislative solutions on this point regarding civil measures to be taken (see e.g. the Belgian, German, Dutch or Polish reports). Some of the comments made also mention the criminal proceedings suitable for asking for these measures (e.g. the Czech report).

182 R. Castillejo Manzanares and I. Rodríguez Martínez, 'La tutela jurisdiccional de los derechos de autor y la propiedad industrial en el ámbito comunitario y nacional', *Actas de Derecho Industrial*, no. 27, 2006–2007, pp. 39–70.

We should add at this point a comment regarding the duties of Internet service providers. Do they have the duty to control the legal use of the works they hold for their customers? Do they have to respond to the request by the authors to provide any personal data in civil proceedings? The Spanish Law 34/2002 of 11 July, on services of the information society and electronic commerce (LESICE) states in its Article 12 that personal data can only be provided in criminal proceedings or to guarantee public safety. These issues have been dealt in the CJEU's *Promusicae* decision. The ruling affects the metalegal formants on Modifications 1 and 2. The facts were as follows. Promusicae (a non-profit organisation whose members are authors) applied for preliminary measures against Telefónica SAU (a commercial company whose activities include the provision of Internet access services) alleging possible IP rights infringements by Telefónica Internet users. The Spanish Civil Court admitted the preliminary measures applied for by Promusicae, consisting in the disclosure by Telefónica SAU of the identities and physical addresses of certain persons whom it provided with Internet access services, whose IP address and date and time of connection were known. Telefónica appealed the order, considering that these data could only be provided in some cases, for instance criminal proceedings, or for the purpose of safeguarding public safety and national security, as stated in Article 12 LESICE. The exchange of works was based on a P2P system and Promusicae alleged that there was an infringement of the exploitation rights of the authors. The Spanish Court referred a question to the CJEU regarding the interpretation of the limit of the above-mentioned exceptions to the disclosure of personal data in the context of the information society.

The CJEU's decision determines the limits of authors' rights and their protection in the information society context. The ruling shows the relationship that should exist between IP rights and personal data protection in the information society. To reach its conclusion, the CJEU reviewed the following Directives: Directive 2000/31/EC, Directive 2000/29/EC, Directive 2004/48/EC and Directive 2002/58/EC. In sum, the CJEU gave a global interpretation of some Community legislation transposed into the Spanish legislation. The CJEU pointed out that the above-mentioned Directives do not require a member state to adopt of interim measures like the obligation for an Internet service provider to disclose personal data in civil proceedings. However, the CJEU's ruling recognised the fact that the transposition of the Directives should satisfy an equal balance between opposing rights: the recognition of IP rights and the right to the protection of personal data. In consequence, we understand that member states must decide how to protect the rights infringed, and courts should take into account each interest on a case-by-case basis. Regarding the Spanish regulation, some premises should be kept in mind: Article 12 LESICE was abolished by Law 25/2007. However, Law 25/2007 admits the possibility to obtain that data if a criminal offence has followed and criminal proceedings have begun. Therefore, it is difficult to affirm at this point that all the data required in civil proceedings, like releasing the names and addresses of private users, would be justified.

Some authors consider that the transposition of the Directives into the Spanish civil order has gone beyond the contents of the Directives in order to give broad protection to authors' rights.[183] In consequence, it could be stated that some measures of protection of authors' rights are not excluded in the civil procedure, but a balance with personal data protection should be found.[184]

(16) UNITED KINGDOM

I. *Operative Rules*

'String' will succeed with its first claim (the injunction), but most probably not with the second (the delivery of names).

II. *Descriptive Formants*

In *Newzbin II*,[185] the High Court ordered British Telecommunications to block a website used to distribute infringing copies of films. The legal base for injunctions is section 97A, as long as the service provider has actual knowledge of the infringement. This knowledge requirement refers to the rightholder notifying the ISP about the details of the infringement – they then need to be blocked. If the ISP does not comply, it is liable for sanctions under the secondary infringement provisions. Since the ISP would be communicating the work illegally, it can be subject to the criminal sanctions under section 107(2A) as long as it knows or should reasonably have known that the activity is an infringement and the infringement is in the course of business or negatively affecting the rightholder in the course of business. The sanctions for this are a fine, imprisonment (a maximum of two years depending on the circumstances) or both.

With regard to the issue of whether 'String' can be given the names and addresses of 33 subscribers who are suspected of downloading mass quantities of

183 See J.A. Gómez Segade, 'En torno a la Directiva sobre el derecho de autor y los derechos afines en la sociedad de la información', *Actas de Derecho Industrial*, no. 26, 2005–2006, pp. 1430–1447; J.A. Gómez Segade, 'El derecho de autor en el entorno digital', *Revista General de Legislación y Jurisprudencia*, no. 3, 1999, pp. 309–330.

184 See M. Soto García, 'TJCE – Sentencia de 29 January 2008, Promusicae C-275/06 – Sociedad de la información, protección de datos personales, deber de divulgación de proveedores de servicios, protección de los derechos de autor', *Revista de Derecho Comunitario Europeo*, no. 31, septiembre/diciembre 2008, pp. 867–883.

185 *Twentieth Century Fox and Others v. British Telecommunications plc (Newzbin II)* [2011] EWHC 1981 (Ch).

illegal material, there is some English authority on the issue. The High Court did give a judgment in October 2004 permitting the British Phonographic Industry to be given the details of individual 'file-swappers' by ISPs. The proposed prosecutions of a number of the 'file-swappers', who downloaded approximately 8,000 songs each, all ended in out-of-court settlements.[186] If 'String' wishes to take action against the 33 'file-swappers', the best course of action might be to ask the British Phonographic Industry to seek the details of the infringing parties via the courts under section 97A CDPA 1988.[187] The new powers in the CDPA 1988 allow for the High Court to grant an injunction against an ISP 'where that service provider has actual knowledge of another person using their service to infringe copyright.' As yet, however, the power has been relatively untried in the courts. It should also be noted that the cases concerned prolific infringers, which cannot be presumed in the scenario given.

III. Metalegal Formants

Although the UK is bound by EU legislation (*Promusicae*,[188] supra Editorial Note), the UK discussion is heavily influenced by the two seminal cases from American law as to peer-to-peer file-sharing networks.

In *A & M Records Inc. v. Napster Inc.*,[189] the court considered whether Napster, comprising of a central database of music files available for public download, could be liable for wholesale copying and distribution of copyrighted materials. Napster argued that neither it nor its users infringed copyright because they were sharing music for non-commercial purposes. However, the court held that a global system of 20 million users went beyond any fair use defence, particularly as 'the host user sending a file cannot be said to engage in a personal use when distributing that file to an anonymous requester'.[190] Moreover, because Napster users were getting something for free for which they would otherwise have had to pay, they were obtaining an economic advantage through the use of Napster. The file-sharing network was therefore allowing the conversion of non-commercial use to commercial use.

The second and most significant decision from American case law is *Metro-Goldwyn-Mayer Studios Inc. v. Grokster Ltd.*[191] The Supreme Court of the United States held that the operators of the Grokster and Morpheus P2P networks, although completely decentralised, had still infringed copyright. The defendants initially argued they should not be liable because they had no

---

186 N. Hopkins, 'Fans to walk plank over pirating on the Internet', *The Times*, 8 October 2004.
187 Implementing Council Directive 2001/29/EC.
188 *Promusicae v. Telefonica de Espana SAU* Case C-275/06.
189 239 F.3d 1004 (9th Cir. 2001).
190 Ibid., p. 1015.
191 125 S. Ct. 2764 (U.S.S.C. 2005).

control over the content passing through the network and could not prevent continued file-sharing even if the systems were taken offline. The Supreme Court overruled the lower courts and held that the court cannot protect a party which has intentionally infringed or promoted the infringement of copyright. Justice Souter, in particular, held that anyone who distributes a product which is primarily intended to infringe copyright, as demonstrated by clear evidence of such an intention, cannot avoid being liable for copyright infringement in the event that a user of that product uses it to infringe copyright.

B.4. COMPARATIVE REMARKS

The comparative remarks on this case are aggregated in section E.3 below.

C.1. MODIFICATION 2

Carla has a monthly subscription to OD2, an Internet site where you can legally download popular songs for €30 per month. Each song bought via OD2 is encrypted so that no copy can be made nor distributed to anyone else over the Internet. This technological protection measure makes it impossible for Carla to burn a CD of the songs that she just paid for and to listen to them on her way to school every day. Carla finds this unacceptable: she circumvents the technological lock and burns a CD of the songs for her own private use.

Can the record company 'String' object to this?

C.2. EDITORIAL NOTE ON EU LAW

The base case established that the law generally recognises a private copying exception to the benefit of natural persons, as long as the protected content is not obtained from an illegal source. The first modification also established that rightholders can, in most cases, ask for injunctive relief against ISPs to stop widespread infringement from taking place. The rights owners' power to enforce their rights against individuals who use peer-to-peer file-sharing software most often does not extend to gaining access to the names and addresses of private individuals, however. Through Article 6 of Directive 2001/29/EC, rights owners have been granted yet another layer of protection to help them combat (online) piracy or control the use made of their works. With the implementation of this provision, it has become unlawful for anyone to circumvent effective technological protection measures (TPMs) or to offer devices the main purpose of which is to circumvent such TPMs. By enacting Article 6, the European legislator has made an attempt to address the conflict between the IP holder's interest in preventing illegal copies by way of a TPM, and the users' right to exercise certain statutory exceptions. Unfortunately, Article 6(4) has turned out to be extremely complex and has ended up leaving member states broad discretion on how to respond to this conflict.

In the specific case of the private copying exception, member states are under no obligation to take action in respect to the private copying exception. Moreover, if the rightholder designs his/her TPM in such a way that private copies are possible, then member states are not allowed to intervene on the basis of Article 6(4). And, as the text of Recital 52 states, rightholders may in any case use TPMs to control the number of reproductions in accordance with Article 5(2)(b) and (5).[192] TMPs that are used to control the number of reproductions receive equal protection according to Article 6(4), third paragraph. The result is that member states have adopted a rather strict stance on where to draw the line between the respective interests of rights owners and end users, to the benefit of rights owners.

C.3. COUNTRY REPORTS

(1) BELGIUM

I. Operative Rules

No, 'String' cannot do anything about this.

II. Descriptive Formants

- Articles 22§1 5°, 79bis and 87bis BCA (Arts. XI.190 9°, XI.291 and XI.336 BCEL).

When implementing the Copyright Directive 2001/29/EC[193] in the BCA in 2005, the Belgian legislator introduced a new Article 79bis (Art. XI.291 BCEL) to regulate technical protection measures. Article 79bis §1 BCA (Art. XI.291§1 BCEL) stipulates that anyone who knowingly circumvents effective technical measures or reasonably should know that his/her actions could circumvent these measures *and* knows or reasonably should know that this circumvention

192 M. M. M. van Eechoud, P. B. Hugenholtz, N. Helberger, L. Guibault and S. van Gompel, *The Harmonization of European Copyright Law – The Challenges of Better Lawmaking* (Alphen aan den Rijn: 2009).

193 Directive 2001/29/EC of the European Parliament and of the Council of 22 May 2001 on the harmonisation of certain aspects of copyright and related rights in the information society, OJ L 167, 22 June 2001, 10–19.

facilitates copyright infringement is guilty of copyright infringement and is held liable both civilly and criminally. Two conditions are therefore required for the circumvention to constitute an act of infringement. First, a material act of circumvention is necessary. Second, the act must be conducted with a particular 'double' knowledge.[194]

Since it is required that the circumventor knowingly infringes a copyright,[195] Carla will not be held liable. By paying the monthly subscription to OD2, she may assume that she is legally downloading songs. According to Article 22§1 5° BCA (Art. XI.190 9° BCEL) she can therefore not be held liable for making a home copy. Since she never knowingly infringed copyright law, 'String' cannot object.

III. Metalegal Formants

This specific variant of the case is to be situated in the discussion on whether or not making home copies is a subjective right. Belgian legal doctrine is more or less divided over this question.[196] Some authors argue that allowing home copying is merely tolerated due to market failure or the technical impossibility of exercising control in people's homes.[197] Others take the view it is simply a defence against prosecution and liability, simply an exception.[198]

Yet others suggest that home copying is a real subjective right[199] and that industry would not be allowed to construct protection mechanisms to prevent home copying. Article 87bis BCA (Art. XI. 336 BCEL) allows going to court when the industry's technical protection measures hinder normal use. However, the Belgian legislator chose not to include the home copy exception in the list of exceptions that had to be guaranteed (Art. 79bis §2 BCA, now Art. XI.291§2 BCEL).[200]

---

194 S. Dussolier, 'Les nouvelles dispositions belges en matière de protection technique des oeuvres' [The New Belgian Provisions Relating to the Technical Protection of Works], *Auteurs & Medias* 2005, 532–549.

195 M.-C. Janssens, 'De Belgische auteurswet doet zijn intrede in het tijdperk van de informatiemaatschappij' [The Belgian Copyright Act Enters the Era of the Information Society], *Computerrecht* 2006, no. 2, 6–8 and 11.

196 T. Faell, 'La copie privée malmenée' [The Private Copy Badly Managed], *I.R.D.I.* 2006, no. 1, 46–53.

197 J. Deene, 'Recht op privé-kopie van een muziek-CD' [Right to a Homecopy of a Music CD?], note under Court of Appeal Brussels, 9 September 2005, *NjW* 2005, no. 124, 1063–1064.

198 Pres. Court of 1st Instance Brussels [Voorz. Rb. Brussel], 25 May 2004, *A&M* 2004, no. 4, 338, note S. Dussolier, 'Copie privée versus mesures techniques de protection: l'exception est-elle un droit?' [Private Copy versus Technical Protection Measures: Is The Exception a Right?].

199 For an excellent overview of the various positions, see S. Dusollier, *Droit d'auteur et protection des œuvres dans l'univers numérique. Droits et exceptions à la lumière des dispositifs de verrouillage des œuvres* [Copyright and the Protection of Works in the Digital Age. Rights and Exceptions in the Light of Technical Protection Measures], in collection Création Information Communication [Creation Information Communication] (Brussels: 2005), 477–494.

200 Nor are these exemptions guaranteed for online applications: see Art. 79bis §3 BCA.

During the parliamentary debates on the BCA, it was decided that the home copy exception would continue to have the status of an exemption and not become a right. As 'compensation' for the lack of explicit inclusion of the exception in this provision, a condition was added to Article 79bis §1 BCA (Art. XI.291§1 BCEL), providing that in order to be guilty of circumventing technical measures, knowingly infringing or helping to infringe copyright was required (i.e. the second knowledge element).[201] Additionally, under Article 79bis §2 BCA (Art. XI.291§2 BCEL), it is possible for the government via a royal decree, to add the private copy exception to the list of exceptions. However, at the time of writing, this possibility has not been used. These two mechanisms (i.e. the 'double' knowledge requirement and the possibility of a royal decree) have been considered ambiguous as they do not clearly stipulate whether circumventing technical measures for the purpose of making a private copy would be authorised.[202]

(2) CZECH REPUBLIC

I. Operative Rules

'String' is entitled to object to this.

II. Descriptive Formants

According to section 43(1) Copyright Act, anyone who is circumventing effective technological measures infringes copyright. Technological measures are defined in section 43(3) Copyright Act *inter alia* as any technology which is intended to prevent or limit acts related to the works to which the author did not grant a licence. The above-mentioned technological measures which are intended to prevent users from burning songs on CD perfectly meet the above-mentioned requirements of section 43(3) of the Copyright Act and Carla's act is copyright infringement according to section 43(1).

---

201 Report Bill on the Implementation in Belgian Law of the European Directive 2001/29/EC of 22 May 2001 on the Harmonisation of Certain Aspects of Copyright and Neighbouring Rights in the Information Society, *Parl. Doc.*, Chambre, 2003–2004, DOC 51 1137/013, 85 [Verslag Wetsontwerp houdende de omzetting in Belgisch recht van de Europese richtlijn 2001/29/EG van 22 mei 2001 betreffende de harmonisatie van bepaalde aspecten van het auteursrecht en de naburige rechten in de informatiemaatschappij, *Parl. St.*, Kamer, 2003–2004, DOC 51 1137/013, 85], available at: www.dekamer.be (last consulted 5 May 2019).

202 S. Dussolier, 'Les nouvelles dispositions belges en matière de protection technique des oeuvres' [The New Belgian Provisions Relating to the Technical Protection of Works], *Auteurs & Medias* 2005, 532–549.

According to the above-mentioned section 40(1)(b) Copyright Act, an injunction shall be granted to prohibit Carla from circumventing the technological block and burning songs on CD. In addition, an injunction to remedy the consequence of the infringement shall be granted according to section 40(1)(d)(3) Copyright Act – i.e. the CD shall be destroyed, and if her burner and/or her computer is used mainly for the production of unauthorised CDs, then her burner and/or her computer shall also be destroyed according to section 40(1)(d)(4) Copyright Act. Of course, radical measures such as the destruction of the burner and/or the computer will not take place if Carla burned only a few songs from OD2, because such measures would not be proportionate to that breach of the law.

Furthermore, it is necessary to keep in mind that to standing in such proceedings 'String' must meet the requirements set out in section 41 Copyright Act – i.e. it must be exclusively authorised by the author to use the work or to be entrusted by statute to exercise property rights. Otherwise, an injunction will not be granted by reason of lack of standing.

III. Metalegal Formants

Answer omitted.

(3) DENMARK

I. Operative Rules

'String' can probably object to this.

II. Descriptive Formants

Technological protection measures (TPMs) which are 'effective' are subject to a prohibition against circumvention pursuant to DCA §§75b–e (implementing Article 6 of the European Copyright Directive 2001/29/EC).

The DCA allows for circumvention in certain limited and specifically listed instances, but copying for personal use is not on the list.

The Act does not contain any special rules regarding the activity undertaken by Carla ('platform shifting'). According to the preparatory work, it is legal to circumvent region codes on DVDs etc. if this is necessary in order to enjoy the movie. The reason given for this is that the viewing of a movie as 'personal enjoyment' of the movie is an activity which is not covered by the exclusivity afforded by the DCA. Even if a Danish court were to uphold such a reading of the rules, the principle would seem not to cover platform shifting, which is not strictly 'necessary' for Carla's 'personal enjoyment' (as she can enjoy the music in the format in which she downloads it). Circumvention via time or space shifting would seem to be generally illegal too.

III. Metalegal Formants

The Danish legislator, as opposed, for example, to the Norwegian, has not been much concerned with the (im)balances between rightholders' and users' interests that may follow from the broad legal protection of technical protection measures provided for in the Copyright Directive.

(4) ESTONIA

I. Operative Rules

Unlawful removal of a technological lock is punished as a crime. 'String' can object to removal of the technological lock.

II. Descriptive Formants

Pursuant to §80^3(1) Copyright Act, '[a]uthors and holders of related rights may, in order to protect their rights, add technological measures to a work or object of related rights'. In this case, OD2 has exercised that right and added a technological measure to its copyrighted materials. However, there is a complex set of limitations attached to this right. A relevant provision to this case is §80^3(5) Copyright Act, which provides that the limitations do not 'apply to such works and objects of related rights which have been made available to the public on the basis of an agreement in such a way that persons can use them from a place and at a time individually chosen by them'. This means that if copyrighted materials protected by technological measures which restrict copying, etc. have been made available through the Internet, then the right to add technological measures is not restricted. Consequently, OD2 is entitled to add technological measures and has no obligation to remove them itself or tolerate their removal by other individuals. In fact, unlawful removal of a technical measure is punishable as a crime. Subsection 225(1) of the Penal Code provides:

> Unlawful removal of a of technical means of protection preventing violation of copyright and related rights, or manufacture, transfer or possession, or advertising for commercial purposes of a device or equipment intended for removal of such means of protection is punishable by a pecuniary punishment or up to 3 years' imprisonment.

Additionally, OD2 can demand that Carla refrain from violating its rights in the future.[203]

III. Metalegal Formants

H. Pisuke points out that the implementation of Directive 2001/29/EC into the Copyright Act provided authors and holders of related rights with two additional economic rights: the right to add technological measures to a work or object of related rights (§80^3) and the right to add information on the exercise of rights to published works or objects of related rights (§80^4).[204] The present case concerns enforcement of these rights. The introduction of possibilities to control the copyrighted material via technical measures raised certain expectations. For instance, according to Estonian legal literature, the private copying exemption was established due to the impossibility to control private copying. Technological developments, however, offer possibilities to control copying by individuals.[205] Although a possibility to add technological measures to protect one's intellectual property has been introduced, it has not caused considerable legal disputes in Estonia.

(5) FRANCE

I. Operative Rules

'String' may object the circumvention of the technological lock.

II. Descriptive Formants

Article L. 331-5 of the French Intellectual Property Code provides adequate legal protection against the circumvention of any effective technological measures. According to Article 6 of Directive 2001/20/EC of 22 May 2001 on the harmonisation of certain aspects of copyright and related rights in the information society, the expression 'technological measures' means: 'any technology, device or component that, in the normal course of its operation, is designed to prevent or restrict acts, in respect of works or other subject matter, which are not authorised by the rightholder of any copyright or any right related

---

203 Law of Obligations Act §1055(3).

204 H. Pisuke, *Autoriõiguse alused* (Copyright Basics) (Tallinn: 2006), pp. 43–44.

205 E. Vasamäe, 'Fonogrammitootja reprodutseerimisõigus ja infoühiskonna mõju sellele (Right of Reproduction for a Producer of Phonograms, and the Impact of the Information Society Thereon)', (2006) 10 *Juridica*, pp. 683–691, p. 687.

to copyright as provided for by law'.[206] Nevertheless, the rightholder, according to Article 6(4) of Directive 2001/20/EC, has to take the necessary measures to guarantee the private use exception (Arts. L. 331-8 and L. 331-9 of the French Intellectual Property Code), unless reproduction for private use has already been made possible by rightholders to the extent necessary to benefit from the exception. But necessary measures to guarantee the exercise of the private copy exception shall not apply to works or other subject matter made available to the public on agreed contractual terms in such a way that members of the public may access them from a place and at a time individually chosen by them (Art. 6(4) of Directive 2001/20/EC and Art. L. 331-10 of the French Intellectual Property Code).

Carla can listen to the songs downloaded on her computer, thus at a time and from a place chosen by her. The private use exception is guaranteed by OD2. Carla is therefore not allowed to circumvent the technological lock and she risks being condemned to pay a fine of €3,750.

III. Metalegal Formants

Answer omitted.

(6) GERMANY

I. Operative Rules

'String' has a claim for injunction against Carla.

II. Descriptive Formants

As in the base case, it is Carla's right to private use (§53 UrhG) which could limit the copyright of 'String'. Theoretically, private use prevails over technical locks (§95b sec. 1 No. 6 UrhG). The latter are explicitly permitted (§95a UrhG), provided that they allow for rights listed in §95b UrhG. However, the private use scope of §95 b sec. 1 No. 6 UrhG is *not* equal to §53 UrhG: it does *not* extend to digital private copies (§95 b sec. 1 No. 6 UrhG). Thus, neither OD2 nor 'String' are obliged to provide access. (Notwithstanding the fact that the law does provide for remedies (and does *not*, according to the prevailing (although contested) academic opinion, allow for self-help).) In terms of German dogmatic legal terminology, private copying is *not* a subjective right but only a privilege.

---

[206] Directive 2001/20/EC of the European Parliament and of the Council of 22 May 2001 on the harmonisation of certain aspects of copyright and related rights in the information society, OJ L 167, 22 June 2001, 10.

III. Metalegal Formants

Private copying (contested in its dogmatic structure) as a restriction to copyright has become a tiger without teeth– especially with technical protection measures in place. Remedies are too complicated. Only a gifted few have (if it were legal anyway) the individual skills to circumvent technical protection measures. Thus, the property has expanded at the expense of collective and competing individual interests.[207] Private use is restricted to a minimum of access (binary yes/no), which does not include a degree of discretion (downloading/burning). The conditions are controlled by the owner. Access is no longer defined by privileges (private use), nor by the privileged user.

(7) GREECE

I. Operative Rules

'String' may object to the forbidden circumvention of technical measures.

II. Descriptive Formants

The circumvention of technological measures is prohibited according to the provisions of Article 66A of the Law 2121/1993. Of course, the legal protection of the technological measures does not prevent the legal 'private use' of the work according to Article 18 of the Law 2121/1993. In this framework, the aforementioned analysis under point (1) in the base case fits here as well. In any event, Carla is not prohibited from circumventing the technical measures if the agreed contractual terms contain a different solution.

III. Metalegal Formants

Answer omitted.

(8) IRELAND

I. Operative Rules

'String' may object to this and seek an injunction.

---

[207] Further reading: P. Rott, 'Die Privatkopie aus der Perspektive des Verbraucherrechts', in: R.M. Hilty and A. Peukert (eds.), *Interessenausgleich im Urheberrecht* (Baden-Baden: 2004), pp. 267–287; E.I. Obergfell, 'Freier Werkzugang versus Urheberrechtsschutz', in: A. Halfmeier,

II. *Descriptive Formants*

Section 39(1)(a) CRRA 2000 provides that copying includes references to storing the work in any medium. Electronic capture and storage of a work, without the permission of the copyright owner, will infringe. However, the mere possession of infringing copies does not appear to be an offence, if *Minister for Justice v. Hogyi*[208] is followed. There is little commercial damage.

The right of private copying is very limited in Ireland and the fair dealing provisions are narrow. With regard to the circumvention of technological locks, it is not clear what device Carla uses to circumvent the protection. Section 370 of the CRRA 2000 defines a rights protection measure as any process treatment, mechanism or system which is designed to prevent or inhibit the unauthorised exercise of any of the rights conferred by this Act, under section 2.

Digital infringement tools are prohibited by the following provision, which states that an offence will be committed by a person who:

> makes, ... sells, rents or lends ... or has in his or her possession, custody or control, a protection-defeating device, knowing or having reason to believe that it has been or is to be used to circumvent rights protection measures, or provides information, or offers or performs any service, intended to enable or assist a person to circumvent rights protection measures.

III. *Metalegal Formants*

Answer omitted.

(9) ITALY

I. *Operative Rules*

Yes, 'String' can object to Carla circumventing the technological lock. According to Article 71sexies, any private copy must be made without violating the technological measures used to regulate access to the copyrighted work. The same article states that copyright holders are not allowed to use technological measures to prevent legitimate users from making a backup copy, but that requirement is fulfilled by the possibility of making an analogue copy.

P. Rott, A.C. Ciacchi, O. Deinert, T. Koller and S. Thalheim (eds.), *Zugang und Ausschluss als Gegenstand des Privatrechts* (Stuttgart: 2006), pp. 101–121.

208 [2006] IEHC 373.

II. Descriptive Formants

While the simple removal of a technological lock is not specifically addressed by the Italian legislation, Article 174ter considers to be an administrative infraction any abusive use which is not specifically considered a crime by other provisions.

III. Metalegal Formants

Answer omitted.

(10) LITHUANIA

I. Operative Rules

'String' has a claim for injunction against Carla. Carla can ask 'String' to remove the protection so that she can make a private copy.

II. Descriptive Formants

On the one hand, according to the Article 74 of the Copyright Act, the copyright holder is authorised to take technological measures to prevent the work from being reproduced. The circumvention of any effective technological measures, which the person concerned carries out in the knowledge, or with reasonable grounds to know, that he/she seeks to circumvent the technological measures applied by the owners of copyright, related rights or *sui generis* rights, shall be regarded as violation of the technological measures.

On the other hand, the copyright holder's exclusive rights do not include the right to prevent others from making socially beneficial use (fair use) of the owner's work.[209] Article 20 provides for the private copy exception.

Article 75 establishes the limitations on the application of technological measures, copies for private use being one of them. The users of the rights must be provided with conditions enabling them to use legitimately accessible objects of copyright to the extent necessary for them to benefit from the limitations of copyright. Thus, Carla could not circumvent or hack a technological measure (digital lock) to make the copy.

If 'String' rejects to remove the technical protection, Carla may apply to the Lithuanian Copyright and Related Rights Commission for mediation in such dispute. If the parties do not accept the proposal of the mediator(s), the dispute

---

209 Directive 2001/29/EC of 22 May 2001 on the harmonisation of certain aspects of copyright and related rights in the information society.

shall be settled by the Vilnius regional court. So far, not one dispute of this kind has been brought before the Vilnius regional court or has reached the pre-trial investigation stage.

III. Metalegal Formants

The private copy exception, even if it is not a right but just an exception, is still law. The private copy exception is not *per se* at the disposal of private parties, such as CD producers; they still must abide by the law, even if consumers have no corresponding right.

Therefore, it could be asserted that the application of the technical protection measures changes the role of exceptions in the system of copyright in the sense that the user of rights has to take active steps in order to benefit from the exceptions, or, otherwise stated, exemptions will become devoid of their earlier purpose and meaning.[210]

(11) NETHERLANDS

I. Operative Rules

Yes, 'String' may object to the circumvention of the technological lock.

II. Descriptive Formants

The Netherlands has implemented the provisions of Article 6 Directive 2001/29/EC in Article 29a of the Dutch Copyright Act. Deliberately circumventing technological protection measures (TPMs) is a wrongful act according to Article 29a of the Dutch Copyright Act, assuming the work is still protected by copyright. According to the explanatory memorandum, this provision is only applicable in the case of copyrighted works and not for works which fall in the public domain.[211] However, with respect to the intersection between the application of TPMs and the exercise of exceptions and limitations, the Dutch legislator was less forthcoming. Article 6(4) of the Directive was implemented in Article 29a(4) of the Copyright Act, which essentially leaves it to the government to adopt rules by order in council that oblige the author to provide the user of a work, for the purposes described in Articles 15i, 16, 16b, 16c, 16h, 16n, 17b and 22

---

210 V. Mizaras, 'Lithuanian Copyright: Historical and Modern Aspects and Trends of Development', *Journal of Copyright Society of the USA*, 2006, vol. 54, No. 4, p. 851; S. Dusolier, 'Exceptions and Technological Measures in the European Copyright Directive of 2001 – An Empty Promise', *I.I.C.*, 2003, vol. 34, p. 68.

211 *Kamerstukken II* 2001–2002, 28 482 nr. 3 (MvT), p. 55.

of this Act, with the means necessary to benefit from these restrictions, provided that the user has lawful access to the work protected by technological measures. The private copying exception is listed among the limitations enumerated. To date, no order in council has been issued with respect to this provision of the Copyright Act. Dutch users have nowhere to go if the rights owner does not provide the means to exercise the limitations listed in this article.

Article 29a(4), last sentence, further states that the provisions in the preceding sentence do not apply when, under contractual terms, works are made available to users at a place and at a time individually chosen by them.

In Carla's specific case, if she circumvents the protection measure to make a private copy, she commits an unlawful act against which 'String' may object, either because no mechanism has been put in place to allow her to exercise the private copy exception pursuant to Article 29a(4), or because the works she is accessing may have been made available to her under contractual terms, which could prevent her from circumventing.

III. Metalegal Formants

As a consequence of Article 6 of the Information Society Directive, the Dutch legislator had to adapt the Dutch Copyright Act to provide adequate legal protection against the circumvention of any effective technological measures. In the explanatory memorandum to the Dutch Copyright Act, the Minister of Justice points out several important topics in the implementation of the Directive, among which the protection against the circumvention of TPMs and against the manufacture, sale and trade of devices and the providing of services which make circumvention possible. Another important topic was the authority of the government to take measures if the use of TPMs goes against certain interests of users.[212] The implementation resulted in Article 29a of the Dutch Copyright Act. During the lawmaking process, the discussion focused on the copyright exceptions and the scope of the protection against the circumvention of TPMs. Questions were asked about the effects for users, especially consumers.[213]

The explanatory memorandum firstly points out the development of technologies. On the one hand, new technologies make it possible for rightholders to use TPMs to prevent or to restrict infringements of copyright. On the other hand, new technologies also make it possible to make perfect copies of copyrighted works. Therefore, Article 29a of the Dutch Copyright Act is an important provision, according to the explanatory memorandum. It states that the possibility to act against the circumvention of TPMs and against

212 Ibid., p. 4.

213 L. Guibault and G.J.H.M. Mom, *Evaluatie van de artikelen 29a en 29b van de Auteurswet 1912*, Onderzoek in opdracht van het WODC (Ministerie van Justitie), October 2007, p. 13.

the provision of circumventing devices is a new form of protection besides copyright, neighbouring rights and database rights. This new form of protection is justified for several reasons: the investments which are necessary to develop TPMs at a Community level, the problems around the enforcement of copyright in the digital environment, and the wish to make as much use as possible of the new technologies.[214]

The first paragraph of Article 29a defines TPMs as measures which are intended to prevent or restrict acts regarding protected material which are not permitted by the rightholder. Examples are encryption techniques and copy control methods, which prevent the user from copying the protected work. The explanatory memorandum emphasises that TPMs may not disturb the normal functioning of the equipment which plays the protected works.

(12) NORWAY

I. *Operative Rules*

No, 'String' (probably) cannot object to this.

II. *Descriptive Formants*

Technological protection measures (TPMs) are subject to a prohibition against circumvention pursuant to NCA §53a, first paragraph (New Act §99, first paragraph), implementing Article 6 of the European Copyright Directive 2001/29/EC. However, the Norwegian legislator found that the prohibition should not apply to cases where the TPM prevented a user from playing a legally acquired copy of the work on relevant playback equipment, the example used by the Ministry of Culture being that a purchaser of a CD should be entitled to circumvent a TPM in order to play the CD in his/her car stereo. On the other hand, the Ministry added that an MP3 player should not be considered 'relevant playback equipment' for CDs. Hence, according to the Ministry's proposal, a TPM could not be circumvented in order to be able to transfer material from CDs to MP3 players. On this very point the proposal led to an intense discussion in the press and Parliament, which amended it in order to permit circumvention of TPMs for the sake of transferring material from CDs to MP3 players. NCA §53a, third paragraph, second sentence (New Act §99, fourth paragraph, first sentence) was therefore phrased as following: 'Nor shall the [prohibition] in the first paragraph prevent private users from gaining access to legally acquired

[214] *Kamerstukken II* 2001–2002, 28 482 nr. 3 (MvT), pp. 26–27.

works on what is generally understood as relevant playback equipment.' In the same way as MP3 players are accordingly to be 'generally understood' as relevant playback equipment for CDs, it could be argued that a Discman is generally understood as relevant playback equipment for files legally downloaded from an Internet site. The same space and time shifting argument that justifies the 'MP3 situation' should apply in this case, provided that there are no 'agreed contractual terms' to the contrary. As the facts are silent on this point, the conclusion is that Carla's circumvention complies with §53, third paragraph, second sentence (New Act §99, fourth paragraph, first sentence). It is possible to claim that the result is hard to reconcile with Article 6 of the Directive. The Directive, however, is far from clear on this point, so a Norwegian court would likely follow the Norwegian statutory provision in this case.

III. Metalegal Formants

It follows from the foregoing that the Norwegian legislator has been much concerned with the imbalance between rightholders' and users' interests that may follow from the broad legal protection of technical protection measures provided for in the Copyright Directive. The provision in NCA §53, third paragraph, second sentence (New Act §99, fourth paragraph, first sentence) seeks to safeguard users' interests; however, at the same time it reflects a fear that the Directive does not leave much room in this respect. The result is a rather unclear provision which leaves as many questions unanswered as it solves.

(13) POLAND

I. Operative Rules

'String' has no claim against Carla.

II. Descriptive Formants

The result may be surprising, but it follows directly from incorrect implementation of the Directive 2001/29/EC of the European Parliament and of the Council of 22 May 2001 on the harmonisation of certain aspects of copyright and related rights in Poland. The characteristic feature of this Directive with regard to technological protection measures (TPMs) is that it has severed the link between TPMs and fair use (still present in the WIPO 1996 Treaties). In other words, according to the Directive, circumvention of TPMs is not allowed, even if the circumventing person intends to use the work within the copyright exceptions and limitations. Although the Directive (and national implementing legislation) leaves many legal issues unanswered,[215] this effect of the Directive is obvious (although not always welcome).[216] The Polish Copyright Act, perhaps unintentionally, follows the WIPO Treaties and not the Directive. TPMs have been defined as means the purpose of which is to restrict or make impossible infringing uses. This has been reinforced by Article 79(6) of the Copyright Act, which sanctions circumvention only if it has been undertaken to illegally use the work. The consequence of these provisions is simple: since fair use is not illegal, circumventing TPMs in order to use the work in a way covered by copyright limitations and exceptions is not illegal either. The majority view in Polish doctrine is of the opinion that even an EU law-friendly interpretation of the Copyright Act may not help to bring it in line with Article 6(1) of the Copyright Directive.[217] [The editor, LG, opposes this opinion with reference to Article 4 of the Directive, which provides some leeway to the member states.]

III. Metalegal Formants

TPMs protected independently of fair use pose huge problems for the coherence of the copyright law system. Copyright exceptions and limitations are embedded in the very nature of copyright, just like the term of protection. These exceptions provide for the only practical way to grant access to works for the benefit of the society and culture and have been carefully crafted by legislators in such a way as to balance the interests of the righholders and the interests of the general public. By accepting protection of TPMs even in situations where the resulting use of copyright works would be legal destroys this balance of interests and must be perceived as a privatisation of law. It also has further-reaching consequences. For example, it may be argued, with good reason, that if it is possible to unilaterally circumscribe the scope of fair use, the same should be admissible in contracts. If this tendency were to continue, copyright exceptions in the way we have known them would cease to have any practical relevance. What is most interesting, however, is that the development the law has taken has not been apparently worth the price that had to be paid. TPMs have not limited the amount of illegal copies available for download, as for expert users it is easy to circumvent them.[218] What they do is to restrict legitimate users who have paid to use copyright works. It seems that the idea TPMs may replace copyright law and allow for purely private ordering has been from the beginning very naïve and has not been accepted by consumers.

---

215 For example as regards the legal nature of TPMs or who may pursue claims against the infringers.

216 A. Matlak, *Charakter prawny regulacji dotyczących zabezpieczeń technicznych utworów* (Kraków: 2007), pp. 19 f., 67.

217 Ibid., pp. 134 ff.; J. Barta, R. Markiewicz, in: M. Bukowski et al., *Prawo autorskie i prawa pokrewne. Komentarz* (Kraków: 2005), p. 613.

218 Which makes it difficult to differentiate 'effective' and 'normal' TPMs.

(14) SLOVENIA

I. *Operative Rules*

'String' has a claim for injunction against Carla.

II. *Descriptive Formants*

It is Carla's right to private use (Art. 50 CRRA) which could limit the right of reproduction of 'String'. However, as stated above, there is a significant possibility that the definition of the private use exemption in Slovenian legislation is too narrow to allow for downloading of music files.

If downloading music files were allowed as an example of private use and the music files were protected using technological measures, the Slovenian Copyright Act (Art. 166c CRRA) would give Carla the right to demand that the rightholder remove the protection. Namely, the rightholder who uses technological measures must make available to persons with legal access to the subject matter of the rights, at their request and without delay, appropriate means on the basis of which they can enforce the limitations to copyright, amongst which is included private and other internal reproduction.

If the rightholder fails to secure the means which would enable Carla to use the music files, she could request mediation of the dispute (Art. 166c(2) CRRA). However, such mediation is in practice completely ineffective.

III. *Metalegal Formants*

The Slovenian legislator has enacted the private use exemption very narrowly. See the explanation in Modification 1 above.

(15) SPAIN

I. *Operative Rules*

'String' can ask Carla not to remove the technological protective measures but, in turn, if Carla has legally obtained the music, she can ask 'String' to remove the protection so that she can make a copy for private use.

II. *Descriptive Formants*

In this hypothetical case, as well as the initial assumption, we assume that OD2 acts with the authorisation of the legitimate holder of the copyright, the record company 'String'.

The Spanish LPI provides for the so-called private copy, in contrast to the author's right of reproduction. As has been mentioned in the cases above, the LPI recognises the right of the copyright holder to reproduce the work. It also authorises the copyright holder to take technological measures to prevent the work from being reproduced without the authorisation of the copyright holder.

At this point, we should focus on the transposition of the InfoSoc-Dir. 2001/29/EC to the Spanish legal system. With this transposition, the Spanish legislation recognises the right to apply technological measures, but this right is limited to authors and copyright holders (Art. 161 LPI). In brief, the rights of authors and the interests of third parties will be appraised to determine whether the behaviour of a third party is licit in a given scenario. In Article 6.4.1, the InfoSoc-Dir. 2001/29/EC recognises that when a work is made available to the public and also technologically protected to prevent copying, the end user who legally acquires the work has no right to make a copy.[219] Therefore, the content of the Directive indicates that the protection applied to the work cannot be ignored, independently of how the work has been acquired. However, the InfoSoc-Dir. 2001/29/EC made it possible for the member states to set limits on the application of these technological measures: that is to say, it authorises states to remove possible overprotection of the copyright holders by setting limits. Various authors consider that this 'overprotection' derives from the reproduction right and the 'public communication' right, which in conjunction enable the imposition of technological security measures. Article 161 LPI limits the measures that can be taken by the authors and one of these limits is the private copy exception. Therefore, one of the limits on the use of technological lock measures by copyright holders is that third parties have the right to make private copies. We consider that member states could provide to copyright holders procedures to remove these limits on private copies[220] in that case.

Article 160 LPI allows copyright holders to take action against those who evade technological measures to protect their rights. Nevertheless, Article 161 recognises – and therefore acknowledges the facultative limitation of the InfoSoc-Dir. 2001/29/EC – that copyright holders who technologically protect their work must provide those who benefit from copyright limits with the necessary mechanisms to be able to enjoy the exceptions. If a third party has legal access to the work and is covered by the private copy exception of Article 31.2 LPI, the

219 See J.A. Gómez Segade, 'El derecho de autor en el entorno digital', *Revista General de Legislación y Jurisprudencia*, no. 3, 1999, pp. 309–330; F.J. Cabrera Blázquez, 'Regulación de la copia privada a nivel europeo y jurisprudencia reciente en materia de redes P2P', *Autor y Derecho*, Ciberrevista sobre propiedad intelectual, February 2006.

220 It should be pointed out that not all the doctrine regards private copying as the user's enforceable right: it is simply an exception to copyright. If it is understood to be an exception or limit that cannot be appealed to, the attitude towards the author's rights is more protectionist and the defence of legal mechanisms that allow the technological protective measures imposed by the author to be lifted is not so lax.

copyright holder must provide access to the work and remove any limitations on access. Article 161 LPI recognises that the copyright holder who uses protection technology must provide legitimate third party users with the means to be able to enjoy the work. In connection with this, Article 31.2 LPI accepts that authors do not have to give permission to those who wish to reproduce a work that is already on the market if it is reproduced by a physical person, it is for private use and it is non-profit-making, as long as the provision of fair compensation (Art. 25 LPI) is upheld. If the so-called fair compensation for reproducing the work is satisfied and the aforementioned requirements are respected, the holder of the copyright is obliged to guarantee that users can access the work.

In accordance with the InfoSoc-Dir. 2001/29/EC and Articles 160 and 161 LPI, Carla cannot decrypt the work. Even so, if the download is licit and the copy is for private use with no profit-making purpose, private copying is an exception to the limitation applicable to the technological measures. In this case, we consider that 'String' should authorise or facilitate the lifting of the technological measures that protect the work (Art. 161 LPI).

III. Metalegal Formants

To date, there has been no case law on this issue. Spain has opted to protect copyright not only by recognising intellectual property rights, but also by allowing copyright holders to protect their work with the option provided by the InfoSoc-Dir. 2001/29/EC. Nevertheless, each case should be studied so that it can be determined whether these security measures are in favour of the beneficiaries of the copyright limitations, which we understand would give rise to a variety of interpretations and possible conflicts between the copyright holders and the beneficiaries of the limitations. Whatever the case may be, we understand that from a practical point of view it is difficult to establish the mechanism by which copyright holders can authorise the technological protection to be removed for each legitimate user in a digital environment.

(16) UNITED KINGDOM

I. Operative Rules

Yes, 'String' may object to Carla circumventing the technological protection measures.

II. Descriptive Formants

The record company can object to this because, although Carla is paying a monthly subscription to OD2 in order to legally download popular songs for

€30 per month, this does not give Carla the right to circumvent the technological protection measures put in place to protect the copyright of the works. Under section 296ZF CDPA 1988, technological measures are defined as 'any technology, device or component that is designed, in the normal course of its operation, to protect a copyright work other than a computer programme'. The encryption put in place over the songs by the record company 'String' evidently comes within an access control or protection process under section 298ZF(2) CDPA 1988.

Carla has paid for the downloaded songs in order to personally listen to them, but she must do so in a format chosen by 'String'. However, the act of successfully circumventing the technological lock on the downloaded songs is deemed illegal under section 296ZA CDPA 1988. The section gives specified persons civil rights of action where a person knowingly does anything which circumvents technological measures or has reasonable grounds to know that they are pursuing that objective. Despite Carla purchasing the various songs through OD2, a legal Internet site for downloading songs, Carla has still purposefully circumvented the technological measures on the downloaded songs and clearly cannot rely on the defence of accidental circumvention. As the record company has put the technological protection measure on the downloaded songs, it can object to the circumvention of its encryption of the songs and opt for civil sanctions on Carla if deemed necessary.

Aside from the issue of circumventing the technological protection measure, Carla has also copied and transferred the downloaded songs onto a different format – CDs. Even though Carla is solely listening to the copied songs on the daily bus ride to school, only the copyright owner has the exclusive right to copy their work from a downloadable format to a CD under section 16(1) CDPA 1988 and, in particular, section 17(2) CDPA 1988. Therefore, Carla seems to have infringed the owner's exclusive rights over their work as there is no legal defence for 'format-shifting' downloaded songs to hard copy CDs at this current time.

III. Metalegal Formants

The UK discussion on circumventing technological protection measures is firmly based on the CDPA 1988, and takes little account of considerations which influenced the European InfoSoc and Enforcement Directives.

C.4. COMPARATIVE REMARKS

The comparative remarks on this case are aggregated in section E.3 below.

D.1. MODIFICATION 3

Would Carla have an extra argument by saying that she does not want to pay twice (the subscription price at OD2 and the levy on the blank CD in the framework of the home copying regime) for a song that she cannot copy?

D.2. EDITORIAL NOTE

Article 5(2)(b) of Directive 2001/29/EC allows member states to introduce a private copy exception, provided that fair compensation is paid to the rightholder. The size of the compensation should take technological measures into account. This standard leaves broad discretion to member states.

D.3. COUNTRY REPORTS

(1) BELGIUM

I. Operative Rules

No, Carla does not have an extra argument.

II. Descriptive Formants

As confirmed by case law, the payment of a levy on CDs does not authorise the circumvention of technical protection measures (for more comments see Modification 4 below).[221]

III. Metalegal Formants

See Modifications 2 and 4.

(2) CZECH REPUBLIC

I. Operative Rules

Carla does not have an extra argument.

221 Pres. Court of 1st Instance Brussels [Voorz. Rb. Brussel], 25 May 2004, *A&M* 2004, no. 4, 338, note S. Dussolier, 'Copie privée versus mesures techniques de protection: l'exception est-elle un droit?' [Private Copy versus Technical Protection Measures: Is The Exception a

II. Descriptive Formants

Carla would not have an extra argument by saying that she does not want to pay twice. Paying a levy is an obligation imposed by section 25 Copyright Act, without any possibility for her not to pay (with the only exceptions being those laid down in section 25(8) for export and persons acting as an enterprise who make reproductions based on licence contracts). According to the doctrine, levies were introduced to '[s]olve results of rapid technological development ... which affords to users an opportunity to make an uncontrollable number and a qualitatively perfect number of copies'.[222] She is not paying twice; she is paying for songs and she is paying levies too.

III. Metalegal Formants

Answer omitted.

(3) DENMARK

I. Operative Rules

No, Carla would have no such extra argument in law.

II. Descriptive Formants

Denmark operates a blank CD levy system (for most CDs), cf. DCA §39 (the levy is about €0.2575 per CD). The levy compensates for the legal copying and in principle should correlate to the value of the copying for the user. Payment of the levy does not result in any contractual or other right to use the media for copying.

III. Metalegal Formants

The 'double payment' argument is valid in a political context. It would make no sense if the DCA did not in fact leave any room for producing the private copies for which the levy compensates the rightholders. To the extent that TPMs provide for effective protection against copying and individual negotiation

Right?]; A. Beerenboom, *Le nouveau droit d'auteur et les droits voisins* [The New Copyright and the Neighbouring Rights], in collection Création Information Communication [Creation Information Communication] (Brussels: 2005), 153.

222 J. Kříž, I. Holcová, J. Kordač, V. Křesťanová, *Autorský zákon komentář a předpisy související* (Copyright Act, Commentary and related regulations) (2nd ed., Prague: 2005), p. 116.

between buyers and sellers of music, the justification for blank media levy schemes, therefore, would be reduced and they would eventually disappear.

(4) ESTONIA

I. Operative Rules

No, Carla does not have an extra argument.

II. Descriptive Formants

The Copyright Act allows private use of audio-visual works and sound recordings of works and entitles the rightholders to obtain equitable remuneration for such use.[223] The Copyright Act provides a list of when the remuneration shall be repaid.[224] The list does not include the situation of the storage media being used by a private individual to copy material for which he/she has already paid or to copy works created by him/her. Consequently, Carla has to pay twice.

III. Metalegal Formants

The regulation concerning the levy on blank CDs might be changed to some extent in the future. It is hard to say what the specific regulation would be.

(5) FRANCE

I. Operative Rules

Carla might be justified in saying that she does not want to pay twice for a song that she cannot copy.

II. Descriptive Formants

The purchase of songs must not be confused with the private use exception. The levy on the blank CD compensates for the loss of income due to the private use exception,[225] whereas the price of the subscription to OD2 concerns the use of downloaded songs.

---

223 Copyright Act §26(1).

224 Copyright Act §27(5).

225 Art. L. 122-5 2° of the Intellectual Property Code (rights of the author), Art. L. 211-3 2° of the Intellectual Property Code (rights of the producer) and Art. L. 311-1 et seq. of the Intellectual Property Code.

III. *Metalegal Formants*

Answer omitted.

(6) GERMANY

I. *Operative Rules*

No, Carla does not have an extra argument.

II. *Descriptive Formants*

The current system is a double-track system. The consumer also pays twice: when listening to the radio (the radio charge covers the levy imposed on each radio transmission; §20 UrhG, collected by the German Collecting Society [GEMA][226]), and the levy imposed on home copying (§54 UrhG, collected by the Zentralstelle für private Überspielungsrechte). The system conceives these levies as complementary. However, the answer would have been yes, when considering the former §13 sec. 4 Urheberrechtswahrnehmungsgesetz (UrhWG, Copyright Administration Act, in effect until 2008).[227] It obliged collecting societies to take technical measures (DRM) into account when determining the amount of the levy. Thus, the levy on home copying is linked to DRM. As long as the levy does not take into account protection measures, Carla would have a counter-argument. Yet with §13 sec. 1 sentence 2 UrhWG in place, it is up to the collecting society to negotiate with producers *prior* to setting the levies. Thus, Carla has no individual right.

III. *Metalegal Formants*

The contingent answer is caused by the fact that systems converge – mirrored by a shift in concepts. Formerly, there was a clear-cut distinction between the property right and the private use right of the consumer. As compensation, the owner was given claims against collecting societies set up to correct

---

226 GEMA = Gesellschaft für musikalische Aufführungs- und mechanische Vervielfältigungsrechte.

227 §13 sec. 4 Urheberrechtswahrnehmungsgesetz read: 'Bei der Gestaltung von Tarifen, die auf den §§54 und 54a des Urheberrechtsgesetzes beruhen, ist auch zu berücksichtigen, inwieweit technische Schutzmaßnahmen nach §95a des Urheberrechtsgesetzes auf die betreffenden Werke oder die betreffenden Schutzgegenstände angewendet werden.' It was deleted and substituted by §13a UrhWG enacted on 26 October 2007 (BGBl. I S. 2513). The law was replaced in 2016 by the Verwertungsgesellschaftengesetz (which transposes EU Directive 2014/26/EU). §40 sec. 1 sentence 2 VGG now reads more generally: 'Die Verwertungsgesellschaften stellen hierfür Tarife auf Grundlage einer empirischen Untersuchung aus einem Verfahren gemäß §93 auf.'

market failures. And various uses appeared to be distinct, for example making available and coping. In the digital environment, however, there is no 'market failure' anymore. Nor can the clear-cut distinction between the property right and the consumer's private use right be upheld (because the private sphere becomes the main market). Bilateral contracts are possible due to technical measures. With the dissolving of a mere private sphere, the consumer's right cannot be defined by private use: we lose the distinction between public and private use. We also lose the idea of two different rights, which triggers the double levy. With the expansion of the property right (the owner decides the scope of use), the subscriptions mirror the breadth of the conveyed use rights. Thus, an additional levy does not seem to be justified. Carla has an additional argument. With the reform of 2003 (transposing Directive 2001/29/EC), German law shifted to the second concept (broad property right, narrow user rights).

(7) GREECE

I. Operative Rules

It is extremely uncertain that Carla will have such an extra argument.

II. Descriptive Formants

Answer omitted.

III. Metalegal Formants

If we stick to the letter of the law, we can only give a negative answer. This is an obligation of citizens towards the state and towards the intellectual creator. In spite of this, the provisions of Law 2121/1993 on payment could be included, on certain conditions, in the evaluation to assess the abusiveness of the injunction.

(8) IRELAND

No levies apply in Ireland.

(9) ITALY

I. Operative Rules

No, Carla does not have an extra argument.

II. Descriptive Formants

The levy, which is defined by Article 71-septies ICL, is compensation for the right, granted to the end user, to make an exclusively personal copy. We have already seen that Carla still has the possibility to make an analogue copy and so, according to the wording of the provision, the compensation is justified. The ministerial decree, which determines the compensation, must take into account, according to Article 71-septies c. 2, the presence of technological protection measures. Still, the presence of such measures does not exclude the compensation.

III. Metalegal Formants

Answer omitted.

(10) LITHUANIA

I. Operative Rules

No, Carla cannot argue that she does not want to pay twice.

II. Descriptive Formants

Essentially, consumers are required to pay once for a physical CD and once for the digital music file. The restrictions for online subscription services and physical CDs are part of a music-industry-wide attempt to stop online music piracy.

III. Metalegal Formants

Here, an important decision of the Supreme Court should be discussed. The Court in the *LATGAA v. Trajektorija* case[228] upheld the extended copyright levies on all blank media introduced into Lithuania (regardless of whether the media was imported from outside of the EU or introduced from another EU country, and irrespective of the purpose for which the media is intended or used). The Court assumed that the EU Copyright Directive requires 'fair compensation' in all cases where the 'right to private copy is provided'. The Court also assumed that the government had rightfully imposed the levies on all blank media introduced

---

228 Supreme Court Decision of 3 March 2008, No. 3K-3-4/2008, *LATGAA v. Trajektorija*.

into the country, regardless of whether they are intended for personal purposes (the law itself is moot on this issue). Even though it was accepted that media may be used for non-personal purposes (such as broadcasting, to meet the needs of the hearing/vision impaired, public administration, public security, scientific research), the general levy on all media with a limited right to a refund was upheld.

The Court sidestepped practical aspects of collecting the copyright levies, thus leaving the door open for further litigation. The Court recognised that there are no rules on how the levies shall be reported and paid if the levied media are brought into the country from another EU country (and no customs procedures are performed), although it failed to acknowledge the lack of such rules as an implication of the import-only nature of the levies. In the intra-EU situation, the Court suggested that the parties (a collecting society, as well as a wholesaler) should deal with this by means of a contract (if this was not already obvious). In the decision, no mention was made of the double levying of the blank media in several EU countries and accompanying distortions of competition.

(11) NETHERLANDS

I. *Operative Rules*

No, she does not have this argument.

II. *Descriptive Formants*

Articles 16c–16g of the Dutch Copyright Act govern the making of private copies of works by fixing them on an object which is intended to show the images or play the sounds recorded upon it, and the conditions for payment of fair compensation to the rightholder. The compensation is mandatory and owed to rights owners by the manufacturer or the importer of devices. The fee is usually passed down to the end consumer. None of these statutory provisions make any accommodation for the fact that TPMs can be applied to a work, thereby preventing the making of a copy of that work, and that, as a consequence, a levy should logically not be paid.

III. *Metalegal Formants*

The argument Carla uses is dealt with in Article 5(2)(b) of the Information Society Directive. Where levies co-exist with TPMs, consumers run the risk of paying twice for the right to make a private copy of a work. Consumers would have to pay once by paying the levy and once again by paying the rightholder for the right to copy the work.[229] Recital 35 of the Directive shows that the legislator tried to prevent double payment by consumers. Article 5(2)(b) of the Directive, which deals with the private copy exception, specifically refers to TPMs. The article prescribes that in calculating the fair compensation for private copying, the application or non-application of TPMs should be taken into account.

The Dutch Copyright Act does not specifically refer to the requirement in Article 5(2)(b) of the Directive. The Minister of Justice states in the explanatory memorandum that 'the current private copying regime should be applied to analogue and digital storage media, since the reasons initially invoked for the creation of such a regime are still valid and since there are no practical alternatives currently available'. He continued that 'it is to be expected that the technology will in the future allow the regulation of private copying activities so that there will then be little or no need for a levy system'.[230]

While Carla's argument is 'valid', this does not create a right to circumvent a TPM in an individual case or to refuse to pay the levy on the blank CD.

(12) NORWAY

I. *Operative Rules*

No, Carla would have no such extra argument.

II. *Descriptive Formants*

Norway no longer has a blank CD levy system. The obligation pursuant to Article 5(2)(b) of the Copyright Directive to provide for fair compensation for private use was implemented by the introduction of an obligation to compensate rightholders by means of the state budget, cf. NCA §12, first paragraph, third sentence (New Act §26, fourth paragraph). Thus, Carla has no relevant 'double payment' argument under Norwegian law. The general obligation to pay taxes for the benefit of the state budget is too remote to be legally relevant.

III. *Metalegal Formants*

The issue at hand concerns the requirement in Article 5(2), cf. Recital 35, of the Copyright Directive, to take TPMs into consideration when providing for fair compensation for private copying. Due to the Norwegian solution for fair compensation – the state budget solution – the impact of TPMs with regard to

[229] P.B. Hugenholtz, L. Guibault and S. van Geffen, *The Future of Levies in a Digital Environment* (final report), Institute for Information Law Amsterdam, March 2003, p. 1.

[230] Ibid., pp. 28–29; *Kamerstukken II*, 2001–2002, 28 482 Nr. 3, p. 46.

fair compensation will have to be decided on a more general level than is the case for levy-based systems.

(13) POLAND

I. Operative Rules

No, she does not have that argument.

II. Descriptive Formants

Since Carla did not infringe copyright and did not illegally circumvent TPMs, no additional arguments are necessary.

III. Metalegal Formants

Here the problem arises from the co-existence of solutions belonging to different generations. Copyright levies by their very nature must be wholly independent of the use of a concrete blank media. The very idea of levies relies on the assumption that it is impossible to track down uses requiring payment to the rightholder and therefore they have been imposed on products that are often used in such a way. TPMs and digital management rights are based on an entirely different assumption: it is believed that what was impossible in the past has become feasible now thanks to new digital technologies, which make it possible to contract around every single use of a copyright work. The rationales for copyright levies and DRMs are therefore irreconcilable. Because of this, the impact of the more widespread use of DRMs on copyright levies may be evaluated in only one way: namely, based on market data on how often DRMs are used, the copyright levies on blank media could be reduced.

(14) SLOVENIA

I. Operative Rules

No, Carla does not have that argument.

II. Descriptive Formants

The use of effective technological measures should, according to the new Directive, be taken into account when setting the amount of remuneration. However, the analysis of the Decree of the Slovenian Intellectual Property Office

(SIPO) on amounts of remuneration for private and other internal reproduction (DARPOIR)[231] reveals that the Slovenian legislator has not considered this properly. A suitable modification of the Decree and adjustment of the remuneration amounts could be demanded.

III. Metalegal Formants

Directive 2001/29/EC introduced a new concept and 'equitable remuneration' was replaced by 'fair compensation'. One of the factors that also has to be considered when adopting the model for setting the levy rate is the applicability of technological measures.

(15) SPAIN

I. Operative Rules

Carla's argument would not be valid for what she intends.

II. Descriptive Formants

All the comments made in the previous section are also applicable to the current scenario. However, it should be pointed out that if the third user decides to use the exceptions to the limitations on copyrights, he/she may be within his/her right to have the copyright holder remove the technological protection. Under no circumstances can he/she just remove the technological protection.

However, the fact that Carla has paid tax on a blank CD is not an argument in her favour, insofar as the whole issue (the levy payment) revolves around the rights of the title holder, the limitations on these rights and how the exceptions to the limitations are formulated.

III. Metalegal Formants

The payment of tax on blank CDs and CD-ROMs in Spain has been the subject of considerable debate. The issue of the payment of a tax and those subjects who are obliged to pay has been studied by civil and administrative courts. Regarding the administrative bodies, the Spanish Authority on Competition (TDC), in response to a formal complaint made by various consumer associations, reviewed an agreement to fix the amount of tax for fair compensation between copyright

[231] Official Gazette RS, nos. 63/1998, 103/2006.

management associations and manufacturers of equipment for reproducing the works, because it allegedly infringed regulations on competition. The TDC considered that it was not an anti-collusive pact.[232]

Regarding civil proceedings, the legal confrontation in the civil courts was settled on various fronts after the *TRAXDATA* court decision in 2003. The main argument put forward by the critics of paying a tax on blank CDs and CD-ROMs was that the copyright management associations assumed that these media were to be used to infringe intellectual property rights. The results of these legal conflicts have been varied, and in some cases legal bodies have only been able to reach a decision by considering the use given to the CD by the consumer. Some court decisions, then, considered that consumers had been wrongfully charged if they were going to use the CD for something that did not involve infringing intellectual property rights. In addition, since the aim of the tax is to compensate the author, if there is no infringement, there is no need for compensation and there is no need to pay the tax. Even so, quite different court decisions have also been reached, so it is clear that it is a controversial issue that does not have an easy solution. But at this point, it is possible that there will be a change in the interpretation on the levy. We refer to the CJEU judgment on the fairness of the levy relative to the subjects affected and the uses of the digital equipment to reproduce authors' works. See the comments below in the metalegal formants for Modification 4 on the CJEU decision about the levy.

(16) UNITED KINGDOM

I. *Operative Rules*

At present, the cost of a subscription to OD2 and the levy on the blank CD in the framework of the home copying regime would not provide an extra argument because the UK does not have a levy system.

II. *Descriptive Formants*

As discussed above, the private copying exemption does allow format-shifting but it was not accompanied by a levy, giving rise to debates about the compliance with the relevant InfoSoc Directive provision. In any case, implementing the 'format-shifting' exception (s. 28B(5)(b)) does not affect technological protection measures and, as a result, full liability for infringement applies.

---

232 TDC Ruling of 31 May 2007 (among other previous rulings, TDC Ruling 634/04, SGAE-ASIMELEC of 24 November 2005).

III. Metalegal Formants

The UK IPO proposal, following Recommendation 8 of the Gower Review, had proposed the creation of a new exception, which would allow consumers to make a copy of a work they legally own in order to make it accessible in another format for playback on devices in their lawful possession – CD players and iPods.

Certain limitations would however be imposed on the potential exception. For example, the owner would not be permitted to lend, sell or give away the copy made, or share it with others through an online peer-to-peer network. Another main element of the proposed 'format-shifting' exception is that it is not to be coupled with a corresponding levy on devices like CDs. Legal commentators had promoted this position because the relevant industries can price works like songs to include the recognition that the consumer will be able to transfer the format of the work, and that the proposed exception is narrow enough to avoid significant harm to the holder of the copyright.

D.4. COMPARATIVE REMARKS

The comparative remarks on this case are aggregated in section E.3 below.

E.1. MODIFICATION 4

Carla downloads and burns onto a CD songs that are distributed under a Creative Commons licence, on a royalty-free basis, allowing users to freely reproduce and distribute the works for non-commercial purposes.

Would Carla have a cause of action for reimbursement of the levy on the blank CD against the collecting society administering the home copying regime?

E.2. COUNTRY REPORTS

(1) BELGIUM

I. Operative Rules

No, Carla would not have a cause of action for reimbursement of the levy.

II. Descriptive Formants

- Articles 1, 22§1 5° and 55–58 BCA (Arts. XI.165, XI.190 9° and XI.229–234 BCEL);

- Article 2 Royal Decree on the Home Copy Levy of 28 March 1996[233] (at present the Royal Decree is no longer in force; Articles XI.229–XI.239 BCEL provide for a new framework, which is far less worrisome than in the past).

Articles 55–58 BCA (Arts. XI.229–234 BCEL) regulate the levy on blank storage devices and equipment and the remuneration for private reproductions. The Royal Decree on the Home Copy Levy of 28 March 1996 (as updated in 2003) implements these provisions. Article 2 of this Royal Decree prescribes that the current levy on a blank CD is €0.12. This legal levy has to be paid by those bringing the CDs into circulation on the national territory (Art. 55§2 BCA) and *because of* this bringing into circulation.[234] It is not the final user who has to pay the levy, but obviously the sellers of the blank CDs will keep the levy in mind when setting the market price. The levy is due because of the bringing into national circulation, regardless of the use that is made of the blank CDs later on. It does not matter whether the consumer uses the CD for copying (protected or unprotected) content; the levy is paid for and will not be reimbursed, as confirmed by the Belgian Constitutional Court.[235] (Art. 55§2 BCA has been replaced by Article XI.229, which sets forth that the levy has to be paid by those who make, import or acquire within the Union storage devices which are manifestly used for private copy or devices manifestly used for this reproduction when these storage devices and copying equipment are put on the national territory.)

III. Metalegal Formants

Article 1 BCA (Art. XI.165 BCEL) attributes to the author the right to exploit his/her work. Private copying on the other hand is in the interest of the consumer. Whether it is a right or not, whether it is technically possible to prevent or control it or not, private copying is a fact. As a compromise, the Belgian legislator has decided to allow private copying (Art. 22§1 5° BCA, now Art. XI.190 9° BCEL),

233 Royal Decree on the Home Copy Levy, 28 March 1996, *Official Gazette*, 6 June 1996 [K.B. 28 maart 1996 betreffende het recht op vergoeding voor het kopiëren voor eigen gebruik voor de auteurs, de uitvoerende kunstenaars en de producenten van fonogrammen en van audiovisuele werken, *B.S.*, 6 juni 1996].

234 M.-C. Janssens, 'Art. 55', in: F. Brison and H. Vanhees (eds.), *Huldeboek aan Jan Corbet. De Belgische Auteurswet. Artikelsgewijze Commentaar [Homage to Jan Corbet. The Belgian Copyright Act. Commentaries Article per Article]* (Brussels: 2006), 281–283.

235 Belgian Constitutional Court [Grondwettelijk Hof], no. 152/2008, 6 November 2008, available at: www.grondwettelijkhof.be (last consulted 13 November 2008), reported on by J. Deene, 'Heffing op lege cd's en dvd's is geen discriminatie' [A Levy on Empty CDs and DVDs does not Constitute a Discrimination], *De Juristenkrant*, 26 November 2008, 1. For comments, see F. de Visscher and B. Michaux, *Précis du droit d'auteur et des droits voisins [Manual Copyright and Neighbouring Rights]* (Brussels: 2000), 337–378. For a commentary on Arts. 55–58 Copyright Act, see M.-C. Janssens, in: F. Brison and H. Vanhees (eds.), *Huldeboek aan Jan Corbet. De Belgische Auteurswet. Artikelsgewijze Commentaar [Homage to Jan Corbet. The Belgian Copyright Act. Commentaries Article per Article]* (Brussels: 2006), 279–293.

but to compensate the rightholders for the resulting financial loss by creating a legal licence system comprising levies on blank storage devices and copying equipment (Arts. 55–58 BCA, now Arts. XI.229–234 BCEL).[236]

Recently the Belgian Constitutional Court confirmed that the levy did not constitute discrimination between users who copy protected content and users using CDs or DVDs for other purposes than making private copies of copyright-protected content. For practical reasons, the Court deemed the fixed levy to be a proportional measure.[237]

In Recital 35 and Article 5(2)(b) of the Copyright Directive 2001/29/EC, member states are invited to take into account the technical measures hindering private copying when deciding on fair compensation for home copying. The future Article 56 BCA[238] (Art. XI.232 BCEL) suggests accounting for technical measures that restrict copying when calculating fair compensation. For now, the Belgian legislator will not help Carla in her frustrations about paying for these levies when she is not copying protected content or when she is prevented from copying by technical measures.[239]

(2) CZECH REPUBLIC

I. Operative Rules

Carla would not be entitled to reimbursement of the levy from the collecting society.

II. Descriptive Formants

The collecting society is collecting levies according to section 25 Copyright Act and, as shown above, there are only two exceptions to the payment of levies

---

236 D. Baervoets, 'Kopiëren voor eigen gebruik en reprografie na de wet van 22 mei 2005 houdende de omzetting in Belgisch recht van richtlijn 2001/29/EG betreffende de harmonisering van bepaalde aspecten van het auteursrecht en de naburige rechten in de informatiemaatschappij. Enkele beschouwingen aangaande het toepassingsgebied van deze uitzonderingen en de 'compensatie' stelsels (augustus 2005)' [Home Copying and Reprography after the Law of 2005 on the Implementation of Directive 2001/29/EC. A Few Observations on the Applicability of These Exceptions and the 'Compensation' Systems (August 2005)], *I.R.D.I.* 2006, 10.

237 Belgian Constitutional Court, no. 152/2008, 6 November 2008.

238 Introduced by Art. 15 Act on the Implementation of the Copyright Directive 2001/29/EC, 22 May 2005, *Official Gazette*, 27 May 2005 [Wet 22 mei 2005 houdende de omzetting in Belgisch recht van de Europese Richtlijn 2001/29/EG van 22 mei 2001 betreffende de harmonisatie van bepaalde aspecten van het auteursrecht en de naburige rechten in de informatiemaatschappij, *B.S.*, 27 mei 2005]. According to Art. 40 of the same Act, this article will enter into force at a date yet to be determined by the King.

239 M.-C. Janssens, 'De Belgische auteurswet doet zijn intrede in het tijdperk van de informatiemaatschappij' [The Belgian Copyright Act Enters the Era of the Information Society], *Computerrecht* 2006, no. 2, 7.

recognised by the Copyright Act. Levies are paid by the importer, producer or consignee of blank CDs and the Copyright Act does not entitle anyone to reimbursement.

III. Metalegal Formants

Answer omitted.

(3) DENMARK

I. Operative Rules

No, Carla would not have a cause of action.

II. Descriptive Formants

The Danish rules do not allow for any reimbursement.

III. Metalegal Formants

Answer omitted.

(4) ESTONIA

I. Operative Rules

No, Carla would not be entitled to reimbursement.

II. Descriptive Formants

The amount of remuneration for private use of audio-visual works and sound recordings of works is 8% of the value of the goods in the case of storage media (§27(7) clause 1 Copyright Act).

The list of storage media on which the levy is imposed is established by a regulation of the Government of the Republic.[240] The list includes *inter alia*

[240] Audiovisuaalse teose ja teose helisalvestise isiklikeks vajadusteks kasutamise kompenseerimiseks tasu maksmise kord, salvestusseadmete ja -kandjate loetelu ning muusika- ja filmikultuuri arendamiseks ning koolitus- ja teadusprogrammide finantseerimiseks või kasutamiseks muudel analoogsetel eesmärkidel tasu taotlemise kord. Vabariigi Valitsuse 17. jaanuari 2006. a määrus nr 14. Entered into force on 30 January 2006 – RT I 2006, 5, 23 (in Estonian).

the following storage media: VHS, CD-R, CD-RW, DVD-R and DVD-RW. As a result, it can be concluded that the levy is imposed on different kinds of CDs.

Subsection 27(5) Copyright Act provides that:

> The remuneration shall be repaid on the storage media and recording devices:
>
> 1) which, due to their technical characteristics, do not enable the reproduction of audio-visual works and sound recordings of works as single copies;
> 2) exported or transported from Estonia into the Community customs territory;
> 3) which are used in the course of the activities specified in the articles of association of the undertaking;
> 4) which are used in an activity in the case of which the result of the main activity of the person who makes the recording requires the manufacture of an audio or video recording as an intermediate stage;
> 5) which are intended for recording activities in educational and research institutions for the purpose of teaching or scientific research;
> 6) used for making recordings for the benefit of disabled persons.

As has been seen, the list does not include the situation where the CD is used for one's own creations, music under CC licences, etc. Therefore, Carla does not have the right to a reimbursement of the levy on the blank CD.

III. Metalegal Formants

The regulation concerning the levy on blank CDs might be changed to some extent in the future. It is hard to say what the specific regulation would be.

(5) FRANCE

I. Operative Rules

Carla does not have a cause to file for reimbursement of the levy on the blank CD against the collecting society administering the home copying regime.

II. Descriptive Formants

The French Commission of Private Copy decided on 4 January 2001 that the levy for private copying is applicable to all digital recording formats used for private copying of works fixed on phonograms and videograms, whatever their format and presentation (sound, picture and all other data).[241] The authors and

[241] Council of State, 11 July 2008, case no. 298779.

performers of works fixed on phonograms or videograms and the producers of such phonograms or videograms shall be entitled to remuneration for the reproduction of those works made in accordance with the private use exception (Art. L. 311-1 of the French Intellectual Property Code). The remuneration for private copying shall be refunded when the recording medium is acquired for their own use or production by audio-visual, phonogram or videogram producers and persons who carry out the reproduction of phonogram or videograms on behalf of producers, publishers of works published on digital mediums, and legal persons or bodies – a list of which shall be established by the Minister of Culture – that use recording mediums for the purpose of assisting persons with vision or hearing disabilities (Art. L. 311-8 of the French Intellectual Property Code). Therefore, Clara does not have a cause to file for reimbursement of the levy on blank CDs against the collecting society administering the home copying regime.

III. Metalegal Formants

Answer omitted.

(6) GERMANY

I. Operative Rules

No, Carla is not entitled to reimbursement.

II. Descriptive Formants

While the levy on blank CDs is fixed by statute (Annex to §54d UrhG, unchanged since 1985), the home copying regime builds on the private copy exemption. It is conceived as a legislative licence. The claim for compensation arises by law. Whereas an author can, in principle, provide for a cost-free licence to everyone (§32 sec. 3 UrhG), the statutory exemption cannot be set aside (§63 a UrhG). Therefore, the author can also not renounce the statutory compensation. (Thus, the author can renounce pay (property rule), but not compensation (liability rule)). Carla has no claim for reimbursement.

III. Metalegal Formants

The legitimation of the home coping regime (the levy on blank CDs as compensation for private use – liability rule) stems from the idea of market failure. The author cannot collect the compensation him/herself. With the market failure in the digital world disappearing, this argument may cease to exist. Therefore, if DRM were to become the rule in the future, the levy on CDs would need to take gratuitous licences into account. Then Carla would have a claim for reimbursement.

(7) GREECE

I. Operative Rules

Carla has no action for reimbursement.

II. Descriptive Formants

Downloading and burning songs for other users constitutes a *res inter alios acta* vis-à-vis the collecting company. Thus, it does not influence the legal relations between this company and Carla.

III. Metalegal Formants

Answer omitted.

(8) IRELAND

In Ireland, there are no levies.

(9) ITALY

I. Operative Rules

No, Carla is not entitled to reimbursement (see Modification 3).

II. Descriptive Formants

The compensation is related to the possibility of using a blank CD for making a private copy, regulated by Article 71-sexties, of works whose licence is more restrictive than Creative Commons licences, and not to the actual use of the blank CD for that specific purpose.

III. Metalegal Formants

Answer omitted.

(10) LITHUANIA

I. Operative Rules

No, Carla has no right to reimbursement.

II. Descriptive Formants

A Creative Commons licence does not mean giving up a copyright. It means offering some of the rights to any member of the public. The claim for compensation arises by law.[242]

III. Metalegal Formants

Answer omitted.

(11) NETHERLANDS

I. Operative Rules

No, Carla is not entitled to reimbursement.

II. Descriptive Formants

When determining the size of the levy, the possibility of royalty-free use of blank CDs was taken into account. The percentage of royalty-free use is investigated every two years. The only cause for reimbursement of the levy is if the blank CDs are used for professional purposes. In that case, the levy will be reimbursed to the producer or importer of the blank CDs, who has paid the levy to the collecting society. The producer or importer will then pay back the levy to the professional user.

III. Metalegal Formants

According to the Dutch legislation, it does not matter whether the CD is used for copyright-protected material or not. The reproduction devices and storage media which fall under the levy system are noted in a Decree.[243] To decide which

242 See the Spanish country report.

243 *Besluit van 23 oktober 2012, houdende aanwijzing van de voorwerpen, bedoeld in artikel 16c van de Auteurswet, en tot vaststelling van nadere regels over de hoogte en de verschuldigdheid van de vergoeding, bedoeld in artikel 16c van de Auteurswet* – Staatsblad 2012, 505, p. 1.

devices should fall under the levy system, the purpose of the device is relevant. For example, tapes used for dictating are excluded from the levy system because they are not meant to record protected works. In the case of CDs, these are likely being used for private copying of protected material.[244]

Article 16c was modified as a consequence of the implementation of the Information Society Directive. The Directive prescribes that rightholders should receive fair compensation because of the disadvantages they experience due to private copying. There has been some discussion on how to interpret 'fair compensation'. It is unclear whether the fair compensation is meant to compensate damages suffered by rightholders or is meant as a compensation for the use of the work even when rightholders are not harmed by the act of private copying. If fair compensation is to be seen as compensation for damages, users should not have to pay if there are no damages. This would for instance be the case if a CD is used for material which is not protected by copyright.[245]

(12) NORWAY

I. Operative Rules

No, Carla would not have a cause of action.

II. Descriptive Formants

See under Modification 3. The lack of a blank CD levy under Norwegian law renders the argument for a cause of action irrelevant.

III. Metalegal Formants

As under Modification 3.

(13) POLAND

I. Operative Rules

No, Carla is not entitled to reimbursement.

---

244 *Nota van Toelichting bij Besluit van 17 februari 2007, houdende de aanwijzing van de voorwerpen, bedoeld in artikel 16c van de Auteurswet 1912* – Staatsblad 2007, 75, p. 4.

245 C. Gielen and D.W.F. Verkade, *Intellectuele eigendom* (Deventer: 2005), pp. 477–478. See also P.B. Hugenholtz, L. Guibault and S. van Geffen, *The Future of Levies in a Digital Environment* (final report), Institute for Information Law Amsterdam, March 2003, para. 5.3.

II. Descriptive Formants

The most obvious answer would be that the system of copyright levies operates on the basis of the law in force and the law does not provide for such exceptions. The practicability of copyright levy schemes would be called into serious doubt if it were possible to demand refunds for those blank CDs (or other blank media) that were not used in any copyright-relevant way.

III. Metalegal Formants

On the metalegal level, the problem revolves around similar questions as in Modification 3. The case demonstrates that the legitimacy of copyright levies may be regarded as dubious, as there is no direct connection between payment of the levy and a copyright-relevant use. It is very often argued that such schemes may be justified only as a response to market failures and when the latter can be remedied (e.g. by DRM systems) this justification ceases to exist. In this line of reasoning, copyright levies should be gradually withdrawn and replaced by DRMs. It seems, however, that such a view is overly simplistic. In essence it is based on the assumption that the sphere of fair use itself is justified only by market failure, which is a controversial statement to say the least.

(14) SLOVENIA

I. Operative Rules

No, Carla is not entitled to reimbursement.

II. Descriptive Formants

The amount of remuneration is set by the Decree on Remuneration (DR). Carla cannot demand reimbursement from the collective society.

III. Metalegal Formants

When setting the amount of remuneration, the copyright office has to take into account multiple factors. Directive 2001/29/EC introduced a new concept. The former concept of 'equitable remuneration' was replaced by the new concept of 'fair compensation'. One of the factors is therefore also the fact that rightholders are allowing for reproduction on a larger scale. Along with the allowed private use, which represents the basis for compensation, many works are made available online under conditions which do not oppose free reproduction. This could present a reason for a decreasing number of reproductions committed pursuant to the private use provisions, and for a decreased amount of compensation paid upon the sale of every blank CD. However, this reasoning is not reflected by the amounts of the levies set by the DR.

(15) SPAIN

I. Operative Rules

It would be difficult for Carla to have the tax on the CD refunded because no distinction is made as to the origin of reproductions at the moment in Spain. All CDs, as equipment available to reproduce an author's work, are subject to the payment of the levy.

II. Descriptive Formants

Creative Commons licences in Spain regulate the rights that authors have over their work and allow them to retain some specific rights. However, they do not deal with the issue of the taxes levied on blank CDs. These licences cite the protection that the LPI provides to the holders of intellectual property rights on those issues that are not regulated or that are subject to greater protection than that given by the Creative Commons system. At the present time, the LPI states that a tax must be levied on all equipment that can reproduce a work as fair compensation for the right to make private copies.

III. Metalegal Formants

With respect to Creative Commons licences, we should consider the possibility that if an author acts under a Creative Commons licence and authorises the reproduction of his/her work, as stated in the facts of the present case, a private user could ask for a reimbursement of the levy, particularly after the CJEU case *Padawan S.L. v. Sociedad de autores y editores de España (SGAE) et al.*[246] As is stated in the CJEU's decision, it is important to study the possibility that if the levy is a system to compensate authors for the harm suffered as a consequence of the avoidance of their reproduction right, where this harm does not exist because the author has published his/her work under a Creative Commons licence, the levy on the blank CD would not be justified and it would not accomplish its goal. As a consequence, a reimbursement of the levy could have a legal justification.

---

246 CJEU judgment of 21 October 2010, *Padawan S.L. v. Sociedad de autores y editores de España (SGAE)*, C-467/08.

We consider it worthwhile to comment on the CJEU's judgment in *Padawan*. Some of the rulings contained in this judgment could be applicable in Modifications 3 and 4. The CJEU's decision reviews the concept of the private copy levy applied to digital reproduction equipment, devices and media. The CJEU states the need to harmonise fair compensation for authors in those state regulations that recognise private copying as an exception to the author's reproduction right. On this point, the CJEU recognises that the compensation for authors is a response to the possible harm caused to them as a consequence of the existence of the private copying exception. The CJEU states that the levy system is a valid system to compensate for this harm so long as it is not applied indiscriminately. The Court's decision states that the levy generates discrimination where the levy taxes all types of digital reproduction equipment, devices and media, 'including those acquired by persons other than natural persons for purposes clearly unrelated to private copying'.

It is on that point that some comments could be made. In our case, Carla buys equipment capable of copying music and that fact, according to the ruling in the CJEU's decision, gives rise to compensate the author – the levy must be paid for the possible copies that would be made due to private use and, in consequence, it is necessary to compensate the possible harm done to the authors or rightholders. The first question that arises relates to the CJEU's statement on the *iuris tantum* presumption regarding private end users. This presumption means that a third user who acquires digital reproduction equipment (in a broad sense) has the possibility to reproduce protected works, even if that function is not going to be used. These premises sustain the use of the private copying exception. But on the contrary, if the third user is a natural person and the use of the equipment is not directed to reproducing works, this natural person should not be considered to be subject to the fair compensation obligation. In consequence, it should be considered that new litigation scenarios will probably occur and the evidence about the use of the equipment will be an issue to ponder. On the one hand, it will be for the private user to prove that the equipment is not used to make copies of the works, and on the other hand, it will be for the collective societies or authors to prove that natural persons are indeed using the reproduction equipment to reproduce works that are protected under an IP right in concrete cases. The second question that could be considered is the one advanced some paragraphs before regarding the reimbursement of the levy against a collecting society in a Creative Commons licence scenario. Arguably, a revision regarding the object of the levy, the protection provided by Creative Commons licences and the practical difficulties that imply a discriminative application of the legal exempted uses of the works by third parties would result in a possible refund of the levy.

A final comment could be made regarding a possible double imposition of the levy when a private consumer buys a blank CD and also reproduction equipment. The mere fact of being a private user implies a *iuris tantum* presumption that the consumer will use all the media he/she purchases to reproduce works. We consider that if the private user is able to prove that he/she is not making reproductions, the reimbursement of the levy could be justified. On the contrary, unjust enrichment of the author could occur with the double imposition of the levy. We consider that this could be an open question after the CJEU decision's in *Padawan*.

In conclusion, we believe that the Spanish private coping regime, which is seen as an exception to the reproduction right, should be reviewed with respect to the levy concept and its execution. At the moment, the practical application of the Spanish levy system appears incompatible with the interpretation of Directive 2001/29/EC in the CJEU's ruling in *Padawan*. The interpretation by the Spanish legislator supports the discriminatory imposition of the levy on all users and for all types of uses. In consequence, a reform of the LPI is needed or a new interpretation by the courts, but the levy system should be implemented taking account of the conditions stated in the ruling: (1) the end user and (2) the type of use.

At this point we should indicate that the Audiencia Provincial de Barcelona (hereinafter the Court of Appeal) took a decision on the conflict which was at the source of the CJEU's preliminary ruling in the *Padawan* case. This decision was adopted on 2 February 2011 (JUR\2011\68191). The conflict in the main proceedings related to a claim brought by the SGAE against the company Padawan, S.L. The SGAE is the administrative body responsible for the collective rights of authors. The SGAE claimed the amount based on the private copying levy applied to digital media (CD-Rs, CD-RWs, DVD-Rs, MP3 players). The amount was claimed for the period from September 2002 to September 2004. Padawan marketed digital products to natural persons, professional entities and also to private users. Private users could buy these products because Padawan had a store that was open to all kinds of customers. The Barcelona First Instance Court concluded that Padawan was obliged to pay €16,759.25 plus interest under the copying levy as applied to the digital media Padawan was selling. Padawan appealed the First Instance Court's decision and asked the Court of Appeal to apply for a preliminary ruling from the CJEU concerning the interpretation of the concept of 'fair compensation' contained in Article 5(2)(b) Directive 2001/29/EC to be paid to copyright holders in respect of the 'private copying exception'.

The Spanish Court of Appeal, taking account of the CJEU's ruling, considers two important legal issues. First, the Court decision admits that the bodies responsible for the collective rights of the authors can claim the levy payment. This is mainly because the levy is a system to compensate authors due to the existence of the private copy exception. The Court decision admits that this levy is applicable to all digital equipment that allows reproductions of a work without the consent of the author. The mere fact of allowing the reproduction justifies the economic compensation that protects the author. The second question – different to the previous one – is the possible indiscriminate application of the levy to digital equipment used for other purposes than private copying. The Court of Appeal maintains, and we agree, that an indiscriminate application of the canon could violate the European autonomous legal concept of fair compensation. The reason is clear: the levy system does not distinguish between the end users of the media as it is recognised in the Spanish legislation. On the contrary, Spanish legislation establishes the levy system based on whether or not the media allow the reproduction of the works protected by authors' rights. In this sense, the Court of Appeal insists on the following key issue: if the levy is charged on all digital equipment without distinguishing the end users, there would not be a link between the fair compensation of the author and the private copy limitation (point 10 of the legal findings). In consequence, the Court of Appeal distinguishes between the different users – private users and natural persons – in order to make a presumption of use. The Court of Appeal states that private users can use digital equipment to make copies of works protected by the authors' rights. On the other hand, the Court states that natural persons or public bodies are considered professionals which would not use the digital equipment for copying protected works. Finally, the Court of Appeal states that if there is no difference between the users, a lack of distinction could lead to an indiscriminate application of the private copying levy.

The Court of Appeal states that if there is no link between the end uses of the digital equipment, it could give rise to an indiscriminate application of the levy, according to the interpretation given by the CJEU of the fair compensation concept and the fair balance as to the amount of the levy. The Court of Appeal decided that Padawan would not have to pay any amount because the company had proved that the majority of its customers were natural persons, not private users. An interpretation that would lead to the conclusion that all digital equipment is used to make reproductions of works protected by authors' rights would not be justified. In consequence, the Court of Appeal annulled the First Instance Court's decision.

At this point, we would like to remark that the Court of Appeal in this decision does not consider whether the amount of the levy maintains the so-called 'fair balance' between the different interests established by the CJEU. We want to point out that taxes are determined by the Spanish government in a ministerial ruling. Several decisions by the Audiencia Nacional (Administrative Court of Appeal) have declared null and void the Orden (ministerial ruling) 1743/2008 dated 18 June.[247] The ministerial ruling established the equipment that should be subject to the levy and the amounts applicable. The repeal of the ministerial ruling does not relate to the tax rates, but rather to the non-fulfilment of the formal requirements to its approval. In consequence, now the

---

247 Decisions dated 22 March 2011 (JUR\2011\94695; JUR 2011\94694; JUR\2011\94692; JUR\2011\94693; JT\2011\202).

Spanish government is in the process of approving a new ministerial ruling to rectify this failure. The previous regulation regarding tax rates is now in force. We should point out that even the Spanish government, administrative courts and civil courts have considered the possibility that the tax rate will maintain the fair balance of the different interests involved (cultural consumers and authors).

(16) UNITED KINGDOM

I. Operative Rules

Carla has no claim.

II. Descriptive Formants

It took a while until the UK government acted on Recital 35 of the Copyright Directive, which states that owners 'should receive fair compensation to compensate them adequately for the use of their protected works.' It obliged the United Kingdom to implement a well-balanced levy system with exceptions. As early as 1985, the imposition of a blank tape levy on audio and video tapes was recommended in a consultative document on copyright for audio-visual material presented to the British Parliament by the Secretary of State for Trade and Industry, to which the government's 1986 White Paper on Intellectual Property Innovation referred. Nevertheless, these recommendations were eventually rejected as a result of pressure from tape manufactures and consumers.[248] Yet in October 2014, the government introduced a private copying exception permitting individuals to make personal copies of copyright work for private use (e.g. for format-shifting CDs to MP3 players). Two decisions in 2015 (the first on 19 June 2015,[249] the second on 17 July 2015),[250] the High Court quashed the exception, with the effect that acts of private copying which would have fallen under the exception now constitute acts of infringement. The government did not take further action to reintroduce an exception.

III. Metalegal Formants

The UK music industry opposed a private copying exception without a levy system.[251]

---

248 'UK Government locks European levy' (1992) 2 *Music & Copyright* (29 September) 5.
249 [2015] EWHC 1723 (Admin).
250 [2015] EWHC 2041 (Admin).
251 https://www.gov.uk/government/news/quashing-of-private-copying-exception (last accessed 2022).

E.3. COMPARATIVE REMARKS

Of all the exceptions recognised under copyright law, one of the most fundamental to the public interest relates to the possibility given to individuals to make a copy of a copyright-protected work for their own private purposes. This case focuses on the boundaries set by the European copyright regime as a means to balance the respective interests of the rights owners and the end users of copyright-protected works. It also examines how these boundaries shift along with changes in digital technology and with the legislator's evolving perception of the balance of interests. The private copying exception, as portrayed in the different modifications in this case, is governed by two main European legislative instruments: Directive 2001/29/EC on Copyright in the Information Society,[252] and Directive 2000/31/EC on Electronic Commerce.[253] While the norms laid down in these Directives, as subsequently interpreted by the Court of Justice of the EU, have contributed to the harmonisation of the exception across Europe, member states still enjoy a relative degree of latitude to decide on the specifics of the regime. This explains the variations in the member states' implementing legislation and judicial interpretation, relating for example to the conditions required for the application of the private copying exception, the level of liability incurred by Internet intermediaries who facilitate access to illegal content, the application of technological protection measures to works distributed online and the payment of fair compensation to the rights owners.

1. Making a private copy

The basic factual situation deals with two commonly occurring activities among the general public: (1) the downloading of songs from the Internet; and (2) the exchange of CDs with a friend. In principle, both acts fall within the scope of Directive 2001/29/EC, pursuant to Article 5(2)(b), which regulates the private copying exception, or Article 4(1), which grants owners a right of distribution of copies of their works, and Article 4(2), which codifies the exhaustion doctrine. More specifically, Article 5(2)(b) of Directive 2001/29/EC states that member states may:

> provide for exceptions or limitations to the reproduction right provided for in Article 2 in respect of reproductions on any medium made by a natural person for private use and for ends that are neither directly nor indirectly commercial, on condition that the rightholders receive fair compensation which takes account of the application

252 Directive 2001/29/EC of the European Parliament and of the Council of 22 May 2001 on the harmonisation of certain aspects of copyright and related rights in the information society, OJ L 167, 22 June 2001 10–19.

253 Directive 2000/31/EC of the European Parliament and of the Council of 8 June 2000 on certain legal aspects of information society services, in particular electronic commerce, in the Internal Market ('Directive on electronic commerce'), OJ L 178, 17 July 2000, 1–16.

or non-application of technological measures referred to in Article 6 to the work or subject-matter concerned.

In turn, Article 4(1) of the same Directive provides that 'member states shall provide for authors, in respect of the original of their works or of copies thereof, the exclusive right to authorise or prohibit any form of distribution to the public by sale or otherwise'. The applicability of these provisions depends concomitantly on the wording of the national legislative provision and on the interpretation given by the national reporters to the facts of the case.

a) Downloading songs from the Internet

All reports identified Carla's acts of downloading songs as a private copying issue. At the outset, those reports that mention it are unanimous in saying that if the peer-to-peer file-sharing software used by Carla to download the songs entails an automatic upload, that upload qualifies as a form of communication to the public that is not covered by the private copying exception and therefore requires 'String's' authorisation. Article 5(2)(b) of Directive 2001/29/EC being optional, the lawfulness of Carla's downloading activities varies from one country to the next. Two member states have opted not to implement this provision at all: Ireland and the United Kingdom. In these two countries, downloading for private use without prior permission constitutes, in most circumstances, an act of infringement of the owner's right of reproduction.

In the remaining member states, the main factor to be taken into consideration in the analysis of the legality of Carla's downloading activity is not mentioned in Article 5(2)(b) of the Directive. This deals with the question of whether the songs copied were lawfully disclosed to the public prior to the download. This condition has been added in the implementing legislation of several member states (Denmark, Estonia, Germany, Greece, Poland, Slovenia) or has been recognised through judicial interpretation (France, the Netherlands) or majority opinion of the legal doctrine (Belgium). The approach taken by the Dutch representative organisation of rightholders not to sue individuals that engage in illegal downloads is undoubtedly the most pragmatic: if, in theory, downloads from illegal sources no longer qualify as private copies following the CJEU's decision in the *ACI Adams* case,[254] it does not mean that such widespread practices can be easily monitored or stopped without jeopardising the social acceptability of the copyright regime.

In Carla's case, two correspondents made the assumption that the download taking place through peer-to-peer file-sharing had an unlawful origin. They consequently concluded that the exception would not apply.[255] But most correspondents either assumed that the songs were uploaded on the website

[254] CJEU judgment of 10.4.2014, *ACI Adams*, C-435/12, ECLI:EU:C:2014:254.
[255] See the reports of Estonia and Slovenia.

lawfully or refrained from questioning the origin of the download and accepted that Carla's downloading activity fell within the scope of the private copying exception in their jurisdiction.[256] The Greek report suggests that Carla's downloading of songs from the Internet may run counter to the three-step test and therefore be unlawful.

b) Exchanging CDs with a friend

The facts of the case did not specify whether Carla burned the songs that she downloaded from the Internet onto the CDs that she exchanges with her friend or whether those CDs were acquired lawfully from another source. In the former case, while the act of reproduction could arguably be covered by Article 5(2)(b) of the Directive, the exchange of the CDs with a friend may not, since the provision requires that copies made pursuant thereto be for the sole benefit of the natural person making them. Some countries tolerate a broad reading of the beneficiaries of the exception. But if Karen does not fall within the scope of the private copying exception, Carla would in fact be seen as engaging in an act of unauthorised distribution of the works that she burned onto the CDs, contrary to Article 4(1) of the Directive. In the latter case, by contrast, where the CDs were acquired lawfully from another source, once the CDs are put on the market with the consent of the rightholder, the owners of the rights on the songs could not prevent the further alienation of those CDs pursuant to Article 4(2) of Directive. If Carla bought the CDs from a lawful source, she would be committing no infringement by exchanging them with her friend, since the exhaustion doctrine would apply.

Not all country reports have considered the possibility that the CDs could have been acquired from a lawful source, which would give rise to the application of the exhaustion doctrine. Where exhaustion was deemed to apply, the reports conclude that Carla's act does not infringe the owners' rights.[257] Most correspondents focused on the CDs as being a prolongation of Carla's act of downloading and examined whether the exchange with Karen fell within the scope of their national private copying exception. In France, Germany and Poland, family and friends belong to the group of persons that is included within the private use exception. Thus, an exchange with Karen would be allowed. In Belgium, the exception is probably restricted to family members only, which would not extend to Karen. If Carla's friend does not qualify under the private use exception, then the act amounts to an infringement. The Czech Republic, Ireland, Lithuania, Slovenia and the United Kingdom have the strictest rules, as exchanging of CDs is in all cases an act of distribution that would require the rightholder's authorisation.

---

256 See reports of Belgium, Czech Republic, Denmark, France, Germany, Lithuania, the Netherlands, Norway, Poland, and Spain.

257 See the reports of Denmark, Estonia, Ireland, the Netherlands, Norway and Spain.

2. Preventing illegal downloads

Internet service providers (ISPs) are the motor of online technological development. They continue to play an essential role in granting the public access to content, whether legal or illegal. As intermediaries in the chain of online distribution of content, ISPs are all too often caught arbitrating the different interests of authors, publishers, web content offerers and end users. Their situation requires that they navigate between such conflicting interests as freedom of information, the right to conduct business, IP ownership and privacy. In this iteration of the case, two different questions arise: first, whether an ISP can be held liable for facilitating the downloading of illegal copyrighted content; and second, whether the ISP can be compelled to disclose the names and addresses of the private individuals who allegedly download illegal content. The constant evolution of digital technology, including an increasing sophistication of peer-to-peer file-sharing software (e.g. from Napster to BitTorrent), adds to the difficulty of finding the proper response to this legal conundrum.

a) Liability of the Internet service provider

The reports show a remarkable degree of consensus over the fact that 'String' would most likely be able to obtain an injunction ordering 'Keep Movn'n' to stop the illegal activities. A number of reporters consider that 'String' could invoke the general rules of copyright law, claiming that 'Keep Mov'n' engages in direct copyright infringement, since it reproduces the works and makes them available to the public.[258] Some do observe that if the ISP is not itself committing the acts of downloading, but only facilitating its subscribers in doing so, it might not be directly liable. In such circumstances, most national laws do not provide for a remedy, as secondary or contributory liability is not a known concept in most civil law jurisdictions.[259] Secondary liability exists in common law countries, like Ireland and the United Kingdom, as well as in Lithuania. General principles of Polish tort law could support a claim of indirect tortfeasance in this case.

A number of reports examine the issue of liability incurred by ISPs for the activities carried out by their subscribers from the perspective of the safe haven rules for information society services, laid down in Articles 12–14 of the E-Commerce Directive 2000/31/EC.[260] Generally, the national reports that take this approach consider that 'Keep Mov'n' qualifies either as a hosting provider or a content provider, rather than as a mere conduit or caching service. Those who view 'Keep Mov'n' as a content provider conclude that the service may be deemed directly liable for the infringing acts of its subscribers, because it has both knowledge and control over the content of its service.[261]

---

258 See the reports of Czech Republic, Denmark, Estonia, Greece, Italy and Spain.
259 See the report of Czech Republic.
260 See the reports of Belgium, France, the Netherlands, Norway and Poland.
261 See the reports of France, Poland and Slovenia.

Those who qualify 'Keep Mov'n' as a hosting provider recall that the service would not be liable, according to Article 14 E-Commerce Directive, for the information stored at the request of a recipient of the service, on the condition that:

1. it does not have actual knowledge of illegal activity or information and, as regards claims for damages, is not aware of facts or circumstances from which the illegal activity or information is apparent; or
2. upon obtaining such knowledge or awareness, it acts expeditiously to remove or to disable access to the information.

The real question therefore is whether 'Keep Mov'n' meets the criterion under (1) of absence of actual knowledge about or control over the illegal activity taking place through its services in order to escape liability. In the opinion of most reporters, the ISP probably does not. The situation in the UK seems to be a little bit vague, but there are grounds to believe that 'String' could also file for injunctive relief to prevent further copyright infringement in the UK.

As the Belgian report points out, ' if there is no control and knowledge of the content, the exoneration of liability for ISPs does not restrict the possibility for judicial authorities to oblige ISPs to terminate or prevent a specific infringement'. In other words, irrespective of whether 'Keep Mov'n' should be qualified as a mere conduit, a caching, hosting or content provider, 'String' can ask for an injunction on the basis of the national implementation of Article 8(3) of Directive 2001/29/EC. Article 8(3) of Directive 2001/29/EC indeed provides that 'Member States must ensure that rightholders are in a position to apply for an injunction against intermediaries whose services are used by a third party to infringe a copyright or related right'.

b) Disclosure of users' personal data

In the second part of this modification, the arbitration at the national level takes place between allowing rights owners to enforce their IP rights against specific alleged infringers, and protecting the privacy of the latter by not disclosing their names and addresses. The solution to this conflict leads to various outcomes across member states, from an outright refusal to disclose,[262] to a grant of the request,[263] with some countries where the situation is uncertain.[264]

Two European legislative provisions underpin such a request for information. The first one lies in Article 15 E-Commerce Directive, which specifies that:

> Member States may establish obligations for information society service providers promptly to inform the competent public authorities of alleged illegal activities

262 See the reports of Germany, Greece, Italy, Poland, Slovenia and Spain.
263 This would be true for Czech Republic, Estonia, France, Lithuania and the UK. In Ireland there must be proof of wrongdoing in order to be able to request the information.
264 See the reports of Belgium, Denmark, the Netherlands and Norway.

> undertaken or information provided by recipients of their service or obligations to communicate to the competent authorities, at their request, information enabling the identification of recipients of their service with whom they have storage agreements.

If read literally, Article 15 concerns the 'identification of recipients of their service with whom they have *storage agreements*'. If 'Keep Mov'n' users were merely downloading songs, rather than storing them on the server, then no identification data would need to be released.

A similar provision concerning the obligation to provide information was introduced in Article 8 of Directive 2004/48/EC on the enforcement of intellectual property rights.[265] This provision states:

> Member States shall ensure that, in the context of proceedings concerning an infringement of an intellectual property right and in response to a justified and proportionate request of the claimant, the competent judicial authorities may order that information on the origin and distribution networks of the goods or services which infringe an intellectual property right be provided by the infringer and/or any other person who: ...
>
> (c) was found to be providing on a commercial scale services used in infringing activities;

The Enforcement Directive generally aims at reinforcing the rights owners' recourses and remedies to curb infringement on a commercial scale. This is also apparent from the information provision, which concerns 'the origin and distribution networks' where the infringer 'was found to be providing on a commercial scale'. This wording likely does not cover the alleged infringing activities of individual subscribers of the services, such as the 33 users mentioned in the case.

Because of the highly sensitive nature of the information requested and the high status of the right to privacy in Europe, some member states are reluctant to give IP holders the possibility to obtain personal information too easily. It is wise to balance the interests of IP holders and private persons (probably active in infringing) before allowing a release of information. It should also be kept in mind that the CJEU decided in *Promusicae* that member states can, but do not have to, implement a duty to disclose personal information.[266] However, member states must ensure that a fair balance is struck between the various fundamental rights at stake.[267]

---

265 Directive 2004/48/EC of the European Parliament and of the Council of 29 April 2004 on the enforcement of intellectual property rights, OJ L 157, 30 April 2004, 45–86.

266 CJEU judgment of 29 January 2008, *Promusicae*, C-275/06, ECLI:EU:C:2008:54, para. 54 et seq.

267 Ibid., para. 68.

In several member states, the names and addresses of alleged infringers will not be released without the fulfilment of further special requirements, like an infringement on a commercial scale.[268] The release of information may also not be disproportionate[269] or the interests of the rightholder must be more important in this situation than the interests of the users after weighing them against each other.[270]

3. Circumventing a technological protection measure

Not all member states have implemented Article 6(4), second paragraph, of Directive 2001/29/EC to provide users with recourse in the event that the work they wish to copy for private purposes is protected by a TPM. If the law is silent on the issue, then Carla would be committing an unlawful act by circumventing the TPM in order to play the songs on a portable device.[271] As a consequence, String would be entitled to object to her action. Obviously, beyond Article 6(4) of the Directive, if Irish and UK law do not provide for a private copying exception in the first place, there is no argument to support the lawfulness of an act of circumvention of TPMs for the purpose of exercising this non-existent exception.

The majority of member states do not allow the circumvention of TPMs for the purposes of private use. These jurisdictions have in effect decided to strengthen the position of the copyright holder, rather than that of the user. In Estonia, the removal of a technological measure is even punished by criminal law. The German provision is worth mentioning. With respect to technological protection measures, the permission to circumvent a TPM only applies for making copies on paper or on a similar medium and not for digital copies. Carla's situation therefore falls outside of the parameters of the German provision.

In those member states that have implemented Article 6(4), second paragraph, users are not always better off, as the states have taken different routes to deal with the issue. Whether Carla's act of circumvention of the TPM is lawful or not depends on the relevant provision in the national legislation. Indeed, some countries have simply granted the head of government the power to adopt further measures regulating the issue, power which has remained unexercised.[272] Such wording leaves users like Carla empty handed: in the absence of government measure, there is no mechanism in place to allow users to exercise their private copying exception and any act of circumvention is deemed to amount to an unlawful act.

In other countries, the national legislation reproduces word for word the text of the Directive, saying that if reproduction for private use has already been made

268 See the reports of Lithuania and Spain.
269 See the German report.
270 See the report of the Netherlands.
271 See the reports of Czech Republic, Denmark, Estonia, Greece, Ireland, Italy and the UK.
272 See the reports of Belgium and the Netherlands.

possible by rights owners to the extent necessary to benefit from the exception, then no additional measure needs to be taken. The law is usually silent on the type of accommodations that will have been made possible by the rights owner to relieve them from having to provide greater copying opportunities.

Other states have developed their law in favour of the private user's interest.[273] In Lithuania, Slovenia and Spain, the removal of a technological lock is indeed generally forbidden, but Carla would have a right to ask 'String' for authorisation in order to burn the songs for her private use. Norway's approach to the issue is unique. The Norwegian legislator found that the prohibition should not apply to cases where the TPM prevented a user from displaying a legally acquired copy of the work on relevant playback equipment. As MP3 players and car stereos have been categorised under this term, there is a significant probability that Discmans would also fall under the exception.

On the issue of the accommodation of user exceptions, the exercise of which is hindered by the application of TPMs, one last word must be said about the last paragraph of Article 6(4) of the Directive. The fourth paragraph states that the obligation to accommodate the exercise of the limitations listed in the first or second paragraphs (i.e. the private copying exception) do not 'apply to such works and objects of related rights which have been made available to the public on the basis of an agreement in such a way that persons can use them from a place and at a time individually chosen by them'. This means that if copyrighted materials subject to anti-copy mechanisms have been made available through the Internet pursuant to the terms of a contractual agreement, then neither the rights owner nor the member state has the obligation to take measures to ensure that the private copying exception can be exercised. Arguably, a subscription service, like OD2, is most likely governed by an agreement that regulates the extent of the permitted use of works made available via this service. As a consequence, neither 'String' nor the individual member state has any obligation to remove the TPM or to tolerate its removal by other individuals.

4. Obligation to pay a levy for copy-protected works

The two last modifications to the base case relate to the obligation to pay rights owners fair compensation as a condition for making a lawful private copy, pursuant to Article 5(2)(b) Directive 2001/29/EC. According to this provision, all member states but three (Ireland, the UK and Norway) have set up a levy system designed to implement this obligation. In short, manufacturers and importers of blank recording media and/or equipment must pay a fixed amount on the sales price of such media and equipment. This amount is passed down to the user as part of the purchase price; the money is collected by a local collective rights management organisation, which then distributes it to the rights owners.

---

273 See the Polish report.

This modification follows from the previous one. Let us recall that in most cases, the intersection between the application of TPMs and the private copying exception leaves users in an unsatisfactory predicament. A logical argument could be made that if a user is not authorised to circumvent a TPM in order to make a private copy of a work, then there is no point in paying the levy on the blank recording media. This is presumably the rationale behind the sentence in Article 5(2)(b) specifying that the condition that 'the rightholders receive fair compensation [must] take account of the application or non-application of technological measures referred to in Article 6 to the work or subject-matter concerned'. Otherwise, end users like Carla would end up paying twice, once for the acquisition of a copy-protected work and once for the blank media, without the possibility of realising a private copy.

The legal situation is quite similar throughout the member states. While national reporters agree that Carla's argument is understandable,[274] it cannot be used as a legal ground to refuse payment. So, Carla has to pay twice in almost all the member states, except for Ireland, the UK and Norway. At the moment there is no system of paying a levy on blank CDs in Ireland and in the UK. In comparison to that, Norway has a compensation system, but it does not function through levies. Rightholders are compensated out of the state budget (namely through tax revenue). Consequently, it is fair to say that, on basis of the Directive, a strong protection for copyright holders is achieved in most of the member states. As a result, the outcome for consumers can be unfair under certain circumstances, as double payment is possible.

5. Obligation to pay a levy for freely licensed works

With new ways of preventing private copying (technical measures) and new forms of dealing with individuals' own rights (Creative Commons licensing on a royalty-free basis), the idea of the levy system is becoming vulnerable. In the same line of reasoning as in the above modification, the definition of what constitutes fair compensation for the rights owner, pursuant to Article 5(2) of the Directive, is given in Recital 35 of the same Directive. This Recital states:

> In certain cases of exceptions or limitations, rightholders should receive fair compensation to compensate them adequately for the use made of their protected works or other subject-matter. When determining the form, detailed arrangements and possible level of such fair compensation, account should be taken of the particular circumstances of each case. When evaluating these circumstances, a valuable criterion would be the possible harm to the rightholders resulting from the act in question. In cases where rightholders have already received payment in some other form, for instance as part of a licence fee, no specific or separate payment may be due. The level of fair compensation should take full account of the degree of use of technological

[274] See the Danish, German, Dutch and Spanish reports.

> protection measures referred to in this Directive. In certain situations where the prejudice to the rightholder would be minimal, no obligation for payment may arise.

This Recital establishes a direct link between the possible harm incurred by the rights owner due to private copying activities. The CJEU has repeatedly considered the meaning of the concept of fair compensation in relation to the private copying exception, always referring to Recital 35. All cases heard by the Court, including in the *Padawan v. SGAE* case cited in several reports,[275] examine the issue from the perspective of the user: if the user is not engaging in a 'private' copy, then there can be no harm relating to private copying activities, and therefore no compensation should be due.

The reports show that Carla is not entitled to a reimbursement in any member state. Nevertheless, the court proceedings in Belgium and in Spain show how contested this issue is. The CJEU's decision in *Padawan v. SGAE* has emphasised that a levy on devices which are not bought by a natural person and which are used for clearly other purposes than making private copies is not in conformity with EU law. If a device is bought by a natural person for private purposes, it is not necessary to show that the person in fact has made private copies, which have led to harm for the rightholder.[276] The legal assumption that the person will use the device for private copying is sufficient. In principle, the levy imposed on Carla is compatible with the CJEU's decision.

Some national reports point out that there was no justification to claim a reimbursement of the levy before the CJEU's decision in *Padawan v. Telefónica SAU*. But it is very interesting how the different reports show the possibility that this point could change in the future, like the Estonian and the Danish reports. The Dutch report suggests going back to considering the origin of the levy system in trying to determine its current appropriateness. The German report emphasises the need to improve the digital market in order to satisfy the author's right, advocating for a disappearance of the private copy exception. A global revision of the author's protection system in the digital era (massive distribution, copies, etc.) should probably be made in order to avoid an unfair system for both authors and cultural consumers.

Carla's situation should actually be considered from the author's perspective. Not one report put its finger on the main argument available in this particular circumstance, which is that if authors opt to distribute their work under a Creative Commons licence, thereby allowing anyone to freely reproduce and distribute the works for non-commercial purposes, then no harm occurs to the author when users make a private copy. If no harm arises, no levy should

---

275 CJEU judgment of 21 October 2010, *Padawan v. SGAE*, C-467/08, ECLI:EU:C:2010:620, para. 53.

276 Ibid., para. 54 et seq.

be payable, according to Recital 35. The question of reimbursement in such a situation has not been addressed by the court for the simple reason that such a set of circumstances has not made its way there yet. In reality, the levy system lacks any kind of sophistication: not only do users need to pay the levy whether they actually use a CD for making private copies or not, but they also need to pay the levy even when authors have chosen to distribute their works on a royalty-free basis. The practicability of the system would otherwise collapse. But this should not be an argument to allow an unfair system to persist.

CASE 4. PUBLIC DATA/DATABASE PROTECTION OF A PUBLIC INSTITUTION

A.1. CASE

The Royal Institute of Meteorology of country X (RIM) is a 100% publicly owned and funded entity whose statutory mission is to gather, organise and interpret meteorological data. In the course of the last century, RIM has developed a comprehensive database, containing all the relevant statistics for the meteorological events that occurred during the period in its own country and across Northern Europe. Realising the immense commercial value of the information included in its database, RIM has recently decided to start licensing its use to the public for a substantial fee. The private research company CLIMATE seeks a licence for use. Referring to its *sui generis* database right, RIM reserves to itself the right to extract and re-utilise substantial and insubstantial parts of its database. CLIMATE objects to this contractual clause, referring to the public financing of the database and claims free and unrestricted access to RIM's data bank.

If CLIMATE proceeds to use the data without the licence, does RIM have a claim for injunction?

A.2. EDITORIAL NOTE ON EU LAW

The case is governed by two European Directives, Directive 1996/9/EC and Directive 2003/98/EC.[1] The first Directive created a *sui generis* right for producers of databases; the second contains requirements for the re-use of information held by public sector bodies.

[1] Directive 1996/9/EC of the European Parliament and of the Council of 11 March 1996 on the legal protection of databases, OJ L 77, 27 March 1996, 20–28; and Directive 2003/98/EC of the European Parliament and of the Council of 17 November 2003 on the re-use of public sector information, OJ L 345, 31 December 2003, 90–96.

A.3. COUNTRY REPORTS

(1) BELGIUM

I. Operative Rules

CLIMATE needs to obtain a licence. If it uses the database without such a licence, then RIM has a claim for injunction. However, RIM has to be careful not to abuse its dominant position; therefore, it cannot simply refuse licences on reasonable and non-discriminatory terms.

II. Descriptive Formants

- Directive 96/9/EC on the Legal Protection of Databases;[2]
- Article 3 Directive 2003/98/EC on the Re-use of Public Sector Information[3] (amended by Directive 2013/37/EU);[4]
- Article 94/3 of the Belgian Commercial Practices Act[5] (Art. VI.104 BCEL);
- Belgian Database Protection Act of 31 August 1998[6] (Book XI, Title VII BCEL);
- Article 5 Belgian Act of 7 March 2007 on the re-use of public sector information[7] (now Art. 4 Act of 4 May 2016 on the re-use of public sector information).

Originally, Belgian legislation explicitly prohibited the commercial re-use of public sector information.[8] This position was mitigated by case law and

---

2 Directive 96/9/EC of the European Parliament and of the Council of 11 March 1996 on the legal protection of databases, OJ L 77, 27 March 1996, 20–28.

3 Directive 2003/98/EC of the European Parliament and of the Council of 17 November 2003 on the re-use of public sector information, OJ L 345, 31 December 2003, 90–96.

4 Directive 2013/37/EU of the European Parliament and of the Council of 26 June 2013 amending Directive 2003/98/EC on the re-use of public sector information, OJ L 175, 27 June 2013, 1–8.

5 Act on Trade Practices and Consumer Information and Protection, 14 July 1991, *Official Gazette*, 29 August 1991 [Wet 14 juli 1991 betreffende de handelspraktijken en de voorlichting en bescherming van de consument, *B.S.*, 29 augustus 1991].

6 Act on the Implementation of Directive 96/9/EC on the Protection of Databases, 31 August 1998, *Official Gazette*, 14 November 1998 [Wet 31 augustus 1998 houdende omzetting in Belgisch recht van de Europese richtlijn van 11 maart 1996 betreffende de rechtsbescherming van databanken, *B.S.*, 14 november 1998].

7 Act of 7 March 2007 on the Implementation of Directive 2003/98/EC on the Re-Use of Public Sector Information, *Official Gazette*, 19 April 2007 [Wet tot omzetting van de richtlijn 2003/98/EG van het Europees Parlement en de Raad van 17 november 2003 inzake het hergebruik van overheidsinformatie, 7 maart 2007, *B.S.*, 19 april 2007]. This Act concerns only the federal level. Leading us too far, we will not treat here the different government levels and therefore the other implementation legislations for the federal entities.

8 Art. 10 Government Transparency Act, 11 April 1994, *Official Gazette*, 30 June 1994 [Wet betreffende de openbaarheid van bestuur, 11 april 1994, *B.S.*, 30 juni 1994].

legal doctrine arguing that the prohibition only concerned the re-use of the information as such. Commercialisation was allowed after processing and if some value was added to the information as such.[9]

The regulatory framework changed after the introduction of the Directive on the Re-use of Public Sector Information.[10] The Directive leaves a lot of room to manoeuvre but it obliges member states to allow commercial re-use, when non-commercial re-use is permitted (Art. 3). This commercial re-use can be subject to a remuneration.

The Directive has been implemented in Belgian law by the Act of 7 March 2007 on the re-use of public sector information,[11] which entered into force on 6 November 2007[12] (now Act of 4 May 2016 on the re-use of public sector information). Following the general idea of the Directive, the Act does not impose a general obligation to make public sector documents available for re-use, but stipulates that where non-commercial re-use is allowed, commercial re-use has to be allowed as well (Art. 5, now Art. 4). The decision about whether or not to make public sector documents available for re-use will remain with the government.[13] In line with Article 8 of the Directive, the federal government had proposed a model standard licence.

Both the Directive and the Belgian Act exclude educational and research institutions from the scope of the *re-use* legislation, as well as 'documents the supply of which is an activity falling outside the scope of the public task of the

---

9 B. Michaux, *Droit des bases de données [Database Law]* (Brussels: 2005), 88. Not so convinced of this position, J.J.C Kabel and K. Janssen, 'Commercialisering van overheidsinformatie door de overheid: rechtspraak en wetgeving in België en Nederland. De honden blaffen, maar de karavaan trekt voort' [Commercialisation of Public Information by the Government: Caselaw and Legislation in Belgium and The Netherlands. The Dogs Bark, but the Caravan Moves Forward], *Computerrecht* 2005, no. 3, 121–122.

10 Directive 2003/98/EC of the European Parliament and of the Council of 17 November 2003 on the re-use of public sector information, OJ L 345, 31 December 2003, 90–96.

11 Act of 7 March 2007 on the Implementation of Directive 2003/98/EC on the Re-Use of Public Sector Information, *Official Gazette*, 19 April 2007 [Wet tot omzetting van de richtlijn 2003/98/EG van het Europees Parlement en de Raad van 17 november 2003 inzake het hergebruik van overheidsinformatie, 7 maart 2007, *B.S.*, 19 april 2007]. This Act concerns only the federal level. Leading us too far, we will not treat here the different government levels and therefore the other implementation legislations for the federal entities.

12 Art. 12 Royal Decree of 29 October 2007, *Official Gazette*, 6 November 2007 [Koninklijk besluit tot bepaling van de behandelingsprocedure en -termijnen voor een aanvraag voor hergebruik van overheidsinformatie alsook het toezicht op de verplichting om bestuursdocumenten beschikbaar te stellen, 29 oktober 2007, *B.S.*, 6 november 2007].

13 K. Janssen, 'Richtlijn inzake hergebruik van onverheidsinformatie omgezet in België' [The Directive on the Re-Use of Public Sector Information Implemented in Belgium], *Computerrecht* 2007, 261; C. De Terwangne, 'Réutilisation des informations du secteur public: la directive 2003/98 enfin totalement transposée en droit belge', *R.D.T.I.* 2008, no. 31, 142–143.

public-sector bodies',[14] which means that those institutions are not obliged to allow commercial re-use. Gathering and communicating meteorological data would be RIM's public task.[15] Therefore, the Institute is obliged to abide the legislation on the re-use of public sector information.[16]

The matter might become somewhat more complicated if the documents required for re-use are protected by IP. Recital 22 of the Directive states in this regard that: 'The intellectual property rights of third parties are not affected by this Directive', and:

> The Directive does not affect the existence or ownership of intellectual property rights of public sector bodies, nor does it limit the exercise of these rights in any way beyond the boundaries set by this Directive. The obligations imposed by this Directive should apply only insofar as they are compatible with the provisions of international agreements on the protection of intellectual property rights, in particular the Berne Convention for the Protection of Literary and Artistic Works (the Berne Convention) and the Agreement on Trade-Related Aspects of Intellectual Property Rights (the TRIPS Agreement). Public sector bodies should, however, exercise their copyright in a way that facilitates re-use.

The latest version of the Re-use of Public Sector Information Directive did not keep this Recital as it is. However, the basic idea was included in Recitals 9 and 18 of Directive 2013/37/EU.

The *sui generis* part of Directive 96/9/EC[17] has been implemented by the Belgian Database Protection Act of 31 August 1998 (now Book XI, Title VII BCEL).[18] In the present case, we assume that RIM's database fulfils the requirements for this *sui generis* protection, meaning that the substantial

---

14 Art. 1(2)(a) and (e) Directive and Art. 3(2) (2° and 5°) Implementation Act of 7 March 2007 (now Art. 3(2) (2° and 7°) Act of 4 May 2016). For comments, see N. Poupaert and K. Janssen, 'La directive du 17 novembre 2003 concernant la réutilisation des informations du secteur public' [The 17 November 2003 Directive on the Re-use of Public Information], *R.D.T.I.* 2004, no. 19, 33–34.

15 Art. 3 Royal Decree on the Organic Regulation of the Royal Observatory and the Royal Meteorological Institute of Belgium, 8 April 2002, *Official Gazette*, 23 April 2002 [Koninklijk besluit tot wijziging van het koninklijk besluit van 31 juli 1913 betreffende het organiek reglement van de Koninklijke Sterrenwacht van België en van het Koninklijk Meteorologisch Instituut van België, 8 april 2002, *B.S.*, 23 april 2002].

16 Also in the Report to the King (i.e. the explanatory memorandum, to be consulted under the decree itself on www.juridat.be) of Royal Decree of 8 April 2002 stating its mission, there is a clear emphasis on the role RIM has to play in the information society, the commercial re-use of its information being of course a proper way to realise this aim.

17 Directive 96/9/EC of the European Parliament and of the Council of 11 March 1996 on the legal protection of databases, OJ L 77, 27 March 1996, 20–28.

18 Act on the Implementation of Directive 96/9/EC on the Protection of Databases, 31 August 1998, *Official Gazette*, 14 November 1998 [Wet 31 augustus 1998 houdende omzetting in Belgisch recht van de Europese richtlijn van 11 maart 1996 betreffende de rechtsbescherming van databanken, *B.S.*, 14 november 1998].

investment relates not only to the creation of the meteorological data, but also to the collection, verification and presentation of that data in the database.[19]

According to Recital 22 of the Re-use of Public Sector Information Directive, the exercise of IP rights by public sector bodies is not limited beyond the boundaries set by the Directive. Public sector bodies should, however, exercise their copyright and related rights (including *sui generis* forms of protection) in a way that facilitates re-use.[20] Parliamentary history reveals the intention of the Belgian legislator to allow public sector bodies to charge fees high enough to account for a reasonable return on investment and to consider self-financing. On the other hand, public sector bodies should be encouraged to ask for fees that are not higher than the mere cost of reproduction and distribution.[21]

Although the Belgian Act on the Re-use of Public Sector Information does not exactly prescribe how to reconcile the re-use obligations with IP concepts, we tend to believe that a refusal to make documents available for re-use on the sole ground that they are covered by government-held IP rights is not in line with the objectives of both the European and the Belgian legislators. Not only would this affect the idea and objectives of the Re-use of Public Sector Information Directive, it could also run counter to competition law in certain circumstances (prohibition on abuse of dominance – see Case 1). On the other hand, accounting for the value of IP in the fees charged would be perfectly acceptable, since this is compatible with the idea of a 'reasonable return on investment' and the 'requirement of self-financing'.

Since RIM is performing an economic activity that goes beyond the scope of its *public service*, it has to abide by competition law.[22] In general terms, this comes down to an application of the *Magill* and *IMS Health* principles.[23]

There is some relevant and interesting Belgian case law on this issue. In the *Teleatlas* case,[24] the Belgian National Institute of Geography (NGI)[25] tried to

---

19 CJEU judgments of 9 November 2004, *Fixtures Marketing Ltd v. Oy Veikkaus Ab.*, C-46/02, ECLI:EU:C:2004:694; *The British Horseracing Board Ltd et al. v. William Hill Organisation Ltd*, C-203/02, ECLI:EU:C:2004:695; *Fixtures Marketing Ltd v. AB Svenska Spel*, C-388/02, ECLI:EU:C:2004:696; *Fixtures Marketing Ltd v. OPAP*, C-444/02, ECLI:EU:C:2004:697.

20 Recital 22 of the Re-Use of Public Sector Information Directive.

21 Explanatory Memorandum, Bill on the implementation of Directive 2003/98/EC on the Re-use of Public Sector Information, *Parl. Doc.*, Chambre, 2006–2007, DOC 51 2634/001, 11 [M.v.T., Wetsontwerp tot omzetting van de richtlijn 2003/98/EG van het Europees Parlement en de Raad van 17 november 2003 inzake het hergebruik van overheidsinformatie, *Parl. St.*, Kamer, 2006–2007, DOC 51 2634/001, 11], available at: www.dekamer.be (last consulted 5 May 2019).

22 For more on this, for instance: Court of Appeal Brussels (9th Chamber bis), 31 January 2006, *T.B.M.* 2006, no. 2, 154–156, note F. Tuytschaever, 'Meer over het begrip onderneming in het mededingingsrecht' [More on the Concept of 'Undertaking' in Competition Law], 157–158.

23 See Case 1.

24 Court of Appeal Gent, 1 November 1995, *A&M* 1997, 54, note A. Strowel, 'Des cartes aux bases de données géographiques' [Maps and Geographical Databases], 56–57.

25 Nationaal Geografisch Instituut, www.ngi.be (last consulted 5 May 2019).

prevent Teleatlas from using its data to commercialise digitalised and enriched products. As the suit was based on Article 94(3) of the Belgian Commercial Practices Act[26] (unfair competition, now Art. VI.104 BCEL), and not the BCA, no question of copyright was dealt with.[27] Even so, the Court took the view that Teleatlas' behaviour was not parasitic since it did not make a mere copy. The real objective of NGI was to receive some remuneration, but the Court decided that no remuneration could be based on the Belgian Commercial Practices Act. The Court added that NGI should not exaggerate about its investments with regard to commercial use, in view of the public funding it was already receiving for its public services.[28] In the same line, Belgacom could not prevent the re-use of its phone book on a CD-ROM by Kapital Trading.[29] The terminology and reasoning in this judgment was clearly inspired by *Magill*.[30] There is some more case law applying those principles, although not specifically regarding access to information.[31]

Although the examples discussed above often conclude that there was no IP infraction or unfair competition, this does not mean RIM cannot ask for royalties. In view of the *sui generis* database protection, RIM merely has to be in line with the *Magill, IMS Health* and *Microsoft* principles.

The Belgian RIM allows re-use of its data on the basis of the standard licences and price lists developed by ECOMET.[32] Although the licensing and pricing

---

26 Act on Trade Practices and Consumer Information and Protection, 14 July 1991, *Official Gazette*, 29 August 1991 [Wet 14 juli 1991 betreffende de handelspraktijken en de voorlichting en bescherming van de consument, *B.S.*, 29 augustus 1991].

27 The case dates from before the Database Directive 96/9/EC and its implementation. Under copyright law the requirement of originality would of course difficultly be fulfilled.

28 B. Michaux, *Droit des bases de données [Database Law]* (Brussels: 2005), 83–84.

29 Pres. Commercial Court Brussels, 19 July 1995, *R.D.C.* 1995, 747 criticised by: A. Strowel and E. Derclaye, *Droit d'auteur et numérique: logiciels, bases de données, multimédia. Droit belge, européen et comparé [Copyright and the Numeric: software, databases and multimedia. Belgian, European and Comparative Law]* (Brussels: 2001), 341.

30 A. Strowel and E. Derclaye, *Droit d'auteur et numérique: logiciels, bases de données, multimédia. Droit belge, européen et comparé [Copyright and the Numeric: software, databases and multimedia. Belgian, European and Comparative Law]* (Brussels: 2001), 341.

31 As explained by B. Michaux, *Droit des bases de données [Database Law]* (Brussels: 2005), 86–87 and J.J.C. Kabel and K. Janssen, 'Commercialisering van overheidsinformatie door de overheid: rechtspraak en wetgeving in België en Nederland. De honden blaffen, maar de karavaan trekt voort' [Commercialisation of Public Information by the Government: Caselaw and Legislation in Belgium and The Netherlands. The Dogs Bark, but the Caravan Moves Forward], *Computerrecht* 2005, no. 3, 117–129; Pres. Commercial Court Brussels, 14 August 1992, *R.D.C.* 1993, 28 et seq.; Court of Appeal Brussels, 7 December 1995, *Ann. Prat. Comm.* 1995, 676; Court of Appeal Gent, 21 January 2004, *R.A.B.G.* 2004, no. 11, 679, note Y. van Gerven, 'Overheidsmonopolies die niet aan de marktvraag voldoen' [Government monopolies which do no satisfy the market demand].

32 The economic interest grouping of some European meteorological institutes. For more information: www.ecomet.eu (last accessed 5 May 2019).

practices[33] seem to be coherent with the objectives of the Re-use Directive and national legislation, the collective price setting by the different European meteorological institutes might raise other competition law issues.[34]

III. Metalegal Formants

While performing their public tasks, governments and administrations have gathered a huge amount of information in lots of domains. Since the computer era, this information constitutes a precious source for the development of new products (e.g. TomTom using the data of the geographic institutes).[35]

Although access has to be granted to all information held by the administration, the Belgian legislator had at one point chosen not to allow the commercial re-use of this information.[36] The *ratio legis* was that the accessibility of public sector information serves a democratic purpose, namely allowing for control and transparency. The legislator did not want private companies to abuse this objective and tried to avoid providing a cheap right of access for the companies' benefit.[37] In addition, the administrative institutions realised the economic potential of the data they had collected over the years, and wanted to exploit this themselves, or at least receive remuneration for it.

In view of the head start of the United States with regard to the information industry, the European Commission decided that the commercial re-use of public sector information could enable Europe to catch up, resulting in Directive 2003/98/EC.[38]

---

33 Consultable on their website: www.ecomet.eu.

34 There were hopes that the Belgian Competition Council would deal with issues on price discrimination, cross-subsidies and price setting in a complaint filed in 2004 (*Royal Meteorological Institute v. Meteoservices*), but the Council never treated the case, not considering it to be a priority; see K. Janssens, 'PSI in Belgium: A Slow Journey Towards Open Data?', ESPSI Platform Topic Report No. 2011/1, available at: https://www.europeandataportal.eu/sites/default/files/2011_belgium_psi_in_belgium_a_slow_journey_towards_open_data.pdf (last consulted 31 July 2019).

35 J.J.C. Kabel and K. Janssen, 'Commercialisering van overheidsinformatie door de overheid: rechtspraak en wetgeving in België en Nederland. De honden blaffen, maar de karavaan trekt voort' [Commercialisation of Public Information by the Government: Caselaw and Legislation in Belgium and The Netherlands. The Dogs Bark, but the Caravan Moves Forward], *Computerrecht* 2005, no. 3, 117–118.

36 Former Art. 10 Administration's Transparency Act, 11 April 1994, *Official Gazette*, 30 June 1994 [Wet betreffende de openbaarheid van bestuur, 11 april 1994, *B.S.*, 30 juni 1994].

37 J. Pas, 'De richtlijn 2003/98/EG inzake het hergebruik van overheidsinformatie – een kritische analyse' [Directive 2003/98/EC on the Re-use of Public Sector Information – a Critical Analysis], *A&M* 2005, no. 2, 113.

38 N. Poupaert and K. Janssen, 'La directive du 17 novembre 2003 concernant la réutilisation des informations du secteur public' [The 17 November 2003 Directive on the Re-use of Public Information], *R.D.T.I.* 2004, no. 19, 29.

(2) CZECH REPUBLIC

I. *Operative Rules*

RIM will be granted an injunction if CLIMATE makes use of substantial parts of the database without obtaining a licence.

II. *Descriptive Formants*

Protection of databases was adopted in the Czech Republic as part of the new Copyright Act in 2001 and is based on Directive 96/9/EC on the legal protection of databases. The relevant provisions of the Copyright Act on protection of databases are section 2(2)[39] and sections 88–94.

Sui generis rights to a database belong to the creator of the database (section 88(1)). The maker of the database is the natural person or legal entity who, on his/her own motion and risk, has compiled the database or who has had a database compiled by another person or entity (section 89).

The content of the *sui generis* rights of the creator of the database is specified in section 90. The creator has the right to extraction or re-utilisation of qualitatively or quantitatively the whole content or part of the database, and the right to grant to another person the authorisation to execute that right (section 90(1)). A person without the authorisation of the creator of the database is not allowed to extract the whole content or substantial parts of the database.

Limitations of the *sui generis* rights are stipulated in section 91, which copies Article 8 of Directive 96/9/EC.[40] A user is allowed to extract or re-utilise qualitatively or quantitatively insubstantial parts of the content of the database or of its part.

The basic requirements for licence contracts are specified in section 46 et seq. According to the provisions of section 50, the maker of the database may grant a restricted licence to the user. A licence may be restricted to extracting or utilising insubstantial parts of the database.

The Copyright Act does not include any provision obliging public institutions to grant a free access to its database. But as a public institution, RIM is bound by the Act on Freedom of Access to Information 106/1999 Coll. According to section 2, this Act applies *inter alia* to public institutions. The right to information is *inter alia* restricted in section 11(5) of the Act. This restriction

---

39 The provisions of section 2(2) establish the conditions for a database to be considered a work.

40 See also J. Kříž, I. Holcová, J. Kordač, V. Křesťanová, *Autorský zákon komentář a předpisy související* (Copyright Act, Commentary and related regulations) (2nd ed., Prague: 2005), p. 239.

shall apply to information which is the subject of copyright protection or related rights protection and if it is in tenancy of *inter alia* a public institution which is a recipient of subventions from public funds to support research and development. The definition of research and development can be found in section 2(1) of the Act on Support of Research and Development 130/2002. The definition says that research and development is systematic creative work made for the purpose of acquisition of knowledge or utilisation of knowledge.

The key point is to stipulate whether RIM meets the above-mentioned definition of a research institution. If not, then section 14a(1) and (2) of the Act on Freedom of Access to Information shall apply. If section 14a applies, then RIM is obliged to provide the required database to CLIMATE. The limits and restrictions on the licence should be the subject of a licence contract between RIM and CLIMATE.[41] In that case the remuneration will be, in accordance with section 17 of the Act on Freedom of Access to Information, an amount not exceeding the costs of providing copies and of postage to the applicant.

RIM is a public institution whose statutory mission is to gather, organise and interpret meteorological data. This gathering, organising and interpretation of meteorological data is, according to above-mentioned section 11(5) of the Act on Freedom of Access to Information, research. All the conditions for the restriction of the right to information stipulated by the Act on Freedom of Access to Information are met because RIM is a public institution which is a recipient of subventions from public funds to support its research, and so the Act on Freedom of Access to Information does not apply.

RIM has the *sui generis* rights and is therefore allowed to set conditions for users to use the database and ask for remuneration for access to the database. However, according to section 91 of the Copyright Act, a lawful user of the database is entitled to extract or re-utilise insubstantial parts of the database. RIM cannot prohibit the extraction of insubstantial parts of the database because a user is authorised to carry out such extraction directly by the Copyright Act and a clause restricting this would not be valid[42] because it contravenes section 91 Copyright Act.

RIM is entitled to restrict access to the data bank and is entitled to ask for a fee. RIM is not entitled to reserve to itself the right to extract insubstantial part of the data bank. CLIMATE is entitled, *ex lege* as a lawful user, to extract insubstantial parts of RIM's data bank.

---

41 According to the explanatory report to section 14a of the Act on Freedom of Access to Information, such a licence contract shall take into account whether information shall be used only for personal use or for business activities.

42 According to section 39 of the Civil Code: 'A legal act whose content or purpose contravenes an act, circumvents an act or contravenes good manners shall be invalid.'

III. *Metalegal Formants*

Answer omitted.

(3) DENMARK

I. *Operative Rules*

RIM has a claim for injunction, provided that the fee entails no more than a 'reasonable return' on the investments involved and that the refusal to license does not conflict with the competition rules.

II. *Descriptive Formants*

A public database enjoys database protection under DCA §1 (work) or §71 (*sui generis*) if the general requirements for protection are fulfilled. The DCA does not preclude database protection for public institutions – only works concerning the exercise of public authority (legal statutes, court decisions, administrative regulations, etc.) are exempted from copyright or neighbouring rights protection (DCA §9).

As far as the *sui generis* protection for databases is concerned, it has been disputed whether meteorological data are 'existing' or 'created' data according to the CJEU's interpretation of the 'substantial investment' criteria in Article 7(2) of the Database Directive (Directive 96/9/EC). However, it is to be assumed in any case that the database in question enjoys protection due to the investments concerned with the collection, verification and presentation in the database. Moreover, as in the other Nordic countries, the *sui generis* protection in DCA §71 also applies to databases that compile a large amount of data, regardless of the fact that this criterion has been criticised as being incompatible with the Database Directive.

Provided that the database in question is protected, there is an issue of compliance with the Directive on re-use of public information (Directive 2003/98/EC). The Directive's principles of governing charges (Art. 6) and transparency (Art. 7), requiring the public-sector body in question to divulge the basis for calculation of the public charge as well as the factors taken into account in the calculation charges, is implemented by way of §8 of the Danish Public Information Act (DPIA, 24 June 2005). This provision states that for institutions covered by the Re-use Directive, their total income from delivery of information must not exceed the factual costs involved in collection, production, reproduction and dissemination of information, with the addition of a reasonable reimbursement for the investments. Consequently, the provision sets limits on how 'substantial' a fee RIM can charge for access to its database.

III. Metalegal Formants

Access to public goods and information is important, but it is not a given that the public, and in particular commercial undertakings, should be able to benefit from public investments without contributing financially.

(4) ESTONIA

I. Operative Rules

Presumably, competition law obliges RIM to grant access, but not necessarily free of charge.

II. Descriptive Formants

It is possible to protect databases containing, for example, meteorological data under Estonian law. Chapter VIII^{1} of the Copyright Act[43] was adopted to 'provide independent protection for databases by establishing special rights for makers of databases to protect investments made by them'.[44] A database which enjoys protection under this regulation is defined as 'a collection of works, data or other [material] arranged in a systematic or methodical way and individually accessible by electronic or other means'.[45] The maker of a database who has the exclusive rights in respect of a database is defined as 'a person who has made a substantial investment, evaluated qualitatively or quantitatively, in the collecting, obtaining, verification, arranging or presentation of data which constitutes the contents of the database'.[46]

RIM has developed a database by gathering, organising and interpreting meteorological data. Obviously, RIM also qualifies as the maker of the database. The fact that RIM is a public agency complicates the case to some extent. The problem is that the provisions on the rights of makers of databases are not very clear on whether public authorities enjoy *sui generis* database protection.

---

43 Chapter VIII^{1} of the Copyright Act entered into force on 6 January 2000 – Autoriõiguse seaduse ja sellega seonduvate seaduste muutmise seadus. Entered into force on 6 January 2000 – RT I 1999, 97, 859 (in Estonian). Official text available at https://www.riigiteataja.ee/ert/act.jsp?id=77999 (4 February 2009).

44 Copyright Act §75^{1}.

45 Copyright Act §75^{2}.

46 Copyright Act §75^{3}(1).

According to the Copyright Act the provisions of Chapter VIII^1 establishing and regulating rights of makers of databases

> apply if:
>
> 1) the maker of a database or rightholder is a citizen or permanent resident of the Republic of Estonia;
> 2) the maker of a database or rightholder is a company which is founded in accordance with the law of the Republic of Estonia and has its registered office, central administration or principal place of business within the territory of the Republic of Estonia. If such company has only its registered office in the territory of the Republic of Estonia, its operations must be genuinely linked on an ongoing basis with the economy of Estonia;
> 3) a database must be protected in accordance with an international agreement of the Republic of Estonia.[47]

The fact that the list only concerns private persons gives rise to a question of whether public authorities and public agencies are excluded from *sui generis* database protection. The systematic and teleological interpretation of the Copyright Act, however, supports the position that public authorities and public agencies are not excluded. It is more likely that if the intent of the legislator had been to exclude someone from *sui generis* database protection, there would be a provision in the Copyright Act saying it directly. Still §75^3(2) of the Copyright Act may cause some confusion. For the purpose of the analysis of this case, it was assumed that public agencies are not excluded from *sui generis* database protection.

According to §75^4(1) Copyright Act, '[t]he maker of a database has the exclusive right to authorise or prohibit the use of the database'. The following limitations to rights of makers of databases are provided in §75^6 Copyright Act:

> [a] lawful user of a database which is lawfully made available to the public in whatever manner may, without the authorisation of its maker and without payment of remuneration, extract or re-utilise a substantial part of the database in the case of:
>
> 1) extraction for private purposes of the contents of a non-electronic database;
> 2) extraction for the purposes of illustration for teaching or scientific research, as long as the source is indicated and to the extent justified by the non-commercial purpose to be achieved;
> 3) extraction or re-utilisation for the purposes of public security or an administrative or judicial procedure to the extent justified by the purposes of public security or an administrative or judicial procedure.

47 Copyright Act §75^3(2).

Even if we say that CLIMATE as a private research company is seeking access for scientific research, the limitation would not be applicable for two reasons. Firstly, the database has to be lawfully made available to the public before limitations apply. Nothing in the case indicates that RIM has made its database available to the public. Secondly, the research exemption requires a non-commercial purpose. As said in the case, CLIMATE is a private company which means it is profit-orientated. Consequently, we can say that the Copyright Act does not give CLIMATE access to RIM's database.

It is still necessary to analyse whether other regulations oblige RIM to grant access to its database.

Since RIM is a public agency (a legal person in public law), it has obligations under the Public Information Act,[48] which was adopted 'to ensure that the public and every person has the opportunity to access information intended for public use, based on the principles of a democratic and social rule of law and an open society, and to create opportunities for the public to monitor the performance of public duties' (§1 Public Information Act). The central question is whether the Public Information Act obliges holders of information[49] to grant unrestricted continuous access to their databases. The Public Information Act provides that '[a] holder of information may refuse to comply with a request for information if the request for information cannot be complied with by a single release of information' (§23(2) clause 4 Public Information Act). In the present case, CLIMATE seeks free, continuous and unrestricted access to RIM's database, which does not qualify as a single request for the information. Consequently, it seems that RIM can refuse to grant access to the database. Still, the question is very complicated and there is no clear answer.

The database developed by RIM might constitute an essential facility for the purposes of the Competition Act. The fact that RIM is a legal person in public law does not exclude it from the regulatory impact of the Competition Act. According to §2(2) of the Competition Act, '[t]he provisions concerning undertakings apply to persons who perform functions in public law and to the state and local governments if they participate in a goods market'.

Section 15 of the Competition Act provides:

> An undertaking is deemed to control essential facilities or to have a natural monopoly if it owns, possesses or operates a network, infrastructure or any other essential facility which other persons cannot duplicate or for whom it is economically inexpedient to

---

48 Avaliku teabe seadus. Entered into force on 1 January 2001 – RT I 2000, 92, 597; 2008, 35, 213 (in Estonian).

49 Legal persons in public law are also considered to be holders of information – Public Information Act §5(1) clause 2.

duplicate but without access to which or the existence of which it is impossible to operate in the goods market.

Undertakings in control of essential facilities are undertakings in a dominant position (§13(2) Competition Act).

They have specific obligations. Pursuant to the Competition Act, an undertaking in control of an essential facility is obliged to 'permit other undertakings to gain access to the network, infrastructure or other essential facility under reasonable and non-discriminatory conditions for the purposes of the supply or sale of goods' (§18(1) clause 1 Competition Act).

Based on the analysis above, it can be concluded that competition law might oblige RIM to grant access to its database. Competition law does not require that the access be granted free of charge.

III. Metalegal Formants

The case concentrates on the possibility to control access to data collected by public authorities and agencies. On the one hand, citizens are entitled to information, but on the other hand, public authorities have to have some control over data. The reasons to control access to data may relate to personal data protection (e.g. the Personal Data Protection Act[50] was adopted to protect the fundamental rights and freedoms of natural persons with regard to processing of personal data)[51] and proprietary interests. As a general rule, separate legal acts are adopted to regulate the utilisation of the databases created by public authorities. For instance, the Human Genes Research Act[52] *inter alia* regulates the establishment and maintenance of a Gene Bank[53] and organises the genetic research necessary therefor.[54] Section 6 of the Land Cadastre Act[55] regulates access to cadastral data. Due to the maxim *lex specialis derogat legi generali*, it is always necessary to determine whether specific regulation exists on databases developed by public authorities before we turn to more general acts (the Copyright Act, the Public Information Act, etc.).

---

50 Isikuandmete kaitse seadus. Entered into force on 1 January 2008 – RT I 2007, 24, 127 (in Estonian). Available at https://www.riigiteataja.ee/ert/act.jsp?id=12909389 (last accessed 5 May 2019).

51 Personal Data Protection Act §1(1).

52 Inimgeeniuuringute seadus. Entered into force on 8 January 2001 – RT I 2000, 104, 685; 2007, 22, 111 (in Estonian).

53 Gene Bank is 'a database established and maintained by the chief processor consisting of tissue samples, descriptions of DNA, descriptions of state of health, genealogies, genetic data and data enabling the identification of gene donors' – Human Genes Research Act §2 clause 10.

54 Human Genes Research Act §1(1).

55 Maakatastriseadus. Entered into force on 8 November 1994 – RT I 1994, 74, 1324; 2007, 69, 425 (in Estonian).

(5) FRANCE

I. Operative Rules

RIM does not have a claim for injunction.

II. Descriptive Formants

This case deals with the *sui generis* right of the creators of databases (Arts. L. 341-1 et seq. of the French Intellectual Property Code – which translate Directive 96/9/EC of 11 March 1996 on the legal protection of databases). According to Article L. 341-1 of the French Intellectual Property Code: 'The producer of a database, understood as the person who takes the initiative and the risk of the corresponding investments, benefits from protection of the contents of the database when its constitution, verification or presentation shows that there has been a substantial financial, technical or human investment.' Is RIM a creator of a database?

A database is a collection of independent works, data or other materials arranged in a systematic or methodical way and capable of being individually accessed by electronic or other means (Art. L. 112-3 of the French Intellectual Property Code).

RIM's database contains meteorological data and 'all the relevant statistics for the meteorological events that occurred during the period in its own country and across Northern Europe'. RIM's database is therefore a database according to Article L. 112-3 of the French Intellectual Property Code.

RIM must also prove that there has been a substantial investment qualitatively and/or quantitatively in either the obtaining, verification or presentation of the contents of a meteorological database.

RIM's statutory mission is to gather, organise and interpret meteorological data. RIM's employees have to collect the data over a certain period of time.[56] There is therefore a human investment in the obtaining and verification of the meteorological data.

However, substantial investment must be directed toward research and gathering of data in a database; it should not concern work on statistics.[57] RIM must therefore prove that the obtaining, verification or presentation of

---

56 Commercial Court of Nanterre, 16 May 2000, C.C.E. 2000, comm. 85, note Ch. Caron.

57 CJEU judgments of 9 November 2004, *Fixtures Marketing Ltd v. Oy Veikkaus Ab.*, C-46/02, ECLI:EU:C:2004:694; *The British Horseracing Board Ltd et al. v. William Hill Organisation Ltd*, C-203/02, ECLI:EU:C:2004:695; *Fixtures Marketing Ltd v. AB Svenska Spel*, C-388/02, ECLI:EU:C:2004:696; *Fixtures Marketing Ltd v. OPAP*, C-444/02, ECLI:EU:C:2004:697.
See D. 2005, somm. p. 1495, obs. P. Sirinelli, R.T.D.Com. 2005, p. 90 ff., obs. F. Pollaud-Dulian, C.C.E. 2005, comm. 2, note Ch. Caron; M. Vivant, 'L'investissement rien que l'investissement', R.L.D.I. 2005, p. 41 f.

the contents of the meteorological database is independent of the work on meteorological statistics.

If RIM is a producer of a database, it has the right to prohibit the extraction by the permanent or temporary transfer of all or a substantial part, qualitatively or quantitatively, of the contents of the database to another medium, by any means or in any form. It has also the right to re-use, by making available to the public, all or a substantial part, qualitatively or quantitatively, of the contents of a database, in any form whatsoever (Art. 342-1 of the French Intellectual Property Code). RIM may also prohibit the repeated and systematic extraction or re-use of insubstantial parts, qualitatively or quantitatively, of the contents of the database when such operations manifestly go beyond the conditions of normal use of the database (Art. L. 342-2 of the French Intellectual Property Code).

CLIMATE is a lawful user; it has free access to RIM's database.[58] RIM cannot reserve for itself the right to extract and to re-use insubstantial parts of its database, because when a database is made available to the public by the rightholder, he/she may not prohibit the extraction or the re-use of an insubstantial part, evaluated qualitatively or quantitatively, of the contents of the database, by a person having lawful access (Art. L. 342-3 of the French Intellectual Property Code). But RIM can reserve for itself the right to extract and to re-use *substantial* parts of its database.

Finally, it should be noted that the public financing of the database has no impact on RIM's *sui generis* rights.[59]

III. Metalegal Formants

Answer omitted.

(6) GERMANY

I. Operative Rules

No, RIM has no right to injunction. CLIMATE can demand access; however, not for free.

II. Descriptive Formants

The first question at hand is whether RIM's collection of data qualifies as a 'database' under §87a UrhG. Yet, the case raises three distinct legal questions.

---

58 'The private research company CLIMATE seeks a licence for use.'

59 'The State can receive right privatives on the occasion of the communication of public data with the aim of their marketing.' Council of State, 29 July 2002, case no. 200886.

What about the public dimension ('100% publicly funded entity') when the institution is 100% tax-funded? German law does not exclude public agencies from database protection *per se*.[60] Neither does it preclude 'public data', nor databases established by public finances, nor investments made primarily for non-commercial purposes.[61] However, there was debate on whether the exclusion of public data under copyright protection (§5 UrhG) is to be expanded to the *sui generis* system (§§87a UrhG et seq.). The regional court (*Oberlandesgericht*) of Dresden inferred from the lack of an exemption in German law and the lack of regulatory discretion of the member states (Art. 9 Directive 96/9/EC) that *sui generis* protection has to be granted.[62] However, the Supreme Court, in a case dealing with telephone book information after privatisation, has left this question open.[63] In principle, public agencies have always claimed control over generated and collected data, for example satellite data, land registries, meteorological and environmental measurements, telecommunication (telephone books). Transfer, access and commercial use has been publicly regulated[64] since 2006 by regulation[65] transposing the EC Public Sector Information (PSI) Directive.[66] Still, collections protected by intellectual property rights enjoy potential exemption under §2a IWG, but access has to be regulated (and might be overlayed by a listing under Art. 14 Directive 2019/1024[67]). Under the reasoning of *Tele-Info-CD*, copyright and data bank protection is granted for privatised agencies.

The second question is whether RIM's activity of 'gathering, organising, and interpreting meteorological data' qualifies as 'database protection'. Is RIM primarily 'creating' these data or 'verifying' them for the compilation in the data bank?

60 See T. Dreier, in: T. Dreier and G. Schulze (eds.), *UrhG-Commentary* (6th ed., Munich: 2018), §87 a, No. 20 – in contrast, laws and regulations etc. are exempt from normal copyright protection, §5 UrhG.

61 M. Vogel, in: U. Loewenheim, M. Leistner and A. Ohly (eds.), *Urheberrecht*, (6th ed., Munich: 2020), §87a, No. 15.

62 OLG Dresden, decision of 18 July 2001, ZUM 2001, 595 at 597.

63 GRUR 1999, 923 – *Tele-Info-CD*.

64 Access to land registries is regulated by federal state (*Länder*) laws on surveying, cadastral information and mapping: they provide for simple access rules for a fee. The licensed use for commercial purposes for share in profits is distinguished. For access to information in telephone books, the system is proceduralised, §12 TKG. The international order for satellite data is rudimentary and so far governed by national copyright rules (see M. Höpfl, *Rechtsrahmen für die wirtschaftliche Nutzung des Weltraums durch Privatunternehmen* (Würzburg: 2003)), lacking *lex specialis* rules for privileged access.

65 Informationsweiterverwendungsgesetz (IWG), OJ (BGBl.), 18 December 2006, 2913; First revision: BGBl., 15 July 2015, 1162.

66 Directive 2003/98/EC on the re-use of public sector information, OJ L 345, 31 December 2003, 90–96.

67 Annex 1 of Directive (EU) 2019/1024 of the European Parliament and of the Council of 20 June 2019 on open data and the re-use of public sector information, OJ L 172, 26 June 2019, 56, explicitly mentions 'meteorological' datasets as possible 'high-value datasets' as referred to in Article 13(1) Directive 2019/1024. If listed, access shall be granted free of charge.

Being a scientific institute, it was thinkable that it created the data, which then were possibly covered by copyright content protection. In *British Horse Racing Board* from 2004,[68] the CJEU clearly distinguished these activities ('spin-off theory'). In contrast, under an earlier, much broader wording of the German Supreme Court (BGH) in *Tele-Info-CD* from 1999[69] there would be no doubt that the collection as such is covered by the *sui generis* investment protection. The problem is with institutions, like in this case, which do both.[70] Here, RIM is claiming protection for the gathering and selection of the existing data. The investment is not geared to generating new content. This activity is 'creating the data bank' and therefore covered by database protection. Thus, RIM enjoys data bank protection.

The third question that finally stirs the operative rules is whether competition law requires RIM to provide unconditional access to CLIMATE (bottleneck theorem, essential facility).[71] Applying the two-step approach (see Case 1), it would seem that access has to be provided (however not for free): the data bank leverages market power to a second market; the severe restrictions have the potential to block research and thus ultimately the development of a novel product. One could also argue with the BGH *Spundfass* reasoning that the database right protects more than the investor has given due to the fact that the database was established with public money. Therefore, unrestricted access has to be granted, though not for free.

III. Metalegal Formants

The central legal question of this case revolves around public data. Does it enjoy property protection and to what extent? This issue is under pressure from two sides. On the one hand, the privatisation of agencies and public functions is pressing for commodification of data, thus exclusive rights.[72] On the other hand, the notion that agencies provide *service* to citizens, the movement towards 'Open Data', and various acts which provide citizens with information rights against agencies are pressing for Open Access.[73] Prior to this debate, the state has

---

68 CJEU combined judgments of 9 November 2004, *The British Horse Racing Board Ltd and Others v. William Hill Organisation Ltd*, C-203/02, [2004] ECR I-10415; C-46/02, *Fixtures Marketing Ltd v. Oy Veikkaus AB*, [2004] ECR I-10365; C-338/02, *Fixtures Marketing Ltd v. Svenska Sopel AB*, [2004] ECR I-10497; C-444/02, *Fixtures Marketing Ltd v. Organismos pronostikon agonon podosfairou (OPAP)*, [2004] ECR I-10549.

69 GRUR 1999, 923 (scanning of telephone books).

70 T. Dreier, in: T. Dreier and G. Schulze (eds.), *UrhG-Commentary* (6th ed., Munich: 2018), §87a No. 13 with further references to the discussion.

71 Originally the political motivation for the EU and the Member States to enact the PSI Directive in 2003.

72 This stance is not only taken by the respective agency but also by corporations interested in protected limited access.

73 Catching up a democratisation process which began in the US with the Freedom of Information Act in 1967.

claimed control over its data due to its sovereign right; access has been regulated according to the governmental purpose. The claim for access to information first became legally acknowledged in the transposition of the PSI Directive in Germany in 2006, by the transposition of the Åarhus Convention of 1998,[74] in Germany in 2004,[75] and by the Freedom of Information Acts.[76] Yet third party IP-protected interests in data and trade secret protection (claiming protection under Art. 39 TRIPS) enjoy priority over access rights (PSI-claims, freedom of information claims as regulated in freedom of information acts, environmental information acts).[77] Yet, the relationship between these acts has remained tense.[78] Finding the right balance continues to be a challenge.

(7) GREECE

I. *Operative Rules*

The use of the database for research is legitimate in principle, but not totally unrestricted.

II. *Descriptive Formants*

Directive 96/9/EC on the legal protection of databases was transposed in Greece by Law 2819/2000. The maker of the database has the right to prevent extraction

---

[74] ECE/CEP/43, in force since 30 October 2001. The EC reacted by improving its Directive 90/313/EEC (OJ L 158, 7 June 1990, 56–58) by enacting Directive 2003/4/EC (OJ L 41, 28 January 2003, 26–32). Interestingly, the claim to release information is directed not only to public agencies but also to private entities with public functions, Art. 2(2) (definition of 'agency') Directive 2003/4/EC. In Germany, this Directive is to be transposed on each administrative level; the respective transformation laws are in progress within the legislative process. Due to the vertical split, the claim for information will not only be regionally different, but also different vis-à-vis the nature of data (as regional administrations execute not only their own tasks but also federal ones), see F. Scholles, 'Das Umweltinformationsrecht – Paradebeispiel deutscher Kleinstaaterei', *UVP-Report* 2004, vol. 18, 157; A. Scheidler, 'Der Anspruch auf Zugang zu Umweltinformation – zur Neufassung des Umweltinformationsgesetzes', *Umwelt- und Planunsgrecht (UPR)* 2006, vol. 26, 13–17.

[75] Environmental Information Act (Umweltinformationsgesetz, UIG), first enacted in 2004 on the federal level, revised in 2017, supplemented by the environmental information acts by the states.

[76] Federal Freedom of Information Act of Germany (IFG) enacted 5 September 2005 (BGBl. I, 2722), revised by regulation of 19 June 2020 (BGBl. I, 1328); complemented by the Freedom of Information Acts of the German states.

[77] §1 sec. 2 No. 4 Public Sector Information Act of the Federal State Germany (2003/2015); revised Directive (EU) 2019/1024 of the European Parliament and of the Council of 20 June 2019 on open data and the re-use of public sector information awaits is transposition in Germany (deadline 17.6.2021). §6 Federal Freedom of Information Act, §9 sec. 1 No. 2 Federal Environmental Information Act.

[78] E.g. for the PSI transposition, H. Richter, *Information als Infrastruktur* (Tübingen: 2021), 150.

and/or re-utilisation of the whole or of substantial part of the database under the conditions of Article 45A para. 1 of Law 2121/1993 (Art. 7 Directive 96/9/EC). The lawful user of a database may extract and/or re-utilise a substantial part of its content for reasons of public safety (Art. 45A para. 6). Of course, the 'using' of the data contained in this database, if the database is available to the public, should be considered a permitted act.

Consequently, in accordance with both mandatory Community and Greek law, a clause which deprives the lawful user of the right to download and re-use non-essential parts of the database available to the public will be null and void. The same will hold good in the case of essential parts of the database if the downloading and re-use of them is for public security, scientific purposes, for example research, or other similar purposes. In this framework arises the question of whether private research is covered by the term 'research', without the recognised academic guarantees, or even without any guarantee of credibility.

A central question also to be investigated here is the extent of the compulsory (further) commercialisation of the public domain, when its 'establishment' as such is affected by a private act. To this question, the law probably gives a negative answer, insofar as a database available to the public free of charge is at issue. The lawful user has a right to freely access, download and re-use as regards the non-essential parts. As to the essential parts, there appears to be no grounds for a compulsory licence for their exploitation by third parties (as CLIMATE is here), as the database is already accessible to the public. On the other hand, if a consideration (albeit an affordable one) is demanded from the public for access to the database, then the answer will resemble that in Case 1, that is, the granting to the user of a compulsory licence to exploit the essential part of the database with the parallel payment of a reasonable fee to the creator, since the contrary could constitute abuse of the dominant position of the creator of the database in the relevant market.

III. Metalegal Formants

The ratio of the provision is to provide public access to intellectual property. Viewed in this way, the criteria of the relevant options of the Community legislator do not seem to be identical: see, for example, the differences between the regulations governing public databases (Art. 45A Law 2121/1993) and those governing libraries, public performances of audio-visual works (Art. 23 Law 2121/1993 etc.), differences which do not seem always to be justified by the equivalent in the means of incorporation of the non-material good. A similar provision on real possession is contained in Article 970 of the Civil Code, which lays down that the ceding of the exploitation of a thing in common use to private citizens is not precluded, provided that its common use is not affected.

Furthermore, the distinction between essential and non-essential parts of the database should be understood as enhancing the qualitative criterion of the distinction between private and non-private use with a quantitative one. In fact, regardless of whether the non-material good of another is used by the third party for his/her personal satisfaction or for the circle of the individuals closely associated with him/her, the extent of this use would seem to be crucial: if it is isolated in terms of time (e.g. reproduction of a song at a social gathering, even of those who are not acquaintances or friends; leafing through a book) or in terms of the object (e.g. re-broadcasting of extracts from a work), then it seems more likely that it does not concern and does not prejudice the right of exploitation of the work except non-essentially, even if it does not involve the circle of those individuals closely associated with the user. On the other hand, even if it is addressed only to this close circle, the use of the non-material good of another, if this involves the whole of the non-material good or the essential part of it, will be unlawful.

(8) IRELAND

I. *Operative Rules*

RIM probably cannot prevent CLIMATE from using the contents of the database, but this facility will not be provided for free.

II. *Descriptive Formants*

Directive 96/9/EC was passed into Irish law by means of the CRRA 2000 and this occasioned some change to the previous law. Under the Copyright Act 1963, most, if not all, databases were protected by copyright as 'compilations' and of note is the fact that the threshold of originality in Irish copyright law was very low. The Directive addressed this disparity between common and civil law jurisdictions and provided that the threshold of originality for original databases would be raised throughout the EU, whereas the *sui generis* right would be applied to databases which did not have a creative spark, but which had involved the creator in substantial investment and labour. It introduced a sort of 'sweat of the brow' test for non-original databases and lowered to term of protection substantially to a period of 15 years instead of the 70 years *post mortem auctoris*.

Section 17(3) CRRA makes it clear that copyright does not extend to the contents of a database, as distinct from the selection or arrangement of the database.

The CRRA 2000 refers to the *sui generis* right in the legislation as the 'database right'. A rather odd feature of the legislation is that the right is described as a property right,[79] which surely extends the potential ambit of the protection to constitutional rights. This does not appear to have been the purpose of the Directive, which roots the legislation in unfair competition law. Under section 321, the right applies to databases where there has been a substantial investment in obtaining, verifying or presenting the contents of the database. Investment can involve financial, human or technical resources, under section 320(1), and must be substantial, either or both quantitatively or qualitatively.

Infringements of the database right may take place where the exclusive rights of the database maker, which comprise the right to undertake or authorise others to undertake the extraction or reutilisation of a substantial part of the contents of the database, under section 324(1), are conducted without authorisation.[80] Repeated and systematic extraction or re-utilisation of insubstantial parts of the contents of the database, where this conflicts with the normal exploitation of the database or which prejudices the interests of the maker of the database, will be treated as extraction or re-utilisation of a substantial part of those contents.[81]

Under section 329, private study is an additional legitimate purpose for extraction, in addition to extraction for scientific research, as defined by the Directive. Section 330 replicates other 'teaching' exceptions in the Directive.

Under section 333, there will be no infringement of the database right where all or a substantial part of the contents of a database which are open to public inspection are extracted or re-utilised. However, section 334 appears to muddy this otherwise clear water. This permission is subject to the authority of either the person who maintains the records or the person who is required to make the contents of the database open to public inspection. However, this authority cannot be abused or used arbitrarily, but it may be invoked to prevent such utilisation or extraction as is permitted. The person seeking the inspection will need to make a declaration that no other use will be made of all or a substantial part of the contents without first seeking a licence from the owner of the database right, under section 334(3).

Section 334 sets out how the contents of a database which is open to public inspection may be extracted and re-utilised and section 334(5) provides that where the contents of a database which are open to public inspection pursuant to a statutory requirement contain information about matters of a commercial interest, the database right in the database is not infringed by the extraction or re-utilisation of all or a substantial part of the contents for the purpose of disseminating that information, with permission of the aforementioned persons. Lawful users cannot be prevented from extracting or reutilising insubstantial parts of a database and any terms or conditions to the contrary are void.

---

79 Section 321(1).
80 Section 324(2).
81 Section 324(3).

The Minister may prescribe conditions which must be complied with before the contents of a database are made available to the public, under section 334(6).

In total, the provisions relating to the *sui generis* right in the Irish CRRA 2000 number 41, although no offences are provided for in the legislation in relation to this right.

III. Metalegal Formants

Answer omitted.

(9) ITALY

I. Operative Rules

Yes, with regard to the substantial parts of the database, RIM has a claim for injunction, according to the *sui generis* database right.

As for the insubstantial parts, it seems that RIM would have no claim for injunction, because the lawful user has the full right to extract and re-utilise insubstantial parts of the database without any authorisation, unless the activities of extraction or re-utilisation of insubstantial parts of the database by CLIMATE appear not only to be repetitive and systematic, but also to presuppose operations which are in contrast with the normal administration of the database or unjustifiably prejudice the creator of the database.

II. Descriptive Formants

As a general rule, the producers of databases involving consistent investments of resources,[82] whether they are private or public entities, are entitled to forbid the extraction and re-utilisation of substantial parts of their databases. According to Article 102bis c. 3 ICL (which translates the provision contained in Article 7 of Directive 96/9/EC on the legal protection of databases), a maker of a database who shows that there has been qualitatively and/or quantitatively a substantial investment in either the obtaining, verification or presentation of the contents, has the right to prevent extraction and/or re-utilisation of the whole or of a

---

[82] The juridical nature of the right recognised to the creator of a database first by Directive 96/9/EC and later by the ICL is similar to one of the other connected rights that the Italian legal system provides for the protection of products, activities and goods which do not necessarily meet the requirements for classic copyright or patent protection. The purpose of such a *sui generis* protection is the remuneration of the economic investment made by the database producer. See Marchetti, Ubertazzi, *Commentario breve al diritto della concorrenza* (Padova: 2007), p. 1810.

substantial part, evaluated qualitatively and/or quantitatively, of the contents of that database.

With regard to the aforementioned information, it is therefore possible to affirm that as developer of a database of 'immense commercial value' (so such a database has been described), RIM has the undeniable right to reserve to itself the extraction and the re-utilisation of substantial parts of the database at issue, notwithstanding any objection raised by CLIMATE. No limitations are applicable to the above-mentioned right. Notwithstanding the fact that the Database Directive recognises the faculty of every state to create specific limitations on the *sui generis* right,[83] the Italian implementing law does not authorise any form of free utilisation of a substantial part of the database. Therefore, even though CLIMATE can be defined as a research company (and so, according to Article 9(b) of the Directive, it could theoretically have the right to 'extract or re-utilise a substantial part of the database contents without the authorisation of its maker in the case of extraction for the purposes of illustration for teaching or scientific research, as long as the source is indicated and to the extent justified by the non-commercial purpose to be achieved'), under Italian law such an exception to the *sui generis* right is not applicable, due to the absence of a specific norm on this point.[84]

Whether the extraction and the re-utilisation of substantial parts of the database protected by the *sui generis* right is subject to the authorisation of the creator of the database itself, when it comes to the extraction and re-utilisation of *insubstantial* parts, a distinction has to be made between the general rule and the exceptions to it. According to Article 102ter c. 3 ICL, the activities of extraction or re-utilisation of insubstantial parts (evaluated qualitatively and/or

---

83 See Art. 9 Directive: 'Exceptions to the *sui generis* right

Member States may stipulate that lawful users of a database which is made available to the public in whatever manner may, without the authorisation of its maker, extract or re-utilise a substantial part of its contents:

(a) in the case of extraction for private purposes of the contents of a non-electronic database;
(b) in the case of extraction for the purposes of illustration for teaching or scientific research, as long as the source is indicated and to the extent justified by the non-commercial purpose to be achieved;
(c) in the case of extraction and/or re-utilisation for the purposes of public security or an administrative or judicial procedure'.

84 A different approach to the topic of free utilisation is the one illustrated by Art. 64sexies ICL, according to which, under classical copyright protection, access and consultation of the database for the purposes of illustration for teaching or scientific research – as long as the source is indicated and the extent justified by the non-commercial purpose to be achieved – are not subject to the authorisation of the database maker. In Bertani's opinion, as described in the comment contained in Marchetti, Ubertazzi, *Commentario breve al diritto della concorrenza* (Padova: 2007), p. 1811, free utilisation *ex* Art. 64sexies should also apply to the connected *sui generis* right *ex* Art. 102bis. However, such an opinion is not widely held.

quantitatively) of a database,[85] for any purpose, by a lawful user are not subject to the authorisation of the producer of the database and any contractual clause to the contrary is to be considered void.[86]

However, the right assured to the lawful user by Article 102ter c. 3 ICL does have some limitations, which have necessarily been taken into account for a complete analysis of the case at issue.

The first exception to the general rule illustrated above is contemplated in Article 102ter, which states that, in any case, the lawful user of the database cannot extract or re-utilise parts of the database, even if insubstantial, when those activities are in contrast with the normal administration of the database or when they prejudice the interests of the creator of the database or of the holders of connected rights.

The second exception to the right of the lawful user to the extraction and re-utilisation of insubstantial parts of the database is connected to the right recognised to the creator of the database, by Article 102bis c. 9 ICL, to forbid repetitive and systematic activities of extraction or re-utilisation of insubstantial parts of the database when, once again, they presuppose operations which are in contrast with the normal administration of the database or unjustifiably prejudice the creator of the database.

As regards the fact that RIM is a 100% publicly owned and funded entity (something that, according to CLIMATE's objection, would have as a consequence the free and unrestricted access to RIM's database for everyone), Italian law implementing the Database Directive does not make any distinction between databases produced by a private or a public entity. According to c. 4 and 5 of Article 102bis ICL, the right described in c. 3 of the same article is equally applicable to all those databases whose producers are citizens of a member state of the European Union (and, more generically, residents in the EU territory), as well as companies and societies constituted under the law of a member state of the European Union and having their registered office, their central administration or the centre of their main activity within the European Union.

As can be seen, in defining the subjects with the right to *sui generis* database protection, Italian law does not expressly allocate the right at issue to private and public entities in a different way. The only necessary requirement for being considered a rightholder is having made those investments which were indispensable for the constitution, the verification and the presentation of the database. In conclusion, even if it is a public entity and not a private

---

[85] The Tribunale di Catania, 8 January 2001 (as reported in Marchetti, Ubertazzi, *Commentario breve al diritto della concorrenza* (Padova: 2007), p. 1811) defines an 'insubstantial part' as that irrelevant percentage of data contained in a database (following the quantitative principle) which does not present any systematic coordination (under a qualitative criterion) in a way that, alone, it can be defined and utilised as an independent database.

[86] See Art. 102ter c. 4 ICL.

entrepreneur, RIM (by force of the significant investment which was necessary for the development of the whole database) has the right, stated in Article 102bis c. 3, to reserve to itself both the right to extract and re-utilise substantial parts of the its own database and the right to forbid repetitive and systematic extraction and re-utilisation of insubstantial parts of the database, when such activities are contrary to the normal management of the database itself or unjustifiably prejudice the legitimate interests of the original rightholder.

III. Metalegal Formants

Answer omitted.

(10) LITHUANIA

I. Operative Rules

No, RIM does not have a claim for injunction.

II. Descriptive Formants

The situation should be considered from the point of view both of *sui generis* database protection and of the re-utilisation of public sector information. Directive 1996/9/EC of the European Parliament and of the Council of 11 March 1996 on the legal protection of databases was implemented into Lithuanian law as Chapter IV of the Copyright Act. The previous Directive 2003/98/EC of the European Parliament and of the Council of 17 November 2003 on the re-use of public sector information was replaced by Directive (EU) 2019/1024 of the European Parliament and of the Council of 20 June 2019 on open data and the re-use of public sector information. Accordingly, from 17 July 2021 the old Lithuanian regulation on the re-use of public information was amended and new regulation implemented by the Law on the Right of Information and Data Re-use. Considering the *sui generis* database right, the following remarks should be made. First, although it depends on particular facts of the case, RIM's database most likely meets the requirements of a database, such as independency of the works, data or other materials constituting the content of a database, the systematic or methodical arrangement of the content, and its individual accessibility (Art. 2(7) of the Copyright Act).

The second step is to check whether RIM made, qualitatively and/or quantitatively, a substantial investment in either the obtaining, verification or presentation of the contents of its database (Art. 61(1) of the Copyright Act). The requirement to prove qualitatively and/or quantitatively a substantial investment is normally easily met, because, according to the EU and Lithuanian regulation, investment is understood broadly, encompassing financial, human, technical, time, effort and energy resources. But there is uncertainty as to whether the investment was made in either the obtaining, verification or presentation of the contents of its database. As explained by the European Court of Justice,[87] the investment must be understood to refer to the resources used to seek out existing independent materials and collect them in the database, and it does not cover the resources used for the creation of materials which make up the contents of a database. In this way, the CJEU created a distinction between the creation of data and its collection, verification and presentation. With this distinction a degree of uncertainty arises over which data are created and which are merely collected. In particular, and with regard to the present case, some legal scholars have expressed doubt about whether meteorological data is 'objective' and merely collected by the database maker (in this case, by RIM), or whether it is created.[88] It remains true, however, that even if meteorological data is considered to be created, RIM probably can show separate substantial investment in, for example, presenting the database content and in this way prove its eligibility for *sui generis* database protection.

Even maintaining that RIM's database meets the requirements for *sui generis* database protection, there is a clear problem with its licence agreements. If the said conditions for *sui generis* database protection are met, the maker of a database has the right to prevent the extraction and/or re-utilisation of the whole or of a substantial part, evaluated qualitatively and/or quantitatively, of the contents of that database (Art. 61(1) of the Copyright Act). The scope of protection (the whole or a substantial part, evaluated qualitatively and/or quantitatively, of the contents of that database) is mirrored by the right of a lawful user of the database to extract and/or re-utilise insubstantial parts of its contents for any purposes whatsoever (Art. 62(1) of the Copyright Act). Importantly, this provision is mandatory and any contractual clause to the contrary is void (Art. 62(5) of the Copyright Act). Therefore, RIM's reservation of the right to extract and re-utilise insubstantial parts of its database is invalid and CLIMATE, as long as it is considered a lawful user, can extract and re-utilise insubstantial parts of RIM's database.

Analysing the situation from the perspective of the re-utilisation of public sector information, as has already been stated, Lithuania amended its regulation

---

87 See CJEU cases *Fixtures Marketing v. Organismos prognostikon agonon podosfairou AE*, C-444/02; *Fixtures Marketing v. Svenska Spel AB*, C-338/02; *Fixtures Marketing v. Oy Veikkaus Ab*, C-46/02; *The British Horseracing Board Ltd and Others v. William Hill Organization Ltd*, C-203/02.

88 M. Davison, P.B. Hugenholtz, 'Football fixtures, horse races and spin-offs: the ECJ domesticates the database right', *EIPR.*, 2005, vol. 3, pp. 113–118. The same concerns were expressed in Lithuania as well – R. Birštonas, *The Legal Protection of Databases*, Doctoral Dissertation, Vilnius, 2007, p. 115.

concerning public sector data. The relationship between the *sui generis* database protection and re-use of public data is dealt with in Article 2(3) of the Law on the Right of Information and Data Re-use, which states:

> If other laws governing the rights of database producers provide for an authorization to prohibit the re-use of data or restrict the re-use of data to a greater extent than provided for in this Law, the provisions of other laws shall apply to the extent that they do not conflict with this Law.

Therefore, the Law on the Right of Information and Data Re-use takes priority over the Copyright Act.

The main focus and aim of the new regulation is open data, which presupposes not only availability of data for re-use, but also its availability without payment. In particular, the basic rule is that data for re-use shall be provided to applicants free of charge, unless otherwise provided by the laws of the Republic of Lithuania or legal acts of the European Union (Art. 8 Law on the Right of Information and Data Re-use). Even if in exceptional cases, a fee is provided for, the amount of the fee is normally restricted to the recovery of the marginal costs. Therefore, it is doubtful whether the 'substantial fee' imposed by RIM would satisfy this requirement.

Furthermore, the Law on the Right of Information and Data Re-use has a special provision that high-value datasets for re-use shall be provided free of charge (Arts. 8(8), 16(4)). While so far there is no special regulation specifying which particular datasets are regarded as 'high-value datasets', it is officially understood that meteorological data is covered by this category.[89] Therefore, relying on this special norm, meteorological data should in any case be provided free of charge.

To summarise the regulation of public sector data (including meteorological data), the current regulation establishes free use of such data and specifically stresses that other laws (in particular, provisions of the Copyright Act regulating the *sui generis* database right) cannot restrict this possibility. Therefore, RIM could not impose such licensing conditions and cannot claim an injunction.

III. Metalegal Formants

The current Lithuanian law and policy stresses the huge benefits of open data, including the new commercial perspectives. That is why even commercial re-use of public data is fostered and encouraged. For this reason, the state is ready to

---

[89] Press release of the Ministry of the Economy and Innovation of the Republic of Lithuania concerning the open data, 30 June 2021, available at: https://eimin.lrv.lt/lt/naujienos/atveriami-dideles-vertes-duomenys-paskatins-nauju-produktu-kurima.

abandon the legal restrictions, *inter alia sui generis* database protection, which would normally be available.

(11) NETHERLANDS

I. Operative Rules

RIM may successfully claim an injunction, unless the court rules that because of public funding there is no substantial investment in the collection of data by the public authority.

II. Descriptive Formants

According to the Dutch Database Act, RIM is the producer of the database. RIM would therefore be able to reserve the right to extract and re-utilise substantial parts of its database. With regard to the use of insubstantial parts of the database, it only owns the exclusive right to allow others to repeatedly and systematically extract and re-utilise insubstantial parts, unless this obstructs the normal exploitation of the database or causes unjustified damages to its (RIM's) lawful interests (Art. 2(1) Dutch Database Act). RIM can never prevent a lawful user from extracting and re-utilising insubstantial parts of the database, if the database is made available to the public (Art. 3 Dutch Database Act).

RIM is a public authority. Article 8(2) Dutch Database Act denies a public authority the right to exercise its exclusive database rights, unless the database right is reserved explicitly in general by law, order or ordinance, or in a specific case by notification on the database itself or while the database is made available to the public. Since RIM has indeed reserved its rights explicitly in the licence, CLIMATE cannot invoke the application of this provision to its advantage.

In this context, the decision of the Dutch Council of State must be mentioned. The case involved the interpretation of a statutory provision governing the re-use of public sector information. Landmark, a private company specialising in geographical information, had filed a request for environmental information from the local authorities. Part of the requested information was a list of addresses where soil research had been conducted. The question in this case was whether the local authorities of Amsterdam were authorised to impose conditions and restrictions for the re-use of the list of addresses. Former Article 11a(1)(a) of the Government Information Act establishes two conditions for the re-use of information held by the public body. First, the collection of information must qualify as a database, and second, the public-sector body must qualify as the producer of the database. The Council notes that the definition of 'database' and 'producer of the database' should be interpreted in the same way as in the context of the Dutch Database Act.

The Council of State comes to the conclusion that the data collection did take a substantial investment, and that therefore it qualified as a database in the sense of Article 11 of the Government Information Act. In answering the second question, whether the public-sector body was the producer of the database, the Council refers to European law, specifically Recitals 40–41 of the Database Directive. It follows from these Recitals that the producer of the database is the person that takes the initiative and carries the risk of the investments to collect, verify and present the content of the database.

The Council states that the database was made with the intention of simplifying/facilitating the public task of the local authorities. Furthermore, the production of the database was initiated and financed by the local authorities of Amsterdam. A large part was financed by the Ministry of Housing, Spatial Planning and the Environment to fulfil the task of mapping the local soil pollution. In these circumstances, the Council of State finds that the local authorities did not carry the risk of the substantial investment for the production of the database and therefore could not be qualified as the producer of the database that contained the list of addresses.[90]

While this case concerned a request for the re-use of public sector information and did touch on elements of the Dutch Database Act, it did not discuss Article 8(2).

III. Metalegal Formants

The Dutch lawmaker has always approached European database protection with a good dose of circumspection. Part of the reason for this is that the Dutch copyright regime already contained a rule granting minimal protection to non-original writings (*geschriftenbescherming*) and that therefore any additional form of protection was unnecessary. The Dutch Copyright Act contains in Article 15b, a rule similar to Article 8(2) of the Database Act, which reads as follows:

> The further communication to the public or reproduction of a literary, scientific or artistic work communicated to the public by or on behalf of the public authorities shall not be deemed an infringement of the copyright in such a work, unless the copyright has been explicitly reserved, either in a general manner by law, decree or ordinance, or in a specific case by a notice on the work itself or at the communication to the public. Even if no such reservation has been made, the author shall retain the exclusive right to have appear, in the form of a collection, his works which have been communicated to the public by or on behalf of the public authorities.

---

90 ABRvS, 29 april 2009, nr. 07/786, *AMI* 2009/6 (*College B&W Amsterdam v. Landmark*), m.nt. M.M.M. van Eechoud.

When transposing the Database Directive into Dutch law, the Dutch legislator did not want to put the makers of a database in a better position than authors of copyright protected works.

Coming back to the *Landmark* case, the Council of State uses several arguments in support of denying local authorities the status of producer, based on the Database Directive and the case law of the European Court of Justice. The preamble of the Database Directive notes that the Directive aims to remove current differences which disturb the internal market. The European Court of Justice, in *Directmedia Publishing*, highlighted the purpose of the *sui generis* database right as follows:

> to guarantee the person who has taken the initiative and assumed the risk of making a substantial investment in terms of human, technical and/or financial resources in the obtaining, verification or presentation of the contents of a database a return on his investment by protecting him against the unauthorised appropriation of the results of that investment by acts which involve in particular the reconstitution by a user or a competitor of that database or a substantial part of it at a fraction of the cost needed to design it independently.[91]

The Council of State reaffirms the internal market considerations at the root of the Database Directive, which were emphasised in the explanatory memorandum of the Dutch Database Act. In light of this background, the conclusion that local authorities do not qualify as producers of a database is unsurprising. In a case note to the *Landmark* decision, a commentator points out that, in relation to public-sector information, the public interest is better served by increasing the access and re-use of information that is created in the context of public-service purposes, rather than by restricting it. This coincides with the outcome of the *Landmark* case, whereby the information contained in the database can be re-used. While this case did receive some criticism, authors sympathised with the outcome of the judgment because they believed the purpose of the database right is not served with the protection of data collected primarily for the exercise of public tasks. Furthermore, the Directive on the Re-use of Public Sector Information is based on the idea that it is good for the economy if public-sector data is freely available for new products and services. However, the construction whereby there is a protected work but no rightholder is not ideal. The Council of State in the *Landmark* case seems to suggest that, for protection to arise, the public authority must carry the risk of the investment. It seems doubtful whether the European legislator would interpret this criterion in the same way. The European legislator did decide to treat public database producers

---

91 CJEU judgment of 9 October 2008, *DirectMedia Publishing*, C-304/07, ECLI:EU:C:2008:552, para. 33.

in the same way as private database producers. In the Netherlands, the public-sector producers of databases seem to be treated differently.

(12) NORWAY

I. Operative Rules

RIM has a claim for injunction, provided that the fee entails no more than a 'reasonable return' on the investments involved and that the refusal to license does not conflict with the competition rules.

II. Descriptive Formants

A public database enjoys database protection under NCA §1 (work) or §43 (*sui generis*) (New Act §§2 and 24, respectively) if the general requirements for protection are fulfilled. The NCA does not preclude database protection for public institutions – only works concerning the exercise of public authority (legal statutes, court decisions, administrative regulations, etc.) are exempted from copyright or neighbouring rights protection (NCA §9; New Act §14).

As far as the *sui generis* protection for databases is concerned, it has been disputed whether meteorological data are 'existing' or 'created' data according to the CJEU's interpretation of the 'substantial investment' criteria in Article 7(2) of the Database Directive (Directive 9/96/EC).[92] However, it is to be assumed in any case that the database in question enjoys protection due to the investments relating to the collection, verification and presentation of information in the database.[93]

Provided that the database in question is protected, there is an issue of compliance with Directive 2003/98/EC on re-use of public information. The Directive's principles of governing charges (Art. 6) and transparency (Art. 7), requiring the public-sector body in question to divulge the basis for the calculation of the public access charge as well as the factors taken into account in the calculation of charges, is implemented by way of §8, fourth and fifth paragraphs, of the Norwegian Public Information Act (NPIA, 19 May 2006). The former provision states that for institutions covered by the Re-use Directive, their total income from delivery of information must not exceed the factual costs involved in collection, production, reproduction and dissemination of

[92] Cf. for two different views M. Davison/B. Hugenholtz, 'Football fixtures, horse races and spin-offs: The CJEU domesticates the database rights', *EIPR* 2005, pp. 113–118 at p. 115 and E. Derclaye: 'Databases "*Sui generis*" Right: Should we Adopt the Spin-off Theory?', *EIPR* 2004, p. 402 at pp. 441–412.

[93] Cf. the Belgian report.

information, with the addition of a reasonable reimbursement of the investments. Consequently, the provision sets limits on how 'substantial' a fee RIM can charge for access to its database.

Here, too, it is possible to challenge the rightholders' exercise of their rights under the competition rules, cf. the *Magill/IMS Health* doctrine.[94] However, it is far from clear from the facts that RIM's refusal to license will constitute an abuse of a (supra-)dominant position. In any event RIM, will not be entitled to access for free.

III. Metalegal Formants

Access to public goods and information is important, but it is not a given that the public, and in particular commercial undertakings, shall benefit from public investments without contributing financially. For information of the kind dealt with in this case, NPIA §8, fourth paragraph seeks to ensure, apart from transparency, that public bodies may receive a return on their investments in information databases, while on the other hand taking into consideration public information concerns, since the public bodies are entitled only to recover costs plus a *reasonable* return on investments.

(13) POLAND

I. Operative Rules

CLIMATE may not demand free access.

II. Descriptive Formants

The answer to this question depends on whether RIM may rely on a *sui generis* database right. It is rather obvious on the facts of the case that because of the nature of the data, this is a more appropriate legal ground than copyright, although because of rather low thresholds for originality and creativity under Polish law, it cannot be excluded that the arrangement of the database may qualify for copyright protection. However, as regards information contained in this database, it would seem rather unlikely. As database protection has been harmonised within the EU, the conditions of protection under Polish law are the same as in the Directive 96/9/EC of the European Parliament and of the Council of 11 March 1996 on the legal protection of databases. It would be reasonable to assume that RIM has made a substantial investment to create the database

---

[94] See, for example, the Belgian report.

(and not just the content of the database)[95] and thus would enjoy a *sui generis* right in this database. Since extraction and re-utilisation of data is covered by the *sui generis* right,[96] CLIMATE may use the data only on the conditions authorised by RIM.

In Poland, there is no provision that would exclude public bodies from holding a *sui generis* right (or other IP rights). General conditions of protection must apply, and this means that the right will be vested in the producer of the database. The producer may be a public body.

Because of the importance of the database, it should be considered whether refusal to license the database does not constitute an abuse of dominant position on the part of RIM. In this respect, the remarks concerning Case 1 remain valid. However, certainly competition law would not allow CLIMATE to demand free access to the database.

III. Metalegal Formants

This case raises interesting questions about the scope of IP protection for public bodies. It is obvious that public bodies using public funding (i.e. in effect taxes collected from all taxpayers) may become owners of various IP rights (patents, copyright, *sui generis* database right, sometimes even trademarks).[97] In some areas of IP law, the relevant statutes have at least identified the problem. It is, for example, common to limit copyright protection of certain public works such as statutes, court judgments or other official documents.[98] Where no special provisions have been enacted, it must be assumed that public bodies enjoy, as a rule, the same scope of protection as private persons (natural or legal). However, it is of course problematic if public bodies demand fees for access to IP subject matter since the creation of this subject matter has already been paid for by the public (in the form of tax revenues). Nevertheless, it is open to question whether this problem is really about IP law. As the open source and Creative Commons movements have proven, IP law itself allows IP subject matter to be made available to the public on reasonable conditions. Therefore, it rather seems to be a problem of democratic influence on public bodies that would make them provide access to such subject matter on acceptable conditions. This solution is preferable for at least two reasons. Firstly, tampering with IP legislation would be complicated and would not always produce the desired results. For example, it would be wrong to assume that public bodies must always provide access for

---

95 S. Stanisławska-Kloc, 'Ochrona baz danych', *ZNUJ PWiOWI*, 2002, vol. 82, p. 232.

96 Art. 6(1) of the Law on the Protection of Databases, Journal of Laws 2001, No. 128, pos. 1402; J. Barta, R. Markiewicz, *Ustawa o ochronie baz danych* (Kraków: 2002), p. 106.

97 There is even a tendency to create special procedures the purpose of which is to take advantage of IP rights. Such procedures are implemented for example by municipalities.

98 E.g. Art. 4 points 1–2 of the Polish Copyright Act.

free or that they may not impose any conditions on use. Secondly, even if public bodies could not invoke IP rights, they could use their factual monopoly (civil property rights) to the same purpose.[99]

(14) SLOVENIA

I. Operative Rules

CLIMATE has the right to consult RIM's database without restriction and free of charge. RIM may deny a request by CLIMATE for a transcript, photocopy or electronic record of all or of a qualitatively or quantitatively significant part of the database, and under specific conditions also a qualitatively or quantitatively insignificant part of the database. If the database is accessible online, consulting the database is free of charge.

CLIMATE has the right to re-use parts of the database (information) in return for the payment defined by the act on access to public information. If RIM makes the database accessible online, it cannot charge for re-use. CLIMATE must state the source of the data in case of re-use.

If CLIMATE wants to acquire a meteorological product that does not constitute national meteorological information, it must cover the prescribed costs for that product, which relate to its preparation and production.

II. Descriptive Formants

The description of the problem indicates that RIM is 100% state-owned, and 100% financed by the state. Legislation on meteorological activities is therefore applicable.

1. Consulting the database and reproduction of the database

According to Articles 10 and 27 of the Meteorological Activities Act (MAA), the provider of a national meteorological service shall keep a compilation of data or a database of national meteorological information and meteorological observations from registered meteorological stations, comprising:

- meteorological observation data from the national network of meteorological stations;
- national meteorological information;[100] and

[99] For example, RIM could simply block access to its database.

[100] Art. 17(7) MAA: 'National meteorological information is a meteorological product prepared as part of the national meteorological service from meteorological observation data from the national meteorological station network.'

- meteorological data acquired from the international exchange of meteorological data.

This data is public, in accordance with the act regulating access to public information.

The Access to Public Information Act (APIA)[101] states that public information is information:

1. arising from the working sphere of an institution;
2. which an institution holds (has produced itself or acquired from a third party); and
3. in the form of a document, files, dossiers, registers, records or other documentary material. (Art. 4(1) APIA).

Given the description of the case and the provisions of the MAA on the tasks of the national meteorological service set out above, RIM acquired data and created a database within its field of work. This fulfilled the first precondition for RIM's database to be deemed public information. At the same time, the second precondition was also fulfilled, as RIM has a database. The third precondition is met if the institution keeps information in the form of a document, files, dossiers, registers, records or other documentary material. The list of categories given in the MAA is not exhaustive, as indicated by the term 'and other documentary material' in Article 4 of the MAA. The listed forms should not be understood as exclusive, since technological development will produce new forms of information carriers.[102] The concept of a document therefore must be explained as any material record.[103] This criterion is met by a database. All the preconditions for RIM's database to be deemed public information have therefore been met.

The principle of free access applies to databases as repositories of public information (Art. 5 APIA). The fact that according to the case description RIM's database is subject to related rights pursuant to Article 141a of the CRRA,[104] does not affect public access in this specific case. The APIA defines in detail the exceptions to access to public information in Article 6, but this does not include an exception based on copyright legislation. The APIA provisions on permitting access to public information state that if requested information is

---

101 Official Gazette RS, nos. 24/2003, 61/2005, 96/2005-UPB1, 109/2005-ZDavP-1B, 113/2005-ZInfP, 28/2006, 51/2006-UPB2, 117/2006-ZDavP-2.

102 S. Pličanič, G. Perenič, U. Prepeluh, B. Bugarič, N. Pirc Musar, T. Pucelj Vidović, V.J. Vazzaz, *Komentar Zakona o dostopu do informacij javnega značaja s pravom EU in primerjalno pravno prakso*, Institute of Public Administration, Faculty of Law (Ljubljana: 2005), pp. 83, 84.

103 Ibid.

104 Official Gazette RS, nos. 21/1995, 9/2001, 30/2001, 43/2004, 17/2006, 139/2006, 68/2008.

protected in accordance with an act regulating copyright, the body may only permit the applicant to consult the data, and not to transcribe,[105] photocopy or take an electronic record (hereinafter: reproduction) of the information. RIM's database therefore is subject to the principle of free access, but RIM may deny reproduction of the information it holds. However, it must be stated that this restriction only applies if CLIMATE requests reproduction of:

- all or a qualitatively or quantitatively significant part of the database content; or
- a qualitatively or quantitatively insignificant part of the database content, when used repeatedly and systematically, and in contravention of normal use of the database, or unreasonably prejudicing the legitimate interests of the database producer.

According to Article 141b CRRA, protection only applies in these cases listed above.

Also relevant in this regard are the provisions of the MAA, which as a more specialist regulation (compared to the APIA and the CRRA) states that the body (RIM) must also permit access to its databases produced in accordance with Articles 10 and 27 of the MAA.

Given all the above, RIM must permit CLIMATE to consult its database, but it retains the option of denying CLIMATE the right to reproduction in the cases listed above.

1.1. Costs of consultation or reproduction

The MAA states that an individual wanting to acquire data from a body, who does not use the data to create meteorological products (Art. 17(14) MAA) and does not issue them to third parties, is only required to cover the prescribed costs of the provision of this data, in accordance with the act regulating access to public information (Art. 30(1) MAA).

Consulting the requested information is free of charge, pursuant to Article 34(1) MAA. According to the Decree on the Provision and Re-use of Public Information, RIM cannot charge CLIMATE for consulting the database, for provision of information by telephone, for provision of information by e-mail or for submission of information by fax, if it does not exceed five pages (Art. 18(2) of the Decree). It may, however, charge for the material costs of communicating a reproduction of the requested information to the applicant (Art. 34(2) APIA). Of course, as stated above, under certain conditions it has the option of refusing to reproduce the database or parts thereof, and hence also its communication by e-mail or fax.

---

105 According to Art. 18(1)(1) of the Decree on the Provision and Re-use of Public Information (see below), 'the production of any type of copy by technical means' is deemed to be a transcription.

RIM may charge for:

- conversion of information from electronic to physical form, if the information exists exclusively in electronic form and the applicant has requested that the information be in physical form;
- conversion of information from physical to electronic form, if the information exists exclusively in physical form and the applicant has requested that the information be in electronic form; and
- postage costs (Art. 18(1) of the Decree).

The Decree provides for the maximum permitted material costs that may be charged (Art. 19), and the method of payment (Art. 20).

If RIM has a database available online (in certain cases publishing information online is obligatory, Article 10(1) APIA) then access must be free of charge (Art. 10(2) APIA).

Any party wanting to acquire a meteorological product that does not constitute national meteorological information pursuant to the MAA must cover the prescribed costs for that product, which relate to its preparation and production (Art. 30(3)).

2. Re-use

The MAA states that an individual wanting to use the body's data to create meteorological products or provide them to third parties must cover the prescribed costs of acquiring the data (Art. 30(2)). The level of costs should be defined in implementing regulations (Art. 30(4) MAA). Implementing regulations of this type have not yet been adopted.

The production of meteorological products means the processing of meteorological data (Art. 14(3) MAA) and therefore constitutes the re-use of public information pursuant to Article 4(3) APIA. The payment rules for the re-use of public information – which includes RIM database – are defined in the APIA. The provisions of the APIA therefore apply to determining the costs of re-use of a database or parts thereof.

As already stated, the principle of free access applies to the database and parts thereof, which means that each applicant has the right, under the same conditions as any other person, to acquire the right to re-use information for commercial or non-commercial purposes (Art. 5(3) APIA). The APIA also defines exceptions to the re-use rules (Art. 6(6)), but none of these applies in this specific case. The APIA defines, for example, an exception in the event that information is protected by the intellectual property rights of third parties (Art. 6(6)). In this specific case, the database is protected by the rights of the body itself (RIM) rather than a third party, so that exception cannot be enforced. It follows from the above that the principle of free access also applies to re-use in the case of RIM's database.

RIM must permit the re-use of information at the same price and under the same conditions to all applicants and cannot restrict their number. Furthermore, RIM cannot enable a form of re-use that would exclude the re-use of information by third parties (Art. 36a(3) APIA). If it were found necessary and unavoidable for the performance of a public service or other services in the public interest, RIM could grant an exclusive right to re-use of information (Art. 35a(4) APIA).

2.1. Costs of database re-use

RIM may charge a price for the re-use of information for commercial prices (Art. 34a(1) APIA), which:

- cannot exceed the costs of collecting, preparing, reproduction and dissemination of information and the typical return on invested funds;
- must be cost-reflective;
- must be set for a normal accounting period, and in accordance with the prescribed accounting rules for RIM;
- must have a cost-calculation method that is public information and that RIM must provide to any applicant on request.

RIM generally must publish online all conditions regarding re-use of information, the normal price for re-use and the cost-calculation method that will be used for special re-use requests (Art. 36(2) APIA). It also must notify every applicant – including CLIMATE – of the payment requirement, and if so requested, provide the applicant with an estimate in advance of the costs it will be charged for information provision (Art. 36(3) APIA). If CLIMATE's request relates to a large amount of information, RIM may demand a deposit, which will be set as a percentage of the total assessed amount for information provision (Art. 36(4) APIA).

RIM cannot charge for the re-use of information, if:

- it provides the information online free of charge (Art. 34a(3) APIA);
- the purpose of use is providing information, ensuring freedom of expression, culture and art, or the re-use of information by the media (Art. 34a(1) APIA);
- the Decree defines more detailed criteria and conditions for re-use pricing (Arts. 20, 23, 24 and 25 of the Decree).

2.2. Re-use conditions

CLIMATE's request for re-use of the database must include a definition of the commercial or non-commercial purpose of re-use, primarily by describing the following circumstances:

- legal and organisational form or status of the applicant and its line of business or activity; and
- the anticipated method of re-use of the information, including conditions for communication of the information to the public.

As a condition of re-use of database contents, RIM must require an attribution of the data source that includes the title '*Javne informacije Slovenije*' (public information of Slovenia) and RIM's title. RIM may also define other conditions of use, if necessary:

- to ensure public information is up-to-date and correct;
- for a proper understanding of public information;
- to provide feedback for users or the body; or
- for official procedures or public tasks for the purposes of which the public information was provided.

CLIMATE must respect Article 29 MAA, which requires it to state the source of the data, if it publishes or in any other way enables public access to a meteorological product or any other product prepared on the basis of acquired data.

In every case, RIM must use the funds collected to facilitate consultation, reproduction and re-use of information to improve the quality of services of acquiring, producing and providing data (Art. 30(5) MAA).

III. Metalegal Formants

The APIA states that the body may deny a request to reproduce public information, if it represents work protected by the CRRA. The body can therefore refuse to reproduce public information, even if it is the holder of copyright or related rights to a work itself. At the same time, even if it is the holder of copyright for that work, it cannot prevent the *re-use* of public information that is copyrighted. The APIA therefore leads to an absurd situation, where an applicant is prevented from reproducing information, but is permitted to re-use the information.

The purpose of the APIA was not to protect copyrighted work when its author is a public body, but only in cases where the holder of a copyright or related right is a third party. An exception of this kind also applies in the event of re-use (as stated above) – the APIA permits an exception from the principle of accessibility if an applicant requests the re-use of information for which a third party holds an intellectual property right. In a case of this kind, the body may refuse to grant an applicant permission to re-use information.

The Information Commissioner of the Republic of Slovenia has therefore already proposed an appropriate amendment to the APIA that would enable the reproduction of public information when the holder of the copyright (or related right) is the public body itself.

(15) SPAIN

I. Operative Rules

CLIMATE has no right to object the validity of the clause by arguing that the database has been financed with public capital.

CLIMATE, as a legitimate user of the database, has only the right to request to extract and re-use non-substantial parts of the database.

II. Descriptive Formants

According to what Article 12 LPI determines, databases consist of 'the collections of works, data or other independent elements that are prepared in either a systematic or a methodical way and that are accessible by electronic or other means'. In this sense, the law provides for the protection of all of the database, either because it constitutes a work or because it constitutes a substantial investment susceptible of receiving temporal protection, i.e. the so-called *sui generis* protection regulated in Book II, Title VIII of the LPI (Arts. 133–137). The two forms of legal protection are exclusive rights over the creation that can be exercised separately or together.

In the assumption of specific fact, we are trying to solve the scope of legal protection that the law grants to the entitled of a database rightholder, not because they are the author of it but because of the substantial investment, valued in terms of quality or quantity, that was necessary for the obtaining, verifying and presentation of its content (Art. 133.1 LPI).

There is no need to show an investment in economic or financial terms, but it will be valued in terms of time used, effort, energy or anything of a similar nature.[106] The CJEU has had the opportunity to pronounce on this principle, by means of three judgments issued on 9 November 2004.[107] In these judgments, the Court lays the foundations for the doctrine by which the *sui generis* right over a database aims to promote access to knowledge through the system of information.

It is thus not a matter of protecting the production of knowledge inside the database, but rather the effort devoted to summarising the knowledge in a single tool.

---

106 R. Bercovitz Rodríguez-Cano (coord.), *Manual de Propiedad Intelectual* (3rd ed., Valencia: 2006), p. 265.

107 CJEU judgments of 9 November 2004, *The British Horseracing Board Ltd et al. v. William Hill Organisation Ltd*, C-203/02, ECLI:EU:C:2004:695; *Fixtures Marketing Ltd v. OPAP*, C-444/02, ECLI:EU:C:2004:697; and *Fixtures Marketing Ltd v. AB Svenska Spel*, C-338/02, ECLI:EU:C:2004:696.

To conclude, the criteria of originality is replaced by the criteria of investment, recognising the *sui generis* database right over other copyright, such as the rights over industrial inventions. The objective is then to promote the introduction of storing and processing systems for already existing information, by giving temporal exclusivity to the manufacturer in a negative way, that is, forbidding the use by third persons without prior consent.

The content of the exclusive right is not an absolute one. It is limited to the possibility of forbidding the extraction or re-use of the whole or of a substantial part of the content of the database by a legitimate user, valued in terms of quantity and quality whenever the obtaining, verifying or presentation of the content may represent a substantial investment (Art. 133.1 LPI). We shall add to this disposition another one, to the benefit of the manufacturer of databases, whose objective is to avoid the illegal abuse that legitimate users may engage in, seeking protection in the definition of 'substantial'. Thus, Article 133.2 LPI establishes 'the repeated or systematic extraction and/or re-utilization of non-substantial parts of the contents of a database which involve acts contrary to the normal exploitation of the database or which unreasonably prejudice the legitimate interests of the database maker shall not be authorized'. On the contrary, the users of a database will have the right to extract or re-use non-substantial parts of the database. This right arises in the same way as the protection of databases collides with the protection of the market of information, so there is a tendency to prevent the constitution of obstacles to free competition.

According to the faculty granted to the member states by Directive 96/9/EC in its Article 9 to establish exceptions, the Spanish legislator decided to establishes a series of assumptions that shall be unnecessary to submit to the prohibition described in the previous paragraph. That is, Article 135 LPI describes three different situations in which a legitimate user will be able to extract or re-use substantial parts of the database without the authorisation of the database author. These three situations are:

1. whenever the extraction of the database content is for private use only;
2. whenever the extraction has either illustrative or teaching objectives, or is for the purpose of scientific research with a justified non-commercial objective and always indicating the source; and
3. whenever the extraction has public security aims, in terms of legal or governmental processes.

These three exceptions are a reiteration of those mentioned in Article 34.2 LPI and that are described in Chapter II (Limits) of Title III (length, limits and safeguarding of other legal dispositions) of Book I (Copyright) of the LPI. As shown, the common denominator in these three exceptions is the non-commercial character, because the aim is to avoid economic damage and prejudice for the manufacturer of the database. He/she shall be the only person permitted to commercially exploit the database.

In conclusion, the LPI does not distinguish between types of manufactures. They are all protected by the same *sui generis* right over the database, no matter whether this database has been created with public or private capital.[108] The law aims to protect the investment, so it does not matter who makes the investment. As a consequence, the argumentation used by CLIMATE cannot be accepted, except to the extent that as a legitimate user they have the right to extract non-substantial parts of the content of the database.

III. Metalegal Formants

Answer omitted.

(16) UNITED KINGDOM

I. Operative Rules

RIM has no claim for injunction, if CLIMATE qualifies as a lawful user.

II. Descriptive Formants

Legal position
In order to determine whether RIM has a claim for an injunction against CLIMATE, it is firstly necessary to determine whether RIM's database will qualify for (1) copyright protection under the CDPA 1988 or (2) under the *sui generis* 'database right' as introduced through Directive 96/9/EC. Secondly, if RIM's database qualifies for protection under these two concepts, it will be necessary to determine whether CLIMATE commits an infringing act by claiming free and unrestricted access to RIM's data bank.

An existence of a 'database' is the precondition to claiming protection under any of the above-mentioned concepts. Databases are defined in section 3A CDPA 1988 as 'a collection of independent works, data or other materials which are arranged in a systematic or methodical way and individually accessible by electronic or other means.' RIM's database is most likely to satisfy this definition.

1. Copyright
For copyright to subsist, the work must be (1) covered by copyright, (2) recorded in material form, (3) original, (4) sufficiently connected to the UK

108 In the same sense, the Czech Copyright Law does not include any specific provision applicable to public institutions.

to qualify for protection under UK law, and (5) not excluded from protection on public policy grounds. According to section 1(1) CDPA 1988, copyright in its biggest part covers 'original literary, dramatic, musical or artistic works.' Databases are considered as literary works as per section 3(1) CDPA 1988 and as held in the *Ladbroke (Football)*[109] case. Therefore, RIM's database satisfies the first criterion for copyright protection.

Secondly, in order to satisfy the 'fixation' requirement, it is necessary that RIM's database has been recorded in writing or otherwise. It can be easily presumed that RIM has indeed recorded its database over the course of a century's worth of development.

The originality requirement normally represents the biggest obstacle for acquiring copyright protection under UK law, as it depends largely on the facts of the case and must in each case be a question of degree. Under UK law, in order to establish originality, it is necessary to show that the author has put a significant amount of labour, skill or effort into creating the work in question (*Ladbroke*). However, the standard of originality required in the EU is somewhat different and requires that the work is the 'author's intellectual creation'. When it comes to databases, Directive 96/9/EC introduced a new and harmonising test for originality of databases which states that 'where originality derives from the *quality of the labour* used in either the *selection or arrangement* then this is likely to be regarded as an author's intellectual creation.' The leading case on copyright protection for databases is *Feist*,[110] where it was stated that 'assuming the absence of original written expression, only the compiler's selection and arrangement may be protected; the raw facts may be copied at will.' Moreover, *Feist* makes clear that the degree of copyright protection for factual databases is thin and covers only the selection and arrangement.

Therefore, following this reasoning, it may be possible to argue that RIM's selection and arrangement of the meteorological data has the potential to satisfy the higher originality standard to be protected by copyright, bearing in mind that it most likely required a substantial level of labour to be put in by RIM in order to ensure it is of an 'incredible' commercial and general value, as stated in the problem question. However, it is unlikely that the very contents of the database will be protected under copyright and especially so if the information was already in the public domain (RIM is a body that gathers, organises and interprets existing meteorological data, rather than being a creator of new information), thereby failing to satisfy the higher originality criteria. This information could however be protected under the *sui generis* right, as explained below.

The third criterion for copyright protection requires that the work is sufficiently connected to the UK. According to section 153 CDPA 1988,

---

109 *Ladbroke (Football) Ltd v. William Hill (Football) Ltd* [1964] 1 All ER 465.

110 *Feist Publications v. Rural Telephone*, 499 U.S. 340 (1991).

qualification can occur by way of authorship, first publication and transmission. Moreover, section 9(1) CDPA 1988 states that an author is a person who creates the work. Since RIM is the creator of the database as such and presuming that it is a UK company, it could qualify by way of authorship for copyright protection.

Finally, copyright protection will not be granted for obscene, blasphemous or immoral works. It is highly unlikely that this criterion will represent problems for RIM's database qualifying for copyright protection.

Bearing in mind what was said above, it can be argued that RIM's database, i.e. its arrangement and selection, will qualify for protection under UK copyright law.

CLIMATE seeks free and unrestricted access to this database, notwithstanding the fact that RIM seeks to impose a substantial licence on everyone who wishes to access the data bank. In order to determine whether this conduct will amount to *infringement* and hence support RIM's claim for an injunction, it is necessary to look at the copyright infringement criteria under UK copyright law.

According to section 16 CDPA 1988, the claimant must show on the balance of probabilities that: (1) the defendant carried out an activity that falls under copyright owner's control; (2) there is a causal link between the defendant's work and the copyrighted work, i.e. that the defendant derived his/her work from the claimant's work; and (3) that the restricted act was carried out in relation to the work or substantial part thereof.

Restricted activities are listed in section 16(1) CDPA 1988 and include copying the work, issuing copies of the work to the public, renting or lending the work to public, performing, showing or playing the work in public, making adaptations of the work, and authorising anyone else to carry out any of the activities mentioned above. In this case, it is not precisely clear what CLIMATE seeks to do with the database if free and unrestricted access is granted to it. However, if it seeks to copy a substantial part of the database, including the way the information was arranged or selected, or if it seeks to make an adaptation of the existing arrangement and selection of the information for its own purpose and contrary to the licensing conditions imposed by RIM, CLIMATE will be conducting a restricted activity. It has to be however noted again that if CLIMATE only seeks to copy, adapt or make available to the public the contents of the database, it is unlikely that it will be infringing under UK copyright law.

The causal connection between the two works is a matter of fact and the burden falls on the claimant to show copying. The main thing to pay attention to when determining the causal connection is the similarities between the two works, including the evidence demonstrating that the defendant had access to the work and an opportunity to copy the work (the latter was stated in the case of *Bron*).[111]

[111] *Francis Day v. Bron* [1963] Ch 587.

It was stated in *Ibcos Computers*[112] that the more numerous the similarities are, the higher the likelihood that the work has been copied. Moreover, the mistakes copied from the original to the copied work will also demonstrate the causal connection between the two works, as held in *Rose*.[113] With this in mind, it can be argued that if there is a causal connection between the work that CLIMATE seeks to produce with the help of having free and unrestricted access to RIM's data bank, i.e. if there are actual similarities between the way RIM's database was arranged and the information selected, then there may be a possibility that CLIMATE is indeed acting in infringement of RIM's copyright.

Finally, in order to establish infringement, it is necessary to determine whether CLIMATE would have taken all or a substantial part of the copyright work. For this element to be determined, it is necessary to examine the parameter of the work and the depth of protection, and to distinguish between the protected and non-protected parts of the work. In determining the parameter of work, it is necessary to examine what falls under copyright and what does not. In *Hyperion Records*[114] and *Newspaper Licensing Agency*,[115] it was held that the whole of the works in question will be protected by copyright and that copying individual parts will not be sufficient to amount to copyright infringement. Similarly, the protected and non-protected parts of a work are distinguished. Non-original (*Designers Guild*)[116] and irrelevant elements, including ideas, will not be included in the depth of protection provided under copyright.

Bearing the above elements in mind, if CLIMATE conducted a restricted activity over the contents of the database, this will not amount to infringement as it does not fall under the parameter of the copyright work and it is a part of the work which is not protected under copyright due to lack of originality. On the other hand, the selection and arrangement of the data falls under the parameter of the work and will be protected by copyright.

The next question that needs to be answered is whether the defendant utilises the whole of the claimant's work or a substantial part thereof. This will depend on the facts of the case and the relative importance of the part that is taken to be the claimant's work. In determining this, different types of evidence will be taken into account to assess the quality of the part that was taken by the defendant.

Therefore, in this case much will depend on the quality of the part that is to be taken for free, i.e. the labour and the skill RIM invested in choosing the data and the arrangement of that part of the database (*Newspaper Licensing Agency*), notwithstanding the size of the part that is taken. Assuming that CLIMATE seeks

---

112 *Ibcos Computers v. Barclays Mercantile Highland Finance* [1964] FSR 275.
113 *Waterlow Publishers v. Rose* [1995] PSR 409.
114 *Hyperion Records v. Warner Music* (unreported).
115 *Newspaper Licensing Agency v. Marks and Spencer* [2003] 1 AC 559.
116 *Designers Guild v. Williams* [2000] 1 WLR 2416.

to utilise the whole or a part of RIM's database that represents a qualitatively important part of its originality without complying with its licensing conditions, it can be argued that CLIMATE is at risk of commit copyright infringement.

Having in mind what was said above, it can be argued that CLIMATE will be infringing RIM's copyright over the database if it seeks to utilise the way its database was arranged and the information selected for the purpose of its own research without paying the substantial fee imposed by RIM. If this argument is accepted by the UK courts, an injunction may be granted (s. 96 CDPA 1988) to prevent free and unrestricted access to the database.

Presuming that infringement can be demonstrated, it is necessary to examine whether any of the *defences* to copyright infringement apply in this case, thereby relieving CLIMATE of liability.

The first defence that may apply is fair dealing for the purposes of research or private study as defined in section 29(1) CDPA 1988. This defence is normally very limited under UK law. In order for this defence to be granted, it is necessary that the dealing, i.e. using the work, is fair. Several factors are taken into account when determining whether the dealing is fair, including whether the work has been published, how the work was obtained, the amount of the work that was taken, the use of the work, whether there was sufficient acknowledgment of the author, the motives behind taking the work, and the consequences of using the copyright work. Moreover, it will be necessary to show that the work will be used for non-commercial research and that there will be sufficient acknowledgement of the author where appropriate.

With this in mind, it is unlikely that CLIMATE will be allowed to claim this defence, due to the fact that it is a private research company which is most likely doing research for commercial purposes. Moreover, an argument exists that if CLIMATE is seeking to achieve commercial advantage rather than contributing to the public domain, it may be justifiable for RIM to impose a substantial fee for institutions like CLIMATE.

The second defence that may be available to CLIMATE is the possibility of challenging RIM's decision to impose a substantial licensing fee on everyone wishing to access the database and on the basis that the disclosure of the data is in the public interest. This is endorsed in section 171(3) CDPA 1988, where it is stated that 'nothing … affects any rule of law preventing or restricting the enforcement of copyright, on grounds of public interest or otherwise.' The existence and the scope of this defence depend on the following three Court of Appeal cases. The public interest prevailed in *Lion Laboratories*,[117] where it was held that the information from an internal company memo was of such nature that its publication was justifiable. The *Hyde Park*[118] case reinforces the

[117] *Lion Labaratories v. Evans* [1985] QB 526.
[118] *Hyde Park v. Yelland* [2000] EMLR 363.

inherent jurisdiction of the courts to refuse a claim for infringement of copyright where the enforcement of copyright would offend against the policy of the law. In *Ashdown*,[119] the Court of Appeal in the end concluded that 'there may be circumstances in which the public interest required the verbatim publication of copyright material. However, these are rare'. The public interest defence for the infringement of copyright was affirmed for the first time in the *Beloff*[120] case. Although the defence of public interest did not apply in the case, Ungoed-Thomas J stated that 'public interest is a defence outside and independent of statutes, is not limited to copyright cases and is based on a general principle of common law.'[121]

In addition to the arguments proposed above, Waelde and McGinley argue against licensing as a way of regulating access to a database due to its tendency of 'constraining the already limited public domain at the behest of the copyright owner or database maker.'[122] On the contrary, there is a strong public interest in the works created through funding with public money and these databases should be free and in the public domain for maximum public benefit.

Bearing these academic arguments in mind and the legally enforceable concept of 'public interest', it may be possible to argue that the licence imposed by RIM contradicts the public interest in having the information freely accessible for further research development (which arguably CLIMATE seeks to achieve) and the nature and purpose of RIM as a 100% publicly owned institution. If this argument is accepted by the courts, CLIMATE will most probably be allowed to defend itself on grounds of public interest in disclosing the database information.

However, in order to cover both possibilities, it is necessary to mention and note the argument that CLIMATE remains a private research company whose purpose is arguably not providing benefit to the public through using RIM's database and publishing additional research, but rather private commercial advancement. There is a possibility that RIM's copyright work (the method of selecting or arranging the database) will be used for achieving results which will then be 'drawn into and exploited by the private sector to the detriment of both advancement of science and public interest'.[123] Bearing this argument in mind, it may be possible to argue that a licensing fee should be and is justifiably imposed on institutions such as CLIMATE who only seek to achieve private commercial advancements.

---

119 *Ashdown v. Telegraph* [2001] 3 WLR 1368.

120 *Beloff v. Pressdram Ltd* [1973] All ER 241–273.

121 T. Guanhong, 'Comparative Study of Copyright and the Public Interest in the United Kingdom and China' (2004) 1(2) *SCRIPTED, A Journal of Technology and Society* 273–300.

122 C. Waelde and M. McGinley, 'Public Domain; Public Interest; Public Funding: focussing on the "three Ps" in scientific research' (2005) 2(1) *SCRIPTED, A Journal of Technology and Society* 71–97.

123 Ibid.

Moreover, as RIM is 100% publicly owned, it can also be argued that the licensing fee should be imposed, as the proceeds will go back into the public domain. Whether CLIMATE will be allowed to claim the public disclosure interest defence will depend on the court's interpretation of what will be the best solution for satisfying the public interest in free information and providing benefit to the public through motivating new scientific research and breakthroughs.

2. Sui generis database protection

The aim of Directive 96/9/EC is to 'remove existing differences in the legal protection of databases by harmonising the rules that applied to copyright protection, safeguard investment of database makers and ensure that the legitimate interests of users to access information compiled in databases are secured.'[124] In England and Wales, the Database Directive was implemented by the Copyright and Rights in Databases Regulations 1997. Under Regulation 13 of the 1997 Regulations, database rights subsist in a database if 'there has been a *substantial investment* in obtaining, verifying or presenting the contents of the database.' This right is mainly intended to protect non-original databases which fail the normal copyright tests.

Therefore, even though the contents of RIM's database cannot be protected under copyright law, it may be possible to establish qualification under this right if there has been substantial investment in obtaining, verifying or presenting the contents of database. The European Court of Justice in the *British Horseracing Board*[125] case held that 'the investment in the selection, for the purpose of organising horse racing, of the horses admitted to run in a race related to the creation of the data which make up the lists for those races which appear in the BHB database.'[126] Thus the investment by BHB in that activity was not relevant when considering the '*sui generis* right.'[127] The rule that seems to come out of this case is that even publicly available information could be protectable, provided that significant investment in the collation of the information can be shown.

In this case, it is not exactly clear whether RIM as a company only gathers, organises and interprets meteorological data or whether it also creates the data to produce the contents for the database. If RIM creates this data, it may be possible to qualify for protection under standard copyright rules. On the other

---

124 J. Jenkins, 'Database rights' subsistence: under starter's orders' (2006) 1(7) *Journal of Intellectual Property Law & Practice* 467–480, available at https://doi.org/10.1093/jiplp/jpl059 (last accessed 2021).

125 *The British Horseracing Board Ltd and Others v. William Hill Organization Ltd*, A3/2001/0632, 13 July 2005.

126 C. Waelde and M. McGinley, 'Public Domain; Public Interest; Public Funding: focussing on the "three Ps" in scientific research' (2005) 2(1) *SCRIPTED, A Journal of Technology and Society* 73.

127 Ibid.

hand, if RIM's primary activity is to obtain, verify or present the existing data to create a database for which it had to make substantial investments, it can qualify for *sui generis* database protection under the Directive.

The database right gives the owner the right to prevent copying and unauthorised use of the database. Under Regulation 16(1) of the 1997 Regulations, 'a person infringes database right in a database if, without the consent of the owner of the right, he *extracts* or *re-utilises* all or a *substantial* part of the contents of the database.' (Emphasis added.) 'Extraction' is defined in Regulation 12 of the 1997 Regulations as 'the permanent or temporary transfer of the contents of the database to another medium by any means or in any form.' 'Re-utilisation' is defined in the same section as 'making the contents of the database available to the public by any means' and 'substantial' is defined 'in terms of quantity or quality or a combination of both.' Therefore, in order for CLIMATE to be infringing the *sui generis* database right, it is necessary that it extracted or re-utilised a substantial part of RIM's database for free and without any restrictions, i.e. not complying with the licensing requirements.

Finally, it is necessary to determine the *defences* for infringement of the *sui generis* database right. Regulation 20(1)(a) of the 1997 Regulations endorses the defence of extraction by a 'lawful user', whereby it is allowed to extract or re-utilise insubstantial parts of the database for any purpose. The term 'lawful user' is unsatisfactorily left undefined in the Directive. However, 'it appears from the European decisions on this issue that most uses of parts of a database will be determined qualitatively rather than quantitatively and may be deemed to be substantial by virtue of their perceived benefit to the end-user'.[128] Bearing this in mind, it may be possible to argue that CLIMATE will avoid liability on grounds that it extracted or re-utilised an insubstantial part of the database without RIM's consent. This will consequently depend on the way the courts interpret the term 'insubstantial'.

In conclusion, assuming that RIM's database satisfies the strict originality criteria, copyright protection can be established and hence an injunction may be claimed. This will once again depend on the court's discretion in deciding whether to enforce the public interest in free information over copyright protection. On the other hand, the broad *sui generis* right can provide protection for the contents of the database against substantial extraction or re-utilisation unless CLIMATE qualifies as a lawful user, in which case RIM cannot claim an injunction.

---

128 *The British Horseracing Board Ltd and Others v. William Hill Organization Ltd*, A3/2001/0632, 13 July 2005 and S. Corbett, 'A Human Rights Perspective on the Database Directive' [2006] 28(2) *European Intellectual Property Review* 83–91.

III. *Metalegal Formants*

This problem question raises the issue of the longstanding debate between protecting the public interest in free information and ensuring that sufficient incentives are provided to researchers and investors through copyright law.

UK copyright law has proved to be particularly unsatisfactory in establishing a balance between these two competing values due to a strict originality test and limited exceptions to copyright infringement. Corbett argues that 'traditional copyright protection for databases, while offering the advantages of limited public interest access and a finite term of protection, has been demonstrated to be unsatisfactory owing to its uncertainty and international inconsistency'.[129] Besides this, as was seen in the *Feist* decision, the copyright protection for factual databases is very thin due to the inability to satisfy the high creativity criteria. On the other hand, copyright has to be noted 'for a near complete lack of procedural formalities'[130] because it arises simultaneously with the emergence of the work without any registration requirements, which is 'one of the attractions of copyright.[131]

The aim of the Directive was to harmonise the protection of databases across the board and strike a balance between 'the interests of the manufacturers of databases and the legitimate interests of their users'.[132] Indeed, the *sui generis* database right provides protection for non-original databases (thereby enforcing the interests of the manufacturers and guaranteeing an appropriate return on their investments), but at the same time allows insubstantial extractions or re-utilisations of database contents, whereby it seeks to satisfy the public interest in having free access to information.

However, 'a key concern in relation to the Directive has been a perception that the *sui generis* right seems close to grant of an intellectual property right in data and information *per se*, allowing only limited extractions for the purposes of non-commercial research'.[133] The result is somewhat similar to the case in question, where scientists such as those at CLIMATE[134] 'may suffer restrictions on access to the raw data necessary for scientific progress'. Indeed, scientists, researchers, teachers and librarians call the Directive 'one of the least balanced and most potentially anti-competitive intellectual property rights ever'.[135]

---

129 Corbett, ibid., p. 7.

130 S. Klein, 'Search engines and copyright: an analysis of the Belgian Copiepresse decision in consideration of British and German copyright law' [2008] 39(4) *International Review of Intellectual Property and Competition Law* 451.

131 T. Dworkin, *Blackstone's Guide to the Copyright, Designs and Patents Act 1988* (Oxford: 1989).

132 C. Waelde and M. McGinley, 'Public Domain; Public Interest; Public Funding: focussing on the "three Ps" in scientific research' (2005) 2(1) *SCRIPTED, A Journal of Technology and Society* 73.

133 Ibid.

134 Ibid.

135 S. Corbett, 'A Human Rights Perspective on the Database Directive' [2006] *European Intellectual Property Review* 6.

As a solution to this problem, academics suggest repealing the whole Directive, withdrawing the *sui generis* right or amending the *sui generis* provision. Moreover, Corbett suggests that the right approach is a human rights property approach, which will promote coherent and balanced legal norms that enhance both individual rights and economic welfare.[136] Whichever approach is adopted, it is necessary to ensure a 'balance between private interests and public rights while ensuring the commercial needs of database producers, access to information and prevention of unfair commercial competition',[137] a balance very difficult to achieve in almost every area of law.

A.4. COMPARATIVE REMARKS

The reports mirror the European influence. All jurisdictions see RIM as the producer of the database with an exclusive right.[138] The laws do not differentiate between public or private institutions in this regard. In many countries, the public issue comes in with the limitation on fees.[139] Still, incurring costs for passing on the information and a reasonable return on investment is the bottom line for which Article 6 Directive 2003/98/EC is the basis.[140] Although public sector information as such can be protected, the European legislator has recognised that some special requirements are needed in comparison to information gathered by private entities. In Germany, it is debated whether the scope of §5 II UrhG (no copyright for official/public creations) should be applied to databases. In the UK and Lithuania, one could possibly demand free and unrestricted access to RIM's database on grounds of public interest. The Slovenian situation is exceptional. It has its own Act that applies to the given case, namely the Meteorological Activities Act. This statute orders that the data concerned shall be made public. RIM would nevertheless have a claim for a fee, if CLIMATE wants to re-use the information. Some states have also considered that CLIMATE could, depending on the specific circumstances, claim a licence on the basis of competition law, but surely not for free.[141]

---

136 M.J. Davison, *The Legal Protection of Databases* (Cambridge: 2003) and P. Vandrevala, 'A Study on the Impact of Protection of Unoriginal Databases on Developing Countries: The Indian Experience', WIPO SCCR 7/5, 2002.

137 A. Mazumdar, 'Information, copyright and the future' [2007] *European Intellectual Property Review* 1.

138 The kind of the right seems to be different. The UK approach is unusual, as the right can be a classic copyright as well as a *sui generis* right.

139 See the reports of Belgium, Czech Republic, Denmark, Germany, Norway and Slovenia.

140 Nevertheless, it is difficult to define what 'reasonable' means in a concrete case. It is an open term, which can be interpreted in different ways by different parties. Thus, the effectiveness of the limitation given by Directive 2003/98/EC can be questioned.

141 See the reports of Belgium, Estonia, Germany, Norway and Poland.

CASE 5. THE RIGHT TO BE NAMED (MORAL RIGHTS)

A.1. CASE

Richard, a scientist with the renowned pharmaceutical company IPC, buys a computer programme, the top-selling product of IT-Company (ITC), which organises his article database. The programme has been written by the renowned Professor Higgens at Y-University. A specific algorithm, developed by him, is the core of the programme. This is widely known in the relevant community. In order to strengthen its marketing position, ITC markets the programme enclosing a licence agreement that obliges commercial users to cite the company's name (ITC) when improving the programme; explicitly, any reference to Professor Higgens is forbidden. The contract between Higgens and ITC is silent about the original personality right of Prof. Higgens.

Does Prof. Higgens have the right to be named if Richard adapts ITC's programme to the needs of pharmaceutical companies? Can Higgens claim an injunction if IPC markets the improved product making reference only to ITC?

A.2. COUNTRY REPORTS

(1) BELGIUM

I. Operative Rules

Yes, Prof. Higgens has the right to be named and can claim an injunction to stop marketing the improved product without mentioning his name.

II. Descriptive Formants

- Article 6bis Berne Convention;[1]
- Software Directive 91/250/EC;[2]

1 Berne Convention of 9 September 1886 for the Protection of Literary and Artistic Works, as approved by the Act of 25 March 1999, *Official Gazette*, 10 November 1999.

2 Council Directive 91/250/EEC of 14 May 1991 on the legal protection of computer programs, OJ L 122, 17 May 1991, 42–46.

- Articles 3 and 4 BSA[3] (Arts. XI.296 and XI.297 BCEL);
- Articles 1§2, 3, 86ter and 87 BCA (Arts. XI.165§2, XI.167, XI.334 and XVII.14 BCEL).

The starting assumption to solve the present case is that the algorithm developed by Prof. Higgens is protectable under copyright law, more particularly under the BSA, which implements the Software Directive 91/250/EC[4] (now Book XI, Title VI BCEL).

a) Does Prof. Higgens have the right to be named?
According to Article 4 of the BSA (Art. XI.297 BCEL), the moral rights on computer programmes are regulated by Article 6bis of the Berne Convention. Article 6bis Berne Convention stipulates that: 'Independently of the author's economic rights, and even after the transfer of the said rights, the author shall have the right to claim authorship of the work and to object to any distortion, mutilation or other modification of, or other derogatory action in relation to, the said work, which would be prejudicial to his honour or reputation.'

Although the scope of the moral rights of an author of a computer programme seems *less* than the scope of the moral rights of other authors (as laid down in Art. 1§2 BCA,[5] now Art. XI.165§2 BCEL), the author of a computer programme clearly has the right to claim authorship of the work.[6]

It is still open for debate whether or not this moral right is inalienable (as stipulated in Art. 1§2 BCA, now Art. XI.165§2 BCEL), in the sense of whether a global transfer or renunciation would be possible or not.[7] Belgian legal doctrine takes the view that well-defined consent to a specific exploitation of the moral right is valid.[8] The case clearly indicates that the contract is silent about the

3 Software Act, 30 June 1994, *Official Gazette*, 27 July 1994 [Wet 30 juni 1994 houdende omzetting in Belgisch recht van de Europese richtlijn van 14 mei 1991 betreffende de rechtsbescherming van computerprogramma's, *B.S.*, 27 July 1994].

4 For more information: A. Strowel and E. Derclaye, *Droit d'auteur et numérique: logiciels, bases de données, multimédia. Droit belge, européen et comparé* [Copyright and the Numeric: software, databases and multimedia. Belgian, European and Comparative Law] (Brussels: 2001), 192.

5 A. Strowel and E. Derclaye, *Droit d'auteur et numérique: logiciels, bases de données, multimédia. Droit belge, européen et comparé [Copyright and the Numeric: software, databases and multimedia. Belgian, European and Comparative Law]* (Brussels: 2001), 210–213.

6 Y. van den Brande and J. Keustermans, 'Open source software: een analyse naar Belgisch recht' [Open Source Software: an Analysis according to Belgian Law], *I.R.D.I.* 2007, 375–376.

7 A. Strowel and E. Derclaye, *Droit d'auteur et numérique: logiciels, bases de données, multimédia. Droit belge, européen et compare [Copyright and the Numeric: software, databases and multimedia. Belgian, European and Comparative Law]* (Brussels: 2001), 212–213.

8 Art. 1§2 BCA (*a contrario*) as explained by F. Gotzen, 'Art.1', in: F. Brison and H. Vanhees (eds.), *Huldeboek aan Jan Corbet. De Belgische Auteurswet. Artikelsgewijze Commentaar [Homage to Jan Corbet. The Belgian Copyright Act. Commentaries Article per Article]* (Brussels: 2006), 15 – referring to the Report De Clerck, Bill on Copyright and Neighbouring Rights, *Parl. Doc.*, Chambre, Special Session 1991/1992, DOC 48 473/33, 70–71 [Verslag De Clerck bij het wetsontwerp betreffende het auteursrecht en de naburige rechten, *Parl. St.*,

personality rights. Hence no transfer of moral rights has been negotiated nor can such transfer be presumed (not as an employee, nor as a contractor or a licensor) (Art. 3 BCA and Art. 3 BSA).[9] Therefore, Prof. Higgens is still in possession of all moral rights on his programme.

b) Can Higgens claim an injunction when IPC markets the improved product making reference only to ITC?
Taking a look at Articles 5a) and b) of the BSA (Arts. XI.298a) and b) BCEL) and given the fact that Prof. Higgens' algorithm will undoubtedly be re-used,[10] it becomes clear that the improved programme will still be covered by ITC's economic rights:

> the economic rights [of a computer programme] shall comprise:
>
> (a) the permanent or temporary reproduction of a computer program by any means and in any form, in part or in whole. Insofar as loading, displaying, running, transmission or storage of the computer program necessitate such reproduction, such acts shall be subject to authorisation by the rightholder;
> (b) the translation, adaptation, arrangement and any other alteration of a computer program and the reproduction of the results thereof, without prejudice to the rights of the person who alters the program.

Since ITC merely possesses the economic rights,[11] Prof. Higgens can exercise the moral rights on the improved programme. Thus, at any given time, Prof. Higgens can claim that the copies of his programme have to be marketed under his name.[12] If his request is not granted, he could ask a judge to forbid the marketing of the programme without mentioning his name (on the basis of e.g. Arts. 86ter and 87 BCA, now Arts. XI.334 and XVII.14 BCEL).

Contrary to 'general' copyright,[13] no specific case law is known to us.

Kamer, B.Z. 91/92, DOC 48 473/33, 70–71], available at: www.dekamer.be (last consulted 5 May 2019).

9 For a good understanding, for the issues left open by the Software Act, it is supplemented by the 'general' Copyright Act: A. Strowel and E. Derclaye, *Droit d'auteur et numérique: logiciels, bases de données, multimédia. Droit belge, européen et comparé [Copyright and the Numeric: software, databases and multimedia. Belgian, European and Comparative Law]* (Brussels: 2001), 175–176.

10 The aim of this project in mind, we assume the algorithm is protectable under copyright law. For more information: A. Strowel and E. Derclaye, *Droit d'auteur et numérique: logiciels, bases de données, multimédia. Droit belge, européen et comparé [Copyright and the Numeric: software, databases and multimedia. Belgian, European and Comparative Law]* (Brussels: 2001), 192.

11 See above under a): no transfer of the moral rights has been negotiated, nor can such a transfer be presumed.

12 H. Vanhees, 'Art. 1–14 Wet Bescherming Computerprogramma's (Art. 4)' [Art. 1–14 Software Act (Art.4)], in H. Swennen (ed.), *Handels- en economisch recht. Commentaar met overzicht van rechtspraak en rechtsleer [Commercial and Economic Law. Commentary and Overview of Case Law and Doctrine]* (Brussels: 1995), 1–2.

13 Belgian Supreme Court [Cass.] (1st Chamber), 22 May 1980, *Ing. Cons.* 1981, 354, note M. Demeur; Court of Appeal Brussels, 29 March 1991, *R.W.* 1991–92, 814; Court of Appeal

III. Metalegal Formants

The Software Directive 91/250/EC does not regulate authors' moral rights. Following some discussion,[14] the Belgian legislator chose to refer to Article 6bis Berne Convention. Following the Berne regime leaves the author of computer programmes with only a few moral rights compared to a conventional author subject to the BCA. In this regard, the integrity right is far less extensive and a possible divulgation right for software is disputed.[15] The paternity right, however, is foreseen in Article 6bis Berne Convention and thus applies to software in Belgium.

Since 1994, employees developing software are presumed to have transferred their economic rights to their employers (Art. 3 BSA, now Art. XI.296 BCEL). The rationale was to avoid some practical complications and to give some guarantees to software companies who are deemed to be the economic actors taking the real initiative in specific software development. The moral rights, however, have never been included in this presumption. This was subject to criticism during the parliamentary debates on the BSA.[16] The same applies to licensors and contractors, for whom not even the presumption above exists. Therefore, careful drafting of contracts is necessary, and to a large extent feasible.[17]

(2) CZECH REPUBLIC

I. Operative Rules

Professor Higgens has a right to be named. An injunction will be granted in his favour.

Mons, 2 October 1997, *J.T.* 1998, 168. For more information F. de Visscher and B. Michaux, *Précis du droit d'auteur et des droits voisins [Manual Copyright and Neighbouring Rights]* (Brussels: 2000), 154–156.

14 Report, Bill on the Implementation of European Directive 91/250/EEC, *Parl. Doc.*, Chambre, 1992–1993, DOC 48 1078/6, 11–15 [Verslag bij wetsvoorstel houdende omzetting in Belgisch recht van de Europese richtlijn van 14 mei 1991 betreffende de rechtsbescherming van computerprogramma's, *Parl. St.*, Kamer, 1992–1993, DOC 48 1078/6, 11–15].

15 A. Strowel and E. Derclaye, *Droit d'auteur et numérique: logiciels, bases de données, multimédia. Droit belge, européen et comparé [Copyright and the Numeric: software, databases and multimedia. Belgian, European and Comparative Law]* (Brussels: 2001), 210–213.

16 Report, Bill on the Implementation of European Directive 91/250/EEC, *Parl. Doc.*, Chambre, 1992–1993, DOC 48 1078/6, 11–15 [Verslag bij wetsvoorstel houdende omzetting in Belgisch recht van de Europese richtlijn van 14 mei 1991 betreffende de rechtsbescherming van computerprogramma's, *Parl. St.*, Kamer, 1992–1993, DOC 48 1078/6, 11–15].

17 J.A. Keustermans (ed.), *Informatica & Recht [Informatics & Law]* (Brussels: 1997), 93–97.

II. Descriptive Formants

In this case, it will be necessary to discover what part of computer programme was made by Professor Higgens. According to section 2(2) Copyright Act, a computer programme shall be deemed to be a work if the programme is original in the sense of being the author's own intellectual creation; otherwise, a pure algorithm is not protected according to section 2(6) Copyright Act.

A more concrete legal basis, in respect of computer programmes, is section 65 Copyright Act, which is based on Article 1 of Council Directive 91/250/EEC. Section 65 Copyright Act says that computer programmes shall be protected as literary works. This includes preparatory design material but not ideas and principles which underlie any element of a computer programme. An algorithm as such is deemed to be an idea and principle on which a computer programme is based.[18]

If Professor Higgens developed just an algorithm for the computer programme or any other idea or principle, and not more than that, then the injunction will not be granted. But in the present case, Professor Higgens wrote more and the computer programme is his own intellectual creation. This would be a typical example where the author has the right to be named. The right to be named is expressed in section 11(2) Copyright Act. Traditionally, according to the doctrine, this right is called the right to author's indication.[19] The first part of section 11(2) Copyright Act must be interpreted as the author's absolute right to claim authorship.

In respect of the adapted version of the computer programme, Professor Higgens has just as much a right to be named as he had in relation to former version. As mentioned above, the computer programme is protected as a literary work and the analogical relation in this case is the same as that between the author of a literary work and the author of an adapted version of that literary work.

The injunction will be granted in this case.

III. Metalegal Formants

Answer omitted.

---

18 See further J. Kříž, I. Holcová, J. Kordač, V. Křesťanová, *Autorský zákon komentář a předpisy související* (Copyright Act, Commentary and related regulations) (2nd ed., Prague: 2005), p. 190.

19 Ibid., p. 82.

(3) DENMARK

I. Operative Rules

Professor Higgens would probably not have a right to be named. No injunction would thus be granted.

II. Descriptive Formants

A computer programme is protected as a work pursuant to DCA §1, provided that it fulfils the originality criteria. Prof. Higgens has a right to be named as author of the work 'in accordance with proper usage', cf. DCA §3, first paragraph. It follows, however, from DCA §59 that the copyright to a computer programme which has been produced in the course of employment passes to the employer. This transfer includes the moral rights.

It is not entirely clear whether or not §59 applies to university professors etc. The traditional position would be that the 'professor's privilege' which can be said to apply to traditional scientific and scholarly works would also include computer programmes. Some remarks made by the legislator in passing a statute which revoked the 'privilege' for patentable inventions in 2000 seem to indicate, however, that DCA §59 should be understood as including all employees, including professors and other research personnel at universities. There is no case law on this matter, but it would seem most likely that a Danish court would find that Prof. Higgens is covered by §59. The right to the programme, therefore, passes to the University and this would seem to also include the right to be named. The legal position is, however, not completely clear and courts may argue that for an author to lose his/her right to be named according to DCA §3, a more precise legal foundation than the present one would be needed.

III. Metalegal Formants

Danish copyright law, like the other Scandinavian laws, is based on the *droit d'auteur* tradition. The right to be named (paternity right) and the right to respect (*droit au respect*) are based on the obligations from Article 6bis of the Berne Convention. The *droit moral* aspect is emphasised, in that the paternity right as such is inalienable – only use limited in nature and extent can be waived. Against this background, it is very peculiar that the work-for-hire rule in DCA §59 includes the moral rights. The wording of the present rule is from the Directive on Computer Programs (Directive 91/250/EC), but the principles predate that Directive. The reason given for the very broad transfer of the rights is the special circumstances involved in the production of computer programmes (capital-intensive production and work by teams of technicians) and the 'non-artistic' character of such programmes. The automatic transfer of moral rights would seem to be troublesome in the light of the obligations imposed by the Berne Convention. Furthermore, the assumptions behind the rule, especially the general notion that computer programmes *per se* are non-artistic, would seem to be of a rather dubious nature. On balance, §59 does not represent a highlight in the history of Danish copyright lawmaking.

(4) ESTONIA

I. Operative Rules

Prof. Higgens enjoys the right to be named and can successfully claim an injunction.

II. Descriptive Formants

The case concerns the rights of a person who has created a computer programme. Computer programmes are protected as literary works (§4(3) clause 3 Copyright Act). According to §11(1) Copyright Act, '[c]opyright in a work arises upon the creation of the work by the author of the work. Moral rights and economic rights constitute the content of copyright'. The central issue of the case concerns the possibility to exercise certain moral rights (the right of authorship and the right of author's name). The right of authorship is defined as 'the right to appear in public as the creator of the work and claim recognition of the fact of creation of the work by way of relating the authorship of the work to the author's person and name upon any use of the work' (§12(1) clause 1 Copyright Act) and the right of author's name as 'the right to decide in which manner the author's name shall be designated upon use of the work – as the real name of the author, identifying mark of the author, a fictitious name (pseudonym) or without a name (anonymously)' (§12(1) clause 2 Copyright Act).

The general term of protection of the copyright in Estonia is 70 years *post mortem auctoris* (§38 Copyright Act). This means that after this period a work comes into the public domain, and everyone is entitled to use it. However, the right to use a work in the public domain is not without limitations. Some rights of the author are protected without a time limit. Subsection 44(1) Copyright Act provides: '[t]he authorship of a certain work, the name of the author and the honour and reputation of the author shall be protected without a term'. The reason to protect authorship without a term has been explained by H. Pisuke as follows: '[a]uthorship is a notion that expresses the relation between the creator and the result of his or her specific creative activity (work). Authorship is a link over time; as long as a work exists, we can speak about authorship'.[20]

It appears from the case that Prof. Higgens created the computer programme to fulfil his contractual obligations. It is not specified whether it was an employment contract or not. If the programme was created during the employment, then the following regulation applies (§32(5) Copyright Act):

> The author of a computer programme or the author of a database who creates the programme or database in the execution of his or her duties or following the instructions given by his or her employer shall enjoy a copyright in the programme or database but the employer has the exclusive licence[21] to exercise all economic rights unless otherwise provided by contract.

The Estonian Supreme Court has taken a wider approach to the concept of employment than a literal interpretation of the Copyright Act. The Supreme Court has emphasised that §32 Copyright Act is also applicable to other lasting contractual relationships, but not to the fulfilment of a single order. For instance, a contract between a company and a board member could constitute a lasting contractual relationship.[22] In the present case, nothing mentions that there was a continuous working relationship between Prof. Higgens and ITC. Even if we could say that there is an employment or a continuous working relationship between Prof. Higgens and ITC, it would only mean that ITC has the exclusive licence to use the economic rights. The moral rights belong to an author regardless of whether a work is created under an employment contract or in fulfilment of a single contractual obligation (e.g. writing a specific computer programme). It is always necessary to address the issue of the moral rights in a licensing agreement. Otherwise, an author has the exclusive right to exercise them. The existing case law on problems related to the ownership of IP is not very extensive in Estonia. However, there is some literature.[23]

---

20 H. Pisuke, 'Moral Rights of Author in Estonian Copyright Law', (2002) 1 *Juridica International*, pp. 166–175, p. 169.

21 The Copyright Act differentiates computer programmes and other works created within employment. According to §32(1) of the Copyright Act, '[t]he author of a work created under an employment contract or in the public service in the execution of his or her direct duties shall enjoy copyright in the work but the economic rights of the author to use the work for the purpose and to the extent prescribed by the duties shall be transferred to the employer unless otherwise prescribed by contract'. As seen, the economic rights are usually transferred (not exclusively licensed) to the employer. However, the situation is different with computer programmes.

22 Judgment of Civil Chamber of Supreme Court, 23 May 2003 (3-2-1-39-03) – RT III 2003, 20, 196, clause 23.

23 See. J. Ostrat, 'Töösuhtes või muu lepingu täitmisel tehtud leiutise õigusliku reguleerimise probleeme. Kas lepinguvabadus või eraldi seadus?' (Problems in the Legal Regulation of an Employment-Relationship Invention. Freedom of Contract or a Separate Law?), (2007) 3 *Juridica*, pp. 189–198 (in Estonian); A. Kelli, 'Some Issues of the Estonian Innovation and Intellectual Property Policy', (2008) 15 *Juridica International*, pp. 104–114.

There is one additional legal issue which needs to be highlighted. The right of integrity of the work is a moral right of the author. The Copyright Act defines it as 'the right to make or permit other persons to make any changes to the work, its title (name) or designation of the author's name and the right to contest any changes made without the author's consent' (§12(1) clause 3 Copyright Act). If the right of integrity of the work is not licensed to ITC, then no changes are allowed to the programme.

As is given in the case, the contract is silent about the moral rights. This means that ITC is not allowed to exercise them. According to §81^3(1) Copyright Act, violation of the moral rights is punishable by a fine of up to 300 fine units.

Civil remedies are available to Prof. Higgens as well. Subsection 81^7(1) Copyright Act provides that in the case of the unlawful use of a work or an object of related rights, the author or holder of related rights may, *inter alia*, claim compensation for damages and termination of the unlawful use of a work or an object of related rights.

III. Metalegal Formants

The impact of the moral rights on possibilities to utilise a work should not be underestimated. If the moral rights are ignored, many potential problems may arise.

Some of the moral rights may interfere with the economic exploitation of a work. One aspect concerns the right of authorship and the right of author's name. The other is connected with the possibilities to change the work (e.g. a computer programme). The catalogue of the moral rights (§12(1) Copyright Act) includes *inter alia* the right to:

1. 'make or permit other persons to make any changes to the work, its title (name) or designation of the author's name and the right to contest any changes made without the author's consent (right of integrity of the work)';
2. 'permit the addition of other authors' works to the author's work (illustrations, forewords, epilogues, comments, explanations, additional parts, etc.) (right of additions to the work)'; or
3. 'supplement and improve the author's work which is made public (right of supplementation of the work)'.

It can be concluded from the provisions that changing, improving, etc. a work violates moral rights.

Whereas the economic rights are transferable (§11(3) Copyright Act), that is not the case with the moral rights. The Copyright Act[24] explicitly provides

[24] Section 39 of the Constitution of the Republic of Estonia also provides the following principle: '[a]n author has the inalienable right to his or her work'. A literal interpretation of this section

that '[t]he moral rights of an author are inseparable from the author's person and non-transferable' (§11(2) Copyright Act). This provision gives rise to the question of whether it is possible to license the moral rights. The general understanding is that licensing moral rights is allowed.[25] The wording of some provisions of the Copyright Act supports this approach. For instance, pursuant to §12(1) clause 3 of the Copyright Act, '[t]he author of a work has the right to make or *permit other persons to make* any changes to the work, its title (name) or designation of the author's name and the right to contest any changes made without the author's consent (right of integrity of the work)' (emphasis added). As indicated, the provision allows the author to 'permit other persons to make …'. Such permission could probably be formalised as a licence agreement (author's contract).[26]

Based on the above, it can be said that it is presumably possible to license at least some of the moral rights. Many aspects relating to licensing of the moral rights remain a controversial issue in Estonian legal literature. For instance, H. Pisuke suggests: 'for the purposes of Estonian law, moral rights cannot be assigned. However, it is possible to issue an exclusive licence and a non-exclusive licence for exercising any moral right'.[27] There are differing opinions. M. Rosentau argues that licensing the moral rights *in corpore et in genere* is not allowed. It is essential to agree on how every single moral right will be exercised. Some moral rights are not licensable at all.[28]

In the context of the analysed case, it does not matter if we adopt a wider or narrower approach to licensing of the moral rights. In both instances there has to be an agreement,[29] which in this case does not exist. Another issue is how to license the right of authorship and the right of author's name. H. Pisuke is of opinion that 'it is possible to issue an exclusive licence and a non-exclusive licence for exercising any moral right. … Thus, in Estonian law, the issues related

could mean that it is not allowed to transfer or license the moral and economic rights. This, however, is not the case. The problem has been analysed by H. Pisuke. See H. Pisuke, 'Kas autori õigusi saab võõrandada?' (Are the author's rights inalienable?), (1994) 4 *Juridica*, pp. 89–90.

25 See A. Kalvi, 'Autorilepingu uus kuub' (New skin of author's contracts), (2003) 4 *Juridica*, pp. 250–260, p. 258.

26 An author's contract is defined as 'an agreement between the author or his or her legal successor and a person who wishes to use the work for the use of a work on the basis of which the author or his or her legal successor transfers the author's patrimonial rights to the other party or grants to the other party an authorisation to use the work to the extent and pursuant to the procedure prescribed by the conditions of the contract' – Copyright Act §48(1).

27 H. Pisuke, 'Moral Rights of Author in Estonian Copyright Law', (2002) 1 *Juridica International*, pp. 166–175, p. 170.

28 M. Rosentau, 'Intellektuaalse omandi õigused infotehnoloogias. Autori isiklikud õigused' (Intellectual Property Rights in Information Technology. The Personal (Moral) Rights of the Author), (2007) 9 *Juridica*, pp. 651–666, p. 654.

29 A general licence or detailed licence with defined terms for exercising every licensed moral right.

to the so-called "ghost authors", authors of trademark and other issues that may come up in practice have been settled'.[30] M. Rosentau specifies that if the right of authorship and the right of author's name are licensed, then it is important to have a detailed agreement on how these rights will be exercised.[31] In order to avoid problems, ITC should conclude a licensing agreement which would *expressis verbis* allow marketing of the computer programme without naming Prof. Higgens as an author and improving the programme.

(5) FRANCE

I. Operative Rules

Assuming that Professor Higgens' computer programme was protectable by copyright laws, he has a right to be named and can claim an injunction.

II. Descriptive Formants

The question that immediately comes to mind is related to the existence of moral rights, and more precisely authorship rights, as far as computer programmes are concerned.

Therefore, it is of crucial importance to clarify the current framework relating to the intellectual property legislation applicable to computer programmes, before providing an answer to the aforementioned question.

Computer programmes are protectable in French law by patent or copyright laws. Under patent law, Article L. 611-10 of the French Intellectual Property Code provides that:

1. Inventions which are susceptible of industrial application, which are new, and which involve an inventive step shall be patentable.
2. The following in particular shall not be regarded as inventions within the meaning of the first paragraph of this Article:
   a) discoveries, scientific theories and mathematical methods;
   b) aesthetic creations;
   c) schemes, rules and methods for performing mental acts, playing games or doing business, and programs for computers;
   d) presentations of information.

---

30 H. Pisuke, 'Moral Rights of Author in Estonian Copyright Law', (2002) 1 *Juridica International*, pp. 166–175, pp. 170–171.

31 M. Rosentau, 'Intellektuaalse omandi õigused infotehnoloogias. Autori isiklikud õigused' (Intellectual Property Rights in Information Technology. The Personal (Moral) Rights of the Author), (2007) 9 *Juridica*, pp. 651–666, pp. 660–661.

In addition, Article 52 of the European Patent Convention (EPC) also rejects the patentability of mathematical methods and computer programmes.

In the present context, Prof. Higgens originally conceived of both the programme and the algorithm, a core component of the programme. However, neither the former nor the latter is eligible for protection conferred by means of a patent. Indeed, the algorithm, which may be considered as a mathematical method, cannot in any case be patented. Moreover, in regard to computer programmes as a whole, Article L. 611-10 of the French Intellectual Property Code expressly rejects the patentability of computer programmes. Thus, the computer programme in question is not patentable and as a result authorship claims lack any legal grounds. Moreover, case law confirms this. A decision of the French Supreme Court dating back to 28 May 1975 rejected a patent application seeking protection for a computer programme and stated that computer programmes are not patentable.[32] Thus, the computer programme of Prof. Higgens cannot be patented. As a result, the case of IP rights eventually conferred by copyright laws has to be examined.

Under copyright law, Article L. 112-2 of the French Intellectual Property Code states that computer programmes, including materialised preparatory concepts, can be considered to be intellectual works, protected by copyright laws. As a result, a computer programme which conforms to the definition of an intellectual work may be copyrightable. Therefore, both computer programmes and underlying algorithms may be protected by copyright laws, if the following two criteria are fulfilled.

First, the intellectual work has to be fixed in an original form. Such a condition excludes from protection any non-materialised idea, given that ideas are free and that only a work's creation confers on an author the very quality of author. As a result, whatever resembles an idea and is not fixed is not protected by copyright laws. As far as computer programmes are concerned, Article 1(2) of Directive 91/250/EEC of 14 March 1991 on the legal protection of computer programmes[33] makes clear that the exclusive rights conferred by copyright laws do not cover non-materialised ideas. In that sense, Recital 13 of the aforementioned Directive clarifies that 'ideas, underlying algorithm principles as well as computer programme languages' are not protected. This general principle has not been explicitly transposed into French law. However, according to the hierarchy of laws, the Directive in question, like any other EU Directive, is of capital importance and superior to the national legislation of the member states.

Secondly, the work in question has to be original. For a long time, originality was subjectively perceived as the mark of the author's personality. However,

---

32 Court of Cassation (commercial section), 28 May 1975, PIBD 1975, n°155, III, p. 345.

33 Directive 2009/24/EC of the European Parliament and of the Council of 23 April 2009 on the legal protection of computer programs (Codified version), OJ L 111, 5 May 2009, 16–22.

since the *Pachod* decision, the concept of originality has become increasingly explicit. Indeed, since *Pachod* the concept of originality has been increasingly understood as a personalised effort and intellectual contribution. Directive 91/250/EEC on the legal protection of computer programmes clearly expresses in its Article 3(1) that computer programmes are original under one and only one condition: such computer programmes have to be the fruit of an author's own intellectual work. Thus, the resulting protection applies only to original computer programmes, meaning programmes that carry the mark of the personal intellectual contribution of their author. In this sense, computer programmes can notably be considered to be original creations when they 'operate a specific choice in a particular configuration, a particular presentation of headings, or organization of titles or windows architecture, or a combination of colours or different character typesets'.[34]

In the present case, the algorithm of Professor Higgens, seen from the point of view of copyright law as being purely an idea, is excluded from protection. Thus, no authorship rights may be claimed for such an algorithm.

However, Professor Higgens is the author not only of the underlying algorithm, but also of the programme at issue. Unfortunately, no further detailed information is given. It is only known that Professor Higgens' computer programme is the work of a well-known university professor and a best-seller in its category. However, this sparse information is not sufficient enough to establish the programme's originality or the required intellectual contribution of its author. However, if we take for granted that Professor Higgens' computer programme is protectable by copyright laws as fulfilling the aforementioned conditions, it is now necessary to examine whether Professor Higgens has the right to claim authorship of the computer programme in question.

Paternity rights

The author of an intellectual work is the holder of both patrimonial and extra-patrimonial prerogatives. In theory, these extra-patrimonial prerogatives are the right to disclose, to withdraw or to repent, to demand respect for the work, and finally to claim paternity or authorship of the work.

It is advisable to first examine the existence of a paternity or authorship right and subsequently to study the possible sanctions in the event of the non-respect of such a right.

The existence of paternity rights

More than one scenario may be foreseen. But first the general principles have to be set forth in order to then study the exceptions that could apply in particular to the present case.

---

34 Paris Court of Appeal, 4 February 2004, Expertises 2004, p. 156.

Principle: In France, paternity rights made their way very early into case law.[35] Nowadays, they are established in Article L. 121-2 of the French Intellectual Property Code, according to which a work's author enjoys a protection covering his/her name, capacity and work. However, the content of authorship rights is not defined by law, but by doctrine. The latter defines authorship rights as an author's faculty to be made known or not as the creator of a published work. Moreover, paternity rights are also established in Article 6bis of the Berne Convention. Thus, the author of a published work can demand that his/her work be accompanied by a mention of his/her name. Therefore, the person exploiting the work is obliged, no matter what the circumstances are, to mention the name of the author. The absence of such a mention infringes the moral rights[36] of the author, which have to be respected both by publishers and producers[37] involved in the exploitation of the work. It should be noted though that the person exploiting the work cannot be held responsible for a violation of paternity rights if the author omitted to sign his/her work.[38] Moreover, the respect due to such rights also binds both transferees and subcontractors.

As a result, Professor Higgens should have grounds to demand that his paternity rights be respected and thus refuse to have his name omitted not only when there is an alteration of the initial computer programme but also when marketing it in either its original or altered form. The general principles being set, it is now convenient to proceed to an analysis of both the details and exceptions concerning moral rights as set out above.

Foreseeable exceptions

Computer programmes: The intellectual work in question is a computer programme. Moreover, it may be the result of the effort of several people. Last but not least, Professor Higgens might have signed a contract whose terms amount to a relinquishment of his paternity rights.

In regard to computer programmes, Article L. 121-7 states that the right to the integrity of the work and the right to repent are suspended in favour of the transferee of the rights of use, unless stated otherwise. Some case law has even gone so far as to consider that moral rights are limited to paternity rights when it comes to computer programmes.[39] In any case, it seems that paternity rights are applicable to computer programmes.

---

35 Paris Court of Appeal, 20 March 1826, D. 1827, 2, p. 55; Paris Court of Appeal, 8 August 1837, Dalloz, jurispr. gén., 1857, t. 37, PLA n°194.

36 Paris Court of Appeal, 27 September 1996, D. 1997, somm. p. 94, obs. Colombet; Court of Cassation (criminal section), 16 December 1976, J.C.P. C.I. 1976, I, 5114; Court of Cassation (1st chamber, civil section), 12 December 2000, D. 2001, jurispr. p. 1532, n°7.

37 Paris Court of Appeal, 12 December 1995, RIDA 1996, n°3, p. 372.

38 Paris Court of Appeal, 22 December 1987, Cah. dr. auteur, January 1988, p. 15.

39 Douai Court of Appeal, 1 July 1996, J.C.P. E. 1997, I, 657, n°1, obs. Vivant and Le Stanc.

Therefore, given this analysis of the weak legal status of computer programmes, Professor Higgens should have the right to seek enforcement of his paternity rights in regard to the computer programme in question and thus ask the latter to be accompanied by a mention of his name as the original creator.

Furthermore, even in the case of open source computer software, developed under the CeCILL licence, all rights conferred by copyright laws should be respect. Thus, a licensee, such as Richard, would be authorised to contribute to the software on the condition that he mentions the name of the original author.

Collaboration and collective work: The computer programme in question could however be either a collaborative work or a collective work.

According to Article L. 113-2 al. 1 of the French Intellectual Property Code, a collaborative work is the result of the effort of more than one physical person. Each of the co-authors enjoys in such a case the moral rights resulting both from the work as a whole and from his personal contribution. As a result, paternity rights remain.

It is already known that Professor Higgens took part in the creation of the computer programme at issue. It is not known though what his actual participation in the creation of the computer programme in question was. Maybe Professor Higgens participated only in the creation of the algorithm. In this case, since algorithms are not protected by copyright law, Professor Higgens would not be eligible to claim any authorship rights. If his contribution was larger, he could enjoy authorship rights for the work as a whole as well as for his personal contribution and could require that his name be attached to the programme.

The computer programme in question may also be a collective work.[40] According to Article L. 113-2 al. 3 of the French Intellectual Property Code:

> 'Collective work' shall mean a work created at the initiative of a natural or legal person who edits it, publishes it and discloses it under his direction and name and in which the personal contributions of the various authors who participated in its production are merged in the overall work for which they were conceived, without it being possible to attribute to each author a separate right in the work as created.

It appears that as far as paternity rights are concerned, the contributor of a collective work is in the best position to preserve his/her prerogatives. Moreover, contractual clauses cannot call into question paternity rights. The case law has upheld contributors' paternity rights in a decision dating back to 15 April 1986.[41] Once more, author's paternity rights are not questioned. Therefore, Professor Higgens,

---

40 Paris Court of Appeal, 9 June 2004, PIBD 2005, 801, III, p. 95; Prop. ind. n°4 April 2005, comm. 34.

41 Court of Cassation (1st chamber, civil section), 15 April 1986, RIDA, 1986, n°130, p. 143; see Y. Basire, 'Le droit moral dans les œuvres collectives', mémoire de DEA Droit de la propriété intellectuelle, CEIPI, sous la direction du Pr. T. Hassler, p. 24.

even as a simple contributor to a collective work, has the right to demand that his name be attached in one way or another to the programme. However, this solution has to be clarified: his contribution must not be solely limited to the algorithm.

In the case of a contract: For a more complete analysis, the case of a contract under the terms of which Professor Higgens waived his paternity rights should also be examined. The right to waive the paternity of a work is one of the prerogatives offered to the author who wishes not to see his/her name attached to his/her work. But what is the fate of such a convention when an author ultimately wishes to see his/her name associated with his/her work? An author's moral rights are inalienable and imprescriptible. Moreover, this general principle is one of public order. As a result, even if the author initially waives his/her paternity rights, such a waiver is not definitive and as such the author may at any time reconsider his/her initial decision. Furthermore, according to case law: 'the authorization not to mention his name on the goods reproducing his works given by an author to a transferee who received a right of use, does not result in alienating the author from his paternity rights, since he conserves the faculty to demand the mention of his name'.[42]

In the present case, Professor Higgens still has the faculty to reconsider such a choice even if he initially waived his paternity rights. Thus, a clause stipulating a prohibition on mentioning the name of Professor Higgens would be decisive in such a case.

Once again, the paternity rights of Professor Higgens cannot be questioned. As a result, anyone who buys and uses the programme at issue should not take into account a clause prohibiting a mention of Professor Higgens' name at a later time.

Composite work: Last but not least, it is necessary to consider paternity rights insofar as the programme, when modified, results in the creation of a new work.

This is the case of a composite work. A composite work incorporates a pre-existing one. The author of the pre-existing work does not participate in the creation of the composite one. However, Article L. 113-4 of the French Intellectual Property Code states that a composite work is the property of its author without prejudice to the rights of the pre-existing work's author. Thus, respect is also due to the paternity rights of the latter.

Therefore, Professor Higgens has the right to require the company IPC which markets the improved version of the computer programme in question to make reference not only to ITC, the holder of the rights, but also to him, the author of the programme.

---

42 Court of Cassation (1st chamber, civil section), 13 February 2007, JurisData n°2007-037342; Comm. com. électr. 2007, comm. 53, note Ch. Caron, Propr. intell. 2007, p. 207, J.M. Bruguière, J.C.P. G. 2005, IV, 1580.

In the above, it has been clearly demonstrated that there is almost no exception to paternity rights. Thus, Prof. Higgens, regardless of whether he is in the capacity of a single author, joint author or contributor, has the right to claim authorship of his work. Such a right cannot be indefinitely compromised on a contractual basis. As a result, Prof. Higgens has the right to see his name associated with his work, irrespective of the manner in which such a connection is made. However, given the complexity of the current issue, it is necessary to examine thoroughly all the possible alternatives available for Prof. Higgens to ensure the enforcement of his paternity rights.

According to Prof. Higgens' wishes, paternity rights can be enforced in all possible cases, namely in the event of marketing of the software at issue, modification of the software by a third party for exclusive in-house use, and finally modification of the basic programme and marketing of this modified new version as such.

Proceedings and sanctions

It is now necessary to consider the options available to Prof. Higgens if IPC refuses to associate his name with the programme in question.

The action brought to enforce respect of paternity rights is an infringement lawsuit. This action can be tried under civil law as well as under criminal law.

In regard to criminal proceedings, the limitation period for which is three years, Article L. 335-3 of the French Intellectual Property Code stipulates that the offence of forgery includes reproduction, representation or diffusion of any intellectual work and by any means, resulting in a violation of copyright rights, defined and regulated as such by law. According to case law, it is possible to be found guilty under criminal law of the infringement of moral rights.[43] Besides the legal element and the material element, it is important to dwell on the moral element. In criminal proceedings, the offence of forgery implies a guilty intention. It has always been admitted by the courts that the materiality of the act of counterfeiting establishes a presumption of the bad faith of the perpetrator.[44] It is thus up to the defendant to reverse this presumption by establishing his/her good faith. However, jurisprudence makes a distinction between direct counterfeiters and indirect counterfeiters (an example of the latter being importers of counterfeited merchandise).

Counterfeiting can be punished with three years of imprisonment and a fine of €300,000. The cessation of any counterfeiting acts will also be ordered by the court and the holder of the infringed rights will be able to obtain compensation for the damages suffered.

---

43 Paris Court of Appeal, 25 January 1968, RIDA, July 1968, p. 17; Court of Cassation (1st chamber, civil section), 13 December 1995, RIDA, July 1996, p. 307; RTD com., 1996, p. 462, obs. Françon; Court of Cassation (criminal section), 24 September 1997, Gaz. Pal., 1998-2-259, note Leclerc.

44 Court of Cassation, 11 April 1889, Annales 1892, p. 190.

If criminal proceedings are instituted, evidence of counterfeiting will need to be established, given that in the absence of a contract, ITC cannot pretend to be unaware of Professor Higgens' moral rights. ITC was indeed fully aware that it was not respecting Professor Higgens' paternity rights, and as a result, ITC's criminal responsibility will be upheld by the court. If Professor Higgens signed a contract waiving his authorship rights, the criminal responsibility of ITC will also be upheld once Professor Higgens has expressed his will to see his name associated with the programme he originally conceived. Moreover, and in addition to eventual criminal sanctions, ITC will be obliged to respect Professor Higgens' paternity rights.

In the scenario where IPC adapts the programme and then sells a modified version, things appear to be more complex. IPC, given the licence contract signed with ITC, could not have been aware of Prof. Higgens' paternity rights. Thus, if IPC manages to demonstrate its good faith, the court will obviously not hold it to be criminally responsible. However, if Professor Higgens informed IPC directly of his wish to see his name linked to the modified product as the author of the initial version of the computer programme, IPC would certainly be obliged to fulfil such a request. If not, IPC will be unable to prove its good faith and it will be held to be criminally responsible.

On the other hand, a civil action will not only result in an order to cease and desist from all infringing acts but also in an adjudication of damages. Contrary to criminal proceedings, the good faith is immaterial. As a result, only the material existence of infringing acts is sufficient to justify a judgment in favour of Professor Higgens.

Thus, ITC and IPC can be sanctioned under civil law for not having associated the name of the author with the programme as they should have done in all cases other than the one governed by a contract stipulating that Professor Higgens had given up his paternity rights. In this case, ITC and IPC will be held liable from the moment Professor Higgens notified them of his wish to see his name associated with the final product in his capacity as the initial author. As a result, a judgment under civil law will not only contain an order to cease and desist from all prohibited counterfeiting acts but also an adjudication of damages and interests covering the period after Professor Higgens notified ITC and IPC of his wishes in the event that the latter did not conform to his request.

Professor Higgens' paternity rights allow him to decide whether or not he wishes to be associated with the computer programme in question as its initial author. ITC's and IPC's failure to comply with such a wish constitutes reprehensible counterfeiting acts under both civil and criminal law.

III. Metalegal Formants

Answer omitted.

(6) GERMANY

I. *Operative Rules*

Higgens has a right to be named and can claim an injunction against the marketing of the products without his name.

II. *Descriptive Formants*

An algorithm, if determining a specific computer programme, is protected under §69a UrhG. Algorithms are not protected if they are generally well-known mathematical rules (§69a sec. 2 UrhG). If those programmes are created under commission or in a work relationship, then the intellectual property is directly assigned to the principal or employer respectively (§69b UrhG). Higgens, however, was not employed by ITC. Thus, he is the initial holder of the copyright. In his contract with ITC, he transfers the economic rights to ITC, but his moral right to be named (§13 UrhG) is not negotiated. The right to be named is conceptualised as a rule in principle, any restriction requires explicit recognition.[45] As the contract is silent on this matter, Higgens' moral right to be named is not compromised. His right covers replications,[46] but not 'improvements' and artistic use.[47]

III. *Metalegal Formants*

The right to be named is a strong rule in principle which serves various functions. It protects not only the individual interests in respect of the assignment of rights and promotion. The public interest is also protected because it informs the consumer. It derives from the moral right of the creator. However, the right to be named is limited and bound to the copyright. This is the consequence of the fact that the notion of 'dependency' is foreign to copyright law. 'Using' or 'modifying' copyrighted material is not covered by copyright, in contrast to a patent (§15 UrhG, §9 German Patent Code). There is only an either/or between publishing 'the same' (right to injunction and right to be named) or an 'original modification' (no right to injunction, no right to be named) – and the line between them is a fine one.

---

45 If nothing is negotiated, the owner can insist on his/her right to be named afterwards (G. Schulze, in: T. Dreier, in: T. Dreier and G. Schulze (eds.), *UrhG-Commentary* (6th ed., Munich: 2018), §13, No. 8). A waiver can be revoked (any waiver in advance cannot extend beyond five years in analogy to §41 sec. 4 sentence 2 UrhG).

46 Ibid., §13, No. 8.

47 For artistic parody see BGH, judgment of 20 March 2003, GRUR 2003, 956 – *Giesadler*; for literary transformative use, BVerfG, decision of 20 June 2000, GRUR 2001, 149 – *Germania 3*.

(7) GREECE

I. Operative Rules

Prof. Higgens may claim the restoration of his name as the true creator, but not an injunction.

II. Descriptive Formants

Greek legislation has always recognised the moral right which safeguards the personal connection between the author and his/her work (Art. 4 Law 2121/1993), without any need to recognise this right in the licence contract. Computer programmes are protected as literary works according to Directive 91/250/EEC (= Arts. 40–45A Law 2121/1993). Prof. Higgens has developed a specific algorithm which is the core of the programme. Even if the pecuniary rights on the programme belonged from the beginning *ex lege* to ITC as the employer of Prof. Higgens according to Article 8 Law 2121/1993, nevertheless the initial rightholder of the programme is still Prof. Higgens, since he has the paternity right over the algorithm and therefore he has the right to be named on the copy of the work.

From a procedural point of view, Prof. Higgens is self-evidently legitimated to exercise his moral right against ITC and IPC, since according to Law 2121/1993 in the case of computer programmes the natural or legal person whose name or title appears on a copy of the work is presumed to be the rightholder of the copyright (Art. 11 Law 2121/1993). This presumption may be rebutted by evidence to the contrary. The moral right of the author is reinforceable by pronouncing judicial penalties in the case of its infringement, according to Article 946 Greek Code of Civil Procedure (CCPr). Instead of this reinforcement, claiming an injunction against the licensee might seem disproportionate (Art. 116 CCPr; Art. 25 of the Constitution) and it is not provided by the law in general, unless, of course, in case of an emergency (Arts. 682, 732 CCPr).

III. Metalegal Formants

The moral right not only seems to correspond to the inalienable hard core of the creator's personality, but the acknowledgment of paternity would seem to constitute the establishment of an actual fact necessary for the judicial resolution of the dispute (even if the waiver of the creator were to be regarded as valid and irrevocable). In this sense, a commitment to conceal the true origin of the work will contravene both Article 20 of the Constitution (right to the protection of law) and a series of penal provisions relating to the examination of witnesses, etc., and, in general, the litigant's duty to tell the truth. In the last analysis, the creator has at any time the right to rescind a contract ceding a licence to exploit his/her property right over the work under Law 2121/1993, and *a fortiori* his/her right to rescind the contract/license, that is, to revoke his/her consent as regards his/her moral right, should be recognised.

According to Article 16 of Law 2121/1993, the written granting of consent by an author for an action or an omission which would otherwise constitute an infringement of his/her moral right shall be deemed to be a form of exercise of his/her moral right and shall be binding upon him/her. Naturally, any clause between third parties (as in the present case) is not binding upon the creator. Furthermore, there is a question as to whether the 'binding' of the creator by his/her waiver of his/her moral right will develop only obligational action, or whether it will deprive him/her of the claim for recognition of his/her paternity of his/her work. The first solution seems more convincing, since it deviates from Article 177 Civil Code, which stipulates that 'subject to any different legal provision, an act whereby the ability to dispose of an alienable right is restricted, shall only entail a personal obligation'.

(8) IRELAND

I. Operative Rules

Under sections 127 and 137 CRRA, damages or other relief may be sought where copyright and moral rights are infringed. Injunctions to prevent future infringements may be granted by the court, providing that the work can be copyrighted.

II. Descriptive Formants

Under section 17 CRRA, copyright is a property right and subsists in original literary works, which include computer programmes. It does not extend, however, to ideas and principles which underlie any element of a work and, therefore, it may not extend to this computer programme if it is only classified as a mathematical concept.

Under the CRRA 2000, moral rights are protected and encompass the paternity right, or the right to be named; the integrity right, or the right not to have one's work distorted; the right against false attribution; and a limited right of privacy for photographs, under Chapter VII of the Act.

The paternity right gives the author a right to be identified as the author of his/her work and this right also extends to any adaptation of the work, under section 107(1). Moral rights also extend to computer programmers, unlike in the UK. It would appear that ITC is seeking to exert a moral right which it does not have and despite the fact that Professor Higgens has not assert his moral right, this does not matter in Ireland, unlike in the UK, as Irish law complies with the absence of formalities required by the Berne Convention, in this instance.

Prof. Higgens probably does have a right to be named in any adaption of the work. He can also claim an injunction when ITC markets the improved product both because of the copyright infringement and because of the infringement of his moral rights. His moral rights can only be waived in writing and, clearly, this has not been achieved in this case.

III. Metalegal Formants

Answer omitted.

(9) ITALY

I. Operative Rules

Yes, Prof. Higgens has the right to be named as author of the programme every time someone fails to disclose the identity of the author. In addition, he can claim that the nexus of derivation from the programme he has created be reported whenever IPC markets the improved product.

II. Descriptive Formants

Assuming that there is an employment relationship between the ITC and Higgens, ITC is presumed by law to be the initial owner of the economic rights on the software. Article 12bis of ICL establishes that, unless the contract provides otherwise, the owner of a software programme created by an employee in the exercise of his/her duties or upon instructions given by his/her employer is the employer. However, the right to be recognised as the author remains with the author (Arts. 20 et seq. ICL). Article 20 c. 1 ICL indeed states that regardless of the exclusive rights of exploitation, and also after they are transferred (thus including the case of transfer in an employment relationship, ex Art. 12bis ICL), the author retains the right to be named. Although he has transferred the economic rights on the programme, under Italian law Professor Higgens still retains the inalienable right[48] to be recognised as the author of the work and he can claim it whenever someone fails to disclose the identity of the author. On the other hand, the person who holds the rights of economic exploitation of the work is obliged to indicate the author's name when the work is marketed.[49]

---

48 See Art. 22 c. 1 ICL.

49 See Tribunale di Milano, 14 December 1998, *Stefano Babic v. Moon Shadow S.P.A.*, in *AIDA*, 1999, p. 629.

In order to distribute moral rights between the original work and the derivative one, courts have coupled the rule contained in Article 20, stated above, with the one contained in Article 7 c. 2 ICL. This states that: 'the author of the development is the "developer", within the limits of his work'. This means that the elaborator owns the economic and moral rights on the derivative only in proportion to his/her creative contribution. For the part of the contribution unrelated to the 'limits of his work' it must be attributed to the person who made it and that is the author of the original work. Consequently, even where the author has transferred his/her economic rights of the original work, he/she retains the moral right to be named as author in the commercialisation of a derivative works.[50] All this translates into the operative rules that the *derivation nexus* must be reported in any communication of the derivative work to the public, which means that the right to be identified as the author includes the right to be identified whenever copies are issued to the public in relation to an improvement of the work as the author of the work from which the improvement was made.[51]

III. Metalegal Formants

From this provision, and from the whole structure and tradition of the ICL, it is a well-accepted principle in Italian copyright law that the author of the original work has the right to be named not only in any use of his/her work, but also in any use of a derivative work. It is in some ways implicit, since the right of adaptation is a form of use of the original work and therefore is reserved to the author of the original work (economic right). With the transfer or licensing of the right to adapt the work, it is just the economic right that is transferred (or licensed), and not the moral one. This sounds quite obvious since under the ICL, moral rights may not be transferred, waived or relinquished. Any disposition to the contrary is deemed void and without any effect (Arts. 20 c. 1, 21 and 22 c. 1). Although this is a minority theory, some leading scholars have argued (especially in the past) that through the creation of a derivative work (which is the creative development of an original work) the corresponding ownership rules will be that of tenancy in common. Doubts on this theory are connected primarily with the rules that Italian law on *comunione* which required unanimity for almost any use (transfer, exclusive licence, and also a non-exclusive licence lasting more than nine years). It obviously favours a situation similar to that of a tragedy of the anticommons.

This debate reveals how the Italian conception of derivative work is strongly dualistic. The derivative work is one unique work, with only one unique author.

---

50 See Cass. 28 February 1997, no. 1807, in *AIDA*, 1998, pp. 506 ff.

51 See Ammendola, Ubertazzi, *Il diritto d'autore* (Torino: 1993), p. 55.

But this author has based her activity on a previous original work which in some ways and to some extent survives in the derivative work. The way, form and extent to which the original work is present – the *nexus of derivation* – must be reported in any use and communication of the derivative work.

(10) LITHUANIA

I. Operative Rules

Prof. Higgens most likely cannot claim an injunction.

II. Descriptive Formants

Article 42 of the Constitution of the Republic of Lithuania declares that the law shall protect and defend the spiritual and material interests of an author which are related to scientific, technical, cultural and artistic work.

Article 27 of the Universal Declaration of Human Rights proclaims that everyone has the right to the protection of the moral and material interests resulting from any scientific, literary or artistic production of which he/she is the author.

Following the concept of the *droit d'auteur*, the Copyright Act treats the moral rights of the author as individual primary initial rights and provides for their priority over economic rights, which are held by the doctrine to be derived from moral rights.

First, Article 14(1) of the Copyright Act establishes that the author's moral rights cannot be subject to transfer to other persons (moral rights are inalienable) and cannot be inherited. Second, the Law provides for the so-called 'minimum' of moral rights as set out in Article 6bis of the Berne Convention. Article 14 provides for three moral rights: the right to claim authorship of the work, the right to be named as author and the right to the inviolability of the work. Finally, moral rights should be protected for an unlimited period of time. This regulation of individual moral rights of the author is in line with the French dualistic concept of the *droit d'auteur*, though it differs from the German system of copyright law.[52]

The author of a work, even after transfer of the economic rights to another person, has the right to claim or prevent the mention of his/her name in connection with any use of the work, or the right to claim that the work be disclosed to the public under a pseudonym (right to the author's name, Article 14(1)).

[52] V. Mizaras, 'Lithuanian Copyright: Historical and Modern Aspects and Trends of Development', *Journal of Copyright Society of the USA*, 2006, vol. 54, No. 4, p. 844.

Algorithms themselves are not protected. It should be noted that in this hypothetical case, the specific algorithm is the core of the computer programme.[53] The subject matter of copyright furthermore is a computer programme (Art. 4(1)(1)). The computer programme must be original (criteria for quality or artistic value do not apply). Article 2 contains the definition of a computer programme:

> a set of instructions expressed in words, codes, schemes or in any other form capable, when incorporated in a computer-readable medium, of causing a computer to perform a particular task or bring about a certain result; this definition also includes preparatory design material of such instructions, provided that the said set of instructions can be created from it.

Article 10 of the Copyright Act prescribes that the author of a computer programme is the natural person or group of natural persons who created the programme. The owner of an author's economic rights in a computer programme created by an employee in the execution of his/her duties or fulfilment of his/her work functions is the employer. Therefore, the right to be named is inalienable;[54] any transaction about these rights is null.

Prof. Higgens can be considered the author of the computer programme (as per Art. 10) and, in principle, has a right to be named (Art. 14(1)). But it is essential to note that the same article provides a special rule concerning the enforcement of moral rights of authors of computer programmes and databases vis-à-vis software producers. In particular, Article 14(3) states:

> The moral rights of an author of computer programs and databases may not be used in a manner which unreasonably prejudices the rights of a holder of the author's economic rights in these computer programs and databases, including the right to carry out adaptation, alteration, and distribution of these works at his discretion, with the exception of the cases when such actions would be prejudicial to the author's honor or reputation.

This provision was added to the Copyright Act in 2006, and the *travaux préparatoires* explain that this addition was introduced to take into account the specific legal nature of computer programmes and databases and the need to safeguard the legitimate interests of software producers. This leads to the conclusion that the protection of moral rights to computer programmes and databases is narrower than for other types of works.

---

53 The same conclusion seems to be given in the German and Spain country reports.

54 Supreme Court Decision of 5 April 2000, No. 3K-3-415/2000, *R. Sileika v. UAB 'Faris'*. In this case, the employer displayed the pictures taken by the employee without mentioning the author's name. The Court considered it an infringement of moral right.

It is important to note that even in cases not connected to computer programmes or databases, the established case law of the Supreme Court of Lithuania requires finding a balance between the moral rights (including the right to the author's name) and legitimate interests of other parties. In particular, this balancing exercise is required when an author creates work on commission or has other contractual relationships with a holder of economic rights. In such circumstances, the Supreme Court of Lithuania has stated that an author cannot enforce his/her moral rights to the prejudice of the economic rightholders or other users.[55] Accordingly, there are cases in which claims based on the infringement of a moral right were rejected even when a user did not indicate the author's name.[56] Notably, these cases dealt with so-called utilitarian works (to which computer programmes also belong). The same arguments are *a fortiori* applied in the case of computer programmes, taking into account the special rule of Article 14(3). As can be seen from the formulation of Article 14(3), the moral rights of an author can be enforced only if the actions of the holder of the author's economic rights would be prejudicial to the author's honour or reputation. But there is nothing in the facts of the case which allows us to state that distribution of the computer programme without indicating Prof. Higgens' name prejudices his honour or reputation. Such prejudice could probably be established if false authorship were to be attributed, but this is not the case here, as IPC cannot be considered the author, only a holder of economic rights (Art. 10).

Therefore, most likely, Prof. Higgens's claim would be rejected either because there is no violation of the moral right at all or alternatively because the claim for an injunction would be considered a disproportionate measure.

Of course, the final evaluation is fact-dependent and different modalities are possible. For example, if the duty to indicate the name of Prof. Higgens had been agreed in a contract, or if he had instantly raised the issue of the violation of his moral right with IPC, the answer could be different. And *vice versa* – long delays from the author's side to enforce his moral rights usually are considered proof that there was no prejudice.

III. Metalegal Formants

In the early stages of Lithuanian copyright doctrine, the concept of the *droit d'auteur* was often referred to. Jurisprudential judgments recognised the author's right to be mentioned, which connects the author with his/her work.[57] According

55 Supreme Court Decision of 25 June 2008, No. 3K-3-160/2008.

56 Ibid. See also the Supreme Court Decision of 30 June 2016, No. 3K-3-339-690/2016.

57 Supreme Court Decision of 19 February 2003, No. 3K-3-273/2003, *J. Jakstas v. UAB 'Musu gaires'*. Court of Appeal Decision of 8 June 2006, No. 2A-248/2006, *L.J. v. K.J. Vasiliausko imone*. The Courts held that the right to the inviolability of a work cannot be treated in isolation because a creative work is a process of spiritual experience that pertains to very

to the Supreme Court, every infringement of moral right gives the author the right to claim non-pecuniary damages.[58]

However, it was argued that this jurisprudence was caused less by the adoption of the *droit d'auteur* concept, but by the inertia of the Soviet copyright legacy. Later and current legal doctrine do not support the absolute protection of moral rights any longer. The Copyright Act says nothing about the priority of moral rights. Both on a regulatory level and on the level of practical application, the imperative to balance the author's rights, including his/her moral right to be named, with the interests of other parties is proclaimed. As stated above, this imperative works primarily at the stage of considering whether the violation occurred in the first place. Second, the balance of interests test is applied when deciding whether to enforce a particular remedy (including injunctions) and, if so, to what extent. In doing that, all relevant factors are considered, such as the type of work, the relationship and the previous actions of the parties.

Lithuania has not availed itself of the opportunity envisaged in Article 2 of Directive 91/250/EEC for the member states to extend the scope of authorship of computer programmes to legal entities. As follows from the current national copyright legislation, legal entities cannot be considered authors or initial rightholders. Legal entities can, in the cases provided by law, enjoy economic rights.[59]

(11) NETHERLANDS

I. *Operative Rules*

Yes, Professor Higgens has the right to be named and can claim an injunction against products marketed without his name.

II. *Descriptive Formants*

This case concerns the author's moral right of paternity, i.e. the right to be named as creator of the work, as laid down in Article 25(1)(a) Dutch Copyright Act: 'Even after assignment of his copyright, the author of a work has the following rights: a. the right to oppose the communication to the public of the work

sensitive feelings and the experience of the author and that certain alterations or distortions, although minor in their extent, might be painful to the author.

58 Supreme Court Decision of 8 January 2003, No. 3K-3-2/2003, *B.V. – F. v. UANB 'Fodio', Kauno valstybinis M.K. Ciurlionio dailes muziejus*; Supreme Court Decision of 19 February 2003, No. 3K-3-273/2003, *J. Jakstas v. UAB 'Musu gaires'*.

59 V. Mizaras, 'Lithuanian Copyright: Historical and Modern Aspects and Trends of Development', *Journal of Copyright Society of the USA*, 2006, vol. 54, No. 4, p. 842.

without acknowledgement of his name or other indication as author, unless such opposition would be unreasonable'. Article 25(3) Dutch Copyright Act explicitly provides for the possibility of waiving the entitlement of the acknowledgement of the author's name: 'The right referred to in paragraph 1, sub a, may be waived'. It is to be assumed that Professor Higgens did not waive his moral right of acknowledgement of his name, since the agreement between ITC and Professor Higgens is silent on this point.

This case also touches upon the moral right of integrity, i.e. the right to oppose an alteration or impairment of the work, as laid down in Article 25(1)(c) Dutch Copyright Act: 'Even after assignment of his copyright, the author of a work has the following rights: ... c. the right to oppose any other alteration of the work, unless the nature of the alteration is such that opposition would be unreasonable'. It is defendable to say that improvements to a computer programme made by its user cannot be frustrated by reasonable objections of the makers of the programme, unless there are special circumstances.[60] Professor Higgens will have to tolerate the improvements made by IPC.

Accordingly, Professor Higgens can successfully invoke the right to oppose the communication to the public of his work without acknowledgement of his name or other indication as author, unless such opposition would be unreasonable. With this 'unless formula' the legislator sought to prevent the introduction of a right of paternity that is uncommon in a specific sector of the industry or that is overly burdensome on the publisher of the work. Examples thereof are publications of reports in daily newspapers by freelance correspondents and publications of old photographs.[61] This does not seem to be the case at present, although the – unknown – specific circumstances of this case might lead to another conclusion. The fact that, in the respective community, it is widely known that the core of the programme consists of a specific algorithm, developed by Professor Higgens, might carry some weight in this respect.

III. Metalegal Formants

This case involves two moral rights of the author: the right of paternity and the right of integrity. Moral rights protect the immaterial interests an author has when his/her work is being 'used'. Moral rights are described as securing the

---

[60] J.H. Spoor, D.W.F. Verkade and D.J.G. Visser, *Auteursrecht. Auteursrecht, naburige rechten en databankenrecht* (Deventer: 2005), p. 371.

[61] C. Gielen and D.W.F. Verkade, *Tekst en Commentaar Intellectuele Eigendom* (Deventer: 2005), p. 57, Art. 25(1) Dutch Copyright Act, annotation 2; J.H. Spoor, D.W.F. Verkade and D.J.G. Visser, *Auteursrecht. Auteursrecht, naburige rechten en databankenrecht* (Deventer: 2005), p. 386.

bond between an author and his/her work through legal ties. It follows from Article 25 of the Dutch Copyright Act that the moral rights of the author remain unaffected by the transfer of rights. In the Netherlands, moral rights last as long as the economic rights. This guarantees that the author (or his/her heirs) can still exercise control over his/her creation even after the transfer of rights. This is important because both moral right attributes, paternity and integrity, contribute to the reputation of the author.[62]

Moral rights are inalienable and cannot be generally waived in advance. However, in some circumstances, the exercise of moral rights is not always advantageous. For example, in the publishing sector, it may be necessary, for the successful exploitation of a work, to make adaptations to it. Therefore, the Dutch Copyright Act makes it possible to waive certain moral rights.

The right to paternity entails the right of the author to object to the publication of his/her work without his/her name unless the objection is unreasonable. The author has to prove that the omission of his/her name is unfair.[63] The same applies to the right to adaptation. The author has the right to object to changes of his/her work unless this objection would be unreasonable.[64] The key issue is to decide what constitutes an unreasonable objection to an alteration. Depending on the outcome of the reasonable test, Professor Higgens could be entitled to claim an injunction.

The Dutch Copyright Act acknowledges the importance of moral rights to the author. For example, it is not possible to waive the right to object to distortion and mutilation of the work. On the other hand, the Dutch Copyright Act also factors in the practical needs of publishers. Therefore, it is possible to waive the right to paternity and the right to integrity. The Dutch Copyright Act protects both interests.

(12) NORWAY

I. *Operative Rules*

Yes, Professor Higgens has a right to be named and can claim an injunction against IPC for marketing the improved product without making a reference to his name.

---

62 C. Gielen, *Kort begrip van het intellectuele eigendomsrecht* (Deventer: 2007), p. 458.

63 M. Salokannel and A. Strowel, *Report concerning moral rights in the context of the exploitation of works through digital technology*, Commissioned by European Commission's Internal Market Directorate-General, 2000, p. 99.

64 H.D.J Jongen, 'The Netherlands', in: H.D.J. Jongen and A.P. Meijboom, *Copyright software protection in the European Community* (Deventer/Boston: 1993), no. 1.6.

II. Descriptive Formants

A computer programme is protected as a work pursuant to NCA §1 (cf. the explicit list in the second paragraph, lit. 12; New Act §2(2) l), provided that it fulfils the originality criteria. It is to be assumed that this will apply in the case of Prof. Higgens' 'specific algorithm', although it is not further explained what is meant by this expression. On the premise that the expression refers to the computer programme itself and not the general ideas behind it, so that it constitutes a work, Prof. Higgens has a right to be named as author of the work 'in accordance with proper usage', cf. NCA §3, first paragraph (New Act §5, first paragraph). According to NCA §3, third paragraph (New Act §5, third paragraph), the author may not waive his/her right under the first paragraph, unless the use of the work in question is limited in nature and extent. As the contract with ITC is silent with regard to the right to be named, Prof. Higgens has not waived any right, and it is therefore not necessary to decide whether the use of the work is limited (which it probably is not). When deciding what is 'proper usage', due account must be taken *inter alia* of normal practice and the practical possibilities that the use has for citing the author's name. From the facts it seems doubtful that mentioning Prof. Higgens' name will cause any practical inconvenience to ITC, and it is natural to conclude that 'proper usage' will be to cite Prof. Higgens' name in this situation.

III. Metalegal Formants

Norwegian copyright law is based on the *droit d'auteur* tradition, and the right to be named (paternity right) is, together with the right to respect (*droit au respect*), a fundamental *droit moral* (cf. Article 6bis of the Berne Convention), although the right indeed may have economic value. The *droit moral* aspect is emphasised in that the paternity right as such is inalienable – only use that is limited in nature and extent can be waived. It should also be noted that, contrary to what is stipulated in, for example, Swedish law, the moral rights also pertain to the author in situations where computer programmes are created under employment. NCA §39g (New Act §72) states that copyright in a computer programme which is created by an employee in the execution of duties for which he/she is employed or in accordance with the instructions of his/her employer shall, *subject to the limitation ensuing from §3 (§5)*, devolve to the employer. In other words, whereas the 'economic rights' by way of this provision are transferred, unless otherwise agreed, to the employer, the right to be named stays with the employee as the original author.

(13) POLAND

I. *Operative Rules*

Prof. Higgens must be named and would be entitled to an injunction if this obligation was not met.

II. *Descriptive Formants*

The Polish copyright law is based on a dualistic model and differentiates between economic and moral rights. The right to be named as the author of the work has been explicitly mentioned in Article 16 point 2 of the Copyright Act. Computer programmes are as a rule protected like literary works (Art. 74(1) Copyright Act). The specific characteristics of computer programmes as a subject matter of copyright has, however, been recognised – Article 77 Copyright Act lists general provisions of copyright law that are not applicable to computer programmes. This list includes Article 16 of the Act, but only with regard to points 3–5.[65] Consequently, Article 16 point 2 (paternity right, the right to be named) is fully applicable. Moral rights cannot be set aside by contracts and cannot be transferred. Even when economic rights are acquired contractually or by force of law (e.g. when an employer acquires copyright in works created by employees),[66] moral rights remain with the author. Of course, in practice the exercise of moral rights (especially the right to integrity) becomes the subject matter of contracts in which authors undertake not to exercise their moral rights or not to exercise them in a certain way.[67] On the facts of the case it may be established that the moral right to be named as the author of the computer programme[68] lies with Prof. Higgens. The contract between Higgens and IPC could not transfer this right to IPC. Neither was it possible for Higgens to renounce the paternity right. Since the contract is silent about this issue, we may assume that Prof. Higgens has not undertaken not to exercise his paternity right, although it must be added that even if he had done so, and even if such a clause could be regarded as valid, this would only grant a contractual right to IPC, for example to claim damages from Higgens for not complying with his promise.[69]

---

65 The integrity right, the right to decide about making the work available to the public for the first time, the right to control the use of the work.

66 With respect to software, the employer acquires copyright automatically (Art. 74(3) Copyright Act), whereas for other types of works the employer must accept the work.

67 The validity of such contracts is a controversial issue. J. Barta, R. Markiewicz, in: M. Bukowski et al., *Prawo autorskie i prawa pokrewne. Komentarz* (Kraków: 2005), p. 229.

68 We must assume that Prof. Higgens created more than the algorithm since algorithms as such are not covered by copyright protection.

69 In other words, a purely contractual regulation may not completely override the statutory regulation of moral rights. Therefore, even if Higgens undertakes not to exercise his moral

The licence agreement ITC applies would force the licensees to infringe upon Prof. Higgens' paternity right. In any event, such a contract could not have any effect on Prof. Higgens' rights – this results from the basic principles of contract law, i.e. that contracts as a rule bind only the parties.[70] Besides, it would be correct to assume that such a contract would be at least partly invalid (invalidity would cover the clause forbidding naming Prof. Higgens) as this obligation is contrary to the law (Art. 58 Civil Code) – it must be regarded as inadmissible to contractually bind one's contractual partner to commit illegal actions (and that would be the case if the licensee failed to properly indicate the authorship of Prof. Higgens).

Prof. Higgens may demand that the infringement of his paternity right be stopped, and the effects of the infringement removed. Prof. Higgens may therefore apply for an injunction against ITC and may also demand that the copies already put on the market be withdrawn.

III. Metalegal Formants

The question is about the scope of the so-called moral rights, in this case the paternity right. It may be argued that the current regime of moral rights, at least in some countries, stems from the times when copyrights mostly protected works of literature, music and art. Sometimes very strict, usually non-negotiable rules on moral rights seem to be not entirely appropriate for works of purely utilitarian nature, sometimes on the borderline between industrial property and copyright. What is particularly interesting (although not directly relevant for the facts of Case 5) is whether moral rights should always be excluded from contractual freedom. Current legislation on computer programmes takes this perspective into account when it does not recognise certain moral rights with regard to computer programmes (especially the integrity right).

(14) SLOVENIA

I. Operative Rules

Higgens has the right to attribution (recognition of authorship). Higgens has grounds to sue if ITC markets an improved – adapted – product and fails to

---

right, he may still relay on statutory protection. This however could be regarded as a breach of contract.

70 Exceptions allow granting rights to third parties but never depriving them of their rights or imposing obligations on them.

mention him as the author of the original work and only attributes ITC. If the product is a completely new copyright work and not a result of adaptation, Higgens does not have grounds to sue.

II. Descriptive Formants

Algorithms generally have copyright protection as they constitute the core of a computer programme (Art. 111(3) CRRA).[71] A distinction is made between general and implementation algorithms. General algorithms are as such not copyright protected due to their general and standardised nature, while implementation algorithms do enjoy protection, since they provide specific descriptions of procedures within a programme.[72] The algorithm developed by Professor Higgens constitutes the core of the programme and is therefore deemed to be an implementation algorithm.

According to the CRRA, copyright encompasses the economic, moral and related rights of an author. An author acquires the copyright in a work at the moment of the work's creation. Professor Higgens therefore acquired the copyright in the work in question, and hence also the moral rights, at the moment he created the algorithm (Art. 14 CRRA).

An author's right to attribution of authorship is, in principle, taken into account for all categories of copyrighted works and all forms of expression of copyright, including computer programmes.[73]

The CRRA, which includes special provisions on computer programmes, does not, however, include special provisions that would constitute an exception from the general rights that moral copyright confers. The general provisions of Article 69 CRRA, stating that copyright cannot be assigned in its entirety, also apply to computer programmes. In the contract in question, Professor Higgens was only able to assign his economic and other rights to ITC, but not his moral rights. The CRRA explicitly stipulates that moral rights cannot be assigned to another party (Art. 70(1) CRRA). If a contract contains a provision assigning moral rights, the provision is null and void according to Article 79(2).

In the case in question, the relevant issue is the attribution of the author's moral rights. According to Article 18 of the CRRA, this covers the right to be identified as the author of a work, the right to disclosure of true authorship and the right to prevent others from identifying themselves as the authors of a work.

---

71 Official Gazette RS, nos. 21/1995, 9/2001, 30/2001, 43/2004, 17/2006, 139/2006, 68/2008, Art. 111(3)(3): 'Computer programmes shall be protected if they are individual works, in the sense that they are their author's own intellectual creations.'

72 M. Trampuž, B. Oman, A. Zupančič, 'Zakon o avtorski in sorodnih pravicah (ZASP) s komentarjem' (1997) *Gospodarski vestnik*, p. 267.

73 Ibid., p. 77.

This right is independent from economic rights, and an author retains the right even if he/she has waived the economic rights. The right to attribution of authorship is a non-assignable and inalienable right. An author may exercise the right by demanding an attribution of authorship or even by prohibiting attribution. Authorship is attributed in accordance with good business practice,[74] which may result in an author waiving a claim to attribution in a contract. A distinction must be made between the non-assignable core of the moral right to attribution of authorship and the methods of exercising the right.[75]

If Professor Higgens is deemed to be employed by ITC, all the original author's economic and other rights in the work are exclusively assigned to the employer without restriction, unless otherwise stated by a contract (Art. 112 CRRA). In the case of computer programmes, moral rights remain non-assignable.

Professor Higgens was not employed by ITC, since it is explicitly stated that he concluded a special contract with the company. Professor Higgens could only assign the economic and other copyright-related rights to ITC, but not his moral rights. Even if the contract included a provision assigning the moral rights, that provision would be null and void.[76] In the case in question, the contract does not mention attribution of authorship. According to the general principle that in case of doubt decisions shall be made in favour of the author, it is thus deemed that Professor Higgens did not waive his right to attribution of authorship and retained that right when Richard adapted the computer programme to meet the requirements of pharmaceutical companies.

Higgens can sue if ITC markets an improved product and attributes ITC, but only if the improved programme is just a mechanical or technical continuation of Higgens' programme. If the improvement constitutes creation of a new individual copyright work, Higgens' action will not be successful.[77]

III. Metalegal Formants

According to Slovenian legislation, an infringement of moral copyright is a criminal act, which is prosecuted on request. Advocates of these legal arrangements emphasise that they indicate the high level of legal protection for copyright in Slovenian law, but in our opinion this is a disproportionate arrangement, with few equivalents in foreign legal systems.

---

74 Ibid., p. 78.

75 Ulmer 40, IV, 2.

76 Art. 70(1) CRRA: 'An author may not assign his moral rights to other persons.'

77 M. Trampuž, B. Oman, A. Zupančič, 'Zakon o avtorski in sorodnih pravicah (ZASP) s komentarjem' (1997) *Gospodarski vestnik*, p. 268.

(15) SPAIN

I. *Operative Rules*

Higgens has a right to be named and can claim an injunction against programmes marketed without his name.

II. *Descriptive Formants*

- Revised Text of the Law of Intellectual Property, regularising, clarifying and harmonising the applicable statutory provisions (approved by Royal Legislative Decree 1/1996 of 12 April 12, and amended by Law 5/1998 of 6 March 6, incorporating Directive 96/9/EC of the European Parliament and of the Council of 11 March 1996 on the legal protection of databases).

The right to be recognised as the author of an intellectual creation is part of the so-called moral rights of the author expressly stipulated in the Revised Text of the Law of Intellectual Property of 1996.

The first time that the expression 'the moral right of the author' was recognised by Spanish legislation was in Law 17/1966 of 31 March on the rights of intellectual property in cinematographic works. Likewise, it was one of the main novelties of the Law of Intellectual Property of 11 November 1987, which for the first time regulated in detail the moral right of the author, putting an end to the vague protection of these rights before the enactment of the law. After the modification of the 1987 Law, the Revised Text of the Law of Intellectual Property (Royal Decree Law 1/1996 of 12 April), the same regulation is maintained in Article 14, with the only novelty that a title was added under the heading 'content and characteristics of moral law'.[78]

The first question that we have to consider when discussing the existence of the moral right of the author is the relationship between moral rights and patrimonial rights, as part of copyright. Article 2 LPI, after the partial reform of 2006, indicates that the copyright includes personal and patrimonial rights that attribute to the author the exclusive right to the exploitation of his/her work, without more limitations that the ones established by the law.[79]

Spanish law adopts an integrated legal recognition of copyright which includes moral and economic rights.[80]

---

78 See R. Bercovitz Rodríguez-Cano (coord.), *Comentarios a la Ley de Propiedad Intelectual* (2nd ed., Madrid: 1997), p. 216.

79 See Art. 3 Consolidated Text of the Law of Intellectual Property.

80 See Spanish Supreme Court Decision of 23 May 1975. The Court considered that '[n]o matter which is the nature of copyright, this right grants to the author two types of faculties, some that we could name as faculties of use that confer on him exclusively the right to publish his work and obtain economic profits by reproducing it, executing it, or introducing it at the market, that constitute real patrimonial rights, and another ones that we could name faculties

Article 14 of the Law of Intellectual Property establishes that the moral right of the author is non-renounceable and inalienable, and also considers that one of the faculties that makes up the moral right[81] is the right to be recognised as the author of the work. It also speaks of highly personal rights, which it considers to be non-renounceable and inalienable. The preamble to the Law of Intellectual Property also mentions this aspect and points out that the moral right 'consists of a set of rights inherent to the person of the author that are non-renounceable and inalienable, and which constitute the clearest manifestation of the author's sovereignty over his work'.[82]

Moral rights cannot be transferred *inter vivos* to third persons gratuitously or onerously, and, for this reason, those contracts that transfer to someone other than the author the various rights that Article 14 LPI mentions as moral rights of the author must be considered to be null.

Another of the characteristics of the moral right of the author is its non-renounceability.[83] In a contract or clause, an author cannot wholly or partly renounce his/her moral rights.[84] The right to the paternity of the work is expressly recognised in the aforementioned Article 14 and consists of the right that the author has that a work be recognised as the result of his/her invention or intellectual labour. It is the right of the author that connects him/her to his/her work, which recognises his/her status as author.

The right of paternity also has its negative side. The author may wish his/her identity to remain concealed, by using a pseudonym or simply remaining anonymous (Art. 14.2 LPI). Of course, the author can change his/her mind and wish that his/her identity be known (Art. 14.3 LPI).

The LPI shows other manifestations of the right of paternity. For example, Articles 6.2 and 27 govern the right of the author of an anonymous work and the duration of the rights of these works.[85] Article 64.1 obliges the publisher to include the name, signature or sign that identifies the author in all copies.[86]

---

of exclusion, which confer to the author the right to defend his moral rights and the integrity of his work, and that make possible to claim against any modification'.

81 Also recognised by German, Czech and Greek law.

82 See R. Bercovitz Rodríguez-Cano (coord.), *Comentarios a la Ley de Propiedad Intelectual* (2nd ed., Madrid: 1997), p. 219.

83 Likewise for Czech and Greek law. By contrast, German law seems to allow that a moral right could be transferred if it is expressly negotiated in the contract, and seems not to be separated from copyright.

84 See H. Desbois, *Le droit d'auter: droit francais convention de Berne revisée* (Barcelona: 1990), p. 470.

85 Art. 6.2 Consolidated Text of the Law of Intellectual Property establishes that: 'Where the work is disclosed anonymously or under a pseudonym or sign, the exercise of the intellectual property rights shall accrue to the person, whether natural person or legal entity, who reveals it with the author's consent for as long as the latter does not reveal his identity'. Art. 27 adds: '(1) The exploitation rights in anonymous or pseudonymous works referred to in Article 6 shall last for 70 years following the lawful disclosure thereof. Where, before the said period expires, the author becomes known either because the pseudonym adopted by him leaves no

There have been many jurisprudential judgments that recognise the author's right to be mentioned as such and which consequently oblige the various cultural agents to connect the authors with their work.[87]

The issue raised in Case 5, however, is not so simple, since Professor Higgens is the author not of a whole computer programme but at least of the most important part of it. In Spanish law, algorithms themselves are not protected; they are excluded from the scope of patent law, and so the only way to recognise them is if they are essential to the creation of a computer programme.

In the Spanish Law of Intellectual Property, the rights on computer programmes are specifically provided for in Articles 95–104. Article 96 prescribes that, 'for the purposes of this law, "computer programme" means any sequence of instructions or data intended for either direct or indirect use in a data processing system to perform a function or task or to obtain a specific result'. Article 97, in particular, stipulates who can be the holder of the rights of intellectual property on computer programmes. Computer programmes can be created by one or several people and, in this latter case, they can be considered as a collaborative or collective work (Art. 97, paragraphs 1, 2 and 3).

The law makes no mention of the moral rights of the authors of computer programmes. When the author is a single person, this issue raises no problems because it is governed by the general regulations specified in Article 14 and Professor Higgens could make a legal claim to his right to be recognised as the author of the programme and to be compensated for moral damages. Jurisprudence recognises compensation for moral damage, even when economic harm cannot be proved, on the basis of Article 135 Law of Intellectual Property. Once a moral right – in this case the right to be recognised as author of a work – has been infringed, it is assumed that that this infringement produces moral damage.

The second paragraph of the aforementioned article indicates that the assessment of the moral damage will take into account the circumstances of the infringement, the severity of the infringement and the degree of illicit diffusion

---

doubt as to his identity or because he himself reveals it, the provisions of the foregoing article shall apply. (2) The exploitation rights in works that have not been lawfully disclosed shall last for 70 years following the creation thereof in cases where the term of protection is not calculated as from the natural or declared death of the author or authors.'

86 The publisher shall be under the obligation to reproduce the work in the agreed form, without making any alteration to which the author has not consented, and with the inclusion on the copies of the name, by-line or sign that identifies him/her.

87 Decision of the Provincial Court of Madrid no. 668/2004 of 14 October, and Decision of the Provincial Court of Madrid of 26 September 2000. The Court established that the 'moral right of the author is unrenounceable and inalienable', and also considered that one of the faculties that make up the moral right is the right to be recognised as the author of the work. Decision of the Provincial Court of Madrid of 26 September 2000 recognises both moral and patrimonial rights. Moral right is unrenounceable and inalienable.

of the work. It is clear that the terms in which the Law is expressed leaves a wide margin for discretion in determining the quantity of the compensation.[88]

Numerous rulings state that the right of the author must be recognised as such and that authors have a right to receive compensation for moral damage.[89]

The amount of the compensation for infringing any of the moral rights of the author has gone from one end of the compensatory scale to the other, to such an extent that some offenders have been sentenced to symbolic compensation of one peseta (ruling of the Supreme Court of 23 February 1989), while others have been obliged to return all the earnings obtained (ruling of the Supreme Court of 7 December 1995).

Article 2 of the new Law 19/2006 of 5 June, which extended the protection of the rights over intellectual and industrial property and established procedural regulations to facilitate the application of various community regulations, modifies the revised text of the Law of Intellectual Property of 1996. Article 140 regulates compensation for infringements of the right of the author. Article 140 paragraph 2 a) refers to the moral damage in the same terms as Article 135 did.

The way in which Case 5 is expressed leads us to understand that although Professor Higgens seems to be the author of an essential part of the computer programme, he is not the only author. As has been mentioned above, in those cases in which a computer programme is the work of several people, it can be a collaborative work or a collective work. Determining whether it is one or the other is of extreme importance if it is to be decided who has the moral rights.

In practice, in many cases it is difficult to identify the author of a computer programme. Hardly any computer programmes are sold to the public with any indication of the person by whom they were created, largely because they are often not created by a single person but by a team of professionals with different qualifications and responsibilities.

Article 97.1 establishes that the author of a computer programme is considered to be the person or group of natural persons who have created it, or the legal person who is the holder of the author's rights in the cases expressly envisaged by law. Paragraphs 1 and 3 indicate who is considered to be the author in the case of collective works and who holds the author's rights when the computer programme is a collaborative work.

The law does not state who should hold the moral rights in those cases in which the computer programmes are created by several people, because

---

88 'Moral prejudice shall afford entitlement to indemnification even where there is no evidence of economic prejudice. The amount of the indemnification shall be determined according to the circumstances of the infringement, the seriousness of the harm done and the extent of unlawful dissemination of the work'.

89 Examples are the Decision of the Provincial Court of Barcelona, Section 15, of 22 January 2000; the Decision of the Provincial Court of Madrid, Section 15, of 26 September 2000; and the Decision of the Provincial Court of Barcelona, Section 15, of 10 September 2003.

according to the general principles of the Law of Intellectual Property they are held by whoever is the legal author. Therefore, it seems necessary to determine whether the computer programme in whose creation Professor Higgens played a decisive role is a collective work or a collaborative work.

Collaborative works are the result of ideas or contributions from several authors. This is stated in Article 7.3 LPI and is also expressly recognised for computer programmes in the aforementioned Article 97. The creation of these sorts of works involves a wide range of contributions, which vary in the extent of their separability from other contributions by other participants. In some cases, the contributions made by each one of the authors are indistinguishable and the authors cannot be attributed a specific part.

In other cases, separability is possible because the contributions of each of the individual authors[90] can be clearly distinguished. This seems to be the case envisaged in the question because it is stated that the scientific community is well aware that the fundamental part of the programme was created by Professor Higgens.

Article 7 LPI contains highly heterogeneous cases, with very few regulations. By recognising that the rights belong to all of the authors, it merely states that there is a special community of all the co-authors with respect to the work.

The majority doctrine considers that the reference that the law makes in Article 7.3 and 7.4 LPI to what the parts agree is decisive as far as the exploitation rights are concerned, but does not affect the moral rights of the author. For this reason, the professor has the right to be mentioned as the co-author of ITC's programme that is subsequently adapted by Richard to the needs of the pharmaceutical company. Likewise, he can claim compensation for moral damages because the fact that IPC does not mention him as co-author of the original programme infringes his moral right of paternity to the work. Compensation for moral damages had already been envisaged, as we have described above, in Article 135 of the Revised Text of thc LPI of 1996, as well as in Law 19/2006 of 6 June that reforms part of the Law of Intellectual Property of 1996.

The fact that the contract drawn up between IPC and ITC expressly prohibits the professor from being mentioned does not absolve them of their obligation to cite him as co-author of the original programme because it is an non-renounceable right, and even if the contract between the professor and ITC were to say nothing on this point, under no circumstances can this mean that the professor renounces his right, because the law expressly states that the moral rights of the author are non-renounceable and inalienable. Therefore, the clause that ITC includes in the contract with IPC expressly prohibiting that Professor Higgens be mentioned would be null.

---

90 See R. Bercovitz, *Comentarios a la Ley de Propiedad Intelectual* (2nd ed., Madrid: 1997), p. 80.

The answer to the question would not be the same if the computer programme could be qualified as a collective work. Article 97.2 of the Revised Text of the Law of Intellectual Property establishes that when a computer programme is a collective work, and unless there is some agreement to the contrary, the natural or legal person who publishes it and under whose name it is distributed will be considered to be the author.

Article 97.2 makes no reference to the requisites for a computer programme to be considered as a collective work. Therefore, we must resort to the general rules established by Article 8 of the Law of Intellectual Property for collective works. It should be borne in mind that it is possible for a computer programme to be considered a collective work whatever the legal relation between those who distribute the work and the authors whose contributions have led to a single creation. It makes no difference whether the individuals are subject to a labour relation or any other sort of relation, such as a building contract when the relation has been determined by agreement, even though some are employees and other outsiders.[91]

Article 8 of the Revised Text of the Law of Intellectual Property establishes that:

> a collective work is considered to be one that is created on the initiative of a natural or legal person who publishes it and under whose name it is distributed. It consists of several contributions by different authors which are fused in a single, autonomous creation for which a right has been conceived on the work as a whole, because it is impossible to attribute a separate right to each of them. Unless there is an agreement to the contrary, the rights on the collective work will belong to the person who publishes it and under whose name it is distributed.

In a collective work, coordinated by a third party, several authors provide contributions that together make up the resulting work, which belongs to none of the authors in particular. The final form and content of the collective work is decided by the publisher and distributor.

Collective works have certain special features:

1. a natural or legal person coordinates and gathers together the contributions of the various authors;
2. the personal contribution of each of the authors has been conceived for the resulting common work;
3. the personal creation of each author is fused into a single, autonomous creation that is the result of the coordination;
4. rights cannot be attributed separately to any of the authors on the work as a whole; the defining feature may be that the various authors who

[91] Ibid., p. 82.

collaborate in the work cannot decide on the final content of the collective work; and
5. the collective work must be published and distributed.

Although there is not sufficient data for us to know what type of work the computer programme produced by the company ITC is, it does not seem to be a collective work, because the essential part of the work was produced exclusively by Professor Higgens and it is perfectly distinguishable and separable from the rest of the programme. Neither does it seem that ITC's contribution, commercialisation aside, has been fundamental to the creation of the work.

Assuming that the case was about a collective work, in the case of computer programmes, Article 97.2 LPI determines that '[i]n the case of a collective work, unless otherwise agreed, the person, whether natural person or legal entity, who edits and discloses it under his name shall have the status of author'.

Some considerable doctrinal sectors criticise the fact that a legal person can be recognised as the author, to such an extent that some authors distinguish between authorship and ownership of the rights on a work. The exploitation rights would belong to the person who publishes and distributes the work, but the same cannot be said of the moral rights.

In the case of a collective work, and unless there is no agreement to the contrary, other authors consider that Article 97.2 clearly attributes authorship to the natural or legal person who publishes the work and under whose name it is distributed. There is nothing in the moral rights to prevent them from being attributed to the person who publishes and distributes the work, even if this is a legal person.

Therefore, and according to the most authoritative doctrine, if it were a collective work, the moral rights would belong to ITC, and Professor Higgens would have no rights at all to be recognised as author or, as a result, to claim compensation for moral damages.

The little information provided suggests that the computer programme mentioned is a collaborative work of which Professor Higgens is one of the co-authors. He is therefore entitled to be recognised as co-author. The author's moral rights are stipulated in Article 14 of the Revised Text of the Law of Intellectual Property. Likewise, the infringement of this right legitimates a claim for compensation for moral damages (Art. 140 of the Law of Intellectual Property, after the reform introduced by Law 20/2006 of 5 June).

III. Metalegal Formants

The moral right of author links the creator to his/her work and is independent from the economic rights. Whereas the exploitation rights may be transferred by transaction, moral rights are non-renounceable and inalienable. Any transaction of these rights is null.

(16) UNITED KINGDOM

I. *Operative Rules*

In principle, Professor Higgens cannot assert moral rights in the computer programme he has written or claim an injunction when the product containing the programme is marketed without making any reference to him as the author.

If the algorithm is considered to represent a separate literary work, however, Higgens may assert his right to be named as author and claim an injunction against IPC.

II. *Descriptive Formants*

This problem question deals with protection of Professor Higgens' moral rights with respect to the computer programme and the algorithm written and developed by him. 'The term "moral rights" refers to the rights of authors – meaning all creative workers – to have their work attributed and not subjected to prejudicial changes.'[92] In the UK, moral rights are regulated by the CDPA 1988, which grants four different rights: the right to be identified as the author or director (s. 77 CDPA 1988), the right to object to derogatory treatment of work (s. 80 CDPA 1988), the right against false attribution of work (s. 84 CDPA 1988), and the right to privacy of certain photographs and films (s. 85 CDPA 1988).

It is firstly necessary to examine whether Professor Higgens has a right to be identified as an author of ITC's programme when Richard adapts it to the needs of pharmaceutical companies. Normally, computer programmes are considered to be literary works, the author of which 'has the right to be identified as the author of the work, but the right is not infringed unless it has been asserted in accordance with section 78' (s. 77(1) CDPA 1988). However, there are exceptions to this right. According to section 79(2) CDPA 1988, the right to be identified does not apply in relation to a computer programme. Therefore, following the clear position in UK copyright law, Professor Higgens cannot assert moral rights in the computer programme he has written nor claim an injunction when the product containing the programme is marketed without making any reference to him as the author.

However, the problem question sets out that Professor Higgens also develops a specific algorithm for the computer programme. An algorithm can be defined as a rule or procedure for solving a logical or mathematical problem. Therefore, at least in theory, it is possible to write an algorithm to solve a particular

---

92 D. Vaver, 'Moral rights yesterday, today and tomorrow' (1999) 7(3) *International Journal of Law and Information Technology* 270–278, 270, available at https://doi.org/10.1093/ijlit/7.3.270 (last accessed 2022).

problem and then write the computer programme to implement the algorithm. It is therefore possible to see the algorithm as a literary work over which it may be possible to assert moral rights.

Working under this assumption, in order to have a right to be named, Professor Higgens has to comply with certain requirements. As stated above, under section 77 CPDA 1988, the right has to be asserted. Section 78 CDPA 1988 explains that there are several ways to assert this right, such as, 'on assignment of copyright in the work, by including in the instruments effecting the assignment a statement that the author or director asserts in relation to that work his right to be identified' (s. 78(2)(a)) or by instrument in writing signed by the author or director (s. 78(2)(b)). Therefore, seeing that Professor Higgens is most likely to be the author of the algorithm, he could have a right to be named if he issues an instrument in writing signed by him asserting this right.

It is important to note that moral rights can be waived 'by an instrument in writing signed by the person giving up the right' (s. 87(2) CDPA 1988) It is, therefore, possible to argue that the contract between Professor Higgens and ITC, which is silent as to his original personality rights, represents a waiver of the professor's right to be named. If this is the case, Professor Higgens cannot assert his right to be named and there can be no infringement when the algorithm is adapted and marketed for commercial purposes.

However, in the event that this contract does not fully satisfy the requirements of a 'waiving instrument', infringement arises (1) where the author is not properly identified, (2) in the circumstances where attribution is required, and (3) where no defences or exceptions apply. It can therefore be argued that when Richard adapts ITC's programme to the needs of pharmaceutical companies, attribution to Professor Higgens is required, as the algorithm will be used for commercial purposes and as an integral part of the programme. Moreover, it is also arguable that when IPC markets the product making reference only to ITC and not Professor Higgens, IPC in theory fails to properly identify the author of the core of the programme.

Assuming that the contract is not 'precise' enough to act as a waiver instrument, as explained above, it is necessary to look at other exceptions and defences. Firstly, this right does not apply when it concerns a work produced in the course of employment (s. 79(3) CDPA 1988). Professor Higgens is not an employee of ITC but is with Y-University, which renders this exception inapplicable. Defences such as fair dealing for the purpose of reporting current events and incidental use in artistic work, sound recording or film broadcast (s. 79 CDPA 1988) are inapplicable in this case. Following this approach and bearing in mind the caveats emphasised above, Professor Higgens may be able to claim an injunction to prevent marketing of the computer programme making reference only to ITC. This can be achieved under section 103 CDPA 1988, which states that 'an infringement of moral rights is actionable as a breach of statutory duty owed to the person entitled to the right.'

Finally, it is also worthwhile examining whether the fact that IPC improves the product invokes Professor Higgens' right to object to derogatory treatment of his work as prescribed under section 80 CDPA 1988. Computer programmes in themselves are also excluded from protection under this moral right, as stated in section 81 CDPA 1988. However, following the assumption set out above, it is possible to argue that Professor Higgens' moral rights could be protected if one looks at the algorithm as a separate literary work. In order to assert a moral right under section 80 CDPA 1988, it is necessary to show there was (1) treatment of the work and that this treatment was (2) derogatory. According to section 80(2)(a) CDPA 1988, 'treatment of a work means any addition to, deletion from or alteration or adaptation of the work.' It can therefore be argued that the fact that Richard adapts the programme, and with that the algorithm itself, could amount to treatment of the work. However, this treatment needs to be derogatory, i.e. 'it amounts to distortion or mutilation of the work or is otherwise prejudicial to the honour or reputation of the author' (s. 80(2)(b) CDPA 1988).

UK law seems to take an objective interpretation of this term as it was held in the cases of *Tidy*,[93] *Pasterfield*[94] and *Confetti*,[95] where the courts were prepared to find that there was treatment of the work but could not infer that it was derogatory. The courts based these judgments on the reasoning that even though the alterations and the adaptation could have been seen as derogatory from the subjective viewpoint of the authors, they were only trivial and minor from an objective standpoint and therefore there could not have been a breach of moral rights.

However, in *Morrison*[96] and the Canadian case of *Snow*,[97] it was held that taking and adding bits to the work and putting them into different context could amount to distortion or mutilation, as it was seen by the author himself. These cases seem to demonstrate that better protection of an author's right to integrity should be given in certain circumstances. Whether the UK courts are more likely to take the objective stance of the 'right thinking member of the society' or follow the subjective overtones of the terms 'honour' and 'reputation' this right seeks to protect remains unclear.

Going back to the situation at hand, if Richard has made trivial amendments to the programme and potentially the algorithm to adapt it to the needs of pharmaceutical companies, it is highly likely that the UK courts will follow the judgments in *Tidy* and *Pasterfield*, to decide that there was no derogatory treatment of the work. However, it is also, at least theoretically, possible that – depending on the alterations and whether they affect the algorithm – the courts

93 *Tidy v. Natural History Museum* [1998] 39 IPR 503.
94 *Pasterfield v. Denham* [1999] FSR 168.
95 *Confetti Records v. Warner Music UK* [2003] ECDR 33.
96 *Morrison Leahy Music Limited and Another v. Lightbond Limited and Others* [1991] Ch D.
97 *Snow v. Eaton Centre* [1982] 70 CPR 105.

will decide to side with Professor Higgens and find derogatory treatment of the algorithm. If this is the case, IPC could be infringing Professor Higgens' moral rights by marketing the article in the course of business, as stated in section 83(1)(b) CDPA 1988. Moreover, according to section 103(2), the court has the discretion to grant whichever remedy it finds adequate, including an 'injunction on terms prohibiting the doing of any act.'

III. Metalegal Formants

UK IP law provides limited protection to moral rights, with many considerably detailed restraints, exemptions and 'uncontrolled waiver provisions'[98] built into the statute. This 'common law antipathy to moral rights'[99] is due to several factors, some of which may be because of the potential impact the exercise of moral rights may have on 'economic exploitation of creative works'.[100] Moreover, moral rights are largely associated with the ideal of 'romantic authorship':[101] 'the view that works protected by copyright are produced by those tucked away in their lonely garrets, labouring long and hard over creative work'.[102] In fact, the situation today is very much different, where authorship and creativity are associated with wealth and the desire to reap the economic advantages resulting from a work. Dworkin argues that the protection afforded to moral rights under UK law was an attempt by the government to 'modify, some would say to emasculate, moral rights in the light of business reality'.[103]

Some authors, such as Eagles and Longdin, mention further that this trend is particularly evident in the area of software authorships. They take the exclusion of computer programmes as an example and argue that 'software designers will use moral rights to pursue financial objectives which have nothing to do with preserving the creativity expressed in the programme.'[104] Additionally, to allow moral rights for these works would lead to problems of identification

---

98 H. Zhonglin, 'Author's Moral Rights in UK and China', School of African and Oriental Studies, 2002, p. 19, available at: http://www.ciplawyer.com/Copyright4/136196.jhtml (last accessed 2019).

99 D. Vaver, 'Moral rights yesterday, today and tomorrow' (1999) 7(3) *International Journal of Law and Information Technology* 270–278, 275, available at https://doi.org/10.1093/ijlit/7.3.270 (last accessed 2022).

100 C. Waelde and L. de Souza, 'Moral Rights and the Internet: Squaring the Circle', p. 11, available at: https://www.era.lib.ed.ac.uk/bitstream/1842/2306/1/moralrightsandtheinternet.pdf. (last accessed 2019).

101 L. Bently and B. Sherman, *Intellectual Property Law* (2nd ed., Oxford: 2004).

102 Ibid., p. 9.

103 G. Dworkin, 'Moral Rights and the Common Law Countries', in: *The Moral Right of the Author* (Paris: 1993), p. 105.

104 I. Eagles and L. Longdin, 'Technological Creativity And Moral Rights: A Comparative Perspective', (2004) 12(2) *International Journal of Law and Information Technology* 209–236, 217, available at https://doi.org/10.1093/ijlit/12.2.209 (last accessed 2022).

and assertion because there are too many people having a say in preserving the work's integrity.[105]

However, it can be argued that there are several reasons why moral rights should be taken more seriously in the UK. First of all, 'the integrity and authenticity of an author's work is of importance to society as a whole. Unless moral rights are preserved there is a danger that the original work will be modified to make it commercially successful.'[106] If this is allowed, the diversity of different cultures could degenerate into something that is simply easy to sell. Moreover, Vaver rightly points out that 'moral rights provide authors with a bargaining chip which, given the greater power generally wielded by entrepreneurs, allows authors some say over the manner in which their work is later exploited.'[107]

Furthermore, there are no sufficiently persuasive reasons to treat software creators differently from other authors of literary works. Computer programmes are accepted as copyright subject matter and 'moral rights should apply across all the categories of copyright'.[108] Bearing this in mind, it is reasonable to suggest that UK moral rights should be more comprehensive, with stricter control over the waivers and exemptions employed. However, it seems unlikely that these changes will be introduced in the near future.

A.3. COMPARATIVE REMARKS

In principle, all jurisdictions provide strong support for moral rights in copyright, especially the right to be named.[109] Interestingly, the right to improvement or alteration of the author's work is in some jurisdictions a moral right (Estonia and the Netherlands), in others an economic right (Germany). Therefore, in most countries Prof. Higgens can claim an injunction.[110] If there is a contract, only economic rights are transferred and not moral ones.[111] The Danish and the Lithuanian systems are the only exceptions. In Denmark, economic *and* moral rights are transferred to the employer (but it is not wholly clear whether this also

105 Ibid.

106 M. Holderness, 'Moral Rights and Authors' Rights: The Keys to the Information Age' (1988) *JILT* 16.

107 D. Vaver, 'Moral rights yesterday, today and tomorrow' (1999) 7(3) *International Journal of Law and Information Technology* 277–278, 277, available at https://doi.org/10.1093/ijlit/7.3.270 (last accessed 2022).

108 I. Eagles and L. Longdin, 'Technological Creativity And Moral Rights: A Comparative Perspective', (2004) 12(2) *International Journal of Law and Information Technology* 209–236, 217, available at https://doi.org/10.1093/ijlit/12.2.209 (last accessed 2022).

109 Divergences can be found in the Belgian and Estonian reports.

110 See the reports of Belgium, Czech Republic, Estonia, France, Germany, Ireland, Italy, Lithuania, the Netherlands, Norway, Poland, Slovenia and Spain.

111 See the reports of Estonia, Norway, Slovenia and Italy.

applies to professors and research personnel of universities). Therefore, Prof. Higgens probably cannot claim an injunction in Denmark. In the UK and in Lithuania, the situation is special. Moral rights under copyright law are explicitly not granted for computer programmes. But British law provides copyright protection for algorithms. Consequently, Prof. Higgens could have the right to be named with regard to the algorithm. Concerning the improved programme, the situation is not entirely clear, as there is diverging case law by the British courts. Many national statutes provide for certain limitations on the right to be named (although not applicable in the present case). In Greece, the injunction may not be disproportionate. In the Netherlands, the author can demand to be named, unless this would be unreasonable in a specific case. In Norway, the right must be 'in accordance with proper usage', which means that one has to examine whether there are any practical inconveniences for the other party.

CASE 6. FARMERS' RIGHTS

A.1. CASE

Assume that your country has accepted GM food: the company CaMon is marketing seeds of a tomato plant that looks fresh on the shelf for longer than others. This feature of the tomato has been patented. Paul, a farmer of vegetables and legumes, is looking for better marketing opportunities. He heard about this plant and hopes to win more customers by expanding his distribution system. It seems that the new tomato plant has the potential to be a building block for his new strategy. He buys the seed – enough to plant 100 acres. However, the delivery of the seed is accompanied by a licence contract that obliges him to sell the whole harvest to a big food processing company (FPC), located 700 km away. Any violation will give rise to contractual penalties.

Paul ignores the licence and sells the harvested tomatoes to regional customers. In September, he receives a letter from CaMon reminding him only to sell to FPC and announcing a lawsuit. Since Paul pursues his own marketing strategies, they meet in court one year later.

Is CaMon entitled to contractual penalties?

A.2. COUNTRY REPORTS

(1) BELGIUM

I. Operative Rules

In case of breach of contract, CaMon would, in theory, be entitled to the agreed contractual penalties. However, some difficulties arise in this case.

We may ask whether Paul can be deemed to have consented to the licence contract. If not, the contract is not valid.

The contract clause containing the penalties might be invalid. Real penalty clauses, with the objective of private punishment instead of compensation for potential damages, are invalid.

The penalty clause could be invalid from a competition law perspective.

Although the validity of the contract depends on the detailed circumstances, it seems probable in the present case that CaMon would not be entitled to the contractual penalties.

II. *Descriptive Formants*

- Article 16 Regulation (EC) No. 2100/94 on Community plant variety rights;[1]
- Article 10 Biotechnology Directive 98/44/EC;
- Article 27quater BPA (Art. XI.32 BCEL);
- Article 21 Belgian Plant Variety Protection Act[2] (the Belgian Plant Variety Protection Act of 1975 was replaced by the Plant Variety Protection Act on 10 January 2011, the latter implementing the UPOV Convention of 19 March 1991. The 2011 Plant Variety Protection Act is now stipulated in Book XI BCEL, specifically Arts. XI.104–162).

a) Patent law or plant breeders' rights perspective

In 2005, Article 27quater (now Art. XI.32 BCEL) was inserted in the BPA,[3] implementing Article 10 of the Biotechnology Directive:

> The protection referred to in Articles 8 and 9 [now Arts. XI.30 and XI.31 BCEL] shall not extend to biological material obtained from the propagation or multiplication of biological material placed on the market in the territory of a Member State by the holder of the patent or with his consent, where the multiplication or propagation necessarily results from the application for which the biological material was marketed, provided that the material obtained is not subsequently used for other propagation or multiplication.

Paul's tomatoes will not be covered by CaMon's patent. Paul's actions would only fall under the scope of the patent if he were to use the tomatoes to propagate, in other words to use the seeds for further multiplication, or to sell the seed.[4]

The present case is about a feature of the tomato plant which is protected by a patent. However, the above would also be valid if the tomato plant had been protected as a plant variety under the Belgian Plant Variety Protection Act.[5] The scope of the current Belgian plant variety protection is limited to breeding material and does not extend to the end product. In addition, under

1 Council Regulation (EC) No. 2100/94, 27 July 1994, on Community plant variety rights, OJ L 227, 1 September 1994, 1–30.

2 Belgian Plant Variety Protection Act, 20 May 1975, *Official Gazette*, 5 September 1975 [Wet tot bescherming van kweekproducten, 20 mei 1975, *B.S.*, 5 september 1975].

3 Introduced by Art. 9 Act on Biotechnological Inventions, 28 April 2005, *Official Gazette*, 13 May 2005 [Wet 28 april 2005 tot wijziging van de wet van 28 maart 1984 op de uitvindingsoctrooien, wat betreft de octrooieerbaarheid van de biotechnologische uitvindingen, *B.S.*, 13 mei 2005].

4 E. de Gryse, 'Licentieovereenkomsten' [Licence Agreements], in: *Bijzondere overeenkomsten. Commentaar met overzicht van rechtspraak en rechtsleer [Special Agreements. Commentaries with Overviews of Case Law and Doctrine]* (Antwerpen: 1985), 25–27.

5 Belgian Plant Variety Protection Act, 20 May 1975, *Official Gazette*, 5 September 1975 [Wet tot bescherming van kweekproducten, 20 mei 1975, *B.S.*, 5 september 1975].

the Community Plant Variety Right Regulation, Paul's actions would not fall under the scope of the exclusive rights, since CaMon would have exhausted its breeder's right by selling the tomato seeds within the European Union.[6]

b) Contract law perspective

Does this mean that Paul is free to do whatever he wants with the harvested tomatoes?[7] If he has closed a contract in advance to sell his harvest to a particular client, the contract binds him and is enforceable (Art. 1134 Civil Code). According to general principles of contract law, Paul then has no right to sell his tomatoes to regional customers and therefore CaMon will be entitled to contractual penalties as foreseen in the freely consented contract.[8]

It is doubtful in the present case, however, whether the contract is valid. Articles 1108–1133 Civil Code impose four conditions for contracts to be valid: mutual consent, contractual capacity, an object or purpose of the contract, and, finally, a lawful cause. Has the condition of mutual consent been met? It is said that 'the delivery of the seed is accompanied by a licence contract'. We can ask whether due consent to this licence contract has been given by Paul. A lot will depend on the specific circumstances, but, in general, the accompanying contract will not be binding upon Paul,[9] unless he would consent to this, even silently. According to Article 25 Commercial Code, the absence of protest could amount to an acceptance of the accompanying licence contract. The latter will not be accepted, however, when the clauses of the accompanying contract deviate from the original contract or when the accompanying contract contains unusual or excessive clauses.[10] The same issues regarding these shrink-wrap licences have arisen in the software business.[11]

Second, we need to keep in mind that stipulating real penalty clauses is not allowed in Belgium. Such clauses can only account for potential damages, but may not constitute a kind of private punishment. This was confirmed by the

6 Art. 16 Council Regulation (EC) No. 2100/94 of 27 July 1994 on Community plant variety rights, OJ L 227, 1 September 1994, 1–30.

7 Except using them for further propagation, of course.

8 For more information on these general principles: S. Stijns, *Verbintenissenrecht [Contract Law]* (Brugge: 2005), 37–42.

9 For instance: Court of Appeal Brussels, 23 November 2001, *D.A.O.R.* 2002, 244.

10 For instance: Commercial Court Brussels [Kh.], 16 January 2004, *R.W.* 2005–06, 872; More on this: K. Vanderschot, 'Instemming met algemene voorwaarden: kennisname- en aanvaarding clausules (Hoofdtstuk 1)' [Consent of Standard Agreements], in: S. Stijns and K. Vanderschot (eds.), *Contractuele clausules rond de (niet-)uitvoering en de beëindiging van contracten [Contractual Clauses on the (Non-)Execution and the Termination of Contracts]* (Antwerpen/Oxford: 2006), 1–39.

11 M.W. Cheltema and T.F.E. Tjong Tjin Tai, 'Overeenkomsten sluiten door openen en klikken?' [Contracting by Opening and Clicking?], *Computerrecht* 2003, no. 4, 244–248; P.H. Blok and T. De Weerd, 'Shrink-wrap- en click-wraplicenties zijn aanvaardbaar' [Shrink-Wrap- and Click-Wrap Licences are Acceptable], *Computerrecht* 2004, no. 3, 126–128; R. Westerdijk, 'Openen en klikken: overeenkomst gesloten' [To Open and Click: Contract concluded], *Computerrecht* 2004, no. 6, 280–284.

Belgian Supreme Court in 1970,[12] which considers such clauses null. The Court considered private punishment or the fact that a contract party could be better off in the event of a breach of contract and could therefore speculate on it to be contrary to the public interest. A new Article 1231 was added to the Belgian Civil Code in 1998, confirming this jurisprudential doctrine and allowing the judge to moderate contractual penalties to damages *ex officio*.[13] If CaMon were to go to court, the penalty clause could be adapted, depending on the specific and detailed circumstances.[14]

c) Competition law perspective

Assuming proper consent has been given and the issue of the punitive character of the contractual penalties set aside, contract freedom is limited by a variety of additional provisions. Some of those concern the protection of the consumer, others the protection of traders and/or competition.[15] It is the latter category that can also come into play as well if the conditions are fulfilled.

The particular clause obliging Paul to sell his harvest 700 km away to FPC, and FPC alone, can raise certain objections, in the light of both Article 101 and Article 102 TFEU (Arts. 2 and 3 BCtA, now Arts. IV.1 and IV.2 BCEL). There might be legitimate reasons for the specific behaviour of CaMon, however. A detailed analysis of the specific circumstances would be necessary. Since no particular Belgian case law is available, we will limit ourselves to some general remarks. It should be recalled that Belgian competition law adheres strongly to European competition law and case law.

Article 102 TFEU

In order for Article 102 TFEU (especially subsections (a) and (d))[16] to be applicable, the conditions need to be fulfilled, among which dominance of CaMon on the relevant market. The fact that the tomato might be a building block for Paul's strategy will be relevant, but is, on its own, not enough to establish dominance.

---

12 Belgian Supreme Court [Cass.], 17 April 1970, *A.C.* 1970, 754; *J.T.* 1970, 545.

13 Act on the Modification of the Civil Code, concerning penalty clauses and moratory interest, 23 November 1998, *Official Gazette*, 13 January 1999 [Wet tot wijziging, wat het strafbeding en de moratoire interest betreft, van het Burgerlijk Wetboek, 23 november 1998, *B.S.*, 13 januari 1999].

14 S. Stijns, *Verbintenissenrecht [Contract Law]* (Brugge: 2005), 181–186.

15 See the Commerce Practices Act and the Competition Act (now included in Book IV–VI BCEL). Also: S. Stijns, *Verbintenissenrecht [Contract Law]* (Brugge: 2005), 43–54. For some doctrine on the relevant provisions and how they are connected: J. Stuyck, W. Devroe and P. Wytinck (eds.), *De nieuwe Belgische Mededingingswet 2006 [The New Belgian Competition Act 2006]* (Mechelen: 2007), 260; R. Steennot and S. Dejonghe, *Handboek Consumentenbescherming en Handelspraktijken [Manual Consumer Protection and Trade Practices]* (Antwerpen/Oxford: 2007), 628; D. Dessard and A. de Caluwé, *Les usages honnêtes [Fair Practices]* (Brussels: 2007), 300.

16 Art. 3 1° and 4° BCtA (Art. VI.2 1° and 4° BCEL) being equivalent.

Article 101 TFEU

Article 101 TFEU might provide some possibilities to counter CaMon's behaviour. In this regard, Article 4(b) Vertical Agreements Block Regulation[17] states that 'a restriction of the customers to whom the buyer may sell the contract goods or services' constitutes a hardcore restriction.[18] As we have seen in Case 1, Modification 1, hardcore restrictions are not necessarily excluded from the application of Article 101(3) TFEU, but this is quite likely. Whether or not CaMon can invoke Article 101(3) will depend on the reasons for imposing the disputed contract clauses. In this regard, it remains to be seen whether CaMon's motivation is not mainly related to the quality and publicity function of trademarks.[19] If the purpose of CaMon's behaviour were to try to enter a new market more effectively or to prevent free-riding on promotional efforts, this would be relevant for an evaluation under Article 101(3).[20] The functions of breeder's rights or patents, on the other hand, seem less coherent with CaMon's actions.

According to Article 101(2) TFEU and Article 2§2 BCtA (now Art. VI.1 BCEL), prohibited agreements are automatically void.

III. Metalegal Formants

Conventional patents confer on their owner the right to prevent all third parties not having his/her consent from producing, using or selling an invention. Once put on the market with consent, the patented objects can be resold and freely circulate, as the patent is exhausted with regard to those specific objects. No one other than the patent holder or a possible licensee is allowed to produce the invention and put it on the market him/herself.

With respect to biotechnological inventions, the issue becomes somewhat more complicated.[21] Biotechnological products (e.g. seeds) are easily reproduced. Therefore, it has been provided that the scope of a biotechnological patent covers the materials derived from the original biological material through propagation or multiplication.[22] This will not be the case if the propagation or multiplication (e.g. sowing seeds) necessarily results from the application for

---

17 Commission Regulation (EC) No. 330/2010 of 20 April 2010 on the application of Article 101(3) of the Treaty on the Functioning of the European Union to categories of vertical agreements and concerted practices, OJ L 102, 23 April 2010, 1–7.

18 The Vertical Agreements Block Regulation provides for some exceptions, which do not seem applicable to the present case.

19 J. Verbruggen, 'Merkenrecht functioneel bekeken' [Function of Trademarks], *I.R.D.I.* 2001, 107–118.

20 See also para. 107(1) Guidelines on Vertical Restraints, OJ C 130, 19 May 2010, 1–46.

21 E. de Gryse, 'Licentieovereenkomsten' [Licence Agreements], in: *Bijzondere overeenkomsten. Commentaar met overzicht van rechtspraak en rechtsleer [Special Agreements. Commentaries with Overviews of Case Law and Doctrine]* (Antwerpen: 1985), 25–27.

22 Arts. 8 and 9 Biotechnology Directive and Arts. 27bis and 27ter BPA (Arts. XI.30 and XI.31 BCEL).

which the biological material was marketed. In other words, no patent will cover a farmer's harvests (e.g. Paul's tomatoes), albeit on the condition that the derived materials are not used for further propagation (so he should not sow the seeds of the harvested tomatoes in order to have another harvest).[23]

By imposing the said contract clause, CaMon has been able to extent the scope of its patent *de facto* to the derived materials as well. Contract law is used here to extent the scope of a patent, where patent law had explicitly limited this scope. In this way, CaMon is able to extend the IP-originated monopoly and include a downstream market, namely the market of already harvested tomatoes.

In competitive market conditions, the above does not have to be problematic: Paul could always choose another seed supplier who does not impose such re-sale restrictions. But when there is not an alternative, the situation *can* become problematic. A lot will depend on the necessity/importance of really using this specific type of tomato in order to be successful on the tomato market.

Apart from competition law, the restrictive clause CaMon wants to impose can be criticised from a purer contract/patent law point of view. While recent software and biotechnological developments tend to render the differences between sales and licences obscure, some inherent characteristics of sales should be preserved. In this regard, the liberty to resell or unrestrictedly use the stuff we have bought should be protected. Overly restrictive clauses on re-sale could infringe the *ordre public*[24] just as much as unreasonable use restrictions could. Free circulation of goods is essential for society in the sense that overly harsh restrictions on property (e.g. inalienability clauses) could lead to stagnation.[25] After-sale conditions should not be used to unreasonably broaden patent protection.[26] After all, selling, for instance, a television with the restriction that one cannot sell it on the second-hand market might prove to be subject to criticism as well.

(2) CZECH REPUBLIC

I. Operative Rules

CaMon is not entitled to contractual penalties.

---

23 Art. 10 Biotechnology Directive and Art. 27quater BPA (Art. XI. 32 BCEL). We will not elaborate on the farmers' privilege that could allow for re-sowing to a certain degree in certain situations.

24 Court of Appeal Antwerp, 5th Chamber, 26 March 1984, *R.W.* 1985–1986, 1769–1772; Court of Appeal Gent, 22 Mai 1987, *Pas.* 1987, 175–178.

25 H. de Page and R. Dekkers, *Traité élémentaire de droit civil belge* (Vol. 5, Brussels: 1975), paras. 907–908, 803–805.

26 H. Ghijsen, 'Access to Germplasm for Further Breeding in the Case of Patents and After-Sale Conditions', *BSLR* 2005–2006, no. 2, 91.

II. Descriptive Formants

In Czech law, no specific requirement exists for purchase contracts on buying seed to be in writing. Paul concluded a valid oral purchase contract while buying the seed.

The seed arrived accompanied by the licence contract. According to section 43a(1) of the Civil Code, the licence contract which accompanies the seed is an offer to conclude the contract. According to section 43c(2) of the Civil Code, the contract is concluded at the time when the acceptance is delivered to the offering person. In addition, according to section 44(1) of the Civil Code, inactivity or silence shall not be considered as acceptance of the offer. Paul did not deliver his acceptance to CaMon and so a licence contract was not concluded.

Plant variety rights are protected in the Czech Republic by the Act on the Protection of Plant Variety Rights 408/2000 Coll. According to section 19(1) of the Act, the holder has sole authority to use the protected plant, including the production and sale of protected plants. According to section 19(2) of the Act, the holder of the rights to the plant may grant a licence to a third person via a licence contract, which must be in writing.[27]

However, according to section 20(1) of the Act on the Protection of Plant Variety Rights, the provisions of section 19 do not apply in the case of plant material[28] which was sold by the holder of the rights or with his/her consent.[29] According to section 20, the rights of the holder are exhausted in respect to the material which was sold by the holder or with his/her consent. This provision introduces the principle that the licence charge shall be paid only once per reproduction cycle.[30] There is the assumption that the price of the marketed seed includes a licence charge too.

According to the facts of the case, seed was sold to Paul by CaMon, so that the rights of CaMon were exhausted. Paul was not obliged to conclude the licence contract, and if he ignores the licence contract, no obligations can arise in this respect for him. He was a lawful user of the seed.

---

27 According to the explanatory report to section 19 of the Act on the Protection of Plant Variety Rights, the provisions of section 19 were adopted in the nearly same wording as the Regulation (EC) No. 2100/94 on Community plant variety rights and Art. 14 of the Universal Convention for the Protection of New Varieties of Plants.

28 'Material' is defined in section 20(2) as any propagating material of plant variety or any harvested material of the protected variety.

29 According to the explanatory report to section 20 of the Act on the Protection of Plant Variety Rights, the provisions of section 20 correspond to Art. 16 of Regulation (EC) No. 2100/94 on Community plant variety rights and to Art. 16 of the Universal Convention for the Protection of New Varieties of Plants.

30 See the explanatory report to section 20 of the Act on the Protection of Plant Variety Rights.

III. Metalegal Formants

Answer omitted.

(3) DENMARK

I. Operative Rules

CaMon has no claim as regards the first generation of tomatoes but will have a claim vis-à-vis possible second generations.

II. Descriptive Formants

The point of departure is the exhaustion rule in DPA §3a, fourth paragraph. According to this rule (which stems from the Biotechnology Directive (Directive 98/44/EC)), the patent holder's exclusive right to exploitation shall not include biological material produced on the basis of reproduction of biological material which has been put on the market in the EEA by the patent holder him/herself or with his/her consent, if this reproduction was necessary in order to use the material for the use for which it was sold. The impact of the contract clause depends partly on the nature of the exhaustion rule (mandatory or non-mandatory) and partly on whether it is at all contractually binding. It is not quite settled whether the exhaustion rule in the DPA is mandatory or may be superseded by contract. The starting point, however, would seem to be that the rule of exhaustion cannot be waived by contract and certainly not by a general disclaimer such as the one in the present example. In addition, it is doubtful whether a standard contract clause unilaterally dictated by one party (CaMon) can be regarded as consented to by the other party and thus be legally binding. In relation to trade between EEA states, it will follow from the rules on free movement of goods (Arts. 28 and 30 EC Treaty) that it is mandatory. The conclusion, based on the facts of the case, should be in any event that CaMon is not entitled to 'contractual penalties' for the tomato harvest resulting from the seed bought by Paul.

If Paul, however, uses seeds from the first crop to raise new crops of tomatoes, the situation will be different. The exhaustion rule is not applicable in this situation as these seeds are not put on the market with the consent of the rightholder. On the other hand, DPA §3b, first paragraph, implementing Article 11 of the Biotechnology Directive, contains a 'farmers' privilege' rule: if plant-propagating material is sold or transferred, with the consent of the patent holder, to a farmer for agricultural use, this shall imply authorisation for the farmer to use the product of his/her harvest for propagation or multiplication on his/her own farm. However, pursuant to §3b, second paragraph, the further extent and conditions of the farmer's right are determined in Article 14 of Council

Regulation (EC) No. 2100/94 of 27 July 1994 on Community plant variety rights. This provision enumerates the kinds of plant-propagating material covered by the farmers' privilege. As tomatoes are not listed, the derogation from the patent holders' exclusive rights does not apply. Consequently, Paul cannot use seeds from the plant to raise new crops.

III. Metalegal Formants

The exhaustion rule delimits the scope of the patent in the first place, and it is doubtful whether the rightholder should be entitled to extend the scope through contract provision. The special exhaustion provision on biological material extends the scope of the traditional exhaustion rule to allow the buyer (i.e. farmer) to reproduce the invention as far as the first generation is concerned. In this way, the special rule is evidence of the fact that the inclusion of biological material in the sphere of patent protection sometimes warrants special considerations.

(4) ESTONIA

I. Operative Rules

CaMon is entitled to contractual penalties.

II. Descriptive Formants

The Plant Propagation and Plant Variety Rights Act[31] regulates *inter alia* the rights of the holders of plant variety rights.[32] According to §35(2) of the Plant Propagation and Plant Variety Rights Act, '[b]ased on a plant variety right, the holder of the plant variety right has the exclusive right, and other persons duly authorised by the holder of the plant variety right have the right to' produce, market, import, export and possess the seed, and to propagate and cultivate material of the variety.

CaMon and Paul have concluded an agreement according to which the whole harvest has to be sold to FPC. The fulfilment of this obligation was guaranteed by contractual penalty. Based on the limited facts, the contract is presumably valid under Estonian law. The right to market the harvest was limited to a specific company (FPC). Marketing to other customers was not allowed. Consequently, CaMon is entitled to contractual penalties.

---

[31] Taimede paljundamise ja sordikaitse seadus. Entered into force on 1 January 2006 – RT I 2005, 70, 540; 2009, 3, 15 (in Estonian).

[32] Plant Propagation and Plant Variety Rights Act §1(1).

III. *Metalegal Formants*

Plant variety rights are also protected by criminal law. Subsection 229(1) of the Penal Code provides that '[i]llegal appropriation of rights belonging to the breeder or owner of a protected variety or use of a protected variety without a licence issued by the owner, is punishable by a pecuniary punishment or up to 3 years' imprisonment'. Since Paul did not have a licence to sell the harvest to his customers, his actions might presumably constitute 'use of a protected variety without a licence issued by the owner', which is a criminal offence.

(5) FRANCE

I. *Operative Rules*

Unless the clause is declared invalid on the grounds of competition law, CaMon is entitled to contractual penalties.

II. *Descriptive Formants*

In accordance with the Biotechnology Directive, introduced into the French Intellectual Property Code by Law No. 2004-1338 of 8 December 2004, Article L. 613-2-2 of the French Intellectual Property Code provides that the scope of the protection of a patent concerning a product that includes genetic information extends to the product itself. This means that the right of the patentee concerns the seeds and the plants insofar as they contain the biological information which was patented. To this extent, the exploitation of the plants by the farmer justifies the granting of a licensing agreement.

Regarding the terms, the question concerns only the contractual penalties that CaMon may be entitled to. To this extent, it remains to be determined whether the provision that obliges Paul to sell the harvest to a specific company is valid.

Under French contract law, this clause is not problematic insofar as freedom is the rule. Under competition law, however, this provision may give rise to debate, given that Article 4(1)(c) of Regulation (EC) No. 772/2004 that forbids hardcore restrictions whose object is to allocate markets or consumers (except in the case covered by Art. 4(1)(c)(vii)). To this extent, CaMon is entitled to contractual penalties.

The more problematic question, which is not asked, is whether Paul's behaviour can be considered to be a counterfeiting act. The answer depends on the extent of the rights of the patent owner. We do not know of any case law concerning this point. But, in reference to Article 13(2) of Regulation (EC) No. 2100/94 on Community plant variety rights, which provides that 'the holder may take his authorisation subject to conditions and limitations', we would answer positively. The validity of the provision remains dependent on its conformity with competition law (see above).

III. Metalegal Formants

Answer omitted.

(6) GERMANY

I. Operative Rules

CaMon has no claim.

II. Descriptive Formants

The question to begin with is whether Paul violates CaMon's patent right. If so, one has to ask whether the penalty clause is valid in this regard. If Paul does not violate CaMon's patent right, the question arises whether the delivery obligation is valid.

I argue that Paul does not violate CaMon's patent. He would only violate CaMon's patent if the right to determine to whom the cultivated crop of the patented seed was sold was covered by the patent. I argue that this right is *not* covered by the patent right to seeds under §9a German Patent Law (transposing Art. 11 Biotechnology Directive). The intention of the legislator in 2005 was to bring patent law and seed variety laws in line – by introducing the farmers' privilege in the scope of UPOV 1991 into patent law. UPOV 1991 was transposed to European law through Regulation (EC) No. 2100/94 of 27 July 1994, and to German law in 1997 (anticipating the German ratification of UPOV 1991 in 1998). Through these reforms to seed variety protection, farmers' rights have been drastically curtailed by extending the breeders' right to the second generation, rendering the request for equitable remuneration ('sensibly lower than the amount charged for licensed production') for big-sized farmers (above a size threshold of acres needed to produce 92 tonnes of cereals) possible.[33] Thus, the legislative intent was to bring the second generation into the realm of, conceptually speaking, a liability rule. The intent was remuneration, not proprietary payment. In introducing §9a German Patent Law, the usual patent

[33] This is around 50% of the licence. 80% is excessive, A. Metzger, Artt. 14, 15 GSortV, in: A. Metzger and H. Zech (eds.) *Sortenschutzrecht* (Munich: 2016) paras. 30–33.

scope was curtailed to a liability rule in respect of the relation of breeder and farmer.[34]

Thus, the second generation is not drawn into the property right *per se*. The contrary is true. In bringing the use rights and the remuneration rules from the plant breeders' scheme into patent law, only a claim for remuneration was to be secured. Regulation (EC) No. 2100/94 is perceived as a hard-fought compromise; further restrictions of the farmers' freedoms are illegitimate.

Can a farmer contractually submit to the obligation to transport long distances and deliver to specific customers? Even if he/she does, I would argue that the obligation would be surprising considering the statutory frame and, therefore, would be invalid – at least as standard clause.

III. Metalegal Formants

The case does not deal with the question of farmers' rights. It revolves around the question of how far patent rights reach in the area of self-reproducible material, in this case crops. Can external boundaries (plant variety protection) be activated in patent law (through historic, teleological interpretation of the patenting breeder/farmers interface) in order to fence property rights? Historically, the legal development went into the other direction. Patent law has superseded *lex specialis* rules; double protection schemes have become accepted. The central question is now whether economic freedoms can be protected by recurring to rights which have been spelled out in another, earlier context – here, the farmer's freedom to operate.

(7) GREECE

I. Operative Rules

Most probably, the term providing contractual penalties is invalid.

II. Descriptive Formants

Biopatents are recognised in Greece (Presidential Decree 321/2001= Biotechnology Directive).[35] To the extent they are recognised, CaMon would have, in accordance with Article 10 para. 1(c) Law 1733/1987, the exclusive

---

34 C. Godt, 'Streit um den Biopatentschutz: Stoffschutz, Patente auf Leben und *Ordre public* – nationaler Gestaltungsspielraum bei der Umsetzung der Europäischen Biopatentrichtlinie', ZERP-Diskussionspapier 1/2003, 46 ff.

35 See, for preference, Mikroulea, 'The registration of biotechnological inventions with a patent', *EEmpD* 2000, 245.

right of sale of the products of the invention. This is a matter of the power of economic exploitation of a non-material good (the invention), and this should not be confused with the real right of ownership over the individual products.[36] The the right of intellectual property of the creator shall not be confused with ownership of the material vehicle of his/her work, for example the picture or the copies:[37] the right of intellectual property is single, whereas there are as many rights of ownership as there are material vehicles. Thus, in the present instance, Paul is and remains the owner of the products of the invention as fruits of his/her immoveable property in accordance with the provisions of the law of property (Arts. 1061 et seq. Civil Code), and no question of the protection of the real property of CaMon arises.

On the other hand (to the extent, of course, that biopatents are recognised), a problem of the protection of CaMon would arise, not as the owner, but as the inventor, with an exclusive right to decide on the manner of disposal of the products of his invention. This power CaMon transferred to Paul by a contract for the selective distribution of the products of the invention. The problem of the validity of such contracts remains even when an absolute right is not transferred by them. More specifically, such contracts on selective distribution are regarded as being abusive and prohibited vertical restrictions when they offend the principles of impartiality (equality), transparency, etc., and distort competition (Art. 81 EC Treaty; Arts. 1 and 2A Law 703/1977). This is in accordance with Article 81 EC Treaty, on the condition that any distortion of competition is 'perceptible',[38] a condition which, however, is not set by Greek law (Art. 1 Law 703/1977).[39]

Nevertheless, the agreement between CaMon and Paul is a technology transfer agreement (patent licence); therefore, in order to assess its validity, one must take firstly the Technology Transfer Block Exemption Regulation (TT-BER, Regulation (EC) No. 772/2004, later Regulation (EU) No. 316/2014) into consideration. A basic distinction for the assessment of agreements according to the TT-BER is the one between competitors and non-competitors. It seems that CaMon and Paul are not competing either with regard to the technology or in the relevant product market. Thus, according to Article 4(2) TT-BER the restriction of active sales imposed on Paul is legitimate.

On the other hand, if Paul sells his tomatoes only passively, the sales prohibition clause constitutes a hardcore restriction and the TT-BER is not

36 The prevailing opinion is to the contrary. Feuerlein, *GRUR* 2001, 564; BGH, *GRUR* 1972, 541; BGH, *GRUR* 1996, 109; Mikroulea, *EEmpD* 2000, 279.

37 See e.g. Kallinikou, *The Jurisprudence on Copyright* (1986), pp. 12–13 in contrast with what prevails in the case of patents (see preceding footnote).

38 See e.g. CJEU judgment of 26 November 2008, *Bronner*, C-7/97, ECLI:EU:C:1998:569; Gr Conseil d'Etat 902–909/1998.

39 Nevertheless see Gr Comp Comm 15/1981, 22/1982 et al.

applicable. In this case, the licensing agreement is to be assessed through direct application of Article 81 EC Treaty. Absent any additional pro-competitive effects of the sales restriction clause, the agreement would fail the Article 81(3) test and CaMon would not be able to sustain any claims against Paul. The invalidity of the term cannot involve the whole of the contract on assigning access to the invention in invalidity, since this would entail legitimation of the unjustified refusal to conclude a contract and the consequent blackmailing by CaMon of counterparties who are opposed to the abusive term (Art. 181 Civil Code, in conjunction with Arts. 178, 200 Civil Code). On the other hand, the invalidity of the term will involve the relevant penalty clause, which in any event can also be overturned by the courts as being unreasonable in accordance with Article 409 Civil Code.

III. Metalegal Formants

Answer omitted

(8) IRELAND

Answer omitted.

(9) ITALY

I. Operative Rules

Whether CaMon is entitled to contractual penalties depends on whether there is a breach of contract or not.

II. Descriptive Formants

If the contract is considered to have been lawfully concluded, then CaMon might be entitled to contractual penalties (but only to those, meaning that it could not claim further damages, nor the fulfilment of the obligation, Art. 1383 Civil Code). The amount of the penalty could be reduced if deemed manifestly excessive (Art. 1384 Civil Code).

As to the validity of the contract, Paul could argue that the contract is not binding on him since he has not expressed his consent to it. In that case, no licence contract has ever been concluded. He bought tomato seeds, and they arrived together with a licence contract. The case sounds similar to shrink-wrap licences in software.

III. *Metalegal Formants*

It could be argued whether or not the sale of tomatoes is an activity covered by the patent. Probably not. Paul is planting the seed to grow tomatoes, with the intention of selling the vegetable. He is not reproducing the gene, or developing it further, nor is he selling seeds.[40] However, this does not mean that, still in the absence of an activity violating the patent, the contract – if lawfully concluded – should not be enforced. Perhaps conscious of this exact scenario, CaMon has introduced a penalty clause, which is immediately payable, without the necessity to prove the damage, meaning without the need for a long and costly lawsuit to determine it.

It might also be interesting to analyse whether such limitations are in violation of antitrust law, i.e. whether CaMon has a position of market dominance and is abusing that position, or whether there is other behaviour violating European competition law (Arts. 101 and 102 TFEU).

(10) LITHUANIA

I. *Operative Rules*

Arguably, CaMon is not entitled to contractual penalties

II. *Descriptive Formants*

First of all, the question needs to be answered from the patent law perspective.[41] As the company CaMon holds a patent over a trait of the tomato, i.e. a biotechnological invention, Article 39(4) of the Lithuanian Patent Law applies. This provision stipulates:

> The legal protection … shall not extend to biological material obtained from the propagation or multiplication of biological material placed on the market of the European Economic Area by or with consent the proprietor of the patent, where the multiplication or propagation necessarily results from the application for which the biological material was marketed, provided that the material obtained is not subsequently used for other propagation or multiplication.

[40] See Article 5 and 107 Italian Code of Industrial Property, transposing into Italian legislation Article 10 of the Biotechnology Directive.

[41] Tomatoes can be protected by plant variety protection, but from the facts of the case it can be concluded this not the case here.

This provision is the expression of the fundamental exhaustion rule with regard to biotechnological inventions. It follows that first-generation harvested tomatoes can be sold without infringing the patent holder's rights, because these are exhausted. The answer is different if Paul further uses the patented invention for propagation or multiplication (which is beyond exhaustion). Therefore, Lithuanian patent law creates no obstacles to Paul to sell the first-generation harvest.

The second issue is the formation and validity of the licence, i.e. the contractual expansion of the patent holder's rights. This question, in turn, further splits into two. First, was the licence validly concluded? From the facts of the case, it is not totally clear whether a separate licence contract was agreed by the two parties or whether the licence agreement was presented unilaterally by CaMon and Paul accepted it. According to Lithuanian law, the silence of the other contractual party is *not* considered to be consent and active actions (albeit factual) are needed (Art. 1.64 of the Lithuanian Civil Code).

Even if Paul accepted the licence, the question remains whether such a licence agreement does not contradict the mandatory norms, in particular the exhaustion rule. While there is no Lithuanian case law on this issue, arguably the correct approach would be *not* to enforce such a contractual clause. The exhaustion rule should be considered the mandatory rule, and it would quickly lose its rationale if it were possible to contract around it.

III. Metalegal Formants

The case poses a classical problem of the overridability of various exceptions (in a wide sense) to the exclusive IP rights by contractual arrangements. While the precise boundaries of the extent to which contractual freedom can modify or extend property rights can be difficult to answer in many cases, the clear contractual encroachment on the exhaustion rule should not be tolerated.

(11) NETHERLANDS

I. Operative Rules

CaMon is not entitled to contractual penalties. Paul did not consent to the additional contractual terms or licence contract. Therefore, Paul is not obliged to respect the licence contract. The sale of the harvest is not within the scope of the patent. The licence contract is therefore null and void. The terms of the licence contract are also problematic from a competition law perspective.

II. *Descriptive Formants*

a) Plant breeders' rights perspective

Plant breeders' rights protect new varieties of plants. In accordance with the relevant rules laid down in the Dutch Sowing-seed and Plant Act, a person who develops a new variety with one or more special characteristics acquires an exclusive right for a specific period of time.[42] The regulations of the Dutch Sowing-seed and Plant Act are not applicable in this case, however, since there is no indication of a new variety of plants and the case does not mention an existing breeding right.

b) Patent law perspective

Article 2(1) DPA reads: 'Inventions that are new, that involve an inventive step and that are susceptible of industrial application shall be patentable'. As to Article 2a(2)(c) DPA, this is also the case when the invention concerns a product consisting of or containing biological material or a process by means of which biological material is produced, processed or used, as long as the technical feasibility of the invention is not confined to a particular plant or animal variety (Art. 4(2) Biotechnology Directive). This case concerns a patented product and therefore the owner of the patent has the exclusive right to use the process in or for his/her business, or to use, put on the market, resell, hire out or deliver the product obtained directly as a result of the use of the gene method, in this case the seeds. He/she may otherwise deal, offer, import or stock them for any of those purposes (Art. 53(1)(b) DPA). In contrast with the Harmonisation Treaty and the European Patent Treaty, in Article 53(1) the DPA distinguishes a patented *product* from a patented *process*. This distinction is of importance for the scope of the patent right.

Article 53a(1) DPA provides that the protection conferred by a patent on a biological material possessing specific characteristics as a result of the invention shall extend to any biological material derived from that original biological material through propagation or multiplication in an identical or divergent form and possessing those same characteristics (Art. 8(2) Biotechnology Directive). Therefore one could argue that the protection that is conferred by the patent extends to the tomatoes that grow from the seed. Article 53b DPA provides an exception to this rule: biological material obtained from the propagation or multiplication of biological material placed on the market in the territory of the Netherlands or the Netherlands Antilles by the holder of the patent or with his/her consent, where the multiplication or propagation necessarily results from the application for which the biological material was marketed, provided

42 C. Gielen and D.W.F. Verkade (eds.), *Tekst en Commentaar Intellectuele Eigendom* (Deventer: 2005), p. 643, Introduction remarks, annotation 1.

that the material obtained is not subsequently used for other propagation or multiplication, is not protected by the patent (Art. 10 Biotechnology Directive). An example of such use is genetically modified bacteria that can be used for cleaning up oil stains or water purification. Multiplication of the bacteria is then necessary for fulfilling the purpose of the bacteria.[43] Paul bought an amount enough to plant 100 acres. The multiplication or propagation of the biological material in this case is not a necessary result of the harvesting of tomatoes.

But the DPA does contain a provision that could apply to Paul's actions. Article 53c DPA provides an exception to the exclusive right of the patent owner, which is probably inspired by the farmers' privilege recognised in the UPOV Convention (Art. 11 Biotechnology Directive). Article 53c DPA provides that the sale or other form of commercialisation of plant-propagating material to a farmer by the holder of the patent or with his/her consent for agricultural use implies authorisation for the farmer to use the product of his/her harvest for propagation or multiplication by him/her on his/her own farm. Hence, a farmer is not allowed to sell tomatoes or seed for use in propagation, but a farmer is allowed to sell tomatoes for consumption.[44] In this case, this means that Paul selling the tomatoes to a big food processing company is not an infringement of CaMon's patent.

c) Contract law perspective

The main consideration for the solution of this case is whether the sale of CaMon's seeds, together with a set of licence terms, gives rise to a validly formed contract. An important principle of general contract law is that, to be bound by a contract, both parties must acquiesce to its terms before the conclusion of the transaction.[45] From a contract law perspective, it is unclear whether the licence was presented to Paul before the conclusion of the purchase, so that the terms can be considered binding on Paul. This is especially true of the added condition that any violation of the licence would give rise to penalties. If this condition was added after the purchase took place, it will not be binding. The added contractual term is not included in the contract, unless Paul has manifested his consent either expressly or tacitly.[46] Whether or not Paul consented tacitly depends on specific circumstances,[47] but consenting tacitly is not easily assumed. Since the additional contractual term is not part of the contract, CaMon is not entitled to contractual penalties. If the additional contractual term was part of the contract, and keeping in mind that Paul selling the tomatoes is not within the scope of

---

43 Ibid., p. 542, annotation 2.

44 J.L.R.A. Huydecoper and C.J.J.C. van Nispen, *Industriële eigendom. Bescherming van technische innovatie* (Deventer: 2002) p. 235.

45 A.S. Hartkamp (ed.), *Asser-Hartkamp 4-11* (Deventer: 2005), p. 11.

46 Consenting does not require formalities and can even be implicit: Art. 3:37 Dutch Civil Code.

47 A.S. Hartkamp (ed.), *Asser-Hartkamp 4-11* (Deventer: 2005), p. 134.

CaMon's patent, one could argue that the licence agreement is incompatible with the compelling provisions of the DPA. Therefore, the licence agreement is null and void as Article 3:40 Dutch Civil Code prescribes.

d) Competition law perspective

The additional contractual terms could raise concerns from a competition law perspective. The case, however, does not provide the detailed information needed for a good analysis. Therefore, I will confine myself to a general comment. Since, the Netherlands have the same substantive provisions as EU competition law, I will refer to EU law. In this case both Articles 101 and 102 TFEU could be relevant. The clause that obliges Paul to sell his harvest 700 km away to FPC, and FPC alone, could be prohibited by Article 101 TFEU because it consists of a vertical agreement that affects trade and distorts or restricts competition. In addition, Article 102 TFEU could be applicable if CaMon's actions constitute an abuse of its dominant position.

III. Metalegal Formants

This case deals with the extension of the patent right on biotechnological inventions, which is the effect of the Directive 98/44/EC on the legal protection of biotechnological inventions. A basic principle of patent law is that once a patented object is put on the market, the object can be freely used and circulated (patent exhaustion).[48] However, for biotechnological inventions, the scope of protection has been extended to all biological material derived from that original biological material through propagation or multiplication. There are two restrictions for this extended scope of protection that have both been discussed in the descriptive formants. First, in cases of biological material where the multiplication or propagation necessarily results from the application for which the biological material was marketed, the resulting material is not protected by the patent. This restriction is a novelty in patent law, as it is connected with the introduction of living material in patent law. The second restriction is the farmers' privilege, which provides that the sale or other form of commercialisation of plant-propagating material to a farmer by the holder of the patent or with his/her consent for agricultural use implies authorisation for the farmer to use the product of his/her harvest for propagation or multiplication by him/her on his/her own farm. This restriction is aimed at the protection of a particular professional group. At the same time, this restriction sees to an existing practice that already took place before the introduction of the Directive on the legal protection of biotechnological inventions.[49]

---

48 This is provided for by Art. 53(4) DPA.

49 S. Bostyn, in: C. Gielen and D.W.F. Verkade (ed.), *Tekst en Commentaar Intellectuele Eigendom* (Deventer: 2005), pp. 542–543.

(12) NORWAY

I. Operative Rules

CaMon has no claim as regards the first generation of tomatoes but will have a claim vis-à-vis possible second generations.

II. Descriptive Formants

The point of departure is the exhaustion rule in NPA §3, third paragraph, no. 2, which states that the patent holder's exclusive right to exploitation shall not include products protected by the patent which have been put on the market in the EEA by the patent holder him/herself or with his/her consent. This means that the patent rights are exhausted as far as the seed bought by Paul is concerned. The impact of the contract clause depends partly on the nature of the exhaustion rule (mandatory or non-mandatory) and partly on whether it is at all contractually binding. It is not quite settled whether the exhaustion rule in the NPA is mandatory or may be superseded by contract, but at least in relation to trade between EEA states, it will follow from the rules on free movement of goods (Arts. 11 and 13 EEA Agreement, corresponding to Arts. 34 and 36 TFEU) that it is mandatory. In addition, it is doubtful whether a standard contract clause unilaterally dictated by one party (CaMon) can be regarded as consented to by the other party and thus be legally binding. The conclusion, based on the facts of the case, should be in any event that CaMon is not entitled to 'contractual penalties' for the tomato harvest resulting from the seed bought by Paul.

If Paul, however, uses seeds from the first crop to raise new crops of tomatoes, the situation will be different. The exhaustion rule is not applicable in this situation as these seeds are not put on the market with the consent of the rightholder. On the other hand, NPA §3b, first paragraph, implementing Article 11 of the Biotechnology Directive, contains a 'farmers' privilege' rule: if plant-propagating material is sold or transferred, with the consent of the patent holder, to a farmer for agricultural use, this shall imply authorisation for the farmer to use the product of his/her harvest for propagation or multiplication on his/her own farm. However, pursuant to NPA §3b, third paragraph, the further extent and conditions of the farmer's right are determined in §89 of the Patent Regulation (NPR, 14 December 2007). This provision enumerates the kinds of plant-propagating material covered by the farmers' privilege. As tomatoes are not listed, the derogation from the patent holders' exclusive rights does not apply. Consequently, Paul cannot use seeds from the plant to raise new crops.

III. *Metalegal Formants*

The exhaustion rule delimits the scope of the patent in the first place, and it is doubtful whether the rightholder should be entitled to extend the scope through contract provision. The farmers' privilege delimits the scope of the patent as far as the use of plant-propagating material is concerned, but in Norwegian law it does not have general application.

(13) POLAND

I. *Operative Rules*

CaMon probably will not be able to claim contractual damages.

II. *Descriptive Formants*

There are two questions that have to be answered. First, whether the scope of protection granted to CaMon also encompasses the sale of products (crops) harvested with the seed purchased from that company. Second, if the answer to the first question is in the negative, whether, nevertheless, Paul is not bound by a contractual obligation to deliver the crops to the specific selected processing company (FPC). We assume that CaMon owns a patent and not a plant variety right. If so Article 93(5) point 1 of the Industrial Property Law (IPL) should be relevant. According to this provision, implementing Article 10 of the Directive 98/44/EC of the European Parliament and of the Council of 6 July 1998 on the legal protection of biotechnological inventions, the protection referred to in Article 94(4) does not extend to biological material obtained from the propagation or multiplication of biological material placed on the market in the territory of a member state by the holder of the patent or with his/her consent, where the multiplication or propagation necessarily results from the application for which the biological material was marketed, unless that the material obtained is subsequently used for other propagation or multiplication. This is in essence a regulation concerning the exhaustion of rights.[50] Since the seeds were sold to Paul so that he could grow crops from them, exhaustion will apply and CaMon's patent will not cover the sale of the crops. By selling to other companies than FPC, Paul would not violate CaMon's patent rights. It should also be assumed that the consent CaMon expressed cannot be qualified by the obligation to sell

---

50 M. du Vall, in: *Prawo własności przemysłowej* (Warszawa: 2008), p. 58; T. Szymanek, *Prawo własności przemysłowej. Podręcznik akademicki* (Warszawa: 2008), p. 40.

the resulting products to a selected recipient. Exhaustion is a matter of law and may only be prevented in a limited way by the rightholder.

The question then arises whether a contractual obligation could be enforced. The Polish law recognises the freedom of contract as a basic principle of civil law. Nevertheless, freedom of contract is restricted by statutes. In this case, contractual provisions would impose on Paul an obligation which does not result from CaMon's patent rights. Patent law does not create any obstacles; however, the contractual clause in question may be invalid because of competition law. Licence contracts should be perceived as technology transfer according to the Regulation on technology transfer agreements of 30 July 2007.[51] The regulation exempts technology transfer agreements from the prohibition of agreements restricting competition, provided that the requirements of this regulation are met. The regulation explicitly refers to clauses obligating the licensee to deliver the product to the selected recipient (§6 point 3 e, §7 point 2 d). Such clauses are exempt only when the purpose of the agreement is to create an alternative source of supplies for this buyer. It seems that this is not the case and consequently the obligation to sell solely to FPC would be void (Art. 6(2) of the Act on the Protection of Competition and Consumers).[52]

III. Metalegal Formants

Again, there are two basic issues involved: first, the scope of patent rights and the question of whether the protection granted by statute does not reach too far; and second, the validity of private ordering, i.e. using contracts to achieve the scope of protection not granted by statutory law. Atypical subject matter of protection, such as biotechnological inventions, sometimes requires special regulations that take into account the properties of the protected subject matter and the need to ensure adequate protection for the rightholder. For example, biotech inventions, such as the one belonging to CaMon, require modified rules on exhaustion.

Since IP rights create monopolies, even curtailing the scope of legal protection may prove ineffective, as rightholders are able to circumvent such restrictions. For example, they may (as often the only market source of a patented product) apply contractual restrictions that provide them with in practice the scope of protection the law deliberately limits. How to treat such contracts is a very controversial issue, not only in patent law but also, for example, in copyright law.[53] So far, this problem has been addressed only by competition law.

---

51 Journal of Laws 2007, No. 137, pos. 963.

52 Journal of Laws 2007, No. 50, pos. 331.

53 L. Guibault, *Copyright Limitation and Contracts* (The Hague/London/Boston: 2002).

(14) SLOVENIA

I. Operative Rules

CaMon cannot claim contractual penalties.

II. Descriptive Formants

In Slovenian law, there is a clear demarcation between a plant variety and genetically modified plants. A plant variety is acquired via a biological procedure (through propagation or multiplication, as occurs in nature) and cannot be protected by patent, but only by a plant variety right. A genetically modified plant is acquired using gene technology, which changes genetic material in a manner different to that which occurs in nature. Plant groupings with a higher taxonomic rank than a plant variety defined by an individual gene may be protected by a patent, if the invention relates to one gene that is significant for the entire plant grouping. A plant variety is defined by its entire genome and is protected as such by plant variety rights.[54]

In the case in question, the genetically modified plant is patented. The provisions of the Industrial Property Act (IPA)[55] are therefore relevant, as are the provisions of the Decree on the Legal Protection of Biotechnological Inventions[56] that define detailed conditions on granting patents for biotechnical inventions. The case description does not include details on any other form of protection, particularly protection for new plant varieties. According to the Protection of New Plant Varieties Act (PNPVA), a plant variety right is not acquired automatically, but only on the basis of an application for protection.[57]

On delivery, Paul received a licence agreement that required him to sell his whole harvest to a specified company. In Slovenian law, the licence agreement in the case in question would not be considered valid, and Paul would not be bound by it. According to Article 22(1) of the Code of Obligations (CO),[58] what Paul received on delivery of the goods was only an offer of a licence agreement, as the conclusion of a contract also requires the addressee's acceptance of the offer, in accordance with Article 28 of the CO. Since a licence agreement must

---

54 B. Strel, 'Gensko spremenjene rastline in patentno varstvo', in: B. Bohanec, B. Javornik, B. Strel (eds.), *Gensko spremeljena hrana* (Ljubljana: 2004), p. 149.

55 Official Gazette RS, nos. 45/2001, 96/2002, 7/2003, 37/2004, 102/2004, 20/2006, 51/2006.

56 Official Gazette RS, no. 81/2003.

57 Official Gazette RS, nos. 86/1998, 61/2006, 113/2006, Art. 14: 'A breeder acquires a plant variety right by protecting a variety'; Art. 24: 'The procedure to protect a variety shall commence on the basis of an application filed by the applicant with the competent authority.'

58 Official Gazette RS, nos. 83/2001, 32/2004, 40/2007, 97/2007, Art. 22(1): 'An offer is a proposal made to a specific person for the conclusion of a contract that contains all the essence of the contract, such that through the acceptance thereof a contract could be concluded.'

be made in writing (Art. 705 CO), the acceptance of an offer must be made in the same form (Art. 27 CO). Paul did not respond to the offer, and since silence does not constitute acceptance according to Article 30 of the CO (legal exceptions related only to cases of clients in a fixed business relationship and contracts on the provision or performance of orders, neither of which apply to the case in question), the licence agreement was not concluded. CaMon would not therefore be able to claim contractual penalties on that basis.

The question remains whether this restriction is actually permissible in Slovenian law. The general rule is that the licensee must exploit the subject of the licence in an agreed manner, and within an agreed scope and agreed limits (Art. 713 CO). An agreement of that kind is restricted to the scope of rights included in the patent. According to Article 19 IPA, the rights conferred by a patent do not extend to cases of private use, use for non-commercial purposes and for research and experimental purposes, irrespective of their final purpose (and some further uses that do not come into consideration in the case in question); therefore, those forms of use cannot be limited. The case in question involves an entirely commercial use, so these exceptions are not applicable.

Additional rights that are of relevance to the case are included in the Decree. The Decree states that the protection provided by a patent for biological material also extends to all biological material acquired from that biological material through propagation or multiplication (the protection therefore relates to all generation) (Art. 7(1)), but it permits farmers who have acquired a permit to use the material commercially from the patent holder or, with the patent holder's permission, to use their products for further propagation or multiplication on their own farm (Art. 10(1)). The Decree requires that the rights of any holder of plant variety rights defined in Article 16 of the PNPVA be respected in such cases.

Since there are no other limitations, the licensor is, according to Article 713 of the CO, free to define to whom the licensee may sell patent-protected biological material.

III. Metalegal Formants

If a plant was protected by a plant variety right pursuant to the PNPVA and not by a patent, CaMon would not be able to restrict sale of the product. The PNPVA states that the permission of the plant variety rightholder is not required for offering for sale, selling or other forms of marketing of plants, plant parts or products of a protected variety, if propagating material of that variety has been marketed by the holder or a party with the holder's authorisation (Art. 17). In that case, the sale of the products is completely free of impediment. Any provisions of a licence that contravened the legitimate rights arising from Article 17 of the PNPVA would be null and void (Art. 86(1) CO).

(15) SPAIN

I. Operative Rules

CaMon has no claim.

II. Descriptive Formants

Biotechnological inventions raise special problems which can be understood if it is borne in mind that patent legislation was created and developed to protect inventions of inanimate material, not living material. The protection of living material raises problems that had not been considered previously because the material already exists in nature; it reproduces by itself and it directly affects research on animals and plants that impact on livestock and agriculture.[59]

The special regulations that govern biotechnological patents affect the protection of exclusive right, and in particular the exhaustion of the patent right and the rights of farmers.

In the first place, we should determine whether Paul actually infringes CaMon's patent right. I believe that he does not. It would only be infringed if the exclusive right awarded by the patent were to include the product obtained with the patented seeds: that is to say, the tomato harvest. In this case CaMon could decide who the tomatoes could be sold to. This right is not covered by the patent.[60] According to the Spanish Patent Law, when the use of biological material put on the market by the patent holder or with his/her consent necessarily involves its reproduction (for example, when a seed is commercialised, as is the present case), exhaustion is limited to the first cycle of reproduction and does not extend to subsequent cycles, unless this is expressly stated.

This can be deduced from Article 53.3 of the Patent Law, according to which protection does not extend to the biological matter obtained, where the multiplication necessarily results from the application for which the patented biological material was marketed, provided that the material obtained is not subsequently used for other propagation or multiplication. Thus, it cannot be reproduced or marketed without express authorisation from the title holder.

Assuming that Paul sells the tomatoes on the local market for purposes of consumption and not for purposes of further reproduction, he can market them as he sees fit. CaMon has no exclusive right of any kind on the tomatoes and can therefore exert no control over how they are marketed.

A second constraint on the right of the patent holder, in this case CaMon, is the so-called farmers' right. When the patent holder or someone with his/her

---

59 A. Bercovitz, *Apuntes de Derecho Mercantil* (6th ed., Navarra: 2007), p. 415.

60 The same answer is given by considering the German Patent Law (page 14) and the Czech Act on the Protection of Plant Variety Rights.

permission sells a farmer material for reproduction that contains the protected invention for agricultural use, the farmer has the right to use the product of his/her harvest for further reproduction within the confines of his/her own farm (Art.53.1 Patent Law).[61] In this case, Paul could plant the seed of the tomatoes from his harvest on his farm without violating the patent right. The protection of biotechnological inventions has extended to patents the farmers' privilege that comes from the protection of plant varieties. This regulation protects the legitimate interests of the patent holder or of the plant breeder, and safeguards those of the farmer, since all farms of a certain size have to make a payment to the holder. The aim of the regulation is to generate income for the patent holder, not to pay for a property right.

The holder of the CaMon patent is not the owner of the tomatoes harvested from the seeds because the patent right is exhausted, as we have explained above.

The second issue, once it has been determined that the patent right is not infringed, is whether Paul can be contractually connected to the obligation to sell to a particular buyer 700 km away. In our opinion, this clause would be null because it infringes free market competition.

We believe that the inclusion of the contractual clause is a manifestation of the abuse of power that CaMon has in the market and which derives from the exclusive right provided by the patent. The result of this is that CaMon is the only supplier of genetically modified tomato seeds. The law accepts these situations of structural restriction of competition in which there is only one company supplying a product or a service. However, under no circumstances does it accept that this monopoly be abused by the introduction of further restrictions.

If we assume that CaMon is in a dominant position in the market (though we do not believe that to be the case here) an analysis needs to be made of what the relevant market is, because it is the only company that can market the seeds as a result of the patent it has been awarded. It seems clear that introducing this contractual clause is an abuse of the company's situation of power. If Paul does not accept the clause, he cannot obtain the seeds.

Article 2 of the Law on the Defence of Competition of 3 July 2007 prohibits a company or companies from abusing their dominant position in the market and provides some examples. One of these examples is the limitation of distribution.[62]

---

61 Art. 53.1 Spanish Patent Law states: 'Despite the provisions of Art. 50, should the patent holder sell or market the material of plant reproduction in any other way (or give permission for others to do so) to a farmer for agricultural use, the farmer shall have the right to use the product of his harvest for subsequent reproduction or multiplication on his own holding'. The scope and modalities of this regulation shall be those described in Art. 14 of Regulation (EC) No. 2100/94 of the European Council of 27 July on the Community protection of plant varieties.

62 Art. 6 Spanish Law on the Defence of Competition states: 'One or various companies are forbidden from abusing their dominant position in the market in part or in all of the national territory. In particular, abuse can consist of: … b) Limiting production, distribution or technological development to the unjustified detriment of companies or consumers'.

The obligation to sell the whole harvest to FPC limits the distribution of the tomatoes and unjustifiably harms the interests of both the farmer, who is obliged to transport his harvest 700 km and cannot increase his local clientele, and the local consumers, who will not be able to purchase the tomatoes.

In response to CaMon's claim, Paul can argue that the contractual clause is null because it does not respect the Law on the Defence of Competition.

III. Metalegal Formants

The case deals with the extension of the patent right on biotechnological inventions, particularly those materials that can reproduce by themselves or multiply. The legislation on biotechnological patents is based on the need for these inventions to be effectively protected and on the conviction that this protection should be provided by patents for inventions that require a high level of high-risk investments and which have enormous potential.

(16) UNITED KINGDOM

I. Operative Rules

CaMon is not entitled to contractual penalties.

II. Descriptive Formants

This appears to be a patent law dispute that is dressed up as a contractual dispute by the choice of CaMon.[63] By choosing to control the downstream side of the supply chain by way of a licence contract, CaMon is protecting its investment in the patent by channelling the harvested product of the patented seed back to its own choice of retailer, thereby controlling both the distribution of the seed and the marketing of the end product. Effectively, it is also stripping Paul of the defence of exhaustion of rights as contained in paragraph 10 of Schedule A2 PA 1977 in the UK, because the lawsuit is not framed as a patent infringement.

It is submitted that CaMon's licence contract resembles an unreasonable restraint of trade agreement that is null and void and that CaMon is therefore not entitled to contractual penalties.

This conclusion is reached by investigating firstly the rationale of the Biotechnology Directive and the defences it affords to third parties, and secondly the principles relating to restraints of trade agreements.

---

63 A similar observation was made in A. Hobson and G. Cullis, 'Case Comment, Apple Corps Ltd v Apple Computers Inc: Alleged Breach of Trade Mark Agreement' (2006) 17(8) *European Law Review* 234, 235.

a) Biotechnology Directive

The development of new biological material requires substantial investment in capital and in time and energy. The provision of a proprietary right for the plant breeder or inventor enables him/her to ensure a return on his/her investment when he/she develops a successful new plant variety or biological material. This enables future investment and ensures the continued prosperity of a local plant breeding industry. Improved varieties should lead to greater quantity and quality of production and thereby stimulate the activity of farmers and bring a gain to final consumers. It is therefore common ground that these inventions should receive proprietary protection.[64]

Exactly how this protection should be afforded has been, and continues to be, the subject of heated debate. After 10 years of consideration, the Biotechnology Directive[65] was eventually formally adopted by the European Parliament in 1988. However, questions of morality, monopoly and exclusivity cast a shadow over subsequent case law and public debates.[66] The Directive was implemented in the UK by the Patents Regulations 2000 (SI 2000/2037) and has been in force since 28 July 2000.

In respect of patents relating to plant and animal material, the Biotechnology Directive strives to strike a balance between competing aims, namely that of protecting the rights of the patent owner whilst simultaneously allowing others the use of such patented products. As part of the regime dealing with biotechnological inventions, a few defences have been developed to counter claims of infringement.[67] In light of the current problem, two defences appear at first sight to be relevant, namely the farmers' privilege and the exhaustion of patent rights.

b) Farmers' privilege – a valid defence for Paul?

The acceptance of the Biotechnology Directive raised the concern that patents over seeds would jeopardise traditional farming habits as it would prevent farmers from using part of their harvest to re-sow the seeds, as this activity could infringe a patented product. In light of this, a special defence, the so-called 'farmers' privilege', was introduced into the Biotechnology Directive by way of Article 11.[68] This was mirrored in sections 60(5)(g) and (h) PA 1977 in the UK.

---

64 T. Millet, 'The Community System of Plant Variety Rights' (1999) 24(3) *European Law Review* 231, 231.

65 Directive 98/44/EC on the legal protection of biotechnological inventions.

66 S.J.R. Bostyn, 'The Patentability of Genetic Information Carriers' [1999] *Intellectual Property Quarterly* 1.

67 L. Bentley and B. Sherman, *Intellectual Property Law* (2nd ed., Oxford/New York: 2004), pp. 547–548.

68 S.J.R. Bostyn, 'The Patentability of Genetic Information Carriers' [1999] *Intellectual Property Quarterly* 1, 31.

Section 60(5)(g) provides a defence for a farmer who has used a portion of his/her harvest for propagation and multiplication by him/her on his/her farm, where there has been a sale or other form of commercialisation of plant-propagating material to him/her by the holder of the patent or with the latter's consent.

The farmers' privilege is limited to a certain number of plant species, namely fodder plants, cereals, potatoes, and oil and fibre plants. In the event that the farmer makes use of this defence, he/she must pay an equitable remuneration to the patent owner, but this amount must be lower than the amount charged for the production of the protected material. However, the obligation to pay an equitable remuneration does not arise if the farmer is a 'small farmer'.[69]

The farmers' privilege has been a contentious issue. Bostyn doubts that the defence awarded to farmers can be reconciled with Article 30 TRIPS[70] insofar as it may unreasonably prejudice the legitimate interests of the patent owner.[71] This is not the view of Llewelyn. He is of the opinion that the farmers' privilege does take account of the legitimate interests of all the parties, namely the holders of plant variety rights and the farmers who will make use of the protected material.[72] Bently and Sherman note that it would be interesting to see what impact these defences have on farming practices, as well as on the biotechnology industry, as it might lead to the development of techniques such as terminator genes that operate to ensure that seeds will not re-germinate.[73]

In casu, irrespective of the contentious nature of the farmers' privilege, Paul would not be able to avail himself of this privilege as this defence is plant-specific and does not include tomatoes. Furthermore, the lawsuit is concerned with Paul's subsequent sale of the harvested product and not the re-sowing of the patented seeds.

c) The exhaustion of patents

The principle of exhaustion of rights basically provides that the monopoly rights of the patent holder in relation to the invention come to an end once he/she has placed it on the market or consented thereto. In general, three types of actions are covered: the use, offer for sale and sale of the patented product.

---

69 L. Bentley and B. Sherman, *Intellectual Property Law* (2nd ed., Oxford/New York: 2004), pp. 547–548.

70 Art. 30 of TRIPS allows for exceptions to rights conferred: members may provide limited exceptions to the exclusive rights conferred by a patent, provided that such exceptions do not unreasonably conflict with a normal exploitation of the patent and do not unreasonably prejudice the legitimate interests of the patent owner, taking account of the legitimate interests of third parties.

71 S.J.R. Bostyn, 'The Patentability of Genetic Information Carriers' [1999] *Intellectual Property Quarterly* 1, 33.

72 Ibid., p. 33, para. 159.

73 L. Bentley and B. Sherman, *Intellectual Property Law* (2nd ed., Oxford/New York: 2004), p. 548.

These actions are allowed by anyone who has acquired the product of the invention from the patent holder, or with the latter's consent. The manufacture of the product is not covered by the exhaustion principle.[74]

With regard to biological patents, Article 10 of the Biotechnology Directive, as encapsulated in paragraph 10 of Schedule A2 PA 1977 in the UK, specifically incorporates the exhaustion principle. It provides that:

> the protection conferred by a patent shall not extend to biological material obtained from the propagation or multiplication of biological material placed on the market by the owner of the patent or with his consent where the multiplication or propagation necessarily results from the application for which the biological material was marketed.[75]

For the patent rights to be exhausted under paragraph 10 of Schedule A2, the buyer of the patented product needs to establish that the multiplication or propagation is an incident of the true purpose of the sale, hence not infringing the patent. As mentioned, the manufacture of the product is not covered by the defence, but the action of sowing a patented seed, harvesting the crop and selling the seeds will be protected.[76]

In casu, Paul had sold the harvest of the patented seeds which he had bought from CaMon and as such the exhaustion of rights principle would have constituted a valid defence for Paul had CaMon framed its claim in terms of a patent infringement. However, CaMon is choosing to protect its investment by way of a contractual remedy. By doing so it is moving the dispute out of the realm of intellectual property law and into the realm of contractual law. Therefore, it is necessary to investigate whether there are any contractual remedies available to Paul.

d) Is the contract an unreasonable restraint of trade?

The law with regard to restraint of trade has been considered in various cases. In an early case in 1916, it was held that in applying the doctrine of restraint of trade the courts recognise that there was a public interest in freedom of contract in addition to a public interest in freedom of trade. It was furthermore held that the onus of establishing that the contract was reasonable as between the parties was on the proponent of the contract, while the onus of establishing that, although reasonable between the parties, it was nevertheless contrary to public policy lay on the party challenging the contract.[77]

---

74 S.J.R. Bostyn, 'The Patentability of Genetic Information Carriers' [1999] *Intellectual Property Quarterly* 1, 30.

75 L. Bentley and B. Sherman, *Intellectual Property Law* (2nd ed., Oxford/New York: 2004), pp. 546–547.

76 S.J.R. Bostyn, 'The Patentability of Genetic Information Carriers' [1999] *Intellectual Property Quarterly* 1, 30.

77 *Herbert Morris Ltd v. Saxelby* [1916] 1 AC 688.

A leading case which considers the validity of restraint of trade contracts is *Esso Petroleum Co. Ltd v. Harper's Garage (Stourport) Ltd.*[78] Here Lord Diplock emphasises that the law which applies to restraint of trade contracts are quite different from that which applies to contracts in general. Normally unless a contract can be brought within the areas of duress, fraud or mistake, its terms will be enforceable even though it is harsh and appears unreasonable.[79] In the normal course of events, the doctrine of privity of contract will prevail and the courts will not 'remake' the contract. The duty of the court is to merely construe the contract that the parties have made.[80] However, in the event of a restraint of trade contract, the court will investigate whether the restraint is reasonable based on the facts, the rationale being that the public has an interest in everyone carrying on his/her trade freely and any interference with this liberty, irrespective of whether the individual has agreed to it, must be reasonable, otherwise the obligations would be null and void.[81]

Despite the ancient origins of the doctrine, the areas in which it operates are narrow. Originally the doctrine operated in two distinct categories, namely preventing an apprentice from competing with his/her master after completion of his/her apprenticeship contract, and preventing a seller of a business from competing with the purchaser of this business. Lord Diplock makes it clear that not all contracts which involve 'a derogation from the common law right in virtue of which any member of the community may exercise any trade or business he pleases and in such a manner as he thinks best in his own interests' can necessarily be construed as a restraint of trade contract or can be held to be against public policy.[82]

The categories for restraint of trade agreements have over the years been broadened somewhat. In *McEllistrim v. Ballymacelligott Co-operative Agricultural and Dairy Society Ltd*, the society had changed its rules to prevent members from selling milk to anyone else except the society. This was held to be an unfair restraint of trade. Lord Diplock notes that although the doctrine was expanded from the right to use one's skill and labour to one's own benefit, to the right to sell one's goods to whomever one wishes, this was not necessarily a correct application of the doctrine. He noted that:[83]

> It would seem to mean that every contract by which a man (or a company) agrees to sell his whole output (or even half of it) for any future period to the other party to the contract is a contract in restraint of trade because it restricts his liberty to sell

78 [1967] 2 WLR 871.
79 Ibid., p. 295.
80 *Daewoo Heavy Industries v. Kliprivier Shipping Ltd* (CA) 2003 2 LLR 1, 10.
81 *Nordenfelt v. Maxim Nordenfelt Guns & Ammunition Co. Ltd* [1894] AC 535.
82 Ibid., pp. 293–294.
83 Ibid., p. 296.

> as he pleases and is therefore unenforceable unless his agreement can be justified as being reasonable. There must have been many ordinary commercial contracts of that kind in the past, but no one has ever suggested that they were in restraint of trade. But McEllistrim's case at least establishes that there comes a point at which such a contract can come within the doctrine of restraint of trade.

Lord Diplock is loath to define the line which divides contracts between what are restraints of trade and what are not. However, factors he considered that pointed to a restraint of trade were: a contract that place a positive obligation on one party to act in a specific way as opposed to a negative covenant preventing a prescribed action; a stipulation regulating a person's existing trade as opposed to a new trade; and an obligation to take one's whole supply from one source, as opposed to an obligation to sell to one buyer only.

Furthermore, the test to determine whether a restraint in a contract was justified was confirmed to be that as held in *Nordenfelt v. Maxim Nordenfelt Guns and Ammunition Company Ltd*,[84] namely the reasonableness of the restriction had to be considered from the viewpoint both of the parties and of the public interest.

Schroeder Music Publishing Co. v. Macaulay[85] was the first reported case to apply the long-established common law doctrine of restraint of trade to copyright in the music industry.[86] In *Schroeder v. Macaulay*, the role of bargaining power arose as a factor when considering the reasonableness of a restraint of trade agreement. In this case a young, unknown song writer challenged his contract with a big publishing company on their standard form as being an unfair restraint of trade. It was held that the agreement was on its face unduly restrictive and contrary to public policy and hence null and void. Reasons cited included, amongst others, that it was a one-sided agreement that had not been arrived at as a result of negotiation between parties in an equal bargaining position.

> The court referred to Lord Pierce's test in *Esso Petroleum* for determining whether a restraint of trade is unreasonable or not, as follows: It is important that the court, in weighing the question of reasonableness, should give full weight to commercial practices and to the generality of contracts made freely by parties bargaining on equal terms.[87]

It was furthermore held that there was no evidence of the fact that the agreement was moulded by any pressure of negotiation. This was not surprising as an

---

84 [1894] AC 535.

85 [1974] 1 WLR 1308.

86 J. Enser and D. Zeffman, 'The Impact of UK Competition Law on the Music Industry' (1993) 4(3) *European Law Review* 67, 67.

87 *Esso Petroleum Co. Ltd v. Harper's Garage (Stourport) Ltd* [1967] 2 WLR 871, 1323.

unknown composer could not bargain on equal terms or demand his/her own contracts in the same way as well-established composers could do.

It was further observed that the contract in question fell within the category of standard forms of contract that are the result of the concentration of particular types of businesses in a few hands. The court referred to the classic ticket cases of the 19th century in which:

> The terms of this kind of standard form of contract have not been the subject of negotiation between the parties to it or approved by any organisation representing the interests of the weaker party. They have been dictated by that party whose bargaining power, either exercised alone or in conjunction with others providing similar goods or services, enables him to say: 'If you want these goods or services at all, these are the only terms on which they are obtainable. Take it or leave it'.[88]

It was held that the publishing company's bargaining power was so much stronger than that of the song writer that it enabled the former to adopt this 'take it or leave it' attitude. Although this does not raise a presumption that the company used it to drive an unconscionable bargain with the writer, it does raise awareness that calls for vigilance on the part of the court to see that companies do not.[89]

The findings of both *Esso Petroleum* and the *Macaulay* cases mentioned above were considered and confirmed in another case pertaining to copyright and a restraint of trade, namely *Panayiotou and Others v. Sony Music Entertainment (UK) Limited.*[90] Of significance to the present problem is the reiteration that where standard form contracts are used, the fact that they are widely used by parties whose bargaining powers are evenly matched raises a strong presumption that this is reasonable, whereas this presumption does not apply to standard form contracts where the one party's bargaining power is much stronger than the other party and which entitles them to adopt a 'take it or leave it' attitude.

The notion of 'inequality of bargaining power' is becoming more popular with national courts in Europe and has also been endorsed by the Court of Justice as the underlying rationale of Directive 93/13/EEC, which aims to protect consumers against unfair contract terms.

In *Océano Grupo Editorial SA v. Murciano Quintero, Salvat Editores SA v. Sánchez Alcón Prades,*[91] the Court stated:

> [T]he system of protection introduced by the Directive is based on the idea, that the consumer is in a weak position vis-à-vis the seller or supplier, as regards both his

---

88 A. Pathak, *Legal Aspects of Business* (India: 2007), p. 120.

89 Ibid., p. 1316.

90 [1994] EMLR 229.

91 CJEU judgment of 27 June 2000, *Océano Grupo Editorial SA v. Murciano Quintero, Salvat Editores SA v. Sánchez Alcón Prades*, C-240 to C-244/98, ECLI:EU:C:2000:346.

> bargaining power and his level of knowledge. This leads the consumer agreeing to terms drawn up in advance by the seller or supplier without being able to influence the content of the terms.[92]

In casu, the onus would rest on CaMon to prove that the licence contract was reasonable. In all likelihood, CaMon would claim that it was its standard form contract and that the right of freedom to contract should prevail. Furthermore, the dictum in *Esso Petroleum* that a contract to sell one's whole output does not necessarily constitute a restraint of trade would be in CaMon's favour.

In the event that CaMon succeeds, Paul would have to prove that despite the contract being reasonable between the parties, it is against public policy in that it restricts his freedom to trade. Paul would have to prove that the contract resembles an unreasonable restraint of trade in that: it places a positive obligation on him to sell only to CaMon; he did not have an opportunity to negotiate the terms of the contract and even if he had, the imbalance in negotiating power between him and CaMon would have resulted in a 'take it or leave it' attitude from CaMon; the contract affected his existing trade; his produce was small (only 100 acres); and his market was 700 km away from FPC, and he therefore did not resemble a threat to their business.

III. Metalegal Formants

The UK system values the freedom of contract and the freedom of trade as being equally worthy of protection. Even where individuals do not have any choice but to contract with big business on their standard terms, the judiciary is hesitant to provide protection against the unreasonable exploitation of such a situation, even in circumstances where contracts are used to usurp legitimate statutory defences.

A.3. COMPARATIVE REMARKS

I. Operative Rules

In most jurisdictions, CaMon *would not* be entitled to contractual penalties (Belgium, Czech Republic, Denmark, Greece, Lithuania, the Netherlands, Poland, Slovenia, Spain, the UK). However, in some countries, the prohibition turns into a permission, depending on certain circumstances. CaMon is not

92 M. Schillig, 'Inequality of Bargaining Power versus Market for Lemons: Legal Paradigm Change and the Court of Justice Jurisprudence on Directive 93/13 on Unfair Contract Terms' (2008) 33(3) *European* 336–358. *Océano* (C-240 to C-244/98) [2000] E.C.R. I-4963; [2002] 1 C.M.L.R. 43, 25.

entitled to any claim with regard to the first generation of tomatoes, but *might* have a claim with regard to the second generation of tomatoes (Denmark). CaMon *might* be entitled to contractual penalties, *if* Paul has consented, *if* the penalties are compensatory and not punitive, and *if* the contract clauses are valid from the point of view of competition law (Belgium). In some jurisdictions, CaMon *would* be entitled to contractual penalties (Estonia).

II. Descriptive Formants

Developing a comparative analysis of the applicable rules in the present case has proven to be a real challenge for three reasons.

First, the picture is complex because differing *legal regimes* have been put forward in different country reports to substantiate why CaMon is/is not entitled to contractual penalties. Some country reports have recourse to intellectual property law, more particularly patent law and plant breeders' rights law. Other reports bring contract law to the fore. And, last but not least, a few other countries set competition law on the stage. The present analysis will take into account all three legal regimes.

Second, the picture is obscured, because the various country reports discuss the case at different *hierarchical levels*. The (implicit or explicit) starting point in most country reports is the attribution of a national patent[93] or a national plant breeder's right to CaMon. Some reports look into the possibility that CaMon has been granted a Community plant breeder's right.[94] In order to make sense of this variation, the present analysis will take into account both national and Community intellectual property regimes.

Third, the picture is complicated because various rapporteurs have a different *reading of the facts* of the case, in a twofold way. First, there is divergence when it comes to defining the actual rights of CaMon. Some reports start from the assumption that CaMon has a patent on the plant trait, based on the words of the case description ('This feature of the tomato has been patented'). Other reports start from the idea that CaMon has a patent covering both the genetically modified plant and the specific plant trait, based on the overall context of the case at hand. The present analysis discusses both scenarios and focuses on the (consequences of) patent protection for a transgenic plant and for plant traits.

---

93 In the present analysis, no distinction will be made between national patents resulting from a national application procedure with a national patent office, and national patents resulting from the European application procedure before the European Patent Office. As is sufficiently known, European patents fall apart in a bundle of national rights upon grant.

94 A Community plant breeder's right is based on Council Regulation (EC) No. 2100/94 of 27 July 1994 on Community plant variety rights, OJ L 227, 1 September 1994, 1–30.

Second, there is also variation when it comes to the actual acts committed by Paul. Some reports start from the assumption that Paul sows the seed he bought from CaMon, and then sells the resulting harvested tomatoes to regional customers (so-called *first*-generation seeds – using patent owner seed).

Other reports start from the assumption that Paul sows the seed he bought from CaMon, retains seeds from his harvested crop, plants those seeds to grow new tomatoes, and then sells those tomatoes to regional customers (so-called *second*-generation seeds – using farmer-saved seed). The present analysis zooms in on both assumptions.

Taking into account the various interpretations of the facts of the case in the various country reports leads to six different assumptions (see Table 1). The present analysis will carefully examine all six scenarios.

Table 1. Patents, Plant Breeder's Rights and Farmer's Freedom to Operate

	Use of			Response
Patent on	Plant	Patent owner seed	Scenario 1 (See Belgium, Denmark, France, Greece, the Netherlands, Norway, Poland, Slovenia, Spain, UK)	Exhaustion principle applies – no infringement – transposition Art. 10 Biotechnology Directive
	Plant	Farmer saved seed	Scenario 2 (See Denmark, Germany, the Netherlands, Spain, UK)	Farmers' privilege applies *in principle* – no infringement – transposition Art. 11 Biotechnology Directive Farmers' privilege does not apply *in casu*
	Plant trait	Patent owner seed	Scenario 3	
	Plant trait	Farmer saved seed	Scenario 4	
Plant breeder's right on	Plant variety	Patent owner seed	Scenario 5 (See Belgium, Czech Republic, Estonia, the Netherlands, Slovenia)	Exhaustion principle applies – no infringement – transposition Art. 16 UPOV Convention
	Plant variety	Farmer saved seed	Scenario 6	

1. Intellectual Property Law

a) Patent Law

- *Scenario 1. Patent for a transgenic* plant. *Purchase (and use) of seed from the patent owner (Seed from CaMon)* (see Figure 1 – Top scenario)

The key question in the present scenario relates to the scope of protection patent law offers to the holder of a patent on transgenic plants, and whether the behaviour of a farmer sowing transgenic seeds from this patent holder, then growing transgenic plants, and thereupon selling the harvested crops, infringes the plant patent.

All EU member states have transposed the Biotechnology Directive in their national patent legislation, which in Article 10 Biotechnology Directive introduces the exhaustion principle in the area of patents on biological material. Most rapporteurs support the view that the point of departure to resolve the case at hand is the exhaustion principle (Belgium, Czech Republic, Denmark, Estonia). It is underlined that the legal concept is applicable in the present case: once put on the market with the patent owner's consent, the patented objects can be resold and freely circulate, since the patent is exhausted with regard to those specific objects. No obligation to sell to a particular customer can then be derived from patent law. Paul's use of the crops, more particularly the sale to customers of his choice, was totally legitimate (cf. Belgian report).

Figure 1. Patents for Transgenic Plants and Exhaustion

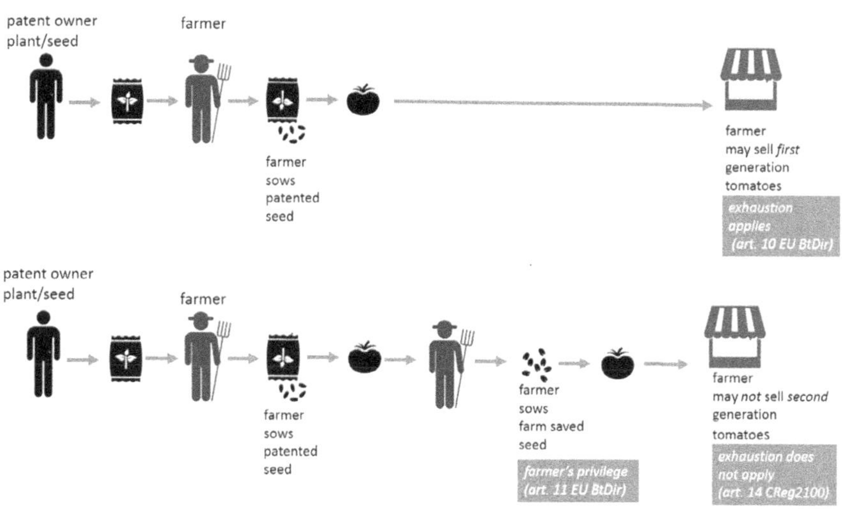

- *Scenario 2. Patent for a transgenic* plant. *Use of farm saved seed (Seed from Paul)* (see Figure 1 – Bottom scenario)

The exhaustion principle, as articulated in Article 10 Biotechnology Directive, does not stretch to the seeds obtained from the harvested material, but only applies if 'the material obtained is not subsequently used for other propagation or multiplication'. In other words, the exhaustion only applies if the tomatoes (= 'material obtained') are not used for multiplication (= sowing). Is Paul only entitled to use the seeds to grow tomatoes which are then sold to customers? Article 11 Biotechnology Directive stipulates that the sale or other form of commercialisation of plant-propagating material to a farmer by the holder of the patent, or with his/her consent, for agricultural use implies authorisation for the farmer to use the product of his/her harvest for propagation or multiplication by him/her on his/her own farm, the extent and conditions of this derogation corresponding to those under Article 14 Regulation (EC) No. 2100/94. The extent and the conditions of the derogation provided for in Article 11 Biotechnology Directive are determined by national laws, regulations and practices.

Some country reports mention the embodiment of the farmers' privilege in patent law (e.g. Spain, the UK). In the event that the farmer makes use of the farmers' privilege, he/she must pay an equitable remuneration to the patent owner, but this amount must be lower than the amount charged for the purchase of the certified material from the patent holder. The obligation to pay an equitable remuneration does not arise if the farmer is a 'small farmer'. Furthermore, the farmers' privilege is often limited to a certain number of plant species, in most cases to fodder plants, cereals, potatoes, and oil and fibre plants.

Yet, since tomatoes are not listed in the enumeration of Article 14. Regulation (EC) No. 2100/94, the derogation from the patent holders' exclusive rights does not apply. Consequently, Paul cannot use seeds from the plant to raise new crops. Paul would not be able to avail himself of this privilege as this defence is plant-specific and does not include tomatoes.

- *Scenario 3. Patent for a plant* trait. *Purchase (and use) of seed from the patent owner (Seed from CaMon)*

We now turn to the plant *trait*, and the related patent. Even though Article 4(1) and (2) of the Biotechnology Directive do not explicitly mention patent protection for plant traits, all EU member states seem to have – indirectly – embraced the patentability of such plant traits.[95]

[95] See G. Van Overwalle, 'Biotechnology and Patents: Global Standards, European Approaches and National Accents', in: D. Wüger and T. Cottier (eds.), *Genetic Engineering and the World Trade System* (Cambridge: 2008), 77–108.

Here, the key question relates to the scope of a patent on a plant *gene*, rather than the scope of a patent on a *crop*. The Court of Justice of the EU concluded this issue.[96]

Yet is the *Monsanto* ruling relevant for the present case?[97] First and foremost, it needs to be said that the CJEU ruling was not available at the time of the writing of the reports and could thus not be taken into account by the country rapporteurs. But let us apply the CJEU ruling to the case at hand, for the sake of completeness. Notwithstanding the fact that Paul's tomatoes carry the patented gene, and that the gene is still able to perform its function, Paul's actions would not fall under the scope of the patent in view of the exhaustion principle.

- *Scenario 4. Patent for a transgenic* trait. *Use of farm saved seed (Seed from Paul)*

Paul's actions would only fall under the scope of the patent if he were to use the tomatoes to propagate, in other words if he were to use the seeds for further multiplication, or to sell the seed.

b) Plant Breeders' Rights Law

- *Scenario 5. Plant breeder's right for a transgenic* plant variety. *Purchase (and use) of seed from the plant breeder (Seed from CaMon)* (see Figure 2 – Top scenario)

Here, the key question is what scope plant breeders' rights law offers to the breeder, and whether the behaviour of a farmer sowing transgenic seeds from the plant variety rightholder, then growing the transgenic plant varieties, and thereupon selling the harvested crops, is infringing the plant breeder's right on the transgenic plant variety (see Figure 2 – Top scenario).

The exclusive right of the breeder under Article 14 of the International Convention for the Protection of New Varieties of Plants (UPOV Convention) does not seem to be applicable in the present case, as the case deals with the sale of harvested material resulting from the authorised use (namely the purchase from the breeder) of the seed. Instead, attention should be given to Article 16 1991 UPOV Convention, which sets forth that the breeder's right shall not extend to acts concerning any material of the protected variety which has been sold or otherwise marketed by the breeder or with his/her consent in the territory of

96 CJEU judgment of 6 July 2010, *Monsanto Technology v. Cefetra*, C-428/08, ECLI:EU:C:2010:402; J. L. R. A. Huydecoper, 'Tot stof zult gij wederkeren', *Bulletin Industriële Eigendom*, 2010, 322–324; M. A. Kock, 'Patent protection for DNA sequences – to be or not to be?', 5 *Journal of Intellectual Property Law and Practice*, 2010, 754–756; G. Van Overwalle, 'The CJEU Monsanto Soybean Decision and Patent Scope: As Clear As Mud', *International Review of Intellectual Property and Competition Law (IIC)*, 2011, 1–3.

97 It is clear that the CJEU verdict would not be applicable in the previous scenario, as the issue at stake relates to the scope of a patent on a *gene*, and not on the scope of a patent on a *crop*.

the contracting party concerned, or any material derived from the said material. Article 16 recognises the exhaustion principle in plant breeders' rights law.

How have the EU member states which have signed the 1991 UPOV Convention dealt with this provision? Most 1991 UPOV signatory states have implemented Article 16 in their national plant breeders' act, embracing the exhaustion principle (see e.g. Belgium, Czech Republic). In those countries, the plant variety breeder is not entitled to a claim against the farmer selling the harvested crops, as the rights of the plant breeder are exhausted in respect of the material which was sold by the plant breeder with his/her consent to the farmer.

So, from a plant breeders' law perspective, Paul was not obliged to conclude a licence contract. If Paul ignores the licence contract, no obligations can arise on the basis of plant breeders' rights law (explicit view in the Belgian and Czech reports).

Figure 2. Plant Breeders' Rights Law and Exhaustion

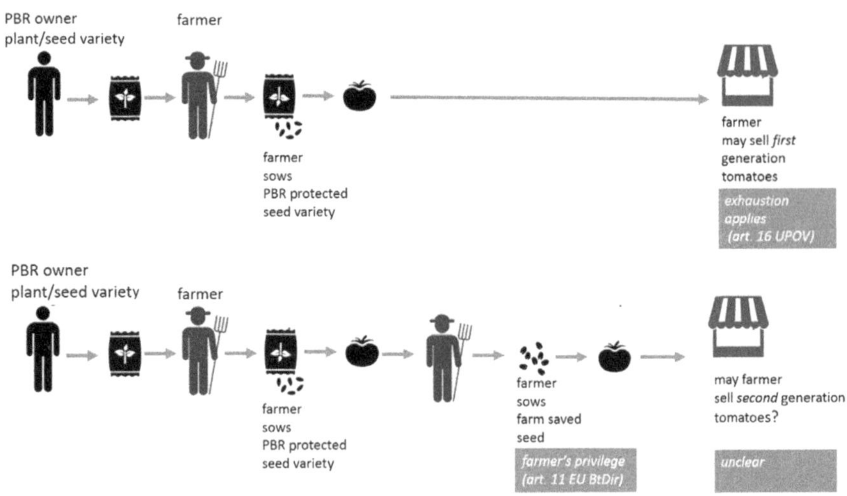

– *Scenario 6. Plant breeder's right for a transgenic* plant variety. *Use of farm saved seed (Seed from Paul)* (see Figure 2 – Bottom scenario)

However, each contracting party *may*, within reasonable limits and subject to the safeguarding of the legitimate interests of the breeder, restrict the breeder's right in relation to any variety in order to permit farmers to use for propagating purposes, on their own holdings, the product of the harvest which they have obtained by planting, on their own holdings, the protected variety (Art. 15(2) 1991 UPOV Convention). Thus, the UPOV regime leaves it up to the member states whether they allow production of propagating material by a farmer for further *planting* on their holdings. Under such a regime, farmers would be able to collect the seeds from their harvest to sow them, and then *sell* the *crops*.

The country reports do not zoom in on this issue. The reason may well be that although the 1991 UPOV Convention has been signed by various member states, implementation measures were not taken at the time of the writing of the reports.

2. Contract Law

In the country reports, two distinct aspects come to the fore. First and foremost, the question arises whether the rule of exhaustion in patent law and/or plant breeders' rights law can be waived by contract. It is not quite settled whether the exhaustion rule is mandatory or may be superseded by contract. In some jurisdictions, the idea prevails that the exhaustion rule cannot be waived by contract and certainly not by a general disclaimer such as the one in the present example (Denmark, Poland).

Secondly, the question comes up whether a contract clause unilaterally dictated by one party (CaMon) can be regarded as consented to by the other party (Paul) and can thus be legally binding. Two distinct scenarios have been scrutinised in the country reports. According to some country reports, Paul closed an *explicit* contract *in advance* with CaMon to sell his harvest to a particular company (see Belgium). In that event, Paul is bound by that contract and no longer has the right to sell his tomatoes to regional customers. CaMon is entitled to contractual penalties as foreseen. However, judging from the facts of the case, it seems quite unlikely that this is the scenario which unfolded.

According to some other country reports, Paul and CaMon did *not* conclude a contract beforehand. In most countries, the contract would be considered valid, as the condition of mutual consent has been met, albeit *tacitly*, when buying the seed (Belgium, Czech Republic). The absence of protest amounts to an acceptance of the accompanying licence contract. This position recalls the viewpoint supported in the software business area, where so-called shrink-wrap licences were generally considered acceptable. The validity will not be accepted, however, when the clauses of the accompanying contract contain unusual or excessive clauses. However, in some other countries, inactivity or silence is not regarded as acceptance of the offer. Hence, the licence contract was not concluded (Czech Republic, Denmark, Slovenia).

Various country reports underline that it is forbidden to stipulate real penalty clauses. Penalty clauses may only account for potential damages but may not constitute a kind of private punishment (Belgium). Such clauses are considered null. In some countries, the judge is allowed to moderate contractual penalties to damages *ex officio* (Belgium). If CaMon were to go to court, the penalty clause could be adapted, depending on the specific and detailed circumstances.

3. Competition Law

The additional contractual terms allude to objections from a competition law perspective, although the case does not provide the detailed information that is needed for a good analysis. Therefore, various country reporters confine themselves to a general comment. Yet the case aims at the question of whether the rationale of Article 4(b) Vertical Agreements Block Exemption Regulation can be applied (by analogy), which outlaws customer restrictions. The reports of Belgium and the Netherlands advocate for this argumentation.

Various country reports underline that, based on the rules on free movement of goods (Arts. 28 and 30 EC Treaty), the exhaustion rule in patent law and/or plant breeders' rights law is mandatory (Denmark).

III. Metalegal Formants

1. Intellectual Property Law

The exhaustion provision is based on the idea that the charge for legitimate use of a protected product shall only be paid once. The special rule for biological material extends the scope of the traditional exhaustion rule to allow the lawful buyer (i.e. farmer) of biological material to reproduce the invention as far as the first generation is concerned, based on the assumption that the price of marketed seed comprises a licence charge. The farmers' privilege implemented in patent law intends to bring the second generation into the realm of, conceptually speaking, a liability rule. The intent is remuneration, not proprietary exclusionary exercise of rights. This special rule demonstrates that inclusion of biological material in the sphere of patent protection sometimes warrants alternative approaches to the property dogma.

2. Contract Law

It is questionable whether the exhaustion principle can be set aside by a contractual provision in order to enable the patent holder to extend the scope of a patent through contract provision. By imposing a contract, patent holders are enabled to extend the scope of their patent *de facto* to the derived materials. Contract law is used here to extend the scope of a patent, where patent law had explicitly limited this scope. In this way, patent holders are able to extend the IP-originated monopoly and include a downstream market. However, after-sale conditions embedded in (explicit or implicit) contracts should not be used to unreasonably broaden patent protection.

CASE 7. PERSONALISED GENOMIC INFORMATION

A.1. BASE CASE

Marc has a unique gene that makes him immune to a specific, but widespread, influenza virus. The Pharmaceutical Company (PhC) screens his genome. As a result of this information, PhC develops a (patented) vaccine against this type of influenza.

Is Marc entitled to veto research on the gene? Does he have *a maiore ad minus* the right not to give consent to experiments that he considers unethical? Could he object to commercial research and restrict the use to 'academic research'?

A.2. EDITORIAL NOTE ON THE GDPR

When the case was drafted and answered, the EC Directive 95/46/EC on Personal Data Protection was still in place, which has since been repealed by the General Data Protection Regulation (EU) No. 2016/679. This Regulation has strengthened patients' rights to medical data.[1] This subsequent fundamental change has to be kept in mind. Reports could not be updated.

The case was conceptualised after the Oviedo Convention on Human Rights and Biomedicine (1997[2]), negotiated by the Council of Europe, came into force under public international law (1999) after five ratifications (Denmark, Slovakia, Slovenia, San Marino and Greece), and prior to Directive 2004/23/EC,[3]

---

1 For instance: E. Wierda, D. C. Eindhoven, M. J. Schalij, C. J. W. Borleffs, G. Amoroso, D. van Veghel, C. R. Mitchell, B. A. J. M. de Mol, A. Hirsch and M. C. Ploem, 'Privacy of patient data in quality-of-care registries in cardiology and cardiothoracic surgery: the impact of the new general data protection regulation EU law', 4 *European Heart Journal – Quality of Care and Clinical Outcomes*, 2018, 239–245, available at: https://doi.org/10.1093/ehjqcco/qcy034 (last visited 9 August 2019).

2 ETS No 164.

3 Directive 2004/23/EC of the European Parliament and the Council of 31 March 2004 on setting standards of quality and safety for the donation, procurement, testing, processing, preservation, storage and distribution of human tissues and cells, OJ L 102, 7 April 2004, 48.

Directive 2006/17/EC,[4] and Directive 2006/86/EC.[5] Depending on when the reports were submitted, transposing national regulations are reported or not.

A.3. COUNTRY REPORTS

(1) BELGIUM

I. Operative Rules

Due to the requirement of a prior informed consent and due to the revocability of it, we believe Marc:

1. would be entitled to veto research on the gene;
2. has the right not to give consent to experiments that he considers unethical; and
3. could object to commercial research and restrict the use to academic research.

II. Descriptive Formants

These and similar issues have not been regulated in Belgium in a general way.[6] There is, however, a significant amount of *ad hoc* legislation,[7] which imposes quite a strong informed consent requirement with regard to human material. The following examples nicely illustrate the principle as embedded in fragmented legislation. Consenting for the purpose of pharmacogenetic analysis would not imply consent for the use of the genetic material for other purposes, as has been advised by both the Belgian Advisory Committee on Bioethics[8] and the

---

4 Commission Directive 2006/17/EC of 8 February 2006 implementing Directive 2004/23/EC of the European Parliament and of the Council as regards certain technical requirements for the donation, procurement and testing of human tissues and cells, OJ L 38, 9 February 2006, 40.

5 Commission Directive 2006/86/EC of 24 October 2006 implementing Directive 2004/23/EC of the European Parliament and of the Council as regards traceability requirements, notification of serious adverse reactions and events and certain technical requirements for the coding, processing, preservation, storage and distribution of human tissues and cells, OJ L 294, 25 October 2006, 32.

6 H. Nys, 'Geneeskunde. Recht en medisch handelen' [Medicine. Law and Medical Practice], *Story-Scientia*, 2005, 505.

7 Organ Transplantation Act, 13 June 1986, *Official Gazette*, 14 February 1987 [Wet 13 juni 1986 betreffende het wegnemen en transplanteren van organen, *B.S.*, 14 februari 1987]; Blood and Blood Derivatives Act, 5 July 1994, *Official Gazette*, 8 October 1994 [Wet 5 juli 1994 betreffende bloed en bloedderivaten van menselijke oorsprong, *B.S.*, 8 oktober 1994]; Patient's Rights Act, 22 August 2002, *Official Gazette*, 26 September 2002 [Wet 22 augustus 2002 betreffende de rechten van de patiënt, *B.S.*, 26 september 2002]; Experiments on Human Persons Act, 7 May 2004, *Official Gazette*, 18 May 2004 [Wet 7 mei 2004 inzake experimenten op de menselijke persoon, *B.S.*, 18 mei 2004].

8 Belgian Bio-ethical Committee [Belgisch Raadgevend Comité voor Bio-ethiek], Advice no. 26, 15 December 2003, on the Introduction of a Pharmacogenetic Part in Research

National Council of the Order of Physicians.[9] Along the same lines, one would keep control over one's blood which had been drawn for transfusion purposes (Art. 14(2) Blood and Blood Derivatives Act). Finally, using DNA material obtained for a criminal investigation for other purposes than this criminal investigation will result in to criminal sanctions.[10] Therefore, one would be able to revoke one's consent, even after the tissue has been separated from one's body, thus illustrating the principle of control over one's own tissue.[11]

Belgian law or case law dealing with the specific issue of the further use of human tissue is not available, which indeed leads to uncertainty.[12] The further use of human tissue therefore falls under the more general Patient's Rights Act, which unfortunately contains no explicit relevant clauses on further use.

In spite of all this, part of the legal doctrine argues that the principles mentioned above also apply when further use is concerned.[13] Therefore, an informed consent requirement and the right to revoke[14] would be applicable

Protocols [betreffende de invoering van een farmacogenetisch luik in onderzoeksprotocollen], available at: https://www.health.belgium.be/en/belgian-advisory-committee-bioethics (last consulted 11 March 2022).

9 National Council of the Order of Physicians [Nationale Raad van de Orde van Geneesheren], Advice 17 July 2004 on DNA Research and Farmacogenetics, 106 TNR, 2004, 4.

10 Art. 6(2) DNA Research in Criminal Case Act, 22 March 1999, *Official Gazette*, 20 May 1999 [Wet 22 maart 1999 betreffende de identificatieprocedure via DNA-onderzoek in strafzaken, *B.S.*, 20 mei 1999]. C. Trouet, *Van lichaam naar lichaamsmateriaal. Recht en het nader gebruik van cellen en weefsels [From Body to Human Tissue. Law and the Further Use of Cells and Tissues]* (Antwerpen/Groningen/Oxford: 2003), 153.

11 Y.-H. Leleu and G. Genicot, 'La maîtrise de son corps par la personne' [The Person's Control over His Body], 5937 *J.T.* 1999, 595–596; C. Trouet, *Van lichaam naar lichaamsmateriaal. Recht en het nader gebruik van cellen en weefsels [From Body to Human Tissue. Law and the Further Use of Cells and Tissues]* (Antwerpen/Groningen/Oxford: 2003), 106.

12 S. Callens, 'Legal Comments on the Further Use of Human Tissue for the Purpose of Research', *BSLR*, 1997, 104 and C. Trouet, *Van lichaam naar lichaamsmateriaal. Recht en het nader gebruik van cellen en weefsels [From Body to Human Tissue. Law and the Further Use of Cells and Tissues]* (Antwerpen/Groningen/Oxford: 2003), 147. Nor has Belgium ratified the Convention on Human Rights and Biomedicine, 4 March 1997, E.T.S. no. 164, available at: http://conventions.coe.int/ (last consulted 5 May 2019).

13 H. Nys, *Geneeskunde. Recht en medisch handelen*, 1991, 383; S. Callens, 'Gezondheidsrechtelijke vragen bij gebruik van cellen, weefsels, coupes en ander lichaamsmateriaal' [Health Law Issues regarding Use of Cells, Tissues, Coupes and Other Human Tissue], in: B. Tilleman and A. Verbeke (eds.), *Actualia Vermogensrecht [Actualia Property Law]* (Brugge: 2005), 268; C. Trouet, *Van lichaam naar lichaamsmateriaal. Recht en het nader gebruik van cellen en weefsels [From Body to Human Tissue. Law and the Further Use of Cells and Tissues]* (Antwerpen/Groningen/Oxford: 2003), 380–400.

14 See also: Belgian Bio-ethical Committee [Belgisch Raadgevend Comité voor Bio-ethiek], Advice no. 26, 15 December 2003, on the Introduction of a Pharmacogenetic Part in Research Protocols [betreffende de invoering van een farmacogenetisch luik in onderzoeksprotocollen], available at: https://portal.health.fgov.be/portal/page?_pageid=56,8546420&_dad=portal&_schema=PORTAL (last consulted 5 May 2019).

to this case. However, this is not accepted unanimously[15] nor is it applied, since there has been a long tradition by which doctors could more or less do as they pleased with separated human tissue.[16]

Marc would have the possibility at any time to revoke his consent and prevent further research on his tissue/genetic data if his conditions are not met. A lot will depend on the specific information he received before giving his consent to extract some blood initially. For instance, if Marc was properly informed of the possibility of the current research, there is no reason why PhC should warn him now and ask for his permission.[17] This brings us to a practical problem, i.e. that very often we will not know it when our tissue is being used for research or activities falling outside the scope of our consent.

III. Metalegal Formants

Human cells, tissue and organs have long been collected, even more so since technological developments increasingly permits their preservation, analysis and use. Various tissue banks have emerged and have proven their enormous potential for scientific and medical research. This explains why limitation of the use of tissue and information is strongly resented by a significant part of the scientific and medicinal community.[18]

However, the use of human material for scientific and therapeutic purposes increasingly evokes criticism. It is argued that people feel their dignity to be violated when they suddenly realise that their tissue, collected a long time ago, has not been destroyed but rather kept, exchanged, used, re-used and sometimes even commercialised (not the tissues themselves but the inventions based upon them).[19]

---

15 H. Nys, 'Het nader gebruik van lichaamsmateriaal en biotechnologische uitvindingen' ['The Further Use of Body Material and Biotechnological Inventions'], in: G. Van Overwalle (ed.), *Patent Law, Ethics and Biotechnology* (Brussels: 1998), 174.

16 H. Nys, *Geneeskunde. Recht en medisch handelen*, 1991, 383; C. Trouet, 'Patiëntenrechten en het onderzoek met lichaamsmateriaal' [Patients' Rights and the Research with Human Tissue], *Leuvense Perspectieven*, 2002, no. 4, 495; C. Trouet, *Van lichaam naar lichaamsmateriaal. Recht en het nader gebruik van cellen en weefsels [From Body to Human Tissue. Law and the Further Use of Cells and Tissues]* (Antwerpen/Groningen/Oxford: 2003), 148.

17 Belgian Bio-ethical Committee [Belgisch Raadgevend Comité voor Bio-ethiek], Advice no. 26, 15 December 2003, on the Introduction of a Pharmacogenetic Part in Research Protocols [betreffende de invoering van een farmacogenetisch luik in onderzoeksprotocollen], available at: https://portal.health.fgov.be/portal/page?_pageid=56,8546420&_dad=portal&_schema=PORTAL (last consulted 5 May 2019).

18 C. Trouet, *Van lichaam naar lichaamsmateriaal. Recht en het nader gebruik van cellen en weefsels [From Body to Human Tissue. Law and the Further Use of Cells and Tissues]* (Antwerpen/Groningen/Oxford: 2003), 74–86.

19 C. Trouet, 'Patiëntenrechten en het onderzoek met lichaamsmateriaal' [Patients' Rights and the Research with Human Tissue], *Leuvense Perspectieven*, 2002, no. 4, 495–497.

There is no doubt that public health and freedom of research have to be safeguarded. However, both these values have to be balanced with other fundamental principles, such as privacy, the right to respect for a private life and the right to self-determination. A broad interpretation of Article 8 ECHR[20] leads to the conclusion that one has a personality right to one's human tissue and genetic information.[21] Following the logic of Article 8(2) ECHR, a careful and proportional balance must be respected when interfering with this personality right on the grounds of public interests like health or freedom of research.

In this debate, an evolution seems to be taking place towards more and more respect for the personality right and thus the requirement of informed consent (even if this consent does not always have to be explicit).[22]

(2) CZECH REPUBLIC

I. *Operative Rules*

Marc is neither entitled to veto research on the gene (including research which he considers to be unethical) nor does he have the right to restrict the use to academic research only.

II. *Descriptive Formants*

Protection of the personality is regulated primarily by the Czech Charter of Fundamental Rights and Freedoms[23] and by the Civil Code 40/1964 Coll. With regard to this case, the Charter grants protection of personality specifically in Article 7(1), where the inviolability of the person is guaranteed. Other provisions of the Charter concerned with personality protections (Art. 10) are specified in section 11 of the Civil Code – a person has the right to protection of his/her personality, in particular his/her life and health. But when a person gives his/her genetic material, for example by the procedure of taking of blood, then the person loses any control over the future use of that material. There is no legal rule requiring the person's consent to manipulation of his/her genetic

---

20 Convention of 4 November 1950 for the Protection of Human Rights and Fundamental Freedoms, ECTS no. 5, www.coe.int (last consulted on 25 October 2007).

21 C. Trouet, *Van lichaam naar lichaamsmateriaal. Recht en het nader gebruik van cellen en weefsels [From Body to Human Tissue. Law and the Further Use of Cells and Tissues]* (Antwerpen/Groningen/Oxford: 2003), 372–400.

22 Ibid., 323–333.

23 The Charter of Fundamental Rights and Freedoms is a part of the Czech constitutional order and is a constitutional act.

material after he/she voluntarily consents, for example, to the taking of his/her blood or body part.[24] If the person agrees to the taking of his/her blood or body part, then, according to section 26 of the Act on Healthcare of the People, such material that has been taken shall be used therapeutic/preventative care, medical science, research and study purposes (this is an exhaustive list).[25] Consent is deemed to be generally given to any kind of use mentioned above. In Czech law, there are only a few exceptions where consent is not assumed to be general. One in the Transplantation Act[26] says that a living donor of an organ must consent to give the organ to a specified recipient. The second exception is in the Stem Cell Act,[27] where consent must be given to the precise purpose for which the embryo shall be used.

III. Metalegal Formants

The central principle is 'non-commercialisation' of the human body and its parts. The Czech Republic is bound by international treaties like the Universal Declaration on the Human Genome and Human Rights of UNESCO or the Convention on Human Rights and Biomedicine of the Council of Europe, which in its Article 21 prohibits profiting financially from the human body. The Transplantation Act,[28] as well as Stem Cell Act, prohibit such profit. But none of the above-mentioned acts distinguish between commercial and academic research.

It will be a question *pro futuro* whether it will be reasonable to develop the law to protect genetic material after the material is taken with consent of the person. On the one hand, we can see that modern law protects any kind of property, in any form (tangible, intangible), gives protection to intellectual property rights, and such protection is granted not only by 'ordinary' law but also by the Constitution. On the other hand, we must also see that, for example, blood is used in the production of many kinds of medical treatments, and if there is to be any law established to protect genetic material after a person voluntarily gives it to medical centres, then we must be sure about the impact of such a law, for example on the production of medical treatments based on human blood.

---

24 Consent to the taking of blood, body parts, etc. is regulated by the Act on Healthcare of the People 20/1966 Coll., the Act on Donation, Taking and Transplantation of Tissues and Organs 285/2002 Coll., etc.

25 See further K. Knap, J. Švestka, O. Jehlička, P. Pavlík, V. Plecitý, *Ochrana osobnosti podle občanského práva* (Protection of personality according to civil law), (4th ed., Prague: 2004), p. 254 et seq.

26 Act on Donation, Taking and Transplantation of Tissues and Organs 285/2002 Coll.

27 Act on Research on Human Embryonic Stem Cells and Related Activities 227/2006 Coll.

28 Act on Donation, Taking and Transplantation of Tissues and Organs 285/2002 Coll.

(3) DENMARK

I. Operative Rules

It depends on the specific circumstances whether Marc is entitled to object to the collection, storage and processing of the gene and to the further research.

II. Descriptive Formants

An individual's right to self-determination in regard to research on human tissue samples is primarily regulated in the Act on Processing of Personal Data (APPD, 31 May 2000), together with the Act on Health (AH, 7 February 2008) and the Act on Biomedical Research Ethics Committee System (ABRECS, 28 May 2003). In general, APPD §10 exempts processing of personal data – including tissue samples – for research purposes from the normal consent requirements stipulated in this Act. However, other laws must also be taken into consideration. If the tissue sample is *collected directly from the donor for research purposes*, the donor (research subject) must give voluntary, express and informed consent, cf. ABRECS §16. The consent may be withdrawn, but it does not follow clearly from the wording of the Act how this affects the further use of the tissue sample for scientific purposes. The further use of the tissue samples for other research projects depends on the scope of the consent. If the tissue sample has not been donated directly for a specific research project, but the pharmaceutical company has obtained *access to the tissue sample from a biobank*, the Research Ethics Committee may derogate from the consent requirement if the research project does not involve any health risks for the individual research subject and will not in any other way in the circumstances cause harm to that person, cf. ABRECS §8, third paragraph. Derogation is also possible if it is impossible or disproportionately difficult to obtain informed consent. In the Research Ethics Committee system's practice, derogation seems to be the rule rather than the exception. In this situation, the tissue donor has no influence on the use of the sample for research purposes. To complicate the question, the AH regulates self-determination with regard to tissue samples which have been *collected in connection with treatment and care in the health care sector*. According to AH §29, patients have a right to veto the use of stored tissue for research purposes by registering in the 'Use of Tissue Register' (Danish: 'Vævsanvendelsesregisteret'). If an individual has signed up in this register, it is illegal to provide his/her or her tissue sample for research purposes. It is not possible to indicate that the tissue may be used for specific kinds of research, for example for non-commercial research. Accordingly, Marc's right to object to and influence further research depends on how the pharmaceutical company has obtained access to his genetic material.

III. *Metalegal Formants*

The Danish attitude to use of personal data and tissue samples for scientific purposes is quite liberal. In general, individual consent is not necessary as long as the research is based exclusively on data files and biobanks. However, in regard to tissue samples, it has been acknowledged that an individual's right to self-determination must also be respected. Consequently, the rules in the AH on the right to 'opt-out' provide patients with some influence on the use of their tissue for research purposes.

(4) ESTONIA

I. *Operative Rules*

Presumably, Marc does not have any of these claims.

II. *Descriptive Formants*

Before PhC can do any research on Marc's gene, it needs a biological sample. Although Estonia has adopted the Human Genes Research Act,[29] it is not applicable to this case.[30] Therefore, the requirements of the Biomedicine Convention[31] have to be complied with. Article 5 of the Biomedicine Convention provides:

> An intervention in the health field may only be carried out after the person concerned has given free and informed consent to it. This person shall beforehand be given appropriate information as to the purpose and nature of the intervention as well as on its consequences and risks. The person concerned may freely withdraw consent at any time.

---

29 Inimgeeniuuringute seadus. Entered into force on 8 January 2001 – RT I 2000, 104, 685; 2007, 22, 111 (in Estonian).

30 Subsection 1(1) of the Human Genes Research Act explains the purpose of this act as follows: '[t]he objectives of this Act are to regulate the establishment and maintenance of a Gene Bank, to organise the genetic research necessary therefor, to ensure the voluntary nature of gene donation and the confidentiality of the identity of gene donors, and to protect persons from misuse of genetic data and from discrimination based on interpretation of the structure of their DNA and the genetic risks arising therefrom'. As seen, the genetic research is only regulated for the purpose of the Gene Bank. The Gene Bank is 'a database established and maintained by the chief processor consisting of tissue samples, descriptions of DNA, descriptions of state of health, genealogies, genetic data and data enabling the identification of gene donors' and the University of Tartu is the chief processor of the Gene Bank (Human Genes Research Act §2 clause 10; §3(1)).

31 Convention for the Protection of Human Rights and Dignity of the Human Being with regard to the Application of Biology and Medicine: Convention on Human Rights and Biomedicine. Entered into force on 1 June 2002 in respect of Estonia – RT II 2002, 1, 2.

The question of whether Marc has any right to determine what kind of research can be done on his biological material is complicated. Marc could have vetoed all research on his gene by not giving his biological sample. Afterwards, Marc's position is not very strong. Based on the facts of the case, it can be assumed that Marc gave his consent to his biological material being used to develop the vaccine. As to the permissibility of the other possible usages of the biological material, there is no clear answer.[32]

III. Metalegal Formants

The case concerns fundamental rights and freedoms guaranteed by the Constitution. Subsection 18 of the Constitution of the Republic of Estonia provides: 'No one shall be subjected to medical or scientific experiments against his or her free will'. It has been emphasised in the legal literature that this provision protects freedom of choice and human dignity.[33] The right not to be subjected to medical or scientific experiments is protected by criminal law. Section 138 of the Penal Code provides:

> Conduct of medical or scientific research on a person who has not granted consent thereto pursuant to the procedure prescribed by law or who before granting such consent was not notified of the essential potential dangers arising from the research is punishable by a pecuniary punishment or up to 3 years' imprisonment. The same act, if committed by a legal person, is punishable by a pecuniary punishment.

Section 139 of the Penal Code provides additionally that:

> removal, for transplantation purposes, of human organs or tissue by a person with the corresponding right arising from law, if the person from whom the organs or tissue are removed has not been notified of the essential potential dangers arising from the removal of organs or tissue before he or she grants consent thereto, or if the person removing the organs or tissue was aware that the person from whom the organs or tissue are removed will receive remuneration therefor, is punishable by a pecuniary punishment or up to one year of imprisonment.

(5) FRANCE

I. Operative Rules

Whether or not Marc may oppose the three claims depends on the degree to which he has been informed about the nature and objective of the research.

---

32 On related issues see A. Nõmper, *Open consent – a new form of informed consent for population genetic databases* (Tartu: 2005).

33 E.-J. Truuväli et al. (eds.), *Eesti Vabariigi põhiseadus. Kommenteeritud väljaanne* (The Constitution of the Republic of Estonia. Commented edition) (Tallinn: 2002), p. 155.

II. Descriptive Formants

In France, there is no general provision for personality rights. However, different laws, court cases and the legal doctrine confirm the existence of personality rights. Especially in the Civil Code, Article 16 and the following provisions provide a strong substantive basis for personality rights. According to the doctrine, personality rights can be seen as the protection of physical integrity, protection of moral integrity and protection of private life.[34]

As far as this case is concerned, the principles of unavailability and non-commercialisation of the human body (physical integrity) are essential. According to the civil law tradition, the data subject has no ownership of the separated elements of his/her body, nor a right to concede those elements, or the associated information data, or the results of research resulting from those elements and data.[35] Otherwise, it risks putting these elements or related information in the commercial circuit.[36]

Nevertheless, one of the fundamental ideas behind the French Bioethics Act of 6 August 2004 is the respect of personal will.[37] The data subject should be fully informed and give his/her consent in any case under French law. Therefore, regarding genetic information, the law stipulates that: 'A genetic examination of the particulars of a person may be undertaken only for medical purposes or in the interest of scientific research'.[38] It also states that:

> The written consent of the person must be obtained before carrying out the study. The person should be fully informed of the nature and the purposes of the process of examination. The objective of the examination should be mentioned in the consent. The consent can be withdrawn at any moment without any form required.[39]

The violation of these articles is liable to prosecution.[40]

The Bioethics Act of 2004 also provides the data subject with the right to oppose re-use of the sampled biological elements for medical or scientific

---

34 F. Terré, *Droit civil* (7e éd., 2005), p. 57.

35 G. Cornu, *Droit civil: les personnes* (13e éd., 2007), p. 29 f.; F. Terré, *Droit civil* (7e éd., 2005), p. 54 f.; H. Mazaud, J. Mazeaud and F. Chabas, *Leçons de droit civil*, t. I, vol. 2, CCNE, 1997, p. 377 ff.; CCNE, Advice n°077: Ethical problems raised by the collected biological material and associated information data: 'biobanks', 'biolibraries', 2003.

36 The French Civil Code states in Art. 16-1, para. 3: 'The human body, its elements and its products may not form the subject of a patrimonial right', and in Art. 16-5: 'Agreements that have the effect of bestowing a patrimonial value to the human body, its elements or products are void.'

37 The word 'consent' (*consentement*) is repeated 57 times in the Bioethics Act of 2004, No. 2004-800.

38 Bioethics Act of 2004, No. 2004-800, Art. 4, 2°; Civil Code, Art. 16-10.

39 Bioethics Act of 2004, No. 2004-800, Art. 4, 2°; Civil Code, Art. 16-10 al. 2.

40 Bioethics Act of 2004, No. 2004-800, Art. 4, 2°; Civil Code, Art. 16-10 al. 2; Penal Code, Art. 226-25.

purposes other than those initially planned.[41] In this case, the data subject must be informed and can oppose this use.[42] More generally, the data subject can withdraw consent and can demand the destruction of the samples and the associated data.

As far as our case is concerned, two situations should be distinguished. If Marc is fully informed about the nature and objective of the research, including the possible research on the gene, the related experiments and the possible commercial development, he can decide not to participate in the said research. However, if he did not receive full information and gave his express consent to the research, or if the research objective is modified at a later stage, Marc has a right to oppose these three claims and can ask for the destruction of his genetic data under the French Bioethics Law.

III. Metalegal Formants

Informed consent is the crucial consideration in the collection of biological elements, such as genes or cells, but there is no general recognition of personality rights over the physical elements of the human body and related data. Personality rights consist only in not being obliged to participate in a collection operation for research by making available physical elements or genetic information.[43] Yet, in the French tradition, the individual's will is of central importance. It is therefore the case that under French law, an individual's change of mind is respected by way of 'opposition to re-use' (yet not retrospectively).

(6) GERMANY

I. Operative Rules

No, Marc has none of these three claims.

II. Descriptive Formants

The Act on Human Genetic Diagnoses (Gendiagnostikgesetz (GenDG), 2009)[44] is not applicable to the case. The law only applies to genetic diagnoses with a

---

41 Bioethics Act of 2004, No. 2004-800, Art. 7, 2°; Public Health Code, Art. L. 1211-2.
42 Bioethics Act of 2004, No. 2004-800, Art. 7, 2°; Public Health Code, Art. L. 1211-2.
43 CCNE, Advice n°077: Ethical problems raised by the collected biological material and associated information data: 'biobanks', 'biolibraries', 2003, p. 17.
44 BGBl. I S. 2529, 3672, revised in 2016 (BGBl. I S. 2460) and changed in 2021 (BGBl. I S. 882).

medical purpose (§2 sec. 1 GenDG), and not to 'research' in general, §2 sec. 2 GenDG.[45] Despite the fact that the distinction between 'medical purpose' and 'research purpose' is fuzzy,[46] in our case the situation is unequivocal: the research conducted is not geared towards a treatment of Marc.

The operating rule is §1004 BGB in conjunction with his personality right (Art. 2 sec. 1 German Constitution). The personality right encompasses the exclusive right to prohibit access to one's own bodily material and the right to control personal data. When the material is separated, however, one's influence transforms according to the transition from the personality right to the 'property/person' hybrid.[47] Legally, the material becomes 'a thing'. Limited personal rights extend to the material, like the interest in sperm stored prior to surgery leading to infertility.[48] In respect of research, it is argued that the personality right only provides for a 'negative' veto right, but not for 'positive' determination rights. Consequently, one could withdraw one's consent to the storage and utilisation of one's own material (claim for delivery, destruction of the material, deletion of data). There is a parallel to §§13, 40 sec. 1 UrhG (cogent law). But the personality right would not encompass the right to determine the nature of the research undertaken, neither ethical/unethical research nor commercial/uncommercial research or commercialisation *per se*.[49] Therefore, Marc has a right not to

---

45 GenDG §2: '(1) Dieses Gesetz gilt für genetische Untersuchungen und im Rahmen genetischer Untersuchungen durchgeführte genetische Analysen bei geborenen Menschen sowie bei Embryonen und Föten während der Schwangerschaft und den Umgang mit dabei gewonnenen genetischen Proben und genetischen Daten bei genetischen Untersuchungen *zu medizinischen Zwecken, zur Klärung der Abstammung sowie im Versicherungsbereich und im Arbeitsleben*. (2) Dieses Gesetz *gilt nicht* für genetische Untersuchungen und Analysen und den Umgang mit genetischen Proben und Daten Nr. 1. *zu Forschungszwecken*' (emphasis added).

46 K. Schillhorm and S. Heidemann, *Gendiagnostikgesetz* (2nd ed., Heidelberg: 2017), p. 26, para. 9. The criteria is 'the primary purpose' (ibid, p. 30, para. 20).

47 For an introduction to the conceptual problem see I. Schneider, *Gesellschaftliche Umgangsweisen bei Keimzellen – Regulation zwischen Gabe, Verkauf und Unveräußerlichkeit*, in: S. Graumann and I. Schneider (eds.) *Verkörperte Technik – entkörperte Technik. Biopolitik und Geschlecht* (Frankfurt/M.: 2003) 41–65; H. Schünemann, *Die Rechte am menschlichen Körper* (Frankfurt: 1985).

48 BGH, judgment of 9 November 1993, BGHZ 124, 52 – sperm.

49 However, there is uncertainty about how to construct principles and legal consequences: A. Krefft, *Patente auf human-genomische Erfindungen: Rechtslage in Deutschland, Europa und den USA* (Cologne: 2003), p. 107, distinguishes between consent to the taking of the material from the body and to commercialisation. He argues that the violation of the duty to inform in respect of the taking from the body always amounts to non-patentability (p. 107). In respect of the consent to commercialisation, he constructs a relation between rule and exception. In principle, the lack of consent to commercialisation in principle has no consequences for patentability. However, if truly unique personal information is to be exploited, then the violation of duties to inform does violate the patient's personality right, and the patentability in respect of this material (based on fraudulent obtained consent which was limited to pure research purposes) would not be given (p. 113). Along the same lines,

participate in a genetic screening if he considers a specific research project unethical. Thus, he has a right to be informed about the research planned. A more problematic case is the question of genetic commercial research. Again, *ex ante* and in principle, Marc has a right not to participate. Anything else is highly contested. It is already contested if he has the right to be informed about the academic or commercial nature of the research planned.[50] However, it is even more contested whether (in cases of personalised data) the lack of consent to commercialisation is a violation of the personality right which amounts to non-patentable subject matter (see Modification 1).

Yet terms are only negotiated contractually (informed consent sheet). There is no case law.

III. Metalegal Formants

The reasoning depends on how far the right to one's own body information shall reach. An academic minority claims that the personality right shall include the determination of which kind of research can be undertaken[51] – and also the question of commercialisation. For the time being, those kinds of restrictions can only be the subject of a contract resulting in contractual duties.

C. Godt, *Eigentum an Information* (Tübingen: 2007), p. 593, fine-tuning however the legal consequences of pre-grant/post-grant lack of consent and the qualities of the genetic information in question. Both authors do not question the internationalised principle of non-commercialisation of the human body *per se*. Godt conceives the inclusion of the disposition about commercialisation as an individualised enforcement measures of the policy principle. As far as commercialisation is possible via patent law, the inclusion of the disposition about use and commercialisation as part of personal autonomy protection functions as a counterweight against the commercial freedoms of researchers and industry. The authors differ in respect of how the non-commercialisation principle comes into play. Krefft (p. 110) argues that when the rule applies (the lack of consent does not interfere with patentability), patients have the possibility to claim benefit-sharing. In contrast, Godt (p. 594) argues that in both cases of rule and exception, benefit-sharing cannot be claimed – for different reasons. When non-individual (collective) genomic information is used, then there is no reason to provide benefit-sharing to an individual who by chance happens to be included in the given research. In the event that the lack of consent amounts to a violation to the autonomy right (individual genomic information), the patient is given the power to prevent commercialisation (via consent), but the principle of non-commercialisation precludes profit-oriented benefit-sharing.

50 J. Taupitz, 'Wem gebührt der Schatz im menschlichen Körper? Zur Beteiligung des Patienten an der kommerziellen Nutzung seiner Körpersubstanzen', (1991) 91 *AcP*, 201–246 argues that one has no right to be informed because of the conflicting research freedom; J. Simon would contradict this, arguing that one has a right because of the overriding personality right which prevails (for his perception, however exemplified in the context of genetic testing required by insurance companies, J. Simon, *Gendiagnostik und Versicherung* (Baden-Baden: 2001), pp. 112–117).

51 Included in the Draft Law on Biobanks proposed by the Green Party Opposition; see F.A.Z., 13 September 2006, No. 213, p. N1.

(7) GREECE

I. *Operative Rules*

The research is subject to Marc's free, informed and specific consent, unless this harms public health (which is probably the case here).

II. *Descriptive Formants*

According to Recital 26 Biotechnology Directive (= Presidential Decree 321/2001), 'if an invention is based on biological material of human origin or if it uses such material, where a patent application is filed, the person from whose body the material is taken must have had an opportunity of expressing free and informed consent thereto'. But instead of containing a specific rule, the Directive refers to national law for this matter. According to Greek law, this is a matter of intervention in Marc's personal data. According to Article 57 of the Civil Code, an offence to an individual's personality gives grounds for a claim for cessation, insofar as it is prohibited by a specific rule of law,[52] which is not the case here. In any event, the consent of the injured party removes the unjust character of the offence, unless it involves grave physical injury (Art. 309 para. 2 Penal Code *e contrario*) or is contrary to a provision of law or to good morals (Arts. 174, 178 Civil Code). The taking and scanning of the gene do not constitute grave physical injury (injury to the body or the health) and thus from this point of view the individual's consent to this and the contract in this connection are in principle valid.

However, they constitute 'processing of data of a personal character' in the sense of Article 2 α Law 2472/1997, since the characteristics of Richard's gene comprise information about his health. Thus, the individual's consent to this is possible, but is subject to the requirement that it be in writing. If it is supposed that this is the way things are, then the following answers should be given.

In Greek law, though it is recognised that consent to the processing of data may be freely revoked (Art. 2 ια, Law 2472/1997), it is at the same time laid down

52 Thus the case law (AP 1508/1988, *NoB* 1990 38, 63; EfAth 12154/1990, *ElDni* 32, 1673; EfAth 10745/1991, *NoB* 40, 290) and the minor opinion in the doctrine (Simantiras, *General Principles of Civil Law* (1980)), in view of the wording of Art. 57 Civil Code ('A person who has suffered an unlawful offence to his personality has the right to claim the cessation of the offence'). The prevailing opinion in the doctrine is to the contrary (Gazis, *General Principles* (1973), §44.II.3; Papantoniou, *General Principles* (1983), §28, p. 134; Georgiades, *General Principles* (2019), §12, no. 18–23); this assumes any offence to the personality to be in principle unlawful, unless there are grounds for the cessation of its unjust character. As a result, the two opinions converge in practice.

that the individual has a 'right of objection' to the processing only if the reason for his/her objection is judged (by the competent authority for the protection of personal data) to be reasonable. The difficult problem of interpretation of the conflict of the two provisions should in the present instance be resolved on the basis of what has been agreed: if the specific experimental research was included within the agreed aim of the processing, Marc has no right of objection. It goes without saying that general consent *en masse* to any experimental processing will not be valid, since the individual should be aware of the more specific aim of the processing of his data, in accordance with Article 2 ια Law 2472/1997. Similarly, if the specific experiments are indeed unethical, then consent will be invalid, in accordance with Article 178 Civil Code. In the last two instances ('general' or unethical consent), Marc will naturally have a right of objection and an obligation to give back any consideration received as unjust enrichment, in accordance with Article 904 Civil Code (the lack of ethicality should not be imputable to either of the parties, in which case the claim is not impeded in accordance with Art. 907 Civil Code). A different solution would be justified only if the experimental research 'derived from exclusively scientific reasons' in accordance with Article 7 para. 2 στ Law 2472/1997.

III. Metalegal Formants

Greece provides strong support for the individual's right to genetic information which is protected under data protection law and general civil law. However, this strong position might only exist on paper. The right to revoke consent is subject to justifying reasons, to be evaluated by the competent authority. In addition, the individual's rights are curtailed for 'experimental research derived from exclusively scientific reasons'. The rationale is that science serves the needs of the people and therefore the inventions should be commercialisable, so that equivalent products can be distributed to anyone.

(8) IRELAND

Answer omitted.

(9) ITALY

I. Operative Rules

Marc is entitled to veto research on the gene, and he can restrict the resulting uses.

II. Descriptive Formants

Genetic data, as everyone knows, are the most sensitive personal information related to an individual (or a group of people: the so-called biological group).[53] Genes are hereditary and can be predictive of individuals' genetic predispositions; thus, they may have a significant impact on a family extending over generations. That is the reason why many Western legal systems have adopted strict regulations concerning the collection, storage and use of human genetic data.[54]

In Italy, the most important rules are laid down in Article 90 Data Protection Code (d.lgs. 196/2003).[55] According to Article 90, any collection and processing of human genetic information requires the prior authorisation of the Data Protection Authority. In February 2007, the Data Protection Authority adopted a general authorisation, setting up the guidelines for the processing of genetic data.[56] According to this regulation, genetic data can be collected and stored only by a limited category of subjects (see Art. 2), acting for well-defined purposes (Art. 3) and respecting a precise set of conditions (Art. 4 et seq.).

One of the most important conditions that makes the processing lawful is the consent of the data subject (Art. 6; in general Art. 23 Data Protection Code). Such a declaration must be in written form and has to be given freely, after having been properly informed about the purposes and the modalities of the processing of the genetic data (Art. 5). Consent may be withdrawn at any time.

These rules – concerning genetic information, though one should not forget that any biological sample can be used to produce human genetic data[57] – are consistent with the general provisions on consent to medical treatment and interference with the human body (in general see Arts. 13 and 32 Constitution; Art. 5 Civil Code). In particular, according to Article 22 of the Oviedo Convention on Biomedicine – ratified by Italy in 2001 (l. 145/2001)[58] – any part

---

53 Genetic data, according to the Council of Europe Recommendation No. R (97) 5 on the Protection of Medical Data, are 'all data, of whatever type, concerning the hereditary characteristics of an individual or concerning the pattern of inheritance of such characteristics within a related group of individuals'.

54 See Anneca, 'Il trattamento dei dati genetici', in: Panetta (ed.), *Libera circolazione e protezione dei dati personali* (Milano: 2006), pp. 1121 ff., p. 1123.

55 See Parisi, *Trattamento dei dati genetici e donatori di midollo osseo*, in Sica, Stanzione (eds.), *La nuova disciplina della privacy* (Bologna: 2004), pp. 385 ff.

56 Provv. 22 February 2007, in *Bollettino*, no. 80, February 2007, doc. web no. 1389918.

57 See Art. 17 UNESCO Declaration on Human Genetic Data (2003); Gruppo di Lavoro per la Tutela dei Dati Personali (Group Art. 29), *Documento di lavoro sui dati genetici*, no. 91 of 17 March 2004, p. 13; E. Mand, 'Biobanken für die Forschung und informationelle Selbstbestimmung', (2005) *Medizinrecht*, p. 566.

58 It has to be clarified that Italy has ratified the Oviedo Convention, but the decrees provided for by this law have not yet been adopted. This raises difficult questions as regards the binding effect – horizontal and vertical – of the Convention. This problem cannot be discussed here; it suffices to say that the Oviedo Convention can *at least* be used as an interpretative tool in order to apply the general clauses of Italian private law, such as 'good faith' or 'good morals'

of the human body removed in the course of an intervention may be stored and used for a purpose other than that for which it was removed, *only after the prior (informed) consent of the person involved has been obtained.* Such permission is required not only for the collection, but also for any other subsequent use: biomedical research, therapeutic use, commercial exploitation.[59] In particular, if the collection of biological material is aimed at research and exploitation, the person has to be informed of the possibility that the results of the research (proteins produced, new screening methods, genetic therapies, etc.) could be patented.

This conclusion, which can be easily inferred from Article 22 Oviedo Convention, is now expressly supported by Article 5 of the d.l. 1 January 2006, no. 3 (implementation of the Biotechnology Directive and harmonisation with duties arising from international treaties, such as the Rio Convention on Biodiversity and the Oviedo Convention).[60] According to this provision, when a patent application is submitted and relates to a biotechnological invention that uses human biological material, the written consent of the person involved is required. The person has to be specifically informed, and consent has to cover not only the collection and storage, but also the intended monopolisation and commercial exploitation of the DNA samples.

Applying these principles to our case, the following conclusions can be drawn.

Marc has a right of veto regarding the collection, storage, research and commercial exploitation of his biological material (DNA samples) and related data (Arts. 23, 90 Data Protection Code, in connection with Article 6 General Authorisation 22 February 2007). He may of course object to experiments that he considers unethical and restrict his permission just to 'academic research'. He may also object to the patent application and it is likely that, having given his consent, he has the right to be named in the patent description (arg. ex Art. 5 d.l. 1 January 2006, no. 3).

It is not easy to say whether Marc could skim off or would be at least entitled to a share of the benefits that are generated by marketing the patented products.

---

in contract law (see on this problem Mantovani, 'Trapianti', in *Digesto/pen., Agg.*** (Torino: 2004), pp. 818–819).

59 See Resta, 'Contratto e persona', in: Roppo (ed.), *Trattato del contratto* (Vol. VI, Milano: 2006), p. 37; Galloux, 'L'utilisation des matériels biologiques humains: vers un droit de destination?', *D.*, 1999, chr., pp. 15 ff.

60 See on this provision, Resta, 'L'accesso al materiale biologico umano a fini di ricerca e sfruttamento industriale: questioni in tema di consenso e responsabilità nella prospettiva del diritto comparato', in: Martins-Costa (ed.), *Bioética e responsabilidade* (Rio de Janeiro: 2008); Germinario, 'L'attuazione della Direttiva n. 8/44/CE in materia di protezione giuridica delle invenzioni biotecnologiche', (2006) *Dir. ind.*, p. 319.

This problem was debated, in a common law context, in the much-renowned *Moore*[61] and *Greenberg*[62] cases.

Looking at this question from a civil law perspective, one has to distinguish between two situations: (1) where there is a contract between Marc and PhC; (2) where PhC has exploited Marc's genetic material without having obtained his consent.

Clearly, in situation (1) the matter will be covered by the contractual terms. It should be noted, however, that the validity of such an agreement could be disputable: depending on the concrete contractual terms, it could be considered void as against public policy.[63]

In situation (2), the remedies available could be damages and restitution. However, under Italian law, the general clause on unjust enrichment (Art. 2041 Civil Code) is subject to the principle of subsidiarity (Art. 2042 Civil Code). Hence, Marc could just recover damages, according to Article 2043 Civil Code. It is worth noting that Italian courts frequently assess damages with the aim of pursuing restitutionary goals. This happens, for instance, in right of publicity and copyright cases (where the parameter adopted is that of foregone royalties).[64] However, it is not likely that such a technique will be applied in our case, because the general principle of *extra-patrimonialité* of body parts and genetic data plays against the recognition of a property right in human biological material (see Art. 21 Oviedo Convention; Art. 3 European Charter of Fundamental Rights; Art. 8 UNESCO Declaration on Human Genetic Data).[65] It is likely that Marc could recover non-pecuniary losses only, for lack of informed consent and violation of his constitutional right to self-determination (Arts. 2 and 13 Constitution). As regards Modification 4, Marc is not entitled *per se* to obtain the product free of charge; this sum could be implied in the general damage award.

III. Metalegal Formants

The most difficult issue involved in this case concerns the nature of the rights one has over one's body parts and genetic data. Traditionally, body parts,

---

61 *Moore v. The Regents of the University of California*, 793 P.2d 479 (Cal. 1990), cert. denied, 111 S. Ct. 1388 (1991).

62 *Greenberg v. Miami Children's Hospital Research Institute, Inc.*, 264 F. Supp. 2d 1064 (S.D. Fla. 2003).

63 Indeed, it could clash – even though it is by no means certain – against the principle of exclusion of monetary gains from the human body: see Rodotà, 'Tra diritto e società. Informazioni genetiche e tecniche di tutela', (2000) *RCDP*, pp. 571 ff., p. 592, p. 594; Resta, 'Contratto e persona', in: Roppo (ed.), *Trattato del contratto* (Vol. VI, Milano: 2006), pp. 36 ff.; Bellivier, Noiville, 'La circulation du vivant humain: modèle de la propriété ou du contrat?', in: Revet (a cura di), *Code civil et modèles. Des modèles du Code au Code comme modèle* (Paris: 2005), pp. 101 ff., p. 118.

64 See Brüggemeier, Colombi Ciacchi, *Personality Rights in Europe* (Cambridge: 2010).

65 See on this point Resta, 'I diritti della personalità', in: Alpa, Resta, *Le persone fisiche e i diritti della personalità, Trattato di diritto civile*, dir. Sacco (Torino: 2006), pp. 603 ff.

organs, cells and tissues were considered personal property, subject to a market-alienability rule.[66] Since the early 2000s, Italian scholars have started looking at these issues from a personality rights perspective, taking more seriously the principle of *extra-patrimonialité*, laid down in Article 21 Oviedo Convention and Article 3(2) European Charter of Fundamental Rights.[67] This shift of paradigms has had important implications not only in terms of (market in)alienability, but also in terms of remedies available for unlawful interference with body parts and information. The debate is open, but there is no relevant Italian case on this matter so far.

Another question that should be considered further – but which goes beyond the scope of this report – relates to the proposed schemas of benefit-sharing, at the individual and collective level.[68]

(10) LITHUANIA

I. *Operative Rules*

Marc can claim an injunction to stop the research (if undertaken against his will, if he considers the research unethical, if he restricted the use to 'academic research' and the research is undertaken for commercial purposes).

II. *Descriptive Formants*

Marc has the personal right to the inviolability and integrity of his body (Art. 21 Constitution, Art. 2.25 Civil Code, Art. 7(1) Law on Patients' Rights and Damage Compensation (3 October 1996, No. I-1562, as amended by Law No. IX-2361)), which guarantees that without the person's will and free consent no scientific or medical research or experimentations may be carried out. Further, Marc's right to the protection of his private life is inviolable (Art. 22(2) Constitution, Art. 2.23(1) Civil Code, Art. 10 Law on Patients' Rights and Damage Compensation) and shall be respected.

---

66 See for references Lenti, *Procreazione artificiale. Genoma della persona e attribuzione della paternità* (Padova: 1993), pp. 110 ff.; Criscuoli, 'L'acquisto delle parti staccate del proprio corpo e gli artt. 820 e 821 c.c.', (1985) *Dir. fam. pers.*, p. 266.

67 See Ferrando, 'Diritto e scienze della vita. Cellule e tessuti nelle recenti direttive europee', in: Aa.Vv., *Il diritto civile oggi. Compiti scientifici e didattici del civilista* (Napoli: 2006), pp. 423 ff.; Resta, 'I diritti della personalità', in: Alpa, Resta, *Le persone fisiche e i diritti della personalità, Trattato di diritto civile*, dir. Sacco (Torino: 2006), pp. 604–605; Forkel, 'Das Persönlichkeitsrecht am Körper, gesehen besonders im Lichte des Transplantationsgesetzes', (2001) *JURA*, p. 73.

68 See Bellievier and Noiville, 'La circulation du vivant humain: modèle de la propriété ou du contrat?', in: Revet (a cura di), *Code civil et modèles. Des modèles du Code au Code comme modèle* (Paris: 2005), pp. 118 ff.

Neither the Law on the Legal Protection of Personal Data (11 June 1996, No. I-1374, the new version of which came into force on 1 January 2009) nor other laws provide for specific regulation on processing the genetic information; therefore, the genetic information is to be regarded as personal data concerning a person's health. All data concerning a person's health is subject to professional secrecy and shall remain confidential even posthumously. Personal information may be collected only with the patient's consent and only if it is necessary for diagnosing, treatment or nursing. Confidential information may not be given to other parties, unless the patient has given his/her written consent, except in cases where it is necessary for the protection of his/her interests or it is explicitly foreseen by law.[69] Thus, the governing principle is that the individual shall have the right to decide him/herself what, to what extent and by whom his/her personal information can be collected and used.

Screening the genome is qualified as biomedical research.[70] Processing of the personal data for the biomedical research is not thoroughly regulated. Therefore, the general principles for processing personal data concerning a person's health and concerning scientific research apply.[71] However, as the research using biological material of human origin (blood, cells, tissue, DNA, etc.) falls under the definition of biomedical research, the principal legal act governing this situation is the Law on the Ethics of Biomedical Research (11 May 2000, No. VIII-1679, as amended on 13 July 2004, No. IX-2362). The law was adopted taking into consideration the Convention for the Protection of Human Rights and Biomedicine (Oviedo Convention),[72] from which the principle of constitutional significance that the interests of the human being prevail over the interests of society and science was transposed.

The Law on the Ethics of Biomedical Research specifies the above-mentioned essential precondition of the legality of any scientific or medical research in relation to humans, establishing that biomedical research may only be undertaken after the subject has given his/her written informed consent. However, the person's consent will only raise legal consequences if the person

---

69 Art. 10(1) Law on the Protection of Personal Data; Art. 10(3) Law on Patients' Rights and Damage Compensation.

70 The legal definition of biomedical research provided by the Law on the Ethics of Biomedical Research is broad: verification of hypotheses of biomedicine by methods of scientific research and development of knowledge about characteristics of human health, and which may be undertaken on human subjects or their groups, a foetus, tissues, organs, cells and genetic material, cadavers and medical documents.

71 Art. 12(1) Law on the Protection of Personal Data reads: provided it is not possible to identify the person whose personal data is being processed, personal data may be processed for scientific research purposes on condition that the data subject has given his/her consent. Without the data subject's consent, personal data may be processed to this end only upon notifying the State Data Protection Inspectorate, which carries out a prior check.

72 Lithuania ratified Law No. IX-1085 on 19 September 2002. According to the Lithuanian legal system, the ratified treaties have the power of statute and are directly applicable.

was informed – in a comprehensible manner and against their signature – about the goal and plan of the research and the methods applied, about decisions of the Lithuanian Bioethics Committee or an appropriate regional committee on ethics of biomedical research, and about the following:

1. the foreseeable benefits of the biomedical research to the subject;
2. the rights, foreseeable risks and inconveniences which the biomedical research may cause to the subject, as well as the compensation available to the subject in the event of the damage incurred by the biomedical research;
3. the right of the subject to revoke his/her consent to participate in the biomedical research in writing at any time, providing to him/her information about the consequences of such discontinuation of the biomedical research; and
4. guarantees of confidentiality of the information.

As the development and application of personalised medicine is highly dependent on obtaining, using and storing samples of biomaterials (DNA in the first place) and personal genetic and health information, the dominant bioethical issue is respect for persons, i.e. protection of an individual's autonomy and dignity, especially by ensuring privacy and confidentiality of his/her personal information. Free and informed consent is a requirement of particular importance and must be obtained at all stages of research in the development of personalised medicine.[73] It should also be noted that voluntariness of consent for the participation in a pharmacogenetic investigation needs consideration, as it is most often discussed just as free agreement or refusal to participate in research made in the absence of coercion, but without more detailed attention to the aspects influencing the person's free will.[74]

Accordingly, if PhC observed the requirement to thoroughly inform Marc about the research and obtained his consent to participate in the research or to carry out research on his biological material/genetic information, Marc has no right to veto the research. However, if a person's right to the inviolability and integrity of his body was infringed by not acquiring the person's consent prior to the research or giving incomplete information[75] based on which he/she

---

[73] V. Kučinskas, D. Steponavičiūtė, G. Andriulionis, 'The value of free and informed consent in personalising medicine (review)', *Acta Medica Lituanica*, 2005, vol. 2, No. 4, p. 7.

[74] Ibid., p. 8.

[75] The Supreme Court has in several cases on health care services ruled that just the informed consent of the patient based on thorough information may have legal consequences (Decision of 30 March 2005, Case No. 3K-3-206/2005, *J. R. and Z. R. v. VŠĮ Vilniaus universiteto Santariškių klinikos*); if it were established that the doctor acted without the patient's consent or with his/her action went beyond the consent obtained or did not properly inform the patient, this is to be regarded as a violation of patients' rights and gives rise to civil liability (Decision of 31 March 2003, No. 3K-3-438, *D. A. v. Vilniaus Universiteto Onkologijos institutas*).

could take his/her decision about whether to participate in the research or not, the injured party may claim compensation for damage – pecuniary as well as non-pecuniary. Besides, the personal right could also be protected by claiming an injunction for the actions that may infringe the personal right, for example requesting to interdict or stop the medical experimentation (Art. 1.138 Civil Code).[76] Therefore, if his personal right would be harmed by research on his genome, Marc could demand the research to be stopped. However, granting the injunction to stop the research should be decided in the light of the principles of fairness, justice and proportionality (Art. 1.5 Civil Code).

Further, taking into consideration Marc's right not to give his consent to experiments that he considers unethical, it should be noted that any biomedical research requires prior approval by the Lithuanian Biomedical Committee or regional committee on ethics of biomedical research which is responsible for the ethical evaluation of the planned research, and that their decisions on the subject are to be communicated to the person before he/she gives his/her consent. Marc – based on all the information he receives – may then take his independent decision on whether it is ethically acceptable for him to take part in the research or not. Furthermore, he may also make use of his right to revoke his consent to participate in the research at any time.

In addition, Marc is free not to give his consent for such research that is conducted for commercial purposes only and restrict his consent to scientific research (if such a distinction is possible in the particular situation), or in general not to give his consent.[77]

However, it will not be possible for Marc to veto research on his gene or to express his disagreement on ethical grounds in cases where it is not necessary to ask for his consent. This is the situation where the Lithuanian Bioethics Committee or a regional committee on ethics of biomedical research takes the decision that consent is not necessary for conducting biomedical research on tissues, organs, a foetus, cell or genetic material which had been obtained from a person for other purposes during medical interventions before applying to undertake research on this person's bodily material (Art. 8(2) Law on the Ethics of Biomedical Research).[78] In this case, the general requirement for biomedical

76 V. Mikelėnas et al., *Commentary on the Civil Code of the Republic of Lithuania. Book Second: Law of Persons* (Vilnius: 2002), p. 78.

77 It should be noted that on 7 March 2005 Lithuania signed the Additional Protocol to the Convention on Human Rights and Biomedicine concerning Biomedical Research of 25 January 2005 (though the ratification procedure has not yet been undertaken), in which it is explicitly foreseen that research participants shall be also informed of any foreseen potential further uses, including commercial uses of the research results, data or biological materials (Art. 13(2)(vii)).

78 At this point, it is worth making reference to Art. 3(5) of the Law on Patients' Rights and Damage Compensation, according to which any part of the human body may only be removed for reasons of medical care of the patient. The removed part of the body may only be stored and used for other purposes if the requirements set by law are observed and only

research shall be observed that the protection of the subject's interests and the confidentiality of information about the subject must be ensured.[79]

The terms of use of biological material of human origin acquired for other purposes before the biomedical research is explicitly mentioned in Article 22 of the Convention on Human Rights and Biomedicine: 'When in the course of an intervention any part of a human body is removed, it may be stored and used for a purpose other than that for which it was removed only if this is done in conformity with appropriate information and consent procedures.' Accordingly, the storage and use of parts of the body which have been removed during an intervention for a specified purpose is illegitimate, unless the relevant conditions governing information and consent have been observed.[80] Referring to the Explanatory Report on the Convention, systematic consent is, however, not needed, thus allowing for particular flexibility. Consequently, according to the Lithuanian model of the appropriate consent and information procedure, it is to be decided on a case-by-case basis whether it is necessary to obtain the person's consent for the further/secondary use of his/her biological or genetic material. The power to decide upon this matter is vested in the Lithuanian Bioethics Committee or a regional committee on the ethics of biomedical research (Art. 8(2) Law on the Ethics of Biomedical Research).

III. Metalegal Formants

The Lithuanian model is Janus-faced. On the one side, it rests on strong personality rights, apparently requiring consent and an appropriate information procedure. The legal consequences of any violation can be both an injunction and damages. The procedure includes an evaluation of whether it is necessary to obtain the person's consent. This implies the other Janus-faced side: consent is subject to administrative oversight. It can be deemed 'unnecessary' in cases of material acquired by prior medical intervention or for further use/re-use. That implies that it is not primarily for the individual to decide; consent can be substituted by the administration. In cases where consent is considered to be

---

if the consent of the patient has been obtained, having previously informed him/her of the consequences of the consent. The relationship between this norm and the above-mentioned norm set out in the Law on the Ethics of Biomedical Research is not completely clear: whether the patient's consent for the particular research will not be necessary provided that the person previously expressed his/her general agreement for any possible further use of his/her biological material (or did not file his/her objection to it), or whether the Committee's decision may supersede the person's will (or the lack of its expression) in particular situations. Although there is no corresponding legal praxis, I would tend to accept the first option as better corresponding to the underlying principles and regulations.

79 Art. 4(2) Law on the Ethics of Biomedical Research.

80 Explanatory report to the Convention on Human Rights and Biomedicine, available at: http://conventions.coe.int/Treaty/en/Reports/Html/164.htm (last accessed 6 May 2019).

needed, its revocation is subject to fairness and proportionality conditions, and thereby becomes an issue to be decided by courts (again not the individual).

(11) NETHERLANDS

I. Operative Rules

Once the gene has been taken, Marc is no longer entitled to veto the research. No *maiore* no *minus*.

II. Descriptive Formants

In order to veto the research, Marc should have a property right. Under Dutch law, several property regimes could be applicable.

First, the private property regime could be considered, although it only applies to pure objects or materials. Private law property (Civil Code Book 5) defines property as confined to material objects (Art. 3:2 in conjunction with Art. 5:1 Civil Code). If 'ownership' of the material can be established, which is unlikely in this case, ownership is still intact when the bodily material has been separated from the body.

Second, the personal property regime comes to mind, as it deals with a person's personal privacy. The gene could be considered as Marc's personal characteristic falling within the scope of personal property. However, this position has not been tested in court. It is worth mentioning that the Netherlands lost its appeal against the European Union regarding the adoption of Directive 98/44/EC on the legal protection of biotechnological inventions. The Netherlands had argued that recognising the patentability of plants and animals would promote genetic manipulation.[81]

Third, the gene could be protected under one of the intellectual property regimes. However, only subject matter that meets the requirements for protection gives rise to the grant of exclusive rights. It is doubtful that the gene itself would meet the requirements of any of the regimes.

Since the gene is in the possession of the company, Marc should have included his veto as a contractual term. The moment he gave his consent for taking and examining his gene, he should have made his wishes (veto or restrictions) explicit.

---

[81] The Netherlands lodged a request for the annulment of the Biotechnology Directive before the CJEU to protest against the Directive because of the infringement(s) of fundamental rights: *Netherlands v. European Parliament and Council*, C-377/98 [2001] ECR I-7079.

III. Metalegal Formants

In 1997, the preparations began for an Act of Parliament in this area.[82] While the first phase concluded with the *Wet Veiligheid en Kwaliteit Lichaamsmateriaal* (Safety and Quality of Body Materials Act), the second phase is still pending in 2021 and concerns the *Wet Zeggenschap Lichaamsmateriaal* (Body Materials Control Act).[83] Key players in its preparation are civil society organisations, including the Dutch Federation of Dutch Medical Scientific Societies (FEDERA) and the Regulatory Committee on Research (COREON).[84] COREON has drawn up a Code of Conduct for Medical Research, which is addressed to researchers and research organisations who collect bodily material from donors.

(12) NORWAY

I. Operative Rules

Marc can object to the collection, storage and processing of the gene but not to the research once consent has been granted for the use.

II. Descriptive Formants

These issues are to be dealt with under chapter 3 of the Biobank Act (NBBA, 21 February 2003). According to NBBA §12, first paragraph, the collection, storage and processing of human biological material for research purposes requires voluntary, express and informed consent by the donor. Such consent may be withdrawn, cf. NBBA §14, first paragraph, but the right of withdrawal does not apply if the material or data is anonymised or if the data has already been used in scientific publications (§14, third paragraph). Given that the information obtained from Marc is used in order to reproduce a synthetic gene, and that the further research is based on this, it seems unlikely that Marc is entitled to veto the research even if it is commercial and, in his opinion, unethical.

---

82 Tweede Kamer, vergaderjaar 1996–1997, 25 284, nr. 1.

83 Regels inzake de veiligheid en kwaliteit van lichaamsmateriaal dat kan worden gebruikt bij een geneeskundige behandeling (Wet veiligheid en kwaliteit lichaamsmateriaal) 27 844; for the second phase see Tweede Kamer, vergaderjaar 2004–2005, 27 543, nr. 8, available at: https://www.rijksoverheid.nl/actueel/nieuws/2021/05/12/wetsvoorstel-zeggenschap-lichaamsmateriaal-naar-tweede-kamer.

84 See http://www.coreon.org/.

III. *Metalegal Formants*

The requirement that the donor must consent to the collection, storage and processing of human biological material for research purposes, and that it has to be an express and informed consent, can be derived from principles of respect for the value of human life, human rights and personal integrity and is in accordance with main principles of Norwegian health law and international conventions.[85] However, if the consent requirement is applied too strictly, it may conflict with the need for research and medical development. The amendment to NBBA §12 in 2006 illustrates this, introducing a deviation from the right to consent as regards persons of full legal age but without legal competence to consent. Prior to the amendment, it was not possible to seek consent from persons lacking competence to consent. The government found that this situation could lead to a great risk of weakening the knowledge and the level of treatment for this group of patients. Therefore, a new provision in §12, sixth paragraph, was introduced that allows the collection, storage and procession of biobank material for research purposes for persons of full legal age but lacking the competence to consent, provided *inter alia* that the person's next-of-kin has consented to the use.

(13) POLAND

I. *Operative Rules*

Marc would probably not succeed.

II. *Descriptive Formants*

No such cases have been decided by courts in Poland. There are currently no doctrinal views available either. In order to solve this case, one must search for a legal ground that would enable Marc to veto the research or to specify the conditions of his consent. There are two such legal grounds (intertwined to a certain extent) that are worthy of further analysis. First, Marc could argue that by conducting this research PhC infringes upon his personality rights. Secondly, Marc could try to rely on personal data protection.

The protection of personality rights is explicitly regulated in the Civil Code. In Poland, the following model has been set up: the law recognises certain personal interests, i.e. values inextricably connected with each human being that merit legal safeguards. The protection of personal interests has been based on a property law model. In consequence, there is a corresponding

85 Cf. the Ministry Proposal, Ot. prp. no. 64 (2004–2005), ch. 5.6.

absolute, subjective personal right to each personal interest. Should this right be infringed, the affected person has several remedies at his/her disposal, one of them being a claim to cease the infringement. Article 23 Civil Code lists the protected personal interest; however, this list is not exhaustive and may be expanded by the judiciary. Among the clearly named personal interests one may find life and health. Physical integrity has also been recognised to constitute a personal interest protected by the corresponding personality right. Infringements of personality rights give rise to civil remedies only when the infringement is found to be illegal. It is commonly accepted that, generally, the consent of the rightholder may negate the illegality of the infringement.[86] Since consent may be qualified as a declaration of intention (or even when one denies such qualification, legal provisions concerning declarations of intention should be applied by analogy) there is no controversy that consent must be free and unforced. With regard to medical treatment and medical experiments, informed consent would be required. Since in order to screen Marc's genome and extract his genes PhC must have made an intrusion upon Marc's physical integrity, his consent was necessary. The question is therefore whether the consent given by Marc must cover not only the very act of physical intervention but also the subsequent applications of the genetic material thus obtained.

There are no legal provisions in Poland deciding this issue, and therefore the answer has to be looked for in the general rules and institutions of civil law. There are serious arguments to be raised in favour of the idea that Marc's consent should not only cover the very act of obtaining biological matter but should also be underpinned by adequate knowledge as to the purpose of these actions. Just as misinformation as to the purpose of physical intervention would certainly justify the view that consent was not validly granted, the same can be said about lack of appropriate information. There would, however, be a lot of controversies surrounding the required scope and content of such informed consent. It seems that if Marc had been informed about the general purpose (medical research), he would later have no legal remedies against specific forms of this research, for example ones he considers unethical. This is because Marc's consent would primarily concern actions directed at his physical integrity – what happens later is only of interest for the validity of consent as no further personality right to gene sequences exists.

However, it is very important to stress that even if PhC were to go beyond what Marc has allowed them to do, and even if therefore the physical intervention would have to be considered infringing, it is another matter whether he may

[86] A. Szpunar, *Ochrona dóbr osobistych* (Warszawa: 1979), p. 161; M. Sośniak, 'Funkcje i skuteczność zgody osoby uprawnionej w zakresie ochrony dóbr osobistych', in: B. Kordasiewicz, E Łętowska (eds.), *Prace z praw cywilnego. Wydane dla uczczenia pracy naukowej Prof. Józefa St. Piątowskiego* (Wrocław: 1985), p. 66; Z. Radwański, 'Koncepcja praw podmiotowych osobistych', *RPEiS*, vol. 2, 1988, p. 13.

demand that the use of his genetic material be stopped, invoking his personality rights. It seems that for such a claim another personal interest would have to be 'discovered'. In other words, Marc could sue, for example, for a solatium, but could not demand that the research he opposes be stopped. In order to do this, there would have to exist another personal interest (let us call it the right to personal genetic resources). Such a right would be difficult to establish, since once the gene has been isolated from Marc's body the link between the gene and Marc's body has been severed. As personal interests are immanently connected to a human person (i.e. internal and not external to it), such a right would be difficult to fit into the underlying civil law concept. Moreover, the desirability of such a solution is very questionable (see under section III below).

An interesting issue would arise if Marc had given his approval only to specific actions (e.g. only academic research) and PhC had not complied with his intentions. The problem is whether in such a case Marc could invoke a breach of contract. It seems that he could, and consequently he could also demand performance (i.e. compliance with contractual conditions).

Personal data protection also seems to be another potentially potent legal weapon. But again, closer analysis sheds some doubt on this assumption. First of all, a gene will normally never constitute personal data since it does not make it possible to establish the identity of a person (Art. 6 of the Law on the Protection of Personal Data).[87] This may of course be different with regard to genetic data (e.g. DNA).[88] Even if a gene is unique, it would normally be too costly and time-consuming to establish the identity of its holder (Art. 6(3) of the Law on the Protection of Personal Data). If so, it must be generally concluded that data protection law would not be of much assistance to Marc.

III. *Metalegal Formants*

A common problem with genetic resources is the fear that by patenting genes certain companies or persons can acquire a monopoly over human beings. This case seems to be the perfect example because it shows that genetic material may be extracted from the human body and later utilised practically without the 'donor's' consent. However, it would seem that in this very case such concern is ill-founded. To begin with, the majority of human genes are shared not only with other people but also with other animals or even insects. Therefore, the very fact that a certain gene has been extracted from someone's body does not and should not give this person any rights to a particular gene sequence. Does this really change when a very rare occurrence (a unique gene) enters the picture? It is tempting to say yes, but in reality, we would be inclined to give the exact

---

87 J. Barta, R. Markiewicz, *Ochrona danych osobowych*, (Warszawa: 1996), pp. 379 ff.

88 Art. 27 of the Law on the Protection of Personal Data explicitly includes genetic data in the catalogue of so-called sensitive data.

opposite answer. Human personality and dignity are not expressed in a single gene,[89] just as they are not expressed in any bodily organ (even if it were true to say that there are no identical hearts or kidneys). There is in fact no connection worthy of extensive protection between a gene and a 'gene holder'. If we look closer, no reasons that were responsible for the current scope of protection of personality rights could justify such an expansion. It is not the subject of the right to physical or moral integrity, it is not a value the essence of which lies in shielding each human person from the unwelcome intrusions of society (privacy), and finally it is not a human or conventional trait that distinguishes the human person in a society (name, image). Of course, intellectual property rights in genetic material are controversial and these controversies are not unfounded, but the alleged deprivation of 'gene donors' is not one of them.

(14) SLOVENIA

I. *Operative Rules*

If Marc consented to the collection of the genetic material for these purposes, he is not entitled to veto research on his gene. He does not have a right to designate the purposes of the research.

II. *Descriptive Formants*

The answer to this question depends on whether Marc participated in this research with his genetic material voluntarily, or if the research was done without his consent. Voluntary participation in such research concerning removal of human cells and tissue (including genetic material) in Slovenia is partially regulated through the Act on the Quality and Safety of Human Tissues and Cells, for the Purposes of Medical Treatment (AQSHTC),[90] which also implements Directives 2004/23/EC, 2006/17/EC and 2006/86/EC, as well as through The Removal and Transplantation of Human Body Parts for the Purposes of Medical Treatment Act (RTHBPA).[91]

In accordance with paragraph I, Article 3 of the AQSHTC, the removal of tissue and cells from a live person is done according to conditions and methods designated by the RTHBPA. The RTHBPA states that the donor must give written consent for removal (Art. 7), for which the nature, intention[92] and procedure of

89 If so, only in the complete DNA sequence.
90 Official Gazette RS, no. 61/2007.
91 Official Gazette RS, no. 12/2000.
92 The legislation does not provide a clear response as to whether or not Marc must be informed about whether the research will be conducted for commercial or academic purposes.

the intervention, as well as eventual risks, must be properly explained to him/her (paragraph I, Art. 10). Such consent may also be revoked at any time until the commencement of the intervention (paragraph IV, Art. 10 RTHBPA). Donation of cells and tissue can only be done on a voluntary and unpaid basis (paragraph I, Art. 13 AQSHTC).

Marc has the sole right of managing his own body, tissue and cells, unless he donates his tissue and cells for the purposes of required research. He therefore has the right to refuse the removal of his genetic material for research purposes and can restrict research on his genome. After Marc has donated his cells, tissue and genetic material on the basis of written consent and suitable explanation of the intention and nature of the procedure, and once the procedure has been completed, he can no longer change his mind and prevent further research, even if the additional experiments would be considered unethical. In the event that he has second thoughts concerning the ethics of the research or economic usage of the results, he must express them before giving consent or during the period before removal has been completed. If he has been properly and completely informed about and having given written consent to the research purposes, Marc may not prevent such research, not even on the grounds of constitutionally guaranteed personal rights, which protect his personality as a set of psychophysical characteristics.[93] The infringement of his rights is done with his consent, which means that his personal rights have not been violated (compare Art. 140 CO[94] – *volenti non fit iniuria*).

Slovenian law does not explicitly deal with the question as to whether or not Marc may lay down conditions to his consenting to the removal of his genetic material, such as not allowing it to be used for commercial purposes, but only for academic research. There is only paragraph III, Article 10 of RTHBPA which states, that it is possible for donations of a living donor to place conditions on the removal of body parts, by demanding they be transplanted to a specific person; however, such legal authorisation cannot be extended to other aspects of person rights by analogy.

A different situation would be the case of removal of genetic material for research purposes without prior consent. Such action and research would mean an unlawful infringement to constitutionally guaranteed personal rights. In such an event, on the basis of Article 134 of the CO, Marc would be able to claim that research be stopped immediately and that any results of this research, which came into being though the unlawful violation of his person, be eliminated. What is most questionable is what would happen in the event that Marc consented to

---

93 Based on Art. 35 of the Constitution of the Republic of Slovenia (Official Gazette RS, no. 33/1991, 42/1997, 66/2000, 24/2003, 69/2004 in 68/2006; URS) the inviolability of the physical and mental integrity of every person, his/her privacy and personality rights are guaranteed.

94 Official Gazette RS, nos. 83/2001, 32/2004, 40/2007, 97/2007.

the removal, but was not adequately informed on the nature, course and purpose of the research. Since Slovenian legislation does not give detailed information regarding the usage of genetic material and there has been no such case in Slovenia to date, it is not possible to give a final answer to this question.

III. Metalegal Formants

Slovenian law protects personal rights, which protect the personality, as absolute and exclusive rights that are above all of a negative nature and shall make illicit interventions in one's person impossible. Yet these rights are only exceptionally recognised as positive rights with the possibility to dispose of the elements of one's person, in the form of consent to removal of blood, body parts, tissue, cells, etc.[95]

(15) SPAIN

I. Operative Rules

Yes, Marc can veto research on the gene and has a right not to give consent to experiments that he considers unethical (unless there is a public interest in the research).

II. Descriptive Formants

- Law 14/2007 of 3 July, on biomedical research;
- Law 29/2006 of 26 July, on guarantees and rational use of medicines and health products;
- Royal Decree 1301/2006 of 10 November, which establishes the regulations governing the quality and safety of giving, obtaining, evaluating, processing, preserving, storing and distributing human cells and tissues, and approves the operating and coordination regulations for use in humans;
- Law 41/2002 of 14 November on patient autonomy and the rights and obligations in the area of information and clinical documentation;
- Law 21/2000 of 29 December on the right to health information, patient autonomy and clinical documentation (Catalan law);
- Royal Decree 561/1993 on Ethical Committees of Clinical Research;
- Civil Code;
- Royal Decree 411/1996 of 1 March on the clinical use of human tissues;
- Patent Law 11/1986 of 20 March; and
- Organic Law 15/1999 of 13 December on Personal Data Protection.

---

[95] A. Finžgar, *Osebnostne pravice*, (Ljubljana: 1985), p. 39.

Although Spanish law accepts patents on biotechnological inventions,[96] it also sets certain limitations: it is, for example, expressly forbidden to patent the human body or the discovery of one of its elements. However, it is possible to patent an element isolated from the human body or otherwise obtained by means of a technical process, including the total or partial sequence of a gene. It is the requirement of a technical process to obtain this element that defines what is patentable and what is not. If no technical process is applied, the biological element cannot be patented. Likewise, the patent application is required to indicate the biological function of the gene that it wishes to patent so that patents are not granted on genes or gene fragments whose function is not already known, as occurs in the US patent system.[97]

To be able to respond, we must define two different situations which depend on the objective of the research.

a) The aim of the research is to study one of Marc's genes, and as a result his genetic material will be made available.

Directive 2004/23/EC and Directive 2006/23/EC[98] state that genetic material donations must respect the conditions of free and informed consent.[99] These Directives were transposed into Spanish law by Royal Decree 1301/2006 of 10 November, which establishes the regulations governing the quality and safety of giving, obtaining, evaluating, processing, preserving, storing and distributing human cells and tissues, and approves the operating and coordination regulations for use in humans. Donation conditions were also developed by Law 14/2007 on Biomedical Research and by Law 41/2002 of 14 November on patient autonomy and the rights and obligations in the area of information and clinical documentation.

These laws are applicable to both public and private medical centres and their essential principle is the need to obtain prior informed consent from the patient for every medical intervention. Patients have the right to receive the necessary and appropriate information about the medical services and medical professionals are obliged to give it to them before acting. So as long as the PhC respects Marc's right to information and he gives his consent in the way prescribed in the cited law, he is not entitled to veto research.[100] In order to give this informed consent, we advise that the following recommendations be followed.

---

96 See the Greek report.

97 B. Salvador Darío, 'Patentamiento de genes y secuencias de genes', *Revista de Derecho y Genoma Humano*, 1998, pp. 31–59.

98 And the recognition of the principle of voluntary and unpaid tissue and cell donations intended for scientific research.

99 See German report, as well as the Italian report, which considers the consent of the patient.

100 The same answer can be found in the Czech report.

Consent should be given in writing. The principle is established that in all biomedical research projects and situations in which donors provide their biological samples, consent must be given in writing. This consent can be revoked at any moment.

The tissue and cell donations will be authorised for a specific aim and in accordance with the use permitted by law. Law 14/2007 deals with the issue of giving consent and accepting that this consent can be revoked at any time, either totally or only for certain purposes. This would necessarily involve the immediate destruction of the material, although the data resulting from any previous investigations would be preserved.

Patients have the right to be informed about the reason why the sample has been taken and any possible uses of the material provided and, if they have given their consent for the material to be used in subsequent research, they must also be informed about patient rights, the consequences and implications of their decisions and the period of time during which the material will be stored or its final destination should permission for storage be refused.

Guarantees must be given that fundamental rights will be protected and the existing framework on personal data protection respected.[101]

All decisions about the material will be confidential and will be guaranteed by an Ethical Committee of the medical centres (regulated by Royal Decree 561/1993 on Ethical Committees of Clinical Research).

The framework in which PhC has to obtain Marc's informed consent makes it possible for him not to give it if he considers the research or the experiments unethical and also for him to forbid any research with a commercial purpose. He can even revoke his consent for this reason at any time.

The donor aside, the existence of Research Ethical Committees in the centres that carry out biomedical research guarantees that the samples obtained are appropriately and legally used. The authorisation and undertaking of any research project on human beings or their biological material will require a favourable prior report. Law 14/2007 has also created the Committee for the Donation and Use of Human Cells and Tissues, which ensures the compliance with the scientific, ethical and legal guarantees in research projects of biological samples from the human embryo.

b) The aim of the research is to use Marc's genetic information.

Chapter III of Law 14/2007 deals with the genetic analyses and processing of personal genetic data. Article 46 of this law establishes the therapeutic purpose of a genetic analysis, which in all circumstances requires the subjects to give their informed consent. Article 50, however, states that these data can be used for epidemiological, public health, research and teaching purposes when

[101] Similar rules have to take in account in Greece.

subjects have given their express consent, or when these data have been made anonymous. This means that Marc must agree to the use to which his genetic information will be put, except when there is a clear public interest case. In these situations, his data can be used without his permission, as long as they cannot be identified with him.

III. Metalegal Formants

Spain provides for a strong protection of the person. Revocation of consent is possible. Yet public interests may supersede the individual's interest in deliberate disposition. The legislator has stipulated the list of grounds for when individual consent is not necessary.

(16) UNITED KINGDOM

I. Operative Rules

In principle, Marc has rights in all three constellations, but these may not be an injunction, only compensation.

II. Descriptive Formants

Marc's right to injunction depends on the terms of consent at the moment when PhC screened his genome (for which reason). If the terms of consent did not cover research and development for influenza vaccination, then *possibly* Marc could argue that this act (screening his genome) was unlawful based on the UK Data Protection Act 1998 (if we assume a relevant date of 2013) or the Data Protection Act 2018 (current law since GDPR took effect), the Human Tissue Act 2004, or section 8 Human Rights Act 1998. Generally speaking, to obtain a sample of tissue, Marc's consent would have been required (in practice mostly obtained in the context of consent to medical treatment). The analysis under UK law needs to discuss the various situations within this legislation *when consent is not required* to use human tissue and personal data acquired from the tissue for the *secondary* purpose of research. Anonymisation is an operative consideration. However, in this case, 'Marc has a unique gene'. So anonymisation might be difficult if this point is well known. There is quite a lot of debate in the UK (especially in and around 2013) about the circumstances in which personal identifiable data can be used for the secondary purpose of important public health medical research without Marc's prior consent. It is additionally difficult for *private* commercial organisations to rely on such arguments.

Supposing Marc established that PhC acted unlawfully when it used his tissue or data in its vaccine research, for example because it was unable to rely on any of the exceptions. Then, the question arises whether Marc could stop PhC marketing and using the influenza vaccine that was developed on the basis of the unlawful act. It is possible that Marc could *only* obtain compensation for the wrongful act, and an injunction to stop future use of his data. He may not have a legal remedy to stop use of the *vaccine* itself *if its repeated use is not considered to rely on his data.* No case law has clarified this point.

The law of negligence would not assist Marc because he has not suffered a recognised 'harm' that can be compensated in the law of negligence, and the law of negligence does not provide declarations of unlawfulness.

It might be possible for Marc to take action by complaining to a professional licensing body, if for example a medical doctor was involved.

As to the question of whether Marc has a right not to give consent to experiments that he considers unethical, the general answer is yes, but there are exceptions. He is also entitled, in principle, to restrict the use to 'academic research', at least as far as PhC requires his consent.

III. Metalegal Formants

The case is governed by considerations of data protection and stipulated exceptions. As regards genomic research data, the UK revolves around the question of whether the patient would be 'identifiable', and to what extent 'important public health medical research' can override the need to request consent for a secondary purpose. This debate takes place in the context of public research. High requirements would apply to *private* commercial organisations.

A.4. COMPARATIVE REMARKS

Of 15 answers submitted, four reports give a 'yes' as the operative rule, seven a 'no', and four give a conditioned answer. This mirrors a spread which might be a superficial indicator, since the individual cautiousness of country reporters does not necessarily reflect the fact that some jurisdictions are stricter than others or give more room for nuances (a special case in this context is France).

The case inquires into how jurisdictions strike the balance between research subjects (as information givers) and researchers (as information users). This conflict is deliberately positioned in genomics and in a health-related setting, providing space for patient-related legislation to apply (e.g. Oviedo Convention on Biomedicine and national laws transposing EC/EU Directives). With regard to the Oviedo Convention, four correlative observations are to be made. Firstly, where respective special laws are reported (Estonia and Lithuania – both Oviedo signatories; Germany – a non-signatory to Oviedo), they are not applicable to our case. General principles have to guide the way. Secondly, of the four countries with a 'yes' operative rule (Italy, Belgium, Lithuania, Spain) and one country with strong protection for the information giver (France), two countries respectively did not or did not properly ratify (Belgium, Italy) and three countries did (France, Spain, Lithuania). Only Lithuania reported a causal relationship. Thirdly, the central questions of the Oviedo Convention (purpose limitation of consent, conditionality, revocation, remuneration) are nevertheless discussed by most reporters. Finally, besides the Oviedo Convention, values embedded in the Biotechnology Directive influence the national answer (the Netherlands, Greece, Spain). I conclude that the ratification of the Oviedo Convention has not a cogent effect on a country's answer. However, the issues discussed during the negotiations structure the answers given. Horizontally across country reports, the contested issues become clear; the national positions are far apart and reflect the fact that national transposition processes drive jurisdictions apart instead of harmonising the law (similar to processes triggered in the transposition processes of EC/EU Directives).

In all jurisdictions, general principles rather than *lex specialis* dominate the case. As for the four 'yes' jurisdictions (Belgium, Italy, Lithuania, the UK), all depart from a different principle. Belgium departs from the *material* to which related information is assigned ('principle of control over one's tissue'). Italy and the UK start out with *information related to the person* to which data protection applies. Lithuania departs from the two principles of inviolability and non-commercialisation of the human being (as in France). In the 'no' jurisdictions (such as the Czech Republic, Germany, Estonia, Poland, Slovenia), research freedoms come out stronger than the rights of data subjects and/or patients. These countries provide for a 'general content' which is irrevocable (= 'revocable until commencement of intervention', 'limited in time', three months for embryo research, see the first footnote in the Czech report for Modification 1), and which cannot be conditioned contractually. Once a person participates (= consents) and gives his/her information away, control elapses. Whereas in Germany the key argument is the importance of research freedom, in Poland the argument is the incompatibility of a 'right to personal genetic resources' with the civil law concept. In contrast to Italy, Poland explicitly does not consider genetic data as establishing the identity of a person.

From a bird's-eye view, it is a rugged landscape. The protection of the individual person has a high value in Southern, Southwestern and Northeastern Europe (France, Belgium, Italy, Spain, Lithuania, the UK). This high value materialises technically in narrow, purpose-bound consent (requiring comprehensive information and new consent for new experiments) and revocability that is unlimited in time. The research subject has to be informed about the possibility of patent applications ('commercialisation') – so that he/she has the possibility not to participate. In Northwestern Europe, the strong research freedom may eventually prompt the interests of research subjects (Denmark, Germany, Poland: materialised in irrevocability). This priority does not govern the law in the UK. In most countries, the research subject shall be informed about the (medical) purpose of research (inducing general consent). However, in the case of mere research-driven inquiries, formal prior informed consent is not even required in Germany. In addition, the possibility to apply for patents is conceived as a liberty purely at the discretion of the researcher (out of the reach of the research subject). A patented gene, even if unique to one person, is not conceived of as 'monopolising' ('gaining control', 'commercialisation of a human being', 'deprivation'). In the middle are countries with strong personality protection, where consent is in principle purpose-bound (*en masse* consent would be invalid) and differentiated (consent to unethical experiments are considered invalid), but the default rule is general consent (e.g. Greece). Others have set up registers for consent (cf. the Netherlands). Even in 'high-protection' countries, consent can be replaced by bioethics committees (Lithuania), or is simply not necessary in the case of a listed public interest (Spain).

B.1. MODIFICATION 1

Is Marc entitled to veto the patent application on the grounds of lacking prior informed consent?

B.2. EDITORIAL NOTE ON THE GDPR

The modification is triggered by Recital 26 Biotechnology Directive. It reads: 'Whereas if an invention is based on biological material of human origin or if it uses such material, where a patent application is filed, the person from whose body the material is taken must have had an opportunity of expressing free and informed consent thereto, in accordance with national law'.

B.3. COUNTRY REPORTS

(1) BELGIUM

I. *Operative Rules*

No, Marc is not entitled to veto the patent application.

II. *Descriptive Formants*

There is no rule in Belgian patent law which would allow Marc to veto a patent application for not having asked his consent. Nor would there be a possibility to refuse the grant of a patent on the ground of a lack of informed consent.

Informed consent, however, requires that the patient is informed about the possible commercial exploitation or patent.[102] When such consent is lacking, a person's personality rights would be infringed. The violation of personality rights constitutes a fault, which can be sanctioned as such, for instance through a claim for reparation of (moral) damages (Art. 1382 Civil Code).[103]

Interestingly enough, when dealing with the implementation of the Biotechnology Directive, the Belgian parliament intended to introduce lack of informed consent as a ground for refusal of a patent.[104] However, in the end, such an informed consent clause was not included in the Biotechnology Act of 2005 (now inserted into Book XI, Titles 1 and 3 BCEL).[105]

Lack of informed consent should not be sanctioned through patent law. Doing so would come into conflict with treaties as TRIPS and the European Patent Convention (EPC), since it is the publication or exploitation of the invention that has to be contrary to *ordre public* or morality in order to refuse the grant of a patent (e.g. Art. 53a EPC) and not the way people have achieved an invention.[106] In addition, Belgian legal doctrine takes the view that introducing informed consent as a patentability requirement is impractical and illogical.[107]

---

102 P. Saelen, 'Biotechnologische uitvindingen, octrooien en informed consent' [Biotechnological Inventions, Patents and Informed Consent], *Vlaamse Raad voor Wetenschapsbeleid*, 2002, 366; C. Trouet, *Van lichaam naar lichaamsmateriaal. Recht en het nader gebruik van cellen en weefsels [From Body to Human Tissue. Law and the Further Use of Cells and Tissues]* (Antwerpen/Groningen/Oxford: 2003), 496; G. Van Overwalle, 'Zonder trommels en trompetten: EU-Biotechnologierichtlijn in het Belgisch octrooirecht' [Without Drums and Trumpets: the EU Biotechnology Directive in Belgian Patent Law], *I.R.D.I.*, 2005, 355–357.

103 C. Trouet, *Van lichaam naar lichaamsmateriaal. Recht en het nader gebruik van cellen en weefsels [From Body to Human Tissue. Law and the Further Use of Cells and Tissues]* (Antwerpen/Groningen/Oxford: 2003), 526–527.

104 Bill to modify the Act of 28 March 1984 on Invention Patents, with Regard to the Patentability of Biotechnological Inventions, *Parl. Doc.*, Chambre, 2003–2004, DOC 51 1886/001, 22 [Wetsontwerp tot wijziging van de wet van 28 maart 1984 op de uitvindingsoctrooien, wat betreft de octrooieerbaarheid van biotechnologische uitvindingen, *Parl. St.*, Kamer, 2003–2004, DOC 51 1886/001, 22], available at: www.dekamer.be (last consulted 6 May 2019).

105 Act on Biotechnological Inventions, 28 April 2005, *Official Gazette*, 13 May 2005 [Wet 28 april 2005 tot wijziging van de wet van 28 maart 1984 op de uitvindingsoctrooien, wat betreft de octrooieerbaarheid van de biotechnologische uitvindingen, *B.S.*, 13 mei 2005]. See G. Van Overwalle, 'Zonder trommels en trompetten: EU-Biotechnologierichtlijn in het Belgisch octrooirecht' [Without Drums and Trumpets: the EU Biotechnology Directive in Belgian Patent Law], *I.R.D.I.* 2005, 355–357.

106 P. Saelen, 'Biotechnologische uitvindingen, octrooien en informed consent' [Biotechnological Inventions, Patents and Informed Consent], *Vlaamse Raad voor Wetenschapsbeleid*, 2002, 354–359.

107 C. Trouet, 'Octrooien en patiëntenrechten: wat de gemiddelde patiënt (nog) niet weet' [Patents and Patients' Rights: What the Average Patient Does Not Know (Yet)], (2000) 17 *De Juristenkrant*, 12–13; P. Saelen, 'Biotechnologische uitvindingen, octrooien en informed consent' [Biotechnological Inventions, Patents and Informed Consent], *Vlaamse Raad voor Wetenschapsbeleid*, 2002, 354–366.

Finally, it is argued that not considering informed consent to be a patentability requirement is in harmony with the fact that informed consent has only been acknowledged in Recital 26 of the Biotechnology Directive.[108]

III. Metalegal Formants

There are numerous reasons and grounds why informed consent is due for the further use of human tissue/genetic data (see the base case). Of course, these arguments apply especially when commercial exploitation or patenting is at stake.

Without informed consent, the doctor–patient confidentiality can be harmed, as has been proven in the past.[109] Furthermore, against the background of the technological evolution in areas like genetics and biotechnology, public discomfort increases. There is a tendency to counter some of the undesired applications or practices of these new technologies in patent law. It seems that granting a patent in a sensitive domain like biotechnology is a real eye-catcher for the public. A distinction should be made, however, between criticism related to patent law as such, and objections raised against the laws and regulations governing the exploitation and commercialisation of a certain technology. In this regard, it is quite obvious that a patent grant for a pharmaceutical product does not authorise the marketing of it. Similarly, allowing patents for bio-engineered plants does not prevent a temporary ban on growing genetically modified organisms in Europe.

It is in this way that lack of informed consent should be sanctioned, not through patent law itself. First of all, the domain of informed consent is much broader than merely the eventual inventions or commercial exploitation.[110] Second, the international patent regulations allow for quite a small scope of possible exceptions to patentability if the legal-technical conditions (invention, novelty, inventiveness, industrial applicability) are met. According to Article 54(a) EPC, 'inventions the publication or exploitation of which would be contrary to "ordre public" or morality shall not be granted a patent'. The urge may exist to counter some practices leading to an invention through this article. This would be contrary to the logic of the patent system and would pose numerous practical problems (e.g. inventions based on research in many countries, the possibility of quickly finding another person with the same 'gene' when the initial source of the tissue or genetic information causes difficulties).[111]

---

108 Ibid., 172.

109 C. Trouet, 'Patiëntenrechten en het onderzoek met lichaamsmateriaal' [Patients' Rights and the Research with Human Tissue], *Leuvense Perspectieven*, 2002, no. 4, 495–496.

110 C. Trouet, 'Octrooien en patiëntenrechten: wat de gemiddelde patiënt (nog) niet weet' [Patents and Patients' Rights: What the Average Patient Does Not Know (Yet)], (2000) 17 *De Juristenkrant*, 12–13.

111 P. Saelen, 'Biotechnologische uitvindingen, octrooien en informed consent' [Biotechnological Inventions, Patents and Informed Consent], *Vlaamse Raad voor Wetenschapsbeleid*, 2002, 354–366.

(2) CZECH REPUBLIC

I. Operative Rules

Marc is not entitled to veto the patent application.

II. Descriptive Formants

Prior informed consent is required in the above-mentioned Transplantation Act and Stem Cell Act, as well as the Act on Healthcare of the People. But if prior consent is given, then with one exception such consent cannot be repealed.[112]

The basic rule of Czech patent protection is that the right to patent belongs, according to section 8 of the Act on Inventions and Rationalisations Proposals 527/1990 Coll., to the inventor or his/her legal successor. In addition, the Act on the Protection of Biotechnological Inventions[113] 206/2000 Coll. is silent on this point.

There is no rule which would apply to veto a patent application based on someone's gene. The Civil Code is also silent in this case. Section 11 of the Civil Code gives protection to personality but not to genetic information as such.

III. Metalegal Formants

Patent law is conceived of as only dealing with the invention attributable to the inventor (defined by the patentability requirements). Anything other than a previous invention or a previous inventor have no influence on patentability.

(3) DENMARK

I. Operative Rules

No, Marc is not entitled to veto the patent application.

II. Descriptive Formants

As in Norwegian law, there is no requirement of prior informed consent for personal information in the Danish patent law currently in force, nor does such a requirement comply with international law (TRIPS, EPC).

---

112 According to section 9 of the above-mentioned Stem Cell Act, consent given to using an embryo for research can be repealed within three months of the day when consent was given and only if that embryo was not yet used for research.

113 This Act transposes into the Czech legal system Directive 98/44/EC on the legal protection of biotechnological inventions.

III. Metalegal Formants

Patent law is immune to faults in private transactions prior to the invention.

(4) ESTONIA

I. Operative Rules

Marc does not have the right to veto the patent application.

II. Descriptive Formants

Pursuant to the Patent Act, '[a]n invention is patentable if it is new, involves an inventive step and is susceptible to industrial application'.[114] This means that if the invention complies with these requirements, it is patentable. Even if Marc's rights were violated, it would not affect the patenting procedure.

III. Metalegal Formants

If the biological material was taken without Marc's consent, he could claim for damages. Marc's bodily integrity is protected by criminal law as well.

(5) FRANCE

I. Operative Rules

Marc is not entitled to veto the patent application.

II. Descriptive Formants

As mentioned in the French report on the base case, the data subject should be informed of the nature and the purpose of the medical or scientific research and give his/her express consent. However, neither the Bioethics Law nor the Intellectual Property Code provide for prior informed consent to the patent application. The provider of the biological element is not qualified as an inventor (Art. L. 611-8 of the Intellectual Property Code).

Recital 26 of the Biotechnology Directive mentions that, for a patent application, the person whose body provides the biological material must give

[114] Patent Act §8(1).

prior informed consent.[115] However, the Recital is not legally binding. It can only be seen as a declaration of intent of the legislators and not as an operative part of the Directive; thus, it was not transposed.

Therefore, Marc is not entitled to veto the patent application.

III. Metalegal Formants

The rationale is that the right to the invention is constitutionally protected. Any interference has to be prevented.

(6) GERMANY

I. Operative Rules

Marc cannot veto.

II. Descriptive Formants

The basic norm would be §1004 BGB which grants an injunction if a propriety right is violated (including a personality right). However, the personality right does not include the determination about someone else's right to patent protection. There is no acknowledged claim in respect of the personality right comparable to the patent vindication claim (§8 German Patent Law). Recital 26 of the Biotechnology Directive[116] was not transposed because it was not regarded as part of patent law.[117] However, it is contended that the violation of the informed consent rule in respect of bodily material can give rise to a claim for invalidity of the patent under Article 53a EPC.[118]

---

115 Recital 26 of the Biotechnology Directive: 'Whereas if an invention is based on biological material of human origin or if it uses such material, where a patent application is filed, the person from whose body the material is taken must have had an opportunity of expressing free and informed consent thereto, in accordance with national law'.

116 OJ L 213, 30 July 1998, 13.

117 Explicitly German Government in BT-Dr. 14/5642, p. 8; for a critical analysis see A. Krefft, *Patente auf human-genomische Erfindungen: Rechtslage in Deutschland, Europa und den USA* (Cologne: 2003).

118 Ibid., pp. 113/114/117, arguing that the validity can be challenged under the condition that the material had high sensitivity to the person's personality right. Any consent or veto to commercialisation, however, were irrelevant in respect of the personality right. This argumentation is inverse to the one of C. Godt, *Eigentum an Information* (Tübingen: 2007), pp. 592 f. She argues that the violation of the prior informed consent rule in respect of the bodily material could only be qualified as an *ex ante* barrier to patentability, not to invalidity of the patent *per se*. This prior informed consent is not directly connected with the patent as such. However, the violation of the patient's veto in respect of commercialisation could amount to invalidity, if the respected data is individual. The veto of the commercial exploitation of the genomic data is connected with the patent's purpose.

III. Metalegal Formants

The conflict between personal information and information property related to personal information is not framed by the law. Prior informed consent is so far only conceptualised in respect of storing bodily material (Directive 2004/23/EC),[119] which Germany transposed as safety regulation into pharmaceutical law, and transplantation and transfusion laws.

(7) GREECE

I. Operative Rules

Marc may not prevent this further use of already anonymised knowledge.

II. Descriptive Formants

Further trading of the patent cannot be prevented by the individual, since this in itself does not constitute further processing of his/her data in the sense of information which concerns him/her, but only of the specific biochemical products and of the methods of their production. On the other hand, the description of their composition (derived from the body of), though constituting processing of the individual's personal data, has now been 'anonymised', since the name of the individual from whom the chemical substances in question (i.e. the gene) came has been suppressed. Nevertheless, a percentage of the company's profits may constitute unjust enrichment resulting from Marc's personal data (see Modification 3 below).

III. Metalegal Formants

The rationale is that the patent shall be shielded from prior (contractual) faults.

(8) IRELAND

Answer omitted.

(9) ITALY

I. Operative Rules

Marc is entitled to veto the patent application.

[119] OJ L 102, 7 April 2004, 48 was to be transposed into national law by 31 March 2004.

II. Descriptive/Metalegal Formants

See the report on the base case.

(10) LITHUANIA

I. Operative Rules

Marc cannot veto the patent application.

II. Descriptive Formants

The requirements and procedure for acquiring legal protection for the invention, including the patent application, is set in the Patent Law (18 January 1994, No. I-372, with subsequent amendments). The Patent Law was amended by the Law of 30 June 2005, No. X-287, transposing Directive 98/44/EC on the legal protection of biotechnological inventions. However, there is no reference in the Law that would make filing the patent application dependent on the consent of the person whose biological material was used.

Provided the subject's consent for biomedical research was obtained, even his/her personal information is not to be regarded as confidential and may be made public without his/her consent so long as his/her identity remains undisclosed after such information is made public (Art. 9 Law on the Ethics of Biomedical Research). It means that the person may not have control over the further use of his/her genetic information obtained in the course of the research as soon as it is impersonalised and it is no longer possible to identify its initial carrier.

III. Metalegal Formants

Answer omitted.

(11) NETHERLANDS

I. Operative Rules

No, there is no provision requiring prior informed consent in Dutch patent law.

II. Descriptive Formants

See Case 10.

III. Metalegal Formants

Answer omitted.

(12) NORWAY

I. Operative Rules

No, Marc is not entitled to veto the patent application.

II. Descriptive Formants

There is no requirement of prior informed consent for personal information in Norwegian patent law currently in force, nor does such a requirement arise from international law (TRIPS, EPC).

III. Metalegal Formants

It may be held that the conflict between personal information and intellectual property rights based on personal information is not to be sanctioned by refusal to grant rights, as it is the use (exploitation) of the personal information and not the granting of the rights *per se* that represents the possible threat to personal integrity.

(13) POLAND

I. Operative Rules

No, Marc is not entitled to veto the patent application.

II. Descriptive Formants

The Polish patent law does not recognise any provisions that would explicitly target this issue. Poland has not implemented Recital 26 of Directive 98/44/EC on the legal protection of biotechnological inventions in any express form.[120] Therefore, the legal ground to 'veto' a patent application would have to be found in general legal provisions on patentability. Consequently, the answer to the base case of this question pre-determines the answer to Modification 1. Firstly, Article 29(1)(1) IPL states that patents should not be granted for inventions

120 See Art. 932(2) IPL.

the use of which would be contrary to *ordre public*, although the very fact that such use would be illegal does not suffice to dismiss a patent application.[121] In the light of this, even if there were doubts about whether Marc had any legal remedies against the use of 'his' gene, there would be no impediment to granting a patent to PhC. This in fact corresponds perfectly to the basic features of the patent system: even if using the invention could infringe on third party rights (e.g. other patents), its patentability as such remains unaffected.

III. Metalegal Formants

The question is whether prior informed consent should be introduced into patent laws as a specific condition of patentability of inventions involving human biological material. The reason for this would be first ethical and second practical, as it has been suggested that otherwise there would be huge public opposition to biotech patents.[122] Legally, however, such a solution does not seem appropriate. If at all, lack of proper consent and the resulting infringement of the personality rights of the 'gene donor' could exert legal effects with regard to the use of the patented invention. Any other answer would be alien to the logic of the patent system.

(14) SLOVENIA

I. Operative Rules

Marc is not entitled to veto the patent application.

II. Descriptive Formants

The issue of patenting biotechnological inventions is handled by the IPA and the RLPBI, which implements the Biotechnology Directive into Slovenian legislation. In accordance with the RLPBI, biological material may also be patented. The provision of paragraph II, Article 5 of this regulation states that a component part, isolated from the human body or obtained otherwise through some technical procedure, including a sequence of or partial sequence of genes, can be an invention, which may be patented, even if the structure of this component part is identical to the structure of a natural component part. It therefore follows that the case in hand deals with an invention, which may be subject to patent protection.

121 Art. 29(1) point 1 IPL; M. du Vall, in: *Prawo własności przemysłowej* (Warszawa: 2008), p. 36.

122 D. Beyleveld, 'Why recital 26 of the E.C. directive on the legal protection of biotechnological inventions should be implemented in national law', IPQ, vol. 1, 2000, pp. 24 ff.

The provision of paragraph I, Article 74 IPA states that the patent is granted to the individual designated as an applicant in the patent application. The conditions required for obtaining a patent are formal and substantive. The first deals with the question of the completed patent application, which contains the request for the patent grant, a description of the invention, patent claims, a summary of the invention, sketches, power of attorney by the representative, the text of the application in the Slovenian language, and evidence of fee payment (Art. 85 IPA).[123] The second refers to the examination of the substance of the patent application. In this regard, it has to be examined whether the subject matter of the claimed invention is patentable and whether the claimed invention, at first sight, meets the requirements of novelty, inventive step and industrial application (Art. 88 IPA). Therefore, in the patent registration procedure, SIPO will not examine whether Marc gave consent for filing a patent application and granting a patent. Besides that, Marc also cannot veto the grant of the patent, as the IPA does not recognise a special procedure of objection during the patent registration procedure, nor does it recognise the reason for refusing patent protection, since an individual who consented to the removal of genetic material did not consent to the subsequent filing of the patent application.

As a result, we think that Marc cannot oppose the granting of the patent, as the IPA contains no provision which would allow vetoing the grant of the patent due to Marc not being informed of the intention of the subsequent patenting of his genetic material, which as a result would mean that he also did not consent to this.

III. Metalegal Formants

Answer omitted.

(15) SPAIN

I. Operative Rules

Marc cannot veto.

II. Descriptive Formants

A patent can be prevented from being taken out if Marc would not have given his consent if he had known about the particular application and he was not duly

[123] The demands are defined in greater detail in the Rules on Contents of Patent Application and on the Division of Patents.

informed by the laboratory. The nullity of the consent must be applied for on the basis of Article 1265 Civil Code and the failure to comply with the conditions in which consent must be given.

Nevertheless, if Marc has been informed about the commercial applications of the research, we have to consider the following conditions.

a) Conditions related to the method for obtaining samples

Article 58 of Law 14/2007 requires that biological samples for purposes of biomedical research be acquired only if the subjects give their prior consent after they have been informed of the consequences and risks that giving the sample may have on their health. This consent will be essential when the samples were obtained for a different purpose and the aim is to use them for research. However, exceptionally, codified or identified samples can be used without the consent of the subject if obtaining consent is not possible or requires an unreasonable effort. This must be approved by the corresponding Research Ethical Committee, which must ensure that all the following conditions are met:

- the research is of general interest;
- the research will be carried out by the same institution that requested the consent for obtaining the samples;
- there is no record of any express objection by the subject; and
- the confidentiality of the personal data is guaranteed.

b) Conditions related to the invention, imposed by patent law

If the research carried out on Marc's samples complies with these conditions, there is nothing to prevent the resulting inventions from being patented,[124] insofar as Marc has no rights over the result of the research, neither economic ones nor the right to be named, as far as the invention that is to be patented complies with the legal requisites.

Therefore, even if Marc had not given his consent, if the object of the invention is patentable in accordance with the requisites of the Patent Law, the biological samples were taken respecting the legal requisites of giving informed consent or the circumstance is one of general public interest and Marc did not expressly state his disconformity, he cannot prevent his biological material from being used to exploit a patent.

III. Metalegal Formants

The rationale is to encapsulate patent law against prior or later legal faults in order to strengthen the legal position of the patent holder.

---

124 By contrast, in Italy Marc will be entitled to veto the patent application.

(16) UNITED KINGDOM

I. *Operative Rules*

Marc can veto the patent application.

II. *Descriptive Formants*

In the UK, Marc would not be entitled to veto the patent application based on data protection or patient protection law, but rather on patent law. There is strong opposition to patents on vaccines. The legal argument rests on vaccines not being patentable subject matter for being contrary to morality and *ordre public*.[125] The reference is *obiter* to this effect in European patent law.

III. *Metalegal Formants*

In the UK, there is a strong conviction that vaccines are peculiar chemical substances. Even where the general patentability requirement would be met, there is strong support for excluding them from protection based on public morality: they (normatively) shall be and (scientifically) need to be accessible to all.

B.4. COMPARATIVE REMARKS

Of 15 answers, 13 report 'no', and only two (Italy and the UK) 'yes' as the operative rule. Only three reports refer explicitly to Recital 26 Biotechnology Directive. The Italian position is of particular interest, especially against the background of those five jurisdictions identified as countries with a high protection standard for the individual genetic subject (France, Belgium, Italy, Spain, Lithuania), requiring purpose-specific information and consent. The UK position expresses an academic position of public health exemptions to patent law which is not shared by the competent patent agencies.

Two countries report regulation triggered by Recital 26 (Belgium, Denmark) requiring prior informed consent in the patent description. While the Belgian Parliament witnessed a debate on patent law consequences when consent is lacking, both countries eventually only stipulated a duty the violation of which will give rise to damages. The Italian answer rests on Article 22 Oviedo Convention, to which Article 5 of the Italian law transposing the Biotechnology Directive refers. These argumentations mirror the conceptual difference between Italy (the

---

125 See only W. Cornish, D. Llewelyn and T. Aplin, *Intellectual Property* (9th ed., London: 2019).

person as autonomous data subject) and Belgium (prior informed consent as a personal interest which might give rise to moral damages, but is not a 'property-type' right). Yet the Italian report is silent about how to enforce the right to opposition. It did not become stipulated black-letter law in the Italian Patent Code. Even if one could speculate about a self-standing, Italian Article 22-type right which allows patent opposition, there is the lingering question of to which patent such a right would apply – to Italian patents only or also to patents granted under the framework of the European Patent Convention (EPC), respectively the future EPC-patents with unitary effect in the EU? In the case of 'Italian patents only', the right would be largely meaningless in the biotech sector. In Germany, the debate remained purely academic.

The Greek and the Lithuanian reports agree in their reasoning that individual patent opposition is precluded once data is anonymised. Norway, Belgium and Poland reason along the lines of the common distinction in IP between the patent granting process and exploitation.

C.1. MODIFICATION 2

Is Marc entitled to be named/not to be named in the patent description?

C.2. EDITORIAL NOTE ON THE GDPR

Note the editorial remark in section A.2 above.

C.3. COUNTRY REPORTS

(1) BELGIUM

I. Operative Rules

Marc is not entitled to be named in the patent description. However, he has the right not to be named in it.

II. Descriptive Formants

a) Right to be named

Nothing in Belgian patent law entitles Marc to be named in the patent description.

b) Right not to be named

Article 10 of the Patient's Rights Act guarantees the right to respect for one's privacy.[126] Article 485 Criminal Code sanctions the violation of medical secrecy.[127] Also relevant is the Personal Data Act of 1992[128] (replaced by the Act on the Protection of Natural Persons with regard to the Processing of Personal Data of 2018, implementing the GDPR in Belgium).[129] All these regulations translate the principle of Article 8 ECHR into their specific contexts.

Based on his right to privacy, Marc is entitled not be named in a patent description because then protected medical data would be made public.

III. Metalegal Formants

According to Article 17 BPA (Art. XI.18 BCEL), the description of the invention has to be sufficiently clear and complete for it to be carried out by a person skilled in the art. The objective of a patent description is the disclosure of the invention to society in return for the grant of exclusive exploitation rights for a limited period of time. The purpose of the patent description is not to acknowledge the role of persons who have provided tissue or genetic information.

On the other hand, some information does have to be mentioned in a patent or patent application. Article 12 BPA (Art. XI.13 BCEL) gives the inventor the right to be mentioned or to oppose the mentioning of his/her name.[130] And according to Article 15§1 6° BPA (Art. XI.16§1 6° BCEL), the patent application shall contain the geographical origin of biological material of plant or animal origin, if known, on the basis of which an invention has been developed.[131]

(2) CZECH REPUBLIC

I. Operative Rules

Marc is not entitled to be named, but his identity is protected.

---

126 H. Nys, *Geneeskunde. Recht en medisch handelen*, 1991, 177.

127 For more information: NIJS, Geneeskunde. Recht en medisch handelen, 524–568.

128 Law on the Protection of Personal Data, 8 December 1992, *Official Gazette*, 18 March 1993 [Wet 8 december 1992 tot bescherming van de persoonlijke levenssfeer ten opzichte van de verwerking van persoonsgegevens, *B.S.*, 18 maart 1993].

129 Law on the Processing of Personal Data of 30 July 2018, *Official Gazette*, 5 September 2018 [Wet van 30 juli 2018 betreffende de bescherming van natuurlijke personen in verband met de verwerking van persoonsgegevens, *B.S.*, 5 September 2018].

130 For more on this see Case 13.

131 For more on this see Case 10.

II. Descriptive Formants

There is no right to be named in the patent description, contrary to section 11 Copyright Act, which includes the moral rights of authors. In addition, PhC must follow the Act on Protection of Personal Data 101/2000 Coll., which protects identity (anonymity) and personal data of donors of, for example, blood, embryos or sperm.

III. Metalegal Formants

Answer omitted.

(3) DENMARK

I. Operative Rules

Marc is not entitled to be named in the patent description, but he can object to it.

II. Descriptive Formants

Marc has not contributed to the invention, and acknowledging the persons providing genetic information is definitively outside the purpose of the patent description. According to §3 of the Danish Patent Regulation (DPR, 29 January 2009), a patent application for an invention involving biological material from the human body must include information on whether the person from whom the material has been derived has given his/her consent to the use of the biological material. A lack of compliance with this does not, however, affect the status of the application or the legality of the issued patent.

Information about the person from *whom* the gene stems from must be considered to be personal data according to the definition in APPD §3, i.e. any information and assessments that may be linked to a natural person, and it must also be considered to be *sensitive* personal information relating to health (§7). The disclosure of this information would require Marc's consent, cf. APPD §7, second paragraph, no. 1. In other words, Marc is entitled not to be named.

III. Metalegal Formants

The rationale is the stabilisation of the legal monopoly.

(4) ESTONIA

I. Operative Rules

Marc does not have to be named in the patent description. On the other hand, naming Marc in the patent description without his consent could violate Marc's rights.

II. Descriptive Formants

The information which a patent application has to include is prescribed by the Patent Act and the regulation on requirements relating to the form and contents of documents included in patent applications[132] adopted by the Minister of Economic Affairs and Communications. For instance, the Patent Act provides that a patent application has to include information concerning the applicant and author and a description of the invention in which the invention must be disclosed in a sufficiently clear and concise manner to enable a person skilled in the art to make the invention (§19(1) clauses 1 and 2 Patent Act).

To sum up, the author of an invention has the right to 'request the disclosure of his or her name as the author' (§13(7) clause 1 Patent Act), but the donor of biological material used in the research which resulted in a patentable invention is not entitled to be named in the patent description.

III. Metalegal Formants

Naming Marc in the patent description without his consent could violate Marc's rights. The Personal Data Protection Act[133] considers data relating to genetic information to be sensitive personal data (§4(2) clause 4 Personal Data Protection Act). As a rule, processing personal data requires the permission of a person whose personal data are processed (§10(1)). Consequently, if PhC is interested in naming Marc in the patent application, it must obtain Marc's consent.

(5) FRANCE

I. Operative Rules

Marc is not entitled to be named, but to protection of his identity.

132 Patenditaotluse sisu- ja vorminõuded ning Patendiametile esitamise kord. Entered into force on 14 January 2005 – RTL 2005, 5, 36 (in Estonian). Official text available at https://www.riigiteataja.ee/ert/act.jsp?replstring=33&dyn=13111167&id=833226 (6 May 2019).

133 Isikuandmete kaitse seadus. Entered into force on 1 January 2008 – RT I 2007, 24, 127; 2007, 68, 421 (in Estonian). Official text available at https://www.riigiteataja.ee/ert/act.jsp?id=12909389 (6 May 2019).

II. *Descriptive Formants*

Limited moral right reserved only to the inventor
Article L. 611-9 of the Intellectual Property Code provides: 'the inventor, whether salaried or not, shall be named as such in the patent; he may also oppose such identification'. Only the inventor is entitled to be named.

Moreover, Article 16-8 of the Civil Code states that no information enabling the identification of the person who donates an element or a product of his/her body may be disclosed. This is to protect the confidentiality of private life. Article 7 of the Universal Declaration on the Human Genome and Human Rights (11 November 1997), regarding the confidentiality of genetic data, could be also taken into consideration.[134]

III. *Metalegal Formants*

The commercial sphere and the protection of persons are to be kept apart.

(6) GERMANY

I. *Operative Rules*

Marc has no right to be named.

II. *Descriptive Formants*

There is no comparable moral right acknowledged by §13 UrhG for the person to his/her personal information.

The personality right limits the disposition about personal data only to prior informed consent of data release, thus is limited to the right to keep information undisclosed, through public law data protection.

III. *Metalegal Formants*

Patent law needs to be shielded from upstream claims for the benefit of title stability.

[134] Art. 7: 'Genetic data associated with an identifiable person and stored or processed for the purposes of research or any other purpose must be held confidential under the conditions set by law'.

(7) GREECE

I. Operative Rules

Only Marc, the subject of personal data, has the right to be named in the patent application. On the other hand, he has the right to seek protection of his identity.

II. Descriptive Formants

Of course, the suppression of the name of the individual from whom the gene on which the chemical composition of the pharmaceutical is based is an effect of the principle of confidentiality in the processing of personal data (Art. 10 Law 2472/1997 = Art. 10 Directive 95/46/EC). However, in this sense the principle of confidentiality of the processing is no more than a promise made by the person responsible for the processing of the data to the individual and, conversely, a right of the latter against the person responsible for the processing. As such, therefore, the principle of confidentiality is effective to the extent that the individual so wishes.

On the other hand, if the individual wishes and requires his/her name to be revealed to third parties during the processing of his/her data, then the person responsible for the processing is under an obligation to reveal the identity of the individual, in accordance with the principle of accuracy (truth) of the processing of the personal data in accordance with Article 4 para. 1 γ Law 2472/1997. This provision, in conjunction with Article 57 Civil Code, thus also legitimates Marc in the present case in seeking from the pharmaceutical company the establishment of the truth in the description of the chemical composition of the product as a processing of his personal data in accordance with Modification 1 above.

III. Metalegal Formants

Answer omitted.

(8) IRELAND

Answer omitted.

(9) ITALY

I. Operative Rules

Marc likely has the right to be named in the patent description.

II. Descriptive/Metalegal Formants

See the report on the base case.

(10) LITHUANIA

I. Operative Rules

Marc does not have the right to be named.

II. Descriptive Formants

There is no right provided by law for Marc to require to be named in the patent description. The requirements of the confidentiality of personal data have to be observed.

III. Metalegal Formants

Answer omitted.

(11) NETHERLANDS

I. Operative Rules

Marc has no entitlement to be named.

II. Descriptive Formants

The Dutch Patent Act only has provisions regarding the rights of the inventor.

III. Metalegal Formants

In the Netherlands, people do not want to stick their heads out. They treasure their privacy. Nobody would want to be mentioned, so nobody will propose a right in this respect.

(12) NORWAY

I. Operative Rules

Marc is not entitled to be named in the patent description, but he can object to being named.

II. Descriptive Formants

Marc has not contributed to the invention, and acknowledging the persons providing genetic information is definitively outside the purpose of the patent description. On the other hand, NPA §8c requires that the patent application for an invention involving biological material from the human body must include information on whether the person from whom the material has been derived has given his/her consent to the use of the biological material, in accordance with the NBBA §12.

Information about the person from whom the gene stems must be considered personal data according to the definition in §2, no. 1 of the Personal Data Act (NPDA, 14 April 2000), i.e. any information and assessments that may be linked to a natural person, and it must also be considered *sensitive* personal information relating to health (§2, no. 8, lit. c). The disclosure of this information would require Marc's consent, cf. NPDA §9, first paragraph, lit. a. In other words, Marc is entitled not to be named.

III. Metalegal Formants

It is hard to see what legitimate interests the provider of genetic information should have in being mentioned in the patent description. On the other hand, the need to protect personal integrity and privacy justifies a veto against disclosure of information concerning the person from whom biological material has been derived, unless strong policy concerns are at stake.

(13) POLAND

I. Operative Rules

No, Marc is not entitled to be named. He is entitled not to be named.

II. Descriptive Formants

Only the inventor has the right to be named in a patent application (Art. 32 IPL). Marc has not made any intellectual contribution to the invention and thus in the current patent law system he may not request to be named in the patent application. However, the opposite right (not to be named) may be easily justified. Firstly, Marc can invoke his right of privacy (personality right), and secondly, naming him against his will would also be contrary to the law on the protection of personal data (a person's name certainly qualifies as such). Since naming the 'donor' is not necessary to disclose the nature of the invention, PhC would have no arguments to oppose such claims.

III. *Metalegal Formants*

It seems that the underlying question again touches upon the problem of 'special rights' that should be bestowed upon those who made genetic research possible by providing the *material*. It should be emphasised that intellectual property is not the appropriate branch of law for such solutions. Marc has made the invention possible, true, but only on the *factual* level. In the same vein, a person who has financed the research or provided the facilities should be able to claim to be named in the patent application.

(14) SLOVENIA

I. *Operative Rules*

Marc is not entitled to claim to be named in the patent description. However, he is entitled to claim not to be named in the patent description.

II. *Descriptive Formants*

Regarding the possibility of claiming that he be named in the patent description, it is possible to conclude that such a right does not exist in this case. Marc is neither the author[135] nor the inventor,[136] and within Slovenian legislation, not even personality rights give him the right to be named.[137]

Marc, however, has the right to claim that he not be mentioned in the patent description. Mentioning Marc would mean disclosing his personal data. Article 15 AQSHTC states that donation centres and institutions for tissue and cells must guarantee anonymity of all data recorded about the donor, including genetic data. In the same way, Article 5 of the Rules on Personal Data Protection of Donors and Recipients of Human Body Parts for Treatment Purposes[138] (passed on the basis of Art. 22 RTHBPA) states that all personal data which might disclose the identity of the donor must be set aside, unless they are absolutely necessary for the execution of procedures in the field of removal of human body parts for treatment purposes. To the greatest possible degree, personal data must be replaced by a special identification code. In accordance with Article 32 of

---

135 The author has the right to demand to be named in accordance with Art. 18 CRRA.

136 The inventor has the right to be named in the application and all other related documents (Art. 73 in relation to Art. 118 IPA).

137 Personality rights are mainly of a negative nature and allow the holder to exclude intervention in the personal sphere. In the given case, it would have to do with positive justification of requesting to be named, which is not one of the justifications that personality rights consist of.

138 Official Gazette RS, no. 75/2003.

the Personal Data Protection Act,[139] an individual has the right to demand the deletion or blocking of all personal data which have been collected or processed in violation of the law, while personal data in the private sector may only be processed if explicitly provided for by legislation or if the individual has given consent. All these provisions allow for the protection of Marc's personal data and demand that he not be named in the patent description.

III. Metalegal Formants

The protection of personal data is better taken care of by a specialised law.

(15) SPAIN

I. Operative Rules

Marc does not have the right to be named.

II. Descriptive Formants

To answer this question, we have to consider Article 58 of Law 14/2007, which states that the identity of the person who donates the biological material is absolutely confidential,[140] so it is very difficult for Marc to ask PhC to include his name in the patent description.

Likewise, the Personal Data Protection Law (Organic Law 15/1999 of 13 December) prevents unauthorised use of personal data.

III. Metalegal Formants

The protection of personal data is better taken care of by a specialised law.

(16) UNITED KINGDOM

I. Operative Rules

Marc has no right to be named.

---

139 Official Gazette RS, nos. 86/2004, 67/2007, 94/2007.

140 As the Czech Copyright Act does.

II. Descriptive Formants

An argument in parallel to the Nagoya Protocol and its UK implementation (Nagoya Protocol (Compliance) (Amendment) (EU Exit) Regulation 2018 (SI 2018/1393)) cannot be made since human genetic resources are exempt. Thus, there is no legal basis to support Marc's claim.

III. Metalegal Formants

While UK law has accepted 'the right to be named in patent applications' for providers of genetic resources under the Nagoya Protocol, there is no equivalent for human beings.

C.4. COMPARATIVE REMARKS

Out of 15 answers, nine provide a dual answer '1: no/2: yes' as the operative rule; six are restricted to a simple 'no' answer to the first part of the question; and provide a 'yes' answer (Italy, Greece).

The Italian reporter's argument is directly based on Italian law. The Greek answer is different. In both parts of the question, it is rooted in strong personality protection. As a matter of principle, the person is protected by the principle of confidentiality. This protection, however, extends only as far as the individual wishes. These positions contrast with the majority, which hold that the right of the data subject 'is of a negative nature' (cf. Slovenia), and that patent law is not the appropriate branch of law to enforce his/her interests (cf. Belgium, Denmark, Poland). The confidentiality principle is conceptualised as absolute (Czech Republic, Spain). All these answers again contrast with the argument submitted by the UK report. It acknowledges the fact that the claim for a 'right to be named in patent claims' by information providers derives from the international debate on patenting of (non-human) genetic resources (and the providers' claim to a share in benefits operationalised by the right to be named in the patent).

D.1. MODIFICATION 3

Is Marc entitled to a share of the benefits that are generated by marketing the patented products?

D.2. COUNTRY REPORTS

(1) BELGIUM

I. *Operative Rules*

No, Marc is not entitled to a share of the benefits.

II. *Descriptive Formants*

Article 21 of the Convention on Human Rights and Biomedicine states that 'the human body and its parts shall not, as such, give rise to financial gain'. Although Belgium has not ratified this Convention, the principle of no financial gain is widely accepted and[141] has been repeated in some legislation (e.g. Art. 4(1) Organ Transplantation Act and Art. 5 Blood and Blood Derivatives Act).

A commercial agreement disregarding the principle of no financial gain would automatically be null.[142]

In the specific context of therapeutic products based on tissues or genetic data, however, there is some criticism in legal doctrine about this principle.[143] Some authors argue that commercialisation of one's specific tissue or genetic data characteristics would be acceptable, similar to the valorisation of scientific, artistic or sports activities or portrait rights (*portretrecht* or *droit à l'image*).[144]

---

141 Belgian Bio-ethical Committee [Belgisch Raadgevend Comité voor Bio-ethiek], Advice no. 5 on the Legal Protection of Biotechnological Inventions, 9 February 1998, available at: https://www.health.belgium.be/en/belgian-advisory-committee-bioethics (last consulted on 11 March 2022); H. Nys, 'Het nader gebruik van lichaamsmateriaal en biotechnologische uitvindingen', in: G. Van Overwalle (ed.), *Patent Law, Ethics and Biotechnology* (Brussels: 1998), 173–175; P. Saelen, 'Biotechnologische uitvindingen, octrooien en informed consent' [Biotechnological Inventions, Patents and Informed Consent], *Vlaamse Raad voor Wetenschapsbeleid*, 2002, 21–22; C. Trouet, *Van lichaam naar lichaamsmateriaal. Recht en het nader gebruik van cellen en weefsels [From Body to Human Tissue. Law and the Further Use of Cells and Tissues]* (Antwerpen/Groningen/Oxford: 2003), 100–103.

142 C. Trouet, *Van lichaam naar lichaamsmateriaal. Recht en het nader gebruik van cellen en weefsels [From Body to Human Tissue. Law and the Further Use of Cells and Tissues]* (Antwerpen/Groningen/Oxford: 2003), 101.

143 For an overview of the positions see H. Nys, 'Het nader gebruik van lichaamsmateriaal en biotechnologische uitvindingen', in: G. Van Overwalle (ed.), *Patent Law, Ethics and Biotechnology* (Brussels: 1998), 173–175; C. Trouet, *Van lichaam naar lichaamsmateriaal. Recht en het nader gebruik van cellen en weefsels [From Body to Human Tissue. Law and the Further Use of Cells and Tissues]* (Antwerpen/Groningen/Oxford: 2003), 100–103.

144 Y.-H. Leleu and G. Genicot, 'La maîtrise de son corps par la personne' [The Person's Control over His Body], 5937 *J.T.* 1999, 598–599.

III. *Metalegal Formants*

The principle of no financial gain for people who donate human tissue seems more or less accepted in Belgium.[145] It seems quite logical to extend this principle to the situation where genetic data of specific persons forms the basis of new therapeutic products. After all, it is the intellectual effort of making an invention out of human tissue or genetic data that is rewarded with a patent, not the tissue or data as such. Besides, it would not seem fair if people are rewarded just for being lucky and having some special genes. Additionally, it is very rare that the invention of a pharmaceutical product can be traced back to one person. Deciding who is entitled to a share will not be easy. Conversely, huge pharmaceutical companies earning money by exploiting knowledge based on this tissue/data does not seem fair either. When preparing its opinion on the Legal Protection of Biotechnological Inventions, not all members of the Belgian Advisory Committee on Bioethics were convinced that sharing profit should be considered illegitimate.[146] The solution might be found in alternatives aiming at returning some of the profit to certain public causes, but not to individual persons as such.[147]

(2) CZECH REPUBLIC

I. *Operative Rules*

Marc is not entitled to a share of the benefits that are generated by marketing the patented products.

---

145 Belgian Bio-ethical Committee [Belgisch Raadgevend Comité voor Bio-ethiek], Advice no. 5 on the Legal Protection of Biotechnological Inventions, 9 February 1998, available at: https://www.health.belgium.be/en/belgian-advisory-committee-bioethics (last consulted on 11 March 2022); H. Nys, 'Het nader gebruik van lichaamsmateriaal en biotechnologische uitvindingen', in: G. Van Overwalle (ed.), *Patent Law, Ethics and Biotechnology* (Brussels: 1998), 173–175; P. Saelen, 'Biotechnologische uitvindingen, octrooien en informed consent' [Biotechnological Inventions, Patents and Informed Consent], *Vlaamse Raad voor Wetenschapsbeleid*, 2002, 21–22; C. Trouet, *Van lichaam naar lichaamsmateriaal. Recht en het nader gebruik van cellen en weefsels [From Body to Human Tissue. Law and the Further Use of Cells and Tissues]* (Antwerpen/Groningen/Oxford: 2003), 100–103.

146 H. Nys, 'Het nader gebruik van lichaamsmateriaal en biotechnologische uitvindingen', in: G. Van Overwalle (ed.), *Patent Law, Ethics and Biotechnology* (Brussels: 1998), 176.

147 C. Trouet, *Van lichaam naar lichaamsmateriaal. Recht en het nader gebruik van cellen en weefsels [From Body to Human Tissue. Law and the Further Use of Cells and Tissues]* (Antwerpen/Groningen/Oxford: 2003), 474–484. For example, Hugo Ethics Committee, *Statement on benefit-sharing*, 9 April 2000, available at: https://www.eubios.info/BENSHARE.htm (last consulted on 11 March 2022).

II. Descriptive Formants

All international treaties, such as the Universal Declaration on the Human Genome and Human Rights of UNESCO or the Convention on Human Rights and Biomedicine of the Council of Europe (Art. 21), prohibit profiting financially from the human body and its parts. The Charter of Fundamental Rights of European Union, in Article 3(2), also prohibits 'making the human body and its parts as such a source of financial gain'. The same prohibition is found in Directive 2004/23/EC on setting standards of quality and safety for the donation, procurement, testing, processing, preservation, storage and distribution of human tissues and cells. Moreover, the national laws are harmonised with international treaties and European law; for example, the Transplantation Act prohibits such profit, as do the Stem Cell Act and the Act on Healthcare of the People.

If Marc asks for a share of benefit, then he would be acting against the concept of non-commercialisation of the human body; however, it could also be argued that human genes should not be defined as a body part as such. However, it is doubtful whether any remuneration will be acceptable *pro futuro* because, in our example, companies like PhC are making a profit on Marc's gene without any remuneration for him. However, we must understand that the principle of non-commercialisation of the human body is an important concept to protect society and its weaker members from the commercialisation of human bodies.

Another problem is that the concept of the protection of personality in the Civil Code is based on moral rights and not on property rights.

III. Metalegal Formants

The principle of non-commercialisation of the human body implies the no-commercial-gain principle.

(3) DENMARK

I. Operative Rules

No, Marc is not entitled to a share of benefits.

II. Descriptive Formants

There are no legal bases for such a claim in Danish law.

III. Metalegal Formants

The commercialisation of the human body and its parts conflicts with international conventions and the no-commercial-gain principle must be considered to be broadly accepted in Denmark.

(4) ESTONIA

I. Operative Rules

Marc is not entitled to a share of the profits.

II. Descriptive Formants

See the response to Modification 4.

III. Metalegal Formants

Answer omitted.

(5) FRANCE

I. Operative Rules

Marc is not entitled to a share of the profits.

II. Descriptive Formants

Legal framework related to sharing the profits of the patented products based on human biological elements in France
Article 4 Universal Declaration on the Human Genome and Human Rights, 1997; Article 3(2) Charter of the Fundamental Rights of the European Union; Convention on Biological Diversity, 1992.

Principle of unavailability and the non-commercialisation of the human body
The principle of non-commercialisation is confirmed in both French law and international law. Article 16-6 of the Civil Code states that no remuneration may be granted to a person who consents to an experimentation on him/herself, to the taking of elements from his/her body or to the collection of products therefrom. Article 1128 of the Civil Code also confirms this principle by providing that only things which may be the subject matter of legal transactions

between private individuals may be the object of agreements. Therefore, even though compensation for expenses may be allowed under French law, genetic data can only be collected as a result of a donation in favour of research, since the human body does not fall within the scope of commercial transactions.

As for the Convention on Biological Diversity (CBD), the consensus is that it does not apply to human tissues. Moreover, although the CBD emphasises the sharing of profits, most of its provisions refer to profits for the source country or its agencies. None of its provisions directly give individual providers or source communities any rights to share in profits.

Therefore, Marc is not entitled to a share of the profits that are generated by marketing the patented products.

III. Metalegal Formants

Answer omitted.

(6) GERMANY

I. Operative Rules

Marc has no right to shared benefits.

II. Descriptive Formants

The personality right is conceived as a moral right, but not as a property right which could be alienated.

III. Metalegal Formants

Commercialisation of the human body and its parts is, in principle, ruled out by international conventions (e.g. for 'the body and its parts': Article 3(2) Charter of the Fundamental Rights of the European Union;[148] for body parts: Article 21 Convention on Human Rights and Biomedicine of the Council of Europe of 1997; in Germany: §17 German Law on Transplantations and §10 German Law on Transfusions (however, with caveat for compensation of expenses, which can be quite high – the transition from compensation to purchase is fluid); *for genetic information*: Article 4 UNESCO Universal Declaration on the Human Genome and Human Rights from 1997; §1a sec. 1 German Patent Act; a principle of the German

148 OJ C 346, 18 December 2000, 1 (2000/C 364/01).

Biobank Law (GendiagnostikG[149])). The Convention on Biological Diversity, which instigated benefit-sharing as an ethical claim, is not applicable to human bodily material. However, the Human Genome Organisation's Ethics Committee has proclaimed benefit-sharing to be 'a civic duty' for companies involved in human health, and claims 1–3% of the net profits to be most reasonable.[150]

(7) GREECE

I. *Operative Rules*

Marc is entitled to claim a sum of money, either as a reasonable consideration for his consent, or as unjust enrichment in the case of absence of such consent.

II. *Descriptive Formants*

Over and above the claim – which is groundless in principle for abstention from trading in the product derived from his body and public recognition of its origin – any other pecuniary claims of Marc against PhC will naturally concern the enrichment of the latter from the biochemical substances from Marc's body. Whether or not the enrichment in question is justified naturally depends on the validity of the contract between Marc and PhC, also in accordance with what is said in the answer to the base case above as to the validity of Marc's consent to the processing of his data.

If Marc's valid consent covered trading in the product, then he is entitled only to what is provided for by his contract with PhC. If consent has been validly given, but no consideration has been concluded for the commercial exploitation of the product on the part of PhC, Marc is entitled to determine the reasonable consideration by a unilateral declaration on his part to PhC according to Articles 371–372, 379 Civil Code, since, in the event of doubt, consent has not been given *gratis* in accordance with Art. 496 Civil Code.

If, again, if there is no valid consent or contract between Marc and PhC, Marc has a right to the profits PhC has realised up to the present (and also over the patent itself), at a percentage, naturally, which corresponds to the adequate (i.e. foreseeable) causal contribution of his gene, and not to the scientific labour of processing it (Arts. 904, 734, in conjunction with 719 Civil Code).

---

149 Gendiagnostikgesetz of 31 July 2009 (BGBl. I S. 2529, 3672), revised 4 May 2021 (BGBl. I S. 882). On the principle of non-commercialisation see National German Council on Ethics, Opinion on Research Biobanks, 17 March 2004, pp. 88, 89 (copies available from the German Council of Ethics: https://www.ethikrat.org/publikationen …).

150 Hugo Ethics Committee Statement on Benefit-Sharing, 9 April 2000; B.M. Knoppers, 'Genetic Benefit Sharing', (2000) 290 *Science* 49. This civil duty, however, is usually proclaimed for information which is collectively shared (see Case 9).

III. *Metalegal Formants*

Answer omitted.

(8) IRELAND

Answer omitted.

(9) ITALY

I. *Operative Rules*

Marc is not entitled to a share of the profits.

II. *Descriptive Formants*

See the report on the base case.

III. *Metalegal Formants*

Answer omitted.

(10) LITHUANIA

I. *Operative Rules*

Marc does not have right to a share of the benefits.

II. *Descriptive Formants*

Participation in the research may only grant the right to compensation for expenses or for pecuniary or non-pecuniary damage incurred by the biomedical research (respectively Arts. 10 and 11 Law on the Ethics of Biomedical Research). The personal right to participate or not participate in the research does not encompass the right to have control over the economical exploitation of the research results. Besides, the governing principle of the non-commercialisation of the human body applies.[151]

---

151 It is explicitly established by law that tissues, cells or organs may not be subject to commercial transactions (Art. 22(1) Law on the Health System of 19 July 1994, No. I-552; Art. 3(5) Law on Patients' Rights and Damage Compensation).

III. Metalegal Formants

The non-commercialisation of the human body also governs the request for remuneration.

(11) NETHERLANDS

I. Operative Rules

Unless Marc had included such terms in the contract, he is not entitled to a share of the benefits.

II. Descriptive Formants

There are no relevant provisions in Dutch law.

III. Metalegal Formants

See the current debate under Modification 2.

(12) NORWAY

I. Operative Rules

No, Marc is not entitled to a share of benefits.

II. Descriptive Formants

There are no legal bases for such a claim in Norwegian law.

III. Metalegal Formants

The commercialisation of the human body and its parts conflicts with international conventions and the no-commercial-gain principle must be considered broadly accepted in Norway.

(13) POLAND

I. Operative Rules

No, Marc is not entitled to a share of the benefits.

II. Descriptive Formants

A special legal ground would have to exist to justify a claim for a share of benefits. It would certainly be lawful to provide for such a solution in a contract (this highlights the importance of prior informed consent). Knowing how unique his gene is, Marc could make his consent dependent on an arrangement granting him a share of benefits. If there is no contract, however, there are no legal grounds to demand such a share. Neither the IPL nor the general institutions of private law could justify Marc's claim.

III. Metalegal Formants

Again, this case shows that the person whose genetic material has been used to create the patented invention may not obtain any economic benefits, whereas the patent holder may reap all the rewards of the commercial success. It will be even more conspicuous when genetic resources of larger groups of people are used and thus 'exploited'. According to the classic principles of IP law (promoting *intellectual* achievements), there is nothing strange with this result. In fact, the sensitive subject matter only aggravates the much more common problem (let us imagine an invention the essential element of which is the use of a unique substance existing only in one state). What should be addressed is simply a question of fairness.

(14) SLOVENIA

I. Operative Rules

Marc is not entitled to a share of the benefits.

II. Descriptive Formants

There are several reasons why it is possible to conclude that, according to the Slovenian legislation, Marc is not entitled to a share of the benefits.

Firstly, in accordance with the provision of Article 18, in relation to Article 74 IPA, patent rights belong to the holder of the patent. Marc is not the holder of the patent and consequently not entitled to any economic rights of the patent. Secondly, both the RTHBPA and AQSHTC state that donating tissue and cells is voluntary and unpaid and that it is not permissible to pay for or accept money for removed parts of the human body, even in the form of pecuniary benefits. In our opinion, receiving a share of the benefits would definitely fall under that category. Thirdly, the legal basis for Marc's claim for a share of the benefits can only be his personality rights, which are non-pecuniary and are above all of a negative nature.[152] This means that Marc is not entitled to any pecuniary claims on the basis of personality rights, nor is he entitled to a share of the benefits. Fourthly, Slovenia ratified the Convention for the Protection of Human Rights and Dignity of Human Beings with regard to the Application of Biology and Medicine (Convention of Human Rights and Biomedicine),[153] which states in Article 21 that the human body and its parts may not be used for pecuniary gain.

III. Metalegal Formants

Answer omitted.

(15) SPAIN

I. Operative Rules

Marc has no right to shared benefits.

II. Descriptive/Metalegal Formants

All donations are governed by the principle of gratuitousness,[154] so donors can receive no economic aid, with the exception of the cost of the medical assistance that they need to recover from the medical intervention.

(16) UNITED KINGDOM

I. Operative Rules

The answer will be yes or no depending on the contract.

II. Descriptive Formants

The claim depends on the terms of consent when the tissue sample and personal information were first collected. If the terms provided for royalty payments, then the answer is clearly 'yes'.

---

152 A. Finžgar, *Osebnostne pravice* (Ljubljana: 1985), p. 39.
153 Official Gazette RS-MP, no. 70/1998.
154 Otherwise in Greece Marc will have a right over economic profits.

If the consent document provided no such right (quite likely), and we assume that the patent is valid (see infra discussion on Case 7, Modification 1 about morality exclusions from patentable subject matter), then the question is (1) whether there was an unlawful act under one of the statutory provisions discussed above: the Human Tissue Act, the Data Protection Act 1998/2018, or the Human Rights Act; and (2) if so, whether courts will award an account of profits as a remedy for breach of statutory duty.

III. Metalegal Formants

Consent forms usually do provide for a humble remuneration, but not by default for royalties. Yet there is no legal principle that an agreement to this effect would be valid.

D.3. COMPARATIVE REMARKS

The reporters answer the case in a ratio of 13 'no' to one 'yes' (Greece) and one 'yes/no' (the UK).

Three issues are interwoven in this case: How to delineate between property and person? What about the validity of a contract? What about 'benefit-sharing'? These questions are triggered by the famous US cases *Moore* and *Greenberg*, and the discussions as part of the European HUGO project.

For the majority, the case is governed by the principle of non-commercialisation of the person. The country reports reflect the influence of the human rights development in the 20th century, which crowded out earlier proprietary default rules. Yet there is dividedness with regard to the destiny of contracts. The Belgian, Danish and Czech (and Italian under certain conditions) reports hold the no-financial-gains principle to be absolute and therefore contracts infringing this principle to be invalid; Poland, Greece and the UK hold them to be valid. To be distinguished is the question of benefit-sharing. *Topos* and concept have triumphed under the Convention on Biological Diversity (which is, however, not applicable to human resources). But while the quest was taken up by the HUGO project, no legally binding rules have emerged (discussed in the Belgian, French, German and Italian reports). The notion is felt to collide with the proprietary concepts of patents, which assign all profits exclusively to the patent holder (cf. Slovenian and Polish reports).

The Greek and the UK reports rest on the notion of a valid contract, based on the valid consent. While the UK report considers a possible money claim based on a breach of statutory duty, the Greek report considers an entitlement: where consent and contract are lacking, the money claim may be based on unjust enrichment.

E.1. MODIFICATION 4

Is Marc entitled to obtain the product free of charge? Does PhC have a right to claim money from Marc for selling him the product?

E.2. COUNTRY REPORTS

(1) BELGIUM

I. Operative Rules

No, Marc is not entitled to obtain the vaccine free of charge. PhC has a right to claim money for selling it to him.

II. Descriptive Formants

There is no rule in Belgian patent law on which a claim to obtain the vaccine for free could be founded. Nor would Marc's personality rights be a suitable ground for such a claim.

In a similar context, it is worth mentioning that Article 19 of the Clinical Experiment Directive[155] and Article 24(7) of the Experiments on Human Persons Act provide for free provision of experimental medicines for patients participating in an experiment *during* the experiment.

III. Metalegal Formants

Remuneration for participation does not imply 'free access to the result'.

(2) CZECH REPUBLIC

I. Operative/Descriptive/Metalegal Rules

Current Czech law does not include any legal rule which could be applied to support Marc to obtain the product free of charge. In addition, to obtain the product for free would be deemed to be against the principle of non-commercialisation of the human body, as mentioned above.

---

155 Directive 2001/20/EC of the European Parliament and of the Council of 4 April 2001 on the approximation of the laws, regulations and administrative provisions of the Member States relating to the implementation of good clinical practice in the conduct of clinical trials on medicinal products for human use, OJ L 121, 1 May 2001, 34–44.

Marc is not entitled to obtain the product free of charge and PhC has a right to claim money from Marc for selling him the product.

(3) DENMARK

I. Operative Rules

Marc is not entitled to obtain the product free of charge. PhC has a right to claim money from Marc.

II. Descriptive/Metalegal Formants

There is no legal foundation in Danish patent law for claims of this kind; see also Modification 3 above.

(4) ESTONIA

I. Operative Rules

Marc cannot demand the product free of charge.

II. Descriptive Formants

The general legal framework on these issues is established by the Biomedicine Convention. Pursuant to Article 21 of the Biomedicine Convention, '[t]he human body and its parts shall not, as such, give rise to financial gain'.

It could be assumed that if there is no agreement concerning Marc's right to receive some compensation, then probably he could not claim any. The legal validity of a contract between PhC and Marc entitling Marc to some share of the benefits is a controversial issue. Section 86 of the General Part of the Civil Code Act provides that '[a] transaction which is contrary to good morals or public order is void'. Section 87 of the General Part of the Civil Code Act provides additionally that '[a] transaction contrary to a prohibition arising from law is void if the purpose of the prohibition is to render the transaction void upon violation of the prohibition, especially if it is provided by law that a certain legal consequence must not arise'. It is not clear how these provisions would be applied if the above-mentioned contract between PhC and Marc had been disputed.

Since nothing in this case indicates that there is any agreement according to which PhC is obliged to pay any compensation, Marc is not entitled to claim any.

III. Metalegal Formants

It has been noted that Estonian law does not regulate explicitly the legal status of human tissue. In principle, property law regulations are applicable. Still, fundamental rights such as human dignity and free self-realisation which form a basis for bodily self-determination have to be honoured. This means that a person has the right to determine the future of his/her removed tissue.[156]

It is also important to bear in mind that inducing a person to donate tissue could be a criminal offence. Section 140 of the Penal Code provides that:

> Inducing a person to consent to the removal of his or her organs or tissue for the purposes of transplantation or genetic research by offering material remuneration or causing damage to the person or by threatening to cause damage to the person is punishable by a pecuniary punishment or up to one year of imprisonment.

(5) FRANCE

I. Operative Rules

Marc has no right to free access to the product

II. Descriptive Formants

Non-commercialisation of the human body
As mentioned in the previous question, no remuneration may be granted to a person who consents to an experiment on him/herself, to the taking of elements from his/her body or to the collection of therefrom. Any form of remuneration should not be granted, except for some small compensation for expenses. Obtaining the product free of charge can be considered as a sort of remuneration. Therefore, Marc is not entitled to obtain the product free of charge.

Moreover, according to Articles L. 611-1 and L. 611-6 of the Intellectual Property Code, the inventor or his/her successor have exclusive rights to the invention, including receiving the profits produced from the invention. Therefore, PhC has a right to claim money from Marc for selling him the product.

III. Metalegal Formants

The remuneration principle does not extend to the future product.

---

156 A. Nõmper, J. Sootak, 'Meditsiiniõigus' (Medical law), (2007) *Juura*, Õigusteabe AS, pp. 162–163.

(6) GERMANY

I. Operative Rules

Marc has neither a claim to demand the (free) delivery of a product nor a defence against the claim for the purchase price.

II. Descriptive Formants

The personality right covers neither access to products produced with the help of the product nor any other sort of benefit-sharing.

III. Metalegal Formants

Hitherto, benefit-sharing in human research has only been discussed as either financial benefits (fed into a fund, like the HUGO proposal) or as financial allowances or a non-financial little something for participating in research given to the patient. Any other schemes of cost/benefit-sharing have been met with resistance as they conflict with the non-commercialisation principle.

(7) GREECE

I. Operative Rules

Since Marc is not named as co-inventor, he has no right to enjoy *gratis* the products of the invention.

II. Descriptive Formants

Marc has in any event a right of cognisance (i.e. exhibition) as against PhC of the new product within the framework of the right, according to Article 11 Law 2472/1997, to be informed as the subject as against the person responsible for the processing of his data. However, simple knowledge naturally does not include the physical use (free of charge) and enjoyment of the product in question. Since according to his contract with PhC Marc is not named as co-inventor, he has no right to enjoy *gratis* the products of the invention and he has to pay in order to buy them.

III. Metalegal Formants

The remuneration principle does not extend to the future product.

(8) IRELAND

Answer omitted.

(9) ITALY

I. Operative Rules

Marc is not entitled *per se* to obtain the product free of charge; this sum could be implied in the general damage award.

II. Descriptive/Metalegal Formants

See the report on the base case.

(10) LITHUANIA

I. Operative Rules

Marc has neither a claim for free delivery of a product nor a defence against a claim for the purchase price.

II. Descriptive Formants

From the personal right, no positive claims for particular benefits can be derived.

III. Metalegal Formants

The essential issue in the given situation concerns the scope of a person's rights regarding his/her genetic information. In the Lithuanian legal system, there is hardly any specific regulation addressing this; therefore, the general principles concerning a person's right to inviolability and integrity of his/her body and the right to the inviolability of his/her private life, as well as the regulation of biomedical research, apply. The person's right to determine the scope of the use of his/her genetic data and his/her participation in the research is exercised by giving consent. The principle of informed consent is mainly analysed from the ethical point of view, where the importance of adhering to this principle is stressed.[157]

---

157 E. Gefenas, 'Biomedicinių tyrimų etika' (Ethics of Biomedical Research), available at: http://bioetika.sam.lt/index.php?-278215049#11; V. Kučinskas, D. Steponavičiūtė, G. Andriulionis, 'The value of free and informed consent in personalising medicine (review)', *Acta Medica Lituanica*, 2005, vol. 2, No. 4, pp. 1–12.

Accordingly, to date, only in few instances of scholarly writing has the importance of a person's consent to participate in biomedical research been touched on. However, the modalities of a person's right in genetic information, and how far this right may reach, as well as the problem of the possible economical exploitation of human genetic information, were not considered. Therefore, it is not clear what legal consequences there would be for non-compliance with the *ethical* principle of obtaining informed consent (or its scope) from the person whose genetic information is concerned.

(11) NETHERLANDS

I. Operative/Descriptive/Metalegal Rules

Marc is not entitled to obtain the product free of charge.

(12) NORWAY

I. Operative Rules

Marc is not entitled to obtain the product free of charge.

II. Descriptive/Metalegal Formants

There is no legal foundation in Norwegian patent law for claims of this kind; see also Modification 3 above.

(13) POLAND

I. Operative Rules

No, Marc is not entitled to obtain the product free of charge.

II. Descriptive Formants

Once more, a special legal ground would have to exist in order to equip Marc with a right to demand that PhC give him the product free of charge, and no such provisions are to be found in Polish law.

III. Metalegal Formants

One may generally refer to what has been said above, noticing of course that the present question goes much farther as far as ethical considerations are concerned. Because of undeniable moral unease, it would be possible to hold under Polish law that PhC's claim for payment should be dismissed as abusive (abuse of right – Art. 5 Civil Code). Unfortunately, it is generally held that the concept of an abuse of right may only serve as a defence. In other words, a civil law claim may not be based on Article 5 Civil Code, but one may defend oneself against claims invoking abuse of right. Therefore, Marc could not use this construct to make PhC provide him with the medicine free of charge.

(14) SLOVENIA

I. Operative Rules

Marc is not entitled to obtain the product free of charge from PhC.

II. Descriptive Formants

Neither personality rights nor non-pecuniary rights entitle Marc to claim the product free of charge. Such a claim would fall under the category of pecuniary gain for donated body parts and tissue, which is in conflict with the notion of donating (gratuitous gift) as well as the principle of non-commercialisation of human body parts as described in Modification 3 above.

If PhC sells the product to Marc, it has the right to demand payment according to the provisions of the law of the contract (Art. 435 CO), as Marc does not have the right to claim the product free of charge.

III. Metalegal Formants

The remuneration principle has to do with the protection of the person, but nothing to do with the developed product.

(15) SPAIN

I. Operative Rules

Marc has neither a claim to demand free delivery of the product nor a defence against a claim for the purchase price.

II. Descriptive Formants

Article 7 of Law 14/2007 stipulates that all donations are governed by the principle of gratuitousness, so donors can receive no economic aid, with the exception of the cost of the medical assistance that they need to recover from the medical intervention.

Article 18 of the same Law guarantees that any damages sustained as a result of participating in a research project that involves an invasive procedure will be covered by a private insurance policy and a system of joint liability of the leading researcher and the hospital or centre in which the research was carried out, when the insurance coverage does not fully cover the damages sustained. As an extra guarantee, compensation for the damages is provided by establishing a *iuris tantum* presumption that the damages are the consequence of the research, as long as they affect the health of the donor and become apparent during the subject's participation or the following year (Art. 18.4).

Therefore, Marc cannot use this law to demand any economic compensation for the donation and use of his biological materials, which are defined in Article 3 as any biological material of human origin that can be conserved, and which can contain information about the genetic endowment characteristic of a person. Likewise, the aforementioned precept stipulates that the donation implies that the donor renounces any claim of an economic or other nature over the results that may derive directly or indirectly from the research carried out on these biological materials.

III. Metalegal Formants

The remuneration principle is bound to the person, and does not extend to the future product developed by someone else.

(16) UNITED KINGDOM

I. Operative Rules

Marc has no claim.

II. Descriptive Formants

There is no basis in UK law for Marc to enforce such an argument. In contrast, he would be guilty of theft if he manages to take a vaccine from its owner (e.g. a doctor, a pharmacist or PhC) without paying for it. There is no legal action upon which the courts would order provision of a product free of charge. Such an outcome can only be negotiated by the parties and agreed contractually.

III. Metalegal Formants

English law does not acknowledge a moral duty to participants beyond remuneration other than those contractually agreed upon.

E.3. COMPARATIVE REMARKS

The operative formants provide for 14 'no' answers, and one 'yes' (Italy). While this result seems to reflect a rather firm legal stance, the answers reveal unease (namely Lithuania, Poland). While the preceding Modification 3 was geared towards a financial remuneration which is in conflict with the non-commercialisation principle, Modification 4 raises the question of non-financial benefits of study participants with a *sine qua non* contribution to the later product. The standing law is clear: the proprietary patent cuts off the link to input contributions. All financial gains are assigned to the patent holder, justified by the remuneration and incentive doctrines. Yet some reports refer to criminal law (Estonia), or to remedies and restitution (the provision of the final product can be part of it: this is the Italian report's technical response).

CASE 8. THE HUMAN BODY AS REPLICATOR

A.1. CASE

Amelie underwent gene therapy. As a result of the successful treatment, she is now producing a protein in her bone marrow that is patented by the company Cellgene. Does Cellgene have the right to prevent Amelie from giving her blood away for free?

A.2. COUNTRY REPORTS

(1) BELGIUM

I. Operative Rules

No, Cellgene cannot prevent Amelie from giving her blood away for free.

II. Descriptive Formants

It is not allowed for donors to make profit by donating their blood, on the basis of Article 5 of the Blood and Blood Derivatives Act.[1]

Therefore, it is excluded in any case that Amelie would be allowed to commercially exploit her blood.

However, depending on the specific circumstances of the case, it might be conceivable that Amelie's donations would fall under the private use and the research exemptions, as expressed in Article 28(1)(a) and (b) BPA (Art. XI.34§1 a) and b) BCEL). In addition, with regard to the proteins produced by Amelie's body, Cellgene's patent might be exhausted on the basis of Article 10 Biotechnology Directive (Art. 27quater BPA, now Art. XI.32 BCEL):

> The protection referred to in Articles 8 and 9 (Arts. XI.30 and XI.31 BCEL) shall not extend to biological material obtained from the propagation or multiplication

[1] Blood and Blood Derivatives Act, 5 July 1994, *Official Gazette*, 8 October 1994 [Wet 5 juli 1994 betreffende bloed en bloedderivaten van menselijke oorsprong, *B.S.*, 8 oktober 1994]. On the no-commercialisation principle of human body material, see Case 7.

> of biological material placed on the market in the territory of a Member State by the holder of the patent or with his consent, where the multiplication or propagation necessarily results from the application for which the biological material was marketed, provided that the material obtained is not subsequently used for other propagation or multiplication.

Even if Amelie's donations fall outside the scope of the exemptions above, Cellgene could not forbid her to donate blood.

III. Metalegal Formants

The right to self-determination over one's body is a widely accepted principle in Belgium.[2] It means that nobody can control someone else's body, or that everybody has the right to freely use his/her body.[3] This right is in no way absolute, but it does include the possibility of blood transfer/donation.[4] Everyone has the right to choose to donate blood or not, provided he/she respects the provisions of the Blood and Blood Derivatives Act. We take the view that the existence of a patent cannot limit this absolutely fundamental personality right. As a result of the treatment, certain proteins have been incorporated in Amelie's blood. The fact that these proteins are patented should not lead to the conclusion that Amelie would have fewer personality rights on her blood than others. Article 5 of the Patient's Rights Act stipulates that the patient has a right to medical treatment in full respect of his/her dignity and self-determination. Agreeing to a certain medical treatment should not have the consequence that his/her personality rights are limited. Suggesting the opposite might come down to an abuse of right, since it could be argued that thus exercising a patent perverts patent law by using it to limit personality rights to an extent contrary to *ordre public* or morality.[5]

(2) CZECH REPUBLIC

I. Operative Rules

Cellgene has no right to forbid Amelie to give her blood away for free.

---

2 P. Senaeve, *Compendium van het personen- en familierecht [Compendium of Persons and Family Law]* (Leuven/Leusden: 2003), 179.

3 Y.-H. Leleu and G. Genicot, 'La maîtrise de son corps par la personne' [The Person's Control over His Body], 5937 *J.T.* 1999, 591–594.

4 P. Senaeve, *Compendium van het personen- en familierecht [Compendium of Persons and Family Law]* (Leuven/Leusden: 2003), 186–199.

5 On the abuse of right theory in relation to patents, see: M. Buydens, *Droit des brevets d'invention et protection du savoir-faire [Patent and Protection of Know-how Law]* (Brussels: 1999), 236–241.

II. Descriptive Formants

First of all, we must consult in this case the Czech Charter of Fundamental Rights and Freedoms, which says that no one shall be subjected to humiliating treatment (Art. 7(2)) and that everyone has right to keep his/her personal honour and human dignity (Art. 10(1)). In addition, protection of civic honour and human dignity is granted by section 11 of the Civil Code. If Cellgene asks the court for an injunction to prohibit Amelie from giving her blood away, the above-mentioned arguments will be enough to dismiss an injunction. To prohibit someone from giving his/her blood away would be considered to be a humiliating treatment and against someone's human dignity and civic honour.

Applying the Patent Act[6] yields the same result. Section 13 Patent Act says *inter alia* that the rights of the proprietor of the patent shall not be infringed by use of the protected invention in acts done for non-commercial purposes. The literature often gives pedagogical purposes as an example of a non-commercial purpose.[7] Giving blood is a non-commercial purpose as well – there is no remuneration at present in the Czech Republic for giving blood.

Reading the Patent Act and the provisions of section 13[8] on the breach of the rights of the patent owner, we can see that the condition for a breach of patent rights is will or intention (in the meaning of to do something, e.g. to make something), and Amelie's body is producing the gene irrespective of her will and intention.

III. Metalegal Formants

In the Czech Republic, it is a basic principle that blood is given for free – the donor does not receive any remuneration for it. The underlying idea is that giving blood is a civic honour. The notion of self-determinacy is secondary. More important are the ideas of ethics, reciprocity and solidarity under liberal

---

6 Act on Inventions and Rationalisations Proposals 527/1990 Coll.

7 R. Horáček, K. Čada, P. Hajn, *Práva k průmyslovému vlastnictví* (Rights to the Industrial Property) (1st ed., Prague: 2005), p. 62.

8 Section 13 reads:

'Nobody shall be allowed without the consent of the proprietor of the patent,

a) to make, offer, put on the market or use a product which is the subject-matter of the patent, or to import or stock the product for this purpose, or to dispose with it by another manner;
b) to use a process which is the subject-matter of the patent or to offer the process for use;
c) to offer, put on the market, use or import or stock for this purpose the product obtained directly by a process, which is the subject-matter of the patent; identical products shall be held to have been obtained by means of the process, which is the subject-matter of the patent, when it is highly probable that the product was obtained by means of the process, which is the subject-matter of the patent, and in spite of reasonable effort, the proprietor of the patent was not able to determinate the really used process; unless the contrary is proved. In proving the contrary, rights conferred by the trade secret protection shall be respected.'

ideals since Kant. The Kantian Imperative requires: 'I behave as I expect others to treat me'. Thus, the societal expectation to give blood ensures that blood is available for all.

(3) DENMARK

I. Operative Rules

No, Cellgene has no right to forbid Amelie to give her blood away for free.

II. Descriptive Formants

According to DPA §3, third paragraph, no. 1, exploitation outside the course of professional activity is not covered by the scope of the patent holder's exclusive rights. For that reason alone, Cellgene cannot object to Amelie giving away her blood for free. It is therefore unnecessary to deal with the issue of whether Amelie is even entitled to charge money for the blood.

III. Metalegal Formants

As in Norwegian law, Danish patent law does not cover private purpose acts like the one in question. The rationale behind the law is that blood is special – no 'commodity' – thus not an object of private transactions, but rather a collective good. Patent claims are conceived as belonging to (and confined to) the commercial world of transactions. The (private) disposition of one's own blood is not covered by the commercial entitlements.

(4) ESTONIA

I. Operative Rules

Cellgene cannot prevent Amelie from donating blood.

II. Descriptive Formants

It is assumed that Cellgene has a valid patent on biological material. Clause 2 of §15(1) Patent Act provides that:

> The exclusive right of the proprietor of a patent means that during the period of validity of the patent and without the permission of the proprietor of the patent no person shall manufacture, use, distribute, sell or offer for sale products protected

> by the patent or acquire (incl. by way of importation) such products for the aforementioned purposes.

This provision, however, should be interpreted in the light of the Directive on the legal protection of biotechnological inventions[9] to determine the exact scope of protection of Cellgene's patent.

In addition, the Patent Act provides that the private non-commercial use of the patented invention does not constitute infringement of the exclusive right of the proprietor of a patent if such use does not harm the interests of the proprietor of the patent (§16 clause 5 Patent Act). The Patent Act does not define the concept of 'private use'. It could be assumed that the private use exception is applicable only if a patented invention is used by a physical person. A controversial issue relating to the private use exception is the question of whether it entitles to use a patented invention only by a physical person him/herself or the use could involve several people. It can be presumed that the private use exception is not limited to only one individual. However, it should be determined on the merits of each case.

According to the Patent Act, the private use exception is not allowed if it harms the interests of the proprietor of the patent (§16 clause 5 Patent Act). In the present case, Cellgene should show how the donation of blood by Amelie harms its interests.

It should be noted that fundamental rights such as human dignity should not be ignored when determining the exact scope of the patent owner's rights and applicability of the private use exception. Based on the above, it could be assumed that the private use exception allows Amelie give blood.

III. Metalegal Formants

Another question is whether Amelie could sell her blood. Pursuant to §3 of the Handling and Transplantation of Cells, Organs and Tissues Act,[10] '[o]ffering reward or seeking financial gain for the donation of cells, tissues or organs shall be prohibited'. Offering reward for the donation of cells, tissues or organs constitutes a criminal offence and seeking financial gain is a misdemeanour.

Section 140 of the Penal Code provides that:

> Inducing a person to consent to the removal of his or her organs or tissue for the purposes of transplantation or genetic research by offering material remuneration

---

9 Directive 98/44/EC of the European Parliament and of the Council of 6 July 1998 on the legal protection of biotechnological inventions, OJ L 213, 30 July 1998, 13–21.

10 Rakkude, kudede ja elundite käitlemise ja siirdamise seadus. Entered into force on 1 September 2002 – RT I 2002, 21, 118; 2008, 25, 163 (in Estonian). Official text available at https://www.riigiteataja.ee/ert/act.jsp?id=12980151 (6 May 2019).

or causing damage to the person or by threatening to cause damage to the person is punishable by a pecuniary punishment or up to one year of imprisonment.

Pursuant to §17 of the Handling and Transplantation of Cells, Organs and Tissues Act, '[d]onation of cells, tissues or organs, if the donor or his or her legal representative has derived financial gain for it, is punishable by a fine of up to 300 fine units'.

(5) FRANCE

I. Operative Rules

Cellgene has no right to forbid Amelie to give her blood away for free.

II. Descriptive Formants

Article 16 of French Civil Code provides a legal basis for personality rights and the autonomy of the human body. In particular Article 16-1 paragraph 3 states that 'the human body, its elements and its products may not form the subject of a patrimonial right'.

Moreover, patent law offers an exclusive right to the owner of an invention. Any violation of the rights as set forth in Articles L. 613-3 to L. 613-6 shall constitute an infringement and should be prohibited. In this case, Amelie's giving blood does not constitute an infringement according to the aforementioned article, since she did not produce, use or sell the 'patented product'.

Therefore, Cellgene has no right to forbid Amelie to give her blood away for free.

III. Metalegal Formants

The principle of non-commercialisation of the human body and non-remuneration for a donation governs the case. Based on these rules, the distribution and utilisation of blood and its components is possible for research purposes.[11] Patent law respects this limit.

(6) GERMANY

I. Operative Rules

Cellgene cannot impede Amelie from giving her blood away for free.

[11] Bioethics Act of 2004, No. 2004-800, Art. 8, 4°; Public Health Code, Art. L. 1221-8-1.

II. Descriptive Formants

Regulatory law requires that the donation of blood shall be without remuneration. Only expense allowances are granted to the extent that the direct investment, time and effort are acknowledged (§10 Transfusionsgesetz of 1998 originally, newly issued 28 August 2007, BGBl. I S. 2169, last amendment 2019).

An injunction on the basis of §9 German Patent Act would require that Amelie 'uses' the patented technology. On this statutory level, one could argue that the law requires a conscious action on the part of the infringer. He/she does not need to know that he/she is violating a patent. But a person must be conscious about acting. In this sense, Amelie is not actively infringing. It is her body which produces the product with the prior informed consent of Cellgene. However, even if one argues that the law does not require a conscious action, constitutional law would bar the exercise of Cellgene's patent right. An injunction would violate Amelie's constitutional personal freedom and her human dignity. This constitutional freedom would not only encompass that Cellgene cannot stop the production of the substance in her. The non-commercialisation principle strengthens her position that she is impeded from selling her blood.

III. Metalegal Formants

Once gene therapy is successful, the non-commercialisation principle will falter. Hitherto, the non-commercialisation principle rests on the basis that the body basically functions on its own. Under this assumption, the weight of human dignity is uncompromised. However, when high investments have been made to achieve a specific result in one individual body, this assumption no longer holds. Then, other parallels could be, and are to be, activated, like Article 52 European Patent Convention, which excludes surgical and therapeutic practices from patentability, and Article 1 German Constitution (human dignity). Investments are otherwise to be recouped.

(7) GREECE

I. Operative Rules

Cellgene has no right to forbid Amelie to give her blood anyway she likes; however, it may claim a sum of money as compensation from Amelie or as unjust enrichment from third parties who received the blood.

II. Descriptive Formants

The combined application of Article 9 and Article 5(1) Biotechnology Directive (= Presidential Decree 321/2001) would lead to the conclusion that substances produced in the human body are not covered by patent, even if they are the direct products of a patented gene. Additionally, by way of deviation from the prevailing (and unconvincing) opinion[12] that tissues removed do not constitute things in law, but simply residues of the personality of their bearer, blood is correctly described as a moveable thing within the meaning of Article 947 Civil Code.[13] However, this does not mean that it is capable of having a real right (e.g. of pledge), nor that it is freely transferable, nor – *a fortiori* – that all promissory contracts concerning it are valid, since any such contract of transfer (and *a fortiori* of trading) of human tissue is subject to stricter control in view of the good morals prevailing for the time being (Art. 178 Civil Code).

In view of the above, the discoverer of the substance which today flows in the bloodstream of Amelie has no property right over it either before or (*a fortiori*) after its removal from the body. The opposite would grossly offend against the constitutional right of each person to *habeas corpus* (Art. 6 Constitution). Thus, in any event, Amelie's blood belongs only to her, and she alone can dispose of it as she pleases. Consequently, no claim can be founded which would oblige the individual to make available or not make available his/her blood at will.

The above conclusion is also reinforced by the following more general observations. To the extent that biopatents are recognised by Presidential Decree 321/2001 (= Biotechnology Directive), Cellgene has, in accordance with Article 10 para. 1(c) of Law 1733/1987, the exclusive right of disposal of the products of the invention. This is a case of power over the economic exploitation of a non-material good (the invention), and in my opinion should not be confused with the real right of ownership over the individual products, since these constitute 'things' in law within the meaning of Article 947 Civil Code.[14] This is just like how the creator's right of intellectual property of the creator should not be confused with ownership of the material vehicle of his/her work, for example the picture or the copies. It should be mentioned once more that the right of intellectual property is undivided, whereas there are as many rights of ownership as there are material vehicles.

---

12 Georgiades, *The Law of Real Property I* (1991), §8, nos. 10–12; Sourlas, *ΕρμΑΚ Introduction to Arts. 57–60*, nos. 46, 50, 50α; Dimakou, in: Georgiades/Stathopoulos, *AK 947*, nos. 7, 17–18 a.a.

13 Georgiades, *General Principles of Civil Law* (4th ed., 2002), §12, no. 6; Karakostas, *AK (General Principles I)* (2005), Art. 57, no. 520 a.a.

14 The prevailing opinion is to the contrary. Feuerlein, *GRUR* 2001, 564; BGH, *GRUR* 1972, 541; BGH, *GRUR* 1996, 109; Mikroulea, *EEmpD* 2000, 279.

III. Metalegal Formants

Over and above the – in principle – groundless requirement of the prohibition of the individual from disposing freely of his/her blood, other pecuniary claims of third parties in connection with the enrichment of people from the biochemical substances of their body which are derived from their own scientific activity should not be precluded. Whether or not the enrichment in question is justified depends, naturally, on the validity of the contract between the discoverer and the person who perceived the invention in his/her body. In greater detail:

- If there is express provision in the contract for freedom of the perceiver to trade the invention, then he/she will owe only the agreed consideration. If the consideration has not been determined, the discoverer will be entitled to determine it according to his/her reasonable judgement by a unilateral declaration to the producer, since in the event of doubt, the contract is not a donation (Art. 496 Civil Code).
- If, again, a valid contract between the producer and the discoverer is totally lacking, then the discoverer will, of course, have a right for compensation against Amelie (as the manager of Cellgene's affairs according to Arts. 719, 734 Civil Code). Concurrently, it may have claim for unjust enrichment as against third parties who have received Amelie's blood *gratis* in relation to the property benefit which they have derived from Cellgene's invention according to Articles 904, 913 Civil Code.

(8) IRELAND

Answer omitted.

(9) ITALY

I. Operative Rules

Cellgene has no right to forbid Amelie from giving her blood away for free.

II. Descriptive Formants

The patent owner has, in general, the right to commercially exploit the invention (Art. 66 d.lgs. 30/2005, Industrial Property Code). Therefore, he/she can forbid any interference with the protected field of activity. In particular, if the invention consists of a process, he/she has a right of veto regarding the application of the process and the disposition of the resulting products (Art. 66, II, b Industrial Property Code). However, this monopoly right is not unlimited.

According to Article 68, I, a Industrial Property Code, the patent does not confer the right to forbid 'pure private acts not made for profit'.[15] This seems to be the case here. It is worth asking whether the solution would be different had Amelie given her blood away for profit. This scenario, however, is not realistic, since the Italian legislation expressly forbids any monetary gain from donation of blood and any other body parts and tissues (see Arts. 2 and 4 l. 219/2005).

It is worth noting that the patentability of any biotech invention is subject to the general requirement that its commercial exploitation should not go against human dignity and public policy (Art. 4 d.l. 1 January 2006, no. 3). Giving a right of veto to a patent owner in our hypothetical case would imply a strong limitation on the fundamental freedom to do with one's body as one wishes; hence, the principle of respect of human dignity would be seriously violated. Therefore, no injunction could be granted by any Italian court to Cellgene.

III. Metalegal Formants

It is necessary to consider that the implementation of the Biotechnology Directive has been quite complicated and has had to overcome many obstacles.[16] Italy was one of the countries that challenged the Directive before the European Court of Justice, assuming that it violated the principle of human dignity and equitable access to genetic resources.[17] It is not by chance that in d.l. 1 January 2006, no. 3 much weight is given to the principle of human dignity and to the goal of avoiding overreaching patent protection.[18] Therefore, it is likely that in the construction of such a statute, judges will be suspicious of any claim by a patentee that conflicts with personality rights.

(10) LITHUANIA

I. Operative Rules

No, Cellgene does not have the right to prevent Amelie from giving her blood away for free.

---

15 See Scuffi, Franzosi, Fittante, *Il codice della proprietà industriale* (Padova: 2005), p. 368; Marchetti, Ubertazzi, *Commentario breve al diritto della concorrenza* (Padova: 2004), p. 719.

16 See Nurra, 'Il recepimento della direttiva comunitaria 98/44/CE sulla protezione legale delle invenzioni biotecnologiche', (2006) *Cont. Imp. Eur.*, p. 609.

17 CJEU judgment of 9 October 2001, *Netherlands v. Parliament and Council*, C-377/98, ECLI:EU:C:2001:523.

18 See Montoleone, 'Protezione giuridica delle invenzioni biotecnologiche e tutela della persona', (2006) *Dir. ind.*, pp. 405 ff.

II. *Descriptive Formants*

The situation can be considered from several perspectives. First, evaluated from a patent law perspective, arguably the actions of Amelie fall under the limitation of the patent holder's right established by Article 35(3) of the Lithuanian Patent Law. This legal provision states that the proprietor of the patent shall have no right to prevent third parties from performing acts which are done privately and for non-commercial purposes and it does not significantly prejudice the economic interests of the proprietor of the patent. The donation of blood is a private and clearly non-commercial act, which does not significantly prejudice the economic interests of the proprietor of the patent. Because of that it falls outside the scope of patent holders' rights.

Secondly, one has to take into account the regulation of blood donation in Lithuania. Lithuanian Civil Code in Article 2.25(5) states: 'The human body, its parts or organs and tissues may not become subjects of commercial contracts. Such contracts shall be deemed null and void.' This provision establishes the general principle prohibiting commercial transactions with one's own body and its parts. Further, blood donation is regulated by the special Law on Blood Donation,[19] which also implements Directive 2002/98/EC of the European Parliament and of the Council of 27 January 2003 setting standards of quality and safety for the collection, testing, processing, storage and distribution of human blood and blood components and amending Directive 2001/83/EC. The Law on Blood Donation clearly indicates that blood donation is a socially beneficial and encouraged activity. The said Law heavily relies on the principle of non-remuneration (Art. 3). These provisions further support the interpretation above, that Amelie's actions cannot be considered commercial activity. In fact, Article 7 of the Law on Blood Donation foresees compensation for donors, although this compensation is considered to be not remuneration for the donor's blood, but instead compensation for the donor's travel and supplementary nourishment expenses. Such compensation is considered not to be contradictory to the general non-remuneration principle.[20]

Last but not least, one should take into account fundamental rights such as the respect for private life and dignity (Arts. 21 and 22 of the Constitution of the Republic of Lithuania). The right to give or not to give away blood is part of a person's self-determination. Expanding the patent holder's right to also cover the possibility to prevent a physical person from giving his/her blood would amount to a very serious intervention in his/her private sphere and clash with the aforementioned human rights. On the other hand, having direct

---

19 Law on Blood Donation of the Republic of Lithuania, 1996, No. I-1611.

20 V. Mikelėnas et al., *Commentary on the Civil Code of the Republic of Lithuania. Bock Second: Law of Persons* (Vilnius: 2002), p. 78.

recourse to human rights is not so indispensable, because the conflict between fundamental rights and patent holders' rights can be balanced using the private use exception, as discussed above.

III. Metalegal Formants

Like in many other European countries (including Estonia, Denmark and Italy), Lithuanian patent law provides a personal use exception, which limits the rights of patent holder. This exception is flexible enough to neutralise the possible negative consequences for personal rights arising from the Cellgene patent.

(11) NETHERLANDS

I. Operative Rules

Cellgene has no right unless Amelie had signed a contract with terms to this effect.

II. Descriptive Formants

Amelie is free to decide to donate blood. She might decide not to give blood to blood collectors if they cannot confirm her restrictions on the way the blood is going to be used. The Rules of Accession, Confusion and Specification (Arts. 5:14–16 Dutch Civil Code) will make Amelie the owner of the material within the private property regime. The patented idea, however, will remain with Cellgene, which is protected by patent law against blood collectors that want to take advantage. Cellgene will have an action against the blood collectors in the event that they harvest, use and commercialise the patented protein.

III. Metalegal Formants

Cellgene, as a commercial company, should not restrict the right of a purchaser who paid for the product (ceded to the health insurance company). The rationale in Dutch law is separate spheres of disposition. Patent law shall be confined to the commercial world. Once a product 'leaves' the commercial sphere and is sold to the end consumer, the manufacturer loses all influence over the product.

(12) NORWAY

I. Operative Rules

No, Cellgene has no right to forbid Amelie from giving her blood away for free.

II. Descriptive Formants

According to NPA §3, third paragraph, no. 1, exploitation outside the course of professional activity falls outside the scope of the patent holder's exclusive rights. For the reason above, Cellgene cannot object to Amelie giving away her blood for free. It is therefore unnecessary to deal with the issue of whether Amelie is even entitled to charge money for the blood.

III. Metalegal Formants

In a Norwegian legal context, the case is actually about the scope of the patent – not the conflict between property rights and human dignity. This conflict is not pushed to its extremes in Norwegian patent law since the exclusive right of exploitation does not cover private purpose acts like the one in question.

(13) POLAND

I. Operative Rules

Cellgene has no claims against Amelie.

II. Descriptive Formants

This case should not pose any problems, although no court decisions handed down in similar matters have been reported in Poland yet. The main reason why any claims by Cellgene would have to fail is that a patent is a right providing the patent owner with exclusivity with regard to the use of the invention in the course of business (Art. 63(1) IPL). Any use which is 'private', i.e. non-commercial, is by definition non-infringing. As giving blood is neither a profession nor a course of business, Amelie's actions could not be treated as relevant in the light of patent law.

III. Metalegal Formants

This case illustrates the danger of appropriating the human body by means of biotechnological inventions. Although in this very case the basic principle of patent law proves sufficient to eliminate the morally reprehensible and absurd result, one may of course envisage situations in which there will be no such obvious answers.

(14) SLOVENIA

I. Operative Rules

Cellgene does not have the right to prevent Amelie from donating her blood for free.

II. Descriptive Formants

Cellgene cannot impose any conditions regarding what Amelie does with her own body, and therefore cannot decide how the blood she has donated be used. Any such attempt would be considered a violation of Amelie's personality rights. In accordance with Article 134 of the CO, she would have the right to demand that Cellgene immediately stop all such violations. Amelie is also free to choose to donate her blood, which under Slovenian regulations can only be done gratuitously, as stated in paragraph I, Article 23 of the Supply of Blood Act.[21]

III. Metalegal Formants

Slovenian private law strictly differentiates between subjects and objects of the law, where only subjects, with the help of rights, may exercise legal authority over objects of the law (things or spiritual creations). A principle that is also valid is that each thing which is permanently united with the subject loses the characteristic of an object and becomes part of the subject (accession). For example, an artificial hip is a thing before being transplanted into a patient; afterwards, it becomes part of the patient's person and body, and therefore part of the subject. The prevention of treating a subject or parts of his/her body as an object can be directly deduced from the provision of Article 35 of the Constitution of the Republic of Slovenia, which guarantees the inviolability of the physical and mental integrity of every person, and his/her privacy and personality rights. As a result, we can determine that the company Cellgene cannot have any authoritative rights over Amelie's body or its parts. Therefore, it also does not have any industrial property rights on the proteins produced by her bone marrow, which is in her body.

(15) SPAIN

I. Operative Rules

Cellgene cannot impede Amelie from giving her blood away for free.

[21] Official Gazette RS, no. 104/2006.

II. *Descriptive Formants*

- Law 29/2006 of 26 July, on guarantees and rational use of medicines and health products;
- Royal Decree 1088/2005 of 16 September, which stipulates the technical requirements and minimal conditions for blood donation and for the centres and transfusion services;
- Patent Law 11/1986 of 20 March; and
- Royal Decree 478/1993 of 2 April, on medicines derived from blood and human plasma.

When the object of the patent is a biological material which, for the purposes of the invention, has particular properties, the rights conferred by the patent will be extended to any biological material obtained from the patented biological material by reproduction or multiplication, identical or different, and which possesses the same properties. So, in application of this rule, Cellgene, as the patent holder, has the right to prevent Amelie from commercialising her blood because it contains the protein patented by the company. It cannot, however, forbid donation.[22] This prohibition affects everyone who receives Amelie's blood.

It is worth pointing out that Spanish law, as well as the Biotechnology Directive, requires the person from whose body the material is taken to give informed consent, but this consent is not a requirement to apply for a patent and will not affect a granted patent, or an application for one.[23]

The answer to Case 7, related to informed consent, has to be considered in this case.

III. *Metalegal Formants*

The case under Spanish law is governed by the principle of non-commercialisation of the human body. It affects the person in which a substance is produced, but also the person who is given the substance. Patent law has to respect this limit.

(16) UNITED KINGDOM

I. *Operative Rules*

Cellgene has no claim against Amelie. She may give away her blood as she pleases.

---

22 The same answer is given in the Czech report.

23 By contrast, in Italy it does not seem possible to patent biotechnological inventions.

II. *Descriptive Formants*

Cellgene has obtained a patent on the protein in Amelie's bone marrow by satisfying the substantive criteria set out in the Patents Act 1977. Thus, we can assume that the requirements for a patent (novelty[24] (by way of isolation),[25] an inventive step,[26] and industrial application)[27] are met. English does not differ from the European Patent Office standard of patentability of DNA sequences (including proteins), considering them to be chemical substances, which suggests that the rules governing patent protection for chemical substances are covered.[28] Cellgene has patented the identified and isolated protein from the bone marrow of Amelie, and cannot patent the naturally occurring substance of her blood in her body.[29] We can also assume that Amelie has given her consent to the patenting of her protein. The central legal question refers to the scope of the patent's claim.

While Cellgene holds a title on how the patented protein is used, these rights may come into conflict with the rights of Amelie. Yet two opposing positions are discussed. Spranger argues that 'the protection of a patent on an isolated substance also covers the naturally occurring substance. This protection may conflict with the rights and interests of third parties, e.g. the compounds' owner.'[30] We oppose this interpretation. The distinction between 'isolation' and 'naturally occurring substances' on the level of patentability implies for the patent's scope that the patent granted over the protein in Amelie's bone marrow does not in any way cover a naturally occurring substance like blood. Amelie is the source of the patent application but cannot be deprived of her rights to use the naturally occurring substances in her body as she wishes. Thus, Amelie can give her blood away for free even though it contains a patented protein owned by Cellgene. Simply put, the patent granted to Cellgene does not extend to the naturally occurring substance of blood or the disposal of the blood containing the patented protein. If Amelie gives away her blood, this is not an infringement of the patent owner's right.

A further point to make regarding the distribution of blood is that the person or institution taking the blood may try to take the patented protein and use it in a commercial product. Although the question does not explicitly state this, it

---

24 Section 2 PA 1977.

25 Recitals 21–22 Biotechnology Directive.

26 Section 3 PA 1977.

27 Section 4 PA 1977.

28 Decision of Technical Board of Appeal 3.3.4 of 23 October 2002, *Relaxin v. Howard Florey Institute*, T-0272/95; Decision of Technical Board of Appeal 3.3.4 of 21 November 1994 *Erythropoietin v. Kirin-Amgen*, T-0412/93 [1995].

29 S.J.R. Bostyn, 'The Prodigal Son: The Relationship Between Patent Law and Health Care' (2003) 11(1) *Medical Law Review* 67.

30 T.M. Spranger, 'C-377/98, *Netherlands/Council and European Parliament*, Judgement of the CJEU of 9 October 2001' (2002) 39 *Common Market Law Review* 1147–1158.

is worth considering within its confines if such a situation were to arise. Where a person or institution wishes to use Amelie's blood in a commercial product, this could warrant an infringement of Cellgene's patent right over the protein. General remedies, in respect of this problem if it did arise, could involve an injunction to stop the protected protein being used,[31] or an action for damages[32] or an account for profits.[33] The infringement particularly depends on whether the patented gene is present in the new commercial product sold by the other company and also performs its function. The question of whether the patent protection could harm the human source of the natural product is an interesting topic, but is evidently beyond the scope and understanding of intellectual property.

III. Metalegal Formants

Patent protection is not available for products of nature and human body products in their natural environment (once identified, isolated and purified). The patent over the specific protein gives the company certain monopoly rights over it, but the naturally occurring substances in the body will remain in the control of the person. Anyone may therefore give their blood away to another person or institution. In contrast to the arguments put forward by Spranger (see supra, descriptive formants), this interpretation is the implication of principles set out in the EPC Guidelines, Biotechnology Directive and Schedule A2 PA 1977. A patent can never extend to a naturally occurring substance in the human body. Therefore, only an isolated and purified substance which is found through a technical process can be patentable, because it is slightly different from the naturally occurring substance.[34]

A.3. COMPARATIVE REMARKS

While all reports deliver pretty much the same descriptive answer ('no right' for Cellgene), the legal consideration differ, and the single Greek deviation ('no right, but …') attracts attention.

Reporters approach the (ubiquitous) principle of non-commodification of blood from different starting points, either singular or combined, patent law (Belgium, Czech Republic, Denmark, Estonia, France, Germany, Italy, Lithuania, Norway, Poland, Spain, the UK), regulatory transfusion/patient rights laws

---

31 Section 61(1)(a) PA 1977.
32 Section 61(1)(c) PA 1977.
33 Section 61(1)(d) PA 1977.
34 M.D. Davis, 'The Patenting of Products of Nature' (1995) 21 *Rutgers Computer & Technology Law Journal* 331 et seq.

(Belgium, Denmark, Estonia, Slovenia, Spain), constitutional law (Belgium, Czech Republic, Denmark, Slovenia), or civil law (Czech Republic, France, Greece, the Netherlands, Slovenia). Argumentation is either individualistic, collective or commercial. However, these differences in argumentation might be attributed to the reporter's speciality, and should therefore not be overstressed. For the purpose of the project, it is important to note that the boundary to the patent claim 'comes from the outside'. Even where the result is purely deduced from patent law ('non-commercial/private use': Denmark, Italy, Lithuania, Norway, the UK), a strong reference is made to 'human dignity' (Italy) or 'the person's autonomy' (the UK). These values, depending on the technical variation, either override (*ex post*) or prevent (*ex ante*) IP claims.

The Greek report's singularity rests on its reflection that the parties to whom the blood was given might be unjustly enriched ('no right, but ...'). The reporter reflects on the factual (contractual) conditions under which the (free) donation can result in an enrichment which can be qualified as 'unjust'.

CASE 9. CONFLICTING INTERESTS IN FAMILIES AND GROUPS IN GENOMIC INFORMATION

A.1. BASE CASE

The Miller family carries a unique gene that is somehow linked to the development of intelligence. 80% of the family enjoys an IQ of 140. The downside of the gene is shortgevity. Those carrying the gene live no longer than 42 years. Lilly, a carrier of the gene, agreed with a pharmaceutical company Genfix to undertake extended experiments on the gene. As compensation, she was promised a 1% share in all product sales made on the basis of the respective gene. Her brother William, who carries the same gene, objects. Does William have the right to veto the whole contract? Does he have the right to veto the payment of 1%?

A.2. COUNTRY REPORTS

(1) BELGIUM

I. Operative Rules

No, William probably has no enforceable right to veto the contract, although he might be able to veto the payment.

II. Descriptive Formants

The informed consent requirement for research has to be respected (see Case 7). The individual consent of Lilly Miller fulfils this requirement. However, the issue becomes somewhat more complex when groups are involved. In this regard, it is recommended by legal doctrine[1] and international declarations[2]

---

1 C. Trouet, *Van lichaam naar lichaamsmateriaal. Recht en het nader gebruik van cellen en weefsels [From Body to Human Tissue. Law and the Further Use of Cells and Tissues]* (Antwerpen/Groningen/Oxford: 2003), 487–488 and 508–509.

2 E.g. UNESCO, International Bioethics Committee, *Universal Declaration on Bioethics and Human Rights (Art. 6(3))*, 19 October 2005. Hereafter the Universal Declaration on Bioethics and Human Rights.

that some sort of consulting, informing and consent of the concerned group be sought. The fact that the family should be informed and consulted does not mean, however, that Lilly's individual consent would be invalid. She obviously has the right to donate her tissue in the hope that research on her shortgevity condition could progress.

With regard to profit-sharing, there is a problem, however. First, it is said to be a generally accepted principle that one cannot individually benefit on the grounds of having donated tissue (although modest compensation for time and expenses is allowed).[3] On the other hand, it is suggested that if biomedical research is successful thanks to certain characteristics specific to 'groups', a certain amount of benefit-sharing is acceptable.[4] Sharing with groups probably needs to be done in a more indirect way since the direct transfer of a percentage of profits might be subject to criticism and legal objections.[5] Therefore, William and the other family members might, perhaps, have the right in principle to see some of the benefits shared in an indirect way.

In a Belgian context, it will be far from easy to enforce benefit-sharing since it is not explicitly foreseen. The principle as such hardly provides for an enforceable entitlement before court, although the concepts of unjust enrichment[6] or civil liability (Art. 1382 Civil Code) could be invoked.

While enforcing the benefit-sharing principle in this context would be quite unlikely, it might be possible to hinder Lilly from receiving 1% of the profits. Since individually benefiting from the donation of one's tissue can be conceived as being contrary to *ordre public*, anyone could claim an injunction.

III. Metalegal Formants

The same conflicts as in Case 7, Modification 3 arise here, with one major difference. Although it is quite generally (though not unanimously)[7] accepted

---

3 For instance, Belgian Bio-ethical Committee [Belgisch Raadgevend Comité voor Bio-ethiek], Advice no. 5 on the Legal Protection of Biotechnological Inventions, 9 February 1998, available at: https://portal.health.fgov.be/portal/page?_pageid=56,8546420&_dad=portal&_schema=PORTAL (last consulted on 6 May 2019).

4 C. Trouet, *Van lichaam naar lichaamsmateriaal. Recht en het nader gebruik van cellen en weefsels [From Body to Human Tissue. Law and the Further Use of Cells and Tissues]* (Antwerpen/Groningen/Oxford: 2003), 476–484; WHO, Human Genetics Programma, Review of Ethical Issues in Medical Genetics. Report of Consultants to WHO Professors D.C. Wertz, J.C. Fletcher, K. Berg, 2003, DOC WHO/HGN/ETH/00.4, 87, available at: https://apps.who.int/iris/handle/10665/68512 (last consulted on 11 March 2022).

5 Art. 15 Universal Declaration on Bioethics and Human Rights; Art. 21 Convention on Human Rights and Biomedicine, 4 March 1997, ETS no. 164, http://conventions.coe.int/ (last consulted on 6 May 2019); Hugo Ethics Committee, *Statement on benefit-sharing*, 9 April 2000, available at: https://www.eubios.info/BENSHARE.htm (last consulted on 11 March 2022).

6 See, in the context of bio prospecting, G. Van Overwalle, 'Protecting and Sharing Biodiversity and Traditional Knowledge: Holders and User Tools', 53 *Ecological Economics*, 2005, 601.

7 H. Nys, 'Het nader gebruik van lichaamsmateriaal en biotechnologische uitvindingen', in: G. Van Overwalle, (ed.), *Patent Law, Ethics and Biotechnology* (Brussels: 1998), 176.

that nobody should make money from his/her tissue or genetic information as such, the prohibition is relaxed for groups, families or communities. Legal doctrine takes the view that benefits should be shared when they are based on the exploitation of genetic information specific to certain communities.[8]

(2) CZECH REPUBLIC

I. *Operative Rules*

William has neither the right to veto the contract nor the right to veto the payment.

II. *Descriptive Formants*

There is no legal rule which could be applied to support William vetoing the contract concluded between Genfix and Lilly. He would be able to refer to the protection of personality provisions of the Civil Code and its section 11, but his personality is not touched by the contract, so this reference will not be helpful. Nor is there any legal rule in the Civil Code which could be applied to veto the payment of 1%.

In this case, we cannot see a legal problem with the contract which could be used to void or veto the contract.[9]

III. *Metalegal Formants*

The principle of non-commercialisation of the human body will be argued here. But if we go through and beyond the written texts of the law prohibiting commercialisation of the human body, we cannot find any analogical provision which should be applied to veto (or to void) the contract. It is clear that the principle of non-commercialisation of the human body was developed to protect the health of people in complicated life situations – in other words, to prohibit people from selling their organs, tissues, etc. to improve their financial situation and by the same act to destroy their health. It is the same with stem cell research – the law prevents people from 'producing' embryos only with the

---

8 For more on this: C. Trouet, *Van lichaam naar lichaamsmateriaal. Recht en het nader gebruik van cellen en weefsels [From Body to Human Tissue. Law and the Further Use of Cells and Tissues]* (Antwerpen/Groningen/Oxford: 2003), 476–484.

9 According to section 39 of the Civil Code, a legal act whose content or purpose is inconsistent with an Act or circumvents the Act shall be invalid.

intention of selling them, but of course research on embryos is a very sensitive problem in and of itself.[10]

(3) DENMARK

I. Operative Rules

No, William can veto neither the contract nor the payment of 1%.

II. Descriptive Formants

The carrier of the gene, Lilly has given her express and informed consent to the use of her gene, cf. ABRECS §16, and Genfix will be entitled to undertake extended experiments on the gene. The fact that William carries the same gene has no influence on that result, the decisive factor being that the *donor* has consented to the use. On the same ground, he will not be in a position to prevent Lilly from receiving payment from her participation in the experiments as he has no legal interest in such a veto.

III. Metalegal Formants

As in Norwegian law, the right to veto use of biological material for research purposes is an individual right. Family affiliations are not relevant in this respect.

(4) ESTONIA

I. Operative Rules

Presumably, William cannot veto either the whole contract or the payment. Still, the contract could be disputed on the grounds of being contrary to good morals or violation of a prohibition arising from the law.

II. Descriptive Formants

The Estonian legislation does not have a specific regulation on the issue described by the case. It is assumed that William could claim that the genetic

---

10 See more E. Burdová, 'Klonování etické aspekty a právní úprava' (Cloning ethical aspects and legal regulation) (2004) 1 *Zdravotnické právo v praxi*, p. 10.

research may violate his right of informational self-determination[11] and the right to the inviolability of private and family life, provided for by §§19 and 26 of the Constitution of the Republic of Estonia. Still, it is not very likely that he would succeed. Therefore, it is presumed that William cannot veto either the whole contract or the payment.

III. Metalegal Formants

Lilly has given informed consent to do research on her gene. Since legal framework of genetic research is not sufficiently developed in Estonia, the principles established in the Biomedicine Convention could be used.

Pursuant to Article 21 of the Biomedicine Convention, '[t]he human body and its parts shall not, as such, give rise to financial gain'. The legal validity of a contract between Lilly and Genfix entitling Lilly to some share of benefits is a controversial issue. Section 86 of the General Part of the Civil Code Act provides that '[a] transaction which is contrary to good morals or public order is void'. Section 87 of the General Part of the Civil Code Act provides additionally that '[a] transaction contrary to a prohibition arising from law is void if the purpose of the prohibition is to render the transaction void upon violation of the prohibition, especially if it is provided by law that a certain legal consequence must not arise'. It is not clear how these provisions would be applied if the above-mentioned contract between Genfix and Lilly had been disputed.

(5) FRANCE

I. Operative Rules

William has the right to veto the payment of 1%, but he cannot veto the contract as a whole.

II. Descriptive Formants

The first Bioethics Act was enacted in France in 1988. It was updated and completed in 1994 and revised again in 2004. The resulting Act, dating from 6 August 2004, covers every field of bioethics and especially biomedical research. This law was integrated into the French Public Health Code.

---

11 For the purpose of the Constitution of the Republic of Estonia the right of informational self-determination means everyone's right to decide whether and to what extent his/her personal data is collected and maintained – E.-J. Truuväli et al. (eds.), *Eesti Vabariigi põhiseadus. Kommenteeritud väljaanne* (The Constitution of the Republic of Estonia. Commented edition) (Tallinn: 2002), pp. 160–161.

Usually, only research carried out on patients is authorised. Nevertheless, the 1994 Act included psychological, behavioural research under Articles L. 1121-3 and L. 1122-1 of the French Public Health Code. Moreover, since the aforementioned Act No. 2004-800 of 6 August 2004, relating to bioethics research and biomedical research, exceeding the therapeutic threshold, it seems that genetic research on individuals is possible. In fact, genetic research on individuals' characteristics for scientific purposes is authorised (Art. 16-10 French Civil Code) and misuse of gathered information is sanctioned under Article 226-26 of the French Criminal Code and Article L. 1132-2 of the French Public Health Code.

The Universal Declaration on the Human Genome and Human Rights (11 November 1997), in its Article 10[12] specifies that research has to be carried out with 'respect for the human rights, fundamental freedoms and human dignity of individuals'. Moreover, Article 5 of this Declaration states that these kinds of research should be 'undertaken only after rigorous and prior assessment of the potential risks and benefits pertaining thereto'.

Following this international declaration, Act No. 94-653 of 29 July 1994 includes a Chapter (III entitled 'genetic studies of individuals' characteristics and identification of individuals through genetic fingerprints'. Article 16-10[13] of the French Civil Code is now included in this Chapter.

The principle enacted by the law and expressed by the French Civil Code is the ban on proceeding with such genetic analysis and research, because of the principle of the integrity of the human body. Therefore, two conditions are absolutely necessary to carry out such studies: medical necessity and the consent of the person concerned.[14]

Moreover, Articles 16-10 and 16-11 added two new scenarios: analysis for medical purposes and genetic identification for inquiries or investigations.

Article 16-10 is not directed at the identification of individuals through genetic fingerprints and a circumvention of this principle should be sanctioned by the French Criminal Code.

---

12 No research or research applications concerning the human genome, in particular in the fields of biology, genetics and medicine, should prevail over respect for the human rights, fundamental freedoms and human dignity of individuals or, where applicable, of groups of people.

13 An examination of the genetic particulars of a person may be undertaken only for medical purposes or in the interest of scientific research. The express consent of the person must be obtained in writing before the carrying out of the examination, after he/she has been duly informed of its nature and purpose. The consent shall specify the purpose of the examination. It may be revoked without form at any time.

14 Art. 16-3 of the French Civil Code: 'There may be no invasion of the integrity of the human body except in case of medical necessity for the person or exceptionally in the therapeutic interest of others' (Act no. 2004-800 of 6 Aug. 2004). 'The consent of the person concerned must be obtained previously except when his state necessitates a therapeutic intervention to which he is not able to assent'.

Nevertheless, the final purpose of the genetic research is immaterial: the research can be carried out for industrial, commercial and personal purposes, or even for reasons pertaining to personal assets. Nevertheless, the results of the studies have to be kept confidential and cannot be used by third parties such as banks, insurance companies, employers or the state itself. The French Criminal Code bans the examination of a person's genetic characteristics for purposes other than medical or scientific research, or for medical or scientific research purposes without having first obtained his/her consent under the conditions provided for in Article 16-10 of the Civil Code. It also prohibits circumventing the original medical or scientific purpose for the purpose of seeking to identify a person by genetic fingerprinting (Art. 226-28 French Criminal Code; Art. L. 145-20 French Public Health Code, which provides for a fine of up to €100,000 and one years' imprisonment).

It must be noted that in the case of an illegal contract, for example an unauthorised analysis, this contract would be declared null and void for reasons of *ordre public* (Art. 6 of the French Civil Code) and for having an illicit object. Moreover, the offenders could be subject to disciplinary and/or administrative sanctions.

Therefore, genetic research is authorised in France even where this research does not have as its only purpose medical or scientific aims. In order for this research to be carried out, the individual whose genetic material is the subject of the research has to give his/her consent (Art. L. 209-9 of the French Public Health Code, sanctioned by Art. 223-8 of the French Criminal Code). This consent has to be written and signed by the individual (Art. L. 145-15 al. 2 French Public Health Code).

Another aspect of genetic research should be considered; this aspect is guided by another principle of French law: the ban on commercial transactions whose object is the human body.[15] Moreover, agreements/contracts attributing a commercial value to the human body are no longer valid (for example, the taking of elements from a body to the collection of products therefrom).[16] The different statutory provisions refer to any form of payment, but only to payment agreed on before the collection of the bodily material. Expenses relating to the research can nevertheless be reimbursed (Art. L. 1211-4 of the French Public Health Code), notably travel and accommodation expenses and loss of salary (Art. R. 665-70-1 of the French Public Health Code). Moreover, both the fact of buying products originating from the human body and the fact of selling products originating from the human body are criminally sanctioned.

---

15 Art. 16-6 of the French Civil Code: 'No remuneration may be granted to a person who consents to an experimentation on himself, to the taking of elements off his body or to the collection of products thereof'.

16 Art. 16-5 of the French Civil Code: 'Agreements that have the effect of bestowing a patrimonial value on the human body, its elements or products are void'.

In our case, Lilly agreed to undertake extended experiments on the gene she carries. She was promised, as compensation, a 1% share in all sales made on the basis of the gene.

III. Metalegal Formants

Experiments on genes are possible, but no remuneration can be obtained either in exchange for these experiments or for the collection of products issuing from the body, such as genes or cells. A payment of 1% of the proceeds would violate the non-commercialisation principle and can be sanctioned under the French Criminal Code. In addition, any contract is immune against the interests of third parties, and modern law considers family members to be 'third parties'.

(6) GERMANY

I. Operative Rules

William has neither a right to veto the contract between his sister Lilly and Genfix nor a right to veto the payment arrangement.

II. Descriptive Formants

William's personality rights do not cover his interests in non-commercialisation. Lilly has no obligation towards her brother or any other family member to ask for consent. She has no obligation to inform him either. Any obligation to inform him is conceived as an encroachment t of his own 'right not to know' (understood as protected by §9 sec. 2 No. 3 GenDG).[17] This is the correlative for the basic rule that insurers (with an economic interest in this information) cannot force a person to do a genetic test, §18 GenDG. However, this right is limited to contracts up to a value of €300,000 (a limit which was perceived as a 'victory of consumer protection').

III. Metalegal Formants

The individualistic concept of rights does not bear any restrictions or powers in relation to family ties. In this respect, family law and the law of succession are conclusive. Relations *between* family members in respect of shared genomic information are not conceptualised.

---

[17] K. Schillhorn and S. Heidemann, *Gendiagnostikgesetz* (2nd ed., Heidelberg: 2017), p. 123, para. 21.

(7) GREECE

I. Operative Rules

The more widespread the characteristics in question are, the less has William the right of veto against the contract or a claim for a percentage of the payment of 1% as unjustified enrichment.

II. Descriptive Formants

Although the human body cannot constitute an object of invention, nevertheless the inclusion in a patent of a feature which has been isolated from it is possible, in accordance with the Biotechnology Directive (= Presidential Decree 321/2001).[18] Therefore, the remaining problem here lies in the question of whether a quality which belongs to more than one person constitutes their common personal datum as individuals, so that each cannot decide alone as to the fate of the datum in question – for example in consenting to its processing. In other words, the question is whether Lilly can consent to the processing of her gene without the agreement of her brother and of the rest of her blood relatives.

In connection with this unprecedented issue, it should be noted that the confidentiality of information of any kind is protected only as 'personal' data of a certain individual. In other words, therefore, it is difficult for this 'joint ownership' of personal data to be made meaningful. Nevertheless, it could be asked whether each carrier of the shared datum could be described as responsible for its processing as against the other carriers. In the present instance, that is, the question is how far Lilly can be regarded as responsible for the processing of the common genetic information of her brother and the rest of her blood relatives, since, naturally, the relationship between them is public knowledge. Any counter-observation to the effect that a family relationship does not prejudge with certainty the identity of the genes of the relatives will prove ineffective, since even the probability of someone bearing specific characteristics itself (may) constitute(s) his/her personal datum. In addition, any counter-argument based on the judgement that human blood could only with difficulty be understood as a 'file' of genetic data of one's relations should also be held to be equally ineffective, since the meaning of a file according to Article 2(c) Directive 95/46/EC = Article 2 ε Law 2472/1997 is very broad.

In spite of the above thoughts, the conclusion that the processing of the personal data of each individual remains exclusively his/her own affair and not that of those who have the same characteristics as him/herself

---

18 See, for preference, Rokas, *Industrial Property* (2004), §6, no. 24.

should, nevertheless, be considered probably more correct, since otherwise self-determination as to information of the individual is frustrated, together with the satisfaction of his/her constitutional right (Art. 9A Constitution), and, consequently, no one is entitled to prevent his/her brother from disposing of his/her tissue at will, nor, *a fortiori*, is anyone entitled to claim commercial percentages from the sale of the tissue of third parties, even if related to him/her.

With greater precision: we should distinguish the biological (e.g. genetic) characteristic as such from the information that it belongs to a specific individual. The latter undoubtedly constitutes a personal datum which is exclusively his/hers. On the other hand, the individual constituents of each biological characteristic as such (for example, of each gene, eye colour (brown, for example), hair colour, gender, etc.) do not belong to a specific person. Thus, for example, it is not, of course, a personal datum that white Indo-European men with dark eyes are more likely to suffer from pigmentary glaucoma, whereas, on the other hand, it is a personal datum that a person belongs to the Indo-European race. Naturally, this information of a major abstract order does not cease to be indirectly personal data of the subject of the primarily analysed data, but not data of third parties directly connected with them. For example, although the identified characteristics, complications and methods of treatment of the patient's pigmentary glaucoma are his/her personal data, as 'constituents' of his/her condition, they are not those of every patient with pigmentary glaucoma on earth.

Of course, given that William might veto the use of his sister's data, he might alternatively claim a percentage of her payment of 1% as unjust enrichment.

III. Metalegal Formants

Of course, the more widespread the characteristics in question are, the less they can be described as 'personal' data, in any constellation. Conversely, the fewer people have the characteristics, the more the personal nature of the data will be emphasised. Sometimes the rarity of the subjects of the data is such that by way of exception the impersonal character of the examination of their characteristics depends finally upon the method of construction of the term 'personal' data in accordance with an understanding of transactions and society (business ethics, good morals and good faith). Thus, the final answer to the question remains open to more detailed factors, for example the number of family members, whether their ancestors have descendants in other families, etc.

(8) IRELAND

Answer omitted.

(9) ITALY

I. Operative Rules

It is likely that William does not have a right to veto the contract – assuming its legal validity – nor to a payment of 1%.

II. Descriptive Formants

As already stated above (Case 7), one of the most important features of genetic data is that this type of information is not related only to an individual but is structurally shared by biological relatives (as well as by members of the same ethnic group). Relatives are part of the so-called 'biological group', which is different from a family in its strict legal meaning (e.g. a spouse is member of a family, but not of the biological group). This characteristic is the source of many difficult legal questions. One of these, first decided in Europe by the Italian Data Protection Authority, is the issue of access to a person's medical and genetic information by one of his/her relatives.[19] Another relates to group consent.[20]

No specific provision can be found on this matter. However, the general principles regarding genetic processing, as stated above (Case 7), have to be taken into account. First of all, it has to be noted that the legal basis of such an agreement is controversial. According to Article 23 Data Protection Code and Article 6 General Authorisation 22 February 2007, consent is valid only if it is given freely without any coercion. Many international documents and guidelines, however, tend to suggest that consent cannot be 'free' if induced by financial or other personal gain (see e.g. Art. 8 UNESCO Declaration on Human Genetic Data).[21] Secondly, if the planned experiments involve the storage and utilisation of William's genetic data as well, his consent is obviously required. However, from the facts of the case, we cannot be sure that the experiments were undertaken using data linked to an identifiable person. It is possible – though unlikely – that an anonymisation process was used.

If no information directly or indirectly linked to William was involved, it is unlikely that he can object to the agreement, assuming that he is co-owner of the unique gene. This issue could be debated, for instance, if the stem cells taken from umbilical cord blood were taken into account: here we have a

19 See DPA, in *Bollettino*, 1999, no. 8, p. 90.

20 See Greely, 'The Control of Genetic Research: Involving the "Groups between"', (1997) 33 *Houston L. Rev.*, p. 1397, pp. 1423 ff.; Cambon-Thomsen, 'The Social and Ethical Issues of Post-Genomic Human Biobanks', (2004) *Nature*, p. 869.

21 See Mand, 'Biobanken für die Forschung und informationelle Selbstbestimmung', (2005) *Medizinrecht*, p. 565, p. 571.

possible co-ownership between mother and son.[22] The situation is different in our case.

The same conclusion could be reached in the modification.

III. Metalegal Formants

Until now, the important issue of group consent has not been studied and debated by Italian scholars. No decision can be found on this matter.

(10) LITHUANIA

I. Operative Rules

William does not have the right to veto the whole contract and most likely does not have the right to veto the payment of 1% either.

II. Descriptive Formants

Article 2.25 of the Lithuanian Civil Code provides:

> 1. A natural person shall be inviolable. No natural person may be made to undergo scientific or medical test or examination against his will and without his free consent (in cases of person's incapability – without consent of his legal representative). Such consent shall be given in writing.

Further, biomedical research is specifically regulated in the Law on the Ethics of Biomedical Research. Like the Civil Code, the Law on the Ethics of Biomedical Research requires the informed consent of the patient for the research (Art. 7).

As long as the consent of the natural person (in this case, Lilly) is given to the research, there is nothing under Lithuanian law that could allow William to block the contract. The closest grounds for invalidity of the contract under civil law are nullity of a transaction that does not correspond to the requirements of mandatory statutory provisions (Art. 1.80 Civil Code) and nullity of a transaction contradicting public order and good morals (Art. 1.81 Civil Code), but neither seems applicable in this case (at least to the whole contract), as, it can be argued, the research has a legitimate and socially beneficial aim (i.e. human life and health).

---

22 See Wahle, *Zivilrechtliche Probleme bei der Gewinnung, Konservierung und Anwendung von Stammzellen aus Nabelschnurblut* (Aachen: 2005), pp. 8 ff., pp. 66 ff.; McIntire, 'Legal Issues of Stem Cell Transplantation and the Family', (2002) 32 *U. Mem. L. Rev.*, p. 727.

Besides, the possibility for William to veto the research contract would intervene with the fundamental rights of Lilly, similarly to the situation described in Case 8. While it could be argued that William indeed has certain privacy concerns, arguably they are outweighed by the possible individual and collective utility of the research, which could lead to the prolongation of life expectancy for Lilly and other members of Miller family.

While the Universal Declaration on Bioethics and Human Rights establishes the principle that the interests and welfare of the individual should have priority over the sole interest of science or society (Art. 3(2)), which is also implemented in Lithuanian law (see e.g. Art. 5(1) Law on the Ethics of Biomedical Research), it is not useful here, as Lilly voluntary agrees to participate in the research.

Regarding the benefit-sharing clause, the situation is not straightforward and depends on the particular facts and the content of the contract. On the one hand, it could be argued that the benefit-sharing agreement violates the non-commercialisation principle, i.e. that no body parts or tissue can be the objects of commercial transactions. The Law on the Ethics of Biomedical Research allows only the reimbursement of expenses for participating in biomedical research (Art. 10). Therefore, it could be argued that the benefit-sharing agreement is void because it contradicts mandatory norms and/or public order.

On the other hand, the final answer regarding the validity of benefit-sharing depends on the particular contractual modalities.

Besides, the agreement is not void *per se*, but should be declared as such either by the court *ex officio*, or upon the request of William. But in the latter case, the legitimate interest of the plaintiff is a precondition for a successful claim. And it is not clear whether William has a legitimate interest to oppose the benefit-sharing agreement, because, arguably, his interests are not negatively affected by the benefit-sharing clause.

III. Metalegal Formants

Lithuanian law at the moment is based on individual consent concerning medical research and does not foresee the veto right from family members or other collectives. Currently, there is no benefit-sharing mechanism either.

(11) NETHERLANDS

I. Operative Rules

As a third party, William cannot veto the contract.

II. *Descriptive Formants*

The material that has been taken and screened is Lilly's. The information, however, is not her property; it belongs to the whole group of carriers. Information, however, is free, unless it leads to group discrimination. William could claim privacy protection under the Medical Research Involving Human Subjects Act.

III. *Metalegal Formants*

In the past, the focus was purely on the development of the wellbeing and health of the people. Nowadays people ask: why would the pharmaceutical company benefit and not the donor?

(12) NORWAY

I. *Operative Rules*

No, William cannot veto either veto the contract or the payment of 1%.

II. *Descriptive Formants*

As long as Lilly, the carrier of the gene, has given her express and informed consent to the use of her gene, cf. NBBA §12, Genfix will be entitled to undertake extended experiments on the gene. The fact that William carries the same gene has no influence on that result, the decisive factor being that the donor has consented to the use. On the same ground, he will not be in a position to prevent Lilly from receiving payment from her participation in the experiments as he has no legal interest in such a veto.

III. *Metalegal Formants*

The right to veto use of biological material for research purposes is an individual right. Family affiliations are not relevant in this respect.

(13) POLAND

I. *Operative Rules*

Most probably, William could not veto the contract.

II. Descriptive Formants

As there are no specific legal provisions concerning such situations, one would have to revert to the general institutions of civil law. It has been already hinted above that the only relevant legal ground could be found in the protection of personality rights. However, one should assume that an action based on the civil law provisions concerning personality rights would have to fail on the facts at hand. In this very case the gene is not unique to one person.[23] Therefore, a collective personal interest would have to be created and this is rather impossible. It is true that Polish law may protect personal interests the essence of which lies in the relation of a given person to a wider group of persons or an institution, but here the problem has to be looked at from a different perspective. Let us explain this using the example of 'family tradition', a personal interest recognised by the Polish Supreme Court.[24] Family tradition may be defined as relations one has with one's ancestors and their achievements. The bond with family achievements and history is however something personal. It may be shared by many living family members, but for each of them this would be a stand-alone personal interest,[25] though defined in relation to something external. Following this logic, the gene specific to the Miller family would have to be recognised as a personal interest of each of the family members. William would thus have to show that this particular gene 'as such' constitutes his personal interest[26] and it would be an extremely weak argument to make. Even if one agreed to such a view, it would still have to be proven that Lilly and Genfix infringed William's personality right to the gene and that this infringement was unlawful. It should definitely be noted that by approving William's claims we would grant to William control over the body and genes of all other family members and this would certainly not be the desired result. If we assume that William cannot challenge the contract between Lilly and Genfix, there would also be no legal ground for him to oppose the 1% share of benefits.

III. Metalegal Formants

Despite different facts of the case, there seems to be a recurring legal/moral problem characteristic of nearly all 'genetic' controversies, namely whether appropriation of genetic resources should be allowed, and if so, who should be entitled to the benefits. The current IP regime remains generally oblivious to

---

23 Although, as presented above, even a gene unique to one person should not be treated as a personal interest protected by personality rights.

24 Supreme Court, 28 February 2003, V CK 308/2002, OSNC 5/2004, pos. 82.

25 As a consequence, each family member could theoretically veto commercialisation attempts.

26 It is clear that his physical integrity will not be affected in any way.

these problems and does not recognise the right of gene 'donors' or 'holders' to a share of profits earned through commercialisation of research results. In this case, the problem is aggravated by the fact that the 'Miller gene' may be provided by each Miller family member and thus (as in the present case) the one who concludes a contract reaps all the benefits, while others are left empty handed. It is interesting to see that the solution could lie in regarding a gene as the subject of property of all persons who carry it.[27] Precisely because of this, such a method should be rejected. If we are to decide who should hold the 'rights in a gene' – the person in whose body the gene has been discovered or the person who isolates it and uses in medical applications – the correct answer (when one considers the entire legal system and the incentive-creating function of law) should be in favour of the latter option.[28]

(14) SLOVENIA

I. *Operative Rules*

William does not have the right to veto either the entire contract or the payment of a 1% share of the product sales.

II. *Descriptive Formants*

William's interests concerning his genetic makeup are protected by his personality rights. These rights are, above all, negative and exclusive in content.[29] According to personality rights, William could demand the cessation of eventual interventions in his personal sphere and the elimination of any consequences of such interventions. However, in the case at hand, no such intervention in William's personal sphere occurred, which is why he cannot make such a demand. Thus, William does not have the (subjective) right to veto the contract between Lilly and Genfix, nor does he have the right to veto the payment of a 1% share of the sale price.

Another question that needs to be answered in this regard is the validity of the contract between Lilly and Genfix. A share of the profit was obviously promised to Lilly in exchange for her cooperation in this research and not as payment for her genome. The latter would not even be possible, as it is not possible to treat her genome as a thing. The prohibition of treating a subject or parts of his/her

27 Of course, if the gene in question is carried by an identifiable group of persons.
28 This solution should be accompanied by fairly restrictive criteria of patentability, for example as regards the functions of a gene.
29 A. Finžgar, *Osebnostne pravice* (Ljubljana: 1985), p. 39.

body as an object can be directly deduced from the provision of Article 35 of the Constitution of the Republic of Slovenia, which guarantees the inviolability of the physical and mental integrity of every person, and his/her privacy and personality rights. Apart from that, Article 21 of the Oviedo Convention[30] stipulates that the human body and its parts shall not, as such, give rise to pecuniary gain. The same is true in the case of donating blood (Art. 23 Supply of Blood Act-1),[31] donating tissue and cells (Art. 13 AQSHTC),[32] and the removal and transplantation of human body parts (Art. 4 RTHBPA).[33] On the basis of these provisions, we can conclude that the principle of non-commercialisation of the human body is exercised under Slovenian law. For this reason, the validity of the contract between Lilly and Genfix is questionable. Article 86 of the CO stipulates that contracts which contradict the Constitution, mandatory regulations or moral principles are void. The courts are obliged to take notice of the voidness of such contracts; all interested parties may also refer to such voidness. The concept of an interested party in this case refers to any individual that has a legal interest.[34] A legal interest means that the legal position of such an individual must be endangered due to uncertainty concerning a certain legal relationship.[35] An individual with legal interest can claim voidness of the contract directly in judicial (and other legal) procedures or individually file a declaratory action based on Article 181 of the Civil Procedure Act[36] and request that the court rule that the contract is null and void. Since William's position in relation to the contract between Lilly and Genfix in principle is not directly affected, William cannot enforce the voidness of the contract or claim it. The only remaining option would be for the court to consider the contract void of its own motion.

There is one field concerning the contract with Genfix which protects William's position. This is the issue of his anonymity as the carrier of this genetic

---

30 The Act Ratifying the Convention for the Protection of Human Rights and Dignity of the Human Being with regard to the Application of Biology and Medicine (Convention on Human Rights and Biomedicine) and the Additional Protocol to the Convention for the Protection of Human Rights and Dignity of the Human Being with regard to the Application of Biology and Medicine, on the Prohibition of Cloning Human Beings, Official Gazette RS, no. 70/1998.

31 The Supply of Blood Act-1, Official Gazette RS, no. 104/2006.

32 Act on the Quality and Safety of Human Tissues and Cells, for the Purposes of Medical Treatment (AQSHTC), Official Gazette RS, no. 61/2007 dated 10 July 2007.

33 The Removal and Transplantation of Human Body Parts for the Purposes of Medical Treatment Act (ZOPDCT), Official Gazette RS, no. 12/2000.

34 A. Polajnar Pavčnik, in: M. Juhart, N. Plavšak (eds.), *Obligacijski zakonik s komentarjem (splošni del)* (vol. 1, Ljubljana: 2003), p. 521.

35 A Galič, in: L. Ude, A. Galič (eds.), *Pravdni postopek – zakon s komentarjem, GV Založba in Založba Uradni list Republike Slovenije* (Ljubljana: 2006).

36 Official Gazette RS, nos. 26/1999, 12/2003, 2/2004, 2/2004-ZDSS-1, 36/2004, 52/2007, 73/2007, 45/2008-ZArbit, 45/2008.

makeup. In the event that his anonymity is in any way affected, he would be entitled to claim protection by filing a legal action based on his personality rights, as well as the provisions of Article 5 of RTHBPA and Article 15 of AQSHTC.

Based on this, it can be concluded that the contract on the sale of the gene would definitely be void, as most likely would the contract concerning Lilly's cooperation in the research on her gene in exchange for payment. Regardless, it is possible to determine that because of this William cannot gain the right to nullify the contract on his own, as he has no legal interest to do so. In the case at hand, a court would notice the voidness of its own motion.

III. Metalegal Formants

The case is positioned at the crossroads of the non-commercialisation paradigm and remuneration, the protection of a person with respect to his/her personal information and the entanglement of a person with his/her family. Slovenian law's restriction to 'negative entitlements' safeguards against intrusion by others. The case brings to light the strong role of personal information protection, which can be used to pursue other interests.

(15) SPAIN

I. Operative Rules

William has no right to veto the whole contract but can demand the respect of the confidentiality of genetic data. Lilly should not receive any economic profit from the donation, so the question of whether her brother can veto any economic gain does not arise.

II. Descriptive Formants

- Royal Decree 1301/2006 of 10 November, which establishes the regulations governing the quality and safety of giving, obtaining, evaluating, processing, preserving, storing and distributing human cells and tissues, and approves the operating and coordination regulations for use in humans;
- Civil Code;
- Royal Decree 411/1996 of 1 March on the clinical use of human tissues; and
- Convention for the Protection of Human Rights and Dignity of the Human Being with regard to the Application of Biology and Medicine: Convention on Human Rights and Biomedicine (Oviedo, 1997).

Genfix holds a patent on the industrial application of Lilly's gene, not on her gene, which is the reason why Lilly has no right on this patent. If she has sold her gene, the contract should be revoked in application of Article 1305 of the Civil Code, because a gene is an extra-commercial object and Article 1271 of the Civil Code forbids it to be the object of a sale.

On the other hand, if Lilly has donated her gene with no profit motive in mind, in accordance with Law 14/2007, her brother William cannot veto her decision and can only demand that the confidentiality of genetic data be respected. This confidentiality is expressly guaranteed by the Universal Declaration of Human Genome and Human Rights. In the Spanish case, the confidentiality of data is an individual concern: only the individual to whom the data belongs can decide who can or cannot be given them and to what extent the results of the research using these data can be made public. Lilly's brother cannot take any decision about the destination of her genetic data: he can only object to anybody else being told that he shares the same data. The decision on access to genetic data is such a personal one that even in the case of the genetic analysis of several members of the same family, the law determines that each member must be individually informed of the results.

Lilly should not receive any economic profit from the donation, so the question of whether her brother can veto any economic gain does not arise.

III. Metalegal Formants

Spanish law calibrates the principle of non-commercialisation of the human body with data autonomy of the individual. The result is that privity of contract is safeguarded. The individual person may stop those data disclosures which intrude on his/her data autonomy.

(16) UNITED KINGDOM

I. Operative Rules

William has no right to veto the contract, but might have a right to obtain an injunction stopping future processing of the gene, including stopping sales.

II. Descriptive Formants

William as a third party cannot affect the contract *per se*.

However, he might have legal rights and remedies in other areas of the law that could affect whether products can continue to be sold.

Under the Human Tissue Act, a person can only use tissue with the consent of the person from whom the tissue was obtained. In this case, Genfix has acquired tissue samples with the consent of Lilly.

Under the UK Data Protection Act 1998 or, now, the Data Protection Act 2018 (DPA), William has a claim if Genfix is processing William's personal data. The central question then is whether Genfix is using information that identifies him, or from which he is identifiable. The answer would be 'no' if the data relates to more than one person; it relates to all members of the family with that gene. So it does not identify *William*. However, we could argue that the data identifies William, and Lilly and every other relative with the gene. The question then is whether Genfix has met all the statutory requirements in order to process William's personal data. The Act provides for many requirements geared towards ensuring that data processing is fair, justified and transparent, but it will be possible for Genfix to meet them all, or nearly all, without William's consent. The issue requiring the closest attention is whether data identifying William can be used for the secondary purpose of medical research without his consent. There are permissions within the DPA 1998 and 2018 for using data for the secondary purpose of medical research, but arguably these permissions are subject to the overriding constraint in Article 8 of the Human Rights Act. Thus, it is arguable that using the personally identifying data without consent interferes with William's right to respect for his private life. In this case, the interference must be justified under section 8(2) DPA 2018. Protection of public health is a legitimate purpose for interference, but the interference must be necessary and proportionate. Whether it is necessary and proportionate for Genfix to proceed with Lilly's explicit consent, *and* William's explicit refusal, is open to debate. As of November 2020, no case law has been published on this issue.

If the UK courts find that it was an unlawful interference in William's right to a private life (or unlawful under the Data Protection Act), then William could obtain an injunction stopping future processing of the gene. Depending on the nature of the product that Genfix is selling, then future sales may be stopped.

III. Metalegal Formants

Under UK law, the case is governed by data protection considerations.

A.3. COMPARATIVE REMARKS

The reports on the base case deliver a differentiated picture. 14 of the 15 answers delivered concur in reporting a 'no' descriptive answer for the initial question ('Can the brother veto the sister's contract with the company?'), while Spain reports a conditional 'no'. Two reports provide a divergent answer for the addendum ('Can the brother object to the royalty payment?'): one report gives an unconditional 'yes' (France), and one a conditional 'yes' (Belgium) against the royalty payment. Yet in the UK it might be possible to stop sales if the violation of data protection laws were to come before a court. Even for reports with an identical descriptive formant, the answers are deduced from different principles. Evidently, the minority answers attract the comparatists' attention.

The differences appear to reflect the national reception of the (non-binding) UNESCO Universal Declaration on Bioethics and Human Rights of 2005 (UDBioethicsHR). Its preparatory process stimulated the drafting of the case in the first place (2001). It was signed by all UNESCO members, but it did not require a national parliamentary ratification. It is probably for this reason that central novel concepts (community consent, Art. 6(3) UDBioethicsHR; collective vulnerability and societal benefit-sharing, Arts. 8 and 15 UDBioethicsHR) do not strongly resonate in legal reasonings. Only four reports (Belgium, Estonia, France, Italy) mention the UDBioethicsHR, and three the Oviedo Convention (Estonia, Slovenia, Spain). Interestingly, constitutional self-determination (Estonia) and data protection (translated as the principle of confidentiality) appear much more prominently (Estonia, Greece, Italy, Slovenia, especially Spain).

Reports depart from basically two different concepts. One camp equates prior informed consent for genetic information with that for tangible tissue and body parts (Belgium, Denmark, Norway, Slovenia, Spain); the counter-position is the parallel to data (Greece, Italy, the Netherlands, Poland, the UK). The former departs from individual discretion; the latter from the public domain. But even where reports start from the same conceptual ground, the arguments refer to two different rationales. In the 'material' camp, one group refers to the widespread argument that DNA is material, a chemical substance, an object of property (Belgium, Spain), which implies the power based on property (regardless of whether the object is later put *extra commercium* (Spain) or if the property assignments get split between the material and the immaterial owner (Belgium, in this isolated regard also Poland)). The other group refers to the liberal legacy that – even in families – individuals are not subject to another family member's will (Greece, explicitly Poland, implicitly Denmark), which implies a power of the person (Estonia). The country reporters acknowledge conflicts which are resolved by regulation. These rules, though, give the (acting) individual priority over the competing (non-acting) individual of the collective (no injunction) or any fictitious collective interest (with basically the same result). The concepts of person and data overlap. Five reports openly discuss the tension between the individual and the group (Belgium, Estonia, Greece, Italy, Poland), more precisely in this case the 'biologically related family members' (Italy). Three take up the wording of the UDBioethicsHR ('collective consent': Belgium, Italy, Poland). One embeds the question as one of constitutional protection of the 'inviolability of family life' (Estonia). One report gave no response with regard to collective considerations (the UK). Two reports frame the conflict as one of 'joint ownership' (Greece)/'co-ownership' (Italy) in which interests in 'data protection' and 'public domain information' may collide – considering the continuum between personal versus public information (Greece). A peculiar situation exists in Spain, Italy and the Netherlands due to the national regulations on human genome research calibrating collective interests (by requiring that related family members are informed) and individual interests (by data protection). These rules may give rise to the brother having a claim against the sister's contract if his right to confidentiality is not respected.

With regard to royalties, two argumentative avenues are taken. The majority simply hold up the non-commercialisation principle, while three ponder 'unjust enrichment' with different connotations. The reports unearth, on the one hand, doctrinal differences regarding the non-commercialisation principle (impacting consent (cf. Italian report for the modification), and impacting *who* may take action (France, Slovenia)). On the other hand, some jurisdictions differentiate between non-commercialisation and benefit-sharing (like Belgium, probably Estonia), and some do not (the majority) – impacting the reflection on financial entitlements.

The non-commercialisation principle can be a general principle either in the public interest (Belgium, Czech Republic, Estonia, France, Lithuania) or a protective device for the individual (Slovenia). All jurisdictions hold violating contracts void. They differ as to who may take action, and as to which content renders contracts void.

Third parties can directly invoke the invalidity of the contract only in France. However, they can trigger a court decision in Slovenia, while the procedural means are unclear in Estonia. In all other countries, neither the (public) interest in non-commodification nor the (private) personal interest override the privacy principle. Also, an *omnibus* right to trigger a criminal investigation appears only to be stipulated in France. The basic reason for actionability in the three above-mentioned countries is not the self-interest of the actor (here the brother, based on the argument of property, person or benefit-sharing), but their representative enforcement in the public interest.[37] Thus, the relational claim is not based on a conflict of two individual rights, but on procedural law, which allows private enforcement of public interests.

[37] A modernistic theory in Romanist countries discussed under the label of '*interesses diffusos*'; until recently rejected *inter alia* by German constitutional theory, but emerging since the 1970s in ever-new forms of 'collective judicial redress'.

How content is qualified is, on the one hand, determined by the distinction between legitimate remuneration and illegitimate profit. It rests on two arguments: the dignity of the person (France), and protection of freedom in the moment of consent (Italy, infra the Belgian report for the modification). The less-evident distinction is between individual and collective benefit-sharing (discussed by the Belgian report). While individual sharing of profits by way of royalties clearly violates the non-commercialisation principle, collective benefit-sharing – as required in Article 15 UDBioethicsHR – asks for a 'more indirect' participation by way of regulation (as spelled out by the examples in Art. 15 UDBioethicsHR).

The difference between individual or collective entitlements is reflected by the differences in reflections about unjust enrichment claims. While the Greek and the Belgian reports reflect on unjust enrichment as a basis for an individual claim by the brother against his sister, the Polish report reflects on the conditions for legitimate collective benefit-sharing (i.e. an identifiable group, which the reporter rejects).

B.1. MODIFICATION

Would it make a difference if the gene was not bound to a specific family but was unique to a specific region? Assume the same factual situation as given in the original case; the names are Ricardo and Guillermo, and the name of the company is Genbest. Does Guillermo have a right to veto the payment clause in the contract between Ricardo and Genbest?

B.2. COUNTRY REPORTS

(1) BELGIUM

I. Operative Rules

The same is true for the modification. Guillermo probably has no enforceable right to veto the contract, although he might be able to veto the payment.

II. Descriptive Formants

The answer will be more or less the same as above. The group in question will be defined by geographical criteria, which makes benefit-sharing even more acceptable than in the case of a family, the latter obviously coming closer to individually benefiting. It should be borne in mind, however, that 'benefits should not constitute improper inducements to participate in the research'[38] and 'benefits (should) not be limited to those individuals who participated in such research'.[39] But, once again, enforcing these ethical recommendations and international soft law principles will not be easy before the Belgian courts. Therefore, a lot remains uncertain.

III. Metalegal Formants

The metalegal formants are comparable to the base case. The principle of non-commercialisation would govern the case, but 'remuneration' (of an individual who contributes more to the public good than he/she gets back immediately) and the sharing of benefits (where communities contribute to private profit) are respected counter-principles. Belgian law does not distinguish between different categories of collectivity (family versus territory). Thus, it remains unclear how the protection of the individual's interests would play out differently in cases where the specific gene is limited to the family or confined to the territory.

(2) CZECH REPUBLIC

I. Operative Rules

Guillermo does not have the right to veto the payment clause in the contract between Ricardo and Genbest, nor the contract as a whole.

II. Descriptive Formants

There is no difference if the gene is bound not to a specific family but to a specific region. Genes are not the subject of ownership or co-ownership, and so if a holder of a unique gene decides to join a research programme, then the other holders of the same gene have no right to veto his/her decision, even though that person will receive remuneration for his/her cooperation.

Another question would be whether, in the case of gene research, the other holders of that gene have the right to be informed about the research. The answer must be yes, because if the aim of such research is to produce medical treatments, then they should be informed about it for health reasons. If the therapy is based on medical treatments developed from human genes, then the result of the therapy for such gene holders would be different from the result of the therapy for a person who is not the holder of such gene.

---

38 Art. 15 Universal Declaration on Bioethics and Human Rights.

39 Recommendation 2, Hugo Ethics Committee, *Statement on benefit-sharing*, 9 April 2000, available at: https://www.eubios.info/BENSHARE.htm (last consulted on 11 March 2022).

There is only one possibility for vetoing the payment clause and that is the principle of non-commercialisation of the human body. If any rule exists which would prohibit the payment in respect of commercialisation of human genes, then the contract will be void, at least in this part, according to the provisions of the Civil Code. But in fact, it will not be a veto of the other holders, but the contract will be void in this part *ex lege*.

III. Metalegal Formants

A difference between the base case (family gene) and a gene which is territorially confined is that the individual will be provided with a right to be informed about the research results if these would have an impact on his/her medical status and possible treatment.

(3) DENMARK

I. Operative Rules

No, it would not make any difference if the gene was bound to a specific region.

II. Descriptive Formants

As in Norwegian law, the same situation as for the Miller family applies to Ricardo and Guillermo. The fact that other citizens in the same region carry the same gene has no relevance as long as the donor has consented to the use of the gene for research purposes.

III. Metalegal Formants

The collectivity of genetic sharing (be it defined by family or territory) has no influence on the legal operation of individual claims.

(4) ESTONIA

I. Operative Rules

The answer is the same as in the base case.

II. Descriptive/Metalegal Formants

The answer is the same as in the base case.

(5) FRANCE

I. Operative Rules

It does not make a difference whether the gene is shared among members of a family or inhabitants of a region.

II. Descriptive Formants

Since genetic research is authorised in France, notably since the Bioethics Act of 2004, the fact that the gene belongs to an individual family or to a whole region does not change anything. The research would still be possible under the same conditions and the same legal framework authorising such research, established by various French national entities that depend on the French Ministry of Health. Finally, the fact that the names of the brothers are different, and that the name of the company is no longer Genfix but rather Genbest, does not change anything. The research on the gene is possible, but the payment clause enclosed in the contract Ricardo signed with Genbest is still illicit and must be considered as being null and void. Both Ricardo and Genbest can be sanctioned under French criminal law (like Lilly and Genfix could be in the other case).

III. Metalegal Formants

Again, the principle of non-commercialisation of the human body governs the case. The issue of collectivity (be it family or territory) is taken care of by the framework of public law.

(6) GERMANY

I. Operative Rules

Guillermo has no right to veto the payment clause in the contract between Ricardo and Genbest.

II. Descriptive Formants

Guillermo's personality right does not cover his interests in non-commercialisation (supra base case).

III. Metalegal Formants

The difference to the base case is socio-political – and hints at the collective *problematique* encompassed in both cases. Two distinct issues intersect.

The first issue, again, is non-commercialisation. When specific genomic information is confined territorially, then traditional concepts bound to (territorial) democratic legitimacy can easily be applied. For the modification, one could reasonably argue that the contract between Ricardo and Genbest requires democratic legitimation based on affirmative regulation towards individualistic modes of benefit-sharing. The second issue raises the question of which collective is the 'right one' to which the right to decide and the right to benefit-sharing are assigned. As long as the specific genetic information shares territorial boundaries, the claim for benefit-sharing is absorbed by traditional tax schemes. However, the notion of benefit-sharing implies that those shall benefit who 'participate' or who carry a specific gene (patient groups, cultural communities). Thus, the privileged group is not identical to the political, territorially defined *demos*. Nor is the very idea of tax law appropriate, as it rests on distributive cross-financing. In Germany, to date the tax system seems to be given priority.[40] This is, again, because of the binary relation between the state and the citizen (*tertium non datur*). The case points at the phenomenon of emerging groups which engage as groups in the formally individualistic rights discourse (being an expression of the diversification and fragmentation of modern society).[41]

(7) GREECE

I. *Operative Rules*

Guillermo does not have the right of veto against a contract *inter alios acta*.

II. *Descriptive Formants*

Since the protection of Guillermo depends on the 'personalisability' of the characteristics of the gene, the answer to the modified question seems to be negative.

III. *Metalegal Formants*

Privity of contract prevails.

---

40 National German Council on Ethics, Opinion on Research Biobanks, 17 March 2004, at p. 89: 'Ein obligatorischer Beitrag zu solchen Fonds dürfte nur schwer durchsetzbar sein, da ein solcher Ausgleich zwischen privatem Gewinn und öffentlichem Nutzen in Konkurrenz zum Besteuerungssystem treten würde.' (copies available from the German Council of Ethics: https://www.ethikrat.org/publikationen …).

41 A *problematique* first raised and conceived by the consumer and environmental movement of the 1970s, see R. d. C. Mancuso, *Interesses Difusos* (2nd ed., Sao Paulo: 1991).

(8) IRELAND

Answer omitted.

(9) ITALY

I. Operative Rules

It does not make a difference if the gene is shared among the inhabitants of a certain region – Guillermo has no right to veto the payment clause.

II. Descriptive/Metalegal Formants

See the report on the base case.

(10) LITHUANIA

I. Operative Rules

Most probably, Guillermo does not have a right to veto the payment clause in the contract between Ricardo and Genbest.

II. Descriptive/Metalegal Formants

The factor that the gene is not bound to a specific family but is unique to a specific region makes no difference. Therefore, the answer is the same as in the base case.

(11) NETHERLANDS

I. Operative Rules

Guillermo has no right to veto the contract.

II. Descriptive/Metalegal Formants

Dutch law acknowledges no difference between family and territorial groups.

(12) NORWAY

I. *Operative Rules*

No, it would not make any difference if the gene was bound to a specific region.

II. *Descriptive Formants*

The same situation as for the Miller family applies to Ricardo and Guillermo. The right to veto use of biological material under NBBA §12 is an individual right on part of the donor of the material. The fact that other citizens in the same region carry the same gene has no relevance as long as the donor has consented to the use of the gene for research purposes.

III. *Metalegal Formants*

Norway's law does not establish differences regarding gene collectivities of families or territory. Any regulatory question is assigned to public law.

(13) POLAND

I. *Operative Rules*

It would not make any difference if the gene was unique to a specific region.

II. *Descriptive Formants*

Under the modified facts, the answer is even more clear-cut, since there would be fewer arguments to the contrary. In the case of a family-specific gene, it could be theoretically entertained whether protection by means of personality rights could not be of some assistance (although this solution has been ultimately discarded); in the case of a region-specific gene, the concept of personality rights would have to be stretched far beyond its limits. Thus, Guillermo cannot veto the contract between Ricardo and Genbest and neither can he claim a share of benefits.

III. *Metalegal Formants*

On the metalegal level, the modified case can show that the 'battle for property in genes' may resurface in many configurations. What it also shows, however, is that sometimes the initial impression of who should 'win' this contest may be incorrect. It is not very obvious why persons who simply happen to carry a certain gene should have any rights in this 'gene as such'. It seems that the problems with 'rights in genes' or other biological subject matter lie somewhere else entirely: what should be carefully considered is how to provide for an adequate sphere of 'fair use' of genes, where these have become wholly or partly 'appropriated' by IP rights so that ethical/moral dilemmas on one hand (e.g. claiming rights to a human body or its parts) and research impediments on the other (patent thickets) can be avoided.

(14) SLOVENIA

I. Operative Rules

Guillermo does not have the right to veto the payment clause between Ricardo and Genbest.

II. Descriptive Formants

This modification does not change the basic rule in any way. The inhabitants of a certain region could also only protect their genome based on personality rights, the contents of which are mostly negative. Since no intervention into their personal sphere occurs in the case at hand, the protection of such rights cannot be brought into action.

A contract on the donation of the gene between Ricardo and Genbest would be entirely valid. The situation would be different with a contract containing a payment clause. Due to the obvious rule and the principle of non-commercialisation of human body parts, the contract would be considered void based on Article 86 of the CO. Of course, in the case at hand, Guillermo would have no legal interest in declaring the contract void and so it cannot be considered that he has the right to veto the conclusion of the contract between Ricardo and Genbest containing a payment clause. The only field of protection in this case is the protection of anonymity.

III. Metalegal Formants

The principles to be applied in this case do not differ from the base case. These are non-commercialisation of the human body and anonymity of the person.

(15) SPAIN

I. Operative Rules

Guillermo has no right to veto the payment clause in the contract.

II. Descriptive Formants

This modification does not involve any changes to the answer previously given. Genbest holds a patent on the industrial application of Ricardo's gene, not on his gene; this is the reason why Guillermo has no right on this patent. If Ricardo has bought his gene, the contract should be revoked applying Article 1305 Civil Code, because a gene is an extra-commercial object and Article 1271 Civil Code forbids it to be the object of a sale.

On the contrary, if Ricardo donates his gene without commercial aim, in accordance with Law 14/2007, his brother Guillermo cannot veto his decision, except from the necessity of observing the confidentiality of genetic data. This respect for human rights is expressly guaranteed in the Convention for the Protection of Human Rights and Dignity of the Human Being with regard to the Application of Biology and Medicine: Convention on Human Rights and Biomedicine (Oviedo, 1997), applicable in Spain since 1 January 2000.

III. Metalegal Formants

The same metalegal formants apply to the modification as to the base case.

(16) UNITED KINGDOM

I. Operative Rules

Guillermo has no right.

II. Descriptive Formants

UK data protection laws do not provide him with a basis for action since the gene is not identifying.

III. Metalegal Formants

Under UK law, the case is governed by data protection considerations. Since a person from a region in which a specific gene is dispersed cannot be distinguished from the members of the group, no individual protection is available.

B.3. COMPARATIVE REMARKS

While the operative formants in the modification appear identical to the base case, the rationales of the reporters' answers cover the whole spectrum of opinions. The only factual difference to the base case is the attribution of the genetic character to territory, as opposed to family (in the base case). On one end of the spectrum stands the Belgian report, which insinuates that benefit-sharing is more acceptable once the genetic character is bound to territory. Then, so the argument goes, the ethical non-commercialisation principle, which is linked to the person, plays a smaller role. On the other end of the spectrum stands the Polish report, which deduces *a minore ad maius*: when the personality argument already deserves to be rebutted in the family context, 'in the case of a region-specific gene, the concept of personality rights would have to be stretched far beyond its limits'. The majority of reports note no descriptive or metalegal difference compared to the base case. Information law is discussed in two reports, but again for different reasons. While not argued for the base case, the Czech report promotes the 'right to be informed' once the gene is territorially distributed. The UK report only discusses data protection from the perspective of the individual. It is thus the case that the territorial embedded genome characteristic is even less related to the person's identity than a family trait.

CASE 10. TRADITIONAL KNOWLEDGE

A.1. BASE CASE

For centuries, the indigenous community ABC has harboured the knowledge of how to treat a specific eye infection with a specific plant. Plant biologist Tobin bioprospects the country where the ABC live, and he consults with the respective 'council of the elderly'. The 'council of the elderly' agrees to show Tobin the plant and how it is to be grown, prepared and applied – on three conditions. Tobin may only use the plant extract for medicinal purposes and he has to safeguard against anyone else pursuing research for different purposes. Any potential patent application shall name the ABC community. In addition, ABC shall obtain a 2% share in any profits that are generated from exploiting the patent. Tobin accepts these conditions in front of the council in a formal meeting.

Assume that your own country's laws apply and that ABC is a legal entity according to the home country's constitution.

At home, Tobin has a laboratory colleague, Walter, who does contract research for the Army searching for a new poison. Walter discovers that the lead component of the plant is highly toxic with specific 'beneficial' characteristics for warfare (the toxin spreads despite unfavourable wind conditions). Walter files and is granted a patent. Does ABC have the right to veto the patent?

A.2. EDITORIAL NOTE

The case revolves around the status of 'traditional knowledge' and of 'traditional knowledge holders'. Even though many European countries have signed the Convention on Biological Diversity of 1992 and agreed to its third objective ('the fair and equitable sharing of the benefits arising out of the utilisation of genetic resources'), specific legislation operationalising this objective has only been put in place at a slow pace. Today's (2021) central regulation (EU Regulation (EU) No. 511/2014) was not yet being discussed when the reports were written; only the Bonn Guidelines had been agreed upon (2002). To date, implementation remains slow; Belgium does not have necessary implementing acts for the EU Regulation in place. The question is: in the legal void, how can reporters concretely argue the claims of traditional communities?

At present, the premises, concepts, interpretation and requirements of patent law are not equipped to fit the concept of 'traditional knowledge' and to accommodate communities which are involved in the identification of therapeutic properties of native plants. The contribution of traditional knowledge from which a pharmaceutical product has been developed cannot be the sort of contribution that will meet current patentability standards. A first obstacle is the notion of invention. Traditional knowledge related to the use of plants for medicinal purposes does not fit into the conventional, technically oriented, invention concept of patent law (Greek report). A second impediment is the novelty requirement. It is often said that indigenous knowledge is existing, transgenerational, communally shared and considered to be in the public domain and, therefore, unprotectable (cf. German and Greek reports). A third obstacle is the notion in contemporary patent law of the inventor as an individual, solitary and original creator, or a group of individuals (so-called joint inventorship), not collective entities (cf. German and Polish reports). It is often claimed that for indigenous peoples, knowledge and determination of the use of resources are collective: custodians of traditional medicinal knowledge, and indigenous peoples in general, do not fit the individuality model and might therefore be denied patent protection. The contemporary concept of joint inventorship is only helpful at times, because it requires that each of the joint inventors must have contributed to the inventive conception, working on the same subject matter and making the same contribution to the inventive thought and to the final result (cf. German report). One does not become a joint inventor by being the first to observe a useful property or effect of an invention. In order to claim joint inventorship, some demonstrable role in the final conception needs to be established. In the case of collaboration with indigenous peoples or shamans, the problem is that their cooperation with ethnopharmacologists may be considered to be too indirect to the process of joint invention.[1]

On the other hand, the introduction of a disclosure of origin requirement in patent law is a possibility for production of evidence in respect of access and benefit-sharing rules (German report). In Europe, the origin requirement was dealt with in the Biotechnology Directive of 1998,[2] in particular in Recital 27. Recital 27 requires that 'whereas if an invention is based on biological material of plant or animal origin or if it uses such material, the patent application should, where appropriate, include information on the geographical origin of such material, if known; whereas this is without prejudice to the processing of patent applications or the validity of rights arising from granted patents'. Although Recital 27 contains a praiseworthy principle, this principle was not actively implemented.

---

1 See G. Van Overwalle, 'Protecting and Sharing Biodiversity and Traditional Knowledge: Holder and User Tools', 53(4) *Ecological Economics*, 2005, 585–607 and the references cited there.

2 Directive 98/44/EC of the European Parliament and of the Council of 6 July 1998 on the Legal Protection of Biotechnological Inventions, OJ L 213, 30 July 1998, 13.

Another attempt to give shape to the expectations and needs of indigenous peoples is the voluntary concluding of contractual arrangements. Various elements should be taken into consideration when concluding those contracts: monetary as well as non-monetary benefits, informed consent as well as disclosure procedures, and, last but not least, bilateral as well as multilateral scope. The weak point of contract law is that contracts come about on a voluntary basis, and the concluding of contracts cannot be enforced between knowledge holders (indigenous communities) and knowledge users (universities, firms), the knowledge holders quite often being the weaker party in the negotiations.

Provisions aiming at including the origin requirement as a substantial rather than just a formal requirement have met with a lot of criticism. It is argued that the obligation to disclose the origin of genetic resources and/or traditional knowledge as a substantial requirement for granting a patent could infringe Article 27 TRIPS Agreement, since such a measure might amount to a '*de facto* or *de jure* additional formal or substantial patentability criterion'.[3] However, if the implementation of benefit-sharing under the framework of the CBD[4] is a matter of vital importance to countries both from an economic and a technological perspective, an origin requirement in patent law might not be contrary to TRIPS. A solution might be to take up the obligation as a procedural requirement, within the meaning of 'reasonable procedures' of Article 62 TRIPS.[5]

One could also wonder whether a severe position would not contravene EU legislation. A communication of the EU and its member states stipulated in 2002 that the 'legal consequence to the non-respect of the requirement should lie outside the ambit of patent law'.[6] The Commission announced on

---

3 Communication from the European Communities and their Member States on the Review of Article 27.3(B) of the TRIPS Agreement, and the Relationship Between the TRIPS Agreement and the Convention on Biological Diversity (CBD) and the Protection of Traditional Knowledge and Folklore: 'A Concept Paper', WTO Doc. IP/C/W/383, 16 September 2002, 2, available at: https://www.timeshighereducation.com/news/working-document-of-the-commission-services-on-the-review-of-article-273b-of-the-trips-agreement-the-relationship-between-the-trips-agreement-and-the-convention-on-biological-diversity-cbd-and-t/170459.article (last visited 5 December 2007).

4 The Convention on Biological Diversity (CBD) was opened for signature on 5 June 1992 and entered into force on 29 December 1993. The CBD has three main objectives: the conservation of biological diversity; the sustainable use of the components of biological diversity; and the fair and equitable sharing of the benefits arising out of the utilisation of genetic resources. For more details, see https://www.cbd.int/convention/ (last visited 25 July 2017).

5 See G. Van Overwalle, 'Protecting and Sharing Biodiversity and Traditional Knowledge: Holder and User Tools', 53(4) *Ecological Economics*, 2005, 585–607 and the references cited there.

6 For instance, Communication from the European Communities and their Member States on the Review of Article 27.3(B) of the TRIPS Agreement, and the Relationship Between the TRIPS Agreement and the Convention on Biological Diversity (CBD) and the Protection of Traditional Knowledge and Folklore: A Concept Paper, WTO Doc. IP/C/W/383, 16 September 2002, 2, available at: https://www.timeshighereducation.com/news/working-document-of-the-commission-services-on-the-review-of-article-273b-of-the-trips-agreement-the-relationship-between-the-trips-agreement-and-the-convention-on-biological-diversity-cbd-and-t/170459.article (last visited 5 December 2007).

12 September 2002 that it welcomes a disclosure of origin requirement and production of evidence in respect of access and benefit-sharing rules, as long as this requirement does not constitute an additional formal or substantial patentability criterion and as long as it has no bearing on the patentability of the invention or the validity of the patent.[7] However, the positions have evolved since then, as shown in proposals of the EU and its member states to WIPO, taking the position that an application should not be further processed if the disclosure of origin information is not given.[8]

The case aims at the discussion about the origin requirement, which is debated as a legal measure echoing the third objective of the CBD ('the fair and equitable sharing of the benefits arising out of the utilization of genetic resources'). This measure is a response to the question of how legal protection of biodiversity and traditional knowledge can be accommodated and how the results from the use and exploitation of biodiversity and traditional knowledge can be shared under current patent law. The disclosure of origin requirement would *not* introduce a *direct* remuneration scheme between holders and users of genetic resources, *but* functions as an *indirect* measure in the sense that it provides a possibility for production of evidence in respect of concrete access and benefit-sharing rules laid down in other types of legislation, such as the Bonn Guidelines.[9]

---

7 Communication by the European Communities and their Member States to the TRIPS Council on the Review of Article 27.3(b) of the TRIPS Agreement, and the Relationship between the TRIPS Agreement and the Convention on Biological Diversity (CBD) and the Protection of Traditional Knowledge and Folklore: A Concept Paper, Brussels, European Commission – Directorate General for Trade (12 September 2002). See also: Submission by the European Community and its Member States on Traditional and Intellectual Property Rights, 3rd Session of the WIPO Intergovernmental Committee on IP and Genetic Resources, Traditional Knowledge and Folklore (13–21 June 2002). See also: Review of Article 27.3(B) of the TRIPS Agreement and the relationship between the TRIPS Agreement and the Convention on Biological Diversity and the Protection of Traditional Knowledge and Folklore: A Concept Paper, submitted by the European Communities under paragraph 32(ii) to the WTO (14 February 2003).

8 For instance, Proposal of the European Community and its Member States to WIPO, 16 December 2004, Disclosure of Origin or Source of Genetic Resources and Associated Traditional Knowledge in Patent Applications, 5, confirmed by e.g. the document submitted by the European Community and its Member States to the Intergovernmental Committee on Intellectual Property and Genetic Resources, Tradition Knowledge and Folklore, 8th Session, Geneva, 6–10 June 2005, on the Disclosure of Origin or Source of Genetic Resources and Associated Traditional Knowledge in Patent Application, WIPO/GRTKF/IC/8/11, 17 May 2005, 3–4, available at: http://www.wipo.int/edocs/mdocs/tk/en/wipogrtkfic8/wipogrtkfic811.doc (last visited 17 January 2008).

9 Although the CBD was adopted in 1992 and entered into force at the end of 1993, it was not until 1999 that work began in earnest to operationalise these provisions. The result is the Bonn Guidelines on Access to Genetic Resources and the Fair and Equitable Sharing of Benefits Arising

A.3. COUNTRY REPORTS

(1) BELGIUM

I. *Operative Rules*

No, ABC cannot veto the patent, since there is no opposition procedure in Belgian patent law.

After the granting of the patent, however, ABC could try to claim for revocation of the patent on the grounds of being contrary to *ordre public*.

II. *Descriptive Formants*

With regard to inventors, Article 9 BPA (Art. XI.10 BCEL) states the following:

> Where an application for the grant of a patent has been made either for an invention unlawfully taken from an inventor or his successors in title or in violation of a legal or contractual obligation, the injured party may, in his/her capacity as owner, claim the transfer of the application or of the granted patent, notwithstanding all other rights or proceedings.[10]

Since ABC cannot, however, be considered either the inventor or the owner of the invention, they will be in no position to base a claim on Article 9 BPA (Art. XI.10 BCEL).

As Belgian patent law does not provide for an opposition or examination procedure, it is the judge who will decide later in the event of a conflict.[11] In a Belgian context, ABC will thus not be able to veto the patent before it is granted, but might afterwards try to base a claim on Article 4(2) BPA (Art. XI.5§4 BCEL) (equivalent of Art. 53(a) EPC), i.e. the commercial exploitation of the patent being contrary to *ordre public* and morality. Weapon systems that are forbidden under international law could therefore be excluded from patentability.[12, 13]

The invention at hand can be considered a toxin typically suited for chemical weaponry, since it 'spreads despite unfavourable wind conditions'.

Out of Their Utilization, so named because of the location of the intergovernmental meeting in October 2001 that prepared the first draft, which was eventually adopted, with some changes, by the Conference of the Parties to the Convention at its sixth meeting, held in The Hague in April 2002 (for more details, see https://www.cbd.int/abs/bonn/, last visited 25 July 2017).

10 English translation from: https://wipolex.wipo.int/en/text/490470 (last consulted 11 March 2022).

11 B. Van Reepinghen and M. De Brabanter, *Les brevets d'invention [Patents]* (Brussels: 1987), 217 et seq.; M. Buydens, *Droit des brevets d'invention et protection du savoir-faire [Patent and Protection of Know-how Law]* (Brussels: 1999), 99–102.

12 R. Moufang, 'The Concept of "*ordre public*" and Morality in Patent Law', in: G. Van Overwalle (ed.), *Patent Law, Ethics and Biotechnology* (Brussels: 1998), 73.

13 The example of anti-personnel mines is given by Art. 4(1), Part C, Chapter 4 of the Guidelines for Examination in the European Patent Office, European Patent Office, December 2007.

The use of chemical weapons is not allowed according to international treaties and international customary law.[14] Belgium, along with 182 other states, is a contracting party to the Chemical Weapons Convention,[15] Article 1 of which states: 'Each State Party to this Convention undertakes never under any circumstances: (a) To develop, produce, otherwise acquire, stockpile or retain chemical weapons, or transfer, directly or indirectly, chemical weapons to anyone; (b) To use chemical weapons; …'.

The fact that an informed consent requirement has been violated does not suffice to exclude the invention from patentability (see Case 7, base case).

If ABC were to deliver evidence of the agreement in court, the breach of contract would make Tobin and perhaps his colleagues and employer liable to lawsuits on that basis alone.

The disclosure of origin requirement is dealt with in Modification 1 below.

III. Metalegal Formants

ABC's claim will not succeed based on the argument they trust in, here legitimate entitlement to their traditional knowledge. However, they may use patent exclusion grounds to invalidate the granted patent.

(2) CZECH REPUBLIC

I. Operative Rules

No legal instrument exists for the ABC community to veto the patent application.

II. Descriptive Formants

The Patent Act[16] sets out only four reasons for revocation of a patent, in section 23.

The first reason is that the invention did not meet the conditions of patentability – patentability of inventions is described in section 3 Patent Act. Section 3 Patent Act contains a list which shows what shall not be regarded as inventions. When an application is submitted to the Patent Office, the Patent

---

14 E. David, *Principes de droit des conflits armés [Principles of Armed Conflict Law]* (3rd ed., Brussels: 2002), 328–333.

15 Convention of 13 January 1993 on the prohibition of the development, production, stockpiling and use of chemical weapons and on their destruction, Paris, approved by Law 20 December 1996, *Official Gazette* [*B.S.*], 6 June 1997, available at: http://www.icrc.org/ihl.nsf/INTRO/553?OpenDocument (last consulted 6 May 2019) [Overeenkomst van 13 januari 1993 tot verbod van de ontwikkeling, de productie, de aanleg van voorraden en het gebruik van chemische wapens en inzake de vernietiging van deze wapens, gedaan te Parijs en goedgekeurd bij wet van 20 december 1996, *B.S.*, 6 juni 1997].

16 Act on Inventions and Rationalisations Proposals 527/1990 Coll.

Office does an *ex officio* preliminary examination of the invention in terms of whether that invention is patentable according to section 3 and also section 4 Patent Act. According to section 4 Patent Act, the exploitation of an invention against public order and public morality is excluded from patentability, among others. It is doubtful whether a substance for use in warfare is against public order and public morality, but no decision or opinion exists to support this doubt. Section 3 and 4 will not be helpful to the ABC community, because even a toxin for use in warfare should be patentable.

The second reason for a patent to be revoked is that the patent is not described precisely, so that a skilled person cannot carry it out. When an application is submitted to the Patent Office, the Patent Office makes an *ex officio* preliminary examination of the formal steps, for example whether the application is complete and the administration fee paid.

A third reason for the revocation of a patent is that the subject matter of the patent extends beyond the patent application.

A fourth reason for the revocation of a patent is that the proprietor of the patent has no right to the patent according to section 8 Patent Act. According to this norm, the right to a patent belongs to the inventor or his/her legal successor. A patent can only be revoked upon the request of an authorised person. An authorised person according to section 29 Patent Act is a person who is, pursuant to the decision of the court, the inventor or his/her legal successor. Since Frank is considered to be the inventor of the patented substance, the ABC community has no right to apply for a revocation of the patent.

The Patent Office will make a full examination of the application upon request or *ex officio*. Anyone may submit comments to the Patent Office, but a person who submits comments does not become a party to the procedure.[17] Walter is the inventor and he has a right to patent.

III. Metalegal Formants

Czech patent law only recognises prior (proprietary) technical information as limiting the patent scope, but not other entitlements of information providers on which the technical teaching might be built.

(3) DENMARK

I. Operative Rules

ABC cannot veto the patent.

---

17 See further R. Horáček, K. Čada, P. Hajn, Práva k průmyslovému vlastnictví (Rights to the Industrial Property) (1st ed., Prague: 2005), p. 127.

II. Descriptive Formants

Walter's illegitimate access cannot be grounds for opposition to the patent. In any event, Walter has created the invention and is therefore entitled to the patent, cf. DPA §1, first paragraph.

III. Metalegal Formants

Danish patent law does not recognise entitlements of providers of information on which the technical teaching is built other than prior technical information protected by patents. Any other knowledge is conceptualised as being in the public domain – regardless of its legal status under the law in the state where the knowledge originates.

(4) ESTONIA

I. Operative Rules

ABC does not have the right to veto the patent application.

II. Descriptive Formants

Pursuant to the Patent Act, '[a]n invention is patentable if it is new, involves an inventive step and is susceptible to industrial application'.[18] This means that if the invention complies with these requirements, it is patentable. Even if ABC's rights were violated, it would not affect the patenting procedure. It should be noted that the patents concerning the plant could be violated due to lack of novelty or inventive step.

III. Metalegal Formants

Estonia is a party to the Convention on Biological Diversity.[19] Article 1 of the Convention on Biological Diversity provides:

> The objectives of this Convention, to be pursued in accordance with its relevant provisions, are the conservation of biological diversity, the sustainable use of its components and the fair and equitable sharing of the benefits arising out of the utilisation of genetic resources, including by appropriate access to genetic resources and by appropriate transfer of relevant technologies, taking into account all rights over those resources and to technologies, and by appropriate funding.

---

18 Patent Act §8(1).

19 Entered into force in respect of Estonia 25 October 1994 – RT II 1994, 13, 41.

The Estonian legal framework for IP does not, however, have provisions to facilitate the fulfilment of these objectives (especially the fair and equitable sharing of the benefits arising out of the utilisation of genetic resources).

(5) FRANCE

I. Operative Rules

ABC has no right to veto the patent.

II. Descriptive Formants

Under French patent law, there are no rules that allow the ABC community to veto Walter's patent.

III. Metalegal Formants

Despite the fact that France is a party to the Convention of Biological Diversity (CBD) and the UN Declaration of the Rights of Indigenous Peoples (UNDRIP), France did not provide for claims of information providers ('traditional knowledge') to be respected and recognised when technical teaching is based on them.

(6) GERMANY

I. Operative Rules

ABC has no right to veto the patent.

II. Descriptive Formants

ABC does not have a right either as the inventor (§8 German Patent Law) or as a co-inventor (§6 sentence 2 German Patent Law).

III. Metalegal Formants

The problem is with the status of 'traditional knowledge'. In Western law, including Germany, it is not attributable to a specific person as individual knowledge. Neither is it perceived to become part of the isolation invention. Nor does it render the patent not novel or does it reduce the measure of inventiveness. Nor does the status of the traditional knowledge under the home country laws impact the confined patentability examination governed by the territoriality principle (other than novelty). A contested way to keep control is the request to be named as co-inventor (see Case 13).[20] But if the contribution amounts qualitatively to co-inventorship, then the position of co-ownership secures control (not necessarily or exclusively financial interests). Another statutory way to control novelty is the proposed mandatory duty to disclose the origin of knowledge in the procedure of the patent application. However, this duty is still highly contested by industrialised countries, including Germany. Yet, as morals shift to acknowledging the status of traditional knowledge,[21] the acceptability will likely rise as well.

(7) GREECE

I. Operative Rules

ABC may not object to or challenge Walter's patent.

II. Descriptive Formants

A traditional cure (here of an eye disease) does not constitute an invention, since it involves no 'leap of invention'[22] towards what becomes established (on the contrary, it is itself a kind of established knowledge),[23] nor does it give grounds for any private right, since it 'belongs' to the local community in question (living and departed). But even if it did give grounds for such a right, this still would not be capable of being pursued in the courts, since any claim arising from it would have been time-barred by reason of the lapse of time immemorial from the date of the manifestation of the invention.[24]

Consequently, ABC derive whatever rights they have in this connection from their contract with Tobin (Art. 361 Civil Code), provided, of course, that they

---

20 In terms of patent law, Case 13 shows that the instrument can work. However, the bilateral contractual duty can be void.

21 UNESCO Convention on the Diversity of Cultural Expressions, signed in 2005, ratified by the EC and 12 Member States on 18 December 2006, and came into effect on 18 March 2007 (https://en.unesco.org/creativity/convention); the UN-Declaration on the Rights of Indigenous Peoples was adopted in 2007 (https://www.un.org/development/desa/indigenouspeoples/declaration-on-the-rights-of-indigenous-peoples.html).

22 According to Art. 5 para. 3 Law 1733/1987, an invention is new when it does not emerge in an obvious manner from the existing level of technique. For an analysis of the meaning of 'new', see Kotsiris, 'The inventive idea as a criterion of the newness of an invention', *Themata Dikaiou* 1982, 184; Antonopoulos, *Industrial Property* (2002), p. 777; AP 1588/1991, *EEmpD* 1992, 146.

23 See Gantini, *The distinction between an invention and a discovery in the context of biotechnology and genetic engineering* (2004).

24 On the right of the prior user see Antonopoulos (2002), p. 810.

have legal personality (otherwise the contract will bind Tobin to the others, according to Arts. 68 para. 2 and 212 Civil Code, and gives rise to a multi-personal relation of obligation). Over and above this contract or in the absence of a valid contract, it will be a matter of a multi-personal obligation between Tobin and the members of the community in question arising from *negotiorum gestio*, insofar, of course, as the traditional remedy is apprehended as their 'affair'.

In view of the above observations, the answer to the base case is the following: as has already been explained, ABC have only contractual rights of obligation in connection with the exploitation of the traditional remedy in question. Their rights are relative, i.e. they may be addressed only to Tobin. Consequently, they have no grounds for addressing themselves to the third party (Walter), who has not entered into a contract with them. On the other hand, the members of this community could probably take action against Walter in accordance with the provisions of Articles 730 et seq. Civil Code over the management of another's affairs (*negotiorum gestio*) or of Article 904 Civil Code for unjust enrichment. The proof of a prejudice would, naturally, be difficult in the penultimate instance, as would the description of the traditional collective technique of treatment as an item of property of each member of ABC.

III. Metalegal Formants

Greek law does not recognise any rights to traditional knowledge; therefore, the case would be judged according to general patent law. Greece has joined the Convention on Biological Diversity of 1992 (Law 2204/1994), which in its preamble states that one of its objectives is 'the fair and equitable sharing of the benefits arising out of the utilisation of genetic resources', but no specific national legislation has been issued to date regarding traditional knowledge issues.

(8) IRELAND

Answer omitted.

(9) ITALY

Answer omitted.

(10) LITHUANIA

I. Operative Rules

No, ABC does not have the right to veto the patent.

II. *Descriptive Formants*

Even leaving aside the question of the validity of the agreement between Tobin and ABC (which is, applying the facts of the case, quite doubtful), there are no grounds and procedure for vetoing the patent which ABC could use.

First of all, there is no opposition procedure available under Lithuanian law. Second, when it comes to the grounds for invalidity of the patent after it was issued, Article 63 of the Lithuanian Patent Law provides:

> On the request of any persons concerned the court may invalidate a patent, in whole or in part, on one of the following grounds:
>
> 1) the invention is not patentable within the meaning of Articles 4–8[25] of this Law;
> 2) the patent does not disclose the invention in a manner sufficiently clear and complete for it to be carried out by a person skilled in the art;
> 3) the disclosure contained in the patent goes beyond what has been disclosed in the application as filed, or if the patent was granted on a divisional application, which goes beyond what has been disclosed in the initial patent application filed;
> 4) the proprietor of the patent has no right to the patent within the meaning of Article 11(1) of this Law.[26]

Arguably, ABC cannot use any of these grounds, at least not pointing to the contract made with Tobin. Possibly ABC could try invalidate the patent using the general grounds of contradiction to public order or lack of novelty or non-obviousness.

It is unclear from the facts of the case whether Walter indicated the name of the ABC community in the application. From the facts of the case, it can be understood that ABC is not necessarily asking to be identified as the inventor (which is not possible under Lithuanian law anyway, because only a physical person can be named as the inventor).[27] Even if ABC is not identified, and presuming that the contract between Tobin and ABC is valid, the most ABC could do is to raise the issue of violation of the contract, but not to ask invalidate the patent.

Another legal mechanism which, at least theoretically, could be used by ABC is trade secrets protection. As long as Tobin (and Tobin's employer) could be regarded as restricted by the contract from disclosing the information received from ABC, all three conditions for trade secrets protections (first, secrecy of information, second, its commercial value and, third, reasonable steps under the circumstances to keep the information secret) are met. ABC, being a legal entity,

---

25 Arts. 4–8 Patent Law establish the general requirements for patentable inventions.

26 Art. 11(1) Patent Law deals with employees' inventions.

27 Art. 2(8) Patent Law.

can be considered to be a trade secret holder. The problem with this argument is that it is not clear whether the contract between ABC and Tobin indeed obliges the latter to keep the information secret. On the contrary, their agreement openly foresees the patenting of invention and this amounts to the public disclosure of information. Yet the parties can agree to keep the information secret until the patent application is submitted.

III. Metalegal Formants

As in the other European countries, Lithuanian patent law is based on an individualistic approach to inventors and the inventive process. Therefore, communities and their interests can hardly be accommodated by the requirements of patent law. Not only can ABC not formally be named as the inventor, arguably the knowledge regarding the plant most probably could not be regarded as an invention either, as rightly stated in the Editorial Note. Protection of traditional knowledge, as experience shows, requires a specifically tailored form of protection, which is currently lacking in Lithuania.

(11) NETHERLANDS

Answer omitted.

(12) NORWAY

I. Operative Rules

ABC cannot veto the patent but may have a claim for damages.

II. Descriptive Formants

It is assumed that Tobin has given Walter access to the plant or the plant extract in breach of the contract with ABC or that Walter has in other ways gained illegitimate access to the material. In neither case will Walter's illegitimate access be grounds for opposition to the patent.[28] In any event, Walter has created the

[28] Editors' note: Not even under Norway's comparably strict Biodiversity Act, which was enacted 2009, after the Norwegian country report was submitted to the BIP editors. For the legal situation regarding access to Norwegian biological resources and use in Norway of biological resources from other countries and traditional knowledge from outside Norway, see M. Tvedt, 'Norwegian Experiences with ABS', in: B. Coolsaet et al. (eds), *Implementing the Nagoya Protocol* (Leiden/Boston: 2015), p. 175.

invention and he is therefore entitled to the patent, cf. NCA §1, first paragraph (New Act §2, first paragraph). However, the use of the illegitimately accessed material may be challenged on other grounds, e.g. the prohibition against unfair trade practices in §25 of the Marketing Act (NMA, 9 January 2009) and the prohibition against unlawful use of trade secrets. If so, ABC may have a claim for damages.

III. Metalegal Formants

Illegitimately acquired input (be it information or material) does not, as a matter of principle, affect the status of the patent. Remedies for illegal behaviour need to be sought in torts or criminal law.

(13) POLAND

I. Operative Rules

No, ABC cannot veto the patent.

II. Descriptive Formants

Walter's invention consists of a different application that, it appears, is new and was not known to the ABC community. Thus, the conditions for patentability have probably been met. Since the ABC community does not hold a patent for the substance, it has no legal remedies to forbid Walter to use the invention without its consent. Depending on the agreement between ABC and Tobin, making the substance available to Walter could be regarded as contract violation, but this could exert no effects vis-à-vis Walter.

III. Metalegal Formants

The protection of so-called traditional knowledge poses a serious problem to the IP system. This problem is of a fundamental nature and currently difficult to solve.[29] The IP system that has been to a large extent promoted and even imposed on many countries (the TRIPS Agreement) is of undeniably Western origin, which also means that it has been from the very outset designed to reflect 'Western' values. For example, it is clearly individualistic. This system defines the

---

[29] It is sufficient to look at the attempts such as the WIPO Draft Provisions for the Protection of Traditional Knowledge to come to this pessimistic conclusion: http://www.wipo.int/edocs/mdocs/tk/en/wipo_grtkf_ic_9/wipo_grtkf_ic_9_5.pdf; see. I.B. Mika, 'W poszukiwaniu instrumentów skutecznej ochrony wiedzy tradycyjnej', *PIPWI*, vol. 100, 2007, pp. 293 ff.

condition for protection and grants rights that are exclusive but limited in time to persons who either created an IP subject matter or acquired the relevant rights from the creators. Exclusivity for a limited time can be understood as a sort of contract between the society and the author/inventor, the purpose of which is to stimulate new works and inventions. However, it appears that some intellectual knowledge (sometimes of significant value) has come into being in societies to which the Western system is alien (for example, they regard knowledge as a common good, even if in our understanding it has crossed the boundary separating knowledge from invention). But because this system now prevails almost all over the world, valuable traditional knowledge can be appropriated[30] using existing IP rights precisely because they have been crafted in a way that is completely oblivious of traditional knowledge's existence. Reconciliation of the two incompatible systems of values is an extremely difficult task, especially since the incompatibility goes to the core and inner logic of these systems. The very fact that a 'Western' legal system would encounter serious trouble even accommodating ABC as a party to the contract serves as the best example.

(14) SLOVENIA

Answer omitted.

(15) SPAIN

I. Operative Rules

ABC does not have a right to veto the patent.

II. Descriptive Formants

With the approval of Law 42/2007 of 13 December on Natural Patrimony and Biodiversity, Spain has adopted the principles and rules of the Convention of Biological Diversity (CBD). Article 68 of this Law states that a Royal Decree shall regulate the access to genetic resources in order to make it subject to prior informed consent in the terms of Article 15 CBD. In that sense, the Autonomous Communities are competent to give consent and to negotiate the terms of this access, including the conditions for preserving the conservation and sustainable use of our natural resources. So, as long as ABC's know-how is part of national biodiversity, access will be subject to the above-mentioned conditions.

[30] Of course, on the condition that the very fundamentals of the system do not prevent it, for example when a patent is denied because of a lack of novelty.

Under Law 10/2002 of 29 April, which transposes Directive 98/44/EC on the legal protection of biotechnological inventions and modifies the Patent Law, ABC has no right to veto the patent. The preamble of this Law states that 'consent will not be required as condition of patentability of the invention; neither its lack nor its inaccuracy will affect the validity of the patent already granted'. However, we argue that this premise is contrary to the purpose of the Law 42/2007 of 13 December on Natural Patrimony and Biodiversity and of the CBD.[31]

ABC could only veto the patent if the conditions for accessing natural resources were the same as the donation conditions set out by Law 14/2007 of 3 July on Biomedical Research and by Law 41/2002 of 14 November on patient autonomy and the rights and obligations in the area of information and clinical documentation.

III. Metalegal Formants

Despite being party to the CBD, Spain rejected the obligatory recognition of traditional knowledge in patent law.

(16) UNITED KINGDOM

I. Operative Rules

ABC probably does not have a right to veto Walter's patent.

II. Descriptive Formants

ABC has no contractual rights against Walter, because Walter was not a party to its contract with Tobin.

ABC would not have any rights under the PA 1977 to have Walter's patent revoked unless it could prove it was co-inventor of the invention claimed by Walter. It probably could not prove this because (1) its traditional knowledge (of producing the eye treatment from that particular plant) does not seems to have made any contribution to Walter's invention of the production of the toxin from the same plant, and (2) even if it had made some contribution, US authority suggests that when a traditional community's traditional knowledge of the properties and application of a particular plant was the origin or basis of a later

31 A study of the scope of the CBD and an international approach to these questions can be found in S. Borrás Pentinat, 'El proceso de regulación del régimen internacional sobre acceso y participación en los beneficios derivados de la utilización de los recursos genéticos (APB-ABS) en el marco del Convenio sobre Diversidad Biológica', *Revista Aranzadi de Derecho Ambiental*, no. 11, 2007, pp. 251–278.

invention, the community's contribution is not an 'inventive' contribution.[32] It seems likely the same conclusion would be reached in the UK.

It is arguable that ABC could have some claim against Walter on the basis either (1) that Walter is in breach of his statutory duty under what is now the Nagoya Protocol (Compliance) Regulations 2015 (SI 2015/821) (the UK's implementation of the Nagoya Protocol), and that this gives ABC a remedy against Walter, or (2) that ABC supplied its information to Tobin conditionally on the conditions set out in their contract, and that this gives rise to a Quistclose trust, which would mean that Tobin and anyone who acquired the information from him, such as Walter (not a good faith purchaser), would, in effect, be bound to use it only subject to those conditions. However, it is not clear that either argument would succeed, or if they did, whether ABC's remedy would be an injunction preventing Walter's use.

III. Metalegal Formants

The UK has implemented the Nagoya Protocol by legislation, which now requires Walter to submit due diligence declarations demonstrating (if this is required by ABC's country) ABC's prior informed consent to access the traditional knowledge on mutually agreed terms for undertaking his research and the development of his invention, and for sharing the benefit of his invention with ABC. This is not a requirement with regard to the patent (neither an obligation for filing, nor an obligatory disclosure of origin), but Walter must show compliance before he can be awarded research funding or obtain the various regulatory approvals for the final development of the product of the invention. The primary objective of the UK legislation (as of the Protocol) was to establish a regulatory system for ensuring that, in practice, the genetic resources and related traditional knowledge of indigenous and local communities is not appropriated by others for commercial gain without their prior informed consent and except in accordance with benefit-sharing agreements on mutually agreed terms. However, the enforcement mechanisms provided by the UK Regulations are exclusively in the hands of the state: it is disputable whether the Regulations also incidentally confer *sui generis* rights on the community (and if so whether they amount to property rights in UK law) which the community can enforce against anyone using its resources in breach of the Regulations (which Walter appears to be doing here).

The Quistclose trust is an equitable device developed by the courts, originating in a court decision in 1970.[33] The general principle is that if property (here, ABC's

32 L. Bentley, B. Sherman et al., *Intellectual Property Law* (5th ed., Oxford: 2018), pp. 627–628.

33 *Barclays Bank Ltd v. Quistclose Investments Ltd* [1970] 2 AC 567; the now accepted analysis is that laid out in *Twinsectra v. Yardley* [2002] 2 AC 164.

traditional knowledge) is transferred by X (here, ABC) to Y (here, Tobin) on the understanding that it will be used only for a specified purpose (here, for medicinal purposes and on condition that ABC is named in the patent and has a 2% share in profits), then Y holds it on trust for X (i.e. Y holds only the bare legal interest in the property and X remains the beneficial owner) until the purpose has been fulfilled. Until that happens, X (ABC) has a right, enforceable in equity against Y (Tobin) and all third parties who are not good faith purchasers (Walter) to prevent its application for any other purpose. The *Quistclose* case itself concerned a loan of money, but it has since been extended to other kinds of property and other kinds of transaction.[34] It is arguable that it could be extended to cover ABC's traditional knowledge (the crucial element, that ABC and Tobin had a mutual understanding that the traditional knowledge was not intended to be at Tobin's free disposal, is present), but there may be doubts whether the traditional knowledge itself is sufficiently certain to give rise to property rights.

All claims ABC might make (other than under the Nagoya Protocol) are also complicated by the fact that ABC is not a legal person. It is not impossible for an unincorporated community to bring legal proceedings in the UK, particularly where there is a clear governing structure (as ABC seems to have), but because it is an intergenerational group of individuals it is very difficult to envisage what its remedies might be (what is its loss?) and what is meant by 'its' property (does it include 'its' traditional knowledge?). These problems should not arise in relation to the Nagoya Protocol UK legislation because it is based on the presumption that traditional communities have *sui generis* and actionable rights. However, until we get clarification from legislative bodies or from the courts, we do not know how the problems might be resolved.

A.4. COMPARATIVE REMARKS

In all jurisdictions under review, ABC has *no* right to veto the patent (application). In some jurisdictions, ABC *may have* a claim for damages (Norway, the UK) or to economic compensation (Spain). ABC cannot revoke Walter's patent, neither by starting opposition proceedings, nor via revocation proceedings.

1. Opposition proceedings

None of the national jurisdictions under review provide an opposition procedure allowing third parties – *in casu* ABC – to challenge the patent.

[34] Mostly recently in a decision of the eminent trusts commentator Sarah Worthington QC sitting as a judge in the High Court in *Ali v. Dinc* [2020] EWHC 3055. An appeal on procedural grounds against the decision was dismissed by the Court of Appeal without commenting on the legitimacy of the Quistclose trust in this context ([2022] EWCA Civ 34).

2. Revocation proceedings

Most national patent acts under review allow revoking a patent when certain conditions are met. A patent can be revoked when:

1. the subject matter of the patent is excluded, *in casu* subject matter which runs counter to *ordre public* and morality (Belgium, Czech Republic, Estonia);
2. the substantial patentability requirements are not fulfilled (Belgium, Czech Republic);
3. the formal patentability requirements are not met, in other words for reasons of inadequate patent disclosure (Belgium, Czech Republic); or
4. the patent holder was not entitled to obtain the patent (application).

In the case at hand, it is argued that the revocation procedure will *not* be successful, because patenting a toxic component does *not* run counter to *ordre public* and morality (Czech report), and the patentability conditions have been met (Polish report). On the other hand, it has also been suggested that in the actual case the revocation procedure *might* be successful, because a toxic component might be viewed as a chemical weapon, and the use of chemical weapons is not allowed under international law (Belgian report). The latter assertion is based, however, on an incorrect reading of the so-called ethical clause, which explicitly says that commercial exploitation shall not be deemed to be contrary merely because it is prohibited by law or regulation.

While we wished to find argumentation in favour of traditional communities, the country reporters put their energy into arguments to argue that ABC does not have a claim to become an inventor, a joint inventor and/or a patent holder itself, neither indirectly (by transfer of patent/patent application), nor directly (by submitting a patent itself or via the theory of unjust enrichment).

3. Transfer of patent (application)

Various national patent acts stipulate that when the invention has been unlawfully taken from the inventor, or in violation of a legal or contractual obligation, the injured party may, in his/her capacity as the rightful owner, claim the transfer of the patent (application) (e.g. Belgium).

It has been argued that the actual patent holder – Walter – is the inventor and had no contractual relation with ABC. Hence, ABC cannot claim the transfer of the patent (application) (Czech, Greek, Lithuanian and Polish reports). On the other hand, it has been suggested that the court might take into account that (the employer of) Tobin was bound by the contract. In that case, ABC could argue that (the employer of) Tobin can be held liable for Walter's behaviour, and the conditions of the agreement could be enforced (Belgian report).

4. Inventorship and co-inventorship

Under the current patent regime, ABC would have *no* right to be an inventor or a co-inventor (German report).

Under the contract set up between ABC and Tobin, ABC might have claimed a right to be an inventor. But the contract only applies between ABC and Tobin, and does *not* stretch to Walter, who is not contractually bound by the agreement between ABC and Tobin (Greek and Polish reports).

5. Unjust enrichment
It has been suggested that, all other measures failing, ABC could take action against Walter in accordance with the provisions over the management of another's affairs (*negotiorum gestio*) (Greece) or on the basis of unjust enrichment (Greece). However, it would be challenging to provide the existence of a prejudice, as the description of the traditional collective technique of treatment would be difficult to accept as an item of property.

ABC might, however, claim damages. It is argued that Walter gained illegitimate access to the material and that he can therefore be sued for damages on the basis of the prohibition against unfair trade practices, the prohibition against unlawful use of trade secrets, and the prohibition against unlawful use of entrusted technical drawings, descriptions, formulas, models or similar technical aids (Denmark, Norway).

6. Damages
The only jurisdiction where contractual obligations might extend to third parties is in the common law, by way of trust law (here in the form of the *Quistclose* trust). Yet the remedies under trust law (at least to date) appear not to extend to the special enforcement rights under patent law. In addition, doubts as to the standing of the community remain (although the common law appears to be more open to assigning legal capacity to communities).

B.1. MODIFICATION 1

If Q does not name the community in his own patent description, does ABC have a right to correction?

B.2. COUNTRY REPORTS

(1) BELGIUM

I. Operative Rules

ABC will not have the right to have its community's name mentioned in the patent. However, it should be able to enforce the requirement of the geographical origin indication. In other words, the geographical origin of the said plant has to be indicated in the patent application.

II. Descriptive/Metalegal Formants

ABC can base a claim on Article 15§1 6° BPA (Art. XI.16§1 6° BCEL), which states that a patent application has to include a reference to the geographical origin, if known, of the biological material on the basis of which an invention has been developed.[35] The applicant will be asked to state whether or not the invention is directly based on genetic resources or related traditional knowledge, and if so, will be required to disclose the origin. More particularly, it is mandatory to indicate the geographical origin on the patent *application*, not in the patent description. This disclosure of origin requirement, however, concerns the geographical origin of the biological material and not the community's name itself.

On the one hand, it is important to note that the Belgian legislator has made a real normative and enforceable rule of the principle evoked in Recital 27 of the Biotechnology Directive. If an applicant does not fulfil the disclosure requirement, he/she will have a few months[36] to correct this, otherwise the application will be rejected (Art. 20 BPA (Art. XI.21 BCEL) in combination with Art. 15§1 6° BPA (Art. XI.16§1 6° BCEL)).

On the other hand, Article 15§1 6° BPA (Art. XI.16§1 6° BCEL) has its weaknesses, since it is only when the origin is known that the disclosure requirement applies. In addition, discovering afterwards that the origin has not been disclosed will not prevent patentability, i.e. a patent cannot be declared invalid for a lack of disclosure of origin.[37] It is worth mentioning that the opposite was proposed in an earlier bill in 2002, i.e. an invention developed on the basis of biological material obtained in violation of Article 15 CBD would be contrary to *ordre public* and morality, and therefore not patentable.

In conclusion, ABC should have a right to correction with regard to the geographical origin indication, which should be enforceable before the Brussels

---

35 G. Van Overwalle, 'The Implementation of the Biotechnology Directive in Belgium and its Aftereffects. The Introduction of a New Research Exemption and a Compulsory License for Public Health', 37 *I.I.C.* 2006, no. 8, 895–897; G. Van Overwalle, 'Zonder trommels en trompetten: EU-Biotechnologierichtlijn in het Belgisch octrooirecht' [Without Drums and Trumpets: the EU Biotechnology Directive in Belgian Patent Law], *I.R.D.I.*, 2005, 357–358.

36 Two to four months after the applicant has been alerted, Art. 26 Royal Decree on Application Procedure Patents, 2 December 1986, *Official Gazette*, 6 December 1986 [K.B. 2 december 1886 betreffende het aanvragen, verlenen en in stand houden van uitvindingsoctrooien, *B.S.*, 6 december 1986].

37 G. Van Overwalle, 'Protecting and Sharing Biodiversity and Traditional Knowledge: Holders and User Tools', 53 *Ecological Economics*, 2005, 599–600.

Commercial Court (Art. 73 BPA, now Art. XVII.14 BCEL), as it is mandatory to indicate the geographical origin on the patent *application*, not in the patent description.

(2) CZECH REPUBLIC

I. Operative Rules

The ABC community does not have a right to correction.

II. Descriptive/Metalegal Formants

A patent *description* is a strictly technical document. The aim of the description of the invention is to explain the invention to a third person.[38]

The essential question is whether the ABC community can be named as a co-inventor. Under Czech law, there is no adjudication as to when a contribution of a traditional community amounts to 'inventorship' with regard to the technical teaching.

(3) DENMARK

I. Operative Rules

No, ABC has no right to correction.

II. Descriptive/Metalegal Formants

Only individual persons, and not an indigenous community like ABC, can be named as inventors in patent applications. It follows from DPR §3, fourth paragraph that if an invention concerns or uses biological material, the patent application shall include information on the country from which the inventor collected or received the material (the providing country). The lack of such information cannot lead to a rejection of the application or affect the validity of a subsequent patent. In principle, the obligation to supply the information requested is subject to penalty in accordance with the Danish Penal Code.

---

[38] See also R. Horáček, K. Čada, P. Hajn, Práva k průmyslovému vlastnictví (Rights to the Industrial Property) (1st ed., Prague: 2005), p. 78.

(4) ESTONIA

I. *Operative Rules*

ABC cannot require to be named in the patent description.

II. *Descriptive/Metalegal Formants*

The information which a patent application has to include is prescribed by the Patent Act and the regulation on requirements relating to the form and contents of documents included in patent applications[39] adopted by the Minister of Economic Affairs and Communications. For instance, the Patent Act provides that a patent application has to include information concerning the applicant and author and a description of the invention in which the invention must be disclosed in a sufficiently clear and concise manner to enable a person skilled in the art to make the invention (§19(1) clauses 1 and 2 Patent Act). Furthermore, the author of an invention has the right to 'request the disclosure of his or her name as the author' (§13(7) clause 1 Patent Act), but the 'owner' of traditional knowledge used in the research which resulted in a patentable invention is not entitled to be named in the patent description.

Q is not a party to the agreement between ABC and Tobin. Based on the information provided in the description of the case, it seems that Tobin and ABC have a valid agreement which was infringed by Tobin.

(5) FRANCE

I. *Operative Rules*

ABC has no right vis-à-vis Q to be named in the patent application.

II. *Descriptive/Metalegal Formants*

French patent law does not provide a 'right to correction'. But if Q's patent covers the invention of the ABC community, then the ABC community could institute proceedings for the transfer of ownership (action claiming ownership). Article L. 611-8 of the French Intellectual Property Code provides that:

> Where an application for the grant of an industrial property title has been made either for an invention unlawfully taken from an inventor or his successors in title, or

[39] Patenditaotluse sisu- ja vorminõuded ning Patendiametile esitamise kord. Entered into force on 14 January 2005 – RTL 2005, 5, 36 (in Estonian). Official text available at https://www.riigiteataja.ee/ert/act.jsp?replstring=33&dyn=13111167&id=833226 (6 May 2019).

in violation of a legal contractual obligation, the injured party may claim ownership of the application or of the title granted.

The legal action can cover a patent application or a patent. The claimant must prove that his/her invention has been removed or that the patent application has been made in violation of a legal contractual obligation.[40] Actions claiming ownership are barred after three years from publication of the grant of the industrial property title (Art. L. 611-8 al. 2 of the Intellectual Property Code). However, if the bad faith of the owner of the title at the time the title was granted or acquired can be proved, the time limit is three years as from the expiry of the title (Art. L. 611-8 al. 3 of the Intellectual Property Code). If the action succeeds, the court will order the transfer of the patent to its legal owner.

French patent law is applicable when the patent is a French patent, but it does not matter whether the parties are foreign nationals or not residing in France.[41] So, the ABC community could institute proceedings for the transfer of ownership (action claiming ownership) even if Q applied for a European patent.[42] The ABC community has to prove that Q's application has been made in violation of Tobin's agreement. The second condition of this agreement specifies that 'any potential patent application shall name the ABC community'.

(6) GERMANY

I. Operative Rules

ABC does not have a right to correction.

II. Descriptive Formants

ABC is in legal terms not the 'inventor' (§37 German Patent Law). §34a German Patent Law stipulates a non-mandatory duty to disclose ('*soll*' means 'ought to') for biological material of plant and animal origin only. The text is silent about (plant-related) traditional knowledge. Furthermore, in respect of traditional knowledge, problems are exacerbated by assigning the 'property' to a person or a group.

---

40 Court of Cassation (1st chamber, civil section), 22 March 2005, PIBD 2005, n°810, III, 356, the claimant must prove that all elements of the invention have been removed.

41 Paris Court of Appeal, 28 April 1976, Dalloz 1977.511.

42 Court of Strasbourg, 4 January 1983, Dossiers Brevets, 3 November 1983.

III. Metalegal Formants

The case inquires whether reference duties based on a self-standing entitlement similar to a personality right are recognised in patent law. Is there a citation duty *for the description* of a patent (of which a violation might be actionable)? Black-letter patent law does not acknowledge such a right. Patent law is focused on the inventor and the technical teaching. Any mentioning of prior knowledge only clarifies the scope of the claim. Patent law only acknowledges 'dependency' in the technical sense (the claimed technical teaching build on a prior patent teaching). No further referencing is built into the system. The right *to* the patent and the right to be mentioned are considered to be manifestations of 'one' right (here, the right *to* the patent).

(7) GREECE

I. Operative Rules

ABC has no right of correction directly against the patent office, but it may sue Tobin to achieve this by any legal means.

II. Descriptive/Metalegal Formants

ABC have in fact a right of obligation as against Tobin[43] that he should name them in the relevant patent (if it is supposed that the legal conditions are fulfilled, and he succeeds in obtaining it). It goes without saying that this right cannot be satisfied by their own direct application to the patent office (that is, in Greece to the Industrial Property Organisation (OBI)), but only following an application of the obligor Tobin. Tobin may be judicially ordered to make such an application following an action by ABC, grounded either on the contract between ABC and Tobin, or – most probably – on the infringement of ABC's (or its members') personality right. The court judgment replaces the relevant declaration-application of Tobin in accordance with Art. 949 Code of Civil Procedure, and at Tobin's expense, moreover, since in this way the claim of ABC against Tobin tends towards being an act capable of being undertaken by anyone (Art. 945 Code of Civil Procedure).

(8) IRELAND

Answer omitted.

---

43 Editors' note: The Greek report misleadingly focuses on the relation between ABC and Tobin. However, the case question refers to the rights ABC has with regard to the patent.

(9) ITALY

Answer omitted.

(10) LITHUANIA

I. Operative Rules

No, ABC does not have a right to correction.

II. Descriptive/Metalegal Formants

According to Lithuanian patent law and regulations, only the patent owner, applicant or their representatives can ask to make corrections and/or amendments to the patent description (e.g. Art. 30(1) of the Lithuanian Patent Law). As ABC is neither the patent owner nor the applicant or their representative, it cannot ask for a correction. Besides, as mentioned earlier, ABC cannot be considered an inventor or co-inventor.

(11) NETHERLANDS

Answer omitted.

(12) NORWAY

I. Operative Rules

No, ABC has no right to correction.

II. Descriptive/Metalegal Formants

Only individual persons, and not an indigenous community like ABC, can be named as inventors in patent applications. However, according to NPA §8b, first paragraph, if an invention concerns or uses biological material, the patent application shall include information on the country from which the inventor collected or received the material (the providing country). In the Biodiversity Act (Ministry Proposal, 3 April 2009),[44] it is proposed to amend this provision so as to explicitly include traditional knowledge. The fact that such information is not included, however, has no implication for the validity of the patent and there

---

[44] Enacted 19 June 2009, after the submission of this report.

is no procedure for adding the missing information in the patent description after the patent has been granted. On the other hand, breach of the obligation to disclose information is a criminal offence and is subject to penalties in accordance with §166 of the General Penal Code (22 May 1902), cf. NPA §8b.

(13) POLAND

I. Operative Rules

No, ABC has no right to correction.

II. Descriptive/Metalegal Formants

There is simply no legal ground to name ABC in the description, since it is neither the inventor nor the prospective rightholder.

(14) SLOVENIA

Answer omitted.

(15) SPAIN

I. Operative Rules

ABC probably does not have a right to correction.

II. Descriptive/Metalegal Formants

The possibility has to be considered that patents submitted by ABC or third parties do not fulfil the patent's application requirements, because a traditional cure or well-known application of traditional knowledge could be included in the scope of the closest prior art as long as they are included in the Spanish National Catalogue (but we still do not know if it will be just a list or will include medicinal properties or characteristics of the natural resources).

(16) UNITED KINGDOM

I. Operative Rules

None of the above gives ABC a right to have its name mentioned in Q's patent, even if it could show that its traditional knowledge was sufficiently implicated in Q's invention.

II. Descriptive Formants

ABC would have a right to be named if it could demonstrate that it was a co-inventor, but for the reasons given in the base case it is unlikely that it could do this.

It might have a right to be named if it could show that Q is bound by Tobin's contractual promises, but the only way this could be done would be via a Quistclose trust (see the base case above).

III. Metalegal Formants

Under English patent law, no one other than an 'inventor' or co-inventor is entitled to be named in the patent. Therefore, the answers to the base case and the modification are identical.

B.3. COMPARATIVE REMARKS

In all jurisdictions under review, ABC has *no* right to correction, *nor* a right to be named in the patent (application). However, in some jurisdictions, ABC has the right to *claim* that reference be made in the patent (application) to the geographical origin in their region of the genetic resource on the basis of which the invention was developed.

Specific legislation operationalising this objective has been put in place at a very slow pace and in a fragmented way (cf. Estonian, Germany, Greek and Norwegian reports).[45]

The ABC community has no right to be named, since ABC is not the inventor of the lead component (see section A.4 above), nor is ABC an individual person (see section A.4 above). Subsequently, ABC cannot institute proceedings for correction of the patent application, nor for the transfer of ownership (see section A.4 above). ABC cannot claim a right to be named based on the agreement with Tobin, as Q is not party to that agreement, and ABC has no contractual relationship with Q (see section A.4 above).

---

45 At the time of the drafting of the national reports, no specific measures had been put in place. However, in the meantime, the Nagoya Protocol on Access to Genetic Resources and the Fair and Equitable Sharing of Benefits Arising from their Utilization to the Convention on Biological Diversity has been undersigned. The Nagoya Protocol is a supplementary agreement to the CBD and provides a transparent legal framework for the effective implementation of the third objective of the CBD: the fair and equitable sharing of benefits arising out of the utilisation of genetic resources. The Nagoya Protocol was adopted on 29 October 2010 in Nagoya (Japan) and entered into force on 12 October 2014. For more details, see https://www.cbd.int/abs/, last visited 25 July 2017.

Some countries have introduced an *explicit* origin indication requirement (Belgium, Denmark, Norway), in an attempt to give legal effect to the rather non-committal language of the principle laid down in Recital 27 Biotechnology Directive. Recital 27 requires that 'whereas if an invention is based on biological material of plant or animal origin or if it uses such material, the patent application should, where appropriate, include information on the geographical origin of such material, if known; whereas this is without prejudice to the processing of patent applications or the validity of rights arising from granted patents'. However, the named countries differ in the enforcement regime of said origin indication requirement. Some countries opt for a rather fierce approach and set forth that non-fulfilment of the requirement will result in rejection of the patent application (e.g. Belgium). Other countries underline that the non-fulfilment of the requirement may affect the patent's validity, but may only result in measures outside patent law, such as criminal penalties (e.g. Denmark, Norway).

C.1. MODIFICATION 2

Q develops a derivative from the substance. The new substance is easily produced chemically in large quantities. Q is granted a patent. Is ABC entitled to a share of the profits?

C.2. COUNTRY REPORTS

(1) BELGIUM

I. Operative Rules

ABC is not entitled to a share of the profits.

II. Descriptive Formants

Article 15(7) CBD states that benefits arising from genetic resources should be shared in a fair and equitable way and that contracting parties shall for this purpose take legislative, administrative or policy measures.[46] The disclosure of origin as imposed by Article 15§1 6° BPA (Art. XI.16§1 6° BCEL) is a first step towards this aim.[47] The definitive positive consequence of introducing the

46 Convention on Biological Diversity, 5 June 1992, www.cbd.int (last consulted on 6 May 2019).

47 G. Van Overwalle, 'The Implementation of the Biotechnology Directive in Belgium and its Aftereffects. The Introduction of a New Research Exemption and a Compulsory License for Public Health', 37 *I.I.C.* 2006, no. 8, 895; G. Van Overwalle, 'Zonder trommels en trompetten:

disclosure of origin requirement is that the patent applicant needs to publicly take a position on whether or not he/she has used biological material of plant or animal origin, and if so, where it came from. Lying at this point could, perhaps, trigger the civil liability regime (Art. 1382 Civil Code), potentially allowing for compensatory damages for moral or material damages. It can hardly be accepted that a *bonus pater familias* would completely disregard prior informed consent, the disclosure of origin requirement or the benefit-sharing principle.

One could, on the basis of international private law, also be held liable for damages arising from ignoring foreign law. According to Article 99 of the Belgian International Private Law Code,[48] the law of ABC's country could, under certain conditions, be applicable.[49] Of course, a lot will then still depend on the degree to which ABC's country has implemented the CBD.

Even if the CBD has no direct effect, and even if the national legislator has not implemented its principles, judges can interpret national regulations in conformity with international law.[50] In this regard, the benefit-sharing principle might play a role in applying certain theories, such as unjust enrichment.[51] However, in conclusion, a judicial verdict enforcing the benefit-sharing principle under current law would be quite remarkable

A 2% share of the benefits was negotiated between the 'council of the elderly' and Tobin, but it is conceivable that ABC would not succeed in delivering evidence of the agreement in court.

III. Metalegal Formants

The way to actually realise the principle of fair and equitable sharing, as expressed in an international legally binding text, remains far from clear.[52]

EU-Biotechnologierichtlijn in het Belgisch octrooirecht' [Without Drums and Trumpets: the EU Biotechnology Directive in Belgian Patent Law], *I.R.D.I.* 2005, 357.

48 International Private Law Code, 16 July 2004, *Official Gazette*, 27 July 2004 [Wet houdende het wetboek van internationaal privaatrecht, 16 juli 2004, *B.S.*, 27 juli 2004].

49 Assuming first that regular residence is not the same for ABC and Tobin, second that the wrongful act and damage itself are not easily situated in one country, and third that ABC's country is deemed to be the country with which the tort is more connected. For interesting comments, see J. Verlinden, 'Artikel 99 Recht toepasselijk op verbintenissen uit onrechtmatige daad' [Article 99 Law Applicable on Tort Obligations], in: J. Erauw et al. (eds.), *Het Wetboek Internationaal Privaatrecht becommentarieerd [The International Private Law Code Commented]* (Brussels: 2006), 507–514.

50 E. David and J. Salmon, *Droit des gens [International Law]* (Vol. 1, Brussels: 2004), 135–139.

51 Application of this theory would be quite uncertain. For an overview on the principles of unjust enrichment according to Belgian law: C. Marr, 'L'enrichissement sans cause. Un fondement d'équité sous une apparante rigueur ...' [Unjust Enrichment], in: S. Stijns and P. Wéry (eds.), *De bronnen van niet-contractuele verbintenissen [The Sources of Non-Contractual Obligations]* (Brugge: 2007), 209–257.

52 See for an overview: G. Van Overwalle, 'Protecting and Sharing Biodiversity and Traditional Knowledge: Holders and User Tools', 53 *Ecological Economics*, 2005, 585–607. Also see V. Ost, 'Les brevets portant sur les inventions biotechnologiques' [Patents on Biotechnological

The CBD should be considered more as a framework agreement[53] and the benefit-sharing principle does not seem to fulfil the conditions to have direct effect under international law, i.e. conferring rights to individuals and being precise and complete.[54] And even if the origin requirement is implemented and the origin is properly disclosed, the challenging task remains enforcing real benefit-sharing.

(2) CZECH REPUBLIC

I. Operative Rules

The ABC community is not entitled to a share of the profits.

II. Descriptive Formants

The Patent Act does not include any provision which could be applied to support the ABC community's entitlement to a share of the profits.

The agreement concluded between the ABC community and Tobin says that the ABC community shall obtain a 2% share in any profits that are generated from exploiting the patent. The agreement is clear in this case and there is no possibility for an interpretation that Tobin is obliged to pay a share of the profits to the ABC community when he patents a new substance, even though that substance is based on a former ABC community substance.

III. Metalegal Formants

Answer omitted.

(3) DENMARK

I. Operative Rules

ABC is not entitled to a share of the profits.

Inventions], in: B. Remiche (ed.), *Brevet, innovation et intérêt général. Le Brevet : pourquoi et pour faire quoi ? [Patent, Innovation and Public Interest. Patents: Why and Wherefore?]* (Brussels: 2007), 160–163.

53 G. Van Overwalle, 'Traditional Medicinal Knowledge, Patents and the Convention on Biological Diversity', *Ing.-Cons.*, 2001, nos. 5-6-7, 182.

54 Court of Cassation [Cass.], 27 May 1971, *Fromagerie Franco-Suisse 'Le Ski'*, *J.T.* 1971, 471, following the logic of European case law: CJEU judgment of 5 February 1963, *Van Gend & Loos*, C-26/62, ECLI:EU:C:1963:1.

II. Descriptive Formants

Given that Q has created a new and independent invention, ABC has no right to a share of the profits from it. If Q's patent, however, is dependent on Tobin's invention, ABC will have a contractual right to a share of Tobin's profit from the licensing agreement with Q.

III. Metalegal Formants

The principle of a fair and equitable sharing of benefits derived from genetic resources, cf. Article 15(7) of the Convention on Biological Diversity, is not reflected in patent law to date as a ground for giving the owner of the resources any claim to a share of the profits resulting from inventions based on the resources.

(4) ESTONIA

I. Operative Rules

ABC cannot require any remuneration from Q.

II. Descriptive Formants

It can be assumed that Q receives the information about the plant from Tobin. Still, the contract is between Tobin and ABC. Consequently, ABC cannot require any remuneration from Q.

III. Metalegal Formants

Answer omitted.

(5) FRANCE

I. Operative Rules

The ABC community is not entitled to a share of the profits.

II. Descriptive Formants

Q's patent covers a derivative of the substance. The agreement specifies that: 'ABC shall obtain a 2% share in any profit that is generated from exploiting the patent'. But the agreement refers to the profits that are generated from exploiting the patent granted on the application of the ABC community's plant extract.

It does not refer to the profits that are generated from exploiting the patent granted on a derivative from this substance.

III. Metalegal Formants

Answer omitted.

(6) GERMANY

I. Operative Rules

ABC has no claim to a share in profits.

II. Descriptive Formants

Articles 1 and 15(7) Convention on Biological Diversity (CBD) were not transposed mandatorily. The general rule of §812 I 1, case 2 BGB (*'in sonstiger Weise erlangen'*) requires an encroachment on a legal position (*'Eingriff in den Zuweisungsgehalt eines fremden Rechts'*). As traditional knowledge is not yet accepted as a 'legal position', ABC has no claim under §812 sec. 1 BGB.

III. Metalegal Formants

The problem relates to the non-existence of a proper concept of benefit-sharing. This is similar to problems raised in human genetics (Case 7). Negotiations on a global regime to find more equitable solutions are underway in WIPO and the CBD. Thus far, Germany has not stood out in pushing the discussion forward and has not acted nationally (other than hosting the conference which brought about the Bonn Guidelines). Beyond some isolated projects funded by the GIZ (Gesellschaft für Internationale Zusammenarbeit, Agency for Foreign Aid), there is no concerted action to bring about a model for benefit-sharing contracts.

(7) GREECE

I. Operative Rules

ABC may claim a sum of money if the contract[55] covered the producing of derivatives or otherwise to the extent that the production of the derivative was due to ABC's instructions.

---

[55] Editors' note: The Greece report is misleading, as it focuses on the contract, whereas the contract between ABC and Tobin does not stretch out to Q.

II. *Descriptive Formants*

The answer to the question depends in principle on the will of the parties. If the creation of a derivative and the subsequent trading in it is included in the contract between ABC and Tobin, then ABC will only be entitled to what is provided for by their contract with Tobin (2%). If the interpretation of the contract between Tobin and ABC leads to the conclusion that the permission for the production of the derivative has been given, but an agreement on a consideration has not been concluded for the commercial exploitation of the product on the part of Tobin, then ABC are entitled to determine appropriate consideration in their reasonable judgement by a unilateral declaration to Tobin according to Articles 371–372, 379 Civil Code.

If, again, the contract between ABC and Tobin does not cover the incident at all, then the members of ABC have rights over the profits realised up to the present and over Tobin's invention itself, at a percentage, naturally, which corresponds to the 'adequate' (i.e. foreseeable) causal contribution of ABC's instructions and not to Tobin's own scientific labour (Arts. 904, 734 and 719 of the Civil Code).

III. *Metalegal Formants*

Answer omitted.

(8) IRELAND

Answer omitted.

(9) ITALY

Answer omitted.

(10) LITHUANIA

I. *Operative Rules*

No, ABC is not entitled to a share of the profits (except where a contractual obligation is established).

II. Descriptive/Metalegal Formants

First, it is not clear what the relationship between Q and Tobin is. Presumably, Q is an independent person, having no direct relationship with ABC and Tobin. Even if Q and Tobin are working for the same employer, Q is the owner of patent, and not the employer. As ABC is not an inventor, it has no rights with respect to the substance, nor, *a fortiori*, to the derivative. Any contractual obligation between Q and ABC is also absent.

ABC could be entitled to a share of the profits only indirectly, if Q's invention relies on the previous patent issued to Tobin and the latter is bound by contract to share the profits with ABC.

(11) NETHERLANDS

Answer omitted.

(12) NORWAY

I. Operative Rules

ABC is not entitled to a share of the profits.

II. Descriptive Formants

Given that Q has created a new and independent invention, ABC has no right to a share of the profits from it. If Q's patent, however, is dependent on Tobin's patent, ABC will have a contractual right to a share of Tobin's profit from the licensing agreement with Q.

III. Metalegal Formants

The principle of a fair and equitable sharing of benefits derived from genetic resources, cf. Article 15(7) of the Convention on Biological Diversity, is not reflected in patent law to date as grounds for giving the owner of the resources any claim to a share of the profits resulting from inventions based on the resources.

(13) POLAND

I. Operative Rules

ABC is probably not entitled to a share of the profits.

II. Descriptive/Metalegal Formants

The law on industrial property (and all other imaginable statutes from the area of IP law or general civil law) does not provide a legal ground for such a claim. If ABC were a party to the contract with Q (or formed an organisation capable of being one), there could be a purely contractual legal basis for a share of benefits.

(14) SLOVENIA

Answer omitted.

(15) SPAIN

I. Operative Rules

ABC could claim economic profits from the patent.

II. Descriptive Formants

Article 70 of the Law 42/2007 of 13 December on Natural Patrimony and Biodiversity recognises this right by obliging the Spanish authorities to ensure that benefits arising from the commercial and other utilisation of genetic resources will be shared in a fair and equitable way.

III. Metalegal Formants

Answer omitted.

(16) UNITED KINGDOM

I. Operative Rules

ABC almost certainly does not have a right to a share of Q's profits, except possibly under the UK legislation implementing the Nagoya Protocol.

II. Descriptive Formants

ABC has no contractual rights against Q.

If it could show that Tobin held the information he acquired under the contract under a Quistclose trust (base case above), ABC could claim a share in Q's profits provided (1) Q was not a good faith purchaser and (2) that there was a sufficient connection between ABC's traditional knowledge and Q's product (above, but even less likely here because Q developed a derivative from the plant substance).

The UK Nagoya legislation does not give a supplier of traditional knowledge a direct right to a share of profits, but it may be a remedy for ABC that the courts would be willing to develop. But again, ABC's major problem would be showing a sufficient connection between its traditional knowledge and Q's invention.

III. Metalegal Formants

The difficulty of proving that the development of a derivative is attributable to an earlier appropriation of traditional knowledge will make it impossible for a community to prove a Quistclose trust in most cases. However, if that difficulty can be overcome, the Quistclose trust may be operable for many of the current forms of appropriation of traditional knowledge where the user has notice of breach of an earlier agreement.

C.3. COMPARATIVE REMARKS

In all jurisdictions under review, except one (Spain), ABC is *not* entitled to a share of the profits. In some jurisdictions, ABC *might have* a claim for damages (Belgium).

On a contractual basis, no jurisdiction awards a share of the profits to ABC, because the agreement in the present case has been concluded between ABC and Tobin, to which Q is not party (see section A.4 above). However, if Q's patent is dependent on Tobin's invention, ABC might have a contractual right to a share of Tobin's profit from the licensing agreement with Q (Denmark, Norway).

The right to claim that reference be made to the geographical origin of the genetic resource on the basis of which the invention was developed might be argued based on the Biotechnology Directive, in particular Recital 27 (see section B.3 above). We identify three ways of argumentation. First, it has been argued that the patent applicant, Q, might trigger application of the civil liability regime, allowing for compensatory damages for moral or material damages for ABC, *if* he had been lying about the geographical origin when applying for the patent (Belgium). Second, the patent applicant could be held liable *if* his/her behaviour is considered to ignore foreign law (which must be demanded to be respected by domestic law), *in casu* the law implementing the CBD in ABC's country (Belgium). Along these lines, it has been suggested that the ABC community might try to request sharing of the benefits on the basis of the theory of unjust enrichment (Belgium). The outcome of such a request will be most uncertain at this point in time. Third, a claim might emerge under common law trust principles.

The reports reveal that the third objective of the CBD (the principle of 'fair and equitable sharing of the benefits arising out of the utilisation of genetic resources') has not been transposed and operationalised in most jurisdictions, with the exception of Spain. Without regulation in place, the CBD principle alone cannot serve to invest the owner of a genetic resource with a claim for the profits resulting from inventions developed on the basis of that resource.

CASE 11. GRANT-BACK AND REACH-THROUGH (PUBLIC RESEARCH INSTITUTIONS)

A.1. BASE CASE

After years of in-house research, the large IT-Company (ITC) outsourced its research facilities in the beginning of the 1990s. By now, it contracts not only with its own subdivision but also with a diverse range of universities and public and private research institutions, including spin-offs. ITC contractors are obliged to transfer future intellectual property rights to ITC. In breach of this contractual obligation, Prof. Brain of M-University applies for a patent in the name of M-University. M-University transfers the granted patent to a group of students undertaking a start-up.

Can ITC challenge the patent?

A.2. COUNTRY REPORTS

(1) BELGIUM

I. Operative Rules

ITC can claim the transfer of the patent.

II. Descriptive Formants

Article 9 BPA (Art. XI.10 BCEL) states that:

> Where an application for the grant of a patent has been made either for an invention unlawfully taken from an inventor or his successors in title or in violation of a legal or contractual obligation, the injured party may, in his capacity as owner, claim the transfer of the application or of the granted patent, notwithstanding all other rights or proceedings.[1]

---

[1] M. Buydens, *Droit des brevets d'invention et protection du savoir-faire [Patent and Protection of Know-how Law]* (Brussels: 1999), 85–86.

The BPA does not foresee explicit clauses on commission contracts (e.g. research contracts). Therefore, the specific wording of such a contract is decisive for the ownership of any inventions or patents. Clearly Prof. Brain and M-University applying for this patent are in breach of their contractual obligations, since they were required to transfer all IP to ITC, which can therefore demand the transfer of the application on the basis of Article 9 BPA (Art. XI.10 BCEL).[2]

III. Metalegal Formants

The BPA does not regulate situations of inventions of employees or on commission. This is somewhat strange, since a large majority of patent applications concern inventions made in the context of research carried out in (larger) firms. It is even more remarkable given that these situations are regulated in all other domains of intellectual property rights, for example Article 3 BCA (Art. XI.4 BCEL). The reasons for this lacuna lie in the fact that the obstinate positions of employer and employee organisations could not be reconciled.[3] Given the current legal vacuum, solutions should be sought in contract law and doctrine.[4]

(2) CZECH REPUBLIC

I. Operative Rules

ITC can challenge the patent.

II. Descriptive Formants

The contract between ITC and M-University is governed by sections 536–565 of the Commercial Code 513/1991 Coll. as a contract on work. Section 558 of the Commercial Code is based on the principle that a contractor is the owner of the industrial rights and the client has a licence to use the work. But this is a non-mandatory provision and thus can be excluded by the agreement of the parties.

2 M.-C. Janssens, 'Uitvindingen in dienstverband met bijzondere aandacht voor uitvindingen aan universiteiten' [Employee and University Inventions], *CIR series Katholieke Universiteit Leuven* no. 12 (Brussels: 1995), 281–288; M. Buydens, *Droit des brevets d'invention et protection du savoir-faire [Patent and Protection of Know-how Law]* (Brussels: 1999), 91–92. For a case law example: Court of 1st Instance, Antwerp [Rb. Antwerpen], 30 June 2006, *Ing.-Cons.* 2006, no. 3, 303.

3 M.-C. Janssens, 'Uitvindingen in dienstverband met bijzondere aandacht voor uitvindingen aan universiteiten' [Employee and University Inventions], *CIR series Katholieke Universiteit Leuven* no. 12 (Brussels: 1995), 215–221.

4 For an overview: M.-C. Janssens, 'Uitvindingen in dienstverband met bijzondere aandacht voor uitvindingen aan universiteiten' [Employee and University Inventions], *CIR series Katholieke Universiteit Leuven* no. 12 (Brussels: 1995), 213–299; M. Buydens, *Droit des brevets d'invention et protection du savoir-faire [Patent and Protection of Know-how Law]* (Brussels: 1999), 87–92.

The obligation to transfer future intellectual property rights is in accordance with the provisions of the Commercial Code.

The contract between M-University and the students' start-up is governed by the provisions of sections 409–470 of the Commercial Code as a purchase contract. The problem is that according to section 409(1) of the Commercial Code, a seller is obliged to transfer moveable property to a purchaser. The industrial rights are not moveable property, so provisions on the purchase contract shall be applied only by the principle of *analogia legis*. According to section 546 of the Commercial Code, a purchaser may obtain goods from the seller even if the seller is not the owner of goods. But if the purchaser knows, had known or should know, then the transfer of goods is not valid. According to the doctrine, a restrictive interpretation shall apply.[5] It is doubtful whether the students were acting *bona fide* because they had known and should have known that M-University was working on research for ITC. This exception to the principle *nemo plus iuris ad alium transferre potest quam ipse habet* does not apply in this case.

According to the provision of section 8(1) Patent Act, the right to patent belongs to the inventor or his/her legal successor. If ITC concluded a contract with M-University with the obligation to transfer future intellectual property rights to ITC, then ITC is the legal successor of the inventor.

According to section 29 Patent Act, the Patent Office shall transfer the patent to the person whom the court decides is the proprietor of the patent. In this case, ITC is the legal successor of the inventor and the court should confirm this. The Patent Office is then obliged to replace the name of the students' undertaking with the name of ITC.

If the aim of ITC is only to revoke the patent, then ITC is allowed to revoke the patent in accordance with section 23(1)(d) Patent Act. But first, ITC needs a court decision that it is the legal successor of the inventor and that it has the right to the patent.

III. Metalegal Formants

There are no special rules on the transfer of inventions before the inventions are patented, thus no special safeguards for public research. The general rules of civil and commercial law apply.

(3) DENMARK

I. Operative Rules

Yes, ITC can challenge the patent.

5 Judgment of the Constitutional Court of 13 June 2006, Pl. ÚS 75/04.

II. *Descriptive Formants*

Provided that the contract is valid and that it can be interpreted as comprising the patent in question, ITC will have the right to apply for and be granted the patent (DPA §1). Consequently, Prof. Brain's application is in conflict with DPA §1 and the granted patent is void. Even though the students have acquired the rights from the University in good faith, it will not affect ITC's patent rights. ITC can demand that the rights be transferred from the students under DPA §18, which states that if anyone proves before the Danish Patent Office that he/she, and not the applicant, is entitled to the invention, the Patent Office shall, instead of refusing the application for that reason, transfer the patent to the real owner if he/she so requests.

III. *Metalegal Formants*

The case revolves around the tension in contract research between the true inventor (and his/her institution) and the institution which commissions the resolution of a technical problem: Who owns the technical teaching? Can public research institutions be made subject to ordinary 'grant-back clauses' used in industrial business? Danish law, in these constellations, takes back the control from the inventor and resolves the tension in favour of the research sponsor.

(4) ESTONIA

I. *Operative Rules*

ITC has the right to register the patent in its name or to revoke the patent.

II. *Descriptive Formants*

ITC and M-University have concluded a research contract according to which M-University is obliged to transfer future all IP rights. The contract is presumably valid.

Pursuant to §12(1) Patent Act, '[t]he right to apply for a patent and to become the proprietor of a patent is vested in the author of the invention and a legal successor of the author'. This principle is made more specific by §12(2) Patent Act: '[i]f an invention is created in the performance of contractual obligations or duties of employment, the right to apply for a patent and to become the proprietor of the patent is vested in the author or other person pursuant to the contract or employment contract'.

Based on the above, it can be said that the research contract gives ITC the right to apply for the patent. Subsection 49(1) Patent Act provides:

> Any person who finds that the right to a patent belongs to the person pursuant to §12 of this Act may, after the publication of a patent application pursuant to the provisions of §24 of this Act, file an action in court against the applicant or proprietor of the patent for recognition of the person's rights. If the action is satisfied in the case of a patent application, the person has the right to continue applying for the patent in the person's name, revoke the patent application and file a new patent application with the same filing date concerning the same invention or revoke the patent application. In the case of a patent, the person has the right to register the patent, unamended or subject to amendments, in the person's name or revoke the patent.

III. Metalegal Formants

The Principles of Legal Regulation of Industrial Property Act[6] was adopted *inter alia* to regulate the status of industrial property registers.[7] Section 18 of the Principles of Legal Regulation of Industrial Property Act provides a general principle according to which '[a] person who submits data shall be responsible for the correctness thereof. Persons who submit false information shall be liable for damage wrongfully caused'. It has been explained that according to this provision the state does not guarantee the correctness of the data in the industrial property registers. Consequently, acquisition in good faith on the basis of information entered in the registers is not possible.[8]

(5) FRANCE

I. Operative Rules

While ITC cannot challenge the patent, it may claim for damages for breach of contract.

II. Descriptive Formants

Under IP law, two situations must be distinguished. French law states the reasons for which a patent can be challenged (Art. L. 613-25 of the French Intellectual

---

6 Tööstusomandi õiguskorralduse aluste seadus. Entered into force on 1 May 2004 – RT I 2003, 18, 98; 2009, 4, 24 (in Estonian). Official text available at https://www.riigiteataja.ee/ert/act.jsp?id=13122234 (6 May 2019).

7 Principles of Legal Regulation of Industrial Property Act §1(1).

8 V. Kõve, *Varaliste tehingute süsteem Eestis* (System of proprietary transactions in Estonia), Doctoral Thesis, Supervisor Professor I. Kull, p. 213.

Property Code). These reasons concern the lack of patentability of the invention, an inadequate description of the patent, the extent of the object of the patent beyond the original application's content and, finally, a specific reason concerning the extent of the scale of protection of the patent when this has been limited. The breach of a contractual provision cannot be used to challenge the patent. It plays no role whether the applicant filed a French or a European application since the reasons for challenging a patent are similar (Art. 138(1) EPC).

The situation would have been different if the contract had stipulated that the results of the research belonged to ITC. This would have meant that ITC would have contractually been the only entity that could have filed the application. In this case, ITC could challenge a European patent as far as Article 138(1)(e) EPC provides for this possibility (if the proprietor of the patent is not the entitled one). This solution is not available under French law, which implies that, in this case, a French patent cannot be challenged.

Under Article L. 611-8 of the French Intellectual Property Code, for an application to be issued as a patent, the patentee must be either the inventor or a successor according to Article L. 611-6 of the French Intellectual Property Code. If, however, the invention was removed from the inventor or from his/her successors, or the filing was realised in violation of a legal or contractual provision, then ITC could vindicate the patent.

We read the contractual term of the case as an obligation of Professor Brain to transfer future intellectual property rights, not as an obligation to allow ITC to file a patent. Assuming that filing the patent was legal, the violation of a contractual provision which provides the obligation to transfer the patent after its issuance cannot be sanctioned by invalidating the patent.

Under contract law, damages can be obtained by ITC.

III. Metalegal Formants

French law respects grant-back clauses. A research contract can, of course, provide various clauses concerning the property of the research results. From the perspective of patent law, the given case does not raise the question of who the owner of the research result is, but only who the owner of a granted patent is. This question is purely translational; any provision which stipulates ownership is not, *per se*, in any breach of a legal provision. A breach of those stipulations can be considered a violation of a contract, resulting in damage claims.

(6) GERMANY

I. Operative Rules

ITC cannot challenge the patent, but can claim damages.

II. *Descriptive Formants*

a) IP law provides no remedy

Two remedies are to be considered. First, there is the 'everybody's right' of §§59, 21 German Patent Code, which provides that a challenge to an issued patent has to be justified by patentability arguments (reasons listed in §21 German Patent Code).[9] The authority to file for a patent is not a reason listed. Secondly, under §8 German Patent Code, the 'entitled person' can vindicate the patent from the non-entitled one. 'Entitled' is the inventor and his/her successor. ITC is contractually authorised to become successor, but yet succession has not taken place. Neither the right to file for the patent (as e.g. given to the employer as '*Anmelder*', §7 German Patent Code) nor a contractual right to the patent is sufficient. Thus, ITC has no right to claim the vindication of the patent.

b) Contract law

The underlying question rests on contract law. Were Prof. Brain/M-University obliged to transfer the rights to the patent to ITC? Is the contract clause valid? If it were possible to become the owner of the patent, ITC has a right under §8 German Patent Code.

Under former German law, grant-back clauses in licensing contracts were generally held invalid as a violation of competition law (§17 sec. 2 No. 2 German Antitrust Code).[10] However, the contract between ITC and M-University is a research contract, not a licence. Since §17 German Antitrust Code was abolished in June 2005, one needs to consider whether EU competition law applies. However, even supposing it does,[11] Article 5(1)(b) Regulation (EC) No. 772/2004 (now Art. 5(1) Regulation (EU) No. 314/2014)[12] only applies to obligations in licensing contracts. In the given case, the contract is a paid research contract, not a licence. Most probably, the rationale cannot be transferred.

One could think of a violation of the *ordre public* (§242 BGB) considering that the freedom of research could be impaired. However, Article 5 sec. of the German Constitution does not provide a full-fledged protection against appropriation in paid research. The contract is valid. Prof. Brain and M-University are liable for breach of a contractual duty. As long as the right is still in the hands of

9 Equivalent to Art. 99 EPC.

10 R. Kraßer, *Patentrecht* (5th ed., Munich: 2004), p. 980. The exception rule of §17 sec. 2 German Antitrust Code was narrowly interpreted: only the obligation to grant back dependent improvement inventions was considered to be legal.

11 In any case, the applicable norm would be Art. 82 EC Treaty/Art. 102 TFEU. However, Regulation (EC) No. 772/2004 is conceived of as an exception of Art. 81 EC Treaty/Art. 101 TFEU.

12 OJ L 123, 27 April 2004, 11, substituted by Regulation (EU) No. 316/2014, OJ L 93, 28 March 2014, 17. Art. 5(1)(b) Regulation (EC) No. 772/2004 became integrated in Art. 5(1)(a) Regulation (EU) No. 314/2014. The content remained the same.

Prof. Brain and M-University, they would be obliged to transfer the title. After transferring the title to the students, ITC is entitled to damages (§§283, 275, 249 et seq. BGB).

III. Metalegal Formants

To what extent can industry exercise control over commissioned research by *ex ante* ownership arrangements and to approximate it to an employer/employee relationship via a prior transferral clause (so-called 'grant-back clause')? The issue is contentious since it touches on basic rationales of 'inventor's law' and on assumptions of how innovation takes place in modern industrialised societies. Two rationales dominate the analysis. First, can the sceptical stance of competition law towards grant-back clauses be transposed as a yardstick to evaluate contract clauses outside the domain of competition law? Second, can the rationale of employees' inventions be transposed to contract research? In the relationship between an employer and an employee, it is necessary to expressly claim and compensate the employee for the invention made. The concurring concept where the property right to the employee's invention is directly assigned to the employer is historically discredited in Germany.[13] From an innovation standpoint, the economic situation is at least comparable. Despite these evident tensions, German law has remained silent about the tensions in what has become labelled 'technology transfer' (meaning transfer of commodified research from public research institutions to industry).

(7) GREECE

I. Operative Rules

ITC may not challenge the patent of third parties not contractually related to ITC.

II. Descriptive Formants

Prof. Brain is an independent contractor and not an employee of ITC and therefore his inventions would not belong *ipso jure* and without further formality to ITC (hence Art. 6 Law 1733/1987 *e contrario*; Art. 177 Civil Code). Towards ITC he has only a contractual obligation of the further re-transfer of percentages on the patents, etc. (Art. 683 Civil Code). Thus, the relevant claim of ITC can be addressed directly only against Prof. Brain, and not against third parties. Such third parties are, for example, the original beneficiary, M-University as the

13 Notwithstanding continuous efforts to reform the system.

employer of Prof. Brain, who made the relevant 'in-house' invention; in-house inventions belong *ipso jure* to the employer of the inventor according to Article 6 para. 4 Law 1733/1987.[14] Likewise third parties are the students to whom the new biopatent will belong in full following the transfer from M-University.

III. Metalegal Formants

Under Greek law, there is no specific governance frame for technology transfer. Usual civil and commercial law apply.

(8) IRELAND

I. Operative Rules

Yes, ITC will have a right to challenge the patent.

II. Descriptive Formants

Under section 16(1) of the Patents Act 1992, 'the right to a patent shall belong to the inventor or his successors in title' and, according to Clark, Smyth and Hall, the leading academic writers in this area, this possibly includes employers.[15] Anyone can, under section 15, apply for a patent. Section 2 stipulates that the inventor is the 'actual deviser of an invention'.

Section 57(1) provides that 'any person may apply to the Court or the Controller for revocation of a patent'. One of the grounds for revocation of a patent is to be found in section 58(e), which states that an application for revocation of a patent may be made on the grounds that 'the proprietor of the patent is not entitled thereto under section 16(1)'. In other words, the patent owner is neither the inventor nor a successor in title of the inventor; therefore, ITC would have to establish that they are the successor in title of the inventor in order to succeed. The applicant entitled under section 58(e) would have to seek to have the patent revoked by a court, pursuant to section 81(2), which provides that an application for a patent revocation on this ground may only be made by a

---

14 On the contrary, as 'free invention' is characterised by the one lying outside of the scope of his labour relation (Rokas, *Industrial Property* (2004), no. 12; Antonopoulos, *Industrial Property* (2002), p. 813). On inventions of employees see, for preference, Hatzinikolaou/Angelidou, 'The new regulation on inventive activity of employees', in *Volume in Honour of N. Deloukas I* (1989), pp. 19 ff. On the notion of 'in-house inventions' as inventions made within the scope of employment, and devised on the orders of the employer, see for preference Rokas, *Industrial Property* (2004), no. 13; Antonopoulos, *Industrial Property* (2002), p. 814.

15 R. Clark, S. Smyth and N. Hall, *Intellectual Property Law in Ireland* (3rd ed., Dublin: 2010), p. 187.

person found by the court to be entitled to be granted that patent. The time limit in which the challenger must act after the grant of the patent is two years under section 81(2), unless it can be demonstrated that the patent holder knew that he/she was not entitled to the patent.

If the court finds that a patent was granted to a person who was not so entitled, under section 81(4), it may permit a new patent application. Under section 82(1), where there is such a change of proprietorship of a patent, when the name of the new patent owner is entered on the register, licences which had been in force before the transfer lapse.

We are not sure whether the students knew that Prof. Brain was in breach of his contractual rights, but if they were acting in good faith and had either used or had made serious preparations to use the invention within the state, they can apply for a non-exclusive licence from the new patent owner.

III. Metalegal Formants

According to the leading academic commentators on this area,[16] there are no legislative criteria for ownership in Ireland in a situation where the inventor is an employee. This area, therefore, is governed by the common law and, given the dearth of Irish case law, Irish courts look to the UK for guidance.[17] However, it is of note that they will have to consider section 39 of the UK Patents Act 1977, which reflects the then contemporaneous common law position regarding ownership of inventions made by employees. Such inventions will belong to an employer where they have been made in the course of the employee's normal duties. This is as far as the guidance will go, as the relevant provision in the UK Patents Act is now determinative and UK courts no longer follow the common law in this area. Therefore, Ireland will follow an out-of-date position in UK law. Unless there is an express provision to the contrary, there is an implied common law term that an employee is a trustee of his/her employer where the invention has been made in the course of the employee's duties.

(9) ITALY

I. Operative Rules

Yes, ITC can challenge the patent, once it is settled that it has the exclusive right to file the patent.

---

16 Ibid., p. 92.

17 In the absence of a binding precedent in Ireland, normally judges consider judgments of other common law jurisdictions, especially that of our nearest neighbour, the UK.

II. Descriptive Formants

Article 64 c. 1 Industrial Property Code[18] states that if an invention is made in the course of an employment relationship or in the execution of a contract where the inventive activity is explicitly provided for and compensated, the rights originating from the invention belong to the employer, with the exception of the right to be named as the inventor. Therefore, the specific wording and conditions agreed to between ITC and its contractors are necessary to establish who the right to file the patent belongs to.

If all the conditions of c. 1 are met, except for the provision of a specific compensation, the right to file the patent belongs to the employer, but he/she is obliged to award a 'fair (monetary) prize' to the inventor. This reward is calculated by considering the importance of the protection given to the invention, the role played by the inventor and his/her general compensation, and the contribution that the inventor has obtained from the employer organisation (Art. 64 c. 2 Industrial Property Code).

Finally, if none of the conditions are met, but the invention is relevant in the field of the employer, the latter has an 'option right' for the exploitation of the invention. A market price has to be paid for such exploitation. If the price is not fully paid within the agreed term, all the rights derived from the exercise of the option become automatically void (Art. 64 c. 3 Industrial Property Code).

III. Metalegal Formants

Italian law treats employee inventions and contracted inventions alike, and thus provides for a particularly strong position for the research sponsor. This situation is in some tension with the reform of 2001, which introduces the professor's privilege and aimed at enhancing technology transfer by strengthening the position of university professors.

(10) LITHUANIA

Answer omitted.

(11) NETHERLANDS

I. Operative Rules

Under the current circumstances, it seems quite unlikely that ITC can challenge the patent on the basis of the Dutch Patent Act.

---

[18] The current Industrial Property Code was created by d.lgs. 10 February 2005, no. 30, which systematised previous fragmentary dispositions.

II. *Descriptive Formants*

It is assumed that M-University is the contractor of ITC and Prof. Brain is an employee of M-University. According to Article 75(1) DPA, there are two reasons on the basis of which the patent can be invalidated. The first ground for any person to challenge the patent is the failure of the invention to meet the patentability requirements (Art. 75(3) DPA). The second ground to start an invalidation proceeding is when another person than the holder of the patent is entitled to the patent by virtue of the provisions of Chapter 1 DPA.

In principle, by virtue of Article 8 DPA the first person to file a patent application is deemed to be entitled to the patent. However, the subsequent articles of Chapter 1 DPA encompass a limited set of exceptions to this principle, according to which parties other than the patent applicant are entitled to the patent. First, according to Article 12 DPA, employees are entitled to the patent if they invented the patented invention while in employment, unless the nature of their employment or a contractual clause states otherwise.[19] The contractual relationship between ITC and M-University cannot be qualified as a contract of employment but is rather a contract of commission to conduct research, which falls outside the scope of Article 12 DPA.[20] Entitlement on the basis of priority (Arts. 9 and 10 DPA) or on the basis that the content has been obtained unlawfully from the subject matter made or applied by another person without their consent (Art. 11) is not applicable in the current case either.

If the patent or entitlement to the patent has already been transferred to ITC, it can – as the legal successor to the patent or entitlement to the patent – exercise all the rights of the legal predecessor (Art. 64 DPA), and hence challenge the patent by virtue of Article 75 DPA.[21] Legal succession to the patent or entitlement to the patent requires authority to dispose of property, a valid title and a deed of transfer of title (Art. 3:84, 3:95 Civil Code in conjunction with Art. 65(1) DPA). Transfer of title in advance is not necessarily prohibited *per se* by Dutch law.[22] The main question is whether the grant-back clause can be considered a valid deed of transfer of title in advance and whether the title sufficiently determines the future objects to be transferred.

---

19 In the case of an invention by an employee while under employment of a university or research institution, the entitled entity is, by virtue of Art. 12(3) DPA, the other way around: in principle the employer is entitled to the patent.

20 J. Huydecoper and C. van Nispen, *Industriële eigendom: bescherming van technische innovatie, Deel 1* (Deventer: 2002), p. 288.

21 The legal predecessor – in this case M-University – was initially entitled to the patent, hence had the authority to dispose of the patent by virtue of Art. 12(3) DPA. J. Huydecoper and C. van Nispen, *Industriële eigendom: bescherming van technische innovatie, Deel 1* (Deventer: 2002), pp. 288 and 297.

22 The Dutch Civil Code accepts the transfer of title in advance of future goods (Art. 3:97 Civil Code).

The answer to the latter issue seems to be negative, due to the indefiniteness of the clause to transfer 'all' future IP rights. The validity of the clause could be determined in the light of European competition law.[23] Despite the fact that Regulation (EC) No. 772/2004 regarding the transfer of technology only applies to licences, one could argue that the grant-back clause is analogous to the hardcore restriction of Article 5(1)(b) of this Regulation. However, this provision concerns the prohibition to oblige a licensee to transfer the rights to its own severable improvements to the licensor or to a third party. Whether the grant-back clause is contrary to reasonableness and fairness (Art. 6:248 Civil Code), if one takes the rationale – to protect incentives to innovate[24] – of the aforementioned hardcore restriction into account, is under debate. There is no Dutch case law concerning the validity of such clauses.

Even if the clause is considered to be valid and sufficiently determines the future objects to be transferred, and thus succession of the patent or entitlement to the patent has taken place, ITC cannot challenge the patent against third parties – in this case the group of students – as long as the deed of transfer of title has not yet been registered in the patent register (Art. 65(3) DPA) and the third parties do not and should not know about the initial transfer.[25]

If the patent has not been transferred yet, ITC is not entitled to the patent within the meaning of Chapter 1 DPA and therefore cannot institute an invalidation proceeding under Article 75(1)(e).[26] ITC would have to rely on the general rules of contract law and demand fulfilment of the contractual obligation to transfer the patent. To determine whether M-University is contractually obliged to transfer the patent to ITC, the reader is referred back to what has been said before about the validity of the grant-back clause.

If the grant-back clause is considered to be valid but transfer of the patent did not take place, ITC could claim damages (Art. 6:74 Civil Code), since M-University transferred the patent to a group of students and is therefore unable to perform the contractual duty to transfer the patent to ITC. If M-University did not transfer the patent to the group of students, it would be obliged to fulfil the contractual obligations and thus transfer the patent to ITC (3:296 Civil Code).

III. Metalegal Formants

Besides the ability to challenge a patent on the basis of patentability requirements, the grounds to challenge a patent are limited to the specific reasons as described

---

23 According to the foreword of the Dutch Competitive Trading Act, the national rules should be interpreted in the light of EC competition law.

24 Recital 14 Regulation (EC) No. 772/2004.

25 HR, 15 december 1950, *NJ* 1951, 469.

26 J. Huydecoper and C. van Nispen, *Industriële eigendom: bescherming van technische innovatie, Deel 1* (Deventer: 2002), p. 288.

in Chapter 1 DPA, due to the third-party effect of the right to challenge (Art. 75 DPA) or claim (Art. 78 DPA) the patent.[27] However, the DPA does not exclude other legal actions based on contract law. In practice, it will be hard to determine whether a party is contractually entitled to succession or whether succession has taken place and the party is – as the legal successor – entitled to the patent. With regard to commissioned research, the contractor who made the invention and – against his/her contractual obligation – applied for the patent is in principle entitled to the patent. The validity of general clauses of *ex ante* transfer of ownership will be determined within the light of (EC) competition law and the general rules of reasonableness and fairness.

(12) NORWAY

I. Operative Rules

Yes, ITC can challenge the patent.

II. Descriptive Formants

Provided that the contract is valid and must be interpreted as comprising the patent in question, ITC will have the right to apply for and be granted the patent, cf. NPA §1. Consequently, Prof. Brain's application is in conflict with NPA §1 and the granted patent is void. Even though the students have acquired the rights from the University in good faith, it will not affect ITC's patent rights. ITC can demand that the rights be transferred from the students, cf. NPA §18, which states that if anyone proves before the Norwegian Patent Office that he/she, and not the applicant, is entitled to the invention, the Patent Office shall, instead of refusing the application for that reason, transfer it to him/her if he/she so requests. Alternatively, IPC can raise an objection pursuant to the opposition procedure in NPA §25, cf. §24.

III. Metalegal Formants

The question is whether a contractual successor to an invention is entitled to the patent and whether he/she is entitled to have the patent transferred to him/herself. The Norwegian patent law solves this problem in favour of the successor.

[27] Ibid., pp. 288 and 297.

(13) POLAND

I. Operative Rules

Whether ITC can challenge the patent depends on the details of the transfer, but probably ITC is the lawful owner of the patent and can challenge it.

II. Descriptive Formants

There are two legal issues involved. First, it may be controversial whether a *contract* provision obliging Prof. Brain to transfer all IP rights to ITC is valid. Second, it would matter how this obligation was formulated and especially whether it could be understood as assignment of a future IP subject matter or simply an obligation to assign this subject matter once it comes into existence. Starting from the end, if the second option is the correct one, Prof. Brain would 'only' infringe ITC's contractual rights and thus be liable for damages. This is because as the inventor Brain has the right to obtain the patent and therefore if this right is not transferred, he is entitled to file the patent application. If, on the other hand, the contract between ITC and Prof. Brain were to be understood as falling under Article 11.3 or 11.4 ILP, the answer could be different.[28] According to Article 11.3 IPL, '[w]here an invention … has been made by a creator in the course of employment duties or in the *execution of any other contract*, the right referred to in paragraph (1) (right to obtain a patent) shall belong to the employer or the commissioner, unless otherwise agreed by the parties concerned.' Article 11.4 stipulates that '[a]greements concluded between entrepreneurs may designate the entity to which the rights referred to in paragraph (1) shall belong where an invention, a utility model or an industrial design has been made *in connection with the execution* of such agreement.' It does not follow from the facts of the case whether the invention was created *in execution* of the contract with ITC or *in connection with the execution* of this agreement. In the second case, the only problem would be whether the University could be qualified as an entrepreneur for the purpose of Article 11(4) IPL. It seems that according to the prevailing view this is possible.[29] If ITC validly acquired the right to obtain the patent, it could challenge the patent granted to Prof. Brain (Art. 74 IPL).[30]

The validity of a contractual clause establishing the obligation to transfer all IP rights may be challenged under competition law.[31] Such clauses may be

---

28 See A. Szewc, G. Jyż, *Prawo własności przemysłowej* (Warszawa: 2003), pp. 118 f.

29 E. Nowińska, U. Promińska, M. du Vall, *Prawo własności przemysłowej* (Warszawa: 2008), pp. 127, 129.

30 Ibid., p. 134.

31 K. Kohutek, in: K. Kohutek, M. Sieradzka, *Ustawa o ochronie konkurencji i konsumentów. Komentarz* (Kraków: 2008), p. 78.

regarded as restricting competition (see §8 point 2 of the Technology Transfer Regulation) and consequently void (Art. 6(2) Polish Competition Act). However, the relevant regulations refer to technology transfer (licence) contracts and not research contracts. It seems that for such a clause to be invalid in a research contract, an abuse of dominant position would have to be proven.

III. Metalegal Formants

The main issue here seems to be the all-encompassing transfer clause and the scope of contractual freedom in this field. Because of competition law, the current regime limits the exploitation of market power, but only partially.

(14) SLOVENIA

I. Operative Rules

Yes, ITC can challenge the patent.

II. Descriptive Formants

There are two remedies provided by the Industrial Property Act (IPA) regarding patent disputes. According to Articles 111 and 112 IPA, any interested party may bring an action in the court of competent jurisdiction to declare the nullity of a patent for one or more of the prescribed reasons. An action may be filed if the invention did not meet all requirements on the date of the filing of the application (patentability, Arts. 10 and 11 IPA; novelty, Art. 12 IPA; inventive step, Art. 14 IPA; industrial application, Art. 15 IPA), if the invention does not disclose the invention in a manner sufficiently clear and complete for it to be carried out by a person skilled in the art to which the invention relates, if the content of the protection extends beyond the content of the first received application, or if the patent was granted on a divisional application, beyond the content of the initial application. An action to declare the nullity of a patent may also be filed in the event that the patent has lapsed. However, this remedy is not relevant in the case at hand.

The second remedy would be to contest the right to a patent. Accordingly, an inventor, his/her heir or other successor in title may, at any time during the validity of a patent, file an action requesting that he/she be declared owner of the patent, if the patent has been granted in the name of a person who is not the inventor, his/her heir or other successor in title (Art. 115(1) IPA). Additionally, this action may also be filed by a person who is entitled to the rights conferred by a patent if the patent was granted in the name of the inventor or a third person, which the inventor unjustifiably authorised that the patent be granted in his/her name (Art. 115(3) IPA).

ITC and Prof. Brain, an employee of M-University, entered into a valid paid research contract which required Prof. Brain to transfer to ITC all intellectual property rights resulting from research financed by ITC. Such contracts are governed by Article 22(1) of the Employment Related Industrial Property Rights Act (ERIPRA),[32] which states that contracts between public higher education establishments and third parties providing funds for research activities determine who resulting inventions belong to, define the rights regarding use of the inventions, and set possible additional payment. Accordingly, ITC was entitled to the rights conferred by the patent, yet Prof. Brain registered the patent in the name of M-University. ITC has the right to challenge the patent and request ownership, since the situation represents a case of the entitled person filing an action pursuant to Article 115(3) IPA for the patent being unjustifiably granted in the name of a third party.

III. Metalegal Formants

There is no case law yet in Slovenia regarding this matter. But it is notable that there is a provision in the Slovenian Copyright and Related Rights Act which states that any contractual stipulation is considered null and void if the author undertakes to assign with it economic rights with respect to all his/her future works (Art. 79). However, there are no such provisions in the Industrial Property Act.

Additionally, it has to be noted that it is common practice in Slovenia for employees of higher education institutions (professors, lecturers, researchers, etc.) to independently enter into paid research contracts, without the authorisation of their respective employing institutions. Moreover, many members of faculty are running private research and are consulting institutes in order to make a profit. There are some newly arisen initiatives by major universities in order to change this situation.

(15) SPAIN

I. Operative Rules

If we assume that the invention was made by Prof. Brain during his working relation with ITC and the activity of research was the object of the contract, ITC can challenge the patent according to Article 15 of the Spanish Patent Law.

---

32 Official Gazette RS, no. 15/2007, Art. 22(1): 'Contracts concluded between public higher education institutions or public research institutions and third parties regarding the financing or co-financing of research determine who resulting inventions belong to, define the rights regarding use of the inventions and set possible additional payment. Contractual obligations of all participating subjects have to be taken into account.'

II. *Descriptive Formants*

This case fulfils both the conditions required by the Spanish Patent Law for ownership to be attributed to the company. First, the invention was made by the worker during his/her working relation with the company, and second, the activity of research was the object of the contract. The Spanish Patent Law considers that inventions made as a result of a work contract between the worker and the company belong to the company (Art. 15.1 of the Patent Law). Likewise, any inventions made as the result of providing a service, as in this case, also belong to the company. In this respect, the judgment of the Supreme Court of 31 December 1999 (RJ 1999/9757) points out that Article 15 of the Patent Law considers that all those inventions made by workers who are involved in 'a service relationship with the company' belong to the company and, therefore, it includes the provision of services in general.[33] The second fundamental point of law on which the judgment is based explains that the service relationship with the company involves not only the services provided by the wage earners but also the services provided by other workers.[34] In fact, Article 19 of the Spanish Patent Law states that even a year after the work relation or the service relationship has finished, the company is entitled to challenge the patent.

In this case, Professor Brain works for a university. This may generate some doubts about the solution proposed above, because Article 20.2 of the Spanish Patent Law accepts that 'the inventions made by the professor should belong to the University because of his research and teaching functions there.'[35] However, it should be borne in mind that Article 20.7 of the Spanish Patent Law determines that 'when the professor invents something as the result of a contract with a private or public institution, the contract must specify to which of the parts it belongs'. That is to say, in this case the contract is decisive because it will make it possible to determine to whom the invention belongs. In this case, it seems that the contract clearly established that the invention belonged to ITC and, therefore, Professor Brain could not apply for the patent.[36]

---

33 Interestingly, the Dutch report states the opposite position: 'the contractual relationship between ITC and M-University cannot be qualified as a contract of employment but is rather a contract of commission to conduct research, which falls outside the scope of Art. 12 DPA'. The Belgian report says that the Belgian Patent Act does not foresee explicit clauses on commission contracts. The Greek report considers that Prof. Brain is an independent contractor and not an employee of ITC and therefore his inventions do not belong *ipso jure* and without further formality to ITC.

34 See the differences between the Czech and the Spanish systems on inventions made at work.

35 See also Spanish Organic Law 6/2001 of 21 December on Universities (LOU), Art. 83 of which accepts the possibility that contracts may be entered into with third parties and refers to the statutes of each university to determine the details of how this can be authorised.

36 The same solution is stated in the Slovenia report, which refers to the contracts between public higher education establishments and third parties providing funds for research activities that determine who resulting inventions belong to.

The solution would be the same if ITC had contracted a public research institution. In this case, we have to consider Royal Decree 55/2002 of 18 January, which states that the inventions made by the workers of public research institutions belong to those public research institutions (Art. 2). However, when there is a contract, as in the case submitted, between the public research institution and a company, then the contract must specify to which of the parts it belongs (Art. 5 Royal Decree 55/2002).

ITC could oppose the granting of the patent because, according to Article 10 of the Patent Law, the right to a patent shall belong to the inventor or his/her successor in title. This right is transferable according to what the Law establishes.

On the one hand, ITC could claim ownership of the patent on the basis of Article 12 of the Patent Law. This establishes the procedure when the patent has already been granted. In this case, the person who has the right to the patent is entitled to claim the transfer of the patent within two years from the date of the publication of the patent concession. Moreover, if the owner of the patent is not entitled to the right to the patent according to Article 10, the inventor can ask for it to be revoked (Art. 112.1.d) Spanish Patent Law).

On the other hand, Article 36.1 of the Patent Law establishes that in the general procedure for granting the patent, anybody can make duly reasoned and documented observations on the report on the state of the art. In the granting procedure that involves a prior exam, Article 39.4 of the Law states that interested parties can oppose the granting of the patent by alleging the lack of either of the requisites for it to be granted. In any case, Article 47 of the Law provides for the possibility of lodging a contentious-administrative appeal.

It should also be borne in mind that once the patent has been granted, its holder, ITC, can bring any necessary action, whatever its nature, in the ordinary courts, against those who infringe its right (Prof. Brain) and demand that measures be taken so that it can be safeguarded.

The answer could be different if the contractor were not a physical person like Prof. Brain but a legal person (a university, a public or private research institution or a spin-off) because, if this were to be the case, one cannot apply Article 15 of the Spanish Patent Law or, in general, Title IV of the Law on Work Inventions.[37] In this case, if the contract proposed by ITC and signed by the public or private institution expressly included the clause about the transfer of patent rights to ITC, then the company could claim the patent. This is envisaged in Article 23 of the Patent Law: 'The application for the patent must name the inventor. Should the applicant not be the inventor or not the only inventor, then there should also be a statement explaining how the applicant has come to hold the right of patent.' In this case, the inventor, that is to say the public or private

37 M. Pérez Pérez, *Invenciones laborales de trabajadores, profesionales universitarios y personal investigador* (Madrid: 1994), p. 136.

institution, would have the right to be mentioned as the inventor in the patent (Art. 14 Patent Law).

The issue is the same if M-University transfers the granted patent to a group of students involved in creating a start-up. In this case, according to Article 13 of the Spanish Patent Law, any change in the ownership of a patent as the result of a legal ruling annuls all licences granted to third parties.[38] The only right granted to the licence holders is that that they are allowed to ask the new owner registered in the Patent Register for a non-exclusive licence to continue – or start – exploiting the invention. Licences must be granted for an appropriate period of time and in reasonable conditions, which will be determined, if necessary, by the procedure established in the Spanish Patent Law for compulsory patents.[39]

The other issue raised in this case is the obligation to transfer future property rights to ITC. This is not related to the right to be granted a licence or the ownership of the patent: it is a purely contractual issue. That is to say, it raises the issue of the validity of this sort of clause in a service contract. We consider that in this case the clause is valid as long as a time limit is stipulated, since Article 1583 of the Spanish Civil Code states that 'leasing for a lifetime is null.'

III. Metalegal Formants

Besides the ability to challenge the patent on the basis of the relationship between the employer and the employee according to Articles 15–19 of the Spanish Patent Law, it is important to take into account that the invention may be made by professors belonging to a university. In this case, according to Article 21 of the Spanish Patent Law, the contract between the inventor and the company should establish to whom the invention belongs.

The licence of the granted patent to a third party is regulated by virtue of Article 13 of the Spanish Patent Law, which determines that any change in the ownership of a patent as the result of a legal ruling annuls all licences granted to third parties.[40] Moreover, it is important to take into account Article 77 of the Spanish Patent Law.

The obligation to transfer future property rights to ITC is a contractual issue. We consider that the clause is valid as long as a time limit is stipulated according to Article 1583 Spanish Civil Code.

---

38 The same solution is defended by the Slovenian report. See the differences with the Greek report. The Dutch report protects third parties. The Czech report is interesting because it applies the provisions of the Commercial Code on purchase contracts via the principle of *analogia legis*. The solution of the case will depend on of the *bona fide* of third parties.

39 P. Martín Aresti, *La licencia contractual de patente* (Pamplona: 1997), pp. 141–142.

40 See the differences with the Greek report.

(16) UNITED KINGDOM

I. *Operative Rules*

ITC cannot challenge the patent. But in a two-year time frame, ITC can demand to be registered as the owner of the patent.

II. *Descriptive Formants*

While the UK rules on *entitlement to a patent* are set out in section 7 PA 1977, the *determination of right to a patent after grant* is set out in section 37. It can only lead to a remedy for ITC if it brings the case within two years of the patent grant, unless it is shown that the person registered as a proprietor of the patent knew at the time of the grant or, as the case may be, of the transfer of the patent to him/her that he/she was not entitled to the patent. The policy rationale is that ostensible patent ownership is largely reliable. According to standing case law, the two-year rule does not apply if there has been a failing under section 7.

Section 7(2) provides that:

> (2) A patent for an invention may be granted –
> (a) primarily to the *inventor* or joint inventors; [note that Prof Brain is the inventor]
> (b) in preference to the foregoing, to any person or persons who, by virtue of any *enactment or rule of law* [see s. 39 about the entitlement of an employer], or any foreign law or treaty or international convention, *or* by virtue of an *enforceable term of any agreement entered into with the inventor before the making of the invention, was or were at the time of the making of the invention entitled to the whole of the property in it* (other than equitable interests) in the United Kingdom [see the ITC contractors contract];
> (c) in any event, *to the successor or successors in title of any person or persons* mentioned in paragraph (a) or (b) above or any person so mentioned and the successor or successors in title of another person so mentioned; and to no other person.

The implication of section 7(2)(b) is that it was probably lawful *under the PA 1977* for the patent to be granted to M-University. It would *also* have been lawful for the patent to be granted to ITC.

(Perhaps ITC could argue that Prof. Brain did not make the invention in the course of his employment with M-University (see s. 39 for the circumstances when an employer is entitled to a patent for an invention devised by its employee), for example if he carried out the experiments in his own time, without using M-University equipment. But with Prof. Brain and M-University both arguing that it was during the course of his authorised employment, that sounds like a tenuous argument and one which can be put to one side.)

If ITC complains under section 37 within two years of the grant, or it can show that the student start-up company which is now registered as a proprietor of the patent knew at the time of the transfer of the patent to it that it was not entitled to the patent, then the Comptroller of Patents (the head of the UK Patents Office) can decide under section 37(1)(c) whether ITC should have been given priority over M-University. The Comptroller can also refer such a question to a court. There is a strong argument that ITC should have been given priority. The Comptroller and the court can make such order as they think fit to give effect to this determination, including that the ownership of the patent should be transferred to ITC. Although the argument is strong, counter-arguments may also exist. For instance, there may be clauses in Prof. Brain's employment contract with M-University about its entitlement to inventions made during the course of employment. This might mean M-University has a strong claim to priority *if* Prof. Brain did not have the University's permission when he signed the research contract with ITC.

If ITC complains outside the two-year period referred to in section 37 (and its limited exception), then the student start-up company would remain the owner of the patent. However, ITC could bring a claim for breach of contract against Prof. Brain or (vicariously) against M-University. Unless Prof. Brain is a wealthy man, ITC might prefer to sue the University. However, breach of contract might give rise to damages (compensation for reasonably foreseeable loss, including contributory reduction), but not provide access to the property of the patent. Remedies under equity are beyond the scope of this inquiry.

III. Metalegal Formants

The case raises the question of the proprietary assignment of patents generated in public research institutions under conditions of contract research. Can conventional rules of commissioned research apply? While English law is flexible, at least in the time frame of two years post-grant, permitting the Comptroller of Patents to assign the ownership of the patent, the situation here is purely contractual. A further factor that should be considered, based on the innovation rationale, is the material covered in the patent application, often referred to as 'teaching'. If the 'teaching' is not narrowly technical, but in fact foundational, one possible solution is to assign the patent to the public research institution but require a royalty free licensing regime, thus recognising the importance of the foundational technology. The black-letter law is still silent about this important question.

A.3. COMPARATIVE REMARKS

The conflict addresses a core question of the modern innovation society: How to design the relation between public research and private industry (i.e. 'technology transfer')? How is the distinction between 'basic' and 'applied' research embedded in legal institutions of contract, patent and competition law? Have 'basic' (publicly financed) research institutions become a 'workbench' of the modern supply chain? Can basic research simply be 'commissioned' and exclusively appropriated?

The basic case asks the question: What remedies does an ordering party have if a university applies for a patent in breach of grant-back duties and transfers the property right to third parties?

The answers diverge. In most countries, ITC can challenge the patent on the basis of patent law, and it can claim damages because of breach of contract.[41] A few countries, such as Germany and France, do not provide patent-law-based remedies, but refer to contractual remedies. In most European countries, the assignment of a future patent is possible.[42] Nowhere can the breach of a contractual provision with regard to a patent be used as a means to challenge the patent. It is interesting that in the Czech Republic a court decision is needed which states that ITC is the legal successor.

The core of all the answers is that although a grant-back clause could be invalid under EU competition law, if two companies have made such an agreement, a company can oblige a university to transfer all future patents![43] Research freedom arguably cannot be made operational in these cases. The rationale of competition law cannot be transposed to the industry–university constellation. It is questionable whether this is appropriate.

It is noteworthy that differences in property transfer systems play no role (abstract versus causal systems). Under German law, the assignment of IPRs follows the same legal rules as the assignment of receivables. In such a situation, the two requirements needed for the assignment of the patent can be fulfilled through one contract.[44]

B.1. MODIFICATION 1

Would it make a difference if ITC did not demand the transfer of future intellectual property rights but rather demanded to be named as co-inventor?

---

41 See the reports of Belgium, Denmark, Estonia, Greece, Italy, the Netherlands, Norway, Poland, Slovenia and Spain. In Germany, only contract remedies apply.

42 Although in some countries there is the requirement that the future invention must be sufficiently determined (see the German and Dutch reports).

43 According to Art. 5(1)(b) of Regulation (EC) No. 772/2004 it is forbidden to oblige the licensee to transfer all future IPRs to the licensor; see also CJEU judgment of 6 October 1994, *Tetra Pak v. Commission*, C-333/94 P, ECLI:EU:C:1996:436, para. 135.

44 Normally the duty to assign an object plus a separable transfer of the object is needed (see the German report).

B.2. COUNTRY REPORTS

(1) BELGIUM

I. Operative Rules

ITC cannot be co-inventor.

II. Descriptive Formants

The right of the inventor to be named has been acknowledged since 1934 in Article 4ter Paris Convention[45] and included in Article 12 BPA (Art. XI.13 BCEL). The right to be named is an inalienable right: it remains with the actual inventor, whatever has happened with the patrimonial rights. Logically, it can only belong to natural persons.[46] Therefore, ITC cannot obtain the right to be named as the inventor. However, the above is not unanimously accepted in Belgian legal doctrine. Some authors claim that the right to be named can be partially alienated on the basis of an interpretation of Article 12 BPA (Art. XI.13 BCEL) by analogy with Article 1§2 BCA (Art. XI.165§2 BCEL).[47] The argument is then that this would be required by economic reality due to the fact corporations would rather withhold the fact that their research results have not been achieved within the company.[48]

III. Metalegal Formants

The conceptualisation of the right to be named as moral right is thought to provide particular protection to the inventor. It is inalienable. Only the real inventor is entitled. To date, Belgian law has resisted both economic interests and philanthropic interests to be named as co-inventor for the sake of receiving inventor's protection.

---

45 Paris Convention for the Protection of Industrial Property, 20 March 1883, available at: www.wipo.int (last consulted 6 May 2019).

46 M.-C. Janssens, 'Uitvindingen in dienstverband met bijzondere aandacht voor uitvindingen aan universiteiten' [Employee and University Inventions], *CIR series Katholieke Universiteit Leuven* no. 12 (Brussels: 1995), 18–21.

47 B. de Vuyst and L. Steuts, 'De notie morele rechten in een internationale, vergelijkende en transactionele context' [The Notion of Moral Rights in an International, Comparative and Transactional Context], *I.R.D.I.* 2005, 14–15.

48 Ibid.

(2) CZECH REPUBLIC

I. Operative Rules

ITC does not have the right to be named as co-inventor.

II. Descriptive Formants

The inventor, according to section 8(2) Patent Act, is the person who made the invention by means of his/her own creative work. Reading this definition, it is clear that only a natural person may be an inventor.

III. Metalegal Formants

The right to be named is individualistically conceptualised as a specific protection of the inventor's personality. Any other interest cannot trump it.

(3) DENMARK

I. Operative Rules

ITC will have no claim to being named as co-inventor.

II. Descriptive Formants

A right to be named cannot be validly agreed upon. Only the original inventor(s) have a claim to be named (DPA §8(4)) as only natural persons can be inventors in the legal sense. On the other hand, failing to name the original inventor is grounds neither for opposition to nor for invalidity of the patent – but merely serves as grounds for a claim to be named.

III. Metalegal Formants

The right to be named is a moral right, cf. Article 4ter of the Paris Convention, and belongs to the inventor, not the successor.

(4) ESTONIA

I. Operative Rules

ITC has no claim.

II. *Descriptive Formants*

Pursuant to §13(1) Patent Act, '[t]he author of an invention ... is a natural person who has created an invention as a result of his or her inventing activities'. If several natural persons create an invention, then they are called joint or co-inventors (§13(2) Patent Act). An inventor has the right to request the disclosure of his/her name as the inventor (§13(7) clause 1 Patent Act). ITC is a legal entity and cannot therefore be named as the inventor.

Another issue is whether a manager or other employee of ITC could be named as a co-inventor. Nothing in this case indicates that ITC had actually contributed to creation of any invention. The obligation to name a certain employee of ITC as a co-inventor would be created by a contract. Subsection 13(6) Patent Act provides that '[a]uthorship is inalienable and unspecified in term'. Of course, specifically here, in this hypothetical scenario, this is not the case because in addition to an actual inventor, someone else would be named as a co-inventor. It is hard to estimate whether the obligation to name someone as a co-inventor is valid. Presumably, it is a valid obligation. However, there is no established practice in Estonia.

III. *Metalegal Formants*

The idea behind restricting the right to be named to natural persons is rooted in the idealistic view of the inventor. He/she deserves particular protection.

(5) FRANCE

I. *Operative Rules*

ITC (being a legal entity) cannot be named as co-inventor.

II. *Descriptive Formants*

Article L. 611-9 of the French Intellectual Property Code provides that the inventor is named in the patent. This article provides a moral right, *a minima*, for the physical inventor. As a matter of fact, the right to be named inventor of a patent cannot be owned by a legal entity. This moral right, being non-alienable, cannot be transferred from an inventor to somebody else either.

One more question remains concerning the possibility of naming as co-inventor a natural person such as the representative of ITC. More precisely, the question concerns the validity of a contractual clause which provides that a person who did not participate in the realisation of the invention shall be named as co-inventor. We do not know of any legal provision or case law concerning this particular problem.

Some may say that the fact that the true inventor is named in the patent sufficiently protects his/her moral right no matter who else is named. The fact that a person is named as the co-inventor does not constitute a reason for revoking the patent. Article L. 611-9 of the French Intellectual Property Code provides that the inventor is named in the patent. This article provides a moral right, *a minima*, for the physical inventor. By comparison with the French author's right, which provides an enlarged moral right of the authors, we argue that the moral right is available for the inventor. The author can agree to renounce his/her prerogatives or to accept that a third person be named as co-author. In this case, such a contract must be considered as valid. But the author can, at any time, vindicate his/her moral right, which means that he/she can ask for and obtain recognition as the only author of the work.

We argue that the contract providing that ITC is named as co-inventor remains valid. But the real inventor can change his/her mind at any time and ask the judge to recognise him/her as the real and only inventor.

III. Metalegal Formants

The right to be named is rooted in the idealistic view of the inventor. As a subject, he/she deserves particular protection.

(6) GERMANY

I. Operative Rules

ITC will not be named co-inventor.

II. Descriptive Formants

As a matter of concept, ITC cannot be named as the 'inventor', as inventorship is conceived of as '*höchstpersönlich*' (highly personal). The right can only be transferred to it. Considering this, the clause is to be interpreted as 'transfer to' as under the base case.

It is a distinct question whether the legal obligation to name the executive director of ITC is valid. One might argue that such an agreement would diminish the position of the (only) true inventor. And the moral right of the inventor is strongly protected as a non-alienable right. However, the moral right to be named is satisfied when the name is on the patent. The obligation to name someone in one's patent is not invalid.

III. Metalegal Formants

The potential co-ownership arrangement would amount to a powerful position. If sole ownership cannot be acquired, it is second best to get in control of outsourced research.

However, like prior transferral, co-inventorship may not be in the best interest of research institutions. The situation can be complicated if the contractor brings in his/her own competence, prior know-how and own financial interests. If it is the contractor who conceives of the invention, then his/her impact may outweigh the input of the company's agents and its financial commitment. Even philanthropic motives may not undermine the protection of the inventor.

(7) GREECE

I. Operative Rules

No, the right of ITC is relative and non-addressable against third parties.

II. Descriptive Formants

The profile of the problem in the base case does not change even when the action of ITC aims at partial rather than full acquisition of the powers over the patent. Thus, here too, the rights out of patent must be transferred by the law of obligations and not transferred directly or *ipso jure* to ITC, with the result that ITC is not legitimated to object or to sue directly third parties (for example, the students as special successors of M-University).

III. Metalegal Formants

Greek law on inventors protects their creative personality and shields it, at least in the scope of the moral right, from economic pressures.

(8) IRELAND

I. Operative Rules

Under current law, ITC has no claim to be named.

II. Descriptive Formants

Under section 81(1) of the Patents Act, anyone can refer to a court the question whether, by operation of law or otherwise, he/she is entitled (alone or jointly with any other person) to any patent granted, or about to be granted, in the state. The court may make such order (including an order of apportionment) to give effect to its decision as it considers expedient.

If an applicant is not the inventor, under the Patent Rules it will still be necessary to identify the inventors within 16 months of the earliest priority date and to indicate the title's origin – Patents Act 1992, section 17(2); Patents Rules 1992, rule 6(1) as amended by the Patents (Amendment) Act 2006 – otherwise the patent application will be considered abandoned.

Under section 17(1) and (3) of the Patents Act 1992, one or more inventors may be mentioned and such names may also be deleted. Where a person alleges that they should have been named or that an inventor is erroneously mentioned, he/she bears the onus of proof and must establish the full facts on which the claim is based, under the Patent Rules 1992, rule 7(1).

Under section 79 of the Patents Act 1992, the rules of law applicable to the ownership and devolution of personal property apply also to patent applications and patents.

III. Metalegal Formants

Patents are protected as choses in action. Property rights in Ireland are generally regarded as natural rights and they are protected by the Constitution. However, in recent years the courts have started to shy away from the natural law position in other rights arenas and this is likely to apply also in the case of property rights.

(9) ITALY

I. Operative Rules

ITC has no claim to be named.

II. Descriptive Formants

The right to be named as the inventor is a moral right and can be attributed only to the physical person who actually performs the inventive activity. As a moral right, it is not possible to waive it, or to transfer it in its entirety or partially (Art. 62 Industrial Property Code).

III. Metalegal Formants

Italy subscribes to a strong natural law position. The underlying assumption is to protect the subjective rights of the inventor.

(10) LITHUANIA

Answer omitted.

(11) NETHERLANDS

I. Operative Rules

Whether ITC will succeed with its claim depends on whether it merely requests to be named as co-inventor in the patent application or demands to be considered the co-inventor of the patent.

II. Descriptive Formants

If ITC only demands to be named as co-inventor in the patent application, its demand cannot be satisfied. Although the first applicant for the patent is considered to be entitled to the patent, the invention itself is the juridical fact. The first applicant is merely presumed to be the inventor. The right to be named as the inventor of a patent is a moral right (Art. 4ter Paris Convention) and cannot be transferred. If the inventor is not entitled to the patent, the right to be named as the inventor of a patent cannot be excluded by the contract, according to Article 14 DPA. However, the inventor can opt out of being named as the inventor in a written declaration attached to the patent application (Art. 24(1)(a) DPA). It logically follows that ITC, which did not give rise to the juridical fact of invention, cannot demand to be named as the co-inventor on the patent.

If the clause is considered to have the effect that ITC and M-University agreed to be jointly entitled to the patent, ITC is entitled by virtue of Article 13 DPA, and hence can challenge the patent by virtue of Article 75 DPA. This provision does not require all the parties involved to make an inventive contribution to the resulting invention. There only has to be a 'determined technical cooperation'[49] between the parties, and the agreement needs to have the purpose of granting the cooperating parties joint entitlement to the patent.[50] The clause seems to satisfy the latter requirement, but whether the contract of commissioned research including the co-inventorship clause can be considered a 'determined technical cooperation' between ITC and M-University is debatable. In the current circumstances, it seems unlikely that the contract and its clause qualify as such, since they do not constitute any quantitative or qualitative cooperation between the parties.

---

49 OR (Dutch Patent Board), 29 september 1994, *BIE* 1995, 48.

50 J. Huydecoper and C. van Nispen, *Industriële eigendom: bescherming van technische innovatie, Deel 1* (Deventer: 2002), p. 295; C. Gielen (ed.), *Kort begrip van het intellectuele eigendomsrecht* (Deventer: 2007), p. 53.

III. *Metalegal Formants*

The threshold for *ex ante* joint entitlement to the patent on the basis of a contractual relationship by virtue of Article 13 DPA is quite low. The requirement of a 'determined technical cooperation' seems to be the decisive factor for the determination of a possible co-entitlement to a patent and is mostly influenced by the circumstances of the particular case. The validity of such a clause could, again, be evaluated in the light of (EC) competition law and general rules of reasonableness and fairness.[51]

With regard to the right to be named as the (co-)inventor, it is generally accepted that only the real inventor, who gave rise to the juridical fact, has this personal right, which cannot be transferred to anyone else.

(12) NORWAY

I. *Operative Rules*

ITC will have no claim to being named as co-inventor.

II. *Descriptive Formants*

A right to be named cannot be validly agreed upon. Only the original inventor(s) has a claim to be named, cf. NPA §8, fourth paragraph. In other words, only natural persons can be inventors in legal sense. On the other hand, failing to name the original inventor is grounds for neither opposition to nor invalidity of the patent – but merely serves as grounds for a claim to be named.

III. *Metalegal Formants*

The right to be named is a moral right, cf. Article 4ter Paris Convention, and lies with the inventor, not the successor.

(13) POLAND

I. *Operative Rules*

A claim to be named as co-inventor will not be successful.

---

[51] Though it should be noted that the legislator has chosen to generally accept these kinds of clauses by virtue of Art. 13 DPA.

II. Descriptive Formants

It is essential what has actually happened: a partial transfer (a transfer of the share in the exclusive right to obtain a patent) or the establishment of co-inventorship. Article 11(3) and (4) IPL may justify not only the transfer of all rights but also, *a maiore ad minus*, a contractual regulation of shares. Inventorship, however, is first a question of fact and secondly gives rise to a personal right to be named as the inventor.

III. Metalegal Formants

This right is vested only in the inventor him/herself and is non-transferable.

(14) SLOVENIA

I. Operative Rules

ITC cannot be named as co-inventor.

II. Descriptive Formants

It has to be noted that inventorship and ownership of the patent are two separate categories. In the Slovenian legal order, only natural persons may be named as inventors. Therefore, ITC does not have the right to demand to be named as co-inventor.

III. Metalegal Formants

The construction of the right to be named is a moral right, protecting the inventor.

(15) SPAIN

I. Operative Rules

If the inventor is Professor Brain, only the inventor (Professor Brain) would have the moral right to be considered as such vis-à-vis the owner of the patent. We can take into account that the Spanish Patent Law envisages the issue of co-invention.

II. Descriptive Formants

In general terms, we can take into account that the Spanish Patent Law envisages the issue of co-invention. Article 10.2 of the Patent Law establishes that 'if the invention has been jointly made by various people, the right to obtain the patent will belong to all of them'. This means that all the inventors should make a joint application for the patent. If one of them were to apply by him/herself, he/she would be obliged by law to state how he/she has acquired the right of patent. Thus, Article 23 of the Patent Law states that '[i]f the applicant ... is not the only inventor, he must also provide a statement of how he has acquired the right of patent'. This means that if Prof. Brain were to apply for the patent *de motu proprio* without presenting the justification required by law, the co-inventor could oppose it on the same grounds as we have seen in the previous case.

Specifically, the main question is whether ITC could merely request to be mentioned on the patent as the inventor.[52] In this case, the inventor would have the moral right to be considered as such before the owner of the patent.[53] This possibility is described in Article 14 of the Patent Law: 'The inventor shall have the right, vis-à-vis the applicant or proprietor of a patent, to be mentioned as such before the Patent Office.'[54] In our opinion, in accordance with the regulation that the Patent Law contains on inventions at work, it would neither be legitimate nor make sense for ITC to request to be mentioned as the inventor.[55] The moral right to be mentioned as the inventor belong to the inventor, while ITC can only claim that the patent be granted to them for exploitation.[56] That is to say, in accordance with Article 15.1 of the Patent Law, the entrepreneur has the patrimonial rights of the invention since the non-patrimonial right to be recognised as the author of the invention, known as the moral right, can only be the inventor's.[57]

---

52 It is interesting to read judgment 196/2009 of 1 April (JUR 2009/221245), where the main issue resolved by the Audiencia Provincial of Zaragoza, Section 5, is the recognition of the moral right of the inventor of the mop (*fregona*).

53 The Audiencia Provincial of Murcia, Section 2, judgment 332/2006 of 12 December (Ac 2007/162) in a case on labour inventions distinguishes clearly between the right to be considered as the inventor, who corresponds to the person who invents, and the right to be the owner of the patent, which in this case also was granted to the inventor.

54 See Rule 62 of the Munich Convention of 1973 (revised in 1991). See also Art. 4ter Paris Convention for the Protection of Industrial Property.

55 The same solution is proposed in the Belgian report.

56 In the same sense, see M. Pérez Pérez, *Invenciones laborales de trabajadores, profesionales universitarios y personal investigador* (Madrid: 1994), p. 169. See also the Dutch report with regard to the right to be named as the (co-)inventor. The Slovenian report and the Czech report determine that ITC does not have the right to demand to be named as co-inventor because only natural persons may be named as inventors.

57 R. Estupiñán Cáceres, *Las invenciones laborales en la empresa* (Madrid: 2003), p. 213. See the different solution proposed by the French report: 'the author can agree to renounce his prerogatives or to accept that a third person be named as co-author. In this case, such a contract must be considered as valid'.

III. Metalegal Formants

If the invention has been jointly made by various people, then it would be possible to demand to be named as co-inventor. However, according to this case the inventor is Professor Brain. Only the inventor would have the moral right to be considered as such before the owner of the patent.

(16) UNITED KINGDOM

I. Operative Rules

ITC cannot demand to be named as co-inventor.

II. Descriptive Formants

The definition of an inventor or joint inventor is covered by section 7(3) PA 1977. It states: 'In this Act "inventor" in relation to an invention means the actual deviser of the invention and "joint inventor" shall be construed accordingly.'

The case is similar to the English case law on this (e.g. University of Southampton's application about a bug trap). In that case, the deviser/s of the invention provided the inventive concept (but not the invention). Even if we assumed that ITC provided not only resources, but also background information and the problem identification, the law would solely accept Prof. Brain as the inventor since he provided the inventive concept (the non-obvious technical solution/concept). Under English law, the default rule is that there is only one inventor, no joint inventors.

III. Metalegal Formants

The narrow focus of inventorship on the creative person protects the inventor's subjective rights.

B.3. COMPARATIVE REMARKS

The case is about the right to be named as co-inventor: can co-inventorship be bought? The impetus for designing this case modification was the possibility to juxtapose this clause in a normal industrial setting with a philanthropic motive, such as in the famous US case *PXE*, on which Case 13 is modelled.

Unanimously, all European countries come to the same result: ITC cannot claim to be named as co-inventor. The reason for this is that inventorship is a moral right which can only be granted to natural, and not judicial, persons.[58] Therefore, neither the University nor ITC can be named as co-inventor.[59] In the Netherlands there exists an exclusion under which a company can also be recognised as co-inventor. In this case, the contractual clause must have the aim that both parties are jointly entitled to the patent and there must be a 'determined technical cooperation' between them.

Some reporters changed the facts of the case, assuming that the director of ITC wanted to be named as co-inventor. In Estonia, such a situation has not yet been decided by a court, so the answer to the question under Estonian law remains uncertain. In comparison, the French report states that the contract clause would probably be valid and the director could be named as co-inventor. Nevertheless, the real inventor would still have the possibility to change his/her mind and ask a judge to recognise him/her alone on the patent. Under German law, there is a possibility to name another natural person as co-inventor, but the real inventor can claim a correction, if he/she wants to.

The answers to the case show that the moral right of the inventor has a high status in all countries. It is not transferable and can, in general, only be obtained by natural persons. This rationale ensures that the real inventor has the power to decide in the first place what to do with his/her patent. He/she can assign it, exploit it on his/her own or license it. In countries where he/she is obliged to tender it to his/her employer and the latter has no interest, he/she remains the owner. Because of today's growing need to cooperate in many fields of research, there seem to be some loopholes. In the Belgian literature, co-authorship is discussed as a means to counteract the suppression of the inventor's name. The common constellation is that one party provides only the financial resources for R&D and does not take part in the actual inventive activity. In particular, the provisions in Dutch and German law open the possibility for the funder to be recognised as a co-inventor.

C.1. MODIFICATION 2

Assume that ITC is a biotech company whose basic business is breeding patented laboratory mice. It licenses 100 mice to Prof. Brain under the condition that he transfer all future inventions resulting from experiments with the mouse model to ITC.

If Brain ignores the clause, which he regards invalid, and applies for a patent for an invention based on experiments with the mouse model, is ITC entitled to challenge the patent on the ground that it is the owner of the patent?

58 This rationale can be seen throughout the reports.

59 In Germany, ITC could even be accused of unfair trading (see the German report).

C.2. COUNTRY REPORTS

(1) BELGIUM

I. Operative Rules

No, ITC is not entitled to challenge the patent.

II. Descriptive Formants

The European Commission tends to condemn grant-back clauses, which require the licensee to extensively transfer intellectual property rights to the licensor or a third party.[60]

Although Regulation (EC) No. 772/2004[61] (now Regulation (EU) No. 316/2014)[62] does not cover 'the technological research tool used in the process of further research activity',[63] its Article 5(1)(b) is illustrative, since it excludes grant-back clauses which oblige the licensee to transfer his/her own severable improvements from the block exemption. The exclusion of such clauses from the block exemption merely means an individual assessment is needed, but it should be noted these clauses are excluded because of their likeliness to reduce the incentives of the licensees to innovate.[64]

It is likely that the grant-back clause of the present case would infringe Article 2§1 BCtA (equivalent to Art. 81(1) EC Treaty) without being suitable for exemption under Art. 2§3 BCtA (Art. 81(3) EC Treaty). Therefore, according to Article 2§2 BCtA (Art. 81(2) EC Treaty), Prof. Brain can invoke the automatic nullity of this specific clause.[65]

Belgian courts tend to be guided strongly by European competition law and its case law (see Cases 1 and 6). The provisions of the Commission Guidelines on the application of Article 81 EC Treaty to technology transfer agreements and the relevant decisions constitute strong arguments, but are not legally binding

60 For instance: Commission Decision of 12 July, *Velcro SA v. Aplix SA*, 85/410/EEC, OJ L 233, 30 August 1985, 29 and 31. For some comments, see I. van Bael and J.F. Bellis, *Competition Law of the European Community* (The Hague: 2005), 640–641; V. Korah, *Intellectual Property Rights and the EC Competition Rules* (Oxford/Portland, Ore.: 2006), 41–42.

61 Commission Regulation (EC) No. 772/2004 of 27 April 2004 on the application of Article 81(3) of the Treaty to categories of technology transfer agreements, OJ L 123, 27 April 2004, 11–17.

62 Commission Regulation (EU) No. 316/2014 of 21 March 2014 on the application of Article 101(3) of the Treaty on the Functioning of the European Union to categories of technology transfer agreements, OJ L 93, 28 March 2014, 17–23.

63 Commission Notice: Guidelines on the application of Article 81 of the EC Treaty to technology transfer agreements, OJ C 101, 27 April 2004, 9, para. 45.

64 Ibid., paras. 107–111.

65 I. van Bael and J.F. Bellis, *Competition Law of the European Community* (The Hague: 2005), 82.

instruments in this case. However, the Guidelines are likely to influence the national courts and the Commission's decisions should be taken into account by them insofar as they indicate the Commission's practice.[66] It should be noted that, in Belgium, the group exemption regulations, amongst which Regulation (EU) No. 316/2014, are directly applicable to purely national situations, i.e. which do not affect trade between member states (Art. IV.4 BCEL).[67]

III. Metalegal Formants

The European institutions frequently and categorically consider overly strong grant-back clauses to be anti-competitive, since they reduce the incentives for the licensee to put further effort into innovation.[68] A balanced royalty agreement could perhaps compensate for this effect. However, such a provision was ignored by the Commission in *Velcro SA v. Aplix SA*.[69]

(2) CZECH REPUBLIC

I. Operative Rules

ITC is entitled to challenge the patent.

II. Descriptive Formants

The licence contract is governed by sections 508–515 of the Commercial Code, which comprise provisions on licence contracts on the subject of industrial property. When Professor Brain patents his invention, he is breaching the licence contract, and for this breach of the licence contract ITC shall have the right to damages according to sections 373–386 of the Commercial Code. In addition, according to section 366 of the Commercial Code, ITC may insist on the proper fulfilment of Prof. Brain's obligation – to transfer his inventions to ITC. Then ITC shall be the owner of the patent as the legal successor of the inventor.

---

66 V. Korah, *Intellectual Property Rights and the EC Competition Rules* (Oxford/Portland, Ore.: 2006), 21–26.

67 J. Stuyck, 'Hoofdstuk II. Restrictieve mededingingspraktijken', in: J. Stuyck, W. Devroe and P. Wytinck (eds.), *De nieuwe Belgische Mededingingswet 2006 [The New Belgian Competition Act 2006]* (Mechelen: 2007), 32–34.

68 Commission Notice: Guidelines on the application of Article 81 of the EC Treaty to technology transfer agreements, 20–21, paras. 107–111; V. Korah, *Intellectual Property Rights and the EC Competition Rules* (Oxford/Portland, Ore.: 2006), 69.

69 Commission Decision of 12 July 1985, *Velcro SA v. Aplix SA*, 85/410/EEC, OJ L 233, 30 August 1985, 22–32; V. Korah, *Intellectual Property Rights and the EC Competition Rules* (Oxford/Portland, Ore.: 2006), 69.

III. Metalegal Formants

Modern innovation rests on the distinction between (moral) inventorship and (economic) ownership. In order to secure the functioning of capitalistic market institutions, general civil law rules apply to the property in patents.

(3) DENMARK

I. Operative Rules

ITC will probably not be entitled to challenge the patent.

II. Descriptive Formants

ITC's entitlement to challenge the patent depends on whether Prof. Brain's obligation to transfer the invention in question is valid. This must be decided on the grounds of contract law and competition law. As far as competition law is concerned, the arrangement must be considered under DCompA §6 or Article 101 TFEU.

III. Metalegal Formants

Under Modification 2, the case concerns the competition controversy of strong grant-back clauses. Economic theory rejects reach-through claims as a way of curbing the incentive function of the patent regime, therefore slowing down innovation. There is a double problem. The concept is still contested, and invalidity can only be argued where competition law is applicable.

(4) ESTONIA

I. Operative Rules

Presumably, ITC is entitled to challenge the patent. However, EU competition law could render Prof. Brain's obligation invalid.

II. Descriptive Formants

Subsection 12(2) Patent Act provides: '[i]f an invention is created in the performance of contractual obligations or duties of employment, the right to apply for a patent and to become the proprietor of the patent is vested in the author or other person pursuant to the contract or employment contract'. In the present case, it can be assumed there is a contract which entitles ITC to apply for a patent. Of course, another issue is whether experiments with the mouse model constitute the performance of contractual obligations. The Patent Act, in §12(3), provides that the right to apply for a patent is transferrable.

Subsection 49(1) Patent Act provides:

> Any person who finds that the right to a patent belongs to the person pursuant to §12 of this Act may, after the publication of a patent application pursuant to the provisions of §24 of this Act, file an action in court against the applicant or proprietor of the patent for recognition of the person's rights. If the action is satisfied in the case of a patent application, the person has the right to continue applying for the patent in the person's name, revoke the patent application and file a new patent application with the same filing date concerning the same invention or revoke the patent application. In the case of a patent, the person has the right to register the patent, unamended or subject to amendments, in the person's name or revoke the patent.

III. Metalegal Formants

In addition to the Estonian legal framework, it would be appropriate to analyse the respective EU regulations, such as Commission Regulation (EC) No. 772/2004 of 27 April 2004 on the application of Article 81(3) of the Treaty to categories of technology transfer agreements.

(5) FRANCE

I. Operative Rules

ITC can challenge the patent.

II. Descriptive Formants

The situation differs from the scenario discussed above. Actually, ITC does not oblige Professor Brain to transfer the IP rights he may obtain but to transfer the future inventions he may realise. This means that the research agreement could be considered as containing a provision which stipulates that ITC owns the results of the research.

If Professor Brain filed a French patent, ITC could vindicate it under Article L. 611-8 of the French Intellectual Property Code (see above). This vindication can be obtained whether the patent has already been granted or not and concerns the patent or the application. The vindication can be undertaken up to three years after the grant of the patent was published in the BOPI (Official Report of the Industrial Property). In the case of insincerity of the applicant at the moment when the patent was granted, this period of time runs from the date when the patent has expired.

If Prof. Brain filed a European patent, ITC can ask for the revocation of the patent before a national court (Art. 138(1)(e) EPC) or vindicate the patent as if it was a French patent.

Under contract law, the question is whether the clause is valid. Contractual freedom leads to a first positive answer. Regarding competition law, no specific provision seems to forbid this contractual provision. As a consequence, this clause must be considered valid. This implies that ITC can challenge the patent to the extent mentioned above.

III. Metalegal Formants

Contractual freedom reigns the case.

(6) GERMANY

I. Operative Rules

ITC cannot challenge the patent.

II. Descriptive Formants

The norms to consider are §§59, 21 and §8 German Patent Code. Neither norm applies for the same reasons discussed above.

The distinct contractual question is whether the obligation to grant back the invention made with the licensed technology is valid. Superficially, Article 5(1)(b) Regulation (EC) No. 772/2004 (now Regulation (EU) No. 316/2014) might apply – considering that it is a licence. However, Article 5(1)(b) Regulation (EC) No. 772/2004 only dealt with severable improvements and new applications. The given case deals with inventions made 'with' the licensed technology.

There is no case law yet. Legal intuition tends to qualify those clauses as invalid. Norms potentially resulting in invalidity are §1 UWG, the rationale of Article 5(1) 1 Regulation (EC) No. 772/2004, §§305 c and §242 BGB. The interpretation of these norms may refer to the rationale of §§903/1004 BGB and be strengthened by a reflection of the economic underpinnings of Article 5 sec. 3 German Constitution.

III. Metalegal Formants

Modern research-based technologies have brought about the development of highly competent, independent private research firms marketing research tools.

As they cannot expect to participate in profits via patent dependency (as the tool only enables the new invention, but the latter is not based on the former), research companies try to secure their profits by 'reach-through clauses'. Grant-back promises for future inventions are highly questionable – both under constitutional property considerations and under competition rules.

(7) GREECE

I. Operative Rules

In dubio, the right of ITC is still relative and non-addressable against third parties.

II. Descriptive Formants

In the second modification, the solution ought not to differ either, unless Prof. Brain's invention was not simply tested but was based on the invention of ITC's mice (e.g. on the technical process of their production). In this exceptional instance, ITC will have, over and above the relevant contractual right of obligation against Prof. Brain, a right of action for (partial) annulment of the patent to the extent that this does not recognise ITC as co-inventor in accordance with Article 15 para. 3 Law 1773/1987. In virtue of its 'constitutive nature', this right may be opposed, not only against Prof. Brain, but *erga omnes*.

III. Metalegal Formants

If, by way of an exception to the rule of Article 177 Civil Code, the agreement between ITC and Prof. Brain entails not only a personal obligation, but also a restriction of Prof. Brain's ability to dispose of the patent rights, then the major dogmatic issue to be faced here is the problem of prior transfer of a future patent or the right over the invention not *ex lege* but by virtue of the contract. The IP right shall pass to the employer from the employee's property 'within an ideal second', without any sufficient publicity (to the detriment of third parties), nor even an announcement to the third parties involved, by analogy to the cession of claims, as Article 470 Civil Code would require for any cession of non-specifically regulated rights.

(8) IRELAND

I. Operative Rules

No, ITC is not entitled to challenge the patent.

II. Descriptive Formants

Section 43 Patent Act states that '[t]he rights conferred by a patent shall not extend to any act which, pursuant to any obligation imposed by the law of the Treaties establishing the European Communities, cannot be prevented by the proprietor of the patent.' Nominally, at least, Irish patent law will not trump competition law.

European Union law tends not to favour grant-back clauses, which require the licensee to transfer substantial intellectual property rights to the licensor or to a third party. However, the academic writers in this area[70] observe that the circumstances where an abuse of a dominant position by copyright holders will be found may be broader than for patentees.

III. Metalegal Formants

Irish courts tend to be very protective of property rights and in copyright cases, for example, several judges have speculated that there are sources of copyright which exist outside the statute, effectively potentially extending the rights far beyond that which the statute recognises.

(9) ITALY

I. Operative Rules

ITC cannot challenge the patent, since in all probability it is not the owner of the patent.

II. Descriptive Formants

The provision set out in the case description ('to transfer all future inventions coming out of experiments with the mouse-model to ITC') presumably conflicts with Article 2 of the ICL (mirroring Art. 81(1) EC Treaty).[71]

It could be argued that Regulation (EC) No. 772/2004 provides for a series of exemptions in the field of technological transfer agreements and the proposed case has the potential to fit into the block exemption. However, the particularly broad conditions of the present case ('to transfer all future inventions') likely fall outside the field of application of the Regulation.

---

70 R. Clark, S. Smyth and N. Hall, *Intellectual Property Law in Ireland* (3rd ed., Dublin: 2010), p. 150.

71 The Italian Antitrust Law is Act no. 287 of 10 October 1990, 'Norme per la tutela della concorrenza e del mercato'.

Article 5[72] Regulation (EC) No. 772/2004 provides that 'any direct or indirect obligation on the licensee to assign, in whole or in part, to the licensor ... rights to its own severable improvements to or its own new applications of the licensed technology' falls outside the block exemption provided for by Article 2.

If such a restriction falls outside Article 2 Regulation (EC) No. 772/2004, then it is void and without any effect. Consequently, Prof. Brain is entitled to file for the patent.

III. Metalegal Formants

An interesting issue to bear in mind is that the new Industrial Property Code, unlike the previous legislation and the consolidated European trend, states that in the case of university professors and researchers, the owner of the patent is not the institution but the professor or researcher who legitimately filed it in his/her own name. This is the case only inside academic institutions.

Interestingly, universities continue to hold the right to determine their own share or royalties in the licences granted to third parties, which in any case must respect the protected quota reserved to the inventor (not lower than 50%), and in the absence of any contractual determination is set at 30%.[73]

(10) LITHUANIA

Answer omitted.

(11) NETHERLANDS

I. Operative Rules

No, ITC cannot challenge the patent on the ground that it is the owner of the patent.

II. Descriptive Formants

Despite the fact that a licence is in principle governed by the freedom of contract, the clause in the licence seems to be a prohibited hardcore restriction

72 Art. 5 Regulation (EC) No. 772/2004 concerns the 'excluded restrictions'; also relevant in this case is Art. 4 regarding 'hardcore restrictions'.

73 See Art. 65 Industrial Property Code.

of Article 5(1)(b) Regulation (EC) No. 772/2004.[74] It could be argued, though, that the restriction of Article 5(1)(b) does not cover the licensee's own severable inventions that are invented using the licensed technology. The rationale for this provision – to encourage innovation – seems to indicate that the phrase 'new applications of the licensed technology' could be interpreted more freely, insofar as it also covers inventions that are invented using the licensed technology. This would make the grant-back clause null according to Article 101(2) TFEU. Therefore, ITC cannot be considered to be the owner of the patent.

III. Metalegal Formants

This case shows a potential conflict between the intellectual property rules and the competition rules. Both sets of rules can contribute to an increase in innovation. On the one hand, the market profits from a fast dissemination of new technical information to as many participants as possible as fast as possible. For example, too far-reaching restrictions of technology transfer are forbidden by competition law. On the other hand, the market also profits from continued innovation as fast as possible. Therefore, innovators need an incentive to invest in research and development. Innovators are rewarded by the traditional way of intellectual property. Intellectual property allows them exclusive market positions when it comes to the commercialisation of inventions.[75] In this case, a balance needs to be found between on the one hand protecting the interests of the rightholder and on the other hand limiting the dissemination of technical information too much.

The member states are strongly guided by the developments of European competition law through Regulations and the case law of the European Court of Justice. Articles 12 and 13 of the Dutch Competition Act specifically refer to the applicability of the European Regulations concerning Article 101 TFEU. While Regulation (EC) No. 772/2004 does not apply to this case, it may still be relevant for the individual assessment of this case in the competition law context. Recital 5 of the Regulation notes the importance of technology transfer agreements for economic efficiency and the stimulation of competition. These agreements can 'reduce duplication of research and development, strengthen the incentive for the initial research and development, spur incremental innovation, facilitate

---

74 The reader is referred to what has been said regarding EC competition law in the descriptive formant of the base case. Art. 5(1)(b) Regulation (EC) No. 772/2204 states that: 'Any direct or indirect obligation on the licensee to assign, in whole or in part, to the licensor or to a third party designated by the licensor, rights to its own severable improvements to or its own new applications of the licensed technology'.

75 I.B. Orstavik, 'Technology transfer agreements: grant backs and no challenge clauses in the new EC Technology Transfer Regulation', 36(1) *International Review of Intellectual Property and Competition Law* (2005) 84–85.

diffusion and generate product market competition'.[76] Essentially, technology transfer agreements can stimulate competition. However, the conditions in a technology transfer agreement can also restrict competition. In principle, the rightholder of a patent is free to set the conditions in a licence agreement. However, the rightholder does have to stay within the competition law rules. In the Regulation, one of the hardcore restrictions which is excluded from the exemption in Article 2 of the Regulation is the grant-back clause. The grant-back clause can have severe restrictive effects on competition. Strong grant-back clauses can leave little incentive to innovate for the licensee since there is little room to exploit the innovation. The Commission has been very sceptical about grant-backs, since the incentive to innovate is an important element for increasing competition.[77] The question in this case is whether the grant-back clause complies with the competition rules. Although the Regulation does not apply to this case, the fact that a grant-back clause is qualified as a hardcore restriction in the Regulation is an indication that this could be a forbidden clause in the licence agreement in this case. Of course, there are also arguments for grant-back clauses. One of the arguments is that the grant-back clause is necessary for the rightholders to cover some of the investments in R&D. Another argument used is that if it was not for the grant-back clause, the licence would not have been granted at all. The grant-back clause might make a licence acceptable which otherwise would have been refused. The burden of the grant-back clause could be reduced by lowering the price for the licence. However, in practice this is not always the way it works.[78]

When assessing the validity of a grant-back clause under Article 101 TFEU, all the relevant elements have to be looked at. A relevant element in this case would be that the patented mice are being used as a research tool. If the grant-back clause would apply to inventions where the patented technology was only used as a research tool in an experiment, this would leave little incentive for Prof. Brain to innovate. The patented mice probably have nothing to do with the technology of Prof. Brain's invention. The rationale behind the exclusion of grant-back clauses from the block exemption in the Regulation is to encourage innovation. To apply the grant-back clause in this case would seriously contradict the rationale of the provision.

---

76 S.C. van Es and P.M.A.L. Plompen, 'De nieuwe Groepsvrijstelling voor technologie-licenties (Verordening 772/2004)', 4 *Markt & Mededinging* (2004) 133.

77 I.B. Orstavik, 'Technology transfer agreements: grant backs and no challenge clauses in the new EC Technology Transfer Regulation', 36(1) *International Review of Intellectual Property and Competition Law* (2005) 89; and *The Commission Evaluation Report on the Transfer Technology Block Exemption Regulation Nr. 240/96 – Technology Transfer Agreements under Article 81* (Brussels: 2001), paras. 25 and 166.

78 I.B. Orstavik, 'Technology transfer agreements: grant backs and no challenge clauses in the new EC Technology Transfer Regulation', 36(1) *International Review of Intellectual Property and Competition Law* (2005) 89–90.

(12) NORWAY

I. Operative Rules

ITC will probably not be entitled to challenge the patent.

II. Descriptive Formants

ITC's entitlement to challenge the patent depends on whether Prof. Brain's obligation to transfer the invention in question is valid. This must be decided on the grounds of contract law and competition law. As far as competition law is concerned, the arrangement must be considered under NCompA §10 or Article 53 EEA Agreement, both corresponding to Article 101 TFEU. As pointed out in other country reports,[79] it is highly questionable whether the strong grant-back obligation complies with Article 101, cf. Article 5 Regulation (EC) No. 772/2004,[80] and – given that Norwegian courts apply the competition provisions correctly – the result will not be any different in Norway than in the EU countries.

III. Metalegal Formants

Under Modification 2, the case concerns the competition controversy of strong grant-back (so-called 'reach-through') clauses. To date, the rationale has not been applied as a 'general rule' beyond the confines of competition law.

(13) POLAND

I. Operative Rules

ITC cannot challenge the patent.

II. Descriptive Formants

If Article 11.4 IPL is applicable and the clause is valid, ITC has acquired the right to obtain a patent. If so, the registration for Prof. Brain has violated this right. Article 74 IPL allows ITC to demand that the patent-granting proceeding be discontinued or the patent granted be revoked. ITC may also demand that a

79 Cf. for example the Belgian and the German reports respectively.

80 Cf. the corresponding Art. 5 of the Norwegian Regulations 964 (4 December 1992) ch. IV and 922 (6 July 2006).

patent be granted in its favour or that the patent already granted be transferred to it against reimbursement of the incurred costs of filing the application or of granting the patent. However, a grant-back clause in a licence contract encompassing all inventions would most probably be invalid because of infringement of competition law (Art. 6(2)) Competition Act in connection with §8 point 2. of the Technology Transfer Regulation).[81]

III. Metalegal Formants

The case involves the issue of reach-through clauses by means of which holders of IP rights use their factual and legal monopoly to acquire, on very favourable terms, the rights to inventions created by third parties using subject matter protected by IP rights.

(14) SLOVENIA

I. Operative Rules

Yes, ITC can challenge the patent.

II. Descriptive Formants

ITC and Prof. Brain concluded a valid licence agreement. ITC is consequently entitled to the rights conferred by the patent and may, similarly to the base case, file an action pursuant to Article 115(3) IPA. Namely, Article 115(3) IPA allows a person who is entitled to the rights conferred by a patent to request that he/she be declared owner of the patent if the patent was unjustifiably granted in the name of the inventor.

III. Metalegal Formants

Freedom of contract governs the outcome of the case.

(15) SPAIN

I. Operative Rules

The obligation imposed on Prof. Brain is prohibited under competition law.

---

81 K. Kohutek, in: K. Kohutek, M. Sieradzka, *Ustawa o ochronie konkurencji I konsumentów. Komentarz* (Kraków: 2008), p. 78.

II. Descriptive Formants

This case raises the issue of the licensee's obligation to share the results of exploiting the patent with the licensor. When the obligation is reciprocal, it is in the contractors' and the community's interests because it makes it possible to perfect the patented invention.[82] Nevertheless, the competition authorities have analysed this clause to prevent it from being abusive and leading to unjust results that do not defend the improvement of technology. Regulation (EC) No. 240/96 of 31 January 1996 on the application of Article 85 of the Treaty (the precedent of Regulation (EU) No. 316/2014 of 21 March 2014 on the application of Article 101(3) TFEU) considered that these clauses should be prohibited when they are unilateral, as they are in the given case. In agreement with Article 3(6) of Regulation (EC) No. 240/96, the exemption for categories of agreements will not be applied when the licensee is obliged to transfer to the licensor all or some of the rights on the improvements or new applications of the technology. In this sense, the clause is abusive and, therefore, the agreement is prohibited in accordance with the stipulations of current competition law. The clause is not reciprocal and, therefore, the obligation imposed on Prof. Brain to grant the rights on improvements made to the technology under licence is not lawful.

This issue has not been legally dealt with in Spain, nor is there any case law.

III. Metalegal Formants

Reach-through clauses risk undermining the patent incentive and may therefore stifle innovation. These clauses should therefore, at least in their unilateral form, be subject to abuse scrutiny.

(16) UNITED KINGDOM

I. Operative Rules

ITC has no stronger case to be recognised as the owner of the patent than in the base case.

II. Descriptive Formants

The difference in this scenario is that the research contract involves mice (patented mice), not just financial support. Accordingly, there may be a patent licence as well as the research contract.

[82] P. Martín Aresti, *La licencia contractual de patente* (Pamplona: 1997), p. 249.

ITC might argue that Prof. Brain breached the patent licence. A patent licence is a contract, also subject to the rules of contract law. Establishing that Prof. Brain breached the mouse licensing contract is unlikely to provide the level of financial compensation that ITC seeks, unless Prof. Brain is a very wealthy man. So again, the issue is whether M-University could be linked to the breach in a way that made it legally responsible, and if the liability was in contract and/or negligence, one needs to consider the extent to which ITC could recover consequential loss or a share of profits.

III. Metalegal Formants

English contract law tends to be sceptical towards far-reaching claims which may impede competition and innovation.

C.3. COMPARATIVE REMARKS

The case raises the topic of future transfer of IPRs between private and public research institutions (so-called 'reach-through claims').

The answers of the country reports paint a rather heterogeneous picture. Most countries have analysed the contractual obligation under competition law and concluded that the clause is probably invalid.[83] Therefore, ITC would not be entitled to challenge the patent. In other countries, such as the Czech Republic, France and Slovenia, ITC is, as the owner of the patent, entitled to challenge it.

The current situation is not satisfying because the civilising constraints of competition law are not directly applicable to contracts between public and private research institutions. This has the contradictory effect that industry may be allowed to intrude more upon a public research institution than upon a private research institution. Yet public research institutions are financed by public money, committed to serving the general public interest. In the light of the ever-growing importance of public research for the innovation process, it would be reasonable to devise a framework for industry and public research collaboration, ranging from patent law stipulations (earmarked as foundational patents or patents of public research origin) to contractual restrictions (limits to exclusive agreements, invalidation of reach-through clauses).

---

83 See the reports of Belgium, Denmark, Estonia, Italy, the Netherlands, Poland, Spain and the UK.

CASE 12. USE RESTRICTIONS

A.1. CASE

Dr Grey, the director of a private research institution, undertakes research projects with a variety of sponsors. She receives a licence for 100 EMC4 rats from White Corp. for a research project headed by her employee, Dr Black. The licence obliges the institute only to use the rat model in the identified experiment conducted by Dr Black. The use of the rat model in experiments sponsored by White's competitor, Yellow Corp., is expressly forbidden.

Two years later, Dr Black is entrusted with an in-house research project sponsored by Yellow Corp. He continues using the rat model EMC4 and patents his results.

Does White Corp. have a right to a share in profits as damages on the basis of breach of contract?

A.2. EDITORIAL NOTE ON THE EUROPEAN FRAMEWORK

The EU competition law framework is set by the Research and Development Block Exemption Regulation (Regulation (EU) No. 1217/2010)[1] and the Technology Transfer Regulation (EC) No. 772/2004[2] (now Regulation (EU) No. 316/2014).[3] In addition, Article 13 Directive 2004/48/EC (issued after the cases were designed in 2000) may play a role.[4] Accordingly, courts can set damages by looking at different aspects like negative economic consequences, lost profits and unfair profits made by the infringer or, as an alternative, may set a lump sum on the basis of the royalties that would have been paid in the case of a valid licensing agreement between the parties (Art. 13(a) and (b)

1 Regulation (EU) No. 1217/2010 of 14 December 2010 on the application of Article 101(3) TFEU to certain categories of research and development agreements, OJ L 335, 18 December 2010, 36–42.

2 Regulation (EC) No. 772/2004 of 27 April 2004 on the application of Article 81(3) of the Treaty to categories of technology transfer agreement, OJ L 123, 27 April 2004, 11–17.

3 Commission Regulation (EU) No. 316/2014 of 21 March 2014 on the application of Article 101(3) of the Treaty on the Functioning of the European Union to categories of technology transfer agreements, OJ L 93, 28 March 2014, 17–23.

4 Directive 2004/48/EC of 29 April 2004 on the enforcement of intellectual property rights, OJ L 195, 30 April 2004, 16–25.

Directive 2004/48/EC). If the infringer did not knowingly, or with reasonable grounds to know, infringe the IP, member states may allow the courts to decide the recovery of profits (Art. 13(2)). Yet Case 12 asks for a share of profits based on the violation of a contract. Thus, Directive 2004/48/EC was not directly applicable, but may influence the reasoning.

A.3. COUNTRY REPORTS

(1) BELGIUM

I. Operative Rules

No, White Corp. does not have a right to a share in the profits as damages on the basis of breach of contract since the contract clause at stake will probably be invalid.

II. Descriptive Formants

The contractual obligation not to use the rat model in experiments sponsored by competitors might not be valid, due to incompatibility with Article 2 BCtA (Art. IV.1 BCEL, equivalent to Art. 101 TFEU) in conjunction with applicable Regulation (EU) No. 316/2014.

Field of use restrictions are, if certain conditions are met, block exempted under Regulation (EU) No. 316/2014. The pro-competitive aspects of field of use restrictions are to be seen in the context of licensors who cannot or will not exploit their technology in a specific field and can, through such licence restrictions, allow others to do this without the licensees entering into the field the licensor would like to reserve for him/herself.[5] However, the Commission Guidelines on the application of Article 81 EC Treaty to technology transfer agreements, in paragraph 209, warn about clearly distinguishing field of use restrictions from consumer restrictions. In this regard, Article 4(b) Vertical Agreements Block Exemption Regulation states that 'a restriction of the customers to whom the buyer may sell the contract goods or services' constitutes a hardcore restriction (unless for some specific circumstances),[6] which means that the customers cannot be exempted. The explicit clause not to do business with Yellow Corp. is quite suspicious in this regard.

---

5 Commission Notice: Guidelines on the application of Article 81 of the EC Treaty to technology transfer agreements, OJ C 101, 27 April 2004, 32–33, paras. 179–185.

6 Commission Regulation (EC) No. 330/2010 of 20 April 2010 on the application of Article 101(3) of the Treaty on the Functioning of the European Union to categories of vertical agreements and concerted practices, OJ L 102, 23 April 2010, 1–7. The Vertical Agreements Block Regulation provides for some exceptions, which do not seem applicable to the present case.

The agreement of Case 12 could also fall under a hardcore restriction under Article 5(1)(a) of the R&D Block Exemption Regulation (Regulation (EC) No. 2659/2000, now Regulation (EU) No. 1217/2010), which excludes research and development agreements which have as their object 'the restriction of the freedom of the participating undertakings to carry out research and development independently or in cooperation with third parties in a field unconnected with that to which the research and development relates or, after its completion, in the field to which it relates or in a connected field'. Therefore, the contract between Dr Grey and White Corp. cannot be exempted under block exemption Regulations.[7]

Since the agreement does not fall under a block exemption, an individual analysis will be needed. Even then, the principles behind these block exemption Regulations can be useful and illustrative for this purpose. Black-listed or hardcore restrictions as included in block exemption Regulations – in the present case Article 4(b) Regulation (EC) No. 2790/1999[8] (now Art. 4(a) Regulation (EU) No. 330/2010) and Article 5(1)(a) Regulation (EC) No. 2659/2000[9] (now Regulation (EU) No. 1217/2010) – are generally considered to infringe *per se* Article 101(1) TFEU. They are not automatically excluded from the application of Article 101(3) TFEU, but, generally, it is quite unlikely that the four conditions of Article 101(3) TFEU would be met for these hardcore restrictions.[10] The four conditions that have to be met for an exemption under Article 101(3) are: efficiency gains or the promoting of technical or economic progress, indispensability of the restrictions, a fair share for consumers, and no elimination of competition.[11] We believe that the disputed contract clause in the present case would not fulfil those conditions, since White Corp. seems to aim intentionally at restricting competition and limiting innovation.

Belgian courts tend to be guided very strongly by European competition law and its case law. In addition, the block exemption Regulations are directly applicable to purely national (Belgian) situations (Art. 5§1 BCtA, now Art. IV.4 BCEL).

---

7 For some general Belgian doctrine on the competition law analysis of research and development agreements: I. van Bael and J.F. Bellis, *Competition Law of the European Community* (The Hague: 2005), 487–509; D. Vandermeersch, *De Mededingingswet [The Competition Act]* (Mechelen: 2007), 155–158.

8 Commission Regulation (EC) No. 2790/1999 of 22 December 1999 on the application of Article 81(3) of the Treaty to categories of vertical agreements and concerted practices, OJ L 336, 29 December 1999, 21–25.

9 Commission Regulation (EC) No. 2659/2000, 29 November 2000, on the application of Article 81(3) EC of the Treaty to categories of research and development agreements, OJ L 304, 5 December 2000, 7–12.

10 Commission Notice: Guidelines on the application of Article 81(3) of the Treaty, OJ C 101, 7 April 2004, 97–118, paras. 20 and 46; and Commission Notice: Guidelines on the applicability of Article 81 of the EC Treaty to horizontal cooperation agreements, OJ C 3, 6 January 2001, 2-30, para. 70. For some comments, see I. van Bael and J.F. Bellis, *Competition Law of the European Community* (The Hague: 2005), 69–71 and 507–508.

11 Commission Notice: Guidelines on the application of Article 81(3) of the Treaty, OJ C 101, 7 April 2004, 97–118, paras. 38–116.

We can therefore conclude that the disputed clause would infringe Article 2 BCtA (Art. IV.1 BCEL, equivalent to Art. 101 TFEU) and is therefore invalid and automatically void (Art. 2§2 BCtA, now Art. IV.1§2 BCEL).

III. Metalegal Formants

The transaction between Dr Grey and White Corp. essentially concerns a sale of research tools, not a licence to produce or apply patented inventions. It is an accepted principle that IP on individual items expires when they are put on the market in the European Union.[12] On the other hand, there is of course the acknowledged principle of contract freedom.[13] From this perspective, we can ask to what degree such after-sale use restrictions as in this case are valid (see also the metalegal formants of Case 6).

(2) CZECH REPUBLIC

I. Operative Rules

White Corp. probably has a right to a share in profits.

II. Descriptive Formants

Damages can be based on sections 373–386 of the Commercial Code (for the breach of a licence contract on a subject of industrial property, sections 508–515 Commercial Code), or they can be based on the Civil Code. The main difference is that in the Commercial Code the construction of liability for damages is based on objective liability (liability for an effect, but not absolute),[14] whereas under the Civil Code liability is strictly subjectively based on culpability.[15]

Since White Corp. and Yellow Corp. did not conclude a contract, there is no contractual obligation based on the Commercial Code; therefore, the provisions of the Commercial Code on compensation for damages do not apply. Instead, compensation would be based on section 420 et seq. of the Civil Code.

---

12 B. Van Reepinghen and M. De Brabanter, *Les brevets d'invention [Patents]* (Brussels: 1987), 173–180; E. De Gryse, 'Licentieovereenkomsten' [Licence Agreements], in: *Bijzondere overeenkomsten. Commentaar met overzicht van rechtspraak en rechtsleer* [Special Agreements. Commentaries with Overviwes of Case Law and Doctrine] (Antwerpen: 1985), 53 et seq.

13 S. Stijns, *Verbintenissenrecht [Contract Law]* (1st ed., Brugge: 2005), 38.

14 S. Plíva, in: Pelikánová et al., *Obchodní právo 2. díl* (Commercial Law volume 2) (2nd ed., Prague: 1998), p. 239.

15 J. Fiala, J. Hurdík, V. Korecká, *Občanský zákoník – Komentář* §420 (Commentary on Civil Code Section 420) as published in the legal database ASPI.

White's claim against Yellow is governed by section 420(1) Civil Code. It stipulates that one shall be liable for the damage caused by the violation of a legal duty. According to the doctrine, liability for damages shall occur if four criteria are met: breach of a legal duty, occurrence of damage, chain of causation between the breach of the legal duty and the occurrence of damage, and culpability.[16] Yellow Corp. did not breach any legal duty, so liability for damages shall not arise. Yellow Corp. is not responsible for damages.

The relationship between White Corp. and Dr Grey's institute is governed by the Commercial Code, since the licence stipulates the subject of industrial property (including damages for breaching a licence contract governed by section 373 Commercial Code). The industrial right in question is a patent right. According to section 8(1) Patent Act,[17] the right to a patent belongs to the inventor or his/her legal successor. White Corp. owns the patent on the rats. Dr Black is the inventor of a subsequent patent. According to section 11(1) Patent Act, the proprietor of the patent has the exclusive right to use the invention or to authorise others to use the invention. The proprietor of the patent is, according to section 34(3) Patent Act, the person to whom the Patent Office has granted the patent.

III. Metalegal Formants

Czech patent law does not secure unconditional research freedom, in the sense that researchers do not have to observe IP rights or respect licence clauses. Contractual freedom governs the case. Czech law does not recognise any principle which may set aside contractual use restrictions in the scientific environment.

(3) DENMARK

I. Operative Rules

White Corp. probably does not have a right to share in the profits.

II. Descriptive Formants

As a point of departure, the private research institution (Grey), as the employer of Dr Black, has breached its licence obligation, which will result in a patent infringement, unless the institute has a valid defence. One possible defence could be the experiment exemption of DPA §3, third paragraph, no. 3. It states that the exclusive right to the patent does not include exploitation by experiment relating

[16] Ibid.
[17] Act on Inventions and Rationalisations Proposals 527/1990 Coll.

to the subject matter of the invention. As is widely accepted, the experimental clause in patent law only protects research related to the invention *itself*. Based on the facts of the case, it is doubtful whether this condition is met. The exemption will not apply. Another possible defence, one that is more likely to succeed, is that the licence obligation is contrary to DCompA §6 and Article 101 TFEU.

III. Metalegal Formants

The case concerns the scope of the licensed patent and the impact of contractual obligations to refrain from competitive use of the patent. Field of use restrictions may be critical under competition law.

(4) ESTONIA

I. Operative Rules

White Corp. is not entitled to a share in profit but can claim damages on the basis of breach of contract.

II. Descriptive Formants

A key issue for the case is the question of whether the obligation to use the rats for particular purposes is valid. The rats are licensed, not sold, and therefore the principle of exhaustion[18] is of no great help. The Patent Act allows experimental use, which is defined as 'the use of the patented invention in testing related to the invention itself' (§16 clause 3 Patent Act). In our case, the exception is not applicable because the testing does not concern the rats themselves.

If one concludes that the obligation to use the rats for a particular purpose is valid, then White Corp. can claim damages because the institute has breached the obligation. Pursuant to §127(6) of the Law of Obligations Act, in the event of IP infringement the amount of compensation could also be determined by the court on the basis of an assessment of how much the infringer would have paid to acquire the permission to use the respective IP. It has been explained in Estonian legal literature that this rule is based on the Enforcement Directive[19]

18 The principle of exhaustion of rights provided by §171 Patent Act reads: '[t]he proprietor of a patent has no right to prohibit acquisition (including import), use, distribution, sale or offer for sale of a product containing the patented invention when the product has been put on the market in the territory of the Republic of Estonia or a State party to the Agreement on the European Economic Area by the proprietor of the patent or with the proprietor's consent'.

19 Directive 2004/48/EC of the European Parliament and of the Council of 29 April 2004 on the enforcement of intellectual property rights (Text with EEA relevance), OJ L 157, 30 April 2004, 45–86.

and its objective is to facilitate the determination of damage caused by IP infringement. The profit received by the infringer cannot be considered damage. Still, the regulation on unjust enrichment could be applicable. The fact that the infringer profited is not sufficient ground to claim damages. The injured party can claim damages if he/she had suffered any. This, however, might be complicated to prove. Therefore, the potential royalty could be the best basis for the establishment of the damage.[20]

To sum up, White Corp. is not entitled to a share in profit. Earned profit is just one possible factor facilitating the assessment of damage.

However, it is not obvious that the use restriction is valid. If White Corp. could be considered an undertaking in a dominant position on the market controlling an essential facility, the restriction of the use of the rats could be forbidden based on the Competition Act.[21] It could also be argued that the use restriction is a standard term which causes unfair harm to the other party. Subsection 35(1) of the Law of Obligations Act defines a standard term as follows:

> A contract term which is drafted in advance for use in standard contracts or which the parties have not negotiated individually for some other reason, and which the party supplying the term uses with regard to the other party who is therefore not able to influence the content of the term, is deemed to be a standard term.

According to §42(1) of the Law of Obligations Act:

> A standard term is void if, taking into account the nature, contents and manner of entry into the contract, the interests of the parties and other material circumstances, the term causes unfair harm to the other party, particularly if it causes a significant imbalance in the parties' rights and obligations arising from the contract to the detriment of the other party or if the standard term is contrary to good morals.

As the case is not detailed enough, it is hard to predict whether competition law or the Law of Obligations Act would render the clause invalid.

III. Metalegal Formants

Estonian civil standard contract law is critical of exploitative uses of contracts, especially in the light of significant imbalances between parties. While the freedom of contracts is the default rule, overarching principles of fairness secure good morals in business life.

---

20 P. Varul, I. Kull, V. Kõve, M. Käerdi, *Võlaõigusseadus I, Kommenteeritud väljaanne* (Law of Obligations Act I. Commented edition), General Part (§§1–207) (Tallinn: 2006), p. 449.

21 Clause 2 of §16 of the Competition Act provides: 'Any direct or indirect abuse by an undertaking or several undertakings of the dominant position in the goods market is prohibited, including limiting production, service, goods markets, technical development or investment'.

(5) FRANCE

I. Operative Rules

White Corp. has no right to a share in profits, but it can claim damages.

II. Descriptive Formants

The contract between White Corp. and Dr Grey's institute could, as one possibility, be considered a patent licence agreement.[22] The Intellectual Property Code admits the possibility of licensing the rights attached to a patent (Art. L. 613-8 Intellectual Property Code), but it does not deal with the regime of these contracts. Beside the regular obligations emanating from this type of contract (obligations of delivery, a guarantee for which the patentee is responsible, payment of the licensing fees, obligation of use by the licensee), the contracting parties can insert collateral obligations. The Intellectual Property Code does not actually impose limits on the freedom of contract (except for computer programme contracts in Art. L 122-6-1 Intellectual Property Code).[23] Thus, nothing appears to forbid the considered restriction, at least as regards special law.

Another possibility could be to qualify (against the wording chosen by the parties) the contract as a sales contract of a patented product. In this case, the theory of exhaustion, codified in Article L. 613-6 Intellectual Property Code, is relevant, since it limits the monopoly of the patent right. The rule of exhaustion prevents the holder of a patent and the one who puts the patented product on the market from controlling acts posterior to the marketing of the product, and more specifically as regards the use of the product made by the buyer. In this very case, all limitations added concerning the exploitation of the product by the patent owner are not subject to patent law, but to competition law or to ordinary contract law.[24]

Thus, in principle, it is through ordinary law that the validity of the clause at issue should be examined, and the principle of freedom of contract should be respected. It allows parties to determine freely the contents of the contract.

---

22 To be compared to the debate on 'qualification' as regards contracts known as '*licence d'utilisation de logiciels*', sometimes also called '*cession de droit d'usage*', which some of the doctrine doubt can be included in the category of contracts of exploitation of an intellectual property right ('*ce qui fait l'économie de l'opération n'est pas l'attribution par le fournisseur du logiciel d'un droit sur une œuvre de l'esprit, mais la mise à disposition d'un outil*': A. Lucas and H.-J. Lucas, *Traité de la propriété littéraire et artistique* (2006), p. 549, n°776.). See on the whole discussion: A. Lucas, J. Devèze and J. Frayssinet, *Droit de l'informatique et de l'Internet* (2001), n°746 and 816.

23 Art. L. 122-6-1 prohibits any provision of a contract which would be against legal provisions on the backup copy, the analysis and the decompilation of the software. The clause would then be 'null and void'.

24 J. Azéma and J-C. Galloux, *Droit de la propriété industrielle* (2006), p. 175, n°256.

However, it can be restrained by exceptions. One may wonder whether the clause is in conflict with public policy provisions and more specifically with the freedom to conduct a business[25] to which the concept of freedom of research is closely connected.[26] But this obstacle does not seem, at first sight, decisive, because even non-competition clauses, which yet have the effect of restricting this freedom, are considered valid in principle (although strictly defined). Besides, the clause does not forbid Dr Black to conduct research, but only to use the rat model in experiments sponsored by a competitor. Therefore, the infringement of fundamental freedoms does not seem disproportionate with regard to the objective pursued by the co-contracting party, that is, to prevent its competitor from benefiting indirectly from the patented technology. Thus, there appears to be no crippling obstacle to the validity of the clause.

Consequently, the question concerning the sanction of the breach of the clause by Dr Black can be raised. The failure to recognise the clause restricting the use of the patented product brings to light the contractual liability of the research institute and leads to the right to compensatory damages to the benefit of White Corp. (Art. 1142 Civil Code). Compensatory damages aim to compensate for no more and no less than the entire prejudice caused, but they should not be looked at as a share in profits earned from Dr Black's patented invention. As a defendant, one could take advantage of provisions in Article L. 442-6 Commercial Code enabling incurring the contractual liability of the commercial partner, if the clause aims to create a significant imbalance between the rights and obligations of the parties concerned.[27]

Since there is no contractual relationship between White Corp. and its competitor, Yellow is a third party to the breached contract. However, would it be possible to incur the tortious liability of Yellow Corp.? A consequence of the principle of relative effect of contracts (Art. 1165 Civil Code) is that the contract has an effect vis-à-vis third parties. It implies that the contract generates a legal position which third parties cannot ignore. Although third parties are not obliged to honour obligations stipulated in the contract, they are nevertheless obliged to refrain from any behaviour which could impede the contract. They have to respect rights emanating from the contract. As a result, third parties who, aware of these facts, help the debtor to avoid performing his/her contractual

25 This freedom is not expressly guaranteed by the French Constitution, but its assimilation to the constitutional principles was deduced from Art. 4 Déclaration des Droits de l'Homme et du Citoyen by the Constitutional Council (decision n°81-132 DC of 16 January 1982, *Nationalisations*).

26 The same concern to protect this freedom can be found in Art. L. 613-5 b) Intellectual Property Code: 'the rights afforded by the patent shall not extend to … acts done for experimental purposes relating to the subject matter of the patented invention'. The term 'experimental purpose' is narrowly interpreted by the courts.

27 Art. L. 442-6 I. 2° Commercial Code.

obligations commit a fault and can be held liable.[28] In the light of this analysis, if Yellow Corp. was aware of the existence of such a clause (supposing it to be valid),[29] that raises tortious liability and Yellow Corp. can be ordered to pay damages to White Corp.[30]

III. Metalegal Formants

The French reasoning strongly relies on the assumption that property and contract in conjunction with the principle of privacy bring about the 'right' result. Therefore, interfering means (through competition law or competing fundamental rights like freedom of research) are subject to justification which meets the yardstick of necessary exceptions. In this sense, research freedom is conceptualised as a limitation to property. As current theory shows, its limitations are spelled out in the experimentation clause. Freedom to manoeuver has to step back so that scientists can do further research.

(6) GERMANY

I. Operative Rules

White Corp. has no right to damages.

II. Descriptive Formants

A claim for a share in profits of White *against Grey* depends on the answer to two questions. First, is the restriction valid? Only then might both a contract claim and a patent violation be possible (unless exempt under the research exemption).[31] Second, did Grey generate any profits to be shared (considering that the employee Black only filed the patent: was Grey promised a share in profits made by Yellow (camouflaging the fact that the patent which is dependent on White's patent will eventually benefit Yellow)?

---

28 For example: Court of Cassation (commercial section), 23 April 1985, Bull. civ. IV, n°124 (third party accomplice of the breach of a non-competition clause).

29 This is true only under this scenario, as such knowledge cannot be assumed (Court of Cassation (Commercial Chamber), 12 March 1963, D. 1963.367, note J. Robert).

30 On the basis of Art. 1382 Civil Code, the possibility of joint and several liabilities (*in solidum* liability) of the party and of the third party accomplice (Court of Cassation (1st chamber, civil section), 16 July 1970, Bull. civ. I, n°241).

31 §11 No. 2 German Patent Code; yet the clause was narrowly interpreted, see BGH, BGHZ 130, 259; BGHZ 135, 217 – *Klinische Versuche I und II (clinical trials I and II)*; in further depth C. Godt, *Eigentum an Information* (Tübingen: 2007), pp. 126 et seq.

A claim for a share in profits of White *against Yellow* depends on the preliminary question of whether the restriction is valid, *and* whether the contract between White and Grey has an effect on Yellow. Otherwise, the rights with regard to the use of the mice would be considered exhausted.

In both cases, the central *legal* question is whether the contract restriction is invalid due to a violation of competition rules.

Grey is a private, commercially operating research institution, therefore the primary prerequisite ('an undertaking') for competition law to apply is fulfilled. One could question whether competition law is applicable to contracts between industry and research institutions, and argue that these contracts are 'pre-competitive', for the reason that – as a matter of principle – they cannot exert effects on competition. Yet EU and German competition law control contracts between non-competitors for their structural effect on competition. §1 GWB makes clear that any collusion is forbidden which prevents, restricts or hampers competition. The question is whether the clause restricts competition or whether White legitimately *exercises* the patentee's rights.

The thin line between competition and patent law is drawn by various regulations (see supra section A.2). In principle, field of use restrictions are allowed. However, some restrictions are regulated, for example by Article 5 Technology Transfer Block Exemption Regulation. Forbidden are restrictions which hinder parties from conducting their own R&D, unless the restriction is necessary in order to prevent the disclosure of the licensed know-how to third parties. Article 5(1)(a) Research and Development Block Exemption Regulation says that restrictions on carrying out R&D independently or in cooperation with third parties in a field unconnected with that to which the R&D agreement relates or, after the completion of the joint R&D or the paid-for R&D, in the field to which it relates or in a connected field, are forbidden. These provisions are not directly applicable, but they could be indicators in order to conclude that White's contract clause is invalid, arguing that the restriction unduly restricts the freedom to operate. These considerations have to be weighed against the differences between the block exemption rules and the agreement in Case 12: (1) the private research institute is still allowed to do R&D with third parties (the prohibition only concerns the use of the rats in such R&D);[32] and (2) Grey is still allowed to do research in fields not connected to a direct use of the rat model.

Referring to the case at hand, I would argue that the restriction is overly restrictive since the object of the licence is a research tool. Thus, it is broadly used. In the daily practice of a research laboratory, even if private, a use restriction which is unlimited in duration, indifferent as to the position of the competitor and does not differentiate between sectors (sic: privileging the research sector)

---

32 A hardcore restriction would only exist if the institute would not be allowed to do any research at all (S. Gehring, 'Vereinbarungen über gewerbliche Schutzrechte', in: T. Mäger (ed.), *Europäisches Kartellrecht* (2nd ed., Baden-Baden: 2011), paras. 86 et seq.

appears overly restrictive. Therefore, it is concluded that the contractual clause violates competition law, is therefore invalid and cannot give rise to contractual liability.

The result is supported by a parallel consideration under conventional sales law. The clause can be held invalid under general civil law (taking resort to patent law rationales) by distinguishing the case from traditional manufacture. If 'Grey' (the research institution) 'buys' (not 'licenses') the patented research tool to perform its business, the right (patents and copyright alike) to the technology as incorporated in the given object would have expired as a result of the sale. Today, research tools are explicitly licensed – due to the informational value, which is far higher than the value of the material.[33] Therefore, the intellectual right to the marketed kit is not directly exhausted,[34] enabling use restrictions which travel with the product and restrict the commercial activity of contract partners.

Those restrictive use restrictions are subject to an intense debate as far as they impede exhaustion[35] (such as 'no exhaustion *as conditio sine qua non*', conditional use permit (CUP) clauses, ban on further transfers, or a ban on maintenance).[36]

Yet I submit that the underlying rationale can be transferred. There are three arguments. Firstly, one could argue that exhaustion occurs by analogy ('functional equivalent') – thus withdrawing the legal basis for use restrictions.[37] Secondly, if the clause can be qualified as a standard clause, use restrictions could be classified as invalid under §307 sec. 2 Nos. 1 and 2 BGB ('*Abweichung vom wesentlichen Grundgedanken der gesetzlichen Regelung*'), or as 'unusual' (§305c BGB), or as a disproportional burden on the other party (§307 sec. 1 BGB).[38] The central argument is that the clause restricts the constitutionally secured freedoms of Article 12 (professional freedom) and Article 5 sec. 3 (research freedom) of the German Constitution. Thirdly, if the clause is not to be qualified as standard clause, the reasoning could apply *mutatis mutandis* to the general rule of §242 BGB (*bona fide* principle).

To conclude, the clause is (most probably) invalid under German law.

---

33 For a fully fledged analysis of the analogy see C. Godt, *Eigentum an Information* (Tübingen: 2007), p. 28.

34 Explicitly codified in copyright law in §69c No. 3 German Copyright Code, and strictly interpreted by OLG Munich, decision of 3 August 2006 (6 U 1818/06) – *Oracle*.

35 Most notably discussed with regard to CJEU judgment of 3 July 2012, C-128/2011, *UsedSoft*, ECLI:EU:C:2012:407.

36 Early on conceptualised by T. Hoeren, 'Urheberrecht und Vertragsfreiheit: Kritische Überlegungen am Beispiel der Verwendungsbeschränkungen im IT-Bereich', in: D. Klumpp, H. Kubicek, A. Roßnagel and W. Schulz (eds.), *Medien, Ordnung und Innovation* (Berlin/Heidelberg: 2006), pp. 273–282.

37 Comparable to Hoeren's argumentation as to the transfer of computer programmes, see ibid., p. 275.

38 M. Coester, in: *Staudinger BGB-Kommentar*, §§305–310 BGB (4th ed., 2006), §307, No. 159; S. Roloff, in: *Ermann BGB Kommentar, 1. Band* (§§1–811 BGB) (11th ed., 2004), paras. 8 and 9.

III. *Metalegal Formants*

Information property and licences profoundly transform the market place and provide tools which enhance private control over the business of others (besides grant-back, various restrictions are imposed on use, transfer, sharing and cooperation). These restrictions not only endanger the traditional form of open academic research, economic and private autonomies are also at stake. Confronting these impairments of freedoms in the modern information society, courts are entrusted with a special responsibility. They are required to set reasonable boundaries to intellectual property employed in contracts. Currently, the courts' reasoning is still bifurcated by the formal applicable contract model, which is at the discretion of the IP owner. Yet the line between the two normative models of sale and licence in the transfer of information is blurring – and the normative models do not provide appropriate guidance. There are two ways for courts to deal with the complex interface of property and contract which is at stake. They either limit the scope of property (either via exhaustion or in a limited way via restricting the scope of injunction),[39] or they balance the equitability of contract clauses – as induced by the European influence.

(7) GREECE

I. *Operative Rules*

White Corp. can only claim its own lost profits, unless the prohibition of using the rats constitutes a resolutive condition of Dr Black's licence.

II. *Descriptive Formants*

The transfer of the licence (or its powers) to a third party (sub-licensee) is prohibited in cases of doubt (Art. 12 para. 4 Law 1733/1987 – a solution preferred in cases of doubt according to Art. 177 Civil Code). Thus, if the term of the non-use of the rats in other experiments is simply an obligation and not a condition of the licence, then Black's permission is taken as given even after the infringement of this term.

Consequently, any profits (of Black and of the new firm which collaborates with him) do not constitute unjust enrichment from the property of White Corp., and it would be difficult for them to correspond to damages to it of the same value, since its activity does not justify such *lucrum cessans*. If, however, it is a

---

[39] E.g. by submitting the injunction to a proportionality test, see OLG Hamburg, decision of 8 February 2006 (5 U 78/05) – *Cybersky*.

resolutive condition of the licence, any profits will constitute unjust enrichment from the property of White Corp.

However, the validity of the term that the rats should not be used in experiments sponsored by the competing company is with the reservation that it does not satisfy the conditions for a prohibited vertical restriction. Indeed, the Technology Transfer Block Exemption Regulation (TT-BER) is sceptical about such restrictions. If the parties are competitors, then according to Article 4(1)(d) the licensing contract containing such a restriction does not benefit from the TT-BER. If the parties are non-competitors, as is probably the case here, then only this clause is to be assessed individually according to Articles 101(3) TFEU, and Article 5(2) TT-BER. If the use restriction of the mice is general, as is stated in the case, then its chances of validity from a competition law point of view are lower than if it were specific (e.g. no use only in experiments sponsored by White Corp.'s competitors).

Damages for breach of contract do not amount to a share of profits according to Greek law. The same goes for damages based on tort, which, contrary to the law in other countries (e.g. Germany), allow the plaintiff to claim the profits of the infringer instead of (or as a form of) damages. The plaintiff can only claim his/her own lost profits due to the infringement (Arts. 330, 335 Civil Code by analogy).[40]

III. Metalegal Formants

Greece cautions against overstretching IP rights. Not only is it open to transposing competition law rationales to contexts not technically governed by competition law, it also does not respect the extended profit calculation as damages for an IP infringement.

(8) IRELAND

I. Operative Rules

Most probably, White Corp. is granted a limited damage claim.

II. Descriptive Formants

This is something of a grey area. On paper, Irish courts are compliant with EU competition law policy but it may be that in practice patent rights appear too strong and infringement is decently sanctioned.

[40] *Positive Vertragsverletzung* as a form of frustration of the licence contract.

Assuming that White Corp. has a patent over the rats and therefore is competent to grant the licence, in all likelihood White Corp. would have a remedy against Dr Black and Yellow Corp.

The remedies for patent infringement are listed in section 47 of the Patents Act 1992. Either the patent owner or an exclusive licensee can initiate proceedings in the High Court under section 51 in relation to any infringement which he/she alleges has occurred under sections 40–43 and 45. The remedies include an injunction, an order to deliver up or destroy any infringing product, damages, an account of profits and a declaration that the valid patent has been infringed by the defendant.

The once equitable remedy of account of profits is now on a statutory footing, but under section 47(2), the court will only award damages or an account of profits and not both remedies in relation to the same infringement.

Licence conditions which come within Article 101 TFEU are potentially void on the basis of being contrary to competition law, where the agreement is not covered by a block exemption. Regulation (EC) No. 772/2004 is a block exemption regulation which applies to some restrictive licence terms in technology transfer agreements, which, nonetheless, may not fall outside Article 101(3) TFEU, due to some positive aspects. This Regulation does not have a white list of permitted clauses but anything which is not on the black list is permitted, unless there is a particular reason to consider the clause on a case-by-case basis.

Regulation (EC) No. 2659/200 may also be considered where intellectual property rights intersect with results of research and development.

III. Metalegal Formants

In Ireland, little litigation occurs in the area of competition law and patents. In all likelihood, this case would therefore be analysed on licence/contract principles under the Patents Act, not under competition principles. Under these premises, the court would not have access to competition analogies. Yet, in contrast to other jurisdictions, Irish courts are careful in not overstretching patent liability.

(9) ITALY

I. Operative Rules

No, White Corp. has no right to a share in profits.

II. Descriptive Formants

If the contractual obligation not to use the rat model in experiments sponsored by Yellow Corp. is valid, then it represents a typical case of breach of contract and damages can be granted to White Corp. (Art. 1218 Civil Code). However, this does not mean a share in profits.

Another possibility arising from such a situation would be that Yellow can use Grey's patented results, which are dependent on White's. In this case, Yellow may manufacture only after authorisation granted by White. In this case, without a specific licence, Yellow may not produce and sell its products (Art. 71 Industrial Property Code). If Yellow asked for a licence, but it was not granted, Yellow may apply for a legal licence. Article 71 Industrial Property Code provides for this eventuality in dependency cases. However, the dependent invention has to represent important technological progress of significant economic relevance. In this much delimited case, a kind of share in profits may be envisioned. In fact, Article 72 c. 2 Industrial Property Code states that the legal licence can be granted only upon payment of 'fair compensation'. The concept of fairness is not defined, but it is quite likely that in determining a fair amount, courts will also take into consideration the amount of profits that the downstream licence is able to generate.

A third and last possibility would be that such a contractual obligation will be deemed void according to Article 2 ICL[41] (mirroring Art. 101 TFEU), because it represents a use restriction in the market. If this was the case, such a possible violation of competition should be checked against Regulation (EC) No. 772/2004 on the application of Article 101(3) TFEU to categories of technology transfer agreements. If such a clause represents a use restriction and is not block-exempted, then it is automatically void (Art. 2 c. 3 ICL) and consequently the patent filed by Dr Black would be valid.

III. Metalegal Formants

So far, there is no case law in Italy regarding such a specific situation. The different possible legal consequences depend on the presence – and specific wording – of the employment agreement or commission contract, on the kind of employment between the different parties, and on the industrial and commercial workflow of the productive entities involved.

As a rule of thumb, in the third scenario dealing with use restrictions, it must be borne in mind that the Commission has an 'ontological' antipathy for those agreements that are capable of limiting competition in the internal market. This is solemnly declared in Article 101 TFEU and may also be inferred *a contrario* from Regulation (EC) No. 772/2004. In the proposed case, there is no evidence that the restriction that White Corp. imposes is intended to foster technological development or competition. On the contrary, it seems to be intended only in the direction of limiting competition with Yellow Corp.

---

41 It is the Act of 10 October 1990, no. 287 'Norme per la tutela della concorrenza e del mercato'.

(10) LITHUANIA

Answer omitted.

(11) NETHERLANDS

I. Operative Rules

White Corp. probably has no right to a share in the profits.

II. Descriptive Formants

Using the 100 EMC[4] rats constitutes a breach of the licence. This, in principle, means a patent infringement, unless an exception is applicable.

One possible exception could be the research exception in Article 53 DPA, which aim exclusively is to research the patented invention.[42] However, in this case Dr Black has a different aim. The focus of Dr Black will probably not be related to the patented rats. The research exception does not apply in this case.

A more likely possibility is that the exclusivity clause in the licence is not compatible with competition law rules. Articles 101 and 102 TFEU prohibit certain acts which limit or restrict competition. The same rules on a national level can be found in Articles 6 and 24 of the Dutch Competition Act. However, restrictions can be justified under Article 101(3) TFEU, and Regulation (EC) No. 772/2004. Articles 12 and 13 of the Dutch Competition Act specifically refer to exemptions made by European Regulations. Article 2 of Regulation (EC) No. 772/2004 exempts technology transfer agreements between two undertakings in which permission is given to produce contract products. Contract products are the products produced with the licensed technology.

In this case, it seems the patented rats are used for the purpose of an experiment and not for the production of goods. The Regulation does not apply to agreements licensing technology enabling the licensee to carry out research and development, for example research tools used in the process of further research activity.[43] §45 of the Guidelines on the application of Article 81 of the EC Treaty (now Art. 101 TFEU) to technology transfer agreements states that the framework of the Regulation is based on the premise that there is a direct link between the licensed technology and an identified contract product. The analytical framework of the Regulation may not be appropriate in cases where no such link exist. This would be the case if the main object of the agreement is research and development as opposed to bringing a particular product to the

---

[42] C. Gielen and D.W.F. Verkade, *Intellectuele eigendom* (Deventer: 2005), p. 59.

[43] J.D.C. Turner, *Intellectual Property and EU Competition Law* (Oxford: 2010), p. 139.

market. Here, the rats are used in an experiment as a research tool. Furthermore, the licensee is a private research institute. The case seems to indicate that White Corp. is a sponsor; it therefore seems unlikely that there is a direct link between the patented rats and an identified contract product.

Since the agreement is not covered by the Regulation, the licence must be examined individually for compliance with Articles 101 and 102 TFEU (namely, whether it falls within the scope of Arts. 101 or 102 TFEU and whether an exception applies). The application of national (Arts. 6 and 24 of the Dutch Competition Act) or European competition rules depends on the effect on trade between member states.

The licence probably does not comply with the competition rules if the conditions set out in Article 101(1) TFEU are fulfilled. First of all, the licence granted by White Corp. constitutes an agreement between undertakings. The agreement could restrict and/or distort competition, although the case does not give all the necessary information in order to assess this. The restriction (only use the rats for this specific experiment) might fall under Article 101(1)(b) TFEU ('limit or control technical development'). While it is common for a licence agreement to contain restrictions on use, a restriction on use for only experiments is rare and could limit competition.

The exemption in Article 101(3) TFEU will not save White Corp. because its conditions are not fulfilled. The agreement does not contribute to improving the production or distribution of goods or to promoting technical or economic progress. On the contrary, the licence condition probably hinders technical progress.

The licence agreement could also possibly be an abuse of a dominant position according to Article 102 TFEU. The case does not state that White Corp. holds a dominant position. If it does and if it refuses to grant a licence which is essential for a certain experiment, this could be an abuse. By restraining the dissemination of innovation, competition could be restricted.[44]

The condition set out in the licence agreement does not comply with competition rules. Therefore, the condition will be automatically void according to Article 101(2) TFEU. White Corp. will have no right to a share in profits.

III. Metalegal Formants

In this case the same interests as in Case 11, Modification 2 are involved. In principle, the rightholder is free to set the conditions for a licence. Because of the freedom of contract, parties can in principle agree to use restrictions. It is common for a licence to come with certain use restrictions. However, the conditions have to stay within the limits of the competition rules. While this

44 S.C. van Es and P.M.A.L. Plompen, 'De nieuwe Groepsvrijstelling voor technologie-licenties (Verordening 772/2004)', 4 *Markt & Mededinging* (2004) 133.

use restriction is not as far-reaching as the grant-back clause and therefore not a hardcore restriction, it could still restrict competition. This would especially be the case if the patented technology is essential for further innovation because this could limit competition. In this case, it makes it interesting that the patented technology is a research tool. It would strongly affect the progress of innovation if the use of (essential) research tools were to be restricted too much.

(12) NORWAY

I. Operative Rules

White Corp. probably does not have a right to share in profits.

II. Descriptive Formants

As a point of departure, the private research institution, as the employer of Dr Black, has breached its licence obligation, which will result in patent infringement, on the assumption that EMC^4 is patented, unless it has a valid defence. One possible defence is the experiment exemption in NPA §3, third paragraph, no. 3, which states that the exclusive right to the patent does not include exploitation by experiments relating to the subject matter of the invention. Based on the facts of the case, it is doubtful whether the research carried out can be considered to relate to the invention itself and in that case the exemption will not apply. Another possible defence, one that is more likely to succeed, is that the licence obligation is contrary to NCompA §10 and Article 53 EEA Agreement and is void on that ground alone. This is a field of use restriction which is likely to restrict competition without being exempted under NCompA §10(3), cf. §53(3) (cf. Art. 4(c) Regulation (EC) No. 772/2004).[45] The result in that case is that the obligation is void, so that Dr Black's behaviour will not constitute a patent infringement. If so, White Corp. will not have a claim for damages in the form of a share of the profits. But even if there were an infringement of White Corp.'s patent, the right to damages is limited to the consequences of exploitation of the patent, i.e. the use of the patented model, and not from the exploitation of the new invention, which is a result of the use of the model.

III. Metalegal Formants

The case concerns the scope of the licensed patent and the impact of contractual obligations to refrain from competitive use of the patent. Field of use restrictions may be critical under competition law.

---

45 Cf. the Belgian report.

(13) POLAND

I. *Operative Rules*

White Corp. is entitled to damages, though not necessarily as a share in profits.

II. *Descriptive Formants*

The question boils down to the validity of the contractual clause in the licence agreement and its meaning. If the clause is valid, the contract has been breached and the prejudiced party may sue for damages (Art. 471 Civil Code). However, there is no legal ground to find that the damages should be adjudicated as a share in profits earned from the new invention. It is also possible to hold that by going beyond the scope of the licence the institute has infringed EMC's patent. In that case, all legal remedies (including disgorgement of profits) available in the case of a patent infringement would be at EMC's disposal.

Competition law could intervene if EMC refused to grant another licence, this time concerning the second research project.[46] The very obligation to use the licensed subject matter only for a specific purpose should on the other hand be regarded as valid unless the licensor enjoys a dominant position on the relevant market.

III. *Metalegal Formants*

Polish law attempts to balance the IP property entitlement and the needs of free competition. Yet it is difficult for a civil judge to translate competition considerations into general private law. As the default rule, the freedom of contract prevails. Limits will most likely be translated into limitations on damage claims.

(14) SLOVENIA

I. *Operative Rules*

White Corp. does not have the right to demand a share in profits as damages on the basis of a breach of contract. Nevertheless, when it comes to making a judgment on financial compensation, White Corp. can claim its right to a share in the profit as the subject of execution.

[46] Relevant markets can be defined narrowly in such cases.

II. *Descriptive Formants*

In Slovenian legislation, a licensing contract is regulated by the CO.[47] According to the provision of Article 704 CO, the licensor has the obligation to transfer, in whole or in part, his/her right to use the patented invention, know-how, trademarks, and industrial designs to the licensee. In return the licensee has to pay the licensor a licence fee. The licence can be exclusive or non-exclusive. An exclusive licence can be obtained only in the event that it is specifically agreed upon by the contracting parties; otherwise, a non-exclusive licence is considered to have been granted, through which the holder maintains the right to use the licensed technology, just as he/she can transfer the use of this right to other parties (Art. 707 CO).[48]

The contracting parties can precisely determine their mutual rights and obligations in a licensing contract. The licensee has to exploit the licensed right in the agreed-upon manner and within the agreed-upon scope and limits (Art. 713 CO). The contract between the research institution and White Corp. contained an explicit ban of the use of the EMC[4] model in research ordered by the rival company White Corp. Through a contractual provision, White Corp. sought to prevent rival companies from using the licensed patent or its effect for their own benefit without payment. The provision in the contract seems reasonable, since it is the only way to protect the interests of White Corp. from its competitors. However, such a contractual restriction of a licensee is regulated neither by Slovenian intellectual property law nor by contract law. There is no previous practice on such issues in the Republic of Slovenia.

Individual restrictive clauses in licensing agreement are regulated by competition law. According to the provision of Article 6 of the Prevention of Restriction of Competition Act (PRCA), agreements between undertakings which have as their object or effect the prevention, restriction or distortion of competition in the Republic of Slovenia shall be prohibited and shall be void. The sanction of the voidness of a contract (agreement) and its consequences are regulated by the CO in Articles 86–93, where on the basis of Article 88, voidness can also be only partial. As a result, the contract is not completely void due to the voidness of an individual contractual provision, if the contract can remain without it. Therefore, insofar as it is possible to determine that the concerned clause is void according to the rules of competition law (which means that all conditions from Article 6 of the PRCA will have to be fulfilled, among others that both parties can be treated as undertakings in the meaning of the rules of competition law), White Corp. does not have the right to damages. If the clause

47 Official Gazette RS, nos. 83/2001, 32/2004, 40/2007, 97/2007.

48 See K. Podobnik, in: N. Plavšak et al., *Obligacijski zakonik s komentarjem (posebni del)*, book 4 (Ljubljana: 2004), pp. 67–69.

does not violate the rules of competition law and is consequently not void, the research institute is violating the licensing contract concluded with White Corp.

Neither the IPA nor the provisions of the special section of the CO which regulates the licensing contract contain special provisions concerning compensation claims due to violation of the contract. The general provisions of the CO on compensation claims have to be used (Art. 164 et seq.). In accordance with this, the wronged contracting party may claim compensation of actual damages and lost profits.

Under Slovenian law, a court may only grant pecuniary damages. Which assets payment of pecuniary damages shall be awarded to is a question of the choice of the subject matter of execution. If the creditor so wishes, payment of pecuniary damages may also be asserted as a right share of the profit of the debtor.

III. Metalegal Formants

Slovenian law strikes a balance between property entitlement and competition; however, in cases of doubt, the property entitlement and the freedom of contract will prevail.

(15) SPAIN

I. Operative Rules

White Corp. has no right to a share in profits as damages on the basis of breach of contract.[49]

II. Descriptive Formants

Firstly, patent licences are regulated specifically in Articles 74–80 of the Spanish Patent Law. As far as the content of the licence is concerned, the Law states that the whole of the patent or some of the powers that make up the exclusive right of the title holder should be the object of the licence. Likewise, the Law establishes that, unless otherwise agreed, the holder of a licence has the right to carry out all those acts that make up the exploitation of the patented invention, in all its applications.

At this point, the validity of the clauses that impose limits on the licence holder can be raised. This issue is not expressly regulated by Spanish patent

49 See the differences with the Poland report.

law and the Spanish courts have made no pronouncement either. However, the little doctrine there is on this topic uses European law to consider these clauses anti-competitive as long as they involve restrictions in competition.[50] In fact, it should be borne in mind that this sort of clause can limit research into and development of eventual processes or technologies that are alternatives to the patent. Likewise, it must also be considered whether this type of clause conceals the purpose of sharing clients.[51] The issue raised here is important, particularly if it is borne in mind that it can be difficult to determine whether a clause agreed on under the principle of autonomy of intention is accepted or prohibited by European law.[52]

Moreover, it is important to take into account that patent law should be subject to a restrictive interpretation because the patent is an exclusive right and it creates a legal monopoly which constitutes an important exception to the free enterprise principle.[53] The idea is to avoid the overprotection on the holder of the patent.[54]

Secondly, issues related to the payment of damages for breach of contract are regulated by the Civil Code.[55] This question belongs to contractual law and is, therefore, the law applicable to the licence as a contract. Yellow Corp. could have a right to claim damages for breach of contract by Dr Grey and the private research institute's employee, Dr Black, who did not respect the contractual terms. But it has no claim against White Corp. because there was no contract between them.

III. Metalegal Formants

The title holder and the licensee are free to agree the conditions of the contract. However, competition law must be borne in mind. This means that if a clause affects the progress of innovation, it may be considered an anti-competitive measure, and so it will be removed from the contract.

---

50 P. Martín Aresti, *La licencia contractual de patente* (Pamplona: 1997), p. 219. See also the Dutch report or the Belgian report.

51 J. Massaguer, *El contrato de licencia de know-how* (Barcelona: 1989), p. 228.

52 P. Martín Aresti, *La licencia contractual de patente* (Pamplona: 1997), p. 227.

53 See Decision of the Juzgado de lo Mercantil no. 6 of Madrid, of 27 July 2007, on the right of patent of a product, the seed called 'roundup ready soybeans'. This resolution is commented by J.A. Gómez Segade, *Actas de Derecho Industrial*, 2007–2008, no. 28, pp. 723–752.

54 This idea is well expressed by Vicenzo di Cataldo, 'El uso experimental de la invención patentada: ¿uso libre o violación de la patente?', *Actas de Derecho Industrial*, 2007–2008, no. 28, p. 147: 'when we interpret the Intellectual Property law, we should avoid any overprotection on the holder of the patent'. This means 'not to attribute to the holder of the patent rights and prerogatives which are not consistent with the objectives of the Patent Law'.

55 On this issue, see e.g. Arts. 1101, 1122.2 and 4, and 1124 of the Civil Code.

(16) UNITED KINGDOM

I. Operative Rules

White Corp. has a claim to a share in profits against Dr Grey's research institute.

II. Descriptive Formants

The key issue is that Dr Black, an employee of Dr Grey's research institute, devised an invention using rats that he used in breach of the contract between his employer and White Corp. The legal issues in this scenario are very similar to some of the issues raised by Case 11.

Dr Black is entitled to the patent under section 7(2)(a) PA 1997. His employer, Dr Grey's research institute, is probably entitled under section 7(2)(b). Since White Corp. claims a share of the profits, we assume that the patent is generating profits for Dr Grey's research institute.

If White Corp. brings an action for breach of contract against Dr Grey's research institute, it must establish that the institute is vicariously liable for the action of its employee (this should be possible unless the employee, Dr Black, was acting on his own volition, unknown to his employer).

The question then is what sort of remedies are available under contract law for breach of contract. Under patent law, these are generally quite generous (compared with tort law, human rights law, etc.). Further remedies under torts or equity might be possible, but are beyond the scope of inquiry.

III. Metalegal Formants

Field of use restrictions are widely used and acknowledged. Contract freedom prevails. There appears to be no principle which might invalidate the restrictive contract term.

A.4. COMPARATIVE REMARKS

The country reports are heterogeneous with regard to the operative formants. This is not only due to the fact that the rapporteurs discussed whether a private research institution is an undertaking as a prerequisite for competition law to apply. Some country reports hold competition law to be applicable (Belgium, Denmark, the Netherlands, Norway, Slovenia, Spain), while others do not (Greece, the UK) or not directly (Germany). The reasons why competition law is held to be inapplicable diverge remarkably. This reflects deep insecurities on how to deal with industry–basic research contracts which are not 'contractual research'. The striking observation to be made here is that the outcome (descriptive formant) does not depend on the chosen field of law (cf. Belgium and Germany)! Where competition law is found not to be applicable, the very rationales of competition law are incorporated into patent law and civil law rules (cf. France, Germany, Greece).

Almost all reports qualify the behaviour of Dr Black as an infringement of White Corp.'s right. However, whether a claim covers a share in profits depends on various factors, for example the national bifurcation between civil law in general and IP remedies (Estonia (based on torts), Greece, France, Slovenia; in contrast to DE (where a share in profits is stipulated in IP laws)).[56]

The *core of the case* is *how* national jurisdictions develop restrictions against expanding property. Some have resort to competition rationales; some apply competition law without even discussing its applicability; others interpret civil law by referring to its rationale (e.g. using provisions for standard terms in the Estonian and German reports). Others have resort to limiting doctrines of IP law (exhaustion principle,[57] cf. France (considering but denying), Germany (considering analogy)). Others consider 'experimental exceptions' (Denmark/Norway, Estonia, the Netherlands). Few consider openly public policies, especially the impediment of research freedom (France, Germany). The result of these deliberations depends on the basic value decision. The 'solution' following the analysis of the descriptive formants is reflected in surprisingly similar considerations within the metalegal formants.

---

56 Differences occur with regard to the construction of combining the potential profits generated by Yellow. The French report considers a (contract) liability of Yellow as a third party for its (knowingly) inducing the breach of the contractual obligation between White and Grey not to use the rats in experiments sponsored by Yellow. The German report analyses a (proprietary) claim of patent infringement against Yellow based on the fact that the future patent of Grey is dependent on the patent of White (resulting in enhanced profits generated by Yellow). A contractual claim is not possible in Germany due to the strict privacy principle (restricting the influence of third parties).

57 This is in line with the US Supreme Court decision of 30 May 2017 (Dec. No. 15-1189, 2017 WL 2322830), *Impression Products v. Lexmark*.

CASE 13. CO-INVENTORSHIP, CO-OWNERSHIP (MODELLED ON *PXE*)

A.1. BASE CASE

PXZ is a patient organisation representing 200 families with a disposition of a malignant form of cancer. Its mission is to sponsor wide research on this form of cancer. It raises money, obliges the researchers it sponsors to identify the director of PXZ as a co-inventor in any future filings for patents, and has a strong interest in having a say in future licensing negotiations.

The big pharmaceutical company BPC is close to coming up with a chemotherapy for this form of cancer. A gene-based therapy developed by a researcher sponsored by PXZ could cut profits on the final chemical cocktail. It considers a challenge to the gene patent as part of its business strategy. Can BPC challenge the patent on grounds of false inventorship?

A.2. COUNTRY REPORTS

(1) BELGIUM

I. Operative Rules

No, BPC cannot challenge this patent on the grounds of false inventorship.

II. Descriptive Formants

Inventorship, i.e. the right to be named as inventor, is a personal moral right, which cannot be transferred (this inalienability is not unanimously accepted, however).[1] The specific clause obliging identifying the director of PXZ as a

[1] B. de Vuyst and L. Steuts, 'De notie morele rechten in een internationale, vergelijkende en transactionele context' [The Notion of Moral Rights in an International, Comparative and Transactional Context], *I.R.D.I.* 2005, 14–15; M.-C. Janssens, 'Uitvindingen in dienstverband met bijzondere aandacht voor uitvindingen aan universiteiten' [Employee and University Inventions], *CIR series Katholieke Universiteit Leuven* no. 12 (Brussels: 1995), 18–21. See also Case 11, Modification 1.

co-inventor will therefore be invalid,[2] but only the real inventor will be able to object to this on the basis of Article 12 BPA (Art. XI.13 BCEL).

Whether or not the real inventor is identified in the patent has no influence on the validity of the patent itself.[3]

Therefore, BPC cannot challenge this patent on grounds of false inventorship.

III. Metalegal Formants

Due to the personal bond between an inventor and his/her creation, the moral right to be named as inventor is personal, inalienable[4] and absolute. This does not mean that the patrimonial right of ownership of an invention cannot be transferred. Indeed, PXZ might very well have validly obtained the ownership or co-ownership of any future inventions.

If, however, a patent is applied for without consent of the real inventor or his/her subsidiary, he/she can either reclaim the patent (Art. 9 BPA, now Art. XI.10 BCEL) or make a claim for its nullity (Art. 49§1 4° BPA, now Art. XI.57§1 4° BCEL). Anybody who has a legitimate interest could ask for the latter (Art. 17 Judicial Code). The interest of, for instance, mere consumers, is considered to be too general, but perhaps BPC might fulfil the requirements of Article 17 Judicial Code.[5]

(2) CZECH REPUBLIC

I. Operative Rules

BPC does not have the right to challenge the patent.

II. Descriptive Formants

According to section 23 Patent Act,[6] there are four reasons for which the Patent Office may revoke a patent. This list of reasons is exhaustive. In the case of false inventorship, section 23(1)(d) Patent Act shall apply. Revocation of the patent is possible if the proprietor of the patent has no right to the patent according to section 8(1) Patent Act. According to section 8(1) Patent Act, the right to the patent and invention belongs to the inventor or his/her legal successor.

---

2 Ibid., 19.

3 Ibid.

4 Although this is not unanimously accepted, see Case 11, Modification 1.

5 B. van Reephinghen and M. De Brabanter, *Les brevets d'invention [Patents]* (Brussels: 1987), 217–218.

6 Act on Inventions and Rationalisations Proposals 527/1990 Coll.

Revocation of a patent is to be done only upon the request of an authorised person. An authorised person is, according to section 29 Patent Act, a person who is, pursuant to a court decision, the inventor or his/her legal successor.

BPC is neither 'the inventor' nor a successor; therefore, it has no right to challenge the patent.

III. Metalegal Formants

Inventorship as a moral right is exclusively assigned to the inventor, and is personal and inalienable. No one else can claim this right. The option to influence the exploitation of an invention is exclusively attributed to the owner/s. At least not incontestably, (even) a philanthropic organisation cannot ensure further influence via inventorship.

(3) DENMARK

I. Operative Rules

No, BPC cannot challenge the patent on grounds of false inventorship.

II. Descriptive Formants

As pointed out in Case 11, Modification 1 supra, the right to be named as inventor is not a ground for invalidity or annulment of the patent. No differentiation is permissible for philanthropic organisations.

III. Metalegal Formants

The right to be named is a personal and non-economic right of the inventor. A third party challenging the patent has no claim whatsoever to this right.

(4) ESTONIA

I. Operative Rules

No, BPC cannot challenge the patent on grounds of false inventorship.

II. Descriptive Formants

Pursuant to §13(1) Patent Act, '[t]he author of an invention … is a natural person who has created an invention as a result of his or her inventing activities'.

Subsection 13(2) Patent Act specifies that '[i]f an invention is created as a result of the joint inventing activities of several natural persons, such persons are joint authors'. An inventor is entitled to request the disclosure of his/her name as the inventor (§13(7) clause 1). If the inventor's right to be acknowledged as the inventor is violated, then he/she is entitled to remedies. Subsection 48(2) provides that:

> Any natural person who finds that he or she is the author of an invention pursuant to the provisions of subsection 13(1) or (2) of this Act may file an action in court against the applicant or, after the issue of a patent, the proprietor of the patent for certification of his or her authorship. Authorship may also be contested by the successor of such person.

It should be emphasised that the right to contest the authorship belongs to a person who claims to be an actual inventor. Therefore, BPC cannot challenge the patent on grounds of false inventorship.

III. Metalegal Formants

Pursuant to the Patent Act, '[a]uthorship is inalienable and unspecified in term'.[7] An inventor is entitled to

> a pseudonym and he or she may:
>
> 1) request the disclosure of his or her name as the author;
> 2) prohibit the disclosure of his or her name as the author;
> 3) revoke at any time the prohibition to disclose his or her name.[8]

An inventor may file an action to guarantee these rights. Subsection 51(1) Patent Act provides: 'The author of an invention may file, without a limitation period, an action in court upon infringement of the rights provided for in §13(7) of this Act and for the resolution of other non-proprietary disputes arising from authorship'. As seen, an inventor or co-inventor can enforce his/her right to be named. Still, a person has to prove that he/she has contributed to the creation of the invention. The situation is complicated if there is no actual ground to name the director of PXZ as a co-inventor (there is no actual contribution) and the obligation is contractual. Of course, the question is not very practical because the fact that someone is named as an inventor does not mean that the same person is a patent owner. The interest of PXZ is to control the utilisation of the patented invention, which could be facilitated if PXZ were a co-owner of the patent.

---

7 Patent Act §13(6).
8 Patent Act §13(7).

(5) FRANCE

I. Operative Rules

BPC cannot challenge the patent on the grounds of false inventorship.

II. Descriptive Formants

According to Article R. 611-15 of the Intellectual Property Code: 'The National Institute of Industrial Property shall not verify the correctness of designation of inventor referred to in Article R. 612-10'.

An error concerning the inventor's identity in a French patent is not sanctioned by cancellation.[9] Only a correction of the patent may be requested. The consent of the person wrongly designated or the consent of the owner of the patent are required (Art. R. 611-17 Intellectual Property Code).[10] BPC, who wants to challenge the patent, neither has the required quality to ask for a correction nor is it the true owner.

Could BPC take action claiming ownership? According to Article L. 611-8 of the Intellectual Property Code:

> Where an application for the grant of an industrial property title has been made either for an invention unlawfully taken from an inventor or his successors in title, or in violation of a legal contractual obligation, the injured party may claim ownership of the application or of the title granted.

This action is taken by the one who claims to be the true owner of the patent. BPC does not assert that it is the true owner of the patent. It cannot take this action.

---

9 J. Schmidt-Szalewski and J.-L. Pierre, *Droit de la propriété industrielle* (4e éd., 2007), n°51. The solution would be different if the patent was European. It could be cancelled. According to Art. 138(1)(e) EPC, a European patent may be revoked 'if the proprietor of the European patent is not entitled under Article 60, paragraph 1', in other words if he/she is not 'the inventor or his successor in title'.

10 'The designation of inventor may be corrected only by a request accompanied by the consent of the person wrongly designated and, if the request is not submitted by the applicant or the owner of the patent, the consent of either one of those persons. The provisions of Article R. 612-10 shall apply. If a mistaken designation of inventor has been entered in the National Patent Register or published in the Official Bulletin of Industrial Property, the entry or publication shall be corrected. The mention of the mistaken designation of inventor shall be corrected in the copies of the publications of the patent application or the patent specification not yet distributed. The provisions of the preceding paragraph shall apply in the event of the designation of inventor being annulled by a court' (Art. R. 611-17 Intellectual Property Code).

III. Metalegal Formants

Inventorship is a moral right, inalienable and not transferable. Therefore, only the true inventor may prompt a patent challenge on the ground of inventorship.

(6) GERMANY

I. Operative Rules

No, BPC has no right to challenge the patent.

II. Descriptive Formants

The central question is if BPC has a legal right to oppose the patent on the ground of false inventorship. §59 German Patent Code provides for an everybody's right for a period of three months running from the day of publication. The eligible reasons on which an opposition can be based are, however, restricted to those listed in §21 German Patent Code. False inventorship is not one of them. Only the true inventor has a legal claim against the wrongly indicated person in the patent (§8 German Patent Code: '*Patentvindikation*'). As BPC is not the true inventor, it has no right to challenge the patent. (Only the true inventor employed by the hospital could.) However, where the contributor is not the 'inventor' and the inventorship is misleadingly used in marketing, this could amount to an 'unfair practice' forbidden under the German Unfair Trading Act (§5 I 1 No. 3 UWG).

It is a distinct question whether PXZ could be qualified as a 'co-inventor' at all. In principle, a person only qualifies as a 'co-inventor' who has contributed to the technical teaching *per se*. However, the profession has observed a lowering of the premises for becoming a co-inventor. Thus, if the managerial contribution (formulating the research question, raising money, organising patients, motivating them to donate tissue, founding a tissue bank, building up a database and organising public discourse) is a qualitative contribution and a *conditio sine qua non*, it might amount to co-inventorship. If it is not, a promise to name somebody as inventor is not invalid (§306 BGB). However, under property law, the true inventor keeps the right to correction (§8 German Patent Code).

Yet another question is whether the promise could be enforced. The contractual obligation could be invalid if the proprietary position of the true inventor were impaired (§§138, 242 BGB).

III. Metalegal Formants

The question of the identity of the true inventor of the patented idea is purely personal. The public at large and the competitors are not conceded a legal interest in the true inventorship. Thus, the question of inventorship cannot be exploited by competitors to challenge the patent.

However, considering that the threshold had been lowered (the USPTO accepted the contribution of the head of the PXE patient organisation Genetic Alliance as inventor),[11] the tools can be used to secure the interests of those who have made the research possible and who have an interest in having a continuous say in future licensing policies like an interest in a broad availability of the information covered by the patent. In the case of PXE, the US agency accepted this because PXE's input went well beyond merely financial contributions – that might also be possible in Germany. However, in general, German law is reluctant to mix the personal input of the genuine inventor and the material input of someone else. The (historic) reason is the protection of the employed inventor (considering the historically based reluctance with regard to '*Betriebserfindungen*' in Germany). From a legal point of view, there is no pressing need to distinguish patient organisations (tissue donors)[12] from any other employer. The material input is supposed to be reflected by ownership (not by inventorship). However, the debate about 'intermediaries' (third entities between inventors and owners) might prompt further debate about conditions under which non-governmental organisations might enjoy the privilege of being qualified as 'inventors'.

(7) GREECE

I. Operative Rules

BPC is not legitimated to challenge the inventorship concerning a different scientific method.

II. Descriptive Formants

Indeed, the actual inventor can seek judicially the cancellation of a patent which has been given to another person without his/her consent (Art. 15 para. 1a, Law 1733/1987),[13] but BPC is not the inventor of PXZ's gene therapy. BPC's

---

[11] E. Marshall, 'Patient Advocate Named Co-Inventor on Patent for the PXE Disease Gene' (2004) 305 *Science*, 1226.

[12] This reasoning is in line with background papers submitted to WIPO, where the same problem has been put forward with regard to gene banks, see WIPO Life Sciences Program (2007), 'Patent issues related to influenza viruses and their genes; An overview', Background paper to A/PIP/IGM/3.

[13] See Rokas, *Industrial Property* (2004), §7, nos. 4 et seq. Generally, on the principle of the actual inventor, see Rokas, *Industrial Property* (2004), §7, nos. 1–3; Liakopoulos, *Industrial Property* (2000).

chemotherapy seems to be a different (competitive) method leading to the same result as PXZ's gene therapy. Indeed, two related inventions can be characterised either as one single (co-invention), or as two separate 'parallel' inventions,[14] (or even one main/initial and one dependent). It is evident that a biopatent does not cease to be effective only because there are other such patents with the same final purpose, nor, naturally, may it prevent their circulation and use.

Of course, it remains an open question whether the ownership (or even more the personality right) of the parts of an individual's own body may entail co-inventorship for every gene method based on his/her body. Although the human body cannot constitute an object of invention, nevertheless the inclusion in a patent of a feature which has been isolated from it is possible, in accordance with the Biotechnology Directive (= Presidential Decree 321/2001).[15] In any event, the more widespread the characteristics in question are, the less they can be considered to be a personal contribution to the production of the invention. In the latter case, the contribution of PXZ might be challenged as non-patentable, in the sense that there is no personal contribution of PXZ's members, but only a common knowledge, upon which the gene therapy was based. Nevertheless, even if this case, it should be taken into account that not only the patent but also the simple right over the invention is transferable (Art. 12 para. 1 Law 1733/1987). Thus, since the true inventor has consented to identify PXZ as a co-inventor in the patent of his/her own invention, it is obvious that no third party (such as BPC) is entitled to challenge the inventorship of the patent.

III. Metalegal Formants

The case raises the question of whether this personal right can be instrumentalised to ensure the patient organisation's influence on exploitation. Under Greek law, inventorship is a right strictly tailored to the inventor. It credits his/her creative achievement. Any other contribution has to be recognised in other ways (usually acquisition), but does not become part of the invention. When this rationale applies to the individual originator of the genomic material, the exclusion applies *a fortiori* for an organisation representing several patients. The appropriate tool to control exploitation is ownership, not inventorship.

(8) IRELAND

Answer omitted.

---

14 Rokas, *Industrial Property* (2004), §7, nos. 8–9; Antonopoulos, *Industrial Property* (2002), pp. 806–810.

15 See, for preference, Rokas, *Industrial Property* (2004), §6, no. 24.

(9) ITALY

I. Operative Rules

BPC might invalidate the patent, but only that part of the patent's inventorship which is unlawfully reported.

II. Descriptive Formants

Article 76 §1, lit. d Industrial Property Code provides that a patent is void if the owner did not have the right to file for it. Moreover, it establishes that if the causes which determine the patent to be void affect the patent only partially, then the court should rule accordingly (§2).

Article 118 Industrial Property Code establishes that if two years after the patent has been granted the inventor has not taken any step toward the protection of his/her interest (in inventorship or ownership), then any interested person can file a suit (§4). Therefore, it is likely that a court will recognise BPC's interest in making public the fact that PXZ has not participated in the invention and thus has no title to be named co-inventor. It should be noted, however, that the patent will not be invalidated at all. Only the part that the court holds not valid (in that case the co-inventorship of PXZ) will be declared void, and the patent will be consequently modified.

III. Metalegal Formants

Under Italian law, the problem of inventorship is solved in a person-oriented way. In fact, Article 62 Industrial Property Code says that inventorship may be claimed only by the inventor (and after his/her death by his/her heirs). The same situation is observable in the field of copyright, where only a physical person may be indicated as the author of a work. This is usually the general rule in civil law countries, but it does not necessarily hold true in common law ones. Article 63 Industrial Property Code tells us that the rights emerging from the invention (the right to be granted a patent for an invention and those that derive from the patent itself) are transferable (c. 1), but at the same time it reaffirms (c. 2) that the right to be named as the inventor is not transferable nor can it be waived or relinquished.

(10) LITHUANIA

I. Operative Rules

BPC cannot challenge this patent on the grounds of false inventorship.

II. Descriptive Formants

In Lithuania, the right to be named as inventor is a personal and non-assignable right. In an application, the name of the inventor or – in the case of co-inventors – names of the inventors should be indicated (Art. 12(1) of the Lithuanian Patent Act). The inventor can only be a physical person (Art. 2 of the Lithuanian Patent Act). This leads to the conclusion that a contractual clause which obliges identifying the director of PXZ as a co-inventor is invalid.

But these circumstances do not provide BPC with a right to challenge the patent. First, BPC is not and cannot be an inventor and, therefore, has no legal standing. Second, the Lithuanian Patent Act provides only limited grounds for the invalidation of patent (see Case 10). None of these grounds is connected to the issue of inventorship. To summarise, the question of (false) inventorship has nothing to do with the validity of the patent.

III. Metalegal Formants

The right to be named as an inventor in the patent, which is also an international standard (Art. 4ter of the Paris Convention), is considered to be a non-pecuniary right of the inventor. Only the physical person who came up with a technical solution using his/her intellectual efforts can be considered an inventor, but not a person providing financial, technical and organisational input.[16] Certainly, the real inventor can defend his/her rights against the false inventor or false co-inventor. But this defence of personal interest is conceptually different from the patentability of an invention and the validity of a patent.

(11) NETHERLANDS

I. Operative Rules

No, it is not possible to challenge the patent on grounds of false inventorship.

II. Descriptive Formants

Article 14 of the Dutch Patent Act (DPA) states that an inventor can always require recognition of his/her invention, even when law or contract exclude him/her from claiming the related patent.[17] This is a moral right that cannot

16 R. Birštonas et al., *Intelektinės nuosavybės teisė* (Intellectual Property Law) (Vilnius: 2010), p. 413.

17 C. Gielen and D.W.F. Verkade, *Intellectuele eigendom* (Deventer: 2005), p. 480.

be waived or transferred by agreement (Art. 14(2) DPA). Therefore, the real inventor can always oppose a false or omitted statement in this regard. This article, however, is designed to protect the inventor's right of recognition and shall not be taken as a constitutive element of a valid patent. Moreover, this right of recognition can only be invoked by its holder and not by third parties, such as BPC. To effectively challenge the patent, BPC has to bring up other objections, based on grounds mentioned in Article 75 DPA.

III. Metalegal Formants

Notwithstanding the intimate relationship between the inventor and his/her invention, it is important to distinguish between rules regarding the former and the latter. The right of recognition exists to the benefit of the inventor and it can therefore not be used for claims regarding the validity of the patent. To challenge the patent, BPC must put forward more 'intrinsic' arguments, such as a lack of novelty or industrial applicability (Art. 75 DPA). Or, if opportune, it can try to reclaim the patent on the grounds mentioned in Article 78 DPA. A suit based on the moral rights of the inventor, however, is doomed to failure.

(12) NORWAY

I. Operative Rules

No, BPC cannot challenge the patent on grounds of false inventorship.

II. Descriptive Formants

As pointed out in Case 11, Modification 1 supra, the right to be named as inventor is not a ground for invalidity or annulment of the patent. This is the central argument of the case: BPC, as a third party, has no actionable argument. It is a different matter if PXZ can be legitimately registered as co-inventor.

III. Metalegal Formants

The central legal argument which governs the case is that the right to be named is a personal and non-economic right of the co-inventor: no third party can challenge the patent on those grounds, only the 'true' inventor. Yet it is a different question if inventorship can be strategically instrumentalised for raising public visibility or for securing influence over the exploitation of the patent. Under Norwegian law, it appears that inventorship is only attributable to natural persons, not to organisations.

(13) POLAND

I. Operative Rules

No, BPC cannot challenge the patent on the grounds of false inventorship.

II. Descriptive Formants

Probably, naming the director of PXZ as a co-inventor is incorrect, since co-inventorship should be generally acknowledged when two or more persons contributed intellectually to the invention.[18] However, this particular question does not have to be probed into in more detail here, since even if co-inventorship of PXZ's director were legally unfounded, this would not mean that any third party could demand the invalidation of the patent. False attribution of the invention may indeed give rise to several legal remedies (invalidation being one of them); however, they can only be used by the actual rightholder (i.e. the true inventor or co-inventor, Art. 74 IPL). Since BPC can claim no right to the invention, the rights defined in Article 74 IPL are not applicable.

III. Metalegal Formants

Under Polish law, the concept of inventorship is purely personal. It is actionable only for the true inventor, not third parties. If the director of PXZ gets registered, the registration will be exposed to the risk of the inventive researcher opposing it. Thus, for the organisation, a strategy which relies on registered inventorship might be a risky undertaking.

(14) SLOVENIA

I. Operative Rules

BPC can challenge the patent, if it were entitled to do so.

II. Descriptive Formants

Patent applications in Slovenia are submitted at SIPO, which administers the patent registration procedure. This procedure is governed by the IPA and the rules on the

---

18 Supreme Court, 11 December 1979, IV PR 346/79 (quoted by T. Szymanek, 'Przegląd orzecznictwa sądowego w sprawach ochrony własności przemysłowej', in: *Naruszenie praw na dobrach niematerialnych*, PIRzP (Warszawa: 2000), p. 128); Supreme Court, 21 March 1974, I PR 53/74, OSPiKA 1976, No. 10, pos. 195; M. du Vall, in: *Prawo własności przemysłowej* (Warszawa: 2008), p. 126.

contents of patent applications and the divisional patent procedure.[19] According to Article 73 IPA, the inventor mentioned as such in the application shall be deemed to be the actual inventor. It is an assumption that can be contested, as the court can decide otherwise. SIPO otherwise does not check the accuracy of data on the individual inventor. Besides the inventor, the applicant is also listed in the patent application, wherein the inventor and the applicant are not necessarily the same person. The patent will be granted to the individual or individuals designated as the applicants in the patent application (Art. 74(1) IPA). During this process, SIPO also does not verify whether the applicant is also entitled to the patent. Through the granting of the patent, the applicant becomes the owner of the patent and obtain all the exclusive rights associated with this title.

Since abuse can occur during the patent registration procedure, the IPA contains special provisions for such cases to protect the 'rightful' inventor. Article 115 IPA allows the 'rightful' inventor to file an action to challenge the right to the patent before a competent court only if the patent has been registered in the name of a person who is not the inventor. Under Slovenian law, besides the inventor, his/her heir or another successor in title are also entitled to file action. Apart from the individuals already mentioned, action may also be filed by a person who is neither the inventor nor the heir, but who is entitled to the rights conferred by the patent if the patent was granted in the name of the inventor or a third party, which the inventor unjustifiably authorised that the patent be granted in his/her name (Art. 115(3) IPA). Filing an action is not bound by the preclusive time limit or the statute of limitations. The action may be filed at any time during the validity of the patent. If BPC can be considered among those entitled to sue, it can challenge the right to the patent and vice versa. Within three months from the receipt of a final judgment that rules favourably on the action of challenging the right to the patent, the plaintiff may request to be entered in the register as the new owner of the patent. Thus, challenging does not necessarily mean the cessation of the patent as a consequence. Only in the event that the plaintiff does not submit a request to be entered as the owner within the prescribed time limit will SIPO *ex officio* remove the patent from the register, which results in the cessation of the patent (Art. 117(2) IPA).[20]

In the Slovenian legislation, registration of a patent in the name of a person who is not entitled to the patent is not a reason to declare the nullity of the patent.[21]

---

19 Official Gazette RS, no. 102/2001.

20 Reasons for the validity of industrial property rights to cease are listed in the provision of Art. 77 IPA, and are as follows: if the owner renounces his/her right; if the prescribed fees have not been paid; and pursuant to a final decision of the court or a decision of SIPO in those cases provided for by this Act, on the date specified in such a decision.

21 According to the provision of Art. 112 IPA, actions to declare nullity of a patent may be filed on one or more of the following grounds: if on the date of filing the application the invention did not meet all the patent requirements; if the invention is not disclosed in a manner sufficiently clear and complete for it to be carried out by a person skilled in the art to which the invention relates; if the content of the protection extends beyond the content of the first received application; or if the patent was granted on a divisional application, beyond the content of the initial application.

For this reason, an action contesting the right to a patent may only be filed by the individuals whom the IPA individually specifies, and not by all interested parties. Therefore, this means that if an action is not filed by a justified individual, the owner of the patent remains the individual who is not entitled to it.

III. Metalegal Formants

Inventorship under Slovenian law is a peculiar concept. In contrast to many European countries, it is not conceived of as a purely moral right. The law acknowledges that legitimate third parties can challenge inventorship. If their claim is successful, the patent will not automatically cease to exist. Only in the event that the third party (after a successful lawsuit) does not request to be entered into the register as the owner of the patent will the patent expire.

(15) SPAIN

I. Operative Rules

No, BPC has no right to challenge the patent.

II. Descriptive Formants

In this case, we are considering whether BPC may oppose the grant of a patent on the ground of false inventorship. The Spanish Patent Law states that during the two months following the publication of the examination request (at the revision stage of the procedure for granting the patent with prior examination), any interested party may oppose the grant of the patent on the grounds of the absence of any of the requirements laid down for such a grant. Therefore, the opposition is restricted to the absence of patentability conditions for the invention. Any other reason, like the one examined in this case (false inventorship), is a matter for the ordinary courts. In this case, the patent shall be declared invalid according to Article 112d Patent Law if the owner of the patent had no right to obtain the patent because he/she was not the inventor or his/her successor. Article 10.4 establishes that 'it shall be assumed that the applicant is authorised to exercise the right to a patent'. So, if the person who applies for a patent is not the inventor, the actual inventor may claim for a transfer of ownership of the patent at the ordinary courts, as well as any other corresponding rights or actions. In order to provide for the validity of the registration of industrial property, Spanish patent law requires a judgment of an ordinary court to invalidate rights to a patent.

Another issue is the concept of 'co-inventorship'. It has to be stressed that the inventor is an individual who contributes to the conception of the invention, setting forth at least one claim in a patent application. Someone who just follows instructions about how to develop an invention or who supervises work done by the inventor cannot him/herself be considered inventor.

A different matter is analysing financial or technical contributions to an invention. They might be considered in a similar way as employee inventions; if a contribution has been substantial to the development of an invention, the contributor is to be considered the co-inventor.[22]

III. Metalegal Formants

Article 10.3 Patent Law makes the right to a patent subject to a 'time criterion'. The right to a patent belongs to the person whose application bears the first date of registration in Spain. The declaration of invalidation of the patent is restricted to the cases regulated in Article 112, so competitors cannot challenge the patent apart from in these cases.

(16) UNITED KINGDOM

I. Operative Rules

BPC cannot apply for the patent to be revoked.

II. Descriptive Formants

PXZ does not meet the rules for joint inventor status per section 7(3) PA 1997, since PXZ is not the 'actual deviser of the invention' nor can they seek to revoke the patent under section 72 PA 1977 as they do not meet the required criteria.

Section 72(1)(b) PA 1997 states that a patent can be revoked if it was granted to a person who was not entitled to the patent. However, there is an important limitation in section 72(2)(a) PA 1997. This subsection provides that only a party entitled to be granted the patent can seek to have the patent revoked. BPC does not meet this requirement. Furthermore, section 72(2)(b) PA 1997 provides that the application must be made within two years of the grant, unless it is shown that any person registered as a proprietor of the patent knew at the time of the grant or of the transfer of the patent to him/her that he/she was not entitled to the patent.

---

22 See AAVV, *La copropiete des brevets* (Paris: 1973), p. 81; M.A. Perot-Morel, 'Copropiété des brevets d'invention', *Juris-classeur périodique*, 1986, fascículo 350, p. 6. See the similar solution put forward in the German report.

III. *Metalegal Formants*

In the absence of the moral rights doctrine in English law, the PA 1997 stipulates the limitations on who can bring an action regarding false inventorship and ownership. However, an important consideration must be whether ownership of the patent is a truly viable strategy for a philanthropic organisation. The best way to exploit a patent is through licensing or joint ventures. A philanthropic organisation may not be in the best position to maximise exploitation of the invention.

A.3. COMPARATIVE REMARKS

The case is modelled on the famous *PXE* case.[23] The main question in this case is whether a contractual partner of a financial sponsor can challenge the sponsor's patent based on the argument of false inventorship.

The majority of reports conclude that BPC cannot challenge the patent. Their arguments are different. Most reports depart from the eligibility to raise the argument, since only the true inventor or the true co-inventor, and in some cases his/her successor, are entitled to challenge the patent based on inventorship.[24] (Here it should be clarified that this is not the problem in the base case, since the true inventor is employed by BPC.) Yet in France, Germany, Italy, Slovenia and the UK, one cannot claim the cancellation of the patent, only a correction. In French law, the person who was wrongly named is eligible, and the owner of the patent is authorised to claim a correction. In contrast, Italian law is broader. On the condition that two years have passed after the granting of the patent, any party with an interest can file a suit. The German and the Spanish reports go further. They suggest that PXZ could probably be qualified as the true co-inventor under a wide interpretation. In both countries, the financial, technical and organisational input which PXZ made could qualify as an important contribution to the invention. Such a point of view gives sponsors of research the standing of an 'inventor' and thus a possibility to influence the licensing policies of the economic owner.

B.1. MODIFICATION 1

PXZ and Prof. Marlow hold a patent as co-inventors, owned jointly by PXZ and M-University. After years have passed and contacts have become less frequent,

---

23 Described by G. de Wert, T. ter Meulen, R. Mordacci et al., *Ethics and Genetics: A Workbook for Practitioners and Students* (Oxford: 2003), 89; C. Godt, *Eigentum an Information* (Tübingen: 2007), 599.

24 See the reports of Belgium, Czech Republic, Estonia, Greece, the Netherlands, Slovenia, Norway, Poland and Spain.

M-University licenses the invention exclusively to the transnational chemical company TransChem without prior informed consent on the part of PXZ. As TransChem denies any access to third parties, PXZ objects to the licence. Is PXZ entitled to challenge the contract between M-University and TransChem?

B.2. COUNTRY REPORTS

(1) BELGIUM

I. Operative Rules

Yes, PXZ can challenge the contract between M-University and TransChem.

II. Descriptive Formants

The moral right of inventorship can only belong to natural persons (see Case 11, Modification 1).[25] Although PXZ cannot properly be considered to be co-inventor, they can indeed be co-owner of the patent. The Belgian legislation on co-ownership is quite clear in Article 43§2 BPA (Art. XI.49§2 BCEL): 'No co-owner may burden a patent application or a patent with a right, grant a licence to exploit or institute infringement proceedings without the agreement of the other co-owner or, failing agreement, the authorization of a court.'[26] This seems not to be the case here.

Co-owners can, however, deviate from this legal provision by agreement (Art. 43§1 BPA, now Art. XI.49§1 BCEL).[27]

PXZ can challenge the contract between M-University and TransChem and take the matter to the Commercial Court (Rechtbank van Koophandel) on the basis of Article (Art. XI.49 BCEL) in combination with Article 73 BPA (Art. XVII.14 BCEL).

III. Metalegal Formants

The rationale is that matters would become too complex if co-owners could suddenly be faced with competing third parties who obtained a licence from

25 M.-C. Janssens, 'Uitvindingen in dienstverband met bijzondere aandacht voor uitvindingen aan universiteiten' [Employee and University Inventions], *CIR series Katholieke Universiteit Leuven* no. 12 (Brussels: 1995), 18–21.

26 Translation available at: https://wipolex.wipo.int/en/main/home (last consulted 11 March 2021).

27 B. Van Reepinghen and M. De Brabanter, *Les brevets d'invention [Patents]* (Brussels: 1987), 167–169; Buydens, *Droit des brevets d'invention et protection du savoir-faire [Patent and Protection of Know-how Law]* (Brussels: 1999), 188.

other co-owners without their consent. Imposing agreement or authorisation would therefore avoid tensions between the co-owners.[28]

(2) CZECH REPUBLIC

I. Operative Rules

PXZ is entitled to challenge the contract between M-University and TransChem.

II. Descriptive Formants

Joint ownership of a patent is governed by section 16 Patent Act. According to section 16(3), unless agreed otherwise, consent of all proprietors is required as a condition for the validity of the licence contract.

If not all joint proprietors consent to a licence contract, then the licence contract is not valid *ex lege.*

It does not make a difference whether the contract is exclusive or non-exclusive.

III. Metalegal Formants

Czech law respects the equal right of co-ownership. Even if the exclusive licensing would have been economically 'a good deal', the law forces joint owners into a joint decision about exploitation. If a (tacit) agreement does not exist, the contract is invalid.

(3) DENMARK

I. Operative Rules

Yes, PXZ is entitled to challenge the contract.

II. Descriptive Formants

Denmark has no specific legislation on joint ownership. If the contract is silent, the starting point would be that any important decisions affecting the patent

---

28 B. Van Reepinghen and M. De Brabanter *Les brevets d'invention [Patents]* (Brussels: 1987), 168; Explanatory Memorandum to the Patent Bill, *Parl. Doc.*, Chambre, 1980–81, DOC 919/1, 37–38 [M.v.T. bij het wetsontwerp op de uitvindingsoctrooien, *Parl. St.*, Kamer, 1980–1981, nr. 919/1, 37–38], available at: www.dekamer.be (last consulted 5 May 2019).

require unanimity between the parties.[29] Absent such unanimity, M-University is unable to enter into the licensing agreement. Granting an exclusive licence is obviously an important transaction, which the University was unable to perform unilaterally. PXZ may, therefore, challenge the validity of the agreement. TransChem cannot base any rights on the agreement with the University vis-à-vis PXZ, but would be able to claim damages from the University (as would PXZ).

III. Metalegal Formants

The principle that you may not transfer more rights than you are entitled to is a fundamental one in Danish property law and there is no case law on instances when this pressure for unanimity was reduced.

(4) ESTONIA

I. Operative Rules

The contract between M-University and TransChem is valid and PXZ is not entitled to challenge the contract. Still, the utilisation of the invention by TransChem would constitute a patent infringement.

II. Descriptive Formants

The Patent Act does not have any regulation on how joint patent owners can exercise their rights. In the present case where PXZ and the University own the patent jointly, it would be necessary to determine their agreement about the utilisation of the patented invention. If the utilisation conditions are not explicitly agreed upon, then we could turn to analogy of law and general principles of contract law on interpretation of contracts.

In our case, the Copyright Act and the Law of Property Act[30] could be used in applying the principle of analogy.

Subsection 30(4) Copyright Act provides that '[r]elations between joint authors in the exercise of copyright, including the distribution of remuneration, shall be determined by an agreement between them. In the absence of such agreement, all authors shall exercise copyright in the work jointly and

29 M. Koktvedgaard and J. Schovsbo, *Lærebog I Immaterialret* (7th ed., Copenhagen: 2005) (in Danish), p. 253.

30 Asjaõigusseadus. Entered into force on 1 December 1993 – RT I 1993, 39, 590; 2008, 59, 330 (in Estonian).

remuneration shall be divided equally between them'. Subsection 72(5) Law of Property Act provides that:

> A co-owner[31] has the right to demand from the other co-owners that possession and use of a thing in common ownership be affected according to the interests of all co-owners. Co-owners shall act in good faith in their relations with one another and they shall refrain, in particular, from damaging the rights of other co-owners.

Regardless of whether we apply copyright or property regimes as analogous, they both require that rights have to be exercised jointly. Therefore, even a non-exclusive licence would require consent from all owners.

In addition, we could try to determine the possible agreement between PXZ and M-University. Subsection 29(1) of the Law of Obligations Act provides that '[a] contract shall be interpreted according to the actual common intention of the parties'. This principle, however, does not help to determine whether PXZ and the University had agreed to license the invention separately. We could assume that PXZ and the University, by applying jointly for a patent, had concluded a contract of partnership. According to §580(1) of the Law of Obligations Act, '[i]n a contract of partnership, two or more persons (partners) undertake to act to achieve a mutual objective and to help to achieve the objective in the manner established by the contract, above all by making contributions'. Subsection 582(2) of the Law of Obligations Act provides that '[t]he partners shall manage the partnership jointly and the consent of all partners is needed for any transaction to be concluded'. Subsection 583(1) of the Law of Obligations Act specifies that '[t]he right to manage a partnership may be granted by the contract of partnership to one or several partners'. Nothing in the case indicates that PXZ had granted the University this right.

Based on the above, it could be concluded that the situation is legally uncertain. It is highly unlikely that M-University had the right to exclusively or even non-exclusively license the invention without the consent of PXZ. The University has to prove that the right to license the invention was contractually given to the University by PXZ.

If we assume that the University did not have the right to conclude the licence agreement, then this gives rise to the question of whether the contract is valid or whether PZX is entitled to challenge it. Subsection 12(1) Law of Obligations Act provides the following principle: 'The validity of a contract is not affected by the fact that, at the time of entry into the contract, performance of the contract was impossible or one of the parties did not have the right to dispose of the thing or right which is the object of the contract'. Based on this provision we could say that the contract between the University and TransChem is valid and PXZ is

[31] Pursuant to §70(6) of the Law of Property Act, '[p]rovisions concerning common ownership apply to joint ownership'.

not entitled to challenge the contract. Still, when TransChem starts to use the invention, PXZ could demand compensation for damage caused by unlawful use of the invention, the transfer of that which is received as a result of the unlawful use of the patent, termination of the unlawful use of the patent, and refraining from further violation (§53(1) Patent Act). Of course, these obstacles would mean that the University had not fulfilled its contractual obligation to make the utilisation of the invention possible. Consequently, TransChem could use legal remedies against M-University. However, it has been pointed out in Estonian legal literature that the application of legal remedies (e.g. compensation of damage) may be influenced by the fact that the injured party was aware that the fulfilment of the contract might be impossible.[32]

III. Metalegal Formants

Some Estonian patent law experts have suggested that due to the unity of an invention (an invention is an indivisible whole), joint owners of a patent or utility model should exercise their rights together. It is not excluded that the law should be amended to entitle every patent or utility model owner the right to issue non-exclusive licences. Preferably, however, these issues should be regulated by joint owners in a contract.[33] To sum up, a detailed contract could avoid legal disputes concerning the exercise of rights by joint patent owners.

(5) FRANCE

I. Operative Rules

PXZ has the right to challenge the contract between Prof. Marlow and TransChem.

II. Descriptive Formants

The patent is owned jointly by PXZ and M-University. Texts about joint ownership must be applied.

According to Article L. 613-29 of the Intellectual Property Code: '[j]oint ownership of a patent application or of a patent shall be governed by the following provisions ... d) An exclusive licence may only be granted with the agreement of all the joint owners or by the authorisation of the court'.

32 P. Varul, I. Kull, V. Kõve, M. Käerdi, *Võlaõigusseadus I. Kommenteeritud väljaanne* (Law of Obligations Act I. Commented edition), General Part (§§1–207) (Tallinn: 2006), p. 54 (in Estonian).

33 The author's personal communication with R. Kartus (e-mail, 11 February 2009).

M-University has licensed the invention exclusively to TransChem without the consent of PXZ. This consent was, however, required by the above article.

III. Metalegal Formants

Answer omitted.

(6) GERMANY

I. Operative Rules

Yes, PXZ can oppose the contract between M-University and TransChem.

II. Descriptive Formants

§6 sentence 2 German Patent Code provides that co-owners own their patent in common.[34] As a default rule, the norm refers to §741 BGB, unless the patent is held jointly (§705 BGB). Thus, joint inventorship does not automatically result in joint ownership. This is the legislative purpose of §6 sentence 2 German Patent Code. The bar for joint patent ownership is set higher ('for the achievement of a joint purpose'). The reason is §743 sec. 2 BGB in conjunction with §§747 and 749 BGB.

When property is held *in common*, §741 BGB applies. Then, the law differentiates between 'using' (§743 sec. 2 BGB) and 'transfer' (§747 BGB). The transfer of the whole property requires the consent of every owner; the use of property held in common is permitted to every common owner as long as the use of the others is not impaired (§743 sec. 2 BGB). Exclusive licensing to a third party is qualified as a 'transfer' and requires the agreement of every owner.[35] The *factual* exclusive use by one co-owner (which does not exclude the other partner) is qualified as 'use'.[36] Disagreement with the use of one partner allows for the claim to terminate the community under §749 BGB.

Here, PXZ and Prof. Marlow invented together. It can be assumed that they *intended* to commercially exploit together. This intention would create an assumption that the owners wanted to form a company/civil partnership

---

34 §6 sentence 2 German Patent Code: 'Haben mehrere gemeinsam eine Erfindung gemacht, so steht ihnen das Recht auf das Patent gemeinsam zu'. Art. 60(1) EPC: 'The right to a European patent shall belong to the inventor or his successor in title.' The problems related to European patents are the same: Art. 60 EPC does not regulate joint or plural inventorship. A potential regulation was dropped in 1962 with the argument that it interferes with national sovereignty, see B. Homma, *Der Erwerb des Miterfinderrechts* (Baden-Baden: 1998), p. 177.

35 K.-J. Melullis, in: G. Benkard (ed.), *Patentgesetz* (10th ed., Munich: 2006), §6, para. 35e.

36 BGH, decision of 22 March 2005 (X ZR 152/03), BGHZ 162, 342 – *Gummielastische Masse II*.

(joint ownership). PXZ seeks a strong position in which they have a say in future licence agreements. Prof. Marlow of M-University knew, agreed and acted upon it. This is an indication of an intention of partnership (joint ownership).

The operative answer (yes), however, does not depend on the qualification as joint or common ownership. Since exclusive licences also require the consent of all owners of property held in common ownership, the contract remains pending and without effect until approval ('*schwebend unwirksam*', §177 sec. 1 BGB) and can be challenged by PXZ.

III. Metalegal Formants

(Co-)inventorship can strategically be used in the 'public interest'. Exclusive licensing always requires the agreement of every owner of either joint or common property in German law.[37]

(7) GREECE

I. Operative Rules

PXZ may challenge the licence of TransChem, but only as far as it releases TransChem from having to obtain PXZ's consent for the exploitation of the invention, or as it harms PXZ's own licensees.

II. Descriptive Formants

This is a case of a joint patent, actually a form of co-ownership. In this sense, according to Article 787 Civil Code (a rule implementable in any form of co-ownership), each co-inventor may enjoy the use of the whole work on his/her own, under the condition that his/her use does not harm the other co-inventor's use. If each co-inventor exploits the invention on his/her own, or sells the products of it without the consent of the others, then the other co-inventors will be seriously harmed since there will remain nothing for them to sell. It thus seems that no co-inventor may use the invention without the consent of the others.

Nevertheless, each co-inventor is entitled to dispose alone (only) his/her own ideal portion. In this sense the licence is valid, but TransChem may not exploit the invention without PXZ's consent. Furthermore the exclusivity clause is valid only between the parties to the licence contract (*inter partes*), namely only against M-University and its successors, but not *erga omnes*, i.e. against the other

[37] K.-J. Melullis, in: G. Benkard (ed.), *Patentgesetz* (10th ed., Munich: 2006), §6, para. 35e.

co-inventor (here, PXZ) or its successors/licensees. Of course, TransChem has the right (and the equivalent duty of care) to object to any use of the invention by any third party, i.e. any person not legitimated by the other inventor (PXZ), exactly as with co-ownership of moveables according to Article 1116 Civil Code.

III. Metalegal Formants

In every other respect, the term requiring selective distribution is in all probability void in accordance with Article 181 Civil Code as a non-impartial vertical restriction harmful to substantive interests (health) of the consumer public (Art. 1 Law 703/1977; Art. 101 TFEU).The nullity of the term may affect TransChem's licence, since its wish is to have an exclusive monopoly over the control and retail sales of the pharmaceutical product.

(8) IRELAND

Answer omitted.

(9) ITALY

I. Operative Rules

Yes, PXZ is entitled to challenge the contract, and the same would happen even if TransChem did not deny access to third parties.

II. Descriptive Formants

Article 6 Industrial Property Code establishes that in the case of joint ownership the Civil Code rules on tenancy in common (*comunione*) apply (Arts. 1100 et seq. Italian Civil Code).

In this context, a joint owner cannot exclusively license something owned jointly, because this behaviour would interfere with other joint owners' titles. Therefore, any disposition which may reduce the right of the joint owners, and especially an exclusive licence, is to be considered void and without effect.

III. Metalegal Formants

The application of the Civil Code joint ownership rule (originally meant for real property, family or inheritance law) to the field of inventions may be easily criticised. This is especially true in a timeframe when the inventive activity is to be understood as an industrial and financial-based activity and not in the sense of handcrafting, as it was decades ago. Strong criticisms may also be levelled at the 'new' Article 65 Industrial Property Code, which, by regulating derogatorily the field of ownership of public researchers' inventions, is a perfect application of the anticommons theory.[38] Article 65 is not applicable to the present case because of §5, which states that the provisions of Article 65 do not apply if the research has been fully or partially funded by private subjects or entities.

(10) LITHUANIA

I. Operative Rules

Yes, PXZ is entitled to challenge the contract between M-University and TransChem.

II. Descriptive Formants

Article 44(4) of the Lithuanian Patent Act states: 'The joint proprietors may only jointly surrender the legal protection conferred by a patent *or conclude a licensing agreement with third parties*.' As PXZ and M-University are joint proprietors (holders) of the patent, the licensing agreement with TransChem can be concluded only jointly. As a statutory norm was violated, PXZ is entitled to challenge the contract. Apparently, the fact that PXZ and Prof. Marlow hold a patent as co-inventors is not relevant is this case.

III. Metalegal Formants

Joint patent ownership presupposes equal rights of all holders and the requirement to reconcile their wills when entering into contracts with third parties. One of the joint owners cannot be burdened by the unilateral actions of another joint owner. While the Lithuanian Patent Law is silent on how to settle possible disagreements between the joint owners concerning licensing the invention, it is evident that any owner can ask the court to determine the issue.

---

38 The theory of the anticommons, developed by Michelman, 'Ethics, Economics and the Law of Property', (1982) 24(3) *NOMOS* and Heller, 'The Tragedy of the Anticommons: Property in the Transition from Marx to Markets', (1998) 111 *Harvard Law Review*, p. 621. says that in presence of too many property rights belonging to different holders, the economical value of the good object of property tends to zero. The theory may be, and has been, applied to different case studies like store-fronts in Moscow and patents in pharmaceutical drugs.

(11) NETHERLANDS

I. Operative Rules

Yes, PXZ is probably entitled to challenge the contract between M-University and TransChem.

II. Descriptive Formants

First, it is important to determine what the precise position of PXZ is. Article 13 DPA states that a patent can be claimed by two or more inventors if they have cooperated by agreement. Such an agreement does not necessarily have to meet strict formal requirements.[39] A deliberate cooperation will suffice, but solely financial support, on the other hand, will not constitute a joint invention.[40] This means that PXZ is unlikely to have the status of co-inventor.

In spite of that, PXZ can be the co-owner if the parties have so agreed by contract. Since the case seems to suggest that PXZ and M-University are co-owners, their relationship is subject to Article 66 DPA. Unless the parties have agreed otherwise (Art. 66(1) DPA), one of them can only issue a licence by common consent (Art. 66(2) DPA). It therefore depends on the contractual relationship between PXZ and TransChem whether the licence can be challenged.

III. Metalegal Formants

In the case of co-ownership, licensing affects more than one rightholder (i.e. from a competitive point of view). Therefore, it is justified that the consent of all rightholders is required when a licence is issued. This ensures that the construction of co-ownership remains workable. Otherwise, rightholders could at any time face the unexpected or even detrimental consequences of the uncoordinated management of their patent.

(12) NORWAY

I. Operative Rules

Yes, PXZ is entitled to challenge the contract.

---

39 C. Gielen, *Kort begrip van het intellectuele eigendomsrecht* (Deventer: 2007), p. 53.

40 OR, 1 september 1941, *BIE* 1943, 140; OR, 7 april 1960 *BIE* 1961, 78; OR 19 juli *BIE* 1978, 220.

II. Descriptive Formants

M-University, pursuant to §10 of the Act of Joint Ownership (NJOA, 18 November 1965), is entitled to transfer its share of ownership, wholly or in part. Limitations on this right may follow from the implied assumptions of the parties, but in the present case we have no information that sheds light on whether or not this is the case. A co-owner may not, however, transfer more rights than he/she possesses, cf. NJOA §4 para. 3, and is therefore not entitled to grant an exclusive right to a third party. In the present case, this means that PXZ is not obligated to respect the exclusivity clause. But it has to accept that TransChem holds a non-exclusive right to exploit the patent, unless the opposite may be deduced from the implied assumptions of PXZ and M-University.

III. Metalegal Formants

The principle that one may not transfer more rights than one is entitled to is a fundamental principle in Norwegian property law. There is no indication or case law as to why the principle should not apply as regards patents and other IP rights.

(13) POLAND

I. Operative Rules

Yes, PXZ can challenge the contract.

II. Descriptive Formants

Setting aside the issue of co-inventorship, the problem here is whether a joint owner may grant an exclusive licence to the invention without the other co-inventors' consent. Generally, the answer to this question is negative. The Polish IPL does not decide this issue directly, but it orders that the provisions of the Civil Code on joint property be applied accordingly. Under this regulation, the crucial differentiation is between usual management of the right and actions going beyond the scope of usual management. Because of its consequences (which may be close to the consequences of assignment, for example the patentee may not use his/her own right), an exclusive licence usually goes beyond the scope of 'usual management' and requires the consent of all joint owners. Absent such consent, the exclusive licence would be invalid. However, the majority of co-owners (as regards shares) may apply to the court to grant permission (Art. 199 Civil Code).

III. *Metalegal Formants*

It seems that the main issue is the arrangement of rights between co-owners and the ability of co-owners to block the exploitation of the invention.

(14) SLOVENIA

I. *Operative Rules*

PXZ can challenge the licensing contract between M-University and TransChem.

II. *Descriptive Formants*

In accordance with Article 74 IPA, SIPO grants the patent to the person who is designated as the applicant in the patent application. When several persons are designated as joint applicants, the patent is granted to all of them, making them all patent owners. However, the law explicitly stipulates that SIPO does not determine mutual relations between joint applicants. This raises the question of the mutual relations between the patent owners, as their right to assign the patent and the right to license the patented invention depend on this.

According to the Slovenian legislation, the joint applicants (joint patent owners) in such a case have to be considered a civil law community,[41] and specifically a community by shares. Articles 1003–1011 CO must be used.[42] In accordance with Article 1004 CO, each participant has an equal share in the object of the community in the case of doubt. Each participant has free disposal of his/her share, while the object of the community as a whole can only be disposed of all participants unanimously. The concept of disposal is not defined in the CO. However, it must be understood within the meaning of substantive law, where disposal of a right refers to its transfer, modification, encumbrance or cancellation (cf. Art. 23 Law of Property Code).[43]

---

41 B. Zabel, in: N. Plavšak, B. Zabel, V. Kranjc et al., *Obligacijski zakonik s komentarjem (posebni del)*, book 4 (Ljubljana: 2004), p. 996.

42 On the issue of civil law community, see T. Keresteš, *Priložnostna družba v sodobnem pravu (problematika konzorcijskega pravnega razmerja)*, PhD thesis (Maribor: 2003), pp. 52 ff.

43 Official Gazette RS, no. 87/2002. This provision explains the content of legal transacting concerning real estate, but similarly offers a response to the content of the concept of having the disposal of a right.

In the case at hand, an exclusive licence was granted.[44] Because of the *erga omnes* effect of the exclusive licence,[45] such a transfer of a right to use can be aligned with the concept of disposal explained above. The granting of an exclusive licence does not change the ownership of the right. However, in our opinion, the content of the right does change. For this reason, the grant of an exclusive licence in the case at hand is subject to paragraph IV, Article 1004 CO, according to which all participants unanimously have the community object as a whole at their disposal.

According to the Slovenian legislation, M-University does not have the right to independently grant an exclusive licence for the patent, which belongs to more persons. Such a grant of an exclusive licence would be possible only if the prior consent of all the owners of the patent was given.

III. Metalegal Formants

Co-owners have to make a unanimous decision. This is the purpose of this legal institution. Slovenia does not subscribe to two distinct concepts of ownership (common vs. joint).

(15) SPAIN

I. Operative Rules

PXZ can oppose the contract.

II. Descriptive Formants

Article 72.3 Patent Law establishes that 'a licence to a third party to work the invention shall be granted by the parties jointly, unless the judge deems that, for reasons of equity given the particular circumstances, one of the parties should be authorised to grant the said licence'. Therefore, unless an ordinary court grants an authorisation to dispose of the patent individually, M-University cannot license the invention without prior consent of PXZ. When a patent application or patent belongs to a number of persons in undivided parts, the co-ownership is governed

---

44 In accordance with the provision of Art. 120a IPA, the right to file an action against infringement of industrial property rights also belongs to the recipient of the exclusive licence, to the extent that the rights have been transferred to him/her by law or through a legal transaction.

45 Compare K. Podobnik, in: N. Plavšak et al., *Obligacijski zakonik s komentarjem (posebni del)*, book 4 (Ljubljana: 2004), p. 67.

on the terms agreed upon by the parties,[46] or in the absence of such agreement, the Patent Law and the Civil Code (Art. 392) apply. Article 392 Patent Law prevents one co-inventor from disposing of a patent without the authorisation of the other co-inventors. The licence agreement might be declared invalid because the object (rights conferred by the patent) belongs to all the parties jointly and can only be transferred should all the parties consent.[47]

III. Metalegal Formants

Joint ownership secures the say of any co-owner and forces the parties into an agreement. Only courts can overcome a stalemate.

(16) UNITED KINGDOM

I. Operative Rules

PXZ can object to the exclusive licence.

II. Descriptive Formants

Regardless of PXZ's status as co-inventor, in the case of Modification 1 PXZ and the University institute jointly own the patent.

The question is whether the law requires the consent of both patent owners for the exclusive licence to be valid. Under section 36(3) PA 1977, the answer is that consent of all patent owners is required before granting a licence. It says:

> Subject to the provisions of sections 8 and 12 above and section 37 below and to any agreement for the time being in force, *where two or more persons are proprietors of a patent one of them shall not without the consent of the other or others*; ... (b) *grant a licence under the patent* ...

The effect of section 36(3)(b) PA 1997 is that the University unlawfully created the exclusive licence. Under section 37, the Comptroller of Patents and the

---

46 It seems interesting to remark that on this issue, the Spanish Patent Law differs from the German report because when Art. 10. 2 establishes that '[w]here an invention has been made jointly by a number of persons, the right to obtain a patent shall belong to them jointly', it seems that the purpose of the law is to recognise an automatic joint ownership and that is why Art. 72.1 Patent Law states that, if there is no contractual agreement between them, the relationship between co-inventors shall be governed by the common law provisions on joint ownership.

47 See T. Vazquez Lépinette, *La cotitularidad de los bienes inmateriales* (Valencia: 1996), pp. 372–374, as well as the Report of the Spanish Group of AIPPI (Singapore: 2007) on the question Q 194: '*El impacto de la cotitularidad de los derechos de propiedad industrial e intelectual en su explotación*'. The same solution can be found in the German and Czech reports.

courts have wide powers to make orders to address this. Potentially, they could order that a licence be granted to the parties identified by PXZ. In effect, this would mean that TransChem no longer has an *exclusive* licence. TransChem would probably then seek to renegotiate the terms of its licence or abandon it.

III. Metalegal Formants

English patent law stipulates the applicability of joint tenancy to co-ownership of co-owned patents (in contrast to tenancy in common).[48] This implies the idea of a unity of interest, which requires consent with regard to exploitation.

B.3. COMPARATIVE REMARKS

Joint co-inventorship and joint ownership are the central topics of this case. The question is: what rights does a co-inventor and co-owner have with regard to the licensing of a patent?

In none of the jurisdictions examined does a co-owner or co-inventor have the right to grant an exclusive licence on his/her own. He/she must have the approval of all the other co-owners or co-inventors respectively. Almost everywhere, the co-owner can challenge the contract between the University and the company TransChem. Estonia is the only exception.

There are, however, other interesting differences between the legal systems. In some jurisdictions, the provisions concerning co-ownership of a patent are placed in the IP law itself (Belgium, France, the Netherlands, the UK). Interestingly, they all stipulate joint ownership. In others, civil code rules about joint ownership/common ownership apply (Germany, Italy, Poland, Slovenia, Spain). The Polish rules somewhat stand out in that, concerning the question of whether permission is needed or not, it must be determined whether the case affects the usual management of the patent. Co-owners only have to accept all actions falling within the term 'usual management' (in Germany also '*factual* exclusive use'), otherwise permission is needed.

Norway has a separate statute for joint ownership. It is worth mentioning that in Danish law no written rules are applicable. However, it is commonly known that for important decisions concerning a patent unanimity among the different patent owners is needed.

Apart from having the approval of the other co-owners, there is another route to be allowed to license a patent in Belgium, France, Spain and the UK. In these countries, one can try to get the authorisation of a court. In the UK, the Comptroller of Patents (the head of the UK Patents Office) also enjoys wide discretion.

48 For an explanation of the concepts under English law see A. Clarke, *Principles of Property Law* (Cambridge: 2020), pp. 339–345.

C.1. MODIFICATION 2

Would it make a difference if M-University had only granted a simple licence?

C.2. EDITORIAL NOTE

The case is interested in the *national* legal situation. It might be helpful to describe the national rules against the background of the EU ones. The EU crafts its own rules for intellectual property deriving from collaborative research funded under the EU Research Framework Programme. Depending on the programme, the European Commission advises using model contracts for consortium agreements with a mix of elements,[49] from which partners can deviate. However, if *no* agreement is made, participants own the results jointly (Art. 40(1) Regulation (EC) No. 1906/2006, Art. 38(1) Regulation (EU) 2021/695).[50] In principle, each co-owner is authorised to grant simple licences (without the right to sub-license), partners are to be informed in advance, and fair and reasonable remuneration is to be paid. Any owner is allowed to transfer the property, but is obliged to ensure that obligations are passed on.[51]

---

49 Which are described in adjacent tools to each regulation. In principle, these follow a three-step (allegedly *French*) approach: (1) The right to grant *exclusive licences* requires the consent of all. The consortium agreement shall ease future negotiation by stipulating that when exclusive licences are granted, compensation/remuneration will be given to every co-owner. (2) Co-owners should contractually opt for the right of each co-owner to grant *non-exclusive licences* (including the use of everybody), provided that the first option rights for exclusivity have been honoured (allegedly the *Belgian* status quo). (3) In the event that one joint owner obtains significant benefits from the use of the *non-exclusive* licence, the other parties receive an equitable share of benefits. Originally laid out in European Commission, *Joint Ownership in Intellectual Property Rights* (Brussels: 2004), 16 (originally posted as pdf on the webpage of the 'IPR-helpdesk' of the EC Commission; it was removed in the meantime); for a comparative account of co-ownership in patent law see also C. Heath, 'Harmonising Scope and Allocation of Patent Rights in Europe', *Intellectuelle Rechten, Droits Intellectuels (IRDI)*, 2001, 211 f.

50 For Horizon-2020 (2014–2020), it was Art. 41 Regulation (EU) No. 1290/2013, OJ L 347, 20 December 2013, 81–103; For Horizon Europe (2021–2027), it is Regulation (EU) 2021/695, OJ L 170, 12 May 2021, 1. The legal set-up corresponds to the Anglo-American model (except Scotland) – see the UK report. In the US, each common owner is entitled to grant non-exclusive licence for the patent, but is not entitled to file a suit without the other's consent, H. Stumpf and M. Groß, *Der Lizenzvertrag* (8th ed., Frankfurt/M: 2005), 40 (12th ed., Frankfurt/M: 2020). For an introduction to the evolution (and the rationale) of these rules to the basic and the special programmes see C. Godt, 'Forschungs-, Wissenschafts- und Technologiepolitik (Kap. N.)', in: M. Dauses (ed.), *Handbuch des EU-Wirtschaftsrechts* (1st ed., Munich: 2006), para. 31–37 (revised in: M. A. Dauses and M. Ludwigs (eds.), *Handbuch des EU-Wirtschaftsrechts* (Munich: 2018), nos. 45, 50).

51 Art. 40(1) Reg. (EU) 2021/695 clearly states: 'Beneficiaries may transfer ownership of their results. They shall ensure that their obligations also apply to the new owner and that the latter has the obligation to pass them on in any subsequent transfer.'

While, formerly, the focus was, for example, on confidentiality (Art. 42 Regulation (EC) No. 1906/2006, Art. 44 Regulation (EU) No. 1290/2013), the emphasis has shifted towards access rights and that these access rights are also safeguarded for third parties after transfer. Beyond these mandatory rules, the European Commission advises that the contract provide for a pre-emptive right of partners, both in the case of one partner wanting to pull out[52] and in the case of the insolvency of one. It further advises majority voting and transfer rules in the event the invention is licensed.

C.3. COUNTRY REPORTS

(1) BELGIUM

I. Operative/Descriptive/Metalegal Rules

It would not make a difference if M-University had merely granted a simple licence; also in addition, for a simple licence, co-proprietors of a patent need to agree unanimously (Art. 43§2 BPA, now Art. XI.49§2 BCEL).

(2) CZECH REPUBLIC

I. Operative Rules

No, it would not make a difference if M-University had only granted a simple licence.

II. Descriptive/Metalegal Formants

It does not matter whether the licence is exclusive or non-exclusive. PXZ is entitled to challenge the contract between the M-University and TransChem.

(3) DENMARK

I. Operative Rules

A simple licence will probably not make a difference, but to answer the question in a meaningful way more detailed facts would be needed.

52 So-called *ius accrescendi* – as provided for in §738 BGB.

II. Descriptive/Metalegal Formants

The answer depends on whether the granting of a simple licence can be qualified as an 'important' decision which requires unanimity according to Danish law on joint ownership. It would seem to be impossible to generally state that simple licences are unimportant compared with exclusive licences. Even simple agreements may affect the future value of the patent or other market options gravely. For an exact answer, the detailed content of the specific licence agreement would be needed.

(4) ESTONIA

I. Operative Rules

It would not make a difference whether the licence issued was exclusive or non-exclusive.

II. Descriptive/Metalegal Formants

See the response for the base case.

(5) FRANCE

I. Operative Rules

Yes, the situation would be different if PXZ had been informed about the agreement.

II. Descriptive Formants

Could M-University, the co-owner of the patent, have granted a simple licence? According to Article L. 613-29 Intellectual Property Code, the consent of every co-owner is not needed to grant a simple licence. However, each co-owner must be informed to be able to eventually contest it. M-University would have been able to grant a simple licence without PXZ's consent if it had previously notified the draft licensing agreement. But this procedure seems not to have been followed. If a simple licence had been granted to TransChem, the result would not differ. PXZ would also be able to contest it.

III. Metalegal Formants

The rationale of the French law for simple licences is to reverse the substantive burden to act. The party which wishes to give out a simple licence is only required to notify, thus giving the other party the possibility to object. If the other party is silent, consent is assumed. The purpose is to make licensing easier, and to enhance the availability of the invention.

(6) GERMANY

I. Operative Rules

No, it would not make a difference if only a simple licence was granted.

II. Descriptive Formants

Assuming joint ownership (§705 BGB), the result would not differ to Modification 1 (supra).

Yet, assuming common property (§741 BGB), the status of the contract depends on the question of whether a simple licence is to be qualified as 'non-impeding use' of the patent right in the sense of §743 sec. 2 BGB. There is some discussion as to the qualification of a simple licence.[53] However, the prevailing opinion in the literature is that a common owner can give out neither a simple nor an exclusive licence, whereas one of the common owners can sell his/her share (§747 sentence 1 BGB). In respect of 'use', they argue, the legislative purpose of §743 sec. 2 BGB is to regulate the *factual* use among co-owners. The case of a commonly shared car is the prototype and this rationale was transferred to patents held in common.[54] Yet the BGH case on this issue in 2005 was on factual use only. It remains an open question whether the simple licence to a third party is comparable to a factual use of one co-owner. Here, for reasons of clarity, we argue with the literature. The argument is that *factual* use is not comparable to *contractual* duties which affect the legal status of the right as such and therefore both partners (§749 sec. 2 BGB). Under this rationale, the simple licence is not covered by the scope of §743 sec. 2 BGB.

III. Metalegal Formants

While German property law is geared towards the protection of property control, attenuation has occurred for the sake of innovation. In a constellation on the factual use of patents held in common ownership, the German Supreme Court allowed in 2005 exploitation by one of the owners without prior consent of the co-owner. Once the other co-owner finds out and disapproves, he/she

---

53 References to this literature is found in H. Stumpf and M. Groß, *Der Lizenzvertrag* (8th ed., Frankfurt/M.: 2005), p. 40.

54 BGHZ 162, 342 – *Gummielastische Masse II.*

might terminate the community (§749 BGB). Profits made during that time are not to be shared. The BGH decision builds on the rationale of patent law: the technology shall be worked and disseminated.

(7) GREECE

I. Operative Rules

PXZ may challenge the licence of TransChem, but only as far as it releases TransChem from having to obtain PXZ's consent for the exploitation of the invention.

II. Descriptive Formants

This too is a case of a joint patent, but the licence given by the one co-inventor is simple. If the co-inventor or its licensee exploits the invention, or sells the products of it, without the consent of PXZ (the other co-inventor), then PXZ will be seriously harmed, because there will remain nothing for it to sell. In this frame, it seems that any co-inventor (or its licensees) may not use the invention without the consent of the other. Therefore, PXZ may challenge the licence of TransChem, but only as far as it releases TransChem from the duty of obtaining PXZ's consent for the exploitation of the invention.

III. Metalegal Formants

The core is that a co-inventor (or its licensees) may not use the invention without the consent of the other co-inventor.

(8) IRELAND

Answer omitted.

(9) ITALY

I. Operative Rules

Yes, it would make a difference if M-University had only granted a simple licence.

II. Descriptive/Metalegal Formants

Following, again, the Civil Code rules on tenancy in common, it can be argued that in the case of a non-exclusive licence, as no other joint author would be affected by the exploitation of the good (each one can grant an additional non-exclusive licence), there would be no remedy directed to the invalidation of the licence.

(10) LITHUANIA

I. Operative Rules

No, it would not make a difference if M-University had only granted a simple licence.

II. Descriptive/Metalegal Formants

Lithuanian law (Art. 44(4) of the Lithuanian Patent Act) does not differentiate between exclusive and non-exclusive licences. Thus, in both cases an agreement should be reached between the two co-owners.

(11) NETHERLANDS

I. Operative Rules

No, any licence or permission (as referred to in Art. 73(2) DPA) requires common consent.

II. Descriptive Formants

It follows from Article 66(2) DPA that a licence can only be granted by common consent, unless the rightholders agreed otherwise. There is no exception to this rule in the case of a simple licence. The common consent rule applies to every licence.

III. Metalegal Formants

See Modification 1.

(12) NORWAY

I. Operative Rules

Yes, M-University is entitled to grant TransChem a simple licence.

II. Descriptive Formants

See Modifications 1 and 2 supra.

III. Metalegal Formants

Answer omitted.

(13) POLAND

I. Operative Rules

It may make a difference if M-University had only granted a simple licence.

II. Descriptive Formants

Unlike exclusive licences, non-exclusive licences do not deprive the patent holder of the possibility of granting further licences or using the invention him/herself. Therefore, a non-exclusive licence may stay within the boundaries of 'usual management' of rights, although the opposite view has also been expressed.[55] Under Article 201 Civil Code, the consent of the majority of co-owners is required (majority with regard to shares). If such consent is not reached, each co-owner may apply to the court for permission. If the University had the majority of shares, it could grant a non-exclusive licence. If not, it would have to apply to the court for permission. If PXZ and the University are not able to agree on managing the patent rights, they could ask the court to appoint a court caretaker.

III. Metalegal Formants

Answer omitted.

(14) SLOVENIA

I. Operative Rules

If M-University had only granted a simple licence, PXZ would still have the right to challenge the licensing contract.

---

55 A. Szajkowski, in: J. Szwaja (ed.), *System prawa własności intelektualnej. T III Prawo wynalazcze* (Wrocław: 1990), p. 243.

II. Descriptive Formants

Unlike an exclusive licence, a simple licence does not have *erga omnes* effect. It only represents a relative right, thus a right which is only valid between the licensor and licensee.[56] Therefore, the definition given above of disposal of the right does not include the non-exclusive transfer of a use of a right, as in our opinion it does not make any changes to either in the ownership of the right or its content. For this reason it is necessary to use the provisions of Article 1006 of the CO concerning the use of the community object, which is not of a divided kind. In such a situation, each participant in the community exercises his/her right in accordance with its purpose and in such a way that it does not damage the simultaneous use of other participants and the right as a whole. The rights of the owners may not be limited without the consent of all participants involved (Art. 1006(2) and (3) CO).

It can be determined that the grant of a simple licence by one patent owner does not prevent the other owners from using the patent; however, it does harm the object as a whole. It has to be stressed that the patent represents a legal monopoly of its owner (or owners). Each grant of a licence represents a 'weakening' of the monopolistic position. For this reason, it can be claimed with certainty that upon the grant of a simple licence by one of the owners, the position of the other owners becomes worse, or the right (patent) that belongs to them becomes weaker.

III. Metalegal Formants

Answer omitted.

(15) SPAIN

I. Operative Rules

It would not make a difference if a simple licence had been granted.[57]

II. Descriptive/Metalegal Formants

Article 72.3 Patent Law does not make distinctions between exclusive licences and simple licences. Therefore, the answer is the same as in Modification 1.[58]

56 See M.S. Marković, *Patentno pravo* (Beograd: 1997), p. 319.
57 See the same conclusion in the German and Czech reports.
58 See AAVV, *La modernización del derecho español de patentes* (Madrid: 1984), p. 238.

(16) UNITED KINGDOM

I. Operative Rules

PXZ can object also to the basic licence.

II. Descriptive/Metalegal Formants

There is no difference.

C.4. COMPARATIVE REMARKS

The case differs from Modification 1, as it concerns the granting of a *non-exclusive* licence by a co-owner of a patent. The reports show great divergences.

In many states, it is of no importance whether the licence is exclusive or not. The co-owner needs the approval of the other co-owners, regardless of the nature of the licence.[59] However, in some jurisdictions the difference actually matters. In Denmark, where no special legislation exists, the approval is only necessary if the licence is non-exclusive and can be qualified as an 'important' decision. If not, the licence cannot be challenged.[60] In France, it is sufficient to inform the co-owner about the licensing agreement. In Italy, a non-exclusive licence is seen as not affecting the interests of the co-owner in exploiting the patent at all.[61] Therefore, no consent is needed. In Germany, the difference would matter for the default rule of common property, had the reporter not assumed 'joint property' for the given case constellation. Polish law differentiates between (1) the usual management of a right and (2) actions that go beyond such usual management. In the first situation the consent of the *majority* of the rightholders is required, whereas in the second situation *all* co-owners have to approve. Academic literature broadly qualifies non-exclusive licensing as usual management (thus, if a university had a bigger share in a patent, the other partner could not challenge the contract). In Norway (where a special law on joint ownership has been enacted), co-owners cannot grant an exclusive licence *because* they themselves are not entitled to use the patent exclusively (rationale: 'one cannot dispose more than one has').

---

59 See the reports of Belgium, Czech Republic, Estonia, Germany, Greece, the Netherlands, Slovenia and Spain.

60 This would depend on the actual facts of the case.

61 Whether this is true is doubtful. It is right that the co-owner can still exploit the patent him/herself and can grant non-exclusive licences. But one has to bear in mind that in general every licensee is a potential competitor.

Differences are based on divergent perspectives on (1) how much one co-owner is restricted by giving out a simple licence to a third party, and (2) by different perspectives on innovation. With regard to (1), some countries do not regard simple licences as restrictive, since the co-owner is still able to exploit the patent on his/her own, whereas other countries consider it to be burdensome that the co-owner will be faced by another competitor.

D.1. MODIFICATION 3

Assume that an invention has been made jointly. M-University *refuses to patent* the invention because of the University Guidelines on 'Specifically Important Developments'. These require that scientific inventions with the utmost importance and potential broad use be put into the public domain. PXZ and M-University argue about how far these guidelines are binding on PXZ and if the invention is 'scientifically of utmost importance'. Ultimately, PXZ files for a patent on its own. Can M-University challenge the patent?

D.2. COUNTRY REPORTS

(1) BELGIUM

I. Operative Rules

PXZ can apply for a patent on its own (thus M has no claim).

II. Descriptive Formants

Belgian patent law does not explicitly foresee such a situation, nor do general principles of co-ownership. To our knowledge, there is no case law. But we can deduce the probable solution from various provisions and principles of the BPA.

The moral right of the inventor is quite limited and consists mainly of the right to be named (Art. 12 BPA, now Art. XI.13 BCEL).[62] Therefore, it will not include something like 'respect for one's invention' or 'the right not to have patented one's invention'.

62 M.-C. Janssens, 'Uitvindingen in dienstverband met bijzondere aandacht voor uitvindingen aan universiteiten' [Employee and University Inventions], *CIR series Katholieke Universiteit Leuven* no. 12 (Brussels: 1995), 18–21.

With regard to the patrimonial rights, M-University has the right to apply for a patent or not. Since M-University is merely a co-owner, the other co-owner, PXZ, will also have the right to apply for the patent or not (Art. 8 BPA, now Art. XI.9 BCEL). If PXZ were to apply on its own, the only thing M-University could do is to revindicate its part of the patent application or patent on the basis of its co-ownership of the invention (Art. 9§§1–2 BPA, now Art. XI.10§§1–2 BCEL)

Once co-owners of the patent, they must agree unanimously on the licensing and suing policy, unless there are any contractual provisions to the contrary (Art. 43§§1–2 BPA, now Art. XI.49§§1–2 BCEL). It would then be theoretically possible for M-University to block any infringement proceedings. On the other hand, PXZ would be able to block any open-source licences as well. If co-owners have no valid reason for their refusals, it is up to a Commercial Court to authorise (or not) any lawsuits or licences (Arts. 43§2 2° and 73 BPA, now Arts. XI.49§2 and XVII.14 BCEL).[63] Therefore, M-University's ideal of putting important inventions into the public domain cannot discard PXZ's patrimonial right as co-owner to apply for a patent and exploit it.

III. Metalegal Formants

An inventor has fewer moral rights than an author of an artistic or literary work. The difference lies in the fact that an author supposedly puts more of his/her personality into his/her work. Therefore, an author will have the right to object to disrespectful modifications of his/her work. An inventor, on the other hand, has 'merely' resolved a technical problem. His/her personality is less likely to be harmed by publications, exploitations or modifications of his/her invention, as long as his/her right to be named or not is respected. In any case, the inventor will have the right to apply for a patent regardless of what the other inventor feels about that.[64]

The moral rights being so limited, they do not include the right to impose one's wishes or preferences with regard to licensing policy or the further use of an invention.

(2) CZECH REPUBLIC

I. Operative Rules

PXZ does not have a right to apply on its own. M-University may object.

---

[63] B. van Reepinghen, and M. De Brabanter, *Les brevets d'invention [Patents]* (Brussels: 1987), 168.

[64] A. Braun, 'Sous l'attraction de deux sphères juridiques : les inventions d'employés' [Under the Atttraction of Two Legal Spheres: Inventions of Employees], *T.S.R.* 1967, no. 4, 151–152; H. Buckinx, 'De uitvindingen van de werknemers' [Inventions of Employees], *R.W.* 1970, no. 14, 635–638.

II. Descriptive Formants

The right to patent belongs to the applicant. If there are co-owners, then all of the co-owners must sign the application. According to the doctrine, if any of the co-inventors are not applicants, then a document on the acquisition of the right to submit an application must be enclosed.[65]

The rights of co-owners of the patent, according to section 16(1) Patent Act, are governed by general regulations on joint ownership. Analogically, rights before the invention is patented shall be also governed by general regulations on joint ownership. Joint ownership is governed by sections 137–142 of the Civil Code. According to section 139(2) of the Civil Code, the dispute is to be settled by the court if the size of shares and the votes on management of the property are equal. The court should take into account the intention of the parties when they were concluding the contract on support for research. The intention of the parties was to improve the medical treatment for a malignant form of cancer. PXZ wants to have a say in the licensing negotiation and as such the invention must be patented before the licensing negotiation. The intention of the parties is to introduce inventions.

III. Metalegal Formants

The provisions of the contract, and not the internal rules of M-University, are binding on the parties.

(3) DENMARK

I. Operative Rules

M-University can probably challenge the patent.

II. Descriptive Formants

According to the DPA, inventors or those with a legal right have a right to apply for a patent. The DPA does not contain any rules on co-ownership. As mentioned in Modification 1, Danish law generally requires unanimity for important decisions relating to inventions owned jointly. In the case at hand, applying for patent protection is undoubtedly an 'important decision' and as

---

65 R. Horáček, K. Čada, P. Hajn, *Práva k průmyslovému vlastnictví* (Rights to the Industrial Property) (1st ed., Prague: 2005), p. 76.

such unanimity is required. PXZ, therefore, does not have the right to apply for a patent on its own.

III. Metalegal Formants

Danish law forces co-inventors and co-owners into a consensual decision, and – as the case shows – accepts that a co-inventor may not be able to apply for a patent if the other party disagrees.

(4) ESTONIA

I. Operative Rules

Presumably, PXZ might apply for a patent. The University could file an action to be acknowledged as a joint owner.

II. Descriptive Formants

Subsection 13(3) Patent Act provides that '[i]n the case of joint authorship, all rights arising from the authorship are exercised by the authors jointly, including the right to apply for a patent and to become the proprietor of the patent, unless they have entered into a written agreement which prescribes otherwise'. The situation is, however, different because PXZ and the University had agreed that inventions which are developed to fulfil the research contract between PXZ and the University are patented and both parties are joint owners. Subsection 12(2) Patent Act provides that '[i]f an invention is created in the performance of contractual obligations or duties of employment, the right to apply for a patent and to become the proprietor of the patent is vested in the author or other person pursuant to the contract or employment contract'. The Patent Act does not have sufficient regulations to cover situations where two or more persons should be joint patent owners but some are not named as joint owners. Presumably, however, they could file an action to be acknowledged as a joint owner.

III. Metalegal Formants

If PXZ had applied for a patent and the University filed an action to be named as a joint owner, then in the absence of a contract regulating the exercise of patent rights we would face the difficulties described in the previous section.

Another issue is that the University is in breach of its contractual obligations. Presumably it is not a sound defence that the University had adopted internal regulations which are in conflict with its contractual obligations.

(5) FRANCE

I. Operative Rules

Yes, M-University can probably challenge the patent.

II. Descriptive Formants

We know PXZ is not a true co-inventor [Note of the editor C. Godt in 2019: compare the case text: 'assume PXZ and M are co-inventors'. Yet, as a matter of copyright policy, submitted texts are not changed by the editorial team]. It only raises money for research. It could apply for a patent but would nevertheless be exposed to a claim from the true inventor, M-University.

Article L. 611-8 of the Intellectual Property Code states:

> Where an application for the grant of an industrial property title has been made either for an invention unlawfully taken from an inventor or his successors in title, or in violation of a legal contractual obligation, the injured party may claim ownership of the application or of the title granted.

To succeed, the University should prove PXZ has no right on the patent because PXZ is not the inventor. By contracting with PXZ under the named conditions, M-University committed to identify the director of PXZ as a co-inventor. Did the University through this commitment oblige itself to apply for a patent? Judges would have to seek the will of the parties. If they think M-University has obliged itself implicitly or explicitly to apply for a patent owned jointly by it and PXZ, the University's claim should not succeed.

III. Metalegal Formants

The exact content of the contract between PXZ and the University is not well known. We do not know if PXZ knew about the University Guidelines on 'Specifically Important Developments'. PXZ could not ask for joint ownership in good faith if it knew about the University Guidelines. Under these conditions, if PXZ applied for a patent, the claim from the true inventor, M-University, should succeed.

(6) GERMANY

I. Operative Rules

M-University cannot challenge the validity of the patent. It may, however, (1) request vindication for half of the patent, and (2) require the declaration of patent waiver.

II. Descriptive Formants

Since the German Patent Agency only examines the patentability requirements (and not material inventorship, the inventor must only be named), the co-inventor has no right to challenge the validity of the patent.

The co-inventor might request vindication on the base of §8 German Patent Law.

The case, however, revolves around the guidelines which oblige M-University *not* to patent. Since the guidelines precede the contract in time, they became part of the contract, and are therefore also binding on PXZ. They mimic public declarations of industry which aspire to bind the contractual chain up- and downstream. Consequently, the University has an obligatory claim against PXZ to waive the patent (§241 Civil Code, §20 German Patent Law), if the invention qualifies as 'essential'. The qualification as 'utmost importance and potential broad use' is a contractual term which is liable for trial in a court of law.

III. Metalegal Formants

At the heart of the case is the collision of how to deal with knowledge and innovation. Is technological diffusion fostered by property rights (monetary incentive to innovate) or accelerated by putting knowledge into the public domain (free use for both the inventive idea as such and the work on follow-on inventions)? With regard to the former, the patient organisation not only has its belief on how to foster innovation, but also has an interest in (co-)controlling the exploitation and reserving privileges for its members. The latter aspect is based on traditional research norms (to uphold this rationale, the guidelines were adopted), and in essence also the rationale of the exclusion of discoveries and theory (Art. 52(2) EPC). The case highlights that the intent to put knowledge into the public domain is not protected by the patent system in Germany. Parties, however, may have resort to internal self-regulation. If the other party is aware of that, the terms become part of the cooperation contract and thus enforceable.

(7) GREECE

I. Operative Rules

PXZ can apply for a patent and the University can only claim co-ownership of it.

II. Descriptive Formants

The contractual term dealing with a mandatory joint patent is valid, since it does not prevent without any other formality broad public access to the pharmaceutical product, which is required by Article 102 TFEU and Article 2 Law 703/1977. Whether, all things being equal, the retail sales of the product to be manufactured and the licensing of any commercial distributors of it will be mandatory is another issue.

Since the University agreed with PXZ to a common research programme and the result is a patentable invention, both parties are under a duty of loyalty to the other party (Art. 288 Civil Code). The extent of this duty of loyalty is a matter of interpretation of the contract. If the contract refers to the possibility that the result of the research is a patentable invention, which is apparently the case here, and the University did not object before signing, then its loyalty obligation prohibits it from disclosing the invention to the public and thus ruining its patentability. PXZ can apply for a patent and the University can only claim co-ownership of it, according to Article 6 para. 3 Law 1733/1987. Additionally, Article 12 para. 2 specifies that each co-owner of a patentable (but not yet patented) invention can freely dispose of their part of the invention. This speaks for the obligation of co-owners to respect the commonly owned right even before it is patented. The legislator has specified in Article 5 paras. 6 and 8 what is excluded from patentability (healing processes, animal and plant varieties, *ordre public*, etc.); therefore, every other invention is entitled to patentability.

III. Metalegal Formants

M-University cannot invoke the University Guidelines on 'Specifically Important Developments', unless these Guidelines are stipulated by a law of the state. Neither may it invoke the importance of the invention for public health in order to overcome its contractual obligations towards PXZ. A different issue is the use of the patent after it has been granted (e.g. abusive refusal to licence, etc.), which is to be judged *ad hoc*; however, it seems most probable that the University may not make a claim for the co-invention to be made available to the public for free.

(8) IRELAND

Answer omitted.

(9) ITALY

I. Operative Rules

Yes, M-University can challenge the patent.

II. Descriptive/Metalegal Formants

If PXZ is to be considered the co-inventor (Modification 1), it would be possible for it to apply for its own patent (Art. 63 Industrial Property Code).

(10) LITHUANIA

I. Operative Rules

No, M-University cannot challenge the patent.

II. Descriptive Formants

The Lithuanian Patent Act does not contain provisions directly dealing with such issue. The general norm is Article 10(1) of the Lithuanian Patent Act, which states:

> The right to a patent shall belong to the inventor or his successor in title, or the employer, in the case of a service invention. If an invention is made by a person who carries out scientific research, designing, construction works and other works of creative character under contract with a client who finances an appropriate work, the right to a patent for the invention shall be established by such contract. Joint inventors shall, unless they agree otherwise, have equal rights to the patent.

As a matter of principle, the actions of M-University in refusing to patent amounts to the refusal to enforce its right to patent. But such refusal does not create obstacles to another person having the equal right.

III. Metalegal Formants

The traditional rationale for the patent system is to provide legal protection for inventions, not to put them in the public domain. To achieve the latter goal, an inventor is normally free to make his/her invention public without patenting it. The possible solution for dealing with such conflicts as presented in the current case is that parties should use contractual arrangements.

(11) NETHERLANDS

I. Operative Rules

No, M-University cannot challenge the patent.

II. *Descriptive Formants*

According to Article 8 DPA, the party who applies for a patent is presumed to be the inventor and can therefore claim the patent. If M-University wants to prevent PXZ from exploiting the patent, it cannot block the application, but it may try to revoke (Art. 75 DPA) or reclaim (Art. 78 DPA) the patent. Because of the contractual relation between PXZ and the University, the latter can hardly state that PXZ was not entitled to apply and ask subsequently for revocation (Art. 75(1)(e) DPA). Nor can the moral rights, which stay with the real inventor, effectively impede PXZ. The inventor can, for example, require attribution, but he/she does not have the discretion to approve or to reject a patent application. Therefore, the only remaining option for the University to frustrate the commercial exploitation of the therapy will be to (partially) reclaim it. According to the contract, M-University can become a co-owner of the patent (if necessary by submitting such a request to the court under Article 78 DPA). This strategy, however, will be of little help to M-University, since PXZ can object to any (free) licence issued by the University (see the answer to Modification 1). On the other hand, the University is not entitled to veto possible lawsuits instigated by PXZ, since every (co-)owner of the patent may individually sue infringers (Art. 66(2) DPA). Therefore, M-University will always need the cooperation of PXZ to make the therapy freely available.

III. *Metalegal Formants*

The presumption of inventorship, laid down in Article 8 DPA, ensures that the application process does not become unnecessarily complicated. As compensation, the possibility to challenge an unjust application remains unaffected. In this particular example, however, the contractual conditions agreed upon by M-University have weakened its case. It is therefore justified that M-University has to content itself with co-ownership, instead of complete control. Otherwise, M-University should have acted earlier by not entering into the contract.

With regard to the other aspect – the limited scope of moral rights in the field of patent law – one should consider the bond between inventor and invention. In comparison with an artistic work, the personality of the maker is supposed to be less dominantly present in patents. Inventions contain, so to speak, 'technological ingenuity' rather than 'personal expression'. Therefore, the moral rights attached to an invention are less extensive and do not include the possibility to revoke a just application.

(12) NORWAY

I. *Operative Rules*

M-University can probably not challenge the patent, but will co-own it.

II. *Descriptive Formants*

The situation is not regulated in Norwegian patent law, but general principles of co-ownership are presumed to apply in that case. The NJOA §8, second paragraph, which obliges each and every co-owner to provide for the maintenance of the property, can probably be invoked as a legal ground for a right to apply for a patent without having to obtain consent from the other co-owners.[66] But if so, all inventors will be entitled to the patent. In the present situation, it may be strategically smarter for the University not to abandon its patent rights, as co-ownership will enable it to exert influence on the exploitation of the patent.

III. *Metalegal Formants*

The patent right in NPA §1 is formulated as a right to *apply for* a patent. In situations of co-inventorship, this means that the main rule or principle is that all the inventors are applicants unless the right to apply is transferred to a third party. However, there is no indication that general property principles will not apply to patents.

(13) POLAND

I. *Operative Rules*

No, M-University cannot challenge the patent.

II. *Descriptive Formants*

The provisions of the Civil Code on co-ownership are accordingly applicable to the right to obtain a patent (Art. 72(4) IPL). The decision to file the patent application is considered to exceed the boundaries of usual management[67] and thus requires the consent of all co-owners. The exception applies when the application may be treated as an action undertaken in order to save the joint right (Art. 209 Civil Code), which is mostly the case when a danger of disclosure (destroying patentability) is looming.[68] However, it is questionable whether acting contrary to the wishes of the other co-owners may be qualified as falling under Article 209 Civil Code.

---

66 Cf. A. Stenvik, *Patentrett* (2nd ed., Oslo: 2006), p. 271.

67 A. Szajkowski, in: J. Szwaja (ed.), *System prawa własności intelektualnej. T III Prawo wynalazcze* (Wrocław: 1990), p. 242.

68 Ibid.

III. Metalegal Formants

There is a very interesting question of whether in the case of co-inventorship the co-inventors who do not wish the invention to be patented may, in accordance with the law, effectively oppose registration.

(14) SLOVENIA

I. Operative Rules

M-University cannot object to the granting of the patent; it allegedly has legal means after the patent has been granted.

II. Descriptive Formants

PXZ contributed money to the research. In exchange for funding the research, the parties agreed that M-University would list the manager of PXZ as one of the inventors in the patent application. It is assumed that the research was conducted by the employees of M-University, who contributed to the creation of the invention with their intellectual work, while PXZ did not actively cooperate at the research stage, but was only involved through financial donations. Taking this into consideration, it can be understood that on this basis alone, PXZ does not have the right to file a patent application.

According to Article 74(1) IPA, a patent shall be granted to the person who is designated as the applicant at the time of the grant. In this case, the inventor is the person at the institute who actually created the invention, as well as the manager of PXZ based on the contractual relationship between them. Under Slovenian patent law, there are actually no obstacles that would prevent PXZ from filing a patent application and obtaining the patent, of course, as long as it would be able to compose a complete or correct patent application, including a description of the invention, sketches and the like. A patent application may be filed by any legal entity or private individual, who can subsequently also be the owner of the patent. For the granting of a patent, there are important substantial requirements prescribed by the law[69] (Art. 10 IPA and Art. 3 RLPB), among which there are no substantive or other requirements, which apply to the actual inventor or applicant. During the procedure of granting the patent, SIPO examines all formal and substantial requirements. In accordance with the formal requirements, SIPO must examine whether the application contains all the required items (request for the granting of the patent, a description of the invention, patent claims, a summary of the invention, sketches), power of attorney of a representative, the

[69] Provisions of Art. 10 IPA and Art. 3 RLPBI.

text of the application in Slovenian, and evidence of fee payment (Art. 85 IPA).[70] In accordance with the so-called simplified registration procedure, SIPO examines whether the subject matter of the claimed patent is patentable and whether the claimed invention meets, at first sight, the requirements in terms of novelty, inventiveness and industrial application (Art. 88 IPA).[71] If all the requirements are met, the patent application is published and the patent is granted. Because of the simplified patent registration procedure, there is no objection procedure in the Slovenian legislation. Therefore, M-University cannot prevent the patent from being granted for the sole reason that under the provisions of University Guidelines particularly significant inventions shall remain in the public domain and be used to the greatest extent possible.

The true inventor may file an action once the patent has been granted. To avoid abuse, the IPA gives protection to the true inventor, who may, on the basis of Article 115(1) IPA, challenge the ownership of the patent. The inventor (the individual who created the invention) or his/her heir or legal successor in title – thus, also M-University – is able to challenge the ownership of the patent, as long as PXZ is not the inventor,[72] his/her heir or legal successor in title. In the event that the lawsuit is successful, the institute shall be entered into the register as the owner of the patent, through which it will be able to renounce the enforcement of patent rights and, through this, achieve extensive use of the invention. Of course, there is also the possibility to renounce not only the enforcement but the patent itself (subparagraph a, Art. 77IPA). Alternatively, on the basis of Article 117 IPA, the right may also be removed from the register, if the successful plaintiff does not submit a request to be entered in the register within three months from the receipt of the final judgment. In this event, SIPO shall *ex officio* remove the right from the register (Art. 117(2) IPA).

III. Metalegal Formants

Patent law's goal is to incentivise inventions. The regulatory system assumes the ubiquitous desirability of holding a patent. While the option of renouncement is reflected in the freedom not to apply and in the regulations on fees, the system as a whole assumes the desirability as a rule.

---

70 These requirements are defined in more detail in the Rules on the Contents of the Patent Application and on the Division of Patents.

71 Owners of patents or exclusive rights from patents shall submit to SIPO no later than the end of the ninth year of the patent term written evidence that the patented invention satisfies all the substantive requirements prescribed by the IPA. A Slovenian translation of a European patent or several European patents granted for the same invention by the European Patent Office, or if no application for a European patent has been filed for the same invention, the Slovenian translation of a patent for the same invention granted following substantive examination by another authority which under Art. 32 of the Patent Cooperation Treaty enjoys the status of an International Preliminary Examining authority or by any other patent office with which a relevant treaty has been concluded, shall be considered as such evidence (Arts. 91 and 92 IPA).

72 An individual who only financially contributes to the creation of an invention is not the inventor. M.S. Marković, *Patentno parvo* (Beograd: 1997), p. 140.

(15) SPAIN

I. Operative Rules

M-University may challenge the patent.

II. Descriptive Formants

As a basic principle, Article 20.1 Patent Law provides that 'ownership of inventions made by a professor as a result of his research responsibilities in a university and which come within the scope of his teaching and research functions shall belong to the university'. In the present case, the invention is a property held in common by M-University and PXZ, thus parties have the right to obtain and exploit a patent jointly.

When M-University refuses to apply for a patent, a conflict arises between the parties. Article 10.2 Patent Law recognises that the right to obtain a patent shall belong to them jointly. In order to grant a licence, an agreement between the parties is required by Article 72.3 Patent Law. Therefore, it has to be concluded that M-University had a claim against PXZ because the consent of M-University is required.[73] Should the parties not reach an agreement to solve this issue, M-University may take its claim to the courts of law.[74]

III. Metalegal Formants

Spanish patent law is silent about the conflict at hand. On face value, it gives priority to the co-inventor as far as the application is concerned, but it then forces them to find agreement when it comes to licensing. While patent law provides exclusions to patentability (theories, discoveries, etc.), deliberate non-patenting of patentable subject matter for the sake of wide distribution would be protected as 'individual will' under general rules of private law.

(16) UNITED KINGDOM

I. Operative Rules

If PXZ is 'co-inventor' in law, it is entitled to apply for a patent; however, it is not entitled to exploit it without the consent of the University.

---

73 See T. Vazquez Lépinette, *La cotitularidad de los bienes inmateriales* (Valencia: 1996), p. 86.

74 Ibid., p. 87.

II. Descriptive Formants

Supposing PXZ's contribution to the patented invention did not meet the statutory definition of a joint inventor (see s. 7(3) PA 1977), PXZ does not have the right to apply for a patent on its own.

The University can ensure that 'Specifically Important Developments' are not patented by deliberately putting relevant information into the public domain. Since the UK does not recognise a 'grace period', any information publicly made available destroys the invention's 'novelty' and/or an 'inventive step'.

Supposing PXZ was a co-inventor of the inventive concept, and the University had forgotten to disclose the information of the Guidelines on 'Specifically Important Developments', then the question is whether PXZ can apply for a patent without the consent of the University as co-inventor.

Section 7(1) PA 1977 states that any person can apply for a patent (without the consent of another person), and the patent can then be granted to the co-inventors, or persons entitled via section 7(2), for example their employers. In that circumstance, the University might find itself the owner of a patent which it did not want. Noting that section 36(3)(b) provides that a licence can only be granted with the consent of all owners, the University could prevent PXZ from licensing the invention unless the University also agrees to the terms of the licence. For example, the University might agree to a licence similar to an Open Access licence for research in the public interest.

Supposing PXZ and the University are at a stalemate and no licences are agreed:

- the University itself can use the patented invention without PXZ's consent (see s. 36(2) PA 1977);
- PXZ can use the patented invention with the University's consent (see s. 36(2) PA 1977). But since it is merely a patient organisation, it probably does not have the ability to research with, develop or commercialise the invention;
- PXZ can bring infringement proceedings against *other persons* it alleges have infringed the patents (see s. 66(2) PA 1997). PXZ is required to make the University a party to the proceedings. The University is not required to put in an appearance or to take part. If it does not, it is not liable for costs orders. This is the relevant provision, section 66(2):

> One of two or more joint proprietors of a patent may without the concurrence of the others bring proceedings in respect of an act alleged to infringe the patent, but shall not do so unless the others are made parties to the proceedings; but any of the others made a defendant or defender shall not be liable for any costs or expenses unless he enters an appearance and takes part in the proceedings.

III. Metalegal Formants

Unless PXZ agreed to the said University Guidelines, it remains free to apply for a patent (as the co-inventor). The law thus secures the inventor's rights. But since the exploitation of co-owned patents requires consent from all parties, an agreement will still be required to exploit the patent.

D.3. COMPARATIVE REMARKS

As to the operative formants, M-University can challenge the patent in four jurisdictions; in 11 jurisdictions, it can only – against its expressed interest – claim joint ownership in the patent (but contractual remedies might help). One report did not submit an answer to this case. The reports are largely silent about the normative standing of their jurisdiction towards the collision of the interests of the two non-economic actors involved. PXZ aspires to patent property for strategic reasons as a patient organisation; the University aspires to live up to its mission as a knowledge-diffusing institution. Many reports, however, focus narrowly on co-ownership. The central question of how the internal University Guidelines (co-inventorship assumed) affect the eligibility to file a patent application is seldomly discussed. The German report argues that the internal guidelines of the public University enjoy precedence over PXZ's freedom to file for a patent, based on the argument that PXZ must have known about this restriction since these guidelines are publicly available. However, this argument can only be brought as a contractual agreement, not as an argument to invalidate the patent. While both actors have no direct exploitive interest – the presumed core of the statutory incentive of IP – they pursue interests on the fringes of their own institutional interest and public interests. PXZ wants to hold the patent in order to have a say in future pharmaceutical exploitation to improve patients' rights. The University believes in the classical academic norm of a beneficial public domain. The UK report mentions that the university can sabotage the application if it publishes relevant information before the application is filed. It seems that neither patent law nor contract law provide a language to reflect the normative conflict embedded in this modification.

CASE 14. OPEN ACCESS – CREATIVE COMMONS

A.1. BASE CASE

From 1980 to 2004, Dr Silver and his colleagues have published their scientific articles in the periodicals of 'Big Publishing House, Inc.'. For the publication of each article, 'Big Publishing House, Inc.' required that the authors transfer 'all rights with respect to modes of exploitation now known or to be discovered' to the publisher. In 2004, Dr Silver, along with several of his colleagues, stopped publishing their scientific findings with 'Big Publishing House, Inc.' in reaction to the publisher's very strict licensing conditions. They now decide to make all their publications available on their institute's webpage under a Creative Commons Attribution-NonCommercial-ShareAlike licence. Not only do they make their most recent articles available on the website, they also include the full text of the articles that were previously published by 'Big Publishing House, Inc.'. On the website, the papers are freely accessible, provided that the user accepts the licence conditions by clicking 'I agree' in the dialogue box on their screen. Contrary to the licence used by 'Big Publishing House, Inc.', the Creative Commons licence allows authors to publish their work on the Internet, and to use it for any purpose, including for educational purposes. The licence also allows anyone to reproduce, modify and communicate the paper freely for strictly non-commercial purposes, provided that proper credit is given, and that any redistribution of the paper occurs under the same licence conditions.

'Big Publishing House, Inc.' has got wind of Dr Silver's action and claims an injunction against the making available of the articles on the website. Will an injunction be granted?

A.2. COUNTRY REPORTS

(1) BELGIUM

I. Operative Rules

'Big Publishing House, Inc.' will not be granted an injunction.

II. *Descriptive Formants*

The final paragraph of Article 3§1 BCA (Art. XI.167§1 6° BCEL) states: 'Notwithstanding any provision to the contrary, the assignment of rights in respect of as yet unknown forms of exploitation shall be null and void.' The clause obliging authors to transfer their rights on modes of exploitation yet to be discovered will therefore be null in Belgium. It depends on the specific wording of the contract whether or not online publishing is foreseen. In addition, and according to Article 3§1 3° BCA (Art. XI.167§1 3° BCEL), 'contractual provisions relating to copyright and to its modes of exploitation shall be interpreted restrictively' in favour of the author.[1] It can be debated when exactly online publishing became a known form of exploitation, but chances are that in 1980, at least, online publications would not have constituted such a known form of exploitation.

Under the old Copyright Act of 1886,[2] however, clauses assigning rights for unknown forms of exploitation were possible. Therefore, contracts falling under the scope of the old Copyright Act, i.e. contracts dating from before 1 August 1994 (when the new Copyright Act entered into force), can validly transfer the rights on future forms of exploitation.[3]

Therefore, if the contract had been concluded before 1994, 'Big Publishing House, Inc.' would be entitled to claim an injunction against Dr Silver's actions. If the contract was concluded after 1994, the clause transferring 'all rights with respect to modes of exploitation now known *or to be discovered*' would be invalid. Post-1994, however, it is possible online publication would already be considered a known form of exploitation.

In any event, under current Belgian copyright law, a clause transferring the rights on modes of exploitation yet to be discovered would be null.

III. *Metalegal Formants*

The Belgian rule prohibiting the transfer of future modes of exploitation has to be seen in the context of the differences in negotiating power between author and publisher. Authors being traditionally the weaker party, the Belgian legislator has deemed it necessary to protect them. In pursuit of this objective, Article 3 BCA (Art. XI.167 BCEL) contains some provisions which are intended

---

1 F. de Visscher and B. Michaux, *Précis du droit d'auteur et des droits voisins [Manual Copyright and Neighbouring Rights]* (Brussels: 2000), 316–328.

2 Copyright Law, 22 March 1886, *Official Gazette*, 26 March 1886 [Auteurswet, 22 maart 1886, *B.S.*, 26 maart 1886].

3 A. Berenboom, *Le nouveau droit d'auteur et les droits voisins [The New Copyright and the Neighbouring Rights]*, collection Création Information Communication [Creation Information Communication] (Brussels: 2005), 43–44 and 217–218.

to help authors negotiate a 'good deal'. The aim is to respect contract freedom, but to also ensure that authors are fully aware of the implications of a contract and to avoid the author giving a 'blank cheque' to the publisher.[4] In this regard, all contracts need to be in written format in order to prove the agreed upon provisions. Moreover, the author's contractual obligations need to be interpreted restrictively. In addition, for each mode of remuneration of exploitation, the scope and duration of the assignment has to be set out explicitly. Finally, the assignment of rights in respect of as yet unknown forms of exploitation shall be null and void, notwithstanding any provision to the contrary.[5] These principles are well confirmed by Belgian case law.[6]

Concerning the legal provision on the assignment of as yet unknown forms of exploitation, Belgian copyright law is quite strict in comparison with, for example, France and the Netherlands, although the consequences are mitigated to some extent, since employees, commission contracts and audio-visual works fall under the more flexible provisions of Article 3§3 BCA (Art. XI.167§3 BCEL).[7]

An advantage of Article 3 BCA (Art. XI.167 BCEL) is that when a publisher is exploiting a work in a way that is not satisfactory to the author, the latter can always decide to start exercising the other modes of exploitation still in his/her possession.[8]

(2) CZECH REPUBLIC

I. Operative Rules

The injunction will be granted.

---

4 Report De Clerck, Bill on Copyright and Neighbouring Rights, *Parl. Doc.*, Chambre, Special Session 1991/1992, DOC 48 473/33, 90 [Verslag De Clerck bij het wetsontwerp betreffende het auteursrecht en de naburige rechten, *Parl. St.*, Kamer, B.Z. 91/92, DOC 48 473/33, 90], available at: www.dekamer.be (last consulted 6 May 2019).

5 For instance: F. de Visscher and B. Michaux, *Précis du droit d'auteur et des droits voisins [Manual Copyright and Neighbouring Rights]* (Brussels: 2000), 319–320.

6 Court of Appeal Brussels (9th Chamber), 28 October 1997 ('Central Station'), *A&M* 1997, 383, note Voorhoof, *I.R.D.I.* 1998, 44, note Janssens, *Pas.* 1996, II, 94; and Court of Appeal Brussels (9th Chamber), 25 September 2001, *A&M* 2004, no. 4, 327.

7 A. Berenboom, *Le nouveau droit d'auteur et les droits voisins [The New Copyright and the Neighbouring Rights]*, collection Création Information Communication [Creation Information Communication] (Brussels: 2005), 217–218.

8 Report De Clerck, Bill on Copyright and Neighbouring Rights, *Parl. Doc.*, Chambre, Special Session 1991/1992, DOC 48 473/33, 90 [Verslag De Clerck bij het wetsontwerp betreffende het auteursrecht en de naburige rechten, *Parl. St.*, Kamer, B.Z. 91/92, DOC 48 473/33, 90], available at: www.dekamer.be (last consulted 6 May 2019), 93.

II. *Descriptive Formants*

a) Contracts concluded within the period 1980 to 30 November 2000

First of all, it will be necessary to find out whether the contracts concluded between Dr Silver and 'Big Publishing House, Inc.' on or before 30 November 2000 met mandatory legal requirements as provided by the Copyright Act 35/1965 Coll. If the contracts did not meet strict legal requirements as mentioned above, then the contracts are invalid *ex tunc* and 'Big Publishing House, Inc.' would not be able to claim an injunction.

It will also be necessary to establish the duration of the contractual relations, distinguishing the time period when the mode of distribution of the articles by means of the Internet was not known from the period when this mode of distribution was known.

In the period when the Internet was not known as a mode of distribution of the articles, the contracts concluded between Dr Silver and 'Big Publishing House, Inc.' shall not be applicable. As mentioned above, Dr Silver is not entitled to transfer rights which may arise in future. In this case, the contracts are invalid in relation to the mode of exploitation to be discovered and 'Big Publishing House, Inc.' has no right to distribute articles via the Internet (by publishing the articles on a website). An injunction shall not be granted against making the articles available on the website.

Ever since the Internet was known as a mode of distribution of the articles and the contracts were concluded in accordance with mandatory provisions of the Copyright Act 35/1965 Coll., then 'Big Publishing House, Inc.' would be able to claim an injunction in accordance with section 494 of the Civil Code. According to this provision, the author is in the position of the debtor[9] and he/she has to refrain from distributing his/her articles. In this case, an injunction shall be granted against making the articles available on the website.

b) Contracts concluded within the period 1 December 2000 to 2004

In this period, without a doubt, distribution of the articles via the Internet is a known mode of distribution, so it will not be a question here. Moreover, the mandatory provisions of the Copyright Act are not such a burden for parties to meet the legal requirements to conclude a valid contract. It will only be necessary to have a contract in writing; otherwise, according to section 46(4) Copyright Act, the licence will be a non-exclusive licence and under section 50 Copyright Act will expire after one year.

According to the provisions of section 47(2) Copyright Act, Dr Silver has to refrain from exercising his right to use the work in the way for which he granted a licence to 'Big Publishing House, Inc.'. Dr Silver is also not entitled to grant a

[9] Dr Silver is in the position of the debtor in this case and 'Big Publishing House, Inc.' is in the position of the creditor – Dr Silver was paid for the transfer of rights (credit) and now he has to refrain from distributing his articles (debt).

licence to any third person. In fact, Dr Silver transferred exclusive rights to use the work in any known method of exploitation and accordingly an injunction will be granted against making the articles available on the website.

III. Metalegal Formants

Czech copyright law is all about the freedom of contract. Thus, broad contractual transfers are accepted. Little protection against power imbalances is granted.

(3) DENMARK

I. Operative Rules

'Big Publishing House, Inc.' possibly has a claim for injunction.

II. Descriptive Formants

'All rights' transfers may be challenged under the general prohibition against unreasonable contracts in §36 of the Act relating to Conclusion of Contracts (DACC, 26 August 1996). Moreover, principles of interpretation of contracts, including the so-called specification principle (DCA §53(3)), may lead to a narrowing of the scope of the contract. Danish courts have been rather reluctant to apply §36 to set aside copyright contracts as long as the obligations are not blatantly unreasonable or highly unusual. Even though the present contract is arguably far reaching, it would seem to be rather unlikely that a Danish court would find the present agreement to be invalid.

III. Metalegal Formants

Danish copyright law does not seem to regulate the imbalance of negotiating strength between the original author and publishers, with a few exceptions. In 2006, a proposal to amend the DCA to include 'German-style' contractual provisions to strengthen the contractual position of authors vis-à-vis publishers was put forward (Report No. 1480 to the Parliament on the revision of the DCA). So far, the proposal has had no effect.

(4) ESTONIA

I. Operative Rules

'Big Publishing House, Inc.' will be granted an injunction against Dr Silver.

II. *Descriptive Formants*

According to the Copyright Act, '[a]n author shall enjoy the exclusive right to use the author's work in any manner, to authorise or prohibit the use of the work in a similar manner by other persons'.[10] The Copyright Act also provides that '[t]he economic rights of an author are transferable as single rights or a set of rights for a charge or free of charge'.[11]

Dr Silver and his colleagues transferred their economic rights to 'Big Publishing House, Inc.' from 1980 to 2004.[12] The right of making the work available to the public[13] was included in the catalogue of an author's economic rights on 29 October 2004.[14] This poses the question of whether the broad transfer including future exploitations is allowed. Estonian copyright experts support the position that it is possible to transfer and license the right to use a work in a way which is unknown at the time of the conclusion of the author's contract.[15] Therefore, the transfer of 'all rights with respect to modes of exploitation now known or to be discovered' to the publisher is legally valid under the Copyright Act.

By making all their publications available on their institute's webpage, Dr Silver and his colleagues violate the publisher's rights. Publications in respect of which rights have not been transferred can freely be used (e.g. uploaded in the Internet) by Dr Silver and his colleagues.

'Big Publishing House, Inc.' has several options for how to react. Making publications available on the webpage involves uploading. Uploading is deemed to be a criminal offence. Pursuant to §222(1) of the Penal Code, '[r]eproduction, with the intention of distribution, of a work or an object of copyright without the permission of the author of the work, the holder of the copyright or the holder of the related rights is punishable by a pecuniary punishment or up to 3 years' imprisonment'.

---

10 Copyright Act §13(1).

11 Copyright Act §11(3).

12 The analysis of the case is limited to the legal framework created by the Estonian Copyright Act, which entered into force on 12 December 1992.

13 Pursuant to §13(1) clause 9^1 of the Copyright Act, '[t]he author's rights shall include the right to authorise or prohibit making the work available to the public in such a way that persons may access the work from a place and at a time individually chosen by them (right of making the work available to the public)'. H. Pisuke characterises the right of making the work available to the public as an Internet environment right which was included in the Copyright Act as a requirement of the Directive 2001/29/EC – H. Pisuke, *Autoriõiguse alused* (Copyright Basics) (Tallinn: 2006), p. 41.

14 Autoriõiguse seaduse muutmise seadus. Entered into force on 29 October 2004 – RT I 2004, 71, 500 (in Estonian). Available at https://www.riigiteataja.ee/ert/act.jsp?id=807257 (5 May 2019).

15 See A. Kalvi, 'Autorilepingu uus kuub' (New skin of author's contracts), (2003) 4 *Juridica*, pp. 250–260, pp. 251, 257 (in Estonian); P. Varul, I. Kull, V. Kõve, M. Käerdi, *Võlaõigusseadus II. Kommenteeritud väljaanne* (Law of Obligations Act II. Commented edition), Parts 2–7 (§§208–618) (Tallinn: 2007), p. 337 (in Estonian).

The violation of the right of making the work available to the public (an economic right) constitutes a misdemeanour. According to §81^4(1) Copyright Act, violation of the economic rights is punishable by a fine of up to 300 fine units.[16]

'Big Publishing House, Inc.' can also use civil remedies to address the issue of unauthorised publication of the articles on the web. Subsection 81^7(1) Copyright Act provides that in the case of the unlawful use of a work or an object of related rights, the author or holder of related rights may, *inter alia*, claim compensation for damages, termination of the unlawful use of a work or an object of related rights, and delivery of that which was received by way of the unlawful use of a work or an object of related rights. These claims are made pursuant to the Law of Obligations Act.

III. Metalegal Formants

The Estonian Copyright Act entered into force on 12 December 1992. The legal issues related to works created before that date are very complicated. Although the Copyright Act also extends to works which were created before 12 December 1992 (§88(1) Copyright Act), this has not solved all problems. It is important to bear in mind that Estonia regained its independence on 20 August 1991. Before that time, the legal and economic systems were completely different.

(5) FRANCE

I. Operative Rules

The clause assigning the author's rights is not valid; an injunction will not be granted.

II. Descriptive Formants

'Big Publishing House, Inc.' considers that Dr Silver has infringed its rights. The issue that may be discussed concerns the assignment's validity. Indeed, the fact that the authors transfer 'all rights with respect to modes of exploitation now known or to be discovered' to the publisher may be considered as being contrary to French copyright law.

The transfer of author's rights must respect some legal forms. Article L. 131-3 of the French Intellectual Property Code provides: 'Transfer of authors' rights shall be subject to each of the assigned rights being separately mentioned in the instrument of assignment and the field of exploitation of the assigned rights

16 Pursuant to §47(1) of the Penal Code, a fine unit is equal to 60 Estonian kroons.

being defined as to its scope and purpose, as to place and as to duration.' Thus, Dr Silver may argue that the contract transferring his rights is null because the assignment is not specific enough about which right is transferred, and as to which place and duration. In particular, one may consider that the field of exploitation is not defined.

But the 'modes of exploitation now known or to be discovered' stipulation may be valid considering Article L. 131-6, which provides that '[a]ny assignment clause affording the right to exploit a work in a form that is unforeseeable and not foreseen on the date of the contract shall be explicit', under the condition that it 'stipulate(s) participation correlated to the profits from exploitation.'

III. Metalegal Formants

Under the French Intellectual Property Code, the author's rights assignment will be considered null, particularly because the field of exploitation is not defined strictly enough.

(6) GERMANY

I. Operative Rules

'Big Publishing House, Inc.' has no right to an injunction for articles published between 1984 and 1995 but does have a right to an injunction for articles published between 1995 and 2004. (After 2013, the publisher's right is limited in duration to one year if the publication resulted from research activities at least half of which were financed by public funds – information which is not included in the base case.)

II. Descriptive Formants

The rights to reproduce, to publish and to make available were transferred to 'Big Publishing House, Inc.' by Dr Silver (§§15, 16, 17 UrhG). The right to make available, since 2003 explicitly recognised in §19a UrhG, was covered by §15 UrhG. However, two different questions are to be distinguished. Was the right to publish the articles on the Internet also transferred at that time – despite the fact that the possibility was not yet even envisioned? Does such a broad transfer of rights amount to a 'future right' of which the transfer is restricted (§40 UrhG: indispensable right to terminate after five years) or an 'unknown use' which cannot be transferred at all (§31 sec. 4 UrhG)?

According to the so-called '*Zweckübertragungslehre*' (doctrine of transfer tied to the purpose), rights are only transferred as far as necessary for the purpose of the contract. Internet publication is an independent way of making use of one's copyright, available only since 1995.[17] The purpose was the publication of periodicals. Online publication in science became widespread no earlier than 1995. Acknowledging the principle that 'in doubt the right rests with the author',[18] at least for the articles dating from between 1980 and 1995 the right to publish on the Internet was not transferred.[19]

For the time period between 1995 and 2004, things are different. 'Big Publishing House, Inc.' had required the transfer of all rights for each article. At that time, digital publication was a known and viable form of publication. The transfer was necessary for the purpose of the contract (the exploitation of the copyright), and the digital publication did not come as a surprise to the author. Therefore, the rights for online publication were transferred.

After 2013, the legal situation changed due to the newly introduced §38(4) UrhG,[20] which limits the right of the publisher to one year if the 'scientific contribution resulted from research activities at least half of which were financed by public funds *and* which was reprinted in a collection which is published periodically at least twice per year'. Then, the author 'has the right, if he has granted the publisher or editor an exclusive right of use, to make the contribution available to the public upon expiry of 12 months after first publication in the accepted manuscript version, unless this serves a commercial purpose. The source of the first publication must be cited. Any deviating agreement to the detriment of the author shall be ineffective.'

III. Metalegal Formants

With Internet publication conceived of as a 'new use', German law pressures publishers to renegotiate old, persistent contracts.[21]

---

17 Acknowledged timeline for digital newspaper in OLG Hamburg, ZUM 2000, 870 – *digitaz*; less precise in respect of a time threshold: LG München, I ZUM 2003, 64 – *Pumuckl*; for a timeline open to interpretation OLG Hamburg, decision of 24 February 2005 (5 U 62/04), No. 21 et seq. – *Yachtarchiv*. See for this *problematique* in general T. Dreier, in: T. Dreier and G. Schulze (eds.), *UrhG-Commentary* (6th ed., Munich: 2018), §19a, No. 12.

18 G. Schulze, in: T. Dreier and G. Schulze, in: T. Dreier and G. Schulze (eds.), *UrhG-Commentary* (6th ed., Munich: 2018), §31, No. 110; BGH, GRUR 1984, 119 – *Synchronisationsspeicher*; BGH, ZUM 1998, 500 – *Comic Übersetzungen*.

19 This reasoning is in line with cases like background music vis-à-vis concert rights: BGH, GRUR 1971, 480 – *Schwarzwaldfahrt*.

20 BGBl. 2013 I S. 3728.

21 For the transfer of collecting societies this renegotiation has been done through the adjustment of their constitions, see T. Dreier, in: T. Dreier and G. Schulze (eds.), *UrhG-Commentary* (6th ed., Munich: 2018), §19a, No. 12.

(7) GREECE

I. Operative Rules

The publisher may claim an injunction against the author.

II. Descriptive Formants

The publication in question on the part of the author of an intellectual work for which he/she has already given a licence for exploitation to another party is prohibited. Naturally, the clause to the effect that the author (Dr Silver) transfers to 'Big Publishing House, Inc.' any right over his intellectual ownership of his articles is invalid, since it is not permitted for the creator to be totally alienated from his/her intellectual property, but only to the extent that the alienation serves the purpose of the licence ('principle of the purpose').[22] However, this does not mean that it is not permitted for exclusive rights over specific methods of exploitation of the work to be transferred. The question is whether or not making an electronic version of the article available on a scientific website constitutes a form of exploitation tantamount to publication in a scientific journal. An affirmative reply seems more likely, since the consumer public has access alternatively and on the same terms to either the one or the other means of publication (journal or website).

III. Metalegal Formants

The publisher will be legitimated in claiming an injunction against the author, probably both by virtue of the absolute right of exploitation ceded to him/her and contractually for compliance with the obligation of trust entailed according to Article 288 Civil Code, that is, here, the obligation of non-competition.

(8) IRELAND

I. Operative Rules

An injunction will be granted.

II. Descriptive Formants

Dr Silver is entitled to publish any new works under a Creative Commons licence, which will bind users both under contract and copyright law, also encompassing

[22] Koumantos, *Copyright Law* (Athens/Komotini: 1991), pp. 57, 169, 204–205, 228; Kotsiris, *Copyright Law*, (2017), p. 75; Kallinikou, *The Fundamental Issues of L. 2121/1993 for the Law of Copyright* (Athens: 1994), nos. 121, 128; Goldbaum, *Urheberrecht und Urhebervertragsrecht* (Baden-Baden: 1961), pp. 75 ff.

moral rights, in Ireland. Copyright owners may make a full or partial copyright assignment under CRRA 2000, section 120. However, Dr Silver is violating the copyright which he assigned to 'Big Publishing House, Inc.' in his previous work. BPH will be entitled to an injunction.

Anyone seeking to rely on fair dealing for educational purposes under the CRRA 2000 would be advised to bear in mind that simultaneous distribution of more than one copy is not permitted under section 50(4). Moreover, in order to avail of this exception, the work would have to have been made available lawfully in the first place, which is not the case here.

III. Metalegal Formants

While copyright law got adapted to digitalisation in various forms, the technology has not changed basic rules of property assignment and contracts.

(9) ITALY

I. Operative Rules

No injunction may be granted, especially for the oldest articles.

II. Descriptive Formants

First of all, the provision on transferring every IP right relating to modes of exploitation yet to be discovered is to be considered completely invalid under Italian law (see Article 119 c., 3 ICL). The principle of independence of rights states that only the rights required to fulfil the contractual obligations are intended to be transferred, while any other right remains in the author's domain (Art. 19 ICL). It is assumed that the parties did not intend to transfer digital reproduction rights and that they did not know about the Internet as a form of dissemination of content when they started their contract. The point is to know (or state) when the internet can be considered to be a normal medium of communication. Thus, for the articles published in the periodicals of 'Big Publishing House, Inc.' between the date when the Internet became a normal medium of exploitation and 2004, there is some chance that the publishing house might have a remedy based on breach of contract, but without a specific contractual provision it will not be easy to prove it.

Furthermore, it is worth noting that a publishing contract without any time limit is *ex lege* integrated with a maximum term of 20 years (Art. 122 c.5, ICL). If the contract's object is works to be created, then the term is reduced to 10 years (Art. 120 c.2 ICL). So, again, it is quite likely that the article published in the 1980s is freely re-publishable by the authors.

Finally, if not *explicitly* stated, the publishing contract does not transfer any right to derivative works or transformation of the work, including adaptations to cinematography, broadcasting and recordings on mechanical devices (Art. 119 c.4 ICL). Accordingly, as far as the digitalisation of a work can be considered a derivative work or a transformation of the work, we can discount 'Big Publishing House, Inc.' ever having owned any such rights if not explicitly mentioned in the contract.

III. Metalegal Formants

Scholars are debating whether or not digitalisation should be considered a transformation-derivation of a work. Because the Internet is a relatively new medium in Italy – much more so than in other countries – this debate is strictly connected with Italian idiosyncrasies. In any case, any transfer of exploitation rights under Italian law (the LDA) is to be interpreted restrictively in terms of which rights are transferred. In fact, only the rights strictly necessary for the achievement of the scope of the contract are intended to be transferred, while any other right remains at the author's disposal.[23]

(10) LITHUANIA

I. Operative Rules

'Big Publishing House, Inc.' possibly has a claim for injunction with respect to some publications, published after 1999.

II. Descriptive Formants

While the precise answer is heavily dependent on the facts, in particular on the content and concrete circumstances of the contracts made between Dr Silver and 'Big Publishing House, Inc.' (which also means that each separate agreement should be analysed individually and the outcomes will not necessarily lead to the same result), some generalisations can be made.

It is important to note that during the time period provided in the description of the case, the Lithuanian regulation has radically changed due to the transition from the collapsed Soviet system to a market-oriented one. Therefore, it is important to make a distinction between the regulation in force from 1980 to 9 June 1999 and from 9 June 1999 to 2004.

---

[23] See Art. 119 §5 ICL, which reflects in our system the so-called *Zweckuebertragungstheorie*.

a) Period from 1980 to 9 June 1999

During the first period, copyright contracts, including, in particular, publishing contracts, were regulated by the Lithuanian Civil Code of 1964, Chapter 45. Under the Civil Code (Art. 543), two types of copyright contracts were possible: (1) copyright contracts regarding the use of a work; and (2) licence contracts. The situation under discussion should be qualified as a copyright contract regarding the use of a work, more specifically as publishing contract, which was defined separately in Article 544 of the Lithuanian Civil Code.

It could be argued that the old regulation did not contain the special norms preventing transfer of rights with respect to unknown forms of exploitation, and that in principle such a contractual clause was valid. Arguably, however, that position is not accurate and the more correct approach is that during the Soviet period (i.e. until 1990), copyright contracts were always limited to particular identified uses needed to achieve the purpose of the contract. In addition, it should be noted that all publishing contracts were based on standard contracts, affirmed by the Soviet government (it should also be recalled that during the Soviet period all publishers were state-owned and private publishers were non-existent). Furthermore, Article 549 of the Lithuanian Civil Code prescribed that the author was only temporarily restricted from authorising third persons to use the work in the same manner (by default, three years). This leads to the conclusion that authors never really assigned their rights to publishers. As a result, even without the special restrictive provisions, the copyright/publishing system as a whole operated in this way, which led to the restricted scope of contracts (the formula 'all rights with respect to modes of exploitation now known or to be discovered' itself would have been highly unlikely in this period) and rights to unknown forms of exploitation could not be contractually transferred to a publisher. As publication on the Internet was unknown during most of this period, it could not be included in the contract between Dr Silver and 'Big Publishing House, Inc.'. Therefore 'Big Publishing House, Inc.' has no right to publish on the Internet and, accordingly, no valid claim against Dr Silver.

b) Period from 9 June 1999 to 2004

During the second period, the regulation significantly changed. Chapter 45 of the Civil Code was repealed and the Copyright Act entered into force. On the one hand, the total transfer of exclusive rights was clearly recognised (Art. 38(2) of the Copyright Act). On the other hand, a wide spectrum of restrictions was introduced, aimed at strengthening the position of authors. These provisions included the impossibility of transferring the rights with respect to unknown forms of exploitation. Another important provision of the Copyright Act is the purpose-based interpretation rule of copyright contracts, which states: 'It shall be presumed that under a copyright agreement only as many rights are transferred as are necessary for the accomplishment of the purposes of a concrete agreement'.[24] This rule is accepted and elaborated in the Lithuanian case law, which points to the narrow reading of copyright transfers and prioritises the interests of authors.[25] Therefore, the clause of 'Big Publishing House, Inc.' concerning the transfer of all future and unknown uses would be invalid and cannot be enforced.

Importantly, Lithuanian courts also apply the above-mentioned rules of contract interpretation to the copyright contracts concluded before 9 June 1999.

c) General assessment

As it is clear that publication on the Internet (and the possibility to make a work available on the Internet in general) was not known during most of the period, rights to such uses could not be transferred to 'Big Publishing House, Inc.' and the courts will not enforce the contractual clause against Dr Silver.

Having said that, some chances remain that towards the end of the period, when Internet publishing started to emerge and the right of making available to the public was introduced in Lithuanian copyright law in 1999, the courts *may* have considered this new mode of exploitation to be included in the contract (explicitly or implicitly). In the latter scenario, 'Big Publishing House, Inc.' has a right to claim violation of its public communication right (of which making available to the public is a part) and ask for an injunction.[26]

III. Metalegal Formants

Despite having a very similar history to Estonia and, to a lesser degree, Poland or the Czech Republic, after 1990 significant regulatory differences started to emerge. One of these is a more author-protective view (similarly to Poland, but differently from Estonia). Therefore, both before the Copyright Act was enacted and after, Lithuanian copyright contract law contains many elements which protect the interests of authors and their position is relatively well protected.

(11) NETHERLANDS

I. Operative Rules

No injunction will be granted for the articles published before 1993 and, depending on the facts, no injunction would be granted at all if the articles are the result of publicly funded research.

---

24 Art. 40(2) Copyright Act.

25 Ruling of 27 December 2012 of the Civil Division of the Supreme Court of Lithuania in case No. 3K-3-610/2012.

26 Art. 77 Copyright Act.

II. Descriptive Formants

In any case, 'Big Publishing House, Inc.' would be denied an injunction to stop the online publication of all articles published before 1993. The court's decision would be based on Article 2 of the Dutch Copyright Act, which states that 'the assignment shall comprise only such rights as are recorded in the deed or necessarily derive from the nature or purpose of the title'. This provision is regarded as establishing in Dutch law the German doctrine known as *Zweckübertragungstheorie.* According to the District Court of Amsterdam in the *Volkskrant* case,[27] Article 2 of the Copyright Act should be interpreted as not encompassing forms of exploitation that were still unknown at the time of conclusion of the contract. In practice, courts and scholars have agreed that the forms of online exploitation of works were unknown prior to 1993. As they are deemed known after 1993, the transfer of rights in favour of 'Big Publishing House, Inc.' in the more recent articles would be valid and an injunction would be available.

If applicable, Article 25fa of the Dutch Copyright Act could be invoked to block an injunction by 'Big Publishing House, Inc.' against Dr Silver. This provision states:

> The author of a short scientific work, the research for which was paid for in whole or in part from Dutch public funds, is entitled to make that work available to the public for no consideration following a reasonable period of time after the work was first disclosed to the public, provided that clear reference is made to the source of that first disclosure of the work to the public.

Even if Dr Silver has granted 'Big Publishing House, Inc.' a full transfer of rights in the articles, he has the right, pursuant to Article 25fa Dutch Copyright Act, to make them available on his institutional repository, provided that the research which led to the publication of these articles was paid for in whole or in part from Dutch public funds. The source of financing for Dr Silver's research is not mentioned in the case. If Dr Silver wrote his articles thanks to a research grant offered by the government, he would definitely be able to invoke this provision. On the other hand, if he wrote his articles on the basis of his regular salary paid by the University, his research would most likely qualify as being paid from Dutch public funds, since universities in the Netherlands are all publicly funded. A last requirement of Article 25fa Dutch Copyright Act is that Dr Silver must make a clear reference to the source of that first disclosure of the work to the public, i.e. 'Big Publishing House, Inc.' The case does not specify whether Dr Silver has complied with this requirement.

III. Metalegal Formants

In 1997, the question of whether a transfer of rights covered forms of exploitation still unknown at the time of conclusion of the contract arose before a Dutch court,

[27] Rb. Amsterdam, 24 september 1997 (*De Volkskrant*), in *Informatierecht/AMI* 1997, p. 194.

in a matter relating to the distribution of newspaper articles on the Internet. In the *Volkskrant* case,[28] three freelance journalists brought a copyright infringement action against a major daily newspaper, *De Volkskrant*, for having posted a selection of articles from its printed version on its website and having produced quarterly CD-ROM compilations containing all newspaper copy in full – without securing the journalists' permission. The Amsterdam District Court held for the plaintiffs. According to the Court, the unauthorised republication of articles on CD-ROM and over the World Wide Web constituted restricted acts, subject to the rightholders' prior authorisation. The Court rejected the principal argument put forward by *De Volkskrant*, that the journalists had implicitly granted permission for electronic uses by submitting their articles for publication in the newspaper. In the 1980s, when the licences where initially granted, the plaintiffs could not have foreseen that their contributions would be included on a CD-ROM or website. Interestingly, the Court found infringement not only of the authors' pecuniary rights.

Article 25fa was added to the Copyright Act by amendment to the Proposal for an Act amending the Copyright Act for the strengthening of the contractual position of the author.[29] This provision expressly promotes Open Access for scientific or scholarly publications by enabling authors to deposit articles in their institutional repositories, if the conditions stated in the statute are met. The government explained the rationale behind this amendment in the following terms:

> Open access promotes the exchange of knowledge. That contributes to it innovative capacity of the Netherlands. For the publisher to earn back his investments, this is only permitted after the reasonable period of time just discussed, which starts after the first publication, has expired. Parties together determine what is reasonable. That can vary per scientific discipline, as in the explanation of the amendment. The amendment fits in well with the outspoken educational vision of State Secretary Dekker, who wants to regulate open access via the Higher Education and Scientific Research Act. In the eyes of the VVD [Volkspartij voor Vrijheid en Democracie], this amendment contributes to the recognition of Netherlands as a knowledge country and to promotion of an innovation-oriented economy.[30]

(12) NORWAY

I. Operative Rules

'Big Publishing House, Inc.' may have a claim for injunction, but the scope of the claim is uncertain.

---

28 Ibid.
29 Auteurscontractenrecht, Document nr. 33308, Tweede Kamer, 52-24-1, 10 februari 2015.
30 Ibid., p. 52-24-2, remarks by Van Wijngaarden (VVD).

II. *Descriptive Formants*

As a point of departure 'all rights' transfers may be challenged under the general prohibition on unreasonable contracts in §36 of the Act relating to Conclusion of Contracts (NACC, 31 May 1918), although the courts in Norway, as well as in other Scandinavian countries, have hitherto shown some reluctance in applying §36 to copyright contracts. Moreover, principles of interpretation of contracts, including the so-called specification principle (NCA §39a; New Act §67), may lead to a narrowing of the scope of the contract. Either way, it is not likely that the transfer as such will be deemed null and void. The solution opted for in the German report – that the contract gives 'Big Publishing House, Inc.' a right to make articles created after the emergence of Internet (i.e. after approximately 1995) available on the net – is a possible solution in Norwegian law as well.

III. *Metalegal Formants*

The imbalance of negotiating power between the original author and publishers, with a few exceptions, is not sought to be regulated in Norwegian copyright law. Prior to 1983, the NCA contained a specific prohibition against unreasonable copyright contracts, but it was abandoned due to the introduction of the general prohibition applying to all contracts in NACC §36. The problem with the application of general contract principles, besides their being very broadly formulated, thereby providing a low degree of predictability, is that the courts are often not sufficiently aware of the specific conditions in the copyright field.

(13) POLAND

I. *Operative Rules*

'Big Publishing House, Inc.' will not succeed with regard to works assigned by contracts concluded after 24 May 1994.

II. *Descriptive Formants*

The Polish Copyright Act contains very author-friendly regulations concerning transfers of copyright and other copyright contracts. According to Article 41.2 Copyright Act, the assignment contract must specify the so-called fields of exploitation on which the transfer is to take effect. The interpretation of this provision is controversial; it is in particular not entirely clear whether a clause covering all existing fields of exploitation (without explicitly naming them) is valid.[31] If we concur with the view closer to the literal construction of Article 41.2 Copyright Act, the negative answer is more probable. However, because the cooperation between 'Big Publishing House, Inc.' and Dr Silver began in 1980 and the assignment clause always referred to a specific article, we would also have to go back to the previous Polish Copyright Act of 10 July 1952.[32] This Act did not contain such a restrictive solution and therefore an all-encompassing clause could be regarded as valid. Thus, the legal situation concerning contracts with 'Big Publishing House, Inc.' would be different dependent on their date. Contracts concluded after 24 May 1994 (the date of entry into force of the currently binding Copyright Act) are invalid from the very outset. Even if we considered the more rigorous interpretation to be incorrect, there would be another legal impediment. According to Article 42.4 Copyright Act, assignment of copyright may only cover fields of exploitation known on the day the contract is concluded. Applying this rule to the present case, we would have to establish when publishing works on the Internet became a new and separate field of exploitation. Probably the correct time would be around 1995. Therefore, only contracts concluded after this date could legally transfer copyright to 'Big Publishing House, Inc.', and only with regard to the works subject to these later contracts could 'Big Publishing House, Inc.' apply for an injunction. Contracts concluded before 24 May 1994 would, on the other hand, be valid.

III. Metalegal Formants

Transfer of copyright on unspecified or future fields of exploitation is invalid. On the one hand, the protective provisions of the Copyright Act may seem too far-reaching as they allow the authors to exploit publishers as soon as new technologies are made available. Very often, due to the length of copyright protection, this also causes serious problems in communicating the work in question to the public using 'new' but already established and sometimes crucial channels. For example, it is common in practice for rightholders to be difficult to trace after some time has passed, and thus valuable copyright works cannot be made available in modern electronic databases (often serving as a standard tool of work in a given field), since consent of the rightholders (e.g. heirs) cannot be obtained. On the other hand, however, it is a long tradition of continental law to protect the author in relations with usually economically more powerful market participants.

---

31 J. Barta, R. Markiewicz, 'Obowiązek wymienienia pól eksploatacji w umowie licencyjnej', *PIPWI*, 2007, vol. 100, pp. 15 ff.

32 Journal of Laws 1952, No. 34, pos. 234 with subsequent amendments.

(14) SLOVENIA

I. Operative Rules

Whether 'Big Publishing House, Inc.' has a legal basis to file a claim for an interim injunction depends on the circumstances of the case. First of all, one should differentiate between a case concerning works for which the means of use was known at the time the publishing rights were assigned to 'Big Publishing House, Inc.', and a case concerning works for which the means of use was unknown at the time the publishing rights were assigned to 'Big Publishing House, Inc.' Furthermore, in the first case, two situations are to be differentiated (see below descriptive formants).

II. Descriptive Formants

The facts of the case are not detailed enough to provide a substantiated answer under Slovenian law; therefore a number of assumptions were made, as follows.

a) The subject is works for which an assignment of rights has been made
According to the applicable Slovenian legislation, material copyright cannot be assigned for all of an author's future works.[33] For this reason, the responses are given on the assumption that the subject is works for which an assignment of rights has been made.

b) There was an assignment of rights without time limit and the conditions of Article 83 or Article 93 of the CRRA did not apply
The responses for works for which rights have been assigned are given on the assumption that the assignment of rights was without a time limit. At the same time, it has also been assumed that the conditions from Articles 83 or 93 of the CRRA, according to which the author can revoke an assigned economic right, were not fulfilled, or that the reasons for termination of a publishing contract pursuant to Article 92 of the CRRA were not satisfied.

c) The assignment of rights was exclusive
Since it is a publishing contract, exclusivity of the assignment of rights to reproduce and distribute pursuant to Article 88(1) of the CRRA is presumed. Furthermore, the same responses apply to the case of a non-exclusive assignment of rights as when an author has made no assignment of rights. In both cases, the author is still entitled to the use of his/her works and can publish them online or

---

33 Copyright and Related Rights Act (CRRA), Official Gazette RS, nos. 21/1995, 9/2001, 30/2001, 43/2004, 17/2006, 139/2006, 68/2008, Art. 79(3).

offer them under various licences, since a non-exclusive assignment entitles the holder to use the works in an agreed manner *in addition* to the author or other holders (Art. 74(1) CRRA).

d) The author does not have a contract with a copyright collecting society to manage his/her rights relating to written copyrighted works

The responses are given on the assumption that the author is not a member of a collecting society and is not party to a contract on the management of his/her rights, since the author could not assign his/her rights to 'Big Publishing House, Inc.' if he/she were a member of a collecting society, and he/she also could not publish his/her own works online without permission from the collecting society.

According to Slovenian law, the assignment of economic rights for copyrighted works is not possible via an unknown means of use (Art. 79(4) CRRA). A distinction is therefore made between responses for works for which the rights were assigned when communicating works to the public online was an unknown means of use (response 2.1), and responses for works for which rights were assigned when this means of use was known (responses under 1.1 and 1.2).

1. Works for which the means of use was known at the time the publishing rights were assigned to 'Big Publishing House, Inc.'

According to Article 75(2) CRRA, in cases in which a contract does not specify which individual rights are assigned, it is presumed that only the rights essential to the realisation of the contract's purpose are assigned and only to the extent required for that realisation. The text indicates that one is dealing with a publishing contract, the purpose of which is the publication of articles in 'Big Publishing House, Inc.' periodicals.[34] The responses under point 1 therefore differ according to whether the assignment of the right to communicate to the public was essential to realising the purpose of the contract (response 1.1) or not (response 1.2).

1.1. Contracts where the right to communicate works to the public online is essential to realising the purpose of the contract

If the right to communicate to the public online is essential to realising the purpose of the contract, it is deemed to have been assigned to 'Big Publishing House, Inc.' 'Big Publishing House, Inc.' can therefore enforce all claims for infringement of these rights, including claims against the author.

---

34 Although Art. 85 CRRA states that by means of a publishing contract the author undertakes to assign the publisher the right to reproduce his/her or her work in printed form, and the right to distribute copies of the work, one must consider the fact that in the case being studied the assignment of rights was broader, since it was agreed for all known means of use. The purpose of the contract is therefore still essential in the response to the question of whether the right to online publication has been assigned.

1.2. Contracts where the right to communicate works to the public online is not essential to realising the purpose of the contract

If the right to communicate works to the public online is not essential to realising the purpose of the contract at the time it is agreed, this right will be deemed not assigned, since it was not provided for by the contract. In that case, this right remains within the exclusive domain of the author, and the author can therefore decide to publish said works online under whatever licence he/she chooses.

2. Works for which the form of use was not yet known at the time the publishing rights were assigned to 'Big Publishing House, Inc.'

The assignment of economic rights is not possible for means of use of an author's works that are as yet unknown (Art. 79(4) CRRA). The contract includes the provision that the author assigns the right to use the work in means that are subsequently discovered – that is, unknown at the time the contract was concluded. The provision on the assignment of rights to means of use unknown at the time of agreement is therefore null and void. The author retains the right to communicate to the public online any works for which an assignment contract was agreed at a time when communication online was not yet a known means of use.

III. Metalegal Formants

Since 1995, the Slovenian legal system has included provisions on mandatory collective management that even apply in cases not considered as lawful licences or free use or that are not regulated as substantive restrictions on the exclusive rights defined in Articles 46–57 of the CRRA. The CRRA provides a similar legal regime for publishing.

The Slovenian legal system has a provision, which provides for mandatory collective management in the management of publishing rights for non-theatrical musical works and literary works. An analysis of amendments to the CRRA indicates that in all probability there is an error in relation to publishing rights, which are of particular relevance to individual rights management with Creative Commons licences. In 2001 Article 22 of the CRRA, which defines economic copyright and in the second paragraph also defines public communication, was amended,[35] so that it included the right to publish among the rights covered under public communication, but this amendment was not consistent with the provision regulating mandatory collective management in Article 147. This state of affairs requires urgent adaptations to the CRRA or implementing regulations that will rectify the error, but this must include thorough consideration of whether it is reasonable to fully overturn a legislative basis that offers a solution to managing copyright online.

[35] ZASP-A (CRRA-A), Official Gazette RS, no. 9/2001.

(15) SPAIN

I. Operative Rules

Until 1987, 'Big Publishing House, Inc.' has the right to appeal in court, requesting that the author respect the transfer of the rights as agreed in the contracts.

With regard to publications issued after 1987, 'Big Publishing House, Inc.' no longer can rely on the effectiveness of the contract, since the clause in question is null for contravening compelling law.

II. Descriptive Formants

Dr Silver and his colleagues have agreed a series of bilateral contracts with 'Big Publishing House, Inc.' successive bilateral contracts. These contracts are described as agreements of collaboration in periodical publications under the LPI and they are subtypes of publishing contracts.

Regarding the publishing contract, it can be stated that it is the typical contract of transfer of copyright by which the author realises a temporary transfer of his/her copyright for the benefit of a third person, the publisher, starting between them a relationship without interruption. It is stated that autonomy of intentions plays a basic role within this contract because this reference is imposed in the contract's own legal definition, but some limits must be respect.

Among all the existing limits, one of them can be highlighted to give an accurate legal answer to the suggested problem. We refer to the limit included in Article 43.5 LPI, which bans the use of media that were non-existent or unknown when the cession of copyright was agreed. This means that we must be accurate in the definition of the exact moment when the electronic format appears and whether Dr Silver and his colleagues have access to it. The cession of copyright for the reproduction and distribution of the work agreed in the contract will only include those formats that exist at the very moment of the signature of the contract. From this moment on, the clause will be null in cases of unknown modes, but it will still be valid for the cession of copyright in known electronic formats including the website.

In addition to this, we shall mention another limitation expressly included in the LPI, specifically in the same Article 43.2. This states that a contract of cession shall express, in a specific and concrete way, the modes of exploitation of the work. Clauses that refer to the general form, like the one presented in this case, shall be considered invalid, for example, the clause by which an author hands over 'all the copyright'. Assuming this, the article penalises the agreement, interpreting the clause to the author's benefit and limiting the cession to what is strictly necessary to comply with the aim of the contract.

In conclusion, the clause is not valid because it does not contain the specific rights that the author hands over to the publisher. This absence of express content determines that only the essential rights are transferred for the sake of complying with the contract, that is, the rights of distribution and reproduction. The right of public communication is not included, and this is the way in which Dr Silver and his colleagues work via their website.

This idea is confirmed when referring to Article 52 LPI, regarding the regulation of the copyright in periodicals. In this case, the law attributes the rights of exploitation, reproduction and reproduction to the right's owner of the publication. The author then preserves the right to exploit the work by any other means (public communication, for instance) that use his or her work in any format that does not prejudice the normal course of the publication in which the work has been included.

The explanation offered above regarding the regulation applicable in the case is valid in temporal terms from 1987, when Law 22/1987 on Copyright came into force, combining existing legal reforms. However, the contractual relationship between Dr Silver and his colleagues dates back to 1980, so until 1987 their relationship was governed by the Copyright Law of 1879.

Article 5 of the Law of 1879 stated that copyright would be under the rule of common law, without any other limitations than those of one's own law. In this sense, the regulation of the contract of cession of copyright of Dr Silver and his colleagues will be governed by the rules of the Spanish Civil Code, establishing all the agreements, clauses, and condition that they may consider convenient.

In conclusion, according to the applicable regulation until 1987, all the contracts including a clause by which Dr Silver and his colleagues were forced to hand over the exploitation of copyright in any known or unknown format would not be contrary to law because of the parties' own regulative autonomy in the private contract.

III. Metalegal Formants

Spain recognises the liberty of agreements in contracts. To ensure the balance of interests between the author and the publisher, the cession of rights will be controlled.

(16) UNITED KINGDOM

I. Operative Rules

Yes, the publisher can get an injunction for all of the texts it holds the rights for.

II. Descriptive Formants

There has been no litigation on this and so the normal contract rules apply. Under UK law, copyright is assignable in full as personal and moveable property

(s. 90 CDPA). The assignment has to be writing – a condition that is clearly met in this scenario.

The only real debate is about the use online, which would be considered an unknown use for any transfer prior to the late 1990s. There is no clear cut-off point for this and case law does not exist. The UK has no special provisions on the assignment of rights and a global assignment is permissible, as long as it is writing. Future rights can also be assigned, but the intent to do so needs to have been clearly stated.[36] However, the scope of the assignment of new uses is also shaped by the purpose of the assignment, in the sense that new uses are included to the extent that they are necessary to give the contract effect.[37] In general, the case law tends to favour the authors, so the scope should be interpreted narrowly.[38] In conclusion, for older items, Dr Silver may still own the right to his article that is available online, although the impact this has on the publisher would be taken into account.

III. Metalegal Formants

The UK is a liberal country. As a matter of principle, it leaves the arrangement over the assignment of rights and its use to the parties. The only condition is that it has to be in writing.

A.3. COMPARATIVE REMARKS

The base case inquires whether in the different jurisdictions a full transfer of the author's rights encompasses new modes of exploitation, regardless of whether these modes of exploitation were known at the time of transfer. The answers differ to a large extent.

In some countries, the right is fully transferred, so that 'Big Publishing House, Inc.' has the right not only to publish on paper but also to make available online.[39] In most countries, the answer depends on the circumstances prevailing at the time the contracts were concluded. In the Czech Republic, Italy and Slovenia, any clause about future forms of exploitation is void. Consequently, unknown modes of exploitation are not transferred. The author may him/herself

36 N. Caddick, G. Davies and G. Harbottle, *Copinger and Skone James on Copyright* (17th ed., UK: 2016), para. 5-113; *Redwood Music Ltd v. B. Feldman & Co. Ltd* [1979] RPC 385, 394.

37 *Robin Ray v. Classic FM* [1998] ECC 488, 489; *Gribrook v. MGN* [2011] ECDR 4, 104–105. In particular it was held that the amount of people reached by a certain exploitation plays a role in the impact on the value of the work in other markets.

38 M. Kretschmer, 'Copyright and Contract Law: Regulating Creator Contracts: The State of the Art and a Research Agenda' (2010) 18(1) *Journal of Intellectual Property Law* 155.

39 See the reports of Estonia, Germany, Greece, Ireland, Lithuania and the UK.

publish older articles on his/her website. For known forms of exploitation, the assignment of the rights is assumed. Italian law has a further interesting aspect. If such a contract, as in the given case, is concluded without having an explicit time limit, the law allows only a maximum duration of 20 years. Belgium and Spain have changed their laws in recent years in this respect. Such a clause is today void, but it was not under the old law.[40] Belgian and Spanish law now dictate that the contract of transfer of rights will be interpreted as of the moment of its conclusion. Once the Internet has become a known form of exploitation, 'Big Publishing House, Inc.' has a right to an injunction; prior to that, no claim exists. France and Poland share a similar view. Yet their reasoning departs from the statutory requirement that the field of exploitation must be precisely defined.[41] Yet where modes of exploitation are unknown, the legal clause remains valid. In the Netherlands, the publication of old articles would be possible under the *Zweckübertragungstheorie*, but a more recent legislative amendment would allow the deposit of scientific articles in an institutional repository. There are different theories regarding the transfer of rights for new exploitation modes, but the issue never reached the Dutch Hoge Raad for a final determination on the matter. For Scandinavian states, the solution is identical, though based on very different law. They depart from the prohibition of unreasonable contracts and the specification principle regarding the contents of a contract. In Denmark, a proposal was drafted in order to strengthen the author's rights and possibilities vis-à-vis publishers in general. Interestingly, Eastern European states differ as to the protection granted to authors.

All in all, authors face rather different legal situations throughout Europe.

B.1. MODIFICATION

Dr Cooper works for a pharmaceutical company. He downloads Dr Silver's latest paper, makes small modifications and publishes it in the company's online newsletter without mentioning the conditions of the Open Access licence. Dr Silver brings a court action for violation of his copyright and breach of contract and demands the removal of the article from the online newsletter. Will he succeed?

---

40 In Belgium the new law has been in force since 1994 and in Spain since 1987.

41 In addition to that, Polish law emphasises that today only assignments concerning fields of exploitation already known at the moment of conclusion are valid. But the publisher has a claim for injunction with regard to the articles published before 1994, as according to old Polish copyright law the clause was valid.

B.2. COUNTRY REPORTS

(1) BELGIUM

I. Operative Rules

Dr Cooper and his pharmaceutical company will indeed be liable for violation of Dr Silver's copyright.

II. Descriptive Formants

The actions of Dr Cooper are in violation of Article 4(a)–(d) of the Creative Commons Attribution-NonCommercial-ShareAlike licence.[42] Dr Cooper had to distribute the adaptation under the same conditions. In addition, a copy of this licence also needed to be somehow included.

Secondly, we tend to believe that Dr Cooper has used the work of Dr Silver in a commercial way, since such a newsletter would constitute, perhaps indirectly, a means of publicity. Therefore, Dr Cooper and his company had commercial intents in adapting and distributing Dr Silver's article.[43]

Since the Creative Commons licence is not respected, Dr Silver's copyright is infringed, which entitles him to ask for an injunction and compensation (e.g. Arts. 86ter and 87 BCA, now Arts. XI.334 and XVII.14 BCEL).

III. Metalegal Formants

The Creative Commons ideas have been developed following the example of open software.[44] Encouraging people to use your creations as much as possible should not imply, however, that they can simply steal your effort and put it to their advantage. In this regard, it is important to realise that Creative Commons does not come down to giving up one's copyright, but instead constitutes a specific exercise of it. The free access licences need to be respected, which

---

42 S. Carneroli, *Les contrats commentés du monde informatique. Logiciels, bases de données, multimédia, internet [Commented Contracts of the IT World. Software, Databases, Multimedia, Internet]* (Brussels: 2007), 75–77.

43 More on the topic of 'commercial use' in the context of Creative Commons licences: P. Laurent, 'Premières réactions des juges face aux licences Creative Commons' [First Reactions of the Judges towards Creative Commons Licences], *R.D.T.I.* 2006, no. 26, 329–336, note under Civil Court Amsterdam (summary proceedings), 9 March 2006.

44 Y. Cool and P. Laurent, 'Introduction générale: repères pour comprendre le mouvement du logiciel libre' [General Introduction: Beacons for Better Understanding of the Open Source Movement], in: E. Montero (ed.), *Les logiciels libres face au droit [Legal Viewpoints on Free Software]* (Brussels: 2005), 9–10.

means that, depending on the licence, reference to the original author should be made, no commercial benefits can be pursued and the further distribution of (possibly) adapted versions needs to happen under the same type of licences.[45] If the conditions of the Creative Commons licence are not observed, general copyright applies, which means the unauthorised use of the protected content constitutes a violation of copyright.

(2) CZECH REPUBLIC

I. *Operative Rules*

An injunction will be granted.

II. *Descriptive Formants*

The licence contract was validly concluded by clicking 'I agree' in the dialogue box on the screen according to section 46(5) and (6) Copyright Act. In an Internet environment, the dialogue box with 'I agree' on the screen shall be recognised as offer within the meaning of section 46(5) Copyright Act. Clicking 'I agree' is recognised as a legal act – acceptance is made in accordance with the offer and comes into force at the moment it is carried out in accordance with section 46(6) Copyright Act. This has been recognised by Czech law as a new method of concluding licence contracts since the amendment of the Copyright Act 216/2006 Coll. came into force on 1 January 2007. Before 1 January 2007, a legal act like clicking 'I agree' was governed by the general conditions on the conclusion of contracts in the Civil Code. According to section 44(1) of the Civil Code, a contract is concluded at the moment when acceptance of the offer becomes effective. According to section 43c(2) of the Civil Code, acceptance of the offer to conclude a contract becomes effective when the expression of consent to such an offer is delivered to the person making the offer. The problem was, as in the given case, that the author was never able to find out that someone had clicked 'I agree' and hence the licence contract was not concluded.

The question which arises is whether the company's newsletter should be deemed a non-commercial manner of use of the author's work. Newsletters are made by companies not only to inform clients about new developments in their field of work, but also – indeed mainly – to advertise the company.

---

45 For Belgian doctrine on the adjacent domain of open source: Y. Van Den Brande and J. Keustermans, 'Open source software: een analyse naar Belgisch recht' [Open Source Software: an Analysis according to Belgian Law], *I.R.D.I.* 2007, 369–381.

The court action will be granted in line with the provisions of section 40(1)(b) and (d)(1) Copyright Act. The court will prohibit distribution of Dr Silver's article in the company's online newsletter according to section 40(1)(b) Copyright Act. Distribution of the article in the company's online newsletter is unauthorised distribution according to the contract on distribution concluded between Dr Silver and Dr Cooper. By clicking 'I agree' in the dialogue box – as mentioned above – using the article in the company's newsletter is not non-commercial use of work. Withdrawal of such unauthorised reproduction is to be ordered by the court according to section 40(1)(d)(1), so the company will have to withdraw the online newsletter and before distributing it further the company will have to remove the article from it.

III. Metalegal Formants

Creative Commons were initiated to foster the use of content, but the concept is still firmly built on contract. Once the terms are evidently violated, remedies are available.

(3) DENMARK

I. Operative Rules

Dr Silver would seem to have a claim for breach of contract and may demand the removal of the article on that ground.

II. Descriptive Formants

The validity of the click-wrap contract is subject to some doubt under Danish law, but arguably a court would find a contract to have been concluded. The Danish legal position is similar to that in Norway: there is no doubt that Dr Cooper has breached his contractual obligations under the Open Access licence. It may even be held that there is a substantial breach of contract so that the general condition for revocation of contracts (here: *ex nunc*) is fulfilled. If so, Dr Silver may demand that the article be removed from the online newsletter and it will therefore be unnecessary to invoke the claim of copyright infringement.

III. Metalegal Formants

Open Access licences are tools predicated on the author's ability to open the sphere of the public domain. The contractual and copyright implications of such contracts remain the subject of much debate.

(4) ESTONIA

I. Operative Rules

Dr Silver may require that the conditions of the Open Access licence be added. If Dr Cooper fails to do that, Dr Silver has the right to cancel the contract. After the cancellation, any use of the article by Dr Cooper would be unlawful.

II. Descriptive Formants

It is assumed that the economic and moral rights in respect of the article that Dr Cooper uses belong to Dr Silver. As the holder of the author's rights, Dr Silver is entitled to license his works under the Creative Commons licence. The licence conditions are accepted by clicking 'I agree'. According to the Copyright Act, '[t]he granting of a non-exclusive licence may also be made in a format which can be reproduced in writing'.[46] H. Pisuke explains that 'a format which can be reproduced in writing' does not require the contract to be signed. The exchange of e-mails and SMSs would be enough to consider the contract concluded.[47] Consequently, it can be said that Dr Silver and Dr Cooper have a legally binding contract and Dr Cooper has failed to perform his contractual obligations. Therefore, Dr Silver may *inter alia* require performance of the obligation, demand compensation for damage and cancel the contract.[48]

Dr Silver demands the removal of the article from the online newsletter. The problem is that the Creative Commons licence allows publishing articles on the Internet. The fact that Dr Cooper is in breach of the contract (he did not mention the conditions of the Open Access licence) does not make the contract automatically invalid. However, according to §196(1) Law of Obligations Act, Dr Silver may cancel the contract. Subsection 196 (2) specifies the grounds for the cancellation:

> If non-performance of a contractual obligation by the other party provides good reason for cancelling the contract, the contract may only be cancelled if the other party fails to render a conforming performance within the term granted therefor. Such term need not be granted in the cases provided for in clauses §116(2) 2)–4) of this Act.

To avoid complicated legal dispute about the nature of non-performance, Dr Silver could give Dr Cooper additional time to add the conditions of the Open Access licence to the article. If Dr Cooper fails to do so, then Dr Cooper could cancel

---

46 Copyright Act §49(1).

47 H. Pisuke, *Autoriõiguse alused* (Copyright Basics) (Tallinn: 2006), pp. 63–64.

48 Law of Obligations Act §101(1).

the contract. After the cancellation of the contract, Dr Cooper would not have any legal ground to use Dr Silver's article. Further use of the article by Dr Cooper would be considered unlawful. Dr Silver could demand that the behaviour which is causing damage be terminated (§1055 Law of Obligations Act).

III. *Metalegal Formants*

The Creative Commons licence attached to articles could constitute information on the exercise of rights. Information on the exercise of rights *inter alia* defines the work, the terms of its use and identifies the author (§802 Copyright Act). H. Pisuke points out that the implementation of Directive 2001/29/EC into the Copyright Act provided authors and holders of related rights with two additional economic rights: the right to add technological measures to a work or object of related rights (§80^3) and the right to add information on the exercise of rights to published works or objects of related rights (§80^4).[49] Removal or alteration of information on the exercise of rights is punished as a misdemeanour. Subsection 81^2(1) Copyright Act provides

> Removal or alteration of electronic information on the exercise of the rights of authors or holders of related rights; and distribution, communication, communication to the public or making available to the public of works, objects of related rights or databases from which information concerning the exercise of rights has been removed without authorisation or the information has been altered, is punishable by a fine of 300 fine units.

Still, it is up to case law to establish whether failure to attach a Creative Commons licence to a modified work will be punishable under the Copyright Act.

(5) FRANCE

I. *Operative Rules*

Though Dr Silver's court action for breach of contract will not succeed due to the invalidity of the share-alike clause, Dr Cooper may be faced with claims of counterfeiting.

II. *Descriptive Formants*

Dr Cooper has expressed his consent by clicking the 'I agree' dialogue box. The Attribution-NonCommercial-ShareAlike Creative Commons licence stipulates: 'If you distribute, publicly display, publicly perform, or publicly digitally perform

---

[49] H. Pisuke, *Autoriõiguse alused* (Copyright Basics) (Tallinn: 2006), pp. 43–44.

the Work or any Derivative Works or Collective Works, you must keep intact all copyright notices for the Work' (Art. 4d). Thus, a French court may accept Dr Silver's demand and recognise the breach of contract.

Dr Silver may consider his authorisation 'to create and reproduce Derivative Works' (Art. 3b) to be invalid because it is contrary to his moral rights, in particular the respect for his work (Art. L. 121-1: 'An author shall enjoy the right to respect for his name, his authorship and his work'). Indeed, this right is 'inalienable'.

Dr Cooper, as a defendant, may respond with many arguments, in particular that the Open Access contract is invalid. Indeed, the Creative Commons licence does not define the field of exploitation according to Article L. 131-3 (supra).

The 'share-alike' clause by which Dr Cooper has accepted to 'distribute, publicly display, publicly perform, or publicly digitally perform a Derivative Work only under the terms of this License' (Art. 4b) is null and void, as in French law 'total transfer of future works shall be null and void.' (Art. L. 131-1 of the Intellectual Property Code). [Note of the editor L. Guibault in 2019: This is incorrect: the CC BY-NC-SA does not operate a total transfer of future works since it is a non-exclusive licence on an existing work. This statutory provision is not applicable.]

But Dr Cooper has no interest in seeing the licence declared null: the breach of contract would not be recognised, but he would then be a counterfeiter. In other words, Dr Cooper's demand for invalidating the Creative Commons licence implies that he himself be recognised as a pirate!

III. Metalegal Formants

The author's principle upon which French copyright laws are built respects internal limits to transfer and use of copyright. This weighing process also influences the interpretation of Creative Commons licences (and respective violations).

(6) GERMANY

I. Operative Rules

Silver has a claim for removal as long as Cooper does not add the caveat of 'redistribution only under the same licence condition'.

II. Descriptive Formants

German courts have acknowledged the validity of Open Access-type licences, including the 'share-alike clause', which is a typical clause found in general public licences and in Creative Commons licences alike.[50] Its legal foundation is §32 sec. 3 sentence 3 UrhG (the so-called Linux clause of 2002). In not complying with the clause, Cooper breaches his contractual duty. Under §241 sec. 1 BGB, Silver can claim that a reference to the licence be added. However, whether Cooper also violates Silver's right under §19a UrhG depends on the question of whether the failure to attach the same licence terms to the newly distributed work amounts to a violation of the right of making available. The problem is that this omission does not directly affect the 'right of making available'. As the Creative Commons licence explicitly allows for modifications, Cooper waived his right under §62 UrhG (conditioned by the attribution clause).

III. *Metalegal Formants*

The interesting thing about Creative Common licences is that they successfully re-open the public domain in creating publicly accessible creative commons. The growing movement for open public space, both on the Internet and in the creative commons area, is a challenging phenomenon. It is irritating that it is the licence which opens up this new public space – just the very method of exploitation of intellectual property which is notoriously suspected of extending proprietary control as far as is just about legal. Creative Commons licences, however, do both: they create public space, and at the same time protect the work against appropriation. Legally, Creative Commons licences bind the works on a continuous basis to the creator – yet extending his/her influence. In the old world, with one act of publication governed by contract law, the right to publish did expire. In the digital environment, exhaustion does not take place (explicitly declared non-applicable in the digital environment, Article 3(3) Directive 2001/29/EC). We see this traditional boundary vanishing in other fields of intellectual property as well (Case 6). However, we also see an expanding use of licences in the public interest, re-creating new boundaries to information property (see Case 10).

(7) GREECE

I. *Operative Rules*

Dr Silver may claim the restoration of his name as the true creator; he may also claim an injunction, as well as any profit gained by Dr Cooper due to Dr Silver's creative activity.

---

50 For so-called 'general public licences' LG München, decision of 19 May 2004, Computerrecht 2004, 774–776 – *Netfilter v. Sitecom*.

II. Descriptive Formants

Dr Cooper and his pharmaceutical company very probably infringe the rights of Dr Silver in three ways. First of all, the former is (most likely) appropriating the intellectual work of another, presenting it as his own, in which case he, and the pharmaceutical company, owe Dr Silver the restoration of his true name as the intellectual creator, since this is an inalienable right of the latter. Furthermore, they are altering the intellectual work, in which case they owe to it Dr Silver to make good the integrity of the work, since this remains a non-assignable right of the creator/author.

Finally, Dr Cooper and his company must abstain from what is very probably a non-scientific, but rather advertising – and thus business – use of the article in the online newsletter of the pharmaceutical company. More specifically, Dr Silver has a corresponding claim for an injunction against Dr Cooper and the company, since he has a right to defend his intellectual property, which is here being used without his permission. He also has a contractual claim against Dr Cooper arising from the Open Access contract, the terms of which Dr Cooper has infringed. Any claim (of Dr Cooper or his company) for a compulsory licence seems to be self-evidently precluded by the terms of the Creative Commons licence.

Furthermore, according to Article 904 Civil Code, Dr Silver may also claim as unjustified enrichment any profit made by Dr Cooper due to Dr Silver's own creative activity. In this sense, of course, the creator may not claim the profit made by Dr Cooper to the extent that this is due to the latter's own efforts.

III. Metalegal Formants

Regardless of the more general question of whether the disputed terms of the Open Access contract are abusive or not, the violation of the term prohibiting the professional use of the work means *ex ea ipsa* that the person who accedes to the term in question is not the final recipient of the work and thus is not a consumer within the meaning of Article 1 para. 4 Law 2251/1994. Thus, the term is considered not to fall within the scope of Law 2251/1994 for the Protection of the Consumers, and therefore not legitimated to invoke the abusiveness or invalidity of the disputed term. Of course, the question remains open whether Dr Cooper's claim for a compulsory licence according to Article 102 TFEU should be considered as deviating from mandatory law.

(8) IRELAND

I. Operative Rules

An injunction will likely be granted.

II. Descriptive Formants

There is no case law in Ireland in relation to Open Access licences. In *Ryanair dac v. SC Vola.ro srl*[51] the Irish High Court recognised the enforceability of a 'click-wrap' agreement.

However, it is likely that Dr Cooper has violated Dr Silver's moral rights, as these have not been waived by the Creative Commons licence. Moreover, he may not modify or publish the letter without mentioning the licence, as he is bound under contract law to do so. It has always been the position of the Free Software Foundation that where the licence had not been complied with, copyright owners could rely on this right to bind users who had failed to comply with the licensing conditions.

III. Metalegal Formants

Ireland's policy on the digital industry is supportive. This stance is not restricted to proprietary models, but also supports innovative uses. Thus, Creative Commons are respected, and the violation of their licence terms can be adjudicated.

(9) ITALY

I. Operative Rules

Dr Silver has a claim against Dr Cooper, both for removal and for damages.

II. Descriptive Formants

As in any other type of online contract (click-wrap licences), provisions and obligations originating from this Creative Commons licence are binding on the parties. Moreover, authorship is also a moral right that cannot be transferred or waived. So the remedies at Dr Silver's disposal are for copyright infringement and breach of contract.

III. Metalegal Formants

So far in Italy, there has been no case law involving the validity of a Creative Commons licence (or other Open Access/Content licences). Nevertheless, there is no reason to believe that a court would not consider such contracts binding, at least as far as courts consider other (and very widespread) online contracts to be valid.

---

51 [2019] IEHC 239.

However, it is worth noting that in Italy any transfer of copyright (including simple licences) needs to be proven in written form (validity *ad probationem*). Up to now, the only technology legally recognised is digital signature (asymmetric pair of keys) with a Certification Authority (CA) stamp, which is explicitly regulated by the Digital Administration Code.[52] In this case, the effectiveness of the signature is even stronger than that of a handwritten signature. In fact, while for a handwritten signature one can disregard his/her own signature in the ordinary course of a trial, in the case of a digital signature one has to file a special complaint (*querela di falso*), which is a new and special procedure that suspends the original trial. This special procedure was originally meant to invalidate signatures of 'public faith' like those of notaries and other public officials. Therefore, a digital signature that meets the required conditions has stronger legal validity than a handwritten one.

Any other electronic (not digital in the above sense) signature (so for example a digital signature without a CA stamp) is to be evaluated by courts taking into consideration aspects such as the reliability and modifiability of the text.

So far, transfer of copyright through written form is still an open issue among scholars, who are awaiting the courts' opinion.

(10) LITHUANIA

I. Operative Rules

An injunction will be granted.

II. Descriptive Formants

Open licences (including Creative Commons licences) so far have no direct regulation in Lithuania and no clear explanation in the national case law. Having said that, there are a few decisions of the lower instance courts recognising the validity of open licences (mostly indirectly). As there are no reasons to think otherwise, Dr Silver's Creative Commons licence is valid and enforceable. Click-wrap licences are directly regulated as a possible mode of contract for computer programmes and databases in the Copyright Act (Art. 42) and could be extrapolated to cover other types of works as well.

With regard to the consequences of the violation of the Creative Commons conditions by Dr Cooper (which is quite obvious), the Lithuanian courts would most likely recognise both contract and copyright violations. In the earlier version of the Copyright Act, the use of the work violating the contractual arrangements

[52] See Arts. 20–21 and 71 of d.lgs. 7 March 2005, no. 82, as modified by d.lgs. 4 April 2006, no. 159, entitled 'Codice dell'Amministrazione Digitale' (Digital Administration Code).

was directly named as a copyright infringement. While the statutory wording currently is different (the Copyright Act no longer provides a particular list of infringing activities), the decisions of the Lithuanian Supreme Court[53] confirm that use of the work in violation of the contract amounts to a copyright violation. In such a case, regular remedies apply, including the possibility for an injunction, covering the removal of the article from the online newsletter. It can be added that courts have a duty to weigh the proportionality of the remedy requested by the plaintiff and may refuse or restrict the particular remedy if it can cause disproportional harm to the defendant. Arguably, such disproportional harm is not likely here and an injunction would most likely be granted.

III. Metalegal Formants

Because Creative Commons licences can be conceptualised as contracts, there are no real difficulties in accepting them in legal practice and enforcing them. It is worth mentioning that Creative Commons licences do not deny copyright protection but, on the contrary, rely on it. While the case law in Lithuania is scarce, these licences are already widely used in specific sectors, such as universities or memory institutions (libraries, museums, archives, etc.).

(11) NETHERLANDS

I. Operative Rules

Yes, this is a breach of Dr Silver's copyright.

II. Descriptive Formants

In the *Curry v. Weekend* case, the Creative Commons licence was declared valid and the conditions of the licence were applied.[54] In an annotation of the decision, Koelman posits that the judge assumed that by using the material offered under a Creative Commons licence, the conditions were accepted, and the licence agreement was concluded.[55] In the decision, no attention was paid to the formation of the agreement; the licence agreement and its conditions were just applied. Dr Cooper has explicitly agreed with the conditions of the licence, so there is no problem with the validity of the licence.

---

53 For example, see the ruling of 26 March 2020 of the Civil Division of the Supreme Court of Lithuania in case No. e3K-3-77-687/2020, where the violation of contract was considered to be copyright infringement.

54 Rb. Amsterdam (vzr.), 9 maart 2006, *AMI* 2006, 87–92.

55 Rb. Amsterdam (vzr.), 9 maart 2006 (*Curry/Weekend*), *AMI* 2006/3, m.nt. K. Koelman.

The permission Dr Silver has given is limited to use under the above-mentioned conditions. Dr Cooper has not given proper credit and has not redistributed the paper under the Creative Commons conditions. Because of this omission, Dr Cooper has already breached Dr Silver's copyright. Dr Silver should also have included the 'non-commercial' restriction.

III. Metalegal Formants

This question involves the enforcement of a Creative Commons licence. With a Creative Commons licence, the author can decide under which conditions his/her work will be disclosed.[56]

In the *Curry v. Weekend* case, the question arose regarding the consequences of a breach of the contractual obligations in the Creative Commons licence. The question was whether this constituted an infringement of copyright. In *Curry v. Weekend*, this question is not explicitly answered. The court states that the conditions of the licence were not applied by the magazine. Therefore, Curry's claim could be granted. Weekend was not permitted to copy or publish the photos without permission of the rightholder unless the conditions of the Creative Commons licence are complied with. But the court does not explicitly state that by not complying with the conditions of the Creative Commons licence Weekend infringed Curry's copyright. Nor do the case notes on this case have a clear answer. In the above-mentioned case note by Koelman, he comes to the conclusion that the Court decided Weekend did not comply with the conditions in the Creative Commons licence, and that therefore there was an infringement of copyright.[57] However, in another note by Kabel, doubt is raised as to whether the court actually finds an infringement of copyright or just breach of contract.[58]

(12) NORWAY

I. Operative Rules

Dr Silver has a claim for breach of contract and may demand the removal of the article on that ground.

---

[56] N. Elkin-Koren, 'Exploring Creative Commons: a skeptical view of a worthy pursuit', in: L. Guibault and P.B. Hugenholtz (eds.), *The future of the public domain: Identifying the commons in information law*, Information Law Series No. 16 (The Hague: 2006), p. 15.

[57] Rb. Amsterdam (vzr.), 9 maart 2006 (*Curry/Weekend*), *AMI* 2006/3, m.nt. K. Koelman.

[58] Rb. Amsterdam (vzr.), 9 maart 2006 (*Curry/Weekend*), *IER* 2006/40, m.nt. J. Kabel.

II. *Descriptive Formants*

There is no doubt that Dr Cooper has breached his contractual obligations under the Open Access licence. It may even be held that there is a substantial breach of contract, so that the general condition for revocation of contracts (here: *ex nunc*) is fulfilled. If so, Dr Silver may demand that the article be removed from the online newsletter and it is therefore unnecessary to invoke a claim of copyright infringement. Whether breaches of contractual obligations of this kind also lead to a copyright infringement is settled in neither the NCA nor the case law, but it may be maintained – in line with what is considered in German law[59] – that the obligations in the Creative Commons licence do not affect the right to make available, cf. NCA §2 (New Act §3). On the other hand, it is open to discussion whether or not making the material available to the public for other purposes than those set out in the licence indeed *does constitute* a violation of the right to make available.

III. *Metalegal Formants*

Open Access licences are tools predicated on the author's private autonomy to open the sphere of the public domain. As with other contractual obligations, some uncertainty exists as to whether breaches of the obligations may be considered to be copyright infringements. The practical and principal impact of this problem, however, should not be exaggerated.

(13) POLAND

I. *Operative Rules*

Dr Silver will succeed.

II. *Descriptive Formants*

The Creative Commons and open source movements have become the subject of considerable interest for the Polish copyright doctrine (the courts, however, have not had the opportunity to test these legal concepts in practice). The prevailing view is that Creative Commons licences (which have been adapted to Polish law) are valid,[60] and that if the conditions of use stipulated in such a licence are breached, this constitutes copyright infringement (usually the licence expires). Copyright infringement makes it possible to motion for an injunction (Art. 79 Copyright Act).

---

59 Cf. the German report.
60 J. Barta, R. Markiewicz, *Prawo autorskie* (Kraków: 2008), pp. 170 ff.

III. Metalegal Formants

On the metalegal level, there are several interesting questions: (1) the interrelation between breach of contract and infringement of copyright; (2) the privatisation of law; and (3) the use of IP rights to actually curtail the scope of protection granted by statutory provisions.

(14) SLOVENIA

I. Operative Rules

The responses are provided based on the same assumptions as for the base case. A further assumption is that it involved the adaptation of copyrighted work. [Editors' note: This modification was *not* modelled on the base case! The differentiation was 'upstream' versus 'downstream'. Thus, the following reporter's answers are of relative weight.]

II. Descriptive Formants

The grounds for the use of the same assumptions as in the responses to the base case are the same as the grounds stated under the base case.

First, one must distinguish between situations involving an adaptation of the author's work and situations where changes to the original work are so minimal that they cannot be deemed to be the adaptation of the author's work. Since it is not clear from the text whether an adaptation of the author's work was involved, the responses have been provided on the assumption that the use was a derivative work and then published on the company website.

In cases of adaptation of the author's work, the author of the original work retains the exclusive right to the use of his/her work in the adapted form, unless otherwise stated by the CRRA or by contract (Art. 33(3) CRRA). Since the contract between the author and 'Big Publishing House, Inc.' does not stipulate whether the right to use of the adapted work is assigned to 'Big Publishing House, Inc.', one must again base the argument on the purpose of the contract, and hence whether assignment of the right to use adaptations of the works was essential to the purpose of the contract. The issue in this specific case is the right to communicate adaptations of the work to the public, so one must determine whether that right has been assigned. The grounds are the same as those given for the base case.

1. The works for which communication to the public online was a known means of use at the time the publishing rights were assigned to 'Big Publishing House, Inc.'

The responses to the modification of the base case again distinguish between contracts in which the right to communicate to the public online is essential to realising the purpose of the contract (point 1.1) and contracts in which that right is not essential (point 1.2).

1.1. Contracts where the right to communicate works to the public online is essential to realising the purpose of the contract

As in the grounds for the base case, if the right to communicate to the public online is essential to realising the purpose of the contract, it is deemed to have been assigned to 'Big Publishing House, Inc.' and to no longer be held by the author. As a consequence, only 'Big Publishing House, Inc.', as the exclusive holder of the right to communicate the adapted work to the public online, can enforce any claims for infringement of rights. In that case, even the offer by the author of such adaptations online under a Creative Commons licence is null and void, since the author is not the rightholder and therefore cannot act as licensor. It is irrelevant, therefore, whether or not the user upholds the conditions of the Creative Commons licence; in any case, only 'Big Publishing House, Inc.' is entitled to enforce claims against a user in the event of an infringement of economic rights.

1.2. Contracts where the right to communicate works to the public online is not essential to realising the purpose of the contract

If the right to communicate adaptations of works to the public is not essential to realising the purpose of a publishing contract with 'Big Publishing House, Inc.', then the right was not assigned to 'Big Publishing House, Inc.' and the author remains the holder of that right. According to the given Creative Commons licence, the author only permitted the communication of the adaptation to the public for non-commercial purposes[61] and under the same conditions as the user received the original.[62] The user therefore infringed the CRRA,[63] and the author can enforce a claim for infringement of the right pursuant to general copyright law.

At the same time, the author cannot file an action for breach of contract, since in the specific case no contract was agreed, as the author simply published the licence online. To resolve the issue of whether free access licences (such as the Creative Commons licence) constitute a licence or a licence contract,[64]

61 Creative Commons licence 2.5 Attribution-NonCommercial-ShareAlike, Art. 4(c).

62 Ibid., Art. 4.

63 See also M. Damjan, 'Pravni temelj prostega programja' (2004) nos. 4–6 *Pravnik*, pp. 292, 293.

64 As a unilateral legal transaction, a licence does not require a licence contract and the user's consent to be legally valid. Granting a licence therefore entails a unilateral legal transaction (statement) with which the rightholder permits the user to exploit the right within a defined scope. This may be done by means of a licence contract, a bilateral legal transaction, with which the licensor may undertake to grant the user a licence (permit to exploit a right), while the licensee undertakes to meet the obligations defined in the licence contract. A licence does not have to be granted with a licence, since – as a statement – a licence may also be valid as an independent act. See also M. Damjan, 'Pravni temelj prostega programja' (2004) nos. 4–6 *Pravnik*, p. 285.

the characteristics of free access licences must be taken into account. The granting of a licence is a unilateral legal transaction – a statement by the author permitting the use of his/her work in a specific manner. A licence does not encroach on a user's rights (as a licence contract, as a bilateral legal transaction, usually does), but grants rights, expanding the possibility of use. The restrictions defined by a free access licence relating to specific means of use do not therefore represent substantive restrictions on a right, but rather a resolutory condition, since the licence terminates on infringement of the conditions.[65] The user therefore cannot refer in defence to the Creative Commons licence as the author's permission to use his/her work,[66] since the user has infringed the provision of the licence on mandatory attribution.[67] An infringement of this kind leads to termination of the licence, i.e. fulfilment of the resolutory condition. This case must therefore be deemed to constitute a licence and not a licence contract. Since a licence contract was not concluded, the author cannot file an action against the user for breach of contract. As stated, the author can file an action for infringement of copyright pursuant to the CRRA.

2. Works for which the means of use was not yet known at the time the publishing rights were assigned to 'Big Publishing House, Inc.'

As in the grounds for the base case under point 2, the author did not assign the right to communicate such works (or adaptations) to the public online and is therefore entitled to offer the work to the public by such means. The author therefore also has the right to enforce a claim for infringement of that right. The user infringed the licence conditions, and cannot claim to have the author's permission (as in point 1.2), since the Creative Commons licence is no longer valid in this case, for the same reasons as given in point 1.2. For the same reasons as in the grounds for point 1.2, the author cannot enforce any claims for breach of contract.

In all three cases, the author could enforce claims for infringement of the moral right to respect for his/her work, if the adaptation by Dr Cooper constituted an encroachment that could be prejudicial to his/her person (Art. 19 CRRA). If the user fails to credit the author of the original work when publishing an adaptation, the author could also enforce a claim for infringement of the moral right to recognition of authorship (Art. 18 CRRA). The author can exercise both rights despite the exclusive assignment of economic rights, since moral rights cannot be assigned and remain outside an author's exclusive domain (Art. 70(1) CRRA).

---

65 Summarised from M. Damjan, *Prosta licenca kot pravni temelj odprte vsebine*, Doctoral Dissertation, Faculty of Law, University of Ljubljana, January 2007, pp. 129–134; see also ibid., p. 137: 'In March 2006 a Dutch court … decided that a Creative Commons licence could also be valid if the user has not explicitly consented to it, or even if the user was not aware of the conditions.'

66 Creative Commons licence 2.5 Attribution-NonCommercial-ShareAlike, Art. 7.

67 Ibid., Art. 4.

III. *Metalegal Formants*

On the metalegal level, what was explained in the report on the base case also applies for Modification 1.

(15) SPAIN

I. *Operative Rules*

Dr Silver will be able to successfully bring legal action against Dr Cooper, requesting legal protection over the copyright of his works because he is the author of the works and because of non-fulfilment of the contract of the Creative Commons licence.

II. *Descriptive Formants*

The origin of the conflict resides in the validity that the Spanish legislation can grant to a contract named 'Creative Commons licence'. One of the parties, named as the assignor author, transfers the copyright of a finished work to an assignee, the receiver of the assignment, with the purpose of exploiting the licence as far as possible.

By means of the system of Creative Commons licences, the author who creates a work and wishes to exploit it through the Internet can choose from among the possibilities that the licence offers and confirms it once the work is placed on the network. This means that the user that would like to access to the work will be able to easily identify the conditions of use the author has imposed. Whenever a user decides to use a work under a Creative Commons licence, he/she becomes licensed and he/she commits to accept and respect the conditions of the licence defined by the author.

The clauses of the licence are predefined. By default, the licence authorises the reproduction, distribution, transformation and public communication of the work for every type of objective and for all the modes of exploitation, for free and during all the period of protection. From this starting point, the author will limit the characteristics of the authorisation, excluding commercial uses and allowing its distribution under the licence.

Since the contract is of the type known as 'between absents', offer and demand do not converge in the same agreement, so the competition for the offer and the acceptance take place at different moments and in different places. On this point, both Article 1262 Civil Code and Article 54 *in fine* Commercial Code establish that there will be consent in contracts concluded by means of automatic devices from the very moment of the acceptance. Therefore, consent formalised through the acceptance by the receiver of the work shown by clicking 'I agree' on his/her electronic device will finalise the agreement that gives the right of the exploitation of the work, including the limitations under the Creative Commons licence, referring to Article 1258 Civil Code.[68]

However, it should be mentioned that every contract should be subject to a general legal benchmark which establishes compulsory limits to contractual will, so we must evaluate if the Creative Commons licence is, according to this benchmark, determines whether Dr Cooper has to be subject to its limitations.

The Spanish jurisprudence has not had the opportunity to create a solid argument in relation to this issue. However, it has stated in some minor decisions the validity of Creative Commons licences, although not always in a unified way. As an example, there is the sentence of the Audiencia Provincial of Pontevedra of 29 November 2005.[69] In this decision, enacted on appeal requested by the defendant, the court states that the Creative Commons for free use licence is nothing but 'a mere informative leaflet lacking a signature, so with no possibility of attributing a value to it'.[70]

On the other side, we find the Court of First Instance of Badajoz, in its sentence 17 February 2006.[71] The judge argues that the author, as the person exclusively entitled to the moral and economic rights over his/her creation, has the power to decide on the management of the rights that he/she considers appropriate, whether he/she allows free use as a whole or partially.

In this case, the defendant used the right of public communication of musical works under the distinctive Creative Commons licences. These licences are different types of authorisations that the author gives to his/her works to allow free use. Therefore, the judge confirms that there are several types of licences that allow handing over the economic rights to a greater or lesser extent. In this case, the defendant was able to show with documents that he had used music that had been previously freely handed over by the authors through the above-mentioned licences, giving legal effect to the assignment established by the Creative Commons licences.

In conclusion, the truth is that there is a contractual relationship between two subjects based on the principle of contractual autonomy with legal effects because it does not breach any compulsory norm.

---

68 Art. 1258 Civil Code states: 'Contracts are perfected by mere consent, and from then on are binding, not only to the performance of what has been expressly agreed, but also to all the consequences which, according to their nature, are in accordance with good faith, usage and the law'.

69 Decision of the Provincial Court of Pontevedra, Section 1, of 29 November 2005, Ponente Ilmo D. Francisco Javier Valdés Garrido.

70 By contrast, German courts have acknowledged their validity.

71 Decision of the Court of First Instance of Badajoz no. 6 of 17 February 2006, Magistrado-Juez, D. Luis Cáceres Ruiz.

III. Metalegal Formants

The vast majority of conflicts in Spain which are related to Creative Commons licences are about claims made by the SGAE, AGEDI and AIE, private entities devoted to the defence and collective management of intellectual property rights. There have been no cases involving the validity of a Creative Commons licence.

(16) UNITED KINGDOM

I. Operative Rules

Yes, Dr Silver can sue for infringement and breach of contract.

II. Descriptive Formants

There is no specific litigation on Creative Commons licences, so the discussion is based on the general contract principles. There is also no reason to believe that Creative Commons licences would be treated differently. In the scenario, the first key question is whether the internal use by a commercial company makes the use as such commercial by default. The UK has an exemption for research and private study, and since Creative Commons licences leave all of the national exemptions untouched, the question needs to be answered via this route. In addition, the scope of the exemption overrides any contractual terms to the contrary (s. 29(4B)).

The current case may fall under the fair dealing exemption (s. 29). The interpretation follows the InfoSoc Directive, Recital 42 of which makes it clear that the non-commercial nature of the activity in question should be determined by the activity and not by the establishment's organisational structure or means of funding. Before this change, the UK did not have any restrictions on the purpose at all. The inclusion of the article in the news latter does not have a money-making motive as such and therefore would most likely be considered non-commercial under the law. It would therefore also meet the Creative Commons licensing requirement – which in turn covers the modifications made. The second key consideration refers to not displaying the licensing terms. Section 29 provides guidance, as it has the same requirement, with the proviso 'where this would be impossible for reasons of practicality or otherwise' (s. 29(1)(1B)). There is no reason why a digital newsletter cannot have the Creative Commons badge and/or a link to the licensing terms. As a result, this condition has been breached, the exemption does not apply and the activity needs to be assessed under the Creative Commons terms alone.

The result would be the same: not displaying the licensing terms is unreasonable and therefore also in breach of the Creative Common licence.

This in turn removes the authorisation for use and makes Dr Cooper's behaviour infringing. In practical terms, he would be infringing through copying the article (s. 17), modifying it (adaptation, s. 21) and communicating the adapted work to the public (s. 20). In all of these cases, Dr Cooper is committing direct infringement under section 96, which includes injunctions. The article would therefore have to be removed from the newsletter. The employer may also be liable, but this is not part of the scenario.

III. Metalegal Formants

The liberal approach of the UK respects the licensing terms, but at the same time acknowledges that not any contractual violation (especially with regard to payments of the licence fee) may automatically result in a property infringement. Case law defines the boundaries. 'Repudiatory breach' is conceptualised as an exception to the 'two areas' principle, resulting in both contractual and proprietary remedies for the violation.

B.3. COMPARATIVE REMARKS

The case combines two questions. First, is the Creative Commons licence accepted in the selected jurisdictions? Second, does a contractual breach automatically constitute a copyright infringement?

The first question is resolved easily. All reports acknowledge this type of copyright licensing. The central difference between legal jurisdictions is only revealed when considering the UK report. Under the monistic approach, the relinquishment of the personal right is a non-issue because it is impossible as a matter of principle. In the dual copyright systems of continental Europe, the issue of the relinquishment of the creator's personal right is unsettled. Some states have come to see no problem with this;[72] others have acknowledged Creative Commons licences by way of Supreme Court decisions.[73] Some reporters have cautioned that there is no case law yet.[74] In Spain, differing court decisions render the legal situation rather unclear.

Yet the reports differ to a great extent with regard to the relationship between the contractual breach and a copyright infringement. In Greece, Italy, Ireland and Spain, both claims exist. In some countries, only one violation seems to be present.[75]

---

72 This seems to be the case in the reports of Belgium, Czech Republic, Denmark, Estonia, Lithuania, Greece, Italy and Norway.

73 See the reports of Germany and the Netherlands.

74 See the reports of Ireland and Poland.

75 See the reports of Belgium (copyright infringement), Czech Republic and Estonia (breach of contract).

In Denmark, Germany, the Netherlands, Norway, Poland and the UK, the connection between the contractual breach and a copyright infringement appears vague and requires clarification by case law.

The reports reflect the early days of Creative Commons; some answers are very tentative.[76] It is interesting how restrained lawyers have been in their reactions to the social Creative Commons movement.

[76] See the reports of France and Greece.

INDEX